Joseph D. Suddes

Began read "consistently" 11/7/20

Impt. ☆ Jeremiah 17: 7-10

☆ Genesis 18:25

!! ☆ Deuteronomy 31:6

! ☆ I Chron. 21  God's question

! ☆ II Chron 10:15  Our human event

☆ II Chron. 20:12  We don't know what
to do, but our eyes are
on You!

Very Small ! ☆  Nehemiah 8:10
↓
! ☆ Psalm 88:5  THE ONE WHO SHARES
94:19  Jan 17, 2022  THE EVE

JOHN GOLDINGAY

# THE *first* TESTAMENT

*A NEW TRANSLATION*

IVP Academic

An imprint of InterVarsity Press
Downers Grove, Illinois

InterVarsity Press
P.O. Box 1400, Downers Grove, IL 60515-1426
ivpress.com
email@ivpress.com

InterVarsity Press® is the book-publishing division of InterVarsity Christian Fellowship/USA®, a movement of students and faculty active on campus at hundreds of universities, colleges, and schools of nursing in the United States of America, and a member movement of the International Fellowship of Evangelical Students. For information about local and regional activities, visit intervarsity.org.

Cover design: David Fassett
Images: black slate: © kyoshino/iStockphoto

ISBN 978-0-8308-5199-7 (print)
ISBN 978-0-8308-8796-5 (digital)

Printed in the United States of America ∞

InterVarsity Press is committed to ecological stewardship and to the conservation of natural resources in all our operations. This book was printed using sustainably sourced paper.

**Library of Congress Cataloging-in-Publication Data**
A catalog record for this book is available from the Library of Congress.

| P | 23 | 22 | 21 | 20 | 19 | 18 | 17 | 16 | 15 | 14 | 13 | 12 | 11 | 10 | 9 | 8 | 7 | 6 | 5 | 4 | 3 | 2 | 1 |
| Y | 37 | 36 | 35 | 34 | 33 | 32 | 31 | 30 | 29 | 28 | 27 | 26 | 25 | 24 | 23 | 22 | 21 | 20 | 19 | 18 |

# CONTENTS

# MAPS

# PREFACE

We usually call the first three-quarters of the Bible the 'Old Testament', but that name wasn't introduced until a century or more after Jesus's day. For him, it was simply the 'Scriptures' or the 'Torah', the 'Prophets', and the 'Other Writings'. Calling it the 'Old Testament' can make it sound something antiquated and out-of-date that has nothing much to do with Christian faith. Actually it's utterly up-to-date and hugely significant for Christian faith, a really important 'First Testament'.

The publication of this translation issued from writing a series of little commentaries called *The Old Testament for Everyone* which tried to reflect something of that truth about the significance of the 'First Testament'. But the idea of an Old Testament for everyone in English goes back at least to William Tyndale, the first great figure of the English Reformation, who was executed in 1536. It was a few decades after the printing press came into use in Europe, and Tyndale made it his ambition to produce a translation of the Bible that could be printed and made available to the 'boy that driveth the plough' (so John Foxe's *Book of Martyrs*, published a few decades after Tyndale's death). In other words, it could be available to everyone. Tyndale completed the New Testament and started on the Old, which Miles Coverdale later completed. The Old Testament for everyone is thus a long-running project.

The present translation brings together the translation sections from that series of commentaries and fills the gaps in them. I have substantially revised the translation which appears in the commentaries, partly because I hadn't worried about consistency of style and approach between them as I went along, whereas it seemed necessary to aim at consistency in this complete translation. On reflection, I suspect Tyndale was unrealistic about the accessibility of his translation, and I myself wasn't thinking about people like the ploughboy when I was completing this translation project. If anything, I had in mind people who are familiar with some standard translations but might appreciate something a bit different.

There are many ways of going about translation, and sometimes people try to argue that such and-such an approach is right and others wrong. I don't think that one approach is necessarily better than all others, and there's no such thing as the best translation of the Old Testament. All translations are more or less accurate, but producing a faithful equivalent of any piece of writing in another language is an impossible undertaking; all approaches involve compromise. Translations thus have varying strengths and weaknesses according to the way they choose to prioritize the principles of translation.

I had three or four principles in mind when I began this work, and I formulated three or four more in the course of completing it. There is some tension between these principles, and where my translation is jerky, the jerkiness probably reflects one or other of them. I have finally aimed to produce a translation that as far as possible has the following characteristics.

- It sticks close to the way the Hebrew (and Aramaic) works rather than paraphrasing it, so that readers can get as close as possible to the details of the original text. Sometimes when I've added words to make the meaning clearer, I've put these words in square brackets. Nowadays translations are more inclined to aim at translating sentence by sentence, which has opposite advantages and disadvantages to translating word by word. My translation moves in that older direction, in rendering more word by word. It's consequently more suitable for a slow read than for a quick read, and more suitable for reading on one's own than for reading out loud. And where a sentence may make sense but you're not sure what it refers to or how it fits into the context, it's probably because the text itself doesn't make it clear, and I've left it that way. As a further consequence, although I myself prefer to use gender-inclusive language, I've let the translation stay gendered where inclusivizing it obscures whether the text is using singular or plural – in other words, the translation often uses 'he' when the text refers to a man or a woman and where in my own writing I would thus say 'they' or 'he or she'.
- It stays with the traditional Hebrew text (like the New Jewish Publication Society Version) rather than emending it. When I was making the translation I thus started from that traditional

text itself, but I did refer to some existent translations, and sometimes adopted expressions from them. These other translations also occasionally made me see where I had slipped up, by missing out some words or misreading a word, just like an ancient scribe. I noticed, too, that sometimes they had slipped up in similar ways. I expect I have not eliminated all my mistakes, and you are welcome to let me know at johngold@fuller.edu where you notice one. At johngoldingay.com, under OT Introduction – OT for Everyone, I will post any corrections that come to my notice and any other comments I think of regarding my reason for translating particular verses the way I have.

- It uses everyday English in the sense that it often employs abbreviations such as 'I'll' and 'we'll' for 'I will' and 'we will'. In addition, for some common Hebrew words it generally avoids traditional English translations such as salvation, holiness, eternity, covenant, justice and righteousness, where these translations don't correspond well to the Hebrew words and/ or where the English words are misleading when used to translate Hebrew words that have different connotations.

- In the poetic sections, I've laid out the lines so that they correspond to the way I think the poetry works. Poetic lines commonly comprise two parts (sometimes three) that link with each other to form a complete sentence. In the translation, the second part (and the third, if there is one) appears indented as a second (or third) line.

- It tries to use the same English word to translate any one Hebrew word, so that one can see points of connection between texts. Translations of Exodus, for instance, commonly use the words slavery, bondage, servant and worship to render forms of the same Hebrew word, and part of the point of the story depends on our being able to see the links between the occurrences of this word. So in this example I try to use 'serve' and related words for all occurrences of the related Hebrew words. This principle is also different from the one taken by modern translations that focus on the meaning of words in individual sentences.

- It uses the name for God that God invited Israel to use, the name Yahweh, rather than replacing it by the expressions 'the LORD' or 'GOD'. 'Yahweh' is the name God gave Moses to share with the Israelites. It's God's personal name. For many centuries Israelites thus used this name, and it comes very frequently in the First Testament. But late on in First Testament times, people were less inclined to use the name, perhaps for two reasons. On one hand, if it's important not to take Yahweh's name in vain, it might be safer not to take it at all. On the other, using this name could give the impression that Israel's God was just a little local god, whereas in reality he's the Creator and Lord of the whole world. So Jews started replacing the name Yahweh by the word for 'Lord' or 'God', and they added marks to the text of the Scriptures to remind people to read out one of those other words in place of the name. When the Bible got translated into other languages, the name was then replaced by the equivalents of those words. The snag is that the alteration often spoils the sense of passages. So I have accepted Yahweh's invitation to call him by his personal name. (People sometimes ask me whether this practice is offensive to Jews. The general answer is that they are not offended by other people using the name. As with prescriptions in the Torah, not to do so is simply their vocation or discipline.)

- It translates some other names rather than just transliterating them, or it provides an equivalent English expression for them. English forenames and place names such as Hope or Grace or Wells or Orange County are ordinary words as well as names, and English-speakers are sometimes aware of the resonance about such a name. Other names such as John and Sheffield also have ordinary words behind them, but English-speakers are less likely to be aware of these. Something similar applies to Hebrew names. So I occasionally translate such names when it seems likely that an Israelite would have been aware of their meaning (e.g. 'The Height' for the place transliterated as Ramah, which has 'the' on the front of it in Hebrew). In some other cases I provide the English meaning of the name in square brackets after the name, especially where the context implies an awareness of the name's meaning (e.g. Adam means 'human being').

- Another consequence of the translation of the First Testament into Greek, then of the Greek into Latin, then of the Latin into English, was that Mosheh became Moses, Yesha'yahu became

Isaiah, Yerushalaim became Jerusalem, and so on (and Yohanan became John). I have left such names in their original form, but sometimes added in square brackets the familiar English form of a name – especially the first time it occurs. By using more precise transliterations (without being too technical) I hope also to make it a bit easier to work out the pronunciation of names (e.g. 'Jehoiachin' gives the impression that the name includes a 'j' sound and a 'ch' sound, neither of which is true: 'Yehoyakin' is less misleading). I have represented Hebrew letters as follows:

- zayin becomes z (rather than s);
- kaph becomes k (rather than ch);
- qoph becomes q (rather than k);
- tsade becomes ts (rather than z);
- he and het both become h (sorry not to distinguish these);
- sameq and sin both become s (sorry not to distinguish these);
- when aleph or ayin comes in the middle of names, both become ' (sorry not to distinguish these), like an apostrophe in English, so as to help with pronouncing them. But when they come at the beginning or end of names, I ignore them.

- There is one further aspect of the appearance of names that may seem surprising to Western readers. As William Shakespeare had a number of ways of spelling his name, so the First Testament uses several forms of some names. For instance, Hizqiyyahu, Hizqiyyah and Yehizqiyyahu are all ways of referring to the king who usually appears in English translations as Hezekiah. The place we know as Bethel can be called Bet-el or Bet El. I have preserved these differences rather than smoothed them out, so where such differences appear in the translation, it probably means they are examples of this inherent diversity rather than mistakes.

The Old Testament for Everyone series and this translation were the brainchild of Philip Law, with whom I've worked both at SPCK and at Westminster John Knox. I'm grateful to him for our longstanding and relaxed partnership; as I am to my agent Pieter Kwant, whom I ask for advice about possible projects, and whose enthusiasm for the Old Testament for Everyone commentary series was important to my agreeing to embark on that undertaking. I am also grateful to Mollie Barker for her exceedingly careful editing work, which saved me from many slips.

I've tried to work out how long the translation took, and the nearest I have to an answer is an hour or two a day for about five years, plus the revision time which took me the best part of a year. The commentary took another hour or two a day for about five years.

# INTRODUCTION

'The Old Testament' is the usual Christian name for the collection of Scriptures dating from before the time of Jesus that Jews and Christians have in common. But the actual title 'The Old Testament' comes from a century or more after Jesus and links with the fact that by then the Church had acquired some further Scriptures which it came to call 'The New Testament'. As well as pairing the Old Testament Scriptures with the New Testament Scriptures, Christian Bibles have the First Testament Scriptures in a different order.

In this order, the First Testament unfolds as follows.

1. Genesis, Exodus, Leviticus, Numbers, Deuteronomy
   – the 'Pentateuch' or the 'Torah', traditionally 'The Five Books of Moses', telling the story of the world's beginnings and of the beginnings of Israel;

2. Joshua, Judges, Ruth, 1 and 2 Samuel, 1 and 2 Kings
   – the continuation of Genesis to Deuteronomy, relating Israel's story from its arrival in Canaan to the fall of Jerusalem to the Babylonians;

3. Chronicles, Ezra, Nehemiah, Esther
   – a retelling of the entire story in Genesis to Kings followed by a continuation that relates the restoration of Jerusalem, and by a story about Jewish experience in Persia itself;

4. Job, Psalms, Proverbs, Ecclesiastes, Song of Songs
   – books that are nearly all poetry and that relate more directly to everyday life, worship and prayer, sometimes in confident affirmations, sometimes in questions;

5. Isaiah, Jeremiah, Lamentations, Ezekiel, Daniel, the Twelve Shorter Prophets
   – mostly collections of short messages that challenge and encourage Israel about its present life and circumstances and about the future that lies ahead of it.

## *What was the First Testament for?*

Why is the First Testament this kind of collection of works? What were they supposed to do for the Israelites for whom they were written and for the Jewish community that first came to recognize them as their Scriptures? And what are they supposed to do for the Christian Church?

Their very nature suggests what they were designed to be for Israel and for the Jewish people. First they tell them the beginning of their story, and they thus help them understand who they are. Then they continue that story into subsequent centuries, which adds to this effect. They collect the expectations regarding their lives that God enabled them to formulate over the centuries, which are also therefore expected to shape their life on an ongoing basis. They speak in the present about how life works, how praise and prayer are designed to be, and how to wrestle with some of life's key problems. And they record some of God's nightmares and dreams about the people's future.

When some Jews came to believe in Jesus and to see his coming as the climax of Israel's own story, they naturally used these resources to help them understand Jesus. The 'New Testament' did not regard the 'Old Testament' as 'old' in the sense of antiquated or out-of-date; hence my referring to it as the First Testament rather than the Old Testament. For Jesus and the New Testament writers, these Scriptures were a living resource for understanding God, God's ways in the world and God's ways with us. Every part of them was useful 'for teaching, reproving, correcting, and training in righteousness, so that anyone who belongs to God can be proficient, equipped for every good work' (2 Timothy 3.16–17). They were for everyone, in fact. So it's strange that Christians don't read them very much

1. The first three sequences as the First Testament unfolds are stories or histories. Calling them histories implies that they are talking about things that happened. They helped Israel understand itself by talking about where it came from. Calling them stories points to the fact that they are not just talking about things that happened; they have lessons written into them. Sometimes they pass on traditional stories that are simply good stories to illustrate a point, but more often they are stories with a basis in things that happened.

   That fact points us to a significant aspect of the significance of these stories for Israel. Christians sometimes assume that the basic thing about their faith is that it is a challenge to live the right kind of life and pursue peace and justice, and that the stories in the First Testament are there to give us good examples (or warning examples). But the stories themselves rarely have moral evaluations built into them, and people reading the stories may disagree about the moral evaluation we should come to. This points us to the fact that the stories are more about what God has been doing than about what human beings have been doing. God is pursuing a project – to bring into being a world that fulfils his creation purpose. He can sometimes achieve things by means of the human beings he gets involved with; he sometimes has to pursue his objectives despite the actions of the people he gets involved with. But the propriety of their actions is not the main point. The main point is that God is at work.

2. God's expectations of human beings do come into focus within the first sequence, the Torah, which incorporates considerable material telling Israel about how its life is to be lived. It mixes up moral challenges, social policy and instructions for worship. It connects the teaching on these topics to the story by describing the kind of lifestyle that God has a right to expect in light of what he's done for Israel. It also warns Israel of trouble to follow if people take no notice of the teaching.

   Jesus suggests several clues for interpreting this material. One is that the entirety of the Torah and the Prophets depends on the two commands to love God and love one's neighbour. So of any of the commands (especially the puzzling ones) one may ask how it is an outworking of either of these basic commands. Another clue is that sometimes the Torah is expounding God's creation vision, while sometimes it is making allowance for the human stubbornness that resists this creation vision. Paradoxically, even when it is making allowance in this way, it is an expression of love; the particular circumstance that Jesus mentions is the requirement that a man who divorces a wife must provide her with papers that lay out her legal position.

3. The books from Joshua to Kings relate how Israel put the teaching into practice – or more often failed to do so. So by the time you get to the end of Joshua to Kings, what the books are doing is explaining how things went wrong in Israel's life and why Israel ended up being put down by two successive superpowers, Assyria and Babylon. So they draw Israel to face facts and turn back to God.

   The books from Chronicles to Esther then do two things. They retell the story from Genesis to Kings, in a bit the way that (say) Matthew retells the story in Mark. In both cases, the assumption is that a story needs to be told in a way that will help its readers see what it has to say to them. The people for whom Chronicles is written are not under God's judgement like the people for whom Joshua to Kings are written. They need encouragement more than rebuke. So the story is told in a way designed to encourage them.

   Ezra-Nehemiah and Esther then take the story on into the time of people living later, whether in Jerusalem or in the Dispersion. They make explicit some of the reasons why people in their day needed encouragement, and they also thereby indicate something of the ongoing significance of the books from Chronicles to Esther. The Church in the West, at least, lives in discouraging times. And the Church in other parts of the world often lives in dangerous times, the kind of times about which Esther speaks.

4. The books from Job to Song of Songs more explicitly focus on the present. Psalms provides us with 150 examples of things you can say to God in praise, in prayer and in thanksgiving. It's been said that the book of Psalms used to be where Christians learned to pray, but if it was so in the past, it's isn't so now. We could try reverting to it. Proverbs, Job, Ecclesiastes and Song of Songs all start from everyday life outside the context of worship and share with their readers insights that the writers have gained from their experience of life or through considering the wisdom of other people who have reflected on life. On the whole, Proverbs does so in a positive way, telling people how life works and how to make it work. Job and Ecclesiastes do so in a more questioning way. Job starts from the fact that bad things happen to good people and wrestles with various ways of living with that reality. Ecclesiastes starts from the more general fact that it's hard to make sense of life in the world (especially given that we all die), and seeks to help readers live with that fact. The Song of Songs takes an enthusiastic but realistic look at the wonder of relationships between the sexes and at the pressures that come on those relationships.

5. The background of the Prophets is the time when the great powers start to dominate Israel's life, the time of Assyria and Babylon, then of Persia and Greece. The Prophets seek to get Israel to see how God is involved in this development, initially to bring God's chastisement because of Israel's rebellion and unfaithfulness (in the time of Assyria and Babylon), then to bring God's restoration (by means of Persia), then to bring agents of persecution from which God needs to rescue his people (in the Greek period). They challenge Israel to turn back to God and to live by trust rather than by the assumption that they control their own destinies. The Prophets' messages about the empires provide the Church with ways of thinking about empires and superpowers in the modern world.

   A minor theme in the Prophets is the articulation of a hope for a better king to come – the figure later called the Messiah (but the word does not come in this connection in the First Testament). That promise is part of the broader theme that chastisement and persecution will not be God's last word. There is going to be a new heavens and a new earth in the sense of a new Jerusalem, one characterized by mutual commitment rather than by people taking advantage of one another and by joy and fulfilment, where everyone will be able to sit under their vine or fig tree. Some aspects of the Prophets' promises found fulfilment in Israel's life, some illumine what Jesus was and did, some continue to promise us the fulfilment of God's creation purpose.

## How did the First Testament come into being?

The books in the First Testament were written in the form that we have them between about the eighth and the second centuries before Christ. (Like most things in this Introduction, there could be arguments about those dates – and the same applies to the translation that follows – but I don't think anything here is an idiosyncratic view of mine.)

Most of the First Testament is of anonymous authorship, and we don't know who wrote the books or when. The King James Version has some introductions such as 'The First Book of Moses, Called Genesis' or 'The Lamentations of Jeremiah', but these are not part of the text. The first books that give us names and dates are those associated with prophets such as Hosea, Amos and Micah, and these give us dates in the eighth century, which is the reason for mentioning the eighth century. The last event directly referred to is the great crisis in Jerusalem in the 160s bc. when a Greek Seleucid king banned proper worship in Jerusalem, which the visions in Daniel refer to, so that's the reason for mentioning the second century. We also don't know much about the process whereby the Jewish community came to accept these books as their Scriptures.

The book of Ezra does speak of a priest-theologian called Ezra bringing 'the Torah' from Babylonia to Jerusalem in 458 bc, and 'The Torah' or 'The Law' is the later name for the books from Genesis to Deuteronomy. It wouldn't be surprising if this story in Ezra tells us when 'The Torah' came to be accepted as Scripture in Jerusalem. Later, again in the second century, the preface to a work variously called Ecclesiasticus or Ben Sira or Sirach refers to 'The Law and the Prophets and the rest of the books', which is quite similar to the later expression 'The Torah, the Prophets and the Writings', a common title in the Jewish community for what Christians call the Old Testament.

And as far as Jesus and the New Testament writers were concerned, these were the Scriptures. In putting it that way, I cut a corner a bit, as the New Testament never gives us a list of these Scriptures, but the body of writings that the Jewish people accept is as near as we can get to identifying the collection that Jesus and the New Testament writers would have worked with.

We don't have any record of a meeting 'deciding' that these books and no others would count as the Scriptures. It wouldn't surprise me if it just happened; nobody exactly decided it. These writings compelled themselves on the Jewish people one by one. And it wouldn't surprise me if the last time something compelled itself on the Jewish people with this kind of force was that crisis in Jerusalem in the 160s when the visions in Daniel promised God's deliverance of his people, and were proved true.

The Church also came to accept some extra books such as Maccabees and the aforementioned Ecclesiasticus. They were traditionally called the 'Apocrypha', the books that were 'hidden away', but that name came to imply 'spurious'. They're now often known as the 'Deutero-canonical Writings', which is more cumbersome but less pejorative. It simply indicates that these books have less authority than the Torah, the Prophets and the Writings. The precise list of them varies among different churches. By the 'First Testament' I mean the Scriptures accepted by the Jewish community, though in the Jewish Bible they come in that different order as the Torah, the Prophets and the Writings.

## An outline of the First Testament story

Here is an outline of the story that emerges from the First Testament books (I give no dates for events in Genesis, which involves too much guesswork).

| | |
|---|---|
| 1200s | The Israelites are state serfs in Egypt; God enables them to get out of Egypt under Moses and to settle in Canaan under Joshua |
| 1100s | The 'judges' |
| 1000s | The Israelites decide to become a monarchic state; King Saul, King David |
| 900s | King Solomon; Israel splits into two nations, Ephraim and Judah |
| 800s | Elijah, Elisha |
| 700s | Amos, Hosea, Isaiah, Micah; Assyria the superpower; the Assyrians terminate the life of Ephraim (722) |
| 600s | Jeremiah, King Josiah; Babylon the superpower |
| 500s | Ezekiel; the Babylonians terminate the independent life of Judah (587) |
| | Persia the superpower; Judahites free to return home (537) and rebuild the temple |
| 400s | Ezra brings the Torah to Jerusalem (458); Nehemiah rebuilds its walls (445) |
| 300s | Alexander (333) puts Jerusalem under the authority of Greece as the superpower |
| 200s | Syria (the Seleucids) and Egypt (the Ptolemies) pull Judah one way or the other |
| 100s | Judah rebels against Seleucid domination and persecution and gains independence (164) |
| 000s | Rome the superpower |

Ancient Near East

©Karla Bohmback

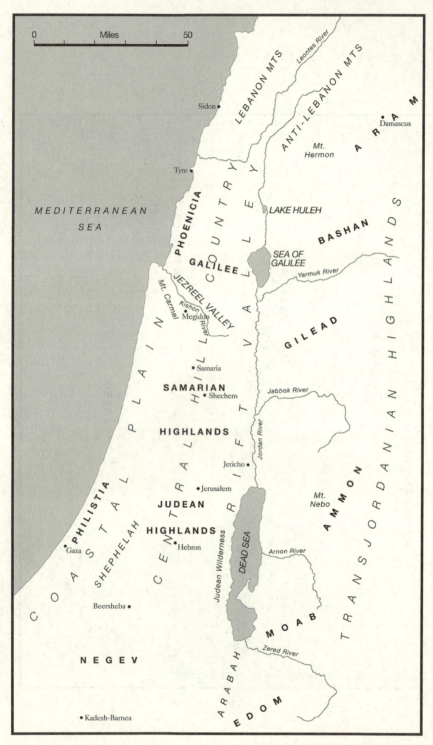

**Ancient Israel**

©*Karla Bohmback*

*Scale:* 0 — Miles — 50

Sidon

LEBANON MTS

Leontes River

ANTI-LEBANON MTS

Damascus

ARAM

Mt. Hermon

Tyre

LAKE HULEH

PHOENICIA

HILL COUNTRY

BASHAN

MEDITERRANEAN SEA

GALILEE

SEA OF GALILEE

Yarmuk River

TRANSJORDANIAN HIGHLANDS

JEZREEL VALLEY

Mt. Carmel

Kishon River

Megiddo

JORDAN RIFT VALLEY

GILEAD

Samaria

SAMARIAN

Jabbok River

Shechem

HIGHLANDS

Jordan River

COASTAL PLAIN

Jericho

AMMON

Jerusalem

Mt. Nebo

JUDEAN

PHILISTIA

HIGHLANDS

CENTRAL RIFT

Gaza

Hebron

DEAD SEA

SHEPHELAH

Judean Wilderness

Arnon River

Beersheba

MOAB

NEGEV

ARABAH

Zered River

Kadesh-Barnea

EDOM

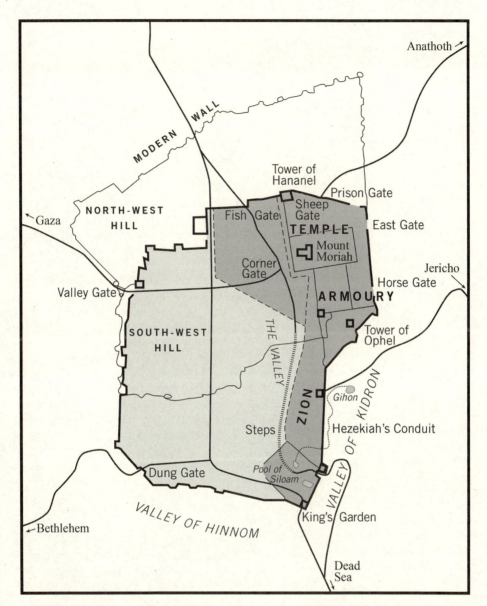

*City of Jerusalem*　　　　　　©*Westminster John Knox Press*

# GENESIS

Genesis provides the people of God with two aspects of the back story to its own story. Chapters 1—11 go back to the beginning of the world as a whole. They thus invite the people of God to see their own story against the broadest and longest backcloth. Then chapters 12—50 tell them about their particular prehistory in God's bringing their ancestors from Mesopotamia to Canaan with the intention of settling them there permanently in due course.

By its nature, then, Genesis tells a story about actual events of the past. Yet a reading of the story makes us hesitate to take it as simply historical. Noah putting specimens of every animal species into a giant box in which they survive a worldwide flood? Lot's wife turned into a column of salt? Genesis is like other histories from its world such as the works of the Greek historians Herodotus and Thucydides. They combine reminiscences of historical events, traditional stories and works of imagination, and comment on what it all means and what readers should make of it. In inspiring Genesis, God let its authors write in the way that was natural to them, and used their way of telling a story to instruct Israel and us about ourselves and about him.

Indeed, rather than comparing Genesis with the kind of history that we might try to write, we do better to compare it with Shakespeare or with historical novels or with the kind of Hollywood movie that's 'based on fact'. In understanding such works, we miss the point if we focus too much on what actually happened. What makes them instructive is the way a creative team has turned them into an illuminating story. It's this kind of story that God inspired his team to write.

The plot of the story is as follows. Act One describes how God set the world going but how it soon went wrong, which made God wonder whether the whole thing had been a mistake; that's Scene One. God starts again, but things again go wrong, and you wonder whether there is no way this project can be a success. That's Scene Two.

One can imagine an intermission at chapter 11 before the beginning of Act Two, which occupies the rest of the book. Its three scenes focus on the story of three families. First God summons Abraham and Sarah from Mesopotamia and promises to give them such blessing that the whole world will pray to be blessed as they are blessed. So God is indeed continuing with his original purpose to bless the entire world. Much of the drama of the first scene focuses on whether Abraham and Sarah will ever have a son through whom God's blessing can find fulfilment. This son, Isaac, is the focus of Scene Two. In turn, much of his story focuses on his two sons, and the conflict between them. Scene Three tells of the family of one of these sons, Jacob, which also becomes a story of conflict. By the end of Genesis, Jacob's family has grown to quite a size, so that one element in God's promise has found fulfilment. But because of a famine it has had to take refuge in Egypt, which is not the country that had been promised to it.

So the end of the story is not really the end of the story. It's more like the cliffhanger at the end of the first series in a television drama. We have to read on into Exodus.

Readers often assume that the point of the stories about people such as Abraham and Sarah is to give us examples of how to live or how not to live our lives. This assumption doesn't make sense of the stories. They're more about God and about God as seeking to fulfil his purpose for the world and for his people, which often works despite the actions of human beings rather than via them. They're stories that help us understand who we are rather than stories that tell us what to be.

## In the beginning (days one to three)

**1** At the beginning of God's creating the heavens and the earth, ²when the earth was an empty void, with darkness over the face of the deep, and God's breath sweeping over the face of the water, ³God said, 'Light!' and light came into being. ⁴God saw that light was good, and God made a distinction between light and darkness. ⁵God called the light 'day'; the darkness he called 'night'. And there was evening and there was morning, day one.

⁶God said, 'A dome in the middle of the water to make water distinct from water!' ⁷And God made the dome and made a distinction between the water that was under the dome and the water that was above the dome. So it came to be. ⁸God called the dome 'heavens'. And there was evening and there was morning, a second day.

⁹God said, 'The water under the heavens is to come together into one place so the dry land may appear!' So it came to be. ¹⁰God called the dry land 'earth'; the coming together of water he called 'seas'. God saw that it was good. ¹¹God said, 'The earth is to put forth vegetation: plants generating seed, fruit trees producing fruit by its species, with its seed in it, on the earth!' So it came to be. ¹²The earth brought forth vegetation, plants generating seed by its species, and trees producing fruit with its seed in it by its species. God saw that it was good. ¹³And there was evening and there was morning, a third day.

## Filling in the outline (days four to six)

¹⁴God said, 'Lights in the dome of the heavens to make a distinction between day and night! They'll be for signs and set times and days and years, ¹⁵and they'll be lights in the dome of the heavens to give light on the earth!' So it came to be. ¹⁶God made the two big lights (the bigger light to rule the day and the smaller light to rule the night) and the stars. ¹⁷God put them in the dome of the heavens to give light on the earth, ¹⁸to rule over the day and over the night, and to make a distinction between light and darkness. God saw that it was good. ¹⁹And there was evening and there was morning, a fourth day.

²⁰God said, 'The water is to teem with living creatures, and birds are to fly over the earth, over the face of the dome of the heavens!' ²¹God created the big sea monsters and every living creature that moves, with which the water teems, by their species, and every winged bird by its species. God saw that it was good. ²²God blessed them: 'Be fruitful, be numerous, fill the water in the seas; birds are to be numerous on the earth.' ²³And there was evening and there was morning, a fifth day.

²⁴God said, 'The earth is to bring forth living creatures by their species – animals, moving things and the living things of the earth, by their species!' So it came to be. ²⁵God made the living things of the earth by their species, animals by their species and all the things that move on the ground by their species. God saw that it was good.

## The week's work completed

²⁶God said, 'Let's make human beings in our image, as our likeness, so they can hold sway over the fish in the sea, over the birds in the heavens, over the animals, over all the earth and over all the things that move on the earth.' ²⁷So God created human beings in his image. He created them in the image of God. He created them male and female. ²⁸God blessed them, and said to them, 'Be fruitful, be numerous, fill the earth and subjugate it, hold sway over the fish in the sea, over the birds in the heavens and over every creature that moves on the earth.'

²⁹God said, 'Here, I give you all the plants that generate seed that are on the face of all the earth, and every tree with fruit that generates seed. These will be food for you, ³⁰for all the creatures of the earth, for all the birds in the heavens and for all the things that move on the earth that have living breath in them, all the green plants as food.' So it came to be.

³¹God saw all that he had made, and there – it was very good. And there was evening and there was morning, the sixth day.

**2** So the heavens and the earth were finished, with all their forces. ²On the seventh day God had finished his work that he had been doing, so on the seventh day he stopped from all his work that he had been doing. ³God blessed the seventh day and made it sacred, because on it God stopped from his entire work of creation that he had been doing.

## To put it another way . . .

⁴These are the lines of descent of the heavens and the earth when they were created.

When Yahweh God made the earth and the heavens, ⁵and no bush of the wild was on the earth yet and no plant of the wild had grown yet (because Yahweh God had not made it rain on the earth, and there was no human being to serve the ground, ⁶though a stream would go up from the earth and water the entire face of the ground), ⁷Yahweh God shaped a human person [adam] with earth from the ground [adamah] and blew into its nostrils living breath, and the human person became a living being.

⁸Yahweh God planted a garden in Eden ['Lavishness'], in the east, and put there the human being he had shaped. ⁹Yahweh God made to grow up from the ground every tree that's desirable to look at and good for food, with the life-tree in the middle of the garden, and the good-and-bad-knowledge tree.

¹⁰There was a river going out of Eden to water the garden, and from there dividing and becoming four headwaters. ¹¹The name of the first was Pishon; it was the one going round the entire Havilah region, where the gold is. (¹²The gold of that region is good; pearl and onyx stone are there.) ¹³The name of the second river was Gihon; it was the one going round the entire Kush [Sudan] region. ¹⁴The name of the third river was Tigris; it was the one going east of Ashshur. The fourth river was the Euphrates.

## The helper

¹⁵Yahweh God took the human being and set him down in Eden Garden to serve it and keep it. ¹⁶Yahweh God ordered the human being: 'From every tree in the garden you may definitely eat. ¹⁷But from the good-and-bad-knowledge tree you will not eat, because on the day you eat from it, you will definitely die.'

¹⁸Yahweh God said, 'It's not good for the human being to be on his own. I'll make

him a helper suitable for him.' ¹⁹Yahweh God shaped from the ground every creature of the wild and every bird in the heavens, and brought them to the human being to see what he'd call it. Whatever the human being called a living being, that became its name. ²⁰The human being gave names to all the animals, to the birds in the heavens and to all the creatures of the wild. But for a human being he didn't find a helper suitable for him.

²¹So Yahweh God made a coma fall on the human being so he slept, took one of his ribs and closed up its place with flesh. ²²Yahweh God built the rib that he'd taken from the human being into a woman, and brought her to the human being. ²³The human being said: 'This, now, is bone from my bones and flesh from my flesh! This one will be called Woman [ishshah], because from a man [ish] this one was taken.' ²⁴That's why a man abandons his father and his mother and attaches himself to his woman and they become one flesh.

²⁵The two of them were naked, the man and his woman, but they felt no shame.

## Creation asserts itself

**3** Now the snake was the shrewdest of all the creatures of the wild that Yahweh God had made. It said to the woman, 'Did God really say you will not eat from any tree in the garden?' ²The woman said to the snake, 'We may eat of the fruit from the trees in the garden, ³but from the fruit of the tree that's in the middle of the garden God said, "You will not eat of it and you will not touch it, so that you don't die."'

⁴The snake said to the woman, 'You won't die at all. ⁵Rather, God knows that on the day you eat of it, your eyes will open and you'll become like gods, knowing good and bad.' ⁶The woman saw that the tree was good to eat and that it was an object of longing to the eyes, and the tree was desirable for giving insight. So she took of its fruit and ate, and also gave some to her man with her, and he ate. ⁷The eyes of the two of them opened and they knew that they were naked, so they sewed fig leaves together and made themselves loincloths.

⁸They heard the sound of Yahweh God walking about in the garden in the breezy time

of the day, so the man and his woman hid from the face of Yahweh God among the trees in the garden. [9]Yahweh God called to the man and said to him, 'Where are you?' [10]He said, 'I heard the sound of you in the garden, and I was afraid because I was naked, so I hid.' [11]He said, 'Who told you that you were naked? Have you eaten from the tree that I ordered you not to eat from?' [12]The man said, 'The woman you put with me – she gave to me from the tree, and I ate.' [13]Yahweh God said to the woman, 'What is this that you've done?' The woman said, 'The snake – it deceived me, and I ate.'

## The consequences

[14]Yahweh God said to the snake, 'Because you've done this, you're cursed, away from all the animals and the creatures of the wild. On your stomach you'll go and soil you'll eat all the days of your life. [15]I shall put enmity between you and the woman, and between your offspring and her offspring. He'll hit you on the head; you'll hit him on the heel.'

[16]To the woman he said, 'I shall make very great your pain in connection with pregnancy. In painfulness you'll give birth to children. Towards your man will be your desire, but he – he'll rule over you.'

[17]To Adam he said, 'Because you listened to the voice of your woman and ate from the tree I ordered you, "You will not eat from it", the ground is cursed because of you. In pain you'll eat from it all the days of your life. [18]Thorn and thistle it will grow for you and you'll eat plants of the wild. [19]By the sweat of your face you'll eat bread, until you go back to the ground, because you were taken from it. Because you were earth, and you'll go back to earth.'

[20]The man named his woman Havvah [Eve], because she became the mother of every living person [hay]. [21]Yahweh God made for Adam and his woman leather coats, and clothed them. [22]But Yahweh God said, 'Here, the man has become like one of us in knowing good and bad. So now, he mustn't put out his hand and also take from the life-tree and eat, and live permanently.' [23]So Yahweh God sent him off from Eden Garden to serve the ground from which he'd been taken.

[24]So Yahweh God drove the man out and made the sphinxes dwell east of Eden Garden, with a sword-like flame whirling, to keep the way to the life-tree.

## The first family, the first worship, the first acceptance, the first rejection

**4** Now the man slept with his woman, Havvah, she got pregnant, and she gave birth to Qayin [Cain]. She said, 'I've acquired [qanah] someone with Yahweh.' [2]She went on to give birth to his brother, Hebel ['Breath'; Abel]. Hebel became one who kept sheep, while Qayin became one who served the ground. [3]After some time, Qayin brought some of the fruit of the ground as an offering for Yahweh, [4]while Hebel, too, brought some of the firstborn of his flock, some of the fat parts. Yahweh recognized Hebel and his offering, [5]but Qayin and his offering Yahweh did not recognize. It really enraged Qayin and he went into a huff. [6]Yahweh said to Qayin, 'Why does it enrage you? Why have you gone into a huff? [7]If you do what's good, there'll be honouring, won't there? But if you don't do what's good, wrongdoing is crouching at the entrance. Towards you will be its desire, but you – you're to rule over it.'

[8]Qayin said to Hebel his brother . . . And while they were in the open country, Qayin set upon Hebel his brother and killed him.

[9]Yahweh said to Qayin, 'Where's Hebel, your brother?' He said, 'I don't know – am I the one who keeps my brother?' [10]He said, 'What have you done? A sound! Your brother's spilt blood is crying out to me from the ground. [11]There, you are cursed, away from the ground that has opened its mouth to receive your brother's spilt blood from your hand. [12]When you serve the ground, it will no more give its energy to you. A drifter, a vagrant, you'll be on the earth.'

## The protection

[13]Qayin said to Yahweh, 'My waywardness is too big to carry. [14]Here, you've driven me away today from the face of the ground, and from your face I'm to conceal myself, and I'm to be a drifter, a vagrant on the earth – and anyone

who finds me can kill me.' ¹⁵But Yahweh said to him, 'Therefore, anyone who kills Qayin, sevenfold it's to be redressed.' And Yahweh put a mark on Qayin so no one who found him would strike him down. ¹⁶So Qayin went out from being before Yahweh's face and lived in the country of Nod ['Drifting'], east of Eden.

¹⁷Qayin slept with his woman, she got pregnant, and she gave birth to Hanok. He was building a town, and he named the town after his son Hanok. ¹⁸To Hanok was born Irad, Irad fathered Mehuyael, Mehiyael fathered Metusael, and Metusael fathered Lemek. ¹⁹Lemek got himself two women; the name of one was Adah, the name of the second Tsillah. ²⁰Adah gave birth to Yabal; he was the ancestor of everyone who lives with a tent and livestock. ²¹His brother's name was Yubal; he was the ancestor of everyone who plays guitar or pipe. ²²Tsillah, she too gave birth, to Tubal Qayin, forger of all copper and iron. Tubal-qayin's sister was Na'amah.

²³Lemek said to his women,

Adah and Tsillah, listen to my voice;
    as Lemek's women, give ear to my word.
Because I've killed someone for wounding me,
    a young man for injuring me.
²⁴If for Qayin it's to be redressed sevenfold,
    for Lemek seventy-sevenfold.

²⁵Once more Adam slept with his woman and she gave birth to a son. She named him Set, because 'God has granted me [*sit*] another offspring in place of Hebel, because Qayin killed him'. ²⁶To Set, too, a son was born, and he named him Enosh. At that time a beginning was made to calling in Yahweh's name.

## Then he died

**5** This is the document with Adam's lines of descent. On the day God created human beings, it was in the likeness of God that he made them. ²Male and female he created them, and he blessed them, and named them 'human beings', on the day he created them. ³When Adam had lived 130 years, he fathered someone in his likeness, as his image, and named him Set. ⁴Adam's days after fathering Set came to 800 years, and

he fathered sons and daughters. ⁵So all the days that Adam lived came to 930 years. Then he died.

⁶When Set had lived 105 years, he fathered Enosh. ⁷Set lived 807 years after fathering Enosh, and he fathered sons and daughters. ⁸So all the days of Set came to 912 years. Then he died.

⁹When Enosh had lived 90 years, he fathered Qenan. ¹⁰Enosh lived 815 years after fathering Qenan, and he fathered sons and daughters. ¹¹So all the days of Enosh came to 905 years. Then he died.

¹²When Qenan had lived 70 years, he fathered Mahalalel. ¹³Qenan lived 840 years after fathering Mahalalel, and he fathered sons and daughters. ¹⁴So all the days of Qenan came to 910 years. Then he died.

¹⁵When Mahalalel had lived 65 years, he fathered Yared. ¹⁶Mahalalel lived 830 years after fathering Yared, and he fathered sons and daughters. ¹⁷So all the days of Mahalalel came to 895 years. Then he died.

¹⁸When Yared had lived 162 years, he fathered Hanok [Enoch]. ¹⁹Yared lived 800 years after fathering Hanok, and he fathered sons and daughters. ²⁰So all the days of Yared came to 962 years. Then he died.

²¹When Hanok had lived 65 years, he fathered Metushalah. ²²Hanok walked about with God 300 years after fathering Metushalah, and he fathered sons and daughters. ²³So all the days of Hanok came to 365 years. ²⁴Hanok walked about with God, and then he was no more, because God took him.

## The need and the promise

²⁵When Metushalah had lived 187 years, he fathered Lemek. ²⁶Metushalah lived 782 years after fathering Lemek, and he fathered sons and daughters. ²⁷So all the days of Metushalah came to 969 years. Then he died.

²⁸When Lemek had lived 182 years, he fathered a son, ²⁹and named him Noah ['Settling Down'], saying: 'This man: he'll relieve us [*niham*] from our work, from

the pain of our hands, from the ground that Yahweh cursed.' [30]Lemek lived 595 years after fathering Noah, and he fathered sons and daughters. [31]So all the days of Lemek came to 777 years. Then he died. [32]When Noah had lived 500 years, Noah fathered Shem, Ham and Yephet.

**6** When humanity started to be numerous on the face of the ground and daughters were born to them, [2]the sons of the divine beings saw that the daughters of the human beings were good-looking and they took women for themselves, any one that they chose.

[3]Yahweh said, 'My spirit will not dwell in humanity permanently, because it's flesh. Its time will be 120 years.' [4]Now the Nephilim ['Fallen'] were on the earth at that time, and also afterwards, when the sons of the divine beings had sex with the daughters of human beings, and they gave birth for them. These were the strong men that were of old, famous men.

[5]Yahweh saw that humanity's bad state on the earth was great. The entire inclination of its mind's intentions was simply bad, all day. [6]Yahweh regretted that he had made humanity on the earth. It pained his heart. [7]Yahweh said, 'I shall wipe out the humanity that I created from the face of the ground, from humanity to animals to moving things to birds in the heavens, because I regret that I made them.' [8]But Noah found grace in Yahweh's eyes.

[9]These are Noah's lines of descent. Now Noah was someone who was faithful and a person of integrity among his generations. It was with God that Noah walked about. [10]Noah fathered three sons, Shem, Ham and Yephet.

## Filled with violence

[11]So the earth had become devastated before God; the earth was full of violence. [12]God looked at the earth: there, it had become devastated, because all flesh had devastated its way on the earth.

[13]So God said to Noah, 'The end of all flesh has come before me, because the earth is full of violence through them. Here, I'm going to devastate them, with the earth. [14]Make for yourself a chest of gopher wood. With rooms you're to make the chest, and cover it inside and outside with pitch. [15]This is how you're to make it: the length of the chest 150 metres, its width 25 metres and its height 15 metres. [16]You're to make a skylight for the chest, to finish it to half a metre above, and to put the entrance of the chest in its side. You're to make it with bottom, second and third levels.

[17]And I: here, I'm bringing a deluge, water on the earth, to devastate all flesh in which there is living breath, from under the heavens. Everything on the earth will breathe its last. [18]But I shall implement my pact with you. You're to come into the chest, you, your sons, your wife and your sons' wives with you. [19]And of everything living, of all flesh, bring two of each into the chest to keep them alive with you. They're to be a male and a female. [20]Of the birds of each species, of the animals of each species and of everything that moves on the ground of each species, two of each are to come to you to keep them alive. [21]And you: get yourself some of all food that's eaten and gather it for yourself. It will be food for you and for them.'

[22]Noah acted in accordance with all that God ordered him. So he did.

## The great deep breaks out

**7** Yahweh said to Noah, 'Go into the chest, you and your entire household, because I've seen that you're a person who is faithful before me in this generation. [2]Of every pure animal take with you seven of each, a male and its mate, and of an animal that's not pure, two, a male and its mate, [3]also of the birds in the heavens seven of each, male and female, to keep offspring alive on the face of the entire earth. [4]Because in seven more days I'm going to make it rain on the earth for forty days and forty nights and wipe out everything that exists that I made, from on the face of the ground.' [5]Noah acted in accordance with all that God ordered him.

[6]Noah was a man of 600 years when the deluge happened, as water on the earth. [7]Noah, his sons, his wife and his sons' wives with him came into the chest because of the water of the deluge. [8]Of the pure animals, of the animals that are not pure, of the birds and of everything that moves on the ground, [9]two

of each came to Noah into the chest, male and female, as God ordered Noah; [10]and after the seven days the water of the deluge came on the earth. [11]In the six hundredth year of Noah's life, in the second month, on the seventeenth day of the month, on that day all the springs in the great deep broke out and the apertures in the heavens opened. [12]The rain came on the earth forty days and forty nights.

### And God shut him in

[13]On this particular day Noah, with Shem, Ham and Yephet, Noah's sons, and Noah's wife and his sons' three wives, came into the chest, [14]they and every living thing by its species, every animal by its species, everything that moves on the earth by its species and everything that flies by its species, every bird and every winged creature. [15]They came to Noah into the chest, two each of all flesh in which was living breath. [16]So the ones who came, male and female from all flesh, came as God ordered him. And Yahweh shut him in.

[17]The deluge went on for forty days on the earth, and the water increased and lifted the chest, and it rose up from on the earth. [18]The water grew strong and increased greatly on the earth, and the chest moved on the face of the water. [19]When the water grew very, very strong on the earth, all the lofty mountains under the entire heavens were covered. [20]Seven metres higher the water grew strong; the mountains were covered. [21]All flesh moving on the earth breathed its last: birds, animals, living things, all the things teeming on the earth, and all humanity. [22]Everything that had living breath in its nostrils, everything that was on the dry land, died. [23]It wiped out everything that existed that was on the face of the ground, from human beings to animals to moving things to birds in the heavens. They were wiped out from the earth. Only Noah and those with him in the chest remained. [24]And the water grew strong on the earth for 150 days.

### But God remembered Noah

**8** But God was mindful of Noah and all the living things and the animals that were with him in the chest, and God made a wind pass over the earth, and the water abated. [2]The springs in the deep and the apertures in the heavens were blocked up, the rain from the heavens held back [3]and the water gradually withdrew from on the earth. The water decreased at the end of 150 days, [4]and the chest came to a stop in the seventh month, on the seventeenth day of the month, on the Ararat mountains. [5]As the water gradually decreased until the tenth month, in the tenth month on the first day of the month the tops of the mountains appeared.

[6]At the end of forty days, Noah opened the window in the chest that he had made [7]and sent out a raven. It continued to go out and come back until the water dried up from on the earth. [8]He sent out a dove from being with him to see if the water had diminished from on the face of the ground, [9]but the dove didn't find a place to alight for the sole of its foot and it came back to him to the chest, because there was water on the face of the entire earth. So he put out his hand and took it and brought it to him into the chest.

[10]He waited again seven more days and once more sent out the dove from the chest. [11]The dove came to him at evening time, and there, in its mouth a plucked-off olive leaf. So Noah knew that the water had diminished from on the earth. [12]He waited again seven more days and sent out the dove, and it didn't come back to him again.

### Never again

[13]In the six hundred and first year, in the first month, on the first of the month, the water dried up from on the earth. Noah removed the chest's cover and looked: there, the face of the ground was dry. [14]In the second month, on the twenty-seventh day of the month, the earth was dried out. [15]God spoke to Noah: [16]'Get out of the chest, you, your wife, your sons and your sons' wives with you. [17]Every living thing that's with you from all flesh, birds, animals and everything that moves on the earth: get them out with you, so they may teem on the earth and be fruitful and be numerous on the earth.'

[18]So Noah got out, he, his sons, his wife and his sons' wives with him. [19]Every living thing, everything that moves and every bird, everything that moves on the earth got out of the chest by their families.

[20]Noah built an altar for Yahweh, took some of every pure animal and of every pure bird, and offered up burnt offerings on the altar, [21]and Yahweh smelled the nice smell. Yahweh said to himself, 'I won't ever again slight the ground on account of humanity, because the inclination of the human mind is bad from its youth. I won't ever again strike down everything living, as I did. [22]Never again, for all earth's days, will seedtime and harvest, cold and heat, summer and winter, day and night, stop.'

## The renewed creation blessing and the first pact or covenant

**9** God blessed Noah and his sons and said to them, 'Be fruitful, be numerous, fill the earth. [2]Reverence towards you and awe towards you will be on all the living things on the earth, on all the birds in the sky, on everything that moves on the ground and on all the fish in the sea; they're given into your hand. [3]Everything that moves, that's alive, will be yours as food. As I gave you green plants, everything is yours. [4]Yet flesh with its life, its blood, you will not eat.

[5]And indeed, your blood, for your life, I shall require. From every living thing I shall require it, and from a human being I shall require a human life, an individual for his brother. [6]One who sheds human blood, by means of a human being his blood will flow, because it was in God's image that he made humanity. [7]But you: be fruitful, be numerous, teem on the earth, be numerous on it.'

[8]And God said to Noah and to his sons with him: [9]'Here, I myself am going to implement my pact with you, with your offspring after you [10]and with every living being that's with you: birds, animals and every living thing on the earth with you, all that got out of the chest, every living thing on the earth. [11]I shall implement my pact with you and all flesh will not be cut off again by the water of a deluge. Never again will there be a deluge to devastate the earth.'

## The bow laid aside (but things go wrong again)

[12]And God said, 'This is the sign of the pact that I'm putting between me and you and every living creature that's with you, to the generations, permanently. [13]I've put my bow in the clouds. It will be a sign of the pact between me and the earth. [14]When I bring clouds on the earth and the bow appears in the clouds, [15]I shall be mindful of my pact that's between me and you and every living creature among all flesh, and the water will never again become a deluge to devastate all flesh. [16]The bow will be in the clouds and I shall see it, being mindful of the permanent pact between God and every living creature among all flesh that's on the earth.' [17]God said to Noah, 'This will be the sign of the pact that I've implemented between me and all flesh that's on the earth.'

[18]Noah's sons who got out of the chest were Shem, Ham and Yephet; Ham was the father of Kena'an [Canaan]. [19]These three were Noah's sons, and from them the entire earth dispersed.

[20]Noah, a man of the ground, as his first act planted a vineyard. [21]He drank some of the wine and got drunk, and exposed himself inside his tent. [22]Ham, Kena'an's father, saw his father's nakedness and told his two brothers outside. [23]Shem and Yephet took a cover, put it on both their shoulders, walked backwards and covered their father's nakedness, with their faces turned backwards so they didn't see their father's nakedness.

[24]Noah woke up from his wine and came to know what his youngest son had done to him. [25]He said, 'Cursed be Kena'an ['Bow Down']: he'll be the lowest servant to his brothers.' [26]And he said, 'Yahweh, the God of Shem, be blessed. May Kena'an be a servant to them. [27]May God extend [yapht] Yephet and may he dwell in Shem's tents. May Kena'an be a servant to them.'

[28]Noah lived after the deluge 350 years. [29]So all Noah's days came to 950 years. Then he died.

## The nations

**10** These are the lines of descent of Noah's sons, Shem, Ham and Yephet. Sons were born to them after the deluge.

²The sons of Yephet: Gomer, Magog, Maday [Media], Yavan [Greece], Tubal, Meshek and Tiras. ³The sons of Gomer: Ashkenaz, Riphat and Togarmah. ⁴The sons of Yavan: Elishah, Tarshish, Kittites and Dodanites. ⁵From these, the nations on far shores parted into their countries, each with its language, by their kin-groups among their nations.

⁶The sons of Ham: Kush [Sudan], Misrayim [Egypt], Put and Kena'an. ⁷The sons of Kush: Seba, Havilah, Sabtah, Ra'mah and Sabteka. The sons of Ra'mah: Sheba and Dedan. ⁸Kush fathered Nimrod, who was the first to become a strong man on the earth. ⁹He became a strong man as a hunter before Yahweh; that's why it's said, 'Like Nimrod, a strong man as a hunter before Yahweh'. ¹⁰The beginning of his kingdom was Babel, Erek, Akkad and Kalneh, in the region of Shin'ar. ¹¹From that region Ashshur went out and built Nineveh and the town squares, Kalah, ¹²and Resen between Nineveh and Kalah: that's the big town. ¹³Misrayim fathered Ludites, Anamites, Lehabites, Naphtuhites, ¹⁴Patrusites, Kasluhites (from whom the Pelishtites [Philistines] went out) and Kaphtorites. ¹⁵Kena'an fathered Tsidon his firstborn, Het, ¹⁶the Yebusites, the Amorites, the Girgashites, ¹⁷the Hivvites,the Arkites, the Sinites, ¹⁸the Arvadites, the Tsemarites and the Hamatites. Later, the Kena'anite kin-groups dispersed ¹⁹and the Kena'anite border reached from Tsidon until you come to Gerar, near Azzah [Gaza], until you come to Sedom, Amorah, Admah and Tseboyim, near Lasha. ²⁰These are the descendants of Ham by their kin-groups, by their languages, in their countries, by their nations.

## Babel becomes Babble-on

²¹Sons were also born to Shem, the ancestor of all the descendants of Eber, and Yephet's older brother. ²²The descendants of Shem: Elam, Ashshur, Arpakshad, Lud and Aram. ²³The descendants of Aram: Uts, Hul, Geter and Mash. ²⁴Arpakshad fathered Shelah; Shelah fathered Eber. ²⁵Two sons were born to Eber: the name of the first was Peleg, because in his time the earth divided [palag], and the name of the second was Yoktan. ²⁶Yoktan fathered Almodad, Sheleph, Hatsarmavet, Yerah, ²⁷Hadoram, Uzal, Diklah, ²⁸Obal, Abima'el, Sheba, ²⁹Ophir, Havilah and Yobab. All these were descendants of Yoktan. ³⁰Their settlements went from Mesha until you come to Sephar, the eastern highland. ³¹These are the descendants of Shem by their kin-groups, by their languages, in their countries, by their nations. ³²These are the kin-groups of Noah's sons by their lines of descent according to their nations. From these the nations parted in the earth after the deluge.

**11** Now the entire earth was of one language and common words. ²As people moved on in the east they found a valley in the region of Shin'ar and lived there. ³They said, one to his neighbour, 'Come on, let's make bricks and bake them thoroughly'; so they had brick in place of stone, and tar in place of cement. ⁴They said, 'Come on, let's build ourselves a town and a tower with its top in the heavens, and make a name for ourselves, so we don't disperse over the face of the entire earth.'

⁵But Yahweh went down to see the town and the tower that the human beings had made. ⁶Yahweh said, 'Here, one people with one language for all of them, and this is the first thing they do. So now nothing that they may scheme to do is closed off from them. ⁷Come on, let's go down and make a babble of their language there, so one person won't be able to hear his neighbour's language.'

⁸So Yahweh dispersed them from there over the face of the entire earth and they left off from building the town. ⁹That's why it was named Babel, because there Yahweh made a babble of the language of the entire earth, and from there Yahweh dispersed them over the face of the entire earth.

## The tragedies of family

[10]These are Shem's lines of descent.
 When Shem had lived 100 years, he fathered
  Arpakshad, two years after the deluge.
  [11]After fathering Arpakshad, Shem
  lived 500 years and fathered sons and
  daughters.
[12]When Arpakshad had lived 35 years, he
  fathered Shelah. [13]After fathering Shelah,
  Arpakshad lived 403 years and fathered
  sons and daughters.
[14]When Shelah had lived 30 years, he
  fathered Eber. [15]After fathering Eber,
  Shelah lived 403 years and fathered sons
  and daughters.
[16]When Eber had lived 34 years, he fathered
  Peleg. [17]After fathering Peleg, Eber lived
  430 years and fathered sons and daughters.
[18]When Peleg had lived 30 years, he fathered
  Re'u. [19]After fathering Re'u, Peleg lived 209
  years and fathered sons and daughters.
[20]When Re'u had lived 32 years, he fathered
  Serug. [21]After fathering Serug, Re'u lived
  207 years and fathered sons and daughters.
[22]When Serug had lived 30 years, he fathered
  Nahor. [23]After fathering Nahor, Serug
  lived 200 years and fathered sons and
  daughters.
[24]When Nahor had lived 29 years, he
  fathered Terah. [25]After fathering Terah,
  Nahor lived 119 years and fathered sons
  and daughters. [26]When Terah had lived
  70 years, he fathered Abram, Nahor and
  Haran.
[27]So these are Terah's lines of descent.
Terah fathered Abram, Nahor and Haran,
and Haran fathered Lot. [28]Haran died before
Terah his father in the country that was his
homeland, Ur of the Kasdites [Babylonians].
[29]Abram and Nahor got themselves wives; the
name of Abram's wife was Sarai and the name
of Nahor's wife was Milkah daughter of Haran,
the father of Milkah and of Yiskah. [30]But Sarai
was infertile; she had no child.

## Get yourself out of here

[31]Terah took Abram his son, Lot ben Haran,
his grandson, and Sarai his daughter-in-law,
the wife of Abram, and they left Ur of the
Kasdites together to go to the country of
Kena'an, but they came as far as Harran and
lived there. [32]Terah's days came to 205 years,
and Terah died in Harran.

**12** Yahweh said to Abram, 'Get yourself
from your country, from your
homeland and from your father's household,
to the country that I shall enable you to see,
[2]and I shall make you into a big nation. I shall
bless you and make your name big and you'll
become a blessing. [3]I shall bless the people
who bless you, but the person who slights you
I shall curse. All the kin-groups on the earth
will bless themselves by you.' [4]Abram went as
Yahweh spoke to him, and Lot went with him.
Abram was a man of seventy-five years when
he left Harran.

[5]So Abram took Sarai his wife, Lot his
brother's son, all the property that they
had acquired and all the people that they had
produced in Harran, and left to go to
the country of Kena'an. When they came to the
country of Kena'an, [6]Abram passed through
the country as far as the site at Shekem, as
far as Moreh Oak. The Kena'anites were then
in the country. [7]Yahweh appeared to Abram
and said, 'To your offspring I shall give this
country.' He built an altar there for Yahweh
who had appeared to him. [8]He went on from
there to the mountain country on the east of
Bet-el [Bethel], and spread his tent, Bet-el on
the west, Ha'ay [Ai, 'The Ruin'] on the east. He
built an altar there for Yahweh and called in
Yahweh's name.

[9]Abram moved on, moving on gradually to
the Negeb.

## The fear and the lie

[10]A famine came in the country, and Abram
went down to Misrayim to reside there,
because the famine was heavy in the country.
[11]When he was near coming into Misrayim, he
said to Sarai his wife, 'Here, please: I know that
you're a woman who's attractive in appearance.
[12]When the Misrayimites see you and say,
"She's his wife", they may kill me and let you
live. [13]Please say that you're my sister, in order
that things may be good for me on account
of you and I myself may live on by means of
you.' [14]When Abram came to Misrayim, the

Misrayimites saw that the woman was very attractive. [15]The officials of Par'oh [Pharaoh] saw her and praised her to Par'oh, and the woman was taken into Par'oh's household. [16]For Abram things were good because of her; he had flock, herd, male and female donkeys, servants, maidservants and camels.

[17]But Yahweh touched Par'oh and his household with serious epidemics on account of Sarai, Abram's wife. [18]Par'oh called for Abram and said, 'What is this that you've done to me? Why didn't you tell me that she was your wife? [19]Why did you say "She's my sister", so I got her for myself as a wife? Now, here's your wife; take her and go.' [20]Par'oh gave men orders concerning him and sent him off, him and his wife and all that he had.

**13** So Abram went up from Misrayim, he and his wife and all that he had, and Lot with him, to the Negeb.

[2]Now Abram was a man of great substance, with livestock, with silver and with gold. [3]In his moving on he went from the Negeb as far as Bet-el, as far as the place where his tent had been formerly, between Bet-el and Ha'ay, [4]the site of the altar that he had made there at first. There Abram called in Yahweh's name.

## The implausible promise

[5]Lot, who went with Abram, also had flock and herd and tents, [6]and the region couldn't support them living together, because their property was great. So they couldn't live together. [7]There was argument between the herdsmen of Abram's livestock and the herdsmen of Lot's livestock (and the Kena'anite and the Perizzite were then living in the country). [8]So Abram said to Lot, 'Please, there mustn't be arguing between me and you and between my herdsmen and your herdsmen, because we're brothers. [9]The entire country is before you, isn't it? Part from me, please: if you go north, I'll go south, but if you go south, I'll go north.'

[10]Lot lifted his eyes and looked at the entire plain of the Yarden [Jordan], that it was well-watered, all of it, before Yahweh devastated Sedom and Amorah [Sodom and Gomorrah], like Yahweh's garden, like the country of Misrayim as you come to Tso'ar; [11]and Lot chose for himself the entire Yarden plain.

So Lot moved on east, and they parted, each from his brother. [12]Abram lived in the country of Kena'an, and Lot lived in the towns of the

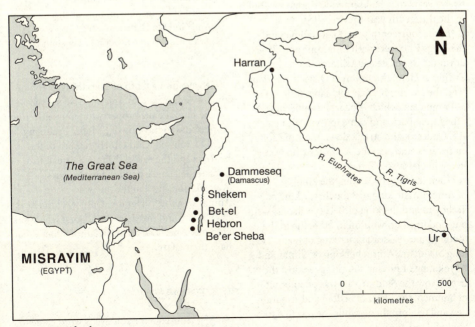

*Genesis 13: Abraham*

plain and put up his tents near Sedom. <sup>13</sup>Now the people of Sedom were bad, wrongdoers in relation to Yahweh, greatly. <sup>14</sup>But Yahweh said to Abram after Lot parted from him, 'Lift your eyes and look, please, from the place where you are, to the north, to the south, to the east and to the west, <sup>15</sup>because the entire country that you're looking at I shall give to you and to your offspring, permanently. <sup>16</sup>I shall make your offspring like the earth's soil, so if a person can count the earth's soil, your offspring will also be counted. <sup>17</sup>Set off, walk about in the country, through its length and its width, because I shall give it to you.'

<sup>18</sup>So Abram moved his tents and came and lived by the Mamre oaks, which are at Hebron, and built an altar for Yahweh there.

## Sedom not such a safe place

**14** In the time of Amraphel king of Shin'ar, Aryok king of Ellasar, Kedorla'omer king of Elam and Tid'al king of Goyim, <sup>2</sup>they did battle with Bera king of Sedom, Birsha king of Amorah, Shin'ab king of Admah, Shem'eber king of Tseboyim, and the king of Bela (i.e. Tso'ar). <sup>3</sup>All these joined together in Siddim Vale (i.e. the Salt Sea). <sup>4</sup>For twelve years they had served Kedorla'omer, but in the thirteenth year they rebelled.

<sup>5</sup>In the fourteenth year, Kedorla'omer and the kings who were with him came and struck down the Repha'ites at Ashterot Karnayim, the Zuzites at Ham, the Emim at Qiryatayim Plain <sup>6</sup>and the Horites in their highland, Se'ir as far as Pa'ran Oak, which is near the wilderness. <sup>7</sup>They went back and came to Ayin Mishpat (i.e. Qadesh), and struck down the Amaleqites' entire area, and also the Amorites who were living in Hatsatson Tamar.

<sup>8</sup>Then the king of Sedom, the king of Amorah, the king of Admah, the king of Tseboyim and the king of Bela (i.e. Tso'ar) went out, and lined up with them for battle in the Siddim Vale: <sup>9</sup>Kedorla'omer king of Elam, Tidal king of Goyim, Amraphel king of Shin'ar and Aryok king of Ellasar, four kings against the five. <sup>10</sup>Now the Siddim Vale was pit after pit of bitumen; the kings of Sedom and Amorah fled and fell into them, while the rest fled to the highland.

## And a time for war

<sup>11</sup>They took all the property of Sedom and Amorah and all their food, and went. <sup>12</sup>So they took Lot, the son of Abram's brother, and his property, and went; he was living in Sedom. <sup>13</sup>Someone who had escaped came and told Abram the Hebrew. He was dwelling by the oaks of Mamre the Amorite, brother of Eshkol and brother of Aner; these were partners in a pact with Abram.

<sup>14</sup>So Abram heard that his brother had been taken captive and mustered his trained men, people born in his household, 318 of them, and went in pursuit as far as Dan. <sup>15</sup>He and his servants split up against them by night, struck them down and pursued them as far as Hobah, which is north of Dammeseq [Damascus]. <sup>16</sup>He took back all the property, and took back both his brother Lot and his property, and also the women and the company. <sup>17</sup>The king of Sedom went out to meet him after he got back from striking down Kedorla'omer and the kings that were with him, in the Shaveh Vale (i.e. the King's Vale), <sup>18</sup>and Melkitsedeq king of Salem brought out bread and wine (he was priest of God On High) <sup>19</sup>and blessed him, saying,

Blessed be Abram by God On High,
   Lord of the heavens and the earth,
<sup>20</sup>And God On High be blessed,
   who has delivered your attackers into your
     hand.

He gave him a tenth of everything. <sup>21</sup>The king of Sedom said to Abram, 'Give me the people but take the property for yourself.' <sup>22</sup>But Abram said to the king of Sedom, 'I raise my hand to Yahweh, God On High, Lord of the heavens and the earth: <sup>23</sup>"From a thread to a bootstrap, if I take anything that's yours . . ."  You will not say, "I'm the one who made Abram wealthy." <sup>24</sup>Not me. Only what the boys have eaten, and the share of the men who went with me, Aner, Eshkol and Mamre – they are to have their share.'

## How can you know?

**15** Subsequently, Yahweh's word came to Abram in a vision: 'Don't be afraid,

Abram. I will be your deliverance, and your wages will be very big.' ²Abram said, 'Lord Yahweh, what will you give me, when I'm going to die childless, and the heir to my household will be a man from Dammeseq, Eli'ezer?'

³So Abram said, 'Here, you haven't given me offspring. Here, someone from my household will come into possession from me.' ⁴But here, Yahweh's word came to him: 'This man won't come into possession from you. No, only someone who comes from inside you – he'll come into possession from you.' ⁵He took him outside and said, 'Look at the heavens, please, and count the stars, if you can count them.' He said to him, 'That's what your offspring will be like.'

⁶He trusted in Yahweh, and he deemed it as faithfulness on his part. ⁷He said to him, 'I am Yahweh who brought you out from Ur of the Kasdites to give you this country as a possession.'

⁸But he said, 'Lord Yahweh, how may I know that I shall take possession of it?' ⁹He said to him, 'Get me a heifer of three years, a goat of three years, a ram of three years, a pigeon and a baby bird.' ¹⁰He got him all these, cut them in half and put one half opposite its neighbour, but didn't cut the birds in half. ¹¹Birds of prey came down on the carcases, but Abram drove them away. ¹²As the sun was about to go, a coma fell on Abram, and there, a great dark dread was falling on him.

### Yahweh confirms a pact or covenant (but will they believe it?)

¹³He said to Abram, 'You can know for sure that your offspring will be residents in a country not theirs. They will serve them, and they will humble them for 400 years. ¹⁴But the nation that they serve I'm indeed going to judge. After this they will get out with much property. ¹⁵But you: you will go to your ancestors with things being well. You'll be buried in a good old age. ¹⁶In the fourth generation they'll come back here, because the Amorites' waywardness is not yet complete.'

¹⁷The sun went and it was dark, and there, a smoking firepot, a blazing torch, that passed between those pieces. ¹⁸On that day Yahweh solemnized a pact with Abram, saying 'To

your offspring I'm giving this country, from the Misrayimite river to the big river (the River Euphrates): ¹⁹the Qenite, the Qenizzite, the Qadmonite, ²⁰the Hittite, the Perizzite, the Repha'ites, ²¹the Amorite, the Kena'anite, the Girgashite and the Yebusite.'

**16** Now Sarai, Abram's wife, had not borne children for him. She had a Misrayimite maidservant; her name was Hagar. ²Sarai said to Abram, 'Here, Yahweh has held me back from giving birth to children. You have sex with my maidservant; maybe I can be built up through her.'

Abram listened to Sarai's voice. ³Sarai, Abram's wife, got Hagar the Misrayimite, her maidservant (after Abram had been living in the country of Kena'an for ten years), and gave her to Abram her husband as a wife. ⁴He had sex with Hagar and she got pregnant. When she saw that she was pregnant, her mistress became of slight worth in her eyes.

### Hagar names God

⁵Sarai said to Abram, 'The violence done to me rests on you. I myself put my maidservant in your arms, she's seen that she's pregnant, and I've become of slight worth in her eyes. Yahweh decide between me and you!' ⁶Abram said to Sarai, 'Here, your maidservant is in your hand. Do to her what's good in your eyes.' Sarai humbled her, and she took flight from her.

⁷Yahweh's envoy found her by a spring of water in the wilderness, by the spring on the Shur road. ⁸He said, 'Hagar, maidservant of Sarai, where have you come from and where are you going?' She said, 'From Sarai, my mistress – I'm taking flight.' ⁹Yahweh's envoy said to her, 'Go back to your mistress. Let yourself be humbled under her hand.' ¹⁰But Yahweh's envoy said to her, 'I shall make your offspring very numerous; they won't be able to be counted because of the large number.'

¹¹Yahweh's envoy said to her, 'There, you're pregnant and you'll give birth to a son. You're to name him Yishma'e'l [Ishmael], because Yahweh has listened [shama] to your humbling. ¹²And he – he'll be a wild donkey of a man, his hand against everyone and everyone's hand against him, and he'll dwell over against all his brothers.'

¹³She named Yahweh who spoke to her, 'You are "God Seeing Me" [El Ro'i]', because (she said), 'Did I really see here, after he was seeing me?' ¹⁴That's why they called the well 'The Well of the Living One Seeing Me' [Be'er Lahay Ro'i]. There, it's between Qedesh and Bered.

¹⁵So Hagar gave birth to a son for Abram, and Abram named his son, to whom Hagar gave birth, Yishma'e'l. ¹⁶Abram was a man of 86 years when Hagar gave birth to Yishma'e'l for Abram.

## God renames Abram and Sarai

**17** Abram was a man of ninety-nine years. Yahweh appeared to Abram and said to him, 'I am God Shadday. Live your life before me and be a person of integrity. ²I shall make my pact between me and you, and make you very, very numerous.' ³Abram fell on his face.

God spoke with him: ⁴'I myself – here is my pact with you. You'll become the ancestor of a horde of nations. ⁵You'll no longer be named Abram. Your name will be Abraham, because I'm making you the "ancestor of a horde" [ab-hamon] of nations. ⁶I shall enable you to be very, very fruitful and I shall make you into nations. From you kings will come. ⁷I shall implement my pact between me and you and your offspring after you, through their generations, as a permanent pact, to be God for you and for your offspring after you. ⁸I shall give to you, and to your offspring after you, the country in which you're residing, the entire country of Kena'an, as a permanent holding, and I shall be God for them.'

⁹God said to Abraham, 'And you, you're to keep my pact, you and your offspring after you, through their generations. ¹⁰This is my pact that you're to keep, between me and you and your offspring after you: the circumcising of every male you have. ¹¹You're to circumcise the flesh of your foreskin. It will be the sign of a pact between me and you. ¹²As a child of eight days, every male among you is to be circumcised, through your generations. The person born in the household or acquired for silver from any foreigner, who doesn't belong to your offspring: ¹³he's definitely to be circumcised, the one born in your household

and the one acquired for silver. My pact in your flesh will be a permanent pact. ¹⁴But a foreskinned male who does not circumcise the flesh of his foreskin: that person will be cut off from his kin. He's contravened my pact.'

¹⁵And God said to Abraham: 'Sarai, your wife: you're not to name her Sarai, because her name is Sarah ['Princess']. ¹⁶I shall bless her. There, I'm giving you a son from her. I shall bless her and she'll become nations; kings of peoples will come from her.'

## A promise for Yishma'e'l

¹⁷Abraham fell on his face, laughed and said to himself, 'Can a child be born to a man of a hundred years, or can Sarah give birth to a child as a woman of ninety years?' ¹⁸Abraham said to God, 'If only Yishma'e'l might live before you.' ¹⁹God said, 'Well: Sarah your wife, she's going to give birth to a son for you, and you're to name him Yitshaq [Isaac]. I shall implement my pact for him as a permanent pact for his offspring after him.

²⁰As for Yishma'e'l: I've listened. There, I'm blessing him, and making him fruitful and making him very, very numerous. Twelve leaders he will father, and I shall make him a big nation. ²¹But my pact I shall implement with Yitshaq, to whom Sarah will give birth for you at this set time next year.' ²²When he had finished speaking with him, God went up from Abraham.

²³So Abraham took Yishma'e'l his son and all those born in his household and all those bought with his silver, every male among the people in Abraham's household, and circumcised the flesh of their foreskin, on that very day, as God had spoken with him. ²⁴Abraham was a man of ninety-nine years at the circumcising of the flesh of his foreskin, ²⁵while Yishma'e'l his son was a boy of thirteen years at the circumcising of the flesh of his foreskin. ²⁶On that very day Abraham and Yishma'e'l his son were circumcised, ²⁷and all the men in his household, those born in the household and those acquired with silver from a foreigner, were circumcised with him.

**18** Yahweh appeared to him by the Mamre oaks, when he was sitting at the tent entrance as the day grew hot. ²He lifted his eyes and looked, and there, three men were standing opposite him. When he saw them, he ran to meet them from the tent entrance, bowed to the ground, ³and said, 'Sirs, please, if I've found grace in your eyes, don't pass by your servant, please. ⁴May someone please get a little water? Bathe your feet. Rest under the tree. ⁵I shall get a bit of bread. Sustain your heart, then you can pass on, since you've passed near your servant.' They said, 'Yes, you may do as you have spoken.'

## Entertaining angels unawares

⁶Abraham hurried to the tent to Sarah and said, 'Hurry, three measures of fine flour, meal, knead it, make bread.' ⁷Abraham ran to the herd, got a nice, tender calf, and gave it to a boy, and he hurried to prepare it. ⁸He got curds and milk and the calf that he'd prepared and set it before them. He stood opposite them under the tree as they ate.

⁹They said to him, 'Where's Sarah your wife?' He said, 'There, in the tent.' ¹⁰He said, 'I shall definitely come back to you at [nature's] reviving time. There, Sarah your wife will have a son.' Sarah was listening at the tent entrance, which was behind him. ¹¹Now Abraham and Sarah were old, going on in years; the way women menstruate had left off from happening for Sarah.

¹²So Sarah laughed to herself, saying 'After I'm withered is there going to be enjoyment for me, with my lord old?' ¹³Yahweh said to Abraham, 'Why did Sarah laugh, saying "Shall I truly give birth, when I'm old?" ¹⁴Is a thing too extraordinary for Yahweh? At this set time I shall come back to you at reviving time and Sarah will have a son.' ¹⁵Sarah lied, saying 'I didn't laugh', because she was afraid. He said, 'No, you laughed.'

¹⁶From there the men set off, and they looked down at Sedom, with Abraham going with them to send them off.

¹⁷Now Yahweh had said, 'Am I going to hide from Abraham what I'm doing, ¹⁸when Abraham is indeed to become a big, numerous nation, and all the nations on the earth are to bless themselves by him? ¹⁹Because I've acknowledged him in order that he may order his children and his household after him

so they may keep Yahweh's way by showing faithfulness in the exercise of authority, in order that Yahweh may bring about for Abraham what he's spoken concerning him.'

## The cry from and for Sedom

²⁰So Yahweh said, 'The outcry of Sedom and Amorah, it's big. Their wrongdoing, it's very grave. ²¹I must go down and see whether they have acted totally in keeping with the outcry that has come to me. If not, I must acknowledge it.'

²²The men turned their face from there and went to Sedom, while Abraham was still standing before Yahweh. ²³Abraham came up and said, 'Will you really sweep away the faithful with the faithless? ²⁴Maybe there are fifty faithful people within the town. Will you really sweep it away and not bear with the place for the sake of the fifty faithful people within it? ²⁵Far be it from you to do a thing like this, putting to death the faithful with the faithless, so the faithful and the faithless are the same. Far be it from you. Isn't the one who exercises authority over the entire earth to exercise authority?'

²⁶Yahweh said, 'If I find in Sedom fifty faithful people within the town, I shall bear with the entire place on account of them.' ²⁷Abraham answered: 'There, please: I've resolved to speak to my Lord, when I'm soil and ash. ²⁸Maybe the fifty faithful will be five short. Will you devastate the entire town because of five?' He said, 'I won't devastate it if I find there forty-five.'

²⁹He spoke yet again to him: 'Maybe forty will be found there.' He said, 'I won't act, on account of the forty.' ³⁰He said, 'May it please not enrage my Lord, and I shall speak. Maybe thirty will be found there.' He said, 'I won't act if I find there thirty.' ³¹He said, 'There, please: I've resolved to speak with my Lord. Maybe twenty will be found there.' He said, 'I won't devastate it on account of the twenty.' ³²He said, 'May it please not enrage my Lord, and I shall speak one last time. Maybe ten will be found there.' He said, 'I won't devastate it on account of the ten.'

³³Yahweh went when he had finished speaking to Abraham, and Abraham went back to his place.

## Sex and violence in Sedom

**19** The two envoys came to Sedom in the evening, and Lot was sitting at the gateway of Sedom. Lot saw them, and got up to meet them. He bowed low, his face to the ground. ²He said, 'Here, sirs, please do turn aside to your servant's house so you can stay the night and bathe your feet. Then you can start early and go on your way.' They said, 'No, because we can stay the night in the square.' ³But he pressed them hard, so they turned aside to him and came into his house. He made a banquet for them and baked flatbread, and they ate.

⁴Before they could go to bed, the men of the town, the men of Sedom, surrounded the house, from young right to old, the entire people, from every part. ⁵They called to Lot and said to him, 'Where are the men who came to you tonight? Bring them out so we can have sex with them.' ⁶Lot went out to them at the entrance but shut the door behind him.

⁷He said, 'My brothers, don't do this wrong, please. ⁸So, please: I have two daughters who haven't had sex with a man. Let me bring them out to you and you can do to them whatever is good in your eyes. Only don't do anything to these men, because this is why they've come under the shelter of my roof-beam.'

⁹But they said, 'Get over there.' They said, 'The man came to reside, and he's actually exercising authority. Now we'll deal badly with you, worse than with them.' They pressed hard against the man (against Lot) and came up to break the door. ¹⁰But the men put out their hand and got Lot to come to them, into the house, and they shut the door. ¹¹As for the men who were at the entrance of the house, they struck them down with a daze, from young right to old, so they became weary of trying to find the entrance.

## Don't look back

¹²The men said to Lot, 'Who else do you have here, sons-in-law, sons, daughters, anyone who belongs to you in the town? Take them out of the place. ¹³Because we're going to devastate this place, because the outcry before Yahweh against them has become so big that Yahweh has sent us to devastate it.' ¹⁴So Lot went out and spoke to his sons-in-law, who were to get his daughters, and said 'Set off, get out of this place, because Yahweh is going to devastate the town.' But in the eyes of his sons-in-law he was like someone making a joke.

¹⁵As dawn came, the envoys pressed Lot, saying 'Set off, take your wife and your two daughters who are to be found here, so you're not swept away because of the waywardness of the town.' ¹⁶But he delayed, so the men took strong hold of his hand, his wife's hand and his two daughters' hand, by Yahweh's mercy on him, and got him out and set him down outside the town. ¹⁷When they had got them outside, one said, 'Escape for your life, don't gaze behind you, don't halt anywhere in the plain. Escape to the highland, so you're not swept away.'

¹⁸Lot said to them, 'No, please, my Lord! ¹⁹There, please: your servant has found grace in your eyes. You've acted in such great commitment with me in preserving my life. But I – I can't flee to the highland in order that the bad event doesn't attach itself to me and I die. ²⁰Here, please – this town's near for fleeing to, and it's small. I can flee there, it's small, so my life can be preserved.'

²¹He said to him, 'Here, I honour your person in this thing too, in not overthrowing the town that you spoke of. ²²Hurry up and escape there, because I can't do anything till you come there.' That's why the town was named Tso'ar ['Small'].

²³As the sun rose on the earth and Lot arrived at Tso'ar, ²⁴Yahweh rained on Sedom and Amorah burning sulphur from Yahweh, from the heavens. ²⁵He overthrew these towns and the entire plain and all the people living in the towns and what grew in the ground.

## A distasteful aftermath

²⁶But his wife gazed behind him and became a salt pilaster.

²⁷Abraham started early in the morning for the place where he had stood before Yahweh ²⁸and looked out over the face of Sedom and Amorah and over the face of the entire plain region. He saw, and there, smoke from the region went up like the smoke from a

furnace. ²⁹So it was that when God devastated the towns of the plain, God was mindful of Abraham and sent Lot out from the middle of the overthrow, when he overthrew the towns in which Lot lived.

³⁰Lot went up from Tso'ar and lived in the highland, his two daughters with him, because he was afraid to live in Tso'ar. He lived in a cave, he and his two daughters. ³¹The firstborn said to the young one, 'Our father is old and there's no one on earth to have sex with us in the way of the entire world. ³²Come on, let's get our father to drink wine so we can sleep with him and get offspring alive through our father.'

³³So they got their father to drink wine that night, and the firstborn went in and slept with her father. He didn't know when she lay down or when she got up. ³⁴Next day the firstborn said to the young one, 'There, I slept with my father last night. Let's get him to drink wine tonight as well, and you come and sleep with him, so we can get offspring alive through our father.' ³⁵So they got their father to drink wine that night as well, and the young one got up and slept with him. He didn't know when she lay down or when she got up.

³⁶So Lot's two daughters got pregnant through their father. ³⁷The firstborn gave birth to a son and named him Mo'ab. He's the ancestor of Mo'ab until today. ³⁸The younger one also gave birth to a son, and named him Ben-ammi. He's the ancestor of the Ammonites until today.

## Do we ever learn?

**20** Abraham moved on from there to the Negeb region and lived between Qadesh and Shur. When he resided in Gerar, ²Abraham said of Sarah his wife, 'She's my sister.' So Abimelek king of Gerar sent and took Sarah. ³But God came to Abimelek in a dream by night and said to him, 'Here, you're a dead man because of the woman whom you've taken. She's married to someone.'

⁴Now Abimelek had not approached her. He said, 'Lord, would you kill a nation even if it's faithful? ⁵That man said to me, "She's my sister", didn't he. And she herself also said, "He's my brother." It was with integrity in my heart and with freedom of guilt in the palms of my hands

that I did this.' ⁶God said to him in the dream, 'I myself both know that you did this with integrity in your heart, and have also held you back from doing wrong in relation to me. That's why I didn't let you touch her. ⁷So now give the man's wife back. Because he's a prophet, he can intercede for you. Save your life. But if you don't give her back, acknowledge that you will definitely die, you and everything that's yours.'

⁸Abimelek started early in the morning, called for all his servants and spoke all these things in their ears. The men were very frightened. ⁹Abimelek called for Abraham and said to him, 'What have you done to us? How did I do wrong in relation to you that you've brought a big wrong on me and on my entire kingdom? You've done deeds with me that should not be done.'

¹⁰Abimelek said to Abraham, 'What did you see that you did this thing?' ¹¹Abraham said, 'I said, "There's just no awe for God in this place, and they'll kill me on account of my wife." ¹²And also, she truly is my sister, my father's daughter, admittedly not my mother's daughter. So she became my wife, ¹³and when God made me wander from my father's household, I said to her, "This is the commitment with which you're to act towards me: every place we come to, say about me: he's my brother."'

## The promise fulfilled

¹⁴Abimelek took flock and herd, servants and maidservants, and gave them to Abraham, and gave his wife Sarah back to him. ¹⁵Abimelek said, 'Here, my country is before you. Live wherever is good in your eyes.' ¹⁶To Sarah he said, 'Here, I'm giving your brother a thousand pieces of silver. Here, it will be cover over the eyes for you and for everyone who is with you and with everyone, and you will be vindicated.'

¹⁷Abraham interceded with God and God healed Abimelek and his wife and his handmaids, and they gave birth (¹⁸because Yahweh had totally held back every womb belonging to Abimelek's household on account of Sarah, Abraham's wife).

**21** When Yahweh attended to Sarah as he had said, Yahweh did for Sarah as he had spoken, ²and Sarah got pregnant and gave birth to a son for Abraham in his old age, at the set time of which God had spoken to him. ³Abraham named his son, who had been born to him, whom Sarah had borne to him, Yitshaq ['He Will Laugh']. ⁴Abraham circumcised Yitshaq his son when he was eight days old, as God ordered him, ⁵Abraham being a man of a hundred years when his son Yitshaq was born to him.

⁶Sarah said, 'God has made laughter for me, since everyone who hears will laugh for me', ⁷and said, 'Who would have uttered to Abraham, "Sarah has nursed children"? But I've given birth to a son for his old age.'

## On not watching your son die

⁸The child grew and was weaned, and Abraham made a big banquet on the day that Yitshaq was weaned. ⁹But Sarah saw the son of Hagar the Misrayimite, to whom she gave birth for Abraham, laughing. ¹⁰She said to Abraham, 'Drive this handmaid and her son out, because this handmaid's son is not to come into possession with my son, with Yitshaq.'

¹¹The thing was very bad in Abraham's eyes, on account of his son. ¹²But God said to Abraham, 'It isn't to be bad in your eyes about the boy or about your handmaid. Everything that Sarah says to you, listen to her voice, because it's through Yitshaq that offspring will be named for you. ¹³The son of the handmaid: I shall make him into a nation, too, because he's your offspring.'

¹⁴Abraham started early in the morning, got bread and a skin of water, and gave them to Hagar. He put them on her shoulder, and the child, and sent her away. She went, and wandered about in the Be'er Sheba Wilderness. ¹⁵When the water in the skin was finished, she threw the child under one of the bushes ¹⁶and went and sat herself down at a distance, a bowshot away, because (she said), 'I'm not going to watch the child die.'

So she sat down at a distance and lifted up her voice and cried. ¹⁷But God listened to the boy's voice, and God's envoy called to Hagar from the heavens and said to her, 'What's with you, Hagar? Don't be afraid, because God has listened to the voice of the boy where he is. ¹⁸Get up, lift up the boy, take strong hold

of him with your hand, because I'm going to make him into a big nation.' ¹⁹And God opened her eyes and she saw a well of water. She went and filled the skin with water, and got the boy to drink.

²⁰God was with the boy. He grew up and lived in the wilderness, and became a bowman. ²¹He lived in the Pa'ran Wilderness. His mother got a wife for him from the country of Misrayim.

## Testimony to the blessing fulfilled

²²At that time Abimelek and Phikol, his army officer, said to Abraham: 'God is with you in everything that you do. ²³So now, swear to me here by God: if you deal falsely with me or with my offspring or with my posterity . . . You're to act with me and with the country in which you've resided in accordance with the commitment with which I've acted with you.' ²⁴Abraham said, 'I myself swear.'

²⁵Abraham reproved Abimelek concerning a well of water that Abimelek's servants had seized. ²⁶Abimelek said, 'I don't know who did this thing. You didn't tell me; I hadn't heard of it till today.' ²⁷Abraham took flock and herd and gave them to Abimelek, and the two of them solemnized a pact. ²⁸Abraham put seven ewes from the flock on their own. ²⁹Abimelek said to Abraham, 'What are these seven ewes here that you've put on their own?' ³⁰He said, 'You're to take the seven ewes from my hand so it will be a witness for me that I dug this well [be'er].' ³¹That's why that place was called Be'er Sheba, because the two of them swore [shaba] there. ³²So they solemnized a pact at Be'er Sheba, and Abimelek and Phikol, his army officer, set off and went back to the Pelishtites' country.

³³He planted a tamarisk at Be'er Sheba and called there in the name of Yahweh, God For Ever. ³⁴Abraham resided in the Pelishtites' country for a long time.

## The test

**22** Subsequently, God tested Abraham. He said to him, 'Abraham!' He said, 'I'm here.' ²He said, 'Please take your son, your only one, the one you love, Yitshaq, get yourself out to the Moriyyah region and offer him up as a burnt offering there, on one of the mountains that I shall say to you.'

³Abraham started early in the morning, saddled his donkey and took two of his boys with him, and Yitshaq his son. He cut the wood for the burnt offering, set off and went to the place that God said to him. ⁴On the third day, Abraham lifted his eyes and saw the place from a distance. ⁵Abraham said to his boys, 'You stay here with the donkey. The boy and I will go over there and bow low, and come back to you.' ⁶Abraham took the wood for the burnt offering and put it on his son Yitshaq, and took in his own hand the fire and the knife, and the two of them walked together.

⁷Yitshaq said to Abraham his father, 'Father!' He said, 'I'm here, son.' He said, 'Here are the fire and the wood, but where's the sheep for the burnt offering?' ⁸Abraham said, 'God will see for himself to the sheep for the burnt offering, son.' The two of them walked together ⁹and came to the place that God had said to him. There Abraham built the altar, laid out the wood, bound his son Yitshaq and placed him on the altar on top of the wood. ¹⁰Abraham put out his hand and got the knife to slaughter his son.

¹¹But Yahweh's envoy called to him from the heavens and said, 'Abraham, Abraham!' He said, 'I'm here.' ¹²He said, 'Don't put out your hand to the boy, don't do anything to him, because now I acknowledge that you live in awe of God; you haven't held back your son, your only son, from me.'

¹³Abraham lifted his eyes and looked: there, a ram caught in a thicket by its horns. Abraham went and got the ram and offered it up as a burnt offering in place of his son. ¹⁴Abraham named that place 'Yahweh Sees' [*Yahweh yir'eh*], so it's said today, 'On Yahweh's mountain it's seen.'

## The promise and the loss

¹⁵Yahweh's envoy called to Abraham a second time from the heavens ¹⁶and said, 'By myself I swear (Yahweh's declaration) that since you've done this thing and not held back your son, your only one, ¹⁷I shall bless you abundantly and make your offspring very numerous,

like the stars in the heavens and like the sand that's on the seashore; your offspring will take possession of their enemies' gateway. ¹⁸All the nations on the earth will bless themselves by your offspring, on account of the fact that you listened to my voice.'

¹⁹Abraham went back to his boys and they set off and went together to Be'er Sheba. Abraham lived at Be'er Sheba.

²⁰Subsequently, it was told to Abraham: 'Here, Milkah has given birth to children for your brother Nahor, too: ²¹Uts his firstborn, Buz his brother, Qemu'el the father of Aram, ²²Kesed, Hazo, Pildash, Yidlaph and Betu'el'; ²³and Betu'el fathered Ribqah. To these eight Milkah gave birth for Nahor, Abraham's brother. ²⁴His secondary wife – her name was Re'umah – also gave birth to Tebah, Gaham, Tahash and Ma'akah.

**23** Sarah's lifetime was 127 years (the years of Sarah's life). ²Sarah died at Arba Township (i.e. Hebron) in the country of Kena'an. Abraham came to lament for Sarah and bewail her.

³Abraham set off from being in the presence of his dead and spoke to the Hittites: ⁴'I'm a resident, a settler, living with you. Give me a burial holding with you, so I may bury my dead away from my presence.' ⁵The Hittites answered Abraham, ⁶'Hear us, sir. You're an almighty leader among us. Bury your dead in the choicest of our burial places. None of us would withhold his burial place from you for burying your dead.'

## The polite negotiation

⁷Abraham got up and bowed low to the people of the country, to the Hittites, ⁸and spoke with them: 'If it's your desire that I should bury my dead away from my presence, hear me and intercede for me with Ephron ben Tsohar, ⁹so he may give me the cave at Makpelah which is his and which is at the edge of his field. May he give it to me for the full silver as a burial holding among you.' ¹⁰Ephron was sitting among the Hittites.

Ephron the Hittite answered Abraham in the ears of the Hittites, all who came to the town gateway: ¹¹'No, sir, listen to me. The field – I give it to you, and the cave that's in it. I give it to you, before the eyes of the members of my people I give it to you. Bury your dead.' <sup>12</sup>Abraham bowed low before the people of the country <sup>13</sup>and spoke with Ephron in the ears of the people of the country: 'But if you yourself would please listen to me: I give you the silver for the field. Take it from me, so I may bury my dead there.' <sup>14</sup>Ephron answered Abraham, <sup>15</sup>'Sir, listen to me: land worth 400 sheqels – between me and you, what's that? Bury your dead.' <sup>16</sup>Abraham listened to Ephron.

So Abraham weighed out to Ephron the silver that he had spoken of in the ears of the Hittites, 400 sheqels of silver, as current for the merchants. <sup>17</sup>And Ephron's field which is at Makpelah, which is close to Mamre (the field and the cave that was in it and all the trees that were in the field, which were in all its border around) passed <sup>18</sup>to Abraham as his acquisition before the eyes of the Hittites, all who had come to the town gateway.

<sup>19</sup>After this Abraham buried his wife Sarah in the cave in the field at Makpelah, close to Mamre (i.e. Hebron) in the country of Kena'an. <sup>20</sup>The field and the cave that was in it became the sure possession of Abraham as a burial holding, from the Hittites.

## Where to find Yitshaq a wife

**24** Abraham was old, going on in years, and Yahweh had blessed Abraham in every way. <sup>2</sup>Abraham said to his senior servant in his household, who ruled over everything that he had, 'Please put your hand under my thigh, <sup>3</sup>and I'll get you to swear by Yahweh the God of the heavens and the God of the earth that you won't get a wife for my son from the daughters of the Kena'anites among whom I'm living, <sup>4</sup>but go to my country, to my homeland, and get a wife for my son, for Yitshaq.'

<sup>5</sup>The servant said to him, 'Maybe the woman won't be willing to follow me to this country. Should I actually take your son back to the country that you left?' <sup>6</sup>Abraham said to him, 'Keep watch so that you don't take my son back there. <sup>7</sup>Yahweh, the God of the heavens, who took me from my father's household and from the country that is my homeland and spoke to me and swore to me: "To your offspring I shall give this country" – he will

send his envoy before you and you'll get a wife for my son from there. <sup>8</sup>If the woman is not willing to follow you, then you'll be free from this oath to me. Only don't take my son back there.'

<sup>9</sup>The servant put his hand under the thigh of Abraham his lord and swore to him concerning this thing. <sup>10</sup>The servant took ten camels from his lord's camels and went, with all the good things belonging to his lord in his possession. He set off and went to Aram of the Two Rivers, to Nahor's town, <sup>11</sup>and got the camels to kneel outside the town at the water well, at evening time, at the time when the women who draw water go out.

## Too much of a coincidence

<sup>12</sup>He said, 'Yahweh, God of my lord Abraham, please make things happen for me today. Act with commitment to my lord Abraham. <sup>13</sup>Here, I'm standing by the water spring, and the daughters of the townspeople are going out to draw water. <sup>14</sup>May the girl to whom I say "Please put down your pitcher so I can drink", and she says "Drink, and I'll also water your camels", may she be the one you've decided on for your servant, for Yitshaq. By this I shall acknowledge that you've acted with commitment to my lord.'

<sup>15</sup>Before he had finished speaking, there was Ribqah [Rebekah], who had been born to Betu'el ben Milkah, wife of Nahor, Abraham's brother, coming out with her pitcher on her shoulder. <sup>16</sup>The girl was very good-looking, a young girl that no one had had sex with. She went down to the spring, filled her pitcher and went up.

<sup>17</sup>The servant ran to meet her and said, 'Please may I sip a little water from your pitcher.' <sup>18</sup>She said, 'Drink, sir', and hurried and lowered her pitcher onto her hand and let him drink. <sup>19</sup>When she had finished letting him drink, she said, 'I'll draw water for your camels as well, till they've finished drinking.' <sup>20</sup>She hurried and emptied her pitcher into the trough, ran back to the well to draw and drew for all his camels, <sup>21</sup>while the man was looking at her, staying quiet, to know whether or not Yahweh had made his journey successful.

²²When the camels had finished drinking, the man got a gold nose-ring (its weight a half-sheqel) and two gold hand-bracelets (their weight ten sheqels). ²³He said, 'Whose daughter are you? Please tell me, is there room at your father's house for us to stay the night?' ²⁴She said to him, 'I'm the daughter of Betu'el ben Milkah, to whom she gave birth for Nahor.' ²⁵And she said to him, 'There's plenty of both straw and fodder with us, and also a place to stay the night.'

## Meet the family

²⁶The man bent his head and bowed low to Yahweh ²⁷and said, 'Yahweh the God of my lord Abraham be blessed, who hasn't abandoned his commitment and his truthfulness with my lord. I myself – Yahweh has led me on the way to the house of my lord's brothers!' ²⁸The girl ran and told her mother's household all these actual words.

²⁹Now Ribqah had a brother; his name was Laban. Laban ran out to the spring to the man. ³⁰When he saw the nose-ring and his sister's two hand-bracelets and heard the words of his sister Ribqah, 'This is how the man spoke to me', he came to the man. There he was, standing by the camels by the spring. ³¹He said, 'Come in, you who are blessed by Yahweh. Why stand outside when I've cleared the house and a place for the camels?'

³²So the man came into the house and unharnessed the camels. He gave the camels straw and fodder, and water to wash his feet and the feet of the men who were with him. ³³Something to eat was set before him, but he said, 'I won't eat until I've spoken my words.' So he said, 'Speak.'

³⁴He said, 'I'm Abraham's servant. ³⁵As Yahweh has greatly blessed my lord, he's become big. He's given him flock and herd, silver and gold, servants and maidservants, camels and donkeys. ³⁶Sarah, my lord's wife, gave birth to a son for my lord in her old age, and he's given him everything that he has. ³⁷My lord got me to swear, saying "You will not get a wife for my son from the daughters of the Kena'anites among whom I'm living in their country. ³⁸No, you are to go to my father's household, to my kin-group, and get a wife for my son."

## It's from God

³⁹I said to my lord, "Maybe the woman won't follow me." ⁴⁰He said to me, "Yahweh, before whom I've walked – he will send his envoy with you and he will make your journey successful. You'll get a wife for my son from my kin-group. ⁴¹Then you'll be free from the vow to me if, when you come to my kin-group, they don't give her to you. You'll be free from the vow to me."

⁴²So I came today to the spring and I said, "Yahweh, God of my lord Abraham: if you could please be one who makes my journey that I'm going on successful! ⁴³Here, I'm standing by the water spring. May the girl who goes out to draw and to whom I say 'Please let me drink a little water from your pitcher', ⁴⁴and she says to me 'Drink, and I'll also draw for your camels', may she be the woman whom Yahweh has decided on for my lord's son."

⁴⁵Before I'd finished speaking in my mind, there was Ribqah going out with her pitcher on her shoulder. She went down to the spring and drew. I said to her, "Please give me a drink." ⁴⁶She hurried and lowered her pitcher from on her shoulder and said, "Drink, and I'll water your camels as well." So I drank, and she watered the camels as well. ⁴⁷I asked her, "Whose daughter are you?" and she said, "The daughter of Betu'el ben Nahor, to whom Milkah gave birth for him." I put the nose-ring on her nose and the bracelets on her hands. ⁴⁸I bent my head and bowed low to Yahweh and blessed Yahweh the God of my father Abraham, who had led me on a true way to get the daughter of my lord's brother for his son.

## Will you go with this man?

⁴⁹So now: if you're going to act with commitment and truthfulness to my lord, tell me. And if not, tell me, so I may turn my face to the right or to the left.'

⁵⁰Laban and Betu'el answered, 'It's from Yahweh that the thing has issued. We can't speak to you bad or good. ⁵¹Here is Ribqah before you. Take her and go, so she can be a wife for your lord's son, as Yahweh has said.'

⁵²When Abraham's servant heard their words, he bowed low to the ground before Yahweh. ⁵³The servant brought out objects of

silver and objects of gold, and clothes, and gave them to Ribqah, and he gave choice things to her brother and to her mother. ⁵⁴They ate and drank, he and the men who were with him, and stayed the night.

They got up in the morning, and he said, 'Send me off to my lord.' ⁵⁵Her brother and her mother said, 'The girl should stay with us for some days – say ten. Afterwards, she can go.' ⁵⁶He said to them, 'Don't make me delay when Yahweh has made my journey successful. Send me off so I can go to my lord.'

⁵⁷They said, 'Let's call the girl and ask for her bidding.' ⁵⁸They called Ribqah and said to her, 'Will you go with this man?' She said, 'I'll go.' ⁵⁹So they sent Ribqah their sister off, with her nanny and Abraham's servant and his men. ⁶⁰They blessed Ribqah and said to her, 'Our sister, may you become thousands of myriads, and may your offspring take possession of the gateway that belongs to people who are hostile to them.' ⁶¹ᵃRibqah and her girls got up, mounted their camels and followed the man.

## The romantic story finds a satisfactory ending

⁶¹ᵇSo the servant took Ribqah and went. ⁶²Now Yitshaq had come from where you come to The Well of the Living One Seeing Me; he was living in the Negeb region. ⁶³Yitshaq had gone out to think in the open country as evening turned its face. He lifted his eyes and saw: there, camels coming. ⁶⁴And Ribqah lifted her eyes and saw Yitshaq. She jumped down from her camel ⁶⁵and said to the servant, 'Who's that man walking in the open country about to meet us?' The servant said, 'That's my lord.' She took her veil and covered herself, ⁶⁶and the servant told Yitshaq all the things that he'd done. ⁶⁷Yitshaq brought her into the tent of Sarah his mother. He took Ribqah and she became his wife, and he loved her. So Yitshaq found consolation after his mother.

**25** Abraham again took a wife; her name was Qeturah. ²She gave birth to Zimran, Yoqshan, Medan, Midyan, Yishbaq and Shuah for him. ³Yoqshan fathered Sheba and Dedan, while Dedan's descendants were the Ashshurites, the Letushites and the Le'ummites, ⁴and Midyan's descendants were

Ephah, Epher, Hanok, Abida and Elda'ah. All these were Qeturah's descendants.

⁵Abraham gave all that he had to Yitshaq, ⁶but to the sons of Abraham's secondary wives Abraham gave gifts while he was still alive and sent them off away from Yitshaq his son eastward, to the east country.

⁷This is the span of the years in the life that Abraham lived: 175 years. ⁸So he breathed his last. Abraham died at a good age, old and full, and was gathered to his kin. ⁹Yitshaq and Yishma'e'l his sons buried him in the cave at Makpelah in the field of Ephron ben Tsohar the Hittite, which is close to Mamre, ¹⁰the field that Abraham acquired from the Hittites. There Abraham and his wife Sarah were buried.

¹¹After Abraham's death, God blessed Yitshaq his son. Yitshaq lived near The Well of the Living One Seeing Me.

## The hand grasping the heel

¹²These are the lines of descent of Yishma'e'l, Abraham's son, to whom Hagar the Misrayimite, Sarah's maidservant, gave birth for Abraham. ¹³These are the names of Yishma'e'l's sons, by their names according to their lines of descent. Yishma'e'l's firstborn, Nebayot, Qedar, Adbe'el, Mibsam, ¹⁴Mishma, Dumah, Massa, ¹⁵Hadad, Tema, Yetur, Naphish and Qedemah. ¹⁶These are Yishma'e'l's sons and these are their names, by their villages and by their enclosures, twelve leaders for their peoples.

¹⁷These are the years of Yishma'e'l's life: 137 years. So he breathed his last and died, and was gathered to his kin. ¹⁸They dwelt from Havilah as far as Shur, which is close to Misrayim, as you come to Ashshur. He fell close to all his brothers.

¹⁹These are the lines of descent of Yitshaq, Abraham's son. Abraham fathered Yitshaq, ²⁰and Yitshaq was a man of forty years when he got himself as wife Ribqah daughter of Betu'el the Aramite of Paddan Aram, sister of Laban the Aramite. ²¹Yitshaq entreated Yahweh on behalf of his wife, because she was infertile. Yahweh let himself be entreated, and Ribqah his wife got pregnant. ²²The children pressed on one another inside her, and she said, 'If this is how it is, why is it that I exist?'

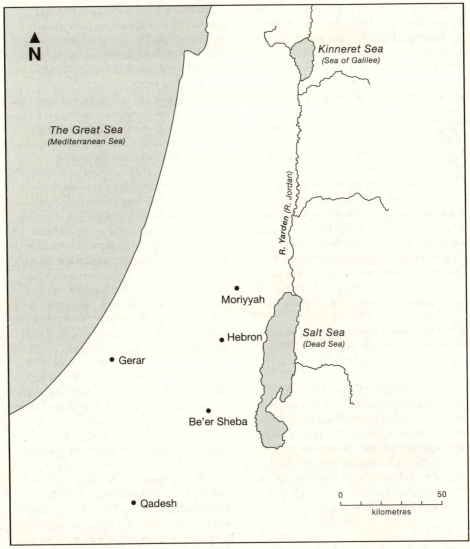

*Genesis 25: Yitshaq (Isaac)*

She went to enquire of Yahweh [23]and Yahweh said to her, 'Two nations are in your womb; two peoples will divide from your body. One people will be stronger than the other people, and the older one will serve the younger one.'

[24]Her time became full for giving birth, and there, twins were in her womb. [25]The first came out red, all of him, like a garment of hair [se'ar]. So they named him Esaw. [26]After that, his brother came out, his hand grasping Esaw's heel [aqeb]. They named him Ya'aqob [Jacob]. Yitshaq was a man of sixty years when they were born.

## The birthright

[27]The boys grew up and Esaw became a man who knew about hunting, a man of the open country, while Ya'aqob was a regular man, staying at the tents. [28]Yitshaq loved Esaw because there was game in his mouth, while Ribqah loved Ya'aqob.

[29]Ya'aqob cooked stew, and Esaw came in from the open country. He was faint. [30]Esaw said to Ya'aqob, 'Please let me wolf down some of the red [adom] stuff, this red stuff, because I'm faint' (that's why they named him Edom).

³¹Ya'aqob said, 'Sell me your birthright today.'
³²Esaw said, 'Here, I'm about to die. What use
is a birthright to me?' ³³Ya'aqob said, 'Swear
to me today.' So he swore to him. He sold
his birthright to Ya'aqob, ³⁴and Ya'aqob gave
Esaw bread and lentil stew. He ate and drank,
and got up and went. So Esaw despised the
birthright.

**26** There was a famine in the country,
apart from the first famine that
happened in Abraham's time, and Yitshaq went
to Gerar, to Abimelek, king of the Pelishtites.
²Yahweh appeared to him and said, 'Don't go
down to Misrayim. Dwell in the country that
I'm telling you about. ³Reside in this country. I
shall be with you and I shall bless you, because
I shall give you and your offspring all these
regions. I shall implement the oath that I
swore to Abraham your father. ⁴I shall make
your offspring as numerous as the stars in the
heavens, and I shall give your offspring all
these regions, and all the nations on earth will
bless themselves by your offspring, ⁵inasmuch
as Abraham listened to my voice and kept
my charge, my orders, my decrees and my
instructions.'

⁶So Yitshaq lived in Gerar. ⁷The people in the
place asked about his wife, and he said 'She's
my sister', because he was afraid to say 'my wife'
in case 'the people in the place kill me because
of Ribqah, because she's good-looking'. ⁸But
when he'd been there some time, Abimelek
king of the Pelishtites looked out through the
window and saw: there was Yitshaq playing
about with Ribqah his wife.

## Do we ever learn? – take two

⁹Abimelek called for Yitshaq and said, 'Here,
really she's your wife! How did you come to
say "She's my sister"?' Yitshaq said to him,
'Because I said, "So I don't die because of her."'
¹⁰Abimelek said, 'What is this that you've done
to us? Almost, someone from the people could
have slept with your wife and brought liability
upon us.' ¹¹Abimelek ordered the entire people:
'Anyone who touches this man or his wife will
absolutely be put to death.'

¹²Yitshaq sowed in that country, and that
year reaped a hundredfold. Yahweh blessed
him. ¹³The man got big, and went on doing

so, until he got very big indeed. ¹⁴He had
livestock, flock and herd, and a large body
of servants, and the Pelishtites were jealous of
him. ¹⁵All the wells that his father's servants
had dug in the time of Abraham his father,
the Pelishtites stopped up and filled with soil,
¹⁶and Abimelek said to Yitshaq, 'Go away from
us, because you're much too numerous for us.'

¹⁷So Yitshaq went from there, camped in
Wadi Gerar and lived there. ¹⁸Yitshaq again
dug the water wells that they had dug in
the time of Abraham his father and that the
Pelishtites had stopped up after Abraham's
death. He named them by the same names as
his father had named them.

¹⁹Yitshaq's servants dug in the wadi and
found there a well of spring water, ²⁰but the
Gerar shepherds got into an argument with
Yitshaq's shepherds, saying 'The water's ours.'
He named the well Eseq ['Contention'] because
they contended with him. ²¹They dug another
well and got into an argument over it, too, and
he named it Sitnah ['Opposition']. ²²He went
on from there and dug another well, and they
didn't argue over it, so he named it Rehobot
['Wide Places'] and said, 'Now Yahweh has
made it wide for us and we'll be fruitful in the
region.' ²³From there he went up to Be'er Sheba.

## We've seen clearly that Yahweh is with you

²⁴Yahweh appeared to him that night and
said, 'I am the God of Abraham your father.
Don't be afraid, because I shall be with you,
and I shall bless you and make your offspring
numerous on account of Abraham my servant.'
²⁵He built an altar there, called in Yahweh's
name and spread his tents there, and Yitshaq's
servants dug out a well there.

²⁶Now Abimelek went to him from Gerar
with Ahuzzat his aide and Phikol his army
officer. ²⁷Yitshaq said to them, 'Why have you
come to me, when you were hostile to me and
you sent me off from being with you?' ²⁸They
said, 'We've seen clearly that Yahweh is with
you, so we said, "There should please be a vow
between us", between us and you. We want to
solemnize a pact with you. ²⁹If you deal badly
with us . . . ! – as we haven't touched you and as
we've done only good with you, and sent you off
in peace. You're now one blessed by Yahweh.'

³⁰So Yitshaq made a banquet for them, and they ate and drank. ³¹They started early in the morning and swore, each to the other. Yitshaq sent them off and they went from being with him in peace. ³²That day, Yitshaq's servants came and told him about the matter of a well that they'd dug, and said to him, 'We've found water.' ³³So he called it Shib'ah ['Sworn Oath']. That's why the name of the town is Be'er Sheba until this day.

³⁴When Esaw was a man of forty years, he got as wife Yehudit daughter of Be'eri the Hittite, and Ba'semat daughter of Elon the Hittite, ³⁵but they became a source of bitterness in spirit to Yitshaq and Ribqah.

## Parents take sides

**27** When Yitshaq was old and his eyes had become too dim to see, he called Esaw his older son and said to him, 'Son!' He said to him, 'I'm here.' ²He said, 'Here, please: I'm old. I don't know the day of my death. ³So now, pick up your equipment, please, your quiver and your bow, and go out to the open country, and hunt game for me. ⁴Make me a dish the way I like, and bring it to me so I can eat, and I will give you my personal blessing before I die.' ⁵Ribqah was listening when Yitshaq was speaking to Esaw his son.

So Esaw went into the country to hunt game to bring, ⁶and Ribqah said to Ya'aqob her son: 'Here, I heard your father speaking to Esaw your brother, saying ⁷"Bring me game and make me a dish so I can eat, and I will bless you before Yahweh before I die." ⁸So now, son, listen to my voice, to what I'm ordering you. ⁹Please go to the flock and get me two choice kid goats from there, and I'll make them into a dish for your father, the way he likes, ¹⁰and you can bring it to your father so he can eat, so he may bless you before he dies.'

¹¹Ya'aqob said to Ribqah his mother, 'Here, my brother Esaw is a hairy man and I'm a smooth-skinned man. ¹²Maybe my father will feel me and in his eyes I shall be like someone playing a trick, and I shall bring on myself slight and not blessing.' ¹³His mother said to him, 'Your slight be on me, son. Just listen to what I say. Go and get them for me.' ¹⁴So he went and got them and brought them to his mother, and his mother made a dish the way his father liked.

## The trick

¹⁵Ribqah got herself the clothes of Esaw her older son, the best ones, which were with her in the house, and put them on Ya'aqob her younger son. ¹⁶The skin of the kid goats she put on his hands and on the smooth part of his neck, ¹⁷and she put the dish, and the bread that she had made, into the hand of Ya'aqob her son.

¹⁸He came to his father and said, 'Father!' He said, 'I'm here. Who are you, son?' ¹⁹Ya'aqob said to his father, 'I'm Esaw your firstborn. I've done as you spoke to me. Please get up, sit and eat some of my game, so you may give me your personal blessing.' ²⁰Yitshaq said to his son, 'How were you so quick in finding it, son?' He said, 'Because Yahweh your God brought it about for me.' ²¹Yitshaq said to Ya'aqob, 'Please come up so I can feel you, son, whether you're really Esaw my son or not.' ²²Ya'aqob came up to Yitshaq his father, and he felt him and said, 'The voice is Ya'aqob's voice, but the hands are Esaw's hands.' ²³He didn't recognize him because his hands were like the hands of Esaw his brother, hairy.

So he blessed him. ²⁴He said, 'Are you really my son Esaw?' He said, 'I am.' ²⁵He said, 'Bring it up to me so I can eat some of my son's game, in order that I can give you my personal blessing.' He brought it up to him and he ate, and he brought him wine and he drank. ²⁶His father Yitshaq said to him, 'Please come up and kiss me, son.' ²⁷He came up and kissed him, and he smelled his clothes.

So he blessed him: 'See: my son's smell is like the smell of the open country that Yahweh has blessed. ²⁸God give you from the dew of the heavens and from the richness of the earth, a large quantity of grain and new wine. ²⁹Peoples are to serve you, nations to bow low to you. Be lord to your brothers; your mother's sons are to bow low to you. Cursed be the people who curse you, blessed be those who bless you.'

## The alternative blessing

³⁰When Yitshaq had finished blessing Ya'aqob and Ya'aqob had scarcely gone right out

from the presence of Yitshaq his father, Esaw his brother came in from his hunting. ³¹He, too, made a dish and brought it to his father and said to his father, 'May my father get up and eat some of his son's game, so you may give me your personal blessing.' ³²Yitshaq his father said to him, 'Who are you?' He said, 'I'm your son, your firstborn, Esaw.' ³³Yitshaq trembled, trembled with force, and said, 'Then who was that who hunted game and brought it to me and I ate of it all before you came, and I blessed him? Yes, he will come to be blessed.'

³⁴When Esaw heard his father's words, he cried out with a very loud and bitter cry. He said to his father, 'Bless me, me as well, father!' ³⁵He said, 'Your brother came with guile and took your blessing.' ³⁶He said, 'He's called "Ya'aqob", isn't he? He's grabbed me [aqab] these two times. He took my birthright, and there, he's taken my blessing now.' And he said, 'Haven't you saved a blessing for me?'

³⁷Yitshaq answered Esaw, 'There, I've made him lord in relation to you. I've given him all his brothers as servants and sustained him with grain and new wine. So what can I therefore do for you, son?' ³⁸Esaw said to his father, 'Do you have one blessing, father? Bless me, me as well, father!' Esaw lifted up his voice and cried.

³⁹Yitshaq his father answered him, 'There, your settlement will be from the richness of the earth and from the dew of the heavens above. ⁴⁰By your sword you'll live, and you will serve your brother. But as you wander you'll break his yoke from your neck.'

⁴¹Esaw was antagonistic to Ya'aqob because of the blessing with which his father had blessed him, and Esaw said to himself, 'When the time for grieving over my father arrives, I shall kill Ya'aqob my brother.'

## Reasons to get out from here

⁴²Ribqah was told the words of Esaw her older son, and she sent and called for Ya'aqob her younger son, and said to him, 'Here, Esaw your brother is going to console himself by killing you. ⁴³Now, son, listen to my voice. Set off, take flight to Harran to Laban my brother ⁴⁴and stay with him for some time till your brother's wrath turns away, ⁴⁵till your brother's

anger with you turns away and he puts out of mind what you've done to him. And I'll send and get you from there. Why should I be bereaved of both of you in one day?'

⁴⁶So Ribqah said to Yitshaq, 'I'm dismayed about my life because of the Hittite women. If Ya'aqob takes a wife from among the Hittite women like these, from the women of this country, what good will life be for me?'

**28** So Yitshaq called for Ya'aqob, blessed him and ordered him, 'You're not to take a wife from among the Kena'anite women. ²Set off for yourself to Paddan Aram to the house of Betu'el, your mother's father, and get yourself a wife from there from among the daughters of Laban, your mother's brother. ³May God Shadday bless you and make you fruitful and make you numerous, so you become a congregation of peoples. ⁴May he give you Abraham's blessing, you and your offspring with you, so you take possession of the country where you're residing, which God gave Abraham.'

⁵So Yitshaq sent Ya'aqob off and he went to Paddan Aram to Laban ben Betu'el, the Aramite, the brother of Ribqah, the mother of Ya'aqob and Esaw.

⁶Esaw saw that his father Yitshaq had blessed Ya'aqob and sent him off to Paddan Aram to get himself a wife from there, and in blessing him had ordered him: 'You're not to take a wife from among the Kena'anite women', ⁷and Ya'aqob had listened to his father and mother and gone to Paddan Aram. ⁸Esaw saw that the Kena'anite women were bad in the eyes of Yitshaq his father. ⁹So Esaw went to Yishma'e'l and got himself as wife Mahalat daughter of Yishma'e'l, Abraham's son, sister of Nebayot, as an addition to his wives.

## The stairway to heaven

¹⁰Ya'aqob left Be'er Sheba and went to Harran. ¹¹He came upon a site and stayed the night there because the sun had gone. He got one of the stones from the site and put it at his head and lay down in that site.

¹²He had a dream. There – a ramp was put up on the earth with its top reaching to the heavens, and there – God's envoys were going up and down on it. ¹³And there – Yahweh was

standing by him. He said, 'I am Yahweh, the God of Abraham your father and the God of Yitshaq. The ground that you're lying on, I shall give to you and to your offspring. ¹⁴Your offspring will be like the earth's soil. You'll break out to the west, to the east, to the north and to the south. All the kin-groups on the earth will bless themselves by you, and by your offspring. ¹⁵There, I shall be with you. I shall keep you wherever you go and bring you back to this land, because I won't abandon you until I've done what I've spoken to you of.'

¹⁶Ya'aqob woke up from his sleep and said, 'Yahweh is definitely here in this site, and I myself didn't know!' ¹⁷He was in awe, and he said, 'How awe-inspiring is this site! This is none other than a house of God, and that is a gateway into the heavens!'

¹⁸Ya'aqob started early in the morning, took the stone where he had put his head, set it up as a column and poured oil on the top of it. ¹⁹He named the site Bet-el [Bethel; 'House of God'] – Luz was the name of the town at first, however. ²⁰And Ya'aqob made a pledge: 'If God will be with me, and will keep me on this journey that I'm going on, and will give me bread to eat and clothes to wear, ²¹and I come back to my father's house with things being well, then Yahweh will be God for me, ²²and this stone that I've set up as a column will be God's house, and of everything that you give me I will rigorously give a tenth to you.'

## Ya'aqob shows his muscle

**29** Ya'aqob took up his journey and went to the country of the Easterners. ²He looked, and there – a well in the fields, and three herds of sheep lying there by it, because people used to water the herds from that well. The stone on the well's mouth was big; ³all the herds would gather there, and people would roll the stone off the well's mouth and water the sheep, and put the stone back in its place on the well's mouth.

⁴Ya'aqob said to them, 'Brothers, where are you from?' They said, 'We're from Harran.' ⁵He said to them, 'Do you know Laban ben Nahor?' They said, 'We know him.' ⁶He said to them, 'Are things well with him?' They said, 'They're well. There – Rahel [Rachel] his daughter is

coming with the sheep.' ⁷He said, 'Here, it's still the middle of the day. It's not time for the livestock to gather. Water the sheep and go pasture them.' ⁸They said, 'We can't, till all the herds gather and people roll the stone from on the well's mouth and we water the sheep.'

⁹While he was still speaking with them, Rahel came with the sheep that belonged to her father, because she was a shepherd. ¹⁰When Ya'aqob saw Rahel daughter of Laban, his mother's brother, and the flock of Laban, his mother's brother, Ya'aqob came up, rolled the stone from on the well's mouth and watered the flock of Laban his mother's brother; ¹¹and Ya'aqob kissed Rahel and lifted his voice and cried. ¹²Ya'aqob told Rahel that he was her father's brother and that he was Ribqah's son, and she ran and told her father. ¹³When Laban heard the report of Ya'aqob, his sister's son, he ran to meet him, kissed him and hugged him, and brought him into his house. He told Laban all these things, ¹⁴and Laban said to him, 'Certainly you're my own bone and flesh.' He stayed with him for a period of a month.

## The deceiver deceived

¹⁵Laban said to Ya'aqob, 'Because you're my brother, are you to serve me for nothing? Tell me: what are your wages to be.' ¹⁶Now Laban had two daughters. The name of the elder was Le'ah and the name of the younger Rahel. ¹⁷Le'ah's eyes were soft, but Rahel was attractive in shape and attractive in appearance. ¹⁸Ya'aqob loved Rahel. So he said, 'I'll serve you seven years for Rahel, your younger daughter.' ¹⁹Laban said, 'For me to give her to you will be better than for me to give her to another man. Stay with me.' ²⁰So Ya'aqob served seven years for Rahel, but in his eyes they were like a few days because of his love for her. ²¹Then Ya'aqob said to Laban, 'Give me my wife, since my time is complete, so I may have sex with her.' ²²Laban gathered all the people of the place and made a banquet, ²³but in the evening he got Le'ah his daughter and brought her to him, and he had sex with her. (²⁴Laban gave her Zilpah his maidservant, to Le'ah his daughter as her maidservant.)

²⁵So in the morning: there, it was Le'ah! He said to Laban, 'What's this that you've done to

me? It was for Rahel that I served with you, wasn't it? Why have you beguiled me?' ²⁶Laban said, 'It's not done like that in our place, giving the younger one before the firstborn. ²⁷Complete the week for the one, and we'll give you the other as well, for the service that you'll give with me for another seven years more.' ²⁸Ya'aqob did so. He completed the week for the one, then he gave him Rahel his daughter as wife. (²⁹Laban gave Rahel his daughter Bilhah his maidservant as her maidservant.)

³⁰So Ya'aqob had sex with Rahel and also loved Rahel more than Le'ah, and he served with him another seven years more.

## I want to know what love is

³¹Yahweh saw that Le'ah was disliked and he opened her womb; whereas Rahel was infertile. ³²So Le'ah got pregnant and gave birth to a son, and named him Re'uben, because (she said), 'Yahweh has seen [ra'ah] my humbling; now my husband will love me [ye'ehabeni].' ³³She got pregnant again and gave birth to a son, and said, 'Yahweh has heard [shama] that I'm disliked and has given me this one as well', so she named him Shim'on [Simeon]. ³⁴She got pregnant again and gave birth to a son, and said, 'Now this time my husband will become attached [lava] to me, because I've given birth to three sons for him.' That's why he named him Levi. ³⁵She got pregnant again and gave birth to a son and said, 'This time I shall confess [yadah] Yahweh.' That's why she named him Yehudah [Judah]. Then she stopped giving birth.

**30** Rahel saw that she couldn't give birth for Ya'aqob. Rahel was jealous of her sister and she said to Ya'aqob, 'Give me children! Otherwise, I'm going to die!' ²Ya'aqob's anger raged at Rahel. He said, 'Am I in the place of God, who has held back the fruit of the womb from you?' ³She said, 'Here's my handmaid Bilhah. Have sex with her, so she can give birth on my knees and I can also be built up through her.'

⁴So she gave him Bilhah her maidservant as wife, and Ya'aqob had sex with her. ⁵Bilhah got pregnant and gave birth to a son for Ya'aqob. ⁶Rahel said, 'God has given judgement [dan] for me; yes, he's listened to my voice and given

me a son.' That's why she named him Dan. ⁷Bilhah, Rahel's maidservant, got pregnant again and gave birth to a second son for Ya'aqob. ⁸Rahel said, 'An almighty wrestling match [naphtulim] I've fought with my sister; yes, I've won.' So she named him Naphtali.

## Wives, sons and a daughter

⁹Le'ah saw that she had stopped giving birth, and she got Zilpah her maidservant and gave her to Ya'aqob as wife. ¹⁰Zilpah, Le'ah's maidservant, gave birth to a son for Ya'aqob, ¹¹and Le'ah said, 'Luck [gad] has come!' So she named him Gad. ¹²Zilpah, Le'ah's maidservant, gave birth to a second son for Ya'aqob, ¹³and Le'ah said 'What good fortune [oshri] I have, because daughters will call me fortunate.' So she named him Asher.

¹⁴In the days of the wheat harvest, Re'uben went and found love-plants in the fields and brought them to Le'ah his mother. Rahel said to Le'ah, 'Please give me some of your son's love-plants.' ¹⁵She said to her, 'Was it a small thing, your taking my husband, and you're also going to take my son's love-plants?' Rahel said, 'Therefore he can sleep with you tonight in return for your son's love-plants.'

¹⁶In the evening Ya'aqob came from the fields, and Le'ah went out to meet him and said, 'I'm the one you're to have sex with, because I've paid a hire charge for you, with my son's love-plants.' So he slept with her that night, ¹⁷and God listened to Le'ah. She got pregnant and gave birth to a fifth son for Ya'aqob. ¹⁸Le'ah said, 'God gave me my hire charge [sakar], because I gave my maidservant to my husband.' So she named him Yissakar [Issachar].

¹⁹Le'ah got pregnant again, and gave birth to a sixth son for Ya'aqob. ²⁰Le'ah said, 'God has given me a good endowment [zebed]; this time my husband will elevate me [yizbeleni], because I've given birth to six sons for him.' So she named him Zebulun. ²¹Later, she gave birth to a daughter, and named her Dinah.

²²But God was mindful of Rahel. God listened to her and opened her womb, ²³and she got pregnant and gave birth to a son, and said, 'God has gathered up [asaph] my reviling.' ²⁴So she named him Yoseph [Joseph], saying 'May Yahweh add [yoseph] another son to me!'

## *The competition to be the shrewdest sheep farmer*

²⁵When Rahel had given birth to Yoseph, Ya'aqob said to Laban, 'Send me off, so I may go to my place, to my country. ²⁶Give me my wives and my children for whom I've served you so I may go, because you yourself know the service that I've given you.' ²⁷Laban said to him, 'Please, if I've found grace in your eyes: I've divined that Yahweh has blessed me because of you.' ²⁸So he said, 'Specify your wages with me and I'll give it to you.' ²⁹He said to him, 'You yourself know how I've served you and how your livestock have been with me, ³⁰because the little that you had before me has broken out so as to become a large number. Yahweh has blessed you wherever I've been. But now, when am I myself also to do something for my household?'

³¹He said, 'What could I give you?' Ya'aqob said, 'You won't give me anything. If you'll do this thing for me, I'll pasture your flock again, I'll keep them. ³²I'll pass through your entire flock today, removing from there every speckled and spotted sheep, and every dark sheep among the lambs, and the spotted and speckled among the goats. It will be my wages. ³³My faithfulness will avow for me on the future day when you come to look at my wages before you. Every one with me that's not speckled or spotted among the goats or dark among the lambs: that one with me will have been stolen.'

³⁴Laban said, 'There, yes, let it be in accordance with your word.' ³⁵But that day he removed the streaked and spotted he-goats and all the speckled and spotted she-goats, every one that had white on it, and every dark one among the lambs. He put them into the care of his sons, ³⁶and put three days' journey between him and Ya'aqob while Ya'aqob was pasturing the rest of Laban's flock.

## *Trouble follows*

³⁷Ya'aqob got for himself fresh canes of poplar, and almond and plane, and peeled white stripes in them, exposing the white that was on the rods. ³⁸The canes that he had peeled he stationed in the troughs, in the water containers that the flock came to drink from, in front of the flock. They were in heat and they came to drink, ³⁹so the flock were in heat by the canes, and the flock gave birth to streaked, speckled and spotted young. ⁴⁰The lambs Ya'aqob divided off, and put the flock's faces towards the streaked and the completely dark animals in Laban's flock. So he put herds for himself each on its own and didn't put them by Laban's flock. ⁴¹Every time the flock was in heat, the well-built females, Ya'aqob would put the canes in the troughs before the eyes of the flock so they would be in heat by the canes. ⁴²But with the feebler in the flock, he didn't put them there. So the feeble ones were Laban's and the well-built ones were Ya'aqob's.

⁴³So the man broke out very greatly. He had a large flock, maidservants, servants, camels and donkeys.

# 31

But he heard the words of Laban's sons: 'Ya'aqob has taken everything that was our father's. It's from what was our father's that he's made all this substance.' ²And Ya'aqob saw Laban's face: there, it wasn't the same with him as it had been in previous days.

³And Yahweh said to Ya'aqob, 'Go back to your ancestors' country, to your homeland. I will be with you.'

## *The divisiveness of stuff*

⁴Ya'aqob sent and called Rahel and Le'ah to the fields, to his flock, ⁵and said to them, 'I see your father's face, that it's not the same towards me as it was in previous days, but my father's God has been with me. ⁶You yourselves know that I've served your father with all my energy, ⁷but your father – he's played about with me and changed my wages ten times. But God didn't let him deal badly with me. ⁸If he would say, "The speckled will be your wages", the entire flock would give birth to speckled. If he would say, "The streaked will be your wages", the entire flock would give birth to streaked. ⁹God has taken away your father's livestock and given them to me.

¹⁰At the time of the flock's being in heat, in a dream I lifted my eyes and looked: there,

the rams that were mounting the flock were streaked, speckled and mottled. ¹¹In the dream God's envoy said to me, "Ya'aqob!" I said "I'm here!" ¹²He said, "There, please lift up your eyes and look. All the rams that are mounting the flock are streaked, speckled and mottled, because I've seen everything that Laban has been doing to you. ¹³I am the God of Bet-el, where you anointed a column, where you made a pledge to me. Now, set off, get out of this country, go back to the country that is your homeland."'

¹⁴Rahel and Le'ah answered him, 'Do we still have a share, a domain, in our father's household? ¹⁵Aren't we deemed outsiders by him, because he sold us and also totally consumed the silver paid for us? ¹⁶Because all the wealth that God has rescued from our father: it belongs to us and to our children. So now, do everything that God has said to you.'

## The secret leaving

¹⁷So Ya'aqob set off. He put his children and his wives on camels ¹⁸and drove all his livestock and all his property that he had gained, the livestock he had acquired, which he had gained in Paddan Aram, to come to Yitshaq his father in the country of Kena'an.

¹⁹Now Laban had gone to shear his flock, and Rahel stole the effigies that belonged to her father. ²⁰Ya'aqob stole away without Laban the Aramite knowing, by not telling him that he was taking flight.

²¹So he took flight, he and all that he had. He set off and crossed the river and set his face towards the highland of Gil'ad. ²²It was told Laban on the third day that Ya'aqob had fled. ²³He took his brothers with him and pursued after him a seven days' journey, and caught up with him in the highland of Gil'ad. ²⁴But God came to Laban the Aramite in a dream by night and said to him, 'Keep watch over yourself so you don't speak anything with Ya'aqob, either good or bad.'

²⁵Laban reached Ya'aqob when Ya'aqob had pitched his tent in the highland, and Laban had pitched, with his brothers, in the highland of Gil'ad. ²⁶Laban said to Ya'aqob, 'What have you done? You stole away without me knowing and you drove my daughters like captives of the sword. ²⁷Why did you secretly take flight and steal away from me and not tell me? I would have sent you off with rejoicing and with singing, with tambourine and with guitar. ²⁸You didn't give me leave to kiss my sons and my daughters. Now you've been idiotic in doing that. ²⁹It's in the almightiness of my hand to deal badly with you. But the God of your father said to me last night: "Keep watch over yourself to avoid speaking anything with Ya'aqob, either good or bad."

³⁰So now: you have indeed gone because you were very keen for your father's household. Why have you stolen my gods?'

## The ironic confrontation

³¹Ya'aqob answered Laban, 'Because I was afraid, because I said, "So that you don't seize your daughters from me." ³²The person with whom you find your gods will not live. In front of our brothers, examine for yourself what I have and take it for yourself.' Ya'aqob didn't know that Rahel had stolen them.

³³Laban came into Ya'aqob's tent, into Le'ah's tent and into the two handmaids' tent, but didn't find them. He went out of Le'ah's tent and came into Rahel's tent. ³⁴Now Rahel had taken the effigies, put them in the camel saddle and sat on them. Laban felt through everything in the tent and didn't find them. ³⁵She said to her father, 'May it not cause rage in my lord's eyes that I cannot get up before you, because a woman's period is upon me.' So he searched but didn't find the effigies.

³⁶It enraged Ya'aqob and he got into an argument with Laban. Ya'aqob avowed to Laban, 'What is my affront, what is my wrongdoing, that you chased after me, ³⁷that you felt through all my possessions? What did you find of all your household possessions? Put it here in front of my brothers and your brothers, so they can decide between the two of us.

³⁸These twenty years I've been with you. Your ewes and your goats haven't miscarried. I haven't eaten rams from your flock. ³⁹I haven't brought you animals that had been killed; I myself dealt with the loss. From my hand you would look for what was stolen by day and what was stolen by night. ⁴⁰I became: by day

heat consumed me and by night frost. My sleep fled from my eyes. ⁴¹I've had these twenty years in your household; I served you fourteen years for your two daughters and six years for your flock, and you changed my wages ten times. ⁴²If the God of my father, the God of Abraham and the Reverence of Yitshaq, had not been mine, now you would have sent me off empty-handed. But God saw my humbling and the weariness of the palms of my hands, and he decided last night.'

## A family divided by miles

⁴³Laban answered Ya'aqob, 'The daughters are my daughters, the children are my children, the flock is my flock. All that you see is mine. But about my daughters: what can I do today about them or about their children to whom they have given birth? ⁴⁴So now, come, let's solemnize a pact, you and I, and it will be a witness between you and me.'

⁴⁵So Ya'aqob took a stone and set it up as a column, ⁴⁶and Ya'aqob said to his brothers, 'Collect stones.' They got stones and made a heap, and they ate there by the heap. ⁴⁷Laban called it Yegar Sahaduta, while Ya'aqob called it Gal'ed ['Witness Mound' in Aramaic and Hebrew]. ⁴⁸Laban said, 'This heap is a witness between me and you today.' That's why he named it Gal'ed, ⁴⁹and 'The Watchtower' [*hammitspah*], because (he said), 'May Yahweh watch between me and you when one is hidden from the other. ⁵⁰If you humble my daughters or take wives on top of my daughters: when there's no one with us, see, God will be a witness between me and you.'

⁵¹And Laban said to Ya'aqob, 'Here is this heap and here is the column that I have thrown up between me and you. ⁵²This heap will be a witness and the column will be a witness that I will not go past this heap to you and you will not go past this heap to me, or this column, to act badly. ⁵³The God of Abraham and the God of Nahor (the God of their ancestor) decide between us.'

Ya'aqob swore by the Reverence of his father Yitshaq, ⁵⁴and Ya'aqob offered a sacrifice at the mountain and invited his brothers to eat bread. They ate bread and stayed the night at the mountain. ⁵⁵Laban started early in the morning, kissed his children and his daughters, and blessed them. Then Laban set off and went back to his place.

## Ya'aqob scared

**32** As Ya'aqob went on his way, God's envoys came upon him. ²When he saw them, Ya'aqob said, 'This is God's camp', and he named that place Mahanayim ['Two Camps']. ³Ya'aqob sent envoys before him to Esaw his brother in the country of Se'ir, in Edom's region. ⁴He ordered them: 'You're to say this to my lord, to Esaw: "Your servant Ya'aqob has said this: 'While I've resided with Laban and remained till now, ⁵oxen, donkeys and flock, and servants and maidservants, have come to belong to me. I've sent to tell my lord so as to find grace in your eyes.'"'

⁶The envoys came back to Ya'aqob, saying, 'We came to your brother, to Esaw, and yes, he's coming to meet you, and 400 men with him.' ⁷Ya'aqob was very fearful. It put pressure on him. He divided the people that were with him, the flock, the herd and the camels into two camps, ⁸and said 'If Esaw comes to the one camp and strikes it down, the remaining camp will escape.'

⁹Ya'aqob said, 'God of my father Abraham, God of my father Yitshaq, Yahweh, you who said to me, "Go back to your country, to your homeland, and I shall do good things with you", ¹⁰I'm too small for all the acts of commitment and all the truthfulness with which you've acted towards your servant. With my cane I crossed this Yarden and now I've become two camps. ¹¹Save me from the hand of my brother, please, from the hand of Esaw, because I'm frightened of him, in case he comes and strikes me down, mother with children. ¹²You yourself said, "I shall definitely do good things with you and make your offspring like the sand of the sea, which cannot be counted because of the large number."'

## Buying off a brother

¹³He stayed the night there that night, then got an offering for Esaw his brother from what had come into his care: ¹⁴two hundred she-goats and twenty he-goats, two hundred ewes and

twenty rams, <sup>15</sup>thirty milch camels and their young, forty cows and ten bulls, and twenty she-donkeys and ten he-donkeys. <sup>16</sup>He put them into the care of his servants, herd by herd on its own, and said to his servants, 'Cross over before me, but put a space between herd and herd.'

<sup>17</sup>He ordered the first: 'Esaw my brother will meet you and ask you, "To whom do you belong? Where are you going? To whom do these belong, before you?" <sup>18</sup>You're to say, "They're your servant Ya'aqob's. They're an offering sent to my lord, to Esaw. Here, he himself is behind us as well."' <sup>19</sup>He ordered both the second and the third and also all the ones who were going behind the herds: 'You're to speak these very words to Esaw when you reach him. <sup>20</sup>You're also to say, "Here, your servant Ya'aqob is behind us"', because (he said), 'I'll mollify his face with an offering that goes ahead of my face, then afterwards I'll face him, and maybe he'll welcome my face.' <sup>21</sup>Thus the offering crossed ahead of his face, while he stayed that night in the camp.

<sup>22</sup>So he set off that night and took his two wives, his two maidservants and his eleven children, and crossed the Yabboq crossing. <sup>23</sup>He took them and got them to cross the wadi and got what belonged to him across.

## God struggles

<sup>24</sup>Ya'aqob was left on his own, and a man wrestled [*aboq*] with him until dawn rose. <sup>25</sup>He saw that he had not overcome him, so he touched him at his hip socket, and Ya'aqob's hip socket was put out as he wrestled with him. <sup>26</sup>He said, 'Let me go off, because the dawn has risen.' He said, 'I won't let you go off unless you bless me.' <sup>27</sup>He said to him, 'What is your name?' He said, 'Ya'aqob'. <sup>28</sup>He said, 'You will no longer be named Ya'aqob, but Yisra'el [Israel], because you have striven [*sarah*] with God and with human beings and have prevailed.' <sup>29</sup>Ya'aqob asked, 'Tell me your name, please.' He said, 'Why is it that you ask my name?' But he blessed him there.

<sup>30</sup>Ya'aqob named the place Peni'el ['God's Face'], 'because I saw God face to face, but my life was rescued.' <sup>31</sup>The sun rose on him as he crossed by Penu'el. He was limping because of his hip. <sup>32</sup>That's why the Israelites don't eat the thigh muscle that's on the hip socket until this day, because he touched Ya'aqob at the hip socket, at the thigh muscle.

**33** Ya'aqob lifted his eyes and looked: there, Esaw was coming, and with him 400 men. He divided the children among Le'ah, Rahel and the two maidservants, <sup>2</sup>and put the maidservants and their children first, Le'ah and her children after them, and Rahel and Yoseph last. <sup>3</sup>He himself passed on before them and bowed to the ground seven times until he came right up to his brother. <sup>4</sup>Esaw ran to meet him, embraced him, threw his arms round his neck and kissed him, and they cried.

## An amicable parting

<sup>5</sup>He lifted his eyes and saw the women and the children, and said 'Who are these of yours?' He said, 'The children with whom God has graced your servant.' <sup>6</sup>The maidservants came up, they and their children, and bowed low. <sup>7</sup>Le'ah also came up, she and her children, and bowed low. Last, Yoseph came up, he and Rahel, and they bowed low. <sup>8</sup>He said, 'What do you mean by this entire camp that I've met?' Ya'aqob said, 'To find grace in my lord's eyes.'

<sup>9</sup>Esaw said, 'I have much, brother. What you have must remain yours.' <sup>10</sup>Ya'aqob said, 'No, please. If I've found grace in your eyes, please, take my offering from my hand, because on account of this I have seen your face, like seeing God's face, and you accepted me. <sup>11</sup>Please take my blessing which has been brought to you, because God has graced me, and because I have everything.' So he urged him, and he took it.

<sup>12</sup>Then he said, 'Let's move on and go. I'll go in front of you.' <sup>13</sup>But he said to him, 'My lord knows that the children are frail and the flock and herd are suckling with me. Should they drive them hard for one day, all the flock will die. <sup>14</sup>My lord should please pass on before his servant. I myself will lead on gently, at the pace of the cattle that are before me and at the pace of the children, until I come to my lord in Se'ir.' <sup>15</sup>Esaw said, 'May I please place with you some of the company that's with me?' He said, 'Why is this? I want to find grace in my lord's eyes.'

<sup>16</sup>So Esaw went back that day on his journey to Se'ir, <sup>17</sup>while Ya'aqob moved on to Sukkot, built himself a house there and made bivouacs

[*sukkot*] for his livestock. That's why they named the place Sukkot.

## The seduction

¹⁸Ya'aqob came with things being well to the town of Shekem, which was in the country of Kena'an, when he came from Paddan Aram, and he camped facing the town. ¹⁹He acquired the plot in the fields where he spread his tent from the sons of Hamor, Shekem's father, for a hundred qesitas. ²⁰He put up an altar there and called it 'God, the God of Yisra'el'.

**34** Dinah daughter of Le'ah, to whom she had given birth for Ya'aqob, went out to see the daughters of the region. ²Shekem ben Hamor, the Hivvite, the leader of the region, saw her, took her and slept with her. He forced her, ³but he himself was attached to Dinah, Ya'aqob's daughter. He loved the girl, and tried to reassure the girl. ⁴Shekem said to Hamor his father: 'Get me this young woman as wife.'

⁵When Ya'aqob heard that he had defiled Dinah his daughter, his sons were with his livestock in the fields, so Ya'aqob remained silent until they came. ⁶Hamor, Shekem's father, went out to Ya'aqob to speak with him. ⁷When Ya'aqob's sons came from the fields, the men were pained when they heard. It deeply enraged them, because he had done something villainous in Yisra'el in sleeping with Ya'aqob's daughter. Such a thing is not done.

⁸Hamor spoke with them: 'Shekem my son, he got attracted to your daughter. Please give her to him as wife. ⁹Make marriages with us: give your daughters to us and take our daughters for yourselves. ¹⁰You can live with us and the region will be before you. Live and move about in it, acquire holdings in it.' ¹¹Shekem said to her father and to her brothers, 'May I find grace in your eyes: what you say to me, I will give. ¹²Set a very large marriage payment and gift upon me, and I will give as you say to me. But give me the girl as wife.'

## The sign of a pact becomes a ploy

¹³Ya'aqob's sons answered Shekem and Hamor his father with guile when they spoke, because he'd defiled their sister Dinah.

¹⁴They said to them, 'We can't do this thing, give our sister to a man who has a foreskin, because that would be a reviling to us. ¹⁵Only on this basis could we consent to you: if you become like us by every male of yours being circumcised, ¹⁶and we will give our daughters to you and take your daughters for ourselves and we will live with you, and we'll become one people. ¹⁷But if you won't listen to us by being circumcised, we'll take our daughter and go.'

¹⁸Their words were good in the eyes of Hamor and in the eyes of Hamor's son Shekem, ¹⁹and the boy didn't delay doing the thing, because he wanted Ya'aqob's daughter.

Now he was the most honoured person in his father's household. ²⁰So Hamor and his son Shekem came to the gateway of their town and spoke to the men of their town: ²¹'These people are peaceable with us. They should live in the region and move about in it. This region – here, it's wide enough for them. We'll take their daughters for ourselves and give our daughters to them. ²²Only on this basis will the people consent to us to live with us, to become one people: by every male of ours being circumcised as they are circumcised. ²³Their livestock and their acquisitions and all their animals: will they not become ours? Let's just consent to them so they will live with us.' ²⁴They listened to Hamor and to Shekem his son, all the people who went out to the gateway of his town; and every male, all the people who went out to the gateway of his town, were circumcised.

## Should our sister be treated like a whore?

²⁵On the third day, when they were hurting, two of Ya'aqob's sons, Shim'on and Levi, Dinah's brothers, got each his sword, came to the town when it was confident, and killed every male. ²⁶Hamor and Shekem his son they killed with the mouth of the sword. They got Dinah from Shekem's house and left, ²⁷while Ya'aqob's sons came on the men who had been run through and plundered the town because they had defiled their sister. ²⁸Their flock, their herd and their donkeys, what was in the town and what was in the fields, they took. ²⁹All their resources, all their little ones and all their women, they captured and plundered, with everything that was in the houses.

³⁰Ya'aqob said to Shim'on and Levi, 'You've brought disaster on me, making me stink to the people who live in the country, the Kena'anite and the Perizzite. I'm few in number. They'll gather against me and strike me down and I'll be annihilated, I and my household.' ³¹But they said, 'Should he treat our sister like a whore?'

# 35

God said to Ya'aqob, 'Set off and go up to Bet-el. Live there and make an altar there for the God who appeared to you when you were taking flight from your brother Esaw.' ²Ya'aqob said to his household and to all who were with him, 'Remove the foreign gods that are among you. Purify yourselves. Change your clothes. ³We shall set off to go up to Bet-el and make an altar there for the God who answered me on the day when I was under pressure and has been with me on the way that I've gone.' ⁴They gave Ya'aqob all the foreign gods that were in their hand, and the rings that were in their ears, and Ya'aqob buried them under the oak that was near Shekem.

## The passing of Ya'aqob's first love

⁵As they moved on, an almighty terror came over the towns that were round about them, and they didn't pursue after Ya'aqob's sons. ⁶So Ya'aqob came to Luz, which is in the country of Kena'an (i.e. Bet-el), he and all the company that was with him. ⁷He built an altar there and called the place 'God of Bet-el', because God had appeared to him there when he was taking flight from his brother. ⁸Deborah, Ribqah's nanny, died, and was buried below Bet-el, beneath the oak. So they named it Wailing Oak. ⁹God appeared to Ya'aqob again when he had come from Paddan Aram, and he blessed him. ¹⁰God said to him, 'Your name is Ya'aqob. You'll no longer be named Ya'aqob; rather, Yisra'el will be your name.' So he named him Yisra'el. ¹¹God said to him, 'I am God Shadday. Be fruitful and numerous. A nation and a congregation of nations will come into being from you. Kings will come out of your insides. ¹²The country that I gave to Abraham and to Yitshaq I shall give to you, and I shall give the country to your offspring after you.' ¹³God went up from him at the place where he spoke with him, ¹⁴and Ya'aqob put up a column at the place where God had spoken with him, a stone column,

and poured out a libation on it and poured oil on it. ¹⁵Ya'aqob named the place where God spoke with him Bet-el.

¹⁶They moved on from Bet El, and there was still a distance in the country so as to come to Ephrat, but Rahel gave birth, and had a tough time in giving birth. ¹⁷When she was having a tough time in giving birth, the midwife said to her, 'Don't be afraid, because this one is a son for you, too.' ¹⁸As her breath was leaving her, because she was dying, she named him Ben-oni ['Son of My Trouble']; but his father called him Binyamin [Benjamin; 'Son of My Right Hand']. ¹⁹So Rahel died and was buried on the road to Ephrat (i.e. Bet Lehem). ²⁰Ya'aqob put up a column over her grave (it's the column at Rahel's grave until today).

## Ya'aqob and Yisra'el, Esaw and Edom

²¹Yisra'el moved on and spread his tent beyond Herd Tower. (²²While Yisra'el was dwelling in that region, Re'uben went and slept with Bilhah, his father's secondary wife; and Yisra'el heard.)

Ya'aqob's sons were twelve:

²³the sons of Le'ah: Ya'aqob's firstborn, Re'uben; Shim'on; Levi; Yehudah; Yissakar; and Zebulun;

²⁴the sons of Rahel: Yoseph and Binyamin;

²⁵the sons of Bilhah, Rahel's maidservant: Dan and Naphtali;

²⁶the sons of Zilpah, Le'ah's maidservant: Gad and Asher.

These were Ya'aqob's sons who were born to him in Paddan Aram.

²⁷Ya'aqob came to Yitshaq his father at Mamre at Arba Township (i.e. Hebron), where Abraham and Yitshaq resided. ²⁸Yitshaq was a man of 180 years. ²⁹Yitshaq breathed his last and died, and was gathered to his kin, old and full of years. Esaw and Ya'aqob, his sons, buried him.

# 36

This is the line of Esaw (i.e. Edom). ²Esaw got his wives from the daughters of Kena'an: Adah daughter of Elon the Hittite, Oholibamah daughter of Anah, the daughter of Tsib'on the Hivvite, ³and Ba'semat daughter of Yishma'el, the sister of Nebayot. ⁴Adah gave birth to Eliphaz for Esaw, Ba'semat gave birth to Re'u'el, ⁵and Oholibamah gave birth to Ye'ush, Yalam and Qorah.

These are the sons of Esaw who were born to him in the country of Kena'an. ⁶Esaw took his wives, his sons and his daughters, and the people in his household, his livestock, all his animals and all his acquisitions that he had gained in the country of Kena'an, and went to a country away from Ya'aqob his brother, ⁷because their property was too big for them to live together and the country where they were residing couldn't support them because of their livestock. ⁸So Esaw lived in the highland of Se'ir (Esaw is Edom).

## Excluded but not forgotten

⁹This is the line of Esaw, the ancestor of Edom, in the highland of Se'ir. ¹⁰These are the names of Esaw's sons:

Eliphaz, son of Esaw's wife Adah;
Re'u'el, son of Esaw's wife Ba'semat.

¹¹The sons of Eliphaz were Teman, Omar, Tsepho, Ga'tam and Qenaz.
¹²Timna was a secondary wife to Esaw's son Eliphaz; she gave birth to Amaleq for Eliphaz.
These were the descendants of Esaw's wife Adah.
¹³These were the sons of Re'u'el: Nahat, Zerah, Shammah and Mizzah.
These were the descendants of Esaw's wife Ba'semat.
¹⁴These were the sons of Esaw's wife Oholibamah daughter of Anah, the daughter of Tsib'on: she gave birth to Ye'ush, Yalam and Qorah for Esaw.
¹⁵These are the clans among Esaw's descendants. The descendants of Eliphaz, Esaw's firstborn:

| | |
|---|---|
| the Teman clan | ¹⁶the Qorah clan |
| the Omar clan | the Ga'tam clan |
| the Tsepho clan | the Amaleq clan |
| the Qenaz clan | |

These are the clans of Eliphaz in the country of Edom; these are the descendants of Adah.

¹⁷These are the descendants of Re'u'el, Esaw's son:

| | |
|---|---|
| the Nahat clan | the Shammah clan |
| the Zerah clan | the Mizzah clan |

These are the clans of Re'u'el in the country of Edom; these are the descendants of Ba'semat, Esaw's wife.

¹⁸These are the descendants of Oholibamah, Esaw's wife:

| | |
|---|---|
| the Ye'ush clan | the Qorah clan |
| the Ya'lam clan | |

These are the clans of Oholibamah daughter of Anah, Esaw's wife.

¹⁹These are the descendants of Esaw and these are their clans (i.e. Edom).

## Kings in Edom

²⁰These are the sons of Se'ir the Horite, the people living in the country: Lotan, Shobal, Tsib'on, Anah, ²¹Dishon, Etser and Dishan. These are the Horites' clans, Se'ir's descendants, in the country of Edom.
²²The sons of Lotan were Hori and Hemam; Lotan's sister was Timna.
²³These are the sons of Shobal: Alvan, Mahanat, Ebal, Shepho and Onam.
²⁴These are the sons of Tsib'on: both Ayyah and Anah (he was the Anah who found the hot springs in the wilderness when he was pasturing the donkeys of Tsib'on his father).
²⁵These are the children of Anah: Dishon and Oholibamah, Anah's daughter.
²⁶These are the sons of Dishan: Hemdan, Eshban, Itran and Keran.
²⁷These are the sons of Etser: Bilhan, Za'avan and Aqan.
²⁸These are the sons of Dishan: Uts and Aran.
²⁹These are the Horites' clans: the clans Lotan, Shobal, Tsib'on, Anah, ³⁰Dishon, Etser and Dishan. These are the Horites' clans by their clans in the country of Se'ir.

³¹These are the kings who reigned in the country of Edom before a king reigned among the Yisra'elites:
³²Bela ben Be'or reigned in Edom; his town's name was Dinhabah.
³³Bela died and Yobab ben Zerah from Botsrah reigned in his place.

³⁴Yobab died and Husham from the Temanites' country reigned in his place. ³⁵Husham died and Hadad ben Bedad, who struck down Midyan in Mo'ab's region, reigned in his place; his town's name was Avit. ³⁶Hadad died and Samlah from Masrekah reigned in his place. ³⁷Samlah died and Sha'ul from Broads on the River reigned in his place. ³⁸Sha'ul died and Ba'al ben Akbor reigned in his place. ³⁹Ba'al Hanan ben Akbor died and Hadar reigned in his place; his town's name was Pa'u, and his wife's name was Mehetabel daughter of Matred, the daughter of Gold Water.

⁴⁰These are the names of Esaw's clans by their kin-groups, by their places, with their names:

| | |
|---|---|
| the Timna clan | the Pinon clan |
| the Alvah clan | ⁴²the Qenaz clan |
| the Yetet clan | the Teman clan |
| ⁴¹the Oholibamah clan | the Mibtsar clan |
| | ⁴³the Magdi'el clan |
| the Elah clan | the Iram clan |

These are the clans of Edom, by their settlements in the country that is their holding (i.e. Esaw, Edom's ancestor).

## The dreamer

**37** Ya'aqob lived in the country where his father had resided, the country of Kena'an. ²This is Ya'aqob's line.

Yoseph, when he was seventeen years of age, was pasturing the flock with his brothers; he was a boy with the sons of Bilhah and Zilpah, his father's wives. Yoseph brought bad criticism of them to their father. ³Now Yisra'el loved Yoseph above all his sons, because he was the son of his old age. He made an ornamented coat for him. ⁴His brothers saw that their father loved him above all his brothers, and they became hostile to him and couldn't speak peaceably to him.

⁵Yoseph had a dream and told his brothers, and they were yet more hostile to him. ⁶He said to them, 'Please listen to this dream that I've had. ⁷There – we were binding sheaves in the middle of the fields. There – my sheaf got up, yes, stood. And there – your sheaves were gathering round and bowing low to my sheaf.' ⁸His brothers said to him, 'Are you really to reign over us? Or are you really to rule over us?' They were yet more hostile to him because of his dreams and because of his words.

⁹He had another dream and recounted it to his brothers. 'Here – I had another dream. There – the sun and the moon and eleven stars were bowing down to me.' ¹⁰He recounted it to his father and to his brothers, and his father reprimanded him and said to him, 'What's this dream that you've had? Are we really to come, I and your mother and your brothers, to bow low to the ground to you?' ¹¹So his brothers were jealous of him, while his father kept the thing in mind.

¹²His brothers went to pasture their father's flock at Shekem. ¹³Yisra'el said to Yoseph, 'Your brothers are pasturing at Shekem, aren't they. Come on, I'll send you to them.' He said to him, 'Here I am.'

## The dreamer walks into a trap

¹⁴So he said to him, 'Go and see if things are well with your brothers, and if things are well with the flock, please, and bring back word to me.' He sent him from the Hebron Vale and he came to Shekem. ¹⁵A man found him: there, he was wandering about in the fields. The man asked him, 'What are you looking for?' ¹⁶He said, 'I'm looking for my brothers. Do tell me, please, where they're pasturing.' ¹⁷The man said, 'They've moved on from here, because I heard them say, "Let's go to Dotan."'

Yoseph followed his brothers and found them at Dotan. ¹⁸They saw him from a distance, and before he got near them they plotted to put him to death. ¹⁹They said one to another, 'Here, that master of dreams is coming! ²⁰So now, come on, let's kill him and throw him into one of the cisterns. We'll say a bad animal ate him. We'll see what will become of his dreams.'

²¹But Re'uben heard them and rescued him from their hand. He said, 'We won't take his life.' ²²Re'uben said to them, 'Don't shed his blood. Throw him into this cistern that's in the

wilderness. Don't lay a hand on him' (in order that he might rescue him from their hand and give him back to his father). ²³So when Yoseph came to his brothers, they stripped Yoseph of his coat, the ornamented coat that was on him, ²⁴and took him and threw him into the cistern. (The cistern was empty; there was no water in it.)

²⁵They sat down to eat bread, but lifted their eyes and looked: there, a caravan of Yishma'e'lites coming from Gil'ad, their camels carrying spices, balm and myrrh, going to take them down to Misrayim. ²⁶Yehudah said to his brothers, 'What's the gain when we kill our brother and cover up his blood? ²⁷Come on, let's sell him to the Yishma'e'lites. Our hands – they shouldn't be on him, because he's our brother, our flesh.' His brothers listened.

### The fate of the famous coat

²⁸So Midyanite men, traders, passed by, and they pulled and got Yoseph up out of the cistern. They sold Yoseph to the Yishma'e'lites for twenty silver pieces, and they brought Yoseph to Misrayim.

²⁹Re'uben went back to the cistern, and there – Yoseph wasn't in the cistern. He tore his clothes ³⁰and went back to his brothers and said, 'The child isn't there! And I – where am I going to go?'

³¹They got Yoseph's coat, slaughtered a goat, dipped the coat in the blood ³²and sent off the ornamented coat so they might bring it to their father, and they said, 'We found this. Please recognize: is it your son's coat, or not?' ³³He recognized it and said, 'My son's coat! A bad animal has devoured him! Yoseph has been torn to pieces!' ³⁴Ya'aqob tore his clothes, put sack round his hips and took up grieving for his son for a long time. ³⁵All his sons and daughters set about consoling him, but he refused to be consoled and said, 'I shall go down to She'ol to my son grieving.' So his father bewailed him.

³⁶Meanwhile the Midyanites sold him into Misrayim, to Potiphar, Par'oh's courtier, the guards officer.

**38** At that time Yehudah went down from his brothers and turned aside

near an Adullamite man; his name was Hirah. ²Yehudah saw there the daughter of a Kena'anite man, whose name was Shua, and he took her. He had sex with her, ³she got pregnant, and she gave birth to a son and named him Er. ⁴She got pregnant again and gave birth to a son, and named him Onan. ⁵Once more she got pregnant and gave birth to a son, and named him Shelah. He was at Kezib when she gave birth to him.

### A daughter-in-law betrayed

⁶Yehudah got a wife for his firstborn, Er. Her name was Tamar. ⁷But Er, Yehudah's firstborn, did what was bad in Yahweh's eyes, and Yahweh let him die. ⁸Yehudah said to Onan, 'Have sex with your brother's wife. Be a brother-in-law to her. Set up offspring for your brother.' ⁹But Onan knew that the offspring would not be his, and when he had sex with his brother's wife he would let it be lost on the ground so he wouldn't give offspring to his brother. ¹⁰But what he did was bad in Yahweh's eyes, and Yahweh also let him die. ¹¹Yehudah said to Tamar his daughter-in-law, 'Live as a widow in your father's household till my son Shelah grows up', because (he said), 'So he doesn't also die, like his brothers.' So Tamar went and lived in her father's household.

¹²Time went on, and Shua's daughter, Yehudah's wife, died. Yehudah was consoled, and went up to the men who were shearing his flock, he and his neighbour Hirah the Adullamite, to Timnah. ¹³It was told Tamar: 'Here, your father-in-law is coming up to Timnah for the shearing of his flock.' ¹⁴Tamar removed her widow's clothes from upon her, covered herself with a veil and wrapped herself up, and sat at the entrance to Two Wells, which is on the road to Timnah, because she saw that Shelah had grown up but she had not been given to him as wife.

¹⁵Yehudah saw her and thought she was a whore, because she had covered her face. ¹⁶He turned aside to her by the road and said 'Come on, can I have sex with you?' because he didn't know that it was his daughter-in-law. She said, 'What will you give me when you have sex with me?' ¹⁷He said, 'I myself will send a kid goat from the flock.' She said, 'If you give

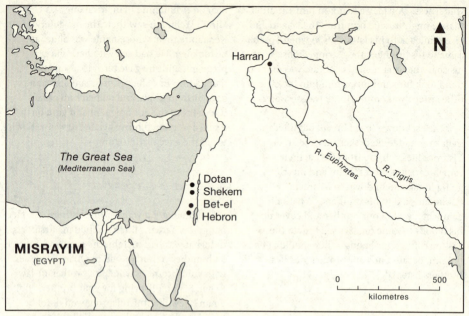

Harran

*The Great Sea*
(Mediterranean Sea)

Dotan
Shekem
Bet-el
Hebron

R. Euphrates
R. Tigris

**MISRAYIM**
(EGYPT)

0                    500
kilometres

N

*Genesis 38: Ya'aqob (Jacob)*

me a pledge till you send it.' ¹⁸He said, 'What's the pledge that I should give you?' She said, 'Your seal and your cord, and the staff that's in your hand.' He gave them to her and he had sex with her, and she got pregnant by him.

### Another deceiver deceived

¹⁹She set off and went, and removed her veil from upon her and put on her widow's clothes. ²⁰Yehudah sent the kid goat by the hand of the Adullamite, his neighbour, to get the pledge from the woman's hand, but he couldn't find her. ²¹He asked the people of her place: 'Where's that hierodule, the one at Two Wells, by the road?' They said, 'There's been no hierodule here.' ²²He went back to Yehudah and said, 'I couldn't find her. Furthermore, the people of the place said, "There's been no hierodule here."' ²³Yehudah said, 'She can have it for herself, so that we don't become an object of contempt. Here, I sent her this kid goat, but you couldn't find her.'

²⁴Some three months later, it was told Yehudah: 'Tamar your daughter-in-law has been whoring. Indeed, there, she's pregnant through whoring.' Yehudah said, 'Bring her out. She should be burned.' ²⁵As she was

being brought out, she sent to her father-in-law, saying: 'It's by the man to whom these belong that I'm pregnant.' So she said, 'Please recognize: who's the one to whom these seal and cord and staff belong?' ²⁶Yehudah recognized them and said, 'She is more in the right than me, because of the fact that I didn't give her to my son Shelah.' He didn't have sex with her again.

²⁷At the time of her giving birth, there – twins were in her womb. ²⁸When she was giving birth, one put out a hand, and the midwife took a red thread and tied it on his hand, saying 'This one came out first.' ²⁹But when he took back his hand, his brother came out, and she said, 'What a breakout you've made for yourself!' So they named him Perets ['Breakout']. ³⁰Afterwards his brother, on whose hand was the red thread, came out. They named him Zerah ['Shining'].

### But Yahweh was with Yoseph

**39** So Yoseph had been taken down to Misrayim and a Misrayimite, Potiphar, Par'oh's courtier, the guards officer, had acquired him from the hand of the Yishma'e'lites who had taken him down there.

²But Yahweh was with Yoseph and he became a successful man. He was in the household of his Misrayimite lord, ³and his lord saw that Yahweh was with him and that everything that he was doing, Yahweh made succeed in his hand. ⁴So Yoseph found grace in his eyes. He ministered to him, and he appointed him over his household and put into his hand everything that belonged to him.

⁵From the time that he appointed him over his household and over everything that belonged to him, Yahweh blessed the Misrayimite's household because of Yoseph. Yahweh's blessing was on everything that belonged to him, in the house and in the fields. ⁶He abandoned everything that he had into Yoseph's hands, and with him he didn't know about anything except the bread that he was eating.

Yoseph was attractive in shape and attractive in appearance, ⁷and subsequently his lord's wife set her eyes on Yoseph and said, 'Sleep with me.' ⁸He refused, and said to his lord's wife, 'Here, with me, my lord doesn't know about what's in the house. Everything that belongs to him he's put into my hand. ⁹There's no one bigger in this household than me. He hasn't held back anything from me except you, because you're his wife. How could I do this massively bad thing, and do wrong in relation to God?' ¹⁰When she spoke to Yoseph day after day he didn't listen to her about sleeping beside her or being with her.

¹¹On such a day he came into the house to do his work. None of the people of the household was there in the house. ¹²She caught hold of him by his coat, saying 'Sleep with me.' He abandoned his coat in her hand, fled and went outside.

## The false allegation

¹³When she saw that he had abandoned his coat in her hand and fled outside, ¹⁴she called the people of the household and said to them: 'Look, he brought us a Hebrew man to fool about with us! He came to me in order to sleep with me and I called out in a loud voice, ¹⁵and when he heard that I raised my voice and called out, he abandoned his coat beside me and fled, and went outside.' ¹⁶She set his coat down beside her until his lord came home, ¹⁷and she spoke to him in the same words: 'The Hebrew servant that you brought to us came to me in order to fool about with me, ¹⁸and when I raised my voice and called out he abandoned his coat beside me and fled outside.'

¹⁹When his lord heard his wife's words that she spoke to him, 'These very things your servant did to me', his anger raged. ²⁰Yoseph's lord took him and put him in the jailhouse, the place where the king's prisoners were imprisoned. So he was there in the jailhouse, ²¹but Yahweh was with Yoseph and he extended commitment to him, and gave him grace in the eyes of the jailhouse officer.

²²The jailhouse officer put into Yoseph's care all the prisoners who were in the jailhouse. Everything that they were doing there, he was the one doing it. ²³The jailhouse official didn't look at any matter that was in his care, because Yahweh was with him and whatever he was doing Yahweh made succeed.

**40** Subsequently, the king of Misrayim's wine waiter and baker did wrong in relation to their lord the king of Misrayim. ²Par'oh was furious with his two courtiers, with the chief wine waiter and with the chief baker, ³and he put them in the keep at the guards officer's house, in the jailhouse, the place where Yoseph was confined.

## Interpretations belong to God

⁴The guards officer appointed Yoseph to them and he ministered to them. They had been some time in the keep, ⁵and the two of them had a dream, each his own dream the same night, each in accordance with the interpretation of his dream – the king of Misrayim's wine waiter and baker, who were confined in the jailhouse. ⁶Yoseph came to them in the morning and saw that they were vexed. ⁷He asked Par'oh's courtiers who were with him in the keep in his lord's house, 'Why are your faces looking bad today?' ⁸They said to him, 'We had a dream, and there's no one to interpret it.' Yoseph said to them, 'Interpretations belong to God, don't they. Please recount them to me.'

⁹The chief wine waiter recounted his dream to Yoseph: 'In my dream: there, a vine before

me. ¹⁰On the vine were three branches. Even as it was budding, its blossom came out and its clusters ripened as grapes. ¹¹Now Par'oh's cup was in my hand, and I got the grapes, pressed them into Par'oh's cup and placed the cup into Par'oh's palm.'

¹²Yoseph said to him, 'This is the interpretation. The three branches are three days. ¹³In yet three days Par'oh will lift up your head and put you back in your position. You'll place Par'oh's cup in his hand in accordance with the former rule when you were his wine waiter.

¹⁴But be mindful of me with you, when things are good for you. Act in commitment with me, please, and make mention of me to Par'oh so you get me out of this house. ¹⁵Because I was actually stolen from the country of the Hebrews, and also I've done nothing here that they should have put me in the cistern.'

## The interpreter forgotten

¹⁶The chief baker saw that he had interpreted it as something good, and he said to Yoseph, 'In my dream, also: there, three wicker baskets on my head, ¹⁷and in the top basket, all kinds of food for Par'oh, the work of a baker. But the birds were eating them from the basket, from on my head.' ¹⁸Yoseph answered, 'This is the interpretation. The three baskets are three days. ¹⁹In yet three days, Par'oh will lift up your head from on you and hang you on a tree, and the birds will eat your flesh from on you.'

²⁰On the third day, Par'oh's birthday, he made a banquet for all his servants, and lifted up the head of the chief wine waiter and the head of the chief baker among his servants. ²¹He put the chief wine waiter back into his wine-waiting so that he placed the cup in Par'oh's palm ²²and the chief baker he hanged, as Yoseph had interpreted to them. ²³But the chief wine waiter was not mindful of Yoseph. He put him out of mind.

**41** At the end of two years, Par'oh himself was dreaming, and there, he was standing by the Ye'or [Nile]. ²There, from the Ye'or seven cows going up, attractive in appearance and sturdy in body, and they pastured among the reeds. ³And there, seven

more cows going up from the Ye'or after them, bad-looking in appearance and thin in body, and they stood beside the cows on the bank of the Ye'or. ⁴The cows that were bad-looking in appearance and thin in body ate the seven cows that were attractive in appearance and sturdy.

Par'oh woke up, ⁵went to sleep and dreamt a second time. There, seven ears of grain growing up on a single stalk, sturdy and good-quality. ⁶And there, seven ears that were thin and scorched by the east wind springing up after them. ⁷The thin ears swallowed the seven sturdy, full ears. Par'oh woke up. There, it was a dream.

⁸In the morning his spirit was agitated, and he sent and called for all Misrayim's diviners and all its experts. Par'oh recounted his dream to them. But no one could interpret them for Par'oh.

## The interpreter remembered

⁹The chief wine waiter spoke with Par'oh: 'I'm going to make mention of my wrongdoings today. ¹⁰When Par'oh was furious with his servants and put me in the keep in the guards officer's house, me and the chief baker, ¹¹we had a dream the same night, I and he. We each dreamt in accordance with the interpretation of his dream. ¹²There with us was a Hebrew boy, a servant of the guards officer. We recounted them to him and he interpreted our dreams for us. Each one in accordance with his dream he interpreted. ¹³As he interpreted it for us, so it happened. I was put back into my position and him they hanged.'

¹⁴So Par'oh sent and called for Yoseph. They got him to run from the cistern, he shaved and changed his clothes, and he came to Par'oh. ¹⁵Par'oh said to Yoseph, 'I had a dream and there is no one to interpret it. I've heard it said about you, that you can listen to a dream and interpret it.' ¹⁶Yoseph answered Par'oh: 'Not me. God is the one who will answer with things that will be well for Par'oh.'

¹⁷Par'oh spoke with Yoseph. 'In my dream: there was I, standing by the bank of the Ye'or. ¹⁸There, from the Ye'or seven cows going up, sturdy in body and attractive in appearance, and they pastured among the reeds. ¹⁹And

there, seven more cows going up after them, poor and very bad-looking in appearance, thin in body. I haven't seen the like of them in the entire country of Misrayim for bad quality. <sup>20</sup>The thin, bad-looking cows ate the first seven sturdy cows. <sup>21</sup>So they came inside them, but it wouldn't have been known that they'd come inside them. Their appearance was as bad as it was at the beginning. And I woke up. <sup>22</sup>Then I saw in my dream, there, seven ears of grain growing up on one stalk, full and good-quality; <sup>23</sup>and there, seven ears of grain springing up after them, withered, thin, scorched by the east wind. <sup>24</sup>The seven thin ears swallowed the seven good ears.

I said it to the diviners but there was no one to tell me.'

## Save first, spend afterwards

<sup>25</sup>Yoseph said to Par'oh, 'Par'oh's dream is one. God has told Par'oh what he's going to do. <sup>26</sup>The seven good cows are seven years and the seven good ears are seven years. It's one dream. <sup>27</sup>The seven empty, bad-quality cows that were going up after them are seven years, as are the seven thin ears of grain, scorched by the east wind. There will be seven years of famine. <sup>28</sup>That's the word that I've spoken to Par'oh.

God has let Par'oh see what he's going to do. <sup>29</sup>There, seven years are coming, great abundance in the entire country of Misrayim, <sup>30</sup>but seven years of famine will arise after them, and the entire abundance in the country of Misrayim will be put out of mind. The famine will finish off the country. <sup>31</sup>The abundance in the country won't be acknowledged in the face of that famine afterwards, because it will be very heavy. <sup>32</sup>And concerning the repeating of the dream to Par'oh, twice: the thing is established by God. God is hurrying to do it.

<sup>33</sup>So now, Par'oh should look for a discerning, smart man and set him over the country of Misrayim. <sup>34</sup>Par'oh should act and set appointees over the country and take a fifth of the country of Misrayim in the seven years of abundance. <sup>35</sup>They should collect all food in these good years that are coming and lay up grain in the towns as food, under Par'oh's care, and keep it. <sup>36</sup>The food will be for appointing for the country

for the seven years of famine that are going to happen in the country of Misrayim, so the country is not cut off by the famine.'

<sup>37</sup>The thing was good in the eyes of Par'oh and in the eyes of all his servants, <sup>38</sup>and Par'oh said to his servants, 'Shall we find a man like this man, in whom is the spirit of God?'

## Yoseph as prime minister

<sup>39</sup>So Par'oh said to Yoseph, 'Given that God has let you know all this, there's no one smart and discerning like you. <sup>40</sup>You – you will be in charge of my household, and to your bidding all my people will acquiesce. Only with respect to the throne will I be greater than you.' <sup>41</sup>So Par'oh said to Yoseph, 'See, I'm putting you in charge of the entire country of Misrayim.' <sup>42</sup>Par'oh removed his signet ring from on his hand and put it on Yoseph's hand, had him clothed in linen robes and put a gold chain on his neck. <sup>43</sup>He had him ride in the chariot of his second-in-command, and they called out before him, 'Bow down!' So he put him in charge of the entire country of Misrayim. <sup>44</sup>Par'oh said to Yoseph, 'I'm Par'oh, but without you no one will raise his hand or his foot in the entire country of Misrayim.'

<sup>45</sup>Par'oh named Yoseph Tsaphenat Pane'ah and gave him Asenat, the daughter of Potiphera, priest in On [Heliopolis], as wife. So Yoseph went out in charge of the country of Misrayim.

<sup>46</sup>Yoseph was a man of thirty years when he stood before Par'oh, the king of Misrayim. Yoseph went out from before Par'oh and passed through the entire country of Misrayim. <sup>47</sup>In the seven years of abundance, the country produced by fistfuls, <sup>48</sup>and he collected all the food of the seven years that passed in the country of Misrayim and put food in the towns; the food of a town's fields that was round it he put in the middle of it. <sup>49</sup>Yoseph laid up the grain like the sand of the sea in vast quantities until he left off from counting, because counting was impossible.

<sup>50</sup>Two sons were born to Yoseph before the famine year came; Asenat, the daughter of Potiphera, priest in On, gave birth to them for him. <sup>51</sup>Yoseph named the firstborn Menashsheh [Manasseh], because 'God has made me forget [*nasha*] all my oppression and

my father's entire household.' ⁵²The second
he named Ephrayim, because 'God has made
me fruitful [*pharah*] in the country of my
humbling.'

### Grain in Misrayim

⁵³The seven years of abundance that passed
in the country of Misrayim finished ⁵⁴and
the seven years of famine started to come, as
Yoseph had said. The famine happened in all the
countries, but in the entire country of Misrayim
there was bread. ⁵⁵When the entire country of
Misrayim was hungry and the people cried out
to Par'oh for bread, Par'oh said to all Misrayim,
'Go to Yoseph, do what he says to you.'

⁵⁶When the famine was over the entire face
of the earth, Yoseph opened all that was in
them and sold grain to the Misrayimites.

So the famine became strong in the country
of Misrayim, ⁵⁷while the entire world came to
Misrayim to Yoseph to buy grain because the
famine was heavy in the entire world,

**42** and Ya'aqob saw that there was grain
in Misrayim. So Ya'aqob said to his
sons, 'Why do you look at one another?' ²He
said, 'Here, I've heard that there's grain in
Misrayim. Go down there and buy us grain
from there, so we may live and not die.' ³So
Yoseph's ten brothers went down to buy grain
from Misrayim. ⁴Binyamin, Yoseph's brother,
Ya'aqob didn't send with his brothers, because
(he said) 'in case harm comes to him'.

⁵So Yisra'el's sons came to buy grain among
the people who came, because the famine
happened to the country of Kena'an. ⁶Now
Yoseph was the prime minister over the
country, the one who sold grain to all the people
of the country. So Yoseph's brothers came and
bowed low to him, their faces to the ground.
⁷Yoseph looked at his brothers and recognized
them, but he acted like a stranger to them and
spoke toughly with them. He said to them,
'Where have you come from?' They said, 'From
the country of Kena'an, to buy food.'

### Yoseph remembers his dream

⁸So Yoseph recognized his brothers but they
didn't recognize him. ⁹Yoseph brought to mind
the dreams that he had about them. He said
to them, 'You're investigating; you've come
to see the country's vulnerability.' ¹⁰They said
to him, 'No, my lord! Your servants – they've
come to buy grain. ¹¹We're all of us sons of one
man. We're honest men. Your servants haven't
been investigating.' ¹²He said to them, 'No, you
came to see the country's vulnerability.' ¹³They
said, 'Your servants, we were twelve brothers,
the sons of one man in the country of Kena'an,
but there, the youngest is with our father at the
moment, and one is no more.'

¹⁴Yoseph said to them, 'It's as I spoke to you:
"You're investigating." ¹⁵By this you'll be tested:
by the life of Par'oh, you won't leave here unless
your youngest brother comes here. ¹⁶Send
one of you so he can get your brother. You,
be imprisoned, so your words will be tested,
whether there is truthfulness in you. And if
not, by the life of Par'oh, you're investigating.'

¹⁷He gathered them in the keep for three
days. ¹⁸On the third day, Yoseph said to them,
'Do this and you'll live; I am in awe of God.
¹⁹If you're honest, one of your brothers must
be imprisoned in the house where you're kept
while you go and bring grain for the famine in
your households, ²⁰and your youngest brother
you're to bring to me so your words may be
shown to be trustworthy and you don't die.'

So they did so, ²¹and said to one another,
'Well, we're paying the penalty for our brother.
We saw the pressure in his spirit when he
pleaded for grace with us and we didn't listen.
That's why this pressure has come to us.' ²²And
Re'uben answered them: 'I spoke to you,
saying: "Don't do wrong in relation to the
child", didn't I, and you didn't listen. Yes, his
blood – there, it's being required.'

### What game is Yoseph playing?

²³Now they didn't know that Yoseph was
listening, because there was an interpreter
between them. ²⁴He turned away from them
and cried, then came back to them and spoke
to them, and took Shim'on from among
them and imprisoned him before their eyes.
²⁵But Yoseph ordered that they should fill
their containers with grain, put back their
silver, each man, into his sack and give them
provisions for the journey.

So he did this for them, ²⁶they loaded their grain on to their donkeys, and they went from there. ²⁷One of them opened his sack to give feed to his donkey at the lodging and he saw his silver. There it was, in the mouth of his bag. ²⁸He said to his brothers, 'My silver has been put back! Really, here it is, in my bag!' Their heart sank. They turned trembling to one another, saying: 'What is this that God has done to us?'

²⁹They came to Ya'aqob their father in the country of Kena'an and told him all that had happened to them: ³⁰'The man who is lord of the country spoke toughly with us and treated us as people who were investigating the country. ³¹We said to him, "We're honest. We haven't been investigating. ³²We were twelve brothers, the sons of our father; one is no more and the youngest is with our father in the country of Kena'an at the moment." ³³But the man who is lord of the country said to us, "By this I shall know that you're honest. Leave one of your brothers with me, take something for the famine in your households and go, ³⁴and bring your youngest brother to me, so I may know that you're not people investigating but are honest. I'll give your brother to you and you can move about in the country."'

³⁵Then, as they were emptying their sacks, there – each man's silver pouch was in his sack. They looked at their silver pouches, they and their father, and they were afraid.

*There's no alternative*

³⁶Ya'aqob their father said to them, 'I'm the one you've bereaved of children. Yoseph is no more and Shim'on is no more and you will take Binyamin. It's all happened to me.' ³⁷But Re'uben said to his father: 'You may put my two sons to death if I don't bring him back to you. Put him into my care and I myself will bring him back to you.' ³⁸But he said, 'My son is not to go down with you, because his brother is dead and he alone remains. If harm comes to him on the journey you're going on, you'll send my grey hair down to She'ol with sadness.'

**43** But because the famine in the country was heavy, ²when they'd finished eating the grain that they'd brought from Misrayim, their father said to them, 'Go back and buy us a little food.' ³Yehudah said to him: 'The man solemnly testified against us: "You shall not see my face unless your brother is with you." ⁴If you do send our brother with us, we'll go down and buy food for you. ⁵But if you don't send him, we won't go down, because the man said to us, "You will not see my face unless your brother is with you."'

⁶Yisra'el said, 'Why did you deal badly with me by telling the man you had another brother?' ⁷They said, 'The man asked and asked about us and about our homeland, saying "Is your father still alive? Do you have a brother?" and we told him these things at his bidding. Could we possibly know that he would say, "Bring your brother down"?'

*When I am bereaved, I am bereaved*

⁸Yehudah said to Yisra'el his father, 'Send the boy with me so we can set off and go, and live and not die, both we and you and also our little ones. ⁹I personally guarantee him. From my hand you can look for him. If I don't bring him back to you and set him before you, I shall have done wrong in relation to you for all time. ¹⁰Because if we had not delayed, by now we could have got back here twice.'

¹¹Yisra'el their father said to them, 'If it's to be so, then, do this. Get some of the country's products in your containers and take them down to the man as an offering: a little balm and a little syrup, spices and myrrh, pistachios and almonds. ¹²And take twice the silver in your hand. Take back in your hand the silver that was put back in the mouth of your bags. Maybe it was a mistake. ¹³And your brother: take him and set off and go back to the man. ¹⁴May God Shadday himself give you compassion before the man so he may release your other brother to you, and Binyamin. And me – when I'm bereaved, I'm bereaved.' ¹⁵So the men took this offering and took twice the silver in their hand, and Binyamin, and they set off and went down to Misrayim and stood before Yoseph.

¹⁶Yoseph saw Binyamin with them and said to the person in charge of his household, 'Bring the men into the house and slaughter an animal and prepare it, because the men will eat with me at noon.' ¹⁷The man did as Yoseph said. The man brought the men into Yoseph's house, ¹⁸but

the men were afraid because they were brought into Yoseph's house. They said, 'It's because of the silver that was put back in our bags the first time that we have been brought in, to overwhelm us and fall on us and take us as servants, with our donkeys.'

## Yoseph can hardly control himself

¹⁹So they came up to the man who was in charge of Yoseph's household and spoke to him at the entrance of the house. ²⁰They said, 'Pardon me, my lord, we only came down the first time to buy food. ²¹But when we came to the lodging, we opened our bags and there, each man's silver was in the mouth of his bag, our silver by its weight. We have brought it back in our hand, ²²while we have brought down other silver with us to buy food. We don't know who put our silver in our bags.'

²³He said, 'Things are well with you. Don't be afraid. Your God, the God of your father, gave you the treasure in your bags, as your silver came to me.' And he brought Shim'on out to them. ²⁴So the man took the men into Yoseph's house, gave them water and they washed their feet, and gave them feed for their donkeys. ²⁵They prepared the offering for when Yoseph came at noon, because they had heard that they were to eat a meal there.

²⁶Yoseph came home and they brought him the offering that was in their hand in the house, and they bowed low to him to the ground. ²⁷He asked them whether things were well: 'Are things well with your aged father of whom you spoke? Is he still alive?' ²⁸They said, 'Things are well with your servant our father. He's still alive', and they bent their head and bowed low. ²⁹He lifted his eyes and saw Binyamin his brother, his mother's son, and said, 'Is this your youngest brother of whom you spoke to me?' And he said, 'God show grace to you, my son.' ³⁰Then Yoseph hurried because his insides burned for his brother and looked for somewhere to cry, and came to a room and cried there.

## Another pressure

³¹He washed his face and went out and controlled himself and said, 'Serve the meal.'

³²They served him on his own and them on their own and the Misrayimites who were eating with him on their own, because Misrayimites couldn't eat a meal with the Hebrews because this would be an offence to Misrayimites. ³³But they sat before him, the firstborn according to his birthright and the youngest according to his being the youngest, while the men looked in astonishment each at his neighbour. ³⁴People carried loads to them from before him, and Binyamin's load was five times bigger than all their loads. They drank and were merry with him.

**44** He ordered the person in charge of his household: 'Fill the men's bags with food, as much as they can carry, and put each person's silver in the mouth of his bag. ²And my chalice, the silver chalice, put in the mouth of the bag belonging to the youngest, with the silver for his grain.' He acted in accordance with the word that Yoseph spoke.

³When morning dawned and the men had been sent off, they and their donkeys, ⁴though they had left the town, they had not gone far when Yoseph said to the person in charge of his household, 'Set off and pursue after the men. Catch up with them and say to them, "Why have you made good with bad for good? ⁵Isn't this the one that my lord drinks from and practises divination with? You've acted badly in what you did."'

⁶He caught up with them and spoke these words to them. ⁷They said to him, 'Why does my lord speak words such as these? Far be it from your servants to do such a thing as this. ⁸Here, the silver that we found in the mouth of our bags we brought back to you from the country of Kena'an. So how would we steal silver or gold from your lord's house? ⁹With whichever of your servants it's found, he will die, and also we will become servants to my lord.'

## Yehudah pleads

¹⁰He said, 'Indeed, now, in accordance with your words, so it will be. The one with whom it's found shall be my servant. You will be free of guilt.' ¹¹So they hurried, each man, and lowered his bag to the ground, and they opened, each man, his bag. ¹²He searched, beginning with the eldest and finishing with the youngest,

and the chalice was found in Binyamin's bag. [13]They tore their clothes, and loaded, each man, his donkey and went back to the town.

[14]Yehudah and his brothers came to Yoseph's house. He was still there. They fell on the ground before him. [15]Yoseph said to them, 'What is this deed that you've done? Didn't you know that a man like me practises divination?' [16]Yehudah said, 'What could we say to my lord? What could we speak? How could we show we are in the right? God has found out your servants' waywardness. Here we are, servants to my lord, both we and the one in whose hand the chalice was found.' [17]But he said, 'Far be it from me to do this. The man in whose hand the chalice was found: he will become my servant. You: go up with things being well to your father.'

[18]Yehudah came up to him and said, 'Pardon me, my lord, can your servant speak a word in my lord's ear and your anger not rage at your servant, because you are like Par'oh. [19]My lord asked his servants, "Do you have a father or brother?" [20]and we said to my lord, "We have an aged father and the child of his old age, the youngest. Since his brother is dead, he alone remains of his mother's, and his father loves him." [21]You said to your servants, "Bring him down to me so I can set my eye on him." [22]We said to my lord, "The boy cannot abandon his father. If he abandons his father, he will die." [23]But you said to your servants, "If your youngest brother doesn't come down with you, you will not see my face again."

## You will send my grey hair down to Sheol with grief

[24]When we went up to your servant my father, we told him my lord's words. [25]Our father said, "Go back, get a little food for us", [26]and we said, "We can't go down. If our youngest brother is with us we can go down, because we won't be able to see the man's face with our youngest brother not being with us."

[27]Your servant my father said to us, "You yourselves know that my wife gave birth to two sons for me. [28]The one went away from me, and I said, 'Yes, he's been torn to pieces.' I haven't seen him until now. [29]Should you take this one from being with me as well, and harm comes,

you will send my grey hair down to She'ol with the bad fortune."

[30]When I now come to your servant my father and the boy is not with us, given that his life is bound up with his life, [31]when he sees the boy is not there, he'll die. Your servants will send your servant our father's grey hair down to She'ol with sadness. [32]Because your servant pledged the boy with my father, saying: "If I don't bring him back to you, I shall have done wrong in relation to my father permanently." [33]So your servant will please now stay as my lord's servant in place of the boy. The boy must go up with his brothers. [34]Because how can I go up to my father with the boy not with me, or I will see the bad fortune that will come on my father.'

## Not you but God

**45** Yoseph couldn't control himself in front of all the people who were stationed by him. He called, 'Get everyone out from being with me!' So no one stood with him when Yoseph made himself known to his brothers. [2]But he raised his voice in crying, and the Misrayimites heard and Par'oh's household heard. [3]Yoseph said to his brothers, 'I'm Yoseph! Is my father still alive?' His brothers couldn't answer him because they were fearful at his presence.

[4]Yoseph said to his brothers, 'Please come up to me', and they came up. He said, 'I'm Yoseph your brother, whom you sold into Misrayim. [5]But now: don't be pained, don't let it make you rage at yourselves because you sold me here, because it was to save life that God sent me before you. [6]Because this has been two years of famine within the country, and there will be five more years in which there will be no ploughing or reaping. [7]But God sent me before you to put in place for you a group remaining on the earth, to keep it alive for you as a big escape group. [8]So now it was not you who sent me here but God. He's made me a father for Par'oh and lord of all his household, and ruling over the entire country of Misrayim.

[9]Hurry and go up to my father and say to him, "Your son Yoseph has said this: 'God has made me into lord of all Misrayim. Come down to me, don't stand waiting. [10]You will live in the

Goshen region and be near me, you and your children and your grandchildren, your flock, your herd and all that's yours. ¹¹I shall provide for you there because there will be five more years of famine, so you and your household and all that's yours doesn't become dispossessed.'"

### 'Yoseph's brothers have come'

¹²Here, your eyes can see and my brother Binyamin's eyes can see that it's my mouth that's speaking to you. ¹³You're to tell my father about all my splendour in Misrayim and all that you've seen, and hurry and bring my father down here.' ¹⁴He fell on his brother Binyamin's neck and cried, and Binyamin cried on his neck, ¹⁵and he kissed all his brothers and cried on them, and after that his brothers spoke with him.

¹⁶When the announcement made itself heard in Par'oh's household, 'Yoseph's brothers have come', it was good in the eyes of Par'oh and in the eyes of his servants. ¹⁷Par'oh said to Yoseph, 'Say to your brothers, "Do this: load your animals and go, come to the country of Kena'an. ¹⁸Get your father and your households and come to me. I shall give you the best of the country of Misrayim and you will eat the fat of the country. ¹⁹You yourself are ordered, do this: get yourselves from the country of Misrayim wagons for your little ones and your wives, and carry your father and come. ²⁰Your eye is not to feel pity about your stuff, because the best of the entire country of Misrayim will be yours."'

²¹Yisra'el's sons did so. Yoseph gave them wagons at Par'oh's bidding and gave them provisions for the journey. ²²To them all he gave changes of clothing for each individual. To Binyamin he gave 300 pieces of silver and five changes of clothing. ²³To his father he sent as follows: ten donkeys carrying some of the good things of Misrayim, and ten she-donkeys carrying grain, bread and provisions for his father for the journey. ²⁴So he sent his brothers off, and as they went, he said to them, 'Don't be agitated on the way.'

### 'My son Yoseph is still alive!'

²⁵So they went up from Misrayim and came to the country of Kena'an to Ya'aqob their father ²⁶and told him: 'Yoseph is still alive, and actually he's ruling over the entire country of Misrayim.' His heart went numb, because he didn't trust them. ²⁷But they spoke to him all Yoseph's words that he had spoken to them, and he saw the wagons that Yoseph sent to carry him, and the spirit of Ya'aqob their father came alive. ²⁸Yisra'el said, 'Great! My son Yoseph is still alive! I must go and see him before I die!'

**46** So Yisra'el moved with all that was his and came to Be'er Sheba. He offered sacrifices to the God of his father Yitshaq, ²and God said to Yisra'el in a great vision at night, 'Ya'aqob, Ya'aqob!' He said, 'I'm here.' ³He said, 'I am God, the God of your father. Don't be afraid of going down to Misrayim, because I shall make you into a big nation there. ⁴I myself will go down with you to Misrayim and I myself will also definitely bring you up from there. Yoseph is the one who will place his hand on your eyes.'

⁵So Ya'aqob set off from Be'er Sheba. Yisra'el's sons carried Ya'aqob their father, their little ones and their wives in the wagons that Par'oh had sent to carry him, ⁶they got their livestock and the property that they had acquired in the country of Kena'an, and Ya'aqob and all his offspring with him came to Misrayim. ⁷His sons and his grandsons with him, his daughters and his granddaughters – all his offspring he brought with him to Misrayim.

### The Seventy

⁸These are the names of the descendants of Yisra'el who came to Misrayim, Ya'aqob and his descendants.

Ya'aqob's firstborn, Re'uben; ⁹Re'uben's sons: Hanok, Pallu, Hetsron and Karmi.

¹⁰Shim'on's sons: Yemu'el, Yamin, Ohad, Yakin, Tsohar and Sha'ul, the son of a Kena'anite woman.

¹¹Levi's sons: Gershon, Qehat and Merari.

¹²Yehudah's sons: Er, Onan, Shelah, Perets and Zerah (but Er and Onan had died in the country of Kena'an); Perets's sons were Hetsron and Hamul.

¹³Yissakar's sons: Tolah, Puvvah, Yob and Shimron.

¹⁴Zebulun's sons: Sered, Elon and Yahle'el.

15These are the sons of Le'ah, to whom she gave birth for Ya'aqob in Paddan Aram, and his daughter Dinah. Every person, his sons and his daughters: thirty-three.

16Gad's sons: Tsiphyon, Haggi, Shuni, Etsbon, Eri, Arodi and Ar'eli.
17Asher's sons: Yimnah, Yishvah, Yishvi and Beri'ah, with Serah their sister. Beri'ah's sons: Heber and Malki'el.
18These are the sons of Zilpah, whom Laban gave to his daughter Le'ah. She gave birth to these for Ya'aqob: sixteen persons.

19The sons of Ya'aqob's wife Rahel: Yoseph and Binyamin. 20To Yoseph were born in the country of Misrayim Menashsheh and Ephrayim, to whom Asenat, the daughter of Potiphera, priest in On, gave birth for him.
21Binyamin's sons: Bela, Beker, Ashbel, Gera, Na'aman, Ehi, Rosh, Muppim, Huppim and Ard.
22These are the sons of Rahel who were born to Ya'aqob. Every person: fourteen.

23Dan's sons: Hushim.
24Naphtali's sons: Yahtse'el, Guni, Yetser and Shillem.
25These are the sons of Bilhah, whom Laban gave to his daughter Rahel. She gave birth to these for Ya'aqob. Every person: seven.
26Every person belonging to Ya'aqob who came to Misrayim, the people who went out of his loins, apart from the wives of Ya'aqob's sons, every person: sixty-six. 27Yoseph's sons who were born to him in Misrayim, the persons: two. Every person belonging to Ya'aqob's household who came to Misrayim: seventy.

## I can die now

28He had sent Yehudah before him to Yoseph, to give directions before him to Goshen. So they came to the Goshen region, 29and Yoseph harnessed his chariot and went up to meet Yisra'el his father in Goshen. He appeared to him, and he fell on his neck and cried on his neck again and again. 30Yisra'el said to Yoseph, 'I can die now, after I've seen your face, that you're still alive.'

31Yoseph said to his brothers and to his father's household, 'I'll go up and tell Par'oh: "My brothers and my father's household, who were in the country of Kena'an – they have come to me. 32The men are shepherds of a flock, because they've been livestock men, and their flock and their herd and all that's theirs – they've brought them." 33So when Par'oh calls for you and says, "What's your work?" 34say "Your servants have been livestock men from our youth till now, both we and our ancestors", so that you may live in the Goshen region, because every shepherd of a flock is an offence to Misrayimites.'

**47** So Yoseph came and told Par'oh, 'My father and my brothers, their flock and their herd and all that's theirs – they've come from the country of Kena'an. There, they're in the Goshen region.' 2He took some of the total number of his brothers, five of them, and presented them before Par'oh. 3Par'oh said to his brothers, 'What is your work?' They said to Par'oh, 'Your servants are shepherds of a flock, both we and our ancestors.' 4They said to Par'oh, 'We have come to reside in the country because there's no pasture for your servants' flock, because the famine is heavy in the country of Kena'an. So now may your servants please live in the Goshen region.' 5Par'oh said to Yoseph: 'Given that your father and your brothers have come to you, 6the country of Misrayim is before you. Get your father and your brothers to live in the best part of the country. They should live in the Goshen region, and if you know that there are capable men among them, make them livestock officials over all that's mine.'

## State provision

7Yoseph brought Ya'aqob his father and got him to stand before Par'oh, and Ya'aqob blessed Par'oh. 8Par'oh said to Ya'aqob, 'What is the span of the years of your life?' 9Ya'aqob said to Par'oh, 'The span of the years of my residing is 130 years. Small and bad has been the span of the years of my life. They haven't reached the span of the years of my ancestors' lives by the span of their residing.'
10Ya'aqob blessed Par'oh and left Par'oh's presence, 11and Yoseph got his father and his brothers to live and gave them a holding in the

country of Misrayim, in the best part of
the country, in the Ra'meses region, as Par'oh
had ordered. ¹²Yoseph provided his father, his
brothers and his father's entire household with
bread by the number of the little ones.

¹³But bread: there was none in the entire
country, because the famine was very heavy.
The country of Misrayim and the country
of Kena'an withered because of the famine.
¹⁴Yoseph collected all the silver that was to be
found in the country of Misrayim and in the
country of Kena'an in payment for the grain
that they were buying. Yoseph brought the
silver into Par'oh's house.

¹⁵When the silver from the country of
Misrayim and from the country of Kena'an
came to an end, all Misrayim came to Yoseph,
saying, 'Give us bread: why should we die
in front of you, because the silver has gone.'
¹⁶Yoseph said, 'Bring your livestock, and I'll
give it to you in exchange for your livestock,
if the silver's gone.' ¹⁷So they brought their
livestock to Yoseph and Yoseph gave them
bread in exchange for the horses, for the
livestock in the flock, for the livestock in
the herd and for the donkeys. He sustained
them with bread in exchange for all their
livestock that year.

## The nationalization of land

¹⁸When that year came to an end, they came
to him the next year and said to him, 'We won't
hide from my lord that the silver has come to
an end, and the animal stocks belong to my
lord: nothing remains before my lord except
our bodies and our land. ¹⁹Why should we
die before your eyes, both we and our land?
Acquire us and our land in exchange for bread.
We ourselves and our land will become serfs to
Par'oh. Give seed, so we may live and not die,
and the land not become a waste.'

²⁰So Yoseph acquired all the land in
Misrayim for Par'oh, because the Misrayimites,
each of them, sold his fields because the
famine was so hard on them, and the country
came to belong to Par'oh. ²¹The people: he got
them to pass over into the towns from one end
of Misrayim's border to its other end. ²²He only
didn't acquire the priests' land, because the
priests had a statutory allotment from Par'oh

and they ate their allotment that Par'oh gave
them. Therefore they didn't sell their land.

²³Yoseph said to the people, 'Here, today I've
acquired you and your land for Par'oh. Here's
seed for you. You are to sow the land, ²⁴and
with the yield you are to give a fifth to Par'oh,
but four-fifths will be yours, as seed for the
fields and as food for you and for those in your
households, and for eating by your little ones.'
²⁵They said, 'You've kept us alive. May we find
grace in the eyes of my lord. We will become
serfs to Par'oh.'

²⁶Yoseph made it a decree, until this day, for
the land in Misrayim: a fifth is Par'oh's. Only
the land of the priests on their own didn't
become Par'oh's.

## Still remembering his first love

²⁷So Yisra'el lived in the country of Misrayim
in the Goshen region. They acquired holdings in
it, they were fruitful and they became very
numerous. ²⁸Ya'aqob lived seventeen years in the
country of Misrayim. Ya'aqob's span, the years of
his life, was 147 years.

²⁹The days drew near for Yisra'el to die, and
he called his son Yoseph and said to him,
'Please, if I've found grace in your eyes, put
your hand under my thigh, please, and act in
commitment and truthfulness with me. Please
don't bury me in Misrayim. ³⁰I shall lie down
with my ancestors and you're to carry me from
Misrayim and bury me in their burial-place.' He
said, 'I will act in accordance with your word.'
³¹He said, 'Swear to me.' He swore to him, and
Yisra'el bowed low at the head of the bed.

# 48

Subsequently, they said to Yoseph,
'Here, your father is ill,' so he took his
two sons with him, Menashsheh and Ephrayim.
²They told Ya'aqob, 'Here, your son Yoseph
is coming to you.' Yisra'el summoned up his
strength and sat up on the bed. ³Ya'aqob said
to Yoseph, 'God Shadday, he appeared to me at
Luz in the country of Kena'an and blessed me,
⁴and said to me, "Here, I'm making you fruitful
and numerous and making you a congregation
of peoples and giving this country to your
offspring after you as a permanent holding."
⁵Now, your two sons who were born to you
in the country of Misrayim before my coming
to you in Misrayim: they're mine. Like Re'uben

and Shim'on, they are to be mine. ⁶Your family that you father after them will be yours. As regards their domain they will be called with the name of their brothers. ⁷I – when I was coming from Paddan, Rahel died, alas, in the country of Kena'an, on the journey, when there was still a distance so as to come to Ephrat, and I buried her there on the road to Ephrat' (i.e. Bet Lehem).

## The younger again ahead of the elder

⁸So when Yisra'el saw Yoseph's sons, he said 'Who are these?' ⁹Yoseph said to his father, 'They're my sons, whom God has given me here.' He said, 'Please get them to me, so I may bless them.' ¹⁰Now Yisra'el's eyes were heavy because of age, and he couldn't see.

He brought them up to him, and he kissed them and hugged them. ¹¹Yisra'el said to Yoseph, 'To see your face! I didn't expect it. And here – God has let me see your offspring as well.' ¹²Yoseph got them off his knees and bowed low, with his face to the ground. ¹³Yoseph took the two of them, Ephrayim with his right hand to Yisra'el's left, and Menashsheh with his left hand to Yisra'el's right, and brought them up to him.

¹⁴Yisra'el put out his right hand and put it on Ephrayim's head (though he was the younger one) and his left hand on Menashsheh's head, crossing his hands, because Menashsheh was the firstborn, ¹⁵and he blessed Yoseph: 'May the God before whom my fathers Abraham and Yitshaq walked, the God who has been shepherding me from whenever until this day, ¹⁶the envoy who has restored me from every bad fortune, bless the boys. May I be named through them, I and my ancestors Abraham and Yitshaq. May they abound so as to become a large number in the middle of the country.'

¹⁷Yoseph saw that his father was putting his right hand on Ephrayim's head and it was bad in his eyes. He took hold of his father's hand to remove it from on Ephrayim's head on to Menashsheh's head. ¹⁸Yoseph said to his father, 'Not like that, father, because this one is the firstborn. Place your right hand on his head.' ¹⁹But his father refused and said, 'I know, son, I know. He will become a people as well, he will become big as well, but nevertheless his younger brother will be bigger than him and

his offspring will become a full number of nations.'

²⁰So that day he blessed them: 'By you Yisra'el will bless, saying: "God make you like Ephrayim and Menashsheh."' But he put Ephrayim before Menashsheh.

## Deathbed promises and predictions (1)

²¹Yisra'el said to Yoseph: 'Here, I'm going to die, but God will be with you and will take you back to the country of your ancestors. ²²I myself am giving you one shoulder [*shekem*] above your brothers, which I took from the hand of the Amorites with my sword and with my bow.'

# 49
Ya'aqob called his sons and said, 'Gather together and I shall tell you what is to befall you in a later time. ²Collect together and listen, sons of Ya'aqob, listen to Yisra'el your father.'

³Re'uben, you're my firstborn,
my energy and the firstfruit of my strength.
Though excelling in dignity and excelling in
vigour,
⁴turbulent as water, you are not to excel.
Because you climbed into your father's bed,
then profaned it; he climbed on to my
mattress.

⁵Shim'on and Levi, brothers,
their pikes are instruments of violence.
⁶May I myself not come into their council,
may I myself not join in their congregation.
Because when they were angry, they killed
people;
when it was acceptable to them, they
hamstrung oxen.
⁷Cursed be their anger because it was vigorous,
their outburst because it was tough.
I will divide them in Ya'aqob,
scatter them in Yisra'el.

## Deathbed promises and predictions (2)

⁸You are Yehudah;
your brothers will confess you.
With your hand on your enemies' neck,
your father's sons will bow low to you.

⁹Yehudah is a lion cub;
  from the prey, son, you've gone up.
He's bent down, lain like a lion,
  like a cougar – who will make him rise?
¹⁰The staff will not depart from Yehudah,
  the sceptre from between his feet,
Until tribute comes to him
  and the submission of the peoples is his.
¹¹He ties his donkey to a vine,
  the offspring of his she-donkey to a choice
    vine.
He washes his apparel in wine,
  his garments in grape-blood.
¹²His eyes are darker than wine,
  his teeth whiter than milk.

¹³Zebulun is to dwell by the sea shore
he's to be by the shore for ships;
  his flank at Tsidon.

¹⁴Yissakar is a sturdy donkey
  lying among the sheepfolds.
¹⁵He saw a place to settle down – how good it was,
  and the country – how lovely.
He bent his shoulder to the labouring,
  became a serf work force.

¹⁶Dan is to give judgement [*yadin*] for his
    people
  as one of Yisra'el's clans.
¹⁷Dan is to be a snake by the road,
  a viper by the path,
One that bites the horse's heels
  so its rider falls backwards.

¹⁸For your deliverance I have waited, Yahweh.

¹⁹Gad: a raiding gang [*gedud*] will raid him,
  but he himself will raid at its heel.

²⁰From Asher: his bread will be rich,
  and he will give a king's delicacies.

²¹Naphtali is a hind set free,
  who gives lovely fawns.

## Deathbed promises and predictions (3)

²²Yoseph is a fruitful branch,
  a fruitful branch by a spring,
  branches that run over a wall.

²³The archers were ferocious
  and shot at him and assaulted him.
²⁴But his bow stayed firm
  and his arms and hands were agile,
Because of the hands of Ya'aqob's Champion,
  because the Shepherd, Yisra'el's Stone, was
    there,
²⁵Because of your father's God, he helps you,
  and Shadday, he blesses you,
With the blessings of the heavens above,
  the blessings of the deep lying below,
The blessings of the breasts and the womb,
  ²⁶the blessings of your father.
They have been stronger than the blessings of
    the ancient mountains,
  up to the bounty of the age-old hills.
May they come on Yoseph's head,
  on the crown of the one who was
    consecrated from his brothers.

²⁷Binyamin is a wolf who tears apart,
  in the morning he eats prey,
  at evening he shares out spoil.

²⁸All these are the twelve Yisra'elite clans and
this is what their father spoke to them. So he
blessed them. Each of them according to his
blessing he blessed them.
  ²⁹He ordered them and said to them, 'I'm
being gathered to my kin. Bury me with my
ancestors in the cave that's in the field of
Ephron the Hittite, ³⁰in the cave that's in the
field at Makpelah which is east of Mamre, in
the country of Kena'an, the field that Abraham
acquired from Ephron the Hittite as a burial
holding ³¹(there they buried Abraham and
Sarah his wife, there they buried Yitshaq and
Ribqah his wife, there I buried Le'ah), ³²an
acquisition (the field and the cave that's in it)
from the Hittites.'
  ³³Ya'aqob finished giving orders to his sons,
gathered his feet into the bed, breathed his last
and was gathered to his kin.

## The great mourning

**50** Yoseph fell on his father's face and
wailed over him and kissed him.
²Yoseph ordered the physicians who were
his servants to embalm his father. When the
physicians embalmed Yisra'el, ³they fulfilled

forty days for him, because that's how they used to fulfil the days for embalming.

The Misrayimites bewailed him seventy days, ⁴and when the days of bewailing him had passed, Yoseph spoke to Par'oh's household: 'Please, if I have found grace in your eyes, please speak in Par'oh's ears: ⁵"My father himself got me to swear: 'Here, I'm dying; in the grave that I dug for myself in the country of Kena'an, there you're to bury me.' So I shall now go up, please, and bury my father, and come back."'

⁶Par'oh said, 'Go up and bury your father as he got you to swear.' ⁷So Yoseph went up to bury his father. All Par'oh's servants went up with him, and the elders in his household, all the elders in the country of Misrayim, ⁸Yoseph's entire household, his brothers and his father's household. Only the little ones, and their flock and their herd, did they abandon in the Goshen region. ⁹Both chariotry and cavalry went up with him. It was a very substantial camp.

¹⁰They came to the Thorn Threshing Floor, which is across the Yarden, and held a very great and heavy lament there. He made seven days of grieving for his father. ¹¹The Kena'anite people living in the country saw the grieving at Thorn Threshing Floor and said, 'This is a heavy grieving on the part of the Misrayimites.' That's why it was named 'The Misrayimite Grieving', which is across the Yarden.

¹²His sons did thus for him, as he had ordered them, ¹³and his sons carried him to the country of Kena'an and buried him in the cave in the field at Makpelah, the field that Abraham acquired as a burial holding from Ephron the Hittite, east of Mamre.

*Am I in the place of God?*

¹⁴Then Yoseph went back to Misrayim, he and his brothers and all the people who had gone up with him to bury his father, after he had buried his father. ¹⁵Yoseph's brothers saw that their father was dead, and said, 'What if Yoseph feels hostile to us and really gets back at us for all the bad fate that we dealt to him?' ¹⁶So they gave order to Yoseph: 'Your father gave order before his death: ¹⁷"Say this to Yoseph: 'Oh, please carry your brothers' affront and their wrongdoing, that they dealt a bad fate to you.'" So now please carry the affront of the servants of your father's God.' Yoseph cried when they spoke to him. ¹⁸His brothers also came and fell before him and said, 'Here are we as servants to you.'

¹⁹Yoseph said to them, 'Don't be afraid. Am I in the place of God? ²⁰Whereas you yourselves thought up something bad for me, God thought it up for good, in order to act today to keep alive a numerous people. ²¹So now, don't be afraid. I myself will provide for you and your little ones.' Thus he consoled them and reassured them.

²²So Yoseph lived in Misrayim, he and his father's household. Yoseph lived 110 years ²³and saw the third generation of Ephrayim; the children of Makir ben Menashsheh were also born on Yoseph's knees. ²⁴Then Yoseph said to his brothers, 'I'm going to die, but God will definitely attend to you and take you up from this country to the country that he swore to Abraham, to Yitshaq and to Ya'aqob.' ²⁵Yoseph got Yisra'el's sons to swear, saying: 'God will definitely attend to you, and you're to take up my bones from here.' ²⁶Yoseph died, a man of 110 years. They embalmed him and put him in a coffin in Misrayim.

# EXODUS

Exodus tells the story of Israel's beginnings as a people. It starts off with the Israelites as state serfs in Egypt, and its first half recounts how Yahweh forces the Egyptian king to release them so they can go and hold a festival for Yahweh. After a further, final showdown between Yahweh and the king at the Reed Sea, they're able to get to the mountain where their leader, Moses, had earlier met with this God.

The second half relates the renewing of the pact or covenant relationship between Yahweh and Israel and Israel's construction of the splendid portable sanctuary whose specifications Yahweh gives Moses. The book first provides all the specifications and then repeats them in its account of how Israel did as Yahweh said. The story ends with Yahweh coming to dwell among Israel in this sanctuary.

The bridge between the two halves of the book is Yahweh's initial meeting with Israel at Mount Sinai. Whereas in Genesis Yahweh didn't explicitly lay down much by way of expectations of his people, his getting Israel out of their serfdom provides a new basis for his laying down expectations of them. These begin with the Ten Commandments, which embody some basic principles for life. The list sums up a number of the concerns that underlie much of the expression of Yahweh's decrees for Israel's life that are expounded in the First Testament as a whole. It combines some basic obligations that most cultures would accept (no murder, no theft, and so on) with some obligations that would raise eyebrows among other peoples (worship only Yahweh, don't make images, stop working one day a week), and it ends with a final *coup de grâce* that sends anyone away with their tail between their legs (no coveting). The further decrees that follow the Ten Commandments spell out these obligations in sample areas of life. Once again, other Middle Eastern peoples would not be surprised to find directives to avoid the ill-treatment of servants, or procedures for resolving conflicts in the community, but would notice the distinctiveness of instructions about Israel's worship of Yahweh alone.

Exodus is a narrative with a beginning, a middle and an end. Yet it's not self-contained. It continues the story begun in Genesis, and the background for Yahweh's getting Israel out of Egypt lies in things Yahweh had promised in Genesis. At the end, it leads into Leviticus, which relates more of what Yahweh told Moses at Sinai, and it leads on further into the subsequent books that will relate how God continued to pursue his project of settling Israel in Canaan.

As is the case with Genesis, we don't know who wrote Exodus or when it was written, but we can see how its story informed Israel over the centuries about what it was as a people, and what it was supposed to be. The fact that Yahweh rescued Israel from Egypt was a basis for continuing to trust him and for being the kind of community that protects people from harsh servitude rather than ill-treating them as servants. Yahweh's putting Pharaoh in his place provided reason for trusting in and submitting to Yahweh as King and not thinking that the imperial power of the day held the real power. The story of Yahweh's laying out the blueprint for a rather different kind of sanctuary from the temple that Israel later built would give food for thought to a people that liked to devise its own worship and its own worship buildings.

Like Genesis, Exodus is more like a movie based on fact than either a piece of pure fiction or a pure historical narrative. One aspect of its genius is the way it discusses complex theological questions as it tells its story. What is the relationship between God's sovereignty and the sovereignty of a political figure like the Pharaoh? What do we mean by talking about the presence of God? How does God cope with the rebelliousness of his own people in a way that does justice to his faithfulness and mercy and to his sacredness and integrity? In telling its story, Exodus walks round questions such as these, looks at them from various angles and thus resources its readers in thinking about them.

*On not rendering to Caesar*

**1** So these are the names of the sons of Yisra'el [Israel] who came to Misrayim [Egypt] with Ya'aqob [Jacob] (each with his household they came): ²Re'uben, Shim'on [Simeon], Levi and Yehudah [Judah]; ³Yissakar [Issachar], Zebulun and Binyamin [Benjamin]; ⁴Dan and Naphtali; Gad and Asher. ⁵Every person of those who came out of Ya'aqob's loins, they were seventy persons, Yoseph [Joseph] being in Misrayim. ⁶Yoseph died, as did all his brothers, and all that generation, ⁷but the Yisra'elites – they were fruitful and they teemed, they became vast and very, very numerous. The country became full of them.

⁸A new king rose up over Misrayim who didn't acknowledge Yoseph. ⁹He said to his people, 'Here, the people of the Yisra'elites is vaster and more numerous than us. ¹⁰Come on, let's act smart with it so it doesn't become so vast that when battle comes, it even gathers together with our enemies and does battle against us, and goes up from the country.' ¹¹So they set workforce officials over it in order to humble it by means of its labours. It built supply towns for Par'oh [Pharaoh], Pitom and Ra'amses. ¹²But as they would humble it, so it would become vaster and break out. They were dismayed about the Yisra'elites.

¹³So the Misrayimites made the Yisra'elites serve with harshness. ¹⁴They made their lives hard with tough servitude, with mortar, with bricks and with every form of servitude in the fields. Every form of the servitude that they had them undertake was with harshness.

¹⁵The king of Misrayim said to the Hebrew midwives (one of whom was named Shiphrah, the second Pu'ah), ¹⁶'When you're delivering the Hebrew women, look at the

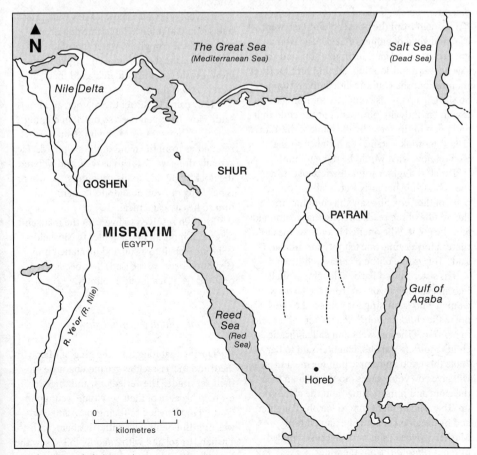

*Exodus 1: Mosheh (Moses)*

stones. If it's a son, put him to death, but if it's a daughter, she may live.' <sup>17</sup>But the midwives lived in awe of God and didn't do as the king of Misrayim had spoken to them. They let the boys live. <sup>18</sup>The king of Misrayim called for the midwives and said to them, 'Why have you done this thing and let the boys live?' <sup>19</sup>The midwives said to Par'oh, 'Because the Hebrew women are not like the Misrayimite women, because they're lively. Before the midwife comes to them, they give birth.'

## How some women continue to defeat Par'oh

<sup>20</sup>God was good to the midwives, and the people became vast and very numerous. <sup>21</sup>Because the midwives lived in awe of God, he made households for them. <sup>22</sup>Then Par'oh ordered all his people, 'Every son who's born, you're to throw into the Ye'or [Nile], but every daughter you can let live.'

2 A man from the household of Levi went and got a daughter of Levi. <sup>2</sup>The woman got pregnant and gave birth to a son, and she saw he was good-looking. She hid him for three months <sup>3</sup>but she couldn't hide him any longer. So she got a papyrus container for him, tarred it with tar and with bitumen, put the child in it and put it in the reeds by the bank of the Ye'or. <sup>4</sup>His sister took a stand at a distance so she would know what would be done to him.

<sup>5</sup>Par'oh's daughter went down to bathe in the Ye'or, while her girls were walking on the bank of the Ye'or. She saw the container in the middle of the reeds and sent her handmaid, and she got it. <sup>6</sup>She opened it and saw the child: there, a boy crying. She felt pity for him, and said, 'This is one of the Hebrews' children.'

<sup>7</sup>His sister said to Par'oh's daughter, 'Shall I go and call for a woman from the Hebrew women who is nursing for you, so she can nurse the child for you?' <sup>8</sup>Par'oh's daughter said to her, 'Go!' The girl went and called for the child's mother. <sup>9</sup>Par'oh's daughter said to her, 'Take this child and nurse him for me. I myself will give you your wages.' So the woman took the child and nursed him, <sup>10</sup>and the child grew up. Then she brought him to Par'oh's daughter and he became her son. She named him Mosheh [Moses]; she said, 'Because I pulled him out [*mashah*] from the water.'

## From guerrilla to fugitive

<sup>11</sup>During that time, Mosheh grew up, and he went out to his brothers and saw their labours. He saw a Misrayimite man striking down a Hebrew man, one of his brothers. <sup>12</sup>He turned his face this way and that, saw that there was no one, and struck down the Misrayimite and hid him in the sand.

<sup>13</sup>He went out the next day and there, two Hebrew men were fighting. He said to the one in the wrong, 'Why do you strike down your neighbour?' <sup>14</sup>He said, 'Who made you someone as an official and an authority over us? Are you thinking of killing me as you killed the Misrayimite?' Mosheh was afraid. He said, 'Then the thing has become known!' <sup>15</sup>And Par'oh heard about this thing and sought to kill Mosheh, but Mosheh took flight from before Par'oh and lived in the country of Midyan.

He lived by a well. <sup>16</sup>Now a Midyanite priest had seven daughters. They came and drew and filled the troughs to water their father's flock, <sup>17</sup>but shepherds came and drove them away. Mosheh got up and delivered them, and watered their flock.

<sup>18</sup>They came to Re'u'el their father, and he said, 'How have you been so quick in coming today?' <sup>19</sup>They said, 'A Misrayimite man rescued us from the hand of the shepherds. He actually drew water for us as well, and watered the flock.' <sup>20</sup>He said to his daughters, 'So where is he? Why did you abandon the man? Call him so he can eat a meal.'

<sup>21</sup>Mosheh resolved to live with the man, and he gave Tsipporah his daughter to Mosheh. <sup>22</sup>She gave birth to a son and he named him Gershom, because (he said) 'I've become a resident [*ger*] in a foreign country.'

## It was an ordinary working day

<sup>23</sup>During that long time the king of Misrayim died, and the Yisra'elites groaned because of their servitude. They cried out, and their cry for help because of their servitude went up to God. <sup>24</sup>God listened to their groan, and God was mindful of his pact with Abraham, with Yitshaq [Isaac] and with Ya'aqob. <sup>25</sup>God saw the Yisra'elites. God acknowledged it.

**3** Now Mosheh was shepherding the flock of Yitro [Jethro] his father-in-law, the Midyanite priest. He had driven the flock to the far side of the wilderness and come to God's mountain, to Horeb. ²Yahweh's envoy appeared to him in a fiery flame out of the middle of a bush. He saw, and there, the bush was burning up with fire but the bush wasn't consumed. ³Mosheh said, 'I must turn aside and see this great sight. Why doesn't the bush burn up?' ⁴Yahweh saw that he turned aside to see.

God called to him out of the middle of the bush and said, 'Mosheh, Mosheh!' He said, 'I'm here.' ⁵He said, 'Don't draw near here. Take your boots off your feet, because the place you're standing on is sacred ground.' ⁶And he said, 'I'm the God of your father, the God of Abraham, the God of Yitshaq and the God of Ya'aqob.' Mosheh hid his face, because he was afraid to look at God.

⁷Yahweh said, 'I really have seen my people's humbling in Misrayim, and I've listened to their outcry on account of their bosses, because I've acknowledged their sufferings. ⁸I've come down to rescue it from the hand of Misrayim and take it up from that country to a good, wide country, a country flowing with milk and syrup, to the place of the Kena'anite [Canaanite], the Hittite, the Amorite, the Perizzite, the Hivvite and the Yebusite. ⁹So now, here, the Yisra'elites' outcry has come to me, and I've also seen the affliction that the Misrayimites are imposing on them. ¹⁰So now, go, and I'll send you to Par'oh to get my people, the Yisra'elites, out of Misrayim.'

*Who God will be*

¹¹Mosheh said to God, 'Who am I, that I should go to Par'oh and get the Yisra'elites out of Misrayim?' ¹²He said, 'Because I will be with you. This will be the sign for you that I've sent you. When you get the people out of Misrayim, you'll all serve God on this mountain.'

¹³Mosheh said to God, 'Here, I'm going to come to the Yisra'elites and say to them, "The God of your ancestors – he has sent me to you", and they will say to me, "What is his name?" What shall I say to them?' ¹⁴God said to Mosheh, 'I will be what I will be.' He said,

'Say this to the Yisra'elites, "I will be" sent me to you.' ¹⁵God said further to Mosheh, 'Say this to the Yisra'elites: "Yahweh, the God of your ancestors, the God of Abraham, the God of Yitshaq, the God of Ya'aqob, sent me to you." This is my name permanently; this is my designation to all generations.

¹⁶Go, gather Yisra'el's elders, and say to them, "Yahweh, the God of your ancestors, the God of Abraham, Yitshaq and Ya'aqob, has appeared to me, saying 'I really have attended to you and to what's being done to you in Misrayim. ¹⁷I've said, I will take you up, out from humbling in Misrayim, to the country of the Kena'anite, the Hittite, the Amorite, the Perizzite, the Hivvite and the Yebusite, to a country flowing with milk and syrup.'"

¹⁸They will listen to your voice, and you are to come, you and Yisra'el's elders, to the king of Misrayim and say to him, "Yahweh, the God of the Hebrews – he's met with us. So now, we must please go three days' journey into the wilderness to sacrifice for Yahweh our God."

*People will need evidence*

¹⁹I myself acknowledge that the king of Misrayim won't allow you to go, not even because of a strong hand. ²⁰But I shall put out my hand and strike Misrayim down with all the extraordinary things that I shall do among them. After this he'll send you off, ²¹and I shall give this people grace in the eyes of Misrayim. When you go, you won't go empty-handed. ²²A woman will ask from her neighbour, and from the woman residing in her house, for objects of silver and objects of gold and clothes, and you will put them on your sons and on your daughters. You will strip Misrayim.'

**4** Mosheh answered: 'But there, they won't trust in me, they won't listen to my voice, because they'll say, "Yahweh didn't appear to you."'

²Yahweh said to him, 'What's this in your hand?' He said, 'A staff.' ³He said, 'Throw it on the ground.' He threw it on the ground, and it became a snake. Mosheh fled from before it. ⁴Yahweh said to Mosheh, 'Put out your hand and grasp it by its tail' (so he put out his hand and took strong hold of it, and it became a staff in his fist) ⁵'in order that they

may trust that Yahweh appeared to you – the God of your ancestors, the God of Abraham, the God of Yitshaq and the God of Ya'aqob.'

[6]Yahweh said to him further, 'Put your hand into the fold of your coat, please.' He put his hand into the fold of his coat, and took it out, and there – his hand was scaly, like snow. [7]He said, 'Put your hand back into the fold of your coat' (so he put his hand back into the fold of his coat, then took it out of the fold of his coat – and there, it had gone back like his flesh) [8]so if they don't trust you and listen to the voice of the first sign, they may listen to the voice of the later sign.

## Some final attempts to say 'No'

[9]If they don't even trust in these two signs and listen to your voice, get some of the water of the Ye'or and pour it on the dry ground, and the water that you get from the Ye'or will become blood on the dry ground.'

[10]Mosheh said to Yahweh, 'Pardon me, Lord: I haven't been a man of words in previous days or since you've spoken to your servant, because I'm heavy of mouth, heavy of tongue.' [11]Yahweh said to him, 'Who made the mouth for human beings, or who makes someone dumb or deaf, seeing or blind? Isn't it me, Yahweh? [12]So now go, and I myself will be with your mouth, and I'll instruct you what you're to say.'

[13]He said, 'Pardon me, Lord: please send by the hand [of someone else] you can send.' [14]Yahweh's anger raged against Mosheh, but he said, 'Isn't there Aharon [Aaron] your brother, the Levite? I know that he can really speak. And also – there, he's going to come out to meet you. When he sees you, he'll rejoice in his heart. [15]You're to speak to him and put the words in his mouth. I myself be with your mouth and with his mouth, and I'll instruct you what you're to do. [16]But he's the one who will speak for you to the people. He – he'll be a mouth for you, and you – you'll be God for him. [17]But take in your hand this staff, with which you'll do the signs.'

[18]So Mosheh went and returned to Yitro his father-in-law and said to him, 'I must please go and return to my brothers in Misrayim and see whether they're still alive.' Yitro said to Mosheh, 'Go; may things be well.'

## The migrant returns

[19]So Yahweh said to Mosheh in Midyan, 'Go, go back to Misrayim, because all the people who were seeking your life are dead.' [20]Mosheh took his wife and his sons, mounted them on a donkey and went back to the country of Misrayim.

Mosheh took God's staff in his hand. [21]Yahweh said to Mosheh, 'When you go back to Misrayim, look at all the proofs that I put in your hand and do them before Par'oh. But I myself will make his mind adamant so he doesn't send the people off. [22]You're to say to Par'oh, "Yahweh has said this: 'Yisra'el is my son, my firstborn. [23]I have said to you, "Send my son off so he can serve me", but you've refused to send him off. Here, I'm going to kill your son, your firstborn."'

[24]On the way, at a lodging place, Yahweh met up with him and sought to put him to death, [25]but Tsipporah got a flint and cut off her son's foreskin, touched his feet with it and said, 'Because you're a bridegroom of shed blood to me!' [26]And he slackened his hold on him. (At that time she said 'a bridegroom of shed blood', regarding the circumcision.)

[27]Yahweh said to Aharon, 'Go and meet Mosheh in the wilderness.' He went and met up with him at God's mountain and kissed him. [28]Mosheh told Aharon all Yahweh's words that he had sent him with and all the signs that he had ordered him with, [29]and Mosheh and Aharon went and gathered all the elders of the Yisra'elites. [30]Aharon spoke all the words that Yahweh had spoken to Mosheh, he did the signs before the people's eyes, [31]and the people trusted. They heard that Yahweh had attended to the Yisra'elites and had seen their humbling, and they bent their heads and bowed low.

## I don't acknowledge Yahweh

**5** Afterwards, Mosheh and Aharon went and said to Par'oh, 'Yahweh has said this: "Send my people Yisra'el off so they may hold a festival for me in the wilderness."' [2]But Par'oh said, 'Who is Yahweh that I should listen to his voice about sending Yisra'el off? I don't acknowledge Yahweh and I won't send Yisra'el off, either.'

³So they said, 'In that the God of the Hebrews has met with us, we must please go a three days' journey into the wilderness and sacrifice for Yahweh our God so that he doesn't come on us with epidemic or with sword.' ⁴The king of Misrayim said to them, 'Mosheh and Aharon, why should you release the people from their work? Get to your labours.' ⁵And Par'oh said, 'Here, the people of the country are now vast, and you'll make them stop from their labours?'

⁶That day Par'oh ordered the bosses over the people and its overseers: ⁷'You will not continue to give the people straw for making brick, as in previous days. They themselves can go and collect straw for themselves. ⁸But you're to set for them the quantity of bricks that they were making in previous days. You will not cut it down, because they're slacking. That's why they're crying out, "Let's go and offer sacrifice for our God." ⁹Service should weigh heavy on the men so they may do it and not listen to deceptive words.'

¹⁰So the people's bosses and its overseers went out and said to the people, 'Par'oh has said this: "I'm not giving you straw. ¹¹You go, get straw for yourselves from wherever you may find it, but not a thing is to be cut down from your service."'

## Divide and rule

¹²The people dispersed through the entire country of Misrayim to gather stubble for straw, ¹³while the bosses hounded them: 'Get your work finished, each day's requirement on its day, just like when there was the straw.' ¹⁴The Yisra'elites' overseers, whom Par'oh's bosses had put over them, were struck down: 'Why have you not finished your decreed amount of brickmaking, as in previous days, either yesterday or today?'

¹⁵The Yisra'elites' overseers came and cried out to Par'oh, 'Why do you act like this towards your servants? ¹⁶No straw is given to your servants but they're saying to us, "Bricks! Make them." Here, your servants being struck down, but the wrongdoing is your people's.' ¹⁷But he said, 'You're slacking, slacking. That's why you're saying, "We want to go sacrifice for Yahweh." ¹⁸So now go, serve. Straw will not be given you, but you must give the tally of bricks.'

¹⁹The Yisra'elites' overseers saw that things were bad for them in his saying 'You're not to cut down your bricks, each day's requirement on its day.' ²⁰They came upon Mosheh and Aharon taking their stand to meet them when they went out from Par'oh, ²¹and they said to them, 'May Yahweh look at you and exercise authority, because you made our smell stink in the eyes of Par'oh and in the eyes of his servants, putting a sword in their hand to kill us.'

²²Mosheh went back to Yahweh and said, 'Lord, why have you dealt badly with this people? Why is it that you sent me? ²³From the time when I came to Par'oh to speak in your name, he's dealt badly with this people, and you haven't rescued your people at all.'

**6** Yahweh said to Mosheh, 'Now you'll see what I shall do to Par'oh, because he will send them off by means of a strong hand. By means of a strong hand he will drive them out of his country.'

## My people – your God

²God spoke to Mosheh and said to him, 'I am Yahweh. ³I appeared to Abraham, to Yitshaq and to Ya'aqob as God Shadday, but by my name Yahweh I didn't make myself known to them. ⁴I also implemented my pact with them to give them the country of Kena'an, the country of their residing, in which they were residents. ⁵I have also now personally listened to the groan of the Yisra'elites, whom the Misrayimites are treating as serfs, and I've been mindful of my pact. ⁶Therefore say to the Yisra'elites, "I am Yahweh. I shall get you out from under the labours of Misrayim and rescue you from their servitude. I shall restore you by an outstretched arm and by great acts of authority. ⁷I shall take you for myself as a people and I shall be God for you, and you will acknowledge that I am Yahweh your God, the one who got you out from under the labours of Misrayim. ⁸I shall bring you to the country that I swore to give to Abraham, to Yitshaq and to Ya'aqob. I shall give it to you as a possession. I am Yahweh."'

⁹Mosheh spoke in this way to the Yisra'elites but they didn't listen to Mosheh because of a worn-out spirit and because of tough servitude. ¹⁰Yahweh spoke to Mosheh: ¹¹'Come speak to Par'oh king of Misrayim so he may send off the

Yisraelites from his country.' ¹²Mosheh spoke before Yahweh: 'Here, the Yisraelites didn't listen to me, so how will Par'oh listen to me, when I'm foreskinned of lips?' ¹³But Yahweh spoke to Mosheh and Aharon and gave them orders about the Yisraelites and about Par'oh king of Misrayim, to get the Yisraelites out of the country of Misrayim.

## The family register

¹⁴These are the heads of their ancestral households:

The descendants of Re'uben, Yisrael's firstborn: Hanok and Pallu, Hetsron and Karmi; these are Re'uben's kin-groups. ¹⁵The descendants of Shim'on: Yemu'el, Yamin, Ohad, Yakin, Tsohar, and Sha'ul, the son of a Kena'anite woman; these are Shim'on's kin-groups. ¹⁶These are the names of Levi's descendants by their lines of descent: Gershon, Qehat and Merari (the span of Levi's life was 137 years). ¹⁷The descendants of Gershon: Libni and Shim'i, by their kin-groups. ¹⁸The descendants of Qehat: Amram, Itshar, Hebron and Uzzi'el (the span of Qehat's life was 133 years). ¹⁹The descendants of Merari: Mahli and Mushi.

These are Levi's kin-groups by their lines of descent:

²⁰Amram got himself as wife Yokebed, his aunt. She gave birth to Aharon and Mosheh for him (the span of Amram's life was 137 years). ²¹The descendants of Itshar: Qorah, Nepheg and Zikri. ²²The descendants of Uzzi'el: Misha'el, Eltsaphan and Sitri. ²³Aharon got for himself as wife Elisheba, the daughter of Amminadab and sister of Nahshon; she gave birth to Nadab and Abihu, El'azar and Itamar, for him. ²⁴The descendants of Qorah: Assir, Elqanah and Abi'asaph; these are the kin-groups of the Qorahites. ²⁵El'azar ben Aharon got for himself as wife one of Puti'el's daughters, and she gave birth to Pinhas for him.

These are the heads of the Levites' ancestral households by their kin-groups. ²⁶That was Aharon and Mosheh to whom Yahweh said, 'Get the Yisraelites out of the country of Misrayim by their armies.' ²⁷They were the people who spoke to Par'oh king of Misrayim about getting the Yisraelites out of Misrayim. That was Mosheh and Aharon.

## The stiffening of Par'oh's resolve

²⁸On the day Yahweh spoke to Mosheh in the country of Misrayim, ²⁹and Yahweh spoke to Mosheh: 'I am Yahweh: speak to Par'oh king of Misrayim all that I'm going to speak to you', ³⁰Mosheh said before Yahweh, 'Here, I am foreskinned of lips, so how will Pharoah listen to me?'

**7** But Yahweh said to Mosheh, 'Look, I am making you God to Par'oh, and Aharon your brother will be your prophet. ²You – you are to speak all that I order you, and Aharon your brother is to speak to Par'oh so he may send off the Yisraelites from his country. ³But I myself will toughen Par'oh's mind so I may do my many signs and proofs in the country of Misrayim. ⁴Par'oh won't listen to you, and I shall set my hand against Misrayim, and I shall get my armies, my people, the Yisraelites, out of the country of Misrayim, with great acts of authority. ⁵So the Misrayimites will acknowledge that I am Yahweh when I stretch out my hand over Misrayim and get the Yisraelites out from among them.'

⁶Mosheh and Aharon did as Yahweh ordered them; so they did. ⁷Mosheh was a man of eighty years and Aharon a man of eighty-three years when they spoke to Par'oh.

⁸Yahweh said to Mosheh and to Aharon: ⁹'When Par'oh speaks to you, "Give us a proof for yourselves", you're to say to Aharon, "Get your staff and throw it before Par'oh; it is to become a serpent."' ¹⁰So Mosheh and Aharon came to Par'oh and did so, as Yahweh ordered. Aharon threw his staff before Par'oh and before his servants, and it became a serpent. ¹¹Par'oh, too, called for the experts and the sorcerers, and the Misrayimite wizards did so, too, with their spells. ¹²They threw, each one, his staff and they became serpents. Then Aharon's staff swallowed their staffs. ¹³But Par'oh's mind

was adamant, and he didn't listen to them, as Yahweh had spoken.

## The Ye'or becomes blood

<sup>14</sup>Yahweh said to Mosheh, 'Par'oh's mind is heavy. He refuses to send the people off. <sup>15</sup>Go to Par'oh in the morning. There, he'll be going out to the water. Take your stand to meet him at the edge of the Ye'or. The staff that turned into a snake – take it in your hand. <sup>16</sup>Say to him, "Yahweh, the God of the Hebrews, has sent me to you to say, 'Send my people off so they may serve me in the wilderness.' But here, you haven't listened so far.

<sup>17</sup>Yahweh has said this: 'Because of this you'll acknowledge that I am Yahweh.' Here, I'm going to strike the water in the Ye'or with the staff that's in my hand, and it will turn into blood. <sup>18</sup>The fish that are in the Ye'or – they'll die. The Ye'or will stink. The Misrayimites will be loath to drink water from the Ye'or.'"

<sup>19</sup>Yahweh said to Mosheh, 'Say to Aharon, "Get your staff and stretch out your hand over the water of Misrayim, over its rivers, over its canals, over its ponds, over every body of water, so they become blood. There'll be blood in the entire country of Misrayim, even in wood and stone [containers]."

<sup>20</sup>Mosheh and Aharon did so, as Yahweh ordered. He lifted the staff and struck the water in the Ye'or before the eyes of Par'oh and before the eyes of his servants, and all the water that was in the Ye'or turned into blood. <sup>21</sup>The fish that were in the Ye'or – they died. The Ye'or stank. The Misrayimites couldn't drink water from the Ye'or. There was blood in the entire country of Misrayim.

<sup>22</sup>But Misrayimite experts did so with their spells, and Par'oh's mind was adamant and he didn't listen to them, as Yahweh had spoken. <sup>23</sup>Par'oh turned his face and came to his house. He didn't give his mind to this, either. <sup>24</sup>All Misrayim dug round the Ye'or for water to drink, because they couldn't drink from the Ye'or water.

## Praying for the oppressor

<sup>25</sup>Seven days were fulfilled after Yahweh struck the Ye'or,

**8** then Yahweh said to Mosheh, 'Come to Par'oh and say to him, "Yahweh has said this: 'Send my people off so they may serve me. <sup>2</sup>If you're going to refuse to send them off: here, I'm going to hit your entire border with frogs. <sup>3</sup>The Ye'or will teem with frogs. They'll climb up and come into your house, into your bedroom and into your bed, and into your servants' house, and in among your people, and into your ovens and into your mixing bowls. <sup>4</sup>Yes, on to you and on to your people and on to all your servants the frogs will climb up."'

<sup>5</sup>Yahweh said to Mosheh, 'Say to Aharon, "Stretch out your hand with your staff over the rivers, over the canals and over the ponds, and get the frogs to climb up on to the country of Misrayim."' <sup>6</sup>Aharon stretched out his hand over the water in Misrayim, and the frogs came up and covered the country of Misrayim. <sup>7</sup>But the experts did so with their spells and got the frogs to climb up on to the country of Misrayim.

<sup>8</sup>Par'oh called for Mosheh and Aharon and said, 'Entreat Yahweh to remove the frogs from me and from my people, and I'll send the people off so they may sacrifice for Yahweh.' <sup>9</sup>Mosheh said to Par'oh, 'You may have the honour over me about when I entreat for you, for your servants and for your people, to cut off the frogs from you and from your houses. Only in the Ye'or will they remain.' <sup>10</sup>He said, 'Tomorrow'. He said, 'According to your word, in order that you may acknowledge that there's no one like Yahweh our God. <sup>11</sup>The frogs will depart from you, from your houses, from your servants and from your people. Only in the Ye'or will they remain.'

## An epidemic of lice

<sup>12</sup>Mosheh and Aharon went out from Par'oh, Mosheh cried out to Yahweh about the frogs that he had brought on Par'oh, <sup>13</sup>and Yahweh acted in accordance with Mosheh's word. The frogs died away from the houses, from the courtyards and from the fields. <sup>14</sup>They piled them up, heaps and heaps. The country stank. <sup>15</sup>But when Par'oh saw that there was relief, he firmed up his mind and didn't listen to them, as Yahweh had spoken.

¹⁶Yahweh said to Mosheh, 'Say to Aharon, "Hold out your staff and strike the country's soil so it becomes lice in the entire country of Misrayim."' ¹⁷They did so. Aharon stretched out his hand with his staff and struck the country's soil, and lice were on human beings and on animals. All the country's soil became lice in the entire country of Misrayim. ¹⁸The experts did so with their spells to make lice issue, but they couldn't. So the lice were on human beings and on animals. ¹⁹The experts said to Par'oh, 'This is the finger of God.' But Par'oh's mind was adamant and he didn't listen to them, as Yahweh had spoken.

²⁰Yahweh said to Mosheh, 'Start early in the morning and take your stand before Par'oh. There, he'll be going out to the water. You're to say to him, "Yahweh has said this: 'Send my people off so they may serve me. ²¹Because if you don't send my people off – here, I'm going to send swarms of flies on you, on your servants, on your people and on your houses. The houses of Misrayim will be full of the swarms of flies, and also the ground that they walk on. ²²But on that day I'll make a distinction between the Goshen region on which my people stand, so there's no swarm of flies there, in order that you may acknowledge that I am Yahweh, within the country. ²³I shall put a redemption between my people and your people. Tomorrow this sign will come about.""'

## Swarms of flies

²⁴Yahweh did so. Heavy swarms of flies came into Par'oh's house and into his servants' house. In the entire country of Misrayim the country was devastated in the face of the swarms of flies. ²⁵Par'oh called for Mosheh and Aharon and said, 'Go, sacrifice for Yahweh your God within the country.' ²⁶Mosheh said, 'It isn't established to do so, because what we sacrifice for Yahweh our God is an offence to Misrayimites. If we sacrifice what is an offence to Misrayimites before your eyes, won't they stone us? ²⁷We want to go three days' journey into the wilderness to sacrifice for Yahweh our God, as he says to us.'

²⁸Par'oh said, 'I myself will send you off so you may sacrifice for Yahweh your God in the wilderness. Only don't go any great distance.

Entreat for me.' ²⁹Mosheh said, 'Here I am, going out from before you, and I'll entreat Yahweh so the swarms of flies depart from Par'oh and from his servants and from his people tomorrow. Only, Par'oh must not again play about by not sending the people off to sacrifice for Yahweh.'

³⁰Mosheh went out from before Par'oh and entreated Yahweh. ³¹Yahweh acted in accordance with Mosheh's word and removed the swarms of flies from Par'oh, from his servants and from his people. Not one remained. ³²But Par'oh firmed up his mind this time, too, and did not send the people off.

## *The distinction between Misrayim and Yisra'el*

**9** Yahweh said to Mosheh: 'Come to Par'oh and speak to him: "Yahweh, the God of the Hebrews, has said this: 'Send my people off so they may serve me. ²Because if you refuse to send them off and still keep strong hold on to them, ³here – Yahweh's hand is going to be on your livestock that's in the fields, on the horses, on the donkeys, on the camels, on the herd and on the flock, with a very heavy pestilence. ⁴But Yahweh will make a distinction between Yisra'el's livestock and Misrayim's livestock. Of all that belongs to the Yisra'elites not a thing will die. ⁵Yahweh has fixed a set time: tomorrow Yahweh will do this thing in the country.""'

⁶Yahweh did this thing next day. All Misrayim's livestock died; of the Yisra'elites' livestock, not one died. ⁷Par'oh sent, and there – not even one of Yisra'el's livestock had died. But Par'oh's mind was firm. He didn't send off the people.

⁸Yahweh said to Mosheh and to Aharon, 'Get yourselves fistfuls of kiln ash. Mosheh is to toss it into the heavens before Par'oh's eyes. ⁹It will become dust on the entire country of Misrayim, and on human beings and on animals it will become an inflammation breaking out in blisters in the entire country of Misrayim.'

¹⁰They got the kiln ash and stood before Par'oh. Mosheh tossed it into the heavens and it became an inflammation breaking out in blisters on human beings and on animals. ¹¹The wizards were not able to stand before

Mosheh because of the inflammation, because the inflammation was on the wizards and on all Misrayim. [12]But Yahweh made Par'oh's mind adamant and he didn't listen to them, as Yahweh has spoken to Mosheh.

### The acknowledgement needed

[13]Yahweh said to Mosheh, 'Start early in the morning and take your stand before Par'oh, and say to him, "Yahweh, the God of the Hebrews, has said this: 'Send my people off so they may serve me. [14]Because this time I'm going to send all my blows towards your mind, and on your servants and on your people, in order that you may acknowledge that there's no one like me, in the entire country. [15]Because by now, had I sent my hand and struck down you and your people with an epidemic, you would have been effaced from the country. [16]Yet for this purpose I've let you stand, for the purpose of getting you to see my energy and for the sake of recounting my name in the entire country. [17]You're still exalting yourself over my people so as not to send them off.

[18]Here, this very time tomorrow I'm going to make it rain very heavy hail, such as hasn't happened in Misrayim from the day of its founding until now. [19]So now, send to bring into safety your livestock and everything that you have in the fields. Any human beings or animals that are found in the fields and don't gather in the house, the hail will come down on them and they'll die.""'

[20]Anyone among Par'oh's servants who was in awe of Yahweh's word got his servants and his livestock to flee into their houses, [21]but whoever didn't give his mind to Yahweh's word abandoned his servants and his livestock in the fields. [22]And Yahweh said to Mosheh, 'Stretch out your hand over the heavens so hail may come through the entire country of Misrayim, on human beings and on animals and on all the plants of the wild in the country of Misrayim.'

### Par'oh flip-flop

[23]So Mosheh stretched out his staff over the heavens. As Yahweh sent a great noise, and hail

and fire fell on the ground, Yahweh rained hail on the country of Misrayim. [24]Hail came, with fire flashing about in the middle of the hail, very heavy, such as had not come in the entire country of Misrayim since it became a nation. [25]In the entire country of Misrayim, the hail struck down everything that was in the fields, both human beings and animals. All the plants in the fields it struck down, and all the trees in the fields it broke off. [26]Only in the Goshen region, where the Yisra'elites were, was there no hail.

[27]Par'oh sent and called for Mosheh and Aharon and said to them, 'This time I've done wrong. Yahweh is in the right and I and my people are in the wrong. [28]Entreat Yahweh so this may be plenty of almighty noise and hail, and I shall send you off. You'll stay no longer.' [29]Mosheh said to him, 'As I go out of the town, I shall spread the palms of my hands to Yahweh. The great noise – it will leave off, the hail – it will be no more, in order that you may acknowledge that the country belongs to Yahweh. [30]But you and your servants: I know that you are not yet in awe of Yahweh.' [31]The flax and the barley were struck down, because the barley was ripening and the flax was budding, [32]but the wheat and hulled wheat were not struck down, because they are late-ripening. [33]Mosheh went out of the town from being with Par'oh and spread the palms of his hands to Yahweh, and the great noise and the hail left off and the rain didn't pour on the earth. [34]But Par'oh saw that the rain, the hail and the great noise had left off, and he did wrong again and firmed up his mind, he and his servants. [35]So Par'oh's mind remained adamant and he didn't send the Yisra'elites off – as Yahweh had spoken through Mosheh.

### An epidemic of locusts

**10** Yahweh said to Mosheh, 'Come to Par'oh, because I've hardened his mind and his servants' mind in order to set these signs of mine in his midst [2]and in order that you may recount in the ears of your son and your grandson how I acted abusively against Misrayim, and my signs that I have set among them, so you may acknowledge that I am Yahweh.'

³So Mosheh and Aharon came to Par'oh and said to him, 'Yahweh the God of the Hebrews has said this: "How long do you refuse to humble yourself before me? Send my people off so they may serve me. ⁴Because if you refuse to send my people off – here, I'm going to bring a locust swarm into your border tomorrow. ⁵It will cover the face of the land; people won't be able to see the land. It will eat the rest of what escaped, which remained to you from the hail. It will eat every tree that grows for you, from the fields. ⁶They will fill your houses, all your servants' houses and all Misrayim's houses, something that your fathers and grandfathers didn't see, from the day they came into existence on the land until this day."' And he turned his face and went out from being with Par'oh.

⁷Par'oh's servants said to him, 'How long will this man be a snare for us? Send the people off so they may serve Yahweh their God. Don't you yet acknowledge that Misrayim is lost?' ⁸So Mosheh and Aharon were brought back to Par'oh, and he said to them, 'Go, serve Yahweh your God. Who exactly are going?' ⁹Mosheh said, 'With our young and with our old we will go, with our sons and with our daughters, with our flock and with our herd we will go, because it's Yahweh's festival for us.'

## Repentance and more flip-flop

¹⁰He said to them, 'May Yahweh be with you indeed when I send you and your little ones off! See, you have something bad in view. ¹¹Definitely not. You men do go and serve Yahweh, because this is what you're seeking.' And they were driven out of Par'oh's presence.

¹²Yahweh said to Mosheh, 'Stretch out your hand over the country of Misrayim with the locust swarm, so it may come over the country of Misrayim and eat all the plants in the country, anything that the hail left remaining.' ¹³So Mosheh stretched out his staff over the country of Misrayim and Yahweh drove an east wind through the country all that day and all night. When the morning came, the east wind had carried the locust swarm.

¹⁴The locust swarm came over the entire country of Misrayim and settled down in the entire border of Misrayim, very heavy. There had not been a locust swarm like it before it,

and after it there would not be. ¹⁵It covered the face of the entire country. The country was dark. It ate all the plants in the country and all the fruit on the trees that the hail had left. Nothing green was left of the trees or the plants in the fields in the entire country of Misrayim.

¹⁶Par'oh hurried to call for Mosheh and for Aharon and said, 'I've done wrong against Yahweh your God and against you. ¹⁷But now, please carry my wrongdoing only this time. Entreat Yahweh your God that he only remove this death from me.'

¹⁸He went out from being with Par'oh and entreated Yahweh, ¹⁹and Yahweh changed a very strong west wind. It carried the locust swarm and threw it into the Reed Sea. Not one of the locust swarm remained in the entire border of Misrayim. ²⁰But Yahweh made Par'oh's mind adamant and he didn't send the Yisra'elites off.

## You won't see my face again

²¹Yahweh said to Mosheh, 'Stretch out your hand over the heavens so there may be darkness over the country of Misrayim and so one can feel darkness.' ²²Mosheh stretched out his hand over the heavens and there was thick darkness through the entire country of Misrayim for three days. ²³No one could see his brother and no one could get up from where he was for three days. But for all the Yisra'elites there was light in their settlements.

²⁴Par'oh called for Mosheh and said, 'Go, serve Yahweh. Only your flock and your herd must be laid down. Even your little ones can go with you.' ²⁵Mosheh said, 'You yourself are to give into our hand sacrifices and burnt offerings so we may make them for Yahweh our God, ²⁶and also our livestock will go with us (not a hoof will remain behind) because we shall take some of it to serve Yahweh our God, and we ourselves won't know with what we shall serve Yahweh until we come there.'

²⁷But Yahweh made Par'oh's mind adamant and he was not willing to send them off. ²⁸Par'oh said to him, 'Get away from me! Keep watch over yourself: don't see my face again, because on the day you see my face, you'll die.' ²⁹Mosheh said, 'You've spoken correctly. I shall not see your face ever again.'

## The final threat

**11** Yahweh said to Mosheh, 'There's yet one more blow I shall bring on Par'oh and on Misrayim. After that, he will send you off from here. When he sends you off, it will be complete. He will finally drive you out of here. ²Speak in the ears of the people, please, so they ask for objects of silver and gold, each man from his neighbour and each woman from her neighbour.' ³Yahweh gave the people grace in the eyes of Misrayim. Mosheh himself was also very big in the country of Misrayim in the eyes of Par'oh's servants and in the eyes of the people.

⁴Mosheh said, 'Yahweh has said this: "At midnight, I'm going out among the Misrayimites. ⁵Every firstborn in the country of Misrayim will die, from the firstborn of Par'oh who sits on the throne to the firstborn of the maidservant who is behind the millstones, and every firstborn of the animals." ⁶There will be a loud cry in the entire country of Misrayim such as has not been and will not be again. ⁷But at any of the Yisra'elites a dog won't growl, either at a person or at an animal, in order that you may acknowledge that Yahweh makes a distinction between Misrayim and Yisra'el. ⁸All these servants of yours will come down to me and bow low to me saying, "Get out, you and all your people who follow you." After, that I'll go out.' He went out from Par'oh's presence in an angry rage.

⁹Yahweh had said to Mosheh, 'Par'oh won't listen to you, in order that my proofs may become numerous in the country of Misrayim', ¹⁰and Mosheh and Aharon had performed all these proofs before Par'oh, but Yahweh had made Par'oh's mind adamant and he had not sent the Yisra'elites off from his country.

## Instructions for a solemn celebration

**12** Yahweh said to Mosheh and to Aharon in the country of Misrayim: ²'This month is to be the beginning of the months for you. It's to be the first of the months in the year for you. ³Speak to the entire Yisra'elite assembly: "On the tenth of this month they're to get for themselves, each man, a lamb for the ancestral family, a lamb for the household. ⁴If the household is too small for a lamb, he and his neighbour near his household are to get one, on the basis of a count of the persons. Each person according to what he will eat, you're to calculate for the lamb. ⁵Your lamb is to be whole, male, a year old. You may get it from the sheep or from the goats.

⁶It's to be in your keeping until the fourteenth day of this month, then the entire Yisra'elite assembled congregation are to slaughter it at twilight. ⁷They're to get some of the blood and put it on the two doorposts and on the lintel of the houses where they'll eat it. ⁸They're to eat the meat this night. They're to eat it roasted in fire, with flatbread and bitters. ⁹Don't eat any of it raw or boiled (boiled in water), please, but rather roasted in fire, including its head, with its legs and its innards. ¹⁰You're not to leave any of it until morning. What's left of it until morning, you're to burn in fire.

¹¹This is how you're to eat it: your hips wrapped round, your boots on your feet, your cane in your hand. You're to eat it in haste. It's a Pesah [Passover] for Yahweh. ¹²I shall pass through the country of Misrayim this night and strike down every firstborn in the country of Misrayim, human beings and animals. On all the Misrayimite gods I shall perform acts of authority. I am Yahweh.

¹³But for you the blood will be a sign on the houses where you are. I'll see the blood and pass over you. No blow to devastate will come on you when I strike down the country of Misrayim.

## A reminder

¹⁴This day is to be for you a reminder. You're to observe it as a festival for Yahweh. Through your generations you're to observe it, a permanent decree. ¹⁵For seven days you're to eat flatbread. On the first day you're totally to eliminate yeast from your houses (because anyone who eats leavened bread – that person shall be cut off from Yisra'el), from the first day to the seventh day.

¹⁶On the first day it's a sacred occasion and on the seventh day a sacred occasion for you. No work will be done among you. Only what is to be eaten by a person, that alone may be

prepared by you. ¹⁷You're to keep Flatbread, because on this particular day I got your armies out of the country of Misrayim. You're to keep this day through your generations, a permanent decree. ¹⁸In the first month on the fourteenth day in the evening, you're to eat flatbread, until the twenty-first day of the month in the evening. ¹⁹For seven days yeast is not to be found in your houses, because anyone who eats leavened bread – that person shall be cut off from the Yisra'elite assembly, whether being a resident or a native. ²⁰You will eat no leavened bread. In all your settlements you will eat flatbread.'"

²¹Mosheh called for all Yisra'el's elders and said to them, 'Go out, get yourselves sheep for your kin-groups and slaughter the Pesah. ²²Get a bunch of hyssop, dip it in the blood that's in the basin, and touch the lintel and the two doorposts with the blood that's in the basin. You – you're not to go outside, anyone, from the entrance of his house until morning. ²³Yahweh will pass through to hit Misrayim, but he will see the blood on the lintel and on the two doorposts. Yahweh will pass by the entrance and not let the devastater come into your households to hit them.

## The scream

²⁴You're to keep this word as a permanent decree for yourself and for your descendants. ²⁵When you come into the country that Yahweh will give you, as he spoke, you're to keep this service. ²⁶When your children say to you, "What is this service for you?" ²⁷you're to say, "It's the Pesah sacrifice for Yahweh, because he passed over the Yisra'elites' households in Misrayim, when he hit Misrayim but rescued our households."' The people bent their heads and bowed low.

²⁸The Yisra'elites went and did as Yahweh ordered Mosheh and Aharon; so they did. ²⁹In the middle of the night Yahweh struck down every firstborn in the country of Misrayim, from the firstborn of Par'oh who sat on the throne to the firstborn of the captive who was in the cistern, and every firstborn of an animal. ³⁰Par'oh got up in the night, he and all his servants and all Misrayim, and there was a loud crying out in Misrayim, because

there was no household where there was not someone dead.

³¹He called for Mosheh and Aharon in the night and said, 'Set off, get out from among my people, both you and the Yisra'elites. Go, serve Yahweh in accordance with your word. ³²Both your flock and your herd – take them as you have spoken. Go. But bless me also.'

³³Misrayim was firm with the people, hurrying to send them off from the country, because (they said), 'We're all going to be dead.' ³⁴So the people picked up their dough before it was leavened, their mixing bowls wrapped in their clothes, on their shoulder.

³⁵The Yisra'elites had acted in accordance with Mosheh's word and asked the Misrayimites for objects of silver and gold, and clothes, ³⁶and Yahweh had given the people grace in the eyes of the Misrayimites so they had let them ask. So they stripped the Misrayimites.

## A huge company

³⁷The Yisra'elites moved on from Ra'meses to Sukkot, some 600,000 men on foot apart from little ones. ³⁸A mixed crowd also went up with them, and a flock and herd, very substantial livestock. ³⁹They baked the dough they had brought out of Misrayim into flatbread loaves because it was not leavened, because they'd been driven out of Misrayim and hadn't been able to delay, and also they hadn't made provisions for themselves.

⁴⁰The Yisra'elites' settlement that they had had in Misrayim lasted 430 years. ⁴¹At the end of 430 years, on that particular day all Yahweh's armies came out of the country of Misrayim. ⁴²It was a night of keeping watch for Yahweh, in getting them out of the country of Misrayim. For the Yisra'elites through their generations this night is one of keeping watch for Yahweh.

⁴³Yahweh said to Mosheh and Aharon, 'This is the Pesah decree. While no one born of a foreigner may eat of it, ⁴⁴any person who is a servant, acquired for silver, but you've circumcised him – he may then eat of it. ⁴⁵A settler or employee may not eat of it. ⁴⁶It's to be eaten in one house. You may not take any of the meat outside the house. You may not break any bone of it. ⁴⁷The entire

Yisraʾelite assembly is to do this. [48]When someone is a resident with you and makes Pesah for Yahweh, every male belonging to him is to be circumcised, and then he may draw near to perform it; he'll be like a native of the country. But anyone who is foreskinned may not eat of it. [49]There is to be one instruction for the native and for the person who is a resident among you.'

[50]All the Yisraʾelites did as Yahweh ordered Mosheh and Aharon; so they did. [51]This particular day Yahweh got the Yisraʾelites out of the country of Misrayim by their armies.

## The reminders

**13** Yahweh spoke to Mosheh: [2]'Make every firstborn sacred for me; the one who opens every womb among the Yisraʾelites, human being or animal, is mine.'

[3]Mosheh said to the people, 'Be mindful of this day when you got out of Misrayim, out of a household of serfs, because Yahweh got you out of it by strength of hand. No leavened bread is to be eaten. [4]Today you're going out, in the month of Aviv. [5]When Yahweh brings you into the country of the Kenaʾanites, the Hittites, the Amorites, the Hivvites and the Yebusites, which he swore to your ancestors to give you, a country flowing with milk and syrup, you're to perform this service in this month. [6]For seven days you're to eat flatbread, and on the seventh day there's to be a festival for Yahweh. [7]Flatbread is to be eaten through the seven days. Leavened bread is not to appear among you. Yeast is not to appear among you in your entire border. [8]You're to tell your child on that day, "It's because of what Yahweh did for me when I got out of Misrayim." [9]It will be a sign for you on your hand and a reminder between your eyes, in order that Yahweh's instruction may be in your mouth, because Yahweh got you out of Misrayim with a strong hand. [10]You're to keep this decree at its set time from year to year.

[11]When Yahweh brings you into the country of the Kenaʾanites as he swore to you and to your ancestors, and gives it to you, [12]you're to pass on every opener of the womb to Yahweh. Every opener (the drop of an animal that belongs to you), the males are Yahweh's.

[13]Any donkey's opener you're to redeem with a sheep; if you don't redeem it, you're to break its neck. Every human opener among your children, you're to redeem.

## The long way round

[14]When your child asks in the future "What is this?" you're to say to him, "Yahweh got us out of Misrayim, out of a household of serfs, by strength of hand. [15]When Parʾoh was tough about sending us off, Yahweh killed every firstborn in the country of Misrayim, both human firstborn and animal firstborn. That's why I'm sacrificing for Yahweh every opener of the womb, the males, but I redeem the firstborn among my sons." [16]So it will be a sign on your hand and a symbol between your eyes, because Yahweh got us out of Misrayim by strength of hand.'

[17]When Parʾoh sent the people off, God didn't lead them by the road to the Pelishtites' [Philistines'] country because it was near, because (God said), 'So that the people don't have a change of heart when they see battle, and turn back to Misrayim.' [18]God made the people go round by the wilderness road to the Reed Sea.

The Yisraʾelites went up from the country of Misrayim organized into companies. [19]Mosheh took Yosephʾs bones with him, because he had made the Yisraʾelites solemnly swear, 'God will definitely attend to you, and you're to take up my bones from here with you.' [20]They moved on from Sukkot and camped at Etam at the edge of the wilderness, [21]with Yahweh going before them by day in a cloud pillar to lead them on the way and by night in a fire pillar to give them light, so they could go by day or night. [22]The cloud pillar by day and the fire pillar by night would not move away from before the people.

## One kind of fear turns to another

**14** Yahweh spoke to Mosheh: [2]'Speak to the Yisraʾelites: they're to turn back and camp before Pi Hahirot, between Migdol and the sea. You're to camp before Baʾal Tsephon, opposite it, by the sea. [3]Parʾoh will say of the Yisraelites, "They're lost in the region. The wilderness has closed in on them." ⁴I shall make Par'oh's mind adamant and he'll pursue after them, so I may show my splendour through Par'oh and all his force, and the Misrayimites may acknowledge that I am Yahweh.' They did so.

⁵It was told the king of Misrayim that the people had taken flight, and the mind of Par'oh and his servants towards the people changed. They said, 'What's this that we've done, that we've sent Yisra'el off from serving us?' ⁶He harnessed his chariot and took his people with him, ⁷and took 600 picked chariotry, and the entire Misrayimite chariotry, with adjutants over all of them.

⁸So Yahweh made the mind of Par'oh king of Misrayim adamant and he pursued after the Yisraelites as the Yisraelites were leaving with hand high. ⁹The Misrayimites pursued after them and overtook them camping by the sea, all Par'oh's chariot horses, his riders and his force, near Pi Hahirot, opposite Ba'al Tsephon.

¹⁰As Par'oh got near, the Yisraelites lifted their eyes, and there, the Misrayimites were moving on after them, and they were very fearful. The Yisraelites cried out to Yahweh, ¹¹and said to Mosheh, 'Was it for lack of graves in Misrayim that you took us to die in the wilderness? What's this you've done to us in getting us out of Misrayim? ¹²Isn't this the thing we spoke to you in Misrayim, "Leave off from us and we'll serve the Misrayimites, because serving the Misrayimites is better for us than dying in the wilderness"?'

## Why should you cry out to me?

¹³Mosheh said to the people, 'Don't be fearful. Take your stand and see Yahweh's deliverance, which he'll effect for you today. Because the Misrayimites you've seen today you won't see any more, ever again, permanently. ¹⁴Yahweh – he will do battle for you. You – you can stay quiet.'

¹⁵Yahweh said to Mosheh, 'Why should you cry out to me? Speak to the Yisraelites so they may move on. ¹⁶You yourself, lift up your staff and stretch out your hand over the sea and divide it so the Yisraelites may come into the middle of the sea on the dry ground.

¹⁷And I – here am I, making the Misrayimites' mind adamant so they come after them. I shall show my splendour through Par'oh and through all his force, through his chariotry and through his cavalry. ¹⁸The Misrayimites will acknowledge that I am Yahweh when I show my splendour through Par'oh, through his chariotry and through his cavalry.'

¹⁹God's envoy, who had been going before the Yisraelite camp, moved on and went behind them, and the cloud pillar moved on from before them and stood behind them, ²⁰so it came between the Misrayimite camp and the Yisraelite camp. So there was the cloud and the darkness, though it lit the night.

The one didn't draw near the other all night, ²¹but Mosheh stretched out his hand over the sea and Yahweh caused the sea to go by means of a vigorous east wind, all night, and made the sea into parched ground. So the water split ²²and the Yisraelites came into the middle of the sea on the dry ground, with the water a wall for them on their right and on their left. ²³The Misrayimites pursued, and all Par'oh's horse, his chariotry and his cavalry came into the middle of the sea.

## The good kind of fear returns

²⁴At the morning watch Yahweh looked out at the Misrayimite camp through the fire and cloud pillar, and made the Misrayimite camp turmoil. ²⁵He jammed the wheels of its chariotry so they drove them with difficulty. Misrayim said, 'I must flee from before Yisra'el, because Yahweh is battling for them against Misrayim.'

²⁶Yahweh said to Mosheh, 'Stretch out your hand over the sea, so the water comes back over Misrayim, over its chariotry and over its cavalry.' ²⁷Mosheh stretched out his hand over the sea, and as morning turned its face the sea came back to its regular position while the Misrayimites were fleeing to meet it. So Yahweh shook the Misrayimites off into the middle of the sea. ²⁸The water came back and covered the chariotry and the cavalry. As for all Par'oh's force coming behind them into the sea, not one of them remained. ²⁹But the Yisraelites: they had gone on dry ground in the middle of the sea with the water a wall for them on their right and on their left.

[30]Yahweh delivered Yisra'el that day from the hand of Misrayim. Yisra'el saw Misrayim dead on the shore of the sea. [31]Yisra'el saw the great control with which Yahweh had acted against Misrayim, and they were in awe of Yahweh. They trusted in Yahweh and in his servant Mosheh.

## Yes, Yahweh reigns

**15** Then Mosheh and the Yisra'elites sang this song for Yahweh. They said:

I'll sing for Yahweh because he acted
  majestically, so majestically:
    horse and its rider he threw into the sea.
[2]Yah is my vigour and my strength:
  he became my deliverance.
This is my God – I'll glorify him:
  my father's God – I'll exalt him.
[3]Yahweh is a strong man;
  Yahweh is his name.
[4]Par'oh's chariotry and his force he threw into
    the sea,
  the pick of his adjutants sank in the Reed Sea.
[5]Deeps covered them,
  they went down into the depths like a stone.
[6]Your right hand, Yahweh, was triumphant in
    energy;
  your right hand, Yahweh, smashed the
    enemy.
[7]In the greatness of your majesty you tore down
    those who rose up against you;
  you sent off your rage, it devoured them like
    straw.
[8]At the blast of your nostrils
  water piled up.
Floods stood up as a heap,
  deeps solidified in the heart of the sea.
[9]The enemy said, 'I'll pursue, overtake;
  I'll share out spoil, my appetite will have its
    fill.
I'll bare my sword,
  my hand will dispossess them.'
[10]You blew with your blast, the sea covered
    them;
  they sank like lead in the august water.
[11]Who is like you among the gods, Yahweh,
  who is like you, triumphant in sacredness,
Awe-inspiring in praises,
  doing extraordinary things?

[12]You stretched out your hand,
  earth swallowed them.
[13]In your commitment you've led the people
    that you restored,
  in your vigour you've guided them to your
    sacred abode.
[14]Peoples have heard and shuddered,
  writhing has seized the people living in
    Peleshet [Philistia].
[15]Then Edom's chiefs have become fearful,
  Mo'ab's leaders.
A shudder has seized them,
  all the people living in Kena'an have melted.
[16]Alarm and dread have fallen upon them;
  through your arm's greatness they have
    become as still as stone,
Until your people have passed, Yahweh,
  until the people you acquired have passed.
[17]You've brought them and planted them on the
    mountain that is your domain,
  the established place for you to live in that
    you've made, Yahweh,
The sanctuary, Lord, your hands have
    established:
[18]Yahweh will reign for ever and ever!

## Dancing, singing, protesting

[19]Because Par'oh's horse, his chariotry and his riders came into the sea, and Yahweh let the sea's water come back on them, whereas the Yisra'elites went on dry ground in the middle of the sea. [20]Miryam the prophetess, Aharon's sister, took a tambourine in her hand, and all the women went out after her with tambourines and with dancing. [21]Miryam chanted for them:

Sing for Yahweh, because he has acted
  majestically, so majestically:
    horse and its rider he threw into the sea.

[22]Mosheh got Yisra'el to move on from the Reed Sea and they went out into the Shur Wilderness. They went for three days in the wilderness, and found no water. [23]They came to Marah [Bitter] and couldn't drink water from Marah because it was bitter; that's why they named it Marah. [24]The people protested at Mosheh: 'What are we to drink?' [25]He cried out to Yahweh, and Yahweh pointed

out some wood. He threw it into the water and the water became sweet.

He made a decree, a ruling for them there; he tested them there. 26He said, 'If you listen attentively to the voice of Yahweh your God, do what is right in his eyes, give ear to his orders and keep all his decrees, I won't bring on you any of the diseases that I brought on Misrayim, because I am Yahweh your healer.'

27They came to Elim. There were twelve springs of water there and seventy palms. They camped there by the water.

## Protests in the wilderness

**16** The entire assembly of the Yisra'elites moved on from Elim and came to the Syn Wilderness, which is between Elim and Sinay, on the fifteenth day of the second month after their leaving the country of Misrayim.

2The entire assembly of the Yisra'elites protested against Mosheh and Aharon in the wilderness. 3The Yisra'elites said to them, 'If only we had died by Yahweh's hand in the country of Misrayim when we sat by a pot of meat and ate bread till we were full – because you've brought us out into this wilderness to make this entire congregation die of hunger!'

4Yahweh said to Mosheh, 'Here, I'm going to rain bread for you from the heavens so the people may go out and glean a day's allocation on its day, in order that I may test it, whether it will walk by my instruction or not. 5On the sixth day they will prepare what they bring in and it will be double what they glean each day.'

6Mosheh and Aharon said to all the Yisra'elites, 'In the evening, then you will acknowledge that it was Yahweh who got you out of the country of Misrayim, 7and in the morning, then you'll see Yahweh's splendour, when he listens to your protests against Yahweh. But we – what are we that you protest against us?' 8Mosheh said, 'When Yahweh gives you meat in the evening to eat and bread in the morning till you're full, when Yahweh listens to your protests that you're making against him: what are we? Your protests are not against us but against Yahweh.'

9So Mosheh said to Aharon, 'Say to the entire assembly of the Yisra'elites, "Draw near before Yahweh, because he's listened to your protests."'

## One day at a time

10As Aharon spoke to the entire assembly of the Yisra'elites, they turned their face to the wilderness, and there, Yahweh's splendour appeared in a cloud, 11and Yahweh spoke to Mosheh: 12'I've listened to the Yisra'elites' protests. Speak to them: "At twilight you shall eat meat and in the morning you shall have your fill of bread, and you will acknowledge that I am Yahweh your God."'

13In the evening quail came up and covered the camp, and in the morning there was a layer of dew round the camp. 14The layer of dew came up, and there, on the face of the wilderness something fine, flaky, fine like frost, on the earth.

15The Yisra'elites saw it and said each to his brother, 'What [*maan*] is it?' because they didn't know what it was. Mosheh said to them, 'It's the bread that Yahweh has given you as food. 16This is the thing that Yahweh has ordered. Glean some of it, each of you, as much as he will eat, a gallon per head for the number of persons you are. You're to get it, each individual for the people who are in his tent.'

17The Yisra'elites did so. They gleaned, one person getting much, one getting little. 18But when they measured it by the gallon, the one who got much didn't have excess and the one who got little didn't lack. They had gleaned, each individual, as much as he would eat. 19Mosheh said to them, 'No one is to leave any of it over until morning.' 20But they didn't listen to Mosheh. People left some of it over until morning, and it bred maggots and stank, and Mosheh was furious with them.

## Manna

21So they gleaned it morning by morning, each person, as much as he would eat. When the sun got hot, it would melt. 22On Friday they gleaned double bread, two gallons for a single person. All the assembly's leaders came and told Mosheh. 23He said to them, 'It's what Yahweh spoke. Tomorrow is a stopping, a sacred sabbath [*shabbat*, 'stop'] for Yahweh. Bake what you will bake and boil what you will boil, and lay up for yourselves all that's surplus for keeping until morning.'

[24]They laid it up until morning as Mosheh ordered. It didn't stink and there was no breeding in it. [25]Mosheh said, 'Eat it today, because today is a sabbath for Yahweh. Today you won't find it in the fields. [26]For six days you're to glean, but on the seventh day, the sabbath – there'll be none then.'

[27]On the seventh day some of the people went out to glean, but they didn't find any. [28]Yahweh said to Mosheh, 'How long do you people refuse to keep my orders and my instructions? [29]See that it's Yahweh who's given you the sabbath. That's why he's giving bread for two days on the sixth day. Stay each person where he is. No one's to go out of his place on the seventh day.' [30]So the people stopped on the seventh day.

[31]The household of Yisra'el named it *maan* [manna]. It was like coriander seed, white. Its taste was like wafers with sweetener. [32]Mosheh said, 'This is the thing that Yahweh has ordered: "A full gallon of it is to be for keeping through your generations, in order that people may see the bread that I let you eat in the wilderness when I got you out of the country of Misrayim."' [33]So Mosheh said to Aharon, 'Get a container and put a full gallon of *maan* in it, and lay it up before Yahweh for keeping through your generations.' [34]As Yahweh ordered Mosheh, Aharon laid it up before the Affirmation, for keeping.

## Hit the rock

[35]The Yisra'elites ate the *maan* for forty years until they came to the edge of the country of Kena'an. ([36]A gallon is a tenth of a barrel.)

**17** The entire Yisra'elite assembly moved on from the Syn Wilderness by stages at Yahweh's bidding. They camped at Rephidim, but there was no water for the people to drink, [2]and the people got into an argument with Mosheh. They said, 'Give us water so we can drink!' Mosheh said to them, 'Why argue with me? Why test Yahweh?' [3]But the people were thirsty there for water.

So the people protested against Mosheh: 'Why was it that you brought us up from Misrayim to have me and my children and my livestock die of thirst? [4]Mosheh cried out to Yahweh, 'What shall I do about this people? A little while and they'll stone me!'

[5]Yahweh said to Mosheh, 'Pass before the people, take some of Yisra'el's elders with you and your staff with which you struck the Ye'or in your hand, and go. [6]There, I'll be standing before you there on the crag at Horeb. You're to strike the crag, and water will come out of it, and the people will drink.'

Mosheh did so before the eyes of Yisra'el's elders. [7]He named the place Massah and Meribah ['Testing' and 'Argument'], because of the Yisra'elites' arguing and because of their testing Yahweh by saying, 'Is Yahweh among us or isn't he?'

## The first assailant

[8]Amaleq came and battled with Yisra'el at Rephidim. [9]Mosheh said to Yehoshua [Joshua], 'Choose some men for us and go out and do battle against Amaleq. Tomorrow I'm going to take my stand on top of the hill with God's staff in my hand.'

[10]Yehoshua did as Mosheh told him by battling against Amaleq, while Mosheh, Aharon and Hur went up to the top of the hill. [11]As Mosheh would raise his hand, Yisra'el would prevail, but as he would rest his hand, Amaleq would prevail. [12]So when Mosheh's hands were heavy, they got a stone and put it under him and he sat on it, while Aharon and Hur took hold of his hands, one on this side and one on that. So his hands were trustworthy until sundown [13]and Yehoshua overwhelmed Amaleq and its people with the mouth of the sword.

[14]Yahweh said to Mosheh, 'Write this in a document as a reminder, and put it into Yehoshua's ears, how I shall totally wipe out Amaleq's memory from under the heavens.' [15]Mosheh built an altar and named it 'Yahweh My Banner', [16]and said, 'A hand against Yah's throne! There will be a battle for Yahweh against Amaleq from generation to generation!'

## The first convert

**18** Yitro the Midyanite priest, Mosheh's father-in-law, heard all that God had done for Mosheh and for his people Yisra'el, how Yahweh had got Yisra'el out of Misrayim. [2]So Yitro, Mosheh's father-in-law, got Tsipporah, Mosheh's wife (after her sending away) ³and her two sons (of whom one had the name Gershom because – he said – 'I've been a resident [*ger*] in a foreign country' ⁴and the other had the name Eli'ezer because 'the God of my father has been my help [*ezer*] and rescued me from Par'oh's sword'), ⁵and Yitro, Mosheh's father-in-law, came with his sons and his wife to Mosheh in the wilderness where he was camped at God's mountain.

⁶He had said to Mosheh, 'I, your father-in-law Yitro, am coming to you with your wife and her two sons with her.' ⁷Mosheh went out to meet his father-in-law. He bowed low and kissed him. Each of them asked his neighbour about whether things were well, and they came into the tent.

⁸Mosheh recounted to his father-in-law all that Yahweh had done to Par'oh and to Misrayim for Yisra'el's sake, all the hardship that had befallen them on the way and how Yahweh had rescued them. ⁹Yitro rejoiced over all the good that Yahweh had done for Yisra'el when he rescued them from the hand of Misrayim. ¹⁰Yitro said, 'Yahweh be blessed, who rescued you from the hand of Misrayim and from the hand of Par'oh, who rescued the people from under the hand of Misrayim. ¹¹Now I acknowledge that Yahweh is greater than all gods, because in this matter they asserted themselves against them.' ¹²Yitro, Mosheh's father-in-law, got a burnt offering and sacrifices for God, and Aharon and all Yisra'el's elders came to eat a meal before God with Mosheh's father-in-law.

## On not doing everything yourself

¹³Next day Mosheh sat to decide things for the people, and the people stood round Mosheh from the morning until the evening. ¹⁴Mosheh's father-in-law saw all that he was doing for the people and said, 'What's this thing that you're doing for the people? Why are you sitting on your own with the entire people taking a stand round you from morning until evening?' ¹⁵Mosheh said to his father-in-law, 'Because the people come to me to enquire of God. ¹⁶When they have something, it comes to me and I decide between one person and his neighbour, and I enable them to know God's decrees and his instructions.'

¹⁷Mosheh's father-in-law said to him, 'The thing that you're doing isn't good. ¹⁸You'll totally wear yourself out, both you and this people that's with you, too, because the thing's too heavy for you. You can't do it on your own. ¹⁹So now listen to my voice. I'll give you some counsel. And God be with you! You yourself be near God for the people and you yourself bring the things to God, ²⁰and make clear to them the decrees and the instructions and enable them to acknowledge the way in which they're to go and the action that they're to take. ²¹But from the entire people, you yourself are to behold capable individuals who live in awe of God, truthful individuals, who are hostile to dishonest gain, and to set them over them as divisional officials, section officials, unit officials and group officials, ²²to decide things for the people at all times. Every big thing they'll bring to you but every small thing they'll decide themselves. Make things lighter for yourself; they will carry things with you. ²³If you do this thing (and so God orders you), you'll be able to stand, and also this entire people will come to its place with things being well.'

²⁴Mosheh listened to the voice of his father-in-law and did everything that he said. ²⁵Mosheh chose capable individuals from all Yisra'el and made them heads over the people, divisional officials, section officials, unit officials and group officials. ²⁶They would decide things for the people at all times. The tough thing they'd bring to Mosheh, but every small thing they'd decide themselves.

²⁷Then Mosheh sent his father-in-law off, and he went his way to his own country.

## Two kinds of preparation for meeting God

**19** At the beginning of the third month after the Yisra'elites came out of the country of Misrayim, on that day they came to the Sinay Wilderness. ²They moved on from Rephidim, came to the Sinay Wilderness and camped in the wilderness. Yisra'el camped there in front of the mountain ³and Mosheh went up to God.

Yahweh called to him from the mountain: 'You're to say this to the household of Ya'aqob and to tell the Yisra'elites, ⁴"You yourselves saw what I did to Misrayim. I lifted you on eagles' wings and brought you to me. ⁵So now, if you really listen to my voice and keep my pact, you'll be for me personal treasure from among all the peoples. Because the entire earth is mine, ⁶but you in particular will be a priestly kingdom, a sacred nation, for me." These are the words that you're to speak to the Yisra'elites.'

⁷Mosheh came and called for the people's elders and set before them all these words that Yahweh ordered him. ⁸The entire people answered together, 'Everything that Yahweh spoke we will do.' Mosheh took the people's words back to Yahweh, ⁹and Yahweh said to Mosheh, 'Here, I'm coming to you in a thick cloud, so the people may hear when I speak with you and also may trust in you permanently.'

So Mosheh told Yahweh the people's words, ¹⁰and Yahweh said to Mosheh, 'Go to the people and make them sacred today and tomorrow, and get them to wash their clothes. ¹¹They're to be ready for the third day, because on the third day Yahweh will come down before the eyes of the entire people on Mount Sinay. ¹²You're to set bounds for the people round about, saying "Keep watch over yourselves about going up the mountain or touching its border. Anyone who touches the mountain is absolutely to be put to death. ¹³No hand is to touch him, because he's simply to be stoned or simply to be shot with arrows. Whether it's an animal or a person, he's not to live. When the ram's horn sounds out, they may go up the mountain."'

*Beware the electric nature of a meeting with God*

¹⁴So Mosheh came down from the mountain to the people and made the people sacred, and they washed their clothes. ¹⁵He said to the people, 'Be ready for the third day. Don't approach a woman.'

¹⁶On the third day, when the morning came, there were sounds, lightning-flashes and heavy cloud on the mountain, and the very strong sound of a horn. The entire people that was in the camp trembled. ¹⁷But Mosheh got the people to come out of the camp to meet God, and they took their stand at the bottom of the mountain.

¹⁸Now Mount Sinay smoked, all of it, as a result of the fact that Yahweh had come down on it in fire. His smoke went up like the smoke of a kiln. The entire mountain trembled greatly. ¹⁹The horn's sound was getting stronger and stronger. When Mosheh would speak, God would answer him with the sound.

²⁰So Yahweh came down on Mount Sinay, to the top of the mountain, and Yahweh called Mosheh to the top of the mountain. Mosheh went up, ²¹but Yahweh said to Mosheh, 'Go down, testify against the people so they don't tear through to Yahweh to look, or many of them will fall. ²²The priests also, who come up to Yahweh, must make themselves sacred, so Yahweh doesn't break out against them.' ²³Mosheh said to Yahweh, 'The people cannot come up to Mount Sinay, because you yourself testified against us, "Set bounds for the mountain and make it sacred."' ²⁴But Yahweh said to him, 'Go, get down, then you come up, and Aharon with you, but the priests and the people are not to tear through to come up to Yahweh, so he doesn't break out against them.' ²⁵So Mosheh went down to the people and said it to them.

*A rule of life*

**20** God spoke all these words: ²'I am Yahweh your God who got you out of the country of Misrayim, out of a household of serfs.

³For you there will be no other gods in my presence.

⁴You will not make yourself a sculpture or any shape that's in the heavens above, that's on the earth below or that's in the water under the earth. ⁵You will not bow low to them and you will not serve them. Because I, Yahweh your God, am the passionate God, attending to parents' waywardness in connection with children, with thirds and with fourths, for people who are hostile to me, ⁶but acting in commitment towards thousands for people who are loyal to me and who keep my orders.

⁷You will not lift up the name of Yahweh your God in respect of something empty, because Yahweh will not free of guilt a person who lifts up his name in respect of something empty.

⁸Be mindful of the sabbath day to make it sacred. ⁹For six days you can serve and do all your work, ¹⁰but the seventh day is a sabbath for Yahweh your God. You will not do any work, you, your son or your daughter, your servant or your handmaid, your animal or your resident who is in your communities. ¹¹Because in six days Yahweh made the heavens, the earth, the sea and all that's in them, and settled down on the seventh day. That's why Yahweh blessed the seventh day and made it sacred.

¹²Honour your father and your mother, in order that your time may be long on the land that Yahweh your God is going to give you.

¹³You will not murder.

¹⁴You will not be adulterous.

¹⁵You will not steal.

¹⁶You will not avow false testimony against your neighbour.

¹⁷You will not desire your neighbour's household: you will not desire your neighbour's wife, his servant or his handmaid, his ox or his donkey, or anything your neighbour has.'

## No manufactured gods

¹⁸While the entire people were looking at the sounds, the flashes, the sound of the horn, and the smoking mountain – as the people looked, they hesitated and stood at a distance. ¹⁹They said to Mosheh, 'You speak with us and we'll listen. God mustn't speak with us, or we'll die.' ²⁰Mosheh said to the people, 'Don't be afraid, because God has come in order to test you, and in order that awe for him may be upon your faces, so you don't do wrong.' ²¹But the people stood at a distance, whereas Mosheh went up to the denseness where God was.

²²Yahweh said to Mosheh, 'You're to say this to the Yisraelites: "You yourselves saw how I spoke with you from the heavens. ²³With me you will not make gods of silver and you will not make gods of gold for yourselves. ²⁴An altar of soil you will make for me, and you will sacrifice on it your burnt offerings and your well-being offerings, your flock and your herd. At every site where I cause my name to be commemorated, I'll come to you and bless you.

²⁵If you make an altar out of stones for me, you will not build it of cut stone, because when you've wielded your cutter on them, you'll have made them ordinary. ²⁶You will not go up my altar by steps, so your nakedness will not be exposed on it."

## Treating bondservants properly

**21** These are the rulings that you're to set before them.

²When you acquire a Hebrew servant, he's to serve for six years. In the seventh he's to leave as a free man, for nothing. ³If he comes by himself, he leaves by himself. If he possesses a wife, his wife leaves with him. ⁴If his lord gives him a wife and she gives birth to sons or daughters for him, the wife and her children belong to her lord. He leaves by himself. ⁵If the servant explicitly says, "I am loyal to my lord, my wife and my children. I won't leave as a free man", ⁶his lord is to bring him up to God and bring him up to the door or the doorpost, and his lord is to pierce his ear with an awl. He's his servant permanently.

⁷When someone sells his daughter as a handmaid, she doesn't leave as servants do. ⁸If she is bad in the eyes of her lord, who had designated her for himself, he's to let her be redeemed. He doesn't have the power to sell her to a foreign people, because of his breaking faith with her. ⁹But if he was designating her for his son, he's to deal with her in accordance with the ruling for daughters. ¹⁰If he takes himself another wife, he will not withhold her food, her clothing or her time. ¹¹If he doesn't do these three things for her, she may leave for nothing, without payment.

## An eye for an eye

¹²Someone who strikes a man down, so he dies, is absolutely to be put to death. ¹³Someone who didn't set a trap, but God made him fall into his hand: I shall set a site for you where he may flee. ¹⁴But when someone asserts himself against his neighbour so as to kill him with shrewdness, you're to take him from beside my altar to die.

¹⁵Someone who strikes down his father or his mother is absolutely to be put to death.

¹⁶Someone who kidnaps a person, and he sells him or he's found in his possession, is absolutely to be put to death. ¹⁷Someone who slights his father or his mother is absolutely to be put to death.

¹⁸When people get into an argument and one strikes his neighbour with a stone or with his fist and he doesn't die but he falls into bed, ¹⁹if he gets up and walks about outside on his staff, the one who struck him can be free of guilt, only he's to pay for his sitting around, and definitely to get him healed. ²⁰When someone strikes his servant or his handmaid with a club and he dies under his hand, he's definitely to submit to redress. ²¹Yet if he stands after a day or two, he's not to be subjected to redress, because he's his own silver.

²²When men fight and they hit a pregnant woman and her children come out but there's no harm, he's definitely to make compensation, as the woman's husband may lay on him, or give it by arbitration. ²³If there's harm, you're to give life for life, ²⁴eye for eye, tooth for tooth, hand for hand, foot for foot, ²⁵burn for burn, wound for wound, bruise for bruise. ²⁶When someone strikes his servant's eye or his handmaid's eye and devastates it, he's to send him off as a free person because of his eye. ²⁷If someone makes his servant's tooth or his handmaid's tooth fall out, he's to send him off as a free person because of his tooth.

### The goring ox and the missing ox

²⁸When an ox gores a man or a woman and he dies, the ox is absolutely to be stoned and its flesh is not to be eaten, but the ox's owner can be free of guilt. ²⁹But if the ox has been inclined to gore in previous days, and it's been testified with its owner, and he doesn't keep it in and it causes the death of a man or a woman, the ox is to be stoned and its owner is also to be put to death. ³⁰If a ransom is laid on him, he's to give the redemption price for his life in accordance with all that's laid on him. ³¹Should it either gore a son or gore a daughter, it's to be done to him in accordance with this ruling. ³²If the ox gores a servant or a handmaid, he's to give silver, thirty sheqels, to his lord, and the ox is to be stoned.

³³When someone opens a cistern or when someone digs a cistern and doesn't cover it, and an ox or a donkey falls into it, ³⁴the cistern's owner is to make good. He's to give back silver to its owner, but the dead thing will be his. ³⁵When someone's ox injures his neighbour's ox and it dies, they're to sell the live ox and divide the silver, and also divide the dead thing. ³⁶If it was known that the ox was inclined to gore in previous days and its owner doesn't keep it in, he must definitely make good, ox for ox, but the dead thing will be his.

**22** When someone steals an ox or sheep and slaughters it or sells it, he's to make good with five from the herd for the ox or four from the fold for the sheep. (²If the thief is found while breaking in and he's struck down and dies, no bloodshed is counted in respect of him. ³If the sun had risen on him, bloodshed is counted in respect of him.) He's definitely to make good; if he doesn't have it, he's to be sold for his theft. ⁴If the thing stolen (either ox or donkey or sheep, alive) is actually found in his possession, he's to make good double.

### More problems on the farm

⁵When someone burns up a field or vineyard (or sends off his animals so they burn up someone else's field), he's to make good from the good things of his field or from the good things of his vineyard. ⁶When a fire breaks out and reaches the thorns, so stacked grain or standing grain or the field is consumed, the person who caused the burn is definitely to make good.

⁷When someone gives his neighbour silver or things to keep but it's stolen from the man's house, if the thief is found, he's to make good double. ⁸If the thief isn't found, the owner of the house is to draw near to God [to testify] that he didn't lay hand on his neighbour's work. ⁹Over any breach of trust, over an ox or donkey or sheep or garment or any loss about which someone says, 'This is it', the thing involving the two of them is to come to God. The one whom God says is in the wrong is to make good double to his neighbour.

¹⁰When someone gives his neighbour a donkey or ox or sheep or any animal to keep and it dies or is injured or is taken off, with no one seeing, ¹¹there's to be an oath to Yahweh between the two of them that he hasn't laid his

hand on his neighbour's work. Its owner is to accept it, and he's not to make good. [12]But if it's actually stolen from him, he's to make good to its owner. [13]If it gets mauled at all, he's to bring it as evidence. For something mauled, he's not to make good.

## On taking advantage of people

[14]When someone asks for something from his neighbour and it's injured or it dies, its owner not being with it, he's definitely to make good. [15]If its owner was with it, he's not to make good. If it was a hire, he comes into its hire.
[16]If a man seduces a young girl who's not betrothed and sleeps with her, he's to make the actual marriage payment for her as a wife for himself. [17]If her father absolutely refuses to give her to him, he's to weigh out silver in accordance with the marriage payment for young girls.
[18]A medium: you will not allow her to live. [19]Anyone who has sex with an animal: is absolutely to be put to death. [20]Someone who sacrifices to a god other than Yahweh alone: is to be devoted.
[21]A resident: you will not oppress or afflict him, because you were residents in the country of Misrayim. [22]Any widow or orphan: you will not humble them. [23]If you humble them at all, when they cry aloud to me, I shall listen attentively to their cry. [24]My anger will rage and I shall kill you with the sword. Your wives will become widows, your children orphans.
[25]If you lend silver to my people, to a humble person who is with you, you will not be like a lender to him. You will not make him pay interest. [26]If you take your neighbour's coat as a pledge, before sundown you will give it back to him, [27]because it alone is his covering, his wrapping for his skin. What is he to sleep in? When he cries out to me, I shall listen, because I am gracious.

## You know what it's like to be a resident alien

[28]You will not slight God or curse a leader among your people. [29]Your fullness and the pressing of your grapes: you will not delay them. The firstborn of your sons: you will give him to me. [30]You will do this with your oxen

and with your sheep. It will be seven days with its mother; on the eighth day you will give it to me. [31]You will be sacred people to me. You will not eat meat from an animal mauled in the fields; you will throw it to the dogs.

**23** You will not carry an empty report. Don't put your hand in with a faithless person to become a felonious witness. [2]You will not follow a majority to act badly. You will not avow in an argument so as to bend after a majority, so as to bend it. [3]Neither will you defer to a poor person in his argument.
[4]When you come upon an ox belonging to your enemy or his donkey, straying, you will take it straight back to him. [5]When you see a donkey belonging to someone who is hostile to you lying down under its load and you would refrain from loosening [the load] for it, you will definitely loosen it with him.
[6]You will not bend a poor person's ruling when he is in an argument. [7]A false statement: stay distant from it. Someone who is free of guilt and is in the right: don't kill him, because I do not treat the person who is in the right as in the wrong. [8]A bribe: don't accept it, because a bribe blinds people who can see and overturns the statements of people who are in the right. [9]A resident: you will not afflict him; you yourselves know the feelings of a resident, because you were residents in the country of Misrayim.

## The principle of the seventh

[10]For six years you're to sow your land and gather its yield. [11]The seventh, you're to allow it to lie and leave it alone. The needy among your people may eat, and what they leave the creatures of the wild may eat. So you're to do for your vineyard and for your olive. [12]For six days you can do your work, but on the seventh day you're to stop, in order that your ox and your donkey may find relief and the offspring of your handmaid and the resident may find refreshment.
[13]You're to keep watch concerning everything I've said to you. You will not commemorate the name of other gods. It will not be heard in your mouth.
[14]On three occasions in the year you're to hold a festival for me. [15]You're to keep the Flatbread Festival: for seven days you're

to eat flatbread as I ordered you, at the set time in the month of Aviv [March–April], because in it you left Misrayim; and people are not to appear before me empty-handed;

16the Harvest Festival: the first products of your work, of what you sow in the fields; the Ingathering Festival at the end of the year, when you gather your work from the fields. 17Three times in the year, every male among you is to appear before the Lord Yahweh.

18You will not offer the blood of a sacrifice for me accompanied by leavened bread. The fat from a festival for me will not stay until morning. 19The very first of the first products of your land you're to bring to the house of Yahweh your God.

You will not cook a kid goat in its own mother's milk.

## How to get into the promised land

20Here, I'm going to send an envoy before you to keep you on the way and to bring you to the place that I've prepared. 21Keep watch before him. Listen to his voice. Don't defy him, because he won't carry your rebellions, because my name is within him. 22But if you do really listen to his voice and do everything I speak, I'll be an enemy to your enemies, an adversary to your adversaries, 23because my envoy will go before you and bring you to the Amorite, the Hittite, the Perizzite, the Kena'anite, the Hivvite and the Yebusite, and I shall efface them.

24You will not bow low to their gods, you will not serve them, you will not do as they do, but completely tear them down and completely break up their columns. 25You are to serve Yahweh your God. He will bless your bread and your water, and I will remove illness from among you. 26There'll be no one miscarrying or infertile in your country. I'll bring to completion the number of your days.

27I shall send off a dread of me before you and it will throw into turmoil all the people among whom you come. I shall make all your enemies turn their back before you. 28I shall send a hornet before you, and it will drive out the Hivvites, the Kena'anites and the Hittites from before you.

29I shall not drive them out from before you in one year, in case the country becomes a desolation and the creatures of the wild multiply against you. 30Little by little I shall drive them out from before you until you're fruitful and you have the country as a domain. 31I shall set your border from the Reed Sea to the Pelishtites' Sea and from the wilderness to the River [Euphrates], because I shall give into your hand the people living in the country and you will drive them out from before you. 32You will not solemnize a pact with them or with their gods. 33They won't live in your country, in case they cause you to do wrong in relation to me because you serve their gods, because it would be a snare to you.'

## Seeing God

**24** He said to Mosheh, 'Go up to Yahweh, you and Aharon, Nadab and Abihu, and seventy of the Yisra'elite elders. Bow low from afar. 2Mosheh alone is to come up to Yahweh; they're not to come up and the people are not to go up with him.'

3Mosheh came and recounted all Yahweh's words to the people, all the rulings. The entire people answered with one voice: 'All the things Yahweh spoke of, we will do.' 4Mosheh wrote down all Yahweh's words.

Mosheh started early in the morning and built an altar beneath the mountain, and twelve columns for the twelve Yisra'elite clans. 5He sent the Yisra'elite boys and they offered up burnt offerings and made well-being sacrifices of bulls. 6Mosheh took half the blood and put it in basins, and half the blood he tossed over the altar. 7He got the pact document and read it in the people's ears. They said, 'All that Yahweh spoke of, we will do, we will obey.' 8Mosheh took the blood, tossed it over the people, and said, 'Here is the blood of the pact that Yahweh has solemnized with you on the basis of all these words.'

9Then Mosheh and Aharon, Nadab and Abihu, and seventy of the Yisra'elite elders went up, 10and saw the God of Yisra'el. Under his feet was something like a sapphire pavement, like the actual heavens for purity. 11Against the Yisra'elites' 'pillars' he didn't put out his hand. They beheld God, and they ate and drank.

¹²Yahweh said to Mosheh, 'Go up to me on the mountain and be there. I shall give you the stone tablets with the instruction and the order that I've written, to instruct them.' ¹³So Mosheh and Yehoshua his minister set off, and Mosheh went up to God's mountain. ¹⁴To the elders he said, 'Stay here for us till we come back to you. Here are Aharon and Hur with you. Anyone who has things to raise can come up to them.'

## How to build a sanctuary

¹⁵So Mosheh went up the mountain. The cloud covered the mountain ¹⁶and Yahweh's splendour dwelt on Mount Sinay. The cloud covered it for six days and on the seventh day he called to Mosheh from the middle of the cloud. ¹⁷The appearance of Yahweh's splendour was like devouring fire on the top of the mountain before the eyes of the Yisra'elites. ¹⁸Mosheh came into the middle of the cloud and went up the mountain. Mosheh was on the mountain for forty days and forty nights.

**25** Yahweh spoke to Mosheh: ²'Speak to the Yisra'elites so they get a contribution for me. You're to get the contribution for me from every individual whose heart makes him free. ³This is the contribution that you're to get from them: gold, silver, copper; ⁴blue, purple and bright crimson, linen, goats' [hair], ⁵ram skins dyed red, dolphin skins, acacia wood; ⁶oil for lighting, spices for the anointing oil and the aromatic incense; ⁷onyx stones and stones for the mountings for the chasuble and for the pouch. ⁸They're to make me a sanctuary, so that I may dwell among them. ⁹In accordance with everything that I'm going to let you see, the pattern of the dwelling and the pattern of all the articles in it, so you're to make it.

¹⁰They're to make an acacia wood chest, its length two and a half cubits, its width a cubit and a half, and its height a cubit and a half. ¹¹You are to overlay it with pure gold, overlay it inside and outside, and make a gold moulding on it all round. ¹²You're to cast four gold rings for it and put them on its four feet, two rings on one side of it and two on the other. ¹³You're to make acacia wood poles and overlay them with gold, ¹⁴and insert the poles into the rings on

the sides of the chest, so as to carry the chest by them. ¹⁵The poles are to be in the rings of the chest; they are not to depart from it. ¹⁶Put into the chest the affirmation that I shall give you.

## The expiation cover and the table

¹⁷You're to make an expiation cover of pure gold, its length two and a half cubits and its width a cubit and a half, ¹⁸and to make two gold sphinxes (of hammered work you're to make them) at the two ends of the expiation cover. ¹⁹You're to make one sphinx at one end and the other sphinx at the other end; you're to make the sphinxes issuing from the expiation cover at its two ends. ²⁰The sphinxes are to be spreading their wings upwards, shielding the expiation cover with their wings, and with their faces one towards the other; the sphinxes' faces will be towards the expiation cover. ²¹You're to put the expiation cover on the chest, on top, and put into the chest the affirmation that I shall give you. ²²I shall keep an appointment with you there and speak with you from above the expiation cover, from between the sphinxes that are above the affirmation chest, all that I shall order you for the Yisra'elites.

²³You're to make an acacia wood table, its length two cubits, its width one cubit and its height a cubit and a half. ²⁴You're to overlay it with pure gold and make a gold moulding for it all round. ²⁵You're to make a rim for it, a handbreadth all round, and to make a gold moulding for its rim all round. ²⁶You're to make four gold rings for it and put the rings at the four corners that are at its four legs. ²⁷The rings are to be close by the rim as housing for the poles for carrying the table. ²⁸You're to make the poles of acacia wood and overlay them with gold. The table will be carried by means of them.

²⁹You're to make its dishes, its ladles, its pitchers and its bowls, with which the drink offering will be poured – you're to make them of pure gold. ³⁰You're to put the presence bread on the table before my presence, regularly.

## The candelabrum

³¹You're to make a candelabrum of pure gold. The candelabrum is to be made of hammered

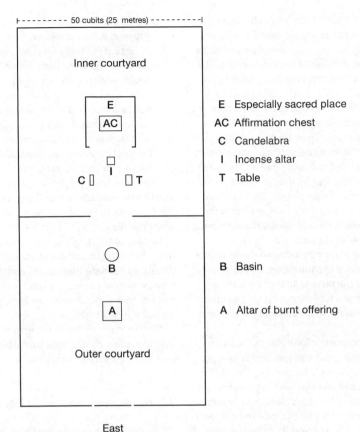

┠- - - - - - - - 50 cubits (25 metres) - - - - - - - - -┨

Inner courtyard

E    Especially sacred place
AC  Affirmation chest
C    Candelabra
I     Incense altar
T    Table

B    Basin

A    Altar of burnt offering

East

*Exodus 25: The sanctuary – Yahweh's dwelling*

work, its base and its stem. Its cups, its flowers and its petals are to come from it; ³²six stems going out from its flanks, three stems of the candelabrum from its one flank and three stems of the candelabrum from its second flank; ³³three cups made like almond blossom on one stem, flower and petal, three stems made like almond blossom on another stem, flower and petal; so for the six stems going out from the candelabrum.

³⁴On the candelabrum four cups made like almond blossom, its flowers and its petals; ³⁵a flower beneath two stems issuing from it, and a flower beneath two stems issuing from it, and a flower beneath two stems issuing from it, for the six branches going out from the candelabrum; ³⁶their flowers and their stems are to come from it, all of it a single hammered work, pure gold. ³⁷You're to make its seven lamps (they are to put up its lamps so they

give light on the area before it) ³⁸and its tongs and its pans of pure gold. ³⁹It will be made of a talent of pure gold, with all these articles.

⁴⁰See that you act by the pattern for them that you're being shown on the mountain.

## How to weave a sanctuary

**26** You're to make the dwelling from ten pieces of woven linen and from blue, purple and bright crimson, and to make them with sphinxes, designer's work. ²The length of each piece, twenty-eight cubits and the width of each piece, four cubits – one size for all the pieces. ³Five of the pieces are to be joining one to the other, and the other five pieces are to be joining one to the other.

⁴You're to make loops of blue on the lip of the one piece at the edge in its joined set,

and to make them in this way at the lip of the edging piece in the second joined set. ⁵You're to make fifty loops on the one piece and make fifty loops at the edge of the piece that's in the second joined set, with the loops holding one to the other. ⁶You're to make fifty gold clasps and to join the pieces one to the other with the clasps so the dwelling becomes one unit.

⁷You're to make pieces from goats' [hair] for a tent over the dwelling; you're to make eleven pieces. ⁸The length of each piece, thirty by the cubit; the width, four by the cubit each piece; one size for the eleven pieces. ⁹You're to join five of the pieces on their own, and six of the pieces on their own, and double the sixth piece near the front of the tent.

¹⁰You're to make fifty loops on the lip of one outermost piece in a joined set, and fifty loops on the lip of the piece in the other joined set. ¹¹You're to make fifty copper clasps and insert the clasps into the loops and join the tent so it becomes one unit.

¹²The overhang that's surplus in the tent's pieces: the half-piece that's surplus is to overhang the back of the dwelling, ¹³while the cubit at one end and the cubit at the other end in the surplus of the tent's pieces will be hung over the flanks of the dwelling on one side and on the other side, to cover it. ¹⁴And you're to make a covering for the tent of ram skins dyed red, with a covering of dolphin skins above it.

## How to build a sanctuary

¹⁵You're to make the planks for the dwelling of acacia wood, standing upright. ¹⁶The length of a plank, ten cubits; the width of a plank, a cubit and a half, each one; ¹⁷two projections for a plank, parallel one to the other. So you're to do for all the dwelling's planks. ¹⁸You're to make the planks for the dwelling: twenty planks for the south (southern) aspect; ¹⁹you're to make forty silver sockets under the twenty planks, two sockets under a plank for its two projections and two sockets under the next plank for its two projections. ²⁰For the dwelling's second side, for the north aspect: twenty planks, ²¹with their forty silver sockets, two sockets under a plank and two sockets under the next plank.

²²For the back of the dwelling, to the west, you're to make six planks, ²³and you're to make two planks for the corners of the dwelling, at the back. ²⁴They're to be double underneath, but together they're to be whole at its top, at the one ring. So it will be for both of them: they'll form two corners. ²⁵Thus there will be eight planks with their silver sockets, sixteen sockets: two sockets under one plank and two sockets under the next plank.

²⁶You're to make bars of acacia wood: five for the planks in one side of the dwelling, ²⁷five bars for the planks in the second side of the dwelling, and five bars for the planks in the side of the dwelling at the back, to the west, ²⁸with the central bar in the middle of the planks running from end to end. ²⁹You're to overlay the planks with gold and to make their rings of gold as housing for the bars, and to overlay the bars with gold.

³⁰You're to set up the dwelling in accordance with the ruling about it that you've been enabled to see on the mountain.

## The curtain, the screen and the altar

³¹You're to make a curtain of blue, purple and bright crimson, and of woven linen. It's to be made as designer's work, with sphinxes. ³²You're to put it on four posts of acacia overlaid with gold, with their gold hooks, on four silver sockets. ³³You're to put the curtain under the clasps and bring the affirmation chest there, behind the curtain. The curtain will make a distinction between the sacred place and the especially sacred place for you. ³⁴You're to put the expiation cover on the affirmation chest in the especially sacred place. ³⁵You're to place the table outside the curtain and the candelabrum in front of the table on the south side of the dwelling, and to put the table on the north side. ³⁶You're to make a screen for the tent entrance, of blue, purple and bright crimson, and of woven linen, embroiderer's work, ³⁷and to make for the screen five posts of acacia and overlay them with gold, with their gold hooks, and to cast for them five copper sockets.

**27** You're to make the altar of acacia wood, five cubits in length, five cubits in width (the altar will be square), and three cubits in height, ²and to make its horns on its four corners (its horns are to come from it), and overlay it with copper. ³You're to make its buckets for clearing it of waste, its shovels, its basins, its forks and its pans: you're to make all its utensils of copper. ⁴You're to make a grating for it, a mesh made of copper, and make on the mesh four copper rings at its four corners. ⁵You're to put it beneath the altar ledge, underneath; the mesh is to be halfway up the altar. ⁶You're to make poles for the altar, poles of acacia wood, and overlay them with copper. ⁷The poles are to be inserted into the rings and the poles are to be on the two sides of the altar when it's carried. ⁸You're to make it hollow, of boards. As it has been shown you on the mountain, so they are to make it.

## The courtyard

⁹You're to make a courtyard for the dwelling: On the south (southern) aspect: hangings for the courtyard, woven linen, a hundred by the cubit the length on the one aspect; ¹⁰its twenty posts and their twenty sockets, copper; the posts' hooks and their clasps, silver. ¹¹So also on the north aspect along the length: hangings, a hundred cubits the length; its twenty posts and their twenty sockets, copper; the posts' hooks and their clasps, silver. ¹²The width of the courtyard on the west aspect: hangings, fifty cubits; their posts, ten; their sockets, ten. ¹³The width of the courtyard on the front aspect, the east, fifty cubits: ¹⁴hangings, fifteen cubits to the shoulder; their posts, three; their sockets, three; ¹⁵for the second shoulder, hangings, fifteen cubits; their posts, three; their sockets, three. ¹⁶For the courtyard gateway: a screen, twenty cubits, of blue, purple and bright crimson, and of woven linen, embroiderer's work; their posts, four; their sockets, four. ¹⁷All the courtyard's posts around: clasped with silver; their hooks, silver; their sockets, copper. ¹⁸The length of the courtyard, a hundred by the cubit; the width, fifty consistently; the height, five cubits; of woven linen. Their sockets, copper; ¹⁹for all the articles

in the dwelling in all its service, and all its pegs and all the courtyard's pegs, copper.

²⁰You yourself are to order the Yisra'elites that they are to get you pure pressed olive oil for lighting, for putting up a lamp regularly. ²¹In the appointment tent, outside the curtain which is over the affirmation, Aharon and his sons are to arrange it from evening till morning before Yahweh, a permanent decree through their generations for the Yisra'elites.

## How to dress a priest

**28** You yourself are to have Aharon your brother presented to you, and his sons with him, from among the Yisra'elites, to act as priests for me: Aharon, Nadab and Abihu, El'azar and Itamar, Aharon's sons. ²Make sacred garments for Aharon your brother, for splendour and for glory. ³You yourself are to speak to all the people who are smart in their thinking, the people I've filled with a smart spirit, so they may make Aharon's garments, for making him sacred to act as priest for me.

⁴These are the garments that they're to make: pouch, chasuble, coat, woven tunic, turban and sash. They're to make the sacred garments for Aharon your brother and for his sons to act as priests for me ⁵when they get the gold, the blue, purple and bright crimson, and linen.

⁶They're to make the chasuble of gold, of blue, purple and bright crimson, and of woven linen, designer's work. ⁷It will have two shoulder pieces joining to its two corners, so it will be joined. ⁸The chasuble's design-work strap, which is on it, is to be like its work, coming from it: of gold, of blue, purple and bright crimson, and of woven linen.

⁹You're to get two onyx stones and engrave on them the names of Yisra'el's sons, ¹⁰six of their names on the one stone and the remaining six names on the second, by their lines of descent. ¹¹As craftsman's work in stone, with seal engravings, you're to engrave the two stones with the names of Yisra'el's sons. You're to make them surrounded by gold braids. ¹²You're to put the two stones on the chasuble's shoulder pieces as reminder stones for Yisra'el's sons. Aharon is to carry their names before Yahweh on his two shoulder pieces for a reminder.

¹³You're to make braids of gold ¹⁴and two chains of pure gold, as plaitings. You're to make them as woven work and to put the woven chains on the braids.

## The decision pouch

¹⁵You're to make a decision pouch, designer's work. You're to make it like the work of the chasuble, of gold, of blue, purple and bright crimson, and of woven linen. ¹⁶It's to be square and folded double, its length a handbreadth and its width a handbreadth. ¹⁷You're to fill it with a filling of stones, four rows of stones:

the first row: a row of carnelian, chrysolyte and emerald;
¹⁸the second row: turquoise, sapphire and amethyst;
¹⁹the third row: jacinth, agate and crystal;
²⁰the fourth row: beryl, onyx and jasper.

They're to be set in gold in their fillings. ²¹The stones will correspond to the names of Yisra'el's sons, twelve corresponding to their names. With seal engravings, each corresponding to its name, they will be for the twelve clans. ²²On the pouch you're to make plaited chains, woven work, pure gold.

²³You're to make two gold rings on the pouch and to put the two rings on the two edges of the pouch. ²⁴You're to put the two gold weavings on the two rings at the edges of the pouch. ²⁵The two ends of the two weavings you're to put on the two braids, and you're to put them on the chasuble's shoulder pieces near its front. ²⁶You're to make two gold rings and put them on the two edges of the pouch at its lip, which is on the side nearer the chasuble. ²⁷You're to make two gold rings and put them on the chasuble's two shoulder pieces underneath, near the front, close by its join, above the chasuble's design-work strap. ²⁸They're to attach the pouch by its rings to the chasuble's rings with a blue cord, so it's on the chasuble's design-work strap and so the pouch doesn't come loose from on the chasuble.

²⁹Aharon is to carry the names of Yisra'el's sons on the decision pouch over his heart when he goes into the sacred place, for a reminder before Yahweh regularly. ³⁰You're

to put into the decision pouch the Urim and Tummim, so they're over Aharon's heart when he comes in before Yahweh. Aharon is to carry the decision-making for the Yisra'elites over his heart before Yahweh regularly.

## The coat and the medallion

³¹You're to make the chasuble coat, all blue. ³²There's to be an opening for the head in the middle of it. The lip for its opening all round is to be weaver's work (it's to be like the opening of a vest for it) so it doesn't tear. ³³On its hems you're to make pomegranates of blue, purple and bright crimson, on its hems all round, and gold bells among them all round, ³⁴a gold bell and a pomegranate, a gold bell and a pomegranate, on the coat's hems all round. ³⁵It's to be on Aharon for ministering so its sound may be heard when he comes into the sacred place before Yahweh and when he goes out, so he does not die.

³⁶You're to make a medallion of pure gold and engrave on it with seal engravings, "Sacred for Yahweh". ³⁷You're to put it on a blue cord so it's on the turban. It's to be near the front of the turban. ³⁸It's to be on Aharon's forehead so Aharon can carry the waywardness associated with the sacred objects that the Yisra'elites make sacred in connection with any of their sacred gifts. It will be on his forehead regularly, for their acceptance before Yahweh.

³⁹You're to weave the tunic of linen, you're to make a turban of linen and you're to make a sash, embroiderer's work.

⁴⁰For Aharon's sons you're to make tunics, and you're to make them sashes and to make mitres for them, for splendour and for glory. ⁴¹You're to put them on Aharon your brother and on his sons with him, and to anoint them, commission them and make them sacred, so they can act as priests for me.

⁴²You're to make cloth shorts for them to cover their naked flesh. They're to go from the hips to the thighs ⁴³and they're to be on Aharon and on his sons when they come into the appointment tent or when they come up to the altar to minister in the sacred place, so that they don't carry waywardness and die. It's a permanent decree for him and for his offspring after him.

## The first ordination offering

**29** This is the thing that you're to do for them in making them sacred to act as priests for me. Get one bull from the herd and two rams, whole, ²and flatbread and loaves of flatbread mixed with oil, and flat wafers spread with oil. You're to make them of fine wheat flour. ³You're to put them in a basket and present them in the basket, with the bull and with the two rams.

⁴Aharon and his sons you're to present at the entrance of the appointment tent and wash them with water. ⁵You're to get the garments and clothe Aharon with the tunic, the chasuble coat, the chasuble and the pouch, to wind the chasuble on him with the chasuble's design-work strap, ⁶place the turban on his head, put the sacred diadem on the turban, ⁷get the anointing oil, pour it on his head and anoint him.

⁸And you're to present his sons, clothe them with tunics, ⁹wrap round them with a sash, Aharon and his sons, and bind mitres on them. The priesthood will be theirs by a permanent decree.

You're then to commission Aharon and his sons. ¹⁰Present the bull before the appointment tent. Aharon and his sons are to lean their hands on the bull's head, ¹¹and you're to slaughter the bull before Yahweh at the entrance of the appointment tent. ¹²You're to get some of the bull's blood and put it on the altar's horns with your finger, and all the rest of the blood you're to pour out at the altar's base. ¹³You're to get all the fat that covers the innards, the lobe on the liver, and the two kidneys and the fat that's on them, and turn them into smoke on the altar. ¹⁴The bull's flesh, its skin and its intestines you're to burn in fire outside the camp. It's a decontamination.

## The second ordination offering

¹⁵You're to get the one ram, Aharon and his sons are to lean their hands on the ram's head, ¹⁶and you're to slaughter the ram, get its blood and toss it over the altar all round. ¹⁷You're to cut up the ram into its parts, wash its innards and its legs, put them along with its parts and along with its head, ¹⁸and turn the entire ram into smoke on the altar. It's a burnt offering

for Yahweh, a nice smell. It's a gift offering for Yahweh.

¹⁹Then you're to get the second ram, Aharon and his sons are to lean their hands on the ram's head, ²⁰and you're to slaughter the ram. You're to get some of its blood and put it on the lobe of Aharon's ear and on the lobe of his sons' right ear, on the thumb of their right hand and on the big toe of their right foot, and toss the rest of the blood over the altar all round. ²¹You're to get some of the blood that's on the altar and some of the anointing oil and spatter it on Aharon, on his garments, on his sons and on his sons' garments with him. So he will become sacred, he, his garments, his sons and his sons' garments with him.

²²You're to get from the ram the fat, the broad tail, the fat covering the innards, the lobe of the liver, the two kidneys, the fat that's on them, and the right thigh, because it's the commissioning ram, ²³and one round of bread, one loaf of bread made with oil and one wafer from the basket of flatbread that's before Yahweh, ²⁴put everything on Aharon's palms and on his sons' palms, and elevate them as an elevation offering before Yahweh. ²⁵Then you're to get them from their hand and turn them into smoke on the altar along with the burnt offering, for a nice smell before Yahweh. It's a gift offering for Yahweh.

## The next generation

²⁶You're to get the breast from Aharon's commissioning ram and elevate it as an elevation offering before Yahweh, and it will be your portion. ²⁷You're to make sacred the breast, the elevation offering and the thigh that was the contribution, which was offered up and which was taken up from the commissioning ram, from what belonged to Aharon and from what belonged to his sons, ²⁸and it will belong to Aharon and to his sons, as a permanent decree from the Yisra'elites, because it's a contribution. It will be a contribution from the Yisra'elites from the well-being sacrifices, their gift for Yahweh.

²⁹Aharon's sacred garments will be for his sons after him, for anointing and commissioning them in them. ³⁰For seven days the one of his sons who acts as priest in his place is to put them on, the one who comes into the

appointment tent to minister in the sacred place. ³¹You're to get the commissioning ram and cook its flesh at the sacred site, ³²and Aharon and his sons are to eat the ram's flesh and the bread that's in the basket, at the entrance of the appointment tent. ³³The people for whom expiation was made with them in commissioning them, in making them sacred, they're to eat them; an outsider is not to eat them, because they're sacred. ³⁴If some of the commissioning flesh or some of the bread is left over until morning, you're to burn what is left over in fire. It's not to be eaten, because it's sacred.

## How to start and end the day

³⁵You're to act towards Aharon and his sons in accordance with all that I've ordered you. For seven days you're to commission them. ³⁶You're to make a bull as a decontamination each day, for total expiation, and you're to decontaminate the altar through your making expiation on it, and to anoint it, to make it sacred. ³⁷For seven days you're to make expiation on the altar and make it sacred, so the altar becomes especially sacred, and anything that touches the altar becomes sacred. ³⁸This is what you're to make on the altar: two sheep, a year old, regularly each day. ³⁹Make one sheep in the morning and make the second sheep at twilight, ⁴⁰with a tenth of fine flour mixed with pressed oil (a quarter of a gallon) and a libation (a quarter of a gallon of wine for the one sheep). ⁴¹You're to make the second sheep at twilight. You're to make it in the same way as the morning grain offering and its libation, for a nice smell, a gift offering for Yahweh, ⁴²a regular burnt offering through your generations at the entrance of the appointment tent before Yahweh, where I shall keep an appointment with you to speak to you there, ⁴³and keep an appointment with the Yisra'elites there. It will become sacred through my splendour. ⁴⁴I will make the appointment tent and the altar sacred, and I will make Aharon and his sons sacred to act as priests for me. ⁴⁵I shall dwell among the Yisra'elites, I shall be God for them, ⁴⁶and they will acknowledge that I am Yahweh their God who got them out of the country of Misrayim to dwell among them. I am Yahweh their God.

## The incense altar

**30** You're to make an altar for burning incense. You're to make it of acacia wood, ²its length a cubit, its width a cubit (square) and its height two cubits, with its horns coming from it. ³You're to overlay it with pure gold – its top, its sides all round and its horns. You're to make a gold moulding for it all round. ⁴You're to make two gold rings for it under its moulding, on its two sides, and to make them on its two flanks so they can be housing for poles to carry it with. ⁵You're to make the poles of acacia wood and overlay them with gold.

⁶You're to put it before the curtain that's over the affirmation chest (before the curtain that's over the affirmation) where I will keep an appointment with you. ⁷Aharon is to burn sweet-smelling incense on it. Morning by morning when he looks after the lamps he's to burn it. ⁸And when Aharon sets up the lamps at twilight he's to burn incense regularly before Yahweh through your generations. ⁹You're not to offer up outside incense on it (either a burnt offering or a grain offering), and you're not to pour a libation on it. ¹⁰Aharon is to make expiation on its horns once a year with the blood of a decontamination for complete expiation. Once a year he's to make expiation on it through your generations. It's especially sacred for Yahweh.'

## The ransom price

¹¹Yahweh spoke to Mosheh: ¹²'When you take the sum of the Yisra'elites in connection with their register, they're to give for Yahweh, each individual, the ransom price for his life, when you register them, so there isn't an epidemic among them when you register them. ¹³This is what they're to give, each person who passes on to the register: a half-sheqel by the sanctuary sheqel (twenty grains to the sheqel) – a half-sheqel contribution for Yahweh. ¹⁴Each person passing on to the register, from the age of twenty years and upwards, is to give the contribution for Yahweh. ¹⁵The wealthy person is not to do more and the poor person is not to do less than the half-sheqel, in giving Yahweh's contribution to make expiation for your lives. ¹⁶You're to take the silver of complete expiation

from the Yisra'elites and give it for the service of the appointment tent. It's to be for the Yisra'elites a reminder before Yahweh, to make expiation for your lives.'

[17]Yahweh spoke to Mosheh: [18]'You're to make a copper basin and a copper stand for it, for washing, and to put it between the appointment tent and the altar. Put water there, [19]so Aharon and his sons may wash their hands and their feet from it. [20]When they go into the appointment tent they're to wash with water so they don't die. Or when they come up to the altar to minister by turning into smoke a gift offering for Yahweh, [21]they're to wash their hands and their feet so they don't die. For them it's to be a permanent decree, for him and for his offspring, through their generations.'

## How to make incense

[22]Yahweh spoke to Mosheh: [23]'You yourself, get yourself the chief spices: liquid myrrh, 500; spiced cinnamon, half that, 250; fragrant cane, 250; [24]cassia, 500 – by the sanctuary sheqel; and olive oil, a gallon. [25]You're to make it into sacred anointing oil, the best blend, blender's work. It will be the sacred anointing oil. [26]With it you're to anoint the appointment tent, the affirmation chest, [27]the table and all its articles, the candelabrum and its articles, the incense altar, [28]the burnt offering altar and all its articles, and the basin and its stand. [29]You're to make them sacred so that they become especially sacred. Anyone who touches them will become sacred. [30]You're to anoint Aharon and his sons and make them sacred to act as priests for me.

[31]You're to speak to the Yisra'elites: "This will be the sacred anointing oil for me through your generations. [32]It's not to be poured on the flesh of anyone, and you're not to make any like it, by its proportions. It's sacred. It's to be sacred for you. [33]Anyone who blends some like it or puts some of it on an outsider shall be cut off from his kin."'

[34]Yahweh said to Mosheh, 'Get yourself aromatic spices – stacte, onyka and galbanum. Of aromatic spices and pure frankincense there's to be equal weight. [35]You're to make them into blended incense, blender's work, salted, pure, sacred. [36]You're to beat some of it into powder and put some of it before the affirmation in the appointment tent where I shall keep an appointment with you. It's to be especially sacred for you. [37]The incense that you make, you're not to make by its proportions for yourselves. For you it's to be sacred for Yahweh. [38]Anyone who makes some like it to smell of it shall be cut off from his kin.'

## The first spiritual gifting

**31** Yahweh spoke to Mosheh: [2]'See, I've called for Betsal'el ben Uri, son of Hur, of the clan of Yehudah, by name. [3]I've filled him with a divine spirit, with smartness, with discernment and with knowledge, in any workmanship, [4]for making designs so as to make things with gold, with silver and with copper, [5]in cutting stone for mountings and in carving wood, for working in any craft.

[6]And I: here, I have put with him Oholi'ab ben Ahisamak of the clan of Dan, and into the mind of everyone who is smart in mind I have put smartness, so they can make everything that I've ordered you: [7]the appointment tent, the chest for the affirmation, the expiation cover that will be on it, all the articles in the tent, [8]the table and its articles, the pure gold candelabrum and all its articles, the incense altar, [9]the burnt offering altar and all its articles, the basin and its stand, [10]the liturgical garments, the sacred garments for Aharon the priest, and his sons' garments for acting as priests, [11]the anointing oil and the aromatic incense for the sacred place. In accordance with all that I've ordered you they are to act.'

[12]Yahweh said to Mosheh: [13]'You yourself, speak to the Yisra'elites: "Nevertheless, my sabbaths you're to keep, because it's a sign between me and you through your generations, for acknowledging that I Yahweh have made you sacred. [14]You're to keep the sabbath because it's sacred for you. The person who treats it as ordinary is absolutely to be put to death. When anyone does work on it, that person shall be cut off from among his kin. [15]For six days work can be done. On the seventh day there is a complete stop [*shabbat shabbaton*], sacred for Yahweh. Anyone who does work on the sabbath day is absolutely to be put to death.

¹⁶The Yisra'elites are to keep the sabbath, making sabbath through their generations, a permanent pact. ¹⁷Between me and the Yisra'elites it will be a permanent sign. Because in six days Yahweh made the heavens and the earth, and on the seventh day he stopped and found refreshment.'"

## Meanwhile, at the foot of the mountain

¹⁸He gave Mosheh (when he had finished speaking with him on Mount Sinai) the two affirmation tablets, stone tablets written by God's finger.

**32** But the people saw that Mosheh was shamefully long about coming down from the mountain. So the people congregated against Aharon and said to him, 'Up, make us gods who will go before us, because this Mosheh, the man who brought us up from the country of Misrayim – we don't know what's happened to him.' ²So Aharon said to them, 'Tear off the gold rings that are in the ears of your wives, your sons and your daughters, and bring them to me.'

³The entire people tore off the gold rings that were in their ears and brought them to Aharon. ⁴He took it from their hand, shaped it with a tool and made it into a bullock figurine. They said, 'Yisra'el, these are your gods who brought you up from the country of Misrayim.'

⁵Aharon saw and built an altar before it. Aharon called out, 'Tomorrow is a festival for Yahweh!' ⁶So they started early next day and offered up burnt offerings and brought up well-being sacrifices. The people sat down to eat and to drink, and set about enjoying themselves.

⁷Yahweh spoke to Mosheh: 'Get yourself down, because your people whom you brought up from the country of Misrayim have acted devastatingly. ⁸They have departed quickly from the way that I ordered them. They've made themselves a bullock figurine, and bowed low to it and sacrificed to it, and said, "Yisra'el, these are your gods who brought you up from the country of Misrayim."'

⁹Yahweh said to Mosheh, 'I've looked at this people. Here, it's a tough-necked people. ¹⁰So now, let me be, so my anger may rage against them and I may finish them off, and make you into a big nation.'

## How to pray for rebels and how to lose your temper

¹¹Mosheh sought the goodwill of Yahweh his God: 'Yahweh, why should your anger rage against your people whom you got out of the country of Misrayim by great energy and by a strong hand? ¹²Why should the Misrayimites say, "It was in connection with something bad that he got them out, to kill them in the mountains and finish them off from on the face of the ground"? Turn back from your angry rage. Relent of bringing something bad to your people. ¹³Be mindful of Abraham, Yitshaq and Yisra'el, your servants, to whom you swore by your own self: "I will make your offspring as numerous as the stars in the heavens, and this entire country of which I spoke I will give to your offspring and they will have it as their permanent domain."' ¹⁴And Yahweh relented of the bad thing he spoke of bringing to his people.

¹⁵Then Mosheh turned his face and went down from the mountain with the two affirmation tablets in his hand, tablets written on both their surfaces. They were written this side and that. ¹⁶The tablets were God's work. The writing was God's writing, cut on the tablets.

¹⁷Yehoshua heard the sound of the people with their shouting and said to Mosheh, 'The sound of battle in the camp!' ¹⁸But he said,

It's not the sound of singing in strength,
  and it's not the sound of singing in weakness,
  the sound of singing that I'm hearing.

¹⁹When he got near the camp, he saw the bullock and dancing. Mosheh's anger raged and he threw the tablets from his hands and broke them up beneath the mountain. ²⁰He got the bullock that they had made and burned it in fire. He ground it until it became fine, scattered it on the face of the water and made the Yisra'elites drink it.

## 'This bullock came out'

²¹Mosheh said to Aharon, 'What did this people do to you that you brought upon it this great wrong?' ²²Aharon said, 'May my

lord's anger not rage. You know this people, that it's the epitome of what is bad. ²³They said to me, "Make us gods that will go before us, because this Mosheh, the man who brought us up from the country of Misrayim – we don't know what has happened to him." ²⁴So I said to them, "Whoever has gold, tear it off." They gave it to me and I threw it into the fire, and this bullock came out.'

²⁵Mosheh saw the people – it was gone wild, because Aharon had let it go wild, with contempt for those who rose up against them. ²⁶Mosheh stood in the camp gateway and said, 'Who belongs to Yahweh – to me!' All the Levites gathered to him. ²⁷He said to them, 'Yahweh, Yisra'el's God, has said this: "Put, each person, his sword on his thigh. Pass through and come back from gateway to gateway in the camp and kill each person his brother, each person his friend and each person the one near to him."'

²⁸The Levites acted in accordance with Mosheh's word, and of the people that day there fell some 3,000 people. ²⁹Mosheh said, 'They've commissioned you today for Yahweh, because each person was against his son and against his brother, to bestow a blessing on you today.'

³⁰Next day Mosheh said to the people, 'You – you've done a great wrong, but I'll now go up to God. Maybe I can make expiation for your wrongdoing.' ³¹So Mosheh went back to Yahweh and said, 'Oh, it was a great wrong this people did when they made gold gods for themselves. ³²But now, if you could carry their wrongdoing . . . But if not, please wipe me out from the document that you wrote.'

³³Yahweh said to Mosheh, 'Whoever did wrong in relation to me, I'll wipe him out from my document. ³⁴So now, get going, lead the people where I spoke you of. There, my envoy – he'll go before you, but on the day I attend to them, I shall attend to them in respect of their wrongdoing.'

*A place where people could check things out with God*

³⁵Yahweh hit the people because they made the bullock, which Aharon made,

**33** and Yahweh spoke to Mosheh: 'Get going, go up from here, you and the people that you brought up from the country of Misrayim, to the country that I swore to Abraham, to Yitshaq and to Ya'aqob, saying "To your offspring I will give it." ²I shall send an envoy before you and drive out the Kena'anite, the Amorite, the Hittite, the Perizzite, the Hivvite and the Yebusite – ³to a country flowing with milk and syrup. Because I shall not go up among you, because you're a tough-necked people, in case I finish you off on the way.' ⁴When the people heard this bad thing, they took up grieving and no one put on his finery.

⁵Yahweh said to Mosheh, 'Say to the Yisra'elites, "You're a tough-necked people. Were I to go up among you for one moment, I could finish you off. So now, take your jewellery off you, so I may know what I should do with you."' ⁶So the Yisra'elites stripped off their jewellery from Mount Horeb onwards.

⁷Now Mosheh would take a tent and spread it for himself outside the camp, some distance from the camp. He called it the appointment tent. Anyone seeking something from Yahweh would go out to the appointment tent that was outside the camp.

⁸When Mosheh went out to the tent, the entire people would get up and stand, each person at his tent entrance, and look at Mosheh until he came into the tent. ⁹As Mosheh came into the tent, the cloud pillar would come down and stand at the tent entrance, and he would speak with Mosheh. ¹⁰The entire people would see the cloud pillar standing at the tent entrance, and the entire people would get up and bow low, each person at his tent entrance. ¹¹Yahweh would speak to Mosheh face to face, as someone speaks to his neighbour, and he would go back to the camp, though his minister, Yehoshua ben Nun, a boy, would not move away from inside the tent.

### Rock of Ages

¹²Mosheh said to Yahweh, 'Look, you're saying to me, "Take this people up", but you yourself haven't made known to me whom you'll send with me. And you yourself said, "I've acknowledged you by name; indeed, you've found grace in my eyes." ¹³So now, please, if I've actually found grace in your

eyes, please let me know your way, so I may acknowledge you, in order that I may find grace in your eyes. Look, because this nation is your people.'

[14]He said, 'My face – it will go, and I'll enable you to settle down.' [15]He said to him, 'If your face doesn't go, don't take us up from here. [16]By what means would it be acknowledged, then, that I've found grace in your eyes, I and your people, unless by your going with us, so we may be distinct, I and your people, from any other people on the face of the ground?' [17]Yahweh said to Mosheh, 'This thing, too, that you've spoken of, I will do, because you've found grace in my eyes and I've acknowledged you by name.'

[18]He said, 'Please let me see your splendour.' [19]He said, 'I myself will pass all my goodness before your face and call out the very name of Yahweh before you: I grace whomever I grace and have compassion on whomever I have compassion.' [20]But he said, 'You can't see my face, because a human being can't see me and stay alive.'

[21]But Yahweh said, 'Here is a place with me. Take your stand on the crag. [22]When my splendour passes, I'll put you in a crack in the crag and lay the palm of my hand over you until I've passed by. [23]Then I'll remove my palm and you'll see my back, whereas my face won't be seen.'

## Now I will confirm the pact

**34** Yahweh said to Mosheh, 'Carve yourself two stone tablets like the first ones, and I'll write on the tablets the words that were on the first tablets, which you broke up. [2]Be ready by the morning, and come up Mount Sinay in the morning and take your stand before me there on the top of the mountain. [3]No one's to come up with you, nor is anyone to appear on the entire mountain, nor are flock or herd to pasture near the mountain.' [4]So he carved two stone tablets like the first ones.

Mosheh started early in the morning and went up Mount Sinay as Yahweh ordered him. He took the two stone tablets in his hand. [5]Yahweh came down in a cloud, took his stand with him there and called out the very name of Yahweh. [6]Yahweh passed before his face.

Yahweh called out, 'Yahweh, God compassionate and gracious, long-tempered, big in commitment and truthfulness, [7]preserving commitment towards the thousands, carrying waywardness, rebellion and wrongdoing; he certainly doesn't treat people as free of guilt, attending to parents' waywardness in connection with children and with grandchildren, with thirds and with fourths.'

[8]Mosheh hurried and bent his head to the ground and bowed low, [9]and said, 'Please, if I have indeed found grace in your eyes, will the Lord, will the Lord please go among us? Because this is a tough-necked people, pardon our waywardness and our wrongdoing. Have us as your domain.'

[10]He said, 'Here, I am going to solemnize a pact. In front of all your people I will do extraordinary things that haven't been created in the entire earth or among all the nations. The entire people among whom you are will see how awe-inspiring is the deed of Yahweh that I'm going to do with you.

## Promises and decrees reaffirmed

[11]See that you keep what I'm ordering you today. Here I am, I'm going to drive out from before you the Amorite, the Kena'anite, the Hittite, the Perizzite, the Hivvite and the Yebusite.

[12]Keep watch over yourself so that you don't solemnize a pact with the people living in the country into which you're coming, so that it doesn't become a snare among you. [13]Because you're to demolish their altars, break up their columns and cut down their totem poles. [14]Because you will not bow low to any god, because Yahweh, whose name is 'Passionate', is the passionate God. [15]You are not to solemnize a pact with the people living in the country. They will whore after their gods and sacrifice for their gods, and someone will call you and you'll eat of his sacrifice. [16]You'll take some of his daughters for your sons, and his daughters will whore after their gods, and get your sons to whore after their gods.

[17]You will not make cast-metal gods for yourself.

¹⁸You're to keep the Flatbread Festival. For seven days you're to eat flatbread, which I ordered at the set time in the month of Aviv, because in the month of Aviv you got out of Misrayim. ¹⁹Every opener of the womb is mine, and all your livestock that's born male, the first offspring of ox and sheep. ²⁰A donkey's opener you're to redeem with a sheep, but if you don't redeem it, you're to break its neck. Every firstborn among your children, you're to redeem.

People may not appear before me empty-handed.

²¹For six days you can serve, but on the seventh day you're to stop. In ploughing and in harvest you're to stop.

## The magnificent presence

²²You're to perform the Shabu'ot Festival for yourself, the first products of the wheat harvest, and the Ingathering Festival, the turning of the year. ²³Three times in the year all your males are to appear before the Lord Yahweh, Yisra'el's God, ²⁴because I shall dispossess nations from before you and widen your border, and no one will desire your land when you go up to appear before Yahweh your God three times in the year.

²⁵You will not slaughter the blood of a sacrifice for me accompanied by leavened bread.

The sacrifice of the Pesah Festival will not stay until morning.

²⁶The very first of the first products of your land you're to bring to the house of Yahweh your God.

You will not cook a kid goat in its mother's milk.'

²⁷Yahweh said to Mosheh, 'Write these words for yourself, because on the basis of these words I solemnize a pact with you and with Yisra'el.'

²⁸He was there with Yahweh for forty days and forty nights; he didn't eat food and he didn't drink water. He wrote on the tablets the words of the pact, the Ten Words.

²⁹When Mosheh came down from Mount Sinay with the two affirmation tablets in Mosheh's hand as he came down from the mountain, Mosheh didn't know that the skin of his face emanated through his speaking with him. ³⁰Aharon and all the Yisra'elites saw Mosheh: there, the skin of his face emanated. They were afraid to come up to him. ³¹Mosheh called to them, and Aharon and all the assembly's leaders came back to him and Mosheh spoke to them. ³²Afterwards, all the Yisra'elites came up and he gave them orders about all that Yahweh had spoken with him on Mount Sinay.

³³When Mosheh had finished speaking with them he put a veil on his face. ³⁴When Mosheh came before Yahweh to speak with him he would remove the veil until he came out. Then he would come out and speak to the Yisra'elites about what he had been ordered. ³⁵The Yisra'elites would see Mosheh's face, how the skin of Mosheh's face emanated, and Mosheh would put back the veil on his face until he came to speak with him.

## The commission

**35** Mosheh got the entire assembly of the Yisra'elites to congregate, and he said to them, 'These are the things that Yahweh has ordered you to do. ²For six days work can be done, but on the seventh day it will be sacred for you, a complete stopping, for Yahweh. Anyone who does work on it is to be put to death. ³You're not to burn a fire among all your settlements on the stopping day.'

⁴Mosheh said to the entire assembly of the Yisra'elites: 'This is the thing that Yahweh has ordered. ⁵Get from among yourselves a contribution for Yahweh. Everyone who's free in heart can bring Yahweh's contribution: gold, silver, copper; ⁶blue, purple and bright crimson, linen, goats' [hair]; ⁷ram skins dyed red, dolphin skins, acacia wood; ⁸oil for lighting, spices for the anointing oil and the aromatic incense, ⁹onyx stones and stones for the mountings for the chasuble and for the pouch.

¹⁰Everyone who is smart of mind among you, they're to come and make everything that Yahweh has ordered: ¹¹the dwelling, the tent and its covering, its clasps and its planks, its bars, its posts and its sockets, ¹²the chest and its poles, the expiation cover and the screen

curtain, [13]the table, its poles and all its articles, and the presence bread, [14]the candelabrum for lighting, its articles, its lamps and the oil for lighting, [15]the incense altar and its poles, the anointing oil and the aromatic incense, the entrance screen for the dwelling entrance, [16]the altar for the burnt offering, the copper grating that it has, its poles and all its articles, the basin and its stand, [17]the hangings for the courtyard, its posts and its sockets, and the screen for the courtyard gateway, [18]the pegs for the dwelling, the pegs for the courtyard and their ropes, [19]the liturgical garments for ministering in the sacred place, the sacred garments for Aharon the priest, and the garments for his sons to act as priests.'

## The enthusiastic giving

[20]The entire assembly of the Yisra'elites went out of Mosheh's presence, [21]then came, every individual whose mind lifted him up and everyone whose spirit made him free, and brought a contribution for Yahweh for the work on the appointment tent and for all its service, and for the sacred garments. [22]They came, men along with women, everyone who was free in heart, and brought brooches, earrings, rings and necklaces – all objects of gold, each individual who brought an offering of gold for Yahweh. [23]Everyone with whom there could be found blue, purple and bright crimson, linen, goats' [hair], ram skins dyed red or dolphin skins, brought them. [24]Everyone who was taking up a contribution of silver or copper brought the offering for Yahweh. Everyone with whom acacia wood could be found for any of the work for the service brought it. [25]Every woman who was smart of mind spun with her hands and brought the spinning, blue, purple and bright crimson, and linen. [26]All the women whose mind lifted them up with smartness spun the goats' [hair]. [27]The leaders brought onyx stones and stones for the mountings on the chasuble and on the pouch, [28]the spice and the oil for lighting, for the anointing oil and for the aromatic incense. [29]Every man and woman whose heart made them free to bring for all the work that Yahweh ordered them to do, through Mosheh – the Yisra'elites brought a free offering for Yahweh.

## The over-enthusiastic giving

[30]Mosheh said to the Yisra'elites: 'Look, Yahweh has called by name for Betsal'el ben Uri, son of Hur, of the clan of Yehudah. [31]He's filled him with a divine spirit, with smartness, with discernment and with knowledge, in any workmanship, [32]for drafting designs to make things with gold, with silver and with copper, [33]in cutting stone for mountings and in carving wood, to make things in any design craft. [34]He's put in his mind how to teach, he and Oholi'ab ben Ahisamak of the clan of Dan. [35]He's filled them with smartness of mind to do any work: the craftsman, the designer, the embroiderer in blue, purple and bright crimson, and in linen, and the weaver, workers in any craft and makers of designs.

**36** So Betsal'el and Oholi'ab and everyone smart of mind, in whom Yahweh has put smartness and discernment so as to know how to do the work for the service in the sacred place, are to do all that Yahweh ordered.'

[2]So Mosheh called for Betsal'el and Oholi'ab and everyone smart of mind, into whose mind Yahweh had put smartness, everyone whose mind lifted him up, to draw near for the work, to do it. [3]They got from before Mosheh every contribution that the Yisra'elites had brought for the work for the service in the sacred place, to do it.

When those people still brought to him a free gift, morning by morning, [4]all the smart people doing all the work in the sacred place came, one by one from his work, which they were doing, [5]and said to Mosheh, 'The people are bringing much, more than enough for the service involved in the work that Yahweh ordered us to do.' [6]So Mosheh made an order and they passed the sound through the camp, 'No man or woman is to do any more work towards the contribution for the sacred place.' So the people finished bringing. [7]The work was enough for the work, to do it. It left some over.

## Hangings for the dwelling

[8]The people who were doing the work, everyone who was smart of mind, made the dwelling of ten pieces of woven linen and blue, purple and bright crimson; with sphinxes,

designer's work, he made them. ⁹The length of each piece, twenty-eight cubits, and the width of each piece, four cubits – one size for all the pieces. ¹⁰He joined five of the pieces one to the other, and joined the other five pieces one to the other. ¹¹He made loops of blue on the lip of the one piece at the edge of its joined set, and in this way made them at the lip of the edging piece in the second joined set. ¹²He made fifty loops on the one piece and made fifty loops at the edge of the piece that's in the second joined set, with the loops holding one to the other. ¹³He made fifty gold clasps, and joined the pieces to one another with the clasps so the dwelling became one unit.

¹⁴He made pieces from goats' [hair] for a tent over the dwelling; eleven pieces he made them. ¹⁵The length of each piece thirty by the cubit; the width four cubits each piece, one size for the eleven pieces. ¹⁶He joined five of the pieces on their own, and six of the pieces on their own. ¹⁷He made fifty loops on the lip of one outermost piece in a joined set, and fifty loops on the lip of the piece in the other joined set. ¹⁸He made fifty copper clasps to join the tent so it became one unit. ¹⁹He made a covering for the tent of ram skins dyed red and a covering of dolphin skins above it.

## The frame for the dwelling

²⁰He made the planks for the dwelling of acacia wood, standing upright, ²¹the length of a plank ten cubits, the width of a plank a cubit and a half, each one, ²²two projections for each plank, parallel one to the other. So he did for all the dwelling's planks. ²³He made the planks for the dwelling:

twenty planks for the south (southern) aspect; ²⁴he made forty silver sockets under the twenty planks, two sockets under the one plank for its two projections and two sockets under the next plank for its two projections.
²⁵For the dwelling's second side, on the north aspect: twenty planks, ²⁶with their forty silver sockets, two sockets under the one plank and two sockets under the next plank.
²⁷For the back of the dwelling, to the west, he made six planks, ²⁸and he made two planks for the corners of the dwelling, at the

back. ²⁹They were double underneath, but together they were whole at its top, at the one ring. So he made it for both of them, for the two corners. ³⁰Thus there were eight planks with their silver sockets, sixteen sockets: two sockets under one plank and two sockets under the next plank.

³¹He made bars of acacia wood: five for the planks in one side of the dwelling, ³²five bars for planks in the second side of the dwelling, and five bars for the planks in the dwelling at the back, to the west. ³³He made the central bar in the middle of the planks running from end to end. ³⁴The planks he overlaid with gold. The rings he made of gold as housing for the bars, and he overlaid the bars with gold.

## The affirmation chest and the expiation cover

³⁵He made the curtain of blue, purple and bright crimson, and woven linen. He made it as designer's work, with sphinxes. ³⁶He made for it four posts of acacia and overlaid them with gold, with their gold hooks, and he cast for them four silver sockets. ³⁷He made a screen for the tent entrance, of blue, purple and bright crimson, and woven linen, embroiderer's work, ³⁸and its five posts with their hooks. He overlaid their tops and their clasps with gold. The five sockets were copper.

**37** Betsal'el made the chest of acacia wood, its length two and a half cubits, its width a cubit and a half, and its height a cubit and a half. ²He overlaid it with pure gold, inside and outside, and made a gold moulding for it all round. ³He cast four gold rings for it, on its four feet, two rings on one side of it and two on the other. ⁴He made poles of acacia wood and overlaid them with gold, ⁵and inserted the poles into the rings on the sides of the chest, for carrying the chest.

⁶He made an expiation cover of pure gold, its length two and a half cubits and its width a cubit and a half, ⁷and he made two gold sphinxes (of hammered work he made them) at the two ends of the expiation cover, ⁸one sphinx at one end and the other sphinx at the other end. He made the sphinxes coming from the expiation cover at its two ends. ⁹The sphinxes were spreading their wings upwards, shielding the expiation cover with their wings, and with

their faces one towards the other; the sphinxes' faces were towards the expiation cover.

## The candelabrum

¹⁰He made the table of acacia wood, its length two cubits, its width one cubit and its height a cubit and a half. ¹¹He overlaid it with pure gold and made a gold moulding for it all round. ¹²He made a rim of a handbreadth for it all round and made a gold moulding for its rim all round. ¹³He made four gold rings for it and put the rings at the four corners that were at its four feet. ¹⁴The rings were close by the rim as housing for the poles for carrying the table. ¹⁵He made the poles of acacia wood and overlaid them with gold. ¹⁶He made the articles that would be on the table – its dishes, its ladles, its pitchers and its bowls, in which the drink offering would be poured – of pure gold.

¹⁷He made the candelabrum of pure gold. He made the candelabrum of hammered work, its base and its stem. Its cups, its flowers and its petals came from it; ¹⁸six stems going out from its flanks, three stems of the candelabrum from its one flank and three stems of the candelabrum from its second flank; ¹⁹three cups made like almond blossom on one stem, flower and petal, three stems made like almond blossom on another stem, flower and petal; so for the six stems going out from the candelabrum.

²⁰On the candelabrum four cups made like almond blossom, its flowers and its petals; ²¹a flower beneath two stems issuing from it, and a flower beneath two stems issuing from it, and a flower beneath two stems issuing from it, for the six branches going out from it; ²²their flowers and their stems came from it, all of it a single hammered work, pure gold. ²³He made its seven lamps, its tongs and its pans of pure gold. ²⁴He made it and all its articles out of a talent of pure gold.

## The altars

²⁵He made the incense altar of acacia wood, its length a cubit, its width a cubit (square) and its height two cubits; its horns came from it. ²⁶He overlaid it with pure gold – its top, its sides all round and its horns. He made a gold moulding for it all round. ²⁷He made two gold rings for it under its moulding, on its two sides, on its two flanks, for housing for the poles to carry it with. ²⁸He made the poles of acacia wood and overlaid them with gold. ²⁹He made the sacred anointing oil and the pure aromatic incense, blender's work.

**38** He made the altar for burnt offering of acacia wood, its length five cubits, its width five cubits (square) and its height three cubits. ²He made its horns on its four corners (its horns came from it) and overlaid it with copper. ³He made all the altar's utensils: the buckets, the shovels, the basins, the forks and the pans; he made all its utensils of copper. ⁴He made a grating for the altar, a mesh made of copper, below its ledge, underneath, halfway up it. ⁵He cast four rings at the four corners of the copper mesh as housing for the poles. ⁶He made the poles of acacia wood and overlaid them with copper, ⁷and inserted the poles into the rings on the two sides of the altar for carrying it with. He made it hollow, of boards.

⁸He made the copper basin and its copper stand with the mirrors of the women who served, who did their serving at the entrance of the appointment tent.

## The courtyard

⁹He made the courtyard:
on the south (southern) aspect: hangings for the courtyard, woven linen, a hundred by the cubit; ¹⁰their twenty posts and their twenty sockets, copper; the posts' hooks and their clasps, silver;
¹¹on the north aspect: a hundred by the cubit; their twenty posts and their twenty sockets, copper; the posts' hooks and their clasps, silver;
¹²on the west aspect: hangings, fifty by the cubit; their posts, ten; their sockets, ten; the posts' hooks and their clasps, silver;
¹³on the front aspect, the east: fifty by the cubit: ¹⁴hangings, fifteen cubits to the shoulder; their posts, three; their sockets, three; ¹⁵for the second shoulder (on each side of the courtyard gateway), hangings, fifteen cubits; their posts, three; their

sockets, three;
16all the courtyard hangings, woven linen, all
round;
17the sockets for the posts, copper; the
hooks and the clasps of the posts, silver;
the overlay of their tops, silver; all the
courtyard posts were clasped with silver;
18the screen for the courtyard gateway,
embroiderer's work: blue, purple and
bright crimson, and woven linen, twenty
cubits in length, its height (by width) five
cubits, close by the courtyard hangings;
19their four posts and their four sockets,
copper; their hooks, silver; the overlay of
their tops and their clasps, silver;
20all the pegs for the dwelling and for the
courtyard all round, copper.
21This is the register of the dwelling,
the affirmation dwelling, which was made
at Mosheh's bidding, the Levites' service at
the hand of Itamar ben Aharon the priest.
22Betsal'el ben Uri, son of Hur of the clan
of Yehudah – he made all that Yahweh had
ordered Mosheh, 23and with him Oholi'ab ben
Ahisamak of the clan of Dan, the craftsman,
the designer, and the embroiderer in blue,
purple and bright crimson, and in linen.

## How much it was!

24All the gold that was made into the work,
in all the work in the sacred place and that was
the gold of the elevation offering: 29 talents
and 730 sheqels (by the sanctuary sheqel).
25The silver in the assembly register: 100
talents and 1,775 sheqels (by the sanctuary
sheqel), 26a fraction per head (a half-sheqel by
the sanctuary sheqel) for each person passing
through the register, from the age of twenty
years and upwards: 603,550 people.
27The 100 talents of silver were for casting
the sockets for the sacred place and the curtain
sockets, 100 sockets for the 100 talents, a talent
for a socket. 28He made the 1,775 sheqels into
hooks for the posts, overlaid their tops and
clasped them.
29The copper of the elevation offering: 70
talents and 2,400 sheqels. 30With it he made
the entrance sockets for the appointment
tent, the copper altar and the copper grating
that it had, and all the altar's utensils; 31the

courtyard sockets all round and the courtyard
gateway sockets; and all the dwelling's pegs and
all the courtyard's pegs all round.

# 39

From the blue, purple and bright
crimson, they made the liturgical
garments for ministering in the sacred place,
and they made the sacred garments that were
for Aharon, as Yahweh had ordered Mosheh.
2He made the chasuble of gold, of blue,
purple and bright crimson, and of woven linen.
3They beat out sheets of gold and cut wires
for working into the middle of the blue, of the
purple, of the bright crimson and of the linen,
designer's work. 4They made joining shoulder
pieces for it; it was joined to two of its corners.
5Its chasuble's design-work strap, which was on
it, came from it; it was made like its work, gold,
blue, purple, bright crimson and woven linen,
as Yahweh had ordered Mosheh.

## The pouch

6They made the onyx stones surrounded
by gold braids, engraved with seal engravings
corresponding to the names of Yisra'el's sons.
7He put them on the chasuble's shoulder pieces
as reminder stones for Yisra'el's sons, as Yahweh
had ordered Mosheh.
8He made the pouch as designer's work like
the work of the chasuble, gold, blue, purple
and bright crimson, and woven linen. 9It was
square. They made the pouch folded double, a
handbreadth its length and a handbreadth its
width, folded double. 10They filled it with four
rows of stones:

the first row: a row of carnelian, chrysolyte
and emerald;
11the second row: turquoise, sapphire and
amethyst;
12the third row: jacinth, agate and crystal;
13the fourth row: beryl, onyx and jasper.

They were surrounded by gold braids in their
fillings. 14The stones corresponded to the
names of Yisra'el's sons, twelve corresponding
to their names, with seal engravings, each
corresponding to its name, for the twelve clans.
15On the pouch they made plaited chains,
woven work, pure gold. 16They made two gold
braids and two gold rings and put the two

rings on the two edges of the pouch. <sup>17</sup>They put the two gold weavings on the two rings at the edges of the pouch. <sup>18</sup>The two ends of the two weavings they put on the chasuble's shoulder pieces near its front.

## As Yahweh had ordered

<sup>19</sup>They made two gold rings and put them on the two edges of the pouch at its lip, which is on the side nearer the chasuble. <sup>20</sup>They made two gold rings and put them on the chasuble's two shoulder pieces underneath, near the front, close by its join, above the chasuble's design-work strap. <sup>21</sup>They attached the pouch by its rings to the chasuble's rings with a blue cord, so it was on the chasuble's design-work strap and the pouch would not come loose from on the chasuble, as Yahweh had ordered Mosheh.

<sup>22</sup>They made the chasuble coat, weaver's work, all blue, <sup>23</sup>the opening of the coat in the middle of it like the opening of a vest, with the lip for its opening all round so it would not tear. <sup>24</sup>On the coat's hems they made pomegranates of blue, purple and bright crimson, woven, <sup>25</sup>and they made bells of pure gold and put the bells in among the pomegranates on the coat's hems all round, <sup>26</sup>a bell and a pomegranate, a bell and a pomegranate, on the coat's hems all round, for ministering, as Yahweh had ordered Mosheh. <sup>27</sup>They made linen tunics, weaver's work, for Aharon and for his sons, <sup>28</sup>the linen turban, ornamental linen mitres, cloth shorts (woven linen), <sup>29</sup>and the sash of woven linen, blue, purple and bright crimson, embroiderer's work, as Yahweh had ordered Mosheh.

<sup>30</sup>They made the medallion, the sacred diadem of pure gold, and wrote on it a seal inscription, 'Sacred for Yahweh'. <sup>31</sup>They put a blue cord on it so as to put it on the turban above, as Yahweh had ordered Mosheh.

## And Mosheh blessed them

<sup>32</sup>So the entire service of the dwelling, the appointment tent, finished. The Yisra'elites did everything in accordance with all that Yahweh had ordered Mosheh, so they did. <sup>33</sup>They brought the dwelling to Mosheh with the tent and all its articles – its clasps, its planks, its bars, its posts, its sockets, <sup>34</sup>the covering of ram skins dyed red, the covering of dolphin skins, the screen curtain, <sup>35</sup>the affirmation chest and its poles and the expiation cover; <sup>36</sup>the table and all its articles and the presence bread; <sup>37</sup>the pure candelabrum, its lamps (lamps in order) and all its articles, and the oil for lighting; <sup>38</sup>the gold altar, the anointing oil, the aromatic incense and the screen for the tent entrance; <sup>39</sup>the copper altar, the copper grating that it had, its poles and all its articles, the basin and its stand; <sup>40</sup>the courtyard hangings, its posts and its sockets, the screen for the courtyard gateway, its cords and its pegs; and all the articles for the service of the dwelling, the appointment tent; <sup>41</sup>the liturgical garments for ministering in the sacred place, the sacred garments for Aharon the priest, and his sons' garments for acting as priests.

<sup>42</sup>In accordance with all that Yahweh had ordered Mosheh, so the Yisra'elites had done the entire service. <sup>43</sup>Mosheh saw all the work: there, they had done it. As Yahweh had ordered, so they had done. And Mosheh blessed them.

## Instructions for assembling and sanctifying

**40** Yahweh spoke to Mosheh: <sup>2</sup>'On the first day of the first month you're to set up the dwelling, the appointment tent. <sup>3</sup>You're to place there the affirmation chest and screen over the chest with the curtain. <sup>4</sup>You're to bring in the table and see to its arrangement, bring in the candelabrum and put up its lamps, <sup>5</sup>put the gold incense altar before the affirmation chest, and place the screen for the courtyard gateway.

<sup>6</sup>You're to put the altar for burnt offering before the entrance of the dwelling, the appointment tent, <sup>7</sup>put the basin between the appointment tent and the altar and put water there, <sup>8</sup>place the courtyard all round, and put in place the screen for the courtyard gateway.

<sup>9</sup>You're to get the anointing oil and anoint the dwelling and everything that's in it, and make it and all its articles sacred, so it may be sacred. <sup>10</sup>You're to anoint the altar for burnt offering and all its articles and make the altar

sacred, so the altar may be especially sacred, [11]and you're to anoint the basin and its stand and make it sacred.

[12]You're to present Aharon and his sons at the entrance of the appointment tent and wash them with water, [13]put the sacred garments on Aharon, and anoint him and make him sacred so he may act as priest for me. [14]You're to present his sons and put tunics on them, [15]and anoint them as you anointed their father so they may act as priests for me. Their anointing will continue to be for them for a permanent priesthood, through their generations.'

[16]Mosheh acted in accordance with all that Yahweh had ordered him, so he did.

### Yahweh's splendour fills the dwelling

[17]In the first month in the second year, on the first of the month, the dwelling was set up. [18]Mosheh set up the dwelling.

He put its sockets and placed its planks and put its bars and set up its posts. [19]He spread the tent over the dwelling and put the tent covering over it, on top, as Yahweh had ordered Mosheh. [20]He got the affirmation and put it in the chest, placed the poles on the chest and put the expiation cover on the chest, on top, [21]brought the chest into the dwelling, placed the screening curtain and screened off the affirmation chest, as Yahweh had ordered Mosheh. [22]He put the table in the appointment tent on the side of the dwelling, northward, outside the curtain, [23]and saw to the arrangement of bread on it before Yahweh, as Yahweh had ordered Mosheh. [24]He placed the candelabrum in the appointment tent in front of the table on the side of the dwelling southward, [25]and put up the lamps before Yahweh, as Yahweh had ordered Mosheh.

[26]He placed the gold altar in the appointment tent before the curtain, [27]and burned aromatic incense on it, as Yahweh had ordered Mosheh.

[28]He placed the screen for the dwelling entrance, [29]and placed the altar for burnt offering at the entrance of the dwelling, the appointment tent, and offered up the burnt offering and the grain offering on it, as Yahweh had ordered Mosheh.

[30]He placed the basin between the appointment tent and the altar and put water for washing there, [31]so that Mosheh and Aharon and his sons could wash their hands and their feet from it, [32]so they could wash when they came into the appointment tent and when they drew near the altar, as Yahweh had ordered Mosheh. [33]He set up the courtyard all round the dwelling and the altar and put in place the screen for the courtyard entrance.

When Mosheh finished the work, [34]the cloud covered the appointment tent, and Yahweh's splendour filled the dwelling. [35]Mosheh couldn't go into the appointment tent because the cloud dwelt over it and Yahweh's splendour filled the dwelling.

[36]When the cloud lifted from over the dwelling, the Yisra'elites would move on, during all their movements. [37]If the cloud didn't lift, they wouldn't move on until the day it lifted, [38]because Yahweh's cloud would be over the dwelling by day and the fire would be in it by night, before the eyes of Yisra'el's entire household during all their movements.

# LEVITICUS

Leviticus takes its name from the Levites, the people who traced their descent back to Jacob's son Levi. Among them were the descendants of Aaron, Levi's great-grandson; they were the priests, people who had responsibility for key aspects of the offering of sacrifices. The other descendants of Levi, the non-priestly Levites, are commonly referred to simply as 'the Levites', for short; they were responsible for the many practical aspects of worship in the sanctuary.

The priests and the (other) Levites also had important responsibility for teaching people about what it means to be a proper Israelite, and much of Leviticus comprises a handbook on matters the Levites need to know about, in order to give such teaching. It also covers matters the priests and Levites themselves need to know about, in order to do their own work.

Chapters 1—7 of the book comprise instructions for them about how to offer the different sacrifices, which can be

- a way of giving something to God as an act of worship;
- a way of sharing in a fellowship meal with God, especially when one had reason to express gratitude to God for some blessing;
- a way of finding purification or decontamination when one was affected by a taboo;
- a way of making reparation for wrongdoing (sacrifice was not directly a means by which one found forgiveness for sins; that came on the basis of God's mercy and grace when one repented).

These opening chapters of the book thus pose challenges to us about worship, about giving to God, about fellowship with God, about purification and about reparation.

Chapters 8—10 recount how Moses ordains Aaron and his sons, how they begin their ministry, but then how things go terribly wrong. Leviticus thus continues the story in Exodus.

Chapters 11—16 revert to detailed instructions. They now concern things that make people taboo and thus forbidden to come into the sanctuary. Many of these are things that clash with Yahweh's own nature, particularly death and sex. The rules in Leviticus can drive readers to face the reality of death and face the way we can make sex into a god. Infringing such taboos would defile the sanctuary and risk making God unwilling to be there. An annual expiation day purifies the sanctuary from the effect of such breaches.

Chapters 17—27 offer miscellaneous instructions about ordinary people's lives, with an underlying concern for Israel to be different, to be sacred as God is sacred. It means maintaining distinctions such as those between God and sex or God and death, and also maintaining distinctions of a moral kind. Behaviour that doesn't match Yahweh's moral character is at least as reprehensible as behaviour that doesn't match other aspects of who God is.

The rules for life cover much of the same ground as Exodus 20—24. Genesis to Deuteronomy as a whole is a compilation of teachings that the Holy Spirit inspired during Israel's history, when different contexts required God to give the people different guidance to match different situations. The teaching in Leviticus suggests a context when Israel had become a nation with a central government, a capital and a 'proper' temple.

Attributing the instructions to Moses then affirms that these instructions are outworkings of principles that Moses would affirm. They're the kind of thing Moses would say if he were living in the time of (say) Hezekiah in the eighth century, 500 years after Moses – though we don't know which particular century Leviticus actually comes from.

*Giving to God: something from your herd*

**1** He called Mosheh [Moses]; Yahweh spoke to him from the appointment tent: ²"Speak to the Yisra'elites [Israelites] and say to them: "When one of you presents an offering of an animal for Yahweh, you may present your offering from the herd or from the flock.

³If his offering is a burnt offering from the herd, he's to present a male that's whole. He's to present it at the entrance of the appointment tent, for his acceptance before Yahweh. ⁴He's to lean his hand on the head of the burnt offering so it may be acceptable for him, to make expiation for him. ⁵He's to slaughter the animal from the herd before Yahweh, and Aharon's [Aaron's] sons, the priests, are to present the blood and toss the blood over the altar that's at the entrance of the appointment tent, all round.

⁶He's to skin the burnt offering and cut it up into its parts. ⁷The sons of Aharon the priest are to put fire on the altar and arrange wood on the fire, ⁸and Aharon's sons, the priests, are to arrange the parts, with the head and with the suet, on the wood that's on the fire that's on the altar. ⁹He's to wash its innards and its legs in water, and the priest is to turn the entire thing into smoke at the altar, a burnt offering, a gift offering, a nice smell for Yahweh.

*Giving something smaller*

¹⁰If his offering as a burnt offering is from the flock, from the sheep or from the goats, he's to present a male that's whole. ¹¹He's to slaughter it before Yahweh at the side of the altar, to the north, and Aharon's sons, the priests, are to toss its blood over the altar, all round. ¹²He's to cut it up into its parts, and the priest is to arrange them with its head and with its suet on the wood that's on the fire that's on the altar. ¹³He's to wash the innards and the legs with water, and the priest is to present the entire thing and turn it into smoke at the altar. It's a burnt offering, a gift offering, a nice smell for Yahweh.

¹⁴If his offering for Yahweh is a burnt offering from the birds, he's to present his offering from doves or from young pigeons. ¹⁵The priest is to present it at the altar, wring its head and turn it into smoke at the altar. Its blood is to be drained out against the side

of the altar. ¹⁶He's to remove its crop with its plumage and throw it beside the altar to the east, to the place for waste. ¹⁷The priest is to tear it open by its wings, not divide it, and turn it to smoke at the altar on the wood that's on the fire. It's a burnt offering, a gift offering, a nice smell for Yahweh.

*The grain offering*

**2** When a person presents as an offering a grain offering for Yahweh, his offering is to be fine flour. He's to pour oil on it and put frankincense on it ²and bring it to Aharon's sons, the priests. He's to scoop from there a fistful from its fine flour and from its oil, along with all its frankincense, and the priest is to turn its commemorative portion into smoke at the altar, a gift offering, a nice smell for Yahweh. ³The rest of the grain offering is for Aharon and his sons, something especially sacred from Yahweh's gift offerings.

⁴When you present as an offering a grain offering baked in an oven: fine flour, loaves of flatbread mixed with oil, or flat wafers spread with oil. ⁵If your offering is a grain offering on a griddle, it's to be fine flour mixed with oil, flatbread; ⁶break it into bits and pour oil on it. It's a grain offering. ⁷If your offering is a grain offering in a pan, it's to be made of fine flour in oil.

⁸You may bring for Yahweh a grain offering that's made from these, and one is to present it to the priest and he will bring it up to the altar. ⁹The priest is to take up from the grain offering its commemorative portion and turn it into smoke at the altar, a gift offering, a nice smell for Yahweh. ¹⁰The rest of the grain offering is for Aharon and his sons, something especially sacred from Yahweh's gift offerings.

*Season with salt*

¹¹No grain offering that you present for Yahweh is to be made with yeast, because all leavened bread and all syrup – you're not to turn any of it into smoke as a gift offering for Yahweh. ¹²You may present them for Yahweh as an offering of the very first [of the harvest], but they may not go up to the altar as a nice smell.

¹³You're to season with salt your every offering that's a grain offering. You're not to let the salt of your pact with God cease from your grain offering. With every offering of yours you're to present salt.

¹⁴If you present a first-products grain offering for Yahweh, you're to present young ears, roasted in fire, kernels from the plantation, as your first-products grain offering. ¹⁵You're to put oil on it and place frankincense on it; it's a grain offering. ¹⁶The priest is to turn its commemorative portion into smoke, some of its kernels and of its oil, along with all its frankincense, as a gift offering for Yahweh.

## The sacrifice shared with Yahweh

**3** If his offering is a well-being sacrifice: if he's presenting something from the herd, whether male or female, he's to present it as one that's whole, before Yahweh. ²He's to lean his hand on his offering's head and slaughter it at the entrance of the appointment tent, and Aharon's sons, the priests, are to toss the blood over the altar, all round. ³He's to present from the well-being sacrifice, as a gift offering for Yahweh, the fat covering the innards, all the fat that's on the innards, ⁴the two kidneys and the fat that's on them, which is on the loins, and the lobe on the liver; he's to remove it along with the kidneys. ⁵Aharon's sons are to turn it into smoke at the altar, along with the burnt offering that's on the wood that's on the fire, a gift offering, a nice smell for Yahweh.

⁶If his offering as a well-being sacrifice for Yahweh is from the flock, whether male or female, he's to present it as one that's whole. ⁷If he's presenting a sheep as his offering, he's to present it before Yahweh, ⁸lean his hand on his offering's head and slaughter it before the appointment tent. Aharon's sons are to toss its blood over the altar, all round.

## All fat belongs to Yahweh

⁹He's to present from the well-being sacrifice, as a gift offering for Yahweh, its fat, the broad tail, whole (which he's to remove close by the backbone), the fat covering the innards, all the fat that's on the innards, ¹⁰the two kidneys and

the fat that's on them, which is on the loins, and the lobe on the liver; he's to remove it along with the kidneys. ¹¹The priest is to turn it into smoke at the altar as a meal, as a gift offering for Yahweh.

¹²If his offering is a goat, he's to present it before Yahweh, ¹³lean his hand on its head and slaughter it before the appointment tent. Aharon's sons are to toss its blood over the altar, all round. ¹⁴He's to present from it as his offering, as a gift offering for Yahweh, the fat covering the innards and all the fat that's on the innards, ¹⁵the two kidneys and the fat that's on them, which is on the loins, and the lobe on the liver; he's to remove it along with the kidneys. ¹⁶The priest is to turn them into smoke at the altar as a meal, as a gift offering, as a nice smell.

All fat belongs to Yahweh. ¹⁷It's a permanent decree through your generations in all your settlements. You will not eat any fat or any blood.'"

## When a priest does wrong by mistake

**4** Yahweh spoke to Mosheh: ²"Speak to the Yisra'elites: "When a person does wrong by mistake in connection with any of Yahweh's orders about what should not be done, and does one of them . . .

³If the anointed priest does wrong and brings liability on the people, for his wrong that he did he's to present for Yahweh a bull from the herd, one that's whole, as a decontamination. ⁴He's to bring the bull to the entrance of the appointment tent before Yahweh, lean his hand on the bull's head and slaughter the bull before Yahweh. ⁵The anointed priest is to get some of the bull's blood and bring it into the appointment tent. ⁶The priest is to dip his finger in the blood and spatter some of the blood seven times before Yahweh, before the curtain of the sacred place.

⁷The priest is to put some of the blood on the horns of the altar of aromatic incense that's in the appointment tent, before Yahweh, and to pour out all the bull's blood at the base of the altar for burnt offering, at the entrance of the appointment tent.

⁸All the fat of the decontamination bull: he's to take up from it the fat covering the innards, all the fat that's on the innards, ⁹the two kidneys

and the fat that's on them, which is on the loins, and the lobe on the liver; he's to remove it along with the kidneys [10]as it's taken up from an ox that's a well-being sacrifice. The priest is to turn them into smoke at the altar for burnt offering. [11]The bull's skin and all its flesh, along with its head, its legs, its innards and its intestines: [12]he's to take the entire bull out to a pure place outside the camp, to where the waste is poured out, and burn it on wood in fire. It's to burn at the place where the waste is poured out.

## When the assembly does wrong by mistake

[13]If the entire Yisra'elite assembly make a mistake and something escapes the eyes of the congregation, and they do something in connection with any of Yahweh's orders about what should not be done, and incur liability, [14]and the wrong that they did in connection with it becomes known, the congregation are to present a bull from the herd as a decontamination. They're to bring it before the appointment tent, [15]the assembly's elders are to lean their hands on the bull's head before Yahweh, and one is to slaughter the bull before Yahweh.

[16]The anointed priest is to bring some of the bull's blood into the appointment tent. [17]The priest is to dip his finger in the blood and spatter it seven times before Yahweh, before the curtain. [18]He's to put some of the blood on the horns of the altar that's before Yahweh, which is in the appointment tent, and to pour out all the blood at the base of the altar for burnt offering, at the entrance of the appointment tent.

[19]All its fat he's to take up from it and turn it into smoke at the altar. [20]He's to do to the bull as he did to the decontamination bull; so he's to do to it, and make expiation for them, and it will be pardoned them. [21]He's to take the bull out, outside the camp, and burn it as he burned the first bull. It's a decontamination for the congregation.

## When a leader does wrong by mistake

[22]When a leader does wrong and does something in connection with any of Yahweh's orders about what should not be done, by mistake, and incurs liability, [23]or someone causes him to acknowledge his wrong that he did, he's to bring as his offering a he-goat from the flock, one that's whole. [24]He's to lean his hand on the goat's head and slaughter it in the place where one slaughters the burnt offering before Yahweh. It's a decontamination. [25]The priest is to get some of the decontamination blood with his finger and put it on the horns of the altar for burnt offering, and to pour out its blood at the base of the altar for burnt offering. [26]All its fat he's to turn into smoke at the altar, like the fat of the well-being sacrifice. So he's to make expiation for him because of his wrongdoing, and it will be pardoned him.

## When an individual does wrong by mistake

[27]If an individual person from the country's people does wrong by mistake, in doing something in connection with any of Yahweh's orders about what should not be done, and incurs liability, [28]or someone causes him to acknowledge his wrong that he did, he's to bring as his offering a she-goat from the flock, one that's whole, a female, for his wrong that he did. [29]He's to lean his hand on the head of the decontamination and slaughter the decontamination in the place of burnt offering. [30]The priest is to get some of its blood with his finger and put it on the horns of the altar for burnt offering, and to pour out all its blood at the altar's base. [31]All its fat he's to remove, as the fat was removed from the well-being sacrifice, and the priest is to turn it into smoke at the altar, as a nice smell for Yahweh. So the priest is to make expiation for him, and it will be pardoned him.

[32]If he brings a sheep as his offering as a decontamination, he's to bring a female that's whole. [33]He's to lean his hand on the head of the decontamination and slaughter it as a decontamination in the place where one slaughters the burnt offering. [34]The priest is to get some of the blood of the decontamination with his finger and put it on the horns of the altar for burnt offering, and to pour out all its blood at the altar's base. [35]All its fat he's to remove, as the fat from the sheep of a well-being sacrifice is removed, and the priest is to

turn them into smoke at the altar over Yahweh's gift offering. So the priest is to make expiation for him for his wrong that he did, and it will be pardoned him.

## Making reparation

**5** When a person does wrong: he heard the sound of a vow and he was a witness (either he saw or he knew). If he doesn't tell, he carries his waywardness. ²Or a person who touches any taboo thing (either the corpse of a taboo creature, the corpse of a taboo domestic animal or the corpse of a taboo teeming creature) and it escapes him, but he's become taboo and he's liable. ³Or when he touches something human that's taboo (in connection with anything taboo for him, by which one becomes taboo) and it escapes him, but he's come to know it and he's liable. ⁴Or when a person swears, blurting with his lips, to act badly or to do good, in connection with anything that a human being may blurt out in an oath, and it escapes him, but he's come to know it and he's liable.

In connection with one of these matters: ⁵when he's liable in connection with one of these matters, he must make confession of what he's done wrong in connection with it, ⁶and bring his reparation to Yahweh for his wrong that he did: a female from the flock, a ewe-lamb or a she-goat from the flock, as a decontamination; and the priest is to make expiation for him in relation to his wrongdoing. ⁷If his hand doesn't extend to enough for a sheep, he's to bring to Yahweh as his reparation for what he's done wrong two doves or two young pigeons, one as a decontamination and one as a burnt offering. ⁸He's to bring them to the priest and he's to present the one that's a decontamination first, wring its head from near its neck, but not divide it, ⁹and spatter some of the decontamination blood against the side of the altar. The remainder of the blood is to drain at the altar's base. It's a decontamination. ¹⁰The second he's to make as a burnt offering in accordance with the ruling.

So the priest is to make expiation for him because of his wrong that he did, and it will be pardoned him.

## More occasions for reparation

¹¹If his hand doesn't stretch to two doves or two young pigeons, he's to bring as his offering for what he did wrong a tenth of a barrel of fine flour as a decontamination. He's not to place oil on it and he's not to put frankincense on it, because it's a decontamination. ¹²He's to bring it to the priest, and the priest is to scoop out of it a fistful as a commemorative portion and turn it into smoke at the altar over Yahweh's gift offering. It's a decontamination. ¹³So the priest is to make expiation for him because of his wrong that he did in connection with one of these matters, and it will be pardoned him. It will be the priest's, like the grain offering.'"

¹⁴Yahweh spoke to Mosheh: ¹⁵'When a person commits a trespass and does wrong by mistake in connection with Yahweh's sacred things, he's to bring his reparation to Yahweh, a ram that's whole from the flock on the basis of the evaluation (in silver by sheqels, by the sanctuary sheqel), as a reparation. ¹⁶For what he did wrong in connection with the sacred thing, he's to make good and add a fifth to it, and give it to the priest. The priest will make expiation for him with the reparation ram, and it will be pardoned him.

¹⁷If a person, when he does wrong and does one of all the things that Yahweh has ordered should not be done, but he didn't know, he'll be liable and he'll carry his waywardness. ¹⁸He's to bring to the priest a ram that's whole from the flock, on the basis of the evaluation as a reparation. The priest will make expiation for him because of his mistake that he made when he didn't know, and it will be pardoned him. ¹⁹It's a reparation. He incurred liability to Yahweh.'

## Wrongdoing against Yahweh and wrongdoing against other people

**6** Yahweh spoke to Mosheh: ²'When a person does wrong and commits a trespass against Yahweh and is deceptive towards his fellow in connection with something entrusted or something deposited with him or by seizing, or he defrauds his fellow, ³or he finds something lost and is deceptive about it and swears in falsehood, regarding one of all the things that a human being may do so as to do wrong by them: [4]when he does wrong and is liable, he's to give back the thing that he seized or the thing that he got by fraud or the thing that was entrusted to him or the lost thing that he found, [5]or anything regarding which he swore in falsehood. He's to make good for it in terms of its total sum and add to it a fifth of it. He's to give it to the person to whom it belongs, on the day of his reparation.

[6]As his reparation he's to bring Yahweh a ram that's whole from the flock, on the basis of the evaluation as a reparation, to the priest. [7]The priest will make expiation for him before Yahweh and it will be pardoned him in respect of the one thing out of all the things that he might do, to incur liability by it.'

[8]Yahweh spoke to Mosheh: [9]'Order Aharon and his sons: "This is the instruction about the burnt offering. The burnt offering is on the hearth, on the altar, all night until the morning. The altar fire is to be kept burning on it. [10]Then the priest is to put on his cloth tunic and put on his cloth shorts over his flesh and take up the waste to which the fire devours the burnt offering on the altar and put it beside the altar. [11]He's then to take off his garments, put on other garments and take out the waste outside the camp to a pure place.

## Priests' instructions about grain offerings

[12]The fire on the altar is to be kept burning on it; it's not to go out. The priest is to burn wood on it morning by morning, arrange the burnt offering on it and turn into smoke the fat parts of the well-being sacrifices on it. [13]A continual fire is to be kept burning on the altar; it's not to go out.

[14]This is the instruction about the grain offering. Aharon's sons are to bring it before Yahweh before the altar. [15]He's to take up from it in his fist some of the fine flour of the grain offering and some of its oil and all the frankincense that's on the grain offering, and burn its commemorative portion into smoke for Yahweh at the altar, a nice smell. [16]The rest of it Aharon and his sons are to eat. It's to be eaten as flatbread in the sacred place; they're to eat it in the appointment tent courtyard.

[17]It's not to be baked with yeast. I've given it to them as their share from my gift offerings. It's especially sacred, like the decontamination and the reparation. [18]Any male among Aharon's descendants may eat it (a permanent decree through your generations) from Yahweh's gift offerings. Anything that touches them becomes sacred."'

[19]Yahweh spoke to Mosheh: [20]'This is Aharon and his sons' offering, which they're to present for Yahweh on the day of his anointing: a tenth of a gallon of fine flour as a regular grain offering, half of it in the morning and half of it in the evening. [21]It's to be made on a griddle, with oil. You're to bring it blended. You're to present it as baked bits of the grain offering, broken pieces, a nice smell for Yahweh.

[22]The priest anointed in his place from among his sons is to make it (a permanent decree) for Yahweh. It's to be turned into smoke, a whole offering. [23]Every grain offering by a priest is to be a whole offering. It will not be eaten.'

## Priests' instructions about the decontamination and reparation

[24]Yahweh spoke to Mosheh: [25]'Speak to Aharon and to his sons: "This is the instruction about the decontamination. In the place where the burnt offering is slaughtered, the decontamination is to be slaughtered, before Yahweh. It's especially sacred. [26]The priest who offers it as a decontamination is to eat it. It's to be eaten in the sacred place, in the appointment tent courtyard. [27]Anything that touches its flesh becomes sacred, and when some of its blood spatters on a garment, you're to wash what it spatters on, in the sacred place. [28]A clay container in which it's boiled is to be broken. If it was boiled in a copper container, it's to be scoured and rinsed with water. [29]Any male among the priests may eat it. It's especially sacred. [30]But no decontamination may be eaten from which some of its blood has been brought into the appointment tent to make expiation in the sacred place. It's to be burned in fire.

**7** This is the instruction about the reparation. It's especially sacred. [2]In the place where they slaughter the burnt offering

they're to slaughter the reparation. Its blood
he's to toss over the altar all round. ³From it
he's to present all its fat: the broad tail, the fat
covering the innards, ⁴the two kidneys and the
fat that's on them, which is on the loins, and
the lobe on the liver; he's to remove it along
with the kidneys. ⁵The priest is to turn them
into smoke at the altar as a gift offering for
Yahweh. It's a reparation. ⁶Any male among the
priests may eat it. He's to eat it in the sacred
place. It's especially sacred.

## The several reasons for a well-being sacrifice

⁷As is the decontamination, so is the
reparation; there's one instruction for them.
The priest who makes expiation by it, it belongs
to him. ⁸The priest who presents an individual's
burnt offering – the skin of the burnt offering
that he presents belongs to the priest; it's to
be his. ⁹Any grain offering that's baked in the
oven, and any that's made in the pan or on a
griddle, belongs to the priest who presents it;
it's to be his. ¹⁰Any grain offering that's mixed
with oil or dry is to belong to Aharon's sons,
each the same as his brother.

¹¹This is the instruction about the well-being
sacrifice that someone presents for Yahweh.
¹²If he presents it as a thanksgiving, along with
the thanksgiving he's to present flat loaves
mixed with oil, flat wafers spread with oil,
and fine flour blended, loaves mixed with
oil, ¹³along with the loaves of leavened bread.
He's to present his offering along with his
thanksgiving well-being sacrifice. ¹⁴From it
he's to present one from each offering as a
contribution for Yahweh, to the priest who
tosses the blood of the well-being sacrifice: it's
to be his.

¹⁵The flesh of his thanksgiving well-being
sacrifice is to be eaten on the day of its offering.
He's not to leave any of it till morning. ¹⁶If the
sacrifice he offers is a pledge or free offering,
it's to be eaten on the day he presents his
sacrifice, though what is left of it may be eaten
on the next day, ¹⁷but what is left of the flesh
of the sacrifice is to be burned in fire on the
third day. ¹⁸If any of the flesh of his well-being
sacrifice is eaten at all on the third day, the one
who presents it won't find acceptance. It won't
be deemed for him. It will be an objectionable

thing. The person who eats of it will carry his
waywardness.

## The priest's allocations

¹⁹Flesh that touches anything taboo will not
be eaten. It will be burned in fire. [Other] flesh:
anyone who is pure may eat flesh. ²⁰But the
person who eats the flesh from a well-being
sacrifice, which is Yahweh's, when his taboo is
on him – that person shall be cut off from his
kin. ²¹A person who touches anything taboo (a
human taboo or a taboo animal or any taboo
atrocity) and eats from the flesh of Yahweh's
well-being sacrifice – that person shall be cut
off from his kin.'"

²²Yahweh spoke to Mosheh: ²³'Speak to the
Yisra'elites: "You will not eat any of the fat of
ox or sheep or goat. ²⁴The fat from a corpse
and the fat from something mauled may be
used for any work, but you will not eat it at all.
²⁵When anyone eats the fat from an animal
from which one may present a gift offering for
Yahweh, the person who eats shall be cut off
from his kin.

²⁶You will not eat any blood in any of your
settlements, of bird or of animal. ²⁷Any person
who eats any blood, that person shall be cut off
from his kin.'"

²⁸Yahweh spoke to Mosheh: ²⁹'Speak to the
Yisra'elites: "One who presents his well-being
sacrifice for Yahweh, he's to bring his offering
for Yahweh from his well-being sacrifice. ³⁰His
hands are to bring Yahweh's gift offerings. He's
to bring the fat along with the breast – the
breast for elevating as an elevation offering
before Yahweh.

³¹The priest is to turn the fat into smoke at
the altar, and the breast is to be for Aharon and
his sons. ³²The right thigh you're to give as a
contribution to the priest from your well-being
sacrifices. ³³The one of Aharon's sons who
presents the blood of the well-being sacrifices,
and the fat: the right thigh is to be his portion,
³⁴because I've taken the breast of the elevation
offering and the thigh of the contribution from
the Yisra'elites from their well-being sacrifices
and given them to Aharon the priest and to
his sons (as a permanent decree) from the
Yisra'elites.'"

## The ordination begins

**35**This is Aharon's anointing share and
his sons' anointing share from Yahweh's gift
offerings on the day he presents them to act as
priests for Yahweh, **36**which Yahweh ordered
to give them on the day of his anointing them
(a permanent decree from the Yisra'elites
through their generations).

**37**This is the instruction for the burnt
offering, for the grain offering, for the
decontamination, for the reparation, for
the commissioning and for the well-being
sacrifice, **38**with which Yahweh ordered
Mosheh at Mount Sinay on the day he ordered
the Yisra'elites to present their offerings for
Yahweh, in the Sinay Wilderness.

**8** Yahweh spoke to Mosheh: **2**'Get Aharon
and his sons with him, and the garments,
the anointing oil, the decontamination bull, the
two rams and the basket of flatbread, **3**and
congregate the entire assembly at the entrance
of the appointment tent.'

**4**Mosheh did as Yahweh ordered him, and
the assembly congregated at the entrance of the
appointment tent. **5**Mosheh said to the assembly,
'This is the thing that Yahweh has ordered to do.'

**6**Mosheh presented Aharon and his sons
and washed them with water. **7**He put the tunic
on him, wrapped him with the sash, clothed
him with the coat, put the chasuble on him,
wrapped him with the chasuble's design-work
strap and wound it to him with it. **8**He placed
the pouch on him and put into the pouch the
Urim and Tummim. **9**He placed the turban
on his head and placed on the turban near
the front of it the gold medallion, the sacred
diadem, as Yahweh ordered Mosheh.

## The vestments

**10**Mosheh got the anointing oil and anointed
the dwelling and everything that was in it, and
made them sacred. **11**He sprinkled some of it
on the altar seven times and anointed the altar
and all its articles, and the basin and its stand,
to make them sacred. **12**He poured some of the
anointing oil on Aharon's head and anointed
him, to make him sacred.

**13**Mosheh presented Aharon's sons, clothed
them in tunics, wrapped them with a sash and

bound mitres on them, as Yahweh ordered
Mosheh. **14**He brought up the decontamination
bull. Aharon and his sons leaned their hands
on the head of the decontamination bull,
**15**and he slaughtered it. Mosheh got the blood
and put it on the altar's horns all round with
his finger and decontaminated the altar, and
poured out the blood at the altar's base. So he
made it sacred for making expiation on it.
**16**He got all the fat that was on the innards,
the lobe of the liver, the two kidneys and their
fat, and Mosheh turned them into smoke at
the altar. **17**The bull, its skin, its flesh and its
intestines he burned in fire outside the camp,
as Yahweh ordered Mosheh.

**18**He presented the ram for the burnt
offering, Aharon and his sons leaned their
hands on the ram's head, **19**and he slaughtered
it. Mosheh tossed the blood over the altar
all round **20**and cut up the ram into its parts.
Mosheh turned the head, the parts and the suet
into smoke, **21**and the innards and the legs he
washed with water.

So Mosheh turned the entire ram into smoke
at the altar. It was a burnt offering, as a nice
smell. It was a gift offering for Yahweh, as
Yahweh ordered Mosheh.

## The commissioning offering

**22**Then he presented the second ram, the
commissioning ram. Aharon and his sons
leaned their hands on the ram's head, **23**and he
slaughtered it. Mosheh got some of its blood
and put it on the lobe of Aharon's right ear, on
the thumb of his right hand and on the big toe
of his right foot. **24**He presented Aharon's sons,
and Mosheh put some of the blood on the lobe
of their right ear, on the thumb of their right
hand and on the big toe of their right foot.

Mosheh tossed the blood over the altar all
round. **25**He got the fat – the broad tail, all the
fat that was on the innards, the lobe of the liver,
the two kidneys and their fat, and the right
thigh – **26**and from the basket of flatbread that
was before Yahweh he got one loaf of flatbread,
one loaf of bread made with oil, and one wafer,
and placed them on the fat parts and on the
right thigh.

**27**He put everything on Aharon's palms and
on his sons' palms and elevated them as an

elevation offering before Yahweh. [28]Mosheh took them from on their palms and turned them into smoke at the altar along with the burnt offering. They were a commissioning offering, as a sweet smell. It was a gift offering for Yahweh. [29]Mosheh got the breast and elevated it as an elevation offering before Yahweh. From the commissioning ram it was Mosheh's portion, as Yahweh ordered Mosheh.

[30]Mosheh got some of the anointing oil and some of the blood that was on the altar and spattered it on Aharon and on his garments, and on his sons and on his sons' garments with him, and made them sacred, Aharon and his garments and his sons and his sons' garments with him.

## Seven days in the appointment tent

[31]Mosheh said to Aharon and to his sons: 'Boil the flesh at the entrance of the appointment tent. You're to eat it there, with the bread that's in the commissioning basket, as I ordered: "Aharon and his sons are to eat it." [32]The rest of the flesh and of the bread you're to burn in fire. [33]You will not go out of the entrance of the appointment tent for seven days until the day when the days of your commissioning are complete, because for seven days he will commission you. [34]As he has done this day, Yahweh has ordered to do, to make expiation for you. [35]You're to stay at the entrance of the appointment tent, day and night, for seven days, and keep Yahweh's charge, so you don't die, because so I've been ordered.'

[36]Aharon and his sons did all the things that Yahweh ordered through Mosheh.

**9** On the eighth day Mosheh called for Aharon and his sons, and Yisra'el's elders, [2]and said to Aharon, 'Get yourself a bullock from the herd as a decontamination and a ram as a burnt offering, ones that are whole, and present them before Yahweh. [3]And speak to the Yisra'elites: "Get a he-goat from the flock as a decontamination, a bullock and a lamb (ones that are a year old, that are whole) as a burnt offering, [4]an ox and a ram as a well-being offering to sacrifice before Yahweh, and a grain offering mixed with oil, because today Yahweh will appear to you."'

## Aharon's offerings

[5]So they took what Mosheh ordered to the front of the appointment tent, and the entire assembly drew near and stood before Yahweh. [6]Mosheh said, 'This is the thing that Yahweh ordered that you do, so Yahweh's splendour may appear to you.'

[7]Mosheh said to Aharon, 'Draw near the altar and make your decontamination and your burnt offering and make expiation for yourself and for the people, and make the people's offering and make expiation for them, as Yahweh has ordered.'

[8]So Aharon drew near the altar and slaughtered the decontamination bullock that was his. [9]Aharon's sons presented the blood to him and he dipped his finger in the blood and put it on the altar's horns, and poured out the blood at the altar's base. [10]The fat, the kidneys and the lobe from the liver from the decontamination he turned into smoke at the altar, as Yahweh ordered Mosheh. [11]The flesh and the skin he burned in fire outside the camp.

[12]He slaughtered the burnt offering, and Aharon's sons passed the blood to him and he tossed it over the altar all round. [13]They passed the burnt offering to him in its parts, with the head, and he turned it into smoke on the altar. [14]He washed the innards and the legs and turned them into smoke along with the burnt offering on the altar.

## Yahweh's splendour appears

[15]Then he presented the people's offering. He got the decontamination goat which was the people's, slaughtered it and made it a decontamination, like the first. [16]He presented the burnt offering and made it in accordance with the ruling. [17]He presented the grain offering, filled his palm from it and turned it into smoke on the altar, apart from the morning burnt offering. [18]He slaughtered the ox and the ram, the well-being sacrifice that was the people's, and Aharon's sons passed the blood to him (and he tossed it over the altar, all round), [19]and the fat parts from the ox and the ram, the broad tail, the covering, the kidneys and the lobe of the liver. [20]They placed the fat parts on the breasts and turned the fat parts into smoke at the altar. [21]The breasts and the

right thigh Aharon elevated as an elevation offering before Yahweh, as Mosheh ordered.

²²Aharon lifted up his hands to the people and blessed them, then came down from making the decontamination, the burnt offering and the well-being sacrifice. ²³Mosheh and Aharon went into the appointment tent, and came out and blessed the people. Then Yahweh's splendour appeared to the entire people, ²⁴and fire came out from before Yahweh and devoured the burnt offering and the fat parts on the altar. The entire people saw, and resounded, and fell on their faces.

## Disaster strikes

**10** But Aharon's sons, Nadab and Abihu, each took his pan, put fire in it, placed incense on it and presented before Yahweh outside fire, which he had not ordered them. ²Fire came out from before Yahweh and devoured them. They died before Yahweh.

³Mosheh said to Aharon, 'It's what Yahweh spoke of:

In the people who draw near me I will show
    myself sacred
and before the face of the entire people I will
    show splendour.'

Aharon was silent, ⁴but Mosheh called for Misha'el and Eltsaphan, sons of Uzzi'el, Aharon's uncle, and said to them, 'Draw near, carry your brothers from before the sacred place, outside the camp.' ⁵They drew near and carried them by their tunics outside the camp, as Mosheh said.

⁶Mosheh said to Aharon and to El'azar and Itamar his sons, 'Don't bare your heads, and you will not tear your clothes, so you don't die and he becomes furious with the entire assembly. Your brothers, Yisra'el's entire household, may bewail the burning that Yahweh has brought about. ⁷You will not go out of the entrance of the appointment tent, so you will not die, because Yahweh's anointing oil is on you.' They did as Mosheh said.

⁸Yahweh spoke to Aharon, ⁹'Don't drink wine or liquor, you or your sons with you, when you go into the appointment tent, so you will not die (a permanent decree, through your generations), ¹⁰so you can make a distinction between the sacred and the ordinary

and between the taboo and the pure, ¹¹and instruct the Yisra'elites in all the decrees that Yahweh has spoken to them through Mosheh.'

## On being careful with the decrees

¹²Mosheh spoke to Aharon and to El'azar and to Itamar, his remaining sons: 'Get the grain offering that's left from Yahweh's gift offerings and eat it as flatbread beside the altar, because it's especially sacred. ¹³You're to eat it in the sacred place, because it's a decree for you and a decree for your sons from Yahweh's gift offerings, because I've been ordered so. ¹⁴The breast of the elevation offering and the thigh of the contribution you may eat in a pure place, you and your sons and your daughters with you, because they have been given (a decree for you and a decree for your children) from the Yisra'elites' well-being sacrifices. ¹⁵They're to bring the thigh of the contribution and the breast of the elevation offering, along with the gift offerings of fat things, to elevate as an elevation offering before Yahweh, and it will be yours and your children's with you (as a permanent decree) as Yahweh has ordered.'

¹⁶Then Mosheh enquired urgently about the decontamination goat. There, it had been burned. He was furious with El'azar and Itamar, Aharon's remaining sons, and said, ¹⁷'Why didn't you eat the decontamination, in the sacred place, because it's especially sacred, and he's given it to you to carry the assembly's waywardness, to make expiation for them before Yahweh? ¹⁸Here, its blood was not brought into the sacred place, inside. You should certainly eat it in the sacred place, as I ordered.'

¹⁹But Aharon spoke to Mosheh: 'Here, today they have presented their decontamination and their burnt offering before Yahweh, and things like these have happened to me. Had I eaten the decontamination today, would it have been good in Yahweh's eyes?' ²⁰Mosheh listened, and it was good in his eyes.

## You are what you eat

**11** Yahweh spoke to Mosheh and to Aharon: ²'Speak to the Yisra'elites: "These are the creatures that you may eat, of all the animals that are on the earth: ³anything that has a divided hoof (that has a cleft in its hoofs) that brings up the cud – among the animals, you may eat it. ⁴This, however, you will not eat, of those that bring up the cud or of those that have a divided hoof:

> the camel, because it brings up its cud but it doesn't have a divided hoof – it's taboo for you;
> ⁵the rock badger, because it brings up the cud but it doesn't have a divided hoof – it's taboo for you;
> ⁶the hare, because it brings up the cud but it doesn't have a divided hoof – it's taboo for you;
> ⁷the pig, because it has a divided hoof (it has a cleft in its hoof) but it doesn't chew the cud – it's taboo for you.

⁸You will not eat of their meat and you will not touch their corpse – they're taboo for you.

⁹This you may eat of everything that's in the water: anything that has fins and scales, in the water, in the seas and in the wadis – you may eat them. ¹⁰But anything that doesn't have fins and scales, in the water and in the wadis, of any teeming things of the water and of any living thing that's in the water – they're an atrocity for you. ¹¹Given that they will be an atrocity for you, from their flesh you will not eat and you're to treat their corpse as an atrocity. ¹²Anything in the water that does not have fins and scales is an atrocity for you.

## How touch produces taboo

¹³These you're to treat as an atrocity from the birds – they're not to be eaten, they're an atrocity:

> the eagle, the vulture, the osprey, ¹⁴the kite, the falcon (any of its species), ¹⁵the raven (any of its species), ¹⁶the ostrich, the nighthawk, the seagull, the hawk (any of its species), ¹⁷the tawny owl, the cormorant, the screech owl, ¹⁸the barn owl, the pelican, the swan, ¹⁹the stork, the heron (any of its species), the hoopoe and the bat.

²⁰Any teeming, flying thing walking on all fours is an atrocity for you. ²¹However, you may eat this: of any teeming, flying thing walking on all fours that has bending legs above its feet to leap with on the earth, ²²of them you may eat these:

> the locust (any of its species), the winged locust (any of its species), the cricket (any of its species), the grasshopper (any of its species).

²³But any other teeming, flying thing that has four legs is an atrocity for you.

²⁴By these you make yourself taboo; anyone who touches their corpse becomes taboo until the evening, ²⁵and anyone who carries their corpse is to wash his clothes and becomes taboo until the evening:

> ²⁶By any animal that does have hoofs but they have no cleft, or that doesn't bring up the cud. They're taboo for you; anyone who touches them becomes taboo.
> ²⁷Any that walks on its hands, among all the creatures that walk on all fours, are taboo for you. Anyone who touches their corpse becomes taboo until the evening.
> ²⁸Someone who carries their corpse is to wash his clothes and become taboo until the evening. They're taboo for you.

## How other contact produces taboo

²⁹This is taboo for you among the things that teem on the earth:

> the mole, the mouse, the lizard (any of its species), ³⁰the ferret, the gecko, the crocodile, the skink and the chameleon.

³¹These are the taboo things for you among everything that teems.

> Anyone who touches them when they're dead becomes taboo until the evening.
> ³²Anything on which one of them falls when they're dead becomes taboo, of any article of wood, clothing, skin or sacking.
> Any article that can be used for work is to be put in water; it becomes taboo until the evening, then it becomes pure.
> ³³Any clay container inside which one of them falls – anything that's inside it becomes taboo, and you're to break it.
> ³⁴Of anything that would be eaten on to which water comes, it becomes taboo.
> Anything that would be drunk in any container becomes taboo.
> ³⁵Anything on which one of their corpses falls becomes taboo.

An oven or a stove is to be smashed; they're taboo, and they're to be taboo for you. ³⁶However, a spring or a cistern (a container for water) continues to be pure, but a person who touches their corpse [in it] becomes taboo. ³⁷When one of their corpses falls on any seed for sowing, which is to be sown, it's pure. ³⁸But when water is put on seed and one of their corpses falls on it, it becomes taboo for you.

## The importance of making distinctions

³⁹When one of the animals that's for eating by you dies, someone who touches its corpse becomes taboo until the evening. ⁴⁰One who eats of its corpse is to wash his clothes; he becomes taboo until the evening. One who carries its corpse is to wash his clothes; he becomes taboo until the evening.

⁴¹Everything that teems on the earth is an atrocity. It's not to be eaten. ⁴²Anything that goes on its belly and anything that goes on all fours, and further anything that has many feet: regarding anything that teems on the earth, you will not eat them, because they're an atrocity. ⁴³You're not to make yourselves into an atrocity through anything that teems. You will not make yourselves taboo through them and become taboo through them, ⁴⁴because I am Yahweh your God. You're to make yourselves sacred and be sacred, because I am sacred. You will not make yourselves taboo through any teeming thing that moves on the earth, ⁴⁵because I am Yahweh who brought you up from the country of Misrayim [Egypt] to be your God. You're to be sacred, because I am sacred.

⁴⁶This is the instruction about animals, birds, and all living creatures that move in the water, and concerning all creatures that teem on the earth, ⁴⁷for making a distinction between the taboo and the pure and between the living things that are eaten and the living things that may not be eaten.'"

## The childbirth taboo

**12** Yahweh spoke to Mosheh: ²"Speak to the Yisra'elites: "When a woman brings forth offspring and gives birth to a male, she becomes taboo for seven days; she becomes taboo as in the days of flowing when she's unwell. (³On the eighth day the flesh of his foreskin is to be circumcised.)

⁴For thirty-three days she's to live in a state of blood purifying. She will not touch anything sacred or go into the sanctuary until the completion of her days of purifying. ⁵If she gives birth to a female, she becomes taboo for two weeks as in her flowing and she's to live for sixty-six days in a state of blood purifying.

⁶At the completion of her days of purifying, for a son or a daughter, she's to bring a year-old lamb as a burnt offering, and a young pigeon or dove as a decontamination, to the priest at the entrance of the appointment tent. ⁷He's to present it before Yahweh and make expiation for her, and she'll become pure from her flow of blood. This is the instruction about someone giving birth to a male or to a female.

⁸If her hand can't find enough for a sheep, she's to get two doves or two young pigeons, one for a burnt offering and one for decontamination, and the priest is to make expiation for her, and she'll become pure.'"

## Scaliness (aka leprosy)

**13** Yahweh spoke to Mosheh and to Aharon: ²"When there is in the skin of a person's body a swelling or rash or spot and it becomes an outbreak of scaliness in the skin of his body, he's to be brought to Aharon the priest or to one of his sons, the priests, ³and the priest is to look at the outbreak in the skin of the body. If the hair in the outbreak has turned white and the outbreak's appearance is deeper than the skin of his body, the outbreak is scaliness. When the priest sees it, he's to pronounce him taboo.

⁴If it's a white spot in the skin of his body, its appearance is not deeper than the skin, and the hair hasn't turned white, the priest is to confine [the person with] the outbreak for seven days. ⁵On the seventh day the priest is to look: there, if the outbreak has stood still, in his eyes, and the outbreak hasn't spread in the skin, the priest is to confine him for a second seven days.

⁶The priest is to look at him on the second seventh day: there, if the outbreak has faded

and the outbreak hasn't spread in the skin, the priest is to pronounce him pure. It's a rash. He's to wash his clothes, and he'll become pure. [7]But if the rash actually spreads in the skin after his appearing to the priest for his purity pronouncement, he's to appear a second time to the priest, [8]and the priest will look, and there, the rash has spread in the skin, the priest is to pronounce him taboo. It's scaliness.

## Dealing with uncertainty

[9]When there's an outbreak of scaliness in a person and he's brought to the priest, [10]if the priest looks, and there, a white swelling in the skin, and it's turned the hair white, with a living growth of live flesh in the swelling: [11]it's dormant scaliness in the skin of his body, and the priest will pronounce him taboo. He won't confine him, because he's taboo.

[12]If the scaliness does break out in the skin and the scaliness covers the entire skin of [the person with] the outbreak, from his head to his feet, everything visible to the priest's eyes, [13]so the priest looks and there, the scaliness has covered his entire body, he'll pronounce [the person with] the outbreak pure. All of him has turned white. He's pure.

[14]But on the day live flesh appears in him, he becomes taboo. [15]When the priest sees the live flesh, he's to pronounce him taboo. The live flesh is taboo. It's scaliness. [16]Or when the live flesh again turns white, he's to come to the priest [17]and the priest is to look, and there, the outbreak has turned white, then the priest is to pronounce [the person with] the outbreak pure. He's pure.

[18]When there's an eruption in the skin of someone's body and it heals, [19]but in the place of the eruption there's a white swelling or a white-reddish spot, he's to appear to the priest [20]and the priest is to look and there, it's lower than the skin and its hair has turned white, then the priest is to pronounce him taboo. It's an outbreak of scaliness that has broken out in the eruption. [21]But if the priest looks at it and there, no white hair is in it, it's not lower than the skin and it's pale, then the priest is to confine him for seven days. [22]If it does spread in his skin, the priest is to pronounce him taboo. It's an outbreak. [23]But if the spot halts in

its place (it hasn't spread), it's the scab from the eruption. The priest is to pronounce him pure.

## Burns and scabies

[24]Or when there's a burn from fire in the skin of a body and the living growth from the burn becomes a white-reddish or white spot, [25]if the priest looks at it, and there, the hair has turned white in the spot and its appearance is deeper than the skin: it's scaliness that's broken out in the burn. The priest is to pronounce him taboo. It's an outbreak of scaliness. [26]But if the priest looks at it and there, in the spot is no white hair, and it's not lower than the skin and it's pale, the priest is to confine him for seven days. [27]The priest is to look at him on the seventh day. If it's actually spread in the skin, the priest is to pronounce him taboo. It's an outbreak of scaliness. [28]But if the spot halts in its place (it hasn't spread in the skin) and it's pale, it's the swelling from the burn. The priest is to pronounce him pure, because it's the scab from the burn.

[29]When there's an outbreak in a man or a woman in the head or in the beard, [30]and the priest looks at the outbreak, and there, its appearance is deeper than the skin and there's thin yellow hair in it, the priest is to pronounce him taboo. It's scabies; it's scaliness in the head or the beard. [31]But when the priest looks at the scabies outbreak and there, its appearance is not deeper than the skin, but there's no black hair in it, the priest is to confine [the person with] the scabies outbreak for seven days. [32]The priest is to look at the outbreak on the seventh day: there, the scabies hasn't spread and no yellow hair has come in it, and the scabies' appearance is not deeper than the skin, [33]the person is to shave, but not shave the scabies, and the priest is to confine [the person with] the scabies for a second seven days.

## Spots and hair loss

[34]The priest is to look at the scabies on the seventh day: there, the scabies hasn't spread in the skin and its appearance is not deeper than the skin, so the priest is to pronounce him pure. He's to wash his clothes, and he'll become

pure. [35]But if the scabies actually spreads after his purity pronouncement, [36]the priest is to look at him. There, the scabies has spread in his skin. The priest will not seek for yellow hair. The person is taboo. [37]But if in his eyes the scabies has halted and black hair has grown in it, the scabies has healed. The person is pure. The priest is to pronounce him pure.

[38]When there are spots in the skin of a man or a woman's body, white spots, [39]and the priest looks, and there, the spots in the skin of their body are pale, white, it's a sore that's broken out in the skin. The person is pure.

[40]When a man's head becomes hairless: he's bald, he's pure. [41]If his head becomes hairless from the side of his face: his hair is receding, he's pure. [42]But when there's a white-reddish outbreak in the bald part or in the receding part, it's scaliness breaking out in his bald part or in his receding part, [43]and the priest is to look at him. There, the swelling from the outbreak is white-reddish in his bald part or in his receding part, like the appearance of scaliness in the skin of the body, [44]the man has been made scaly. He's taboo. The priest is to pronounce him taboo. His outbreak is in his head.

[45]Somone who's been made scaly, who has the outbreak in him: his clothes are to be torn, his head is to be bared, he's to cover his lip and he's to call, "Taboo, taboo". [46]For all the time that the outbreak is in him, he becomes taboo. While he's taboo, he's to live apart. His dwelling will be outside the camp.

## Scaliness in clothing

[47]When there's an outbreak of scaliness in clothing, in wool clothing or in fabric clothing, [48]whether in the warp or in the woof of the fabric or of the wool, or in a skin or in anything worked from skin, [49]and the outbreak is greenish or reddish in the clothing or in the skin, whether in the warp or in the woof, or in any skin article: it's an outbreak of scaliness. It's to be shown to the priest. [50]The priest is to look at the outbreak and confine [the thing with] the outbreak for seven days. [51]He's to look at the outbreak on the seventh day. When the outbreak has spread in the clothing, whether in the warp or in the woof or in the skin, for

any work for which the skin may be used, the outbreak is a malignant scaliness. It's taboo. [52]He's to burn the cloth, whether warp or woof, in wool or in fabric or any skin article in which there is the outbreak, because it's a malignant scaliness. It's to be burned in fire.

[53]But if the priest looks, and there, the outbreak in the clothing, whether in the warp or in the woof or in any skin article, hasn't spread, [54]the priest is to order that they wash the thing with the outbreak in it, and 'confine' it for a second seven days. [55]The priest is to look at the outbreak after it has been washed, and there, the outbreak hasn't changed its appearance, though the outbreak hasn't spread, it's taboo. You're to burn it in fire. It's a fungus, in its bald side or in its receding side.

[56]But if the priest looks, and there, the outbreak is pale after it's been washed, he's to tear it out from the clothing or from the skin, either from the warp or from the woof. [57]If it appears again in the clothing, either in the warp or in the woof, or in any skin article, it's breaking out. You're to burn in fire the thing in which is the outbreak. [58]But the clothing, either the warp or the woof or any skin article that you wash so that the outbreak departs from them, it's to be washed a second time, and it will become pure.

[59]This is the instruction for an outbreak of scaliness in clothing, wool or fabric, either the warp or the woof, or for any skin article, for pronouncing it pure or pronouncing it taboo.'

## Being restored to the assembly

**14** Yahweh spoke to Mosheh: [2]'This is to be the instruction for the person with scaliness, on the day of his purifying. He's to be brought to the priest; [3]the priest is to go outside the camp. The priest is to look, and there, the outbreak of scaliness has healed from the person with scaliness, [4]so the priest is to order that someone get for the person purifying himself two pure live birds, cedar wood, scarlet yarn and hyssop.

[5]The priest is to order that he slaughter one bird in a clay container over fresh water. [6]The live bird he's to take, with the cedar wood, the scarlet yarn and the hyssop, and dip them with the live bird in the blood of the bird that

was slaughtered over the fresh water. [7]He's to spatter it over the person purifying himself from the scaliness, seven times, and purify him, and to send off the live bird over the face of the fields.

[8]The person purifying himself is to wash his clothes, shave all his hair and bathe in water, and he'll become pure. Afterwards, he may go into the camp, but he's to live outside his tent for seven days. [9]On the seventh day he's to shave all his hair – his head, his beard and his eyebrows. He's to shave all his hair, wash his clothes and bathe his body in water, and he'll become pure.

[10]On the eighth day he's to get two sheep that are whole, and one ewe a year old that's whole, three tenths of grain-offering fine flour, mixed with oil, and one pint of oil. [11]The priest who is purifying is to stand the person who's purifying himself with them, before Yahweh, at the entrance of the appointment tent.

## The decontamination rite

[12]The priest is to get one sheep and present it as a reparation, with the pint of oil, and to elevate them as an elevation offering before Yahweh. [13]He's to slaughter the sheep in the place where one slaughters the decontamination and the burnt offering, in the sacred place, because the reparation is like the decontamination; it belongs to the priest. It's especially sacred.

[14]The priest is to get some of the blood of the reparation. The priest is to put it on the lobe of the ear of the person purifying himself (the right), on the thumb of his right hand and on the big toe of his right foot. [15]The priest is to get some of the pint of oil and pour it on to the priest's palm, the left. [16]And the priest is to dip his right finger in the oil that's on his left palm and sprinkle some of the oil with his finger seven times before Yahweh. [17]Some of the rest of the oil that's on his palm the priest is to put on the lobe of the ear of the person purifying himself (the right), on the thumb of his right hand and on the big toe of his right foot, over the blood of the reparation. [18]The rest of the oil that's on the priest's palm he's to put on the head of the person purifying himself. So the priest is to make expiation for

him before Yahweh. [19]The priest is to make the decontamination and make expiation for the person purifying himself from his taboo.

Afterwards, he's to slaughter the burnt offering. [20]The priest is to offer up the burnt offering and the grain offering at the altar. So the priest will make expiation for him, and he'll become pure.

## For someone of limited means

[21]If he's poor and his hand doesn't stretch to it, he's to get one sheep as a reparation, to be an elevation offering to make expiation for him, one tenth of fine flour mixed with oil as a grain offering, a pint of oil, [22]and two doves or two young pigeons, as his hand stretches to it. One will be a decontamination and one a burnt offering.

[23]He's to bring them to the priest on the eighth day for his purifying, to the entrance of the appointment tent, before Yahweh. [24]The priest is to get the reparation sheep and the pint of oil, and the priest is to elevate them as an elevation offering before Yahweh. [25]He's to slaughter the reparation sheep, and the priest is to get some of the blood of the reparation and put it on the lobe of the ear of the person purifying himself (the right), on the thumb of his right hand and on the big toe of his right foot.

[26]The priest is to pour some of the oil on to the priest's palm, the left, [27]and the priest is to spatter some of the oil that's on his left palm with the finger of his right hand seven times before Yahweh. [28]Some of the oil that's on his palm the priest is to put on the lobe of the ear of the person purifying himself (the right), on the thumb of his right hand and on the big toe of his right foot, on the place with the reparation blood. [29]The rest of the oil that's on the priest's palm he's to put on the head of the person purifying himself, to make expiation for him before Yahweh.

[30]He's to make an offering of one of the doves or young pigeons, from whichever his hand stretches to [31](whichever his hand stretches to), one the decontamination and one the burnt offering, along with the grain offering. So the priest is to make expiation before Yahweh for the person purifying himself.

³²This is the instruction for the person on whom there's an outbreak of scaliness, whose hand doesn't stretch, in his purifying.'

## Scaliness in a house

³³Yahweh spoke to Mosheh and to Aharon: ³⁴'When you come into the country of Kena'an [Canaan], which I'm giving you as a holding, and I put an outbreak of scaliness in a house in the country that's your holding, ³⁵the house's owner is to come and tell the priest, "Something like an outbreak has appeared to me in the house." ³⁶The priest is to order that they clear the house before the priest comes to look at the outbreak, so nothing that's in the house becomes taboo. After this, the priest will come to look at the house. ³⁷He will look at the outbreak, and there, if the outbreak in the house's walls is greenish or reddish depressions and their appearance is lower than the wall, ³⁸the priest is to come out from the house to the entrance of the house and confine it for seven days.

³⁹The priest is to come back on the seventh day and look, and there, the outbreak has spread in the house's walls. ⁴⁰The priest is to order that they take out the stones in which is the outbreak and throw them outside the town into a taboo place. ⁴¹He's to get the house scraped, from the house all round, and they're to pour out the earth that they've scraped off, outside the town into a taboo place. ⁴²They're to get other stones and bring them in the place of the stones, and get other earth and coat the house.

⁴³If the outbreak comes back and breaks out in the house after he's pulled out the stones and after the scraping of the house and after the coating, ⁴⁴the priest is to come and look, and there, the outbreak has spread in the house. It's a malignant scaliness. ⁴⁵He's to demolish the house, its stones, its wood and all the soil from the house, and take it out to a taboo place outside the town.

## Purifying a house

⁴⁶Someone who goes into the house through all the time he's confined it becomes taboo until the evening. ⁴⁷Someone who sleeps in the house is to wash his clothes. Someone who eats in the house is to wash his clothes.

⁴⁸If the priest actually comes and looks, and there, the outbreak hasn't spread in the house after the coating of the house, the priest is to pronounce the house pure, because the outbreak has healed. ⁴⁹To decontaminate the house, he's to get two birds, cedar wood, bright crimson and hyssop. ⁵⁰He's to slaughter one bird in a clay container over fresh water. ⁵¹He's to get the cedar wood and the hyssop and the bright crimson and the live bird and dip them in the blood of the slaughtered bird and in the fresh water, and spatter the house seven times. ⁵²He's to decontaminate the house with the bird's blood, with the fresh water, with the live bird, with the cedar wood, with the hyssop and with the bright crimson, ⁵³then send off the live bird outside the town to the fields. So he will make expiation for the house, and it will become pure.

⁵⁴This is the instruction for every outbreak of scaliness, for scabies, ⁵⁵for scaliness in cloth or for a house, ⁵⁶for a swelling, for a rash or for a spot, ⁵⁷to give instruction on the day of becoming taboo and on the day of becoming pure. This is the instruction about scaliness.'

## A man's genital discharge

**15** Yahweh spoke to Mosheh and to Aharon: ²'Speak to the Yisra'elites: "When any man is discharging from his flesh, his discharge is taboo. ³This will be his taboo through his discharge, whether his flesh runs with his discharge or his flesh seizes up because of his discharge – it's his taboo: ⁴any bedding that the man who is discharging lies on becomes taboo. Any object that he sits on becomes taboo. ⁵A person who touches his bedding is to wash his clothes and bathe in water, and he becomes taboo until the evening.

⁶Someone who sits on the object that the man who is discharging sits on is to wash his clothes and bathe in water, and he becomes taboo until the evening. ⁷Someone who touches the flesh of the man who is discharging is to wash his clothes and bathe in water, and he becomes taboo until the evening. ⁸When the man who is discharging spits on someone who

is pure, he's to wash his clothes and bathe in water, and he becomes taboo until the evening. [9]Any saddle that the man who is discharging rides on becomes taboo. [10]Anyone who touches anything that was under him becomes taboo until the evening, and someone who carries them is to wash his clothes and bathe in water, and he becomes taboo until the evening. [11]Anyone whom the man who is discharging touches when he hasn't rinsed his hands in water is to wash his clothes and bathe in water, and he becomes taboo until the evening. [12]A clay object that the man who is discharging touches is to be broken, and any wood object is to be rinsed in water.

### More on genital discharges and emission of semen

[13]When the man who is discharging is pure from his discharge, he's to count for himself seven days for his purifying, wash his clothes and bathe his body in fresh water, and he'll become pure. [14]On the eighth day he's to get himself two doves or two young pigeons and come before Yahweh at the entrance of the appointment tent, and give them to the priest. [15]The priest is to make them as offerings, one as a decontamination, one as a burnt offering. So the priest is to make expiation for him before Yahweh because of his discharge.

[16]When an emission of semen goes out from a man, he's to bathe his entire body in water, and he becomes taboo until the evening. [17]Any clothing or any skin on which the emission of semen comes is to be washed in water, and it becomes taboo until the evening. [18]A woman that the man sleeps with involving an emission of semen, they're to bathe in water and they become taboo until the evening.

[19]When a woman is discharging, if her discharge in her flesh is blood, she's to be in her flowing for seven days. Anyone who touches her becomes taboo until the evening. [20]Anything that she lies on in her flowing becomes taboo, and anything that she sits on becomes taboo. [21]Anyone who touches her bedding is to wash his clothes and bathe in water, and he becomes taboo until the evening. [22]Anyone who touches any article on which she sits is to wash his clothes and bathe in

water, and he becomes taboo until the evening. [23]Whether it's on the bedding or on the article on which she sits, through touching it he becomes taboo until the evening. [24]If a man actually sleeps with her, her flowing comes on him. He becomes taboo for seven days, and any bedding on which he lies becomes taboo.

### On keeping away from taboo

[25]When a woman's discharge of blood flows for many days not during her flowing, or when she discharges beyond her flowing, for all the days of her discharge her taboo will be like the days of her flowing. She's taboo. [26]Any bedding on which she lies all the days of her discharge will be for her like the bedding during her flowing. Any article that she sits on becomes taboo, like the taboo during her flowing. [27]Anyone who touches them becomes taboo. He's to wash his clothes and bathe in water, and he becomes taboo until the evening.

[28]If she's pure from her discharge, she's to count for herself seven days, and afterwards she'll become pure. [29]On the eighth day she's to get herself two doves or two young pigeons and bring them to the priest at the entrance of the appointment tent. [30]The priest is to make one as a decontamination and one as a burnt offering. So the priest is to make expiation for her before Yahweh, from her taboo discharge.

[31]You're to consecrate the Yisra'elites from their taboo, so they won't die through their taboo, through bringing taboo on my dwelling among them.

[32]This is the instruction about someone from whom an emission of semen goes out and who becomes taboo through it, [33]about a woman when she's unwell, about someone who has their discharge, male or female, and about the man who sleeps with a woman who is taboo.'

### The expiation day

**16** Yahweh spoke to Mosheh and Aharon after the death of Aharon's two sons when they drew near before Yahweh and died. [2]Yahweh said to Mosheh: 'Speak to your brother Aharon: he's not to come at any time into the sacred place, inside the curtain, before the expiation cover that's on the chest, so he doesn't die, because I appear in a cloud, over the expiation cover. ³In this way Aharon is to come into the sacred place: with a bull from the herd as a decontamination, and a ram as a burnt offering. ⁴He's to put on a sacred linen tunic, and cloth shorts are to be on his body. He's to wrap on a cloth sash and wind on a cloth turban. They're sacred garments; he's to wash his body in water and then put them on.

⁵From the assembly of the Yisra'elites he's to get two goats from the flock as a decontamination and a ram as a burnt offering. ⁶Aharon is to present the decontamination bull that is his and make expiation for himself and for his household, ⁷and to get the two goats and set them before Yahweh at the entrance of the appointment tent. ⁸Aharon is to put lots on the two goats, one lot for Yahweh and one lot for Azazel. ⁹Aharon is to present the goat on to which the lot came for Yahweh and to make it as a decontamination. ¹⁰The goat on to which the lot came for Azazel is to stand alive before Yahweh, to make expiation on it and to send it off to Azazel to the wilderness.

## Expiation for the sanctuary

¹¹Aharon is then to present the decontamination bull which is his, and make expiation for himself and for his household. He's to slaughter the decontamination bull that is his, ¹²and get a panful of burning coals from on the altar from before Yahweh, and his fistfuls of fine aromatic incense, and bring it inside the curtain. ¹³He's to put the incense on the fire before Yahweh so the incense cloud covers the expiation cover that's on the affirmation, so he won't die.

¹⁴He's to get some of the bull's blood and spatter it with his finger on the surface of the expiation cover to the east, and before the expiation cover he's to spatter some of the blood seven times with his finger. ¹⁵Then he's to slaughter the decontamination goat that's the people's, bring its blood inside the curtain and do with the blood as he did with the bull's blood. He's to spatter it on the expiation cover and before the expiation cover. ¹⁶So he will make expiation for the sacred place

from the Yisra'elites' taboos and from their rebellions, in relation to all their wrongdoings.

So he's to do for the appointment tent, which dwells with them in the middle of their taboos. ¹⁷No human being is to be in the appointment tent when he goes in to make expiation in the sacred place, until his coming out. So he will make expiation for himself, for his household and for the entire Yisra'elite congregation.

## The goat for Azazel

¹⁸Then he's to go out to the altar that's before Yahweh and make expiation on it. He's to get some of the bull's blood and some of the goat's blood and put it on the altar's horns all round. ¹⁹He's to spatter some of the blood on it seven times with his finger. So he will purify it and make it sacred from the Yisra'elites' taboos.

²⁰When he's finished making expiation for the sacred place, the appointment tent and the altar, he's to present the live goat. ²¹Aharon is to lean both his hands on the live goat's head and confess over it all the wayward acts of the Yisra'elites and all their rebellions in relation to all their wrongdoings, put them on the goat's head and send it off by means of an appointed person into the wilderness. ²²The goat is to carry on it all their wayward acts to a region that's cut off. He's to send off the goat into the wilderness.

²³Then Aharon is to go into the appointment tent and take off the cloth garments that he put on when he went into the sacred place, and set them down there. ²⁴He's to bathe his body in water in the sacred place, put on his garments, go out and make his burnt offering and the people's burnt offering, and make expiation for himself and for the people. ²⁵The fat of the decontamination he's to turn into smoke at the altar. ²⁶The person who sent off the goat to Azazel is to wash his clothes and bathe his body in water, and after that come into the camp.

## The discipline of the seventh month

²⁷He's to take out the decontamination bull and the decontamination goat (whose blood was brought in to make expiation in the sacred place) outside the camp, and burn in fire their

skins, their flesh and their intestines. <sup>28</sup>The one who burns them is to wash his clothes and bathe his body in water, and after that come into the camp.

<sup>29</sup>This is to be a permanent decree for you: in the seventh month on the tenth of the month you're to humble yourselves and not do any work, the native and the person who is a resident among you, <sup>30</sup>because on this day he makes expiation for you to purify you from all your wrongdoings; you will become pure before Yahweh. <sup>31</sup>It will be a total stop for you. You're to humble yourselves (a permanent decree).

<sup>32</sup>The priest whom he anoints and commissions to act as priest in his father's place is to make expiation. He's to put on the cloth garments, the sacred garments. <sup>33</sup>He's to make expiation for the sacred sanctuary, to make expiation for the appointment tent and the altar, and to make expiation for the priests and for the entire people of the congregation.

<sup>34</sup>This is to be a permanent decree for you, to make expiation for the Yisra'elites from all their wrongdoings once in the year.'

He did as Yahweh ordered Mosheh.

## Slaughtering animals at the sanctuary

**17** Yahweh spoke to Mosheh: <sup>2</sup>'Speak to Aharon, to his sons and to all the Yisra'elites: "This is the thing that Yahweh has ordered. <sup>3</sup>An individual person from Yisra'el's household who slaughters an ox or sheep or goat in the camp or slaughters it outside the camp <sup>4</sup>and doesn't bring it to the entrance of the appointment tent to present as an offering for Yahweh before Yahweh's dwelling: blood will be deemed for that person. He's shed blood. That person shall be cut off from among his people."

<sup>5</sup>It is in order that the Yisra'elites may bring their sacrifices that they're making on the face of the fields – may bring them to Yahweh at the entrance of the appointment tent, to the priest, and make them into well-being sacrifices for Yahweh, <sup>6</sup>and the priest may toss their blood over Yahweh's altar at the entrance of the appointment tent and turn the fat into smoke as a nice smell for Yahweh, <sup>7</sup>and they may no more make their sacrifices to goat-demons

after whom they're whoring. This is to be a permanent decree for them, through their generations.

<sup>8</sup>You're to say to them: "Anyone, anyone from Yisra'el's household or from the people who reside among you who offers up a burnt offering or a sacrifice <sup>9</sup>and doesn't bring it to the entrance of the appointment tent to make it as an offering for Yahweh, that individual shall be cut off from his kin. <sup>10</sup>And an individual person from Yisra'el's household or from the people who reside among you who eats any blood: I will set my face against the life of the person who eats the blood and cut it off from among its people, <sup>11a</sup>because the life of the body is in the blood."

## It's the blood that makes expiation

<sup>11b</sup>I myself have given it to you on the altar to make expiation for your lives, because it's the blood that makes expiation, by means of the life. <sup>12</sup>That's why I've said to the Yisra'elites, "No person from among you will eat blood, nor will the people who reside among you eat blood."

<sup>13</sup>An individual person from the Yisra'elites or from the people who reside among you who catches a game animal or a bird that may be eaten is to pour out its blood and cover it with soil. <sup>14</sup>Because its blood is the life of all flesh. It simply is its life. So I've said to the Yisra'elites, "You will not eat the blood of any flesh, because its blood is the life of all flesh. Anyone who eats it shall be cut off."

<sup>15</sup>Any person who eats a corpse or something mauled, either a native or a resident, is to wash his clothes and bathe in water, and he becomes taboo until the evening, then he becomes pure. <sup>16</sup>If he doesn't wash them and doesn't bathe his body, he carries his waywardness.'

**18** Yahweh spoke to Mosheh: <sup>2</sup>'Speak to the Yisra'elites: "I am Yahweh your God. <sup>3</sup>You will not act in accordance with the practice of the country of Misrayim in which you lived, and you will not act in accordance with the practice of the country of Kena'an where I'm bringing you. You will not walk by their decrees. <sup>4</sup>You're to act on my rulings and keep my decrees, walking by them. I am Yahweh your God. <sup>5</sup>You're to keep my decrees and my rulings, by which the person who acts on them may live. I am Yahweh.

## Forbidden sexual relationships

⁶No individual person will approach any close relative so as to expose their nakedness. I am Yahweh.

⁷You will not expose your father's nakedness or your mother's nakedness. It's your mother; you will not expose her nakedness.

⁸You will not expose the nakedness of your father's wife; it's your father's nakedness.

⁹You will not expose the nakedness of your sister – your father's daughter or your mother's daughter, born in the household or born outside.

¹⁰You will not expose the nakedness of your son's daughter or your daughter's daughter, their nakedness, because they are your nakedness.

¹¹You will not expose the nakedness of your father's wife's daughter, your father's offspring; she's your sister. You will not expose her nakedness.

¹²You will not expose the nakedness of your father's sister; she's your father's relative.

¹³You will not expose the nakedness of your mother's sister, because she's your mother's relative.

¹⁴You will not expose the nakedness of your father's brother. You will not approach his wife; she's your aunt.

¹⁵You will not expose the nakedness of your daughter-in-law. She's your son's wife; you will not expose her nakedness.

¹⁶You will not expose the nakedness of your brother's wife. It's your brother's nakedness.

¹⁷You will not expose the nakedness of a woman and her daughter. You will not take her son's daughter or her daughter's daughter and expose her nakedness. They're relatives. It's a deliberate wickedness.

## How Kena'an vomited out its inhabitants

¹⁸You will not take a wife alongside her sister so as to cause pressure, so as to expose her nakedness beside her during her lifetime.

¹⁹You will not approach a woman during her taboo flowing, so as to expose her nakedness.

²⁰You will not have sex with the wife of your fellow, so as to become taboo through her.

²¹You will not give any of your offspring for passing across to the Shameful King; you will not treat the name of your God as ordinary. I am Yahweh.

²²You will not sleep with a male as one sleeps with a woman. It's an offensive act.

²³You will not have sex with any animal so as to become taboo by it, and no woman is to present herself before an animal so as to lie down with it. It's a perversion.

²⁴Don't make yourself taboo through any of these things, because by all these the nations that I'm going to send off from before you made themselves taboo. ²⁵The country became taboo and I've attended to it for its waywardness, and the country has vomited out the people living in it. ²⁶You yourselves are to keep my decrees and my rulings; you will not perform any of these offensive acts, the native or the person who is a resident among you, ²⁷because the people who were in the country before you performed all these offensive acts, and the country became taboo. ²⁸The country is not to vomit you out because you make it taboo, as it has vomited out the nations that were before you. ²⁹Because anyone who performs any of these offensive acts – the persons who perform them shall be cut off from among their people.

³⁰You're to keep my charge so you don't perform any of the offensive decrees that were performed before you. You're not to make yourselves taboo through them. I am Yahweh your God.'"

## Be sacred as I am sacred

**19** Yahweh spoke to Mosheh: ²'Speak to the entire Yisra'elite assembly: "You're to be sacred, because I, Yahweh your God, am sacred.

³An individual is to live in awe of his mother and his father and keep my sabbaths. I am Yahweh your God.

⁴Don't turn your face to non-entities and don't make figurine gods for yourselves. I am Yahweh your God. ⁵When you make a well-being sacrifice for Yahweh, make it so it may be for your acceptance. ⁶It's to be eaten on the day you sacrifice it, or the next day. What is left until the third day is to be burned in fire. ⁷If it's actually eaten on the third day, it will be an objectionable thing. It won't find acceptance. ⁸The one who eats it – he will carry his waywardness, because he's treated as ordinary something sacred that belongs to Yahweh. That person shall be cut off from his kin. ⁹When you reap the harvest of your land, each of you will not finish off harvesting the side of your field, and you will not gather the gleanings of your harvest ¹⁰or scour your vineyard or glean your vineyard's windfall. You're to leave them for the humble and for the resident. I am Yahweh your God. ¹¹You will not steal, you will not deceive, and you will not cheat, one individual his fellow. ¹²You will not swear falsely by my name and treat the name of your God as ordinary. I am Yahweh. ¹³You will not defraud your neighbour and you will not seize things.

The wages of an employee will not stay with you until morning. ¹⁴You will not slight the deaf and you will not put an obstacle before the blind but live in awe of your God. I am Yahweh.

## Let creation be

¹⁵You will not do evil in making a decision: you will not honour the person of someone who is poor and you will not respect the person of someone who is big; you will make a decision for your fellow with faithfulness. ¹⁶You will not live as a slanderer among your kin.

You will not take the stand against your neighbour's life. I am Yahweh. ¹⁷You will not be hostile to your brother in your mind; you will firmly reprove your fellow, so you do not carry liability because of him. ¹⁸You will not take redress and you will not hold on to things in relation to members of your people, but be loyal to your neighbour as to yourself. I am Yahweh. ¹⁹You're to keep my decrees.

You will not mate two kinds of animals; you will not sow your field with two kinds; you will not put cloth woven of two kinds on to yourself. ²⁰When a man sleeps with a woman (has sex) and she's a maidservant designated to someone but she hasn't actually been redeemed or given her freedom, there's to be an inquiry. They will not be put to death, because she had not been freed, ²¹but he's to bring his reparation to Yahweh to the entrance of the appointment tent, a ram as a reparation, ²²and the priest is to make expiation for him with the reparation ram before Yahweh for the wrong that he did. So it will be pardoned for him in respect of the wrong that he did. ²³When you come into the country and you plant any edible tree, you're to treat its fruit as its foreskin. For three years it's to be foreskinned to you. It's not to be eaten. ²⁴In the fourth year all its fruit will be sacred, an expression of great praise to Yahweh. ²⁵In the fifth year you may eat its fruit – so as to increase its yield for you. I am Yahweh your God.

## Yisra'el's distinctiveness

²⁶You will not eat anything with the blood. You will not cast spells and you will not practise augury. ²⁷You will not trim the side of your head, you will not do violence to the side of your beard, ²⁸you will not make a gash on your flesh for someone and you will not make the mark of a cut on yourselves. I am Yahweh. ²⁹Don't treat your daughter as ordinary by making her act the whore, so the country doesn't whore and become full of deliberate wickedness. ³⁰You're to keep my sabbaths and live in awe of my sanctuary. I am Yahweh.

³¹Don't turn your face to ghosts and don't seek spirits, so as to become taboo through them. I am Yahweh your God. ³²You're to get up in the presence of the grey-haired, respect the person of the elderly and live in awe of your God. I am Yahweh. ³³When a person is a resident with you in your country, you will not wrong him. ³⁴The person who is a resident with you is to be for you like a native from among you. You're to be loyal to him as someone like you, because you were residents in the country of Misrayim. I am Yahweh your God. ³⁵You will not do evil over a ruling – over length, over weight or over volume. ³⁶You're to have true balances, true weights, a true barrel and a true gallon. I am Yahweh your God who got you out of the country of Misrayim, ³⁷and you're to keep all my decrees and all my rulings, and act on them. I am Yahweh.'"

## Yisra'el's sacredness

**20** Yahweh spoke to Mosheh: ²"Say to the Yisra'elites: "An individual person from the Yisra'elites or from the people residing in Yisra'el who gives one of his offspring to the Shameful King is absolutely to be put to death. The people of the country are to pelt him with stones. ³I myself will set my face against that man and cut him off from among his people, because he's given one of his offspring to the Shameful King, in order to make my sanctuary taboo and treat my sacred name as ordinary. ⁴If the people of the country actually hide their eyes from that man when he gives one of his offspring to the Shameful King, so they don't put him to death, ⁵I myself will set my face against that man and against his kin-group, and cut off him and all those who whore after him, and thus whore after the Shameful King, from among their people.

⁶The person who turns his face to ghosts and to spirits to whore after them: I shall set my face against that person and cut him off from among his people. ⁷You're to make yourselves sacred and to be sacred, because I am Yahweh your God. ⁸You're to keep my decrees and act on them. I am Yahweh who makes you sacred.

⁹When an individual person who slights his father and his mother – he's absolutely to be put to death. He's slighted his father and his mother. His shed blood is against him.

## Rules about sex

¹⁰When someone is adulterous with someone's wife (is adulterous with his neighbour's wife), the adulterer and the adulteress are absolutely to be put to death. ¹¹Someone who sleeps with his father's wife has exposed his father's nakedness. The two of them are absolutely to be put to death. Their shed blood is against them. ¹²Someone who sleeps with his daughter-in-law is absolutely to die. The two of them have committed a perversion. Their shed blood is against them. ¹³Someone who sleeps with a male as one sleeps with a woman – the two of them have performed an offensive act. They are absolutely to be put to death. Their shed blood is against them. ¹⁴Someone who takes a woman and her mother: it's a deliberate wickedness. They are to burn him and them in fire. There will not be a deliberate wickedness among you. ¹⁵Someone who has sex with an animal is absolutely to be put to death, and you're to kill the animal. ¹⁶A woman who approaches any animal to lie down with it: you're to kill the woman and the animal. They are absolutely to be put to death. Their shed blood is against them. ¹⁷Someone who takes his sister, his father's daughter or his mother's daughter, and he sees her nakedness and she sees his nakedness: it's a shameful thing. They shall be cut off before their people's eyes. He's exposed his sister's nakedness. He will carry his waywardness. ¹⁸When a man sleeps with a woman who's unwell and exposes her nakedness, he has bared her flow and she herself has exposed her blood flow. Both of them shall be cut off from among their people. ¹⁹You will not expose the nakedness of your mother's sister or your father's sister, because he's bared his flesh. They will carry their waywardness.

²⁰Someone who sleeps with his aunt has exposed his uncle's nakedness. They will carry their waywardness. They will die childless. ²¹Someone who takes his brother's wife – it's a defilement. He's exposed his brother's nakedness. They will be childless.

## Yisra'el's distinctiveness

²²You're to keep all my decrees and all my rulings, and act on them, so the country where I'm bringing you to live won't vomit you out. ²³You will not walk by the decrees of the nations that I'm sending off from before you because they did all these things. I was dismayed about them ²⁴and I said to you, 'You're the ones who will take possession of their land.' I myself shall give it to you to possess, a country flowing with milk and syrup. I am Yahweh your God, who has made you distinct from the peoples.

²⁵So you're to make a distinction between the pure animal and the taboo, between the taboo bird and the pure. You will not make yourselves into an atrocity through an animal or a bird or anything that moves on the ground, which I've made distinct, for you to treat as taboo. ²⁶You're to be sacred for me, because I Yahweh am sacred, and I've made you distinct from the peoples to be mine.

²⁷When there's a ghost or spirit in a man or a woman, they are absolutely to be put to death. People are to pelt them with stones. Their shed blood will be on their own heads.'"

## The priests' discipline

**21** Yahweh said to Mosheh: 'Speak to the priests, Aharon's sons: "No one is to make himself taboo for a [dead] person among his kin, ²except for his relative who's near to him – for his mother, for his father, for his son, for his daughter, for his brother, ³or for his sister who's a young girl and is near to him, who hasn't yet come to belong to a man; for her he may make himself taboo. ⁴He will not make himself taboo as a husband among his kin, so as to become ordinary.

⁵They will not make a bald patch on their head, they will not shave the side of their beard and they will not make a gash on their flesh. ⁶They are to be sacred for their God and they will not treat the name of their God as ordinary, because they present Yahweh's gift offerings, their God's meal, so they're to be sacred. ⁷They will not take a woman who's a whore and who's ordinary, and they will not take a woman divorced by her husband, because he's sacred for his God. ⁸You're to treat him as sacred, because he presents your God's meal. He's to be sacred for you, because I am sacred, Yahweh who makes you sacred. ⁹When the daughter of an individual priest becomes ordinary by whoring, she makes her father ordinary. She's to be burned in fire.

¹⁰The priest who is greater than his brothers, on whose head the anointing oil has been poured and whom they have commissioned to put on the garments, will not bare his head or tear his clothes. ¹¹He will not go in near any dead people; he will not become taboo for his father or for his mother. ¹²He will not go out of the sanctuary and treat his God's sanctuary as ordinary, because the consecration of his God's anointing oil is on him. I am Yahweh.

¹³That man is to take a woman in her virginity. ¹⁴A widow or divorcee or someone made ordinary by whoring – these he will not take. Rather, he's to take a young girl from his kin, ¹⁵so he doesn't make his offspring among his kin ordinary, because I am Yahweh who makes him sacred."'

## Priestly distinctives

¹⁶Yahweh spoke to Mosheh: ¹⁷'Speak to Aharon: "Through their generations, no individual from your offspring in whom there's a defect is to draw near to present his God's meal. ¹⁸Because no individual in whom there's a defect is to draw near: one blind or lame or disfigured or deformed, ¹⁹or one who has an injury to his leg or an injury to his hand, ²⁰or one who is a hunchback or dwarf or defective in his eye or [has] scab or sore or crushed testicle. ²¹No individual from Aharon's offspring in whom there's a defect will come up to present Yahweh's gift offerings. There being a defect in him, he will not come up to present Yahweh's meal. ²²He may eat his God's meal, from the especially sacred and from the sacred.

²³Nevertheless he will not go to the curtain and he will not come up to the altar, because there's a defect in him. He will not treat my great sanctuary as ordinary, because I am Yahweh who makes it sacred."

²⁴Mosheh spoke to Aharon and to his sons and to all the Yisra'elites.

**22** Yahweh spoke to Mosheh: ²'Speak to Aharon and to his sons so they stay consecrated from the Yisra'elites' sacred things (and don't treat my sacred name as ordinary), which they are making sacred for me. I am Yahweh. ³Say to them: "Through your generations, any one of all your offspring who comes near the sacred things that the Yisra'elites make sacred for Yahweh and his taboo is on him, that person shall be cut off from before me. I am Yahweh."

## Dealing with sacred food

⁴No individual person from Aharon's offspring who has been made scaly or is discharging will eat of the sacred things until he becomes pure. Someone who touches anything taboo through a [dead] person, or an individual from whom there's an emission of semen, ⁵or an individual who touches anything that teems for which he becomes taboo or a human being for whom he becomes taboo: for any taboo of his, ⁶the person who touches it becomes taboo until the evening and will not eat of the sacred things unless he's bathed his body in water ⁷and the sun has gone down, and he's become pure. Afterwards, he may eat of the sacred things, because it's his meal. ⁸He will not eat a corpse or something mauled so as to become taboo through it. I am Yahweh.

⁹They're to keep my charge, and not carry wrongdoing because of it and die through it because they treat it as ordinary. I am Yahweh who makes them sacred. ¹⁰No outsider will eat something sacred. A settler with a priest, or an employee, will not eat something sacred. ¹¹When a priest acquires someone as his own for silver, he may eat of it, and someone born in his household – they may eat of his meal. ¹²When a priest's daughter comes to belong to an individual who is an outsider, she will not eat of the contribution among the sacred things. ¹³But when a priest's

daughter becomes a widow or divorcee and she has no offspring, and comes back to her father's household as in her youth, she may eat of her father's meal. But no outsider may eat of it.

¹⁴When an individual eats something sacred by mistake, he's to add to it a fifth of it and give the priest the sacred thing. ¹⁵They will not treat the Yisra'elites' sacred things as ordinary, which they take up for Yahweh, ¹⁶and make them carry waywardness requiring reparation through their eating their sacred things, because I am Yahweh who makes them sacred.'

## Acceptable sacrifices

¹⁷Yahweh spoke to Mosheh: ¹⁸'Speak to Aharon and to his sons and to all the Yisra'elites: "An individual person from Yisra'el's household or from the residents in Yisra'el who presents his offering in connection with any of their pledges or with any of their free offerings that they present for Yahweh as a burnt offering: ¹⁹for your acceptance, a male – among the herd, among the flock or among the goats – that's whole. ²⁰Any in which there's a defect you will not present because it won't be for acceptance for you.

²¹When someone presents a well-being sacrifice for Yahweh, to fulfil a pledge or as a free offering, among the herd or among the flock, it's to be whole, for acceptance; there will be no defect in it. ²²Blind or injured or disfigured or suppurating or with scabs or sores: you will not present these for Yahweh and you will not put any of them on the altar as a gift offering for Yahweh. ²³You may make into a free offering an ox or sheep that's deformed or stunted, but for a pledge it will not find acceptance.

²⁴You will not present for Yahweh something bruised, crushed, torn or cut. In your country you will not make an offering ²⁵or present as your God's meal any of these from the hand of a foreigner, because their deformity in them is a defect in them. They won't find acceptance for you."'

²⁶Yahweh spoke to Mosheh: ²⁷'When an ox or sheep or goat is born, it's to be under its mother for seven days. From the eighth day onwards, it will find acceptance as an offering, a gift offering for Yahweh. ²⁸You will not

slaughter a cow or sheep with its offspring on the same day. ²⁹When you make a thanksgiving sacrifice for Yahweh, offer it so it may be for your acceptance. ³⁰It's to be eaten on that day. You will not leave any of it until morning. I am Yahweh.

³¹You're to keep my orders and act on them. I am Yahweh. ³²You will not treat my sacred name as ordinary, so I may show myself sacred among the Yisra'elites. I am Yahweh, who made you sacred, ³³the one who got you out of the country of Misrayim to be your God. I am Yahweh.'

## The set times

23 Yahweh spoke to Mosheh: ²'Speak to the Yisra'elites: "These are Yahweh's set times, which you're to call for as sacred occasions. They're my set times. ³For six days, work may be done. On the seventh a complete stop [*shabbat shabbaton*], a sacred occasion. You will not do any work. It's a sabbath for Yahweh in all your settlements.

⁴These are Yahweh's set times, the sacred occasions, which you're to call for at their set time. ⁵In the first month on the fourteenth of the month at twilight, Yahweh's Pesah [Passover], ⁶and on the fifteenth day of this month, the Flatbread Festival for Yahweh. For seven days you're to eat flatbread. ⁷On the first day it's to be a sacred occasion for you; you will not do any servile work. ⁸You're to present a gift offering for Yahweh for seven days. On the seventh day, a sacred occasion, you will not do any servile work."

⁹Yahweh spoke to Mosheh: ¹⁰'Speak to the Yisra'elites: "When you come into the country that I'm giving you and you reap its harvest, you're to bring the first sheaf of your harvest to the priest. ¹¹He's to elevate the sheaf before Yahweh for your acceptance. On the day after the sabbath the priest is to elevate it. ¹²On the day of your elevating the sheaf, you're to make a lamb that's whole, a year old, into a burnt offering for Yahweh, ¹³with its grain offering of two tenths of fine flour mixed with oil, a gift offering for Yahweh, a nice smell, and its libation, wine, a quarter of a gallon. ¹⁴You will not eat bread or roasted grain or plantation-growth until this particular day, until you

bring the offering to your God (a permanent decree through your generations in all your settlements).

## The first harvests

¹⁵You're to count seven sabbaths for yourselves from the day after the sabbath, from the day you bring the elevation sheaf. They're to be whole weeks. ¹⁶You're to count until the day after the seventh sabbath, fifty days, and present an offering of new grain for Yahweh.

¹⁷From your settlements you're to bring two loaves of elevation bread. They're to be two tenths of fine flour. They're to be baked with yeast, as first products for Yahweh. ¹⁸You're to present with the bread seven lambs that are whole, a year old, one bull from the herd and two rams. They're to be a burnt offering for Yahweh, with their grain offering and their libations, a gift offering, a nice smell for Yahweh. ¹⁹And you're to make one he-goat from the flock into a decontamination, and two sheep, a year old, into a well-being sacrifice. ²⁰The priest is to elevate them with the first-products bread as an elevation offering before Yahweh, along with the two sheep. They're to be sacred for Yahweh, for the priest.

²¹You're to call for this particular day. It's to be a sacred occasion for you; you're to do no servile work (a permanent decree in all your settlements through your generations).

²²When you reap the harvest of your land, each of you will not finish off harvesting the edge of your field and you will not gather the gleanings of your harvest. You will leave them for the humble and for the resident. I am Yahweh your God."

²³Yahweh spoke to Mosheh: ²⁴'Speak to the Yisra'elites: "In the seventh month on the first of the month there's to be a stop for you, a reminder with a horn blast, a sacred occasion. ²⁵You will do no servile work. You're to present a gift offering for Yahweh."

## The Day of Complete Expiation

²⁶Yahweh spoke to Mosheh: ²⁷'But then: on the tenth of this seventh month is the Day of Complete Expiation. It's to be a sacred occasion

for you. You're to humble yourselves and present a gift offering for Yahweh. ²⁸You will do no work on this particular day, because it's the Day of Complete Expiation, to make expiation for you before Yahweh your God. ²⁹Because any person who is not humbled on this particular day is to be cut off from his kin, ³⁰and any person who does any work on this particular day – I'll cause that person to perish from among his people. ³¹You will not do any work (a permanent decree through your generations in all your settlements). ³²It's to be a complete stop [*shabbat shabbaton*] for you, and you're to humble yourselves. On the ninth of the month in the evening, from evening to evening, you're to make your sabbath stop.'

³³Yahweh spoke to Mosheh: ³⁴"Speak to the Yisra'elites: "On the fifteenth day of this seventh month is the Sukkot Festival for Yahweh, for seven days. ³⁵On the first day, a sacred occasion; you will do no servile work. ³⁶For seven days you are to present a gift offering for Yahweh. On the eighth day it's to be a sacred occasion for you. You're to present a gift offering for Yahweh. It's an assembly; you will not do any servile work.

³⁷These are Yahweh's set times that you're to call for as sacred occasions for presenting a gift offering for Yahweh: burnt offering and grain offering, sacrifice and libations, a day's allocation on its day, ³⁸apart from Yahweh's sabbaths, from your gift offerings, from all your pledges and from all your free offerings that you give for Yahweh.

## The Sukkot (Tabernacles) Festival and the candelabrum

³⁹But then, on the fifteenth day of the seventh month, when you've gathered in the yield of the country, you're to observe Yahweh's festival, for seven days: on the first day a stop and on the eighth day a stop. ⁴⁰On the first day you're to get yourselves the fruit of magnificent trees, branches of palm, boughs of green trees, and poplars from the wadi, and rejoice before Yahweh your God for seven days. ⁴¹You're to observe it as a festival for Yahweh for seven days in the year (a permanent decree through your generations). In the seventh month you're to observe it. ⁴²You're to live in bivouacs [*sukkot*] for seven days – every native in

Yisra'el, they're to live in bivouacs – ⁴³in order that your generations may acknowledge that I made the Yisra'elites live in bivouacs when I got them out of the country of Misrayim. I am Yahweh your God."'

⁴⁴Mosheh called for Yahweh's set times to all the Yisra'elites.

**24** Yahweh spoke to Mosheh: ²"Order the Yisra'elites that they're to get for you clear pressed olive oil for lighting, for putting up a lamp regularly. ³Outside the affirmation curtain in the appointment tent, Aharon is to order it from evening to morning before Yahweh regularly (a permanent decree through your generations). ⁴On the pure candelabrum he's to order the lamps before Yahweh regularly.

⁵You're to get fine flour and bake it into twelve loaves. One loaf is to be two tenths. ⁶You're to place them in two rows, six in a row, on the pure table before Yahweh. ⁷You're to put pure frankincense with the row. It will be a commemorative portion for the bread, a gift offering for Yahweh. ⁸Sabbath day by sabbath day he's to order it before Yahweh, regularly, a permanent pact on the part of the Yisra'elites. ⁹It's to belong to Aharon and to his sons and they're to eat it in a sacred place, because it's especially sacred for him from Yahweh's gift offerings (a permanent decree).'

## An eye for an eye

¹⁰A Yisra'elite woman's son, who was a Misrayimite man's son, went out among the Yisra'elites, and the Yisra'elite woman's son and a Yisra'elite got into a fight in the camp. ¹¹The Yisra'elite woman's son cursed the name and slighted it. So they brought him to Mosheh (his mother's name was Shelomit bat Dibri, of the clan of Dan) ¹²and they placed him under keep for things to be made clear to them at Yahweh's bidding.

¹³Yahweh spoke to Mosheh: ¹⁴"Take the slighter outside the camp. All the people who heard are to lean their hands on his head, and the entire assembly is to stone him.

¹⁵You're to speak to the Yisra'elites: "An individual person who slights his God will carry his wrongdoing. ¹⁶A person who curses Yahweh's name is absolutely to be put to death. The entire assembly is indeed to stone him. As

with the resident, so with the native, for his cursing the name he's to be put to death. [17]An individual who strikes down any human being is absolutely to be put to death. [18]One who strikes down an animal is to make good for it, life for life. [19]An individual who causes an injury to his fellow: as he did, so it's to be done to him, [20]fracture for fracture, eye for eye, tooth for tooth. As he causes an injury to the person, so it's to be caused to him. [21]One who strikes down an animal is to make good for it, but one who strikes down a human being is to be put to death. [22]There's to be one ruling for you; it's to be as with the resident, so with the native, because I am Yahweh your God.'"

[23]Mosheh spoke to the Yisra'elites, and they took the slighter outside the camp and pelted him with stones. The Yisra'elites did as Yahweh ordered Mosheh.

## Sabbaths for the land

**25** Yahweh spoke to Mosheh at Mount Sinay: [2]'Speak to the Yisra'elites: "When you come into the country I'm giving you, the country is to make a sabbath stop for Yahweh. [3]For six years you may sow your field and for six years you may prune your vineyard and gather its yield, [4]but in the seventh year there's to be a complete stop [*shabbat shabbaton*] for the country, a sabbath for Yahweh. You will not sow your field, you will not prune your vineyard, [5]you will not reap your harvest's aftergrowth, you will not cut the grapes of your free vines. It's to be a year of stopping for the country. [6]The country's sabbath will be food for you, for you yourself, for your servant and for your handmaid, for your employee and for your resident living with you, [7]for your animals and for the creatures that are in your country: all its yield will be for eating.

[8]You're to count seven sabbaths of years for yourselves, seven times seven years, so that the time period of your seven sabbaths of years will be forty-nine years. [9]You're to make a blasting horn pass through in the seventh month, on the tenth of the month; on the Day of Complete Expiation you're to make the horn pass through your entire country. [10]You're to make the fiftieth year sacred and call for a release in the country for all the people living in it. It's to be a ram's horn year for you. You're to go back, each individual, to his holding, and to go back, each individual, to his kin-group. [11]The year, that fiftieth year, is to be a ram's horn year for you: you will not sow, you will not reap its aftergrowth and you will not cut its free vines, [12]because it's a ram's horn year. It's to be sacred for you. You will eat the yield from the field.

## The 'Jubilee', the ram's horn year

[13]In this ram's horn year you're to go back, each individual, to his holding. [14]When you sell something to your fellow, or buy from your fellow's hand, you're not to wrong one another. [15]It's by the count of the years since the ram's horn year that you're to buy from your fellow; it's by the count of the years of yield that he's to sell to you. [16]On the basis of the large number of the years you'll pay a high price to him; on the basis of the low number of the years you'll pay a low price to him, because it's the count of the yields that he's selling to you. [17]You will not wrong one another but live in awe of your God, because I am Yahweh your God.

[18]You're to act on my decrees and keep my rulings and act on them, so you may live on the land in confidence. [19]The land will give its fruit and you'll eat your fill and live in confidence on it. [20]When you say, 'What are we to eat in the seventh year if we don't sow or gather our yield?', [21]I shall order my blessing for you in the sixth year and it will generate the yield for three years. [22]You'll sow the eighth year and eat from the yield of the old; until the ninth year, until its yield comes in, you'll eat the old.

[23]The land will not be sold permanently because the land belongs to me, because you're residents, settlers, living with me. [24]In the entire land that's your holding, you're to grant restoration for the land.

## When your brother does badly

[25]When your brother does poorly and sells part of his holding, his restorer who is near to him is to come to him and restore what his brother has sold. [26]When an individual

doesn't have a restorer, but his means stretch and provide enough for its restoration, <sup>27</sup>he's to think over the years since his sale and give the surplus back to the individual to whom he sold it, and go back to his holding. <sup>28</sup>If his means don't provide enough for giving it back to him, what he sold will be in the possession of the person who bought it until the ram's horn year. It will go out in the ram's horn year and he will go back to his holding.

<sup>29</sup>If an individual sells a dwelling house in a walled town, its restoration may happen up to the completion of a year from its sale. Through the time, its restoration may happen. <sup>30</sup>If it's not restored up to the fulfilling of a whole year for it, the house (which is in a town that has a wall) will transfer permanently to the person who bought it, through his generations. It will not go out in the ram's horn year.

<sup>31</sup>Given that houses in villages that have no wall all round are to be thought of as fields in the country, restoration may happen for it, and it will go out in the ram's horn year. <sup>32</sup>The Levites' towns, the houses in the towns in their holding: there may be permanent restoration for the Levites. <sup>33</sup>Something that one of the Levites may restore (a house sale when the town is in his holding) will go out in the ram's horn year, because the houses in the Levites' towns are their holding among the Yisra'elites. <sup>34</sup>The pastureland fields belonging to their towns will not be sold, because it's a permanent holding for them.

## Not like slaves

<sup>35</sup>When your brother does poorly and his means fall to you, you're to take strong hold of him as a resident, a settler, so he can stay alive with you. <sup>36</sup>You're not to take interest or profit from him; you're to live in awe of your God, so your brother can stay alive with you. <sup>37</sup>You will not give your money to him at interest and you will not give him your food for profit. <sup>38</sup>I am Yahweh your God who got you out of the country of Misrayim to give you the country of Kena'an, to be God for you.

<sup>39</sup>When your brother does badly with you, and he sells himself to you, you will not make him serve with servile service. <sup>40</sup>He's to be with you as an employee, as a settler. Until the ram's horn year he's to serve with you, <sup>41</sup>then he's to go out from you, he and his children with him, and go back to his kin-group, to his ancestors' holding. <sup>42</sup>Because they're my servants, whom I got out of the country of Misrayim, they will not sell themselves as a servant is sold. <sup>43</sup>You're not to hold sway over him with harshness. You're to live in awe of your God.

<sup>44</sup>Your servant and your handmaid who belong to you from the nations that are round you – from them you may buy a servant or a handmaid, <sup>45</sup>and also from the children of the settlers who are resident with you. You may buy from them and from their kin-groups that are with you, that give birth in your country, and they will be your holding. <sup>46</sup>You may have them as a domain for your children after you, to possess as a permanent holding. By means of them you may get service. But over your brothers, the Yisra'elites, over one another you will not hold sway with harshness.

## Servitude to a foreigner

<sup>47</sup>When the means of a resident (a settler with you) stretch, but your brother with him does badly, and he sells himself to the resident (the settler with you) or to an offshoot of a resident's kin-group, <sup>48</sup>after he's sold himself, restoration may happen for him; one of his brothers may restore him, <sup>49</sup>or his uncle or his uncle's son may restore him, or any close relative from his kin-group may restore him. Or when his means stretch, he may restore himself.

<sup>50</sup>He's to think with the person who bought him, from the year when he sold himself to him until the ram's horn year, and the silver for his sale will be in accordance with the number of years. As it would be for the time of an employee he'll be with him. <sup>51</sup>If there are still many years, on the basis of them he's to give back for his restoration some of the silver that was his price, <sup>52</sup>and if few years remain until the ram's horn year, he's to think about himself, and on the basis of his years he's to give back for his restoration. <sup>53</sup>He's to be with him like an employee by the year. He's not to hold sway over him with harshness in your eyes. <sup>54</sup>If he doesn't restore himself in these ways, he's to go out in the ram's horn year, he and his children with him, <sup>55</sup>because the

Yisra'elites are my servants. They're my servants whom I got out of the country of Misrayim. I am Yahweh your God.

**26** You will not make non-entities for yourselves, you will not set up a sculpture or a column for yourselves and you will not put a carved stone in your country to bow low to it, because I am Yahweh your God. <sup>2</sup>You're to keep my sabbaths and to live in awe of my sanctuary. I am Yahweh.

## Promises

<sup>3</sup>If you walk by my decrees, and keep my orders and act on them, <sup>4</sup>I shall give your rains in their time, so the country will give its produce and the trees of the fields will give their fruit. <sup>5</sup>For you, threshing will overtake reaping and reaping will overtake sowing. You'll eat your bread to the full and live in confidence in your country.

<sup>6</sup>I shall put peace in the country and you will lie down with no one making you tremble. I shall eliminate the bad animal from the country and a sword won't pass through your country. <sup>7</sup>You will pursue your enemies and they will fall to the sword before you. <sup>8</sup>Five of you will pursue a hundred and a hundred of you will pursue 10,000. Your enemies will fall to the sword before you.

<sup>9</sup>I shall turn my face to you and make you fruitful and make you numerous. I shall implement my pact with you. <sup>10</sup>You'll eat old stuff stored but then take out the old in favour of the new. <sup>11</sup>I shall put my dwelling among you and my soul won't spurn you. <sup>12</sup>I shall walk about among you. I shall be God for you and you will be a people for me. <sup>13</sup>I am Yahweh your God who got you out of the country of Misrayim, from being servants to them. I broke the bars of your yoke and let you walk tall.

## Warnings

<sup>14</sup>But if you don't listen to me and don't act on all these orders, <sup>15</sup>if you reject my decrees and your soul spurns my rulings so as not to act on all my orders and so as to contravene my pact, <sup>16</sup>I shall also do this to you. I shall appoint terror over you, wasting away and fever,

finishing off the eyes and consuming the life. You will sow your seed with empty results; your enemies will eat it. <sup>17</sup>I shall set my face against you and you will take a beating before your enemies. Your foes will hold sway over you and you will flee when there's no one pursuing you.

<sup>18</sup>And if for all these things you don't listen to me, I shall continue disciplining you sevenfold for your wrongdoings. <sup>19</sup>I shall break the majesty of your vigour. I shall make your heavens like iron and your land like copper. <sup>20</sup>Your energy will be used up with empty results. Your land won't give its produce. The trees in the land won't give their fruit.

<sup>21</sup>If you walk contrary with me and are not willing to listen to me, I shall add a sevenfold calamity against you in accordance with your wrongdoings. <sup>22</sup>I shall send off creatures of the wild against you and they will make you childless and cut off your animals. They will reduce you so your roads become desolate.

<sup>23</sup>And if through these things you don't accept discipline in relation to me, and you walk contrary with me, <sup>24</sup>I myself too will walk contrary with you. I myself will also strike you down sevenfold for your wrongdoings. <sup>25</sup>I shall bring a sword against you, taking the redress in the pact. You'll gather into your towns, and I'll send off an epidemic among you and you'll be given into an enemy's hand. <sup>26</sup>When I break your staff of bread, ten women will bake your bread in one oven, and give back your bread by weight. You'll eat but you won't be full.

## More warnings

<sup>27</sup>And if because of this you don't listen to me and you walk contrary with me, <sup>28</sup>I'll walk with you in contrary wrath. I myself will again discipline you sevenfold for your wrongdoings. <sup>29</sup>You will eat the flesh of your sons and you will eat the flesh of your daughters. <sup>30</sup>I shall annihilate your shrines and cut down your incense stands and put your carcases on your idols' carcases.

I myself will renounce you <sup>31</sup>and make your towns a waste. I'll make your sanctuaries desolate. I won't smell your nice smells. <sup>32</sup>I myself will make your country desolate; your enemies who live in it will be desolate at it. <sup>33</sup>I shall scatter you among the nations and draw a sword after you. Your country will become a desolation. Your towns will become a waste. ³⁴Then the country will make amends for its sabbaths, through all the time of desolation while you're in your enemies' country. Then the country will stop [*shabat*], and make up for its sabbaths. ³⁵All the time of desolation it will stop what it didn't stop during your sabbaths when you were living on it.

³⁶Those who remain among you: I'll bring faintness into their heart in their enemies' countries. The sound of a leaf being blown away will chase them. They'll flee as people do from the sword, and they'll fall when there's no one chasing. ³⁷They'll collapse over one another as if before the sword when there's no one chasing. You won't have the ability to stand before your enemies.

## More promises

³⁸So you will perish among the nations. Your enemies' country will devour you. ³⁹Those who remain among you will rot through their waywardness in your enemies' countries. Yes, through their ancestors' waywardness they will rot with them.

⁴⁰But they will confess their waywardness and their ancestors' waywardness in their trespass that they committed against me; and also they walked contrary with me. ⁴¹When I also walk contrary with them and bring them into their enemies' country, if by chance their foreskinned mind bows down and then they make amends for their waywardness, ⁴²I shall be mindful of my pact with Ya'aqob [Jacob], and also my pact with Yitshaq [Isaac] and also my pact with Abraham. I shall be mindful, and I shall be mindful of the country.

⁴³The country will be left by them so it may make amends for its sabbaths by being desolate without them, and they themselves will make amends for their waywardness because – yes, because they rejected my rulings and their soul renounced my decrees. ⁴⁴But even for this, when they are in their enemies' country I won't reject them and I won't renounce them so as to finish them off, contravening my pact with them, because I am Yahweh their God. ⁴⁵I shall be mindful for them of the pact with the original people whom I got out of the country

of Misrayim before the eyes of the nations, to be God for them. I am Yahweh.'"

⁴⁶These are the decrees, the rulings and the instructions that Yahweh gave between him and the Yisra'elites at Mount Sinay through Mosheh.

## Promises to God

**27** Yahweh spoke to Mosheh: ²"Speak to the Yisra'elites: "When an individual fulfils a pledge to Yahweh on the basis of the evaluation of persons, ³the evaluation is to be:

A male from the age of twenty years until the age of sixty years, the evaluation is to be fifty silver sheqels (by the sanctuary sheqel).

⁴If it's a female, the evaluation is to be thirty sheqels.

⁵If it's someone from the age of five years until the age of thirty years, the evaluation is to be: a male twenty sheqels, for a female ten sheqels.

⁶If it's someone from the age of one month until the age of five years, the evaluation is to be: a male five silver sheqels; for a female the evaluation is to be three silver sheqels.

⁷If it's someone the age of sixty years and upwards: if it's a male, the evaluation is to be fifteen sheqels, and for a female ten sheqels.

⁸If someone has done too badly for the evaluation, they're to get him to stand before the priest and the priest will evaluate him; the priest is to evaluate him on the basis of what the means of the pledge-maker stretch to.

⁹If it's an animal, one of the ones that people may present as an offering for Yahweh, all of what someone gives for Yahweh is to be sacred; ¹⁰he will not exchange it and he will not substitute for it, good for bad or bad for good, and if he does actually substitute one animal for another, it and its substitute will be sacred.

¹¹If it's any taboo animal, one of the ones that people don't present as an offering for Yahweh, he's to get the animal to stand before the priest ¹²and the priest will

evaluate it; whether good or bad, it's to be in accordance with the priest's evaluation, ¹³and if he actually restores it, he's to add a fifth to the evaluation.

## On making things sacred

¹⁴If an individual makes his house sacred, as a thing sacred for Yahweh, the priest is to evaluate it. Whether good or bad, as the priest evaluates it, so it will stand. ¹⁵If the person who makes it sacred restores his house, he's to add to it a fifth of the silver of the evaluation, and it will be his.

¹⁶If an individual makes sacred for Yahweh some of the field that's his holding, the evaluation is to be on the basis of its seed: ten barrels of barley seed to fifty silver sheqels. ¹⁷If he makes his field sacred from the ram's horn year, it will stand in accordance with the evaluation. ¹⁸But if he makes his field sacred after the ram's horn year, the priest is to count the silver on the basis of the years that remain until the ram's horn year, and the evaluation will decrease.

¹⁹If the person who made it sacred actually restores the field, he's to add to it a fifth of the silver of the evaluation, and it will stand for him. ²⁰If he doesn't restore the field, or if he's sold the field to another man, it can't be restored any more. ²¹When the field goes out in the ram's horn year, it will be sacred for Yahweh, like a field that's been devoted. It will belong to the priest as his holding.

²²If he makes sacred for Yahweh a field he bought that's not a field belonging to his holding, ²³the priest is to count for him the proportion of the evaluation until the ram's horn year and he's to give the evaluation on that day as something sacred for Yahweh. ²⁴In the ram's horn year the field is to go back to the one from whom he bought it, to the one whose holding in the country it is.

²⁵Every evaluation is to be by the sanctuary sheqel; the sheqel is to be twenty grams.

## Things that belong to God

²⁶However, a firstborn (which is born first for Yahweh) among animals: an individual will not make it sacred, whether ox or sheep. It belongs to Yahweh. ²⁷But if it's among taboo animals he may redeem it at the evaluation and add to it a fifth of it. If it's not restored, it's to be sold at the evaluation. ²⁸However, anything that an individual devotes to Yahweh from all that belongs to him, from human beings or animals or fields in his holding, will not be sold and will not be restored. Anything that's devoted is especially sacred for Yahweh. ²⁹No one who is devoted from among human beings will be redeemed. He's absolutely to be put to death.

³⁰Every tenth of the land, from the land's seed, from the trees' fruit, belongs to Yahweh. It's sacred for Yahweh. ³¹If an individual actually restores some of his tenth, he's to add to it a fifth of it. ³²Every tenth of herd and flock, every one that passes under the club, the tenth is to be sacred for Yahweh. ³³A person will not seek out between good and bad and he will not exchange it. If he actually exchanges it, both it and the exchanged one will be sacred. It will not be restored."

³⁴These are the orders that Yahweh gave Mosheh for the Yisra'elites at Mount Sinay.

# NUMBERS

The book of Numbers takes its name from the two counts of the assembly's members that almost bookend the work as a whole – they come in chapter 1 and chapter 26. These two chapters give virtually the same report of the assembly's total numbers (603,550 men the first time, 601,730 the second time). Considerable significance attaches to that similarity in light of what happens in-between the two counts.

The story of the first count introduces ten chapters that relate ways in which Yahweh gets the Israelites ready to resume their journey to Canaan. The chapters are Israel's marching orders. They thus both close the account of Israel's stay at Sinai and open the account of that journey. So the whole of the second half of Exodus, the entire book of Leviticus and the first third of Numbers all deal with the time at Sinai, which occupies less than a year in the nation's life. The space given to this year reflects how important the time at Sinai is in the First Testament, and how important are the instructions God gives Israel in connection with its stay at Sinai.

The middle third of Numbers (chapters 11—21) tells of the Israelites' actual journey from Sinai to the edge of Canaan. In contrast to the account of the year at Sinai, this fairly short sequence of chapters covers enough time for a whole generation to pass on. The distance from Mount Sinai to Canaan is only 150 miles, so it should have taken only a couple of weeks, but the Israelites actually took years over it. The reason emerges from the stories that Numbers tells. The journey was characterized by a series of rebellions on Israel's part that led Yahweh to resolve that the generation of Israelites who came out of Egypt should be allowed to die out and not get to Canaan. It would be the next generation that got into the land.

The First and New Testaments see these stories as full of warnings for Israel and for the Church. Psalm 95 reminds enthusiastic worshippers in the temple about their ancestors' rebellions against Yahweh and that whole generation's consequent failure to reach the settled life in Canaan that was their destiny, with the implication that later generations could lose the land if they follow their ancestors' example. Hebrews 3—4 puts the same warning before people who believe in Jesus. In 1 Corinthians 10 Paul refers back to these stories to make the same point. Believers in Jesus, too, need to be wary about worshipping other gods, engaging in sexual immorality, testing Christ, or grumbling, in the way the exodus-wilderness generation did.

The last third of Numbers (chapters 22—36) sees Israel poised finally to enter Canaan, camped just the other side of the River Jordan. These chapters begin with the blessing of Israel by Bil'am [Baalam], which suggests one way in which we are coming near the end of the story that began with Yahweh's promise of blessing and land to Abraham. Balaam restates Yahweh's promise as Abraham's descendants are about to take possession of this land. The significance of Moses' second count of the people then lies in the fact that the people still number approximately the same as they did when they were at Sinai. Yahweh has preserved them despite their rebellion.

The number of 600,000 or so men, which implies two or three million people when one includes their wives and children, is hardly the actual number of people that were there at the time. Deuteronomy will later comment that Israel is rather a small people, and the figure of two or three million is out of proportion to the population of Egypt or Canaan at this time – or to the population of Israel itself over succeeding centuries. It looks as if something odd has happened to the numbers. One plausible explanation is that the word for 'thousand' is also a word for a family or an army division; the word comes with this sense in Numbers 1.16. Behind these figures, then, might be the idea that Israel numbers 600 families – which makes good sense.

## A head count

**1** Yahweh spoke to Mosheh [Moses] in the Sinay Wilderness in the appointment tent, on the first of the second month in the second year after they got out of the country of Misrayim [Egypt]: ²"Take a head count of the entire assembly of the Yisra'elites [Israelites] by their kin-groups, by their ancestral households, according to the number of the names of every male by their heads, ³from the age of twenty years and upwards, everyone in Yisra'el who goes out in the army. You're to register them by their troops, you and Aharon [Aaron]. ⁴An individual person for each clan is to be with you. The individual will be head of his ancestral household.

⁵These are the names of the men who are to stand with you:

for Re'uben, Elitsur ben Shede'ur;
⁶for Shim'on [Simeon], Shelumi'el ben Tsurishadday;
⁷for Yehudah [Judah], Nahshon ben Amminadab;
⁸for Yissakar [Issachar], Netan'el ben Zu'ar;
⁹for Zebulun, Eli'ab ben Helon;
¹⁰for the sons of Yoseph [Joseph] –
    for Ephrayim, Elishama ben Ammihud,
    for Menashsheh, Gamli'el ben Pedahtsur;
¹¹for Binyamin [Benjamin], Abidan ben Gid'oni;
¹²for Dan, Ahi'ezer ben Ammishadday;
¹³for Asher, Pag'i'el ben Okran;
¹⁴for Gad, Elyasaph ben De'u'el;
¹⁵for Naphtali, Ahira ben Enan.'

¹⁶These were the people named from the assembly as leaders of their ancestral clans. They were the heads of the Yisra'elite divisions.

¹⁷Mosheh and Aharon got these men who had been designated by their names, ¹⁸and congregated the entire assembly on the first of the second month. They made their descent known on the basis of their kin-groups by their ancestral household according to the number of the names, from the age of twenty years and upwards, head by head. ¹⁹As Yahweh ordered Mosheh, he registered them in the Sinay Wilderness.

## From Re'uben to Yissakar

²⁰They were:

The descendants of Re'uben, Yisra'el's firstborn
their lines of descent by their kin-groups by their ancestral household
according to the number of the names head by head
every male from the age of twenty years and upwards, everyone who goes out in the army
²¹their register for the clan of Re'uben: 46,500.

²²For Shim'on's descendants
their lines of descent by their kin-groups by their ancestral household
its register according to the number of the names head by head
every male from the age of twenty years and upwards, everyone who goes out in the army
²³their register for the clan of Shim'on: 59,300.

²⁴For Gad's descendants
their lines of descent by their kin-groups by their ancestral household
according to the number of the names
from the age of twenty years and upwards, everyone who goes out in the army
²⁵their register for the clan of Gad: 45,650.

²⁶For Yehudah's descendants
their lines of descent by their kin-groups by their ancestral household
according to the number of the names
from the age of twenty years and upwards, everyone who goes out in the army
²⁷their register for the clan of Yehudah: 74,600.

²⁸For Yissakar's descendants
their lines of descent by their kin-groups by their ancestral household
according to the number of the names
from the age of twenty years and upwards, everyone who goes out in the army
²⁹their register for the clan of Yissakar: 54,400.

## *From Zebulun to Naphtali*

³⁰For Zebulun's descendants
their lines of descent by their kin-groups by
their ancestral household
according to the number of the names
from the age of twenty years and upwards,
everyone who goes out in the army
³¹their register for the clan of Zebulun:
57,400.

³²For Yoseph's descendants:
For Ephrayim's descendants
their lines of descent by their kin-groups by
their ancestral household
according to the number of the names
from the age of twenty years and upwards,
everyone who goes out in the army
³³their register for the clan of Ephrayim:
40,500.

³⁴For Menashsheh's descendants
their lines of descent by their kin-groups, by
their ancestral household
according to the number of the names
from the age of twenty years and upwards,
everyone who goes out in the army
³⁵their register for the clan of Menashsheh:
32,200.

³⁶For Binyamin's descendants
their lines of descent by their kin-groups by
their ancestral household
according to the number of the names
from the age of twenty years and upwards,
everyone who goes out in the army
³⁷their register for the clan of Binyamin:
35,400.

³⁸For Dan's descendants
their lines of descent by their kin-groups by
their ancestral household
according to the number of the names
from the age of twenty years and upwards,
everyone who goes out in the army
³⁹their register for the clan of Dan: 62,700.

⁴⁰For Asher's descendants
their lines of descent by their kin-groups by
their ancestral household
according to the number of the names
from the age of twenty years and upwards,

everyone who goes out in the army
⁴¹their register for the clan of Asher: 41,500.

⁴²For Naphtali's descendants
their lines of descent by their kin-groups by
their ancestral household
according to the number of the names
from the age of twenty years and upwards,
everyone who goes out in the army
⁴³their register for the clan of Naphtali:
53,400.

## *Levi*

⁴⁴This is the register that Mosheh, Aharon and Yisra'el's leaders made (there were twelve, one individual each for his ancestral household). ⁴⁵The entire register of the Yisra'elites by their ancestral household from the age of twenty years and upwards, everyone who goes out in the army in Yisra'el: ⁴⁶the entire register was 603,550.

⁴⁷The Levites were not registered among them by their ancestral clan. ⁴⁸Yahweh had spoken to Mosheh: ⁴⁹'Only, you will not register the clan of Levi or take their head count among the Yisra'elites. ⁵⁰You yourself appoint the Levites over the affirmation dwelling, over all its articles and over everything that belongs to it. They're to carry the dwelling and all its articles and they're to minister to it. They're to camp round the dwelling. ⁵¹When the dwelling sets out, the Levites are to take it down, and when the dwelling camps, the Levites are to set it up. An outsider who comes near is to be put to death.

⁵²The Yisra'elites are to camp each with his camp, each with his standard, by their companies. ⁵³But the Levites are to camp round the affirmation tent, so fury doesn't come on the Yisra'elite assembly. The Levites are to keep the charge of the affirmation dwelling.'

⁵⁴The Yisra'elites acted in accordance with all that Yahweh ordered Mosheh; so they acted.

## *The order for the journey: Levi at the centre*

**2** Yahweh spoke to Mosheh and to Aharon: ²'The Yisra'elites are to camp each by his standard with the ensigns of their ancestral households. They're to camp at a distance round the appointment tent.'

³The people camping to the front, to the east: the standard of Yehudah's camp, by their companies.

The Yehudahites' leader: Nahshon ben Amminadab. ⁴His company, their register: 74,600. ⁵Camping by it, the clan of Yissakar. The Yissakarites' leader: Netan'el ben Tsu'ar. ⁶His company, their register: 54,400. ⁷The clan of Zebulun. The Zebulunites' leader: Eli'ab ben Helon. ⁸His company, their register: 57,400. ⁹The entire register of Yehudah's camp: 186,400 by their companies. They're to move on first.

¹⁰The standard of Re'uben's camp, to the south, by their companies.

The Re'ubenites' leader: Elitsur ben Shede'ur. ¹¹His company, their register: 46,500. ¹²Camping by it, the clan of Shim'on. The Shim'onites' leader: Shelumi'el ben Tsuri-shadday. ¹³His company, their register: 59,300. ¹⁴And the clan of Gad. The Gadites' leader: Elyasaph ben Re'u'el. ¹⁵His company, their register: 45,650. ¹⁶The entire register of Re'uben's camp: 151,450 by their companies. They're to move on second.

¹⁷The appointment tent, the Levites' camp, is to set out in the middle of the camps. As they camp, so they're to move on, each in its own place, by their standards.

### The order for the journey: the arrangement completed

¹⁸The standard of Ephrayim's camp by their companies, to the west.

The Ephrayimites' leader: Elishama ben Ammihud. ¹⁹His company, their register: 40,500. ²⁰By it, the clan of Menashsheh. The Menashshites' leader: Gamli'el ben Pedahtsur. ²¹His company, their register: 32,200. ²²And the clan of Binyamin. The Binyaminites' leader: Abidan ben Gid'oni. ²³His company, their register: 35,400. ²⁴The entire register of Ephrayim's camp: 108,100 by their companies. They're to move on third.

²⁵The standard of Dan's camp, to the north, by their companies.

The Danites' leader: Ahi'ezer ben Ammishadday. ²⁶His company, their register: 62,700. ²⁷Camping by it, the clan of Asher. The Asherites' leader: Pag'i'el ben Okran. ²⁸His company, their register: 41,500. ²⁹And the clan of Naphtali. The Naphtalites' leader: Ahira ben Enan. ³⁰His company, their register: 53,400. ³¹The entire register of Dan's camp: 157,600. They're to move on last, by their standards.

³²This was the register of the Yisra'elites by their ancestral households. The entire register of the camps by their companies: 603,550. ³³The Levites were not registered among the Yisra'elites, as Yahweh ordered Mosheh. ³⁴So the Yisra'elites acted in accordance with all that Yahweh ordered Mosheh. In this way they camped by their standards and in this way they moved on, each by his kin-group according to his ancestral household.

### Yahweh's claim on Levi

**3** These are Aharon's and Mosheh's lines of descent on the day Yahweh spoke with Mosheh at Mount Sinay. ²These are the names of Aharon's sons: the firstborn Nadab, and Abihu, El'azar and Itamar. ³These are the names of Aharon's sons, the anointed priests whom he commissioned to act as priests. ⁴Nadab and Abihu died before Yahweh when they presented outside fire before Yahweh in the Sinay Wilderness. They didn't have sons, so El'azar and Itamar acted as priests in the presence of Aharon their father.

⁵Yahweh spoke to Mosheh: ⁶'Present the clan of Levi and have them stand before Aharon the priest to minister to him. ⁷They're to keep his charge and the charge of the entire assembly before the appointment tent by performing the service of the dwelling. ⁸They're to keep all the articles in the appointment tent, the Yisra'elites' charge, by performing the service of the dwelling. ⁹You're to give the Levites to Aharon and to his sons; they're wholly given to him from among the Yisra'elites. ¹⁰Aharon and his sons you're to appoint to keep watch over their priestly work; the outsider who comes near is to be put to death.'

¹¹Yahweh spoke to Mosheh: ¹²'Here, I myself have taken the Levites from among the Yisra'elites in place of every firstborn, the one who opens the womb, from the Yisra'elites. The Levites are to be mine, ¹³because every firstborn is mine. On the day I struck down every firstborn in the country of Misrayim I made sacred for me every firstborn in Yisra'el, human and animal. They're mine. I am Yahweh.'

¹⁴Yahweh spoke to Mosheh in the Sinay Wilderness: ¹⁵'Register the Levites by their ancestral households, by their kin-groups. Every male from the age of one month and upwards, you're to register them.' ¹⁶So Mosheh registered them at Yahweh's bidding, as he was ordered. ¹⁷These were Levi's sons by their names: Gershon, Qehat and Merari. ¹⁸These were the names of Gershon's sons by their kin-groups: Libni and Shim'i; ¹⁹Qehat's sons by their kin-groups: Amram and Yitshar, Hebron and Uzzi'el; ²⁰ᵃMerari's sons by their kin-groups: Mahli and Mushi.

## Levi's kin-groups

²⁰ᵇThese were Levi's kin-groups by their ancestral households.

²¹Gershon's:
the Libnite kin-group and the Shim'ite kin-group: they were the Gershonite kin-groups. ²²Their register by number, every male from the age of one month and upwards – their register: 7,500. ²³The Gershonite kin-groups were to camp behind the dwelling, to the west.

²⁴The leader of the Gershonite ancestral household was El'asaph ben La'el. ²⁵The Gershonites' charge in the appointment tent: the dwelling and the tent, its covering, the curtain for the entrance of the appointment tent, ²⁶the courtyard hangings, the curtain for the entrance of the courtyard which is next to the dwelling and next to the altar all round, and its ropes, in respect of its entire service.

²⁷Qehat's:
the Amramite kin-group, the Yitsharite kin-group, the Hebronite kin-group and the Uzzi'elite kin-group: they were the Qehatite kin-groups. ²⁸By the number of every male from the age of one month and upwards: 8,600, keeping the charge of the sacred things. ²⁹The kin-groups of the Qehatites were to camp on the side of the dwelling to the south. ³⁰The leader of the ancestral household of the Qehatite kin goups was Elitsaphan ben Uzzi'el. ³¹Their charge: the chest, the table, the candelabrum, the altars, the sacred articles with which people would minister, the curtain and its entire service. ³²The senior Levite leader, El'azar ben Aharon the priest: appointment over the people who keep the charge of the sacred things.

³³Merari's:
the Mahlite kin-group and the Mushite kin-group: they were the Merarite kin-groups. ³⁴Their register by number, every male from the age of one month and upwards: 6,200. ³⁵The leader of the ancestral household of the Mararite kin-groups: Tsuri'el ben Abihayil. They were to camp on the side of the dwelling to the north. ³⁶The appointment regarding the charge of the Merarites: the dwelling's planks, its bars, its posts, its sockets, all its articles and all its service; ³⁷and the courtyard posts all round, their sockets, their pegs and their ropes.

## The count of the firstborn

³⁸The people camping before the dwelling, in front, before the appointment tent, to the

east: Mosheh and Aharon and his sons, having charge of the sanctuary in connection with the Yisra'elites' charge (an outsider who drew near was to be put to death). ³⁹The entire register of the Levites, which Mosheh and Aharon made at Yahweh's bidding, by their kin-groups, every male from the age of one month and upwards: 22,000.

⁴⁰Yahweh said to Mosheh, 'Register every firstborn male belonging to the Yisra'elites from the age of one month and upwards and get the number of their names; ⁴¹and take the Levites for me (I am Yahweh) in place of every firstborn among the Yisra'elites, and the Levites' animals in place of every firstborn among the Yisra'elites' animals.' ⁴²So Mosheh registered, as Yahweh ordered him, every firstborn among the Yisra'elites. ⁴³Every firstborn male by the number of the names from the age of one month and upwards, by their register: 22,273.

⁴⁴Yahweh spoke to Mosheh: ⁴⁵'Take the Levites in place of every firstborn among the Yisra'elites, and the Levites' animals in place of their animals. The Levites are to be mine. I am Yahweh. ⁴⁶As the redemption price for the 273 from the firstborn of the Yisra'elites who are surplus, above and beyond the Levites: ⁴⁷you're to take five sheqels each per head. You're to take it by the sanctuary sheqel (a sheqel is twenty grams). ⁴⁸You're to give the silver to Aharon and to his sons as the redemption price for those who are surplus among them.'

⁴⁹So Mosheh took the redemption silver from those who were surplus, above and beyond those redeemed by the Levites. ⁵⁰From the firstborn of the Yisra'elites he took the 1,365 by the sanctuary sheqel, ⁵¹and Mosheh gave the redemption silver to Aharon and to his sons at Yahweh's bidding, as Yahweh ordered Mosheh.

## Dismantling the camp

**4** Yahweh spoke to Mosheh and Aharon: ²'Take a head count of the Qehatites from among the Levites, by their kin-groups, by their ancestral household, ³from the age of thirty years and upwards until the age of fifty years, everyone coming in for duty to do work in the appointment tent. ⁴This is the service of the Qehatites in the appointment tent: the especially sacred things.

⁵Aharon and his sons are to come in when the camp is setting off, take down the screen curtain and cover the affirmation chest with it. ⁶They're to put a dolphin-skin covering on it, spread an all-blue cloth on top and place its poles. ⁷Over the presence table they're to spread a blue cloth and put on it the dishes, the ladles, the pitchers and the libation bowls; and the regular bread is to be on it. ⁸They're to spread over them a bright crimson cloth, cover it with a dolphin-skin covering and place its poles.

⁹They're to get a blue cloth and cover the candelabrum for lighting, its lamps, its tongs, its pans and all its oil containers with which they minister to it. ¹⁰They're to put it and all its articles into a dolphin skin covering and put them on a frame. ¹¹Over the gold altar they're to spread a blue cloth, cover it with a dolphin-skin covering and place its poles.

## The need to be wary

¹²They're to get all the articles for the ministry in which they minister in the sacred place, put them into a blue cloth, cover them with a dolphin-skin covering and put them on a frame. ¹³They're to clear the altar of waste and spread on it a purple cloth. ¹⁴They're to put on it all the utensils with which they minister on it, the pans, the forks, the shovels and the basins, all the altar's utensils, spread over it a dolphin-skin covering and place its poles.

¹⁵Aharon and his sons are to finish covering the sacred things and all the sacred articles when the camp is moving on, and after that the Qehatites are to come in to carry them. They will not touch the sacred things, and die. These things are for carrying by the Qehatites, in the appointment tent.

¹⁶The appointment of El'azar ben Aharon the priest: the lighting oil, the aromatic incense, the regular grain offering and the anointing oil; appointment over the entire dwelling and everything that's in it – the sacred place and its articles.'

¹⁷Yahweh spoke to Mosheh and to Aharon: ¹⁸'Don't let the clan of Qehatite kin-groups be cut off from among the Levites. ¹⁹Do this for them, and they will live and not die when they come up to the things that are especially

sacred. Aharon and his sons are to go in and place each individual over his service, for his carrying. [20]But they're not to come in to look as people are demolishing the sacred place, and die.'

## The Gershonites and the Merarites

[21]Yahweh spoke to Mosheh: [22]'Take a head count of the Gershonites, them too, by their ancestral household, by their kin-groups. [23]From the age of thirty years and upwards to the age of fifty years you're to register them, everyone coming in to do duty by performing service in the appointment tent. [24]This is the service of the Gershonite kin-groups in serving and in carrying: [25]they're to carry the pieces of the dwelling, the appointment tent and its covering, the dolphin-skin covering that's on it, on top, the curtain for the appointment tent entrance, [26]the courtyard hangings, the curtain for the entrance of the courtyard gateway which is next to the dwelling and next to the altar all round, its ropes, all the articles in their service and everything that's done in connection with them; so they will serve.

[27]It's at the bidding of Aharon and his sons that all the Gershonites' service is to happen, as regards all their carrying and as regards all their service. You're to appoint them over them in having charge of all their carrying. [28]This is the service of the Gershonites' kin-groups in the appointment tent and their charge at the direction of Itamar ben Aharon the priest.

[29]The Merarites: you're to register them by their kin-groups, by their ancestral household. [30]From the age of thirty years and upwards until the age of fifty years you're to register them, everyone coming in for duty, to perform the service of the appointment tent. [31]This is their charge in their carrying, in connection with all their service in the appointment tent: the dwelling's planks, its bars, its posts, its sockets, [32]the courtyard's posts all round, their sockets, their pegs and their ropes. For all their articles and for all their service and by their names you're to register the articles in their charge, their carrying. [33]These are the service of the Merarite kin-groups as regards all their service in the appointment tent at the direction of Itamar ben Aharon the priest.'

## The register of the Levite kin-groups

[34]So Mosheh, Aharon and the assembly's leaders registered the Qehatites by their kin-groups and by their ancestral household, [35]from the age of thirty years and upwards until the age of fifty years, everyone coming in for duty for service in the appointment tent. [36]Their register by their kin-groups was 2,750. [37]This was the register of the Qehatite kin-groups, everyone serving in the appointment tent, which Mosheh and Aharon made at Yahweh's bidding through Mosheh.

[38]The register of the Gershonites by their kin-groups and by their ancestral household, [39]from the age of thirty years and upwards until the age of fifty years, everyone coming in for duty for service in the appointment tent: [40]their register by their kin-groups, by their ancestral household, was 2,630. [41]This was the register of the kin-groups of the Gershonites, everyone serving in the appointment tent, which Mosheh and Aharon made at Yahweh's bidding.

[42]The register of the kin-groups of the Merarites by their kin-groups, by their ancestral household, [43]from the age of thirty years and upwards until the age of fifty years, everyone coming for duty for service in the appointment tent: [44]their register by their kin-groups was 3,200. [45]This was the register of the kin-groups of the Merarites, which Mosheh and Aharon made at Yahweh's bidding through Mosheh.

[46]The entire register that Mosheh and Aharon and the Yisra'elite leaders made, the Levites by their kin-groups and by their ancestral household, [47]from the age of thirty years and upwards until the age of fifty years, everyone coming in to serve (the service of serving and the service of carrying) in the appointment tent: [48]their register was 5,580. [49]At Yahweh's bidding they registered them through Mosheh, each individual according to his service and to his carrying, his register that Yahweh ordered Mosheh.

## Breaking faith

**5** Yahweh spoke to Mosheh: [2]'Order the Yisra'elites that they send off from the camp anyone who's been made scaly, anyone who's discharging and anyone who's taboo through a [dead] person. ³Male and female, you're to send them off. You're to send them off outside the camp so they won't make taboo the camp of the people among whom I'm dwelling.' ⁴The Yisra'elites did so; they sent them off outside the camp. As Yahweh spoke to Mosheh, so the Yisra'elites did.

⁵Yahweh spoke to Mosheh: ⁶'Speak to the Yisra'elites: if a man or a woman does one of all the things that are wrong to a human being, thus breaking faith with Yahweh, the person is liable. ⁷They're to confess their wrong that they did. He's to make reparation for its sum total, add to it a fifth of it and give it to the person to whom he's liable. ⁸If the person doesn't have a restorer to make reparation to, the reparation that's made belongs to Yahweh, to the priest, in addition to the ram of complete expiation with which he makes expiation for him.

⁹Every contribution in connection with all the sacred things belonging to the Yisra'elites that they present to the priest is to be his. ¹⁰Each one, his sacred things are to be his; what the person gives the priest is to be his.'

## Breaking faith in the context of marriage

¹¹Yahweh spoke to Mosheh: ¹²'Speak to the Yisra'elites: "When an individual's wife goes off and breaks faith with him, ¹³and someone has slept with her and they had sex but it was concealed from the eyes of her husband and she's kept it secret, but she has made herself taboo but there's no witness against her and she was not caught, ¹⁴but a jealous spirit has come over him and he's become jealous in respect of his wife when she has made herself taboo; or a jealous spirit has come over him and he's become jealous in respect of his wife when she hasn't made herself taboo: ¹⁵the man is to bring his wife to the priest, and to bring as an offering for her a tenth of a barrel of barley flour; he will not pour oil on it and he will not put frankincense on it, because it's a grain offering of jealousy, a grain offering of mindfulness, which makes someone mindful of waywardness.

¹⁶The priest is to present her and get her to stand before Yahweh. ¹⁷The priest is to get sacred water in a clay container. The priest is to get some of the earth that's on the dwelling floor and the priest is to put it in the water. ¹⁸The priest is to get the woman to stand before Yahweh and to bare the woman's head and put on her palms the grain offering of mindfulness, the grain offering of jealousy. In the priest's hand is to be the bitter water that brings a curse. ¹⁹The priest is to get her to swear: he's to say to the woman, 'If no one has slept with you, and if you haven't gone off in taboo while married to your husband, you can be free of guilt from this bitter water that brings a curse.

## A spirit of jealousy

²⁰But you: when you've gone off while married to your husband and you've made yourself taboo, and a man other than your husband has had sex with you ²¹(the priest is to get the woman to swear the avowed oath, and the priest is to say to the woman), may Yahweh make you a vow and an oath among your people, when Yahweh makes your thigh fall and your womb swell. ²²May this water that brings a curse come into your insides so as to make your womb swell and your thigh fall.' And the woman is to say, 'Yes, yes.' ²³The priest is to write these vows on a document and wipe them off into the bitter water, ²⁴and get the woman to drink the bitter water that brings a curse, so the water that brings a curse may come into her, becoming bitter.

²⁵The priest is to get from the woman's hand the grain offering of jealousy, lift up the grain offering before Yahweh and present it at the altar. ²⁶The priest is to scoop the commemorative portion from the grain offering and turn it into smoke at the altar. Afterwards, he's to get the woman to drink the water.

²⁷When he's got her to drink the water, if she's made herself taboo and broken faith with her husband, the water that brings a curse, becoming bitter, will come into her, her womb will swell and her thigh fall, and the woman will become the exemplar for a vow among her people. ²⁸But if she hasn't made herself taboo and she's pure, she'll be free of guilt and she'll be fruitful.

²⁹This is the instruction regarding incidences of jealousy, when a woman goes off while

married to her husband and becomes taboo, [30]or a jealous spirit comes over a man and he becomes jealous in respect of his wife and gets the woman to stand before Yahweh and the priest acts on this entire instruction toward her. [31]The man will be free of guilt for waywardness when that woman carries her waywardness."'

## The Nazirite pledge

**6** Yahweh spoke to Mosheh: [2]'Speak to the Yisra'elites: "When a man or woman makes himself distinct to make a pledge as a consecrated person, to be consecrated for Yahweh, [3]he's to stay consecrated from wine and liquor. He will not drink wine vinegar or liquor vinegar, he will not drink grape juice and he will not eat grapes, fresh or dried. [4]All the time of his consecration he will not eat anything that's made from the grapevine, either seeds or skin.

[5]All the time of his consecration pledge, no razor will pass over his head; until the fulfilling of the time that he is consecrated for Yahweh, he's to be sacred, growing the locks of the hair of his head. [6]All the time of his being consecrated for Yahweh he will not come in to a dead person. [7]For his father and for his mother, for his brother and for his sister: he will not make himself taboo for them when they die, because his consecration for his God is on his head. [8]All the time of his consecration, he's sacred for Yahweh.

[9]When someone does die near him suddenly, unexpectedly, and makes the head of his consecration taboo, he's to shave his head on the day he becomes pure. He's to shave it on the seventh day, [10]and on the eighth day he's to bring two doves or two young pigeons to the priest at the entrance of the appointment tent. [11]The priest is to make one into a decontamination and one into a burnt offering, and he's to make expiation for him for the wrongdoing in connection with the [dead] person. On that day he's to make his head sacred [12]and put into effect his time of consecration for Yahweh. He's to bring a year-old lamb as a reparation. The previous time will fall away, because his consecration became taboo.

## Yahweh bless you and keep you

[13]This is the instruction for the consecrated person. On the day of the fulfilling of his consecration time, they're to bring him to the entrance of the appointment tent. [14]He's to bring as his offering for Yahweh a year-old lamb, one that's whole, as a burnt offering; a year-old ewe, one that's whole, as a decontamination; a ram, one that's whole, as a well-being sacrifice; [15]a basket of flatbread made from fine flour, loaves mixed with oil; flat wafers spread with oil; their grain offering; and their libations.

[16]The priest is to present them before Yahweh, make the decontamination and its burnt offering, [17]and make the ram a well-being sacrifice for Yahweh, along with the basket of flatbread. The priest is to make its grain offering and its libation. [18]The consecrated person is to shave the head of his consecration at the entrance of the appointment tent. He's to get the hair from the head of his consecration and put it on the fire that's under the well-being sacrifice.

[19]The priest is to get the ram's shoulder, boiled, a loaf of flatbread from the basket and a flat wafer, and put them on the palms of the consecrated person, after his shaving of his consecration. [20]The priest is to elevate them as an elevation offering before Yahweh. It's sacred for the priest, along with the breast of the elevation offering and along with the thigh of the contribution. Afterwards, the consecrated person may drink wine.

[21]This is the instruction concerning the consecrated person. Someone who pledges his offering to Yahweh along with his consecration, apart from what his means stretch to: on the basis of his pledge, that which he pledges, so he's to do, along with the instruction for his consecration."'

[22]Yahweh spoke to Mosheh: [23]'Speak to Aharon and to his sons: "In this way you're to bless the Yisra'elites, saying to them:

[24]Yahweh bless you and keep you!
[25]Yahweh shine his face towards you and be
    gracious to you!
[26]Yahweh lift his face towards you and make
    things be well for you!

[27]They're to put my name on the Yisra'elites so I myself bless them."'

*Provision for the sanctuary*

**7** On the day Mosheh finished setting up the dwelling, he anointed it and made it sacred with all its articles, and the altar with all its articles – he anointed them and made them sacred. ²The Yisraʾelite leaders, the heads of their ancestral household (they were the leaders of the clans, who stood over their register) presented ³and brought their offering before Yahweh: six covered wagons and twelve cattle, a wagon for two leaders and an ox for each. They presented them before the dwelling, ⁴and Yahweh said to Mosheh, ⁵'Receive them from them so they can perform service for the appointment tent, and give them to the Levites, each on the basis of his service.'

⁶So Mosheh received the wagons and the cattle, and gave them to the Levites. ⁷Two wagons and four cattle he gave to the Gershonites on the basis of their service. ⁸Four wagons and eight cattle he gave to the Merarites on the basis of their service, at the direction of Itamar ben Aharon the priest. ⁹To the Qehatites he didn't give any, because the service of the sanctuary was upon them; they would carry it on their shoulder. ¹⁰The leaders presented the altar's dedication gift on the day it was anointed. When the leaders presented their offering before the altar, ¹¹Yahweh said to Mosheh: 'One leader each day, they're to present their offering for the altar dedication.'

*Offerings by Yehudah, Yissakar, Zebulun*

¹²The one who presented his offering on the first day was Nahshon ben Amminadab, of the clan of Yehudah. ¹³His offering: a silver dish, its weight 130 sheqels; a silver basin, seventy sheqels by the sanctuary sheqel; the two of them full of fine flour mixed with oil, for a grain offering; ¹⁴a gold ladle of ten sheqels, full of incense; ¹⁵a bull from the herd; a ram; a year-old lamb as a burnt offering; ¹⁶a he-goat from the flock as a decontamination; ¹⁷and as a well-being sacrifice, two cattle, five rams, five he-goats, five year-old lambs. This was the offering of Nahshon ben Amminadab. ¹⁸On the second day, Netanʾel ben Tsuʾar, leader of Yissakar, presented. ¹⁹He

presented as his offering a silver dish, its weight 130 sheqels; a silver basin, seventy sheqels by the sanctuary sheqel; the two of them full of fine flour mixed with oil, for a grain offering; ²⁰a gold ladle of ten sheqels, full of incense; ²¹a bull from the herd; a ram; a year-old lamb as a burnt offering; ²²a he-goat from the flock as a decontamination; ²³and as a well-being sacrifice, two cattle, five rams, five he-goats, five year-old lambs. This was the offering of Netanʾel ben Tsuʾar. ²⁴On the third day, the leader of the Zebulunites, Eliʾab ben Helon. ²⁵His offering: a silver dish, its weight 130 sheqels; a silver basin, seventy sheqels by the sanctuary sheqel; the two of them full of fine flour mixed with oil, for a grain offering; ²⁶a gold ladle of ten sheqels, full of incense; ²⁷a bull from the herd; a ram; a year-old lamb as a burnt offering; ²⁸a he-goat from the flock as a decontamination; ²⁹and as a well-being sacrifice, two cattle, five rams, five he-goats, five year-old lambs. This was the offering of Eliʾab ben Helon.

*Offerings by Reʾuben, Shimʾon, Gad*

³⁰On the fourth day, the leader of the Reʾubenites, Elitsur ben Shedeʾur. ³¹His offering: a silver dish, its weight 130 sheqels; a silver basin, seventy sheqels by the sanctuary sheqel; the two of them full of fine flour mixed with oil, for a grain offering; ³²a gold ladle of ten sheqels, full of incense; ³³a bull from the herd; a ram; a year-old lamb as a burnt offering; ³⁴a he-goat from the flock as a decontamination; ³⁵and as a well-being sacrifice, two cattle, five rams, five he-goats, five year-old lambs. This was the offering of Elitsur ben Shedeʾur. ³⁶On the fifth day, the leader of the Shimʾonites, Shelumiʾel ben Tsurishadday. ³⁷His offering: a silver dish, its weight 130 sheqels; a silver basin, seventy sheqels by the sanctuary sheqel; the two of them full of fine flour mixed with oil, for a grain offering; ³⁸a gold ladle of ten sheqels, full of incense; ³⁹a bull from the herd; a ram; a

year-old lamb as a burnt offering; ⁴⁰a he-goat from the flock as a decontamination; ⁴¹and as a well-being sacrifice, two cattle, five rams, five he-goats, five year-old lambs. This was the offering of Shelumi'el ben Tsurishadday.

⁴²On the sixth day, the leader of the Gadites, Elyasaph ben De'u'el. ⁴³His offering: a silver dish, its weight 130 sheqels; a silver basin, seventy sheqels by the sanctuary sheqel; the two of them full of fine flour mixed with oil, for a grain offering; ⁴⁴a gold ladle of ten sheqels, full of incense; ⁴⁵a bull from the herd; a ram; a year-old lamb as a burnt offering; ⁴⁶a he-goat from the flock as a decontamination; ⁴⁷and as a well-being sacrifice, two cattle, five rams, five he-goats, five year-old lambs. This was the offering of Elyasaph ben De'u'el.

## Offerings by Ephrayim, Menashsheh, Binyamin

⁴⁸On the seventh day, the leader of the Ephrayimites, Elishama ben Ammihud. ⁴⁹His offering: a silver dish, its weight 130 sheqels; a silver basin, seventy sheqels by the sanctuary sheqel; the two of them full of fine flour mixed with oil, for a grain offering; ⁵⁰a gold ladle of ten sheqels, full of incense; ⁵¹a bull from the herd; a ram; a year-old lamb as a burnt offering; ⁵²a he-goat from the flock as a decontamination; ⁵³and as a well-being sacrifice, two cattle, five rams, five he-goats, five year-old lambs. This was the offering of Elishama ben Ammihud.

⁵⁴On the eighth day, the leader of the Menashshites, Gamli'el ben Pedah-tsur. ⁵⁵His offering: a silver dish, its weight 130 sheqels; a silver basin, seventy sheqels by the sanctuary sheqel; the two of them full of fine flour mixed with oil, for a grain offering; ⁵⁶a gold ladle of ten sheqels, full of incense; ⁵⁷a bull from the herd; a ram; a year-old lamb as a burnt offering; ⁵⁸a he-goat from the flock as a decontamination; ⁵⁹and as a well-being sacrifice, two cattle, five rams, five he-goats, five year-old lambs. This was the offering of Gamli'el ben Pedah-tsur.

⁶⁰On the ninth day, the leader of the Binyaminites, Abidan ben Gid'oni. ⁶¹His offering: a silver dish, its weight 130 sheqels; a silver basin, seventy sheqels by the sacred sheqel; the two of them full of fine flour mixed with oil, for a grain offering; ⁶²a gold ladle of ten sheqels, full of incense; ⁶³a bull from the herd; a ram; a year-old lamb as a burnt offering; ⁶⁴a he-goat from the flock as a decontamination; ⁶⁵and as a well-being sacrifice, two cattle, five rams, five he-goats, five year-old lambs. This was the offering of Abidan ben Gid'oni.

## Offerings by Dan, Asher, Naphtali

⁶⁶On the tenth day, the leader of the Danites, Ahi'ezer ben Ammishadday. ⁶⁷His offering: a silver dish, its weight 130 sheqels; a silver basin, seventy sheqels by the sanctuary sheqel; the two of them full of fine flour mixed with oil, for a grain offering; ⁶⁸a gold ladle of ten sheqels, full of incense; ⁶⁹a bull from the herd; a ram; a year-old lamb as a burnt offering; ⁷⁰a he-goat from the flock as a decontamination; ⁷¹and as a well-being sacrifice, two cattle, five rams, five he-goats, five year-old lambs. This was the offering of Ahi'ezer ben Ammishadday.

⁷²On the eleventh day, the leader of the Asherites, Pag'i'el ben Okran. ⁷³His offering: a silver dish, its weight 130 sheqels; a silver basin, seventy sheqels by the sanctuary sheqel; the two of them full of fine flour mixed with oil, for a grain offering; ⁷⁴a gold ladle of ten sheqels, full of incense; ⁷⁵a bull from the herd; a ram; a year-old lamb as a burnt offering; ⁷⁶a he-goat from the flock as a decontamination; ⁷⁷and as a well-being sacrifice, two cattle, five rams, five he-goats, five year-old lambs. This was the offering of Pag'i'el ben Okran.

⁷⁸On the twelfth day, the leader of the Naphtalites, Ahira ben Enan. ⁷⁹His offering: a silver dish, its weight 130 sheqels; a silver basin, seventy sheqels by the sanctuary sheqel; the two of them full of fine flour mixed with oil, for a grain offering; ⁸⁰a gold ladle of ten sheqels, full of incense; ⁸¹a bull from the herd; a ram;

a year-old lamb as a burnt offering; [82]a he-goat from the flock as a decontamination; [83]and as a well-being sacrifice, two cattle, five rams, five he-goats, five year-old lambs. This was the offering of Ahira ben Enan.

## Mosheh heard God speak

[84]This was the altar's dedication gift on the day of its anointing, from Yisra'el's leaders: silver dishes, twelve; silver basins, twelve; gold ladles, twelve; [85]130 sheqels of silver for each dish; seventy sheqels for each basin; all the silver of the containers, 2,400 sanctuary sheqels; [86]twelve gold ladles full of incense (ten sheqels each ladle by the sanctuary sheqel); all the gold of the ladles, 120 sheqels. [87]All the herd for the burnt offering, twelve bulls; rams, twelve; year-old lambs, twelve (and their grain offering); he-goats from the flock, twelve, as a decontamination. [88]All the herd for the well-being sacrifice: twenty-four bulls; rams: sixty; he-goats: sixty; year-old lambs: sixty. This was the altar's dedication gift after its anointing.

[89]When Mosheh came into the appointment tent to speak with him, he heard the voice speaking to him from above the expiation cover that was on the affirmation chest, from between the two sphinxes. He spoke to him.

**8** Yahweh spoke to Mosheh: [2]"Speak to Aharon: "When you put up the lamps, the seven lamps are to give light near the front of the candelabrum.'" [3]Aharon did so. He put up its lamps near the front of the candelabrum, as Yahweh ordered Mosheh. [4]This was the workmanship of the candelabrum: it was hammered work of gold, hammered work from its base to its petal. In accordance with the picture that Yahweh had let Mosheh see, so he made the candelabrum.

## The dedication of the Levites

[5]Yahweh spoke to Mosheh: [6]"Get the Levites from among the Yisra'elites and purify them. [7]You're to do this to them to purify them. Spatter decontamination water on them, and they are to pass a razor over their entire flesh

and wash their clothes, and they'll become pure. [8]They're to get a bull from the herd and its grain offering, fine flour mixed with oil, and you're to get a second bull from the herd as a decontamination.

[9]You're to present the Levites before the appointment tent and congregate the entire assembly of the Yisra'elites, [10]and present the Levites before Yahweh. The Yisra'elites are to lean their hands on the Levites, [11]and Aharon is to elevate the Levites as an elevation offering before Yahweh from the Yisra'elites, so they may be there to perform service for Yahweh. [12]The Levites are to lean their hands on the bulls' head. Make one as a decontamination and one as a burnt offering for Yahweh, to make expiation for the Levites.

[13]You're to get the Levites to stand before Aharon and before his sons and elevate them as an elevation offering for Yahweh. [14]You're to make the Levites distinct from among the Yisra'elites. The Levites are to be mine. [15]Afterwards, the Levites are to come to serve the appointment tent. You're to purify them and elevate them as an elevation offering, [16]because they're irrevocably given to me from among the Yisra'elites in place of the first issue of every womb, the firstborn of every one of the Yisra'elites. I've taken them for myself. [17]Because every firstborn among the Yisra'elites is mine, of human beings and of animals.

On the day I struck down every firstborn in the country of Misrayim, I made them sacred for myself. [18]I've taken the Levites in place of every firstborn of the Yisra'elites, [19]and given the Levites irrevocably to Aharon and to his sons from among the Yisra'elites to perform the Yisra'elites' service in the appointment tent and to make expiation for the Yisra'elites, so no epidemic will come on the Yisra'elites through the Yisra'elites' coming up to the sanctuary."

## The Levites' service and semi-retirement

[20]Mosheh, Aharon and the entire Yisra'elite assembly acted towards the Levites in accordance with all that Yahweh ordered Mosheh for the Levites. The Yisra'elites did so for them. [21]The Levites decontaminated themselves and washed their clothes, and Aharon elevated them as an elevation

offering before Yahweh, and made expiation for them to purify them. [22]Afterwards the Levites came to perform their services in the appointment tent before Aharon and before his sons. As Yahweh ordered Mosheh concerning the Levites, so they did for them.

[23]Yahweh spoke to Mosheh: [24]"This is how it is to be for the Levites. From the age of twenty-five years and upwards they're to come to do duty in the service of the appointment tent. [25]From the age of fifty years they're to go back from the duty of service. They will not serve any more. [26]One may minister to his brothers in the appointment tent by keeping watch, but they will not perform service. Thus you will do for the Levites regarding their charge.

**9** Yahweh spoke to Mosheh in the Sinay Wilderness in the second year of their getting out of the country of Misrayim, in the first month: [2]"The Yisra'elites are to make the Pesah [Passover] at its set time. [3]You're to make it on the fourteenth day of this month at twilight, at its set time in accordance with all its decrees and in accordance with all it rulings.' [4]So Mosheh spoke to the Yisra'elites about making the Pesah [5]and they made the Pesah in the first [month], on the fourteenth day of the month, at twilight, in the Sinay Wilderness. In accordance with all that Yahweh ordered Mosheh, so the Yisra'elites did.

## God's flexibility

[6]There were some men who were taboo through a [dead] person and couldn't make the Pesah on that day, so they drew near before Mosheh and before Aharon on that day. [7]Those men said to him, 'Though we're taboo through a [dead] person, why should we hold back from presenting Yahweh's offering at its set time among the Yisra'elites?' [8]Mosheh said to them 'Wait so I can listen to what Yahweh orders for you.'

[9]Yahweh spoke to Mosheh: [10]"Speak to the Yisra'elites: "When an individual person becomes taboo through a [dead] person or is on a long journey (one of you or of your future generations) and he makes Pesah for Yahweh, [11]they're to make it in the second month on the fourteenth day at twilight. With flatbread and bitters they're to eat it. [12]They will not let any of

it remain until morning and they will not break a bone of it: in accordance with every decree for the Pesah they will make it. [13]But the individual who is pure or hasn't been on a journey and leaves off from making the Pesah: that person shall be cut off from his kin, because he didn't present Yahweh's offering at its set time. That individual will carry his wrongdoing.

[14]When someone is a resident with you and makes the Pesah for Yahweh: in accordance with the decree for the Pesah and in accordance with the ruling concerning it, so he is to make it. There's to be one decree for you, both for the resident and for the native of the country.""

## The prompting of the cloud

[15]On the day they set up the dwelling, the cloud covered the dwelling belonging to the affirmation tent. In the evening it would be over the dwelling, like the appearance of fire, until morning. [16]So it would be regularly: the cloud would cover it, with the appearance of fire at night. [17]At the bidding of the cloud lifting from over the tent, after this the Yisra'elites would move on, while at the place where the cloud would dwell, there the Yisra'elites would camp. [18]At Yahweh's bidding the Yisra'elites would move on, and at Yahweh's bidding they would camp; through the entire time the cloud would dwell over the dwelling, they would camp.

[19]When the cloud stayed over the dwelling for a long time, the Yisra'elites would keep Yahweh's charge and not move on. [20]When it was the case that the cloud would be over the dwelling for a period of time, at Yahweh's bidding they would camp and at Yahweh's bidding they would move on. [21]When it was the case that the cloud was there from evening to morning, as the cloud lifted in the morning they would move on. Day or night, when the cloud would lift, they would move on.

[22]Whether two days or a month or some time, while the cloud stayed over the dwelling so as to dwell over it, the Yisra'elites would camp and would not move on, and when it went up they would move on. [23]At Yahweh's bidding they would camp and at Yahweh's bidding they would move on. They kept Yahweh's charge at Yahweh's bidding through Mosheh.

## The signal for the journey

**10** Yahweh spoke to Mosheh: ²'Make for yourself two silver trumpets. You're to make them of hammered work and they will be for you for the calling of the assembly and for the camps' moving on. ³They will sound out on them, and the entire assembly is to keep an appointment with you at the entrance of the appointment tent ⁴(if they sound out on one, the leaders – the heads of the Yisra'elite divisions – are to keep an appointment with you). ⁵You will sound a blast, and the camps that are to the east are to move on. ⁶You will sound a second blast, and the camps that are to the south are to move on. They will sound a blast for their setting out. ⁷When you call for them as a congregation, you will sound out but you won't give a blast. ⁸It will be Aharon's sons, the priests, who blow on the trumpets. They will be for you a permanent decree through your generations.

⁹When you come in battle in your country against someone who attacks you, you're to give a blast on the trumpets so you may be remembered before Yahweh your God and be delivered from your enemies. ¹⁰On your day of celebration, at your set times and at the beginning of your months, you're to sound out on the trumpets over your burnt offerings and over your well-being sacrifices. They will be for you a reminder before your God. I am Yahweh your God.'

¹¹In the second year, in the second month, on the twentieth of the month, the cloud went up from above the affirmation dwelling ¹²and the Yisra'elites moved on into their journeys from the Sinay Wilderness. Then the cloud dwelt in the Pa'ran Wilderness.

## The order of the march

¹³They moved on at the beginning at Yahweh's bidding through Mosheh. ¹⁴At the beginning the Yehudahites' standard moved on by their companies. Over its company was Nahshon ben Amminadab. ¹⁵Over the company of the Yissakarites' clan was Netan'el ben Tsu'ar. ¹⁶Over the company of the Zebulunites' clan was Eli'ab ben Helon. ¹⁷The dwelling would be taken down and the Gershonites and the Merarites (who carried the dwelling) would move on.

¹⁸The standard of Re'uben's camp would move on by their companies. Over its company was Elitsur ben Shede'ur. ¹⁹Over the company of the Shim'onites' clan was Shelumi'el ben Tsuri Shadday. ²⁰Over the company of the Gadites' clan was Elyasaph ben De'u'el. ²¹The Qehatites (who carried the sanctuary) would move on; people would set up the dwelling for when they came.

²²The standard of the Ephrayimites' camp would move on by their companies. Over its company was Elishama ben Ammihud. ²³Over the company of the Menashshites' clan was Gamli'el ben Pedah-tsur. ²⁴Over the company of the Binyaminites' clan was Abidan ben Gid'oni.

²⁵The standard of the Danites' camp would move on, bringing up the rear for all the camps by their companies. Over its company was Ahi'ezer ben Ammi Shadday. ²⁶Over the company of the Asherites' clan was Pag'i'el ben Okran. ²⁷Over the company of the Naphtalites' clan was Ahira ben Enan.

²⁸These were the Yisra'elites' ways of moving on by their companies. So they moved on.

²⁹Mosheh said to Hobab ben Re'u'el the Midyanite, Mosheh's father-in-law, 'We're moving on to the place of which Yahweh said, "I shall give it to you." Go with us and we'll bring good to you, because Yahweh has spoken of good things for Yisra'el.' ³⁰He said to him, 'I won't go. Instead I'll go to my country, to my homeland.'

³¹He said, 'Please don't abandon us, because of this: you know where we can camp in the wilderness. You will be our eyes. ³²Because you go with us, that good that Yahweh brings with us we'll bring to you.'

## On missing garlic

³³They moved on from Yahweh's mountain three days' journey, with Yahweh's pact chest moving on before them on the three days' journey to investigate a place to settle down for them, ³⁴and with Yahweh's cloud over them by day as they moved on from the camp. ³⁵When the chest moved on, Mosheh said:

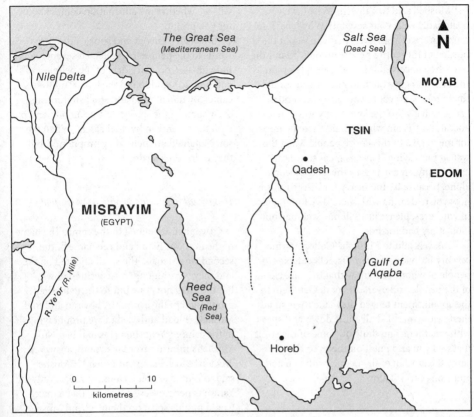

*Numbers 10: The wilderness*

Up, Yahweh, so your enemies disperse,
  so the people who are hostile to you flee from
    before you!

³⁶When it halted, he would say:

Go back, Yahweh,
  to the countless thousands of Yisraʾel!

**11** But the people became veritable complainers in Yahweh's ears about their bad fortune. Yahweh heard, and his anger raged. Yahweh's fire burned up among them and devoured the edge of the camp. ²The people cried out to Mosheh and Mosheh pleaded with Yahweh, and the fire died down. ³They named that place Tabʿerah ['Burning'] because Yahweh's fire had burned up among them.

⁴Now the other people that they had collected, who were among them, were full of longing, and the Yisraʾelites also again wailed and said, 'If only someone would give us meat to eat! ⁵We remember the fish that we could eat in Misrayim for nothing, the cucumbers, the melons, the leeks, the onions and the garlic, ⁶but now our throats are dry. There isn't anything before our eyes except this *maan*.' ⁷The *maan* was like coriander seed; its appearance was like the appearance of resin. ⁸The people went about and gathered it, ground it with millstones or pounded it in a mortar, and cooked it in a pot and made it into loaves. Its taste was like the taste of rich cream. ⁹When the dew came down on the camp at night, the *maan* would come down on it.

*Like a nurse carrying a baby*

¹⁰Mosheh heard the people wailing in their kin-groups, each person at the entrance of his tent. Yahweh's anger raged right up, and it was bad in Mosheh's eyes.

¹¹Mosheh said to Yahweh, 'Why have you dealt badly with your servant? Why have I not found grace in your eyes, that you've put the burden of this entire people on me? ¹²Am I the one who conceived this entire people or am I the one who gave birth to it, that you should say to me, "Carry it in your arms, as a nurse carries a baby", to the land that you swore to its ancestors? ¹³From where could there be meat for me to give to this entire people when they wail at me, saying "Give us meat so we can eat"? ¹⁴I myself can't carry this entire people alone, because it's too heavy for me. ¹⁵If this is how you're dealing with me, if I've found grace in your eyes, please just kill me, so I may not look at my bad fortune.'

¹⁶Yahweh said to Mosheh, 'Collect for me seventy individuals from Yisra'el's elders, people of whom you know that they are elders of the people and overseers of it. Get them to the appointment tent so they take their stand there with you. ¹⁷I shall come down and speak with you there, and draw off some of the spirit that's on you and put it on them, so they can carry the burden of the people with you and you won't carry it alone.

## Is Yahweh short-handed?

¹⁸To the people you're to say, "Make yourselves sacred for tomorrow and you will eat meat, because you've been wailing in Yahweh's ears, 'If only someone would give us meat to eat, because it was good for us in Misrayim.' Yahweh will give you meat, and you'll eat. ¹⁹You'll eat not one day and not two days and not five days and not ten days and not twenty days: ²⁰for a full month, till it comes out of your nose and it's loathsome to you, because you've rejected Yahweh who is among you, and you've wailed before him, saying 'Why oh why did we come out of Misrayim?'"

²¹Mosheh said, 'The people that I'm in the middle of are 600,000 men on foot. You said, "I'll give them meat to eat for a full month." ²²Can a flock and a herd be slaughtered for them so that one could find it for them? Or can all the fish in the sea be collected for them so that one could find it for them?' ²³Yahweh said to Mosheh, 'Is Yahweh's hand short? Now you

will see whether my affirmation comes about for you or not.'

²⁴Mosheh went out and spoke Yahweh's words to the people. He collected seventy individuals from the elders of the people and got them to stand round the tent. ²⁵Yahweh came down in a cloud and spoke to him, and drew some of the spirit that was on him and put it on the seventy individual elders. When the spirit alighted on them, they prophesied, but they didn't do it again.

## If only all Yahweh's people were prophets

²⁶Two men remained in the camp. The name of the first was Eldad and the name of the second was Medad. The spirit alighted on them and they were among those written down, but they had not gone out to the tent. They prophesied in the camp. ²⁷A boy ran and told Mosheh, 'Eldad and Medad are prophesying in the camp.' ²⁸Yehoshua [Joshua] ben Nun, Mosheh's minister from his youth, answered: 'My lord Mosheh, restrain them!' ²⁹Mosheh said to him, 'Are you jealous for me? If only all Yahweh's people were prophets, that Yahweh would put his spirit on them!' ³⁰And Mosheh joined the camp, he and Yisra'el's elders.

³¹Then a wind moved on from Yahweh, brought quail across from the sea and dropped them over the camp, quite a day's journey on one side and quite a day's journey on the other side, all round the camp, and quite a metre deep on the face of the earth. ³²The people set to, all that day and all night and all the next day, and collected the quail. The person who got little collected a hundred barrels. They spread and spread them for themselves all round the camp. ³³But while the meat was still between their teeth, before it was chewed, Yahweh's anger raged against the people, and Yahweh struck the people down in a very great calamity.

³⁴They named that place Qibrot Hatta'avah ['Longing Graves'] because they buried there the people who had been longing. ³⁵From Qibrot Hatta'avah the people moved on to Hatserot ['Settlements'].

**12** They were at Hatserot and Miryam spoke against Mosheh, with Aharon, about the matter of the Kushite [Sudanese] wife he had taken, because he'd taken a Kushite wife. ²They said, 'Has Yahweh really spoken only through Mosheh? He's also spoken through us, hasn't he.' And Yahweh heard. ³Now Mosheh as a man was very ordinary, more so than any human being who has been on the face of the earth.

## Mosheh's supreme authority

⁴Yahweh suddenly said to Mosheh, to Aharon and to Miryam, 'Go out, the three of you, to the appointment tent.' The three of them went out, ⁵and Yahweh came down in the cloud pillar, stood at the tent entrance, and called for Aharon and Miryam. The two of them went out ⁶and he said, 'Listen to my words, please. If there's a prophet of yours, I, Yahweh, make myself known to him in a vision, I speak to him in a dream. ⁷Not so my servant Mosheh. In my entire household he's trustworthy. ⁸I speak to him mouth to mouth, in a vision and not in conundrums. He beholds Yahweh's form. So why were you not afraid to speak against my servant, against Mosheh?' ⁹So Yahweh's anger raged against them and he went, ¹⁰and as the cloud departed from above the tent, there – Miryam was made scaly, like snow. Aharon turned his face to Miryam – there, she was made scaly. ¹¹Aharon said to Mosheh, 'My lord, please, don't hold against us the wrong with which we acted stupidly, the wrong which we did. ¹²Please, she mustn't be like someone dead, whose flesh is half eaten away when he comes out of his mother's womb.' ¹³So Mosheh cried out to Yahweh, 'God, please, heal her, please!' ¹⁴Yahweh said to Mosheh, 'Were her father simply to spit in her face, would she not be in disgrace for seven days? She's to shut herself outside the camp for seven days, and afterwards join.' ¹⁵So Miryam shut herself outside the camp for seven days, but the people didn't move on until Miryam joined. ¹⁶Afterwards the people moved on from Hatserot and camped in the Pa'ran Wilderness.

## A spy story

**13** Yahweh spoke to Mosheh: ²'Send yourself people so they can investigate the country of Kena'an [Canaan], which I'm giving to the Yisra'elites. You're to send one person each per ancestral clan, each one a leader among them.' ³So Mosheh sent them from the Pa'ran Wilderness, at Yahweh's bidding. All of them were people who were leaders of the Yisra'elites. ⁴These are their names:

for the clan of Re'uben, Shammua ben Zakkur;
⁵for the clan of Shim'on, Shaphat ben Hori;
⁶for the clan of Yehudah, Kaleb (Caleb) ben Yephunneh;
⁷for the clan of Yissakar, Yig'al ben Yoseph;
⁸for the clan of Ephrayim, Hoshea ben Nun;
⁹for the clan of Binyamin, Palti ben Raphu;
¹⁰for the clan of Zebulun, Gaddi'el ben Sodi;
¹¹for the clan of Yoseph (for the clan of Menashsheh), Gaddi ben Susi;
¹²for the clan of Dan, Ammi'el ben Gemalli;
¹³for the clan of Asher, Setur ben Mika'el;
¹⁴for the clan of Naphtali, Nahbi ben Vophsi;
¹⁵for the clan of Gad, Ge'u'el ben Maki.

¹⁶These are the names of the people that Mosheh sent to investigate the country. (Mosheh called Hoshea ben Nun 'Yehoshua'.)

¹⁷Mosheh sent them to investigate the country of Kena'an and said to them, 'Go up here into the Negeb, then go up into the highland. ¹⁸You're to look at the country: what's it like? The people that lives in it: is it strong? Is it weak? Is it few or many? ¹⁹What's the country like that it's living in? Is it good or bad? What are the towns that it lives in – in encampments or in fortifications? ²⁰What's the country like? Is it rich or poor? Are there trees in it or are there not? You're to assert your strength, and get some of the country's fruit.' The time was the time of the first of the grapes.

## The good news and the bad news

²¹So they went up and investigated the country from the Tsin Wilderness as far as Rehob (Lebo Hamat). ²²They went up into the Negeb and came as far as Hebron. (Ahiman, Sheshay and Talmay, the descendants of Anaq, were there; Hebron was built seven years before Tso'an in Misrayim.) ²³They came as far as Cluster Wadi, and cut from there a branch

and a cluster of grapes (they carried it on a frame by means of two of them), and some pomegranates and some figs. [24]They called that place Cluster Wadi on account of the cluster that the Yisraelites cut from there. [25]They came back from investigating the country at the end of forty days.

[26]So they went, and then came to Mosheh and to Aharon and to the entire assembly of the Yisraelites at Qadesh in the Pa'ran Wilderness, brought back word to them and to the entire assembly, and let them see the country's fruit. [27]They recounted to him, 'We came to the country that you sent us to. Yes, it flows with milk and syrup, and this is its fruit. [28]Only, the people living in the country is substantial, and the towns are fortified, very large. Also, we saw the descendants of Anaq there. [29]Amaleq is living in the Negeb region, the Hittites, Yebusites and Amorites are living in the highland, and the Kena'anites are living by the sea and by the side of the Yarden [Jordan].'

[30]Kaleb hushed the people before Mosheh. He said, 'Let's simply go up and take possession of it, because we can definitely prevail against it.'

## Listen to the bad news

[31]But the people who went up with him said, 'We can't go up against the people, because it's stronger than us', [32]and they put out criticism of the country that they had investigated to the Yisraelites: 'The country that we passed through to investigate is a country that devours the people living in it, and the entire people that we saw within it are people of stature. [33]We saw the Nephilim ['Fallen'] there (the Anaqites were from the Nephilim). In our eyes we were like grasshoppers, and so we were in their eyes.'

**14** The entire assembly lifted up their voice and gave it out, and the people wailed that night. [2]All the Yisraelites protested against Mosheh and against Aharon. The entire assembly said to them, 'If only we had died in the country of Misrayim or if only we had died in this wilderness! [3]Why is Yahweh bringing us into this country to fall by the sword? Our wives and our little ones will become plunder. Wouldn't it be good for us to go back to Misrayim?' [4]They said one to another, 'Let's appoint a head, and go back to Misrayim.'

[5]Mosheh and Aharon fell on their faces before the entire assembled congregation of the Yisraelites. [6]Yehoshua ben Nun and Kaleb ben Yephunneh from the people who had investigated the country tore their clothes [7]and said to the entire assembly of the Yisraelites: 'The country that we passed through to investigate it is a very, very good country. [8]If Yahweh delights in us, he will bring us to this country and give it to us, a country that flows with milk and syrup. [9]Only you're not to rebel against Yahweh. You're not to be afraid of the people of the country, because they're our bread, their shade has departed from over them, but Yahweh is with us. Don't be afraid of them.'

## Mosheh uses his usual argument

[10]But the entire assembly said to pelt them with stones, while Yahweh's splendour appeared in the appointment tent to all the Yisraelites, [11]and Yahweh said to Mosheh, 'How long will this people disdain me? How long will they not put their trust in me, for all the signs I've done among them? [12]I'll strike it down with an epidemic and dispossess it, and make you into a bigger and more numerous nation than it.'

[13]Mosheh said to Yahweh, 'But the Misrayimites will hear, because you brought this people up by your energy from among them, [14]and they'll tell the people living in this country. They've heard that you, Yahweh, are among this people, you Yahweh who've appeared in plain sight with your cloud standing over them, you who go before them in a cloud pillar by day and in a fire pillar by night. [15]You can put this people to death like one man, but the nations that have heard report of you will say, [16]"Because Yahweh couldn't bring this people into the country that he swore to them, he's slaughtered them in the wilderness."

[17]So now, may my Lord's energy be great as you spoke: [18]"Yahweh, long-tempered and big in commitment, carrying waywardness and rebellion, but he certainly doesn't treat people as free of guilt, attending to parents' waywardness in connection with children, with thirds and with fourths." [19]Please pardon this people's waywardness in accordance with the greatness of your commitment from Misrayim even as far as here.'

*Pardon but punishment*

²⁰Yahweh said, 'I pardon, in accordance with your words. ²¹Yet as I live and as Yahweh's splendour fills the entire world, ²²because all the people who have seen my splendour and my signs that I did in Misrayim and in the wilderness have tested me these ten times and not listened to my voice, ²³if they see the country that I swore to their ancestors . . .

None who disdained me will see it. ²⁴But my servant Kaleb, as a consequence of the fact that there was another spirit with him – he fully followed after me. I shall bring him into the country that he came to, and his offspring will take possession of it. ²⁵Since the Amaleqites and the Kena'anites live in the valley, tomorrow turn your face and move on for yourselves into the wilderness by the Reed Sea road.'

²⁶So Yahweh spoke to Mosheh and to Aharon: ²⁷'How long for this bad assembly that protest against me? I've listened to the Yisra'elites' protests that they utter against me. ²⁸Say to them: "As I live (Yahweh's declaration), if I don't . . .

As you spoke in my ears, so I shall do to you. ²⁹In this wilderness your carcases will fall, the entire register of you by your entire number, from the age of twenty years and upwards, who have protested against me. ³⁰If you come into the country that I lifted up my hand [in an oath] to let you dwell in it, except Kaleb ben Yephunneh and Yehoshua ben Nun . . .

³¹Your little ones whom you said would become plunder – I shall bring them in. They will know the country that you've rejected. ³²But your carcases – you will fall in this wilderness.

*A useless change of mind*

³³While your children are shepherding in the wilderness for forty years, they will carry your whoring, until your carcases come to an end in the wilderness. ³⁴In the wilderness, for the days that you investigated the country, forty, one day each per year you will carry your wayward acts, forty years. You will know my antagonism. ³⁵I, Yahweh, have spoken. If I don't do this to this entire bad assembly that are making an appointment against me . . . In

this wilderness they will come to an end. There they will die."'

³⁶The people whom Mosheh had sent to investigate the country and who had come back and made the entire assembly protest against him by putting out criticism about the country: ³⁷the people who put out the bad criticism of the country died in an epidemic before Yahweh. ³⁸But Yehoshua ben Nun and Kaleb ben Yephunneh lived on, of those people who went to investigate the country.

³⁹Mosheh spoke these words to all the Yisra'elites, and the people took up great grieving. ⁴⁰They started early in the morning and went up to the mountain ridge, saying 'Here we are, we'll go up to the place that Yahweh said, because we did wrong.' ⁴¹Mosheh said, 'Why are you contravening Yahweh's bidding when that won't succeed? ⁴²Don't go up, because Yahweh is not among you. Then you won't take a beating before your enemies. ⁴³Because the Amaleqites and the Kena'anites will be there before you and you'll fall by the sword. Because of the fact that you've turned back from following Yahweh, Yahweh won't be with you.' ⁴⁴They insisted on going up to the mountain ridge, but Yahweh's pact chest and Mosheh didn't move away from within the camp, ⁴⁵and the Amaleqites and the Kena'anites who were living in that highland came down, and struck them down and crushed them as far as Hormah.

*Offerings in the country where they will settle*

**15** Yahweh spoke to Mosheh: ²'Speak to the Yisra'elites: "When you come into the country where you will have your settlements, which I'm giving you, ³and you make a gift offering to Yahweh, a burnt offering or a sacrifice, in fulfilling a pledge or as a free offering or at your set times, to make a nice smell for Yahweh, from the herd or from the flock: ⁴the person presenting his offering to Yahweh is to present a grain offering of fine flour, a tenth, mixed with a quarter of a gallon of oil. ⁵You're also to make wine into a libation, a quarter of a gallon, with the burnt offering or sacrifice, for each sheep. ⁶Or for a ram you're to make a grain offering of fine flour, two tenths, mixed with oil, a third of a gallon, ⁷and you're to present wine for a libation, a third of a gallon, a nice smell for Yahweh.

⁸When you make an animal from the herd into a burnt offering or a sacrifice to fulfil a pledge or a well-being sacrifice for Yahweh, ⁹they're to present with the animal from the herd a grain offering of fine flour, three tenths, mixed with oil, half a gallon. ¹⁰And you're to present wine as a libation, half a gallon, as a gift offering, a nice smell for Yahweh.

¹¹It's to be done in this way with each ox or with each ram or with a young one among the sheep or among the goats, ¹²in accordance with the number that you make. In this way you're to make it for each in accordance with their number. ¹³Every native is to make these in this way in presenting a gift offering, a nice smell for Yahweh.

## The first of the baking

¹⁴When someone who resides with you as a resident, or who is among you through your generations, makes a gift offering, a nice smell for Yahweh: as you make it, so the congregation is to make it. ¹⁵One decree for you and for someone who is a resident, a permanent decree through your generations: it will be the same for you and for the resident, before Yahweh. ¹⁶There will be one instruction and one ruling for you and for the person who is a resident with you."'

¹⁷Yahweh spoke to Mosheh: ¹⁸'Speak to the Yisra'elites: "When you come into the country where I'm bringing you, ¹⁹when you eat of the bread of the country, you're to take up a contribution for Yahweh. ²⁰The first of your baked goods (a loaf) you're to take up as a contribution for Yahweh. Like the contribution from the threshing floor, so you're to take it up. ²¹From the first of your baked goods you're to give a contribution for Yahweh, through your generations.

²²When you make a mistake and don't act on any of these orders that Yahweh has spoken to Mosheh, ²³anything that Yahweh ordered you by means of Mosheh, from the day that Yahweh ordered it and onwards through your generations: ²⁴if it was done by mistake, away from the assembly's eyes, the entire assembly is to make a bull from the herd into a burnt offering, as a nice smell for Yahweh, with its

grain offering and its libation, in accordance with the ruling, and a he-goat from the flock as a decontamination. ²⁵The priest is to make expiation for the entire assembly of the Yisra'elites and it will be pardoned them, because it was a mistake and they've brought their offering as a gift offering for Yahweh and as their decontamination before Yahweh, for their mistake. ²⁶It will be pardoned for the entire assembly of the Yisra'elites and for the person who is a resident among them, because for the entire people it was by mistake.

## The intentional and the unintentional

²⁷If an individual does wrong by mistake, he's to present a year-old she-goat as a decontamination. ²⁸The priest is to make expiation for the person who made the mistake by his wrongdoing (by mistake), before Yahweh, to make expiation for him, so it may be pardoned for him. ²⁹The native among the Yisra'elites, and for the person who is a resident among you: there's to be one instruction for you for one who acts by mistake.

³⁰But the person who acts with hand upraised, from natives or residents: Yahweh is the one he's insulting. That person shall be cut off from among his people, ³¹because it's Yahweh's word he's scorned and Yahweh's order he's contravened. That person shall absolutely be cut off. There's waywardness on him."'

³²The Yisra'elites were in the wilderness and they found someone collecting wood on the sabbath day. ³³The people who found him collecting wood presented him to Mosheh, to Aharon and to the entire assembly, ³⁴and they placed him under keep because it had not been specified what should be done to him. ³⁵Yahweh said to Mosheh, 'The person must absolutely be put to death by the entire assembly pelting him with stones outside the camp.' ³⁶So the entire assembly took him outside the camp and pelted him with stones so he died, as Yahweh ordered Mosheh.

³⁷Yahweh said to Mosheh: ³⁸'Speak to the Yisra'elites and say to them: they're to make themselves a fringe on the corners of their clothes, through their generations. They're to put on the hem's fringe a purple cord. ³⁹You will have the fringe and look at it, and be

mindful of all Yahweh's orders and do them, and not investigate the things you whore after, following your mind and your eyes, [40]in order that you may be mindful and may act on all my orders, and be sacred for your God. [41]I am Yahweh your God who got you out of the country of Misrayim to be God for you. I am Yahweh your God.'

## Ambition

**16** Qorah ben Yitshar, son of Qehat son of Levi, got both Datan and Abiram, sons of Eli'ab, and On ben Pelet, son of Re'uben, [2]and they rose up before Mosheh with 250 men from the Yisra'elites, leaders of the assembly, people called for by the assembly, men with a name. [3]They congregated against Mosheh and against Aharon and said to them, 'You have too much, when the entire assembly, all of them, are sacred, and Yahweh is among them! Why do you raise yourselves above Yahweh's congregation?' [4]Mosheh heard, and fell on his face. [5]He spoke to Qorah and to his entire group: 'In the morning Yahweh can let it be acknowledged who is his and who is sacred, and he can have them draw near to him. The one he chooses is the one he will have draw near to him. [6]Do this. Get yourself pans (Qorah and his entire group) [7]and put fire in them and place incense on them before Yahweh, tomorrow. The person whom Yahweh chooses, he's the sacred one. You have too much, sons of Levi.'

[8]Mosheh said to Qorah: 'Please listen, you Levites. [9]Is it too little for you that Yisra'el's God has made you distinct from the Yisra'elite assembly by having you draw near to him to perform the service of Yahweh's dwelling and to stand before the assembly to minister to them? [10]He's had you draw near, you and all your brothers the Levites with you, and you seek the priesthood also. [11]Therefore you and your entire group are making an appointment against Yahweh. And what is Aharon that you protest against him?'

[12]Mosheh sent to call for Datan and Abiram the sons of Eli'ab but they said, 'We won't go up. [13]Is it too little that you brought us up from a country flowing with milk and syrup to let us die in the wilderness, that you also continue to play the ruler over us? [14]Certainly you haven't brought us into a country flowing with milk and syrup, and given us a domain of fields and vineyards. Will you gouge out these people's eyes? We won't go up.'

## Yahweh must judge

[15]It was very infuriating to Mosheh. He said to Yahweh, 'Don't turn your face to their offering. I haven't taken one donkey from them. I haven't dealt badly with one of them.' [16]Mosheh said to Qorah, 'You and your entire company, be before Yahweh, you and they and Aharon, tomorrow. [17]Get, each person, his pan, put incense on it and present it before Yahweh, each person his pan, 250 pans, and you and Aharon each his pan.' [18]They got, each person, his pan, put fire on them and placed incense on them, and stood at the entrance of the appointment tent, as did Mosheh and Aharon. [19]Qorah congregated the entire assembly against them at the entrance of the appointment tent.

Yahweh's splendour appeared to the entire assembly, [20]and Yahweh spoke to Mosheh and to Aharon: [21]'Make yourselves distinct from among this assembly so I may finish them off in a moment!' [22]They fell on their faces and said, 'God, the God of the spirits of all flesh! One person does wrong. Are you furious with the entire assembly?'

[23]So Yahweh spoke to Mosheh: [24]'Speak to the assembly: "Go up from round the dwelling of Qorah, Datan and Abiram."' [25]Mosheh got up and went to Datan and Abiram, and the Yisra'elite elders followed him. [26]He spoke to the assembly: 'Please move away from near the tents of these faithless people and don't touch anything that belongs to them, so you don't get swept away because of all their wrongdoings.' [27a]So they went up from near the dwelling of Qorah, Datan and Abiram, all round.

## A frightening act of creation

[27b]Now Datan and Abiram had come out, standing at the entrance of their tents, with their wives, their children and their little ones. [28]Mosheh said, 'By this you will acknowledge

that it was Yahweh who sent me to do all these things, that they're not from my mind. ²⁹If these people die as all human beings die, and what is appointed for all human beings comes to them, then it was not Yahweh who sent me. ³⁰But if Yahweh performs an act of creation, and the ground opens its mouth and swallows them and all who belong to them so that they go down to She'ol alive, then you will know that these men have disdained Yahweh.'

³¹As he finished speaking all these words, the ground that was underneath them split, ³²and the earth opened its mouth and swallowed them and their households, all who belonged to Qorah and all the property. ³³Those people and all that belonged to them went down alive to She'ol. The earth covered over them. They perished from among the congregation. ³⁴All Yisra'el that was round them fled at the sound they made, because they said, 'So that the earth doesn't swallow us!' ³⁵And fire came out from Yahweh and devoured the 250 people presenting the incense.

³⁶Yahweh spoke to Mosheh: ³⁷'Say to El'azar ben Aharon the priest that he's to take up the pans from within what is burned and scatter the fire some way away, because they've become sacred. ³⁸The pans of these who did wrong at the cost of their lives: they're to make them into beaten sheets as plating for the altar, because people have presented them before Yahweh and they've become sacred. They're to be a sign for the Yisra'elites.'

## Fury goes out from Yahweh

³⁹So El'azar the priest got the copper pans that the people who had been burned up had presented, and beat them into plating for the altar ⁴⁰as a reminder for the Yisra'elites that no one who is an outsider who is not from Aharon's offspring is to draw near to offer incense before Yahweh, so he won't become like Qorah and his company, as Yahweh spoke through Mosheh.

⁴¹The entire assembly of the Yisra'elites protested against Mosheh and against Aharon next day: 'You put Yahweh's people to death!' ⁴²When the assembly congregated against Mosheh and against Aharon, they turned their face to the appointment tent and there – the cloud covered it and Yahweh's splendour

appeared. ⁴³Mosheh and Aharon came to the front of the appointment tent, ⁴⁴and Yahweh spoke to Mosheh: ⁴⁵'Get up from among this assembly, so I may finish them off in a moment!' They fell on their faces, ⁴⁶and Mosheh said to Aharon, 'Get the pan and put fire on it from on the altar and place incense and take it quickly to the assembly and make expiation for them, because fury has gone out from before Yahweh; the epidemic has started.'

⁴⁷Aharon got it, as Mosheh spoke, and ran into the middle of the congregation. There, the epidemic had started among the people. He put on the incense and made expiation for the people. ⁴⁸He stood between the dead and the living, and the epidemic held back. ⁴⁹The people who were dead through the epidemic were 14,700, apart from the people who were dead on account of Qorah. ⁵⁰Aharon went back to Mosheh at the entrance of the appointment tent when the epidemic had held back.

## The staff that budded

**17** Yahweh spoke to Mosheh: ²'Speak to the Yisra'elites and get from them a staff each per ancestral household from all their leaders, for the ancestral households, twelve staffs. You're to write each individual's name on his staff, ³and write Aharon's name on Levi's staff, because there's one staff for the head of their ancestral household. ⁴Set them down in the appointment tent before the affirmation, where I make an appointment to meet with you. ⁵The individual whom I choose, his staff will bud, and I shall rid myself of the protests of the Yisra'elites which they're uttering against you.'

⁶Mosheh spoke to the Yisra'elites, and all their leaders gave him one staff each per leader, twelve staffs for their ancestral households, with Aharon's staff among their staffs. ⁷Mosheh set the staffs down before Yahweh in the appointment tent. ⁸Next day Mosheh went into the appointment tent and there, Aharon's staff belonging to Levi's household had budded. It had put out buds and issued blossoms and dealt almonds. ⁹Mosheh took out all the staffs from before Yahweh to all the Yisra'elites, and they looked and got each person his staff.

¹⁰Yahweh said to Mosheh, 'Put Aharon's staff back before the affirmation for keeping as a sign for the rebels, so their protests at me may finish, so they don't die.' ¹¹Mosheh did as Yahweh ordered him; so he did. ¹²But the Yisra'elites said to Mosheh, 'Here, we breathe our last, we're lost, all of us are lost! ¹³Anyone who comes near Yahweh's dwelling at all will die. Have we come to an end, breathing our last?'

## Provision for the priests

**18** Yahweh said to Aharon, 'You, your sons and your ancestral household with you carry the sanctuary's waywardness, and you and your sons with you carry your priesthood's waywardness. ²Also, present with you your brothers, the clan of Levi, your ancestral clan, so they may join [lavah] with you and minister to you, as you and your sons with you are before the affirmation tent. ³They're to keep your charge and the charge of the entire tent, yet they're not to draw near to the articles of the sanctuary or to the altar, so both they and you don't die. ⁴They're to join with you and keep charge of the appointment tent, in relation to all the service of the tent. No outsider is to draw near to you. ⁵You're to keep charge of the sanctuary and charge of the altar, so there won't be fury on Yisra'el again. ⁶I myself, I here take your brothers the Levites from among the Yisra'elites for you as a gift given to Yahweh to perform the service of the appointment tent ⁷while you and your sons with you keep your priesthood in relation to every matter involving the altar and what is inside the curtain. So you will serve. I make your priesthood a service that is a gift. But the outsider who comes near is to be put to death.'

⁸Yahweh spoke to Aharon: 'I myself: I here give you charge of my contributions, in relation to all the sacred things belonging to the Yisra'elites. To you I give them in connection with your anointing, and to your sons, as a permanent decree. ⁹This will be yours from the things that are especially sacred, from the fire: every offering of theirs, with every grain offering of theirs, with every decontamination of theirs and with every reparation of theirs, which they render to me as especially sacred things. It belongs to you and to your sons.

¹⁰You may eat of the especially sacred things. Any male may eat it. It's to be sacred for you.

## The sacred gifts

¹¹And this will be yours: the contribution that they give, including every elevation offering by the Yisra'elites, I give them to you and to your sons and to your daughters with you, as a permanent decree. Anyone who is pure in your household may eat it. ¹²All the "fat" of fresh oil and all the "fat" of new wine, and grain: the first of them, which they give to Yahweh, I give them to you. ¹³The first products of everything that will be in their country which they bring to Yahweh will be yours. Anyone who is pure in your household may eat them.

¹⁴Everything devoted in Yisra'el will be yours. ¹⁵Every opener of the womb of any being that people present to Yahweh, among human beings and among animals, will be yours; however, you will definitely redeem the firstborn of a human being, and you will redeem the firstborn of a pure animal. ¹⁶His redemption: at one month old you're to redeem at the evaluation of five silver sheqels by the sanctuary sheqel (it is twenty grams). ¹⁷However, the firstborn of an ox or the firstborn of a sheep or the firstborn of a goat you will not redeem. They're sacred. You're to toss their blood on the altar and burn their fat into smoke as a gift offering, as a nice smell for Yahweh. ¹⁸But their flesh will be yours; like the breast of the elevation offering and the right thigh, it will be yours.

¹⁹Every contribution of things that are sacred that the Yisra'elites take up for Yahweh I give to you, and to your sons and to your daughters with you, as a permanent decree. It's a permanent salt pact before Yahweh for you and for your offspring with you.'

## The tithes

²⁰Yahweh said to Aharon, 'In their country you will not have a domain. There will be no share for you among them. I am your share, your domain, among the Yisra'elites. ²¹And to the Levites I here give every tenth

in Yisra'el as a domain in return for their service that they're performing, the service of the appointment tent. ²²The Yisra'elites will no more draw near the appointment tent, carrying wrongdoing that would mean they die. ²³The Levite – he will perform the service of the appointment tent, but they – they will carry their waywardness (a permanent decree through your generations). But among the Yisra'elites they will not receive a domain, ²⁴because the Yisra'elites' tenth, which they take up for Yahweh as a contribution, I give to the Levites as a domain. That's why I've said regarding them, among the Yisra'elites they will not receive a domain.'

²⁵Yahweh spoke to Mosheh: ²⁶'And to the Levites you're to speak and to say to them: "When you get from the Yisra'elites the tenth which I've given you from them as your domain, you're to take up from it a tenth of the tenth as a contribution for Yahweh. ²⁷It will be deemed for you as your contribution, like the grain from the threshing floor and like the fullness from the vat. ²⁸So you yourselves are also to take up Yahweh's contribution from all your tenths which you get from the Yisra'elites, and you're to give Yahweh's contribution from them to Aharon the priest. ²⁹From all your gifts you're to take up the entire contribution for Yahweh from it, the sacred part of it from all its 'fat.'"

³⁰You're to say to them, "When you take up its 'fat' from it, it will be deemed for the Levites like the yield of the threshing floor and the yield of the vat. ³¹You may eat it in any place, you and your household, because it's wages for you in return for your service in the appointment tent. ³²You won't carry any wrongdoing on account of it when you've taken up its 'fat' from it. But you will not treat the sacred things of the Yisra'elites as ordinary, so you don't die."'

## Death defiles

**19** Yahweh spoke to Mosheh and to Aharon: ²'This is a decree of instruction that Yahweh has ordered: "Speak to the Yisra'elites, so that they get you a red cow that's whole, one in which there's no defect and on which no yoke has come. ³You're to give it to El'azar the priest and they're to take it outside the camp and slaughter it before him.

⁴El'azar the priest is to get some of its blood with his finger and spatter some of its blood seven times in front, before the appointment tent.

⁵They're to burn the cow before his eyes; they're to burn its skin, its flesh and its blood, along with its intestines. ⁶The priest is to get cedar wood, hyssop and scarlet yarn, and throw them into the middle of the fire burning the cow. ⁷The priest is to wash his clothes and bathe his flesh in water, and afterwards to go into the camp. The priest will be taboo until the evening ⁸and the person who burned it – he's to wash his clothes in water and bathe his flesh in water and he'll be taboo until the evening.

⁹A person who's pure is to gather the cow's ashes and set them down outside the camp in a pure place. The assembly of the Yisra'elites is to have them for keeping as water for flowing. It will be a decontamination. ¹⁰The one who gathers the cow's ashes is to wash his clothes and he will be taboo until the evening. It will be a permanent decree for the Yisra'elites and for the person who is a resident among you.

¹¹Someone who touches the dead body of any human person will be taboo for seven days. ¹²If he decontaminates himself with it on the third day and on the seventh day, he will become pure. If he doesn't decontaminate himself on the third day and on the seventh day, he will not become pure. ¹³Anyone who touches the dead body of a human person who dies and doesn't decontaminate himself makes Yahweh's dwelling taboo. That person shall be cut off from Yisra'el. Because the water for flowing hasn't been tossed over him, he will be taboo. His taboo will still be on him.

## Purification from defilement

¹⁴This is the instruction. When a human being dies in a tent, anyone going into the tent and anyone who's in the tent will be taboo for seven days. ¹⁵Every open container with no lid fastened on it is taboo. ¹⁶Anyone who touches on the face of the fields someone run through by the sword or someone who has died or a human bone or a grave will be taboo for seven days.

¹⁷They're to get for the taboo person some of the ashes from the decontamination burning and put fresh water on it in a container.

<sup>18</sup>A pure person is to get hyssop and dip it in the water and spatter it on the tent and on all the containers and on the individuals who were there and on the one who touched the bone or the person run through or the person who died or the grave.

<sup>19</sup>The pure person is to spatter it on the taboo person on the third day and on the seventh day so he will decontaminate him on the seventh day. He's to wash his clothes and bathe in water, and he will become pure in the evening. <sup>20</sup>An individual who becomes taboo and doesn't decontaminate himself: that person shall be cut off from among the congregation, because he has made Yahweh's sanctuary taboo. The water for flowing hasn't been tossed over him. He's taboo. <sup>21</sup>It's to be a permanent decree for them.

The one who spatters the water for flowing is to wash his clothes. One who touches the water for flowing will be taboo until the evening. <sup>22</sup>Everything that the taboo person touches will become taboo and the person who touches him will become taboo until the evening.'"

## Mosheh's one mistake

**20** The Yisra'elites, the entire assembly, came to the Tsin Wilderness in the first month, and the people lived at Qadesh. Miryam died there and was buried there.

<sup>2</sup>But there was no water for the assembly, and they congregated against Mosheh and against Aharon. <sup>3</sup>The people got into an argument with Mosheh: 'If only we had breathed our last when our brothers breathed their last before Yahweh! <sup>4</sup>Why have you brought Yahweh's congregation into this wilderness to die there, us and our animals? <sup>5</sup>Why did you get us to go up from Misrayim to bring us to this bad place, not a place of seed or fig or vine or pomegranate? And there's no water to drink.'

<sup>6</sup>Mosheh and Aharon came from before the congregation to the entrance of the appointment tent and fell on their faces. Yahweh's splendour appeared to them <sup>7</sup>and Yahweh spoke to Mosheh: <sup>8</sup>'Get the staff and congregate the assembly, you and Aharon your brother, and speak to the cliff before their eyes and it will give its water; you will make water come out of the cliff for them and provide drink for the assembly and their animals.' <sup>9</sup>So Mosheh got the staff from before Yahweh as he ordered him, <sup>10</sup>and Mosheh and Aharon gathered the congregation before the cliff, and he said to them, 'Please listen, you rebels! Are we to make water come out of this cliff for you?'

<sup>11</sup>Mosheh lifted up his hand and struck the cliff with his staff, twice. Much water came out, and the assembly and their animals drank. <sup>12</sup>But Yahweh said to Mosheh and to Aharon, 'Because you didn't trust in me so as to make me sacred before the Yisra'elites' eyes, therefore you won't bring this congregation into the country that I'm giving them.'

<sup>13</sup>That's Meribah ['Argument'] Water, where the Yisra'elites got into an argument with Yahweh, and he showed his sacredness among them.

## Seeking to live peacefully

<sup>14</sup>Mosheh sent envoys from Qadesh to the king of Edom: 'Your brother Yisra'el has said this: you yourself know all the hardship that has befallen us. <sup>15</sup>Our ancestors went down into Misrayim and we lived in Misrayim for a long time, but the Misrayimites dealt badly with us and our ancestors. <sup>16</sup>We cried out to Yahweh and he listened to our voice. He sent an envoy and got us out of Misrayim. So here we are, in Qadesh, a town on the edge of your border. <sup>17</sup>May we please pass through your country. We won't pass through field or through vineyard, and we won't drink water from wells. We'll go along the King's Road. We won't turn off right or left till we pass through your border.'

<sup>18</sup>But Edom said to him, 'You're not to pass through me or I'll come out with the sword to meet you.' <sup>19</sup>The Yisra'elites said to him, 'We'll go up by the causeway. If we drink your water, I and my livestock, I'll give you its price. It'll be nothing as we'll pass through only on foot.' <sup>20</sup>But he said, 'You will not pass through.' Edom went out to meet him with a substantial company, with a strong hand. <sup>21</sup>So Edom refused to let Yisra'el pass through its border, and Yisra'el turned from it.

<sup>22</sup>So they moved on from Qadesh and the Yisra'elites came, the entire assembly, to Mount Hor. <sup>23</sup>Yahweh said to Mosheh and to Aharon at Mount Hor, on the border of the country of Edom, <sup>24</sup>'Aharon is to join his kin, because he will not come into the country that I'm

giving to the Yisra'elites, on account of the fact that you [two] rebelled against my bidding about Meribah Water. ²⁵Get Aharon and El'azar his son and take them up Mount Hor. ²⁶Get Aharon to take off his garments, and get El'azar his son to put them on. Aharon will be gathered and die there.'

## Aharon joins his ancestors

²⁷Mosheh did as Yahweh ordered. They went up Mount Hor before the eyes of the entire assembly ²⁸and Mosheh got Aharon to take off his garments and got El'azar his son to put them on. Aharon died there on the top of the mountain, and Mosheh and El'azar came down from the mountain. ²⁹The assembly saw that Aharon had breathed his last, and they bewailed Aharon for thirty days, the entire Yisra'elite household.

**21** The Kena'anite, the king of Arad, who lived in the Negeb, heard that Yisra'el was coming by the Atarim road, and he battled against Yisra'el and took some of them captive. ²Yisra'el made a pledge to Yahweh: 'If you actually give this people into my hand, I will devote their towns.' ³Yahweh listened to Yisra'el's voice and gave the Kena'anites over, and they devoted [haram] them and their towns. So they named the place Hormah.

⁴They moved on from Mount Hor by the Reed Sea road to go round the country of Edom. The people's spirit became short on the way ⁵and the people spoke against God and against Mosheh: 'Why did you bring us up from Misrayim to die in the wilderness, because there's no bread and there's no water and our appetite is dismayed about the pathetic bread?' ⁶Yahweh sent off against the people venomous snakes that bit the people, and a large company from Yisra'el died. ⁷The people came to Mosheh and said, 'We did wrong in that we spoke against Yahweh and against you. Plead with Yahweh to remove the snakes from us.' Mosheh pleaded on behalf of the people ⁸and Yahweh said to Mosheh, 'Make yourself a venomous thing and put it on a standard. Anyone who's bitten but looks at it will live.' ⁹So Mosheh made a copper snake and placed it on a standard, and if a snake bit an individual, he would look to the copper snake and live.

## Sihon king of the Amorites

¹⁰The Yisra'elites moved on and camped at Obot, ¹¹then moved on from Obot and camped at Iyyim in the Regions Across, in the wilderness over against Mo'ab on the east. ¹²From there they moved on and camped by Wadi Zered. ¹³From there they moved on and camped across the Arnon, which is in the wilderness that extends from the Amorite border . . .

(because the Arnon is the border of Mo'ab, between Mo'ab and the Amorites; ¹⁴that's why it's said in the Document about Yahweh's Battles, 'Waheb in Suphah and the wadis; the Arnon ¹⁵and the slope of the wadis that stretches to the Ar settlement and lies at Mo'ab's border')

¹⁶. . . and from there to Be'er ['Well'] . . .

(that's the well of which Yahweh said to Mosheh, 'Gather the people and I'll give them water', ¹⁷then Yisra'el sang this song:

Go up, well – sing for it,
   ¹⁸well that the officials dug,
   That the important ones among the
      people sank,
      with a sceptre, with their staffs)

and from the wilderness to Mattanah, ¹⁹and from Mattanah to Nahali'el, and from Nahali'el to Bamot, ²⁰and from Bamot to the ravine that's in Mo'ab's region, to the top of Pisgah, which overlooks The Wasteland.

²¹Yisra'el sent envoys to Sihon, king of the Amorites: ²²'I want to pass through your country. We won't turn off into your field or into your vineyard. We won't drink water from your well. We'll go by the King's Road till we pass through your border.' ²³But Sihon didn't let Yisra'el pass though his border. Sihon gathered his entire company and went out to meet Yisra'el, into the wilderness. He came to Yahats and battled against Yisra'el. ²⁴But Yisra'el struck him down with the mouth of the sword and took possession of his country from the Arnon as far as the Yabboq, as far as the Ammonites, because the Ammonites' border was strong. ²⁵Yisra'el took all these towns.

## Og king of Bashan

So Yisra'el lived in all the Amorites' towns,
in Heshbon and in all its daughter-towns,
²⁶because Heshbon was the town of Sihon, king
of the Amorites, and he had battled against
the former king of Mo'ab and taken his entire
country from his hand as far as the Arnon.
²⁷That's why the poets say:

Come to Heshbon, which is built up,
    and which is founded, Sihon's town.
²⁸Because fire went out from Heshbon,
    flame from Sihon's township,
Devouring Ar in Mo'ab,
    the masters of the Arnon Heights.
²⁹Ah, you, Mo'ab,
    you were lost, people of Kemosh!
He gave over his sons, the survivors,
    his daughters into captivity,
to the king of the Amorites, Sihon.
³⁰But their dominion is lost,
    Heshbon as far as Dibon.
We wrought desolation as far as Nophah,
    which is as far as Medeba.

³¹So Yisra'el lived in the country of the
Amorites. ³²Mosheh sent people to investigate
Ya'zer, and they captured its daughter-villages
and dispossessed the Amorites who were there.
³³Then they turned the face and went up
the Bashan road, and Og king of Bashan
came out to meet them, he and his entire
company, for a battle at Edre'i. ³⁴Yahweh said
to Mosheh, 'Don't be afraid of him, because I
give him, his entire company and his country
into your hand. You're to do to him as you
did to Sihon king of the Amorites who was
living in Heshbon.' ³⁵They struck down him,
his sons and his entire company until they
let no survivor remain to him, and they took
possession of his country.

**22** Then the Yisra'elites moved on and
camped in the Mo'ab steppes across
the Yarden from Yeriho [Jericho].

## Balaq panics

²Balaq ben Tsippor saw all that Yisra'el
had done to the Amorites, ³and Mo'ab was in
great dread before the people because it was
numerous. So Mo'ab was dismayed about the
Yisra'elites, ⁴and Mo'ab said to the elders of
Midyan, 'The congregation will now lick up
everything around us like an ox licks up the
grass in the fields.'

Balaq ben Tsippor was king of Mo'ab at that
time ⁵and he sent envoys to Bil'am [Balaam]
ben Be'or in Petor, which is by the river, the
country of his kinsfolk, to call for him: 'Here,
a people has come out of Misrayim – here, it
has covered the face of the earth, and it's living
near me. ⁶So now please curse this people
for me, because it's more numerous than me.
Maybe I'll be able to strike it down and drive it
out of the country, because I know that the one
whom you bless is blessed and the one whom
you curse is cursed.'

⁷So Mo'ab's elders and Midyan's elders went
with divination material in their hand, came
to Bil'am and spoke Balaq's words to him. ⁸He
said to them, 'Stay the night here tonight and
I'll bring back word to you as Yahweh speaks
to me.' So the officials from Mo'ab stayed with
Bil'am.

⁹God came to Bil'am and said, 'Who are
these people with you?' ¹⁰Bil'am said to God,
'Balaq ben Tsippor, king of Mo'ab, has sent
to me: ¹¹"Here is the people that came out of
Misrayim, and it has covered the face of the
earth. Come now and damn it for me. Maybe
I'll be able to do battle against it and drive it
out."' ¹²God said to Bil'am, 'You will not go with
them. You will not curse the people, because
it's blessed.'

## Bil'am says no then yes

¹³Bil'am got up in the morning and said to
Balaq's officials, 'Go to your country, because
Yahweh has refused to let me go with you.' ¹⁴So
the officials of Mo'ab set off and came to Balaq
and said, 'Bil'am refused to go with us.'

¹⁵Balaq once again sent officials, more and
more honoured than these. ¹⁶They came to
Bil'am and said to him, 'Balaq ben Tsippor has
said this: please don't hold back from going
to me, ¹⁷because I shall definitely honour
you much, and everything that you say I will
do. Please go and damn this people for me.'
¹⁸Bil'am answered Balaq's servants, 'If Balaq
were to give me his house full of silver and

gold, I couldn't contravene the bidding of Yahweh my God, in doing something small or big. ¹⁹But now, please stay here, you too, tonight, so I may know what Yahweh may further speak with me.'

²⁰God came to Bil'am in the night and said to him, 'If the people have come to call for you, set off, go with them, but only the word that I speak to you – it is what you are to do.' ²¹So Bil'am got up in the morning, saddled his donkey and went with the officials of Mo'ab.

²²But Yahweh's anger raged because he was going, and Yahweh's envoy took his stand on the road as an adversary to him. He was riding on his donkey and his two boys were with him. ²³The donkey saw Yahweh's envoy standing in the road with his drawn sword in his hand, so the donkey turned away from the road and went into the fields. Bil'am struck the donkey to turn it away on to the road. ²⁴Then Yahweh's envoy stood in a vineyards lane, with a barrier this side and a barrier that side. ²⁵The donkey saw Yahweh's envoy and squeezed itself against the wall, and squeezed Bil'am's foot against the wall. He again struck her.

## The donkey speaks

²⁶Again Yahweh's envoy passed on and stood in a narrow place where there was no room to turn away right or left, ²⁷and the donkey saw Yahweh's envoy and lay down under Bil'am. Bil'am's anger raged and he struck the donkey with his stick.

²⁸Yahweh opened the donkey's mouth and she said to Bil'am, 'What have I done to you, that you've struck me these three times?' ²⁹Bil'am said to the donkey, 'Because you've acted abusively to me! If only there were a sword in my hand, because I would now kill you.' ³⁰The donkey said to Bil'am, 'Am I not the donkey that you've ridden on ever since you had me until this day? Have I at all shown myself in the habit of doing this to you?' He said, 'No.'

³¹Yahweh opened Bil'am's eyes and he saw Yahweh's envoy standing in the road with his drawn sword in his hand, and he bent his head and bowed low on his face. ³²Yahweh's envoy said to him, 'Why have you struck your donkey these three times? Here, I'm the one who came out as an adversary, because the journey before me was urgent. ³³The donkey saw me and turned away before me these three times. If she hadn't turned away from before me, then I would rather also have killed you now but kept her alive.' ³⁴Bil'am said to Yahweh's envoy, 'I did wrong, because I didn't know that you were standing to meet me in the road. So now, if it's bad in your eyes, I'll go back.' ³⁵Yahweh's envoy said to Bil'am, 'Go with the people. But you're to speak nothing but the word that I speak to you.' So Bil'am went with Balaq's officials.

## Balaq instructs Bil'am

³⁶Balaq heard that Bil'am was coming and went out to meet him at Mo'ab Town, which is on the Arnon border, which is at the farthest point of the border. ³⁷Balaq said to Bil'am, 'I sent urgently to you to call for you, didn't I. Why didn't you go to me? Am I truly unable to honour you?' ³⁸Bil'am said to Balaq, 'Here, I've come to you now. Am I really able to speak anything? The word that God puts in my mouth: I shall speak it.'

³⁹Bil'am went with Balaq, and they came to Hutstsot Township. ⁴⁰Balaq sacrificed cattle and sheep and sent them off to Bil'am and to the officials who were with him. ⁴¹In the morning Balaq got Bil'am and took him up Master's Heights. From there he looked at the edge of the people.

**23** Bil'am said to Balaq, 'Build me seven altars here and make an offering for me here of seven bulls and seven rams.' ²Balaq did as Bil'am spoke, and Balaq and Bil'am offered up a bull and a ram on each altar. ³Bil'am said to Balaq, 'Take your stand by your burnt offering and I shall go. Maybe Yahweh will come to meet me, and whatever is the word that he lets me see, I shall tell you.'

He went to a bare place. ⁴And God met with Bil'am. He said to him, 'I've laid out seven altars and offered up a bull and a ram on each altar.' ⁵And Yahweh put a thing in Bil'am's mouth and said, 'Go back to Balaq and speak in this way.' ⁶He went back to him. There he was, standing by his burnt offering, he and all the officials of Mo'ab.

## Bil'am's message

⁷He took up his poem:

From Aram Balaq led me,
  Mo'ab's king from the eastern mountains:
'Go, curse Jacob for me;
  go, condemn Yisra'el.'
⁸How can I slight what God has not slighted,
  how can I condemn what God has not
    condemned?
⁹For from the top of the crags I see him,
  from the hills I behold him.
There, a people that dwells apart,
  that does not think of itself as one of the
    nations.
¹⁰Who can count the earth of Ya'aqob [Jacob],
  or the number of Yisra'el's dust cloud?
May I myself die the death of the upright;
  may my future be like his!

¹¹Balaq said to Bil'am, 'What have you done
to me? It was to slight my enemies that I got
you. Here, you've greatly blessed them!' ¹²He
answered, 'It's what Yahweh puts in my mouth
that I keep watch to speak, isn't it.' ¹³So Balaq
said to him, 'Please get yourself with me to
another place where you can see him. From
there you will see only the edge of them. You
won't see all of them. You can slight them for
me from there.' ¹⁴He took him to Lookouts
Field, to the top of Pisgah, built seven altars,
and offered up a bull and a ram on each altar.
¹⁵He said to Balaq, 'Take your stand in this
way by your offering. I myself will seek a
meeting here.'

¹⁶Yahweh met with Bil'am and put a word
in his mouth, and said, 'Go back to Balaq and
speak in this way.' ¹⁷He came to him and there
he was, standing by his offering, the officials of
Mo'ab with him. Balaq said to him, 'What did
Yahweh say?'

## Balaq tries again

¹⁸Bil'am took up his poem:

Get up, Balaq, listen;
  give ear to me, ben Tsippor.
¹⁹God is not a human person so he lies,
  a human being so he relents.

Would he say and not do,
  speak and not implement it?
²⁰Here, 'Bless' I received;
  when he blesses, I can't turn it back.
²¹He has not envisaged trouble in Ya'aqob,
  he has not visualized oppression in Yisra'el.
Yahweh its God is with it,
  the acclamation of a king is in it,
²²God who got them out of Misrayim
  is like an oryx's horns for it.
²³Because there's no spell against Ya'aqob,
  no magic against Yisra'el.
It is said just once about Ya'aqob,
  and about Yisra'el, what God is doing.
²⁴Here – a people that gets up like a cougar,
  raises itself like a lion.
It doesn't lie down until it eats prey
  and drinks the blood of people who have
    been run through.

²⁵Balaq said to Bil'am, 'Neither properly
slight them nor properly bless them.' ²⁶Bil'am
answered Balaq, 'I've spoken to you, haven't I:
"Everything that Yahweh speaks with me, I must
do."' ²⁷Balaq said to Bil'am, 'Please do go, I'll take
you to another place. Maybe it will be all right
in God's eyes to slight them for me from there.'
²⁸So Balaq took Bil'am to the top of Pe'or, which
overlooks the face of The Wasteland. ²⁹Bil'am
said to Balaq, 'Build me seven altars here and
make an offering of seven bulls and seven rams
for me.' ³⁰Balaq did as Bil'am said, and offered
up a bull and a ram on each altar.

## Ya'aqob's good tents

24 Bil'am had seen that it was good in
  Yahweh's eyes to bless Yisra'el, and he
didn't go as on other times to find spells but
set his face towards the wilderness. ²Bil'am
lifted his eyes and saw Yisra'el dwelling by its
clans, and God's spirit came on him.
³He took up his poem:

A declaration of Bil'am ben Be'or,
  a declaration of a man who is opened of eye,
⁴A declaration of one who hears God's words,
  one who beholds Shadday's vision,
  falling, with eyes uncovered:
⁵How good are your tents, Ya'aqob,
  your dwellings, Yisra'el,

⁶Like wadis that spread out,
  like gardens by a river,
Like aloes that Yahweh has planted,
  like cedars by water.
⁷Water will flow from its branches,
  its seed will be in much water.
Its king will rise above Agag,
  its kingdom will go up high.
⁸God who brought it out of Misrayim
  is like an oryx's horns to it.
It will devour nations, its attackers,
  crush their bones, hit with its arrows.
⁹It bent down, lay like a lion,
  like a cougar: who would rouse it?
The people who bless you – such a person is
  blessed,
  the people who curse you – such a person is
  cursed!

¹⁰Balaq's anger raged against Bil'am and he
struck the palms of his hands. Balaq said to
Bil'am, 'I called for you to damn my enemies,
but here, you've actually blessed, these three
times! ¹¹So take flight for your life now to
your own place. I said I would really honour
you, but here, Yahweh has held you back from
honour.'
¹²Bil'am said to Balaq, 'I also spoke to your
envoys whom you sent to me, didn't I: ¹³"If
Balaq were to give me his house full of gold
and silver, I couldn't contravene Yahweh's
bidding by doing good or bad out of my own
mind. What Yahweh speaks, I shall speak." ¹⁴So
now: here I am, going to my people. Come, I
shall counsel you about what this people will
do to your people in a later time.'

*Bil'am's last words*

¹⁵He took up his poem:

A declaration of Bil'am ben Be'or,
  a declaration of a man who is opened of eye,
¹⁶A declaration of one who hears God's words,
  who has knowledge from the One on High,
One who beholds Shadday's vision,
  falling, with eyes uncovered:
¹⁷I see it, but not now;
  I behold it, but not near.
A star has made a way from Ya'aqob,
  a staff has risen from Yisra'el.

It has hit Mo'ab's crown,
  the skull of all the Setites.
¹⁸Edom has become a possession,
  Se'ir has become a possession, of its enemies,
While Yisra'el is acting forcefully;
  ¹⁹from Ya'aqob one will hold sway
  and obliterate what survives of the town.

²⁰He saw Amaleq and took up his poem:

If Amaleq is first among the nations,
  but its future: it will perish permanently.

²¹He saw the Qenites and took up his poem:

Your settlement is powerful,
  your nest placed in the cliff.
²²Yet Qayin will be for burning up,
  for how long will Ashshur take you captive?

²³He took up his poem:

Ah, who will live
  apart from God's determining it?
²⁴Ships from Kittim's shore
  will humble Ashshur.
They will humble Eber,
  but it, too, will perish permanently.

²⁵Bil'am set off and went and turned back to his
place, and Balaq, too, went on his way.

**25** But while Yisra'el lived at Acacias,
the people started whoring with
the Mo'abite women. ²They called the people
to their gods' sacrifices, and the people ate
and bowed low to their gods. ³So Yisra'el
bound itself to Master-of-Pe'or, and Yahweh's
anger raged against Yisra'el. ⁴Yahweh said to
Mosheh, 'Get all the heads of the people and
execute them for Yahweh in the light of the
sun, so Yahweh's angry rage may turn back
from Yisra'el.' ⁵So Mosheh said to Yisra'el's
leaders, 'Each of you kill his men who bound
themselves to Master-of-Pe'or.'

*The passion of Pinhas and of Yahweh*

⁶And there, a man from among the
Yisra'elites came and presented a Midyanite
woman to his brothers before the eyes of
Mosheh and before the eyes of the entire

assembly of the Yisra'elites; they were wailing at the entrance of the appointment tent. [7]Pinhas ben El'azar, the son of Aharon the priest, saw it, got up from among the assembly, took a spear in his hand, [8]came after the Yisra'elite man into the pavilion and thrust the two of them through, the Yisra'elite man and the woman, through to her insides.

The epidemic held back from the Yisra'elites, [9]but the people who died through the epidemic were 24,000.

[10]Yahweh spoke to Mosheh: [11]Pinhas ben El'azar, the son of Aharon the priest – he's turned back my wrath from the Yisra'elites by his showing my passion among them, so I didn't finish off the Yisra'elites in my passion. [12]Therefore say: here, I am giving him my pact that things will be well. [13]It will be for him and for his offspring after him as a permanent priestly pact, on account of the fact that he was passionate for his God and made expiation for the Yisra'elites.'

[14]The name of the Yisra'elite man struck down (the one who was struck down with the Midyanite woman) was Zimri ben Salu, leader of an ancestral household belonging to the Shim'onites. [15]The name of the Midyanite woman who was struck down was Kozbi bat Tsur; he was head of the clans in an ancestral household in Midyan.

[16]Yahweh spoke to Mosheh: [17]Attack the Midyanites, strike them down, [18]because they were attacking you with their wiles which they practised towards you, on account of Pe'or and on account of Kozbi, the daughter of a Midyanite leader, their sister, who was struck down on the day of the epidemic on account of Pe'or.'

*Another head count: Re'uben, Shim'on, Gad*

# 26

After the epidemic, Yahweh said to Mosheh and to El'azar ben Aharon the priest, [2]'Take a head count of the entire assembly of the Yisra'elites from the age of twenty years and upwards by their ancestral household, everyone in Yisra'el who goes out in the army.' [3]Mosheh and El'azar the priest spoke with them in the Mo'ab steppes by the Yarden at Yeriho: [4]'From the age of twenty years and upwards . . .', as Yahweh ordered Mosheh.

The Yisra'elites who came out of the country of Misrayim:

[5]Re'uben, Yisra'el's firstborn – Re'uben's descendants:
of Hanok, the Hanokite kin-group; of Pallu, the Pallu'ite kin-group; [6]of Hetsron, the Hetsronite kin-group; of Karmi, the Karmite kin-group.
[7]These were the kin-groups of the Re'ubenites. Their register was 43,730.
[8]Sons of Pallu: Eli'ab.
[9]Sons of Eli'ab: Nemu'el, Datan and Abiram. Datan and Abiram were the people called for by the assembly who campaigned against Mosheh and against Aharon within Qorah's group when they campaigned against Yahweh, [10]and the earth opened its mouth and swallowed them with Qorah, when the company died, when fire devoured the 250 people and they became a banner. [11](Qorah's sons didn't die.)

[12]Shim'on's descendants by their kin-groups: of Nemu'el, the Nemu'elite kin-group; of Yamin, the Yaminite kin-group; of Yakin, the Yakinite kin-group; [13]of Zerah, the Zarhite kin-group; of Sha'ul, the Sha'ulite kin-group. [14]These were the kin-groups of the Shim'onites. 22,200.

[15]Gad's descendants by their kin-groups: of Tsephon, the Tsephonite kin-group; of Haggi, the Haggite kin-group; of Shuni, the Shunite kin-group; [16]of Ozni, the Oznite kin-group; of Eri, the Erite kin-group; [17]of Arod, the Arodite kin-group; of Ar'eli, the Ar'elite kin-group.
[18]These were the kin-groups of the Gadites. By their register: 40,500.

*Yehudah, Yissakar, Zebulun, Menashsheh, Ephraim*

[19]Yehudah's sons: Er and Onan. Er and Onan died in the country of Kena'an.
[20]Yehudah's descendants by their kin-groups were:
of Shelah, the Shelahite kin-group; of Perets, the Partsite kin-group; of Zerah, the Zarhite kin-group.

²¹Perets's descendants were: of Hetsron, the Hetsronite kin-group; of Hamul, the Hamulite kin-group. ²²These were the kin-groups of Yehudah. By their register: 76,500.

²³Yissakar's descendants by their kin-groups: of Tola, the Tola'ite kin-group; of Puvah, the Punite kin-group; ²⁴of Yashub, the Yashubite kin-group; of Shimron, the Shimronite kin-group. ²⁵These were the kin-groups of Yissakar. By their register: 64,300.

²⁶Zebulun's descendants by their kin-groups: of Sered, the Sardite kin-group; of Elon, the Elonite kin-group; of Yahle'el, the Yahle'elite kin-group. ²⁷These were the kin-groups of the Zebulunites. By their register: 60,500.

²⁸Yoseph's descendants by their kin-groups, Menashsheh and Ephrayim.

²⁹Menashsheh's descendants: of Makir, the Makirite kin-group. Makir fathered Gil'ad; of Gil'ad: the kin-group of the Gil'adites. ³⁰These were Gil'ad's descendants: I'ezer, the I'ezrite kin-group; of Heleq, the Helqite kin-group; ³¹Asri'el, the Asri'elite kin-group; Shekem, the Shekemite kin-group; ³²Shemida, the Shemida'ite kin-group; Hepher, the Hephrite kin-group. ³³Tselophhad ben Hepher – he had no sons, only daughters; the names of Tselophhad's daughters were Mahlah, No'ah, Hoglah, Milkah and Tirtsah. ³⁴These were the kin-groups of Menashsheh. And their register: 52,700.

³⁵These were Ephrayim's descendants by their kin-groups: of Shutelah, the Shutalhite kin-group; of Beker, the Bakrite kin-group; of Tahan, the Tahanite kin-group. ³⁶These were Shutelah's descendants: of Eran, the Eranite kin-group. ³⁷These were the kin-groups of Ephrayim's descendants. By their register: 32,500. These were Yoseph's descendants by their kin-groups.

³⁸Binyamin's descendants by their kin-groups: of Bela, the Bal'ite kin-group; of Ashbel, the Ashbelite kin-group; of Ahiram, the Ahiramite kin-group; ³⁹of Shephupham, the Shephuphamite kin-group; of Hupham, the Huphamite kin-group. ⁴⁰Bela's sons were Ard and Na'aman. The Ardite kin-group; of Na'aman, the Na'amanite kin-group. ⁴¹These were Binyamin's descendants by their kin-groups. And by their register: 45,600.

## Dan, Asher, Naphtali, Levi

⁴²These were Dan's descendants by their kin-groups:
of Shuham, the Shuhamite kin-group.
These were the kin-groups of Dan by their kin-groups.
⁴³All the kin-groups of the Shuhamites, by their register: 64,400.

⁴⁴Asher's descendants by their kin-groups: of Imnah, the Imnahite kin-group; of Yishvi, the Yishvite kin-group; of Beri'ah, the Beri'hite kin-group. ⁴⁵Of Beri'ah's descendants: of Heber, the Hebrite kin-group; of Malki'el, the Malki'elite kin-group. ⁴⁶The name of Asher's daughter was Serah. ⁴⁷These were the kin-groups of Asher's descendants. By their register: 53,400.

⁴⁸Naphtali's descendants by their kin-groups:
of Yahtse'el, the Yahtse'elite kin-group; of Guni, the Gunite kin-group; ⁴⁹of Yetser, the Yitsrite kin-group; of Shillem, the Shillemite kin-group. ⁵⁰These were the kin-groups of Napthali by their kin-groups. And by their register: 45,400.

⁵¹This was the register of the Yisra'elites: 601,730. ⁵²Yahweh spoke to Mosheh: ⁵³"To these people the country is to be shared out as a domain by the number of the names. ⁵⁴For a big group, you're to make its domain big, and for a small group, you're to make its domain small. Each is to be given its domain in

accordance with its register. ⁵⁵Only, the country is to be shared out by lot. By the names of the ancestral clans they're to have a domain. ⁵⁶In accordance with the lot its domain is to be shared out, between big and small.'

⁵⁷This was the register of the Levites by their kin-groups:
of Gershon, the Gershonite kin-group; of Qehat, the Qehatite kin-group; of Merari, the Merarite kin-group.
⁵⁸These were the kin-groups of Levi:
the Libnite kin-group, the Hebronite kin-group, the Mahlite kin-group, the Mushite kin-group, the Qorahite kin-group

Qehat fathered Amram, ⁵⁹and the name of Amram's wife was Yokebed bat Levi, to whom [her mother] gave birth for Levi in Misrayim. She gave birth to Aharon, Mosheh and Miryam their sister for Amram. ⁶⁰To Aharon were born Nadab and Abihu, El'azar and Itamar, ⁶¹but Nadab and Abihu died when they presented outside fire before Yahweh.

⁶²Their register was 23,000, every male from one month and upwards, because they were not registered among the Yisra'elites, because no domain was given to them among the Yisra'elites.

## Five pushy women

⁶³This was the register by Mosheh and El'azar the priest that they made of the Yisra'elites in the Mo'ab steppes by the Yarden at Yeriho. ⁶⁴Among these there was not one person from the register by Mosheh and Aharon the priest that they made of the Yisra'elites in the Sinay Wilderness, ⁶⁵because Yahweh had said to them, 'They will definitely die in the wilderness.' Not one of them remained except Kaleb ben Yephunneh and Yehoshua ben Nun.

**27** The daughters of Tselophhad ben Hepher, son of Gil'ad son of Makir son of Menashsheh, of the kin-group of Menashsheh ben Yoseph, presented themselves. These are the names of his daughters: Mahlah, No'ah, Hoglah, Milkah and Tirtsah. ²They stood before Mosheh, before El'azar the priest, and before the leaders

and the entire assembly, at the entrance of the appointment tent, and said, ³'Our father died in the wilderness. He was not among the group who kept an appointment against Yahweh, in Qorah's group, because he died for his own wrongdoing. He had no sons. ⁴Why should our father's name disappear from among his kin-group because he had no son? Give us a holding among our father's brothers.'

⁵Mosheh presented their case before Yahweh, ⁶and Yahweh said to Mosheh, ⁷'The daughters of Tselophhad are speaking correctly. Do give them a holding, a domain among their father's brothers. Pass their father's domain over to them.

⁸You're to speak to the Yisra'elites: "When an individual dies and he had no son, you're to pass his domain over to his daughter. ⁹If he had no daughter, you're to give his domain to his brothers. ¹⁰If he had no brothers, you're to give his domain to his father's brothers. ¹¹If his father had no brothers, you're to give his domain to the nearest relative he had from his kin-group, and he will take possession of it. It's to be a ruling decree for the Yisra'elites, as Yahweh ordered Mosheh.'"

## Appointing a new leader

¹²Yahweh said to Mosheh, 'Go up this mountain in the Regions Across and look at the country that I'm giving the Yisra'elites. ¹³When you've looked at it, you too will be gathered to your kin as Aharon your brother was gathered to them, ¹⁴as you rebelled against my bidding when the assembly argued in the Tsin Wilderness, in connection with making me sacred in their eyes by means of the water' (i.e. Meribah Water at Qadesh in the Tsin Wilderness).

¹⁵Mosheh spoke to Yahweh: ¹⁶'Yahweh, the God of the spirits of all flesh, must appoint an individual over the assembly ¹⁷who will go out before them and come in before them, who will take them out and bring them in, so Yahweh's assembly won't be like a flock that has no shepherd.' ¹⁸Yahweh said to Mosheh, 'Get yourself Yehoshua ben Nun, an individual who has spirit in him. Lean your hand on him. ¹⁹Stand him before El'azar the priest

and before the entire assembly and give him orders before their eyes, ²⁰and put on him some of your dignity in order that the entire assembly of the Yisraʼelites may listen. ²¹He will stand before Elʼazar the priest and he will ask for the decision of the Urim before Yahweh for him. At his bidding they will go out and at his bidding they will come in, he and all the Yisraʼelites with him, the entire assembly.' ²²Mosheh did as Yahweh ordered him. He got Yehoshua, stood him before Elʼazar the priest and before the entire assembly, ²³leaned his hands on him and gave him orders, as Yahweh spoke through Mosheh.

## Daily and weekly offerings

**28** Yahweh spoke to Mosheh: ²'Order the Yisraʼelites: "You're to keep watch about presenting to me my offering, my bread, as my gift offerings, a nice smell for me, at its set time." ³You're to say to them, "This is the gift offering that you're to present to Yahweh:

lambs a year old that are whole, two per day as a regular burnt offering ⁴(you're to make one lamb in the morning and to make the second lamb at twilight);

⁵a tenth of a barrel of fine flour as a grain offering, mixed with a quarter of a gallon of pressed oil ⁶(the regular burnt offering made at Mount Sinay, as a nice smell, a gift offering for Yahweh);

⁷its libation a quarter of a gallon for the one lamb (pour it in the sanctuary as a liquor libation for Yahweh);

⁸you're to make the second lamb at twilight; like the morning grain offering and like its libation you're to make it, a gift offering, a nice smell for Yahweh.

⁹On the sabbath day:

two lambs a year old that are whole;

two tenths of fine flour as a grain offering, mixed with oil, with its libation;

¹⁰a burnt offering for each sabbath along with the regular burnt offering and its libation.

## New Year and Pesah

¹¹At the beginning of your months you're to present

a burnt offering for Yahweh: two bulls from the herd, one ram and seven lambs a year old that are whole;

¹²three tenths of fine flour as a grain offering, mixed with oil, for each bull;

two tenths of fine flour as a grain offering, mixed with oil, for each ram;

¹³a tenth each of fine flour as a grain offering, mixed with oil, for each lamb:

a burnt offering, a nice smell, a gift offering for Yahweh;

¹⁴and their libations will be half a gallon of wine for a bull, a third of a gallon for a ram and a quarter of a gallon for a lamb.

This is the month-by-month burnt offering for the months of the year. ¹⁵And one he-goat from the flock as a decontamination for Yahweh is to be made, along with the regular burnt offering, with its libation.

¹⁶In the first month, on the fourteenth day of the month, is Pesah for Yahweh, ¹⁷and on the fifteenth day of this month there is a festival. For seven days flatbread is to be eaten. ¹⁸On the first day, a sacred occasion. You will not do any servile work. ¹⁹You're to present

a gift offering, a burnt offering, for Yahweh: two bulls from the herd, one ram, and seven lambs a year old; they're to be ones of yours that are whole;

²⁰their grain offering: you're to make fine flour mixed with oil, three tenths for a bull and two tenths for a ram; ²¹you're to make a tenth for each lamb, for the seven lambs;

²²one he-goat from the flock as a decontamination, to make expiation for you.

²³You're to make these apart from the morning burnt offering, which is for the regular burnt offering. ²⁴You're to make ones like these each day for seven days as a meal, a gift offering, a nice smell for Yahweh. It's to be made along with the regular burnt offering, with its libation.

²⁵On the seventh day it's to be a sacred occasion for you. You will not do any servile work.

## The Shabuʼot Festival and the seventh month

²⁶On the day of the first products, when you present a new grain offering for Yahweh, during your Shabuʼot Festival, it's to be a sacred

occasion for you. You will not do any servile work. ²⁷You're to present

a burnt offering as a nice smell for Yahweh, two bulls from the herd, one ram, seven lambs a year old; ²⁸their grain offering, fine flour mixed with oil, three tenths for each bull, two tenths for each ram, ²⁹a tenth each for each lamb, for the seven lambs; ³⁰one he-goat from the flock to make expiation for you.

³¹You're to make them apart from the regular burnt offering and its grain offering (they are to be ones of yours that are whole), and their libations.

**29** In the seventh month on the first of the month it's to be a sacred occasion for you. You will not do any servile work. It's to be for you the day of a horn blast. ²You're to make

a burnt offering as a nice smell for Yahweh: a bull from the herd, a ram, seven lambs a year old that are whole; ³their grain offering: fine flour mixed with oil, three tenths for the bull, two tenths for the ram ⁴and one tenth for each lamb, for the seven lambs; ⁵one he-goat from the flock as a decontamination to make expiation for you; ⁶apart from the month's burnt offering and its grain offering, and the regular burnt offering and its grain offering and their libations in accordance with the rulings for them, as a nice smell, a gift offering for Yahweh.

## The Pilgrimage Festival celebrations

⁷On the tenth of this seventh month it's to be a sacred occasion for you and you're to humble yourselves. You will not do any work. ⁸You're to present for Yahweh

a burnt offering, a nice smell, a bull from the herd, a ram, seven lambs a year old (they're to be ones of yours that are whole); ⁹their grain offering: fine flour mixed with oil, three tenths for the bull, two tenths for each ram ¹⁰and one tenth for each lamb, for the seven lambs; ¹¹one he-goat from the flock as a decontamination; apart from the decontamination for

complete expiation and the regular burnt offering and its grain offering, and their libations.

¹²On the fifteenth day of the seventh month it's to be a sacred occasion for you. You will not do any servile work. You're to hold a festival for Yahweh for seven days. ¹³You're to present

a burnt offering, a gift offering, a nice smell for Yahweh: thirteen bulls from the herd, two rams, fourteen lambs a year old (they're to be whole); ¹⁴their grain offering: fine flour mixed with oil, three tenths for each bull for the thirteen bulls, two tenths for each ram for the two rams ¹⁵and one tenth for each lamb for the fourteen lambs; ¹⁶one he-goat from the flock as a decontamination; apart from the regular burnt offering, its grain offering, and its libation.

¹⁷On the second day: twelve bulls from the herd, two rams, fourteen lambs a year old (ones that are whole); ¹⁸their grain offering and their libations for the bulls, for the rams and for the lambs, by their number in accordance with the ruling; ¹⁹one he-goat from the flock as a decontamination; apart from the regular burnt offering, its grain offering and their libations.

²⁰On the third day: eleven bulls, two rams, fourteen lambs a year old (ones that are whole); ²¹their grain offering and their libations for the bulls, for the rams and for the lambs, by their number in accordance with the ruling; ²²one he-goat as a decontamination; apart from the regular burnt offering, its grain offering and its libation.

## Days four to eight

²³On the fourth day: ten bulls, two rams, fourteen lambs a year old (ones that are whole); ²⁴their grain offering and their libations for

the bulls, for the rams and for the lambs, by their number in accordance with the ruling;
<sup>25</sup>one he-goat from the flock as a decontamination;
apart from the regular burnt offering, its grain offering and its libation.
<sup>26</sup>On the fifth day:
nine bulls, two rams, fourteen lambs a year old (ones that are whole);
<sup>27</sup>their grain offering and their libations for the bulls, for the rams and for the lambs, by their number in accordance with the ruling;
<sup>28</sup>one he-goat as a decontamination;
apart from the regular burnt offering, its grain offering and its libation.
<sup>29</sup>On the sixth day:
eight bulls, two rams, fourteen lambs a year old (ones that are whole);
<sup>30</sup>their grain offering and their libations for the bulls, for the rams and for the lambs, by their number in accordance with the ruling;
<sup>31</sup>one he-goat as a decontamination;
apart from the regular burnt offering, its grain offering and its libation.
<sup>32</sup>On the seventh day:
seven bulls, two rams, fourteen lambs a year old (ones that are whole);
<sup>33</sup>their grain offering and their libations for the bulls, for the rams and for the lambs, by their number in accordance with the ruling;
<sup>34</sup>one he-goat as a decontamination;
apart from the regular burnt offering, its grain offering and its libation.
<sup>35</sup>On the eighth day it's to be an assembly for you. You will not do any servile work. <sup>36</sup>You're to present
a burnt offering, a gift offering, a nice smell for Yahweh: a bull, a ram, seven lambs a year old (ones that are whole);
<sup>37</sup>their grain offering and their libations for the bull, for the ram and for the lambs, by their number in accordance with the ruling;
<sup>38</sup>one he-goat as a decontamination;
apart from the regular burnt offering, its grain offering and its libation.
<sup>39</sup>These you're to make for Yahweh at your set times (apart from your pledges and your free offerings) as your burnt offerings, your

grain offerings, your libations and your well-being sacrifices.'"
<sup>40</sup>Mosheh said it to the Yisraelites in accordance with everything that Yahweh ordered Mosheh.

## Promises that affect other people

**30** Mosheh spoke to the heads of the Yisraelites' clans: 'This is the thing Yahweh has ordered: <sup>2</sup>when a man makes a pledge to Yahweh or swears an oath to take on an obligation for himself, he will not treat his word as ordinary. He's to act in accordance with everything that comes out of his mouth.
<sup>3</sup>When a woman makes a pledge to Yahweh or takes on an obligation, in her father's household in her youth, <sup>4</sup>and her father hears of her pledge or her obligation that she takes on for herself, and her father is silent towards her, all her pledges stand and every obligation of hers that she's taken on herself stands. <sup>5</sup>But if her father restrains her on the day he hears it, none of her pledges or her obligations that she's taken on for herself stand. Yahweh will pardon her because her father has restrained her.
<sup>6</sup>If actually she comes to belong to a husband when there are pledges binding her or an extravagance that came from her lips that she's taken on for herself, <sup>7</sup>and her husband hears and is silent towards her on the day he hears, then her pledges stand and her obligation that she's taken on for herself stands. <sup>8</sup>But if her husband restrains her on the day he hears and contravenes her pledge that was binding her or the extravagance that came from her lips that she had taken on for herself, Yahweh will pardon her. (<sup>9</sup>But the pledge of a widow or a divorcee, everything that she's taken on for herself, stands in respect of her.)

## Speak now or for ever hold your peace

<sup>10</sup>If in her husband's household she's made a pledge or taken on an obligation for herself by an oath <sup>11</sup>and her husband has heard and has been silent towards her (he hasn't restrained her), all her pledges stand and every obligation that she's taken on for herself stands. <sup>12</sup>But if her husband does contravene them on the day

he hears it, nothing coming from her lips in relation to her pledges or to an obligation that she's taken on for herself stands. Her husband has contravened them and Yahweh will pardon her. [13]Every pledge and every sworn obligation to humble herself, her husband may let stand or her husband may contravene. [14]If her husband remains quite silent towards her from one day to the next, he lets stand all her pledges and all the obligations that are upon her. He lets them stand because he was silent towards her on the day he heard. [15]If he does contravene them after hearing it, he carries her waywardness.'

[16]These are the decrees that Yahweh ordered Mosheh between a husband and his wife, between a father and his daughter in her youth, in her father's household.

## Unfinished business

**31** Yahweh spoke to Mosheh: [2]'Take redress for the Yisra'elites from the Midyanites; afterwards, you will be gathered to your kin.' [3]Mosheh spoke to the people: 'Some men from among you are to equip themselves for war and go against Midyan to carry out Yahweh's redress on Midyan. [4]You're to send off to war a division for each clan, for all the Yisra'elite clans.'

[5]So from the Yisra'elite divisions, a division offered themselves for each clan, twelve divisions equipped for war. [6]Mosheh sent them off to the war, a division for each clan, with Pinhas ben El'azar as the priest for the war, the sacred articles and the trumpets for sounding in his hand. [7]They made war against Midyan as Yahweh ordered Mosheh, slaughtered every male [8]and killed the Midyanite kings: along with the others run through by them, Evi, Reqem, Tsur, Hur and Reba, the five Midyanite kings. And they killed Bil'am ben Be'or with the sword.

[9]The Yisra'elites captured the Midyanite women and their little ones and took as plunder all their animals, all their livestock and all their resources. [10]All their towns among their settlements and all their enclosures they burned in fire. [11]They took all the spoil and all the gains, human beings and animals, [12]and brought the captives, the gains and the spoil to Mosheh and to El'azar the priest, and to the

Yisra'elite assembly at the camp in the Mo'ab steppes by the Yarden at Yeriho.

## The danger of contamination

[13]Mosheh, El'azar the priest and all the leaders of the assembly came to meet them outside the camp. [14]Mosheh was furious with the people appointed over the force, the divisional officers and the section officers, who had come from battling in the war. [15]Mosheh said to them, 'You've let every female live! [16]Here, at Bil'am's word they were the ones who for the Yisra'elites came to be a means of instigating a trespass against Yahweh in the matter of Pe'or, so that the epidemic came on Yahweh's assembly. [17]So now, kill every male among the little ones and kill every woman who has had sex with someone, who has slept with a man. [18]But all the little ones among the women, who haven't had sex, who haven't slept with a man – let them live for yourselves.

[19]You yourselves, camp outside the camp for seven days. Everyone who killed someone and everyone who touched someone who had been run through – you're to decontaminate yourselves on the third day and on the seventh day, you and your captives. [20]All clothing, every skin article, everything made of goats' hair and every wood article – you're to decontaminate yourselves.'

[21]El'azar the priest said to the strong men who had come to the battle, 'This is the decree of instruction that Yahweh has ordered Mosheh. [22]However, the gold and the silver, the copper and the iron, the tin and the lead, [23]every object that goes through fire, you're to pass through fire and it will become pure. However, it's to decontaminate itself with the water for flowing. Everything that doesn't go through fire is to pass through water.' [24]You're to wash your clothes on the seventh day, so you become pure. Afterwards, you may come into the camp.'

## Counting the plunder

[25]Yahweh said to Mosheh: [26]'Take the sum total of the gains that were captured, human beings and animals – you and El'azar the

priest and the ancestral heads of the assembly. ²⁷You're to halve the gains between the people who took part in the battle, who went out to the war, and the entire assembly. ²⁸But you're to take up a levy for Yahweh from the people who were in the battle, the people who went out to the war, one living thing in 500, from human beings, from the herd, from donkeys and from the flock. ²⁹You're to take it from their half and give it to El'azar the priest as Yahweh's gift. ³⁰And from the Yisra'elites' half you're to take one that's withheld from fifty, from human beings, from the herd, from donkeys, from the flock and from all the animals, and give them to the Levites, who keep charge of Yahweh's dwelling.'

³¹Mosheh and El'azar the priest did as Yahweh ordered Mosheh. ³²The gains, above and beyond the plunder that the war company took: flock, 675,000; ³³herd, 72,000; ³⁴donkeys, 61,000; ³⁵human beings (from the women who had not had sex, who had not slept with a man), all the people 32,000.

³⁶So the half share of the people who went out in the war was: the number of sheep 337,500, ³⁷so Yahweh's levy from the flock was 675; ³⁸the herd 36,000, so Yahweh's levy 72; ³⁹donkeys 30,500, so Yahweh's levy 61; ⁴⁰human beings 16,000, so Yahweh's levy 32 people. ⁴¹Mosheh gave the levy, Yahweh's gift, to El'azar the priest, as Yahweh had ordered Mosheh.

## The levy

⁴²From the Yisra'elites' half which Mosheh divided off from the men who went to war, ⁴³the community's half: from the flock, 337,500; ⁴⁴the herd, 36,000; ⁴⁵donkeys, 30,500; ⁴⁶human beings, 16,000. ⁴⁷Mosheh took from the Yisra'elites' half the one withheld from 50 of the human beings and of the animals and gave them to the Levites who keep charge of Yahweh's dwelling, as Yahweh had ordered Mosheh.

⁴⁸The people who had been appointed for the army divisions (the divisional officers and the section officers) drew near to Mosheh. ⁴⁹They said to Mosheh, 'Your servants have taken the sum total of the men who were in the battle who were in our control, and no one has absented himself from us. ⁵⁰We are presenting

Yahweh's offering, each individual who found a gold article: a bangle or a bracelet, a ring, an earring or a necklace, for making expiation for ourselves before Yahweh.' ⁵¹Mosheh and El'azar the priest took the gold from them, all the articles of workmanship. ⁵²All the gold, the gift that they took up for Yahweh, came to 16,750 sheqels, from the divisional officers and from the section officers; ⁵³the people in the army had taken plunder each individual for himself.

⁵⁴So Mosheh and El'azar the priest took the gold from the divisional officers and from the section officers and brought it into the appointment tent as a reminder for the Yisra'elites before Yahweh.

## Cattle country

**32** Now the Re'ubenites and the Gadites had much livestock, very numerous, and they looked at the country of Ya'zer and Gil'ad: there, the place was a place for livestock. ²So the Gadites and Re'ubenites came and said to Mosheh, to El'azar the priest and to the assembly's leaders, ³'Atarot, Dibon, Ya'zer, Nimrah, Heshbon, El'alah, Sebam, Nebo and Be'on, ⁴the region that Yahweh has struck down before the Yisra'elite assembly, is livestock country, and your servants have livestock.'

⁵So they said, 'If we have found grace in your eyes, may this region be given to your servants as a holding. Don't make us cross the Yarden.' ⁶Mosheh said to the Gadites and to the Re'ubenites, 'Are your brothers to come into battle while you people live here? ⁷Why would you restrain the Yisra'elites' mind from crossing into the country that Yahweh has given them? ⁸Your fathers did so when I sent them from Qadesh Barnea to look at the country. ⁹They went up as far as Cluster Wadi and looked at the country but restrained the Yisra'elites' mind so they wouldn't come into the country that Yahweh had given them. ¹⁰And Yahweh's anger raged that day and he swore: ¹¹"If the people who went up from Misrayim, from the age of twenty years and upwards, see the land that I swore to Abraham, Yitshaq and Ya'aqob . . . Because they didn't fully follow after me", ¹²except Kaleb ben Yephunneh the Qenizzite and Yehoshua ben

Nun, because they fully followed after Yahweh. [13]Yahweh's anger raged against Yisra'el and he made them wander in the wilderness for forty years until the entire generation that acted badly in Yahweh's eyes was finished.

[14]So here, you've risen in place of your fathers as a multitude of wrongdoers to add further to Yahweh's angry rage towards Yisra'el. [15]When you turn back from following him, he will once again settle it down in the wilderness, and you'll destroy this entire people.'

## Mutual support

[16]They came up to him and said, 'We'll build sheepfolds here for our livestock and towns for our little ones, [17]but we ourselves will equip ourselves as shock troops before the Yisra'elites till we've enabled them to come to their place, while our little ones live in the fortified towns, because of the people who live in the country. [18]We won't come back to our houses till the Yisra'elites, each one, has entered into his domain. [19]Because we won't have a domain with them across the Yarden yonder, because our domain has come to us across the Yarden on the east.'

[20]Mosheh said to them. 'If you do this thing, if you equip yourselves before Yahweh for battle, [21]and every one of you who is equipped crosses over the Yarden before Yahweh till he's dispossessed his enemies from before him [22]and the country is in subjection before Yahweh, you can come back afterwards and be free in relation to Yahweh and to Yisra'el, and this region will be your holding before Yahweh. [23]But if you don't do so: there, you will have done wrong in relation to Yahweh. Acknowledge the wrongdoing you would do, which will find you. [24]Build yourselves towns for your little ones and folds for your sheep. But what has gone out of your mouth, you're to do.'

[25]The Gadites and Re'ubenites said to Mosheh, 'Your servants will do as my lord is ordering. [26]Our little ones, our wives, our livestock and all our animals will be there in the towns of Gil'ad, [27]while your servants will cross over for battle, everyone equipped for war before Yahweh for battle, as my lord is saying.'

## The region across the Yarden

[28]So Mosheh gave an order about them to El'azar the priest, to Yehoshua ben Nun and to the ancestral heads of the clans of the Yisra'elites. [29]Mosheh said to them, 'If the Gadites and Re'ubenites cross over the Yarden with you, each one equipped for battle before Yahweh, and the country is in subjection before you, you may give them the region of Gil'ad as a holding, [30]but if they don't cross over equipped with you, they will receive holdings among you in the country of Kena'an.'

[31]The Gadites and Re'ubenites avowed, 'What Yahweh has spoken to your servants, so we will do. [32]We ourselves will cross over equipped before Yahweh to the country of Kena'an, but the domain which is our holding will be with us across the Yarden.'

[33]So Mosheh gave to them (to the Gadites, to the Re'ubenites and to the half-clan of Menashsheh ben Yoseph) the kingdom of Sihon king of the Amorites and the kingdom of Og king of Bashan, the country with its towns in the territories of the country's towns, all round. [34]The Gadites built up Dibon, Atarot, Aro'er, [35]Atrot Shophan, Ya'zer, Yogbehah, [36]Bet Nimrah and Bet Haran, as fortified towns and sheepfolds. [37]The Re'ubenites built up Heshbon, El'ale, Qiryatayim, [38]Nebo, Ba'al Me'on (these were changed in name) and Sibmah. They gave names to the towns that they built up.

[39]The descendants of Makir ben Menashsheh went to Gil'ad, captured it and dispossessed the Amorites who were there. [40]Mosheh gave Gil'ad to Makir ben Menashsheh and he lived there. [41]When Ya'ir ben Menashsheh went and captured their villages, he named them Ya'ir's Villages. [42]When Nobah went and captured Qenat and its daughter-towns, he named it Nobah, after his own name.

## The stages of the journey

**33** These were the movements of the Yisra'elites who came out of the country of Misrayim by their troops at the direction of Mosheh and Aharon. [2]Mosheh wrote down their departure points for their movements at Yahweh's bidding. These were the movements by their starting points.

³They moved on from Ra'meses in the first month, on the fifteenth day of the first month. On the day after the Pesah the Yisra'elites went out with hands high before the eyes of all Misrayim ⁴as the Misrayimites were burying the people Yahweh had struck down among them, every firstborn; on their gods Yahweh had performed acts of authority.

⁵The Yisra'elites moved on from Ra'meses and camped at Sukkot.

⁶They moved on from Sukkot and camped at Etam, which is on the edge of the wilderness.

⁷They moved on from Etam and turned back towards Pi Hahirot, which is on the east of Ba'al Tsephon, and camped near Migdol.

⁸They moved on from Pene Hahirot, passed through the middle of the sea into the wilderness, went three days' journey in the Etam Wilderness and camped at Marah.

⁹They moved on from Marah, came to Elim, and at Elim there were twelve springs of water and seventy palms, and they camped there.

¹⁰They moved on from Elim and camped by the Reed Sea.

¹¹They moved on from the Reed Sea and camped in the Syn Wilderness.

¹²They moved on from the Syn Wilderness and camped at Dophqah.

¹³They moved on from Dophqah and camped at Alush.

¹⁴They moved on from Alush and camped at Rephidim, and there was no water for the people to drink there.

## Up to the death of Aharon

¹⁵They moved on from Rephidim and camped in the Sinay Wilderness.

¹⁶They moved on from the Sinay Wilderness and camped at Qibrot Hatta'avah.

¹⁷They moved on from Qibrot Hatta'avah and camped at Hatserot.

¹⁸They moved on from Hatserot and camped at Ritmah.

¹⁹They moved on from Ritmah and camped at Rimmon Perets.

²⁰They moved on from Rimmon Perets and camped at Libnah.

²¹They moved on from Libnah and camped at Rissah.

²²They moved on from Rissah and camped at Qehelat.

²³They moved on from Qehelat and camped at Mount Shepher.

²⁴They moved on from Mount Shepher and camped at Haradah.

²⁵They moved on from Haradah and camped at Maqhelot.

²⁶They moved on from Maqhelot and camped at Tahat.

²⁷They moved on from Tahat and camped at Terah.

²⁸They moved on from Terah and camped at Mitqah.

²⁹They moved on from Mitqah and camped at Hashmonah.

³⁰They moved on from Hashmonah and camped at Moserot.

³¹They moved on from Moserot and camped at Bene Ya'aqan.

³²They moved on from Bene Ya'aqan and camped at Hor Haggidgad.

³³They moved on from Hor Haggidgad and camped at Yotbatah.

³⁴They moved on from Yotbatah and camped at Abronah.

³⁵They moved on from Abronah and camped at Etsyon Geber.

³⁶They moved on from Etsyon Geber and camped in the Tsin Wilderness – i.e. Qadesh.

³⁷They moved on from Qadesh and camped at Mount Hor on the edge of the country of Edom.

³⁸Aharon the priest went up Mount Hor at Yahweh's bidding and died there in the fortieth year after the Yisra'elites left the country of Misrayim, in the fifth month, on the first of the month. ³⁹Aharon was a man of 123 years when he died on Mount Hor.

⁴⁰The Kena'anite, the king of Arad (he was living in the Negeb, in the country of Kena'an), heard about the coming of the Yisra'elites.

## Almost the end

⁴¹They moved on from Mount Hor and camped at Tsalmonah.

<sup>42</sup>They moved on from Tsalmonah and camped at Punon.

<sup>43</sup>They moved on from Punon and camped at Obot.

<sup>44</sup>They moved on from Obot and camped at Iyyim in the Regions Across, within the border of Mo'ab.

<sup>45</sup>They moved on from Iyyim and camped at Dibon Gad.

<sup>46</sup>They moved on from Dibon Gad and camped at Almon Diblatayim.

<sup>47</sup>They moved on from Almon Diblatayim and camped in the mountains of the Regions Across, near Nebo.

<sup>48</sup>They moved on from the mountains of the Regions Across and camped in the Mo'ab steppes by the Yarden at Yeriho. <sup>49</sup>They camped by the Yarden from Bet Hayeshimot as far as Acacias Meadow in the Mo'ab steppes.

<sup>50</sup>Yahweh spoke to Mosheh in the Mo'ab steppes by the Yarden at Yeriho: <sup>51</sup>'Speak to the Yisra'elites and say to them: "When you're crossing the Yarden into the country of Kena'an, <sup>52</sup>you're to dispossess all the people living in the country from before you, obliterate all their carvings, obliterate all their cast images and annihilate all their shrines, <sup>53</sup>and to take possession of the country and live in it, because I am giving the country to you to take possession of. <sup>54</sup>You're to have the country as a domain by lot by your kin-groups. For a large one you're to make its domain large and for a small one to make its domain small. Wherever the lot comes out for it, that's where it will be for it, as you enter into your domain by your ancestral clans.

<sup>55</sup>If you don't dispossess the people living in the country from before you, the ones among them whom you allow to remain will be barbs in your eyes and thorns in your sides. They will attack you in the country where you're living, <sup>56</sup>and what I imagined doing to them I'll do to you."'

### The dimensions of the country

**34** Yahweh spoke to Mosheh: <sup>2</sup>'Order the Yisra'elites: "When you come into the country of Kena'an, this is the country that will fall to you as a domain, the country of Kena'an by its borders.

<sup>3</sup>Your southern aspect will go from the Tsin Wilderness along the sides of Edom. Your southern border will go from the end of the Salt Sea on the east. <sup>4</sup>Your border will be south of Scorpions Ascent and pass on to Tsin and its furthest extent will be south of Qadesh Barnea. It will extend to Hatsar-addar and pass on to Atsmon. <sup>5</sup>The border will go round from Atsmon to the Misrayimite Wadi and its furthest extent will be at the Sea.

<sup>6</sup>The western border: it will be the Great Sea for you. This will be your western border, the Great Sea.

<sup>7</sup>This will be your northern border: from the Great Sea you're to mark out Mount Hor for yourselves. <sup>8</sup>From Mount Hor you're to mark out Lebo Hamat. The border's furthest extent will be Tsedad <sup>9</sup>and the border will extend to Ziphron; its furthest extent will be Hatsar Enan. This will be your northern border.

<sup>10</sup>You're to mark out for yourselves as your eastern border from Hatsar Enan to Shepham. <sup>11</sup>The border will go down from Shepham to Hariblah on the east of Ayin. The border will go down and hit the flank of the Kinneret Sea on the east. <sup>12</sup>The border will go down to the Yarden and its furthest extents will be the Salt Sea. This will be your country in respect of your borders all round."'

<sup>13</sup>Mosheh ordered the Yisra'elites: 'This is the country that you're to enter into as a domain by lot, which Yahweh ordered to give to the nine-and-a-half clans, <sup>14</sup>because the clan of the Re'ubenites by their ancestral household, the clan of the Gadites by their ancestral household and the half-clan of Menashsheh have received their domain, <sup>15</sup>in that the two-and-a-half clans have received their domain across the Yarden at Yeriho on the east, towards the sunrise.'

### Twelve trusted men

<sup>16</sup>Yahweh spoke to Mosheh: <sup>17</sup>'These are the names of the people who will make the country into domains for you: El'azar the priest and Yehoshua ben Nun. <sup>18</sup>You're to get one leader from each clan to make the country into domains. <sup>19</sup>These are the people's names:

for the clan of Yehudah, Kaleb ben Yephunneh;

20for the clan of the Shim'onites, Shemu'el ben Ammihud;

21for the clan of Binyamin, Elidad ben Kislon;

22for the clan of the Danites as leader, Buqqi ben Yogli;

23for the Yosephites:

for the clan of the Menashshites as leader, Hanni'el ben Ephod;

24and for the clan of the Ephrayimites as leader, Qemu'el ben Shiphtan;

25for the clan of the Zebulunites as leader, Elitsaphan ben Parnak;

26for the clan of the Yissakarites as leader, Palti'el ben Azzan;

27for the clan of the Asherites as leader, Ahihud ben Shelomi;

28and for the clan of the Naphtalites as leader, Pedahel ben Ammihud.'

29These are the people whom Yahweh ordered to make the country into domains for the Yisra'elites in the country of Kena'an.

# 35

Yahweh spoke to Mosheh in the Mo'ab steppes by the Yarden at Yeriho: 2'Order the Yisra'elites that they're to give the Levites towns to live in, out of the domain they hold, and they're to give the Levites the towns' pastureland round them. 3The towns will be theirs to live in and their pasturelands will be for their animals, for their property and for all their creatures. 4The pasturelands of the towns that you're to give the Levites will be from the town wall outwards, 500 metres round. 5Outside the town, you're to measure on the east side 1,000 metres, on the south side 1,000 metres, on the west side 1,000 metres and on the north side 1,000 metres, with the town in the middle. This will be the towns' pasturelands for them.

## The asylum towns

6The towns that you give to the Levites will be the six asylum towns that you give a killer to flee to, but you're to give forty-two towns along with them. 7All the towns that you give to the Levites will be forty-eight towns, them and their pasturelands. 8The towns that you give from the Yisra'elites' holding: from a large one make it large and from a small one make it small. Each

in proportion to the domain it receives is to give some of its towns to the Levites.'

9Yahweh spoke to Mosheh: 10'Speak to the Yisra'elites: "When you're crossing the Yarden into the country of Kena'an, 11you're to appoint for yourselves towns that will be asylum towns for you, so a killer who strikes down a person by accident may flee there. 12The towns will be an asylum for you from the restorer. The killer will not die until he's stood before the assembly for a ruling. 13The towns that you're to set: you're to have six asylum towns. 14You're to set three towns across the Yarden and set three towns in the country of Kena'an. They will be asylum towns. 15For the Yisra'elites, for the resident and for the settler among them, these six towns are to be for asylum for anyone who strikes down a person by accident to flee there.

16But if he struck him down with an iron object and he died, he's a killer; the killer is absolutely to be put to death. 17If he struck him down with a stone in his hand by which someone might die and he dies, he's a killer; the killer is absolutely to be put to death. 18Or if he struck him down with a wooden object in his hand by which someone might die and he dies, he's a killer; the killer is absolutely to be put to death. 19The blood restorer himself is to put the killer to death. On coming upon him, he's to put him to death.

## Deciding on responsibility

20If he knocks him down in hostility or he threw something at him with deliberation and he died, 21or he struck him down with his hand in enmity and he died, the one who struck down is absolutely to be put to death. He's a killer. The blood restorer is to put the killer to death on coming upon him.

22But if he knocked him down on meeting him without enmity, or threw any object at him without deliberation 23or with any stone by which he might die, without seeing, but he made it fall on him and he died, but he was not his enemy and was not seeking something bad for him, 24the assembly is to decide between the one who strikes down and the blood restorer. 25The assembly is to rescue the killer from the hand of the blood restorer.

The assembly is to take him back to his asylum town, to which he had fled, and he's to live in it until the death of the great priest whom they anointed with the sacred oil. ²⁶But if the killer actually goes out of the boundary of his asylum town to which he's fled, ²⁷and the blood restorer finds him outside the boundary of his asylum town, and the blood restorer kills the killer, there's no blood attaching to him, ²⁸because he was to live in his asylum town until the great priest's death. After the great priest's death the killer may go back to the region of his holding.

²⁹These are to be the ruling decree for you through your generations in all your settlements.

³⁰Anyone who strikes a person down, it's at the mouth of witnesses that people may kill the killer, and one witness will not avow against a person so he dies. ³¹You will not accept a ransom for the life of a killer who is in the wrong and should die, because he is absolutely to be put to death. ³²And you will not accept a ransom in respect of fleeing to his asylum town, so that he may go back to live in the region before the priest's death. ³³You will not pollute the country where you are, because blood pollutes the country and the country cannot be expiated for blood that has been shed in it except by the blood of the one who shed it. ³⁴You will not make taboo the country in which you're living, within which I'm dwelling, because I am Yahweh dwelling among the Yisra'elites.'"

*The five pushy women pushed back a bit*

**36** The ancestral heads of the kin-group of the descendants of Gil'ad ben Makir, son of Menashsheh, from the kin-groups of the Yosephites, drew near and spoke before Mosheh and before the leaders, the ancestral heads of the Yisra'elites. ²They said,

'Yahweh ordered my lord to give the country to the Yisra'elites as a domain by lot, and my lord was ordered by Yahweh to give our brother Tselophhad's domain to his daughters. ³But they may become wives of someone from the members of the other Yisra'elite clans, and their domain will disappear from our ancestral domain and add to the domain of the clan to which they come to belong; it will disappear from our domain by lot. ⁴And if the Yisra'elites have a ram's horn [year], their domain will add to the domain of the clan to which they belong; from the domain of our ancestral clan their domain will disappear.'

⁵So Mosheh ordered the Yisra'elites at Yahweh's bidding: 'The Yosephite clan are speaking correctly. ⁶This is the thing that Yahweh has ordered concerning Tselophhad's daughters: "They may become the wives of whoever is good in their eyes, yet they're to become wives of a kin-group in their father's clan. ⁷The domain of the Yisra'elites will not go round from clan to clan, because the Yisra'elites are to attach themselves, each individual, to his clan's ancestral domain. ⁸Any daughter who possesses a domain from the Yisra'elites' clans is to become the wife of someone from a kin-group in her ancestral clan, in order that the Yisra'elites may possess, each person, his ancestral domain. ⁹No domain will go round from a clan to another clan because the clans of the Yisra'elites are to attach themselves, each individual, to his domain."'

¹⁰As Yahweh ordered Mosheh, so Tselophhad's daughters did. ¹¹Mahlah, Tirtsah, Hoglah, Milkah and No'ah, Tselophhad's daughters, became wives of their uncles' sons. ¹²They became wives in the kin-groups of the descendants of Menashsheh ben Yoseph, and their domain was in the clan of their ancestral kin-group.

¹³These are the orders and the rulings that Yahweh gave to the Yisra'elites through Mosheh in the Mo'ab steppes by the Yarden at Yeriho.

# DEUTERONOMY

The name 'Deutero-nomy' gives the impression that this document gives us a 'second law', and that's not a bad description of it. The first law is then the teaching Yahweh gave Moses at Sinay, which dominates the second half of Exodus and the whole of Leviticus. Deuteronomy is another version of that teaching, retreading much of the same ground as the first. We noted in the Introduction to Leviticus that the Torah brings together several versions of the way God laid the law down to Israel over the centuries. God guided his people in changing social contexts by means of people such as priests, prophets and writers, who in effect presented their teaching as what Moses would say if he were here now, and people accepted it as such. They recognized that it was Moses' God who had been speaking to them in their new context.

In Deuteronomy as in Leviticus, the social context is more developed and urban than it is in the older teaching in Exodus. But Deuteronomy no longer looks at matters that priests especially need to know about, as Leviticus does. It talks about issues such as the sort of person the king ought to be and the need to tell the difference between a real prophet and a pretend prophet. That last question was a lively one in Jeremiah's day, and it wouldn't be surprising if that period (the seventh century) forms the background to Deuteronomy. One of the kings of that time, Josiah, attempted a brave reform of Judah's life and religion, seeking to remove features that reflected more the way the Canaanites and the Assyrians thought of God than the way the Israelites ought to think of God (you can read his story in 2 Kings 22—23), and there are overlaps between Josiah's reformation and the teaching of Deuteronomy.

Another feature of Deuteronomy that makes sense against this background is its emphasis on the pact between Yahweh and Israel, which it portrays along the lines of the treaty relationship that obtained between the imperial power of Assyria and a little people like Judah. In effect Deuteronomy says, 'You know how the Assyrians expect you to relate to them, with them as the big power and you expected to do what they say? Well, I'll tell you who is really the big power and what *he* expects you to do.'

As a treaty/pact/covenant document, Deuteronomy outlines as follows:

|       |                                                          |
|-------|----------------------------------------------------------|
| 1—3   | The relationship between the two parties in the past      |
| 4—11  | The big power's basic expectations, especially of loyalty |
| 12—26 | The big power's detailed expectations                     |
| 27    | Regulations for the formalizing of the relationship       |
| 28—30 | The blessings of cooperation, and the opposite            |
| 31—34 | Moses' final words                                        |

The long section of detailed expectations compares with another kind of document we know from the Middle East, one in which a king would expound some of his social and legal policies.

Jesus suggests several guidelines for discerning how we learn from Deuteronomy. He takes some key principles for relating to God from Deuteronomy 4—11 (see Matthew 4.1–11). He declares that the Torah as a whole is an exposition of Deuteronomy 6.5 and Leviticus 19.18 (see Matthew 22.37), so that in reading Deuteronomy it's always worth asking how its requirements are an exposition of love for God or love for one's neighbour. Jesus also takes up Deuteronomy's own affirmation that it is written the way it is because it makes allowance for people's stubbornness (Matthew 19.1–8), so that in reading Deuteronomy, it's also worth asking, how is God making allowance for our stubbornness here?

*Mosheh (Moses) begins his last sermon*

**1** These are the words that Mosheh spoke to all Yisra'el [Israel] across the Yarden [Jordan] in the wilderness, in the steppe near Suph, between Pa'ran and Tophel, Laban, Hatserot and Di Zahab. (²It's eleven days from Horeb by way of Mount Se'ir to Qadesh Barnea.) ³In the fortieth year in the eleventh month on the first of the month, Mosheh spoke to the Yisra'elites in accordance with everything Yahweh had ordered him for them, ⁴after he had struck down Sihon king of the Amorites who was living in Heshbon and Og king of Bashan who was living in Ashtarot (in Edre'i). ⁵Across the Yarden, in the country of Mo'ab, Mosheh resolved to expound this instruction.

⁶Yahweh our God himself spoke to us at Horeb: 'Your stay at this mountain has been long. ⁷Turn your face, move yourselves on, come to the highland of the Amorites and to all their neighbours in the steppe, in the highland, in the foothills, in the Negeb, on the sea coast (the country of the Kena'anites [Canaanites]) and the Lebanon, as far as the big river (the River Euphrates). ⁸See, I've put the country before you. Come and take possession of the country that Yahweh swore to your ancestors, to Abraham, to Yitshaq [Isaac] and to Ya'aqob [Jacob], to give to them and to their offspring after them.'

⁹I said to you at that time, 'I can't carry you alone; ¹⁰Yahweh your God has made you numerous. Here you are today, like the stars in the heavens in the large number. ¹¹May Yahweh the God of our ancestors add to you as you are, a thousand times, and bless you as he spoke to you. ¹²Alone, how can I carry the weight of you, the burden of you and your arguing? ¹³Provide for yourselves people who are smart, discerning and knowledgeable for your clans, and I will make them into your heads.'

*Recalling the time in the wilderness*

¹⁴You answered me, 'The thing that you spoke of is good to do.' ¹⁵So I got your clan heads, people who were smart and knowledgeable, and made them heads over you, divisional officials, section officials, unit officials, group officials and overseers for your clans. ¹⁶I ordered the people in authority over you at that time: 'Listen between your brothers and exercise authority faithfully between an individual and his brother and a resident. ¹⁷You will not recognize a person in making a decision. Listen to the small as you listen to the big. You will be in dread of no one's person, because decision-making belongs to God. The thing that's too tough for you, present to me, and I'll listen to it.'

¹⁸I gave you orders at that time about all the things that you should do. ¹⁹We moved on from Horeb and went through that entire great, awe-inspiring wilderness that you saw on the way to the Amorite highland, as Yahweh our God ordered us, and we came as far as Qadesh Barnea. ²⁰I said to you, 'You've come as far as the Amorite highland, which Yahweh our God is giving to us. ²¹See, Yahweh your God has put the country before you. Go up, take possession, as Yahweh the God of your ancestors spoke to you. Don't be afraid. Don't be scared.'

²²You all drew near to me and said, 'Let's send people before us so they can check out the country for us and bring us back word about the way by which we should go up, and the towns that we shall come to.' ²³The thing was good in my eyes, and I got from you twelve people, one individual for each clan. ²⁴They turned their face and went up into the highland and came as far as Cluster Wadi. They investigated it ²⁵and got some of the country's fruit in their hand and carried it down to us. They brought us back word, and said, 'The country that Yahweh our God is giving us is good.'

*Recalling the failure of nerve*

²⁶But you were not willing to go up. You rebelled against the bidding of Yahweh your God. ²⁷You muttered in your tents and said, 'It was because of Yahweh's hostility towards us that he got us out of the country of Misrayim [Egypt] to give us into the hand of the Amorites, to annihilate us. ²⁸Where are we going up to? Our brothers have made our minds melt, saying "It was a people bigger and taller than us, and towns big and fortified to the heavens, and also Anaqites, that we saw there."'

²⁹I said to you, 'You will not be frightened; you will not be afraid of them. ³⁰Yahweh your God is going before you. He will do battle for you, in accordance with all that he did with you in Misrayim before your eyes, ³¹and in the wilderness where you saw how Yahweh your God carried you as a man carries his son, on the entire way that you went until you came to this place. ³²Despite this fact, you don't trust in Yahweh your God ³³who goes before you on the way to investigate a place for you to camp, in fire by night (to enable you to see the way by which you should go) and in a cloud by day.'

³⁴Yahweh heard the sound of your words and he was furious. He swore, ³⁵'If an individual among these people, this bad generation, sees the good country that I swore to give to your ancestors . . . ³⁶Except Kaleb [Caleb] ben Yephunneh, he will see it. To him I'll give the country on which he set foot, and to his descendants, because of the fact that he fully followed after Yahweh.'

## How Mosheh paid a price

³⁷With me, too, Yahweh showed himself angry, on your account, saying 'You too will not come there. ³⁸Yehoshua [Joshua] ben Nun, who stands before you, he will come there. Strengthen him, because he's the one who will enable Yisra'el to take it as a domain.

³⁹Your little ones, who you said would become plunder, and your children who haven't got to know good from bad today, they'll come there. To them I'll give it. They'll take possession of it. ⁴⁰But you, turn your face for yourselves, move on into the wilderness by the Reed Sea road.'

⁴¹You answered, 'We've done wrong in relation to Yahweh. We ourselves will go up and do battle in accordance with all that Yahweh our God ordered us.' And you wrapped on your battle gear, each person, and got ready to go up into the highland. ⁴²But Yahweh said to me, 'Say to them, "You will not go up and you will not do battle, because I will not be among you so that you don't take a beating before your enemies."'

⁴³I spoke to you, but you didn't listen. You rebelled against Yahweh's bidding and asserted yourselves and went up into the highland. ⁴⁴And the Amorites who live in that highland came out to meet you and pursued you as bees do. They crushed you in Se'ir as far as Hormah. ⁴⁵You again wailed before Yahweh, but Yahweh didn't listen to your voice. He didn't give ear to you. ⁴⁶So you stayed at Qadesh for a long time, the very time that you stayed there.

**2** Then we turned our face and moved on into the wilderness by the Reed Sea road, as Yahweh spoke to me. We went round the highland of Se'ir for a long time.

## The beginning of the end

²Then Yahweh said to me: ³'Your going round this highland has been long. Turn your face for yourselves north. ⁴Order the people: "You're going to pass through the border of your brothers, Esaw's descendants, who live in Se'ir. They'll be afraid of you. You're to keep close watch on yourselves: ⁵don't engage them, because I shall not give you any of their country, as much as the sole of a foot treads on, because I gave Esaw Mount Se'ir as a possession. ⁶You may buy food from them for silver so you may eat, and you may also purchase water from them for silver so you may drink. ⁷Because Yahweh your God has blessed you in all the action of your hand. He's known your going through this great wilderness. Yahweh your God being with you these forty years, you haven't lacked anything."'

⁸We passed on, away from our brothers, Esaw's descendants, who live in Se'ir, away from the steppe road, away from Elat and from Etsyon Geber. We turned our face and passed by the Mo'ab Wilderness road. ⁹Yahweh said to me, 'Don't attack Mo'ab. Don't engage them in battle, because I shall not give you any of its country as a possession, because I gave Ar to Lot's descendants as a possession.

(¹⁰The Terrors lived in it before, a big and numerous people, and as tall as the Anaqites. ¹¹They are also thought of as Repha'ites, like the Anaqites, but the Mo'abites call them Terrors. ¹²The Horites lived in Se'ir before, but Esaw's descendants dispossessed them, annihilated them from before them and lived in their place, as Yisra'el did in connection with the country it came to possess, which Yahweh gave them.)

¹³Now, set off, get yourselves across Wadi Zered.' So we crossed Wadi Zered.

### When the old generation is gone

¹⁴The time that we were going from Qadesh Barnea until we crossed Wadi Zered was thirty-eight years, until the entire generation of men of battle came to an end from within the camp, as Yahweh swore about them. ¹⁵Indeed, Yahweh's hand was against them to root them out from within the camp, until they came to an end. ¹⁶When all the men of battle came to an end, dying from within the camp, ¹⁷Yahweh spoke to me: ¹⁸'Today you're passing through Mo'ab's border, through Ar, ¹⁹and you will draw near to the Ammonites. Don't attack them. Don't engage with them, because I shall not give you any of the Ammonites' country as a possession, because I've given it to Lot's descendants as a possession.

(²⁰It is also thought of as the country of the Repha'ites; they lived in it before. The Ammonites call them Zamzummites, ²¹a people big and numerous, and as tall as the Anaqites. Yahweh annihilated them from before them, and they dispossessed them and lived in their place, ²²as he did for Esaw's descendants who live in Se'ir, in that he annihilated the Horites from before them. They dispossessed them and lived in their place, until this day. ²³The Avvites who lived in villages as far as Azzah [Gaza] – the Kaphtorites who came from Kaphtor annihilated them and lived in their place.)

²⁴Set off, move on, cross Wadi Arnon, see, I've given Sihon king of Heshbon, the Amorite, into your hand, he and his country. Start taking possession. Engage them in battle. ²⁵This day I shall start putting dread of you and fear of you on the face of the peoples under the entire heavens, peoples who will hear report of you and tremble and shake before you.'

### An attempt to be peaceful

²⁶I sent envoys from the Easterlies Wilderness to Sihon king of Heshbon with words of peace: ²⁷'I want to pass through your country by the road. I shall go by the road. I shall not turn aside right or left. ²⁸You can sell me food for silver so I may eat, and you can give me water for silver so I can drink. I only want to pass through on foot ²⁹(as Esaw's descendants who live in Se'ir did for me, and the Mo'abites who live in Ar) until I cross the Yarden into the country that Yahweh our God is giving us.'

³⁰But Sihon king of Heshbon was not willing to let us pass through, because Yahweh had toughened his spirit and made his mind firm in order to give him into your hand this very day. ³¹Yahweh said to me, 'See, I've started giving over before you Sihon and his country. Start taking possession of his country.'

³²Sihon came out to meet us in battle, he and his entire people, at Yahats, ³³but Yahweh our God gave him over before us and we struck him down, he and his sons and his entire people. ³⁴We captured all his towns at that time and devoted every town, men, women and little ones. We let no survivor remain. ³⁵Only the animals did we take as plunder for ourselves, and the spoil in the towns that we captured. ³⁶From Aro'er, which is on the edge of Wadi Arnon, and the town that's in the wadi, as far as Gil'ad, there was no township that was too high for us. Yahweh our God gave over everything before us. ³⁷Only, you didn't draw near to the country of the Ammonites, the entire bank of Wadi Yabboq and the towns in the highland – everything that Yahweh our God ordered.

**3** We turned our face and went up the Bashan road. Og king of Bashan came out to meet us in battle, he and his entire company, at Edre'i. ²Yahweh said to me, 'Don't be afraid of him, because I've given him into your hand, him and his entire people and his country. You're to do to him as you did to Sihon king of the Amorites, who was living in Heshbon.'

### The man with the huge iron bed

³So Yahweh our God also gave Og king of Bashan into our hand, he and his entire company. We struck him down until no survivor remained to him. ⁴We captured all his towns at that time. There was no township

that we didn't take from them: sixty towns (the entire Argob area, Og's kingdom in Bashan), ⁵all these towns fortified with a lofty wall, doors and a bar, apart from the country towns, very many. ⁶We devoted them as we did Sihon king of Heshbon, devoting every town: men, the women and the little ones. ⁷But all the animals and the spoil in the towns we took as plunder for ourselves.

⁸So at that time we took from the hand of the two Amorite kings the country that was across the Yarden, from Wadi Arnon as far as Mount Hermon (⁹the Tsidonites call Hermon Siryon and the Amorites call it Senir), ¹⁰all the towns in the flatland, all Gil'ad and all Bashan as far as Salkah and Edre'i, the towns of Og's kingdom in Bashan . . .

(¹¹Because only Og king of Bashan remained of what was left of the Repha'ites. There, his bed, a bed made of iron – it's in Rabbah of the Ammonites, isn't it – was five metres in its length and two metres in its width by the human measure. ¹²So we took possession of this region at that time. From Aro'er, which is near Wadi Arnon, and half the highland of Gil'ad and its towns, I gave to the Re'ubenites and to the Gadites. ¹³The rest of Gil'ad and all Bashan, Og's kingdom, I gave to the half-clan of Menashsheh. The entire Argob area (all that part of Bashan used to be called the region of the Repha'ites): ¹⁴Ya'ir ben Menashsheh received the entire Argob area as far as the border of the Geshurites and the Ma'akatites. He named them after his own name (Bashan), Ya'ir's Villages, until this day. ¹⁵To Makir I gave Gil'ad. ¹⁶To the Re'ubenites and to the Gadites I gave the part of Gil'ad as far as Wadi Arnon, the middle of the wadi, the border and as far as Wadi Yabboq, the Ammonites' border.)

¹⁷. . . the steppe, and the Yarden as the border from Kinneret as far as the Steppe Sea (the Salt Sea) beneath the Pisgah slopes on the east.

## The plea Yahweh will not answer

¹⁸I ordered you at that time: 'Yahweh your God has given you this country, to take possession of it. You're to cross equipped before your brothers, the Yisra'elites, all the forceful men. ¹⁹Only your wives, your little ones and your livestock (I know that you have much livestock) are to stay in your towns which I've given you, ²⁰till Yahweh enables your brothers to settle down like you and they too take possession of the country that Yahweh your God is giving them across the Yarden. Then you may go back each individual to his possession, which I have given you.'

²¹I ordered Yehoshua at that time, 'Your eyes see all that Yahweh your God did to these two kings. So will Yahweh do to all the kingdoms into which you're crossing. ²²You will not be afraid of them, because Yahweh your God – he will do battle for you.'

²³I pleaded with Yahweh for grace at that time: ²⁴'My Lord Yahweh, you yourself started to let your servant see your greatness and your strong hand. Who is the God in the heavens or on the earth who does things like your deeds and your acts of strength? ²⁵I want to cross, please, and see the good country that's across the Yarden, this good highland and the Lebanon.'

²⁶But Yahweh was incensed with me on your account, and wouldn't listen to me. Yahweh said, 'That's plenty for you. Don't ever speak to me again about this matter. ²⁷Go up to the top of Pisgah, lift up your eyes west, north, south and east. Look with your eyes, because you will not cross this Yarden. ²⁸Give Yehoshua orders, get him to be strong and to stand firm, because he's the one who will cross before this people, and he will enable them to take possession of the country you will see.'

²⁹So we stayed in the ravine near Bet Pe'or.

## What nation has a story like Yisra'el's?

**4** Now, Yisra'el, listen to the decrees and to the rulings that I am teaching you to act on, in order that you may live, and go in and take possession of the country that Yahweh the God of your ancestors is giving you. ²You will not add to the word that I'm ordering you and you will not take away from it, in keeping the orders of Yahweh your God that I'm giving you. ³Your eyes are the ones that saw what Yahweh did in connection with Master-of-Pe'or, that Yahweh your God eliminated from among you every individual who followed Master-of-Pe'or, [4]but you who attached yourselves to Yahweh your God are all of you alive today.

[5]See, I am teaching you decrees and rulings, as Yahweh my God has ordered me, so you may act in this way within the country where you're coming to take possession of it. [6]Keep them and act on them, because it will be your smartness and your discernment before the eyes of the peoples, who will listen to all these decrees and say, 'Really, this great nation is a smart and discerning people.'

[7]Because who is a great nation that has gods near to it like Yahweh our God whenever we call to him? [8]Who is a great nation that has decrees and rulings as faithful as this entire instruction that I'm putting before you today? [9]Only keep watch on yourself, keep your own person carefully, so you don't put out of mind the things that your eyes have seen, and so they don't depart from your mind all the days of your life. And get your children and your grandchildren to acknowledge them.

## The attraction of images

[10]The day that you stood before Yahweh your God at Horeb, when Yahweh said to me, 'Congregate the people for me so I may get them to listen to my words, that they may learn to live in awe of me all the time that they live on the land, and may teach their children': [11]you drew near and stood beneath the mountain. The mountain was burning up with fire to the heart of the heavens, dark with cloud and denseness. [12]Yahweh spoke to you from the middle of the fire; you could hear the sound of the words, but you couldn't see a shape, only a sound. [13]He told you about his pact which he ordered you to act on, the ten words, and he wrote them on two stone tablets. [14]And at that time Yahweh ordered me to teach you decrees and rulings for you to act on in the country where you're crossing over to take possession of it. [15]Keep close watch on yourselves, because you didn't see any shape on the day Yahweh spoke to you at Horeb from the middle of the fire, [16]so that you don't act devastatingly and make yourselves a shaped sculpture (any figure, the form of a male or female, [17]the form of any animal that's on the earth, the form of any

winged bird that flies in the heavens, [18]the form of anything moving on the ground, the form of any fish that's in the water below the earth), [19]and so you don't raise your eyes to the heavens and look at the sun, the moon and the stars, the entire army in the heavens, and stray and bow low to them and serve them, when Yahweh your God allocated them to all the peoples under all the heavens. [20]Yahweh took you and got you out of the iron furnace, out of Misrayim, to be a people for him, his domain, this very day.

## Annihilation and restoration

[21]Yahweh showed himself angry with me because of your words, and he swore that I would not cross the Yarden and not come into the good country that Yahweh your God is giving you as a domain. [22]Because I'm going to die in this country. I'm not crossing the Yarden. You're going to cross and take possession of this good country.

[23]Keep watch on yourselves so you don't put out of mind the pact of Yahweh your God, which he solemnized with you, and make yourselves a shaped sculpture of anything, about which Yahweh your God has given you orders. [24]Because Yahweh your God is a devouring fire, a passionate God. [25]When you father children and grandchildren and you become sleepy in the country, and you act devastatingly and make a shaped sculpture of anything, and do what is bad in the eyes of Yahweh your God so as to provoke him, [26]I call the heavens and the earth to testify against you today that you will quickly quite perish from on the country where you're crossing the Yarden to take possession of it. You won't stay a long time on it, because you will be totally annihilated. [27]Yahweh will disperse you among the peoples. Few in number of you will remain among the nations where Yahweh drives you, [28]and there you will serve gods made by human hands of wood and stone, which cannot see, cannot listen, cannot eat and cannot smell.

[29]But you will seek Yahweh your God from there, and you will find, when you enquire of him with your entire heart and with your entire being [30]when you're under pressure. All these things will befall you in a later time, but

you will turn back to Yahweh your God and listen to his voice. ³¹Because Yahweh your God is a compassionate God. He won't let go of you. He won't devastate you. He won't put out of mind the pact with your ancestors, which he swore to them.

### Has the like of it ever been heard?

³²Because do ask about an earlier time, which was before you, from the day when God created humanity on the earth, and from one end of the heavens to the other end of the heavens, whether anything like this great thing has happened or anything like this has made itself heard. ³³Has a people heard a god's voice speaking from the middle of the fire, as you yourself heard, and stayed alive? ³⁴Or has a god tried to come to take a nation for himself from within a nation, by trials, by signs, by proofs, by battle, by a strong hand, by an extended arm and by great awe-inspiring deeds, in accordance with all that Yahweh your God did for you in Misrayim before your eyes? ³⁵You yourselves have been allowed to see, so as to acknowledge that Yahweh is God. There's no other apart from him. ³⁶From the heavens he let you hear his voice to discipline you, and on the earth he let you see his great fire. You heard his words from the middle of the fire. ³⁷On account of the fact that he loved your ancestors, he chose their offspring after them, and got you out of Misrayim by his presence, by his great energy, ³⁸to dispossess bigger and more numerous nations than you from before you, to bring you in to give you their country as a domain this very day, ³⁹so you may acknowledge today and make it come back to your mind that Yahweh is God in the heavens above and on the earth below (there's no other) ⁴⁰and may keep his decrees and his orders which I'm giving you today, so things may be good for you and for your children after you, in order that your time may be long on the land that Yahweh your God is giving you for all time.

### What Yahweh said face to face

⁴¹Then Mosheh made three towns distinct, across the Yarden towards the rising of the sun, ⁴²for a killer to flee there who kills his neighbour without knowing and when he was not hostile to him in previous days, so he could flee to one of the towns and live: ⁴³Betser in the wilderness in the flatland, for the Re'ubenites; Heights-in-Gil'ad, for the Gadites; and Golan, in Bashan, for the Menashshites.

⁴⁴This is the instruction that Mosheh put before the Yisra'elites; ⁴⁵these are the affirmations, the decrees and the rulings that Mosheh spoke to the Yisra'elites when they had got out of Misrayim, ⁴⁶across the Yarden, in the ravine near Bet Pe'or, in the country of Sihon king of the Amorites who had been living in Heshbon, whom Mosheh and the Yisra'elites struck down when they had got out of Misrayim. ⁴⁷They took possession of his country and the country of Og king of Bashan, the two kings of the Amorites, which were across the Yarden towards the rising of the sun, ⁴⁸from Aro'er which is on the bank of Wadi Arnon and as far as Mount Si'on (i.e. Hermon), ⁴⁹and all the steppe across the Yarden to the east and as far as the Steppe Sea, beneath the Pisgah slopes.

**5** Mosheh called all Yisra'el and said to them: Listen, Yisra'el, to the decrees and the rulings that I'm speaking in your ears today. You're to learn them and keep them by acting on them.

²Yahweh our God solemnized a pact with us at Horeb. ³It was not with our parents that Yahweh solemnized this pact but with us ourselves, these people here today, all of us who are alive. ⁴Face to face Yahweh spoke with you on the mountain from the middle of the fire ⁵(I was standing between Yahweh and you at that time to tell you Yahweh's word, because you were afraid of the fire and you didn't go up on the mountain):

### Ten words

⁶'I am Yahweh your God who got you out of the country of Misrayim, out of a household of serfs.

⁷For you there will be no other gods in my presence.

⁸You will not make yourself a sculpture of any shape that's in the heavens above, that's on the earth below or that's in the water under the earth. ⁹You will not bow low to

them and you will not serve them. Because I, Yahweh your God, am the passionate God, attending to parents' waywardness in connection with children and with thirds and with fourths for people who are hostile to me, ¹⁰but acting in commitment towards thousands for people who are loyal to me and to people who keep my orders.

¹¹You will not lift up the name of Yahweh your God in respect of something empty, because Yahweh will not free of guilt a person who lifts up his name in respect of something empty.

¹²Keep the sabbath day so as to make it sacred, as Yahweh your God has ordered you. ¹³For six days you can serve and do all your work, ¹⁴but the seventh day is a sabbath for Yahweh your God. You will not do any work, you, your son or your daughter, your servant or your handmaid, your ox or your donkey or any of your animals, or the resident who is in your communities, in order that your servant and your handmaid may rest like you. ¹⁵You're to be mindful that you were a servant in the country of Misrayim but Yahweh your God got you out of there with a strong hand and an extended arm. That's why Yahweh your God has ordered you to make the sabbath day.

¹⁶Honour your father and your mother as Yahweh your God has ordered you, in order that your time may be long, and in order that things may be good for you, on the land that Yahweh your God is giving you.

¹⁷You will not murder.

¹⁸You will not be adulterous.

¹⁹You will not steal.

²⁰You will not avow empty testimony against your neighbour.

²¹You will not desire your neighbour's wife. You will not long for your neighbour's house or his field, his servant or his handmaid, his ox or his donkey, or anything that your neighbour has.'

## If only . . .

²²These words Yahweh spoke to your entire congregation at the mountain from the middle of the fire (the cloud and the denseness) in a loud voice. He didn't add anything. He wrote them on two stone tablets and gave them to me.

²³When you heard the voice from the middle of the darkness, and the mountain was burning up with fire, you drew near to me, all your clan heads and your elders, ²⁴and said, 'Here, Yahweh our God has let us see his splendour and his greatness, and we've heard his voice from the middle of the fire. This day we've seen that God can speak with a human being and he can live.

²⁵But now, why should we die? Because this great fire will devour us. If we continue to hear the voice of Yahweh our God any more, we will die. ²⁶Because who is there of all flesh that has listened to the living God's voice speaking from the middle of the fire like us and lived? ²⁷You draw near and listen to everything that Yahweh our God says, and you can speak to us everything that Yahweh our God speaks to you, and we will listen and do it.'

²⁸Yahweh listened to the sound of your words as you spoke to me. Yahweh said to me, 'I've listened to the sound of this people's words that they have spoken to you. They've done what is good in everything that they spoke. ²⁹If only this will be their mind, to live in awe of me and to keep all my orders at all times, in order that things may be good for them and for their children permanently. ³⁰Go, say to them: "Get yourselves back to your tents." ³¹But you, stand here with me and I shall speak to you the entire order (the decrees and the rulings) that you're to teach them so they will do them in the country that I'm giving them, to take possession of it.'

## Listen, Yisra'el

³²You're to keep them by acting as Yahweh your God has ordered you. You will not turn aside right or left. ³³You're to walk in every way that Yahweh your God has ordered you, in order that you may live and things may be good for you and you may stay a long time in the country that you're to take possession of.

**6** This is the order (the decrees and rulings) that Yahweh your God has ordered to teach you, to act on in the country where you're crossing over to take possession of it, [2]in order that you may live in awe of Yahweh your God by keeping all his decrees and his orders that I'm giving you – you, your children and your grandchildren – all the days of your life, and in order that your time may be long. [3]You're to listen, Yisra'el, and keep them by acting on them so things will be good for you and so you may become very numerous, as Yahweh the God of your ancestors spoke to you (a country flowing with milk and syrup).

[4]Listen, Yisra'el: Yahweh our God Yahweh one. [5]You're to be loyal to Yahweh your God with your entire mind, with your entire being, with your entire might.

[6]These words that I'm ordering you today are to be on your mind. [7]You're to drive them home to your children and speak of them when you're staying at home and when you're going on a journey, when you lie down and when you get up. [8]You're to tie them as a sign on your hand. They're to be bands between your eyes, [9]and you're to write them on the doorposts of your house and on your gateways.

## When your children ask questions

[10]When Yahweh your God brings you into the country that he swore to your ancestors, to Abraham, to Yitshaq and to Ya'aqob, to give you, great and good towns that you haven't built, [11]houses full of everything good that you haven't filled, cisterns dug that you haven't dug, vineyards and olive groves that you haven't planted, and you eat and are full, [12]keep watch on yourself so you don't put Yahweh out of mind, the one who got you out of the country of Misrayim, out of a household of serfs. [13]You're to live in awe of Yahweh your God, to serve him and to swear in his name. [14]You will not follow other gods from among the gods of the peoples that are round you, [15]because Yahweh your God among you is a passionate God, so that the anger of Yahweh your God doesn't rage against you and he annihilate you from on the face of the land. [16]You will not test Yahweh your God as you tested him at Massah ['Testing']. [17]Keep carefully the orders of Yahweh your God, his affirmations and his decrees which he has given you. [18]You're to do what is right and good in Yahweh's eyes in order that things may be good for you and you may come in and take possession of the good country that Yahweh swore to your ancestors, [19]by driving out all your enemies from before you, as Yahweh has spoken.

[20]When your child asks you in the future, 'What were the affirmations, the decrees and the rulings that Yahweh our God ordered you?', [21]you're to say to your child, 'We were Par'oh's serfs in Misrayim, and Yahweh got us out of Misrayim with a strong hand. [22]Yahweh put great, bad signs and proofs against Misrayim, against Par'oh and against his entire household, before our eyes, [23]and he got us out of there in order that he might bring us in to give us the country that he swore to our ancestors. [24]Yahweh ordered us to act on all these decrees, to live in awe of Yahweh our God for our good at all times, to keep us alive, this very day. [25]It will be our right standing, when we keep this entire order before Yahweh our God by acting on it, as he ordered us.'

## Yahweh's attraction

7 When Yahweh your God brings you into the country where you're coming to take possession of it, and clears away many nations from before you (the Hittite, the Girgashite, the Amorite, the Kena'anite, the Perizzite, the Hivvite and the Yebusite, seven nations bigger and more numerous than you), [2]and Yahweh your God gives them up before you and you strike them down, you're to devote them totally. You will not solemnize a pact with them. You will not grace them. [3]You will not make marriages with them. You will not give your daughter to his son or take his daughter for your son, [4]because he'll turn your son aside from following me and they'll serve other gods, and the anger of Yahweh will rage against you and he'll quickly annihilate you. [5]Rather, you're to do this to them: You're to demolish their altars. You're to break up their columns. You're to cut down their totem poles. You're to burn their statues in fire.

[6]Because you're a people sacred for Yahweh your God. It was you that Yahweh your God chose to become a people that is personal treasure for him from all the peoples on the

face of the ground. ⁷It wasn't because of your larger number than all the peoples that Yahweh got attracted to you and chose you, because you were smaller than all the peoples. ⁸Rather, it was because of Yahweh's loyalty to you, and because of his keeping the oath that he swore to your ancestors, that Yahweh got you out with a strong hand, redeemed you out of a household of serfs, out of the hand of Par'oh king of Misrayim.

⁹You're to acknowledge that Yahweh your God is God, the trustworthy God, keeping the pact and commitment to people who are loyal to him and keep his orders, to a thousand generations, ¹⁰but one who makes good to people who are hostile to him, to the person's face, by obliterating him. He isn't slow with someone who's hostile to him; to his face he makes good to him. ¹¹So you're to keep the order (the decrees and the rulings) that I'm giving you today, by acting on it.

### The hornet

¹²On the basis that you listen to these rulings and keep and act on them, Yahweh your God will keep for you the pact and commitment that he swore to your ancestors. ¹³He will be loyal to you, bless you and make you numerous. He will bless the fruit of your womb and the fruit of your land, your grain, your new wine and your fresh oil, the drop of your domestic animals and the young of your flock, on the land that he swore to your ancestors to give you. ¹⁴You will be blessed above all the peoples. There will not be among you male or female who is infertile, or among your animals. ¹⁵Yahweh will remove from you every illness, and none of the bad illnesses of Misrayim, which you know, will he place on you. He'll put them on the people who are hostile to you. ¹⁶You're to devour all the peoples that Yahweh your God is giving over to you. Your eye will not pity them. You will not serve their gods, because it will be a snare to you. ¹⁷When you say inside, 'These nations are more numerous than me – how will I be able to dispossess them?', ¹⁸you will not be afraid of them. You're to be resolutely mindful of what Yahweh your God did to Par'oh and to all Misrayim, ¹⁹the great tests that your eyes

saw, the signs and the proofs, the strong hand and the extended arm by which Yahweh your God got you out. Yahweh your God will act in that way to all the peoples before whom you're afraid.

²⁰Yahweh your God will also send off a hornet against them until those who remain, and who are hiding from before you, perish. ²¹You will not be frightened before them, because Yahweh your God is among you, a great and awe-inspiring God.

### Little by little

²²Yahweh your God will clear away those nations from before you little by little. You won't be able to finish them off quickly, so the creatures of the wild don't become too numerous for you. ²³But Yahweh your God will give them over before you and throw them into a great turmoil until their annihilation. ²⁴He will give their kings into your hand and you will eliminate their name from under the heavens. No one will take a stand before you until you've annihilated them.

²⁵The statues of their gods you're to burn in fire. You will not desire the silver and gold on them and take it for yourself, so you don't trap yourself by it, because it would be an offensive act to Yahweh your God. ²⁶You will not bring an offensive thing into your house, and become an object for devoting, like it. You're to treat it as totally abominable, totally offensive, because it's an object for devoting.

**8** The entire order that I'm giving you today you're to keep by acting on it, in order that you may live and become numerous, and come and take possession of the country that Yahweh swore to your ancestors. ²You're to be mindful of the entire way that Yahweh your God had you go these forty years in the wilderness, in order that he might humble you by testing you so as to know what was in your mind, whether you would keep his orders or not. ³He humbled you and let you be hungry and fed you the *maan* which you hadn't known and your ancestors had not known, in order that he might get you to acknowledge that human beings don't live on the basis of bread alone but on the basis of everything that comes out of Yahweh's mouth. ⁴Your clothing hasn't worn out from upon you and your foot hasn't swollen these forty years.

## The danger of forgetting

[5]You're to acknowledge in your mind that as someone disciplines his son, Yahweh your God disciplines you, [6]and you're to keep the orders of Yahweh your God by walking in his ways and by living in awe of him. [7]Because Yahweh your God is bringing you into a good country, a country of wadis with water, springs and depths issuing, in valley and in mountain, [8]a country of wheat, barley, vine, fig and pomegranate, a country of olive oil and syrup, [9]a country where you can eat bread without being short, where you won't lack anything, a country whose stones are iron and from whose mountains you can dig copper. [10]You will eat and be full and bless Yahweh your God for the good country that he's given you.

[11]Keep watch on yourself so you don't put Yahweh your God out of mind by not keeping his orders, his rulings and his decrees which I'm giving you today, [12]so you don't eat and get full, and build good houses and live in them, [13]and your herd and your flock increase, and your silver and gold increase, and everything that you have increases, [14]and your mind exalts itself and you put out of mind Yahweh your God who got you out of the country of Misrayim, out of a household of serfs, [15]the one who had you go through the great, awe-inspiring wilderness with venomous snake and scorpion, and desert where there was no water, who got water out of a flint crag for you, [16]who enabled you to eat *maan* in the wilderness, which your ancestors had not known, in order that he might humble you and in order that he might test you, so as to do good to you in your later life, [17]and you say inside, 'My energy and the might of my hand generated these resources for me.'

## The importance of remembering

[18]You're to be mindful of Yahweh your God, that he's the one who is giving you the energy to generate resources, in order to implement the pact that he swore to your ancestors, this very day. [19]If you do put Yahweh your God out of mind and follow other gods and serve them and bow low to them, I testify against you today that you will totally perish. [20]Like the nations whom Yahweh is making perish from before you, so you will perish, since you don't listen to the voice of Yahweh your God.

**9** Listen, Yisra'el. Today you're crossing the Yarden to go in to dispossess nations bigger and more numerous than you: big towns fortified to the heavens, [2]a big and tall people, the Anaqites whom you yourselves know and of whom you've heard it said, 'Who can take a stand before the descendants of Anaq?' [3]You're to acknowledge today that Yahweh your God — he's crossing before you, a devouring fire. He's the one who will destroy them. He's the one who will put them down before you so you'll dispossess them and make them perish quickly, as Yahweh has spoken to you.

[4]Don't say inside, when Yahweh your God has driven them out from before you, 'It's because of my faithfulness that Yahweh brought me in to take possession of this country.' It's because of the faithlessness of these nations that Yahweh is dispossessing them from before you. [5]It's not because of your faithfulness or because of the uprightness of your mind that you're going in to take possession of their country. It's because of the faithlessness of these nations that Yahweh your God is dispossessing them from before you, and in order to implement the word that Yahweh swore to your ancestors, to Abraham, to Yitshaq and to Ya'aqob.

## Not because of your faithfulness

[6]You're to acknowledge that it's not because of your faithfulness that Yahweh your God is giving you this good country, to take possession of it, because you're a tough-necked people. [7]Be mindful, don't put out of mind, how you infuriated Yahweh your God in the wilderness. From the day that you left the country of Misrayim till you came to this place, you've been rebellious towards Yahweh. [8]At Horeb you infuriated Yahweh and he showed himself angry enough with you to annihilate you, [9]when I went up the mountain to get the stone tablets, the tablets of the

pact that Yahweh had solemnized with you. I stayed on the mountain forty days and forty nights. I ate no bread and I drank no water. [10]Yahweh gave me the two stone tablets written on by God's finger, with all the very things on them that God had spoken with you on the mountain from the middle of the fire on the day of the congregation. [11]At the end of forty days and forty nights Yahweh gave me the two stone tablets, the pact tablets.

[12]But Yahweh said to me, 'Get up, go down from here quickly, because your people whom you got out of Misrayim have acted devastatingly. They've departed quickly from the way that I ordered them. They've made a figurine for themselves.' [13]And Yahweh said to me, 'I've looked at this people, and here, it's a tough-necked people. [14]Let me go, so I can annihilate them and wipe out their name from under the heavens, and make you into a more numerous and vast nation than them.'

[15]I turned my face and came down from the mountain (the mountain was burning up with fire) with the two tablets of the pact in my two hands. [16]I looked, and there, you'd done wrong in relation to Yahweh your God. You'd made a bullock figurine for yourselves. You'd departed quickly from the way that Yahweh had ordered you. [17]I took hold of the two tablets and threw them out of my two hands and broke them up before your eyes.

## Effective intercession

[18]I made myself fall before Yahweh. Like the first time, for forty days and forty nights I ate no bread and drank no water on account of all the wrong that you'd committed in doing what was bad in Yahweh's eyes so as to provoke him, [19]because I was in dread before the anger and wrath with which Yahweh was furious towards you so as to annihilate you. Yahweh listened to me that time, too. [20]With Aharon [Aaron], Yahweh showed himself very angry, enough to annihilate him, but I also interceded on Aharon's behalf at that time.

[21]The wrongful thing that you'd made, the bullock, I got it and burned it in fire and crushed it and ground it well until it became fine as powder, and I threw its powder into the wadi coming down from the mountain.

[22]At Tab'erah and at Massah and at Qibrot Hatta'avah you were people who infuriated Yahweh. [23]When Yahweh sent you from Qadesh Barnea, saying 'Go up and take possession of the country that I've given you', you rebelled against the bidding of Yahweh your God. You didn't trust in him and you didn't listen to his voice. [24]You've been rebellious in relation to Yahweh from the day I knew you.

[25]I made myself fall before Yahweh for the forty days and forty nights that I made myself fall, because Yahweh said he would annihilate you. [26]I interceded with Yahweh and said, 'My Lord Yahweh, don't devastate your people, your domain, which you redeemed by your greatness, which you got out of Misrayim with a strong hand. [27]Be mindful of your servants, of Abraham, of Yitshaq and of Ya'aqob. Don't turn your face to the obstinacy of this people, to its faithlessness, to its wrongdoing, [28]so the country from which you got us out doesn't say, "It was because Yahweh couldn't bring them into the country of which he spoke to them and because he was hostile to them that he got them out, to let them die in the wilderness." [29]They are your people, your domain, which you got out by your great energy and your extended arm.'

## The ten words re-inscribed

**10** At that time Yahweh said to me, 'Carve yourself two stone tablets like the first ones, and go up to me on the mountain, and make yourself a wooden chest. [2]I'll write on the tablets the words that were on the first tablets, which you broke up, and you're to put them in the chest.' [3]So I made an acacia wood chest and carved two stone tablets like the first. I went up the mountain with the two tablets in my hand, [4]and he wrote on the tablets the same text as the first, the ten words that Yahweh spoke to you on the mountain from the middle of the fire on the day of the congregation. Yahweh gave them to me [5]and I turned my face and came down from the mountain, and put the tablets in the chest that I had made. So they've been there, as Yahweh ordered me.

[6]The Yisra'elites moved on from Bene-ya'aqan Wells to Moserah. There Aharon died

and he was buried there, and El'azar his son acted as priest in his place. ⁷From there they moved on to Gudgod, and from Gudgod to Yotbat, a region of wadis with water. ⁸At that time Yahweh made the clan of Levi distinct, to carry Yahweh's pact chest, to stand before Yahweh to minister to him, and to bless in his name, until this day. ⁹Therefore Levi hasn't had a share, a domain, with his brothers. Yahweh is his domain, as Yahweh your God spoke to him.

¹⁰So I – I stood on the mountain as at the first time for forty days and forty nights, and Yahweh listened to me once again. Yahweh was not willing to devastate you. ¹¹Yahweh said to me, 'Set off, go, move on before the people, so they may come in and take possession of the country that I swore to their ancestors to give them.'

## Attraction and attachment

¹²Now, Yisra'el, what is Yahweh your God asking of you except to live in awe of Yahweh your God so as to walk in all his ways, to be loyal to him and to serve Yahweh your God with your entire mind and with your entire being, ¹³so as to keep Yahweh's orders and his decrees that I'm giving you today for your good?

¹⁴Here, to Yahweh your God belong the heavens, the highest heavens, the earth and everything that's in it. ¹⁵Only Yahweh got attracted to your ancestors so as to be loyal to them, and chose their offspring after them, you, from all the peoples, this very day. ¹⁶So circumcise the foreskin of your mind. You will not toughen your neck any more. ¹⁷Because Yahweh your God – he's the God over the gods, the Lord over the lords, the God great, mighty and awe-inspiring, who doesn't honour a person and doesn't accept a bribe. ¹⁸He makes a ruling for the orphan and the widow and he is loyal to the resident by giving him bread and clothing. ¹⁹So you're to be loyal to the resident, because you were residents in the country of Misrayim.

²⁰Yahweh your God: you're to live in awe of him, serve and attach yourselves to him, and swear by his name. ²¹He's to be your praise and he's to be your God who did for you these great, awe-inspiring things that your eyes saw.

²²As seventy persons your ancestors went down to Misrayim, but now Yahweh your God has made you like the stars in the heavens in the large number.

## It was you

**11** So you're to be loyal to Yahweh your God and keep his charge, his decrees, his rulings and his orders at all times. ²You're to acknowledge today that it was not with your children, who didn't know and who didn't see the discipline of Yahweh your God, his greatness, his strong hand and his extended arm, ³his signs and his deeds that he did in the middle of Misrayim to Par'oh king of Misrayim and to all his country, ⁴and what he did to Misrayim's force, to its horses and to its chariotry, over whose heads Yahweh made the water of the Reed Sea flow when they pursued after you, and in this way destroyed them until this day, ⁵and what he did for you in the wilderness until you came as far as this place, ⁶and what he did to Datan and to Abiram, the sons of Eli'ab the Re'ubenite, whom the earth opened its mouth and swallowed, them, their households, their tents and everything that existed that was in their company, in the middle of all Yisra'el . . .

⁷Rather it was your eyes that saw every great deed that Yahweh did. ⁸So you're to keep the entire order that I'm giving you today, in order that you may be strong and may go in and take possession of the country where you're crossing over to take possession of it, ⁹and in order that you may stay a long time on the land that Yahweh swore to your ancestors to give to them and to their offspring, a country flowing with milk and syrup.

## A country that drinks water from the heavens

¹⁰Because the country where you're coming to take possession of it is not like the country of Misrayim, from where you got out, where you sow your seed and water it by foot, like a vegetable garden. ¹¹The country where you're crossing over to take possession of it is a country of mountains and valleys, one that drinks water from the heavens' rain,

¹²a country that Yahweh your God enquires after. The eyes of Yahweh your God are on it regularly from the year's beginning until the year's end.

¹³If you really do listen to my orders that I'm giving you today by being loyal to Yahweh your God and by serving him with your entire mind and with your entire being, ¹⁴I will give rain on your country in its time, early rain and late rain, and you'll gather in your grain, your new wine and your fresh oil. ¹⁵I'll give grass in your fields for your animals and you'll eat and be full. ¹⁶Keep watch on yourselves so your mind is not naive and you depart, and serve other gods and bow low to them, ¹⁷and Yahweh's anger rages against you, and he holds back the heavens and there's no rain, and the ground doesn't give its produce, and you quickly perish from on the good country that Yahweh is giving you.

¹⁸You're to put these words on to your mind and on to your person. Tie them as a sign on your hand. They're to be bands between your eyes. ¹⁹You're to teach them to your children by speaking of them when you're staying at home and when you're going on a journey, when you're lying down and when you're getting up, ²⁰and you're to write them on the doorposts of your house and on your gateways, ²¹in order that your days and your children's days may be many on the land that Yahweh swore to your ancestors to give them, as many as the days of the heavens over the earth.

## Blessing or slighting

²²Because if you carefully keep this entire order that I'm giving you by acting on it, being loyal to Yahweh your God by walking in all his ways and by attaching yourselves to him, ²³Yahweh will dispossess all these nations from before you and you will take possession of nations bigger and more numerous than you. ²⁴Every place on which the sole of your foot treads will be yours. From the wilderness and the Lebanon, from the river (the River Euphrates) as far as the Western Sea will be your border. ²⁵No one will take a stand against you. Yahweh your God will put dread of you and fear of you on the face of the entire

country on which you tread, as he's spoken to you.

²⁶Look, I'm putting before you today blessing and slight: ²⁷the blessing because you listen to the orders of Yahweh your God that I'm giving you today, ²⁸and the slight if you don't listen to the orders of Yahweh your God but depart from the way that I'm ordering you today by following other gods that you haven't acknowledged. ²⁹When Yahweh your God brings you into the country where you're coming to take possession of it, you're to put the blessing on Mount Gerizim and the slight on Mount Ebal. ³⁰They're across the Yarden, beyond the sunset road in the country of the Kena'anites who live in the steppe near Gilgal, beside the Moreh Oaks, aren't they. ³¹Because you're crossing the Yarden to go in to take possession of the country that Yahweh your God is giving you so you may take possession of it and live in it. ³²You're to keep all the decrees and the rulings that I'm putting before you today, by acting on them.

## On not following your instincts

**12** These are the decrees and the rulings that you're to keep by acting on them, in the country that Yahweh the God of your ancestors has given you to take possession of it, all the time that you're living on the land. ²You're to obliterate, totally, all the sites where the nations that you're dispossessing have served their gods, on high mountains and on hills and under any verdant tree. ³You're to tear down their altars, break up their columns, burn their totem poles in fire, cut down the statues of their gods and obliterate their name from that site. ⁴You will not act for Yahweh your God in that way.

⁵Rather you're to enquire at the site that Yahweh your God chooses from all your clans, to put his name there for him to dwell. You're to come there ⁶and bring there your whole offerings and your sacrifices, your tenths and the contribution from your hand, your pledges and your free offerings, and the firstlings of your herd and of your flock. ⁷You're to eat there before Yahweh your God and rejoice in every undertaking of your hand (you and your households) in which Yahweh your God has blessed you.

⁸You will not act in accordance with anything that we are doing here today, an individual doing anything that's all right in his eyes, ⁹because until now you haven't come to the place to settle down, to the domain that Yahweh your God is giving you. ¹⁰You're to cross the Yarden and live in the country that Yahweh your God is giving you as a domain. He will enable you to settle down free of all your enemies all round, and you will live in confidence. ¹¹And the site where Yahweh your God chooses to have his name dwell, you're to bring there everything that I'm ordering you: your burnt offerings and your sacrifices, your tenths, the contribution from your hand and every choice thing among the pledges that you make to Yahweh.

## Freedom to 'sacrifice' nearer home

¹²So you're to rejoice before Yahweh your God, you, your sons and your daughters, your servants and your handmaids, and the Levite who is in your communities (because he has no share, no domain with you). ¹³Keep watch on yourself so you don't offer up your burnt offerings at every site that you see. ¹⁴Rather, at the site that Yahweh chooses in one of your clans, there you're to offer up your burnt offerings, and there you're to act on everything that I'm ordering you. ¹⁵Only, at any longing of your appetite you may 'sacrifice' and eat meat in accordance with the blessing of Yahweh your God that he's given you, in all your communities. Taboo and pure people may eat it, like the gazelle and like the deer. ¹⁶Only, the blood you will not eat. You're to pour it on the earth like water. ¹⁷In your communities you will not be able to eat the tenth of your grain, new wine and fresh oil, or the firstlings of your herd and flock, or any pledges that you make, or your free offerings or the contribution from your hand. ¹⁸Rather, you're to eat them before Yahweh your God at the site that Yahweh your God chooses, you, your son and your daughter, your servant and your handmaid, and the Levite who is in your communities, and you're to rejoice before Yahweh your God in every undertaking of your hand. ¹⁹Keep watch on yourself so you don't abandon the Levite all your days on your land.

²⁰When Yahweh your God widens your border, as he spoke to you, and you say, 'I want to eat meat', because your appetite longs to eat meat, at any longing of your appetite you may eat meat. ²¹When the site that Yahweh your God chooses to put his name there is far from you, you may 'sacrifice' from your herd or from your flock that Yahweh has given you as I've ordered you, and you may eat in your communities, at the longing of your appetite.

## Not eating the blood

²²However, as the gazelle and the deer are eaten – in this way you're to eat it. Taboo and pure people may eat it together. ²³Only, be firm about not eating the blood, because the blood is the life. You will not eat the life with the meat. ²⁴Given that you will not eat it, you're to pour it on the earth like water. ²⁵You will not eat it, in order that things may be good for you and for your descendants after you, because you do what's right in Yahweh's eyes. ²⁶Only, your sacred things that you have, and your pledges, you're to take up, and come to the site that Yahweh chooses. ²⁷You're to make your burnt offerings, the meat and the blood, on the altar of Yahweh your God. The blood of your sacrifices is to be poured on the altar of Yahweh your God, but the meat you may eat. ²⁸Keep and listen to all these words that I'm ordering you, in order that things may be good for you and for your descendants after you permanently, because you do what is good and right in the eyes of Yahweh your God. ²⁹When Yahweh your God cuts down the nations where you're coming to dispossess them from before you, and you dispossess them and live in their country, ³⁰keep watch on yourself so you're not trapped into following them after they've been annihilated from before you, and so you don't enquire of their gods, saying 'How do these nations serve their gods, so I may also act in the same way?' ³¹You will not act in this way towards Yahweh your God, because they do for their gods everything that's an offence to Yahweh, that to which he's hostile, because they even burn their sons and their daughters in fire for their gods.

³²Every thing that I'm ordering you, you're to keep by acting on it. You will not add to it and you will not take away from it.

## False prophets

**13** When a prophet or someone who has a dream rises among you, and gives you a sign or a proof ²(and the sign or the proof of which he spoke to you comes about), saying 'Let's follow other gods (which you haven't acknowledged) and serve them': ³you will not listen to the words of that prophet or that one who has the dream, because Yahweh your God is testing you so as to know whether you're people who are loyal to Yahweh your God with your entire mind and with your entire being. ⁴You're to follow Yahweh your God. You're to live in awe of him. His orders you're to keep and to his voice you're to listen. He's the one you're to serve, and you're to attach yourselves to him.

⁵That prophet or that one who has the dream: he's to be put to death, because he spoke defiance against Yahweh your God (who got you out of the country of Misrayim and redeemed you from a household of serfs) to drive you from the way that Yahweh your God ordered you to walk in. So you will burn away the bad thing from among you.

⁶When your brother, your mother's son, or your son or your daughter, or the wife in your arms, or your neighbour who is as close to you as your own self, incites you in secret, saying 'Let's go and serve other gods' (which you yourself and your ancestors haven't acknowledged), ⁷from the gods of the peoples that are round you, the ones near to you or the ones far away from you, from one end of the country to the other end of the country, ⁸you will not agree with him, you will not listen to him.

Your eye will not pity him. You will not spare him or conceal him, ⁹but simply kill him. Your own hand will be the first against him, to put him to death, and the hand of the entire people afterwards. ¹⁰Pelt him with stones so he dies, because he sought to drive you away from Yahweh your God who got you out of the country of Misrayim, out of a household of serfs.

¹¹All Yisra'el will hear and live in awe and will not again do the likes of this bad thing among you.

## When someone leads the town astray

¹²When you hear in one of your towns that Yahweh your God is giving you to live in, ¹³People who are scoundrels have gone out from among you and have driven away the people living in their town, saying "Let's go and serve other gods"' (which you haven't acknowledged), ¹⁴you're to enquire well and search out and ask. And there, the thing is established truthful, this offensive act was done among you. ¹⁵Strike down hard the people living in that town with the mouth of the sword. Devote it, everything that's in it and its animals, with the mouth of the sword. ¹⁶All its spoil you're to collect in the middle of the square, and burn the town and all its spoil with fire as a whole offering for Yahweh your God. It's to become a permanent ruin. It will not be built up again.

¹⁷Not a thing from what was to be devoted will attach itself to your hand, in order that Yahweh may turn back from his angry rage and show you compassion. He will be compassionate to you and make you numerous, as he swore to your ancestors, ¹⁸because you listen to the voice of Yahweh your God by keeping all his orders that I'm giving you today, by doing what is right in the eyes of Yahweh your God.

**14** You are the children of Yahweh your God. You will not cut yourselves or make a bald space between your eyes for a dead person, ²because you're a people sacred for Yahweh your God. Yahweh chose you to be his, a people that is personal treasure, from all the peoples that are on the face of the ground.

## You are what you eat

³You may not eat anything offensive. ⁴These are the animals that you may eat: ox, young one from the sheep, young one from the goats, ⁵deer, gazelle, roebuck, wild goat, ibex, antelope, mountain sheep, ⁶any animal that has a divided hoof (that

has a cleft in its hoofs) that brings up its cud; you may eat it.

⁷This, however, you may not eat: ones that bring up their cud or have a divided hoof (have a cleft in their hoof) – the camel, the hare and the rock badger, because they bring up their cud but don't have a divided hoof; they're taboo for you; ⁸the pig, because it has a divided hoof but doesn't bring up its cud; it's taboo for you.

You will not eat of their meat and you will not touch their corpse.

⁹This you may eat of everything that's in the water: anything that has fins and scales you may eat. ¹⁰But anything that has no fins and scales you may not eat; it's taboo for you.

¹¹Any pure bird you may eat. ¹²This is what you may not eat of them: the eagle, the vulture, the osprey, ¹³the kite, the falcon, the buzzard (any of its species), ¹⁴every raven (any of its species), ¹⁵the ostrich, the nighthawk, the seagull, the hawk (any of its species), ¹⁶the tawny owl, the screech owl, the barn owl, ¹⁷the pelican, the swan, the cormorant, ¹⁸the stork, the heron (any of its species), the hoopoe and the bat. ¹⁹Any teeming, flying thing is taboo for you. It may not be eaten. ²⁰Any pure flying thing you may eat. ²¹You may not eat any corpse (though you may give it to the resident who is in your communities so he may eat it, or sell it to a foreigner), because you're a people sacred for Yahweh your God.

You will not cook a kid goat in its own mother's milk.

## Tithes

²²You're carefully to take a tenth of the entire yield from your seed that your fields produce, year by year. ²³Before Yahweh your God at the site where Yahweh chooses to have his name dwell, you're to eat the tenth of your grain, your new wine and your fresh oil, and the firstlings of your herd and your flock, in order that you may learn to live in awe of Yahweh your God at all times. ²⁴When the journey's too big for you, because you can't carry it (because the site

that Yahweh your God chooses to put his name there is too far for you) because Yahweh your God blesses you, ²⁵you may turn it into silver, tie up the silver in your possession, go to the site that Yahweh your God chooses ²⁶and give the silver for anything that your appetite longs for: herd, flock, wine, liquor, anything that your appetite asks for. You're to eat there before Yahweh your God and rejoice, you and your household, ²⁷and you will not abandon the Levite who's in your communities, because he has no share, no domain with you.

²⁸At the end of three years you will take out the entire tenth of your yield in that year, but set it down in your communities. ²⁹The Levite (because he has no share, no domain of his own with you) and the resident, the orphan, and the widow who is in your communities, will come and eat and be full, in order that Yahweh your God may bless you in all the action of your hand that you perform.

## Helping people get back on their feet

**15** At the end of seven years you're to effect a release. ²This is the thing about the release: anyone in a position to make a loan from his hand who makes a loan to his neighbour is not to exact it of his neighbour, his brother, when the release for Yahweh has been called. ³You may exact it of a foreigner, but whatever of yours is with your brother, your hand is to release.

⁴Yet there won't be a needy person among you, because Yahweh will truly bless you in the country that Yahweh your God is giving you as a domain, to take possession of it, ⁵if only you really listen to the voice of Yahweh your God, by keeping this entire order that I'm giving you today, by acting on it. ⁶When Yahweh your God has blessed you as he spoke to you, you'll lend to many nations but you yourself won't borrow. You'll rule over many nations but over you they won't rule.

⁷When there's a needy person among you, one of your brothers, inside one of your communities in the country that Yahweh your God is giving you, you will not firm up your mind and you will not close your hand against your needy brother, ⁸because you're to open your hand wide to him and generously

lend enough for the lack that he has. ⁹Keep watch on yourself so a thing doesn't come into your scoundrelous mind, 'The seventh year, the release year, is drawing near', so your eye works badly towards your needy brother and you don't give anything to him, and he calls to Yahweh about you and it becomes a wrong done by you. ¹⁰Give generously to him. Your mind must not work badly when you give to him, ¹¹because the needy person won't leave off from within the country. That's why I'm ordering you, 'Open your hand wide to your weak and your needy brother in your country.'

### When servants decline their freedom

¹²When your brother, a Hebrew man or a Hebrew woman, sells himself to you, he may serve you for six years, and in the seventh year you're to send him off from you as a free person. ¹³When you send him off from you as a free person, you will not send him off empty-handed. ¹⁴You're to supply him liberally from your flock, from your threshing floor and from your winepress. With what Yahweh your God has blessed you, you're to give to him. ¹⁵Be mindful that you were a serf in the country of Misrayim and Yahweh your God redeemed you. That's why I'm ordering this thing today.

¹⁶When he says to you, 'I won't go out from you', because he's loyal to you and your household, because things have been good for him with you, ¹⁷you're to get an awl and put it through his ear and through the door, and he'll be your servant permanently. You're also to do this for your handmaid. ¹⁸When you send him off from you as a free person, it shouldn't be tough in your eyes, because he's served you for six years for the equivalent of the wages of an employee. And Yahweh your God will bless you in all that you do.

¹⁹Every male firstling that's born in your herd and in your flock you're to make sacred for Yahweh your God. You will not serve with the firstling of your ox and you will not shear the firstling of your flock. ²⁰You're to eat it before Yahweh your God year by year at the site that Yahweh chooses, you and your household. ²¹But when there's a defect in it, lameness or blindness, any bad defect, you're not to sacrifice it for Yahweh your God. ²²You

may eat it in your communities, taboo and pure together, like the gazelle and the deer. ²³Only, its blood you will not eat. You're to pour it on the earth like water.

### Pesah (Passover)

**16** Keep the month of Abib and make Pesah for Yahweh your God, because in the month of Abib Yahweh your God got you out of Misrayim, by night. ²You're to sacrifice the Pesah for Yahweh your God from flock or herd at the site where Yahweh chooses to have his name dwell. ³You will not eat any leavened bread along with it. For seven days you're to eat flatbread (humble bread) with it, because it was in haste that you got out of the country of Misrayim, in order that you may be mindful of the day you got out of the country of Misrayim, all the days of your life. ⁴Yeast will not appear among you, within your entire border, for seven days, and none of the meat that you sacrifice on the evening of the first day will stay until morning.

⁵You will not be able to sacrifice the Pesah within one of your communities that Yahweh your God is giving you. ⁶Rather, you're to sacrifice the Pesah at the site where Yahweh your God chooses to have his name dwell, in the evening, at sunset, the set time of your getting out of Misrayim. ⁷You're to cook and eat at the site that Yahweh your God chooses, and turn your face in the morning and go to your tents. ⁸For six days you're to eat flatbread and on the seventh day there's to be an assembly for Yahweh your God; you will not do any work.

### Shabu'ot and Sukkot (Weeks or Pentecost, and Tabernacles)

⁹You're to count seven weeks [*shabu'ot*] for yourself; from when you start the sickle in the standing grain you're to start counting seven weeks. ¹⁰You're to make the Shabu'ot Festival for Yahweh your God, by the measure of the free offering from your hand that you give, as Yahweh your God blesses you. ¹¹You're to rejoice before Yahweh your God, you, your son and your daughter, your servant and your handmaid, the Levite who is in your communities and the resident, the orphan and the widow who are

among you, at the site where Yahweh your God chooses to have his name dwell. [12]You're to be mindful that you were a serf in Misrayim, and to keep and act on these decrees.

[13]You're to make the Sukkot Festival for yourself for seven days when you've gathered things in from your threshing floor and from your winepress. [14]You're to rejoice at your festival, you, your son and your daughter, your servant and your handmaid, the Levite and the resident, the orphan and the widow who are in your communities. [15]For seven days you're to hold a festival for Yahweh your God at the site that Yahweh chooses, because Yahweh your God will bless you in your entire yield and in all the action of your hands. You will be simply rejoicing.

[16]Three times in the year every male of yours is to appear before Yahweh your God at the site that he chooses, at the Flatbread Festival, at the Shabu'ot Festival and at the Sukkot Festival. He's not to appear before Yahweh empty-handed: [17]each in accordance with the gift in his possession, in accordance with the blessing of Yahweh your God that he's given you.

## Absolute faithfulness

[18]You're to make yourself authorities and officials in all the communities that Yahweh your God is giving you for your clans. They're to exercise faithful authority for the people. [19]You will not twist the exercise of authority. You will not honour persons. You will not accept a bribe, because a bribe blinds the eyes of smart people and twist the words of faithful people. [20]You're to pursue absolute faithfulness in order that you may live and take possession of the country that Yahweh your God is giving you.

[21]You will not plant for yourself as a totem pole any tree beside the altar of Yahweh your God which you will make for yourself, [22]and you will not set up a column for yourself, to which Yahweh your God is hostile.

**17** You will not sacrifice for Yahweh your God an ox or a sheep in which there's a defect, anything bad, because it's an offensive act to Yahweh your God.

[2]When there is found among you, in one of your communities that Yahweh your God is giving you, a man or a woman who does something bad in the eyes of Yahweh your God by contravening his pact [3]and has gone and served other gods and bowed down to them, to the sun or to the moon or to any of the heavenly army, which I haven't ordered, [4]and it's told to you, you're to listen and enquire well. And there, the thing is established as truthful, this offensive act was done in Yisra'el. [5]You're to take out that man or that woman who did this bad thing, to your gateways, and pelt them with stones so they die.

## Making judgements

[6]At the mouth of two witnesses or three witnesses is a person to be put to death. He will not be put to death at the mouth of one witness. [7]The hand of the witnesses is to be the first against him to put him to death, and the hand of the entire people afterwards, so you burn away the bad thing from among you.

[8]When a matter is too hard for you to decide, between one instance of bloodshed and another, between one judgement and another, or between one assault and another (matters of argument in your communities), you're to set off and go up to the site that Yahweh your God chooses [9]and come to the Levitical priests, to the person in authority that's there at that time, and enquire. They'll tell you the word of decision, [10]and you're to act in accordance with the word that they tell you, from that site that Yahweh chooses. You're to keep it by acting in accordance with everything that they instruct you.

[11]You're to act in accordance with the instruction that they give you and by the ruling that they say to you. You will not turn aside from the word that they tell you, right or left. [12]The individual who acts with assertiveness rather than listening to the priest who stands to minister to Yahweh your God there, or to the person in authority: that individual is to die, so you may burn away what is bad from Yisra'el, [13]and so the entire people may listen and live in awe and not assert themselves again.

## Kings

[14]When you come into the country that Yahweh your God is giving you and you take

possession of it and you're living in it, and you say 'I intend to set a king over me, like all the nations that are round me', ¹⁵you may indeed set over you a king whom Yahweh your God chooses. From among your brothers you may set a king over you. You cannot put over you an individual who's a foreigner, who's not your brother.

¹⁶Only, he will not acquire many horses for himself and he will not get the people to go back to Misrayim in order that he may acquire many horses, when Yahweh has said to you, 'You will never again go back that way.' ¹⁷He will not acquire many wives for himself, so his mind does not turn aside, and he will not make very much silver and gold for himself.

¹⁸When he sits on his royal throne, he's to write for himself a copy of this instruction on a document, from before the Levitical priests. ¹⁹It's to be with him and he's to read out of it all the days of his life in order that he may learn to live in awe of Yahweh his God, by keeping all the words of this instruction and these decrees by acting on them, ²⁰so his mind doesn't rise above his brothers and so he doesn't depart from the order, right or left, in order that he may stay a long time over his kingdom, he and his sons, within Yisra'el.

## Priests and Levites

**18** The Levitical priests, the entire clan of Levi, are to have no share, no domain, with Yisra'el. They will eat Yahweh's gift offerings, as its domain. ²It will have no domain among its brothers. Yahweh is its domain, as he spoke to it.

³This is to be the priests' due from the people, from those who are offering a sacrifice, whether an ox or a sheep: he will give the priest the shoulder, the jaws and the stomach. ⁴You're to give him the first of your grain, your new wine and your fresh oil, and the first shearing of your flock. ⁵Because Yahweh your God has chosen him out of all your clans to stand to minister in Yahweh's name, he and his descendants for all time.

⁶When a Levite comes from one of your communities, from all Yisra'el where he's been a resident, and comes with any longing of his own to the site that Yahweh chooses, ⁷he may minister in the name of Yahweh his God like all his brother Levites who are standing there before Yahweh. ⁸They're to eat equal shares, apart from his assets through his ancestors.

⁹When you come into the country that Yahweh your God is giving you, you will not learn to act in accordance with the offensive practices of those nations. ¹⁰There will be no one present among you who makes his son or his daughter pass through fire, who engages in divination, who practises augury, who casts spells, who practises sorcery, ¹¹who uses enchantment, who asks things of ghosts and spirits, or who enquires of the dead. ¹²Because anyone who does these things is an offence to Yahweh. It's because of these offensive acts that Yahweh your God is dispossessing them before you.

## Prophets

¹³You're to be people of integrity with Yahweh your God. ¹⁴Because these nations that you're dispossessing listen to people who practise augury and to diviners, but you: Yahweh your God hasn't made it so for you.

¹⁵Yahweh your God will make a prophet arise for you from among you, from your brothers, like me. You're to listen to him, ¹⁶in accordance with all that you asked of Yahweh your God at Horeb on the day of the congregation, saying 'I won't any more listen to the voice of Yahweh my God and I won't look any longer at this great fire, so I don't die.' ¹⁷Yahweh said to me, 'They did a good thing in what they spoke. ¹⁸I shall make a prophet arise for them from among their brothers like you. I shall put my words in his mouth and he will speak to them all that I order him. ¹⁹The individual who doesn't listen to my words that he speaks in my name – I myself will enquire of him.

²⁰Moreover, the prophet who presumes to speak a word in my name that I didn't order him to speak or who speaks in the name of other gods: that prophet shall die. ²¹When you say to yourself, "How will we know the word that Yahweh hasn't spoken?": ²²what the prophet speaks in Yahweh's name but the word doesn't come about, come true, that's the word that Yahweh didn't speak. The prophet spoke it presumptuously. You will not be in dread of him.'

## Asylum towns

**19** When Yahweh your God cuts down the nations whose country Yahweh your God is giving you and you dispossess them and you live in their towns and in their houses, ²you're to distinguish for yourself three towns within your country that Yahweh your God is giving you, to take possession of it. ³You're to measure the journey for yourself and divide into three the border of your country that Yahweh your God gives you as a domain, so any killer may be able to flee there.

⁴This is the thing with the killer who flees there so he may live – one who strikes down his neighbour without knowing, and wasn't hostile to him in previous days, ⁵but who comes into the forest with his neighbour to chop wood, and his hand thrusts with the axe to cut down a tree and the iron slips off the wooden part and finds his neighbour and he dies. He can flee to one of these towns so he may live, ⁶so the blood restorer doesn't pursue after the killer when his feelings are hot and overtake him, because the journey is long, and strike him down a fatal blow, when he was not liable to the death sentence because he hadn't been hostile to him in previous days. ⁷That's why I'm ordering you, 'You're to distinguish three towns for yourself.'

⁸If Yahweh your God widens your border as he swore to your ancestors and gives you the entire country that he spoke of giving to your ancestors, ⁹when you keep this entire order that I'm giving you today by acting on it, by being loyal to Yahweh your God and by walking in his ways at all times, you're to add for yourself three more towns along with these three. ¹⁰Thus the blood of the person who is free of guilt will not be shed within your country that Yahweh your God is giving you as a domain so that the shed blood comes on you.

## An eye for an eye

¹¹But when an individual is hostile to his neighbour, lies in wait for him, sets on him and strikes him down with a fatal blow so he dies, and he flees to one of these towns, ¹²the elders of his town are to send and get him from there and give him into the hand of the blood restorer, so he dies. ¹³Your eye will not pity him. You're to burn away from Yisra'el the blood of the person who is free of guilt, so things may be good for you.

¹⁴You will not move aside your neighbour's boundary marker, which previous generations laid down, in your domain which you will have as yours in the country that Yahweh your God is giving you to take possession of it.

¹⁵One witness will not stand up against someone regarding any waywardness or regarding any wrong, in connection with any wrong that he does. At the mouth of two witnesses or at the mouth of three witnesses the thing will stand up.

¹⁶When a felonious witness stands up against someone to avow defiance against him, ¹⁷the two people who have the argument are to take their stand before Yahweh, before the priests or the authorities who are there at that time, ¹⁸and the authorities will enquire well.

There, the witness is a false witness. He has avowed a falsehood against his brother. ¹⁹You're to do to him as he intended to do to his brother, and burn away the bad thing from among you, ²⁰while the remaining people will hear and live in awe, and will never again do the likes of this bad deed among you. ²¹Your eye will not pity: life for life, eye for eye, tooth for tooth, hand for hand, foot for foot.

## How to make war

**20** When you go out for battle against your enemies and you see horse and chariotry, a company bigger than you, you will not be afraid of them, because Yahweh your God, who got you out of the country of Misrayim, will be with you. ²When you're drawing near for battle, the priest is to come up and speak to the company, ³and say to them: 'Listen, Yisra'el. You're drawing near for battle against your enemies today. Your heart is not to be soft. Don't be afraid, don't be in haste, don't be frightened before them, ⁴because Yahweh your God is going with you to do battle for you with your enemies, to deliver you.'

⁵The officials will speak to the company: 'Who is the individual who's built a new house and not dedicated it? He's to go and turn back to his house, so he doesn't die in battle and

another individual dedicate it. ⁶Who is the individual who's planted a vineyard and not initiated it? He's to go and turn back to his house, so he doesn't die in battle and another individual initiate it. ⁷Who is the individual who's betrothed a woman and not taken her? He's to go and turn back to his house so he doesn't die in battle and another individual take her.'

⁸The officials are to speak further to the people and say, 'Who is the individual who's afraid and whose mind is frail? He's to go and turn back to his house so his brothers' mind doesn't melt like his mind.'

⁹When the officials have finished speaking to the company, they're to appoint army officers at the head of the company.

## How to make war impractical

¹⁰When you draw near to a town to do battle against it, you're to call for peace to it. ¹¹If it answers with peace and opens up to you, the entire people that's to be found in it will become yours, as a workforce. They'll serve you. ¹²If it doesn't make peace with you and does battle with you, you're to besiege it, ¹³and Yahweh your God will give it into your hand. You're to strike down all its males with the mouth of the sword. ¹⁴Only, the women, the little ones, the animals and everything that's in the town, all its spoil, you may take as plunder for yourself, and devour your enemy's spoil, which Yahweh your God has given you.

¹⁵So you're to do to all the towns that are very far from you, which are not among the towns belonging to these nations here. ¹⁶Only, from the towns of these peoples that Yahweh your God is giving you as a domain you will not let any person live, ¹⁷because you're to devote them totally (the Hittite, the Amorite, the Kena'anite, the Perizzite, the Hivvite and the Yebusite), as Yahweh your God has ordered you, ¹⁸in order that they may not teach you to act in accordance with all their offensive practices, which they have performed for their gods, and you do wrong towards Yahweh your God.

¹⁹When you besiege a town for a long time in battling against it to capture it, you will not devastate its trees by thrusting an axe against them, because you're to eat from them. You will not cut them down, because are the trees of the open country human beings, to come before you in a siege work? ²⁰Only, trees that you know are not trees for food, them you may devastate and cut down so you may build a siege work against the town that's doing battle with you, until its fall.

## Murder desecrates the land

**21** When a person who has been run through is found, fallen in the fields, on the land that Yahweh your God is giving you to take possession of it, and it's not known who struck him down, ²your elders or your authorities are to go out and take measurements to the towns that are round the person who has been run through. ³The town near the person who has been run through – that town's elders are to get a heifer from the herd that hasn't been made to serve, that hasn't pulled in a yoke. ⁴That town's elders are to take the heifer down to a flowing wadi that has not served, not been sown, and to break the heifer's neck there, in the wadi.

⁵The Levitical priests will come up, because Yahweh your God chose them to minister to him and to bless in Yahweh's name, and every argument and every assault rests on their pronouncement. ⁶All the elders of that town who were near to the person who has been run through will wash their hands over the heifer whose neck has been broken in the wadi. ⁷They will avow: 'Our hands didn't shed this blood; our eyes didn't see. ⁸Make expiation for your people Yisra'el whom you redeemed, Yahweh. Don't put the blood of a person who's free of guilt among your people Yisra'el.' And the blood will be expiated for them. ⁹You yourself will burn away the blood of the person who is free of guilt from among you, because you do what's right in Yahweh's eyes.

## The loved and the unloved

¹⁰When you go out for battle against your enemies, and Yahweh your God gives them into your hand and you take them captive, ¹¹and you see among the captives a woman

who's attractive in appearance, you fancy her, you get her for yourself as wife, ¹²you bring her inside your house, she shaves her head, trims her nails, ¹³removes her captive clothes from her, lives in your house, and bewails her father and her mother for a whole month, and after this you have sex with her and you become her husband and she becomes your wife: ¹⁴if you then don't want her, you're to send her off for herself. You will not at all sell her for silver. You will not do what you like with her, since you've humbled her.

¹⁵When a man has two wives and one is loved and one disliked, and they've borne him sons, the loved and the disliked, and the firstborn son belongs to the disliked one, ¹⁶on the day he gives what he has to his sons as their domain, he cannot treat as firstborn the son of the one who is loved in disregard of the son of the one who is disliked who was the firstborn. ¹⁷Rather he's to treat as the firstborn the son of the one who is disliked, by giving him a double share in all that is found to him, because he's the first of his vigour. The due of the firstborn is his.

¹⁸When an individual has a defiant and rebellious son who doesn't listen to his father's voice or to his mother's voice, and they discipline him but he doesn't listen to them, ¹⁹his father and his mother are to get hold of him and take him out to the town's elders, to the gateway of his place. ²⁰They're to say to the town's elders, 'This son of ours is defiant and rebellious. He doesn't listen to our voice. He's a wastrel and a drunkard.' ²¹All the town's people are to pelt him with stones so he dies. So you will burn away the bad thing from among you; all Yisrael will hear and live in awe.

## Responsibilities

²²When there's a wrong that carries a death sentence against a man and he's put to death, and you hang him up on a tree, ²³you will not let his corpse stay the night on the tree. Rather, you're to make sure you bury him that day, because someone hanged up is a slight to God, and you will not make taboo your land that Yahweh your God is giving you as a domain.

**22** You will not see your brother's ox or his sheep straying, and hide from

them. You're definitely to get them back to your brother. ²If your brother is not near to you or you don't know him, take it home to your house so it may be with you until your brother enquires about it and you can give it back to him. ³You're to act in this way with his donkey and to act in this way with his clothing and to act in this way with anything lost by your brother, which gets lost from him and which you find. You can't hide. ⁴You will not see your brother's donkey or his ox falling on the road and hide from them. You must definitely get it up with him.

⁵A man's things will not be on a woman and a man will not wear a woman's clothing, because anyone who does these things is offensive to Yahweh your God.

⁶When a bird's nest happens to be before you on the road, in any tree or on the earth, with young ones or eggs and the mother sitting on the young or on the eggs, you will not take the mother along with the offspring. ⁷You're absolutely to send off the mother, but you may take the offspring for yourself, in order that things may be good for you and you may stay a long time.

⁸When you build a new house, you're to make a wall for your roof so you don't put shed blood on your household when someone falling down falls from it.

## Accusations against a girl

⁹You will not sow your vineyard with two species, so the full harvest doesn't become sacred (the seed that you sow and the vineyard's yield). ¹⁰You will not plough with ox and with donkey together. ¹¹You will not wear a mixture of wool and linen together. ¹²You're to make yourself tassels on the four corners of your garment with which you cover yourself.

¹³When a man takes a wife and has sex with her, but dislikes her ¹⁴and makes accusations about her and causes her to have a bad name, and says 'I took this woman and had sex with her, and I didn't find in her the evidence of virginity', ¹⁵the girl's father and her mother are to get the evidence of the girl's virginity and bring it out to the town's elders at the gateway. ¹⁶The girl's father is to say to the elders, 'I gave my daughter to this man as wife but he came

to dislike her. <sup>17</sup>Here, that man has made
accusations, saying "I didn't find the evidence
of virginity in your daughter." This is the
evidence of my daughter's virginity.' And they
will lay out the cloth before the town's elders.
<sup>18</sup>Then that town's elders are to get the man,
chastise him, <sup>19</sup>charge him a hundred in silver
and give it to the girl's father, because he caused
a Yisra'elite young girl to have a bad name. And
she can be his wife; he will not be able to send
her off through his entire life.

<sup>20</sup>But if this thing was truthful, if the
evidence of virginity was not found for the girl,
<sup>21</sup>they're to bring the girl to the entrance of
her father's house, and the people of her town
are to pelt her with stones so she dies, because
she's done something villainous in Yisra'el by
whoring in her father's household. So you will
burn away the bad thing from among you.

### Sex in the city and in the country

<sup>22</sup>When a man is found sleeping with a
woman who's married to a husband, they are to
die, both of them, the man who slept with the
woman and the woman. So you will burn away
the bad thing from Yisra'el.

<sup>23</sup>When there's a girl who's a young girl
betrothed to a man, and a man finds her in
the town and sleeps with her, <sup>24</sup>you're to take the
two of them out to the gateway of that town and
pelt them with stones so they die (the girl on
account of the fact that she didn't cry out in the
town, and the man on account of the fact that
he humbled his neighbour's wife). So you will
burn away the bad thing from among you.

<sup>25</sup>But if the man finds the betrothed girl in
the fields and the man takes strong hold of her
and sleeps with her, the man who slept with
her is alone to die. <sup>26</sup>You're not to do anything
to the girl. There's no wrong that deserves
death attaching to her, because this thing is like
an individual who sets upon his neighbour and
kills him, <sup>27</sup>because he found her in the fields.
Should the betrothed girl have cried out, there
was no one to deliver her.

<sup>28</sup>When a man finds a girl who's a young girl
who's not betrothed and takes hold of her and
sleeps with her and they're found out, <sup>29</sup>the
man who slept with her is to give the girl's
father fifty in silver and she can be his wife.

Since he humbled her, he can't send her off
through his entire life.

<sup>30</sup>No individual will take his father's wife. He
will not uncover his father's garment.

### Attitudes to foreigners

**23** No one whose testicles are crushed or
whose penis is cut off will come into
Yahweh's congregation. <sup>2</sup>No one misbegotten
will come into Yahweh's congregation; even his
tenth generation will not come into Yahweh's
congregation.

<sup>3</sup>No Ammonite or Mo'abite will come
into Yahweh's congregation; even their tenth
generation will not come into Yahweh's
congregation ever, <sup>4</sup>because of the fact that
they didn't meet you with bread and with water
on the way, when you got out of Misrayim,
and because he hired against you Bil'am ben
Be'or from Petor in Aram-of-the-Two-Rivers,
to slight you <sup>5</sup>(but Yahweh your God was not
willing to listen to Bil'am, and for you Yahweh
your God turned the slight into blessing,
because Yahweh your God is loyal to you).
<sup>6</sup>You will not enquire after their welfare or
what is good for them through your entire life,
permanently.

<sup>7</sup>You will not take offence at an Edomite,
because he's your brother; you will not take
offence at an Misrayimite, because you were a
resident in his country. <sup>8</sup>Children that are born
to them, their third generation, may come into
Yahweh's congregation.

<sup>9</sup>When you go out as a camp against your
enemies, you're to keep yourselves away
from any bad thing. <sup>10</sup>When there is among
you an individual who is not pure because
of a nocturnal emission, he's to go outside
the camp. He will not come inside the camp.
<sup>11</sup>When evening is turning its face, he's to wash
in water, and as the sun goes down he may
come inside the camp.

<sup>12</sup>There's to be an area for you outside the
camp and you're to go out there, outside.
<sup>13</sup>You're to have a stick along with your
equipment, and when you've sat outside, you're
to dig with it and go back and cover your
excrement. <sup>14</sup>Because Yahweh your God walks
about inside your camp to rescue you and to
give over your enemies before you, your camp

is to be sacred. He's not to see in you something indecent and turn back from following you.

## The runaway servant

¹⁵You will not hand over to his lord a servant who escapes to you from his lord. ¹⁶He's to live with you, among you in the place that he chooses in one of your communities, in one that seems good to him. You will not do him wrong. ¹⁷No one from among Yisra'el's women will become a hierodule, and no one from among Yisra'el's men will become a hierodule. ¹⁸A whore's 'gift' and a dog's fee will not come into the house of Yahweh your God for any pledge, because both of them would be an offence to Yahweh your God.

¹⁹You will not charge interest to your brother: interest on silver, interest on food or interest on anything that can be the subject of interest. ²⁰To a foreigner you may charge interest, but to your brother you will not charge interest, in order that Yahweh your God may bless you in every venture of your hand in the country where you're coming to take possession of it.

²¹When you make a pledge to Yahweh your God, you will not put off making good on it, because Yahweh your God will definitely require it from you, and there will be wrongdoing counted against you, ²²but when you leave off from pledging, there will not be wrongdoing counted against you. ²³What comes out from your lips you're to keep and act on, as you freely made a pledge to Yahweh your God, which you spoke with your own mouth.

²⁴When you come into your neighbour's vineyard, you may eat grapes in accordance with your appetite until you're full, but you will not put them into your container. ²⁵When you come into your neighbour's standing grain, you may pluck ears with your hand, but you will not put a sickle to your neighbour's standing grain.

## The pain and the joy of marriage

**24** When a man takes a wife and becomes her husband, if she doesn't find grace in his eyes because he finds

something indecent in her, and he writes her a divorce document, puts it in her hand and sends her off from his household, ²and she leave his household, goes and comes to belong to another man, ³but the other man dislikes her, writes her a divorce document, puts it in her hand and sends her off from his household, or when the other man who took her as his wife dies, ⁴her first husband who sent her off cannot take her again as his wife after she's been made taboo, because it would be an offence before Yahweh. You will not do wrong to the country that Yahweh your God is giving you as a domain.

⁵When a man takes a new wife he will not go out in the army, and he will not pass over to it for anything. For a year he is to be free for his household so he may enable his wife whom he's taken to rejoice.

⁶Someone may not take a hand mill or an upper millstone as security, because he would be taking a life as security.

⁷When an individual is found kidnapping a person from among his brothers, from among the Yisra'elites, so he can turn him into a slave and sell him, that kidnapper is to die. So you will burn away the bad thing from among you.

⁸Keep careful watch on yourself in an outbreak of scaliness by acting in accordance with everything that the Levitical priests instruct you. As I ordered them, you're to keep watch so as to act. ⁹Be mindful of what Yahweh your God did to Miryam on the journey when you'd got out of Misrayim.

## On sacred inefficiency

¹⁰When you make a loan of any kind to your neighbour, you're not to go into his house to get his collateral. ¹¹You're to stand outside while the individual to whom you're making the loan brings the collateral to you outside. ¹²If he's someone humble, you will not sleep with his collateral. ¹³You're definitely to give his collateral back to him at sunset so he may sleep in his covering and bless you, and there will be faithfulness counted for you before Yahweh your God.

¹⁴You will not defraud a humble and needy employee from your brothers or from your residents who are in your country, in your

communities. [15]You're to give him his payment on the day. The sun will not go down on it, because he's humble and he's basing his life on it, and he will call out to God against you, and there will be wrongdoing counted against you.

[16]Parents will not be put to death for children and children will not be put to death for parents. People are to be put to death, an individual for his own wrongdoing.

[17]You will not twist the exercise of authority in respect of a resident or orphan, and you will not take a widow's coat as security. [18]You're to be mindful that you were a serf in Misrayim and Yahweh your God redeemed you from there. That's why I'm ordering you to do this thing.

[19]When you reap your harvest in your fields and you overlook a sheaf in the fields, you will not go back to get it. It's to belong to the resident, to the orphan and to the widow, in order that Yahweh your God may bless you in all the action of your hands. [20]When you beat your olive tree, you will not go over it after you. It's to belong to the resident, to the orphan and to the widow. [21]When you cut the grapes from your vineyard, you will not pick it over after you. It's to belong to the resident, to the orphan and to the widow. [22]You're to be mindful that you were a serf in the country of Misrayim. That's why I'm ordering you to do this thing.

## Maintaining the family name

**25** [1]When there's an argument between people and they come up for a decision, and they decide for them and pronounce one in the right and the other in the wrong, [2]if the one in the wrong is to be beaten, the one who makes decision is to have him fall down and beaten before him with a number that's enough for his wrongdoing. [3]While he may have him beaten forty times, he will not do more, so he doesn't do more beating on top of these, a huge beating, and your brother is slighted in your eyes.

[4]You will not muzzle an ox when it's threshing.

[5]When brothers live together and one of them dies and has no son, the dead man's wife will not go elsewhere, to a man who's an outsider. Her brother-in-law is to have sex with her; he's to take her as his wife and act as brother-in-law to her. [6]The first son to whom she gives birth will take his place in the name of his dead brother so his name is not wiped out from Yisra'el.

[7]If the man doesn't want to take his sister-in-law, his sister-in-law is to go up to the gateway, to the elders, and say, 'My brother-in-law won't set up a name in Yisra'el for his brother. He's not willing to act as brother-in-law to me.' [8]His town's elders will call for him and speak to him. If he stands firm and says 'I don't want to take her', [9]his sister-in-law will come up to him before the eyes of the elders, pull his boot from on his foot, spit in his face and avow, 'In this way it's done to the man who doesn't build up his brother's household.' [10]It will be named in Yisra'el, 'the household of the man who had his boot pulled off'.

## Not to forget Amaleq

[11]When men fight one another, a man and his brother, and the wife of one comes near to rescue her husband from the hand of the one who is striking him, puts out her hand and takes strong hold of him by his private parts, [12]you're to cut off her fist. Your eye will not pity.

[13]You will not have in your bag two stones, big and small. [14]You will not have in your house two measures, big and small. [15]You're to have a stone that's perfect and faithful, a measure that's perfect and faithful, in order that your days may be many on the land that Yahweh your God is giving you. [16]Because anyone who does these things, anyone who does evil, is an offence to Yahweh your God.

[17]Be mindful of what Amaleq did to you on the journey, when you had got out of Misrayim. [18]He met you on the journey and attacked you from the rear (all the ones who were shattered at the back of you), when you were faint and weary. He was not in awe of God. [19]When Yahweh your God enables you to settle down free of all your enemies all round in the country that Yahweh your God is giving you as your domain, to take possession of it, you're to erase the memory of Amaleq from under the heavens. You will not put it out of mind.

*A refugee has become a great nation*

**26** When you come into the country that Yahweh your God is giving you as a domain, and you take possession of it and live in it, ²you're to get some of the first of all the fruit of the land that you bring in from your country that Yahweh your God is giving you, put it in a basket and go to the site where Yahweh your God chooses to have his name dwell. ³You're to come to the priest who is there at that time and say to him, 'I tell Yahweh your God today that I've come into the country that Yahweh swore to our ancestors to give them.'

⁴The priest will take the basket from your hand and set it down before the altar of Yahweh your God. ⁵You are to avow before Yahweh your God: 'My father was an Aramite refugee and he went down to Misrayim and resided there as a few people, but there he became a big, numerous and substantial nation. ⁶The Misrayimites dealt badly with us, humbled us and put tough servitude on us, ⁷but we cried out to Yahweh the God of our ancestors, and Yahweh listened to our voice. He saw our humbling, our hardship and our affliction. ⁸Yahweh got us out of Misrayim with a strong hand, with an extended arm, with great awe-inspiring action, with signs and with proofs. ⁹He brought us to this place and gave us this country, a country flowing with milk and syrup. ¹⁰So now, here, I've brought the first of the fruit of the land that you, Yahweh, have given me.'

You will set it down before Yahweh your God and bow low before Yahweh your God, ¹¹and rejoice in all the good that Yahweh your God has given you and your household, you, the Levite and the resident who is among you.

*A mutual commitment*

¹²When you finish setting aside the entire tenth of your yield in the third year, the year of the tenth, and give to the Levite, to the resident, to the orphan and to the widow, so they may eat in your communities and be full, ¹³you're to say before Yahweh your God, 'I've cleared out what was sacred from the house. Further, I've given it to the Levite, to the resident, to the orphan and to the widow, in accordance with your entire order that you gave me. I haven't contravened any of your orders.

I haven't put them out of mind.
¹⁴I haven't eaten of it while in sorrow.
I haven't cleared out any of it while taboo.
I haven't given any of it to a dead person.

I've listened to the voice of Yahweh my God, I've acted in accordance with everything that you ordered me. ¹⁵Look out from your sacred abode, from the heavens, and bless your people Yisra'el and the land that you've given us, as you swore to our ancestors, a country flowing with milk and syrup.'

¹⁶This day Yahweh your God is ordering you to act on these decrees and rulings. You're to keep them and act on them with your entire mind and with your entire being. ¹⁷You've got Yahweh to say today that he'll be your God and that you'll walk in his ways, keep his decrees, his orders and his rulings, and listen to his voice. ¹⁸And Yahweh has got you to say today that you'll be a people that is personal treasure, as he spoke to you, that you'll keep all his orders, ¹⁹that he'll put you on high over all the nations that he made, for praise, for fame and for glory, and that you'll be a people sacred to Yahweh your God, as he spoke.

*Inscribed stones*

**27** Mosheh and the Yisra'elite elders ordered the people: 'Keep the entire order that I'm giving you today. ²On the day that you cross the Yarden into the country that Yahweh your God is giving you, you're to set up for yourself big stones. You're to coat them in plaster ³and write on them all the words in this instruction, when you cross in order that you may go into the country that Yahweh your God is giving you, a country flowing with milk and syrup, as Yahweh the God of your ancestors spoke to you.

⁴So when you cross the Yarden you're to set up on Mount Ebal these stones about which I'm ordering you today, and coat them in plaster, ⁵and build an altar there for Yahweh your God, an altar of stones. You will not wield iron on them; ⁶you're to build the altar of Yahweh your God from whole stones. You're to

offer up whole offerings on it for Yahweh your God, [7]and make well-being sacrifices, eat there and rejoice before Yahweh your God. [8]And you're to write on the stones all the words in this instruction. Make it good and plain.'

[9]Mosheh and the Levitical priests spoke to all Yisraʼel: 'Be quiet and listen, Yisraʼel. This day you've become a people belonging to Yahweh your God. [10]You're to listen to the voice of Yahweh your God and act on his orders and on his decrees, which I'm ordering you today.'

[11]Mosheh ordered the people that day: [12]'These are to stand to bless the people on Mount Gerizim, when you cross the Yarden: Shimʼon [Simeon], Levi, Yehudah [Judah], Yissakar [Issachar], Yoseph [Joseph] and Binyamin [Benjamin]. [13]These are to stand for the slight on Mount Ebal: Reʼuben, Gad, Asher, Zebulun, Dan and Naphtali.

## Curses

[14]The Levites will avow to every individual in Yisraʼel, in a loud voice:

[15]Cursed is the individual who makes a sculpture or figurine, an offensive thing to Yahweh, the making of a craftsman's hands, and sets it up in secret.

The entire people are to avow, "Yes!" [16]Cursed is one who slights his father or his mother.

The entire people is to avow, "Yes!" [17]Cursed is one who moves aside his neighbour's boundary marker.

The entire people is to avow, "Yes!" [18]Cursed is one who misdirects a blind person on the road.

The entire people is to avow, "Yes!" [19]Cursed is one who twists the exercise of authority for a resident, an orphan or a widow.

The entire people is to avow, "Yes!" [20]Cursed is one who sleeps with his father's wife, because he's uncovered his father's garment.

The entire people is to avow, "Yes!" [21]Cursed is one who sleeps with any animal.

The entire people is to avow, "Yes!" [22]Cursed is one who sleeps with his sister, his father's daughter or his mother's daughter.

The entire people is to avow, "Yes!"

[23]Cursed is one who sleeps with his mother-in-law.

The entire people is to avow, "Yes!" [24]Cursed is one who strikes down his neighbour in secret.

The entire people is to avow, "Yes!" [25]Cursed is one who accepts a bribe to strike down a person who is free of guilt.

The entire people is to avow, "Yes!" [26]Cursed is someone who doesn't implement the words in this instruction and act on them.

The entire people is to avow, "Yes!"

## Blessings

**28** If you listen attentively to the voice of Yahweh your God so as to keep all his orders which I'm giving you today by acting on them, Yahweh your God will put you on high over all the nations on the earth. [2]All these blessings will come on you and overtake you when you listen to the voice of Yahweh your God:

[3]Blessed are you in the town and blessed are you in the fields.

[4]Blessed is the fruit of your womb, the fruit of your land, the fruit of your animals, the drop of your domestic animals and the young of your flock.

[5]Blessed is your basket and your kneading bowl.

[6]Blessed are you in your coming in and blessed are you in your going out.

[7]Yahweh will make your enemies who set upon you take a beating before you. They will come out against you by one route but flee before you by seven routes.

[8]Yahweh will order blessing on you in your barns and in every venture of your hand. He will bless you in the country that Yahweh your God is giving you. [9]Yahweh will set you up as his sacred people, as he swore to you, because you keep the orders of Yahweh your God and walk in his ways. [10]All the peoples of the earth will see that Yahweh's name has been called out over you and they will live in awe of you. [11]Yahweh will make you more than abound with good things, in the fruit of your womb, in the fruit of your animals and in the fruit of your land, on the land that Yahweh swore

to your ancestors to give them. ¹²Yahweh will open for you his storehouse of goodness, the heavens, to give rain on the earth in its time and to bless every action of your hand. You will lend to many nations but you won't borrow.

¹³Yahweh will make you the head and not the tail, and you will be only on top and not at the bottom, when you listen to the orders of Yahweh your God that I'm giving you today, keeping them by acting on them, ¹⁴and don't turn aside from all the things that I'm ordering you today, right or left, by following other gods to serve them.

## Curses once more

¹⁵But if you don't listen to the voice of Yahweh your God, keeping all his orders and his decrees that I'm giving you today by acting on them, all these slights will come on you and overtake you.

¹⁶Cursed are you in the town and cursed are you in the fields.

¹⁷Cursed is your basket and your kneading bowl.

¹⁸Cursed is the fruit of your womb, the fruit of your land, the drop of your domestic animals and the young of your flock.

¹⁹Cursed are you in your coming in and cursed are you in your going out.

²⁰Yahweh will send off against you curse, turmoil and rebuke in every venture of your hand that you undertake, until you're annihilated and until you perish quickly in the face of the bad nature of your practices by which you've abandoned me. ²¹Yahweh will make epidemic attach itself to you until he finishes you off from upon the land where you're coming to take possession of it. ²²Yahweh will strike you down with wasting, with fever, with inflammation, with heatwave, with drought, with blight and with mildew, and they'll pursue you until you perish. ²³The heavens that are above your head will be copper and the earth that's under you will be iron. ²⁴Yahweh will make the rain of your country dust, and earth will descend on you from the heavens until you're annihilated. ²⁵Yahweh will make you take a beating before your enemies. You will go out against him by one route but flee before him by seven routes. You will become a thing of horror

to all the kingdoms of the earth. ²⁶Your corpse will become food for all the birds of the heavens and for the animals of the earth, with no one to make them tremble.

## Troubles

²⁷Yahweh will strike you down with the inflammation of Misrayim, with haemorrhoids, with sores and with rashes, from which you won't be able to find healing. ²⁸Yahweh will strike you down with madness, with blindness and with confusion of mind. ²⁹You'll be groping at noon as the blind person gropes in darkness. You won't make a success of your journeys. You will only be defrauded and robbed all the time, with no one to deliver. ³⁰You'll betroth a wife but another man will sleep with her. You'll build a house but you won't live in it. You'll plant a vineyard but you won't initiate it. ³¹Your ox slaughtered before your eyes: and you won't eat of it. Your donkey stolen before you: and it won't come back to you. Your flock given over to your enemies: and you'll have no one to deliver. ³²Your sons and your daughters given over to another people, with your eyes looking and spending themselves for them all the time: and there'll be no power in your hand. ³³A people you don't acknowledge will eat the fruit of your ground and all your weariness. You'll be only defrauded and crushed all the time. ³⁴You'll be made insane by the sight that your eyes see. ³⁵Yahweh will strike you down with bad inflammation, on your knees and on your thighs, from which you won't be able to find healing, from the sole of your foot to the crown of your head.

³⁶Yahweh will make you, and the king whom you set over you, go to a nation that you haven't acknowledged, you or your ancestors. There you'll serve other gods, wood and stone. ³⁷You'll be something shocking, an object lesson and a subject of taunting among all the peoples where Yahweh drives you.

## Defeat

³⁸You'll take much seed out to the field but you'll gather little because the locust will

devour it. [39]You'll plant vineyards and serve them but you won't drink wine and you won't gather because the worm will eat them. [40]You'll have olive trees through your entire border, but you won't apply oil because your olive tree will drop off. [41]You'll father sons and daughters but they won't be yours because they'll go into captivity. [42]Insects will take possession of all your trees and the fruit of your ground. [43]The resident who's among you will go up higher and higher above you and you'll descend lower and lower. [44]He'll lend to you and you won't lend to him. He'll be head and you'll be tail.

[45]All these slights will come on you, and they'll pursue you and overtake you until you're annihilated, because you didn't listen to the voice of Yahweh your God, keeping his orders and his decrees which he gave you. [46]They'll be permanent signs and proofs against you and against your offspring. [47]Since you didn't serve Yahweh your God with rejoicing and with a good heart because of the large quantity of everything, [48]you'll serve your enemies whom Yahweh will send off against you, in hunger and in thirst, in nakedness and in lack of everything. He'll put an iron yoke on your neck until he's annihilated you.

[49]Yahweh will bring against you a nation from afar, from the end of the earth, as the eagle swoops, a nation whose tongue you can't listen to, [50]a nation hard-faced that won't honour the person of the elderly and won't show grace to the young, [51]and will eat the fruit of your animals and the fruit of your ground until you're annihilated, that won't leave you grain, new wine or fresh oil, the drop of your domestic animals or the young of your flock, until it has let you perish.

## The horrors of siege

[52]It will besiege you in all your communities until the fall of your lofty and fortified walls on which you're relying, in the entire country. It will besiege you in all your communities in the entire country that Yahweh your God has given you. [53]You'll eat the offspring of your womb, the flesh of your sons and your daughters, whom Yahweh your God has given you, in the siege and in the stress that your enemy puts on you.

[54]The soft individual among you and the one who is very sensitive – his eye will be mean towards his brother and towards the wife in his arms and towards the rest of his children whom he has remaining, [55]so that he won't give one of them any of the flesh of his children that he eats, because he doesn't have anything remaining for himself, in the siege and in the stress that your enemy puts on you in all your communities.

[56]The woman who is soft among you and sensitive, who hasn't ventured to set the sole of her foot on the ground because of being sensitive and soft – her eye will be mean towards the husband in her arms, towards her son and towards her daughter, [57]towards her afterbirth that comes out beneath her feet and towards her children to whom she gives birth, because she will eat them in secret, as a result of her lack of everything, in the siege and in the stress that your enemy puts on you in your communities.

[58]If you don't keep all the words in this instruction that are written in this document by acting on them, so as to live in awe of this honoured and awe-inspiring name, Yahweh your God, [59]Yahweh will bring extraordinary calamities on you and calamities on your offspring, big and lasting calamities, bad and lasting diseases. [60]He will bring back on you every illness of Misrayim before which you were in dread, so that they attach themselves to you.

## No resting place

[61]Yahweh will also bring on you every disease and every calamity that's not written in this instruction document, until you're annihilated. [62]You'll remain as a few people, although you were like the stars in the heavens in your large number, because you didn't listen to the voice of Yahweh your God. [63]As Yahweh delighted over you in doing good to you and in multiplying you, so Yahweh will delight over you in letting you perish and annihilating you. You'll be torn from upon the land where you're coming in to take possession of it.

[64]Yahweh will disperse you among the peoples from one end of the earth to the other end of the earth, and you'll serve other gods

there that you haven't acknowledged, you or your ancestors. [65]And among those nations you won't rest. There'll be no place to settle for the sole of your foot. Yahweh will give you there an anxious mind, spending of eyes and languishing of the entire being. [66]Your life will be hanging at a distance from you. You'll be terrified night and day. You won't trust your life. [67]In the morning you'll say, "If only it were evening", and in the evening you'll say, "If only it were morning", because of dread in your mind that you feel and because of the sight of your eyes that you see. [68]Yahweh will take you back to Misrayim in ships, by a way that I said you would not again see, and you'll sell yourselves there to your enemies as servants and maidservants, but there will be no buyer.'

**29** These are the words of the pact that Yahweh ordered Mosheh to solemnize with the Yisraelites in the country of Mo'ab, apart from the pact that he solemnized with them at Horeb.

### The mystery of obedience and disobedience

[2]Mosheh called all Yisra'el and said to them: 'You yourselves have seen all that Yahweh did before your eyes in the country of Misrayim, to Par'oh, to all his servants and to his entire country, [3]the great tests that your eyes saw, those great signs and proofs. [4]But Yahweh hasn't given you a mind to acknowledge or eyes to see or ears to listen, until this day. [5]I enabled you to go through the wilderness for forty years. Your clothes didn't wear out on you and your boot didn't wear out on your foot, [6]you didn't eat bread and you didn't drink wine or liquor, in order that you might acknowledge that I am Yahweh your God. [7]You came to this place and Sihon king of Heshbon and Og king of Bashan came out to meet you in battle but we struck them down, [8]took their country, and gave it to the Re'ubenites, to the Gadites and to the half-clan of Menashsheh, as their domain. [9]You're to keep the words in this pact and act on them, in order that you may thrive in everything that you do. [10]You're standing today, all of you, before Yahweh your God – your heads, your clans, your elders, your officials, every individual in Yisra'el, [11]your little ones, your wives, your resident who is within the camps, from the person who chops your wood to the one who draws your water – [12]for you to pass over into the pact of Yahweh your God and into its vow, which Yahweh your God is solemnizing with you today, [13]in order that he may set you up today as a people for him and that he may be God for you, as he spoke to you and as he swore to your ancestors, to Abraham, to Yitshaq and to Ya'aqob. [14]Not with you alone am I solemnizing this pact and this vow; [15]rather with the one who is here with us today standing before Yahweh our God, and with the one who is not here with us today.

### Why this angry fury?

[16]Because you yourselves acknowledge the fact that we lived in the country of Misrayim and the fact that we passed through the middle of the nations that you did pass through, [17]and you saw their abominations and their idols, wood and stone, silver and gold, which were with them. [18]Beware that there is not among you a man or a woman, a kin-group or a clan, whose mind is turning about today from Yahweh our God to go to serve those nations' gods. Beware that there is not among you a root sprouting a poisonous and bitter plant. [19]When he hears the words of this vow he may bless himself inside, saying "Things will go well for me when I walk by the determination of my mind, in order to augment the well-watered with the dry." [20]Yahweh will not be willing to pardon him. Rather, Yahweh's anger will then smoke, with his passion, against that man. The entire vow written in this document will descend on him. Yahweh will wipe out his name from under the heavens. [21]Yahweh will distinguish him from all the Yisra'elite clans for bad experiences, in accordance with all the vows in the pact written in this instruction document. [22]The next generation will say – your children who come after you, and the foreigner who comes from a distant country and sees the calamities on that country and its diseases that Yahweh will have brought on it ([23]its entire country, burning with sulphur and salt, won't be sown and won't bloom, and no grass will grow in it, like the overthrow of Sedom and Amorah, Admah and Tseboyim, which Yahweh

overthrew in his anger and in his wrath): [24]all the nations will say, "Why did Yahweh act like this to this country? Why this great angry rage?"

## The things hidden and the things revealed

[25]They will say, "On account of the fact that they abandoned the pact of Yahweh the God of their ancestors which he solemnized with them when he got them out of the country of Misrayim, [26]and went and served other gods and bowed low to them, gods that they had not acknowledged and he had not allocated to them. [27]Yahweh's anger raged at that country so as to bring on it every curse that's written in this document. [28]Yahweh rooted them up from on their land in anger, in wrath and in great rage, and sent them off to another country this very day."

[29]The things that are hidden belong to Yahweh our God, but the things that are revealed belong to us and to our children permanently, to act on all the words of this instruction.

**30** But when all these things come on you (the blessing and the curse that I've put before you) and you bring them back to mind among all the nations where Yahweh your God has driven you away, [2]and turn back to Yahweh your God and listen to his voice in accordance with everything that I'm ordering you today, you and your children, with your entire mind and with your entire being, [3]Yahweh your God will bring back your good fortune. He will have compassion on you and again gather you from all the peoples where Yahweh your God has dispersed you. [4]If your people who've been driven away are at the end of the heavens, from there Yahweh your God will gather you, from there he'll get you. [5]Yahweh your God will bring you to the country that your ancestors took possession of and you'll take possession of it. He'll be good to you and he'll make you more numerous than your ancestors.

## In your mouth and in your mind

[6]Yahweh your God will circumcise your mind and the mind of your offspring so that you are loyal to Yahweh your God with your entire mind and with your entire being, in order that you may live. [7]Yahweh your God will put all these vows on your enemies, on the people who are hostile to you, who have pursued you. [8]You yourselves will come back and listen to Yahweh's voice and act on all his orders that I'm giving you today.

[9]Yahweh your God will make you abound in all the action of your hand, in the fruit of your womb, in the fruit of your animals and in the fruit of your land, for good, because Yahweh will again rejoice over you for good, as he rejoiced over your ancestors, [10]when you listen to the voice of Yahweh your God so as to keep his orders and his decrees that are written in this instruction document, when you turn back to Yahweh your God with your entire mind and with your entire being.

[11]Because this order that I'm giving you today is not too extraordinary for you, and it's not far away. [12]It's not in the heavens, to make you say, "Who will go up to the heavens for us and get it for us, and enable us to listen to it so we may act on it?" [13]It's not across the sea, to make you say, "Who will go across the sea for us and get it for us, and enable us to listen to it so we may act on it?" [14]Because the thing is very near you, in your mouth and in your mind, so as to act on it. [15]See, today I've put before you life and good things, death and bad things. [16]I'm ordering you today to be loyal to Yahweh your God by walking in his ways and by keeping his orders, his decrees and his rulings, so you may live and be numerous, and so Yahweh your God may bless you in the country where you're coming to take possession of it.

## Choose life

[17]But if your mind turns about and you don't listen, and you stray and bow low to other gods and serve them, [18]I tell you today that you will quite perish. You won't stay a long time on the land where you're crossing the Yarden to come to take possession of it. [19]I call the heavens and the earth to testify against you today. I've put life and death before you, blessing and curse. You're to choose life, in order that you and your offspring may live, [20]by being loyal to Yahweh your God by

listening to his voice and by attaching yourself to him, because that means your life and your long stay living on the land that Yahweh swore to your ancestors, to Abraham, to Yitshaq and to Ya'aqob, to give them.'

# 31

Mosheh went and spoke these words to all Yisra'el: [2]'I am a man of 120 years. Today I can no longer go out and come in, and Yahweh has said to me, "You will not cross this Yarden." [3]Yahweh your God – he's crossing before you, and he himself will annihilate these nations from before you so you may dispossess them. Yehoshua is the one who is crossing before you, as Yahweh has spoken.

[4]Yahweh will do to them as he did to Sihon and to Og, the kings of the Amorites, and to their country, whom he annihilated. [5]Yahweh will give them up before you and you're to act towards them in accordance with the entire order that I gave you. [6]Be strong and stand firm. Don't be afraid and don't be frightened before them, because Yahweh your God, he's going with you. He won't let go of you. He won't abandon you.'

## Teaching to read

[7]Mosheh called Yehoshua and said to him before the eyes of all Yisra'el, 'Be strong and stand firm, because you're the one who will go with this people into the country that Yahweh swore to their ancestors to give them, and you'll enable them to have it as their domain. [8]Yahweh himself is going before you. He'll be with you. He won't let go of you. He won't abandon you. You won't be afraid. You won't be scared.'

[9]Mosheh wrote this instruction and gave it to the priests, Levi's descendants who carried Yahweh's pact chest, and to all the Yisra'elite elders. [10]Mosheh ordered them, 'At the end of seven years, at the time set for the release year, at the Sukkot Festival, [11]when all Yisra'el comes to appear before Yahweh your God at the site that he chooses, you're to read out this instruction before all Yisra'el, in their ears. [12]Congregate the people – the men and the women, the little ones and the resident who is in your communities – in order that they may listen, and in order that they may learn and live in awe of Yahweh your God, and keep all the things in this instruction by acting on them.

[13]Their children who haven't acknowledged it – they're to listen and learn to live in awe of Yahweh your God all the time that you're living on the land where you're crossing the Yarden to take possession of it.'

[14]Yahweh said to Mosheh: 'Here, the time for you to die has drawn near. Call for Yehoshua and take your stand in the appointment tent so I may give him my orders.' So Mosheh and Yehoshua went and took their stand in the appointment tent, [15]and Yahweh appeared in the tent, in a cloud pillar. The cloud pillar stood at the entrance of the tent.

## Write down this song

[16]Yahweh said to Mosheh: 'Here, you're going to lie down with your ancestors. This people will set off and whore after the foreign gods of the country where it's coming, within it. It will abandon me and contravene my pact, which I solemnized with it, [17]and my anger will rage against it on that day. I shall abandon them and hide my face from them. It will be for devouring. Many bad experiences and pressures will befall it. On that day it will say, "Isn't it on account of the fact that our God was not among us that these bad experiences have befallen us?" [18]But I myself will quite hide my face on that day because of all the bad things that it has done, because it has turned its face to other gods.

[19]So now write down this song for yourselves and teach it to the Yisra'elites. Place it in their mouths in order that this song may be for me a witness against the Yisra'elites. [20]When I bring it into the land that I swore to its ancestors, flowing with milk and syrup, and it eats and is full and becomes enriched, and turns its face to other gods, and they serve them and disdain me, and it contravenes my pact, [21]and when many bad experiences and pressures befall it, this song will avow before it as a witness, because it won't be put out of mind from the mouth of its offspring. Because I know its inclination, which it's forming today, before I bring it into the country that I swore.' [22]So Mosheh wrote down this song that day and taught it to the Yisra'elites.

[23]He ordered Yehoshua ben Nun, 'Be strong and stand firm, because you're the one who will

enable the Yisra'elites to go into the country that I swore to their ancestors. I will be with you.'

## A truthful God

²⁴When Mosheh had finished writing down the words in this instruction on a document, until it was complete, ²⁵Mosheh ordered the Levites, who carried Yahweh's pact chest: ²⁶'Take this instruction document and place it by the side of the pact chest of Yahweh your God. It's to be there as a witness against you. ²⁷Because I myself know your rebelliousness and the toughness of your neck. There, you've been rebellious with Yahweh while I've still been alive with you, today, and you will certainly be after my death. ²⁸Congregate to me all the elders of your clans and your officials so I may speak these words in their ears and call the heavens and the earth to testify against you. ²⁹Because I know that after my death you will behave in a totally devastating way and depart from the path on which I've ordered you, and that bad fortune will meet you in a later time, because you do what is bad in Yahweh's eyes so as to provoke him by the action of your hands.'

³⁰So Mosheh spoke in the ears of the entire Yisra'elite congregation the words of this song, until it was complete.

**32** Give ear, heavens, so I may speak;
　　　the earth is to listen to the words of my
　mouth.

²May my grasp of things fall like rain,
　my speech drop like dew,
Like showers on grass,
　like a downpour on shoots.
³Because I call out the name of Yahweh:
　ascribe greatness to our God!
⁴The crag: his action is perfect,
　because all his ways are authoritative.
A trustworthy God with whom there's no evil;
　he is faithful and upright.

## Is this the way you repay Yahweh?

⁵They have acted devastatingly with him, not as his children,

with a defect in them, a perverse and
　crooked generation.
⁶Do you deal this to Yahweh,
　as a people that is villainous and not smart?
He's your Father who brought you into being,
　isn't he,
　the one who made you and established
　you.
⁷Be mindful of the time of old,
　consider the years of generation after
　generation.
Ask your father, and he will tell you,
　your elders, and they will say it to you.
⁸When the One on High gave the nations
　domains,
　divided up humanity,
He set the boundaries of the peoples,
　according to the number of the divine
　beings,
⁹Because Yahweh's share is his people,
　Ya'aqob is the allocation that is his domain.
¹⁰He found him in a wilderness region,
　in a howling desert wasteland.
He surrounded him, he looked after him,
　he preserved him like the pupil of his eye.
¹¹Like an eagle that stirs its nest,
　hovers over its young,
He spread his wings, took him,
　carried him on his pinions.
¹²Yahweh alone led him,
　there was no foreign god with him.
¹³He let him ride on the heights of the earth,
　he ate the fruit of the field.
He let him suckle on honey from a cliff,
　on oil from the flint of a crag,
¹⁴Curds from the herd, milk from the flock,
　with the fat of lambs,
Rams of Bashan and he-goats,
　with the kidney fat of wheat,
　and the blood of the grape you drank,
　foaming wine.

¹⁵But Yeshurun got fat and kicked;
　you got fat, heavy and gross.
He took leave of the God who made him,
　despised the crag who delivered him.
¹⁶They aroused his passion with outside gods,
　provoked him with offensive things.
¹⁷They sacrificed to demons, no-god,
　gods they had not acknowledged,
New ones that had come from nearby,
　whom your ancestors didn't recognize.

18You forgot the crag who fathered you,
  put out of mind the God who was in labour
    with you.

## Yahweh saw the provocation

19Yahweh saw and disdained them,
  because of the provocation of his sons and
    his daughters.
20He said, 'I shall hide my face from them,
  and I shall see what is their future.
Because they're a contrary generation,
  children in whom there's no
    trustworthiness.
21Those people aroused my passion with a
    no-god,
  provoked me with their hollow things.
So I – I shall arouse their passion with a non-
    people,
  provoke them with a villainous nation.
22Because a fire has blazed in my anger,
  and burned to lowest She'ol.
It has devoured the earth and its produce,
  set on fire the foundations of the
    mountains.
23I shall gather bad things upon them,
  finish up my arrows against them.
24Wasted by hunger, eaten by fever,
  bitter devastation,
I shall send off against them animal fangs,
  with the venom of creatures that crawl in
    the dirt.
25The sword will bereave outside,
  dread from the rooms,
Both young man and young girl,
  the nursing baby with the grey-haired man.
26I said I would cut them in pieces,
  I would eliminate the memory of them from
    humanity.
27Except that I dreaded the provocation of the
    enemy,
  so that their attackers don't recognize,
So that they don't say, "Our hand is high,
  Yahweh has not done any of this!"
28Because they're a nation lost for counsel;
  there's no insight in them.
29If they were smart, they would understand
    this,
  they would have insight into their future.
30How does one pursue a thousand,
  and two make ten thousand flee,

If it's not that their crag has sold them,
  Yahweh has delivered them up?

## Their crag is not like our crag

31Because their crag is not like our crag –
  our enemies may be the judges.
32Because their vine is from Sedom's vine,
  from Amorah's fields.
Their grapes are poisonous grapes,
  their clusters are bitter for them.
33Their wine is the venom of asps,
  vipers' cruel poison.
34It's laid up with me, isn't it,
  sealed up in my storehouses?
35Redress and making good are mine
  at the time when their foot slips.
Because the day of their calamity is near,
  the things that are destined for them are
    making speed.

36Because Yahweh will act in judgement for his
    people,
  will relent concerning his servants,
When he sees that their hand has failed,
  and there's no one, bound or released.
37He will say, 'Where are their gods,
  the crag in which they took shelter,
38Those who ate the fat of their sacrifices,
  drank the wine of their libations?
They should set off and help you;
  he should become a place to hide for you.
39See, now, that I,
  I am the one.
There's no God beside me;
  I myself put to death and I make alive.
I hit and I myself will heal;
  there's no one rescues from my hand.
40Because I raise my hand to the heavens,
  and I say: "As I live permanently:
41If I sharpen the flashing of my sword,
  and my hand takes hold of authority,
I shall give back redress to my attackers,
  I shall make good to the people who're
    hostile to me.
42I shall make my arrows drunk with blood,
  my sword will devour flesh,
From the blood of the person who's been run
    through and the captive,
  from the long-haired head of the
    enemy."

## The song shared

[43]Resound over his people, you nations,
  because he takes redress for the blood of his
    servants.
He gives back redress to his attackers
  and makes expiation for his land, for his
    people.'

[44]Mosheh came and spoke all the words of
this song in the people's ears, he and Hoshea
ben Nun. [45]Mosheh finished speaking all
these words to all Yisra'el, [46]then said to them:
'Give your mind to all these words that I'm
testifying against you today, which you're
to order your children to keep by acting
on them, all the words in this instruction.
[47]Because it's not an empty thing for you.
Rather, it's your life. Through this thing
you'll stay a long time on the land where
you're crossing the Yarden to take possession
of it.'

[48]Yahweh spoke to Mosheh that very
day: [49]'Climb this mountain in the Regions
Across, Mount Nebo, which is in the country
of Mo'ab, which is facing Yeriho [Jericho],
and look at the country of Kena'an, which
I'm giving to the Yisra'elites as a holding.
[50]You're to die on the mountain where you're
climbing, and you're to be gathered to your
kin, as Aharon your brother died on Mount
Hor and was gathered to his kin, [51]because
of the fact that you trespassed against me
among the Yisra'elites at Meribat Qadesh
Water in the Tsin Wilderness, because of the
fact that you didn't make me sacred among
the Yisra'elites, [52]because you're to look at
the country from a distance, but you will not
come there, to the country that I'm giving to
the Yisra'elites.'

## Mosheh's final blessing: Re'uben, Yehudah, Levi

# 33

This is the blessing that Mosheh, the
supernatural man, gave the Yisra'elites
before his death:

[2]Yahweh came from Sinay,
  rose on them from Se'ir,
  shone from Mount Pa'ran.

He arrived from Sacred Myriads,
  from the south to them at the slope.
[3]As one who indeed holds the people dear,
  all its sacred ones are in your hand.
They themselves bowed at your foot,
  as the one who utters your words.
[4]The instruction with which Mosheh ordered us,
  the possession of Ya'aqob's congregation.
[5]He became king in Yeshurun,
  when the heads of the people gathered,
  Yisra'el's clans together.
[6]Re'uben is to live and not die,
  but it's to become few in number.

[7]This of Yehudah – he said:

Listen to Yehudah's voice, Yahweh,
  bring him to his people.
Make his hands powerful for him;
  may you be a help against his attackers.

[8]Of Levi he said:

Your Urim and Tummim
  be with the one who was loyal to you,
Whom you tested at Massah ['Testing'],
  argued with at Meribah ['Argument'] Water,
[9]The one who said of his father and of his
    mother,
  'I haven't looked at him',
And did not recognize his brothers,
  did not acknowledge his children,
Because they kept your word,
  preserved your pact.
[10]They will instruct Ya'aqob in your rulings,
  Yisra'el in your instruction.
They will place incense before your nose
  and a whole offering on your altar.
[11]Bless his forcefulness, Yahweh,
  may you grace the action of his hands.
Hit the hips of the people who rise up against
    him,
  and the people who are hostile to him, so
    that they cannot rise up.

## Binyamin, Yoseph, Zebulun

[12]Of Binyamin he said:

Yahweh's beloved
  is to dwell in confidence with him.

He will be surrounding him at all times;
  he will be dwelling between his shoulders.

¹³Of Yoseph he said:

His region be blessed by Yahweh,
  from the choice things of the heavens, from
    the dew,
  and from the deep that lies down below,
¹⁴From the choice things of the sun's yield,
  from the choice things of the moon's
    produce,
¹⁵From the top of the ancient mountains,
  from the choice things of the age-old
    hills,
¹⁶From the choice things of the earth and its
    fullness,
  and the acceptance of the one who dwelt at
    the bush.
It's to come on Yoseph's head,
  on the crown of the prince of his brothers.
¹⁷His magnificence is that of a firstling ox,
  his horns the horns of an oryx.
With them he's to gore the peoples,
  the ends of the earth all at once.
They are Ephrayim's myriads,
  They are Menashsheh's thousands.

¹⁸Of Zebulun he said:

Rejoice, Zebulun, as you go out,
  and Yissakar in your tents.
¹⁹They're to call peoples to the highland,
  there they will offer right sacrifices.
Because they will suck on the abundance of
    the seas
  and on the hidden treasures of the shore.

## Gad, Dan, Naphtali, Asher

²⁰Of Gad he said:

Blessed the one who widens Gad,
  dwelling like a cougar!
He will tear an arm, yes a crown;
  ²¹he's seen the best for himself.
Because there is the commander's plot,
    reserved,
  and he's come to the people's heads.
He's put Yahweh's faithfulness into action,
  his acts of authority with Yisra'el.

²²Of Dan he said:

Dan is a lion cub
  that will leap out from Bashan.

²³Of Naphtali he said:

Naphtali, enjoying the acceptance
  and full of the blessing of Yahweh,
  take possession west and south.

²⁴Of Asher he said:

Blessed of sons is Asher,
  may he be accepted by his brothers,
  dipping his foot in oil,
²⁵Your bolts iron and copper,
  your strength as long as your days.

²⁶Yeshurun, there's none like God,
  riding the heavens as your help,
  the skies in his majesty.
²⁷The ancient God is an abode,
  underneath are the age-old arms.
He drove out the enemy from before you,
  and said, 'Annihilate!'
²⁸So Yisra'el dwells in confidence,
  Ya'aqob's spring is left alone,
In a country of grain and new wine;
  yes, its heavens drop down dew.
²⁹Your good fortune, Yisra'el – who is like you,
  a people finding deliverance through
    Yahweh,
Your shield who is your help,
  the one who is your majestic sword?
Your enemies will cower before you,
  and you yourself will tread on their backs.

## Dying outside the promised land

**34** So Mosheh went up from the Mo'ab
steppes to Mount Nebo, to the top of
Pisgah, which is opposite Yeriho, and Yahweh
let him see the entire country, Gil'ad as far as
Dan, ²all Naphtali, the region of Ephrayim and
Menashsheh, the entire region of Yehudah
as far as the Western Sea, ³the Negeb and
the Plain (the Valley of Jericho, the town of
palms) as far as Tso'ar. ⁴Yahweh said to him,
'This is the country that I swore to Abraham,
to Yitshaq and to Ya'aqob, "To your offspring

I will give it." I've let you see it with your eyes, but you will not cross there.'

⁵So Mosheh, Yahweh's servant, died there in the country of Mo'ab at Yahweh's bidding, ⁶and he buried him in a ravine in the country of Mo'ab near Bet Pe'or. No one knows his grave until this day. ⁷Mosheh was a man of 120 years when he died. His eye was not weak and his strength had not gone. ⁸The Yisra'elites bewailed Mosheh in the Mo'ab steppes for thirty days, then the days of grieved bewailing for Mosheh came to an end.

⁹Now Yehoshua ben Nun was full of a discerning spirit because Mosheh had leaned his hands on him, and the Yisra'elites listened to him and did as Yahweh ordered Mosheh. ¹⁰There didn't again rise in Yisra'el a prophet like Mosheh, whom Yahweh acknowledged face to face, ¹¹in all the signs and the miracles that Yahweh sent him to do in the country of Misrayim for Par'oh, for all his servants and for all his country, ¹²and in all the strong hand and in all the great awe-inspiring power that Mosheh showed before the eyes of all Yisra'el.

# JOSHUA

The book of Joshua marks a new beginning to the story of Israel in Canaan. Yet the story continues straight on without a break. Deuteronomy had looked forward to the Israelites occupying Canaan; Joshua describes how they did so. Further back, Genesis had told of God's promise that Abraham's descendants would come to possess this land, and the book of Joshua relates how God fulfilled that promise. So Joshua also marks an end.

There are two stages to its account of the fulfilment. The first half of the book relates how the Israelites came to occupy the land. The second half relates how they allocated it among their clans.

But the story also incorporates two complications. The first half also lists areas of the country that Israel didn't conquer. These were the areas where most of the more powerful Canaanites lived. Israel mostly settled in the highland where hardly anyone else lived. Israelites hearing this story would be unable to suppress a smile, because the areas Israel failed to occupy were the best parts of the country. Sometimes Joshua speaks simply of them not occupying these areas, which might imply it was their fault. Sometimes it speaks of them being unable to occupy them, which implies that God didn't enable them to complete their occupation.

The other complication is that there indeed were a number of spectacular moments when the Israelites did not follow God's instructions: see especially the stories about Achan and about the Gibonites (Joshua 7 and 9). This aspect of the story also points to the implication that, while they are not entirely to blame for their failure to occupy the whole country, they do carry some of the blame.

So the people see all God's promises fulfilled, but they don't; and they live by Yahweh's instructions, but they don't. The book thus epitomizes the dynamic of the portrait of the people of God in both Testaments. It encourages us to rejoice in God's fulfilling his promises but also to face the extent to which he hasn't, yet to live in confident hope that he will do so. It encourages us to be realistic about our own obedience to God and also to commit ourselves anew to keeping our commitment to the pact God has made with us.

Two other aspects of the book often trouble people. The story of how 'Joshua fit the battle of Jericho' is well known. Unfortunately, archaeological investigations suggest that no one lived in Jericho in Joshua's time, nor in Ai, whose conquest follows that of Jericho in the book. So the stories of the Israelites' capture of these towns don't correspond to what happened in these particular places. Why might God have inspired Israelite storytellers to develop imaginative stories about the taking of these towns (whose ruins would be familiar)? What the stories do is give concrete expression to the fact that God did give the country to Israel in an amazing way, and to the fact that the Israelites were always in danger of disobeying God.

The other aspect of the book that often troubles people is the fact that Joshua can look like a story about the Israelites committing genocide. This fact seems not to have troubled the New Testament writers, who didn't see the story of Joshua as incompatible with believing in Jesus. Stephen (in Acts 7) and Hebrews 11 are enthusiastic about Israel's violent occupation of Canaan. They don't assume that the story provides a warrant for subsequent acts of genocide, and neither does the First Testament – Israel didn't regularly go around annihilating people. The occupation of the country by Joshua was a one-off act of judgement by God. The Canaanites were getting what they deserved for practices such as sacrificing children; they were not just innocent victims. Ironically, though, the book itself makes clear that the Israelites actually didn't commit genocide. The Canaanites continued in the country for centuries.

## Just one river to cross

**1** After the death of Mosheh [Moses], Yahweh's servant, Yahweh said to Yehoshua [Joshua] ben Nun, Mosheh's minister: [2]'Mosheh my servant is dead. Set off now, cross this Yarden [Jordan], you and this entire people, into the country that I'm giving to them, to the Israelites. [3]Every place on which the sole of your foot treads I give you, as I spoke to Mosheh. [4]From the wilderness and this Lebanon, as far as the big river (the River Euphrates), all the country of the Hittites, as far as the Great Sea on the west, will be your border. [5]No one will take a stand before you all the days of your life. As I was with Mosheh, I'll be with you. I won't let go of you; I won't abandon you. [6]Be strong, stand firm, because you're the one who'll enable this people to take as their domain this country that I swore to their ancestors to give them. [7]Only be strong, stand very firm, so as to keep by acting in accordance with the entire instruction that Mosheh my servant ordered you. Don't turn aside from it right or left, in order that you may thrive everywhere you go. [8]This instruction document will not move away from your mouth. You're to murmur it day and night in order that you may keep by acting in accordance with everything written in it, because then you'll make your journey successful, then you'll thrive. [9]I've ordered you, "Be strong, stand firm", haven't I? Don't be frightened, don't be scared, because Yahweh your God will be with you everywhere you go.'

[10]So Yehoshua ordered the people's overseers: [11]'Pass through the middle of the camp and order the people, "Prepare provisions for yourselves, because in three days more you're going to cross this Yarden, to go in to take possession of the country that Yahweh your God is giving you, to take possession of it."'

## Another spy mission

[12]To the Re'ubenites, to the Gadites and to the half-clan of Menashsheh, Yehoshua said: [13]'Be mindful of the thing that Mosheh, Yahweh's servant, ordered you: "Yahweh your God is letting you settle down and is giving you this region. [14]Your wives, your little ones, and your livestock can stay in the region that Mosheh gave you across the Yarden, but you're to cross, organized into companies, before your brothers, all the forceful strong men. You're to help them [15]till Yahweh enables your brothers to settle down like you and they also take possession of the region that Yahweh your God is giving them. Then you can go back to the region that you're to take possession of and you can take possession of it, which Mosheh, Yahweh's servant, gave you across the Yarden, to the east."'

[16]They answered Yehoshua: 'All that you've ordered us we'll do. Everywhere that you send us we'll go. [17]Just as we listened to Mosheh, so we'll listen to you. May Yahweh simply be with you as he was with Mosheh. [18]Any individual who rebels against your bidding and doesn't listen to your words regarding everything that you order him is to be put to death. Simply be strong and stand firm.'

**2** From Acacias, Yehoshua ben Nun sent two men to investigate quietly: 'Go and look at the country, and at Yeriho [Jericho].' They went, and came to the house of a woman who was a whore named Rahab, and they slept there. [2]It was told to the king of Yeriho: 'Here, some men came here tonight, some of the Yisra'elites [Israelites], to check out the country.' [3]So the king of Yeriho sent to Rahab: 'Bring out the men who came to you, who've come to your house, because they've come to check out the entire country.' [4]The woman had taken the two men and hidden them. So she said, 'Yes, the men came to me. I didn't know where they were from. [5]The gateway was about to be shut at dark and the men went out. I don't know where the men went. Hurry, pursue after them, because you can overtake them.'

## Meanwhile, in the whorehouse

[6]Now she had taken them up to the roof and hidden them among the flax stalks that she had on the roof, laid out. [7]The men pursued after them on the Yarden road, down to the fords. And after their pursuers had gone out, they shut the gateway.

[8]Before those men went to sleep, she went up to them on the roof. [9]She said to the men, 'I acknowledge that Yahweh has given you the

country, that a dread of you has fallen on us, and that all the people living in the country have melted away before you, ¹⁰because we heard how Yahweh dried up the water of the Reed Sea before you when you got out of Misrayim [Egypt] and what you did to the two Amorite kings who were across the Yarden, to Sihon and to Og, whom you devoted. ¹¹We heard, and our mind melted. There was no spirit rising up in anyone in the face of you, because Yahweh your God is God in the heavens above and on the earth below.

¹²So now, please swear to me by Yahweh, because I've acted in commitment with you, that you'll also act in commitment with my father's household. Give me a truthful sign ¹³that you'll let my father and my mother live, and my brothers and my sisters, and everyone who belongs to them, and that you'll save our lives from death.' ¹⁴The men said to her, 'Our lives in place of yours, to the death, if you don't tell about our business here. When Yahweh gives us the country, we'll act in commitment and truthfulness with you.'

### The scarlet cord

¹⁵She let them down by a rope through the window, because her house was in the fortification, so she was living in the fortification. ¹⁶She said to them, 'Go to the highland so the pursuers don't come upon you, and hide there for three days till the pursuers come back, and afterwards you can go on your way.'

¹⁷The men said to her, 'We'll be free of this oath to you, which you've got us to take: ¹⁸here, when we're coming into the country, you're to tie this line of scarlet cord in the window through which you've let us down, and you're to gather to yourself your father, your mother, your brothers, your entire ancestral household, in the house. ¹⁹Anyone who goes out of the doors of your house outside – his blood will be on his head and we'll be free of guilt. Anyone who's with you in the house, his blood will be on our head if a hand is laid on him. ²⁰But if you tell people about this thing of ours, we will be free from the oath to you which you've got us to

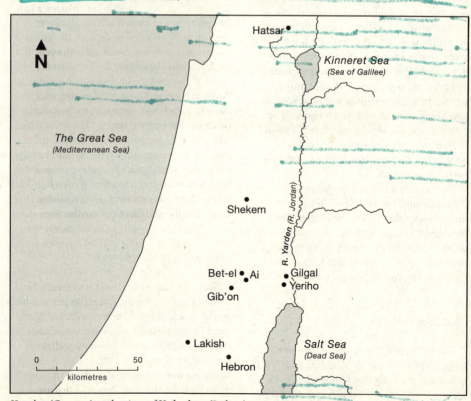

*Kena'an (Canaan) at the time of Yeshoshua (Joshua)*

take.' ²¹She said, 'In accordance with your words, so it will be.' She sent them off and they went, and she tied the scarlet line in her window.

²²So they went, and came into the highland and stayed there for three days until the pursuers came back. The pursuers had searched on the entire road but had not found them. ²³The two men came down again from the highland, crossed over, and came to Yehoshua ben Nun. They recounted to him all the things that had befallen them, ²⁴and said to Yehoshua, 'Yahweh has given the entire country into our hand. What's more, all the people living in the country have melted away before us.'

### On getting your feet wet

**3** Yehoshua started early in the morning and they moved on from Acacias, and came to the Yarden, he and all the Yisra'elites. They stayed the night there before they were to cross over. ²After three days the overseers passed through the middle of the camp ³and ordered the people, 'When you see the pact chest of Yahweh your God, and the Levitical priests carrying it, you yourselves are to move on from your place and follow it ⁴(yet there's to be a distance between you and it, some 1,000 metres by measure – don't go near it), in order that you may know the way whereby you're to go, because you haven't passed this way in previous days.'

⁵Yehoshua said to the people, 'Make yourselves sacred, because tomorrow Yahweh will do extraordinary things among you.' ⁶Yehoshua said to the priests, 'Carry the pact chest and pass through before the people.' So they carried the pact chest and went before the people.

⁷Yahweh said to Yehoshua, 'This day I shall start to make you great in the eyes of all Yisra'el so they may acknowledge that I'm with you as I was with Mosheh. ⁸You yourself are to order the priests carrying the pact chest: "When you come to the edge of the Yarden water, you're to stand in the Yarden."'

⁹Yehoshua said to the Yisra'elites, 'Come up here and listen to the words of Yahweh your God.' ¹⁰Yehoshua said, 'By this you will acknowledge that the living God is among you and that he will totally dispossess from before

you the Canaanite, the Hittite, the Hivvite, the Perizzite, the Girgashite, the Amorite and the Yebusite. ¹¹Here is the pact chest of the Lord of all the earth, passing through the Yarden before you. ¹²Now get yourselves twelve men from the Yisra'elite clans, one man per clan. ¹³When the soles of the feet of the priests carrying the chest of Yahweh, Lord of all the earth, set down in the Yarden water, the Yarden water will break off (the water coming down from higher up) and stand as a single heap.'

### The Yarden stops

¹⁴So when the people moved on from their tents to cross over the Yarden, the priests carrying the pact chest were before the people. ¹⁵As the people carrying the chest came as far as the Yarden and the feet of the priests carrying the chest dipped into the edge of the water (the Yarden overflows all its banks the entire time of harvest), ¹⁶the Yarden water coming down from higher up stood; it rose as a single heap a great way off at Adam, a town near Tsaretan. Going down to the Steppe Sea (the Salt Sea), it completely broke off. So the people crossed near Yeriho. ¹⁷The priests carrying Yahweh's pact chest stood on dry ground in the middle of the Yarden, steady, while all Yisra'el were crossing on dry ground until the entire nation had come to an end of crossing the Yarden.

**4** When the entire nation had come to an end of crossing the Yarden, Yahweh said to Yehoshua: ²'Get yourselves twelve men from the people, one man each from a clan, ³and order them, "Carry yourselves twelve stones from here, from the middle of the Yarden, from the place where the priests' feet stood steady. Take them across with you and set them down at the place where you stay the night tonight."' ⁴So Yehoshua called twelve men whom he settled on from the Yisra'elites, one man for each clan. ⁵Yehoshua said to them, 'Cross before the chest of Yahweh your God, into the middle of the Yarden, and lift up for yourselves, each man, a stone on to his shoulder, corresponding to the number of the Yisra'elites' clans, ⁶in order that this may be a sign among you. When your children ask in the future, "What are these stones of yours?", ⁷you're to say to them,

'The Yarden water broke off before Yahweh's pact chest; when it crossed the Yarden, the Yarden water broke off." These stones will be a permanent reminder for the Yisra'elites.'

## Looking forward and backward

[8]The Yisra'elites did so, as Yehoshua ordered. They carried twelve stones from the middle of the Yarden, as Yahweh spoke to Yehoshua, corresponding to the number of the Yisra'elites' clans, took them across with them to the place where they were going to stay, and set them down there. [9]Yehoshua set up twelve stones in the middle of the Yarden at the place where the feet of the priests carrying the pact chest had stood. They have been there until this day.

[10]The priests carrying the chest were standing in the middle of the Yarden until everything had come to an end that Yahweh had ordered Yehoshua to speak to the people, in accordance with everything Mosheh had ordered Yehoshua. The people hurried and crossed, [11]and when the entire people had come to an end of crossing, Yahweh's chest and the priests crossed before the people.

[12]The Re'ubenites, the Gadites and the half-clan of Menashsheh crossed, organized into companies before the Yisra'elites, as Mosheh had spoken to them. [13]Some 40,000 men equipped for war crossed before Yahweh to the Yeriho steppes for battle. [14]On that day Yahweh made Yehoshua great in the eyes of all Yisra'el. They lived in awe of him as they had lived in awe of Mosheh, all the days of his life.

[15]Yahweh said to Yehoshua: [16]'Order the priests carrying the affirmation chest to go up out of the Yarden.' [17]So Yehoshua ordered the priests: 'Go up out of the Yarden', [18]and when the priests carrying Yahweh's pact chest went up out of the middle of the Yarden and the soles of the priests' feet stepped on to the dry ground, the Yarden water turned back to its place and went over all its banks as in previous days.

## What do these stones mean?

[19]When the people went up from the Yarden on the tenth of the first month, they camped at Gilgal, on the eastern border of Yeriho. [20]These twelve stones that they had got from the Yarden, Yehoshua set up at Gilgal. [21]He said to the Yisra'elites, 'When your children ask their parents in the future, "What are these stones?", [22]you're to let your children know, "On dry land Yisra'el crossed this Yarden", [23]because Yahweh your God dried up the Yarden water before you until you crossed, as Yahweh your God did to the Reed Sea, which he dried up before us until we crossed, [24]in order that all the peoples of the earth might acknowledge how strong is Yahweh's hand, in order that you might live in awe of Yahweh your God for all time.'

**5** When all the kings of the Amorites who were across the Yarden on its western side and all the kings of the Kena'anites [Canaanites] who were near the Sea heard that Yahweh had dried up the Yarden water before the Yisra'elites until they had crossed, their mind melted and there was no longer any spirit left in them because of the Yisra'elites.

## Foreskin Hill

[2]At that time Yahweh said to Yehoshua, 'Make yourself flint knives and circumcise the Yisra'elites again, a second time.' [3]So Yehoshua made himself flint knives and circumcised the Yisra'elites at Foreskin Hill.

[4]This is the reason why Yehoshua circumcised the entire people that got out of Egypt, the males. Every one (the men of battle) had died in the wilderness on the way, when they had got out of Egypt. [5]While the entire people that got out had been circumcised, they had not circumcised the entire people born in the wilderness on the way, when they had got out of Egypt. [6]Because for forty years the Yisra'elites had gone in the wilderness until the entire nation (the men of battle who had got out of Egypt) were gone, the people who had not listened to Yahweh's voice and to whom Yahweh had sworn not to let them see the land that Yahweh had sworn to their ancestors to give us, a land flowing with milk and syrup. [7]In that he had made their sons arise in their place, they are the people Yehoshua circumcised because they were foreskinned, because they had not circumcised them on the way.

[8]When they had come to an end of circumcising the entire nation, they stayed

in their place in the camp until they had recovered. [9]Yahweh said to Yehoshua, 'Today I've rolled away the reviling of Egypt from upon you.' So they've named that place Gilgal ['Rolling'] until this day.

[10]The Yisra'elites camped at Gilgal and made the Pesah [Passover] on the fourteenth day of the month in the evening, in the Yeriho steppes. [11]They ate from the country's produce the day after Pesah, flatbread and roasted grain that actual day. [12]The *maan* stopped the day after they ate from the country's produce. There was no longer any *maan* for the Yisra'elites. They ate from the yield of the country of Kena'an that year.

## Which side are you on?

[13]When Yehoshua was at Yeriho, he lifted his eyes and saw: there, a man standing opposite him, a drawn sword in his hand. Yehoshua went to him and said to him, 'Are you for us or for our attackers?' [14]He said, 'No, because it's as Yahweh's army officer that I've now come.' Yehoshua fell on his face to the ground before him. He bowed low and said to him, 'What is my lord going to speak to his servant?' [15]Yahweh's army officer said to Yehoshua, 'Take your boot off your foot, because the place on which you're standing is sacred.' Yehoshua did so.

**6** Now Yeriho was closed, closed tight, before the Yisra'elites. No one was going out and no one was coming in. [2]Yahweh said to Yehoshua, 'See, I've given Yeriho and its king, the forceful strong men, into your hand. [3]You're to go round the town, all the men of battle circling the town once. You're to do this for six days, [4]while seven priests carry seven ram's horns before the chest. On the seventh day you're to go round the town seven times, while the priests blow on the horns. [5]At the drawing out of a blast on the ram's horn, when you hear the noise of the horn, the entire company is to give a great shout, the town's wall will fall flat, and the company are to go up, each individual straight ahead.'

[6]So Yehoshua ben Nun called the priests and said to them, 'Carry the pact chest, while seven priests carry seven ram's horns before Yahweh's chest.' [7]He said to the company, 'Pass on, go

round the town, while the body equipped for a campaign passes on before Yahweh's chest.'

## Come blow your horn

[8]When Yehoshua had said it to the company, the seven priests carrying the seven ram's horns passed on before Yahweh and blew on the horns, and Yahweh's pact chest followed them, [9]while the body equipped for a campaign was going before the priests blowing the horns, and the rearguard was going behind the chest, with a continuing blowing on the horns. [10]Yehoshua ordered the company, 'You will not shout, you will not make your voice heard, no word will come out of your mouth, until the time I say to you, "Shout!", and you'll shout.'

[11]So he had Yahweh's chest go round the town, circling it once, then they came to the camp and stayed the night in the camp. [12]Yehoshua started early in the morning and the priests carried Yahweh's chest, [13]while the seven priests carrying seven ram's horns before Yahweh's chest were continuing to go and blow on the horns, the body equipped for a campaign was going before them, and the rearguard was going behind Yahweh's chest, with a continuing blowing on the horns. [14]They went round the town once on the second day and came back to the camp. So they did for six days.

[15]On the seventh day they started early, at sunrise, went round the town in accordance with this rule, seven times; only on that day did they go round the town seven times. [16]The seventh time, the priests blew on the horns and Yehoshua said to the company, 'Shout, because Yahweh has given you the town. [17]The town is to be an object devoted to Yahweh, it and everything that's in it, except that Rahab the whore will live, she and everyone who is with her in the house, because she hid the envoys that we sent. [18]Only, you keep yourselves from what's to be devoted so you don't become a thing that's to be devoted, and you take anything from what's to be devoted and make the Yisra'elite camp into a thing that's to be devoted. You will bring disaster on it. [19]All the silver and gold and the objects of copper and iron are sacred to Yahweh. They're to come into Yahweh's treasury.'

### And the walls came tumbling down

²⁰So the company shouted and they blew on the horns, and when the company heard the sound of the horn, the company gave a great shout, the wall fell flat and the company went up into the town, each individual straight ahead. They captured the town ²¹and devoted everything that was in the town, man and woman, young and old, ox and sheep and donkey, with the mouth of the sword.

²²To the two men who had investigated the country Yehoshua said, 'Come into the house of the woman who's a whore and bring out of there the woman and everyone who belongs to her, as you swore to her.' ²³So the young men who'd done the investigating came in and brought out Rahab, her father and her mother, her brothers and everyone who belonged to her. They brought out her entire kin-group, and set them down outside the Yisra'elite camp.

²⁴The town they burned in fire with everything that was in it, except that the silver and the gold and the objects of copper and iron they put in the treasury of Yahweh's house, ²⁵and Yehoshua let Rahab the whore live, with her ancestral household and everyone who belonged to her. She's lived among Yisra'el until this day, because she hid the envoys whom Yehoshua sent to investigate Yeriho.

²⁶At that time Yehoshua swore, 'Cursed before Yahweh be the man who sets about building this town, Yeriho. At the cost of his firstborn may he found it and at the cost of his little one may he put up its doors.'

²⁷Yahweh was with Yehoshua and report of him went through the entire country.

7 But the Yisra'elites committed a trespass in connection with things to be devoted. Akan ben Karmi, son of Zabdi son of Zerah of the clan of Yehudah [Judah], took some of the things that were to be devoted, and Yahweh's anger raged against the Yisra'elites.

### Take it easy

²Yehoshua sent men 'from Yeriho to Ha'ay [Ai, 'The Ruin']', which is by Bet Aven ['Trouble House'], east of Bet-el. He said to them, 'Go up and investigate the region.' The men went up and investigated Ha'ay, ³and came back to Yehoshua and said to him, 'The entire company should not go up. Some two or three thousand men should go up and strike down Ha'ay. You shouldn't make the entire company get weary there, because they are few.' ⁴So some 3,000 of the company went up, but they took flight before the men of Ha'ay. ⁵The men of Ha'ay struck down some thirty-six of them, and pursued them before the gateway as far as the quarries and struck them down on the slope.

The company's mind melted, turned to water. ⁶Yehoshua tore his clothes and fell on his face to the ground before Yahweh's chest until the evening, he and Yisra'el's elders, and they put dirt on their head. ⁷Yehoshua said, 'Oh, Lord Yahweh, why did you bring this people across the Yarden at all, to give us into the hand of the Amorites to obliterate us? If only we had resolved to live across the Yarden. ⁸As for me, Lord, what am I to say after Yisra'el has turned its back before its enemies? ⁹The Kena'anites and all the people living in the country will hear and surround us and cut off our name from the earth, and what will you do about your great name?'

¹⁰Yahweh said to Yehoshua, 'Get yourself up. Why are you falling on your face there? ¹¹Yisra'el has done wrong. Yes, they've contravened my pact about which I gave them orders. They've both taken some of the things that were to be devoted, and they've stolen, and they've acted deceitfully, and they've put things in their bags. ¹²The Yisra'elites won't be able to stand before their enemies, they'll turn their back before their enemies, because they've become something to be devoted. I shall not be with you any more unless you annihilate from among you the thing that's to be devoted.

### Coveting can kill

¹³Get up, make the people sacred. You're to say, "Make yourselves sacred for tomorrow, because Yahweh, the God of Yisra'el, has said this: There's something to be devoted among you, Yisra'el. You can't stand before your enemies until you've removed what is to be devoted from among you."

¹⁴In the morning you're to draw near by your clans. The clan that Yahweh takes is to draw near by kin-groups. The kin-group that

Yahweh takes is to draw near by households. The household that Yahweh takes is to draw near man by man. [15]The one who is taken in the net is to burn in fire, he and everything that belongs to him, because he contravened Yahweh's pact and because he did something villainous in Yisra'el.'

[16]Yehoshua started early in the morning and presented Yisra'el by its clans, and the clan of Yehudah was taken. [17]He presented the kin-group of Yehudah, and he took the kin-group of Zerah. He presented the kin-group of the Zarhites man by man, and Zabdi was taken. [18]He presented his household man by man, and Akan ben Karmi, son of Zabdi son of Zerah of the clan of Yehudah, was taken. [19]Yehoshua said to Akan, 'Son, please give honour to Yahweh, the God of Yisra'el, and make confession to him. Please tell me what you've done. Don't hide it from me.' [20]Akan answered Yehoshua, 'Truly I'm the one who's done wrong against Yahweh, the God of Yisra'el. This actual thing is what I did. [21]I saw in the spoil a fine coat from Shin'ar, and 200 sheqels of silver, and a bar of gold fifty sheqels in weight. I desired them and took them. There, they're buried in the ground inside my tent, with the silver underneath.'

[22]Yehoshua sent envoys and they ran to the tent, and there, it was buried in his tent, with the silver underneath. [23]They took them from inside the tent and brought them to Yehoshua and to all the Yisra'elites, and they laid them out before Yahweh.

## Purging away the trespass

[24]Yehoshua took Akan ben Zerah, the silver, the coat, the gold bar, and his sons, his daughters, his ox, his donkey, his flock, his tent and everything that he had, he and all Yisra'el with him, and brought them up to Disaster Vale. [25]Yehoshua said, 'How you've brought disaster on us! Yahweh will bring disaster on you this day.' All Yisra'el pelted him with stones. They burned them in fire and executed them by stoning, [26]and raised a great heap of stones over them until this day. And Yahweh turned back from his angry burning.

That's why they've named that place Disaster Vale, until this day.

**8** Yahweh said to Yehoshua, 'Don't be afraid. Don't be dismayed. Take the entire battle company with you and set off, go up to Ha'ay. See, I've given into your hand the king of Ha'ay, his town, his people and his region. [2]You're to do to Ha'ay and to its king as you did to Yeriho and to its king, only its spoil and its animals you may treat as plunder for yourselves. Set yourself an ambush for the town, behind it.'

[3]So Yehoshua and all the battle company set off to go up to Ha'ay. Yehoshua chose 30,000 men, forceful strong men, sent them by night [4]and ordered them, 'See, you're going to be men in an ambush for the town, behind the town. Don't be very far from the town, and all of you be ready. [5]I and the entire company that's with me – we'll draw near the town, and when they come out to meet us like the first time, we'll flee before them. [6]They'll come out after us till we've drawn them away from the town, because they'll say "They're fleeing before us like the first time." So we'll flee before them, [7]and you'll get up out of the ambush and take possession of the town. Yahweh your God will give it into your hand. [8]When you've taken the town, set the town on fire. You're to act in accordance with Yahweh's word. See, I've given you orders.'

## The game plan executed

[9]So Yehoshua sent them, they went to the ambush, and they settled down between Bet-el and Ha'ay, west of Ha'ay. Yehoshua stayed the night among the company. [10]Yehoshua started early in the morning and numbered the company, and he and Yisra'el's elders went up before the company to Ha'ay. [11]All the battle company that was with him went up, moved close and came in front of the town, and camped north of Ha'ay. There was a ravine between them and Ha'ay.

[12]So he had taken some 5,000 men and set them as an ambush between Bet-el and Ha'ay, west of the town, [13]and the company set up the entire camp, which was north of the town, and its rearguard west of the town. Yehoshua had gone that night into the middle of the vale. [14]When the king of Ha'ay saw it, the men of the town hurried and started early and went out to meet Yisra'el in battle, he and all his

company, at the set place facing the steppe; he
didn't know that there was an ambush for him
behind the town. [15]Yehoshua and all Yisra'el
let themselves be beaten before them and fled
by the wilderness road. [16]The entire company
that was in Ha'ay cried out to one another
to pursue after them, and they pursued after
Yehoshua and tore out of the town. [17]Not a
man remained in Ha'ay or Bet El who didn't go
out after Yisra'el. They left the town open and
pursued after Yisra'el.

[18]Yahweh said to Yehoshua, 'Hold out the
javelin that's in your hand towards Ha'ay,
because I shall give it into your hand.' Yehoshua
held out the javelin that was in his hand
towards the town, [19]while the ambush quickly
got up out of its place. They ran when he held
out his hand, came into the town and captured
it, and hurried and set the town on fire.

### Ha'ay becomes a ruin

[20]The men of Ha'ay turned their face behind
them and looked: there, smoke from the town
went up to the heavens. There was no capacity
in them to go this way or that when the
company fleeing to the wilderness turned on to
the pursuer, [21]and Yehoshua and all Yisra'el saw
that the ambush had taken the town and that
smoke from the town had gone up, and they
turned back and struck down the men of Ha'ay.
[22]When these [Yisra'elites] came out of the
town to meet them, in relation to Yisra'el they
were in the middle, some [Yisra'elites] on one
side and some on the other. They struck them
down so they didn't let anyone remain to it as
escapee or survivor. [23]The king of Ha'ay they
took alive and presented him to Yehoshua.

[24]When Yisra'el had finished slaughtering
all the people living in Ha'ay in the fields, in
the wilderness where they had pursued them,
and all of them had fallen to the mouth of
the sword until they had come to an end, all
Yisra'el went back to Ha'ay and struck it down
with the mouth of the sword.

[25]All those who fell that day, both men and
women, were 12,000, all the people living in
Ha'ay. [26]Yehoshua didn't take back his hand
with which he held out his javelin until he had
devoted all the people living in Ha'ay. [27]Only the
animals and the spoil in that town did Yisra'el

take as plunder for themselves, in accordance
with Yahweh's word with which he had ordered
Yehoshua. [28]Yehoshua burned Ha'ay and made it a
permanent ruin, a desolation until this day. [29]The
king of Ha'ay he hanged on a tree until the time
of evening. At sunset Yehoshua ordered, and they
took down his corpse from the tree, threw it at
the entrance of the town gateway and set up over
it a great heap of stones, until this day.

### It's over even when it's not over

[30]Then Yehoshua built an altar for Yahweh
the God of Yisra'el on Mount Ebal, [31]as Mosheh
Yahweh's servant ordered the Yisra'elites, as it
is written in Mosheh's instruction document:
an altar of whole stones on which no one
had wielded iron. They offered up on it burnt
offerings for Yahweh and made well-being
sacrifices. [32]He wrote there on the stones a copy
of Mosheh's instruction that he had written,
before the Yisra'elites. [33]All Yisra'el, its elders,
the overseers and its rulers, were standing
on each side of the chest, facing the Levitical
priests who carried Yahweh's pact chest,
resident and native alike, half of them facing
Mount Gerizim and half of them facing Mount
Ebal, as Mosheh Yahweh's servant had ordered
beforehand, to bless the people of Yisra'el.
[34]After this, he read out all the words of
the instruction, the blessing and the slight,
in accordance with all that's written in the
instruction document. [35]There was not a word
of all that Mosheh ordered that Yehoshua
didn't read out in front of Yisra'el's entire
congregation, with the women and little ones
and the residents who were going among them.

**9** When all the kings who were across
the Yarden heard, in the highland, in
the foothills and on the entire coast of the
Great Sea to near the Lebanon (the Hittite,
the Amorite, the Kena'anite, the Perizzite, the
Hivvite and the Yebusite), [2]they gathered
together to battle with Yehoshua and with
Yisra'el, with one accord.

### How to take Yisra'el in

[3]The people living in Gib'on heard what
Yehoshua had done to Yeriho and to Ha'ay,

4and they for their part acted with shrewdness. They went and behaved like envoys, but got worn-out sacks for their donkeys and worn-out wineskins, cracked and mended, 5with worn-out, patched boots on their feet, and worn-out clothes on themselves, and all the bread they had as their provisions was dry and hard. 6They went to Yehoshua in the camp at Gilgal and said to him and to the Yisra'elites, 'We've come from a country far away, so now, solemnize a pact with us.'

7The Yisra'elites said to the Hivvites, 'Maybe you're living among us. How can I solemnize a pact with you?' 8They said to Yehoshua, 'We are your servants.' Yehoshua said to them, 'Who are you? Where do you come from?'

9They said to him, 'Your servants have come from a country very far away by reason of the name of Yahweh your God, because we've heard the report about him, about all that he did in Misrayim, 10and all that he did to the two Amorite kings who were across the Yarden, to Sihon king of Heshbon and to Og king of Bashan who was in Ashtarot. 11Our elders and all the people living in our country said to us, "Get in your hand provisions for the journey and go to meet them and say to them: 'We are your servants, so now, solemnize a pact with us.'" 12This is our bread: we brought it hot as our provision from our houses on the day we left to go to you, but now – here, it's dry and hard. 13These wineskins that we filled new – here, they've cracked. These clothes of ours and boots of ours have worn out from the great length of the journey.'

14The people took some of their provisions and didn't ask for Yahweh's bidding. 15Yehoshua made peace with them and solemnized a pact with them to let them live, and the assembly's leaders swore an oath to them.

### How to swallow your pride

16At the end of three days after they solemnized the pact with them, they heard that they were near them, living among them. 17The Yisra'elites moved on and came to their towns on the third day. Their towns were Gib'on, Qephirah, Be'erot and Ye'arim Township. 18The Yisra'elites didn't strike them down because the assembly's leaders

had sworn to them by Yahweh the God of Yisra'el. The entire assembly protested at the leaders, 19but all the leaders said to the entire assembly, 'We ourselves swore to them by Yahweh the God of Yisra'el. We can't now touch them. 20We'll do this to them: we'll let them live, so that there won't be fury against us because of the oath we swore to them', 21so the leaders said to them, 'They're to live', but they became woodchoppers and water carriers for the entire assembly, as the leaders spoke concerning them.

22So Yehoshua called them and spoke to them: 'Why did you beguile us in saying, "We live very far away from you", and you're living among us? 23You're now cursed. None of you will stop being a servant, both woodchoppers and water carriers for my God's house.' 24They answered Yehoshua, 'Because it had been clearly told to your servants that Yahweh your God ordered Mosheh his servant to give you the entire country and to annihilate all the people living in the country from before you. We were very fearful for our lives from before you, so we did this thing. 25But now, here we are, in your hand. Act towards us in accordance with what is good and with what is right in your eyes to act towards us.'

26He did so to them: he rescued them from the hand of the Yisra'elites, and they didn't slaughter them. 27That day Yehoshua made them woodchoppers and water carriers for the assembly and for Yahweh's altar, until this day, at the site that he would choose.

### Five kings panic

**10** When Adonay-tsedeq king of Yerushalaim [Jerusalem] heard that Yehoshua had taken Ha'ay and devoted it (as he had done to Yeriho and its king, so he had done to Ha'ay and its king), and that the inhabitants of Gib'on had made peace with Yisra'el and were among them, 2people were very fearful, because Gib'on was a big town, like one of the royal towns, and because it was bigger than Ha'ay, and all its men were strong men. 3So Adonay-tsedeq king of Yerushalaim sent to Hoham king of Hebron, to Pir'am king of Yarmut, to Yaphia king of Lakish and to Debir king of Eglon, saying ⁴'Go up to me and help me, and we'll strike down Gib'on, because it's made peace with Yehoshua and with the Yisra'elites.'

⁵So the five Amorite kings, the king of Yerushalaim, the king of Hebron, the king of Yarmut, the king of Lakish and the king of Eglon, they and their entire camp, gathered together, went up, camped against Gib'on and did battle against it. ⁶The people of Gib'on sent to Yehoshua in the camp at Gilgal, saying 'Don't slacken your hands from your servants, go up to us quickly, deliver us, help us, because all the kings of the Amorites, the people living in the highland, have collected together against us.' ⁷So Yehoshua went up from Gilgal, he and the entire battle company with him, all the forceful strong men.

⁸Yahweh said to Yehoshua, 'Don't be afraid of them, because I've given them into your hand. Not one of them will stand before you.' ⁹Yehoshua came on them by surprise; he had gone up all night from Gilgal, ¹⁰and Yahweh put them into a turmoil before Yisra'el. He struck them down in a great rout at Gib'on and pursued them on the road to the Bet-horon ascent, and struck them down as far as Azeqah and as far as Maqqedah.

## No compromise

¹¹While they were fleeing from before Yisra'el (they were on the Bet-horon descent), Yahweh threw big stones at them from the heavens, as far as Azeqah. More died who died through the hailstones than the Yisra'elites slaughtered with the sword.

¹²Yehoshua spoke to Yahweh then, on the day Yahweh gave over the Amorites before the Yisra'elites, and said before the eyes of Yisra'el,

Sun stand still at Gib'on,
   moon at the Ayyalon Vale!
¹³The sun stood still,
   the moon halted,
Until a nation
   took redress from its foes.
(It's written on the Document of the Upright
   One, isn't it.)

The sun stood in the middle of the heavens and didn't hasten to set, the like of a whole day.

¹⁴There hasn't been anything like that day before it or after it for Yahweh's listening to someone's voice, because Yahweh was battling for Yisra'el.

¹⁵Yehoshua and all Yisra'el with him went back to the camp at Gilgal, ¹⁶and these five kings fled and hid in a cave at Maqqedah. ¹⁷It was told Yehoshua, 'Five kings have been found hiding in a cave at Maqqedah.' ¹⁸Yehoshua said, 'Roll big stones to the cave's mouth and appoint men over it to keep them. ¹⁹But you, don't halt; pursue after your enemies and hit them from the rear. Don't let them come to their towns, because Yahweh your God has given them into your hand.' ²⁰When Yehoshua and the Yisra'elites had finished striking them down in a great rout until they had come to an end, though some survivors escaped from them and came to their fortified towns, ²¹the entire company went back to the camp to Yehoshua at Maqqedah in safety. No one loosened his tongue about the Yisra'elites.

## Open the cave

²²Yehoshua said, 'Open the cave mouth and bring these five kings out of the cave to me.' ²³They did so: they brought these five kings out of the cave to him, the king of Yerushalaim, the king of Hebron, the king of Yarmut, the king of Lakish and the king of Eglon. ²⁴When they brought these kings out to Yehoshua, Yehoshua called all the Yisra'elites and said to the commander over the men of battle who had gone with him, 'Draw near; put your feet on the necks of these kings.' They drew near and put their feet on their necks. ²⁵Yehoshua said to them, 'Don't be afraid. Don't be scared. Be strong, stand firm, because Yahweh will act like this to all your enemies with whom you're battling.'

²⁶After this, Yehoshua struck them down. He put them to death and hanged them on five trees. They were hanged on the trees until the evening. ²⁷At the time when the sun went down, Yehoshua gave an order and they took them down from the trees, threw them into the cave where they had hidden, and put big stones on the cave mouth, until this very day.

²⁸That day Yehoshua captured Maqqedah and struck it down, it and its king, with the mouth of the sword. He devoted them, along with every person who was in it. He didn't let a survivor

remain. He did to the king of Maqqedah as he had done to the king of Yeriho. ²⁹Yehoshua and all Yisra'el with him passed on from Maqqedah to Libnah and battled with Libnah, ³⁰and Yahweh gave it, too, into Yisra'el's hand, it and its king. He struck it down with the mouth of the sword, along with every person who was in it. He didn't let a survivor remain in it. He did to its king as he had done to the king of Yeriho.

## Welcome to the wild wild west

³¹Yehoshua and all Yisra'el with him passed on from Libnah to Lakish and camped against it and battled against it, ³²and Yahweh gave Lakish into Yisra'el's hand. He captured it on the second day and struck it down with the mouth of the sword, along with every person who was in it, in accordance with all that he had done to Libnah. ³³Horam king of Gezer had gone up then to help Lakish, but Yehoshua struck down him and his company until he didn't let a survivor remain to him.

³⁴Yehoshua and all Yisra'el with him passed on from Lakish to Eglon and camped against it and battled against it. ³⁵That day they captured it and struck it down with the mouth of the sword. Every person who was in it he devoted that day, in accordance with all that he had done to Lakish. ³⁶Yehoshua and all Yisra'el with him went up from Eglon to Hebron and battled against it. ³⁷They captured it and struck it down with the mouth of the sword, its king and all its towns and every person who was in it. He didn't let a survivor remain, in accordance with all that he had done to Eglon. He devoted it and every person who was in it.

³⁸Yehoshua and all Yisra'el with him went back to Debir and battled against it. ³⁹He captured it and its king and all its towns. They struck them down with the mouth of the sword and devoted every person who was in it. He didn't let a survivor remain. As he had done to Hebron, so he did to Debir and to its king, and as he had done to Libnah and to its king.

## Welcome to the wild wild north

⁴⁰Yehoshua struck down the entire country: the highland, the Negeb, the foothills and the slopes, with all their kings. He didn't let a survivor remain. Anything that breathed he devoted, as Yahweh the God of Yisra'el had ordered. ⁴¹Yehoshua struck them down from Qadesh Barnea to Azzah [Gaza], all the Goshen region, and as far as Gib'on. ⁴²All these kings and their country Yehoshua captured at a single stroke, because Yahweh the God of Yisra'el was battling for Yisra'el. ⁴³Then Yehoshua and all Yisra'el with him went back to the camp at Gilgal.

**11** When Yabin king of Hatsor heard, he sent to Yobab king of Madon, to the king of Shimron, to the king of Akshaph, ²to the kings who were to the north, in the highland, in the steppe south of Kinneret, in the foothills and in the Dor Heights on the west, ³the Kena'anite on the east and on the west, the Amorite, the Hittite, the Perizzite and the Yebusite in the highland, and the Hivvite beneath Hermon in the region of The Watchtower. ⁴They went out, those and their entire camp with them, a company as numerous as the sand that's on the seashore in its large number, with very numerous horse and chariotry. ⁵All these kings arranged to meet, and came and camped together at Merom Water to do battle with Yisra'el.

⁶Yahweh said to Yehoshua, 'Don't be afraid before them, because tomorrow at this very time I'm going to give all of them up, run through before Yisra'el. You're to hamstring their horses and burn their chariots in fire.' ⁷So Yehoshua and all his battle company with him came on them at Merom Water by surprise. They fell on them, ⁸and Yahweh gave them into Yisra'el's hand. They struck them down and pursued them as far as Great Tsidon, as far as Misrephot Water, and as far as Watchtower Valley on the east, and struck them down until they let no survivor remain. ⁹Yehoshua did to them as Yahweh had said to him: he hamstrung their horses and burned their chariots in fire.

## The entire country taken

¹⁰Yehoshua turned back at that time and captured Hatsor, and its king he struck down with the sword, because Hatsor was formerly

head of all these kingdoms. ¹¹They struck down every person who was in it with the mouth of the sword, devoting them. Nothing that breathed was left, while he burned Hatsor in fire.

¹²All these royal towns and their kings Yehoshua captured. He struck them down with the mouth of the sword and devoted them, as Mosheh Yahweh's servant had ordered. ¹³Yet all the towns that were standing on their mound Yisra'el didn't burn, except that Yehoshua burned Hatsor alone. ¹⁴All the spoil in these towns and the animals the Yisra'elites took as plunder for themselves. They struck down only all the human beings with the mouth of the sword until they had annihilated them; they didn't let anything that breathed remain. ¹⁵As Yahweh had ordered Mosheh his servant, so Mosheh had ordered Yehoshua, and so Yehoshua did. He didn't take out anything from all that Yahweh had ordered Mosheh.

¹⁶So Yehoshua took this entire country: the highland, the entire Negeb, the entire Goshen region, the foothills, the steppe, the highland of Yisra'el and its foothills, ¹⁷from Bald Mountain which goes up to Se'ir and as far as Ba'al Gad in the Lebanon Valley beneath Mount Hermon. He captured all their kings, struck them down and put them to death. ¹⁸For a long time Yehoshua did battle with all these kings. ¹⁹There was no town that made peace with the Yisra'elites except the Hivvites living in Gib'on. They took everything in battle, ²⁰because it issued from Yahweh to stiffen their heart to meet with Yisra'el in battle, in order that he might devote them without there being any grace for them – in order that rather he might annihilate them, as Yahweh had ordered Mosheh.

## The kings east of the Yarden

²¹At that time Yehoshua came and cut down the Anaqites from the highland, from Hebron, from Debir, from Anab, from the entire highland of Yehudah and from the entire highland of Yisra'el, with their towns. Yehoshua devoted them. ²²None of the Anaqites were left in the country of the Yisra'elites. Only in Azzah, in Gat and in Ashdod did they remain.

²³So Yehoshua took the entire country, in accordance with all that Yahweh spoke to Mosheh, and Yehoshua gave it to Yisra'el as its domain, in accordance with their divisions, for the clans. And the country was calm from battle.

**12** These are the kings of the country whom the Yisra'elites struck down and whose land they took possession of across the Yarden on the east side, from Wadi Arnon as far as Mount Hermon and the entire steppe, on the east side:

²Sihon king of the Amorites, who lived in Heshbon, ruling from Aro'er, which is on the bank of Wadi Arnon, the middle of the wadi, and half of Gil'ad, as far as Wadi Yabboq, the Ammonites' border; ³and the steppe as far as the Kinneret Sea, on the east side; and as far as the Steppe Sea (the Salt Sea), on the east side, the Bet Hayeshimot road; and on the south side, beneath the Pisgah slopes.

⁴The border of Og king of Bashan, from what was left of the Repha'ites, who lived in Ashtarot and in Edre'i, ⁵ruling over Mount Hermon, over Salkah and over all Bashan, as far as the border of the Geshurites and the Ma'akatites, and half of Gil'ad, the border of Sihon king of Heshbon.

⁶Mosheh Yahweh's servant and the Yisra'elites had struck them down, and Mosheh Yahweh's servant had given it as a possession to the Re'ubenites, to the Gadites and to the half-clan of Menashsheh.

## The kings west of the Yarden

⁷These are the kings of the country whom Yehoshua and the Yisra'elites struck down across the Yarden on the west side, from Ba'al Gad in the Lebanon Valley as far as Bald Mountain, which goes up to Mount Se'ir, which Yehoshua gave to the Yisra'elite clans to be a possession, in accordance with their divisions, ⁸in the highland, in the foothills, in the steppe, in the slopes, in the wilderness and in the Negeb (the Hittite, the Amorite,

the Kena'anite, the Perizzite, the Hivvite and the Yebusite):

| | |
|---|---|
| **9**A king of Yeriho | A king of Hebron |
| A king of Ha'ay, which | **11**A king of Yarmut |
| is near Bet-el | A king of Lakish |
| **10**A king of Yerushalaim | **12**A king of Eglon |
| A king of Gezer | A king of Hatsor |
| **13**A king of Debir | **20**A king of Shimron |
| A king of Geder | Meron |
| **14**A king of Hormah | A king of Akshaph |
| A king of Arad | **21**A king of Ta'nak |
| **15**A king of Libnah | A king of Megiddo |
| A king of Adullam | **22**A king of Qedesh |
| **16**A king of Maqqedah | A king of Yoqne'am |
| A king of Bet-el | in Carmel |
| **17**A king of Tappuah | **23**A king of Dor in |
| A king of Hepher | Dor Height |
| **18**A king of Apheq | A king of Goyim in |
| A king of the Sharon | Gilgal |
| **19**A king of Madon | **24**A king of Tirtsah |

All kings: thirty-one.

*Yehoshua's time is almost over*

**13** Now Yehoshua was old, going on in years. Yahweh said to him, 'You yourself have become old, you have gone on in years, while the country is very great that remains, to take possession of it. **2**This is the country that remains:

All the areas of the Pelishtites [Philistines] and all the Geshurites, **3**from the Shihor, which is east of Misrayim, as far as the border of Eqron to the north, which is thought of as belonging to the Kena'anites (the five Pelishtite lords, the Azzahites, the Ashdodites, the Ashqelonites, the Gittites and the Eqronites); the Avvites **4**on the south; the entire Kena'anite country, Me'arah belonging to the Tsidonites as far as Apheq (as far as the Amorites' border); **5**the country of the Giblites and the entire Lebanon on the east from Ba'al Gad beneath Mount Hermon as far as Lebo' Hamat; **6**all the people living in the highland from the Lebanon as far as Misrephot Water (all the Tsidonites).

I myself will dispossess them from before the Yisra'elites. Only let it fall by lot to Yisra'el as its domain, as I've ordered you. **7**So now share out this country as a domain to the nine clans and the half-clan of Menashsheh.'

**8**With it, the Re'ubenites and the Gadites had taken their domain which Mosheh gave them across the Yarden to the east, as Mosheh Yahweh's servant gave them:

**9**From Aro'er which is on the bank of Wadi Arnon, and the town which is in the middle of the wadi; the entire Medeba flatland as far as Dibon; **10**all the towns of Sihon king of the Amorites who reigned in Heshbon, as far as the Ammonites' border; **11**Gil'ad and the border of the Geshurites and the Ma'akatites; all of Mount Hermon; all of Bashan as far as Salkah, **12**and the entire kingdom of Og in Bashan, who had reigned in Ashtarot and in Edre'i (he remained from what was left of the Repha'ites). Mosheh had struck them down and dispossessed them, **13**but the Yisra'elites didn't dispossess the Geshurites and the Ma'akatites; Geshur and Ma'akah have lived among Yisra'el until this day.

**14**Only to the clan of Levi did he not give a domain. The gift offerings of Yahweh the God of Yisra'el are its domain, as he spoke to it.

*The clans east of the Yarden*

**15**So Mosheh gave to the clan of the Re'ubenites, by their kin-groups, **16**and it became their border:

From Aro'er, which is on the bank of Wadi Arnon, and the town in the middle of the wadi, and the entire flatland, as far as Medeba; **17**Heshbon and all its towns, which are in the flatland; Dibon, Master's Heights, Bet Ba'al Me'on, **18**Yahats, Qedemot, Mepha'at, **19**Qiryatayim, Sibmah, Tseret Shahar on the vale mountain, **20**Bet Pe'or, the Pisgah slopes and Bet Hayeshimot, **21**all the towns of the flatland, the entire kingdom of Sihon king of the Amorites who reigned in Heshbon, whom Mosheh struck down, he and the

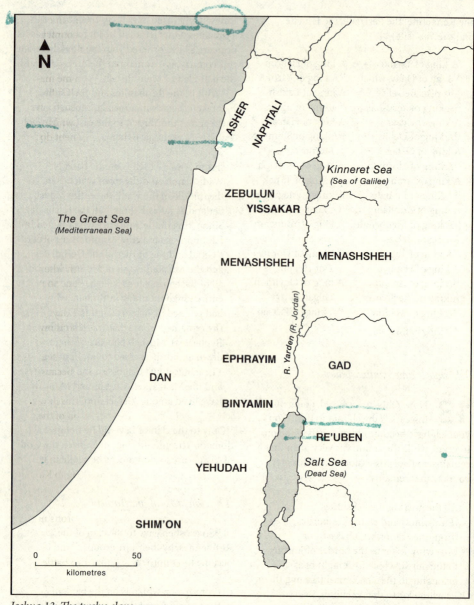

N

ASHER

NAPHTALI

Kinneret Sea
(Sea of Galilee)

ZEBULUN

YISSAKAR

The Great Sea
(Mediterranean Sea)

MENASHSHEH

MENASHSHEH

R. Yarden (R. Jordan)

EPHRAYIM

GAD

DAN

BINYAMIN

RE'UBEN

YEHUDAH

Salt Sea
(Dead Sea)

SHIM'ON

0            50
kilometres

*Joshua 13: The twelve clans*

Midyanite leaders Evi, Reqem, Tsur, Hur and Reba, Sihon's appointees, living in the country. [22]Bil'am ben Be'or the diviner the Yisra'elites killed with the sword, to add to the people run through by them. [23]The Re'ubenites' border was the Yarden and the edge of it. This was the Re'ubenites' domain by their kin-groups, the towns and their villages.

[24]Mosheh gave to the clan of Gad, to the Gadites, by their kin-groups, [25]and it became their border:

Ya'zer; all the towns in Gil'ad; half the Ammonites' country as far as Aro'er which is east of Rabbah; [26]from Heshbon as far as Watchtower Height and Betonim, from Mahanayim as far as the border of Debir; [27]in the vale, Height House, Bet Nimrah,

Sukkot and Tsaphon, the rest of the
kingdom of Sihon king of Heshbon; and
the Yarden and the edge as far as the end
of the Kinneret Sea, across the Yarden
on the east side. <sup>28</sup>This was the Gadites'
domain by their kin-groups, the towns
and their villages.

<sup>29</sup>Mosheh gave to the half-clan of
Menashsheh, so it came to belong to the half-
clan of the Menashshites by their kin-groups,
<sup>30</sup>and it became their border:

From Mahanayim, all of Bashan, the entire
kingdom of Og king of Bashan, all Ya'ir's
Villages in Bashan, sixty towns, <sup>31</sup>half of
Gil'ad, and Ashtarot and Edre'i, Og's royal
towns in Bashan, for the descendants of
Makir son of Menashsheh, for half the
Makirites, by their kin-groups.

## The promise to Kaleb (Caleb)

<sup>32</sup>These are what Mosheh made into domains
in the Mo'ab steppes across the Yarden east of
Yeriho. <sup>33</sup>To the clan of Levi Mosheh didn't give
a domain. Yahweh the God of Yisra'el is their
domain, as he spoke to them.

**14** These are what the Yisra'elites received
as their domain in the country of
Kena'an, which El'azar the priest, Yehoshua ben
Nun and the ancestral heads of the Yisra'elites'
clans made into domains, <sup>2</sup>their domain by lot,
as Yahweh ordered through Mosheh, for the
nine clans and the half-clan, <sup>3</sup>because Mosheh
had given the domain of the two clans and
the half-clan across the Yarden, and to the
Levites he had given no domain among them,
<sup>4</sup>because the Yosephites [Josephites] were two
clans, Menashsheh and Ephrayim, and they
didn't give the Levites a share in the country,
but rather towns to live in and pasturelands for
their livestock and for their cattle. <sup>5</sup>As Yahweh
ordered Mosheh, so the Yisra'elites did, and
shared out the country.

<sup>6</sup>The Yehudahites came up to Yehoshua at
Gilgal, and Kaleb ben Yephunneh the Qenizzite
said to him, 'You yourself know the thing that
Yahweh spoke to Mosheh, the supernatural
man, concerning me and concerning you, at
Qadesh Barnea. <sup>7</sup>I was a man of forty years

when Mosheh Yahweh's servant sent me from
Qadesh Barnea to investigate the country, and
I brought him back word in accordance with
how things were in my mind.

<sup>8</sup>My brothers who went up with me made
the people's mind melt, but I myself fully
followed after Yahweh my God. <sup>9</sup>That day,
Mosheh swore: "If the country on which your
foot trod doesn't become a permanent domain
for you and for your descendants, because you
fully followed after Yahweh my God . . ."

## The country has rest from war

<sup>10</sup>So now, here, Yahweh has kept me alive,
as he spoke, these forty-five years from when
Yahweh spoke this word to Mosheh when
Yisra'el went through the wilderness. So now,
here, I am today a man of eighty-five years.
<sup>11</sup>I'm still as strong today as on the day Mosheh
sent me. As my energy was then, so is my
energy now for battle, both for going out and
for coming in. <sup>12</sup>So now, give me this highland
that Yahweh spoke of on that day, because you
yourself heard that day that Anaqites are there,
and big fortified towns. Maybe Yahweh will be
with me and I shall take possession of them as
Yahweh spoke.'

<sup>13</sup>Yehoshua blessed him and gave Hebron
to Kaleb ben Yephunneh as his domain.
<sup>14</sup>Therefore Hebron came to belong to Kaleb
ben Yephunneh the Qenizzite as his domain,
until this day, because he fully followed
Yahweh the God of Yisra'el. (<sup>15</sup>Hebron's name
formerly was Arba's Township; he was the big
man among the Anaqites.)

And the country was calm from battle.

## Yehudah's borders

**15** The lot fell for the Yehudahites' clan,
by their kin-groups, to the Edomite
border, the Tsin Wilderness to the south the
bottom edge.

<sup>2</sup>Their southern border went from the end
of the Salt Sea, from the tongue that
turns southward, <sup>3</sup>extended to the south
of Scorpions Ascent, passed on to Tsin,
went up south of Qadesh Barnea, passed
on by Hetsron, went up to Addar, turned

to Qarqa, [4]passed on to Atsmon and extended to the Misrayimite Wadi. The border's furthest extents were at the sea. This will be your southern border.
[5]The border to the east: the Salt Sea as far as the edge of the Yarden.

The border on the northern side, from the tongue of the sea, from the end of the Yarden: [6]the border went up by Bet Hoglah and passed north of Bet Ha'arabah. The border went up by Bohan ben-Re'uben Stone. [7]The border went up to Debir from Disaster Vale, and northward turning its face to Gilgal, which is in front of Red Rocks Ascent, which is south of the wadi. The border passed on to Shemesh Spring Water. Its furthest extents went to Treader Spring. [8]The border went up by Ben-hinnom Ravine along the Yebusite flank on the south (i.e. Yerushalaim). The border went up to the top of the mountain which is opposite Hinnom Ravine to the west, which is at the edge of Repha'ites Vale to the north. [9]The border curved from the top of the mountain to Nephtoah Water Spring and extended to the towns of Mount Ephron. The border curved by Ba'alah (i.e. Ye'arim Township). [10]The border turned from Ba'alah westward to Mount Se'ir, passed by the flank of Mount Ye'arim northward (i.e. Kesalon), went down to Bet-shemesh and passed on to Timnah. [11]The border extended to the flank of Eqron northward. The border curved to Shikkeron, passed on to Mount Ba'alah and extended by Yabne'el. The border's furthest extents were at the sea.
[12]The western border: the Great Sea and the border.

This was the border of the Yehudahites all round by their kin-groups.

## Aksah insists

[13]In accordance with Yahweh's bidding to Yehoshua, he gave to Kaleb ben Yephunneh a share among the Yehudahites, Arba's Township, the ancestor of Anaq (i.e. Hebron). [14]Kaleb dispossessed from there the three Anaqites, Sheshay, Ahiman and Talmay, the descendants

of Anaq. [15]He went up from there against the people living in Debir; the name of Debir was formerly Sepher Township. [16]Kaleb said, 'The person who strikes down Sepher Township and captures it: I'll give him Aksah my daughter as wife.' [17]Otni'el ben Qenaz, Kaleb's brother, captured it, and he gave him Aksah his daughter as wife.

[18]When she came, she incited him to ask for some fields from her father. She got down from her donkey and Kaleb said to her, 'What is it?' [19]She said, 'Give me a blessing, because you've given me a region in the south. Give me waterholes.' So he gave her the upper waterholes and the lower waterholes.

## Yehudah's towns

[20]This is the domain of the Yehudahites' clan by their kin-groups.

[21]The towns at the edge of the Yehudahites' clan, near the Edomite border, in the Negeb, were:

Qabtse'el, Eder, Yagur, [22]Qinah, Dimonah, Ad'adah, [23]Qedesh, Hatsor, Yitnan, [24]Ziph, Telem, Be'alot, [25]Hatsor Hadattah, Qeriyyot Hetsron (i.e. Hatsor), [26]Amam, Shema, Moladah, [27]Gaddah Village, Heshmon, Bet Pelet, [28]Shu'al Village, Be'er Sheba, Bizyotyah, [29]Ba'alah, Iyyim, Etsem, [30]Eltolad, Kesil, Hormah, [31]Tsiqlag, Madmannah, Sansannah, [32]Leba'ot, Shilhim, Ayin and Rimmon.

All the towns: twenty-nine, and their villages.

[33]In the foothills:

Eshta'ol, Tsor'ah, Ashnah, [34]Zanoah, Gannim Spring, Tappuah, Enam, [35]Yarmut, Adullam, Sokoh, Azeqah, [36]Sha'arayim, Aditayim, Gederah and Gederotayim.

Fourteen towns and their villages.
[37]Tsenan, Hadashah, Gad Tower, [38]Dil'an, The Watchtower, Yoqte'el, [39]Lakish, Botsqat, Eglon, [40]Kabbon, Lahmas, Kitlish, [41]Gederot, Bet-dagon, Na'amah and Maqqedah.

Sixteen towns and their villages.
[42]Libnah, Eter, Ashan, [43]Yiphtah, Ashnah, Netsib, [44]Qe'ilah, Akzib and Mareshah.

Nine towns and their villages.

[45]Eqron, its daughter-towns, and its villages; [46]from Eqron westward, everything that was in the vicinity of Ashdod and their villages, [47]Ashdod, its daughter-towns, and its villages; Azzah, its daughter-towns and its villages, as far as the Misrayimite Wadi, and the Great Sea and the edge.

[48]In the highland:

Shamir, Yattir, Sokoh, [49]Dannah, Sannah Township (i.e. Debir), [50]Anab, Eshtemoh, Anim, [51]Goshen, Holon and Giloh.
Eleven towns and their villages.
[52]Arab, Rumah, Esh'an, [53]Yanum, Bet-tappuah, Apheqah, [54]Humtah, Arba's Township (i.e. Hebron) and Tsi'or.
Nine towns and their villages.
[55]Ma'on, Karmel, Ziph, Yuttah, [56]Yizre'e'l, Yoqde'am, Zanoah, [57]Qayin, Gib'ah and Timnah.
Ten towns and their villages.
[58]Halhul, Bet-tsur, Gedor, [59]Ma'arat, Bet-anot and Elteqon.
Six towns and their villages.
[60]Ba'al Township (i.e. Ye'arim Township) and Rabbah.
Two towns and their villages.

[61]In the wilderness:

Bet Ha'arabah, Middin, Sekakah, [62]Nibshan, Salt Town and Gedi Spring.
Six towns and their villages.

[63]But the Yehudahites couldn't dispossess the Yebusites, the people living in Yerushalaim, and the Yebusites have lived with the Yehudahites in Yerushalaim until this day.

## The Yosephites

**16** The lot extended for the Yosephites from the Yarden at Yeriho, at the Yeriho water towards the sunrise, through the wilderness, going up from Yeriho into the highland to Bet-el. [2]It extended from Bet-el to Luz and passed on to the Arkites' border at Atarot. [3]It went down to the west to the Yaphletites' border, as far as the border of Lower

Bet-horon and as far as Gezer. Its furthest extents were at the sea. [4]So the Yosephites received their domain – Menashsheh and Ephrayim. [5]The border of the Ephrayimites by their kin-groups, was:

The border of their domain towards the sunrise was Atrot Addar as far as Upper Bet Horon. [6]The border extended to the sea, to Mikmetat on the north. The border turned towards the sunrise at Ta'anat Shiloh and passed by it east of Yanoah. [7]It went down from Yanoah to Atarot and to Na'arat, came to Yeriho and extended to the Yarden. [8]From Tappuah the border extends to the west by Wadi Qanah. Its furthest extents were at the sea. This was the domain of the Ephrayimites' clan by their kin-groups, [9]and the towns distinguished for the Ephrayimites within the domain of the Menashshites, all the towns and their villages.

[10]But they didn't dispossess the Kena'anites who were living in Gezer. The Kena'anites have lived within Ephrayim until this day, but they have been a serf workforce.

**17** The lot fell for the clan of Menashsheh, because he was Yoseph's firstborn.
For Makir, Menashsheh's firstborn and Gil'ad's father (because he was a man of battle): Gil'ad and Bashan had become his. [2]So it fell for the remaining Menashshites by their clans, for the descendants of Abi'ezer, for the descendants of Heleq, for the descendants of Asri'el, for the descendants of Shekem, for the descendants of Hepher and for the descendants of Shemida. These were the male descendants of Menashsheh, Yoseph's son, by their kin-groups.

## Menashsheh (and Tselophhad's daughters again)

[3]Now Tselophhad ben Hepher, son of Gil'ad son of Makir son of Menashsheh, had no sons, but only daughters. These are the names of his daughters: Mahlah, No'ah, Hoglah, Milkah and Tirtsah. [4]They drew near before El'azar the priest, before Yehoshua ben Nun and before

the leaders, saying 'Yahweh himself ordered Mosheh to give us a domain among our brothers.' So he gave them a domain among their father's brothers in accordance with Yahweh's bidding.

⁵Menashsheh's shares fell as ten, apart from the region of Gil'ad and Bashan which are across the Yarden, ⁶because Menashsheh's daughters received a domain among his sons, while the region of Gil'ad belonged to the remaining descendants of Menashsheh.

⁷Menashsheh's border was: from Asher to Mikmetat, which is east of Shekem. The border goes to the south, to the people living in Tappuah Spring (⁸the Tappuah region belonged to Menashsheh, but Tappuah on the border of Menashsheh belonged to the Ephrayimites). ⁹The border goes down by Wadi Qanah. South of the wadi, these towns belonged to Ephrayim, among Menashsheh's towns, with Menashsheh's border north of the wadi and its furthest extents at the sea. ¹⁰To the south belongs to Ephrayim, to the north to Menashsheh, and the sea was its border. They come to Asher on the north and Yissakar [Issachar] on the east, ¹¹but in Yissakar and in Asher, to Menashsheh belonged Bet-she'an and its daughter-towns, Yible'am and its daughter-towns, the people living in Do'r and its daughter-towns, the people living in Dor Spring and its daughter-towns, the people living in Ta'nak and its daughter-towns, and the people living in Megiddo and its daughter-towns (Three Heights).

¹²But the Menashshites couldn't take possession of these towns; the Kena'anites resolved to stay in this region. ¹³When the Yisra'elites became strong, they made the Kena'anites into a workforce, but they didn't dispossess them at all.

## A challenge for Yoseph

¹⁴The Yosephites spoke with Yehoshua: 'Why have you given me as my domain one lot, one allocation, when I'm a numerous people that Yahweh has blessed, up until now?' ¹⁵Yehoshua said to them, 'If you're a numerous people, get yourself up into the forest and clear it for yourself, there in the region of the Perizzite and the Repha'ites, when the highland of Ephrayim is too narrow for you.'

¹⁶The Yosephites said, 'The highland isn't available to us, and there's iron chariotry among all the Kena'anites who live in the vale region, the ones who are in Bet-she'an and in its daughter-towns and the ones who are in the Yizre'el Vale.' ¹⁷Yehoshua said to the household of Yoseph, to Ephrayim and to Menashsheh: 'You're a numerous people. You have great energy. You won't have one lot, ¹⁸because the highland will be yours, because it's forest but you'll clear it, and its furthest extents will be yours because you'll dispossess the Kena'anite when they have iron chariotry, when they're strong.'

**18** The entire assembly of the Yisra'elites congregated at Shiloh and placed the appointment tent there, with the country in subjection before them. ²But there remained seven clans among the Yisra'elites to whom they had not shared out their domain.

## Surveying the land

³So Yehoshua said to the Yisra'elites, 'How long are you going to be slack about coming to take possession of the country that Yahweh the God of your ancestors has given you? ⁴Provide yourselves three men per clan and I'll send them to set off and go through the country, and write it up on the basis of their domain. Then they're to come to me. ⁵They can allocate it for themselves into seven shares. Yehudah is to stay by its border in the south and the household of Yoseph are to stay by their border in the north.

⁶You, you're to write up the country as seven shares and bring it to me here so I can throw lots for you here before Yahweh our God. ⁷Because there's no share for the Levites among you, because Yahweh's priesthood is their domain, and Gad, Re'uben and the half-clan of Menashsheh have received their domain across the Yarden towards the sunrise, which Mosheh, Yahweh's servant, gave them.'

⁸The men set off and went. Yehoshua ordered the men who were going to write up the country: 'Go, go about the country, and write

it up, come back to me, and I'll pitch the lot for you here before Yahweh in Shiloh.' ⁹So the men went and passed through the country, and wrote it up on a document by towns as seven shares. They came to Yehoshua in the camp at Shiloh ¹⁰and Yehoshua pitched the lot for them in Shiloh before Yahweh. So Yehoshua divided up the country before Yisra'el in accordance with their divisions.

## Binyamin (Benjamin)

¹¹The lot of the Binyaminites' clan by their kin-groups went up. The border of their lot extended between the Yehudahites and the Yosephites.
¹²Their border on the north side ran from the Yarden. The border went up to Yeriho's northern flank and went up into the highland westward. Its furthest extents were at the Bet Aven Wilderness. ¹³The border passed on from there to Luz, to the flank of Luz southward (i.e. Bet-el). The border went down to Atrot Addar by the mountain which is on the south of Lower Bet-horon.
¹⁴The border curved and turned on the west side southward from the mountain which is opposite Lower Bet-horon southward. Its furthest extents were at Ba'al Township (i.e. Ye'arim Township), a town of the Yehudahites. This was the west side.
¹⁵The south side: from the edge of Ye'arim Township the border extended westward, and extended to Nephtoah Water Spring. ¹⁶The border went down to the edge of the mountain which is opposite Ben-hinnom Ravine, which is in Repha'ites Vale to the north. It went down Hinnom Ravine to the Yebusite flank on the south and went down to Treader Spring. ¹⁷It curved on the north, extended to Shemesh Spring and extended to Gelilot, which is in front of Red Rocks Ascent. It went down to Bohan ben-Re'uben Stone, ¹⁸passed on to the flank near the steppe, northward, and went down to the steppe. ¹⁹The border passed on to the flank of Bet-hoglah, northward. The border's furthest extents were at the tongue of the Salt Sea to the north, at the end of the Yarden to the

south. This was the southern border. ²⁰The Yarden constituted its border on the east side.
This is the Binyaminites' domain by its borders all round, by their kin-groups. ²¹The towns of the Binyaminites' clan by their kin-groups were:

Yeriho, Bet-hoglah, Qetsits Vale, ²²Bet Ha'arabah, Tsemarayim, Bet-el, ²³Avvim, Parah, Ophrah, ²⁴Ammonah Hamlet, Ophni and Geba.
Twelve towns and their villages.
²⁵Gib'on, The Height, Be'erot, ²⁶The Watchtower, Kephirah, Motsah, ²⁷Reqem, Yirpe'el, Tar'alah, ²⁸Tsela, Eleph and the Yebusite (i.e. Yerushalaim), Gib'ah, Township.
Fourteen towns and their villages.

This is the Binyaminites' domain by their kin-groups.

## Shim'on (Simeon), Zebulun

**19** The second lot went out for Shim'on, for the Shim'onites' clan by their kin-groups. Their domain was within the Yehudahites' domain. ²They had as their domain:

Be'er-sheba (or Sheba), Moladah, ³Shu'al Village, Balah, Etsem, ⁴Eltolad, Betul, Hormah, ⁵Tsiqlag, Bet-markabot, Susah Village, ⁶Bet Leba'ot and Sharuhen.
Thirteen towns and their villages.
⁷Ayin, Rimmon, Eter, Ashan.
Four towns and their villages, ⁸and all the villages that are round these towns, as far as Ba'alat Be'er, Ra'mat Negeb.

This is the domain of the Shim'onites' clan by their kin-groups. ⁹The Shim'onites' domain was part of the Yehudahites' share because the Yehudahites' share was too big for them, and the Shim'onites received a domain within their domain.
¹⁰The third lot went up for the Zebulunites by their clans.
The border of their domain ran as far as Sarid. ¹¹Their border went up westward to Mar'alah, came to Dabbeshet and came to the wadi which is opposite Yoqne'am.

¹²It turned back from Sarid towards the
sunrise, along the border of Kislot Tabor.
It extended to Daberat and went up to
Yaphia.
¹³From there it passed on to the east, towards
the sunrise, to Gat Hepher, to Et Qatsin. It
extended to Rimmon, curving to Ne'ah.
¹⁴It turned (the northern border) to
Hannaton. Its furthest extents were
Yiphtah-'el Ravine, ¹⁵Qattat, Nahalal,
Shimron, Yid'alah and Bet Lehem.
Twelve towns and their villages.
¹⁶This is the Zebulunites' domain by their kin-
groups, these towns and their villages.

## Yissakar, Asher

¹⁷The fourth lot went out for Yissakar, for the
Yissakarites by their kin-groups.
¹⁸Their border was Yizre'e'l, Kesulot,
Shunem, ¹⁹Hapharayim, Shi'on, Anaharat,
²⁰Rabbit, Qishyon, Ebets, ²¹Remet,
Gannim Spring, Haddah Spring and Bet
Patstsets.
²²The border came to Tabor, Shahatsim and
Bet Shemesh.
The Yarden was the furthest extents of their
border.
Sixteen towns and their villages.
²³This is the domain of the Zebulunites' clan by
their kin-groups, the towns and their villages.
²⁴The fifth lot went out for the Asherites' clan
by their kin-groups.
²⁵Their border was Helqat, Hali, Beten,
Akshaph, ²⁶Alammelek, Am'ad and Mish'al.
It came to Karmel on the west and Shihor
Libnat.
²⁷It turned back towards the sunrise, to
Bet Dagon, and came to Zebulun and
Yiphtah-'el Ravine to the north, Bet
Ha'emeq and Ne'i'el.
It extended to Kabul on the north, ²⁸Ebron,
Rehob, Hammon and Qanah, as far as
Great Tsidon. ²⁹The border turned back
to The Height and as far as the fortified
town of Tsor. The border turned back to
Hosah. Its furthest extents were at the sea
in the area of Akzib, ³⁰Ummah, Apheq and
Rehob.
Twenty-two towns and their villages.

³¹This is the domain of the Asherites' clan by
their kin-groups, these towns and their villages.

## Naphtali, Dan

³²The sixth lot went out for the Naphtalites,
for the Naphtalites by their kin-groups.
³³Their border ran from Heleph,
Betsa'anannim Oak, Adami Hanneqeb and
Yabne'el as far as Laqqum, and the Yarden
was its furthest extents.
³⁴The border turned back westward to Aznot
Tabor and went out from there to Huqoq.
It came to Zebulun on the south.
It came to Asher on the west and Yehudah at
the Yarden towards the sunrise.
³⁵Its fortified towns: Tsiddim, Tser, Hammat,
Raqqat, Kinneret, ³⁶Adamah, The Height,
Hatsor, ³⁷Qedesh, Edre'i, Hatsor Spring,
³⁸Yir'on, Migdal-el, Horem, Bet-anat and
Bet Shemesh.
Nineteen towns and their villages.
³⁹This is the domain of the Naphtalites' clan by
their kin-groups, the towns and their villages.
⁴⁰The seventh lot went out for the Danites
by their kin-groups. ⁴¹The border of their
domain was Tsor'ah, Eshta'ol, Shemesh Town,
⁴²Sha'alabbin, Ayyalon, Yitlah, ⁴³Elon, Timnah,
Eqron, ⁴⁴Elteqeh, Gibbeton, Ba'alat, ⁴⁵Yehud,
Bene-beraq, Gat-rimmon, ⁴⁶Yarkon Water,
Raqqon, with the border near Yapho.

⁴⁷But the Danites' border got away from
them, and the Danites went up and battled
with Leshem and captured it. They struck
it down with the mouth of the sword,
took possession of it and lived in it. They
named it Dan in accordance with the
name of their ancestor Dan.

⁴⁸This is the domain of the Danites' clan by
their kin-groups, these towns and their villages.

⁴⁹So they finished making the country into
domains by its borders. The Yisra'elites gave
a domain to Yehoshua ben Nun among them.
⁵⁰At Yahweh's bidding they gave him the town
that he asked for, Timnat-serah in the highland
of Ephrayim. He built up the town and lived in it.
⁵¹These are the domains that El'azar the priest,
Yehoshua ben Nun and the heads of the

ancestral households made for the Yisra'elites' clans by lot in Shiloh before Yahweh at the entrance of the appointment tent. So they finished sharing out the country.

## The asylum towns

**20** Yahweh spoke to Yehoshua: [2]"Speak to the Yisra'elites: "Give yourselves the asylum towns about which I spoke to you through Mosheh, [3]for a killer who strikes a person down by accident (without realizing), to flee there. They will be an asylum for you from the blood restorer.

[4]He will flee to one of these towns, and stand at the entrance of the town gateway and speak in the hearing of that town's elders. They will receive him into the town among them, and give him a place so he can live with them. [5]When the blood restorer pursues after him, they will not surrender the killer into his hand, because he struck down his neighbour without realizing and he was not hostile to him in previous days. [6]He is to live in that town until he stands before the assembly for a decision, until the death of the great priest who is there at that time. Then the killer may go back and come to his town and to his home, to the town from which he fled.'"

[7]So they made sacred Qedesh in Galilee in the highland of Naphtali; Shekem in the highland of Ephrayim; and Arba's Township (i.e. Hebron) in the highland of Yehudah. [8]Across the Yarden (Yeriho) towards the sunrise, they made Betser in the wilderness on the flatland, from the clan of Re'uben; Heights-in-Gil'ad from the clan of Gad; and Golan in Bashan from the clan of Menashsheh. [9]These were the set towns for all the Yisra'elites and for the person who is residing among them to flee there, anyone who struck someone down by accident, so that he would not die by the hand of the blood restorer until he stood before the assembly.

## The Levites' needs

**21** The heads of the Levites' ancestral households came up to El'azar the priest, to Yehoshua ben Nun and to the heads

of the ancestral households of the Yisra'elites' clans. [2]They spoke to them at Shiloh in the country of Kena'an: 'Yahweh himself ordered through Mosheh to give us towns to live in, with their pasturelands for our animals.' [3]So the Yisra'elites gave the Levites part of their domain in accordance with Yahweh's bidding, these towns and their pasturelands.

[4]The lot went out for the Qehatite kin-groups: for the descendants of Aharon [Aaron] the priest, from the Levites, it was from the clan of Yehudah, from the clan of Shim'on, from the clan of Binyamin, by lot, thirteen towns. [5]For the remaining Qehatites: from the kin-groups of the clan of Ephrayim, from the clan of Dan and from the half-clan of Menashsheh, by lot, ten towns. [6]For the Gershonites: from the kin-groups of the clan of Yissakar, from the clan of Asher, from the clan of Naphtali and from the half-clan of Menashsheh in Bashan, by lot, thirteen towns. [7]For the Merarites by their kin-groups: from the clan of Re'uben, from the clan of Gad and from the clan of Zebulun, twelve towns.

[8]The Yisra'elites gave the Levites these towns and their pasturelands, as Yahweh said through Mosheh, by lot.

## The Aharonites and the other Qehatites

[9]From the Yehudahites' clan and from the Shim'onites' clan they gave these towns, which will be named, [10]for the descendants of Aharon from the Qehatite kin-groups of the Levites, because the first lot was for them.

[11]They gave to them Arba's Township, the ancestor of the Anaqites (i.e. Hebron) in the highland of Yehudah, and its pastureland round it. [12]The town's fields and its villages they gave to Kaleb ben Yephunneh as his holding, [13]but to the descendants of Aharon the priest, they gave the killer's asylum town, Hebron, and its pastureland, Libnah and its pastureland, [14]Yattir and its pastureland, Eshtemoa and its pastureland, [15]Holon and its pastureland, Debir and its pastureland, [16]Spring and its pastureland, Yuttah and

*↳ 43) No word of God falls !*

its pastureland, and Bet Shemesh and its pastureland.

Nine towns from these two clans. ¹⁷And from the clan of Binyamin: Gib'on and its pastureland, Geba and its pastureland, ¹⁸Anatot and its pastureland, and Almon and its pastureland.

Four towns.

¹⁹All the towns of the descendants of Aharon, the priests: thirteen towns and their pasturelands.

²⁰For the kin-groups of the Qehatites, the remaining Levites of the Qehatites, the towns in their lot were:

From the clan of Ephrayim, ²¹they gave them the killer's asylum town, Shekem, and its pastureland in the highland of Ephrayim, Gezer and its pastureland, ²²Qibtsayim and its pastureland, and Bet Horon and its pastureland.

Four towns.

²³From the clan of Dan: Elteqe and its pastureland, Gibbeton and its pastureland, ²⁴Ayyalon and its pastureland, Gat-rimmon and its pastureland.

Four towns.

²⁵From the half-clan of Menashsheh: Ta'nak and its pastureland, and Gat-rimmon and its pastureland.

Two towns.

²⁶All the towns: ten, and their pasturelands, for the remaining kin-groups of the Qehatites.

## The Gershonites and the Merarites

²⁷For the Gershonites, of the kin-groups of the Levites:

From the half-clan of Menashsheh, the killer's asylum town, Golan in Bashan and its pastureland, and Be'eshterah and its pastureland.

Two towns.

²⁸From the clan of Yissakar: Qishron and its pastureland, Dobrat and its pastureland, ²⁹Yarmut and its pastureland, and Gannim Spring and its pastureland.

Four towns.

³⁰From the clan of Asher: Mish'al and its pastureland, Abdon and its pastureland, ³¹Helqat and its pastureland, and Rehob and its pastureland.

Four towns.

³²From the clan of Naphtali, the killer's asylum town, Qedesh in Galilee, and its pastureland, Hammot Do'r and its pastureland, and Qartan and its pastureland.

Three towns and their pasturelands.

³³All the towns of the Gershonites by their kin-groups: thirteen towns and their pasturelands.

³⁴For the kin-groups of the Merarites, the remaining Levites:

From the clan of Zebulun: Yoqne'am and its pastureland, Qartah and its pastureland, ³⁵Dimnah and its pastureland, and Nahalal and its pastureland.

Four towns.

³⁶From the clan of Gad, the killer's asylum town, Heights-in-Gil'ad and its pastureland, Mahanayim and its pastureland, ³⁷Heshbon and its pastureland, and Ya'zer and its pastureland.

All the towns, four.

³⁸All the towns of the Merarites by their kin-groups, the remaining kin-groups of the Levites: their lot was twelve towns.

³⁹All the Levites' towns within the Yisra'elites' holding: forty-eight towns and their pasturelands. ⁴⁰These would be the towns, town by town and its pastureland round it – so for all these towns.

## Not one word failed

⁴¹So Yahweh gave Yisra'el the entire country that he had sworn to give to their ancestors. They took possession of it and lived in it. ⁴²Yahweh enabled them to settle down all around in accordance with everything that he had sworn to their ancestors. Not one individual of all their enemies stood against them; all their enemies Yahweh gave into their hand. ⁴³No word fell, of every good word that

God had spoken to the household of Yisra'el. Everything came about.

**22** Then Yehoshua called the Re'ubenites, the Gadites and the half-clan of Menashsheh, [2]and said to them: 'You yourselves have kept everything that Mosheh, Yahweh's servant, ordered you, and you've listened to my voice in everything that I ordered you. [3]You haven't abandoned your brothers this long time until this day. You've kept the charge from the order of Yahweh your God. [4]But Yahweh your God has now enabled your brothers to settle down, as he spoke to them. So now, turn your face and get yourselves to your tents, to the region of your holding which Mosheh Yahweh's servant gave you across the Yarden. [5]Only keep careful watch to act on the order and the instruction that Mosheh Yahweh's servant gave you by being loyal to Yahweh your God, by walking in all his ways, by keeping his orders, by attaching yourselves to him, and by serving him with your entire mind and with your entire being.'

### A little local difficulty

[6]Yehoshua blessed them and sent them off, and they went to their tents. [7]To one half-clan of Menashsheh Mosheh had given [land] in Bashan, and to the other half-clan Yehoshua had given it with their brothers across the Yarden to the west. Further, when Yehoshua sent them off to their tents and blessed them, [8]he said to them, 'Go back to your tents with great riches, with very much livestock, with silver and with gold, with copper and with iron, and with very much clothing. Share out the spoil of your enemies with your brothers.' [9]So the Re'ubenites, the Gadites and the half-clan of Menashsheh turned back and went from being with the Yisra'elites at Shiloh, which is in the country of Kena'an, to go the region of Gil'ad, to the land of their holding, which they had acquired at Yahweh's bidding through Mosheh.

[10]They came to the area of the Yarden which is in the country of Kena'an, and the Re'ubenites, the Gadites and the half-clan of Menashsheh built an altar there at the Yarden, an altar big in appearance. [11]The Yisra'elites heard: 'Here, the Re'ubenites, the Gadites and the half-clan of Menashsheh have built an altar near the land of Kena'an, in the area of the Yarden, across from the Yisra'elites.'

[12]So the Yisra'elites heard, and the entire assembly of the Yisra'elites congregated at Shiloh to go up to war against them. [13]The Yisra'elites sent Pinhas ben El'azar, the priest, to the Re'ubenites, the Gadites and the half-clan of Menashsheh in the region of Gil'ad, [14]and ten leaders with him, one leader for each ancestral household, for all the clans of Yisra'el. They were, each individual, the head of an ancestral household for the Yisra'elite divisions.

### Misunderstanding cleared up

[15]They came to the Re'ubenites, the Gadites and the half-clan of Menashsheh in the region of Gil'ad and spoke with them: [16]'The entire assembly of Yisra'el has said this: "What is this trespass that you've committed against Yisra'el's God in turning back today from following Yahweh, in your building yourselves an altar, rebelling today against Yahweh? [17]Was the waywardness at Pe'or a small thing to us, from which we haven't purified ourselves this day (and an epidemic came on Yahweh's assembly), [18]and you yourselves turn back from following Yahweh today? If you rebel against Yahweh, tomorrow he will be furious with the entire assembly of Yisra'el.

[19]Yet if the land of your holding is taboo, get yourselves across into the land of Yahweh's holding where Yahweh's dwelling is, and hold land among us. Don't rebel against Yahweh and don't rebel against us by your building yourselves an altar other than the altar of Yahweh our God. [20]When Akan ben Zerah trespassed in connection with devoting, fury came on the entire assembly, didn't it. He wasn't the only one who breathed his last for his waywardness."'

[21]The Re'ubenites, the Gadites and the half-clan of Menashsheh answered the heads of the Yisra'elite divisions: [22]'The God over the gods, Yahweh, the God over the gods, Yahweh, he knows, and Yisra'el – it will know: if it was in rebellion or in trespass against Yahweh, don't deliver us today [23]for building ourselves an altar to turn back from following Yahweh. Or if it was for offering up a burnt offering or a grain offering

on it, or if for making well-being sacrifices on it, Yahweh – may he look for it from us. <sup>24</sup>But if it wasn't out of anxiety about something that we did this, saying "Tomorrow your children may say to our children, 'What do you and Yahweh the God of Yisra'el have in common? <sup>25</sup>Yahweh has made the Yarden a border between us and you, Re'ubenites and Gadites. You have no share in Yahweh.'" Your children would make our children stop living in awe of Yahweh.

## A *happy ending*

<sup>26</sup>So we said, "Let's please act for ourselves by building an altar, not for burnt offering and not for sacrifice. <sup>27</sup>Rather it will be a witness between us and you and coming generations, for performing Yahweh's service before him, with our burnt offerings and with our sacrifices and with our well-being offerings, and your children will not say tomorrow to our children, 'You have no share in Yahweh.'" <sup>28</sup>We said, "When they say it to us and to our generations tomorrow, we'll say, 'Look at the pattern of Yahweh's altar which our fathers made, not for burnt offering and not for sacrifice, but it's a witness between us and you.'" <sup>29</sup>Far be it from us for us to rebel against Yahweh and turn back today from following Yahweh by building an altar for burnt offering, for grain offering and for sacrifice, apart from the altar of Yahweh our God that's before his dwelling.'

<sup>30</sup>Pinhas the priest, and the congregation's leaders (the heads of the Yisra'elite divisions) who were with him, listened to the things that the Re'ubenites, the Gadites and the Menashshites spoke of, and it was good in their eyes. <sup>31</sup>Pinhas ben El'azar the priest said to the Re'ubenites, the Gadites and the Menashshites, 'Today we acknowledge that Yahweh is among us, in that you haven't committed this trespass against Yahweh. Therefore you've saved the Yisra'elites from Yahweh's hand.'

<sup>32</sup>Pinhas ben El'azar the priest and the leaders went back from the Re'ubenites and from the Gadites from the region of Gil'ad to the country of Kena'an to the Yisra'elites and took back word to them. <sup>33</sup>The thing was good in the Yisra'elites' eyes and they blessed God. They didn't speak of going up against them to make war, to devastate the land in which the Re'ubenites and the Gadites were living.

<sup>34</sup>The Re'ubenites and the Gadites named the altar, that it was a 'Witness between us that Yahweh is our God'.

## Beware of *the other peoples' faiths*

23 A long time later, after Yahweh had enabled Yisra'el to settle down from all their enemies around, and when Yehoshua was old, going on in years, <sup>2</sup>Yehoshua called all Yisra'el, its elders, its leaders, its rulers and its overseers, and said to them, 'I myself have got old, I've gone on in years. <sup>3</sup>You yourselves have seen everything that Yahweh your God did to all these nations from before you, because Yahweh your God – he's the one who was battling for you. <sup>4</sup>See, I've caused the lot to fall for you on these remaining nations as a domain for your clans, from the Yarden (yes, all the nations I cut off) and the Great Sea in the west.

<sup>5</sup>Yahweh your God – he will push them out from before you and dispossess them from before you so you may take possession of their country as Yahweh your God spoke to you. <sup>6</sup>You're to be very firm about keeping everything written in Mosheh's instruction document by acting on it, without departing from it right or left, <sup>7</sup>and without coming among these nations (these that remain with you). You will not commemorate their gods' name, you will not swear, you will not serve them and you will not bow low to them. <sup>8</sup>Rather, you're to attach yourselves to Yahweh your God, as you've done until this day.

<sup>9</sup>Yahweh has dispossessed great and numerous nations from before you, and you: not one individual stood against you until this day. <sup>10</sup>One individual from among you can pursue a thousand, because Yahweh your God – he has been battling for you, as he spoke to you.

## Beware of *contravening the pact*

<sup>11</sup>You're to keep careful watch for yourselves so as to be loyal to Yahweh your God, <sup>12</sup>because if you do turn back and attach yourselves to what is left of these nations (these that remain

with you) and intermarry with them and have sex with them and they with you, ¹³you're to acknowledge clearly that Yahweh your God won't continue to dispossess these nations from before you. To you they will become a trap and a snare, a whip on your sides and thorns in your eyes, until you perish from on this good land that Yahweh our God has given you.

¹⁴Here I am, going the way of all the earth now. You're to acknowledge with your entire mind and with your entire being that not one word has fallen down of all the good things of which Yahweh your God spoke to you. Everything has come about for you. Not one word of them has fallen down. ¹⁵But as every good thing of which Yahweh your God spoke to you has come about for you, so Yahweh will cause every bad experience to come about for you, until he's eliminated you from on this good land that Yahweh your God has given you. ¹⁶When you contravene the pact of Yahweh your God that he ordered you, and go and serve other gods and bow low to them, Yahweh's anger will rage against you and you will perish quickly from on this good country that he's given you.'

**24** Yehoshua gathered all Yisra'el's clans at Shekem and called Yisra'el's elders, its leaders, its rulers and its overseers, and they took their stand before God.

## Think back over the story

²Yehoshua said to all the people, 'Yahweh, Yisra'el's God, has said this: "Across the river, your ancestors (Terah, Abraham's father and Nahor's father) lived of old and served other gods. ³I got your ancestor Abraham from across the river and enabled him to go through the entire country of Kena'an, and I made his offspring numerous. I gave him Yitshaq [Isaac], ⁴and gave Yitshaq Ya'aqob [Jacob] and Esaw, and I gave Esaw the highland of Se'ir as his domain, while Ya'aqob and his sons went down to Misrayim.

⁵I sent Mosheh and Aharon and I hit Misrayim as I acted in its midst. Afterwards, I got you out. ⁶I got your ancestors out of Misrayim and you came to the sea. The Misrayimites pursued after your ancestors with chariotry and with cavalry, to the Reed Sea.

⁷They cried out to Yahweh and he put darkness between you and the Misrayimites. He made the sea come over them and it covered them. Your eyes saw what I did to the Misrayimites.

You stayed in the wilderness a long time, ⁸but I brought you to the country of the Amorites who were living across the Yarden. They battled with you but I gave them into your hand and you took possession of their country. I eliminated them from before you. ⁹Balaq ben Tsippor king of Mo'ab rose up and battled with Yisra'el. He sent and called for Bil'am ben Be'or to slight you. ¹⁰But I was not willing to listen to Bil'am and he really had to bless you. So I saved you from his hand.

¹¹You crossed the Yarden and came to Yeriho. The Yeriho landowners, the Amorite, the Perizzite, the Kena'anite, the Hittite, the Girgashite, the Hivvite and the Yebusite, battled against you, but I gave them into your hand. ¹²I sent off a hornet before you and it drove them out from before you (two Amorite kings), not by your sword and not by your bow. ¹³I've given you a country for which you didn't get weary, towns that you didn't build but you've lived in, eating from vineyards and olive groves that you didn't plant."

## 'You can't serve Yahweh.' 'Yes we can!'

¹⁴So now, live in awe of Yahweh and serve him with integrity and with truthfulness. Remove the gods that your ancestors served across the river and in Misrayim, and serve Yahweh. ¹⁵If it's bad in your eyes to serve Yahweh, choose for yourselves today whom you'll serve, whether the gods that your ancestors served who were beyond the river, or the gods of the Amorites whose country you're living in. I and my household, we will serve Yahweh.'

¹⁶The people answered, 'Far be it from us to abandon Yahweh to serve other gods, ¹⁷because Yahweh our God – he's the one who got us and our ancestors up from the country of Misrayim, from a household of serfs, and who did before our eyes these great signs, and kept us the entire way that we went and among all the peoples through whom we passed; ¹⁸and Yahweh drove out all the peoples (the Amorites) living in the country from before us. We'll serve Yahweh as well, because he's our God.'

¹⁹Yehoshua said to the people, 'You can't serve Yahweh, because he's a sacred God. He's a passionate God. He won't carry your rebellions and wrongdoings. ²⁰When you abandon Yahweh and serve foreign gods, he'll turn back and bring bad fortune to you and finish you off, after he's been good to you.'

²¹The people said to Yehoshua, 'No, because Yahweh is the one we'll serve.' ²²Yehoshua said to the people, 'You're witnesses against yourselves that you yourselves have chosen for yourselves Yahweh, to serve him.' They said, 'We're witnesses.' ²³'So now remove the foreign gods that are among you and direct your mind to Yahweh the God of Yisraèl.' ²⁴The people said to Yehoshua, 'Yahweh our God we will serve. To his voice we will listen.'

## Confirming the pact anew

²⁵Yehoshua solemnized a pact for the people that day and laid down for them a decree and a ruling, at Shekem. ²⁶Yehoshua wrote these things in God's instruction document. He got a big stone and set it up there under the oak that was in Yahweh's sanctuary. ²⁷Yehoshua said to all the people, 'Here, this stone – it will be a witness against us, because it – it heard all Yahweh's words that he spoke with us. It will be a witness against you, so you don't act deceitfully towards your God.' ²⁸And Yehoshua sent the people off, each to their domain.

²⁹After that, Yehoshua ben Nun, Yahweh's servant, died, a man of 110 years. ³⁰They buried him within the border that was his domain in Timnat-serah in the highland of Ephrayim, north of Mount Gaàsh.

³¹Yisraèl served Yahweh all the time of Yehoshua and all the time of the elders who lived on after Yehoshua and who acknowledged all Yahweh's action that he undertook for Yisraèl. ³²The bones of Yoseph, which the Yisraèlites had brought up from Misrayim, they buried in Shekem on the plot in the fields that Yaʿaqob had acquired from the sons of Hamor, Shekem's father, for a hundred qesitas. It had become a domain of the Yosephites.

³³Elʿazar ben Aharon died and they buried him on the hill of Pinhas his son, which had been given him in the highland of Ephrayim.

# JUDGES

A quick read of Joshua can give one the impression that the story that now follows will relate how everyone lives happily ever after, but the close of Joshua made clear that the Israelites have by no means entered into full possession of the land of Canaan. Moreover, Joshua's challenges to the Israelites at the end of Joshua also raise the question of how faithful Israel will be in fulfilling its own promises.

Judges begins (1.1—2.5) by focusing on the areas of the country over which Israel does not yet have control, and it thus conveys a gloomier impression than the book of Joshua as a whole. Further, the areas that remain under Canaanite control are the most populous areas and the ones most worth possessing. Like Joshua, Judges here moves between 'they didn't gain control' and 'they couldn't gain control' of these areas.

A second introduction to the book (2.6—3.4) then outlines a pattern that runs through much of the book. It introduces a series of stories that relate how Israelites turn away from adherence to Yahweh to serve other deities. Yahweh then himself turns away and leaves them to the mercy of their neighbours. In due course this experience of discipline makes them turn back to Yahweh, and he produces a deliverer who can rescue them from their adversaries.

It is these deliverers who provide the book with its title, 'Judges', though that English word is thus misleading. I use the expression 'exercise authority' to match the rendering elsewhere in this translation. But these leaders are people who don't have an official position like a governor or a king but who by dint of God's spirit coming on them are able to do what needs doing for Israel. Their personalities and gifts are also involved, though they tend to be the kind of people who wouldn't be in positions of official leadership if there were official leaders. God chooses and uses somebody's little brother, somebody who is handicapped, a son of Anat (a name that suggests he is a Canaanite), and then the greatest of the leaders who is – a woman.

Nor are these leaders commonly people of great faith or insight or a high standard of morality. Indeed, there is a troubling arc to the sequence of their stories. As the book unfolds, the leaders become more and more ambiguous figures. They can get the job done, but they lack the moral qualities that one would like to see accompanying their exercise of leadership.

In this respect they mirror the people themselves, and the later chapters in Judges turn it into the most distasteful and disturbing book in the Bible. It becomes a relentless portrayal of human stupidity, failure, and moral and social blindness. Women pay a heavy price in the conflicts and the abuses it reports, though women also exercise remarkable initiatives in different stories in the book.

Its own repeated comment in the closing chapters is that people were doing what was all right in their own eyes, and it adds the further comment that of course there was no king in Israel. The implication is that a king would be able to do something about the situation. The book thus provides some background to the introduction of kings in the next book, 1 Samuel.

If you add up the periods covered by the times of crisis and subsequent quiet in the book, you end up with a history occupying several hundred years. There isn't actually room for that long a period between Joshua (about 1200 BC) and Saul (about 1050 BC). A closer look at the stories, however, reveals that they all concern events and deliverances that are more or less local. They don't involve all the clans. So the periods of years to which the book refers can be overlapping – a time of crisis in one area can be a time of quiet in another. It's then theologically significant that the book portrays all the crises and deliverances as involving 'Israel'. When one suffers, all suffer. Trouble for one part of the body is trouble for the body as a whole.

## Real life is more complicated

**1** After Yehoshua's [Joshua's] death, the Yisra'elites [Israelites] asked of Yahweh, 'Who is to go up for us against the Kena'anites [Canaanites] first, to do battle with them?' ²Yahweh said, 'Yehudah [Judah] is to go up. Here, I am giving the country into his hand.' ³Yehudah said to Shim'on [Simeon], his brother, 'Go up with me into my lot so we can do battle against the Kena'anites, and I'll go with you into your lot as well.' So Shim'on went with him. ⁴Yehudah went up, and Yahweh gave the Kena'anite and the Perizzite into their hand. They struck them down at Bezeq, 10,000 people.

⁵They found Adoni Bezeq at Bezeq and battled against him, and struck down the Kena'anite and the Perizzite. ⁶Adoni Bezeq fled, but they pursued after him. They caught him and cut off his thumbs and big toes. ⁷Adoni-bezeq said, 'Seventy kings, with thumbs and big toes cut off, used to be gleaning under my table. As I have done, so God has made good to me.' They brought him to Yerushalaim [Jerusalem], and he died there.

⁸The Yehudahites battled against Yerushalaim, captured it and struck it down with the mouth of the sword, and the town they sent up in fire. ⁹Afterwards, the Yehudahites went down to battle against the Kena'anites living in the highland, the Negeb and the foothills.

¹⁰Yehudah went against the Kena'anites who were living in Hebron (Hebron's name was Arba's Township before). They struck down Sheshay, Ahiman and Talmay. ¹¹From there, it went against the people living in Debir (Debir's name was Sepher Township before).

¹²Kaleb [Caleb] said, 'The man who strikes down Sepher Township and captures it: I'll give him Aksah my daughter as wife.' ¹³Otni'el ben Qenaz, Kaleb's brother who was younger than him, captured it, and he gave him Aksah his daughter as wife. ¹⁴When she came, she incited him to ask for some fields from her father. She got down from her donkey and Kaleb said to her, 'What is it?' ¹⁵She said to him, 'Give me a blessing, because you've given me a region in the south. Give me waterholes.' So Kaleb gave her the upper waterholes and the lower waterholes.

## Who could and who couldn't

¹⁶The descendants of the Qenite, Mosheh's [Moses'] father-in-law, went up from Palms Town with the Yehudahites into the Yehudah Wilderness that's south of Arad, and he went and lived with the people. ¹⁷Yehudah went with its brother Shim'on and they struck down the Kena'anites living in Tsepat. They devoted it [*haram*], and named the town Hormah. ¹⁸Yehudah captured Azzah [Gaza] and its border, Ashqelon and its border, and Eqron and its border. ¹⁹Yahweh was with Yehudah, and it took possession of the highland, because it couldn't dispossess the people living in the vale because they had iron chariotry. ²⁰They gave Hebron to Kaleb as Mosheh spoke, and he dispossessed the three Anaqites from there. ²¹But the Yebusites living in Yerushalaim the Binyaminites [Benjaminites] didn't dispossess. The Yebusites have lived with the Binyaminites in Yerushalaim until this day.

²²Yoseph's [Joseph's] household, they too, went up to Bet-el; Yahweh was with them. ²³Yoseph's household investigated Bet-el (the town's name was Luz before), ²⁴and the men keeping watch saw a man coming out of the town and said to him, 'Show us the way into the town, will you, and we will act in commitment with you.' ²⁵He showed them the way into the town and they struck down the town with the mouth of the sword, but the man and his entire kin-group they sent off. ²⁶The man went to the Hittites' region and built a town, and named it Luz. That's its name until this day.

²⁷Menashsheh didn't take possession of Bet-she'an and its daughter-towns, Ta'nak and its daughter-towns, the people living in Dor and its daughter-towns, the people living in Yible'am and its daughter-towns, or the people living in Megiddo and its daughter-towns. The Kena'anites were resolved to live in this region. ²⁸When Yisra'el became strong it made the Kena'anites into a workforce, but it didn't dispossess them at all.

## Wailing

²⁹Ephrayim didn't dispossess the Kena'anites who were living in Gezer; the Kena'anites lived among them in Gezer. ³⁰Zebulun didn't

dispossess the people living in Qitron or the people living in Nahalol; the Kena'anites lived among them and became a workforce. [31]Asher didn't dispossess the people living in Akko or the people living in Tsidon, Ahlab, Akzib, Helbah, Aphiq or Rehob. [32]The Asherites lived among the Kena'anites living in the region, because they didn't dispossess them. [33]Naphtali didn't dispossess the people living in Bet-shemesh or the people living in Bet-anat. They lived among the Kena'anites living in the region and the people living in Bet-shemesh and Bet Anat became a workforce for them.

[34]The Amorites forced the Danites into the highland because they didn't let them come down into the vale. [35]The Amorites resolved to stay in Mount Heres in Ayyalon and in Sha'albim. But the hand of Yoseph's household became heavy and they became a workforce. [36]The Amorites' border went from Scorpions Ascent, from Sela, on upwards.

2 Yahweh's envoy went up from Gilgal to Bokim and said, 'I enabled you to go up from Misrayim [Egypt] and I brought you to the country that I swore to your ancestors. I said, "I will not contravene my pact with you, ever. [2]You yourselves will not solemnize a pact towards the people living in this country. You're to tear down their altars." But you didn't listen to my voice. What is this you've done? [3]So I've also said, "I won't drive them out from before you. They'll be at your sides and their gods will be a snare to you."' [4]When Yahweh's envoy spoke these words to all the Yisra'elites, the people lifted up their voice and wailed, [5]and named that place Bokim ['Wailers'], but they sacrificed there to Yahweh.

## The power of forgetting

[6]Yehoshua had sent the company off, and the Yisra'elites had gone each person to his domain to take possession of the country. [7]The people served Yahweh all Yehoshua's time and all the time of the elders who lived on after Yehoshua, who had seen all Yahweh's great work that he did for Yisra'el.

[8]Yehoshua ben Nun, Yahweh's servant, died, a man of 110 years, [9]and they buried him within the border that was his domain at Timnat-heres in the highland of Ephrayim, north of Mount Ga'ash. [10]That entire generation also joined its ancestors, and another generation arose after them who didn't acknowledge Yahweh, or the work he had done for Yisra'el either. [11]The Yisra'elites did what was bad in Yahweh's eyes. They served the Masters [12]and abandoned Yahweh, their ancestors' God, who had got them out of the country of Misrayim. They followed other gods from among the gods of the peoples who were round them, and bowed low to them, and provoked Yahweh. [13]So they abandoned Yahweh and served the Master and the Ashtars, [14]and Yahweh's anger raged against Yisra'el and he gave them into the hand of people who plundered them. He surrendered them into the hand of their enemies all round. They could no longer stand before their enemies. [15]Wherever they went out, Yahweh's hand was against them to make things go badly, as Yahweh had spoken and as Yahweh had sworn to them. It put great pressure on them.

[16]Yahweh made people to exercise authority arise and they delivered them from the hand of their plunderers, [17]but they also didn't listen to the people who exercised authority for them, because they whored after other gods and bowed low to them. They departed quickly from the way that their ancestors had walked by listening to Yahweh's orders. They didn't do so.

## When Yahweh feels sorry for them

[18]When Yahweh made people to exercise authority arise for them, Yahweh would be with the one exercising authority and he would deliver them from the hand of their enemies all the time of the one exercising authority, because Yahweh felt sorry on account of their groan in the face of the people afflicting and crushing them. [19]But when the one exercising authority died, they would go back to acting more devastatingly than their ancestors in following other gods to serve them and bow low to them. They didn't drop any of their practices and their tough-minded way.

[20]So Yahweh's anger raged against Yisra'el. He said, 'Since this nation have contravened the pact with which I ordered their ancestors and haven't listened to my voice, [21]I for my part will not continue to dispossess anyone from

before them, from the nations that Yehoshua left when he died', [22]in order to test Yisra'el by them, whether they're keeping Yahweh's way by walking in them, as their ancestors kept it, or not. [23]So Yahweh had let these nations settle down without dispossessing them quickly, and had not given them into Yehoshua's hand.

**3** These are the nations that Yahweh let settle down, to test Yisra'el by them, all who had not known any of the battles in Kena'an, [2]only in order for Yisra'el's generations to know them, by teaching them about battle – only the people who had not known them before: [3]the five Pelishtite lords and all the Kena'anites, the Tsidonites and the Hivvites living in the highland of the Lebanon from Ba'al Hermon Mountain as far as Lebo Hamat. [4]They were for testing Yisra'el by them, to know whether they would listen to Yahweh's order which he had given their ancestors through Mosheh.

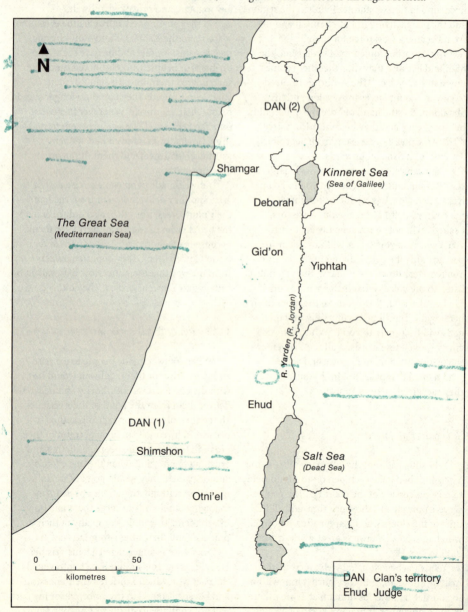

The 'major' judges

## Kaleb's little brother again

[5]So the Yisra'elites lived among the Kena'anite, the Hittite, the Amorite, the Perizzite, the Hivvite and the Yebusite, [6]and got their daughters for themselves as wives and gave their daughters to their sons, and served their gods. [7]The Yisra'elites did what was bad in Yahweh's eyes. They put Yahweh their God out of mind and served the Masters and the Asherahs. [8]Yahweh's anger raged against Yisra'el and he surrendered them into the hand of Kushan Rish'atayim, the king of Aram-of-the-Two-Rivers. The Yisra'elites served Kushan Rish'atayim for eight years.

[9]The Yisra'elites cried out to Yahweh and Yahweh made a deliverer arise for the Yisra'elites and he delivered them: Otni'el ben Qenaz, Kaleb's brother who was younger than him. [10]Yahweh's spirit came on him and he exercised authority for Yisra'el. He went out to battle and Yahweh gave Kushan Rish'atayim, the king of Aram, into his hand. His hand was powerful over Kushan Rish'atayim, [11]and the region was calm for forty years.

Otni'el ben Qenaz died, [12]and the Yisra'elites again did what was bad in Yahweh's eyes. Yahweh made Eglon king of Mo'ab strong over Yisra'el because they did what was bad in Yahweh's eyes, [13]and he got the Ammonites and Amaleq to join him. He went and struck Yisra'el down, and took possession of Palms Town. [14]The Yisra'elites served Eglon king of Mo'ab for eighteen years.

## Another unlikely saviour

[15]The Yisra'elites cried out to Yahweh and Yahweh made a deliverer arise for them, Ehud ben Gera, a Binyaminite, a man restricted in his right hand. The Yisra'elites sent an offering by his hand to Eglon king of Mo'ab. [16]Ehud made himself a sword with two edges, half a metre in length. He wrapped it on under his uniform on his right side, [17]and presented the offering to Eglon king of Mo'ab. Now Eglon was a very stout man.

[18]When he had finished presenting the offering, he sent off the company who had been carrying the gift, [19]but he himself went back from the sculptures that are near Gilgal

and said, 'I have a secret message for you, Your Majesty.' He said, 'Silence', and all the people who stood by him went out from his presence. [20]When Ehud came to him, he was sitting in the cool upper quarters that he had, alone. Ehud said, 'I have a word from God for you.' He got up from his seat, [21]and Ehud put out his left hand, took the sword from on his right side and plunged it into his insides. [22]Even the handle went in after the blade, and the fat closed over the blade, because he didn't pull the sword out of his insides. The dirt came out.

[23]Ehud went out through the porch, shut the doors of the upper quarters on him and locked them [24]as he went out.

His servants came and looked: there, the doors of the upper quarters were locked. They said, 'Yes, he's relieving himself in the cool lounge', [25]and waited until they were shamed. But there – he wasn't opening the doors of the upper quarters. So they got the key and opened them, and there – their lord was fallen on the ground, dead.

[26]Ehud had escaped while they delayed, and had passed the sculptures. He escaped to Se'irah [27]and, when he came, blew on the horn in the highland of Ephrayim. The Yisra'elites went down with him from the highland; he was before them. [28]He said to them 'Pursue after me, because Yahweh has given your enemies, Mo'ab, into your hand.' They went down after him and captured Mo'ab's Yarden [Jordan] crossings, and didn't let anyone cross. [29]They struck down Mo'ab at that time, some 10,000 men, every individual hefty and everyone a forceful man. Not one escaped. [30]So Mo'ab bowed down that day under Yisra'el's hand, and the region was calm for eighty years.

## Shamgar, Deborah, Lapiddot and Baraq

[31]After him there was Shamgar ben Anat. He struck down 600 Pelishtites [Philistines] with an ox goad. He, too, was one who delivered Yisra'el.

**4** The Yisra'elites again did what was bad in Yahweh's eyes when Ehud had died, [2]and Yahweh surrendered them into the hand of Yabin king of Kena'an who reigned in Hatsor. His army officer was Sisera; he was living in

Haroshet Haggoyim. ³The Yisraelites cried out to Yahweh because he had 900 iron chariots, and he had afflicted Yisrael through his strength for twenty years.

⁴Now Deborah, a woman who was a prophetess, the wife of Lapiddot, was exercising authority for Yisrael at that time. ⁵She would sit under Deborah's Palm between The Height and Bet-el in the highland of Ephrayim, and the Yisraelites would go up to her for a decision.

⁶She sent and called for Baraq ben Abino'am, from Qedesh in Naphtali, and said to him, 'Yahweh the God of Yisrael has ordered you, has he not: "Go, march to Mount Tabor, and take with you 10,000 men from the Naphtalites and from the Zebulunites. ⁷I shall march Sisera, Yabin's army officer, to you, to Wadi Qishon, with his chariotry and his horde, and I shall give them into your hand."'

⁸Baraq said to her, 'If you go with me, I'll go, but if you don't go with me, I won't go.' ⁹She said, 'I'll definitely go with you, only it won't be your glory on the journey that you're going on, because it's into the hand of a woman that Yahweh will surrender Sisera.' So Deborah set off and went with Baraq to Qedesh, ¹⁰and Baraq called out Zebulun and Naphtali to Qedesh. Ten thousand men went up after him, and Deborah went up with him. ¹¹Now Heber the Qenite had split from Qayin, from the descendants of Hobab, Mosheh's father-in-law, and spread his tent by the oak at Tsa'anannim, which was near Qedesh.

¹²They told Sisera that Baraq ben Abinoam had gone up to Mount Tabor, ¹³and Sisera called out all his chariotry (900 iron chariots) and all the company that was with him from Haroshet-goyim to Wadi Qishon.

### Ya'el

¹⁴Deborah said to Baraq, 'Set off, because this is the day that Yahweh has given Sisera into your hand. Yahweh has gone out before you, hasn't he.' So Baraq went down from Mount Tabor, with 10,000 men behind him, ¹⁵and Yahweh threw Sisera, all his chariotry and all the camp into confusion at the mouth of the sword before Baraq.

Sisera got down from his chariot and fled on foot, ¹⁶while Baraq pursued after the

chariotry and after the camp as far as Haroshet Haggoyim. Sisera's entire camp fell to the mouth of the sword. Not even one was left.

¹⁷Now Sisera had fled on foot to the tent of Ya'el, the wife of Heber the Qenite, because there was peace between Yabin king of Hatsor and the household of Heber the Qenite. ¹⁸Ya'el came out to meet Sisera and said to him, 'Turn aside, sir, turn aside to me. Don't be afraid.' So he turned aside to her into the tent and she covered him with a rug. ¹⁹He said to her, 'Please give me a little water to drink, because I'm thirsty.' She opened a skin of milk and gave him a drink, and covered him. ²⁰He said to her, 'Stand at the tent entrance. If someone comes and asks you, "Is there anyone here?" you're to say, "There's no one."'

²¹But Ya'el, Heber's wife, got a tent peg and picked up a hammer in her hand. She came to him stealthily and drove the peg through his temple so it went down into the ground; he was in a deep sleep, he was weary. So he died. ²²And there was Baraq, pursuing Sisera. Ya'el went out to meet him. She said to him, 'Come, I'll let you see the man that you're looking for.' He came in to her, and there was Sisera, fallen dead, the peg in his temple.

²³That day God made Yabin king of Hatsor bow down before the Yisraelites. ²⁴The Yisraelites' hand kept getting tougher on Yabin king of Kena'an until they had cut down Yabin king of Kena'an.

### Yahweh's faithful acts

**5** Deborah (and Baraq ben Abino'am) sang that day:

²At people exercising authority who were
    letting themselves go in Yisrael,
  at a company offering itself freely: bless
    Yahweh!
³Listen, kings,
    give ear, sovereigns!
I myself, I shall sing for Yahweh,
    I shall make music for Yahweh the God of
      Yisrael.

⁴Yahweh, when you came out from Se'ir,
    when you marched from Edomite
      country,

Earth trembled,
  yes, heavens poured,
Yes, clouds poured water,
  ⁵when mountains quaked,
Before Yahweh the one of Sinay,
  before Yahweh the God of Yisra'el.

⁶In the time of Shamgar ben Anat,
  in the time of Ya'el,
Journeys left off,
  people going on paths went by roundabout
    ways.
⁷Peasantry left off,
  left off in Yisra'el,
Until I, Deborah, arose,
  arose as mother in Yisra'el.
⁸It chose new gods,
  then there was battling in the gateways.
Shield and spear did not appear
  among 40,000 in Yisra'el.
⁹My heart was with Yisra'el's commanders,
  who offered themselves freely in the company.

Bless Yahweh,
  ¹⁰riders on tawny donkeys!
You who sit on saddle blankets,
  you who go on a journey, talk.
¹¹Above the voice of dealers among watering
  holes,
  there they are to commemorate Yahweh's
  faithful acts,
Faithful acts for his peasantry in Yisra'el;
  then Yahweh's company went down to the
  gateways.

## Who came and who didn't

¹²Stir, stir, Deborah,
  Stir, stir, sound out a song!
Set off, Baraq,
  take your captives, ben Abino'am!
¹³Then those of the august ones who were left
  came down,
  Yahweh's company came down for me
  among the strong men,
¹⁴From Ephrayim people whose root is in
  Amaleq,
  after you, Binyamin with your kin.
From Makir commanders came down,
  from Zebulun people wielding the marshal's
  staff.

¹⁵The officers in Yissakar [Issachar] were with
  Deborah;
  as Yissakar, so was Baraq,
  sent into the vale behind him.
Among Re'uben's divisions,
  great searchings of heart.
¹⁶Why did you sit among the folds
  to listen to the whistlings for the flocks?
Among Re'uben's divisions,
  great searchings of heart.
¹⁷Gil'ad dwelled across the Yarden;
  Dan: why did he stay by the ships?
Asher lived at the sea coast
  and dwelled by its harbours.
¹⁸Zebulun was a people that reviled its life to
  the death;
  Naphtali was on the heights of the fields.

¹⁹Kings came, battled,
  kings of Kena'an battled then.
At Ta'nak by Megiddo's water
  they got no gain of silver.
²⁰From the heavens the stars battled,
  from their causeways they battled with Sisera.
²¹Wadi Qishon swept them away,
  the rushing wadi, Wadi Qishon:
  go on with vigour, my soul!
²²Then horse hoofs pounded,
  with the galloping, the galloping of his
  sturdy ones.
²³'Curse Meroz', Yahweh's envoy said,
  'utterly curse the people living in it,
Because they didn't come when Yahweh was
  helping,
  when Yahweh was helping against the strong
  men.'

## Sisera's mother waits

²⁴Most blessed of women be Ya'el,
  wife of Heber the Qenite,
  most blessed of tent women.
²⁵He asked for water, she gave milk;
  in a bowl fit for august people she presented
  curds.
²⁶She put out her hand for the peg,
  her right hand for the labourers' hammer.
She hammered Sisera, smashed his head,
  hit and pierced his temple.
²⁷Between her feet he bent down,
  he fell, he lay.

Between her feet he bent down, he fell;
    where he bent down, there he fell, destroyed.

²⁸Through the window Sisera's mother peered,
    she gazed through the lattice.
'Why is his chariot taking time to come,
    why have the rumblings of his chariots
      delayed?'
²⁹The smartest of her ladies answer her,
    indeed she gives back her word to herself:
³⁰'They've found and shared out the spoil,
    haven't they,
  a woman, two women, for each man,
Spoil of dyed cloth for Sisera,
    spoil of dyed cloth embroidered,
    two embroidered cloths for the necks as spoil.'

³¹So may all your enemies perish, Yahweh,
    but may his friends be like the sun coming
      out in its strength.

The region was calm for forty years.

## The man hiding to beat out wheat

**6** The Yisraelites did what was bad in Yahweh's eyes and he gave them into the hand of Midyan for seven years. ²The hand of Midyan was powerful over Yisrael. Because of Midyan, the Yisraelites made themselves hideouts that were in the mountains, caves and strongholds. ³If Yisrael had sown, Midyan, Amaleq and the Easterners would go up. They would go up against it ⁴and camp against them, and devastate the region's yield until you come to Azzah. They wouldn't let anything remain alive in Yisrael, either sheep or ox or donkey, ⁵because they and their livestock would go up with their tents. They would come like a locust swarm in their large number. There was no counting them or their camels.

So they came into the region to devastate it, ⁶and Yisrael became very low before Midyan. The Yisraelites cried out to Yahweh. ⁷When the Yisraelites cried out to Yahweh on account of Midyan, ⁸Yahweh sent someone as a prophet to the Yisraelites. He said to them, 'Yahweh the God of Yisrael has said this: "I'm the one who got you up from Misrayim, got you out of the household of serfs, ⁹rescued you from the hand of Misrayim and from the hand of all the people

who afflicted you. I drove them out from before you and gave you their country. ¹⁰I said to you, 'I am Yahweh your God. You will not live in awe of the gods of the Amorites in whose country you're living.' But you didn't listen to my voice."'

¹¹Yahweh's envoy came and sat under the oak at Ophrah that belonged to Yo'ash the Abi'ezrite. His son Gid'on [Gideon] was beating out wheat in the winepress to keep it safe from before Midyan. ¹²Yahweh's envoy appeared to him and said to him, 'Yahweh is with you, forceful strong man.' ¹³Gid'on said to him, 'Pardon me, my Lord: Yahweh is with us? So why has all this befallen us? Where are all his extraordinary acts that our ancestors recounted to us, saying "Yahweh got us up from Misrayim, didn't he"? Yahweh has now left us alone and given us into Midyan's fist.'

## Asking for a sign

¹⁴Yahweh turned his face to him and said, 'Go in this energy of yours and deliver Yisrael from Midyan's fist. I've sent you, haven't I.' ¹⁵He said to him, 'Pardon me, my Lord: how can I deliver Yisrael? Here, my family is the poorest in Menashsheh and I'm the youngest in my father's household.' ¹⁶Yahweh said to him, 'But I'll be with you, and you'll strike Midyan down as if they were one man.'

¹⁷He said to him, 'If I've found grace in your eyes, please perform a sign for me that you're the one speaking with me. ¹⁸Don't move away from here, please, until I come to you and bring my offering out and set it down before you.' He said, 'I myself will stay until you come back.'

¹⁹When Gid'on had come in, he prepared a kid goat from the flock and a barrel of flour into flatbread. When he'd put the meat in a basket and put the broth in a pot, he took them out to him under the oak. So he brought them up ²⁰and God's envoy said to him, 'Get the meat and the flatbread and set them down on this rock, and pour out the broth.' He did so. ²¹Yahweh's envoy put out the end of the staff that was in his hand and touched the meat and the flatbread. Fire went up from the crag and devoured the meat and the flatbread, as Yahweh's envoy went from before his eyes.

²²Gid'on saw that it was Yahweh's envoy. Gid'on said, 'Oh, Lord Yahweh, that therefore

I've seen Yahweh's envoy face to face!' ²³Yahweh said to him, 'Things will be well for you. Don't be afraid. You won't die.'

²⁴Gid'on built an altar there for Yahweh and called it 'Yahweh-things-will-be-well'. Until this day it's still in Ophrah of the Abi'ezrites.

## The mixed-up father

²⁵That night Yahweh said to him, 'Get the ox bullock that belongs to your father and a second bullock of seven years. Tear down the Master's altar that belongs to your father and cut down the totem pole that's by it, ²⁶and build an altar for Yahweh your God on the top of this stronghold, in proper order. Get the second bullock and offer it up as a burnt offering with the wood of the totem pole that you cut down.' ²⁷So Gid'on got ten men from among his servants and did as Yahweh had spoken to him, but as he was too afraid of his father's household and of the people of the town to do it by day, he did it by night.

²⁸The people of the town started early in the morning and there, the Master's altar was demolished, the totem pole that was by it was cut down and the second bull was sacrificed on the altar that had been built. ²⁹They said, one to his neighbour, 'Who did this thing?'. They enquired and sought, and said, 'Gid'on ben Yo'ash did this thing.' ³⁰The people of the town said to Yo'ash, 'Bring your son out: he's to die, because he demolished the Master's altar and because he cut down the totem pole that was by it.' ³¹But Yo'ash said to all who stood round him, 'Do you yourselves argue for the Master? Or do you yourselves deliver him? The person who argues for him should be put to death by morning. If he's a god, he should argue for himself, because someone has demolished his altar.' ³²That day they called him Yerubba'al ('Master-Must-Argue'), saying 'The Master must argue against him, because he demolished his altar.'

## The fleece

³³Now all Midyan, Amaleq and the Easterners gathered together, crossed over and camped in the Yizre'e'l Vale, ³⁴and Yahweh's

spirit clothed itself in Gid'on. He blew on the horn, and the Abi'ezrites had themselves called out to follow him. ³⁵When he sent envoys through all Menashsheh, they too had themselves called out to follow him, and when he sent envoys through Asher, through Zebulun and through Naphtali, they went up to meet them.

³⁶Gid'on said to God, 'If you're really going to deliver Yisra'el by my hand, as you spoke: ³⁷here, I'm placing a wool fleece on the threshing floor. If there's dew on the fleece alone but on all the ground it's dry, I'll acknowledge that you will deliver Yisra'el by my hand as you spoke.' ³⁸So it happened. He started early next day, squeezed the fleece and wrung out dew from the fleece, a full bowl of water.

³⁹Gid'on said to God, 'May your anger not rage against me and I'll speak just one more time. May I please test with the fleece only one more time. May there please be dry on the fleece alone but on all the ground may there be dew.' ⁴⁰God did so that night. There was dry on the fleece alone but on the ground there was dew.

**7** Yerubba'al (i.e. Gid'on) and all the company with him started early and camped above Harod Spring; the Midyanite camp was north of him at Moreh Hill, in the vale. ²Yahweh said to Gid'on, 'The company that's with you is too big for me to give Midyan into their hand, so Yisra'el doesn't take glory for itself over me, saying "My hand delivered me." ³Now call out, please, in the ears of the company, "Whoever is afraid and trembling is to go back and fly from Mount Gil'ad."' Twenty-two thousand of the company went back; 10,000 remained.

## How to increase the odds against yourself

⁴Yahweh said to Gid'on, 'The company is still big. Get them to go down to the water and I'll smelt them for you there. The one of whom I say to you, "This one is to go with you", he's to go with you. Everyone that I say to you, "This one's not to go with you", he's not to go.' ⁵So he got the company to go down to the water. Yahweh said to Gid'on, 'Everyone who laps from the water with his tongue as a dog laps, you're to place apart; and everyone who bends down on his knees to drink.' ⁶The

number of people who lapped with their hand into their mouth was 300. All the rest of the company bent down on their knees to drink water. [7]Yahweh said to Gid'on, 'With the 300 men who were lapping I shall deliver you and give Midyan into your hand, while the entire company are to go each individual to his place.' [8]So they got the company's provisions in their hand, and their horns, while he sent off every Yisra'elite, each one to his tents, but kept strong hold of the 300 men.

The Midyanite camp was below him in the vale. [9]That night Yahweh said to him, 'Set off, go down against the camp, because I've given it into your hand. [10]If you're afraid to go down, you yourself go down to the camp with Purah your boy [11]and listen to what they speak of, and afterwards your hands will be strong and you'll go down against the camp.' So he himself went down with Purah his boy to the edge of where the men organized into companies were in the camp. [12]Midyan, Amaleq and all the Easterners were lying in the vale like a locust swarm in their large number, and there was no counting their camels, like the sea on the seashore in their large number.

## The man with a dream

[13]Gid'on came, and there, a man was recounting a dream to his neighbour. He said, 'Here, I had a dream. There, a loaf of barley bread was rolling against the Midyanite camp. It came to a tent and struck it down, and it fell. It turned it over, upside down. The tent fell.' [14]His neighbour answered, 'This is nothing but the sword of Gid'on ben Yo'ash, the Yisra'elite. God has given Midyan and the entire camp into his hand.' [15]When Gid'on heard the recounting of the dream and its explaining, he bowed low. He went back to the Yisra'elite camp and said, 'Set off, because Yahweh has given the Midyanite camp into your hand.'

[16]He divided the 300 men into three units and put horns into the hand of each of them, with empty pitchers and torches inside the pitchers. [17]He said to them, 'Look at me and do the same. Here am I, coming against the edge of the camp. As I do, so you're to do. [18]I'll blow on my horn, I and everyone who's with me, and you're to blow on your horns, as well, round

the entire camp, and you're to say, "Yahweh's and Gid'on's!"'

[19]So Gid'on and the 300 men who were with him came against the edge of the camp at the start of the middle watch. They had only then actually set up the watchmen. They blew on the horns, with the pitchers to be smashed that were in their hand, [20]and the three units blew on their horns and broke the pitchers and took strong hold of the torches in their left hand while the horns for blowing were in their right hand. They called, 'Yahweh's sword and Gid'on's' [21]and stood each person where he was round the camp. The entire camp ran and shouted and fled. [22]The 300 horns blew and Yahweh set one person's sword against his neighbour in the entire camp. The camp fled as far as Bet Shittim, towards Tsererah, as far as the edge of Meholah Meadow near Tabbat.

## Oreb and Ze'eb

[23]Yisra'elites from Naphtali, from Asher and from all Menashsheh had themselves called out, and pursued after Midyan, [24]while Gid'on sent envoys through the entire highland of Ephrayim saying, 'Go down to meet Midyan and capture their water as far as Bet Barah and the Yarden.' All the Ephrayimites had themselves called out, and they captured the water as far as Bet Barah and the Yarden. [25]They captured two Midyanite officers, Oreb and Ze'eb, and killed Oreb at Oreb's Crag and killed Ze'eb at Ze'eb's Winepress. So they pursued Midyan, and the head of Oreb and Ze'eb they brought to Gid'on from across the Yarden.

**8** But the Ephrayimites said to him, 'Why did you do this thing to us, not calling for us when you went to battle against Midyan?' They argued with him strongly. [2]He said to them, 'What have I done now compared with you? Aren't Ephrayim's gleanings better than Abi'ezer's reaping? [3]Into your hand God gave the Midyanite officers Oreb and Ze'eb. What could I do compared with you?' Then their feelings against him relaxed, when he spoke this word.

[4]Gid'on came to the Yarden. He was crossing, he and the 300 men who were with him, faint as they were pursuing. [5]He said to the people of Sukkot, 'Please give us loaves of bread for the

company that's after me, because they're faint and I'm pursuing after Zebah and Tsalmunna, the Midyanite kings.' ⁶The officials of Sukkot said to him, 'Is the fist of Zebah and Salmunna in your hand now, that we should give your army bread?' ⁷Gid'on said, 'Therefore, when Yahweh gives Zebah and Salmunna into my hand, I'll thresh your flesh with wilderness thorns and with briars.'

⁸From there he went up to Penu'el and spoke to them in this same way, and the people of Penu'el answered him as the people of Sukkot had answered. ⁹So he also said to the people of Penu'el, 'When I come back with things being well, I'll demolish this tower.'

### They were my brothers

¹⁰Now Zebah and Tsalmunna were at Qarqor and their camp with them, some 15,000, all that was left of the entire camp of the Easterners; the fallen were 120,000 men drawing the sword. ¹¹Gid'on went up the tent-dwellers road, east of Nobah and Yogbehah, and struck down the camp when the camp was feeling confident. ¹²Zebah and Tsalmunna fled and he pursued after them. He captured the two Midyanite kings, Zebah and Tsalmunna, and made the entire camp tremble.

¹³Gid'on ben Yo'ash came back from the battle, from Heres Ascent. ¹⁴He captured a boy from among the people of Sukkot and questioned him, and he wrote down for him the officials of Sukkot and its elders, seventy-seven people. ¹⁵He came to the people of Sukkot and said, 'Here are Zebah and Tsalmunna, about whom you reviled me, saying "Is the fist of Zebah and Salmunna in your hand, that we should give bread to your weary men?"' ¹⁶He got the town's elders, and wilderness thorns and briars, and taught the people of Sukkot with them. ¹⁷The tower at Penu'el he demolished, and he killed the town's people.

¹⁸He said to Zebah and to Tsalmunna, 'Where are the men that you killed at Tabor?' They said, 'They were just like you, the very appearance of a king's sons.' ¹⁹He said, 'They were my brothers, my mother's sons. As Yahweh lives, if you had let them live, I would not have killed you.' ²⁰He said to Yeter, his

firstborn, 'Get up, kill them.' But the boy didn't draw his sword, because he was afraid, because he was still a boy. ²¹Zebah and Tsalmunna said, 'You yourself get up and attack us, because "As a man is, so is his strength."' So Gid'on got up and killed Zebah and Tsalmunna, and took the crescents that were on their camels' necks.

### 'I'm not the hero; the hero is God'

²²The Yisra'elites said to Gid'on, 'Rule over us, both you and your son and your grandson, because you've delivered us from the hand of Midyan.' ²³Gid'on said to them, 'I myself won't rule over you and my son won't rule over you. Yahweh is the one who will rule over you.'

²⁴But Gid'on said to them, 'I will ask something of you. Each man, give me the earring that was his spoil' (because they had gold earrings, because they were Yishma'e'lites). ²⁵They said, 'We'll certainly give them.' They spread out a coat and threw there, each man, the earring that was his spoil. ²⁶The weight of the gold earrings that he asked for came to 1,700 in gold, apart from the crescents, pendants and purple robes that were on the Midyanite kings, and apart from the collars that were on their camels' necks. ²⁷Gid'on made it into a chasuble and placed it in his town, in Ophrah. All Yisra'el whored after it there. It became a snare to Gid'on and to his household.

²⁸So Midyan bowed down before the Yisra'elites. They didn't raise their head again. The region was calm for forty years in Gid'on's time.

²⁹Yerubba'al ben Yo'ash went and lived at home. ³⁰Gid'on had seventy sons who issued from his own body, because he had many wives. ³¹His secondary wife who was in Shekem also gave birth to a son for him; he named him Abimelek. ³²Gid'on ben Yo'ash died in a good old age and was buried in his father Yo'ash's tomb in Ophrah of the Abi'ezrites.

### The man who would be king

³³When Gid'on died, the Yisra'elites again whored after the Masters, and they made the Pact Master into god for themselves. ³⁴The Yisra'elites didn't keep Yahweh their God in

mind, the one who rescued them from the hand of all their enemies round them. [35]They didn't act in commitment with the household of Yerubba'al (Gid'on) in accordance with all the good that he had done in Yisra'el.

9 Abimelek, son of Yerubba'al, went to Shekem to his mother's brothers and spoke to them and to the entire kin-group in his mother's ancestral household: [2]'Speak, will you, in the ears of all the Shekem landowners: "Which is better for you, seventy men ruling over you (all the sons of Yerubba'al), or one man ruling over you? Be mindful that I am your own flesh and blood."' [3]His mother's brothers spoke all these things about him in the ears of all the Shekem landowners. Their mind turned away to follow Abimelek, because (they said), 'He's our brother', [4]and they gave him seventy in silver from the house of the Pact Master. With these, Abimelek hired empty-headed and wild men and they followed him. [5]He came to his father's house in Ophrah and killed his brothers, the sons of Yerubba'al, seventy men on one stone. But Yotam, youngest son of Yerubba'al, was left, because he hid.

[6]All the Shekem landowners and the entire Bet Millo gathered, and went and installed Abimelek as king by the oak at the column which was in Shekem.

## A parable about leadership

[7]People told Yotam and he went and stood on top of Mount Gerizim. He lifted his voice and called to them: 'Listen to me, Shekem landowners, so God may listen to you. [8]The trees went with resolve to anoint a king over themselves. They said to the olive tree, "Do reign over us." [9]The olive tree said to them, "Should I leave off from my richness, I by whom people honour God and human beings, and go to wave over the trees?" [10]So the trees said to the fig tree, "You go reign over us." [11]The fig tree said to them, "Should I leave off from my sweetness, my good fruit, and go to wave over the trees?" [12]So the trees said to the vine, "You go reign over us." [13]The vine said to them, "Should I leave off from my new wine, which makes God and human beings rejoice, and go to wave over the trees?"

[14]So all the trees said to the thorn bush, "You go reign over us." [15]The thorn bush said to the trees, "If you're going to anoint me as king over you with truthfulness, come take shelter in my shade. But if not, may fire come out of the thorn bush and devour the cedars of the Lebanon."

[16]So now, if you've acted in truthfulness and integrity and made Abimelek king, and if you've done something good by Yerubba'al and by his household, and if you've acted towards him in accordance with the dealing of his hands – [17]that my father battled on your account and threw his life a distance away and rescued you from the hand of Midyan . . .

[18]But you people have risen up against my father's household today and killed his sons, seventy men on one stone, and made Abimelek, his handmaid's son, king over the Shekem landowners, because he's your brother.

## Ambition rebounds

[19]If you've acted in truthfulness and integrity with Yerubba'al and with his household this day, rejoice in Abimelek, and may he rejoice in you, too. [20]But if not, may fire come out from Abimelek and devour the Shekem landowners and Bet Millo, and may fire come out from the Shekem landowners and from Bet Millo and devour Abimelek!' [21]Then Yotam took flight. He escaped and went to Be'er, and lived there, away from the presence of Abimelek his brother.

[22]Abimelek held office over Yisra'el for three years, [23]but God sent a bad spirit between Abimelek and the Shekem landowners, and the Shekem landowners broke faith with Abimelek, [24]so that the violence against the seventy sons of Yerubba'al might come home and so that the bloodshed be put on Abimelek their brother who killed them and on the Shekem landowners who had strengthened his hands in the killing of his brothers. [25]The Shekem landowners laid ambushes for him on the tops of the mountains and robbed anyone who passed by them on the road, and it was told Abimelek.

[26]Ga'al ben Ebed and his brothers came and passed through Shekem, and the Shekem landowners put their trust in him. [27]They went out to the fields, cut their vineyards and trod them, and made a great celebration.

They came into their god's house and ate and drank, and slighted Abimelek. [28]Ga'al ben Ebed said, 'Who is Abimelek, and who is Shekem, that we should serve him? Isn't he the son of Yerubba'al, and Zebul is his appointee? Serve the men of Hamor, the ancestor of Shekem! Why should we be people who serve him? [29]If only this people were in my hand! I would remove Abimelek. Someone would have said to Abimelek, "Amass your army and go out!"'

## The ambush

[30]Zebul, the town official, heard the words of Ga'al ben Ebed, and his anger raged. [31]He sent envoys to Abimelek at Tormah to say, 'Here, Ga'al ben Ebed and his brothers are coming to Shekem, and here, they're besieging the town against you. [32]So now, set off by night, you and the company that's with you, and make an ambush in the fields. [33]In the morning, at sunrise, you should start early and charge against the town. Here, he and the company that's with him are going to go out against you, and you can do to him whatever your hand finds to do.'

[34]So Abimelek and the entire company that was with him set off by night and laid an ambush against Shekem in four columns. [35]Ga'al ben Ebed went out and stood at the entrance of the town gateway, and Abimelek and the company that was with him arose from the ambush.

[36]Ga'al saw the company and said to Zebul, 'There, a company is coming down from the tops of the mountains!' Zebul said to him, 'You're seeing the shadow of the mountains as if they were men.' [37]Ga'al spoke once again and said, 'There, a company is coming down from the centre of the land, and a company is coming from the Elon Me'onenim road!' [38]Zebul said to him, 'Where then is your mouth with which you say, "Who is Abimelek that we should serve him?" This is the company that you rejected, isn't it! Please go out now, and do battle against it!'

[39]So Ga'al went out before the Shekem landowners and battled against Abimelek, [40]but Abimelek pursued him and he fled from before him. Many people fell, run through, as far as the entrance of the gateway. [41]Abimelek stayed

in Arumah, but Zebul drove out Ga'al and his brothers from living in Shekem.

## Undone by a woman

[42]Next day, the people went out to the fields, and Abimelek was told. [43]He got the company, divided it into three columns and set an ambush in the fields. He looked: there was the people coming out from the town. He set upon them and struck them down. [44]Abimelek and the columns that were with him charged and stood at the entrance of the town gateway. The other two columns charged against everyone who was in the fields and struck them down, [45]while Abimelek was battling against the town all that day. He captured the town and killed the people that were in it, demolished the town and sowed it with salt.

[46]All the Shekem Tower landowners heard, and came into a tunnel at the house of the Pact God. [47]It was told Abimelek that all the Shekem Tower landowners had collected together. [48]Abimelek went up Mount Tsalmon, he and the entire company that was with him. Abimelek got axes in his hand, cut a tree branch, lifted it and put it on his shoulder. He said to the company that was with him, 'What you have seen I did, hurry, do like me.' [49]The entire company also cut a branch each, followed Abimelek, placed them against the tunnel and set fire to the tunnel over them. All the people in the Shekem Tower also died, some thousand men and women.

[50]Abimelek then went to Tebets, camped against Tebets and captured it. [51]There was a strong tower inside the town and all the men and women, all the town's landowners, fled there, shut themselves in and went up on to the tower roof. [52]Abimelek came right up to the tower and battled against it, and drew up close to the tower entrance to burn it in fire. [53]But a woman threw an upper millstone on Abimelek's head and broke his skull. [54]He quickly called to the boy carrying his things and said to him, 'Draw your sword and put me to death, so they don't say of me, "A woman killed him."' So his boy thrust him through, and he died. [55]The Yisra'elites saw that Abimelek was dead, and went each man to his place.

## Peace for a while

⁵⁶So God turned back Abimelek's bad action which he had undertaken towards his father, in killing his seventy brothers, ⁵⁷and God turned back on their head all the bad action of the people of Shekem. The slight by Yotam son of Yerubba'al came true for them.

**10** After Abimelek, there arose to deliver Yisra'el Tola ben Pu'ah, son of Dodo, a Yissakarite. He was living in Shamir in the highland of Ephrayim. ²He exercised authority for Yisra'el for twenty-three years. He died, and was buried in Shamir.

³After him, there arose Ya'ir the Gil'adite. He exercised authority for Yisra'el for twenty-two years. ⁴He had thirty sons riding on thirty donkey colts, and he had thirty towns (they call them Ya'ir's Villages until this day) which were in the region of Gil'ad. ⁵Ya'ir died and was buried in Qamon.

⁶But the Yisra'elites again did what was bad in Yahweh's eyes and served the Masters, the Ashtars, the gods of Aram, the gods of Tsidon, the gods of Mo'ab, the gods of the Ammonites and the gods of the Pelishtites. They abandoned Yahweh and did not serve him. ⁷Yahweh's anger raged against Yisra'el and he surrendered them into the hand of the Pelishtites and into the hand of the Ammonites. ⁸They shattered and crushed the Yisra'elites that year – for eighteen years, all the Yisra'elites who were across the Yarden in the Amorites' country, which was in Gil'ad. ⁹The Ammonites also crossed the Yarden to battle against Yehudah, against Binyamin and against the household of Ephrayim. It put great pressure on Yisra'el.

¹⁰So the Yisra'elites cried out to Yahweh: 'We've done wrong against you, because we've abandoned our God and served the Masters.'

## God finds it hard to be tough

¹¹Yahweh said to the Yisra'elites, 'Isn't it the case that from the Misrayimites, from the Amorites, from the Ammonites, from the Pelishtites . . . ¹²And the Tsidonites and Amaleq and Ma'on, they afflicted you, and you cried out to me and I delivered you from their hand. ¹³But you – you abandoned me and served other gods. Therefore I won't deliver you again.

¹⁴Go and cry out to the gods that you've chosen. They can deliver you in your time of pressure.'

¹⁵But the Yisra'elites said to Yahweh, 'We've done wrong. You yourself, act towards us in accordance with what's good in your eyes. Only please rescue us this day.' ¹⁶They removed the foreign gods from among them and served Yahweh, and his heart was overwhelmed by Yisra'el's oppression.

¹⁷The Ammonites had themselves called out and camped in Gil'ad, and the Yisra'elites gathered and camped at The Watchtower. ¹⁸The company (Gil'ad's officers) said, one to his neighbour, 'Who is the man who will start battling against the Ammonites? He's to be head over all the people who live in Gil'ad.'

**11** Now Yiphtah the Gil'adite was a forceful strong man, but he was the son of a whore. Gil'ad fathered Yiphtah, ²but Gil'ad's wife gave birth to sons for him, and his wife's sons grew up and drove Yiphtah out. They said to him, 'You're to have no domain of your own in our father's household, because you're the son of another woman.' ³So Yiphtah ran away from before his brothers and lived in the region of Good. Empty-headed people collected together to Yiphtah and went out with him.

⁴After a time, the Ammonites battled with Yisra'el, ⁵and when the Ammonites battled with Yisra'el, the Gil'adite elders went to get Yiphtah from the region of Good. ⁶They said to Yiphtah, 'Come, will you, and be our commander, so we can battle against the Ammonites.'

## An invitation Yiphtah can't refuse

⁷Yiphtah said to the Gil'adite elders, 'You're the people who were hostile to me and drove me out of my father's household, aren't you. So why have you come to me now when things are pressing for you?' ⁸The Gil'adite elders said to Yiphtah, 'That's why we've come back to you now, so you can go with us and battle against the Ammonites, and you will be head of all the people living in Gil'ad for us.'

⁹Yiphtah said to the Gil'adite elders, 'If you're bringing me back to battle against the Ammonites and Yahweh gives them over before me, I myself will be your head.' ¹⁰The Gil'adite elders said to Yiphtah, 'Yahweh

himself will be listening between us if we don't act in accordance with your word, just so.' ¹¹So Yiphtah went with the Gil'adite elders, and the people made him head and commander over them. Yiphtah spoke all his words before Yahweh at The Watchtower.

¹²Yiphtah sent envoys to the Ammonites' king to say, 'What is between me and you that you've come against me to battle against my land?' ¹³The Ammonites' king said to Yiphtah's envoys, 'Yisra'el took my land when it went up from Misrayim, from the Armon as far as the Yabboq, and as far as the Yarden. So now do give it back peacefully.'

¹⁴Yiphtah once again sent envoys to the Ammonites' king. ¹⁵He said to him, 'Yiphtah has said this: "Yisra'el didn't take Mo'ab's land or the Ammonites' land, ¹⁶because when they went up from Misrayim, Yisra'el went through the wilderness as far as the Reed Sea, then came to Qadesh. ¹⁷Yisra'el sent envoys to the king of Edom to say, 'Please may I pass through your country', but the king of Edom didn't listen. It also sent to the king of Mo'ab and he wasn't willing. Yisra'el lived at Qadesh, ¹⁸then went through the wilderness and went round the country of Edom and the country of Mo'ab, and came east of the country of Mo'ab. They camped across the Arnon and they didn't come inside Mo'ab's border, because Mo'ab's border is the Arnon.

## How Yisra'el tried to be peaceable

¹⁹Then Yisra'el sent envoys to Sihon king of the Amorites, king of Heshbon. Yisra'el said to him, 'Please may I pass through your country to get to my place.' ²⁰But Sihon didn't trust Yisra'el to pass through his border. Sihon gathered his entire company and camped at Yahats, and battled with Yisra'el. ²¹But Yahweh the God of Yisra'el gave Sihon and his entire company into Yisra'el's hand, and they struck them down. So Yisra'el took possession of the entire country of the Amorites living in that country. ²²They took possession of the entire border of the Amorites from the Arnon as far as the Yabboq, and from the wilderness to the Yarden.

²³So now, Yahweh the God of Yisra'el – he dispossessed the Amorites from before his people Yisra'el, and are you to dispossess it? ²⁴Won't you possess what Kemosh your god enabled you to possess, and we'll possess all that Yahweh our God dispossessed from before us? ²⁵And are you now so much better than Balaq ben Tsippor, king of Mo'ab? Did he argue at all with Yisra'el or battle at all with them? ²⁶While Yisra'el has been living in Heshbon and in its daughter-towns, in Ar'or and in its daughter-towns, and in all the towns that are on the sides of the Arnon for 300 years, why haven't you rescued them during this time? ²⁷I for my part haven't wronged you, but you for your part are dealing badly with me by battling against me. May Yahweh, who exercises authority, decide authoritatively today between the Yisra'elites and the Ammonites."'

²⁸The Ammmonites' king didn't listen to the words of Yiphtah which he sent to him. ²⁹Then Yahweh's spirit came on Yiphtah and he passed through Gil'ad and Menashsheh, passed Watchtower in Gil'ad and from Watchtower in Gil'ad passed on to the Ammonites.

## The man whose promise makes the blood run cold

³⁰Yiphtah made a pledge to Yahweh: 'If you do actually give the Ammonites into my hand, ³¹then the one coming out to meet me, who comes out of the doors of my house when I come back from the Ammonites with things being well, will be Yahweh's. I shall offer this one up as a burnt offering.'

³²So Yiphtah passed on to the Ammonites to do battle against them, and Yahweh gave them into his hand. ³³He struck them down from Aro'er as far as when you come to Minnit, twenty towns, and as far as Keramim Meadow, in a very great rout. So the Ammonites bowed down before the Yisra'elites.

³⁴Yiphtah came home to The Watchtower, and there was his daughter coming out to meet him with a tambourine and with dancing. There was just her, an only child; apart from her he had no son or daughter. ³⁵When he saw her, he tore his clothes and said, 'Oh, my daughter, you've bent me down, bent me down; you yourself have become someone bringing disaster on me. I opened my mouth myself to Yahweh. I can't go back.' ³⁶She said to him,

'Father, you opened your mouth to Yahweh. Do to me as it came from your mouth, after Yahweh has performed full redress for you from your enemies, the Ammonites.'

<sup>37</sup>She said to her father, 'May this thing be done for me. Let me go for two months so I can walk and go down on the mountains and bewail my girlhood, I and my friends.' <sup>38</sup>He said, 'Go', and sent her for two months. She and her friends went and bewailed her girlhood on the mountains. <sup>39</sup>At the end of two months she came back to her father and he performed the pledge that he had made in connection with her. She had not had sex with a man.

It became a decree in Yisra'el: <sup>40</sup>from time to time Yisra'elite girls would go to commemorate the daughter of Yiphtah the Gil'adite, for four days in the year.

*Shibboleth*

**12** Then the Ephrayimites had themselves called out, crossed to Tsaphon and said to Yiphtah, 'Why did you cross over to battle against the Ammonites and not call for us to go with you? We'll burn your house in fire over you.' <sup>2</sup>Yiphtah said to them, 'I was involved in an argument, my people and the Ammonites, seriously. I called out to you and you didn't deliver me from their hand. <sup>3</sup>I saw that you were not a deliverer and I took my life in the palm of my hand and passed over to the Ammonites, and Yahweh gave them into my hand. So why have you gone up against me this day to do battle against me?'

<sup>4</sup>Yiphtah collected all the Gil'adites and did battle with Ephrayim. The Gil'adites struck Ephrayim down, because they said, 'You're Ephrayimite escapees, Gil'ad within Ephrayim – within Menashsheh.' <sup>5</sup>Gil'ad captured Ephrayim's Yarden crossings, and when Ephrayimite escapees would say, 'I want to cross', the Gil'adites said to him, 'Are you an Ephrayimite?', and he said, 'No'. <sup>6</sup>They then said to him, 'Say *shibbolet*, please', and he said *sibbolet*, and couldn't speak in that way. So they took hold of him and killed him by the Yarden crossings. Forty-two thousand Ephrayimites fell at that time.

<sup>7</sup>Yiphtah exercised authority for Yisra'el for six years. Then Yiphtah the Gil'adite died, and was buried in the towns of Gil'ad.

<sup>8</sup>After him, Ibtsan from Bet Lehem exercised authority for Yisra'el. <sup>9</sup>He had thirty sons and thirty daughters whom he sent off abroad, and he brought in thirty girls for his sons from abroad. He exercised authority for Yisra'el for seven years. <sup>10</sup>Ibtsan died, and was buried in Bet Lehem.

<sup>11</sup>After him, Elon the Zebulunite exercised authority for Yisra'el. He exercised authority for Yisra'el for ten years. <sup>12</sup>Elon the Zubulunite died, and was buried in Ayyalon in the region of Zebulun.

<sup>13</sup>After him, Abdon ben Hillel the Pir'atonite exercised authority for Yisra'el. <sup>14</sup>He had forty sons and thirty grandsons, riding on seventy donkeys. He exercised authority for Yisra'el for eight years. <sup>15</sup>Abdon ben Hillel the Pir'atonite died, and was buried in Pir'aton in the region of Ephrayim, in the highland of the Amaleqites.

*Entertaining angels unawares*

**13** The Yisra'elites again did what was bad in Yahweh's eyes and Yahweh gave them into the hand of the Pelishtites for forty years. <sup>2</sup>There was a certain man from Tsor'ah, from the kin-group of Dan. His name was Manoah. His wife was infertile; she had not given birth. <sup>3</sup>Yahweh's envoy appeared to the woman and said to her, 'Here, please, you're infertile, you haven't given birth, but you're going to get pregnant and give birth to a son. <sup>4</sup>So now keep watch, please, so you don't drink wine or liquor and don't eat anything taboo, <sup>5</sup>because here, you're going to get pregnant and give birth to a son, and no razor is to go up on to his head, because the boy is to be a consecrated person for God from the womb. He's the one who will start to deliver Yisra'el from the hand of the Pelishtites.'

<sup>6</sup>The woman came and said to her husband, 'A supernatural man came to me; his appearance was like that of a divine envoy, very awe-inspiring. I didn't ask him where he was from and he didn't tell me his name. <sup>7</sup>He said to me, "Here, you're going to get pregnant and give birth to a son. So now don't drink wine or liquor and don't eat anything taboo, because the boy's to be a consecrated person for God from the womb until the day of his death."'

[8]Manoah entreated Yahweh: 'Pardon me, Lord, may the supernatural man whom you sent please come to us again and instruct us what we're to do for the boy who's to be born?' [9]God listened to Manoah's voice, and God's envoy again came to the woman. She was sitting in the fields and Manoah her husband was not with her. [10]The woman hurried and ran and told her husband, and said to him, 'There, the man who came that day has appeared to me.'

## A logical woman

[11]Manoah got up and followed his wife. He came to the man and said to him, 'Are you the man who spoke to the woman?' He said, 'I am.' [12]Manoah said, 'May your words come true now! What will be the rule for the boy and the work for him?' [13]Yahweh's envoy said to Manoah, 'The woman is to keep watch in connection with everything that I said. [14]Of anything that comes from the grapevine she's not to eat. Wine and liquor she's not to drink. Anything taboo she's not to eat. Everything that I ordered her, she's to keep watch.'

[15]Manoah said to Yahweh's envoy, 'We'll please hold you back and prepare a kid goat from the flock before you.' [16]Yahweh's envoy said to Manoah, 'If you hold me back, I won't eat of your meal, but if you make a burnt offering, you may offer it up for Yahweh' (because Manoah didn't know that it was Yahweh's envoy). [17]Manoah said to Yahweh's envoy, 'What is your name? When your words come true, we will honour you.' [18]Yahweh's envoy said to him, 'Why is it that you ask my name when it's extraordinary?'

[19]Manoah got a kid goat from the flock and a grain offering and offered them up on a crag for Yahweh, and he did something extraordinary as Manoah and his wife were looking. [20]When the flame went up from on the altar to the heavens, Yahweh's envoy went up in the altar flame as Manoah and his wife were looking. They fell on their faces to the earth. [21]Yahweh's envoy didn't appear ever again to Manoah and his wife.

Then Manoah knew that it had been Yahweh's envoy. [22]Manoah said to his wife, 'We'll die, we'll die, because we've seen God!' [23]His wife said to him, 'If Yahweh wanted to put us to death, he wouldn't have received the burnt offering and the grain offering from our hand and he wouldn't have let us see all these things, or just now have let us hear something like this.' [24]The woman gave birth to a son and named him Shimshon [Samson]. The boy grew, and Yahweh blessed him. [25]Yahweh's spirit started to impel him in Dan's Camp between Tsor'ah and Eshta'ol.

## The right one for me

**14** Shimshon went down to Timnah and saw a woman in Timnah among the Pelishtite girls. [2]He went up and told his father and his mother and said, 'I saw a woman in Timnah among the Pelishtite girls, so now, get her for me as wife.' [3]His father and his mother said to him, 'Isn't there a wife among your brothers' girls or among all my people, that you're going to take a wife from the foreskinned Pelishtites?' Shimshon said to his father, 'Get that one for me, because she's right in my eyes.' [4]His father and his mother didn't know that it stemmed from Yahweh, because he was looking for an opportunity from the Pelishtites. At that time the Pelishtites were ruling over Yisra'el.

[5]Shimshon went down to Timnah with his father and his mother and they came as far as the vineyards at Timnah. And there, a lion whelp, roaring as it met him. [6]Yahweh's spirit thrust itself on to him and he tore it apart as one might tear apart a kid. There was nothing in his hand. He didn't tell his father and his mother what he'd done.

[7]He went down and spoke to the woman. She was right in Shimshon's eyes. [8]He went back some time later to get her, and he turned aside to see the remains of the lion. There, a swarm of bees was in the lion's corpse, with honey. [9]He scraped it out into his palms and went on, eating it. He went to his father and to his mother and gave them some, and they ate it. He didn't tell them that he had scraped the honey from the lion's corpse.

[10]His father went down to the woman and Shimshon made a banquet there, because that was what the young men used to do. [11]When they saw him, they got thirty good friends and they came to be with him.

## The conundrum

¹²Shimshon said to them, 'I shall propound a conundrum to you, please. If you can properly explain it to me in the seven days of the banquet and solve it, I'll give you thirty shirts and thirty changes of clothing. ¹³But if you can't explain it, you're to give me thirty shirts and thirty changes of clothing.' They said to him, 'Propound your conundrum and we'll listen.' ¹⁴He said to them:

> From the eater there came out something to
> eat,
> From the vigorous there came out something
> sweet.

They couldn't explain the conundrum for three days.

¹⁵On the seventh day they said to Shimshon's wife, 'Coax your husband so he explains the conundrum for us, or else we'll burn you and your father's household in fire. Was it to dispossess us that you invited us? Wasn't it?' ¹⁶So Shimshon's wife wailed at him and said, 'Really you dislike me. You don't love me. You propounded a conundrum to my people and you haven't explained it to me.' He said to her, 'There, I didn't explain it to my father and to my mother, and am I to explain it to you?' ¹⁷She wailed at him for the seven days that their banquet lasted. On the seventh day he explained it to her, because she pressed him, and she explained the conundrum to the members of her people. ¹⁸So the men of the town said to him on the seventh day, before the sun went down:

> What's sweeter than honey,
> What's more vigorous than a lion?

He said to them,

> If you had not ploughed with my heifer
> You would not have solved my conundrum!

¹⁹Yahweh's spirit thrust itself on to him and he went down to Ashqelon and from them he struck down thirty men. He got their strip and gave the changes of clothing to the men who had explained the conundrum. But his anger raged and he went up to his father's house.

²⁰Shimshon's wife came to belong to his good friend, one who had been his friend.

## Shimshon's redress

**15** After some time, during the time of the wheat harvest, Shimshon visited his wife with a kid goat from the flock. He said, 'I want to come in and have sex with my wife in the room', but her father wouldn't let him come in. ²Her father said, 'I said for sure that you totally disliked her and I gave her to your good friend. Her little sister is better than her. She can be yours in place of her, can't she?' ³Shimshon said to them, 'This time I'm free of guilt in relation to the Pelishtites when I deal badly with them!'

⁴Shimshon went and caught 300 foxes and got torches. He made them face tail to tail and put a torch between two tails, in the middle, ⁵set fire to the torches and sent them off into the Pelishtites' standing grain. He burned up the stacked grain, and both the standing grain and the olive vineyard. ⁶The Pelishtites said, 'Who did this?' And they said, 'Shimshon, the son-in-law of the Timnite, because he took his wife and gave her to his good friend.' So the Pelishtites went up and burned her and her father in fire.

⁷Shimshon said to them, 'If you act like this, I shall definitely have redress against you, and only after shall I leave off.' ⁸He struck them down, leg upon thigh, in a great rout. He then went down and lived in a cleft in Etam Rock. ⁹The Pelishtites went up and camped against Yehudah and ran loose in Lehi, ¹⁰and the Yehudahites said, 'Why have you gone up against us?' They said, 'We've gone up to bind Shimshon, to do to him as he did to us.' ¹¹So 3,000 men from Yehudah went down to the cleft in Etam Rock and said to Shimshon, 'Don't you acknowledge that the Pelishtites are ruling over us? So why have you done this to us?' He said to them, 'As they did to me, so I did to them.'

## Jawbone

¹²They said to him, 'It's to bind you that we've gone down, to give you over into the Pelishtites' hand.' Shimshon said to them,

'Swear to me that you yourselves won't attack me.' ¹³They said to him, 'No, but we'll simply bind you and give you over into their hand. We definitely won't put you to death.' So they bound him with two new ropes and got him to go up from the Rock. ¹⁴As he came to Lehi and the Pelishtites shouted on meeting him, Yahweh's spirit thrust itself on to him and the ropes that were on his arms became like flax that burns up in fire. His bonds melted from on his hands. ¹⁵He found a fresh donkey jawbone, put out his hand and got it, and struck down a thousand men with it. ¹⁶Shimshon said,

> With a donkey jawbone – a donkey-heap, two
>    donkey-heaps;
> With a donkey jawbone I've struck down a
>    thousand.

¹⁷As he finished speaking, he threw the jawbone from his hand. He called that place Lehi ['Jawbone'] Height. ¹⁸He was very thirsty. He called to Yahweh and said, 'You yourself have given this great deliverance by your servant's hand. Now am I to die of thirst and fall into the hand of the foreskinned?' ¹⁹God split the hollow that was at Lehi, and water came out from it. He drank, and his spirit came back and he revived. That's why it has been named Haqqore ['The Caller'] Spring, which is in Lehi, until this day. ²⁰He exercised authority for Yisra'el in the time of the Pelishtites for twenty years.

## Love actually

**16** Shimshon went to Azzah and saw there a woman who was a whore, and he had sex with her. ²Someone said to the Gazites, 'Shimshon has come here.' They came round and laid an ambush for him all night at the town gateway. They were still all night, saying 'At morning light, we'll kill him.' ³But Shimshon lay in bed until midnight, then got up at midnight, took hold of the doors of the town gateway and the two gateposts, pulled them out with the bar, put them on his shoulders and took them up to the top of the mountain that's east of Hebron. ⁴After that he loved a woman in Wadi Soreq named Delilah. ⁵The Pelishtites' lords went

up to her and said to her, 'Coax him and see whereby is his great energy and whereby we can overcome him and bind him, so as to subdue him. We – we'll each give you 1,100 in silver.' ⁶So Delilah said to Shimshon, 'Please tell me whereby is your great energy and whereby you could be bound so as to subdue you.' ⁷Shimshon said to her, 'If they bind me with seven fresh cords that haven't been dried, I'd become weak. I'd be like any human being.' ⁸So the Pelishtites' lords took up to her seven fresh cords that hadn't been dried and she bound him with them, ⁹while the ambush was sitting waiting for her in a room. She said to him, 'Pelishtites are on you, Shimshon!', and he snapped the tendons as a strand of fibre snaps when it smells fire. So his energy didn't become known. ¹⁰Delilah said to Shimshon, 'Here, you've played about with me. You've spoken lies to me. Now, please tell me whereby you could be bound.' ¹¹He said to her, 'If they actually bind me with new ropes with which no work has been done, I'd become weak, I'd be like any human being.' ¹²So Delilah got new ropes and bound him with them, and said to him, 'Pelishtites are on you, Shimshon!', while the ambush was sitting waiting in a room. He snapped them from on his arms like a thread.

### He didn't realize that Yahweh had left him

¹³Delilah said to Shimshon, 'Until now you've played about with me. You've spoken lies to me. Tell me whereby you could be bound.' He said to her, 'If you weave seven braids from my head with the web.' ¹⁴She pinned it with a peg and said to him, 'Pelishtites are on you, Shimshon!' He woke up from his sleep and pulled out the peg (the loom) and the web. ¹⁵She said to him, 'How can you say "I love you" when your mind isn't with me? These three times you've played about with me and not told me whereby is your great energy.' ¹⁶Because she pressed him with her words all the time and begged him, and his spirit was tired to death, ¹⁷he told her everything in his mind. He said to her, 'No razor has gone up on my head, because I've been a consecrated person for God from my mother's womb. If my hair were cut, my energy would depart from me and I'd be weak. I'd be like any human

being.' <sup>18</sup>Delilah saw that he had told her
everything in his mind, and she sent and called
for the Pelishtites' lords: 'Come up this time,
because he's told me everything in his mind.'
The Pelishtites' lords went up to her and took
up the silver in their hand.

<sup>19</sup>She got him to go to sleep on her lap, and
called for a man and cut off the seven braids
on his head. She started to humble him, and
his energy departed from him. <sup>20</sup>She said,
'Pelishtites are on you, Shimshon!' He woke up
from his sleep and said, 'I'll go out as at other
times and shake myself free.' He didn't know
that Yahweh had departed from him.

<sup>21</sup>The Pelishtites took hold of him and
gouged out his eyes. They took him down to
Azzah and bound him in copper shackles, and
he became a grinder in the prison.

### But Shimshon's hair began to grow again

<sup>22</sup>But the hair on his head started to grow,
when it had been cut off.

<sup>23</sup>Now the Pelishtites' lords gathered to offer
a great sacrifice for Dagan their god, and for a
celebration. They said, 'Our god has given
Shimshon, our enemy, into our hand.' <sup>24</sup>The
people saw him and praised their god, because
(they said) 'Our god has given our enemy into
our hand, the one who wasted our country
and multiplied the number of us run through.'
<sup>25</sup>When their heart felt good, they said 'Call for
Shimshon. He must make fun for us.' So they
called for Shimshon from the prison house and
he entertained them.

They stood him between the pillars, <sup>26</sup>and
Shimshon said to the boy who had a strong
hold of him by the hand, 'Let me be and let
me feel the pillars that the house depends on,
so I can lean on them.' <sup>27</sup>The house was full of
men and women. All the Pelishtites' lords were
there. On the roof were some 3,000 men and
women watching Shimshon, making fun.

<sup>28</sup>Shimshon called to Yahweh and said, 'My
Lord Yahweh, please be mindful of me. Please
just this once, God, make me strong so I can
take redress from the Pelishtites, redress for
one of my two eyes.' <sup>29</sup>And Shimshon grasped
the two middle pillars that the house was
established on and leaned on them, one with
his right hand and one with his left. <sup>30</sup>Shimshon

said, 'I myself can die with the Pelishtites', and
he pushed energetically. The house fell on the
lords and on the entire company that was in it.
The people whom he put to death when he died
were more than he put to death when he lived.

<sup>31</sup>His brothers and his father's entire
household went down, lifted him, took him up,
and buried him between Tsor'ah and Eshta'ol
in the grave of Manoah his father. He had
exercised authority for Yisra'el for twenty years.

### Everyone did what was all right in their own eyes

**17** There was a man from the highland
of Ephrayim; his name was Mikah.
<sup>2</sup>He said to his mother, 'The 1,100 in silver that
were taken from you, and you uttered a curse
and also said it in my ears: here, the silver is
with me. I'm the one who took it.' His mother
said, 'May my son be blessed by Yahweh.' <sup>3</sup>He
gave back the 1,100 in silver to his mother, and
his mother said 'I'm definitely making the
silver sacred for Yahweh from my hand for my
son to make a statue and a cast image. I now
give it back to you.' <sup>4</sup>So he gave the silver back
to his mother and she got 200 in silver and
gave it to a smith. He made a statue and a cast
image, and it was in Mikah's house.

<sup>5</sup>This man Mikah had a house of God.
He made a chasuble and effigies, and
commissioned one of his sons and he became
priest for him. <sup>6</sup>At that time there was no
king in Yisra'el. An individual would do what
was all right in his own eyes. <sup>7</sup>But there was
a boy from Bet Lehem in Yehudah, from the
clan of Yehudah. He was a Levite and had
been residing there, <sup>8</sup>but this individual went
from the town, from Bet Lehem in Yehudah,
to reside wherever he could find somewhere,
and he came to the highland of Ephrayim,
as far as the house of Mikah, as he made his
way. <sup>9</sup>Mikah said to him, 'Where do you come
from?' He said to him, 'I'm a Levite from Bet
Lehem in Yehudah but I'm going so as to reside
wherever I can find somewhere.' <sup>10</sup>Mikah said
to him, 'Stay with me. You'll be a father and a
priest for me. I'll give you ten in silver a year,
a set of clothes and your living.' So the Levite
went. <sup>11</sup>The Levite agreed to live with the man,
and the boy became to him like one of his sons.

¹²So Mikah commissioned the Levite, and the boy became priest for him. He was in Mikah's household. ¹³Mikah said, 'Now I know that Yahweh will be good to me, because the Levite has become priest for me.'

## Desperate Dan

**18** At that time there was no king in Yisra'el, and at that time the clan of Dan was looking for a domain for itself to live in, because until that day nothing had fallen to it as a domain among Yisra'el's clans.

²The Danites sent from their kin-group five men from their total number, men of ability, from Tsor'ah and from Eshta'ol, to investigate the country and search it out. So they said to them, 'Go and search out the country', and they came to the highland of Ephrayim, as far as Mikah's house, and stayed the night there.

³When they were near Mikah's house and recognized the young Levite's accent they turned aside there and said to him, 'Who brought you here? What are you doing in this place? What are you here for?' ⁴He said to them, 'Mikah acted like this and like this for me. He hired me and I became priest for him.' ⁵They said to him, 'Please ask of God so we can know if the journey on which we're going will be successful.' ⁶The priest said to them, 'Go, things will be well. The journey on which you're going is in front of Yahweh.'

⁷The five men went and came to Layish. They saw the people that was within it, living in confidence in accordance with the rule of the Tsidonites, calm and confident, with no one in the region possessing them by force, bringing shame regarding anything; though they were far away from the Tsidonites and had nothing to do with anyone.

⁸So they came to their brothers in Tsor'ah and Eshta'ol, and their brothers said to them, 'What did you find?' ⁹They said, 'Set off, let's go up against them, because we've looked at the region; there, it's very good, and you're sitting still! Don't be slow to go, to come and take possession of the region. ¹⁰When you come, you'll come to a people that feels confident, and the region is wide on both sides. Because God has given it into your hand, a place where there's no lack of anything that's in the earth.'

## The unfortunate Mikah

¹¹So 600 men of the Danite clan from Tsor'ah and Eshta'ol, wrapped round with battle equipment, moved on from there ¹²and went up and camped in Ye'arim Township in Yehudah (for that reason they call that place 'Dan's Camp' until this day – there, it's west of Ye'arim Township). ¹³They passed on from there to the highland of Ephrayim and came as far as Mikah's house. ¹⁴The five men who had gone to investigate the region of Layish said to their brothers, 'Do you know that in these houses there is a chasuble and effigies and a statue and a cast image? Now acknowledge what you're to do.'

¹⁵They turned aside there and came into the young Levite's house at Mikah's house and asked him whether things were well with him, ¹⁶while 600 men wrapped round with battle equipment were standing at the entrance of the gateway (the men who were from the Danites). ¹⁷The five men who had gone to investigate the country went up, came in there, took the statue, the chasuble, the effigies and the cast image, while the priest was standing at the entrance of the gateway, with the 600 men wrapped round with battle equipment.

¹⁸When these men came into Mikah's house and took the statue with the chasuble, the effigies and the cast image, the priest said to them, 'What are you doing?' ¹⁹They said to him, 'Quiet. Put your hand on your mouth. Go with us and become a father and a priest for us. Is it better for you to be a priest for the household of one man or to be a priest for a clan, a kin-group in Yisra'el?'

²⁰The priest's heart felt good, so he got the chasuble, the effigies and the cast image, and came among the company. ²¹They turned their face and went, and put the little ones, the livestock and the valuables before them.

## The unfortunate people of Layish

²²When they had gone a distance from Mikah's house, the men who were in the households that were near Mikah's house had themselves called out, caught up with the Danites ²³and called to the Danites. They turned round and said to Mikah, 'What's the

matter with you, that you've had yourself called out?' [24]He said, 'You took my gods that I made, and the priest, and you went. What do I still have? And you say to me, "What's the matter with you?"' [25]The Danites said to him, 'Don't make your voice heard among us, or men who are fierce in spirit may come upon you and gather up your life and the life of your household.'

[26]So the Danites went on their way. Mikah saw that they were stronger than him, turned his face and went back to his house, [27]while they took what Mikah had made and the priest that he had. They came to Layish, to a people calm and confident, and struck them down with the mouth of the sword, and burned their town in fire. [28]There was no one to rescue because it was far away from Tsidon and they had nothing to do with anyone (it was in the vale that belonged to Bet-rehob).

They built up the town and lived in it, [29]and named the town Dan, after the name of Dan, their ancestor, who had been born to Yisra'el (the town's name was Layish originally, however). [30]The Danites set up the statue for themselves, and Yehonatan ben Gershom, son of Mosheh, he and his sons, were priests for the clan of Dan until the time of the country's exile. [31]They put in place for themselves Mikah's statue that he had made, the entire time that the house of God was at Shiloh.

## The broken marriage that might recover

**19** At that time, when there was no king in Yisra'el, a Levite individual residing in the remote parts of the highland of Ephrayim got himself a woman as a secondary wife from Bet Lehem in Yehudah, [2]but his wife whored against him and went from being with him to her father's household in Bet Lehem in Yehudah, and she was there for a full four months. [3]Her husband set off and followed her to speak to her heart to get her to come back. His boy and a pair of donkeys were with him.

She let him come into her father's house, and the girl's father saw him and rejoiced to meet him. [4]His father-in-law, the girl's father, took strong hold of him, and he stayed with him for three days. They ate and drank and stayed the night there.

[5]On the fourth day they started early in the morning and got up to go, but the girl's father said to his son-in-law, 'Strengthen your heart with a bit of bread, and go afterwards.' [6]So the two of them sat down and ate together, and drank. The girl's father said to the man, 'Do resolve to stay the night. Your heart will feel good.' [7]The man got up to go, but his father-in-law pressed him, and he went back and stayed the night there.

[8]They started early in the morning on the fifth day to go, but the girl's father said, 'Do strengthen your heart and wait till the day declines', and the two of them ate. [9]The man got up to go, he and his wife and his boy, but his father-in-law, the girl's father, said to him, 'Here, please, the day is slackening towards evening. Please stay the night. Here, it's the time of day for spreading tents. Stay the night here. Your heart will feel good, and you can start early on your way tomorrow and go to your tent.'

## A foreign town won't be safe?

[10]The man was not willing to stay the night, and he got up and went. He came as far as in front of Yebus (i.e. Yerushalaim). With him were a pair of laden donkeys, and his wife was with him. [11]As they were near Yebus and the day had worn far on, the boy said to his lord, 'Come on, please let's turn aside into this town of the Yebusites and stay the night in it.' [12]His lord said to him, 'We won't turn aside into a foreign town where there aren't any Yisra'elites. We'll pass on as far as Gib'ah.' [13]So he said to his boy, 'Come on, we'll get near one of the places and stay the night in Gib'ah or in The Height.' [14]So they passed on, and as they went, the sun set on them beside Gib'ah which belongs to Binyamin, [15]and they turned aside there to come in to stay the night in Gib'ah.

They came in and sat in the town square, but there was no one gathering them into his house to stay the night. [16]But there, an old man came in from his work, from the fields, in the evening. The man was from the highland of Ephrayim; he was a resident in Gib'ah, while the men of the place were Binyaminites. [17]He lifted his eyes and saw the man on a journey, in the town square.

The old man said, 'Where are you going and where do you come from?' ¹⁸He said to him, 'We're passing through from Bet-lehem in Yehudah as far as the remote parts of the highland of Ephrayim. I'm from there but I went as far as Bet Lehem in Yehudah and I'm going to Yahweh's house. But there's no one gathering me into his house. ¹⁹Our donkeys have got both straw and fodder and I and your handmaid and the boy with your servants have also got bread and wine. There's no lack of anything.' ²⁰The old man said, 'Welcome to you. All your needs are definitely my responsibility. You're definitely not to stay the night in the square.'

## The horrific ending

²¹So he brought him into his house and fed the donkeys, and they bathed their feet and ate and drank. ²²While they were making their heart feel good, there, men from the town, scoundrels, surrounded the house, banging on the door. They said to the man who was the master of the house, the old man, 'Bring out the man who came to your house, so we can have sex with him.' ²³The man who was the master of the house went out to them and said to them, 'No, my brothers, don't do something so bad, will you, after this man has come to my house. Don't perform this villainy. ²⁴Here is my daughter, a young girl, and his wife. I'll bring them out to you, please. Humble them. Do to them what's good in your eyes. But to this man you will not perform this villainy.'

²⁵The men were not willing to listen to him, so the man took strong hold of his wife and made her go out to them, outside. They had sex with her and acted abusively to her all night until morning, and sent her off as dawn came up. ²⁶The woman came as morning turned its face and fell at the entrance of the man's house where her lord was, until daylight.

²⁷Her lord got up in the morning, opened the doors of the house and went out to go on his journey, and there was the woman who was his secondary wife, fallen at the entrance of the house, her hands on the threshold. ²⁸He said to her, 'Get up, let's go.' There was no response, so he got her on to the donkey. The man set off and went to his own place. ²⁹He came to his house and got a knife, took

strong hold of his wife, cut her up limb by limb into twelve parts and sent her off through Yisra'el's entire border. ³⁰Everyone who saw said, 'Such a thing hasn't happened and hasn't been seen from the day the Yisra'elites went up from the country of Misrayim until this day. Apply yourself to this. Take counsel. Speak.'

## The outrage

**20** All the Yisra'elites went out and the assembly congregated as one person, from Dan as far as Be'er Sheba and the region of Gil'ad, to Yahweh at The Watchtower. ²The cornerstones of the entire people, all Yisra'el's clans, took their stand as the congregation of God's people, 400,000 men on foot, drawing a sword. ³The Binyaminites heard that the Yisra'elites had gone up to The Watchtower.

The Yisra'elites said, 'Speak: how did this bad thing happen?' ⁴The man who was a Levite, the husband of the woman who had been killed, said, 'I came, I and my secondary wife, to Gib'ah which belongs to Binyamin, to stay the night. ⁵The landowners in Gib'ah set upon me and surrounded the house against me at night. They thought about killing me and they humbled my wife, and she died. ⁶So I took hold of my wife and cut her in pieces, and sent her off through every area in Yisra'el's domain, because they had committed a deliberate wickedness that's an act of villainy in Yisra'el. ⁷Here, all you Yisra'elites, come up with your word, your counsel, here and now!'

⁸The entire company got up as one man, saying 'We won't go, not one of us, to his tent; we won't depart, not one of us, to his home. ⁹This is the thing that we will now do to Gib'ah, against it, by lot. ¹⁰We'll get ten men per hundred for all Yisra'el's clans, a hundred per thousand, a thousand per ten thousand, to get provisions for the company, to take action by going to Geba in Binyamin in accordance with the total villainy that it's done in Yisra'el.'

## The redress that misfires

¹¹So all the Yisra'elites gathered against the town, united as one man. ¹²The Yisra'elite

clans sent men through all the Binyaminite clans, saying, 'What is this bad thing that has happened among you? [13]So now give us the scoundrels who are in Gib'ah. We'll put them to death and burn away what is bad from Yisra'el.' But the Binyaminites were not willing to listen to the voice of their brothers, the Yisra'elites, [14]and the Binyaminites gathered from the towns to Gib'ah to go out to do battle with the Yisra'elites.

[15]That day the Binyaminites registered from the towns 26,000 men drawing a sword, apart from the people living in Gib'ah, with 700 picked men registered [16]from this entire company, 700 picked men restricted in their right hand, each one able to sling a stone at a hair and not go wrong.

[17]The Yisra'elites apart from Binyamin registered 400,000 men drawing a sword, each one a man of battle. [18]They set off and went up to Bet-el and asked of God: the Yisra'elites said, 'Who's to go up for us first for the battle with the Binyaminites?' Yahweh said, 'Yehudah first'. [19]The Yisra'elites set off in the morning and camped against Gib'ah.

[20]So the Yisra'elites went out to do battle with Binyamin. The Yisra'elites lined up for battle with them at Gib'ah, [21]but the Binyaminites went out from Gib'ah and devastated Yisra'el that day, 22,000 men to the ground. [22]The company (the Yisra'elites) summoned up its strength and again lined up for battle in the place where they had lined up the previous day. [23]The Yisra'elites went up and wailed before Yahweh until the evening and asked of Yahweh, 'Shall we go up again to battle with the descendants of Binyamin my brother?' and Yahweh said, 'Go up against him.' [24]So the Yisra'elites drew near to the Binyaminites on the second day, [25]but Binyamin came out from Gib'ah to meet them on the second day and devastated the Yisra'elites, 18,000 more to the ground, all these men drawing a sword.

## The ambush that succeeds

[26]All the Yisra'elites and the entire company went up and came to Bet-el. They wailed and sat there before Yahweh and fasted that day until the evening, and offered up burnt offerings and well-being sacrifices before Yahweh. [27]The

Yisra'elites asked of Yahweh (God's pact chest was there at that time [28]and Pinhas son of El'azar son of Aharon was standing before him at that time), 'Shall I go out once more to battle with the descendants of Binyamin my brother, or leave off?' Yahweh said, 'Go up, because I shall give them into your hand tomorrow.' [29]Yisra'el put men in ambush against Gib'ah all round. [30]On the third day the Yisra'elites went up against the Binyaminites and lined up against Gib'ah as on other times, [31]and the Binyaminites came out to meet the company. They were drawn away from the town and began to strike down some of the company, run through, as on other times, on the causeways (of which one goes up to Bet-el and one to Gib'ah) in the fields, some thirty men in Yisra'el. [32]The Binyaminites said, 'They've taken a beating before us as before', but the Yisra'elites had said, 'We'll flee and draw them away from the town on to the causeways.'

[33]So while all the Yisra'elites got up from their place and lined up at Ba'al Tamar, the Yisra'elite ambush was breaking out from its place, from the Geba wilderness, [34]and 10,000 picked men from all Yisra'el came from south of Gib'ah. The battle was heavy and they didn't acknowledge that something bad was closing in on them. [35]So Yahweh defeated Binyamin before Yisra'el. That day the Yisra'elites devastated Binyamin, 25,100 men, all these drawing a sword. [36a]The Binyaminites saw that they had taken a beating.

## The terrible slaughter of Binyamin

[36b]The Yisra'elites had given ground to Binyamin, because they relied on the ambush that they set against Gib'ah. [37]While one ambush quickly charged against Gib'ah, the other ambush advanced and struck down the entire town with the mouth of the sword. [38]The set time for the Yisra'elites with the ambush was: make a great uprising of smoke go up from the town [39]and the Yisra'elites would turn about in the battle. While Binyamin started striking down some thirty men in Yisra'el, run through, because (they said) 'It's taking a terrible beating before us like the first battle', [40]when the uprising (the smoke column) started to go up from the town, Binyamin

turned his face behind him, and there, the
entire town had gone up into the heavens.

⁴¹Yisra'el circled round and Binyamin
became fearful because it saw that something
bad had closed in on it. ⁴²They turned their
face before Yisra'el to the wilderness road, but
the battle caught up with it, while the men
from the towns were devastating it inside it.
⁴³They surrounded Binyamin, pursued him to
Menuhah and trod him down as far as in front
of Gib'ah on the east.

⁴⁴There fell of Binyamin 18,000 that day,
all these forceful men. ⁴⁵They turned their
face and fled to the wilderness, to Rimmon
Cliff, but on the causeways they gleaned 5,000
men, then caught up with them at Gid'om,
and struck down 2,000 of them. ⁴⁶So all the
fallen from Binyamin that day were 25,000
men drawing a sword, all these forceful men.
⁴⁷Six hundred men turned their face and fled
to the wilderness, to Rimmon Cliff, and lived
at Rimmon Cliff for four months, ⁴⁸while the
Yisra'elites went back to the Binyaminites
and struck them down with the mouth of the
sword – both the entire town (the people),
and the animals and everything that was to be
found. They also burned in fire all the towns
that were to be found.

## How not to save the situation

**21** Now the Yisra'elites had sworn at The
Watchtower, 'None of us will give his
daughter to Binyamin as a wife.' ²The company
came to Bet-el and sat there before God until
the evening. They lifted up their voice, and
wailed and wailed, loudly. ³They said, 'Why,
Yahweh God of Yisra'el, has this happened
in Yisra'el, so a clan is counted missing today
from Yisra'el?'

⁴Next day the people started early and built
an altar there, and offered up whole offerings
and well-being sacrifices. ⁵The Yisra'elites said,
'Who is there from all Yisra'el's clans that didn't
come up in the congregation to Yahweh?'
Because there had been a great oath regarding
anyone who didn't come up to Yahweh at The
Watchtower: 'He will absolutely be put to death.'
⁶So the Yisra'elites felt sorry towards
Binyamin their brother and said, 'Today a clan
has been cut off from Yisra'el. ⁷What can we do

for them, for wives for those who are left, when
we have sworn by Yahweh not to give them any
of our daughters as wives?'

⁸They said, 'Who is there from Yisra'el's
clans who didn't go up to Yahweh at The
Watchtower?' There, no one had come
from Yabesh-in-Gil'ad to the camp, to the
congregation; ⁹the company had registered, and
there was no one there from the people living in
Yabesh-in-Gil'ad. ¹⁰So the assembly sent 12,000
of the forceful men and ordered them, 'Go and
strike down the people living in Yabesh-in-
Gil'ad with the mouth of the sword, and the
women and little ones. ¹¹This is the thing that
you're to do: you're to devote every male and
every woman who has slept with a male.'

¹²But they found from the people living in
Yabesh-in-Gil'ad 400 young girls who had
not had sex by sleeping with a male, and they
brought them to the camp at Shiloh, which
is in the country of Kena'an. ¹³The entire
assembly sent and spoke to the Binyaminites
who were at Rimmon Cliff and called out peace
to them. ¹⁴So Binyamin came back at that time
and they gave them the women whom they'd
let live from the women of Yabesh-in-Gil'ad.

## *Everyone was doing what was all right in his own eyes*

But they didn't find for them [all] in this
way. ¹⁵As the company felt sorry for Binyamin
because Yahweh had made a breach in Yisra'el's
clans, ¹⁶the elders of the assembly said, 'What
can we do for wives for those who are left,
because the women have been annihilated
from Binyamin?' ¹⁷They said, 'An escape
possession for Binyamin – a clan will not be
wiped out from Yisra'el! ¹⁸But we ourselves can't
give them wives from among our daughters'
(because the Yisra'elites had sworn, 'Cursed is
the person who gives a wife to Binyamin').

¹⁹So they said, 'Here, from time to time it's
Yahweh's festival at Shiloh' (which is north
of Bet-el, east of the causeway going up from
Bet-el to Shekem and south of Lebonah).
²⁰They ordered the Binyaminites, 'Go and
make an ambush in the vineyards ²¹and look.
There, if the daughters of Shiloh go out to join
in the dances, you go out of the vineyards.
Each of you capture a wife for himself from

the daughters of Shiloh, and go to the region of Binyamin. ²²When their fathers or their brothers come to argue with us, we'll say to them, "Be gracious to us over them, because we didn't each get his wife in the battle, because you yourselves didn't give them to them at a time when you would be liable.'"

²³The Binyaminites did so and carried off wives in accordance with their number from the dancers whom they seized. Then they went and returned to their domain, and built up the towns and lived in them.

²⁴The Yisra'elites went off from there at that time, each to his clan and to his kin-group. They left from there, each to his domain.

²⁵At that time there was no king in Yisra'el. Each person would do what was all right in his own eyes.

# RUTH

Ruth is a short story about the aftermath of a series of calamities that befalls an Israelite family. Although Ruth herself may be the book's most prominent character, Naomi is almost as important, and it is worth also reading the story from the angles of Elimelek, Mahlon, Kilyon, Orpah, Boaz, Obed, and other characters who are even more minor.

In the Hebrew Bible Ruth appears in the company of the Song of Songs, Lamentations, Ecclesiastes and Esther. The Jewish community reads each of these 'Five Scrolls' on one main occasion each year. Ruth is used at the Shabu'ot Festival (Pentecost), in the light of its focus on harvest. The story also provides fine examples of commitment to the Torah, and the giving of the Torah became a theme of the Shabu'ot Festival.

In the order of books in the English Bible, Ruth offers a breath of fresh air after the unpleasantness of the later stories in Judges. It contributes to the transition from Judges to 1 and 2 Samuel in another way, in that we discover at the very end of Ruth that we are reading the story of how David acquired his great-grandmother. That note adds extra significance to the fact that the book's heroine is a Moabite. Elsewhere, the Scriptures emphasize the importance of not intermarrying with people such as Moabites who could lead Israelites to serve other gods. Ruth makes explicit that foreigners who come to serve Yahweh are a different matter. Israel is always open to such foreigners. Its faith is not ethnically based.

The book presupposes a cultural context in which the men have the formal authority in society, and it tells a story about how women may nevertheless be able to take responsibility for their destiny. It makes little reference to God directly acting, and it thus reminds readers how God often works via human planning and initiative and through coincidences. And it shows how a traditional culture can provide safety nets for vulnerable people through the expectations laid on the 'restorer' (English translations often use the word *redeemer*). The restorer is a senior member of the extended family who is expected to be willing to use his resources to help members of the family get back on their feet and to restore equilibrium when things get out of order.

## How Na'omi's life falls apart

**1** During the time when the people who exercised authority were doing so, there was a famine in the country and a man went from Bet Lehem in Yehudah [Judah] to reside in Mo'abite country, he, his wife and his two sons. ²The man's name was Elimelek, his wife's name was Na'omi, and his two sons' names were Mahlon and Kilyon – Ephratites from Bet Lehem in Yehudah.

So they came to Mo'abite country and they were there, ³but Elimelek, Na'omi's husband, died. She remained, she and her two sons. ⁴They took up for themselves Mo'abite wives; the name of the first was Orpah and the name of the second, Ruth. They lived there some ten years, ⁵but the two of them, Mahlon and Kilyon, also died, and the woman was left without her two sons and without her husband.

⁶She set off, she and her daughters-in-law, and went back from Mo'abite country, because she had heard in Mo'abite country that Yahweh had attended to his people by giving them bread. ⁷So she left the place where she was, her two daughters-in-law with her, and they went on the road to go back to the region of Yehudah.

⁸But Na'omi said to her two daughters-in-law, 'Go, get back, each one to her mother's household. May Yahweh act in commitment with you as you've acted with the dead men and with me. ⁹May Yahweh grant to you that you find a place to settle down, each one in the household of her husband.' She kissed them and they lifted up their voice and cried. ¹⁰They said to her, 'But we should go back with you to your people.'

## The choice

¹¹Na'omi said, 'Go back, my daughters, why should you go with me? Do I still have sons inside me so they can become husbands for you? ¹²Go back, my daughters, go, because I'm too old to belong to a man. If I said there's hope for me, even if I both belonged to a man tonight and also gave birth to sons, ¹³would you therefore wait until they grew up, would you therefore hold yourself back

from belonging to a man? No, my daughters, because things are much more bitter for me than for you, because Yahweh's hand has gone out against me.'

¹⁴They lifted up their voice and cried again and Orpah kissed her mother-in-law, but Ruth attached herself to her. ¹⁵So she said, 'There, your sister-in-law has gone back to her people and to her gods. Go back after your sister-in-law.' ¹⁶Ruth said, 'Don't press me to abandon you by turning back from following you, because where you go I shall go and where you stay the night I shall stay the night. Your people will be my people and your God will be my God. ¹⁷Where you die I'll die, and there I'll be buried. So may Yahweh do to me, and so may he do more, if death divides between me and you . . .'

¹⁸She saw that she was showing herself firm about going with her, and she left off from speaking to her. ¹⁹So the two of them went on until they came to Bet Lehem. When they came to Bet Lehem, the entire town was astir over them. They said, 'Is this Na'omi?' ²⁰She said to them, 'Don't call me Na'omi ['Lovely'], call me Mara ['Bitter'], because Shadday has made things very bitter for me. ²¹I went full. Yahweh has brought me back empty. Why do you call me Na'omi when Yahweh has humbled me, when Shadday has dealt badly with me?'

## She's a Mo'abite, for goodness' sake!

²²So Na'omi went back, she and Ruth the Mo'abite her daughter-in-law with her, coming back from Mo'abite country. They came to Bet Lehem at the beginning of the barley harvest. **2** Now Na'omi had a relative of her husband's, a forceful strong man, from Elimelek's kin-group. His name was Bo'az. ²Ruth the Mo'abite said to Na'omi, 'Please, may I go to the fields and I'll glean among the ears of grain behind someone in whose eyes I may find grace.' She said to her, 'Go, daughter.' ³So she went.

She came and gleaned in the fields behind the reapers and chance took her to the share in the fields belonging to Bo'az, who was from Elimelek's kin-group. ⁴And there was Bo'az, coming from Bet Lehem. He said to the reapers, 'Yahweh be with you', and they said to him, 'Yahweh bless you.' ⁵Bo'az said to his boy who was standing by the reapers, 'Who does that girl belong to?' ⁶The boy who was standing by the reapers said, 'She's a Mo'abite girl who came back with Na'omi from Mo'abite country. ⁷She said, "Please, may I glean and gather among the sheaves behind the reapers." She came and stood from then, in the morning, until now. Her stay in the house has been short.'

⁸Bo'az said to Ruth, 'Listen, daughter, will you. You're not to go to glean in another field. No, you will not pass on from here. Attach yourself to my girls, ⁹your eyes on the field that they reap. Follow them. I've ordered the boys not to touch you, haven't I. When you're thirsty, go to the containers and drink from what the boys draw.'

## The God of coincidences

¹⁰She fell on her face and bowed low to the ground and said to him, 'Why have I found grace in your eyes, as you're recognizing me, and I'm a foreigner?' ¹¹Bo'az answered her, 'It's been fully told me everything that you've done for your mother-in-law after the death of your husband. You abandoned your father and your mother and the country that was your homeland and went to a people that you had not acknowledged in previous days. ¹²May Yahweh make good for your deed. May your wages be complete from Yahweh the God of Yisra'el [Israel], under whose skirts you've come to take shelter.' ¹³She said, 'May I find grace in your eyes, sir, because you've comforted me and spoken to your maidservant's heart, and I'm not one of your maidservants.'

¹⁴Bo'az said to her at the mealtime, 'Come up here and eat some of the bread and dip your bit in the vinegar.' So she sat by the side of the reapers, he passed her the roasted grain, and she ate and was full, and she had some left over. ¹⁵She got up to glean, and Bo'az ordered his boys, 'She can also glean among the sheaves, and you will not put her down. ¹⁶You can also pull some out for her from the bundles, and abandon them and she can glean. You will not reprimand her.'

¹⁷She gleaned in the fields until the evening and beat out what she'd gleaned. It came to something like a barrel of barley. ¹⁸She picked it up and came to the town, and her mother-in-law saw what she'd gleaned, and she got out and gave her what was left over from when she'd been full.

¹⁹Her mother-in-law said to her, 'Where did you glean today? Where did you work? Blessed be the man who recognized you.' She told her mother-in-law who she had worked with and said, 'The name of the man that I worked with today was Bo'az.'

## How not to leave the initiative to the man

²⁰Na'omi said to her daughter-in-law, 'May he be blessed by Yahweh, who hasn't abandoned his commitment with the living and with the dead.' Na'omi said to her, 'The man is a close relative of ours. He's one of our restorers.' ²¹Ruth the Mo'abite said, 'He also said to me, "You're to attach yourself to my boys until they've finished the entire harvest that belongs to me."' ²²Na'omi said to Ruth, her daughter-in-law, 'Daughter, it will be good that you go out with his girls, and people don't come upon you in another field.' ²³So she attached herself to Bo'az's girls to glean until the finish of the barley harvest and the wheat harvest, and lived with her mother-in-law.

3 Na'omi her mother-in-law said to her, 'My daughter, shouldn't I seek a place for you to settle down that will be good for you? ²So now, Bo'az is our relative, isn't he. You've been with his girls. Here, he's winnowing the barley on the threshing floor tonight. ³Have a bath, put on your make-up, put on your best clothes and go down to the threshing floor. Don't make yourself known to the man until he's finished eating and drinking. ⁴When he lies down and you know the place where he lies down, come in and uncover his feet and lie down. He himself will tell you what you should do.' ⁵She said to her, 'Everything that you say to me, I'll do.'

⁶She went down to the threshing floor and acted in accordance with all that her mother-in-law had ordered her. ⁷Bo'az ate and drank and his heart felt good. He came to lie down at the edge of the heap. She came quietly, uncovered his feet and lay down.

### The obstacle to a happy ending

[8]In the middle of the night the man gave a start and twisted round: there, a woman lying at his feet! [9]He said, 'Who are you?' She said, 'I'm Ruth, your handmaid. You should spread your skirt over your handmaid, because you're a restorer.'

[10]He said, 'May you be blessed of Yahweh, daughter. You've made your last act of commitment better than your first in not following the young men, whether a poor one or a wealthy one. [11]So now, my daughter, don't be afraid; all that you say I will do for you, because everyone at my people's gateway acknowledges that you're a forceful woman. [12]But now, because it's true that I'm a restorer, but there's also a restorer nearer than me, [13]stay the night tonight, and in the morning, if he will act as restorer, good, he may act as restorer. But if he doesn't want to act as your restorer, I myself will act as your restorer, as Yahweh lives. Lie down until the morning.'

[14]So she lay at his feet until the morning but got up before one person could recognize his neighbour. He said, 'It shouldn't become known that the woman came to the threshing floor', [15]but he said, 'Bring the shawl that you have on and hold it.' She held it and he weighed out six measures of barley and put it on her.

He went to the town, [16]and she came to her mother-in-law. She said, 'How are you, my daughter?' She told her all that the man had done for her, [17]and said, 'He gave me these six measures of barley, because he said "Don't come to your mother-in-law empty-handed."' [18]She said, 'Stay, my daughter, until you know how the matter falls, because the man won't relax. Rather he'll finish the thing today.'

### How not to get overextended in property ownership

4 Now Bo'az had gone up to the gateway and sat down there. And there, the restorer of whom Bo'az had spoken was passing. He said, 'Come over, sit down here, so-and-so.' He turned aside and sat down. [2]He got ten men from the town's elders and said, 'Sit down here', and they sat down. [3]He said to the restorer, 'The share in the fields that belonged to our brother, to Elimelek: Na'omi, who has come back from Mo'abite country, is disposing of it. [4]I myself said, "I must open your ear, saying 'Acquire it in the presence of the people who are sitting here, in the presence of the elders of my people. If you're to act as restorer, restore, but (if he's not to restore) do tell me, so I may know, because there's no one to act as restorer apart from you, but I'm after you.'"' He said, 'I'll act as restorer.' [5]But Bo'az said, 'On the day you acquire the fields from Na'omi's hand and from Ruth the Mo'abite, you will have acquired the dead man's wife, to set up the dead man's name over his domain.' [6]The restorer said, 'I can't act as restorer for myself, or I'll devastate my domain. You act as restorer for yourself regarding my position as restorer, because I cannot act as restorer.'

[7]Now this is how it was formerly in Yisra'el, in connection with acting as restorer and with transfer. To make any matter firm, a man took off his boot and gave it to his neighbour. This was the attestation process in Yisra'el. [8]So the restorer said to Bo'az, 'Acquire it for yourself', and took off his boot. [9]Bo'az said to the elders and the entire people, 'You're witnesses today that I've acquired from Na'omi's hand everything that belonged to Elimelek and everything that belonged to Kilyon and Mahlon. [10]I've also acquired Ruth the Mo'abite, Mahlon's wife, for myself as wife, to set up the dead man's name over his domain, so the dead man's name is not cut off from among his brothers and from the gateway of his place. You're witnesses today.'

### How David acquired his grandfather

[11]The entire company that was at the gateway and the elders said, 'Witnesses! May Yahweh make the woman who is coming into your house like Rahel and like Le'ah, both of whom built up Yisra'el's household. Act capably in Ephratah, call out a name in Bet Lehem! [12]May your household be like the household of Perets, to whom Tamar gave birth for Yehudah, through the offspring that Yahweh will give you through this girl.'

[13]So Bo'az got Ruth and she became his wife. He had sex with her and Yahweh enabled her to get pregnant. She gave birth to a son, [14]and the

women said to Naomi, 'Yahweh be blessed, who hasn't held back a restorer for you today. May his name be called out in Yisrael! <sup>15</sup>For you he will be one who gives life back and provides for your old age, because your daughter-in-law who loves you has borne him, she who has been better for you than seven sons.'

<sup>16</sup>Naomi got the child and put him in her arms and became a nurse for him. <sup>17</sup>The neighbours named him, saying 'A son has been born to Naomi', and named him Obed. He was father of Yishay [Jesse], father of David.

<sup>18</sup>This is the family history of Perets. Perets fathered Hetsron. <sup>19</sup>Hetsron fathered Ram. Ram fathered Amminadab. <sup>20</sup>Amminadab fathered Nahshon. Nahshon fathered Salmah. <sup>21</sup>Salmon fathered Boaz. Boaz fathered Obed. <sup>22</sup>Obed fathered Yishay. Yishay fathered David.

# I SAMUEL

In the English Bible, 1 Samuel follows on from Ruth. That story ends by telling us about a line of people descended from Ruth and Boaz, the last of whom is David, and 1 Samuel is another take on David's backstory – on the process that led to David's becoming king. To complement that point, in the Hebrew Bible 1 Samuel directly follows Judges. Judges ends with a rueful comment on how people have been doing what was all right in their own eyes because there was no king in Israel. The implication is that Israel needed someone to exercise ongoing authority and get people to take Yahweh seriously. A king might be able to do so.

It's the first of two books named after Samuel. He did not write them; he dies halfway through 1 Samuel. But he is a huge figure in 1 Samuel, one of the three big men in the book. The account of his birth is a powerful story of a woman's boldness in coming before God with the pain in her life and in challenging God to do something about it, and of this woman's courage in then giving up the son who is the answer to her prayers, so that he can be Yahweh's servant.

Samuel is the last of the 'judges', the leaders of Israel who dominate the book of Judges, people who act effectively and with great authority though without the official position of someone like a king. Samuel is also the first great prophet. It's no coincidence that Yahweh produces him at the same time as kings emerge in Israel. One of the chief responsibilities of a prophet is to be the king's conscience, to challenge him about what he ought to be doing – and more often about what he ought not to be doing. Samuel is responsible for designating and anointing Saul, the second of the three huge figures, and then for pronouncing Yahweh's decommissioning of him. He is then responsible for designating and anointing David. He even reappears at the end of the book, coming back from the dead to meet with Saul on the eve of Saul's last battle.

The background to Samuel's anointing of Saul is the people's desire to have a king like other peoples. This desire fits with that comment at the end of Judges, yet the people are going back on a distinctive aspect of their life, the principle that Yahweh is their king, though humanly speaking it's hard to imagine how they could have gone on as a people without some form of central government to replace the decentralized system whereby no organization holds the clans together. Although asking for a king implies rejecting Yahweh as king, Yahweh accedes to their request and nominates the king. Chapters 8—12 of the book expound all sides of Samuel's and Yahweh's attitude to kingship, which one may infer applies to other forms of leadership. There are advantages and disadvantages to having a leader. It costs people, in varying ways.

Yahweh's mixed feelings about Israel having kings is the background to Saul's having successes but then experiencing Yahweh's rejection for failures that may not seem very culpable. He is a tragic figure, a man enlisted to do a job that Yahweh didn't really want done and that he himself didn't really want, but who becomes attached to the job even as he is making mistakes that lead to his rejection. Eventually Yahweh sends a 'bad spirit' to Saul – not an evil spirit (the First Testament doesn't talk about those) but a depressed and angry spirit, a bad temper.

The third huge figure is David, who is designated by Yahweh as Saul's successor and who shows himself to be someone who always trusts in Yahweh and is a courageous fighter, a faithful subject, a magnetic personality, an energetic campaigner, a ruthless commander, a shrewd compromiser and a magnanimous victor. Although anointed by Samuel in Yahweh's name, before becoming king he has to wait until Yahweh has finished with Saul; he is also a man who is prepared to wait rather than trying to force things. Eventually Saul and his son Jonathan (David's best friend) meet their death in battle, which opens up the future for David.

## The pain of childlessness

**1** There was a man from Twin Heights in Tsophim, from the highland of Ephrayim, whose name was Elqanah ben Yeroham, son of Elihu son of Tohu son of Tsuph, an Ephrayimite. [2]He had two wives; the name of one was Hannah, the name of the second was Peninnah. Peninnah had children, but Hannah had no children.

[3]That man used to go up from his town from year to year to bow low and to sacrifice for Yahweh of Armies at Shiloh. The two sons of Eli, Hophni and Pinhas, were priests for Yahweh there.

[4]A day came when Elqanah sacrificed, and he would give portions to his wife Peninnah and to all her sons and her daughters. [5]To Hannah he would give a portion for two people because he loved Hannah, whereas Yahweh had closed up her womb, [6]and her rival would provoke her greatly to make her fret because Yahweh had closed up her womb. [7]So he would do, year after year. As often as she went up to Yahweh's house, she would provoke her in this way, and she would cry and not eat. [8]Elqanah, her husband, said to her, 'Hannah, why do you cry, why don't you eat, why does your heart feel bad? Aren't I better for you than ten sons?'

[9]Hannah got up after the eating in Shiloh and after the drinking. Eli the priest was sitting on the seat by the doorpost of Yahweh's palace. [10]She was bitter in spirit but she made a plea to Yahweh and cried and cried, [11]and she made a pledge. She said, 'Yahweh of Armies, if you actually look at your handmaid's humbling and you're mindful of me, and you don't put your handmaid out of mind but give your handmaid a male offspring, I'll give him to Yahweh all the days of his life. No razor will go up on his head.'

## A face transformed

[12]Because she was doing much pleading before Yahweh, and Eli was watching her mouth, [13]and Hannah was speaking in her heart (only her lips were quivering, but her voice did not make itself heard), Eli thought she was drunk. [14]Eli said to her, 'How long will you behave like a drunk? Put your wine away from you.' [15]Hannah

answered, 'No, sir, I'm a tough-spirited woman and I haven't drunk wine or liquor. I've poured myself out before Yahweh. [16]Don't make your handmaid into a scoundrelous woman, because it was out of the dimensions of my tetchiness and my provocation that I've spoken until now.' [17]Eli answered, 'Go, things will be well. The God of Yisra'el: he will give the thing that you've asked of him.' [18]She said, 'May your maidservant find grace in your eyes.'

The woman went on her way and ate, and her face was no longer [the same]. [19]They started early in the morning, bowed low before Yahweh, and went back and came to their home in The Height. Elqanah had sex with his wife Hannah and Yahweh was mindful of her, [20]and at the end of the year Hannah had got pregnant. She gave birth to a son and named him Shemu'el [Samuel], because 'I asked [sha'al] for him from Yahweh.'

[21]The man, Elqanah, went up with his entire household to offer Yahweh the yearly sacrifice and his pledge, [22]but Hannah didn't go up, because (she said to her husband) 'When the boy is weaned I'll bring him. We'll see Yahweh's face, and he'll live there permanently.' [23]Elqanah her husband said to her, 'Do what's good in your eyes; stay till you've weaned him. Only, may Yahweh implement his word.' So the woman stayed and nursed her son until she'd weaned him. [24]She took him up with her when she had weaned him, with a three-year-old bull, a barrel of flour and a skin of wine, and brought him to Yahweh's house at Shiloh. He was a boy. [25]They slaughtered the bull and brought the boy to Eli.

## On giving up your son

[26]She said, 'Pardon me, sir, as surely as you live, sir, I'm the woman who stood with you here to make my plea to Yahweh. [27]It was for this boy that I made my plea, and Yahweh gave me what I asked of him. [28]I myself am also giving him to Yahweh; for all the days that he lives he's given to Yahweh.' He bowed low there to Yahweh,

**2** and Hannah made her plea:

My heart has exulted in Yahweh,
my horn has lifted high through Yahweh.

My mouth has opened wide at my enemies,
  because I have rejoiced in your deliverance.
²There's no sacred one like Yahweh,
  because there's no one apart from you,
  there's no crag like our God.
³Don't do much speaking of lofty, lofty speech,
  nor should outspoken speech come out of
  your mouth.
Because Yahweh is a God who knows;
  by him actions are weighed.
⁴The bows of strong men are broken,
  but people who were falling have belted on
  forcefulness.
⁵People who were full have hired themselves
  out for bread,
  but the hungry left off from being hungry.
While the infertile woman has given birth to
  seven,
  the woman with many children is withered.
⁶Yahweh is one who puts to death and brings
  to life,
  sends down to She'ol and brings up.
⁷Yahweh is one who makes poor and makes
  wealthy,
  puts down, also lifts up.
⁸He is one who raises the poor from the dirt,
  lifts up the needy from the dump,
To sit with important people;
  he gives them a seat of splendour as their
  domain.
Because earth's pillars belong to Yahweh;
  he set the world upon them.
⁹He keeps the feet of the people who are loyal
  to him,
  but the faithless go silent into the darkness.
Because it's not by energy that a person
  prevails;
  ¹⁰Yahweh – people who argue with him
  shatter.
The One on High thunders in the heavens;
  Yahweh judges the ends of the earth.
He gives vigour to his king,
  lifts up the horn of his anointed one.

## Ministers who indulge themselves

¹¹Elqanah went home to The Height, while
the boy was ministering to Yahweh in the
presence of Eli the priest. ¹²Now Eli's sons were
scoundrels; they didn't acknowledge Yahweh.
¹³The priests' rule with the people was: when
each person was offering a sacrifice, the priest's
boy would come while the meat was boiling,
with a three-pronged fork in his hand. ¹⁴He
would thrust it into the pan or the kettle or the
cauldron or the pot; all that the fork brought up,
the priest would take with it. In this way they
would act with all Yisra'el [Israel] who came
there to Shiloh. ¹⁵Further, before they turned
the fat into smoke, the priest's boy would come
and say to the individual making the sacrifice,
'Give over some meat for roasting for the
priest; he won't take boiled meat from you, only
raw.' ¹⁶Should the individual say to him, 'They
should actually turn the fat into smoke now,
then take for yourself whatever your appetite
longs for', he would say 'No, but you're to give it
over now, or I'm taking it by force.'
¹⁷The boys' wrongdoing in Yahweh's presence
was very great, because the men disdained
Yahweh's offering.
¹⁸So Shemu'el was ministering in the presence
of Yahweh, a boy wrapped round in a linen
chasuble. ¹⁹His mother would make a little
coat for him and bring it up for him from year
to year when she went up with her husband to
offer the yearly sacrifice. ²⁰Eli would bless
Elqanah and his wife and say, 'May Yahweh give
you offspring from this woman in place of the
one she asked for from Yahweh', and they would
go to their place. ²¹Because Yahweh attended to
Hannah, she got pregnant and she gave birth
to three sons and two daughters, but the boy
Shemu'el grew up with Yahweh.

## Why do you kick at my sacrifices?

²²When Eli was very old, he heard of all that
his sons were doing to all Yisra'el and how they
were sleeping with the women who fulfilled
duties at the entrance of the appointment tent.
²³He said to them, 'Why do you do such actions
as these that I am hearing of, bad actions of
yours, from all these people? ²⁴Don't, my sons,
because the report is not good that I'm hearing
Yahweh's people passing on. ²⁵If an individual
does wrong against an individual, God may
plead for him, but if an individual does wrong
against Yahweh, who will make a plea for
him?' But they wouldn't listen to their father's
voice because Yahweh wanted to put them to
death. ²⁶But the boy Shemu'el was continuing

to grow and seem good both with Yahweh and with people.

²⁷A supernatural man came to Eli and said to him: Yahweh has said this: "Did I clearly reveal myself to your father's household when they were in Misrayim [Egypt], belonging to Par'oh's [Pharaoh's] household? ²⁸I chose him out of all Yisra'el's clans as a priest for me, to go up on my altar, to burn incense, to carry a chasuble before me, and I gave your father's household all the Yisra'elites' gift offerings. ²⁹Why do you kick at my sacrifice and at my offering which I ordered, at my abode? You've honoured your sons more than me in fattening yourselves on the first of every offering of Yisra'el as my people.

## A trustworthy priest

³⁰Therefore (a declaration of Yahweh the God of Yisra'el), I did say that your household and your father's household would go about before me permanently, but now (Yahweh's declaration), far be it from me, because the people who honour me I honour, but the people who despise me will become slight. ³¹Here, a time is coming when I shall cut off your arm and the arm of your father's household, so that there will be no one as an elder in your household. ³²You will look at the pressure that comes on [my] abode, despite all the good that is done to Yisra'el, and there will be no one as an elder in your household for the entire time. ³³While I shall not cut off every individual of yours from my altar, so as to consume your eyes and make your spirit grieve, the entire abundance of your household: people will die. ³⁴This will be the sign for you that will come on your two sons, on Hophi and Pinhas: the two of them will die on one day.

³⁵I shall set up for myself a trustworthy priest. He will act in accordance with what is in my mind and in my spirit. I shall build a trustworthy household for him and he will go about before my anointed one for all time. ³⁶Anyone who is left of your household will come to bow low to him for a payment in silver and a loaf of bread. He will say, 'Assign me to one of the priestly duties so I can eat a bit of bread.'"

## A summons, not a call

**3** The boy, Shemu'el, was ministering to Yahweh in the presence of Eli. Yahweh's word was rare at that time; there was no vision spreading about. ²On a day when Eli was lying

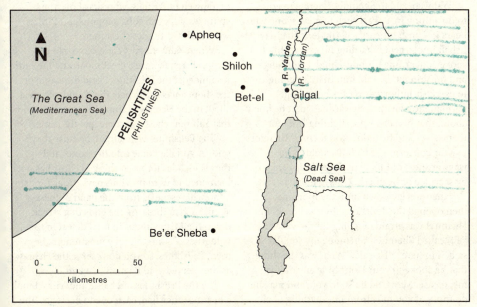

*Yisra'el at the time of Shemu'el (Samuel)*

down in his place (his eyes had started to fail; he couldn't see) ³but God's lamp had not yet gone out, and Shemu'el was lying down in Yahweh's palace where God's chest was, ⁴Yahweh called to Shemu'el.

He said, 'I'm here', ⁵and ran to Eli and said, 'I'm here, because you called to me.' He said, 'I didn't call. Go back, lie down.' He went and lay down. ⁶Yahweh called yet again, 'Shemu'el', and Shemu'el got up and went to Eli and said, 'I'm here, because you called to me.' He said, 'I didn't call, son, go back, lie down.' ⁷Now Shemu'el hadn't yet acknowledged Yahweh; Yahweh's word hadn't yet revealed itself to him. ⁸Yahweh again called Shemu'el, a third time, and he got up, went to Eli and said, 'I'm here, because you called to me.' Eli perceived that Yahweh was calling to the boy. ⁹Eli said to Shemu'el, 'Go, lie down, and if he calls to you, you're to say, "Speak, Yahweh, because your servant is listening."' So Shemu'el went and lay down in his place.

¹⁰Yahweh came and took his stand and called as at the other times, 'Shemu'el, Shemu'el'. Shemu'el said, 'Speak, because your servant is listening.'

### The message no one would want to give

¹¹Yahweh said to Shemu'el, 'Here, I'm going to do a thing in Yisra'el such that everyone who hears it – both his ears will tingle. ¹²That day I shall implement regarding Eli everything I spoke concerning his household, beginning and finishing it. ¹³I told him that I'm going to exercise authority over his household permanently for the waywardness that he knew about, that his sons were slighting [me] for themselves and he didn't stop them. ¹⁴Therefore I swear concerning Eli's household: if the waywardness of Eli's household finds expiation by sacrifice or by offering, permanently . . .'

¹⁵Shemu'el lay down until the morning, then opened the doors of Yahweh's house. But Shemu'el was afraid of telling Eli the vision. ¹⁶Eli called Shemu'el: 'Shemu'el, my son'. He said, 'I'm here.' ¹⁷He said, 'What was the thing that he spoke to you? Don't hide any of it from me, please. May God do so to you, and may he do more, if you hide from me anything of all that he said to you.' ¹⁸Shemu'el told him all the

things and didn't hide it from him. He said, 'He is Yahweh. He will do what is good in his eyes.'

¹⁹Shemu'el grew up, and as Yahweh was with him, he didn't allow any of his words to fall to the ground. ²⁰All Yisra'el from Dan as far as Be'er Sheba acknowledged that Shemu'el was trustworthy as a prophet belonging to Yahweh. ²¹Yahweh again appeared at Shiloh, in that Yahweh revealed himself to Shemu'el at Shiloh with Yahweh's word,

**4** and Shemu'el's word came to all Yisra'el.

### Get the chest

¹ᵇYisra'el went out to meet the Pelishtites [Philistines] in battle, and camped at Help Stone [Eben Ha'ezer], while the Pelishtites camped at Apheq. ²The Pelishtites lined up to meet Yisra'el and the battle spread, and Yisra'el took a beating before the Pelishtites. They struck down some 4,000 men in their line in the fields. ³The company came to the camp and Yisra'el's elders said, 'Why did Yahweh defeat us today before the Pelishtites? Let's get Yahweh's pact chest from Shiloh for ourselves, so he will come among us and deliver us from our enemies' fist.' ⁴So the company sent to Shiloh and carried from there the pact chest of Yahweh of Armies, who sits above the sphinxes. Eli's two sons, Hophni and Pinhas, were with God's pact chest there. ⁵When Yahweh's pact chest came into the camp, all Yisra'el gave a great shout, and the earth resounded. ⁶The Pelishtites heard the sound of the shout and said, 'What's this sound of a great shout in the Hebrews' camp?' They came to know that Yahweh's chest had come into the camp. ⁷The Pelishtites were afraid, because they said, 'A god has come into the camp', and they said, 'Alas for us! A thing like this has not happened to us in previous days. ⁸Alas for us! Who will rescue us from the hand of these august gods? These are the gods that struck down the Misrayimites in total defeat in the wilderness. ⁹Summon up your strength, be men, Pelishtites, so you don't serve the Hebrews as they served you. Be men! Do battle!' ¹⁰So the Pelishtites did battle and Yisra'el took a beating. They fled, each one to his tents. The rout was very great, and from Yisra'el 30,000

men on foot fell, [11]while God's chest was taken, and Eli's two sons, Hophni and Pinhas, died.

### The splendour is gone

[12]A Binyaminite [Benjaminite] man ran from the line and came to Shiloh that day, with his uniform torn and earth on his head. [13]He came, and there, Eli was sitting on a seat by the road, watching, because his heart was trembling for God's chest. When the man came to tell of it in the town, the entire town cried out. [14]Eli heard the sound of the cry and said, 'What's this sound of an uproar?' The man hurried and came, and told Eli.

[15]Eli was a man of ninety-eight years. His eyes were set and he couldn't see. [16]The man said to Eli, 'I'm the one coming from the line. I myself fled from the line today.' He said, 'What was the thing that happened, son?' [17]The man bringing the news replied, 'Yisra'el fled before the Pelishtites. It was both a great disaster to the company, and also your two sons, Hophni and Pinhas, are dead, and God's chest was taken.' [18]When he made mention of God's chest, he fell backwards from on his seat by the side of the gateway. His neck broke and he died, because the man was old and heavy. He had exercised authority for Yisra'el for forty years.

[19]His daughter-in-law, Pinhas's wife, was pregnant, soon to give birth. She heard the report about God's chest being taken and her father-in-law and her husband being dead, and she bent down and gave birth, because her labour pains came over her. [20]At the time of her dying, the women standing by her spoke: 'Don't be afraid, because you've given birth to a son.' She didn't answer. She didn't give her mind to it.

[21]She called the boy Ikabod ['Where Is the Splendour?'], saying 'The splendour has gone into exile from Yisra'el', in connection with God's chest being taken, and with her father-in-law and with her husband. [22]She said, 'The splendour has gone into exile from Yisra'el, because God's chest has been taken.'

### You can't mess with the chest

**5** When the Pelishtites took God's chest, they brought it from Help Stone to Ashdod. [2]The Pelishtites took God's chest and brought it to Dagon's house and set it beside Dagon. [3]The Ashdodites started early next day and there was Dagon, fallen on his face on the ground before Yahweh's chest. So they took Dagon and put him back in his place.

[4]They started early in the morning next day and there was Dagon, fallen on his face on the ground before Yahweh's chest, with Dagon's head and both the palms of his hands cut off, on the threshold. Only [the body of] Dagon remained to him. [5]That's why Dagon's priests and all the people who come to Dagon's house don't tread on Dagon's threshold in Ashdod, until this day.

[6]Yahweh's hand was heavy on the Ashdodites. He desolated them and struck them down with haemorrhoids, Ashdod and its territories. [7]The Ashdodites saw that it was so, and said, 'The chest of Yisra'el's God is not to stay with us, because his hand has been tough with us and with Dagon our god.' [8]They sent and gathered all the Pelishtites' lords to them and said, 'What shall we do with the chest of Yisra'el's God?' They said, 'The chest of Yisra'el's God should get itself round to Gat.' So they took the chest of Yisra'el's God round. [9]After they had taken it round, Yahweh's hand came against the town with a great turmoil. He struck the town's people from young to old, and haemorrhoids broke out on them.

[10]So they sent God's chest off to Eqron. But when God's chest came to Eqron, the Eqronites cried out, 'They've brought the chest of Yisra'el's God round to me to put me and my people to death.' [11]So they sent off and gathered all the Pelishtites' lords and said, 'Send the chest of Yisra'el's God off so it goes back to its place. It will not put me and my people to death', because there was a deathly turmoil in the entire town. God's hand was very heavy there. [12]The men who didn't die were struck down by the haemorrhoids. The town's cry for help went up to the heavens.

### The need for reparation

**6** Yahweh's chest was in the Pelishtites' country for seven months. [2]The Pelishtites called for the priests and for the diviners: 'What shall we do about Yahweh's chest? Let us know what we're to send it off with to its place.' ³They said, 'If you're going to send off the chest of Yisra'el's God, don't send if off empty-handed. Rather, you're definitely to send a reparation back to him. Then you'll find healing. He'll get himself acknowledged by you; why should his hand not depart from you?'

⁴They said, 'What's the reparation that we should send back to him?' They said, 'Five gold haemorrhoids and five gold rats, the number of the Pelishtites' lords, because the same epidemic came to all of them, and to your lords. ⁵You're to make models of your haemorrhoids and models of your rats that have been devastating the country, and give honour to the God of Yisra'el. Maybe he will ease his hand from upon you and from upon your gods and from upon your country. ⁶Why would you harden your mind as Misrayim and Par'oh hardened their mind? When he had acted abusively to them, they sent them off and they went, didn't they.

⁷So now, get and make ready a new cart and two nursing cows on which no yoke has come. Harness the cows to the cart but take their young ones back home, from following them. ⁸Get Yahweh's chest and put it on the cart. The gold articles that you're sending back to him as a reparation you're to put in a receptacle by its side, and send it off so it goes, ⁹and you're to look. If it goes up the road to his border, to Bet Shemesh, he's the one who did this huge bad thing to you. If not, we'll know that it was not his hand touched us. It was a chance that happened to us.'

¹⁰The people did so. They got two nursing cows, harnessed them to a cart, shut up their young ones at home, ¹¹and put Yahweh's chest on the cart, with the receptacle and the gold rats and the models of their haemorrhoids.

## Too hot to handle

¹²The cows went straight by the road, on the Bet Shemesh road. By a causeway they went steadily and lowed and didn't depart right or left, with the Pelishtites' lords following them as far as the Bet Shemesh border. ¹³Bet Shemesh people were reaping the wheat harvest in the vale. They lifted up their eyes and

saw the chest, and rejoiced to see it. ¹⁴The cart came to the fields of Yehoshua of Bet-shemesh and stood there. There was a big stone there. They split the wood of the cart and offered up the cows as a burnt offering for Yahweh. ¹⁵The Levites took down Yahweh's chest and the receptacle that was with it, in which were the gold articles, and put them on the big stone. The people of Bet-shemesh offered up whole offerings and offered sacrifices that day for Yahweh. ¹⁶The Pelishtites' five lords looked, and went back to Eqron that day.

¹⁷These are the gold haemorrhoids that the Pelishtites gave back as a reparation to Yahweh: one for Ashdod, one for Azzah [Gaza], one for Ashqelon, one for Gat, one for Eqron. ¹⁸The gold rats: the number of all the Pelishtites' towns belonging to the Pelishtites' five lords, both fortified town and country hamlet, as far as the big stone on which they set down Yahweh's chest, until this day in the fields of Yehoshua of Bet-shemesh.

¹⁹But he struck down the people of Bet-shemesh because they looked in Yahweh's chest. He struck down seventy individuals (50,000 individuals) among the people. The people took up grieving because Yahweh had struck the people down with a heavy blow. ²⁰The people of Bet-shemesh said, 'Who can stand before Yahweh, this sacred God? To whom might he go up from us?' ²¹So they sent envoys to the people living in Ye'arim Township to say, 'The Pelishtites have sent Yahweh's chest back. Come down, take it up to you.'

**7** The people of Ye'arim Township came and took Yahweh's chest up and brought it into the house of Abinadab, on the hill. They made his son El'azar sacred to keep Yahweh's chest.

## Yahweh helped us as far as this

²From the day the chest lived at Ye'arim Township time went on; twenty years passed. The entire household of Yisra'el grieved after Yahweh, ³and Shemu'el said to the entire household of Yisra'el, 'If with your entire heart you're coming back to Yahweh, remove the foreign gods and the Ashtars from among you. Direct your heart firmly towards Yahweh and serve him alone, and he will rescue you from

the hand of the Pelishtites.' ⁴So the Yisra'elites removed the Masters and the Ashtars and served Yahweh alone.

⁵Shemu'el said, 'Gather all Yisra'el at The Watchtower and I'll plead with Yahweh on your behalf.' ⁶They gathered at The Watchtower and drew water and poured it out before Yahweh. They fasted that day and said there, 'We have done wrong against Yahweh.' So Shemu'el exercised authority for the Yisra'elites at The Watchtower.

⁷The Pelishtites heard that the Yisra'elites had gathered at The Watchtower and the Pelishtites' lords went up against Yisra'el. The Yisra'elites heard and were afraid of the Pelishtites. ⁸So the Yisra'elites said to Shemu'el, 'Don't be deaf to us and not cry out to Yahweh our God so he may deliver us from the hand of the Pelishtites.' ⁹So Shemu'el got a suckling lamb and offered it up as a whole burnt offering for Yahweh. Shemu'el cried out to Yahweh on behalf of Yisra'el, and Yahweh answered him. ¹⁰As Shemu'el was offering up the burnt offering, the Pelishtites were coming up for battle against Yisra'el, but Yahweh thundered with a loud voice that day against the Pelishtites and threw them into a turmoil, and they took a beating before Yisra'el. ¹¹The Yisra'elites went out from The Watchtower, pursued the Pelishtites and struck them down as far as below Bet Kar.

¹²Shemu'el got a stone and put it between The Watchtower and The Tooth, and named it 'Help Stone'. He said, 'As far as this Yahweh helped us.' ¹³The Pelishtites bowed down and didn't any more come within Yisra'el's border again. Yahweh's hand was against the Pelishtites all the days of Shemu'el. ¹⁴The towns that the Pelishtites had taken from Yisra'el came back to Yisra'el, from Eqron as far as Gat. Yisra'el rescued their border from the hand of the Pelishtites, and there was peace between Yisra'el and the Amorites.

## Appoint us a king

¹⁵Shemu'el exercised authority for Yisra'el all the days of his life. ¹⁶He went year by year and travelled round to Bet-el, Gilgal and The Watchtower and exercised authority for Yisra'el at all these sites; ¹⁷then his return to The Height, because his home was there. He

exercised authority for Yisra'el there and built an altar for Yahweh there.

**8** When Shemu'el was old, he made his sons into people who exercised authority for Yisra'el. ²The name of his firstborn son was Yo'el and the name of his second Abiyyah; they were authorities in Be'er Sheba. ³But his sons didn't walk in his ways. They turned after profit and accepted bribes, and overturned the exercise of authority.

⁴So all Yisra'el's elders gathered and came to Shemu'el at The Height, ⁵and said to him, 'Here, you've got old and your sons haven't walked in your ways. Now appoint us a king to exercise authority for us like all the nations.' ⁶The thing was bad in Shemu'el's eyes, when they said 'Give us a king to exercise authority for us', and Shemu'el made a plea to Yahweh.

⁷Yahweh said to Shemu'el, 'Listen to the people's voice in everything that they say to you, because it's not you they've rejected, because it's me they've rejected from being king over them. ⁸In accordance with all the deeds they've done from the day I brought them up from Misrayim and until this day, they've abandoned me and served other gods, so they're doing also to you. ⁹So now listen to their voice. Only testify against them solemnly and tell them about the authority of the king who will reign over them.'

## What a king will be like

¹⁰Shemu'el spoke all Yahweh's words to the people who were asking for a king from him. ¹¹He said, 'This will be the authority of the king who will reign over you. Your sons he'll take and make into his chariotry and into his cavalry for himself and they'll run before his chariotry, ¹²making them divisional officers and unit officers for himself, and for ploughing his fields and reaping his harvest and making his battle equipment and his chariot equipment. ¹³Your daughters he'll take as perfumers, cooks and bakers. ¹⁴Your fields, your vineyards and your olive groves, the best, he'll take and give to his servants. ¹⁵Of your seed and your vineyards he'll take a tenth and give to his courtiers and to his servants. ¹⁶Your servants and your maidservants, your best young men and your donkeys, he'll take and make into his

workforce. <sup>17</sup>Of your flock he'll take a tenth and you yourselves will become servants to him. <sup>18</sup>You will cry out on that day on account of your king whom you've chosen for yourselves, but Yahweh will not answer you on that day.'

<sup>19</sup>The people refused to listen to Shemu'el's voice and said, 'No! Rather, there is to be a king over us, <sup>20</sup>so we can become like all the nations. Our king will exercise authority, and go out before us and fight our battles.' <sup>21</sup>Shemu'el listened to all the people's words and spoke them in Yahweh's ears. <sup>22</sup>Yahweh said to Shemu'el, 'Listen to their voice. Make a king for them.' Shemu'el said to the Yisra'elites, 'Go, each one, to his town.'

## How Sha'ul lost some donkeys

**9** There was a man from Binyamin; his name was Qish ben Abi'el, son of Tseror son of Bekorat son of Aphiah, a Binyaminite – a forceful man. <sup>2</sup>He had a son; his name was Sha'ul [Saul], young and good-looking. There was no one better-looking among the Yisra'elites than him. From his shoulders up, he was loftier than all the people.

<sup>3</sup>Donkeys belonging to Qish, Sha'ul's father, got lost, and Qish said to Sha'ul his son, 'Please take one of the boys with you, and set off and go look for the donkeys.' <sup>4</sup>They passed through the highland of Ephrayim and passed through the region of Shalishah, but they didn't find them. They passed through the region of Sha'alim, but they were not there. They passed through the region of Binyamin and didn't find them. <sup>5</sup>When they came to the region of Tsuph, Sha'ul said to his boy who was with him, 'Come on, let's go back, so my father doesn't leave off from the donkeys and get anxious about us.'

<sup>6</sup>He said to him, 'Here, please, there's a supernatural man in this town. The man is honoured. Everything that he speaks does come about. Let's go there now. Maybe he'll tell us about our journey that we've gone on.' <sup>7</sup>Sha'ul said to his boy, 'But here, we can go, but what are we to bring the man, because the bread is exhausted from our bags and there's no present to bring to the supernatural man. What is there with us?' <sup>8</sup>The boy again answered Sha'ul, 'Here, there's a quarter-sheqel of silver present in my hand. I'll give it to the

supernatural man so he can tell us about our journey.' (<sup>9</sup>Formerly in Yisra'el, an individual said this when he was going to enquire of God: 'Come on, let's go to the seer', because the prophet today was formerly called the seer.)

## An extraordinary coincidence

<sup>10</sup>So Sha'ul said to his boy, 'Your words are good. Come on, let's go.' So they went to the town where the supernatural man was. <sup>11</sup>When they were going up the ascent to the town and they found girls going out to draw water, they said to them, 'Is the seer here?' <sup>12</sup>They answered them, 'He is, there, before you. Hurry now, because today he's come to the town because the people have a sacrifice at the shrine today. <sup>13</sup>As you come into the town, there you'll find him before he goes up to the shrine to eat, because the people won't eat until he comes, because he has to say the blessing for the sacrifice. After that, the people who've been invited will eat. So now, go up, because this very day you'll find him.' <sup>14</sup>So they went up to the town. As they were coming into the middle of the town – there was Shemu'el, going out to meet them, going up to the shrine.

<sup>15</sup>Now Yahweh had had a word in Shemu'el's ear the day before Sha'ul came: <sup>16</sup>'This very time tomorrow I shall send you a man from the region of Binyamin, and you're to anoint him as ruler over my people Yisra'el. He will deliver my people from the hand of the Pelishtites, because I've seen my people, because their cry has come to me.' <sup>17</sup>When Shemu'el saw Sha'ul, Yahweh himself avowed to him, 'Here is the man of whom I said to you, "This is the man who will put some restraint on my people."' <sup>18</sup>Sha'ul went up to Shemu'el in the middle of the gateway and said, 'Please tell me where the seer's house is.'

## An unexpected banquet

<sup>19</sup>Shemu'el answered Sha'ul, 'I'm the seer. Go up before me to the shrine and you can eat with me today. I'll send you off in the morning, but everything that's on your mind I'll tell you. <sup>20</sup>As for your donkeys that got lost three days ago: don't set your mind on them, because

they've been found. And who is the object of all Yisra'el's desire? You and your entire ancestral household.'

²¹Sha'ul answered, 'I'm a Binyaminite, aren't I, from the smallest of Yisra'el's clans, and my kin-group is the littlest of all the kin-groups in the clans of Binyamin. Why have you spoken to me of such a thing?'

²²Shemu'el took Sha'ul and his boy, brought them into the hall and gave them a place at the head of the people who had been invited; they were some thirty individuals. ²³Shemu'el said to the cook, 'Give me the portion that I gave you, about which I said to you, "Put it by you."' ²⁴The cook lifted up the thigh and what was on it and put it before Sha'ul.

He said, 'There is what has remained, put before you. Eat, because it was kept for you for the set time when I said "I am inviting the people."' So Sha'ul ate with Shemu'el that day, ²⁵then they came down from the shrine to the town, and he spoke with Sha'ul on the roof.

### How Sha'ul found more than he bargained for

²⁶They started early, and at break of day Shemu'el called to Sha'ul on the roof: 'Get up, and I'll send you off.' Sha'ul got up, and the two of them, he and Shemu'el, went outside. ²⁷As they were going down to the edge of the town Shemu'el said to Sha'ul, 'Say to the boy that he's to pass on before us' (and he passed on) 'but you stand here this very moment and I shall let you hear God's word.'

**10** Shemu'el got a flask of oil and poured it on his head and kissed him, and said, 'Yahweh anoints you as ruler over his domain, does he not. ²When you go from being with me today, you'll find two men by Rahel's grave within the border of Binyamin at Tseltsah. They'll say to you, "The donkeys that you went to look for have been found. Here, your father's given up on the thing about the donkeys and got anxious about you, saying 'What shall I do about my son?'" ³You're to go on from there, and further on you'll come as far as Tabor Oak. Three men will find you there, coming up to God to Bet-el, one carrying three kid goats, one carrying three loaves of bread and one carrying a skin of wine.

⁴They'll ask you if things are well with you, and they'll give you two loaves of bread. You're to accept them from their hand.

⁵After this you're to come to God's Hill, where the Pelishtites' outpost is. When you come into the town there, you'll come upon a group of prophets going down from the shrine, with mandolin, tambourine, pipe and guitar before them, They'll be prophesying. ⁶Yahweh's spirit will thrust itself on to you and you'll prophesy with them. You'll turn into another person. ⁷When these signs come about for you, do for yourself what your hand finds, because God will be with you.

### Is Sha'ul a prophet, too?

⁸You're to go down before me to Gilgal. There; I'm going to come down to you to offer up burnt offerings and to make well-being sacrifices. You're to wait seven days until I come to you and make known to you what you're to do.' ⁹As he turned his face to go from being with Shemu'el, God gave him another mind.

All these signs came about that day. ¹⁰They came there, to the hill, and here – a group of prophets coming to meet him. God's spirit thrust itself on to him and he prophesied among them. ¹¹Everyone who knew him in previous days looked – and here, he was prophesying with prophets. The people said, one to his neighbour, 'What's this that's happened to ben Qish? Is Sha'ul among the prophets, too?' ¹²One person from there answered, 'And who is their father?' That's why it became an aphorism, 'Is Sha'ul among the prophets, too?' ¹³He finished prophesying and came to the shrine.

¹⁴Sha'ul's uncle said to him and to his boy, 'Where did you go?' He said, 'To look for the donkeys. We saw that they weren't there, and we came to Shemu'el.' ¹⁵Sha'ul's uncle said, 'Please tell me what Shemu'el said to you.' ¹⁶Sha'ul said to his uncle, 'He did tell us that the donkeys had been found.' As for the matter of the kingship, he didn't tell him what Shemu'el said.

### How not to evade being enlisted

¹⁷Shemu'el called out the people to Yahweh at The Watchtower. ¹⁸He said to the Yisra'elites,

'Yahweh the God of Yisra'el has said this: "I am the one who brought Yisra'el up from Misrayim. I rescued you from the hand of Misrayim and from the hand of all the kingdoms that afflicted you", ¹⁹but today you people have rejected your God who was a deliverer for you from all your bad experiences and your pressures. You said to him, "No, rather you're to set a king over us." So now, take your stand before Yahweh by your clans and by your families.'

²⁰Shemu'el presented all the Yisra'elite clans, and the clan of Binyamin was taken. ²¹He presented the clan of Binyamin by its kin-groups and the kin-group of the Matrites arose, and Sha'ul ben Qish was taken. They looked for him but he couldn't be found, ²²so they asked of Yahweh again, 'Has anyone else come here?' Yahweh said, 'There, he's hiding with the things.' ²³They ran and got him from there and he took his stand among the people. He was loftier than all the people, from his shoulders up. ²⁴Shemu'el said to all the people, 'Have you seen the one that Yahweh has chosen, that there's no one like him among all the people?' All the people shouted and said, 'Long live the king.'

²⁵Shemu'el spoke to the people about the rule for the kingship, wrote it in a document and set it down before Yahweh. Then Shemu'el sent all the people off, each to his house. ²⁶Sha'ul also went to his house at Gib'ah, and with him went the force whose heart God had touched. ²⁷When scoundrels said, 'How can this man deliver us?', and despised him and didn't bring him an offering, he was like someone deaf.

## Anger as a fruit of the Spirit

**11** Nahash the Ammonite went up and camped against Yabesh-in-Gil'ad. All the men of Yabesh said to Nahash, 'Solemnize a pact to us and we'll serve you.' ²Nahash the Ammonite said to them, 'On this basis I'll solemnize one to you, on the basis of gouging out the right eye of every one of you. I'll make it a reviling to all Yisra'el.' ³The elders of Yabesh said to him, 'Let us go for seven days and we'll send envoys through all Yisra'el's border. If there's no one who'll be a deliverer for us, we'll come out to you.'

⁴The envoys came to Gib'ah-of-Sha'ul and spoke the words in the people's ears, and the

entire people lifted up their voice and wailed. ⁵And there, Sha'ul was coming in behind the herd from the fields. Sha'ul said, 'What's happened to the people, that they're wailing?' They told him the words of the men from Yabesh.

⁶God's spirit thrust itself on to Sha'ul when he heard these words, and his anger raged right up. ⁷He got a pair from the herd and cut them up and sent them off through the entire border of Yisra'el by the hand of envoys, saying 'Anyone of you who doesn't go out after Sha'ul and after Shemu'el: so it will be done to his herd.' Dread of Yahweh fell on the people and they went out as one person. ⁸He numbered them at Bezeq; there were 300,000 Yisra'elites and 30,000 Yehudahites [Judahites]. ⁹They said to the envoys who had come, 'Say this to the people of Yabesh-in-Gil'ad: "Tomorrow there will be deliverance for you, when the sun gets hot."' The envoys came and told the people of Yabesh and they rejoiced. ¹⁰The people of Yabesh said, 'Tomorrow we'll go out to you and you can act towards us in accordance with everything that's good in your eyes.'

## No redress

¹¹Next day Sha'ul made the company into three units, and they came into the middle of the camp during the morning watch and struck down Ammon until the day got hot. Those who remained dispersed; among them there did not remain two together. ¹²The people said to Shemu'el, 'Who was the person who said "Is Sha'ul to reign over us?" Give the people over and we'll put them to death.' ¹³But Sha'ul said, 'No one is to be put to death this day, because today Yahweh has brought about deliverance in Yisra'el.'

¹⁴Shemu'el said to the people, 'Come, let's go to Gilgal and renew the kingship there.' ¹⁵So all the people went to Gilgal and made Sha'ul king there before Yahweh at Gilgal. They made well-being sacrifices there before Yahweh. Sha'ul and all the Yisra'elites rejoiced greatly there.

**12** Shemu'el said to all Yisra'el, 'Here, I listened to your voice regarding all that you said to me and I made a king reign over you. ²So now, there is your king walking about before you. I myself am old and grey, but my sons – here they are, with you. I myself have walked about before you from my youth until this day. ³Here I am. Vow against me in the presence of Yahweh and in the presence of his anointed. Whose ox have I taken? Whose donkey have I taken? Whom have I defrauded? Whom have I crushed? From whose hand have I taken a ransom so I might close my eyes to him? I'll give it back to you.'

⁴They said, 'You haven't defrauded us, you haven't crushed us, you haven't taken anything from anyone's hand.' ⁵He said to them, 'Yahweh is witness against you, and his anointed is witness this day, that you haven't found anything in my hand.' They said, 'He is witness.' ⁶Shemu'el said to the people, 'Yahweh, who made Mosheh and Aharon [Moses and Aaron] and who brought your ancestors up from the country of Misrayim.

## Take your stand and face facts

⁷So now take your stand so that I may enter into judgement with you before Yahweh on the basis of all Yahweh's acts of faithfulness which he performed with you and with your ancestors. ⁸When Ya'aqob [Jacob] came to Misrayim and your ancestors cried out to Yahweh, Yahweh sent Mosheh and Aharon and got your ancestors out of Misrayim and enabled them to live in this place. ⁹But they put Yahweh their God out of mind and he sold them into the hand of Sisera the army officer at Hatsor, into the hand of the Pelishtites and into the hand of the king of Mo'ab, and they battled against them. ¹⁰They cried out to Yahweh and said, "We've done wrong, because we've abandoned Yahweh and served the Masters and the Ashtars, but now, deliver us from the hand of our enemies and we will serve you." ¹¹Yahweh sent Yerubba'al, Bedan, Yiphtah and Shemu'el, and rescued you from the hand of your enemies all round, and you lived in confidence. ¹²But you saw that Nahash king of the Ammonites was coming against you and you said to me, "No, rather a king must reign over us", when Yahweh your God was your king.

¹³So now, here is the king that you chose, that you asked for. Here, Yahweh has put a king over you. ¹⁴If you live in awe of Yahweh, serve him, listen to his voice and do not rebel against

Yahweh's bidding, and both you and the king who reigns over you follow Yahweh your God . . .

¹⁵But if you don't listen to the voice of Yahweh your God but rebel against Yahweh's bidding, Yahweh's hand will be against you and against your ancestors.

## The sin of not praying

¹⁶Further, take your stand now and see this great thing that Yahweh is going to do before your eyes. ¹⁷It's the wheat harvest today, isn't it. I shall call to Yahweh and he will give thunder and rain. You will acknowledge and see that you did a thing that was extremely bad in Yahweh's eyes, in asking for a king for yourselves.'

¹⁸So Shemu'el called to Yahweh and Yahweh gave thunder and rain that day. All the people were in great awe of Yahweh and of Shemu'el. ¹⁹All the people said to Shemu'el, 'Plead on behalf of your servants to Yahweh your God so we don't die, because we've added something bad to all our wrongdoings in asking for a king for ourselves.'

²⁰Shemu'el said to the people, 'Don't be afraid. You yourselves have undertaken all this bad action. Nevertheless don't turn aside from following Yahweh. Serve Yahweh with your entire mind. ²¹You're not to turn aside, because [it would be] after something empty, things that are no use and cannot rescue, because they're empty. ²²Because Yahweh won't take leave of his people, for the sake of his great name, because Yahweh resolved to make you a people for him. ²³Further, as for me, far be it from me to do wrong against Yahweh by leaving off from pleading for you. I shall instruct you in the way that's good and right. ²⁴Nevertheless, live in awe of Yahweh and serve him in truthfulness with your entire mind, because you can see how he has done great things for you. ²⁵But if you actually do what's bad: both you and your king, you'll be swept away.'

## The king takes decisive action

**13** Sha'ul had been one year reigning and he reigned two years over Yisra'el. ²Then Sha'ul chose for himself 3,000 men from Yisra'el; 2,000 were with Sha'ul at Mikmas and in the highland at Bet-el, and 1,000 were with Yonatan [Jonathan] at Gib'ah-in-Binyamin. The rest of the company he sent off, each one, to his tents.

³Yonatan struck down the Pelishtites' outpost that was at Geba, and the Pelishtites heard. Sha'ul himself blew on the horn throughout the country, saying 'The Hebrews are to hear!' ⁴and all Yisra'el heard: 'Sha'ul has struck down the Pelishtites' outpost, and now Yisra'el has come to stink to the Pelishtites.' The people had themselves called out behind Sha'ul at Gilgal, ⁵while the Pelishtites gathered to battle with Yisra'el: 30,000 chariotry, 6,000 cavalry and a company like the sand that is on the seashore in their large number. They went up and camped at Mikmas, east of Bet Aven. ⁶When the Yisra'elites saw that things were pressing for them, that the company was hard pressed, the company hid in caves, in thickets, in cliffs, in pits and in cisterns, ⁷while Hebrews crossed the Yarden [Jordan] to the region of Gad and Gil'ad.

Sha'ul was still at Gilgal, while the entire company following him trembled. ⁸He waited seven days for the set time that Shemu'el said, but Shemu'el didn't come to Gilgal, and the company was dispersing from him. ⁹So Sha'ul said, 'Bring up to me the burnt offering and the well-being sacrifices', and he offered up the burnt offering. ¹⁰As he finished offering up the burnt offering, there was Shemu'el coming. Sha'ul went out to meet him, to bless him.

## You've been stupid

¹¹But Shemu'el said, 'What have you done?' Sha'ul said, 'When I saw that the company was dispersing from me, and you yourself had not come at the set time, and the Pelishtites were gathering at Mikmas, ¹²I said, "The Pelishtites will now come down to me at Gilgal and I haven't sought to gain Yahweh's goodwill." So I forced myself and offered up the burnt offering.'

¹³Shemu'el said to Sha'ul, 'You've been idiotic. You haven't kept the order of Yahweh your God, which he gave you. Because Yahweh would now have made your kingship over Yisra'el stand permanently, ¹⁴but now your kingship won't stand. Yahweh has sought for himself a man in accordance with his own mind. Yahweh has ordered that he is to be ruler over his people,

because you haven't kept what Yahweh ordered you.' ¹⁵And Shemu'el set off and went up from Gilgal to Gib'ah-in-Binyamin.

Sha'ul numbered the company of those that could be found with him, some 600 men. ¹⁶Sha'ul and Yonatan his son and the company that could be found with them were staying at Geba in Binyamin and the Pelishtites had camped at Mikmas. ¹⁷A group wreaking devastation went out of the Pelishtites' camp in three columns. One column would turn its face towards the Ophrah road, towards the Shu'al region. ¹⁸One column would turn its face towards the Bet Horon road. One column would turn its face towards the border road overlooking Tsebo'im Ravine, towards the wilderness.

¹⁹Now no smith could be found in all the country of Yisra'el because the Pelishtites had said, 'So that the Hebrews cannot make sword or lance.' (²⁰So all Yisra'el went down to the Pelishtites for anyone to sharpen his ploughshare, his pick, his axe and his sickle. ²¹The charge was two thirds of a sheqel for the ploughshare and for the picks, and a third for a fork, for the axes and for setting the goad.) ²²So on a day of battle no sword or lance could be found in the hand of any of the company that was with Sha'ul and with Yonatan, though it could be found belonging to Sha'ul and to Yonatan his son.

## A bright idea on the part of Yonatan (Yehonatan)

²³So the Pelishtites' garrison had gone out to the pass at Mikmas.

**14** A day came and Yonatan ben Sha'ul said to the boy who was his equipment-bearer, 'Come on, let's cross over to the Pelishtites' garrison that's across over there.' He didn't tell his father.

²Sha'ul was staying on the edge of Gib'ah, under the pomegranate tree which is at Migron. The company that was with him was some 600 men, ³with Ahiyyah ben Ahitub, who was brother of Ikabod ben Pinhas, son of Eli, Yahweh's priest at Shiloh, carrying a chasuble; the company didn't know that Yonatan had gone.

⁴Between the crossings by which Yonatan sought to cross to the Pelishtites' garrison

there was a craggy outcrop on one side of the crossing and a craggy outcrop on the other side of the crossing. The name of the one was Swamp and the name of the other was Thorn. [5]The one outcrop was a pillar on the north near Mikmas, the other on the south near Geba.

[6]So Yehonatan said to the boy who was his equipment-bearer, 'Come on, let's cross over to the garrison of these foreskinned men. Maybe Yahweh will act on our behalf, because Yahweh has no difficulty in delivering by many or by few.' [7]His equipment-bearer said to him, 'Do all that's in your mind. Follow your inclination. Here, I'm with you. Just what's in your mind.' [8]Yehonatan said, 'Here, we're going to cross over to the men and we'll show ourselves to them. [9]If they say this to us, "Stay still till we reach you", we'll stand where we are and not go up to them. [10]But if they say this, "Come up to us", we'll go up, because Yahweh will have given them into our hand. This will be the sign for us.'

### Yonatan and his boy

[11]So the two of them showed themselves to the Pelishtites' garrison, and the Pelishtites said, 'There, Hebrews coming out of the holes where they hid themselves.' [12]The men in the garrison avowed to Yonatan and to his equipment-bearer, 'Come up to us and we'll make you acknowledge something.' Yonatan said to his equipment-bearer, 'Come up after me, because Yahweh has given them into the hand of Yisra'el.' [13]Yonatan went up on his hands and his feet with his equipment-bearer behind him. And they fell before Yonatan, with his equipment-bearer putting them to death behind him. [14]The first blow that Yonatan and his equipment-bearer struck was some twenty men, in some half a furlong of an acre of field. [15]There was trembling in the camp, in the field and in the entire company, while the garrison and the group wreaking devastation also trembled, and the earth shook. It became a supernatural trembling.

[16]Sha'ul's lookouts at Gib'ah-in-Binyamin saw: there, the turmoil was surging. It went hither and thither. [17]Sha'ul said to the company that was with him, 'Take a count, will you, and see who's gone from us.' They took a count and there, Yonatan and his equipment-bearer

were not there. [18]Sha'ul said to Ahiyyah, 'Bring up God's chest' (because God's chest was at that time with the Yisra'elites).

[19]But while Sha'ul spoke to the priest, the turmoil that was in the Pelishtites' camp continued to go on and increase, so Sha'ul said to the priest, 'Take away your hand', [20]and Sha'ul and the entire company that was with him had themselves called out and came to the battle. There, one person's sword was against his neighbour, a very great confusion. [21]Some Hebrews had belonged to the Pelishtites in previous days, people who had gone up with them into the camp all round, and they too came to be with the Yisra'el that was with Sha'ul and Yonatan, [22]while all the Yisra'elites hiding in the highland of Ephrayim heard that the Pelishtites had fled, and they too caught up with them in battle. [23a]Yahweh delivered Yisra'el that day.

### A taste of honey

[23b]When the battle passed beyond Bet Aven, [24]the Yisra'elites were hard pressed that day. Sha'ul had got the company to swear, 'Cursed is the man who eats a meal before evening, when I've taken redress from my enemies', and the entire company hadn't tasted a meal.

[25]Now the whole country came into the forest and there was honey on the face of the field. [26]So the company came into the forest, and there, honey flowing. But no one put his hand to his mouth, because the company was in awe of the oath. [27]But Yonatan hadn't heard his father get the company to swear, and he stretched out the end of the cane that was in his hand, dipped it into a honeycomb and brought his hand back to his mouth, and his eyes lit up. [28]Someone from the company avowed, 'Your father actually got the company to swear, "Cursed is the man who eats food today", and the company has got weary.' [29]Yonatan said, 'My father has brought disaster on the country. Please see that my eyes lit up when I tasted this bit of honey. [30]Yes, if only the company had actually eaten of its enemies' spoil that it found today, because now wouldn't the calamity for the Pelishtites have been great.'

[31]They struck the Pelishtites down that day from Mikmas to Ayyalon, but the company

got very weary. ³²So the company pounced on the spoil, got flock, herd and calves, and slaughtered them on the ground. The company ate with the blood.

³³People told Sha'ul: 'There, the company are doing wrong in relation to Yahweh by eating with the blood.' He said, 'You've broken faith. Roll a big stone to me now.' ³⁴Sha'ul said, 'Spread out among the company and say to them, "Bring up to me each one his ox and each one his sheep and slaughter it here, and you can eat. You are not to do wrong in relation to Yahweh by eating with the blood."' So the entire company brought up, each one, his ox in his possession that night and slaughtered it there. ³⁵Sha'ul built an altar for Yahweh. It was the first he built as an altar for Yahweh.

## The fog of war clarified

³⁶Sha'ul said, 'Let's go down after the Pelishtites tonight and plunder among them till morning light, and not let one person remain among them.' They said, 'Do all that's good in your eyes.' But the priest said, 'Let's draw near to God here.' ³⁷So Sha'ul asked of God, 'Shall I go down after the Pelishtites? Will you give them into Yisra'el's hand?' But he didn't answer him that day. ³⁸Sha'ul said, 'Come up to here, all you cornerstones of the company. Get to know and see how this wrong has happened today. ³⁹Because as Yahweh who delivers Yisra'el lives, even if it is through Yonatan my son, he will absolutely be put to death.' From the entire company there was no one answered him. ⁴⁰He said to all Yisra'el, 'You're to be on one side, and I and Yonatan my son will be on the other side.' The company said to Sha'ul, 'Do what is good in your eyes.' ⁴¹Sha'ul said to Yahweh the God of Yisra'el, 'Grant the truth.' Yonatan and Sha'ul were taken and the company came out. ⁴²Sha'ul said, 'Make it fall between me and Yonatan my son.' Yonatan was taken. ⁴³Sha'ul said to Yonatan, 'Do tell me what you've done.' Yonatan told him: 'I just took a taste, with the end of the cane that was in my hand, of a bit of honey. Here I am. I will die.' ⁴⁴Sha'ul said, 'May God do thus and may he do more [to me], because you absolutely must die, Yonatan.' ⁴⁵But the company said to Sha'ul, 'Is Yonatan to die when he brought about this

great deliverance in Yisra'el? Far be it, as Yahweh lives, if a hair of his head is to fall to the ground, because he has acted this day with God.' So the company redeemed Yonatan and he didn't die. ⁴⁶But Sha'ul gave up from following the Pelishtites, and the Pelishtites went to their place.

## The successful king

⁴⁷When Sha'ul had taken the kingship over Yisra'el, he did battle all round against all his enemies, against Mo'ab, against the Ammonites, against Edom, against the kings of Tsobah and against the Pelishtites. Anyone who would turn his face, he treated as faithless. ⁴⁸He acted forcefully, struck down Amaleq and rescued Yisra'el from the hand of its despoiler.

⁴⁹Sha'ul's sons were Yonatan, Yishvi and Malki-shua. The name of his two daughters – the name of the firstborn, Merab, the name of the younger, Mikal. ⁵⁰The name of Sha'ul's wife: Ahino'am bat Ahima'ats. The name of his army officer: Abiner ben Ner, Sha'ul's uncle. ⁵¹Both Qish, Sha'ul's father, and Ner, Abner's father, was Abi'el's son.

⁵²There was fierce battling against the Pelishtites all Sha'ul's time, but Sha'ul would see anyone who was a strong man or any forceful individual and get him to join him.

**15** Shemu'el said to Sha'ul, 'It was me that Yahweh sent to anoint you as king over his people, over Yisra'el. So listen now to the voice (the words) of Yahweh. ²Yahweh of Armies has said this: "I am attending to what Amaleq did to Yisra'el when he set upon them on the way, when they were going up from Misrayim. ³Now go and strike down Amaleq and devote everything that it has. You will not spare it. Put to death both man and woman, both child and baby, both ox and sheep, both camel and donkey."'

⁴Sha'ul got the company to listen, and numbered them at Tela'im, 200,000 men on foot and 10,000 men from Judah. ⁵Sha'ul came as far as the town of Amaleq and lay in wait in the wadi. ⁶Sha'ul said to the Qenites, 'Go, move away, go down from among the Amaleqites, so I don't gather you up with them, given that you acted in commitment with all the Yisra'elites when they went up from Misrayim.' So the Qenites departed from among Amaleq.

### The king who wasn't ruthless enough

[7]Sha'ul struck down Amaleq from Havilah until you come to Shur, which is east of Misrayim. [8]He captured Agag king of Amaleq alive, while the entire company he devoted with the mouth of the sword. [9]But Sha'ul and the company spared Agag and the best of the flock, the herd, the second-born and the lambs, everything that was good. They were not willing to devote them. But every object that was despised and emaciated – they devoted it.

[10]Yahweh's word came to Shemu'el: [11]'I relent of having Sha'ul reign as king, because he's turned from following me and hasn't implemented my words.' It enraged Shemu'el and he cried out to Yahweh all night.

[12]Shemu'el started early in the morning to meet Sha'ul. It was told Shemu'el, 'Sha'ul's come to Carmel. Here, he's been putting up a monument for himself. Then he turned round and passed on, and went down to Gilgal.'

[13]Shemu'el came to Sha'ul, and Sha'ul said to him, 'Blessed are you by Yahweh! I've implemented Yahweh's word.' [14]Shemu'el said, 'So what's this sound of a flock in my ears, and the sound of a herd that I'm hearing?' [15]Sha'ul said, 'They brought them from the Amaleqites, because the company spared the best of the flock and the herd to sacrifice for Yahweh your God. The rest we devoted.'

[16]Shemu'el said to Sha'ul, 'Slow down, and I shall tell you what Yahweh spoke to me last night.' He said to him, 'Speak.' [17]Shemu'el said, 'Though you were small in your eyes, you're the head of Yisra'el's clans. Yahweh anointed you as king over Yisra'el [18]and Yahweh sent you on a journey. He said to you, "Go and devote the wrongdoers, Amaleq. Do battle against them until you've finished them off." [19]Why didn't you listen to Yahweh's voice but pounce on the spoil and do what was bad in Yahweh's eyes?'

### Listening is better than sacrificing

[20]Sha'ul said to Shemu'el, 'I listened to Yahweh's voice! I went on the journey that Yahweh sent me on. I brought Agag king of Amaleq, but Amaleq I devoted. [21]The company took flock and herd from the spoil, the first of what was to be devoted, to sacrifice for Yahweh your God at Gilgal.' [22]Shemu'el said,

Are burnt offerings and sacrifices as pleasing
    to Yahweh
    as listening to Yahweh's voice?
Here, listening is better than sacrificing,
    heeding than the fat of rams.
[23]Because rebellion: the wrongdoing that comes
    from divination,
    arrogance: the trouble that comes from
    effigies.
Since you rejected Yahweh's word,
    he has rejected you from being king.

[24]Sha'ul said to Shemu'el, 'I did wrong, because I transgressed Yahweh's bidding and your words, because I was afraid of the company and I listened to their voice. [25]But now, please carry my wrongdoing. Come back with me and I will bow low to Yahweh.' [26]Shemu'el said to Sha'ul, 'I will not come back with you, because you rejected Yahweh's word and Yahweh has rejected you from being king over Yisra'el.' [27]And Shemu'el turned round to go.

He took strong hold of the corner of his coat, and it tore, [28]and Shemu'el said to him, 'Yahweh has torn the kingship of Yisra'el from you today and given it to a neighbour of yours who is better than you. [29]Further, Yisra'el's Enduring One does not speak falsely and does not relent, because he's not a human being so as to relent.'

[30]He said, 'I did wrong. Now please honour me in the presence of the elders of my people and in the presence of Yisra'el, and come back with me, and I will bow low to Yahweh your God.' [31]So Shemu'el went back after Sha'ul and Sha'ul bowed low to Yahweh.

[32]Shemu'el said, 'Bring up to me Agag king of Amaleq.' Agag went to him in chains. Agag said, 'Yes! The bitterness of death is departing!' [33]But Shemu'el said, 'As your sword made women childless, so your mother will become childless beyond other women.' And Shemu'el cut Agag down before Yahweh at Gilgal.

### Yahweh sees into the heart

[34]Shemu'el went to The Height while Sha'ul went up to his home at Gib'ah-of-Sha'ul. [35]Shemu'el didn't see Sha'ul again until the day

of his death, because Shemu'el took up grieving for Sha'ul when Yahweh had relented that he had made Sha'ul king over Yisra'el.

**16** But Yahweh said to Shemu'el, 'How long are you going to take up grieving for Sha'ul, when I myself have rejected him from being king over Yisra'el? Fill your horn with oil and go: I shall send you to Yishay [Jesse] the Bet-lehemite because I've seen a king for myself among his sons.' ²Shemu'el said, 'How can I go? Sha'ul will hear and kill me.' Yahweh said, 'You're to take a heifer in your possession and say "It's to sacrifice for Yahweh that I've come", ³and invite Yishay to the sacrifice. I myself will let you know what you're to do and you're to anoint for me the one that I say to you.'

⁴Shemu'el did what Yahweh spoke. He came to Bet Lehem, and the town's elders trembled to meet him and said, 'Does your coming mean things are well?' ⁵He said, 'Things are well. It's to sacrifice for Yahweh that I've come. Make yourselves sacred and come with me to the sacrifice.' He made Yishay and his sons sacred and invited them to the sacrifice.

⁶When they came, he saw Eli'ab and said, 'Surely his anointed is in front of Yahweh!' ⁷But Yahweh said to Shemu'el, 'Don't look at his appearance or at the loftiness to which he stands, because I've rejected him, because it's not what a human being sees, because a human being sees what appears to the eyes, but Yahweh sees into the mind.' ⁸Yishay called Abinadab and had him pass before Shemu'el,

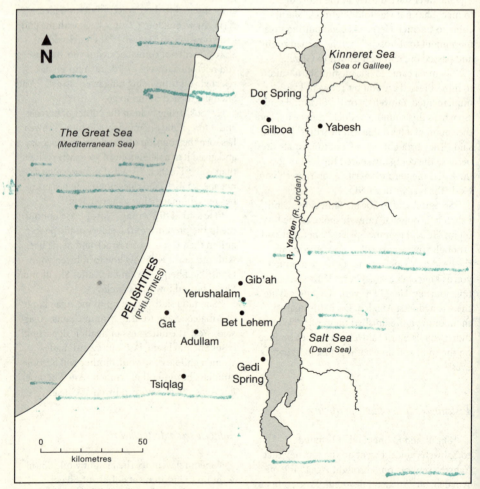

*1 Samuel 16: Sha'ul (Saul) and David*

but he said, 'Yahweh has not chosen this one either.' ⁹Yishay had Shammah pass, but he said, 'Yahweh has not chosen this one either.' ¹⁰Yishay had his seven sons pass before Shemu'el, but Shemu'el said to Yishay, 'Yahweh has not chosen these.'

## Yahweh's good spirit and Yahweh's bad spirit

¹¹Shemu'el said to Yishay, 'Have the boys come to an end?' He said, 'The little one still remains, but there, he's tending the flock.' Shemu'el said to Yishay, 'Send and get him, because we won't sit down till he comes here.' ¹²So he sent and brought him. He was tanned, with lovely eyes, good-looking. Yahweh said, 'Get up, anoint him, because this is the one.' ¹³Shemu'el got the horn of oil and anointed him among his brothers. Yahweh's spirit thrust itself on to David from that day onwards. And Shemu'el set off and went to The Height.

¹⁴Now Yahweh's spirit had departed from Sha'ul and a bad spirit from Yahweh had terrified him. ¹⁵Sha'ul's servants said to him, 'Please, here, a bad spirit from God is terrifying you. ¹⁶Please, our lord should say that your servants who are before you should look for someone who knows how to play the guitar. When the bad spirit from God is upon you, he would play and it would be good for you.' ¹⁷Sha'ul said to his servants, 'Look for someone who is good at playing for me, please, and bring him to me.' ¹⁸One of the boys answered, 'Here, I've seen a son of Yishay the Bet-lehemite who knows how to play. He's a forceful strong man, a man of battle, but smart with words and good-looking, and Yahweh is with him.'

¹⁹So Sha'ul sent envoys to Yishay and said, 'Send me David your son, who's with the flock.' ²⁰Yishay got a donkey, bread, a skin of wine and a kid-goat from the flock, and sent them by the hand of David his son to Sha'ul. ²¹David came to Sha'ul and stood by him. He liked him a lot and he became an equipment-bearer for him. ²²Sha'ul sent to Yishay to say, 'May David please stand before me, because he's found grace in my eyes.' ²³When the spirit from God would come to Sha'ul, David would get the guitar and play by hand, and there would be relief

for Sha'ul. It was good for him. The bad spirit would depart from him.

## The frightening champion

**17** The Pelishtites gathered their camp for battle. They gathered at Sokoh which belongs to Yehudah and camped between Sokoh and Azeqah, at Dammim End, ²while Sha'ul and the Yisra'elites gathered and camped in Oak Vale and lined up for battle to meet the Pelishtites. ³The Pelishtites were standing on a mountain on one side and Yisra'el was standing on a mountain on the other side, with the ravine between them.

⁴A representative went out from the Pelishtites' camps, Golyat [Goliath] his name, from Gat, his height three metres and a handbreadth, ⁵a copper helmet on his head. He was clothed in a coat of mail (the weight of the coat was 5,000 sheqels of copper), ⁶with copper shin guards on his legs, a copper javelin between his shoulders, ⁷the wood of his lance like a weavers' rod, the point of his lance 600 sheqels of iron, and a shield-bearer walking before him.

⁸He stood and called to the ranks of Yisra'el: 'Why should you go out and line up for battle? I'm the Pelishtite, aren't I, and you're Sha'ul's servants. Choose yourselves someone who will go down against me. ⁹If he succeeds in battling with me and strikes me down, we'll become servants to you. If I'm the one who succeeds over him and strikes him down, you'll become servants to us and serve us.' ¹⁰The Pelishtite said, 'I myself revile Yisra'el's ranks this day. Give me a man and we'll do battle together.' ¹¹Sha'ul and all Yisra'el listened to these words of the Pelishtite, and they were scared, very frightened.

## The boy gets the chance to see

¹²Now David was the son of an Ephratite individual from Bet Lehem in Yehudah; his name was Yishay. He had eight sons. In the time of Sha'ul the man was old, going on in age among men. ¹³Yishay's three eldest sons had gone, gone after Sha'ul to the battle. The names

of his three sons who had gone into the battle were Eli'ab the firstborn, his second Abinadab and the third Shammah, [14]while David was the youngest. The three oldest had gone after Sha'ul, [15]while David was going and coming back from being with Sha'ul to shepherd his father's flock in Bet-lehem.

[16]The Pelishtite went up, starting early and doing it in the evening, and took his stand for forty days.

[17]Yishay said to David his son, 'Get a barrel of this roasted grain and ten loaves of this bread, please, and run them to the camp for your brothers. [18]And these ten wedges of cheese, you're to bring to the divisional officer. You're to attend to your brothers, as to whether things are well with them, and get some reassurance from them, [19]while Sha'ul and they and all the Yisra'elites are in Oak Vale doing battle with the Pelishtites.'

[20]David started early in the morning, left the flock to a keeper, picked things up, went as Yishay had ordered him, and came to the encampment when the force was going out to the line and shouting for the battle. [21]Yisra'el and the Pelishtites lined up, line to meet line.

[22]David left the things with him in the hand of the equipment-keeper and ran to the line. He came and asked his brothers whether things were well with them. [23]While he was speaking with them, there, the representative was going up (Golyat the Pelishtite was his name, from Gat) from the Pelishtites' lines. He spoke these same words, and David listened.

## You're too young and inexperienced

[24]When all the Yisra'elites saw the man, they fled from before him. They were very frightened. [25]A Yisra'elite said, 'Have you seen this man going up? Because he's going up to revile Yisra'el. The man who strikes him down, the king will give him great wealth and give him his daughter and make his father's household tax-free in Yisra'el.'

[26]So David said to the men standing with him, 'What will be done for the man who strikes down that Pelishtite and removes reviling from Yisra'el? Because who is this foreskinned Pelishtite that he's reviled the lines of the living God?' [27]The company said to him

this same thing, 'So it will be done for the man who strikes him down.'

[28]Eli'ab, David's older brother, heard him speaking to the men, and Eli'ab's anger raged at David. He said, 'Why is it that you've come down? And who did you leave that little flock alone in the wilderness with? I myself know your assertiveness and the bad inclination in your mind, that you've come down in order to see the battle.' [29]David said, 'What have I done now? Wasn't that just a word?' [30]He turned from being near him towards another man and said this same thing. The company gave word back to him that was the same as the first.

[31]The words that David spoke were heard and they told Sha'ul, and he got hold of him. [32]David said to Sha'ul, 'No one's heart should fail him. Your servant himself will go and battle with this Pelishtite.' [33]Sha'ul said to David, 'You can't succeed in going to this Pelishtite to battle with him, because you're a boy and he's been a strong man from his boyhood.'

## How to recycle your killer instinct

[34]David said to Sha'ul, 'Your servant has been shepherding over the flock for his father. A lion or a bear comes and carries off a sheep from the flock, [35]and I go out after it and strike it down and rescue it from its mouth. It rises up against me and I get strong hold of it by its beard and strike it down and put it to death. [36]Both lion and bear your servant has struck down. This foreskinned Pelishtite will be like one of them, because he's reviled the ranks of the living God.' [37]And David said, 'Yahweh who rescued me from the hand of the lion and from the hand of the bear: he will rescue me from the hand of this Pelishtite.' Sha'ul said to David, 'Go, and Yahweh be with you.'

[38]Sha'ul clothed David in his uniform and put a copper helmet on his head and clothed him in a coat of mail. [39]David wrapped his sword over his uniform and resolved to walk, because he hadn't tried it. But David said to Sha'ul, 'I can't walk in these because I haven't tried them.' So David removed them off him, [40]took his stick in his hand, chose five smooth stones for himself from the wadi, put them in the shepherds' bag which he had, in the pouch,

with his sling in his hand, and went up to the Pelishtite. ⁴¹The Pelishtite kept walking and drawing near to David, with the shield-bearer before him.

⁴²The Pelishtite looked out and saw David, and despised him because he was a boy, tanned and lovely in appearance. ⁴³The Pelishtite said to David, 'Am I a dog that you're coming against me with sticks?' And the Pelishtite slighted David by his gods. ⁴⁴The Pelishtite said to David, 'Come to me, and I'll give your flesh to the birds of the heavens and to the animals of the wild.'

## There is a God in Yisra'el

⁴⁵David said to the Pelishtite, 'You're coming against me with sword, with lance and with javelin, but I'm coming against you in the name of Yahweh of Armies the God of Yisra'el's lines, whom you've reviled. ⁴⁶This day Yahweh will deliver you into my hand and I shall strike you down and remove your head from you. I shall give the carcases of the Pelishtites' camp this day to the birds of the heavens and to the creatures of the earth. All the earth will acknowledge that Yisra'el has a God, ⁴⁷and this entire congregation will acknowledge that it is not by sword or by lance that Yahweh delivers, because the battle belongs to Yahweh and he will give you people into our hand.'

⁴⁸When the Pelishtite got up and walked and drew near to meet David, David hurried and ran to the line to meet the Pelishtite. ⁴⁹David put his hand into the bag, got a stone from there, slung it and struck the Pelishtite on his forehead. The stone sank into his forehead. He fell on his face to the ground. ⁵⁰So David was stronger than the Pelishtite with sling and with stone. He struck the Pelishtite down and put him to death. There was no sword in David's hand, ⁵¹so David ran, stood over the Pelishtite, got his sword, pulled it from its sheath and put him to death. He cut off his head with it.

The Pelishtites saw that their strong man was dead, and they fled. ⁵²The Yisra'elites and Yehudahites got up, shouted, and pursued after the Pelishtites until you come to the ravine and to the gateways of Eqron. The Pelishtites who were run through fell on the Sha'arim road as far as Gat and as far as Eqron. ⁵³The Yisra'elites came back from chasing after the Pelishtites and despoiled their camp. ⁵⁴David got the Pelishtite's head and brought it to Yerushalaim [Jerusalem]. His equipment he put in his own tent.

## Sha'ul has struck down his thousands, David his ten thousands

⁵⁵When Sha'ul saw David going out to meet the Pelishtite, he said to Abner, the army officer, 'The boy, whose son is he, Abner?' Abner said, 'On your life, Your Majesty, if I know.' ⁵⁶The king said, 'You ask whose son the kid is.' ⁵⁷When David came back from striking down the Pelishtite, Abner got him and brought him before Sha'ul, with the Pelishtite's head in his hand. ⁵⁸Sha'ul said to him, 'Whose son are you, my boy?' David said, 'The son of your servant Yishay the Bet Lehemite.'

**18** When he'd finished speaking to Sha'ul, the person of Yehonatan bound itself to David's person. Yehonatan became loyal to him as a person like himself. ²Sha'ul took him that day and didn't let him go back to his father's household. ³Yehonatan and David solemnized a pact because he was loyal to him as a person like himself. ⁴Yehonatan took off the coat that he had on and gave it to David, with his uniform, and along with his sword, with his bow and with his belt.

⁵David went out wherever Sha'ul would send him; as he was successful, Sha'ul set him over the men of battle. It was good in the eyes of the entire company, and also in the eyes of Sha'ul's servants.

⁶But when they had come home, when David got back from striking down the Pelishtite, the women came out from all the towns in Yisra'el for singing and dances to meet King Sha'ul, with tambourines, with celebration and with triangles. ⁷The women who were having fun chanted,

Sha'ul has struck down his thousands,
David his ten thousands.

⁸And it really enraged Sha'ul. This thing was bad in his eyes. He said, 'They've given David ten thousands and given me thousands. Only the kingship will yet be his.' ⁹Sha'ul was eyeing David from that day on.

## Daughters are just political pawns

<sup>10</sup>Next day a bad spirit from God thrust itself on Sha'ul and he prophesied inside the house while David was playing by hand, as he did each day. There was a lance in Sha'ul's hand <sup>11</sup>and Sha'ul threw the lance. He said 'I'll pin David to the wall'; but David turned from before him, twice. <sup>12</sup>Sha'ul was afraid before David because Yahweh was with him and had departed from Sha'ul, <sup>13</sup>and Sha'ul moved him away from being with him and made him a divisional officer, so he went out and came in before the company. <sup>14</sup>David was successful on all his journeys; Yahweh was with him. <sup>15</sup>Sha'ul saw that he was very successful, and he was in dread before him, <sup>16</sup>but all Yisra'el and Yehudah loved David, because he was going out and coming in before them.

<sup>17</sup>Sha'ul said to David, 'Here's my oldest daughter Merab. I'll give her to you as wife. Only be a forceful man for me and engage in Yahweh's battles' (Sha'ul had said, 'My hand must not be against him. The Pelishtites' hand is to be against him'). <sup>18</sup>David said to Sha'ul, 'Who am I and what is my life, my father's kin-group in Yisra'el, that I should become the king's son-in-law?'

<sup>19</sup>Then at the time for giving Merab, Sha'ul's daughter, to David, she was given as wife to Adri'el the Meholatite. <sup>20</sup>But Mikal, Sha'ul's daughter, loved David, and they told Sha'ul. The thing was all right in his eyes. <sup>21</sup>Sha'ul said, 'I'll give her to him and she'll become a snare to him, so the Pelishtites' hand may be against him.' So Sha'ul said to David, 'Through number two you're to become my son-in-law, right now.'

## Twice as many deaths as Sha'ul asks for

<sup>22</sup>Sha'ul ordered his servants, 'Speak to David quietly: "Here, the king delights in you and all his servants love you. So now, become the king's son-in-law."' <sup>23</sup>The king's servants spoke these words in David's ears. David said, 'Is it a slight thing in your eyes, becoming the king's son-in-law, when I am a destitute, slight person?' <sup>24</sup>Sha'ul's servants told him, 'These very words David spoke.'

<sup>25</sup>Sha'ul said, 'Say this to David: "The king will have no delight in a marriage gift except in a hundred Pelishtite foreskins, to have redress on the king's enemies"' (Sha'ul thought to have David fall by the hand of the Pelishtites). <sup>26</sup>His servants told these things to David, and the thing was all right in David's eyes, for becoming the king's son-in-law. The days were not complete <sup>27</sup>but David got up and went, he and his men, and struck down 200 of the Pelishtites. David brought their foreskins and they fulfilled the number for the king so that he might become the king's son-in-law. So Sha'ul gave him Mikal his daughter as wife.

<sup>28</sup>Sha'ul saw and acknowledged that Yahweh was with David, and Mikal Sha'ul's daughter loved him, <sup>29</sup>and Sha'ul grew more afraid of David. Sha'ul became hostile to David all the time.

<sup>30</sup>The Pelishtites' officers went out, and as many times as they went out, David was more successful than all Sha'ul's servants. His name was highly esteemed.

**19** Sha'ul spoke to Yonatan his son and to all his servants about bringing about David's death, but Yehonatan Sha'ul's son delighted in David very much, <sup>2</sup>and Yehonatan told David: 'Sha'ul my father is seeking to bring about your death, so now, please keep watch in the morning, stay in a secret place and hide. <sup>3</sup>I myself will go out and stand at my father's hand in the fields where you are, and I'll speak to my father about you. I'll see what, and tell you.'

## A bad spirit from Yahweh

<sup>4</sup>Yehonatan spoke good things of David to Sha'ul his father. He said to him, 'The king shouldn't do wrong to his servant, to David, because he hasn't done wrong to you, and because his actions have been very good for you. <sup>5</sup>He put his life in the palm of his hand and struck down the Pelishtite, and Yahweh brought about a great deliverance for all Yisra'el. You saw and you rejoiced. Why should you do wrong, shedding the blood of a person who is free of guilt, by bringing about David's death for nothing?' <sup>6</sup>Sha'ul listened to Yehonatan's voice, and Sha'ul swore, 'As Yahweh lives, if he is put to death . . .'

<sup>7</sup>So Yehonatan called to David and Yehonatan told him all these things, and

Yehonatan brought David to Sha'ul and he was before him as in previous days. ⁸Again there was a battle and David went out to battle with the Pelishtites and struck them down in a great rout, and they fled from before him.

⁹But a bad spirit from Yahweh came on Sha'ul. He was sitting in his house with his lance in his hand, and David was playing by hand, ¹⁰and Sha'ul sought to pin David to the wall, but he slipped away from before Sha'ul, and he pinned the lance into the wall. David fled and escaped that night. ¹¹Sha'ul sent envoys to David's house to keep watch on him and put him to death in the morning, but Mikal his wife told David, 'If you don't escape with your life tonight, you'll be put to death tomorrow.'

## Is Sha'ul among the prophets, too?

¹²So Mikal let David down through the window and he went and escaped and took flight. ¹³Mikal got the effigies and put them in the bed, and put a goat's hair quilt at its head and covered it with clothing. ¹⁴Sha'ul sent envoys to get David, but she said, 'He's ill.' ¹⁵So Sha'ul sent the envoys to see David, saying 'Bring him up to me in the bed, to put him to death.' ¹⁶The envoys came and there, the effigies in the bed and the goat's hair quilt at its head. ¹⁷Sha'ul said to Mikal, 'Why did you beguile me like that and help my enemy get away so he escaped?' Mikal said to Sha'ul, 'He himself said to me, "Help me get away. Why should I put you to death?"'

¹⁸When David took flight and escaped, he came to Shemu'el at The Height and told him all that Sha'ul had done to him. He went, he and Shemu'el, and they stayed in the cabins. ¹⁹It was told Sha'ul, 'There, David's in the cabins at The Height.' ²⁰Sha'ul sent envoys to get David. He saw a group of prophets prophesying, and Shemu'el standing presiding over them. God's spirit came on Sha'ul's envoys and they too prophesied. ²¹People told Sha'ul, so he sent more envoys, but they prophesied, too. Sha'ul again sent, the third envoys, and they prophesied, too.

²²So he also went to The Height. He came as far as the great cistern which is at Seku and asked, 'Where are Shemu'el and David?' Someone said, 'There, in the cabins at The

Height.' ²³He went there, to the cabins at The Height, and God's spirit came on him, too. He walked on and prophesied until he came to the cabins at The Height. ²⁴He too stripped off his clothes, and he too prophesied before Shemu'el. He fell down naked all that day and all night. That's why they say, 'Is Sha'ul among the prophets, too?'

## A test of Sha'ul's attitude

**20** David took flight from the cabins at The Height and came and said before Yehonatan, 'What have I done, what is my waywardness, what is my wrongdoing before your father, that he is seeking my life?' ²He said to him, 'Far be it! You will not die. Here, my father doesn't do anything big or anything small but he has a word in my ear. Why would my father conceal this thing from me? This won't be.' ³But David also swore, 'Your father does know that I've found grace in your eyes, and he's said, "Yehonatan isn't to know this, so he won't be pained." Actually, as Yahweh lives and as you yourself live, there's really just a step between me and death.' ⁴Yehonatan said to David, 'What you yourself say, I will do for you.'

⁵David said to Yehonatan, 'Here, tomorrow is the new month. I'm definitely to sit with the king to eat. You should send me off and I'll hide in the fields until the third evening. ⁶If your father does attend to me, you're to say, "David did ask me about running to Bet-lehem, his town, because there's the annual sacrifice for the entire kin-group there." ⁷If he says this: "Good", things are well for your servant, but if it really enrages him, acknowledge that some bad action is certain from him. ⁸You're to act in commitment with your servant because you've brought your servant into a pact before Yahweh with you. If there's waywardness in me, put me to death yourself. Why is it that you should bring me back to your father?'

⁹Yehonatan said, 'Far be it from you! Because if I do get to know that some bad action by my father is certain to come on you, wouldn't I tell you about it?' ¹⁰David said to Yehonatan, 'Who will tell me if your father gives you a tough answer?'

## Loyalty

[11]Yehonatan said to David, 'Come on, let's go out to the fields.' The two of them went out to the fields, [12]and Yehonatan said to David, 'Yahweh the God of Yisra'el! When I search out my father this very time tomorrow or the third day, and there – things are good for David, I shall then send to you and have a word in your ear, won't I. [13]May Yahweh act thus to Yehonatan and act thus again: when some bad action towards you seems good to my father, I will have a word in your ear and send you off, and you can go to where things will be well. And may Yahweh be with you as he was with my father. [14]While I'm still alive, will you not act in Yahweh's commitment with me, and I will not die. [15]And will you not cut off your commitment from my household, ever, not even when Yahweh has cut off David's enemies, each one, from the face of the ground. [16]Yehonatan has solemnized it with David's household. Yahweh will look for it from the hand of (the enemies of) David.' [17]Yehonatan again got David to swear by his loyalty to him, because he was loyal to him with the loyalty of his person.

[18]Yehonatan said to him, 'Tomorrow is the new month and you'll draw attention, because your seat will draw attention. [19]The third day, go right down and come to the place where you hid on the day you did it before, and stay beside the Ezel Stone. [20]When I myself shoot three arrows by the side of it, directing them for myself to a target, [21]there – I shall send the boy, "Go, find the arrows." If I do say to the boy, "There, the arrows are away from you over here, get them", you're to come, because things are well for you, and there's nothing, as Yahweh lives. [22]But if I say this to the kid, "There, the arrows are away from you over there", go, because Yahweh has sent you off. [23]The word that we have spoken, you and I: here, Yahweh is between you and me permanently.'

## Rage and shaming

[24]So David hid in the fields. The new month came and the king sat down to eat for the meal. [25]The king sat on his seat as usual, in the seat by the wall. Yehonatan got up and Abner sat at Sha'ul's side, but David's place drew attention.

[26]Sha'ul didn't speak a thing that day because (he said), 'There's been some chance thing so that he's not pure. Yes, he's not pure.' [27]Then the day after the new month, the second day, David's place drew attention, and Sha'ul said to Yehonatan his son, 'Why didn't ben Yishay come to the meal either yesterday or today?' [28]Yehonatan answered Sha'ul, 'David did ask me about going to Bet Lehem. [29]He said, "Please send me off, because we have a kin-group sacrifice in the town and my brother has given me an order. So now, if I've found grace in your eyes, please, I'll escape and see my brothers." That's why he hasn't come to the king's table.' [30]But Sha'ul's anger raged at Yehonatan. He said to him, 'Son of a perverse, rebellious woman! I know that you're choosing ben Yishay, aren't you, to your shame and to the shame of your mother's nakedness? [31]Because all the days that ben Yishay is alive on the earth, you and your kingship won't be established. So now, send and get him to me, because he deserves death.' [32]Yehonatan answered Sha'ul his father, 'Why is he to be put to death, what has he done?' [33]And Sha'ul threw the lance at him to strike him down. So Yehonatan acknowledged that it was determined by his father to put David to death. [34]Yehonatan got up from the table in an angry rage and didn't eat a meal on the second day of the new month because he felt pain for David because his father had shamed him.

## The play with the arrows

[35]In the morning Yehonatan went out to the fields for the meeting with David, a young boy with him. [36]He said to his boy, 'Run, please find the arrows that I'm shooting.' When the boy ran, and he shot an arrow so that it passed him, [37]the boy came to the location of the arrow that Yehonatan had shot, and Yehonatan called after the boy, 'Isn't the arrow away from you, over there?' [38]Yehonatan called after the boy, 'Hurry, be quick, don't stand there!' So Yehonatan's boy gathered the arrows and came to his lord. [39]The boy didn't know anything. Only Yehonatan and David knew about the thing. [40]Yehonatan gave the equipment to the boy that he had and said to him, 'Go, bring it to the town.'

⁴¹When the boy had come and David had got up from towards the south, he fell on his face to the ground and bowed low three times, and they kissed one another and cried with one another, until David did so greatly. ⁴²Yehonatan said to David, 'Go to where it will be well, because the two of us have sworn in Yahweh's name, "Yahweh be between me and you and between my offspring and your offspring permanently."' So David got up and went, while Yehonatan came to the town.

**21** David came to Nob, to Ahimelek the priest. Ahimelek trembled to meet David. He said to him, 'Why are you alone, and there's no one with you?' ²David said to Ahimelek the priest, 'When the king gave me an order about a matter, he said to me, "No one is to know anything about the matter on which I'm sending you and about which I gave you order." I've let the boys know about such and such a place. ³So now, what do you have at hand? Do put five loaves of bread in my hand, or what can be found.'

## Re-enter Golyat's sword

⁴The priest answered David, 'There's no ordinary bread at hand. Rather, there's sacred bread, if the boys have only kept themselves from women.' ⁵David answered the priest, 'No, women have been withheld from us, as in previous days. When I've gone out, the boys' bodies have been sacred, when it was an ordinary journey. How much more today, when it's sacred, [they are sacred] in body.' ⁶So the priest gave him what was sacred, because there wasn't any bread there except the presence bread that had been removed from before Yahweh so as to put warm bread, at the time when it's taken away.

⁷Now there that day, held back before Yahweh, was one of Sha'ul's servants; his name was Do'eg the Edomite, chief of Sha'ul's shepherds.

⁸David said to Ahimelek, 'Isn't there a lance or a sword at hand here? Because I didn't take my sword or my equipment in my hand, because the king's business was pressing.' ⁹The priest said, 'The sword of Golyat the Pelishtite whom you struck down in Oaks Vale – here, it's wrapped in a cloth behind the chasuble. If you're to take it for yourself, take it, because

there's none other apart from it here.' David said, 'There's none like it. Give it to me.'

¹⁰So David set off and took flight that day from before Sha'ul and came to Akish king of Gat. ¹¹Akish's servants said to him, 'This is David, the king of the country, isn't it. This is the man they chant about during the dances, isn't it:

Sha'ul has struck down his thousands,
David his ten thousands.

¹²David took these words to heart and became much afraid before Akish the king of Gat. ¹³So he disguised his good sense before their eyes and behaved oddly while in their control. He scratched on the gateway doors and let his saliva go down his beard. ¹⁴Akish said to his servants, 'Here, you see a man who's acting crazy. Why do you bring him to me? ¹⁵Am I lacking crazy people, that you bring this one to act crazy for me? Is this man to come into my household?'

## The Adullam Cave

**22** David went from there and escaped to the Adullam Cave. His brothers and his father's entire household heard, and they went down to him there. ²Everyone under pressure, everyone who had a creditor and everyone who was personally bitter collected themselves together to him, and he became their leader. There were some 400 men with him.

³David went from there to The WatchTower in Mo'ab and said to the king of Mo'ab, 'May my father and my mother please come out to be with you until I know what God will do for me.' ⁴So he led them into the presence of the king of Mo'ab and they stayed with him all the time David was at the stronghold. ⁵But Gad the prophet said to David, 'You're not to stay at the stronghold. Go, take yourself to the region of Yehudah.' So David went, and came to the Heret Forest.

⁶Sha'ul heard that David and the men who were with him had been discovered. Sha'ul was sitting at Gib'ah under the oak on the height, with his lance in his hand and all his servants standing by him. ⁷Sha'ul said to his

servants who were standing by him, 'Listen, please, Binyaminites. Will ben Yishay give fields and vineyards to all of you? Will he make all of you divisional officers or section officers? [8]Because all of you have conspired against me. There's no one who has a word in my ear when my son solemnizes things with ben Yishay. There's none of you who's feeling sick for me and has a word in my ear when my son has set up my servant to lie in ambush for me this very day.'

[9]Doeg the Edomite (he was standing with Sha'ul's servants) answered, 'I saw ben Yishay coming to Nob, to Ahimelek ben Ahitub. [10]He asked of Yahweh for him, and gave him provisions, and gave him the sword of Golyat the Pelishtite.' [11]The king sent to call for Ahimelek ben Ahitub the priest, and his father's entire household, the priests who were at Nob. All of them came to the king.

## The danger of being identified with David

[12]Sha'ul said, 'Listen, will you, ben Ahitub.' He said, 'Here I am, my lord.' [13]Sha'ul said to him, 'Why have you conspired against me, you and ben Yishay, in giving him bread and a sword, and asking of God for him, so he can rise up against me and lie in ambush this very day?' [14]Ahimelek answered the king, 'But who among all your servants is as trustworthy as David, the king's son-in-law, the officer over your bodyguard and honoured in your household? [15]Was it today I started asking of God for him? Far be it from me. The king should not lay anything against his servant, against my father's entire household, because your servant didn't know anything small or great about all this.'

[16]But the king said, 'You are definitely to die, Ahimelek, you and your father's entire household.' [17]The king said to the runners standing by him, 'Turn round and put Yahweh's priests to death, because their hand is also with David, and because they knew that he was taking flight and they didn't have a word in my ear.' The king's servants were not willing to put out their hand to attack Yahweh's priests, [18]so the king said to Doeg, 'You turn and attack the priests.' Doeg the Edomite turned and was the one who attacked the priests and put them to death that day, eighty-five men bearing the linen chasuble. [19]He struck down Nob, the priests' town, with the mouth of the sword – both man and woman, child and baby, ox, donkey and sheep, with the mouth of the sword.

[20]One son of Ahimelek ben Ahitub escaped; his name was Ebyatar [Abiathar]. He took flight after David. [21]Ebyatar told David that Sha'ul had killed Yahweh's priests, [22]and David said to Ebyatar, 'I knew that day when Doeg the Edomite was there that he would definitely tell Sha'ul. I was responsible for every life in your father's household. [23]Stay with me. Don't be afraid, because whoever seeks your life will be someone who seeks my life, because you will be in my charge.'

## David on the run

**23** They told David: 'Here, the Pelishtites are battling aginst Qe'ilah, and they're despoiling the threshing floors.' [2]David asked of Yahweh, 'Shall I go and strike down these Pelishtites?' Yahweh said to David, 'Go and strike the Pelishtites down and deliver Qe'ilah.' [3]David's men said to him, 'Here, we're afraid here in Yehudah, and how much more when we go to Qe'ilah against the Pelishtites' lines.' [4]David asked of Yahweh yet again, and Yahweh answered him, 'Set off, go down to Qe'ilah, because I'm going to give the Pelishtites into your hand.' [5]So David went with his men to Qe'ilah and did battle against the Pelishtites, drove off their livestock and struck them down in a great rout. So David delivered the people living in Qe'ilah.

[6]Now when Ebyatar ben Ahimelek had taken flight to David (at Qe'ilah), a chasuble had come down in his hand. [7]It was told Sha'ul that David had come to Qe'ilah. Sha'ul said, 'God has transferred him into my hand, because he's shut himself in by coming into a town with doors and a bar.' [8]Sha'ul got the entire company to listen about a battle, about going down to Qe'ilah to besiege David and his men. [9]David got to know that Sha'ul was devising something bad against him, and he said to Ebyatar the priest, 'Bring up the chasuble.' [10]David said, 'Yahweh, God of Yisra'el, your servant has heard for certain that Sha'ul is seeking to come to Qe'ilah to devastate the town because of me. [11]Will the Qe'ilah landowners deliver me into his hand? Will

Sha'ul come down as your servant heard?
Yahweh, God of Yisra'el, please tell your
servant.' Yahweh said, 'He will come down.'
¹²David said, 'Will the Qe'ilah landowners
deliver me and my men into Sha'ul's hand?'
Yahweh said, 'They will deliver.' ¹³So David and
his men, some 600 people, set off, got out of
Qe'ilah and went about wherever they could
go. It was told Sha'ul that David had escaped
from Qe'ilah and he left off from setting out.

¹⁴David stayed in the wilderness in the
strongholds; he stayed in the highland, in
the Ziph Wilderness. Sha'ul looked for him
all the time but God didn't give him into his
hand.

## Slippery cliff

¹⁵But David saw that Sha'ul had set out
to seek his life when David was in the Ziph
Wilderness at The Forest. ¹⁶Yehonatan, Sha'ul's
son, set off and went to David at The Forest
and strengthened his hand in God. ¹⁷He said
to him, 'Don't be afraid, because the hand of
Sha'ul my father will not find you. You yourself
will reign over Yisra'el and I will be second to
you. Even Sha'ul my father acknowledges it's
so.' ¹⁸The two of them solemnized a pact before
Yahweh, and David stayed in The Forest, while
Yehonatan went home.

¹⁹Ziphites went up to Sha'ul at Gib'ah,
saying 'David's hiding with us, isn't he, in the
strongholds in The Forest, on Hakilah Hill,
which is south of The Wasteland. ²⁰So now,
with all the longing to come down that you
yourself have, Your Majesty, come down and
we'll deliver him into the king's hand.' ²¹Sha'ul
said, 'May you be blessed by Yahweh because
you've spared me. ²²Go, will you, and establish
things further. Get to know and see the place
where his foot goes, who has seen him there,
because they've said to me, "He acts very
shrewdly." ²³Look and get to know of all the
hiding places where he hides, and come back
to me with things established, and I'll go with
you. If he's in the region, I'll search for him
among all the divisions of Yehudah.'

²⁴They set off and went to Ziph before Sha'ul.
David and his men were in Ma'on Wilderness
in the steppe, to the south of The Wasteland.
²⁵Sha'ul and his men went to search, and

people told David. He went down to The Cliff
and stayed in Ma'on Wilderness. Sha'ul heard
and pursued after David to Ma'on Wilderness.
²⁶Sha'ul went on one side of the mountain
while David and his men were on the other
side of the mountain. David was making haste
to get away from before Sha'ul, while Sha'ul
and his men were surrounding David and his
men so as to seize them, ²⁷when an envoy came
to Sha'ul saying 'Hurry, come, because the
Pelishtites have made a raid on the country.'
²⁸So Sha'ul went back from pursuing after
David and went to meet the Pelishtites. That's
why they called that place Slippery Cliff.

## Sha'ul pays a visit in a cave

²⁹David went up from there and stayed in the
strongholds at Gedi Spring.

**24** When Sha'ul came back from
following the Pelishtites, they told him,
'There, David's in the Gedi Spring Wilderness.'
²Sha'ul got 3,000 picked men from all Yisra'el
and went to look for David and his men in the
direction of Ibex Rocks. ³He came to sheepfolds
by the road and a cave there, and Sha'ul came in
to relieve himself, while David and his men were
sitting in the innermost parts of the cave.
⁴David's men said to him, 'Here, it's the day
that Yahweh said to you, "Here, I'm giving your
enemy into your hand and you can do to him
as seems good in your eyes."' David got up and
cut off the corner of Sha'ul's coat quietly, ⁵but
afterwards, David's heart struck him because
he'd cut the corner off that belonged to Sha'ul.
⁶He said to his men. 'Far be it from me by
Yahweh, if I should do this thing to my lord,
to Yahweh's anointed, in putting out my hand
against him, when he's Yahweh's anointed!'
⁷David tore his men apart with the words and
didn't let them rise up against Sha'ul.

When Sha'ul set off from the cave and went
on his way, ⁸David set off afterwards and
went out of the cave. He called after Sha'ul,
'My lord king!' Sha'ul looked behind him and
David bent his head, face to the ground, and
bowed low. ⁹David said to Sha'ul, 'Why do you
listen to people's words, saying "There, David
is seeking something bad for you"? ¹⁰Here, this
day your eyes have seen the fact that Yahweh
gave you into my hand today in the cave, and

they said to kill you, but I had pity on you. I said I wouldn't put out my hand against my lord, because he is Yahweh's anointed.

## A dead dog? A flea?

¹¹My father, look and look some more at the corner of your coat in my hand, because when I cut off the corner of your coat, I didn't kill you. Acknowledge and see that there's nothing bad and no rebellion in my hand. I haven't wronged you, but you're hunting down my life so as to take it. ¹²May Yahweh decide between me and you! May Yahweh take redress from you, whereas my hand will not be against you. ¹³As the old aphorism says, "It's from faithless people that faithlessness comes." Given that my hand will not be against you, ¹⁴after whom has the king of Yisra'el gone out? After whom are you pursuing? After a dead dog? After a single flea? ¹⁵May Yahweh be judge and may he decide between me and you. May he look and settle my argument and decide for me from your hand.'

¹⁶When David finished speaking these words to Sha'ul, Sha'ul said, 'Is this your voice, my son David?' Sha'ul lifted up his voice and wailed. ¹⁷He said to David, 'You're more faithful than me, because you've dealt me good things but I've dealt you bad things. ¹⁸Today you yourself have told of the good that you did to me, the fact that Yahweh delivered me into your hand and you didn't kill me. ¹⁹When someone finds his enemy and sends him off on his way with good . . . Yahweh himself will make good to you with good in return this day for what you've done for me. ²⁰And now, here, I acknowledge that you will definitely reign as king and Yisra'el's kingdom will rise up in your hand. ²¹So now, swear to me by Yahweh, if you cut off my offspring after me, if you annihilate my name from my father's household . . .'

²²David swore to Sha'ul, and Sha'ul went home, while David and his men went up to the stronghold.

## The man with the sheep business

**25** Shemu'el died, and all Yisra'el collected and lamented for him. They buried him at his home, at The Height.

David set off and went down to the Pa'ran Wilderness. ²Now a man in Ma'on with his business in Carmel: this man was very big. He had a flock of 3,000, and 1,000 goats, and he was shearing his flock in Carmel. ³The man's name was Nabal and his wife's name was Abigayil; the woman was good in her insight and attractive in her appearance, but the man was tough and bad in his practices, though he was a Kalebite [Calebite].

⁴David heard in the wilderness that Nabal was shearing his flock ⁵and David sent ten boys. David said to the boys, 'Go up to Carmel and come to Nabal and ask of him in my name whether things are well for him. ⁶Say this: "Long life! May things be well for you, may things be well for your household and may things be well for all that is yours! ⁷So now, I've heard that you have people shearing. Your shepherds have now been with us. We haven't let them be put to shame and nothing of theirs has been counted missing all the time that they were in Carmel. ⁸Ask your boys and they'll tell you. So may the boys find grace in your eyes, because we've come on a good day. Give what your hand finds to your servants, please, and to your son, to David."'

⁹David's boys came and spoke all these very words to Nabal in David's name, and let be. ¹⁰Nabal answered David's servants, 'Who is David, who is ben Yishay? There are many servants breaking away today, each from his lord. ¹¹Should I take my bread and my water and the meat I've slaughtered for my shearers and give them to men who are from I don't know where?'

## Abigayil gets to work

¹²David's boys turned round for their journey and went back, and came and told him all these very words. ¹³David said to his men, 'Wrap on, each one, his sword.' They wrapped on, each one, his sword, and David also wrapped on his sword. Some 400 men went up after David while 200 stayed by the things.

¹⁴One of the boys told Abigayil, Nabal's wife, 'Here, David sent envoys from the wilderness to bless our lord, but he screamed at them, ¹⁵though the men had been very good to us. We weren't shamed and we didn't count anything

missing all the time we were going about with them when we were in the fields, [16]while they were a wall round us both by night and by day all the time we were with them shepherding the flock. [17]So now, acknowledge and see what you should do, because something bad is certain for our lord and for his entire household, but he's a scoundrel to speak to.'

[18]Abigayil hurried and got two hundred loaves of bread, two skins of wine, five prepared sheep, five measures of roasted grain, a hundred raisin blocks and two hundred fig blocks, put them on donkeys [19]and said to her boys, 'Pass on before me. Here, I'm coming after you.' She didn't tell her husband Nabal. [20]While she was riding on the donkey and going down under the cover of the mountain, there, David and his men were going down to meet her. So she ran into them.

[21]Now David had said, 'It really was something false, that I kept watch on everything that belonged to this man in the wilderness and nothing of all that belonged to him has been counted missing, and he has given back something bad to me in return for something good. [22]May God do so to (the enemies of) David and may he do so more if by morning I leave remaining, out of all who belong to him, one person who pisses against a wall.'

### Fool by name and fool by nature

[23]Abigayil saw David, and hurried and got down from on the donkey. She fell on her face before David, and bowed to the ground. [24]So she fell at his feet and said, 'The waywardness is in me myself, my lord. May your handmaid please speak in your ears. Listen to your handmaid's words. [25]My lord should please not give his mind to this scoundrel, to Nabal, because he's the same as his name. "Villain" [nabal] is his name and villainy goes with him. Now I, your handmaid, didn't see my lord's boys whom you sent. [26]But now, my lord, as Yahweh lives, and as you yourself live, Yahweh who has held you back from coming into bloodshed and finding deliverance for yourself by your own hand! Now may your enemies and the people who seek what is bad for my lord be like Nabal! [27]And now may this blessing that your maidservant has brought

for my lord be given to the boys who go about after my lord.

[28]Please bear with your handmaid's rebellion, because Yahweh will definitely make for my lord a trustworthy household, because my lord is engaged in Yahweh's battles, and nothing bad will be found in you through your days. [29]When someone sets about pursuing you and seeking your life, my lord's life will be bound up in the bundle of the living with Yahweh your God, but the life of your enemies he will hurl away, in the middle of a sling's hollow. [30]And when Yahweh acts towards my lord in accordance with everything good that he has spoken concerning you, and charges you to be ruler over Yisra'el, [31]this is not to be a cause of collapsing or stumbling of mind for my lord – to have shed blood for nothing and for my lord to have found deliverance for himself. And when Yahweh has been good to my lord, you are to be mindful of your handmaid.'

### A marriage of convenience

[32]David said to Abigayil, 'Yahweh the God of Yisra'el be blessed, who sent you this day to meet me. [33]Blessed be your good judgement and blessed be you yourself, who restrained me this day from coming into bloodshed and finding deliverance for myself by my hand. [34]Yet, as Yahweh the God of Yisra'el lives, who held me back from dealing badly with you: if you had not hurried and come to meet me, by morning light there would definitely not have been left to Nabal one person who pisses against a wall.'

[35]David took from her hand what she brought for him, and he said to her, 'Go home, things will be well. See, I've listened to your voice and had regard for you.'

[36]Abigayil came to Nabal, and there, he had a banquet in his house, like a royal banquet. Nabal's heart was good in him and he was very drunk, so she didn't tell him anything small or great until morning light. [37]In the morning, when the wine had left Nabal, his wife told him these things, and his heart died inside him. He turned to stone. [38]Some ten days later Yahweh struck Nabal and he died.

[39]David heard that Nabal had died, and said, 'Yahweh be blessed, who has settled the argument over my reviling at the hand

of Nabal, and held back his servant from something bad. Yahweh has made Nabal's bad action come back on his head.' And David sent and spoke with Abigayil in connection with getting her for himself as a wife. ⁴⁰David's servants came to Abigayil at Carmel and spoke to her: 'David has sent us to you to get you for him as a wife.' ⁴¹She got up and bowed low, face to the ground, and said, 'Here is your handmaid, a maidservant to wash my lord's servants' feet.' ⁴²Abigayil hurried and got up, and mounted a donkey with her five girls behind her, and followed David's envoys. So she became his wife.

⁴³As David had got Ahino'am from Yizre'e'l, the two of them also became his wives. ⁴⁴Sha'ul had given Mikal his daughter, David's wife, to Palti ben Layish, who was from Gallim.

## Who can lay hands on Yahweh's anointed?

**26** The Ziphites came to Sha'ul at Gib'ah, saying 'David's hiding on Hakilah Hill, isn't he, over against The Wasteland.' ²Sha'ul set off and went down to the Ziph Wilderness, 300 picked men of Yisra'el with him, to look for David in the Ziph Wilderness. ³Sha'ul camped on Hakilah Hill, which is over against The Wasteland, by the road. David was staying in the wilderness, and he saw that Sha'ul had come after him into the wilderness. ⁴David sent men to investigate and got to know as established fact that Sha'ul had come.

⁵Then David set off and came to the place where Sha'ul had camped. David saw the place where Sha'ul lay down with Abner ben Ner his army officer, Sha'ul lying down in the encampment and the company camping round him. ⁶David avowed to Ahimelek the Hittite and to Abishay ben Tseruyah, Yo'ab's brother, 'Who'll go down with me to Sha'ul, to the camp?' Abishay said, 'I'll go down with you.'

⁷David and Abishay came to the company by night, and there, Sha'ul was lying asleep in the encampment, with his lance stuck in the earth by his head, and Abner and the company lying round him. ⁸Abishay said to David, 'God has surrendered your enemy into your hand today, so now I'll strike him down with the lance, please, with one thrust into the earth. I won't need to do it twice.'

⁹David said to Abishay, 'You're not to do violence to him, because who has put out his hand against Yahweh's anointed and been free of guilt?' ¹⁰David said, 'As Yahweh lives, no, Yahweh will strike him, or his day will come and he'll die, or he'll go down to battle and be swept away. ¹¹Far be it from me by Yahweh to put out my hand against Yahweh's anointed. But now get the lance that's at his head and the water jug, please, and let's take ourselves off.'

## Sha'ul's protectors' failure

¹²So David got the lance and the water jug from by Sha'ul's head and they took themselves off, with no one seeing and no one knowing and no one waking up, because all of them were asleep, because a coma from Yahweh had fallen on them.

¹³David crossed over to the other side and stood on top of the mountain at a distance; the space between them was great. ¹⁴David called to the company and to Abner ben Ner, 'Answer, Abner, won't you!' Abner answered, 'Who are you who've called to the king?' ¹⁵David said to Abner, 'Aren't you a man? Who is like you in Yisra'el? Why haven't you kept watch over your lord the king? Because one from the company came to do violence to the king, your lord. ¹⁶This thing that you've done isn't good. As Yahweh lives, you people deserve death because you haven't kept watch over your lord, over Yahweh's anointed. Look now. Where are the king's lance and the water jar, which were by his head?'

¹⁷Sha'ul recognized David's voice and he said 'Is this your voice, my son David?' David said, 'My voice, my lord king', ¹⁸and he said, 'Why is it that my lord is pursuing after his servant? Because what have I done? What bad action is in my hand? ¹⁹So now my lord the king should please listen to his servant's words. If it's Yahweh who has incited you against me, may he smell an offering, but if it's human beings, may they be cursed before Yahweh, because they've driven me away so I can't attach myself to Yahweh's domain today, saying "Go serve other gods." ²⁰So now may my blood not fall to the ground at a distance from Yahweh's presence, because the king of Yisra'el has gone out to look for a flea, as he might hunt a partridge in the mountains.'

### I've been idiotic

²¹Sha'ul said, 'I've done wrong. Come back,
my son David, because I won't deal badly with
you again, on account of the fact that my life
has been esteemed in your eyes this day. Here,
I've been idiotic and I've made very great
mistakes.' ²²David answered, 'Here's the king's
lance. One of the boys may come across and
get it. ²³Yahweh himself will return a person's
faithfulness and his trustworthiness, in that
Yahweh gave you over into my hand today and
I was not willing to put out my hand against
Yahweh's anointed. ²⁴Here, as your life has been
important in my eyes this day, so may my life
be important in Yahweh's eyes and may he
rescue me from every pressure.' ²⁵Sha'ul said
to David, 'Blessed are you, my son David. May
you both do much and also succeed much.'

David went on his way, while Sha'ul went
back to his place.

**27** David said to himself, 'I shall be
swept away now one day by Sha'ul's
hand. There's nothing good for me but to
make a final escape to the Pelishtites' country.
Sha'ul will despair of me, of looking for me
any more within Yisra'el's entire border, and
I'll escape from his hand.' ²So David set off and
crossed over, he and 600 men who were with
him, to Akish ben Ma'ok, king of Gat. ³David
lived with Akish in Gat, he and his men, each
with his household, David with his two wives
Ahino'am the Yizre'e'lite and Abigayil the wife
of Nabal the Carmelite. ⁴It was told Sha'ul,
'David has taken flight to Gat', and he didn't
look for him any more.

⁵David said to Akish, 'If I've found grace
in your eyes, may they give me a place in one
of the country towns so I can live there. Why
should your servant live in the royal town with
you?' ⁶So that day Akish gave him Tsiqlag.
That's why Tsiqlag has belonged to the kings of
Yehudah until this day. ⁷The length of time that
David lived in the Pelishtites' country was a
year and four months.

### David's ruthless cunning

⁸David and his men went up and made a
raid on the Geshurites, the Gizrites and the
Amaleqites, because they were peoples living

in the country that extends from Olam as you
come to Shur, and as far as the country of
Misrayim.

⁹David would strike down the country and
not let a man or woman live, but take flock and
herd, donkey, camels and clothes, and go back
and come to Akish. ¹⁰Akish would say, 'Whom
did you raid just now?', and David would say,
'The Negeb of Yehudah' or 'The Negeb of the
Yerahme'elites' or 'The Negeb of the Qenites'.
¹¹David wouldn't let man or woman live for
bringing to Gat, saying 'So they don't tell about
us, "David did this."' Such was his rule all the
time that he lived in the Pelishtites' country.
¹²Akish came to trust David, saying 'He's
made himself totally stink among his people,
among Yisra'el. He'll be a servant for me
permanently.'

**28** During that time the Pelishtites
collected their camp for war so as
to battle against Yisra'el. Akish said to David,
'You do know that you're to go out with me in
the camp, you and your men.' ²David said to
Akish, 'Therefore, you yourself will know what
your servant might do.' Akish said to David,
'Therefore I will make you my bodyguard
permanently.'

³Now Shemu'el had died, and all Yisra'el
had lamented for him and had buried him
at The Height, at his town; and Sha'ul had
removed the ghosts and the spirits from the
country. ⁴The Pelishtites collected and came
and camped at Shunem; Sha'ul collected all
Yisra'el and camped at Gilboa. ⁵Sha'ul saw the
Pelishtites' camp and was afraid; his heart
trembled much. ⁶Sha'ul asked of Yahweh but
Yahweh didn't answer him, either by dreams or
by Urim or by prophets.

### What do you do when you're desperate?

⁷So Sha'ul said to his servants, 'Look for a
woman who is a ghost-mistress for me so I can
go to her and enquire through her.' His servants
said to him, 'There, a woman who is a ghost-
mistress is in Dor Spring.' ⁸Sha'ul disguised
himself and put on other clothes and went, he
and two men with him, and came to the woman
at night. He said, 'Please divine through a ghost
for me. Bring up for me the one that I shall say
to you.'

⁹The woman said to him, 'Here, you yourself know what Sha'ul has done, that he's cut off ghosts and spirits from the country. Why are you laying a trap for my life, to bring about my death?' ¹⁰Sha'ul swore to her by Yahweh: 'As Yahweh lives, if waywardness befalls you through this thing . . .'

¹¹So the woman said, 'Who shall I bring up for you?' He said, 'Shemu'el. Bring him up for me.' ¹²The woman saw Shemu'el and cried out in a loud voice. The woman said to Sha'ul, 'Why have you beguiled me? You're Sha'ul.' ¹³The king said to her, 'Don't be afraid. But what have you seen?' The woman said to Sha'ul, 'It's a divine being I've seen coming up from the earth.' ¹⁴He said to her, 'What's he look like?' She said, 'An old man is coming up. He's wearing a coat.' Sha'ul knew that it was Shemu'el. He bent his head, face to the ground, and bowed low.

¹⁵Shemu'el said to Sha'ul, 'Why have you disturbed me by bringing me up?' Sha'ul said, 'Things are very pressing for me. The Pelishtites are battling with me. God has departed from me. He hasn't answered me any more, either by means of prophets or by dreams. I called to you to enable me to know what I should do.'

### Shemu'el still speaks straight

¹⁶Shemu'el said, 'So why do you ask me when Yahweh has departed from you and become your adversary? ¹⁷Yahweh has done to you as he spoke by means of me. Yahweh has torn the kingship from your hand and given it to your neighbour, to David, ¹⁸when you didn't listen to Yahweh's voice and didn't perform his angry rage on Amaleq. That's why Yahweh has done this thing to you this day. ¹⁹Yahweh will also give Yisra'el with you into the hand of the Pelishtites. Tomorrow you and your sons will be with me. Yahweh will also give the Yisra'elite camp into the hand of the Pelishtites.'

²⁰Sha'ul hurried and fell full length on the ground. He was very frightened by Shemu'el's words, while also there was no energy in him because he had not eaten bread all day and all night. ²¹The woman came to Sha'ul and saw that he was very fearful. She said to him, 'Here, your maidservant listened to your voice and I put my life in the palm of my hand. I listened

to your words which you spoke to me, ²²so now please listen to your maidservant's voice as well. I want to put a bit of bread before you. Eat, and there'll be energy in you when you go on your way.' ²³He refused and said, 'I won't eat', but his servants pressed him, as well as the woman, and he listened to their voice. He got up from the ground and sat on the bed.

²⁴The woman had a stall-fed calf in the house. She hurried and slaughtered it, got flour and kneaded it, and baked it into flatbread. ²⁵She brought it up before Sha'ul and before his servants and they ate. Then they got up, and went that night.

29 The Pelishtites collected their entire camp at Apheq, while Yisra'el was camping at the spring which is in Yizre'el ²and the Pelishtites' lords were passing on by sections and by divisions, with David and his men passing on with Akish at the end.

### The Pelishtites' lords are wiser than Akish

³The Pelishtites' officers said, 'What are these Hebrews?' Akish said to the Pelishtites officers, 'This is David, the servant of Sha'ul, king of Yisra'el, isn't it, who's been with me for this time (these years). I haven't found any fault in him from the day he fell away until this day.' ⁴The Pelishtites' officers were furious with him. The Pelishtites' officers said to him, 'Send the man back. He should go back to his place, where you appointed him. He shouldn't go down with us in the battle, so he won't become an adversary to us in the battle. How could this man find acceptance with his lord – it was with those men's heads, wasn't it. ⁵This is the David of whom they used to chant during the dance, isn't it:

Sha'ul has struck down his thousands,
David his ten thousands.

⁶So Akish called for David and said to him, 'As Yahweh lives, you're upright and your going out and coming in with me in the camp is good in my eyes, because I haven't found anything bad in you from the day you came to me until this day. But in the eyes of the lords you're not good. ⁷So now go back, go while things are well, and you won't do anything bad in the eyes of the

Pelishtites' lords.' [8]David said to Akish, 'But what have I done and what have you found in your servant from the day when I came to be before you until this day, that I shouldn't come and do battle with the enemies of my lord the king?'

[9]Akish answered David, 'I acknowledge that you are good in my eyes, like God's envoy. Nevertheless the Pelishtites' officers have said, "He will not go up with us in the battle." [10]So now, start early in the morning, you and your lord's servants who have come with you. Start early in the morning and when you have light, go.'

[11]So in the morning David started early, he and his men, to go to return to the Pelishtites' country, while the Pelishtites went up to Yizre'e'l.

## The disaster while their back was turned

**30** When David and his men came to Tsiqlag, on the third day, the Amaleqites had made a raid on the Negeb and on Tsiqlag. They'd struck down Tsiqlag and burned it in fire [2]and taken captive the women who were in it, from the youngest to the oldest. They hadn't put anyone to death but they'd driven them off and gone on their way.

[3]So David and his men came to the town: there, it was burnt in fire and their wives, their sons and their daughters had been taken captive. [4]David and the company that was with him lifted up their voice and wailed until there was no energy in them to wail. [5]David's two wives had been taken captive, Ahino'am the Yizre'elite and Abigayil the wife of Nabal the Carmelite. [6]It put great pressure on David, because the company said to pelt him with stones, because the entire company's spirit was bitter, each person over his sons and his daughters. But David summoned up his strength through Yahweh his God. [7]David said to Ebyatar the priest, son of Ahimelek, 'Bring up the chasuble for me, please.' Ebyatar brought up the chasuble to David. [8]David asked of Yahweh, 'Should I pursue after this raiding gang, will I overtake it?' He said to him, 'Pursue, because you will indeed overtake and you will indeed rescue.'

[9]So David went, he and 600 men who were with him, and came as far as Wadi Besor. While the people who were to be left halted, [10]David pursued, he and 400 men; 200 men who were too faint to cross Wadi Besor halted.

## The informant

[11]They found a Misrayimite man in the fields and took him to David. They gave him bread and he ate, and they let him drink water, [12]and gave him a piece of a fig block and two raisin blocks. He ate and his spirit came back to him (because he hadn't eaten bread and hadn't drunk water for three days and three nights). [13]David said to him, 'Who do you belong to and where are you from?' He said, 'I'm a Misrayimite boy, the servant of an Amaleqite. My lord abandoned me because I got ill, three days ago, [14]when we had made an incursion against the Negeb of the Keretites and against what belongs to Yehudah and against the Negeb of Kaleb, and we burned Tsiqlag in fire.' [15]David said to him, 'Will you take me down to this raiding gang?' He said, 'Swear to me by God, if you put me to death or if you deliver me into my lord's hand . . . And I will take you down to this gang.' [16]So he took them down and there they were, left to themselves on the face of the ground, eating and drinking and feasting on all the vast spoil that they had taken from the Pelishtites' country and from the region of Yehudah.

[17]David struck them down from dusk until the evening of the next day. Not one of them escaped, except 400 young men who mounted camels and fled. [18]David rescued everything that Amaleq had taken. And David rescued his two wives. [19]Nothing was missing to them, both the young and the old, sons and daughters, and from the spoil and all that they had taken for themselves. David got everything back. [20]David took the entire flock, while they drove the herd before that livestock. They said, 'This is David's spoil.'

## All should share

[21]David came to the 200 men who were too faint to follow David, so that they had let them stay at Wadi Besor. They went out to meet David and to meet the company that was with him. David went up with the company and he asked them whether things were well. [22]Every bad man and scoundrel of the men who had gone with David answered, 'Since they didn't go with me, we shouldn't give them any of the

spoil that we rescued, except an individual his wife and his children, so they can drive them off and go.'

²³David said, 'You will not do so, my brothers, with what Yahweh has given us. He has kept us and given over the raiding gang that came against us, into our hand. ²⁴Who would listen to you regarding this thing? Because as will be the share of the person who went down into the battle, so will be the share of the person who stayed with the things. They will share it out together.' ²⁵From that day onwards he made it a decree and a rule for Yisra'el, until this day.

²⁶David came to Tsiqlag and sent off some of the spoil to the elders of Yehudah, to his friends, saying 'Here's your blessing from the spoil of Yahweh's enemies', ²⁷to the ones in Bet-el, to the ones in the Negeb Heights, to the ones in Yattir, ²⁸to the ones in Aro'er, to the ones in Siphmot, to the ones in Eshtemoa, ²⁹to the ones in Rakal, to the ones in the towns of the Yerahme'elites, to the ones in the towns of the Qenites, ³⁰to the ones in Hormah, to the ones in Ashan Cistern, to the ones in Atak ³¹and to the ones in Hebron, to all the places where David had gone about, he and his men.

## A last act of loyalty to Sha'ul

**31** When the Pelishtites battled against Yisra'el, the Yisra'elites fled from before the Pelishtites and fell, run through, on Mount Gilboa. ²The Pelishtites caught up with Sha'ul and with his sons, and the Pelishtites struck down Yehonatan, Abinadab and Malki-shua, Sha'ul's sons.

³The battle was hard against Sha'ul, and the archers (the bowmen) found him; he was run through by the archers. ⁴Sha'ul said to his equipment-bearer, 'Draw your sword and thrust me through with it, so these foreskinned men don't come and thrust me through and act abusively to me.' But his equipment-bearer wasn't willing because he was very fearful, so Sha'ul took the sword and fell on it. ⁵His equipment-bearer saw that Sha'ul was dead and he too fell on his sword and died with him. ⁶So Sha'ul died, with his three sons, and his equipment-bearer, as well as all his men, all together on that day.

⁷The Yisra'elites who were across the vale and who were across the Yarden saw that the Yisra'elites had fled and that Sha'ul and his sons were dead, and they abandoned their towns and fled (the Pelishtites came and lived in them).

⁸Next day the Pelishtites came to strip the people who were run through. They found Sha'ul and his three sons fallen on Mount Gilboa, ⁹cut off his head and stripped off his equipment. They sent off through the country of the Pelishtites all round to proclaim the news to the house of their idols and to the people. ¹⁰They put his equipment in the house of the Ashtars, and his body they fastened to the wall of Bet Shan. ¹¹But the people living in Yabesh-in-Gil'ad heard about it, about what the Pelishtites had done to Sha'ul, ¹²and they set off, every forceful man. They went all night and got Sha'ul's body and his sons' bodies from the walls of Bet-shan. They came to Yabesh and burned them there, ¹³then got their bones and buried them under the tamarisk at Yabesh, and fasted for seven days.

# 2 SAMUEL

The story in 2 Samuel is a tragedy. In a broad sense a tragedy is any terrible event, but we can also use the word to describe a certain kind of story, one that relates how someone important and successful experiences the collapse of everything that made him or her important and successful. While this collapse may come about through bad luck, it may come about through bad decisions whose terrible consequences could hardly have been foreseen, yet which with hindsight seem inevitable. The tragedy in 2 Samuel is the tragedy of David.

Ironically, the background to David's tragedy is another one, that of Saul. Given the circumstances of Saul's becoming king, it might not seem surprising that his reign ends unhappily. David plays a key role in his downfall, without intending to do so – indeed, David seeks to honour Saul as the king anointed by Yahweh. But Saul's story unravels and he dies in battle, along with Jonathan, his son and David's best friend. Their death opens up the way for David to succeed Saul. He has already been designated by God for this position, but the process whereby he gets there is a human one.

Naturally enough, the people of Judah, David's own clan, are ready to recognize him, but the people of the northern clans are aware of other options from within their own number – specifically, someone from Saul's household might seem a natural choice. But the possible candidates and the party supporting them gradually disappear, so that the northern clans drift into giving their own recognition to David.

David then makes an astute move in conquering Jerusalem. Although it sits in the middle of areas assigned to the Israelite clans, the town is still occupied by the Yebusites. David conquers it and makes it his capital. Its position and its history mean that no clan identifies with it, so it has the potential to be viewed as neutral territory, as David's town. Yahweh later declares that he chose it, but in 2 Samuel, it's David who takes the initiative in choosing it.

The dynamics of this process recur in the decision to build a permanent sanctuary for worship of Yahweh in Jerusalem. Again it is David's idea. Yahweh is not enthusiastic about it, because he doesn't want to be stuck in a fixed place, but he yields to it. He goes on to make a commitment to David that removes some of the ambiguity of his earlier attitude to the idea of having kings. He now promises David that his line will permanently occupy the throne over Israel. His immediate successor will be the king who actually builds the sanctuary in Jerusalem.

In the event, he will be the only successor to reign over the whole of Israel, and after a few centuries Davidic rule over Judah will come to an end. God's promise about David's line thus leads in due course to the hope of a Messiah. The word *Messiah* means *Anointed*, and in the First Testament it applies to actual kings (and priests). But when there are no kings in the present, it comes to refer to the king whom God must surely set up one day.

David wins more spectacular victories but then everything starts to unravel. The second half of 2 Samuel tells of a catastrophic series of events in David's life, for most of which he is directly or indirectly responsible. They centre on his relationships with people inside and outside his family rather than on political or military events. He has shown himself to be a brilliant leader, but he is a disaster as a human being.

It might seem surprising that he is described as a man after God's heart. The description need only mean that he is the man God chose; it doesn't imply that his heart was in tune with God's heart. But in later pages of the First Testament he is viewed as a model who contrasts positively with many other kings. For all his wrongdoing and foolishness, at least he stayed faithful to Yahweh and stayed trusting in Yahweh.

## The fraud that will come unstuck

**1** After Sha'ul's [Saul's] death, and when David had come back from striking down the Amaleqites, David stayed in Tsiqlag for two days, ²and on the third day – there, a man coming from the camp, from being with Sha'ul, with his clothes torn and earth on his head. When he came to David he fell to the ground and bowed low. ³David said to him, 'Where do you come from?' He said to him, 'I escaped from Yisra'el's [Israel's] camp.' ⁴David said to him, 'What was it that happened? Please tell me.' He said how the company fled from the battle and also many of the company fell and died and also Sha'ul and Yehonatan [Jonathan] his son died.

⁵David said to the boy who told him, 'How do you know that Sha'ul is dead, and Yehonatan his son?' ⁶The boy who told him said, 'I just happened to be on Mount Gilboa, and there, Sha'ul was leaning on his lance, and there, chariotry and cavalry caught up with him. ⁷He turned his face behind him and saw me and called to me. I said, "Here I am." ⁸He said to me, "Who are you?" I said to him, "I'm an Amaleqite." ⁹He said to me, "Stand over me, please, and put me to death, because doom has taken hold of me, when my life is still entirely in me." ¹⁰So I stood over him and put him to death because I acknowledged that he would not live after he had fallen. I took the diadem that was on his head and a bracelet that was on his arm and brought them to my lord, here.'

¹¹David took strong hold of his clothes and tore them, he and all the men who were with him as well. ¹²They lamented and wailed and fasted until evening for Sha'ul, for Yehonatan his son, for Yahweh's company and for the household of Yisra'el, because they had fallen by the sword.

## How are the mighty fallen

¹³David said to the boy who told him, 'Where are you from?' He said, 'I'm the son of a resident, an Amaleqite.' ¹⁴David said to him, 'How were you not afraid to put out your hand to do violence to Yahweh's anointed?' ¹⁵David called for one of the boys and said, 'Come up, attack him!' He struck him down and he died.

¹⁶David said to him, 'Your blood is on your own head, because your own mouth avowed against you, "I put Yahweh's anointed to death."'

¹⁷David chanted this elegy over Sha'ul and over Yehonatan his son, ¹⁸and he said to teach the Yehudahites 'The Bow' (there, it's written on the Document of the Upright One):

¹⁹The gazelle, Yisra'el, is run through on your
    heights:
  how have the strong men fallen.
²⁰Don't tell it in Gat,
  don't announce the news in Ashqelon's streets,
Lest the Pelishtites' [Philistines'] daughters
    celebrate,
  lest the daughters of the foreskinned exult.
²¹Mountains of Gilboa, may there be no dew,
  no rain on you or fields of contributions,
Because there the strong men's shield was
    fouled,
  the shield of Sha'ul, no more rubbed with oil.
²²From the blood of the slain,
  from the fat of strong men,
The bow of Yehonatan did not turn back,
  the sword of Sha'ul did not go back empty.
²³Sha'ul and Yehonatan, loved and delighted in,
  in their life and in their death they were not
    parted.
They were swifter than eagles,
  they were stronger than lions.
²⁴Daughters of Yisra'el,
  wail over Sha'ul,
Who clothed you in scarlet and finery,
  who put gold ornaments on your apparel.
²⁵How have the strong men fallen
  in the middle of the battle.
Yehonatan, run through on your heights,
    ²⁶it's depressing for me because of you.
My brother Yehonatan,
  you were very lovely to me.
Your loyalty was extraordinary to me,
  more than the loyalty of women.
²⁷How have the strong men fallen
  and the articles of battle perished!

## Two kings

**2** After this, David asked of Yahweh, 'Should I go up into one of the towns of Judah?' Yahweh said to him, 'Go up.' David said, 'Where should I go up?' He said, 'To Hebron.'

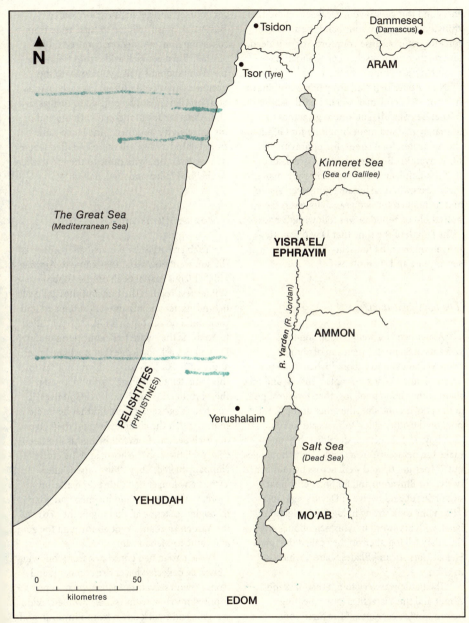

N

Tsidon

Dammeseq
(Damascus)

Tsor (Tyre)

ARAM

The Great Sea
(Mediterranean Sea)

Kinneret Sea
(Sea of Galilee)

YISRA'EL/
EPHRAYIM

R. Yarden (R. Jordan)

AMMON

PELISHTITES
(PHILISTINES)

Yerushalaim

Salt Sea
(Dead Sea)

YEHUDAH

MO'AB

0              50
kilometres

EDOM

*2 Samuel 1: David*

²So David went up there, he and also his two wives Ahino'am the Yizre'elite and Abigayil the wife of Nabal the Carmelite, ³and David took up his men who were with him, each man and his household, and they lived in the Hebron towns. ⁴The Yehudahites [Judahites] came and anointed David as king there over the household of Yehudah.

They told David, 'The people who buried Sha'ul were the people of Yabesh-in-Gil'ad.' ⁵So David sent envoys to the people of Yabesh-in-Gil'ad and said to them, 'Blessed are you by Yahweh because you acted in this commitment with your lord, with Sha'ul, and buried him. ⁶So now may Yahweh act in commitment and truthfulness with you, and I myself will also do this good thing with you, because you did this thing. [7]So now, may your hands be strong, be forceful men, because your lord Sha'ul is dead, and further the household of Yehudah have anointed me as king over them.'

[8]Now Abner ben Ner, army officer for Sha'ul, had got Shameful-man son of Sha'ul [Ish-boshet ben Sha'ul], got him to go across to Mahanayim, [9]and made him king for Gil'ad, for the Ashurites, for Yizre'e'l, for Ephrayim and for Binyamin [Benjamin] – for Yisra'el, all of it. [10]Shameful-man son of Sha'ul was a man of forty years when he became king over Yisra'el and he reigned for two years. However, the household of Yehudah was following David. [11]The length of the time that David was king in Hebron over the household of Yehudah was seven years and six months.

### The boys fight it out

[12]Abner ben Ner went out, he and the servants of Shameful-man son of Sha'ul, from Mahanayim to Gib'on, [13]when Yo'ab ben Tseruyah and David's servants went out and met them at the Gib'on pool, together. One group sat at the pool on one side, the other group at the pool on the other side. [14]Abner said to Yo'ab, 'The boys should get up, shouldn't they, and make fun before us!' Yo'ab said, 'They should get up!' [15]They got up and went across by number, twelve for Binyamin and for Shameful-man son of Sha'ul, and twelve of David's servants. [16]Each one took strong hold of his neighbour's head, with his sword into his neighbour's side; thus they fell together. So they called that place Helqat Hatstsurim ['Blades Share'], which is in Gib'on.

[17]The battle was very tough that day, and Abner and the Yisra'elites took a beating before David's servants. [18]The three sons of Tseruyah were there, Yo'ab, Abishay and Asah'el. Now Asah'el was quick on his feet, like one of the gazelles that are in the wild. [19]Asah'el pursued after Abner, and didn't turn aside as he went, to the right or to the left, from following Abner.

[20]Abner turned his face behind him and said, 'Is it you, Asah'el?' He said, 'It's me.' [21]Abner said to him. 'Turn yourself to your right or to your left and take hold of one of the boys

for yourself and get his strip for yourself.' But Asah'el wasn't willing to turn aside from following him. [22]Abner once more said to Asah'el, 'Turn yourself aside from following me! Why should I strike you down to the ground? How could I lift up my face to Yo'ab your brother?' [23]But he refused to turn aside, and Abner struck him down with the end of his lance, in his abdomen. The lance came out from behind and he fell there and died where he was. Everyone who came to the place where Asah'el had fallen and died, halted.

### The struggle for power

[24]Yo'ab and Abishay pursued after Abner as the sun went down and they came to Ammah Hill, which is east of Giah on the Gib'on Wilderness road. [25]The Binyaminites collected behind Abner and became one company, and they stood on the top of a hill. [26]Abner called to Yo'ab, 'Is the sword to devour permanently? Do you not acknowledge that it will be bitter at the end? For how long will you not say to the company to turn back from following their brothers?' [27]Yo'ab said, 'As God lives, if you hadn't spoken, it would rather be in the morning that the company would then give up, each person, from following his brother.' [28]So Yo'ab blew on the horn, and the entire company halted. They didn't pursue after Yisra'el any longer and didn't do battle any more. [29]When Abner and his men had gone through the steppe all that night, they crossed the Yarden [Jordan], went all through the gorge and came to Mahanayim.

[30]When Yo'ab had gone back from following Abner, he collected his entire company, and from David's servants nineteen men were counted missing, with Asah'el, [31]while David's servants had struck down from Binyamin and among Abner's men 360; they had died. [32]They carried Asah'el and buried him in his father's grave, which is in Bet Lehem. Then Yo'ab and his men went all night, and it got light for them in Hebron.

**3** The battle between Sha'ul's household and David's household was long-drawn-out, though David was growing stronger and Sha'ul's household was growing weaker. [2]Sons were born to David in Hebron. His

firstborn was Amnon, by Ahino'am the
Yizre'e'lite. [3]His second was Kil'ab, by Abigayil,
the wife of Nabal the Carmelite. The third
was Abshalom, the son of Ma'akah bat Talmay,
king of Geshur. [4]The fourth was Adoniyyah,
the son of Haggit. The fifth was Shephatyah, the
son of Abital. [5]The sixth was Yitre'am, by Eglah,
David's wife. These were born to David in
Hebron.

## Abner's power play?

[6]As the battle was going on between Sha'ul's
household and David's household, Abner was
asserting his strength in Sha'ul's household.
[7]Now Sha'ul had a secondary wife; her name
was Ritspah bat Ayyah. [Shameful-man]
said to Abner, 'Why have you had sex with
my father's wife?' [8]It really enraged Abner at
Shameful-man's words. He said, 'Am I a dog's
head that belongs to Yehudah? Today I act in
commitment with the household of Sha'ul your
father, to his brothers and to his friends, and I
haven't let you be found in David's hand, and
today you attribute waywardness to me with
the woman. [9]May God do this to Abner and
may he do more to him, because as Yahweh
swore to David, so I will do for him, [10]to let the
kingship pass over from Sha'ul's household and
establish David's throne over Yisra'el and over
Yehudah, from Dan as far as Be'er Sheba.' [11]He
couldn't say back anything further to Abner,
for fear of him.

[12]Abner sent envoys to David, in place of
himself, saying 'Whose is the country? You
should solemnize your pact with me, and here,
my hand will be with you to get all Yisra'el to
come round to you.' [13]He said, 'Good, I myself
will solemnize a pact with you. I'm going to
ask only one thing from you: you will not see
my face unless beforehand you bring Mikal,
Sha'ul's daughter, when you come to see my
face.' [14]And David sent envoys to Shameful-
man son of Sha'ul, saying 'Give over my wife
Mikal whom I betrothed to myself for a
hundred Pelishtite foreskins.' [15]Shameful-man
sent and got her from being with the husband,
from being with Palti'el ben Layish. [16]Her
husband went with her, wailing as he followed
her as far as Bahurim, but Abner said to him,
'Go, go back', and he went back.

## Abner miscalculates

[17]Abner had word with Yisra'el's elders: 'Even
in previous days, you were seeking David as
king over you. [18]So now, act, because Yahweh
has said of David, "By the hand of David my
servant I will deliver my people Yisra'el from
the hand of the Pelishtites and from the hand
of all their enemies."' [19]Abner both spoke in
Binyamin's ear, and Abner also went to speak
in David's ear in Hebron of all that was good in
the eyes of Yisra'el and in the eyes of the entire
household of Binyamin.

[20]Abner came to David at Hebron, twenty
men with him, and David made a banquet
for Abner and for the men who were with
him. [21]Abner said to David, 'I'll set off and go
and collect all Yisra'el for my lord the king so
they can solemnize a pact with you and you
can reign over all that your appetite longs for.'
David sent Abner off and he went, with things
being well.

[22]But there, David's servants and Yo'ab came
from a raiding gang, and brought much spoil
with them. Abner was not with David in Hebron
because David had sent him off and he had
gone, with things being well. [23]When Yo'ab and
the entire army that was with him came, people
told Yo'ab, 'Abner ben Ner came to the king, and
he sent him off; he went with things being well.'
[24]Yo'ab came to the king and said, 'What have
you done? Here was Abner coming to you.
Why did you send him off? He's totally gone.
[25]You know Abner ben Ner, that he would have
come to deceive you and to know your coming
and your going and to know everything that
you're doing.'

## The elimination of Abner

[26]Yo'ab went out from being with David and
sent envoys after Abner, and they brought him
back from the Sirah cistern. David didn't know.
[27]So Abner came back to Hebron, Yo'ab took
him aside inside the gateway to speak with him
in private, but struck him down there, in the
abdomen. He died for the blood of Asah'el his
brother.

[28]David heard afterwards and said, 'I and
my kingdom are free of guilt before Yahweh
permanently for the shedding of the blood

of Abner ben Ner. <sup>29</sup>May it whirl on the head of Yo'ab and on his father's entire household. May there not be cut off from Yo'ab's household someone with a discharge or someone with scaliness, or a man who takes strong hold of the spindle or falls by the sword or lacks bread.' <sup>30</sup>Yo'ab and Abishay his brother had killed Abner because of the fact that he had put Asahel their brother to death at Gib'on in the battle.

<sup>31</sup>David said to Yo'ab and to the entire company that was with him, 'Tear your clothes and wrap on sack and lament before Abner', while King David was going behind the bier. <sup>32</sup>So they buried Abner at Hebron. The king lifted up his voice and wailed at Abner's grave. The entire company wailed. <sup>33</sup>The king chanted for Abner:

> Should Abner have been dying
>> the death of a villain?
> <sup>34</sup>Your hands were not tied up,
>> your feet were not in chains.
> They were brought together like someone
>> falling –
> before evil men you fell.

So the entire company continued to wail over him.

## The disabled son

<sup>35</sup>The entire company came to get David to eat bread while it was still day, but David swore, 'May God do this to me and may he do more if I taste bread or anything before sunset.' <sup>36</sup>When the entire company recognized, it was good in their eyes, as everything that the king did was good in the eyes of the entire company. <sup>37</sup>The entire company and all Yisra'el acknowledged that day that putting Abner ben Ner to death did not come from the king.

<sup>38</sup>The king said to his servants, 'You acknowledge, do you not, that a leader and a great man has fallen this day in Yisra'el. <sup>39</sup>And I myself am raw today, though anointed king, whereas these men, the sons of Tseruyah, are tougher than me. May Yahweh make good to the person who does what is bad in accordance with the bad thing that he did.'

**4** Ben Sha'ul heard that Abner had died at Hebron, and his hands went slack, while all Yisra'el was fearful. <sup>2</sup>Now ben Sha'ul had

two men who were officers over raiding gangs. The name of one was Ba'anah and the name of the second was Rekab, sons of Rimmon the Be'erotite, of the Binyaminites because Be'erot was also counted with Binyamin. <sup>3</sup>The Be'erotites had taken flight to Gittayim, and they have been residents there until this day.

<sup>4</sup>Now Yehonatan son of Sha'ul had a son who was injured in both feet. He was a boy of five years when the report about Sha'ul and Yehonatan came from Yizre'e'l. His nurse had carried him and fled, and as she was making haste to flee, he fell, so he limped. His name was Mephiboshet ['From-Shame's-Mouth'].

## The elimination of Sha'ul's other son

<sup>5</sup>So the sons of Rimmon the Be'erotite, Rekab and Ba'anah, went and at the very heat of the day came to Shameful-man's house. He was taking a midday lie-down. <sup>6</sup>So there, they came inside the house like people getting wheat and struck him down in the abdomen. Then Rekab and Ba'anah his brother escaped. <sup>7</sup>They had come to the house when he was lying on his bed in his bedroom, struck him down and put him to death, and they removed his head, took his head, went by the Steppe road all night <sup>8</sup>and brought Shameful-man's head to David at Hebron. They said to the king, 'Here is the head of Shameful-man son of Sha'ul, your enemy who sought your life. This day Yahweh has given my lord the king full redress from Sha'ul and his offspring.'

<sup>9</sup>David answered Rekab and Ba'anah his brother, the sons of Rimmon the Be'erotite, 'As Yahweh lives, who has redeemed my life from every pressure: <sup>10</sup>when someone told me, "Here, Sha'ul is dead", and in his eyes he was like someone bringing good news, I seized him and killed him in Tsiqlag, one to whom I might have given something for the news. <sup>11</sup>How much more when faithless men have killed a faithful man in his house on his bed! I will seek his blood from your hand and burn you away from the country, won't I.' <sup>12</sup>So David ordered the boys and they killed them, cut off their hands and their feet, and hanged them over the pool at Hebron. The head of Shameful-man they took and buried in Abner's grave at Hebron.

## David becomes king and Yerushalaim (Jerusalem) becomes his city

**5** Then all the Yisra'elite clans came to David at Hebron and said, 'Here, we are your flesh and blood. ²Further, in previous days, when Sha'ul was king over us, you were the one who took Yisra'el out and brought Yisra'el in. Yahweh said to you, "You're the one who will shepherd my people Yisra'el. You're the one who will be ruler over Yisra'el."

³So all Yisra'el's elders came to the king at Hebron, King David solemnized a pact to them at Hebron before Yahweh, and they anointed David as king over Yisra'el. ⁴David was a man of thirty years when he began to reign and he reigned for forty years: ⁵in Hebron he reigned over Yehudah for seven years and six months, and in Yerushalaim he reigned for thirty-three years over all Yisra'el and Yehudah.

⁶The king and his men went to Yerushalaim against the Yebusites, the inhabitants of the region. They said to David, 'You won't come in here. Actually, the blind and the lame could have removed you' (saying, 'David won't come in here'). ⁷But David captured the Zion stronghold (i.e. David's Town). ⁸David said on that day, 'Anyone striking down the Yebusites (the blind and the lame, treated with hostility by David himself – that's why they say, "A blind or lame person will not come into the house") should take possession of the conduit.'

⁹David lived in the stronghold and named it 'David's Town'. David built it up all round from the Fill to the house. ¹⁰David went on getting bigger and bigger, as Yahweh the God of Armies was with him. ¹¹Hiram king of Tsor [Tyre] sent envoys to David with cedar wood, crafsmen in wood and craftsmen in stone for walls, and they built a house for David.

## For the sake of David's people Yisra'el

¹²David acknowledged that Yahweh had established him as king over Yisra'el and that he had exalted his kingship for the sake of his people Yisra'el. ¹³David took more secondary wives and wives from Yerushalaim after he came from Hebron, and more sons and daughters were born to David. ¹⁴These are the names of the children born to him in Yerushalaim:

Shammua, Shobab, Natan, Shelomoh [Solomon], ¹⁵Yibhar, Elishua, Nepheg, Yaphia, ¹⁶Elishama, Elyada and Eliphelet.

¹⁷The Pelishtites heard that they had anointed David as king over Yisra'el, and all the Pelishtites went up to look for David. David heard, and went down to the stronghold. ¹⁸When the Pelishtites came, they ran loose in Repha'ites Vale. ¹⁹David asked of Yahweh, 'Shall I go up against the Pelishtites? Will you give them into my hand?' Yahweh said to David, 'Go up, because I shall definitely give the Pelishtites into your hand', ²⁰and David came to Ba'al-peratsim. David struck them down there and said, 'Yahweh has broken out on my enemies before me like a breakout of water.' That's why they named that place Ba'al Peratsim ['Master of Breakouts']. ²¹They abandoned their idols there, and David and his men carried them off.

²²The Pelishtites yet again went up and ran loose in Repha'ites Vale. ²³David asked of Yahweh, but he said, 'You will not go up. Make a turn round behind them and come to them from the direction of the weeper trees. ²⁴When you hear the sound of marching in the tops of the weeper trees, then take action, because Yahweh will have gone out before you to strike down the Pelishtites' camp.' ²⁵David did so, as Yahweh ordered him, and struck down the Pelishtites from Geba as far as when you come to Gezer.

## Little things can have terrible consequences

**6** David again gathered every picked man in Yisra'el, 30,000. ²David set off and went, he and the entire company that was with him, from Ba'alim-in-Yehudah to take up from there God's chest over which the name is called out (the name of Yahweh of Armies who sits above the sphinxes). ³They transported God's chest on a new wagon and carried it from Abinadab's house, which was on the hill, with Uzza and Ahyo, Abinadab's sons, driving the new wagon. ⁴So they carried it from Abinadab's house, which was on the hill, with God's chest, with Ahyo going before the chest, ⁵and David and the entire household of Yisra'el made fun before Yahweh with all juniper wood [instruments], with guitars, with mandolins, with tambourines, with rattles and with cymbals.

6But they came as far as Nakon's threshing floor, and Uzza reached out to God's chest and grasped it because the cattle had stumbled, 7and Yahweh's anger raged at Uzzah. God struck him down there because of the blunder. He died there near God's chest.

8It really enraged David that Yahweh had broken out at Uzzah (he called that place Perets Uzzah ['Breakout at Uzzah'], until this day). 9David was afraid of Yahweh that day and said, 'How can Yahweh's chest come to me?' 10So David was not willing to move Yahweh's chest to him, to David's Town. David got it to turn aside to the house of Obed-edom the Gittite.

11Yahweh's chest stayed at the house of Obed Edom the Gittite for three months. Yahweh blessed Obed Edom and his entire household, 12and it was told King David, 'Yahweh has blessed the household of Obed Edom and all that belongs to him on account of God's chest', so David went and brought up God's chest from Obed Edom's house to David's Town with rejoicing.

## How David honoured himself today!

13When the people carrying Yahweh's chest had taken six steps he sacrificed a bull and a fatling, 14with David whirling before Yahweh with all his vigour, and David wrapped round in a linen chasuble, 15and David and all the household of Yisra'el bringing up Yahweh's chest with a shout and with the sound of a horn. 16Yahweh's chest was coming into David's Town as Mikal, Sha'ul's daughter, was looking out through the window. She saw King David jumping and whirling before Yahweh, and she despised him inside.

17They brought in Yahweh's chest and put it in its place inside the tent that David had spread for it. David offered up burnt offerings and well-being sacrifices before Yahweh. 18David finished offering up the burnt offering and the well-being sacrifices, blessed the people in the name of Yahweh of Armies, 19and shared out to the entire people, to the entire Yisra'elite horde, both men and women, to each

individual, a round of bread, a date block and a raisin block.

The entire people went each person to his house, 20and David went back to bless his household. Mikal, Sha'ul's daughter, came out to meet David, but she said, 'How the king of Yisra'el honoured himself today when he exposed himself today before the eyes of his servants' handmaids, as one of the empty-headed people totally exposes himself!'

21David said to Mikal, 'It was before Yahweh, who chose me rather than your father and his entire household to charge me to be ruler over Yahweh's people, over Yisra'el. I'll make fun before Yahweh 22and slight myself yet more than this and be low in my own eyes, but with the handmaids that you speak of, with them I'll find honour.'

23To Mikal, Sha'ul's daughter, no child was born till the day of her death.

## Yahweh doesn't like settling down

7 When the king had gone to live in his house, when Yahweh had given him a settled position in relation to all his enemies around, 2the king said to Natan the prophet, 'Please look: I'm living in a cedar house, but God's chest is living inside a tent.' 3Natan said to the king, 'Go do everything that's in your mind, because Yahweh is with you.'

4But that night Yahweh's word came to Natan: 5'Go and say to my servant, to David, "Yahweh has said this: 'Are you to build me a house to live in? 6Because I haven't lived in a house from the day that I took the Yisra'elites up from Misrayim [Egypt] till this day. I've been going about in a tent as a dwelling. 7Everywhere I went about among all the Yisra'elites, did I speak a word with one of the Yisra'elite clan leaders whom I ordered to shepherd my people Yisra'el, saying "Why have you not built me a cedar house?"'"

8So now you're to say this to my servant, to David, "Yahweh of Armies has said this: 'I myself took you from the pasture, from following the flock, to be ruler over my people, over Yisrael, 9and I've been with you everywhere you've gone. I've cut off all your enemies from before you and I shall make a big name for you, like the name of the big people who are on the earth. <sup>10</sup>I shall make a place for my people, for Yisraèl, and plant them. They will dwell in their place and not tremble again. Evil people won't humble them again as they did previously, <sup>11</sup>from the day that I ordered leaders over my people Yisraèl. I shall give you a settled position in relation to all your enemies.

## A house and a household

Yahweh tells you that Yahweh will make a house(hold) for you. <sup>12</sup>When your days are full and you lie down with your ancestors, I shall set up your offspring after you, who will come out from inside you, and I shall establish his kingship. <sup>13</sup>He is the one who will build a house for my name. I shall establish his royal throne permanently. <sup>14</sup>I myself will become a father to him and he will become a son to me. When he goes wrong, I shall reprove him with a club in the hand of human beings, with the blows of human hands, <sup>15</sup>but my commitment will not depart from him as I removed it from Sha'ul, whom I removed from before you. <sup>16</sup>Your household and your kingship will be trustworthy permanently before you. Your throne will be established permanently."'

<sup>17</sup>In accordance with all these words and in accordance with this entire vision, so Natan spoke to David.

<sup>18</sup>King David came and sat before Yahweh, and said, 'Who am I, Lord Yahweh, and who are my household, that you have brought me as far as this? <sup>19</sup>Moreover, this has been small in your eyes, Lord Yahweh. You've spoken further about your servant's household for the distant future. This is instruction about a human being, Lord Yahweh: <sup>20</sup>what more can David speak to you? You yourself have acknowledged your servant, Lord Yahweh. <sup>21</sup>On account of your word and in accordance with your mind you're doing this entire big thing, making it known to your servant.

## No God like Yahweh, no people like Yisra'el

<sup>22</sup>Thus you are great, Lord Yahweh, because there is no one like you, no God except you, in all that we have heard with our ears. <sup>23</sup>And who is like your people, like Yisraèl, a nation on the

earth that God went to redeem for himself as a people, to make for himself a name, and to do big and awe-inspiring things (for you all) for your country before your people whom you redeemed for yourself from Misrayim (nations and their gods). <sup>24</sup>You established your people Yisraèl for yourself as a people permanently, and you Yahweh became God for them.

<sup>25</sup>Now, Yahweh God, the word that you have spoken about your servant and about his household – establish it permanently and do as you have spoken. <sup>26</sup>May your name be great permanently: "Yahweh of Armies is God over Yisraèl". May your servant David's household be established before you. <sup>27</sup>Because you, Yahweh of Armies, God of Yisraèl, have opened your servant's ear, saying "I will build a household for you." That's why your servant has found his courage to make this plea to you.

<sup>28</sup>Now, Lord Yahweh, you are God, and your words are truthful. You have spoken this good thing to your servant. <sup>29</sup>Now resolve to bless your servant's household so it will be before you permanently, because you, Lord Yahweh, have spoken. May your servant's household be blessed permanently through your blessing.'

## David's victories

**8** Subsequently, David struck down the Pelishtites and made them bow down. David took the reins of control from the hand of the Pelishtites. <sup>2</sup>He also struck down the Mo'abites. He measured them with a length of cord, making them lie down on the ground. He measured two lengths for putting them to death and one full length for letting them live. The Mo'abites became servants to David, bringing offerings. <sup>3</sup>David struck down Hadad'ezer ben Rehob king of Tsobah, when he was going to put back his monument at the River Euphrates. <sup>4</sup>David captured from him 1,700 cavalry and 20,000 men on foot. David hamstrung all the chariotry but of them left a hundred chariotry.

<sup>5</sup>Aramites from Dammeseq [Damascus] came to help Hadad'ezer king of Tsobah, and David struck down 22,000 men in Aram. <sup>6</sup>David put outposts in Aram of Dammeseq and the Aramites became servants to David, bringing offerings. Yahweh delivered David in every place

where he went. ⁷David took the gold quivers that Hadad'ezer's servants had and brought them to Yerushalaim, ⁸and from Betah and from Berotay, Hadad'ezer's towns, King David took very much copper.

⁹To'i king of Hamat heard that David had struck down Hadad'ezer's entire force, ¹⁰and To'i sent Yoram his son to King David to ask him about whether things were well and to bless him, because he had battled against Hadad'ezer and had struck him down, on account of the fact that Hadad'ezer had been involved in battles with To'i. In his hand were objects of silver, objects of gold and objects of copper. ¹¹King David also made them sacred for Yahweh, with the silver and the gold that he made sacred from all the nations that he had subjugated: ¹²from Edom, from Mo'ab, from the Ammonites, from the Pelishtites, from Amaleq and from the spoil of Hadad'ezer ben Rebob king of Tsobah.

### David's best time

¹³David made a name when he came back from striking down the Aramites in Salt Ravine, 18,000. ¹⁴He put outposts in Edom. When he put outposts in all Edom, all Edom became servants to David. Yahweh delivered David wherever he went. ¹⁵David reigned over all Yisra'el and David exercised authority in faithfulness for all his people.

¹⁶Yo'ab ben Tseruyah was over the army. Yehoshaphat ben Ahilud was recorder. ¹⁷Tsadoq [Zadok] ben Ahitub and Abimelek ben Ebyatar were priests. Tserayah was secretary. ¹⁸Benayah ben Yehoyada: both the Keretites and the Peletites. David's sons were priests.

**9** David said, 'Is there anyone still left of Sha'ul's household, so I can act in commitment with him for the sake of Yehonatan?' ²There was a servant belonging to Sha'ul's household; his name was Tsiba. They called for him to David, and the king said to him, 'Are you Tsiba?' He said, 'Your servant'. ³The king said, 'Is there no one at all still left of Sha'ul's household so that I can act

in God's commitment with him?' Tsiba said to the king, 'There's still a son of Yehonatan; he's injured in both feet.' ⁴The king said to him, 'Where is he?' Tsiba said to the king, 'There, he's at the house of Makir ben Ammi'el, in Lo Debar.' ⁵King David sent and got him from the house of Makir ben Ammi'el, from Lo Debar. ⁶Mephiboshet ben Yehonatan, son of Sha'ul, came to David, fell on his face and bowed low. David said, 'Mephiboshet!' He said, 'Here is your servant.' ⁷David said to him, 'Don't be afraid, because I'll definitely act in commitment with you for the sake of Yehonatan your father. I'll give back to you all the fields of Sha'ul, your father, and you yourself may eat bread at my table regularly.' ⁸He bowed low and said, 'What is your servant, that you have turned your face to a dead dog like me?'

### Mephiboshet ('From-Shame's-Mouth')

⁹The king called for Tsiba, Sha'ul's boy, and said to him, 'Everything that belonged to Sha'ul and to his entire household I am giving to your lord's son. ¹⁰You are to serve the land for him, you, your sons and your servants, and bring it so it may be bread for your lord's son, so he may eat it. But Mephiboshet, your lord's son, himself is to eat bread continually at my table' (Tsiba had fifteen sons and twenty servants). ¹¹Tsiba said to the king, 'In accordance with all that my lord the king orders his servant, so your servant will act, "with Mephiboshet eating at my table like one of the king's sons".' ¹²Mephiboshet had a young son; his name was Mika. Everyone who lived in Tsiba's household – they were servants of Mephiboshet, ¹³though Mephiboshet lived in Yerushalaim, because he was eating at the king's table regularly. He was lame in both feet.

**10** Subsequently, the king of the Ammonites died, and Hanun his son began to reign in place of him. ²David said, 'I will act in commitment with Hanun ben Nahash, as his father acted in commitment with me.' So David sent by the hand of his servants to console him over his father. David's servants came to the Ammonites' country, ³but the Ammonites' officials said to Hanun their lord, 'Is David honouring your father, in your eyes, because he sent you people offering consolation? It's for the sake of searching out the town and investigating it so as to overthrow it that David sent his servants to you, isn't it.'

⁴So Hanun got David's servants, clipped off half their beard and cut their clothes in half up to their behinds, and sent them off. ⁵People told David and he sent to meet them, because the men were very ashamed. The king said, 'Stay in Yeriho [Jericho] until your beard grows, then you can come back.' ⁶The Ammonites saw that they stank with David, and the Ammonites sent and hired Aramites from Bet-rehob and Aramites from Tsobah (20,000 men on foot), the king of Ma'akah (1,000 men) and men from Tob (12,000).

## Yo'ab's victories

⁷David heard and sent Yo'ab and the entire army, the strong men. ⁸The Ammonites went out and lined up for battle at the entrance of the gateway, with the Aramites from Tsobah and Rehob, the men from Tob, and Ma'akah alone in the fields. ⁹Yo'ab saw that the face of battle was against him in front and behind. He picked some of all the picked men of Yisra'el and lined them up to meet the Aramites, ¹⁰while he gave the rest of the company into the hand of Abshay his brother and lined them up to meet the Ammonites. ¹¹He said, 'If the Aramites are too strong for me, you'll be my deliverance, and if the Ammonites are too strong for you, I'll go to deliver you. ¹²Be strong, and let's summon up our strength on behalf of our people and on behalf of our God's towns, as Yahweh does what is good in his eyes.'

¹³So Yo'ab went up for the battle against the Aramites, he and his company who were with him, and they fled from before him. ¹⁴When the Ammonites saw that the Aramites had fled, they fled from before Abishay and came into the town. So Yo'ab turned back from fighting the Ammonites, and came to Yerushalaim.

¹⁵The Aramites saw that they had taken a beating before Yisra'el, and they gathered together. ¹⁶Hadad'ezer sent and got the Aramites who were from across the river to go out, and they came to Helam, with Shobak, Hadad'ezer's army officer, at their head. ¹⁷It

was told David, and he gathered all Yisra'el, crossed the Yarden and came to Hela'm, and the Aramites lined up to meet David and did battle with him. ¹⁸The Aramites fled from before Yisra'el. David killed 700 of the Aramite chariotry and 40,000 cavalry, and struck down Shobak, his army officer; he died there. ¹⁹All the kings who were servants of Hadad'ezer saw that they had taken a beating before Yisra'el and they made peace with Yisra'el and served them. The Aramites were afraid to deliver the Ammonites any more.

## The view from the roof

**11** At the turn of the year, at the time when the kings go out, David sent Yo'ab and his servants with him, and all Yisra'el, and they devastated the Ammonites and besieged Rabbah, while David was staying in Yerushalaim.

²During evening time David got up from his bed and walked about on the roof of the king's house, and from on the roof saw a woman bathing. The woman was very good-looking. ³David sent and enquired about the woman. They said, 'She's Bat-sheba bat Eli'am, the wife of Uriyyah the Hittite, isn't she.' ⁴David sent envoys, got her, and she came to him. He slept with her, while she was making herself sacred from her taboo, and she went back to her house.

⁵The woman got pregnant, and she sent and told David, 'I'm pregnant.' ⁶David sent to Yo'ab, 'Send Uriyyah the Hittite to me.' Yo'ab sent Uriyyah to David. ⁷So Uriyyah came to him, and David asked him about how well things were with Yo'ab and how well things were with the company and how well things were with the battle. ⁸Then David said to Uriyyah, 'Go down to your house and bathe your feet.' Uriyyah went out from the king's house, and a present from the king followed him.

⁹But Uriyyah slept at the entrance of the king's house with all his lord's servants. He didn't go down to his house. ¹⁰They told David, 'Uriyyah didn't go down to his house.' David said to Uriyyah, 'Didn't you come from a journey? Why didn't you go down to your house?' ¹¹Uriyyah said to David, 'The chest and Yisra'el and Yehudah are staying at Sukkot, and my lord

Yo'ab and my lord's servants are camped on the face of the fields, and should I myself come to my house to eat and drink and sleep with my wife? By your life, by your very life, if I were to do this thing . . .' ¹²David said to Uriyyah, 'Stay here today, too, and tomorrow I'll send you off.' So Uriyyah stayed in Yerushalaim that day.

## One moral mistake can lead to another

Next day ¹³David called for him, he ate before him and drank, and he got him drunk. But in the evening he went out to lie in his bed with his lord's servants. He didn't go down to his house. ¹⁴So in the morning David wrote a letter to Yo'ab and sent it by the hand of Uriyyah. ¹⁵He wrote in the letter, 'Place Uriyyah near the front of the fiercest battle, and pull back from after him so he may be struck down and die.' ¹⁶So when Yo'ab was keeping watch on the town, he put Uriyyah in the place where he knew that there were forceful men. ¹⁷The men of the town came out and battled against Yo'ab, and of the company some of David's servants fell. Uriyyah the Hittite also died.

¹⁸Yo'ab sent and told David all the things about the battle. ¹⁹He ordered the envoy: 'When you finish speaking all the things about the battle to the king, ²⁰if the king's temper rises and he says to you, "Why did you go up to the town to battle? Didn't you know that they would shoot from on the wall? ²¹Who struck down Abimelek ben Yerubbeshet? Wasn't it a woman who threw down an upper millstone on him from on the wall and he died at Tebets? Why did you go up to the wall?" then you are to say, "Your servant Uriyyah the Hittite also died."'

²²The envoy went, and came and told David all that Yo'ab had sent him with. ²³The envoy said to David, 'The men prevailed against us and came out against us into the fields. Then we were against them as far as the entrance of the gateway. ²⁴But the archers shot at your servants from on the wall and some of the king's servants died; and your servant Uriyyah the Hittie also died.'

²⁵David said to the envoy, 'Say this to Yo'ab: "This thing is not to be bad in your eyes, because the sword devours one way and another way. Make your battle stronger against the town and tear it down." Strengthen him.'

## But the thing David had done was bad in Yahweh's eyes

²⁶Uriyyah's wife heard that Uriyyah her husband was dead, and she lamented over her master. ²⁷The grieving passed, and David sent and gathered her to his house. She became a wife for him, and gave birth to a son for him. But the thing that David did was bad in Yahweh's eyes.

**12** So Yahweh sent Natan to David. He came to him and said to him, 'There were two men in a town, one wealthy, one destitute. ²The wealthy man had a very large flock and herd. ³The destitute man didn't have anything except one small ewe that he had acquired. He had let it live and it had grown up with him and with his children, all together. It used to eat from his bit, drink from his cup and sleep in his arms. It was like a daughter to him. ⁴A traveller came to the wealthy man, but he spared taking something from his flock or from his herd to prepare for the man on a journey who had come to him. He took the destitute man's ewe and prepared it for the man who had come to him.'

⁵David's anger raged right up at the man. He said to Natan, 'As Yahweh lives, the man who did this deserves death. ⁶He should make good fourfold for the ewe on account of the fact that he did this thing, and since he didn't spare.'

⁷Natan said to David, 'You're the man. Yahweh the God of Yisra'el has said this: "I myself anointed you as king over Yisra'el. I myself rescued you from Sha'ul's hand. ⁸I gave you your lord's household and your lord's wives into your arms. I gave you the household of Yisra'el and Yehudah. If that's little, I would have added to you as much again as these. ⁹Why did you despise Yahweh's word by doing what is bad in my eyes? Uriyyah the Hittite you struck down with the sword and his wife you took as your wife. Him you killed, with the sword of the Ammonites. ¹⁰So now the sword won't depart from your household, permanently, because of the fact that you despised me and took Uriyyah the Hittite's wife to be a wife for you."

## The man who has learned how to be a prophet

¹¹Yahweh has said this: "Here, I'm going to make something bad arise for you from your household. I shall take your wives before your eyes and give them to your neighbour. He'll sleep with your wives before the eyes of this sun. ¹²Because you yourself acted in secret, but I myself will do this thing before all Yisra'el and before the sun.'"

¹³David said to Natan, 'I've acted wrongly against Yahweh.' Natan said to David, 'Yes. Because Yahweh has made your wrongdoing pass on, you will not die. ¹⁴Nevertheless, because you've totally disdained (the enemies of) Yahweh by this act, yes, the child born to you will definitely die.' ¹⁵And Natan went home.

Yahweh struck the child to whom Uriyyah's wife gave birth for David, and it became ill. ¹⁶David sought God for the boy. David made a fast and came and stayed the night and lay on the ground. ¹⁷The elders in his household got up over him to make him get up from the ground but he wasn't willing, and he didn't eat a meal with them.

¹⁸On the seventh day the child died. David's servants were afraid to tell him that the child had died, because (they said), 'Here, when the child was alive, we spoke to him and he didn't listen to our voice. How can we say to him, "The child is dead"? He may do something bad.' ¹⁹David saw that his servants were whispering to one another and David perceived that the child was dead. David said to his servants, 'Is the child dead?' They said, 'He's dead.'

## Death and new life

²⁰David got up from the ground, bathed, put on his oils and changed his clothes. He came to Yahweh's house and bowed low. Then he came to his house and asked and they presented him with a meal and he ate. ²¹His servants said to him, 'What's this thing that you've done? When the child was alive, you fasted and wailed. Now that the child is dead, you've got up and eaten a meal.' ²²He said, 'While the child was still alive, I fasted and wailed because I said, "Who knows? Yahweh may be gracious to me. The child may live." ²³But now he's dead, why

on earth should I fast? Can I bring him back again? I'm going to him, but he won't come back to me.'

²⁴David consoled Bat-sheba his wife and had sex with her. He slept with her and she gave birth to a son, and named him Shelomoh [Solomon]. Because Yahweh loved him, ²⁵he sent by means of Natan the prophet and named him 'Beloved-by-Yah', on account of Yahweh.

²⁶Yo'ab battled against Rabbah of the Ammonites and captured the royal town. ²⁷Yo'ab sent envoys to David and said, 'I've battled against Rabbah – yes, captured the water town. ²⁸So now, gather the rest of the company and camp against the town and capture it, so that I myself don't capture the town and my name is called out over it.'

²⁹So David gathered the entire company and went to Rabbah, battled against it and captured it. ³⁰He got their king's crown from on his head (its weight was a talent of gold, with precious stones) and it came on to David's head, while he took out very much spoil from the town. ³¹The people that was in it he took out and put them to saws, iron harrows and iron axes, or transferred them to brickworking. So he would do to all the Ammonites' towns. Then David and the entire company went back to Yerushalaim.

## Amnon's plot

**13** Subsequently: Abshalom, David's son, had an attractive sister; her name was Tamar. Amnon, David's son, was in love with her. ²It was pressing for Amnon, so that he became ill on account of Tamar his sister, because she was a young girl but it was unimaginable in Amnon's eyes to do anything about her.

³Now Amnon had a friend; his name was Yonadab ben Shim'ah, David's brother. Yonadab was a very smart man. ⁴He said to him, 'Prince, why are you down like this, morning by morning? Won't you tell me?' Amnon said to him, 'Tamar, my brother Abshalom's sister – I'm in love with her.' ⁵Yonadab said to him, 'Lie on your bed and act ill. Your father will come to see you and you're to say to him, "May Tamar my sister please come and give me

bread to eat. May she prepare the food before my eyes in order that I may see and eat from her hand.'"

6So Amnon lay down and acted ill, the king came to see him, and Amnon said to the king, 'May Tamar my sister come and make a couple of pancakes before my eyes, so I may eat from her hand.' 7So David sent to Tamar his daughter, saying 'Please go to Amnon your brother's house and make him some food.' 8Tamar went to Amnon her brother's house; he was lying down. She got dough and kneaded it and made pancakes before his eyes, and cooked the pancakes.

9She got the pan and poured them out before him, but he refused to eat. Amnon said, 'Get everyone to go out from me', and everyone went out from him. 10Amnon said to Tamar, 'Bring the food into the room so I can eat from your hand.' Tamar got the pancakes that she'd made, brought them to Amnon her brother in the room 11and brought them up to him to eat, but he took strong hold of her and said to her, 'Come to bed with me, sister.'

## The rape of a sister

12She said to him, 'Don't, brother. Don't humble me, because such a thing is not done in Yisra'el. Don't do this villainous thing. 13I, where would I take my reviling? And you, you'll be just one of the villains in Yisra'el. So now, please speak to the king, because he wouldn't withhold me from you.' 14But he wasn't willing to listen to her voice. He took hold of her and humbled her and bedded her.

15Amnon then felt a very great hostility for her, in that the hostility that he felt for her was greater than the love he had felt for her. Amnon said to her, 'Get up, go.' 16She said to him, 'No, because this bad act is greater than the other that you did with me, sending me away.' But he wasn't willing to listen to her. 17He called the boy who ministered to him and said 'Please send this woman off, away from my presence, outside, and bolt the door after her.'

18She had a long-sleeved gown on, because the young princesses used to dress in such robes. His minister took her outside and bolted the door after her. 19Tamar put earth on her

head, tore the long-sleeved gown that she had on, put her hand on her head and went her way, crying out as she went.

20Abshalom her brother said to her, 'Sister, was it Aminon your brother who was with you? Now, sister, quieten down. He's your brother. Don't set your mind on this thing.' Tamar stayed, a desolate woman, in Abshalom her brother's house. 21When King David heard about all these things, it really enraged him. 22Abshalom didn't speak with Amnon anything bad or good, because Abshalom was hostile to Amnon because of the fact that he had humbled Tamar his sister.

## The strife between brothers

23Two full years later, Abshalom's shearers were at Ba'al Hatsor, which is near Ephrayim, and Abshalom invited all the princes. 24Abshalom came to the king and said, 'Please, here are your servant's shearers. Will the king and his servants please go with your servant?' 25The king said to Abshalom, 'No, son, we won't all of us go, we won't be a burden to you.' He pressed him, but he wasn't willing to go, but he gave them his blessing. 26So Abshalom said, 'But won't Amnon my brother please go with us?' The king said to him, 'Why should he go with you?' 27But Abshalom pressed him, and he sent with him Amnon and all the princes.

28Abshalom ordered his boys, 'Watch when Amnon's heart is good because of the wine, will you, and I'll say to you, "Strike Amnon down": put him to death, don't be afraid. I myself am the one who's given you the order, am I not. Be strong. Be forceful men.' 29Abshalom's boys did to Amnon as Abshalom ordered, and all the princes got up, each one on his mule, and fled.

30While they were on the way, the report came to David: 'Abshalom has struck down all the princes – not one of them was left!' 31David got up and tore his clothes and lay on the ground. All his servants stood, their clothes torn. 32But Yonadab ben Shim'ah, David's brother, avowed, 'My lord should not say that all the young princes are dead, because Amnon alone is dead, because it's been determined at Abshalom's bidding since the day Amnon humbled Tamar his sister. 33So now my lord the

king should not take the thing to heart, saying
"All the princes are dead", because Amnon
alone is dead.'

### The woman from Teqoa

<sup>34</sup>Absalom took flight, and the lookout boy
lifted up his eyes and looked: there, a large
company going from the road behind him,
from the side of the mountain. <sup>35</sup>Yonadab said
to the king, 'There, the princes have come. In
accordance with your servant's word, so it has
happened.' <sup>36</sup>As he finished speaking, there,
the princes came; they lifted up their voice
and wailed. The king and all his servants also
uttered a very great wail. <sup>37</sup>When Absalom
took flight and went to Talmay ben Ammihud
king of Geshur, he took up grieving over his
son all the time.

<sup>38</sup>When Absalom had taken flight and
gone to Geshur, he was there for three years,
<sup>39</sup>then going out to Absalom consumed King
David, because he had found consolation over
Amnon, that he was dead.

**14** Yo'ab ben Tseruyah knew that the
king's mind was on Absalom,
<sup>2</sup>and Yo'ab sent to Teqoa and got a smart
woman from there. He said to her, 'Please act
as someone grieving and dress in grieving
clothes. Don't put on oils; be like a woman
who's been grieving for a long time over
someone who has died. <sup>3</sup>You're to come to the
king and speak to him in this way.' Yo'ab put
the words into her mouth, <sup>4</sup>and the Teqo'ite
woman said them to the king. She fell on
her face to the ground, bowed low, and said,
'Deliver, Your Majesty!'

<sup>5</sup>The king said to her, 'What do you need?'
She said, 'Well, I'm a woman who's a widow;
my husband has died. <sup>6</sup>Your maidservant
had two sons. The two of them fought in the
fields and there was no one to rescue them
from each other. One of them struck the other
down and put him to death. <sup>7</sup>And here, the
entire kin-group has risen up against your
maidservant and said, "Give us the one who
struck his brother down so we may put him to
death for the life of his brother whom he killed.
We'll annihilate the heir, too." So they'll quench
the ember that remains to me, and not give
my husband a name or someone remaining

on the face of the ground.' <sup>8</sup>The king said to
the woman, 'Go home and I'll give an order
concerning you.'

### The parable explained

<sup>9</sup>The Teqo'ite woman said to the king, 'On
me be the waywardness, my lord king, and
on my ancestral household; the king and
his throne be free of guilt.' <sup>10</sup>The king said,
'Anyone who speaks to you, bring him to me,
and he will never touch you again.' <sup>11</sup>She said,
'The king is, please, to be mindful of Yahweh
your God so that the restorer of blood does
not bring more devastation and they do not
annihilate my son.' He said, 'As Yahweh lives, if
one hair of your son's falls to the ground . . .'

<sup>12</sup>The woman said, 'May your maidservant
please speak a word to my lord the king.' He
said, 'Speak.' <sup>13</sup>The woman said, 'So why have
you thought things up in this way against
God's people? By the king's speaking this thing,
he is like someone liable to condemnation,
in that the king does not let his banished son
come back. <sup>14</sup>Because we shall all finally die,
like water poured out on the ground that
cannot be gathered up. But God does not
take up the life of one who thinks of ways so
that someone who is banished does not stay
banished from him.

<sup>15</sup>So now, in that I have come to speak this
word to my lord the king because the people
have frightened me, your maidservant said,
"I must speak to the king; perhaps the king
will act on your handmaid's word, <sup>16</sup>because
the king will listen and rescue his handmaid
from the fist of someone annihilating me and
my son together from God's domain." <sup>17</sup>Your
maidservant said, "May the word of my lord
the king please be for my relief, because my
lord the king is like God's envoy in listening
to what is good and what is bad." May Yahweh
your God be with you.'

### The king won

<sup>18</sup>The king answered the woman, 'Please
don't hide a thing from me of what I am asking
you.' The woman said, 'My lord the king may
please speak.' <sup>19</sup>The king said, 'Is Yo'ab's hand

with you in all this?' The woman answered, 'By your own life, my lord the king, if anyone could go to the right or to the left from all that my lord the king spoke, because your servant Yo'ab – he's the one who gave me orders and who put all these things in your maidservant's mouth. ²⁰It was for the sake of changing the face of the thing that your servant Yo'ab did this thing. My lord is smart with the same smartness as God's envoy in knowing everything that's in the country.'

²¹The king said to Yo'ab, 'Here, I'm going to do this thing. Go and get the boy, Abshalom, back.' ²²Yo'ab fell on his face on the ground and bowed low and blessed the king. Yo'ab said, 'Today your servant acknowledges that I have found grace in your eyes, my lord king, in that the king has acted on your servant's word.'

²³Yo'ab set off and went to Geshur and brought Abshalom to Yerushalaim. ²⁴But the king said, 'He's to go round to his house and not see my face.' So Abshalom went round to his house and didn't see the king's face.

## The field set on fire

²⁵Compared with Abshalom, there was no one in all Yisra'el as attractive, no one to admire so much. From the sole of his foot to the crown of his head there was no defect in him. ²⁶When he shaved his head (at the end of each year when he would shave – because it was too heavy for him, so he would shave it), he would weigh the hair on his head: 200 sheqels by the royal weight. ²⁷There were born to Abshalom three sons and one daughter, and her name was Tamar; she became a woman who was attractive in appearance.

²⁸Abshalom lived in Yerushalaim for two years but didn't see the king's face. ²⁹Then Abshalom sent to Yo'ab so as to send him to the king, but he wouldn't come to him. He sent again, a second time, but he wasn't willing to come. ³⁰So he said to his servants, 'Look, Yo'ab's share is by the side of me and he has barley there. Go and set it on fire.' Abshalom's servants set the share on fire.

³¹Yo'ab got up and came to Abshalom at home and said to him, 'Why did your servants set my share on fire?' ³²Abshalom said to Yo'ab, 'Here, I sent to you, saying "Come here", so I

could send you to the king to say "Why did I come from Geshur? It would be good for me if I were still there." Now, I should see the king's face, and if there is any waywardness in me, he may put me to death.' ³³So Yo'ab came to the king and told him, and he called for Abshalom. He came to the king and bowed low to him, with his face to the ground before the king, and the king kissed Abshalom.

## Abshalom prepares for a coup

**15** Subsequently, Abshalom made ready for himself a chariot and horses, with fifty men running before him. ²Abshalom would start early and stand by the side of the road to the gateway. When anyone had an argument that was to come to the king for a decision, Abshalom called to him and said, 'What town are you from?', and the person said, 'Your servant is from one of the Yisra'elite clans', ³and Abshalom said to him, 'Look, your words are good and straight, but you have no one from the king to listen.'

⁴Abshalom said, 'If only someone would make me an authority in the country so that anyone who had an argument for decision could come to me and I would see he was recognized as in the right.' ⁵When someone drew near to bow low to him, he would put out his hand and take strong hold of him and kiss him. ⁶Abshalom acted in this manner to all Yisra'el who would come to the king for a decision. So Abshalom stole the heart of the Yisra'elites.

⁷At the end of forty years Abshalom said to the king, 'I want please to go and make good my pledge that I made to Yahweh in Hebron, ⁸because your servant made a pledge when I was living in Geshur in Aram, saying "If Yahweh lets me actually go back to Yerushalaim, I will serve Yahweh."' ⁹The king said to him, 'Go; things will be well.' So he set off and went to Hebron.

¹⁰But Abshalom sent followers through all Yisra'el's clans, saying 'When you hear the sound of the horn, you're to say, "Abshalom has become king in Hebron!"' ¹¹Two hundred people from Yerushalaim had gone with Abshalom, invited and going in integrity. They didn't know anything. ¹²And Abshalom

sent for Ahitophel the Gilonite, David's counsellor, from his town, from Giloh, when he was offering sacrifices. The conspiracy became powerful, and the company going with Abshalom was growing.

## David's flight

¹³Someone came telling David, 'The Yisra'elites' mind has gone after Abshalom.' ¹⁴David said to all his servants who were with him in Yerushalaim, 'Get up, let's take flight, because there'll be no escape group for us from before Abshalom. Hurry, go, so he doesn't hurry and catch up with us and hurl something bad upon us and strike the town down with the mouth of the sword.' ¹⁵The king's servants said to the king, 'In accordance with all that my lord the king chooses, here are your servants.' ¹⁶The king went out with his entire household after him, but the king abandoned ten secondary wives to keep the house.

¹⁷So the king went out with the entire company after him, and halted at the farthest house, ¹⁸with all his servants passing on his side, and all the Keretites and all the Peletites, and all the Gittites (600 men who had come after him from Gat), passing on before the king. ¹⁹The king said to Ittay the Gittite, 'Why should you go with us, too? Go back and stay with the king, because you're a foreigner, and also you're an exile in relation to your place. ²⁰You came yesterday. Why should I get you to wander with us today as we go, when I'm going wherever I'm going? Turn back and take your brothers back with you in commitment and truthfulness.'

²¹Ittay answered the king, 'As Yahweh lives and as my lord the king lives, in the place where my lord the king is, whether for death or for life, there will your servant be.' ²²David said to Ittay, 'Go, pass on.' So Ittay the Gittite passed on, with all his men and all the little ones who were with him.

## Turn Ahitophel's advice into stupidity

²³As the entire region was wailing in a loud voice and the entire company was passing on, and the king was passing over Wadi Qidron,

and the entire company was passing on before the wilderness road, ²⁴and there also Tsadoq and all the Levites with him were carrying the chest of God's pact, they put God's chest down (and Ebyatar went up) until the company had finished passing on from the town.

²⁵But the king said to Tsadoq, 'Take God's chest back into the town. If I find grace in Yahweh's eyes, he will let me come back and let me see it and its home. ²⁶But if he says this: "I don't want you", here I am: he can do with me as it is good in his eyes.' ²⁷So the king said to Tsadoq the priest, 'Do you see? You go back to the town and things will go well, with Ahima'ats your son and Yehonatan ben Ebyatar (your two sons) with you. ²⁸See, I'm going to wait in the steppes in the wilderness until word comes from you to tell me.'

²⁹So Tsadoq and Ebyatar took God's chest back to Yerushalaim and stayed there, ³⁰while David was going up the Olives Ascent, wailing as he was going up, with his head covered; he was walking barefoot, while the entire company that was with him covered each one his head. They went up wailing as they were going up. ³¹When David was told, 'Ahitophel is among the conspirators with Abshalom', David said, 'Please turn Ahitophel's counsel into idiocy, Yahweh!'

## Two loyal friends

³²David was coming as far as the top where people would bow low to God, and there was Hushay the Arkite to meet him, his coat torn and earth on his head. ³³David said to him, 'If you pass on with me, you'll be a burden to me. ³⁴But if you go back to the town and say to Abshalom, "I'm your servant, Your Majesty – I used to be your father's servant in the past, but now I'm your servant", you can contravene Ahitophel's counsel for me. ³⁵Tsadoq and Ebyatar the priests will be with you there, won't they. And every word that you hear from the king's house you can tell Tsadoq and Ebyatar the priests. ³⁶There, their two sons, Tsadoq's Ahima'ats and Ebyatar's Yehonatan, are with them. You can send to me through them everything that you hear.' ³⁷So Hushay, David's friend, came to the town as Abshalom was coming to Yerushalaim.

# 16

When David had passed a little beyond the top, there, Tsiba, a servant of Mephiboshet, met him with a pair of donkeys, saddled. On them were two hundred loaves of bread, a hundred raisin blocks, a hundred of summer fruit and a skin of wine. ²The king said to Tsiba, 'Why have you got these?' Tsiba said, 'The donkeys are for the king's household to ride, the bread and the summer fruit are for eating by the boys, and the wine is for drinking by people who are weary in the wilderness.' ³The king said, 'And where is your lord's son?' Tsiba said to the king, 'There, he's staying in Yerushalaim, because he's said, "Today the household of Yisra'el will give me back my father's kingship."' ⁴The king said to Tsiba, 'Here, to you belongs everything that belonged to Mephiboshet.' Tsiba said, 'I bow low. May I find grace in your eyes, my lord king.'

## Shim'i's slighting

⁵King David came as far as Bahurim and there, someone from the kin-group of Sha'ul's household was going out from there. His name was Shim'i ben Gera. As he went out he was slighting ⁶and pelting David and all King David's servants with stones, with the entire company and all the strong men at his right and at his left. ⁷Shim'i said this as he slighted him: 'Get out, get out, you man of bloodshed, you scoundrel! ⁸Yahweh is giving back to you all the bloodshed in the household of Sha'ul, in whose place you became king. Yahweh has given the kingship into the hand of Abshalom your son, and here you are, in a bad situation, because you're a man of bloodshed.'

⁹Abishay ben Tseruyah said to the king, 'Why should this dead dog slight my lord the king? I shall pass on, please, and remove his head!' ¹⁰But the king said, 'What do you and I have in common, you sons of Tseruyah? He can slight in this way because Yahweh has said to him, "Slight David." Who is to say, "Why have you done that?"?' ¹¹David said to Abishay and to all his servants, 'Here, my son who came out from inside me, is seeking my life. How much more now a Binyaminite? Let him be. He can slight, because Yahweh has said it to him. ¹²Maybe Yahweh will look at the waywardness done to me and Yahweh will give back good to me in place of his slighting this day.'

¹³David and his men went on their way, while Shim'i was going along the side of the mountain alongside him, slighting and pelting him with stones alongside him and throwing earth as he went. ¹⁴The king came with the entire company that was with him, faint, and he refreshed himself there.

## Ahitophel's advice

¹⁵Now Abshalom and the entire company, the Yisra'elite men, came to Yerushalaim, and Ahitophel with him. ¹⁶When Hushay the Arkite, David's friend, came to Abshalom, Hushay said to Abshalom, 'Long live the king, long live the king.' ¹⁷Abshalom said to Hushay, 'Is this your commitment to your friend? Why didn't you go with your friend?' ¹⁸Hushay said to Abshalom, 'No, because the one whom Yahweh has chosen, he and this company and all the Yisra'elite men – I shall be for him. I shall stay with him. ¹⁹Second, whom should I serve? Before his son, shouldn't I. As I served before your father, so I shall be before you.'

²⁰Abshalom said to Ahitophel, 'Give your counsel: what shall we do?' ²¹Ahitophel said, 'Have sex with your father's secondary wives whom he left to keep the house. All Yisra'el will hear that you have let yourself stink with your father, and the hands of all the people who are with you will be strong.' ²²They spread a tent for Abshalom on the roof and Abshalom had sex with his father's secondary wives before the eyes of all Yisra'el.

²³At that time the counsel of Ahitophel which he gave was like when one asks of a word from God. So it was with all Ahitophel's counsel both for David and for Abshalom.

# 17

Ahitophel said to Abshalom, 'I should please pick 12,000 men and set off and pursue after David tonight ²so that I come on him when he's weary and weak-handed. I'll make him tremble, and the entire company that's with him will flee. I'll strike down the king alone ³and bring back the entire company to you. When everyone has come back (it's the man you're seeking), the entire people will be at peace.' ⁴The thing seemed right in the eyes of

Abshalom and in the eyes of all Yisra'el's elders, ⁵but Abshalom said, 'Call for Hushay the Arkite as well, please, so we can hear what's in his mouth as well.' ⁶Hushay came to Abshalom and Abshalom said to him: 'This very word Ahitophel spoke. Shall we act on his word? If not, you speak.'

## Good advice treated as folly

⁷Hushay said to Abshalom, 'The counsel Ahitophel has given is not good this time.' ⁸Hushay said, 'You yourself know your father and his men, that they're strong men. They're as fierce-spirited as a bear in the wild that has lost its cubs, and your father is a man of battle. But he won't stay the night with the company. ⁹There, he will now be hiding in one of the pits or in one of the places.

And when some of the men fall at the beginning, a person who hears will hear and say, "Defeat has come on the company that goes after Abshalom!" ¹⁰That man, even if he's a forceful man whose heart's like the heart of a lion, will totally melt, because all Yisra'el knows that your father is a strong man, as are the forceful men who are with him.

¹¹Rather I counsel that all Yisra'el from Dan as far as Be'er-sheba (like the sand on the seashore in numbers) gather together to join you, with you personally going among them. ¹²We'll come against him in one of the places where he may be found and we'll light on him as the dew falls on the ground. None will be left of him and of all the men who are with him, not even one. ¹³If he gathers together into a town, all Yisra'el is to bring ropes to that town and we'll drag it as far as the wadi until not even a pebble is to be found there.'

¹⁴Abshalom and all the Yisra'elite men said, 'The counsel of Hushay the Arkite is better than the counsel of Ahitophel'; Yahweh had ordered the contravening of Ahitophel's good counsel so that Yahweh might bring a bad fate on Abshalom. ¹⁵Hushay said to Tsadoq and to Ebyatar the priests, 'In this and this way Ahitophel counselled Abshalom and the elders of Yisra'el, but in this and this way I myself counselled. ¹⁶Now send off quickly and tell David, "Don't stay the night at the wilderness crossings. Further, cross right over so that he

isn't swallowed up, the king and the entire company that's with him."'

## Ahitophel's suicide

¹⁷Yehonatan and Ahima'ats were halting at Treader's Spring, a maid would go and tell them, and they would go and tell King David, because they couldn't be seen coming into the town. ¹⁸But a boy saw them and told Abshalom. The two of them went quickly and came to the house of someone in Bahurim. He had a well in his courtyard and they went down there. ¹⁹The wife got a length of cloth and spread it over the face of the well, and scattered groats on it, so that nothing would become known. ²⁰Abshalom's servants came to the woman at the house and said, 'Where are Ahima'ats and Yehonatan?' The woman said to them, 'They crossed over the water brook.' They searched, but didn't find them, and went back to Yerushalaim.

²¹After they had gone, they got up from the well and went and told King David. They said to David, 'Set off and cross the water quickly, because Ahitophel has given counsel about you in such-and-such a way.' ²²So David set off, he and the entire company that was with him, and crossed the Yarden before morning light, until not one was missing who had not crossed the Yarden.

²³When Ahitophel saw that his counsel was not acted on, he saddled his donkey, set off and went home to his town. He gave orders concerning his household, and hanged himself. He died and was buried in his father's grave.

²⁴David was coming to Mahanayim when Abshalom crossed the Yarden, he and all the men of Yisra'el with him. ²⁵Abshalom had put Amasa over the army in place of Yo'ab. Amasa was the son of a man whose name was Yitra the Yisra'elite, who had had sex with Abigayil bat Nahash, the sister of Tseruyah, Yo'ab's mother. ²⁶Yisra'el and Abshalom camped in the region of Gil'ad.

## David agrees to stay behind

²⁷When David came to Mahanayim, Shobi ben Nahash from Rabbat of the Ammonites, Makir ben Ammi'el from Lo Debar, and

Barzillay the Gil'adite from Rogelim ²⁸brought up for David and for the company that was with him bedding, basins, potter's containers, wheat, barley, flour, roasted grain, beans, lentils, roasted grain, ²⁹syrup, curds, a flock, and cheese from the herd to eat, because (they said), 'The company's hungry and faint and thirsty in the wilderness.'

**18** David numbered the company that was with him and set over them divisional officers and section officers. ²David sent off the company, a third in the hand of Yo'ab, a third in the hand of Abishay ben Tseruyah, Yo'ab's brother, and a third in the hand of Ittay the Gittite. The king said to the company, 'I myself will definitely go out with you as well.' ³But the company said, 'You're not to go out, because if we do flee, they won't put their mind to us. If half of us die, they won't put their mind to us. Because there are now 10,000 like us. So now, it will be good that you're available to us from the town to help.' ⁴So the king said to them, 'Whatever is good in your eyes I'll do.'

The king stood at the side of the gateway as the entire company went out by sections and by divisions. ⁵The king ordered Yo'ab, Abishay and Ittay, 'Gently for me with the boy, with Abshalom.' The entire company heard the the king ordering all the officers concerning Abshalom.

⁶The company went out to the fields to meet Yisra'el. The battle took place in the Ephrayim Forest ⁷and the Yisra'elite company took a beating there before David's servants. It was a great defeat there that day – 20,000 men. ⁸The battle took place there, spread over the face of the entire region. The forest did more devouring of the company than what the sword devoured that day.

## Abshalom meets his death

⁹Abshalom met up with David's servants while Abshalom was riding on a mule. The mule came under the tangle of a big oak and his head caught hold of the oak. He was given up between the heavens and the earth as the mule that was under him passed on.

¹⁰Someone saw and told Yo'ab, 'Here, I've seen Abshalom hanging in an oak!' ¹¹Yo'ab said to the man who told him, 'Here, you saw, why didn't you strike him down to the ground there? It would have been on me to give you ten pieces of silver and a belt.' ¹²The man said to Yo'ab, 'If I were weighing on my palms a thousand pieces of silver, I wouldn't put out my hand against the prince, because in our ears the king ordered you and Abishay and Gittay, "Keep watch, whoever you are, over the boy Abshalom." ¹³If I'd acted falsely against his life, when nothing hides from the king, you yourself would have taken your stand at a distance.'

¹⁴Yo'ab said, 'I won't wait for you, therefore.' He took three sticks into his fist and plunged them into Abshalom's heart. While he was still alive in the heart of the oak, ¹⁵ten boys, Yo'ab's equipment-bearers, came round, struck Abshalom down and put him to death. ¹⁶Yo'ab blew on the horn, and the company turned back from pursuing after Yisra'el, because Yo'ab held the company back. ¹⁷They took Abshalom and threw him into a big pit in the forest, and put up a very big heap of stones over it, while all Yisra'el fled, each person to his tents.

(¹⁸While he was alive Abshalom himself had got and put up for himself the column that's in King's Vale, because (he said), 'I have no son in order to commemorate my name.' People have named the column 'Abshalom's Monument', until this day.)

¹⁹When Ahima'ats ben Tsadoq said, 'May I run and bring news to the king that Yahweh has acted with authority for him from his enemies' hand', ²⁰Yo'ab said to him, 'You're not to be a man with news this day. You may bring news another day. This day you're not to bring news, because the king's son is dead.'

## The news reaches David

²¹So Yo'ab said to a Kushite [Sudanese], 'Go tell the king what you have seen.' The Sudanese bowed low to Yo'ab and ran. ²²Ahima'ats ben Tsadoq once again said to Yo'ab, 'Whatever happens, may I myself also please run, after the Kushite?' Yo'ab said, 'Why is it that you're going to run, son, when there'll be no reward available for you?' ²³'Whatever happens, I'll run.' So he said to him, 'Run.' Ahima'ats ran by way of the plain, and passed the Kushite.

<sup>24</sup>David was sitting between the two gateways. The lookout at the gateway roof went to the wall. He lifted up his eyes and looked: there, a man running alone. <sup>25</sup>The lookout called and told the king. The king said, 'If he's alone, there's news on his lips.' He continued to draw nearer, <sup>26</sup>and the lookout saw another man running. The lookout called to the gateman, 'There, a man running alone', and the king said, 'He's bringing news, as well.' <sup>27</sup>The lookout said, 'I see the first runner; it's like the running of Ahima'ats ben Tsadoq.' The king said, 'He's a good man; he comes with good news.'

<sup>28</sup>Ahima'ats called out to the king, 'Things are well', bowed low to the king, on his face to the ground, and said, 'Yahweh your God be blessed, who delivered up the men who lifted up their hand against my lord the king!' <sup>29</sup>The king said, 'Is it well with the boy, with Abshalom?' Ahima'ats said, 'I saw a big uproar when the king's servant Yo'ab was sending your servant but I didn't know what it was.' <sup>30</sup>The king said, 'Come round; take your stand there.' He came round and halted, <sup>31</sup>and there, the Kushite was coming. The Kushite said, 'May my lord the king receive the news that Yahweh has acted with authority for you today from the hand of all the people who rose up against you.' <sup>32</sup>The king said to the Kushite, 'Is it well with the boy, with Abshalom?' The Kushite said, 'May my lord the king's enemies and all who rise up against you to do something bad be like the boy.'

### Inconsiderate grief?

<sup>33</sup>The king shook. He went up to the upper story of the gateway and wailed. As he went he said this: 'My son Abshalom, my son, my son Abshalom, if only I had died, I in place of you, Abshalom, my son, my son.'

**19** It was told Yo'ab, 'Here, the king is wailing and has taken up grieving over Abshalom.' <sup>2</sup>The deliverance that day turned to grieving for the entire company when the company heard that day, 'The king is in pain over his son.' <sup>3</sup>The company stole in when they came into the town that day, as a company that has battled steals in ashamed when they've fled in the battle, <sup>4</sup>while the king covered his face. The king cried out in a loud voice, 'My son, Abshalom, Abshalom, my son, my son'.

<sup>5</sup>Yo'ab came to the king at home and said, 'You've made the faces of all your servants ashamed today, people who saved your life today and the life of your sons and your daughters, the life of your wives and the life of your secondary wives, <sup>6</sup>by being loyal to the people who are hostile to you and by being hostile to the people who are loyal to you. Because you've told them today that officers and servants are nothing to you. Because I know today that, were Abshalom alive and all of us dead today, then it would be all right in your eyes.

<sup>7</sup>So now, get up, go out, encourage your servants! Because I swear by Yahweh, when you do not come out – if anyone stays the night with you tonight . . . It will be bad for you, worse than any bad experience that has come upon you from your youth until now.' <sup>8</sup>So the king got up and sat in the gateway, and when they told the entire company, 'Here, the king is sitting in the gateway', the entire company came before the king.

### Bringing David back

When Yisra'el fled, each person to his tents, <sup>9</sup>the entire people was arguing. among all the Yisra'elite clans: 'It was the king who rescued us from our enemies' fist, and he was the one who saved us from the hand of the Pelishtites. He has now taken flight from the country because of Abshalom, <sup>10</sup>but Abshalom, whom we anointed over us, is dead in battle. So now, why are you sitting still with regard to bringing the king back?'

<sup>11</sup>King David himself sent to Tsadoq and to Ebyatar, the priests, saying 'Speak to the elders of Yehudah, saying "Why are you last to bring the king back to his house?"' (when the words of all Yisra'el came to the king at his house). <sup>12</sup>'You're my brothers, you're my flesh and blood. Why should you be last to bring the king back? <sup>13</sup>And to Amasa say, "You're my flesh and blood, aren't you. May God do this to me and may he do more if you do not become officer over the army before me all the time, in place of Yo'ab."'

<sup>14</sup>He turned the mind of all the Yehudahites as one individual, and they sent to the king:

'Come back, you and all your servants.' <sup>15</sup>The king went back and came as far as the Yarden, while Yehudah came to Gilgal to go to meet the king, to bring the king across the Yarden. <sup>16</sup>Shim'i ben Gera, the Binyaminite who was from Bahurim, hurried and came down with the Yehudahites to meet King David, <sup>17</sup>and a thousand Binyaminites with him, while Tsiba, a boy from Sha'ul's household, and his fifteen sons and his twenty servants with him, rushed to the Yarden before the king. <sup>18</sup>The crossing took place to get the king's household across and for him to do what was good in his eyes when Shim'i ben Gera fell down before the king as he was crossing the Yarden.

### Mercy in victory

<sup>19</sup>He said to the king, 'May my lord not think of waywardness in connection with me. Don't be mindful of how your servant was wayward on the day when my lord the king left Yerushalaim, by the king giving his mind to it. <sup>20</sup>Because your servant acknowledges that I myself did wrong, but here – today I have come, the first of all Yoseph's [Joseph's] household to go down to meet my lord the king.'

<sup>21</sup>Abishay ben Tseruyah answered, 'On account of this, will Shim'i not be put to death, because he slighted Yahweh's anointed?' <sup>22</sup>David said, 'What do you and I have in common, sons of Tseruyah, that you should be an adversary to me today? Is an individual in Yisra'el to be put to death today? Because I know that today I'm king over Yisra'el, don't I.' <sup>23</sup>So the king said to Shim'i, 'You will not die', and the king swore to him. <sup>24</sup>Mephiboshet son of Sha'ul also went down to meet the king. He had not done his feet, he had not done his moustache and he had not washed his clothes from the day the king went until the day when he came with things being well.

<sup>25</sup>When he came to Yerushalaim to meet the king, the king said to him, 'Why didn't you go with me, Mephiboshet?' <sup>26</sup>He said, 'My lord king, my servant beguiled me, because your servant said, "I want to saddle my donkey and ride on it and go with the king, because your servant is lame." <sup>27</sup>But he went about [speaking] against your servant to my lord

the king, when my lord the king is like God's envoy.

Do what is good in your eyes. <sup>28</sup>Because there was no one in my father's entire household except people who deserved death before my lord the king, but you put your servant among the people who eat at your table. What right do I have any more to cry out any more to the king?'

<sup>29</sup>The king said to him, 'Why should you speak any more about these things? I say: you and Tsiba are to share out the fields.' <sup>30</sup>But Mephiboshet said to the king, 'He can even take all of it after my lord the king has come home with things being well.'

### Barzillay says 'No thank you'

<sup>31</sup>Now Barzillay the Gil'adite had come down from Rogelim and he crossed over the Yarden with the king, to send him off at the Yarden. <sup>32</sup>Barzillay was very old, a man of eighty years; he was the one who had provided for the king during his stay at Mahanayim, because he was a very big man.

<sup>33</sup>The king said to Barzillay, 'You cross over with me, and I'll provide for you with me in Yerushalaim.' <sup>34</sup>But Barzillay said to the king, 'How many will be the full years of my life, that I should go up to Yerushalaim with the king? <sup>35</sup>I'm a man of eighty years today. Do I know the difference between good and bad? Or can your servant taste what he eats and what he drinks or still listen to the sound of men and women singing? So why should your servant still be a burden to my lord the king? <sup>36</sup>Hardly could your servant cross the Yarden with the king. Why should the king deal this thing to me? <sup>37</sup>May your servant go back, and I shall die in my town near the grave of my father and my mother. But here is your servant Kimham. He should cross with my lord the king. Do for him what is good in your eyes.'

<sup>38</sup>The king said, 'Kimham may cross with me, and I myself will do for him what is good in your eyes. Anything that you choose from me I will do for you.'

<sup>39</sup>So the entire company crossed the Yarden. When the king crossed, the king kissed Barzillay and blessed him and he went back to his place, <sup>40</sup>and the king crossed over to Gilgal; Kimhan crossed with him.

## Tension between Yisra'el and Yehudah

When the entire Yehudahite company took the king across, and also half of the Yisra'elite company, ⁴¹there, all the Yisra'elites were coming to the king. They said to the king, 'Why did our brothers, the Yehudahites, steal you away and take the king and his household across the Yarden, and all David's men with him?' ⁴²All the Yehudahites answered the Yisra'elites, 'Because the king is near to us! Why is it that rage came over you at this thing? Have we actually eaten anything of the king's, or has preference been given to us?'

⁴³The Yisra'elites answered the Yehudahites, 'We have ten shares in the king, so in David as well we have more than you. So why have you slighted us, so that our word wasn't first in connection with bringing our king back?' But the Yehudahites' word was tougher than the Yisra'elites' word.

**20** But a scoundrel happened to be there; his name was Sheba ben Bikri, a Binyaminite. He blew on the horn and said, 'We have no share in David, we have no domain in ben Yishay – each man to his tents, Yisra'el!' ²All the Yisra'elites rose up from following David to follow Sheba ben Bikri, but the Yehudahites attached themselves to their king, from the Yarden to Yerushalaim. ³David came to his house in Yerushalaim. The king got the ten secondary wives whom he had made stay to keep the house, and put them in a house that was under guard. He provided for them but he didn't have sex with them. They were confined until the day of their death, in living widowhood.

⁴The king said to Amasa, 'Call out the Yehudahites for me in three days, and you yourself, stand here.' ⁵Amasa went to call out Yehudah, but he delayed beyond the time that he had set him. ⁶David said to Abishay, 'Now Sheba ben Bikri will make things worse for us than Abshalom. You take your lord's servants and pursue after him so he doesn't find fortified towns for himself, and tear out our eye.'

## Yo'ab deals with Amasa

⁷Yo'ab's men, the Keretites and the Peletites, and all the strong men, went out after him; they went out from Yerushalaim to pursue after Sheba ben Bikri. ⁸When they were near the big stone which is at Gib'on, Amasa himself came before them. Yo'ab was belted in his uniform (his clothing), and over it there was the belt for a sword, fastened on his hips in its sheath. When he went out, it fell down. ⁹Yo'ab said to Amasa, 'Are things well with you, brother?', and Yo'ab's right hand took hold of Amasa's beard, to kiss him, ¹⁰but Amasa didn't keep watch for the sword that was in Yoab's hand, and he struck him down with it in his abdomen and made his insides pour out on to the ground. He didn't do it to him a second time. He died.

While Yo'ab and Abishay his brother pursued after Sheba ben Bikri, ¹¹and one of Yo'ab's boys stood over him and said, 'Whoever delights in Yo'ab and whoever is for David – after Yo'ab!', ¹²and Amasa was rolling in blood in the middle of the causeway, the man saw that the entire company halted. So he took Amasa round from the causeway into the fields and threw a garment over him, because everyone who came on him saw and halted. ¹³When he had been removed from the causeway, everyone passed on after Yo'ab to pursue after Sheba ben Bikri. ¹⁴He had passed through all the Yisra'elite clans to Meadow (Bet Ma'akah). All the Be'erites congregated and came after him also.

¹⁵So they came and besieged him in Bet Ma'akah Meadow. They heaped up a ramp against the town and it stood against the rampart. The entire company that was with Yo'ab were seeking to devastate it to make the wall fall.

## An intelligent woman saves her town

¹⁶But a smart woman called from the town, 'Listen, listen! Please say to Yo'ab, "Draw near here so I can speak to you."' ¹⁷He drew near to her. The woman said, 'Are you Yo'ab?' He said, 'I am.' She said to him, 'Listen to your handmaid's words.' He said, 'I'm listening.' ¹⁸She said, 'People did speak previously, saying "They should just ask at Meadow", and thus they finished things. ¹⁹Whereas I'm among the truthful who are committed to peace in Yisra'el, you're seeking to put to death a town that's a mother in Yisra'el. Why would you swallow up Yahweh's domain?'

²⁰Yo'ab answered, 'Far be it from me, far be it from me, if I should swallow up or devastate. ²¹Things aren't like that. Rather, someone from the highland of Ephrayim, Sheba ben Bikri his name, has raised his hand against the king, against David. Give him alone over, and I'll go from the town.' The woman said to Yo'ab, 'There, his head is going to be thrown over the wall to you.'

²²The woman came to the entire people with her smart thinking, and they cut off the head of Sheba ben Bikri and threw it to Yo'ab. He blew on the horn and the men dispersed from the town, each one to his tents, while Yo'ab went back to Yerushalaim, to the king.

²³Yo'ab was over the entire Yisra'elite army. Benayah ben Yehoyada was over the Keretites and over the Peletites. ²⁴Adoram was over the workforce. Yehoshaphat ben Ahilud was the recorder. ²⁵Sheva was secretary. Tsadoq and Ebyatar were priests. ²⁶Ira the Ya'irite was also a priest for David.

## Mother love

**21** There was a famine in the time of David for three years, year after year. David sought Yahweh's face, and Yahweh said, 'It's in connection with Sha'ul and with the blood-stained household, because he put the Gib'onites to death.' ²So the king called for the Gib'onites and said to them (the Gib'onites were not among the Yisra'elites but rather among what was left of the Amorites, but the Yisra'elites had sworn to them, and Sha'ul had sought to strike them down in his passion for the Yisra'elites and Yehudah) – ³David said to the Gib'onites, 'What shall I do for you? How shall I make expiation, so you can bless Yahweh's domain?'

⁴The Gib'onites said to him, 'We have no [rights to] silver or gold with Sha'ul or with his household and we have no [rights to] put a man to death in Yisra'el.' So he said, 'Whatever you're going to say, I'll do for you.' ⁵They said to the king, 'The man who finished us off and who thought we could be annihilated so we would not take our stand within Yisra'el's entire border: ⁶seven of the men from among his descendants are to be given to us and we will execute them for Yahweh at Gib'ah-of-Sha'ul,

Yahweh's chosen one.' The king said, 'I myself will give them.'

⁷The king spared Mephiboshet ben Yehonatan, son of Sha'ul, because of the oath before Yahweh between David and Yehonatan son of Sha'ul. ⁸The king got the two sons of Ritspah bat Ayyah to whom she gave birth for Sha'ul, Armoni and Mephiboshet, and the five sons of Mikal daughter of Sha'ul, to whom she gave birth for Adri'el ben Barzillay the Meholatite, ⁹and gave them into the hand of the Gib'onites. They executed them on the mountain before Yahweh. The seven of them fell together. These men were put to death during the first days of harvest, during the beginning of barley harvest.

¹⁰But Ritspah bat Ayyah got sack and spread it on a crag for herself from the beginning of harvest until water poured on them from the heavens. She didn't let the birds of the heavens settle on them by day or the creatures of the wild by night.

## A final resting place

¹¹It was told David what Ritspah bat Ayyah, Sha'ul's secondary wife, had done, ¹²and David went and got the bones of Sha'ul and the bones of Yehonatan his son from the Yabesh-in-Gil'ad landowners, who had stolen them from the square in Bet-shan where the Pelishtites had hung them on the day the Pelishtites struck down Sha'ul at Gilboa. ¹³He took up from there the bones of Sha'ul and the bones of Yehonatan his son, and they gathered the bones of the men who had been executed. ¹⁴They buried the bones of Sha'ul and Yehonatan his son in the region of Binyamin in a side chamber in the grave of Qish his father. They did all that the king ordered, and God let himself be entreated for the country subsequently.

¹⁵There was again a battle by the Pelishtites with Yisra'el. David went down, he and his servants with him, and did battle with the Pelishtites. David got weary ¹⁶and Ishbi Benob (who was among the descendants of the Healer, and the weight of whose lance was 300 sheqels, made of copper, and he was belted in new things) thought to strike David down. ¹⁷But Abishay ben Tseruyah helped him, struck down the Pelishtite and put him to death. Then

David's men swore to him, 'You will not go out with us to battle any more, so that you do not extinguish Yisra'el's lamp.'

<sup>18</sup>Subsequently there was again a battle with the Pelishtites at Gob. Then Sibbekay the Hushatite struck down Saph, who was among the descendants of the Healer.

<sup>19</sup>There was again a battle with the Pelishtites at Gob, and Elhanan ben-Ya'are Oregim, the Bet Lehemite, struck down Golyat the Gittite; the wood of his lance was like a weavers' rod.

<sup>20</sup>There was again a battle at Gat. There was a man of stature with six fingers on his hands and six toes on his feet, twenty-four in number; he also was a descendant of the Healer. <sup>21</sup>He reviled Yisra'el, and Yonatan ben Shim'i, David's brother, struck him down.

<sup>22</sup>These four had descended from the Healer in Gat. They fell by the hand of David and by the hand of his servants.

### The God of the storm

**22** David spoke the words of this song to Yahweh on the day Yahweh rescued him from the fist of all his enemies and from the fist of Sha'ul.

<sup>2</sup>Yahweh, my crag,
  my stronghold, the one who enables me to
    survive,
<sup>3</sup>My God, my crag in which I take shelter,
  my shield, the horn that delivers me, my
    turret,
My retreat, my deliverer,
  you deliver me from violence.
<sup>4</sup>As one to be praised, I call on Yahweh,
  and from my enemies I find deliverance.
<sup>5</sup>Because death's waves overwhelmed me,
  Beliyya'al's wadis terrified me,
<sup>6</sup>She'ol's ropes surrounded me,
  death's snares met me.
<sup>7</sup>In my pressure I called on Yahweh,
  to my God I called.
He listened to my voice from his palace,
  my cry for help was in his ears.

<sup>8</sup>And the earth quaked and rocked,
  the heavens' foundations shook.
They quaked because it enraged him;
<sup>9</sup>smoke went up in his anger,

Fire from his mouth consumed,
  coals burned up from him.
<sup>10</sup>He spread the heavens and came down,
  with thundercloud beneath his feet.
<sup>11</sup>He rode on a sphinx and flew,
  he appeared on the wings of the wind.
<sup>12</sup>He made darkness round him a bivouac –
  a mass of water, clouds of mist.
<sup>13</sup>From the brightness in front of him
  fiery coals burned up.
<sup>14</sup>Yahweh thundered from the heavens,
  the One on High gave out his voice.
<sup>15</sup>He sent off arrows and scattered them,
  lightning, and routed them.
<sup>16</sup>The canyons of the sea appeared,
  the worlds' foundations became visible,
Through Yahweh's reprimand,
  at the breath of his angry wind.

### I have kept Yahweh's ways(?)

<sup>17</sup>He sent from on high, he got me,
  he drew me out of much water.
<sup>18</sup>He rescued me from my vigorous enemy,
  from people hostile to me, because they
    stood too firm for me.
<sup>19</sup>They met me on the day of my disaster,
  but Yahweh became my support.
<sup>20</sup>He brought me out into a roomy place;
  he pulled me out because he delighted in
    me.
<sup>21</sup>Yahweh dealt to me in accordance with my
    faithfulness;
  in accordance with the purity of my hands
    he gave back to me.
<sup>22</sup>Because I have kept Yahweh's ways
  and not been faithless to my God.
<sup>23</sup>For all his rulings have been before me;
  his decrees – I haven't departed from them.
<sup>24</sup>I've been a person of integrity with him,
  and I've kept myself from waywardness I
    might have done.
<sup>25</sup>So Yahweh has given back to me in
  accordance with my faithfulness,
  in accordance with my purity before his eyes.
<sup>26</sup>With the committed person you show
    commitment,
  with the man of integrity you show integrity.
<sup>27</sup>With the pure person you show purity,
  but with the crooked you show yourself
    refractory.

²⁸A humble people you deliver,
   but you avert your eyes from exalted people.
²⁹For you, Yahweh, are my lamp;
   it's Yahweh who illumines my darkness.
³⁰For with you I can rush at a barricade,
   with my God I can scale a wall.
³¹God: his way has integrity,
   Yahweh's word is proven.
He is a shield
   to all who take shelter with him.
³²Because who is God apart from Yahweh,
   who is a crag apart from our God?

## I will confess you among the nations

³³God is my stronghold, my forcefulness;
   he released one who had integrity in his way:
³⁴One who fashions my feet like a deer,
   enables me to stand on the heights,
³⁵Trains my hands for battle
   so that my arms could bend a copper bow.
³⁶You gave me your shield that delivered;
   your avowal made me great.
³⁷You widened my step beneath me;
   my ankles did not slip.
³⁸I pursued my enemies and annihilated them;
   I did not turn back until I had finished them
   off.
³⁹I devoured them, hit them, they could not
   get up;
   they fell beneath my feet.
⁴⁰You belted me with forcefulness for battle,
   you bent down beneath me the people who
   rose up against me.
⁴¹My enemies you made turn tail for me,
   the people who were hostile to me – and I
   wiped them out.
⁴²They looked, but there was no deliverer –
   to Yahweh, but he did not answer them.
⁴³I ground them fine like the earth in the
   ground,
   like the mud in the streets I crushed them,
   beat them out.
⁴⁴You enabled me to survive from arguments
   with my people,
   you kept me as head of nations,
A people I did not acknowledge serve me;
   ⁴⁵foreigners cowered before me.
On hearing with the ear, they listened to me;
   ⁴⁶foreigners wilted,
   came quaking out of their strongholds.

⁴⁷Yahweh lives, my crag be blessed,
   may God, the crag who delivers me, be
   exalted,
⁴⁸The God who gives me total redress,
   subjects peoples under me,
⁴⁹Who gets me out from my enemies,
   exalts me above the people who rise up
   against me,
   rescues me from violent men!

⁵⁰Therefore I will confess you, Yahweh, among
   the nations,
   and make music for your name,
⁵¹A tower bringing deliverance to his king,
   acting with commitment to his anointed,
   to David and to his offspring permanently.

## David's last words

**23** These are David's last words.

An utterance of David ben Yishay,
   an utterance of the man set up by the One
   on High,
The anointed of the God of Jacob,
   the delight of Yisra'el's melodies.
²Yahweh's spirit spoke through me,
   his utterance was on my tongue.
³The God of Yisra'el said,
   the crag of Yisra'el spoke to me:
One who rules over people as a faithful man,
   one who rules in awe of God,
⁴Is like the morning light when the sun rises,
   a morning with no clouds;
Because of brightness, because of rain,
   there's growth from the earth.
⁵My household is established with God, is it
   not,
   because he has made a permanent pact for
   me,
   laid out in every respect and secured.
He will bring to accomplishment, will he not,
   all my deliverance and all I delight in.
⁶But scoundrels are like thistles, thrown away,
   all of them,
   because people do not take them in the
   hand.
⁷The person who touches them
   equips himself with iron or the wood of a
   lance,
   and they totally burn up where they lie.

## David's strong men

[8]These are the names of the strong men that David had:

The one who sits in the seat, a Tahkemonite, chief of the Three, was Adino the Etsnite, against 800, run through on one occasion. [9]After him El'azar ben Dodo, son of Ahohi, one of the Three Strong Men with David when they reviled the Pelishtites who had gathered there for battle. The Yisra'elites went up, [10]but he set to and struck down the Pelishtites until his hand got weary. But his hand attached itself to his sword and Yahweh brought about a great deliverance that day. The company came back after him, only to plunder. [11]After him Shamma ben Agee the Hararite. The Pelishtites had gathered at Lahi and there was a plot in the fields there full of lentils. Whereas the company had fled from before the Pelishtites, [12]he took his stand in the middle of the plot and defended it, and struck down the Pelishtites. Yahweh brought about a great deliverance.

[13]Three of the Thirty Heads went down and came at harvest to David at the Adullam Cave. A force of Pelishtites was camped in Repha'ites Vale. [14]David was then in the stronghold and an outpost of Pelishtites was then at Bet Lehem. [15]David had a longing and said, 'If only someone could give me a drink of water from the Bet-lehem cistern that's at the gateway!' [16]The Three Strong Men broke through the Pelishtites' camp, drew water from the Bet-lehem cistern that's at the gateway, carried it and brought it to David. But he was unwilling to drink it. He poured it out for Yahweh [17]and said, 'Far be it from me by Yahweh that I should do this. Should the blood of the men who went at the cost of their lives . . .?' So he was unwilling to drink it. These are things that the Three Strong Men did.

## The Three, the Thirty, the Thirty-Seven

[18]Abishay, the brother of Yo'ab ben Tseruyah, was head of a Three. He was wielding his lance against 300, run through. He had a name among the Three. [19]Of the Three,

he was the most honoured, wasn't he. He became officer for them, but he didn't come to the [other] Three. [20]Benayahu ben Yehoyada was a forceful man, prolific in deeds, from Qabtse'el. He struck down the two of Ari'el of Mo'ab. It was he who went down and struck down a lion inside a cistern on a snowy day, [21]and it was he who struck down a Misrayimite man, an impressive man. In the Misrayimite's hand there was a lance, but he went down to him with a club, seized the lance out of the Misrayimite's hand and killed him with his lance. [22]These things Benayahu ben Yehoyada did, and he had a name among the Three Strong Men. [23]Of the Thirty, he was most honoured, but he did not come to the Three. David put him in charge of his guard. [24]Among the Thirty:

| | |
|---|---|
| Asah-el, Yo'ab's brother | Azmavet the Barhumite |
| Elhanan ben Dodo (Bet Lehem) | [32]Elyahba the Sha'albonite |
| [25]Shammah the Harodite | The sons of Yashen, Yehonatan |
| Eliqa the Harodite | [33]Shammah the Hararite |
| [26]Helets the Paltite | Ahi'am ben Sharar the Ararite |
| Ira ben Iqqesh the Teqo'ite | |
| [27]Abi'ezer the Anatotite | [34]Eliphelet ben Ahasbay, son of the Ma'akatite |
| Mebunnay the Hushatite | Eli'am ben Ahitophel the Gilonite |
| [28]Tsalmon the Ahohite | [35]Hetsray the Carmelite |
| Mahray the Netophatite | Pa'aray the Arbite |
| [29]Heleb ben Ba'anah the Netophatite | [36]Yig'al ben Natan from Tsobah |
| Ittay ben Ribay from Gib'ah-of-the-Binyaminites | Bani the Gadite |
| | [37]Tseleq the Ammonite |
| [30]Benayahu, a Pir'atonite | Nahray the Be'erotite, equipment-bearer for Yo'ab ben Tseruyah |
| Hidday from the Ga'ash Wadis | [38]Ira the Yitrite |
| [31]Abi-albon the Arbatite | Gareb the Yitrite |
| | [39]Uriyyah the Hittite |

Thirty-seven in all.

## When counting was wrong

**24** Yahweh's anger raged against Yisra'el again and he incited David against them, saying 'Go count Yisra'el and Yehudah.' ²So the king said to Yo'ab, the officer over the force that was with him, 'Go round all the Yisra'elite clans from Dan as far as Be'er Sheba, please, and number the company, so I may know the company's count.'

³Yo'ab said to the king, 'May Yahweh your God add to the company a hundred times over compared with what they are, while the eyes of my lord the king are watching, but why does my lord the king want this thing?' ⁴But the king's word was strong toward Yo'ab and over the force's officers, so Yo'ab and the force's officers went out from the king's presence to number the company, Yisra'el.

⁵They crossed the Yarden and camped in Aro'er, to the south of the town, which is in the middle of Wadi Gad, and on to Ya'zer. ⁶They came to Gil'ad and to the region of Tahtim Hodshi and came to Dan Ya'an and round to Tsidon. ⁷They came to the fortress of Tsor and all the towns of the Hivvites and the Kena'anites [Canaanites] and went on to the Negeb of Yehudah (Be'er Sheba). ⁸They went about the entire country and at the end of nine months and twenty days came to Yerushalaim. ⁹Yo'ab gave the king the number for the registration of the company: Yisra'el came to 800,000 forceful men drawing the sword, and the men of Yehudah came to 500,000.

¹⁰David's mind struck him down after he had counted the company, and David said to Yahweh, 'I have acted very wrongly in what I've done. But now, Yahweh, please make your servant's waywardness pass on, because I've been very idiotic.'

## I would rather fall into God's hands than into human hands

¹¹David got up in the morning when Yahweh's word came to Gad the prophet, David's seer: ¹²'Go and speak to David, "Yahweh has said this: 'I'm holding out three things over you. Choose one of them for yourself and I shall do it to you.'"' ¹³Gad came to David and told him.

He said to him, 'Are seven years of famine to come to you in the country, or are you to have three months of flight before your attackers as he pursues you, or are there to be three days of epidemic in your country? Now acknowledge it and see what word I'm to take back to the one who sent me.' ¹⁴David said to God, 'It's very pressurizing for me. We will fall into Yahweh's hands, please, because his compassion is great. I will not fall into a human hand.'

¹⁵So Yahweh put an epidemic on Yisra'el from the morning until the set time, and there died of the company, from Dan as far as Be'er Sheba, 70,000 individuals. ¹⁶The envoy put out his hand to Yerushalaim to devastate it, but Yahweh relented of the bad thing and said to the envoy devastating the company, 'So much! Now slacken your hand!'

Yahweh's envoy was by the threshing floor of Aravnah the Yebusite. ¹⁷David said to Yahweh when he saw the envoy who was striking the company down: 'Here, I'm the one who did wrong. I'm the one who went astray. These people are the flock; what did they do? Your hand should please be against me and against my father's household.'

## I won't offer worship that costs me nothing

¹⁸Gad came to David that day and said to him, 'Go up, set up an altar for Yahweh at the threshing floor of Aravnah the Yebusite.' ¹⁹David went up in accordance with Gad's word, as Yahweh ordered.

²⁰Aravnah looked out and saw the king and his servants crossing to him. Aravnah went out and bowed low to the king, his face to the ground. ²¹Aravnah said, 'Why has my lord the king come to his servant?' David said, 'To acquire the threshing floor from you, to build an altar for Yahweh, so the epidemic may hold back from the company.' ²²Aravnah said to David, 'My lord the king may take it and offer up what is good in his eyes. See, the cattle as the burnt offering and the threshing boards and the cattle's equipment as wood. ²³Aravnah gives everything to the king, Your Majesty.' Aravnah said to the king, 'May Yahweh your God accept you.'

²⁴The king said to Aravnah, 'No, because I will definitely acquire them from you for a

price. I will not offer up for Yahweh my God burnt offerings that cost nothing.' So David acquired the threshing-floor and the cattle for fifty silver sheqels. 25David built an altar there for Yahweh and offered up burnt offerings and well-being sacrifices, and Yahweh let himself be entreated for the country. The epidemic held back from against Yisra'el.

# 1 KINGS

The first book of Kings continues the story from 2 Samuel – indeed, one might have expected the opening chapters to be part of 2 Samuel, because they relate the closing scenes of David's life.

Almost half of 1 Kings then tells the story of the reign of Solomon, the last of the three kings who ruled Israel as a whole. A series of motifs from the stories of Saul and David recur in his story. One is the involvement of God's choice and of human process. In Saul's story, God's choice was the dominant factor, even though it was a choice God never wanted to make (because it wasn't God's idea to have kings). David's story interweaves the fact of God's choosing with a human process whereby much of Israel expects someone from Saul's family to succeed him, an expectation that complicates the process of David's succession. In Solomon's story, the conflictual human process is the dominant factor.

Conflict is more broadly the second motif. Saul's story is dominated by the need to get victory over the Philistines. David is the person who actually achieves this victory, and also deals with peoples such as the Ammonites and Moabites. Solomon thus inherits a kingdom whose international position is stable; it is indeed the dominant force in the region.

The nature of the kings' achievements thus varies. Saul begins with a great deliverance of Jabesh Gilead but achieves little else. David takes Jerusalem and builds on his military victories by making it the nation's capital, and he makes plans for a temple for Yahweh there. Solomon builds this temple and builds up the town in other spectacular ways.

The fourth motif is the trajectory of the kings' reigns. In each case the story unfolds in a way that emphasizes early achievements but then portrays an unravelling. Each king is undone by the pressures and temptations of his position and/or by his personal weaknesses. Whereas for Saul, making his own decisions was his downfall and for David his problem was a wandering eye and a general incompetence in relationships, for Solomon it was the diplomatic marriages that imperilled Israel's faithfulness to Yahweh. Solomon's story thus emphasizes his facilitating of the worship of other deities, which results from the diplomatic move of taking a number of wives from other peoples in order to cement relations with them. But the account of his building achievements also hints at his oppression of the ordinary people who have to pay much of the price for this work, and Solomon fulfils Samuel's warnings about the cost of having kings.

The hints become more explicit statements on the lips of his people after he dies. They want the next king to be less oppressive, but he declines, and this leads to the defection of ten of the Israelite clans and their setting up an alternative state. Because it in fact comprises the bulk of the clans, it retains the name 'Israel'. The state with the Davidic king, centred on Jerusalem, is merely 'Judah'.

The rest of 1 Kings interweaves the stories of Israel and Judah, which often involve conflict between the two states. The first king of Israel sets up an alternative worship structure with sanctuaries at the two ends of the kingdom. It also involves forms of worship that use images of God, flouting the basic principle that Yahweh cannot be imaged. The worship thus follows a regular human instinct to make images of the deity, an instinct that features in the traditional worship of Canaan from which the people of Yahweh were supposed to distance themselves. A dominant theme in the interwoven story of Israel and Judah is then how faithful the two peoples are in their worship of Yahweh: whether they worship Yahweh in inappropriate ways or worship other deities. In general, the worship of Israel is more problematic than that of Judah.

The problematic nature of this worship is important background to the emergence of prophets who confront the nation rather than supporting it (as the prophets did in David's day). These prophets are also involved as Yahweh's agents in initiating coups in Israel.

*David in his dotage*

**1** Now King David was old, advanced in
years. They covered him with clothes but
he couldn't get warm, ²so his servants said
to him, 'They should look for a young girl
for my lord the king so she can stand before
the king and be his caregiver. She can lie in
your arms, and my lord the king will get
warm.' ³So they looked for an attractive girl
in the entire territory of Yisra'el [Israel], and
found Abishag the Shunammite and brought
her to the king. ⁴The girl was very attractive.
She became the king's caregiver and she
ministered to him, but the king didn't have
sex with her.

⁵Now Adoniyyah ben Haggit was elevating
himself, saying 'I shall be king', and he
prepared himself chariotry and cavalry and
fifty men running ahead of him. ⁶His father
had not pained him in all his years by saying
'Why have you acted like this?' Further, he was
very good-looking, and [his mother] had given
birth to him after Abshalom. ⁷He had words
with Yo'ab ben Tseruyah and with Ebyatar
[Abiathar] the priest, and they supported
Adoniyyah, ⁸but Tsadoq [Zadok] the priest,
Benayahu ben Yehoyada, Natan the prophet,
Shim'i, Re'i and David's strong men were not
with Adoniyyah.

⁹Adoniyyah sacrificed sheep and cattle and
fatlings at Zohelet Stone beside Treader Spring,
and called all his brothers, the king's sons, and
all the Yehudahites [Judahites], the king's
servants, ¹⁰but Natan the prophet, Benayahu,
the strong men and Shelomoh [Solomon] his
brother he didn't call.

¹¹Natan said to Bat-sheba, Shelomoh's
mother, 'You've heard, haven't you, that
Adoniyyah ben Haggit has become king,
whereas our lord David has not acknowledged
it? ¹²So now go (may I please give you counsel)
and save your life and the life of your son
Shelomoh. ¹³Go, come to King David and
say to him, "My lord the king, you yourself
swore to your handmaid, didn't you, 'Your
son Shelomoh – he will become king after
me, it's he who will sit on my throne.' So
why has Adoniyyah become king?" ¹⁴There,
while you're still speaking there with the
king, I myself will come after you and fill out
your words.'

*How to manipulate the old man in
order to get things done*

¹⁵So Bat-sheba came to the king in his
room. The king was very old and Abishag
the Shunammite was ministering to the
king. ¹⁶Bat-sheba bent her head and bowed
low to the king. The king said, 'What's on
your mind?' ¹⁷She said to him, 'My lord, you
yourself swore by Yahweh your God to your
handmaid, "Shelomoh your son – he will
become king after me; it's he who will sit on
my throne." ¹⁸But now, here, Adoniyyah has
become king, though my lord the king did not
now acknowledge it. ¹⁹He has sacrificed oxen
and firstlings and sheep in large number and
called all the king's sons and Ebyatar the priest
and Yo'ab the army officer, but Shelomoh your
servant he didn't call. ²⁰So you, my lord king –
the eyes of all Yisra'el are on you to tell them
who is to sit on my lord king's throne after
him. ²¹Or when my lord king lies down with
his ancestors, I and my son Shelomoh will be
[treated as] wrongdoers.'

²²And there, she was still speaking with the
king, and Natan the prophet came. ²³They told
the king, 'Here's Natan the prophet.' He came
before the king and bowed low on his face
to the ground to the king. ²⁴Natan said, 'My
lord king, you yourself have said, "Adoniyyah
will reign after me, he'll sit on my throne!"
²⁵Because he went down today and sacrificed
oxen and fatlings and sheep in large number
and called all the king's sons and the army
officers and Ebyatar the priest. There they
are, eating and drinking before him. They've
said, "Long live King Adoniyyah." ²⁶But me,
myself your servant, and Tsadoq the priest, and
Benayahu ben Yehoyada, and Shelomoh your
servant, he didn't call. ²⁷Did this thing come
from my lord king and had you not made
known to your servant who was to sit on my
lord king's throne after him?'

*Shelomoh enthroned*

²⁸King David answered, 'Call Bat-sheba to
me!' She came before the king and stood before
the king. ²⁹The king swore, 'As Yahweh lives,
who redeemed my life from every pressure,
³⁰indeed as I swore to you by Yahweh the God

of Yisra'el that Shelomoh your son would reign after me, and he would sit on my throne in place of me, so I will do this day.' ³¹Bat-sheba bent her head, face to the ground, and bowed low to the king, and said, 'Long live my lord King David!'

³²King David said, 'Call to me Tsadoq the priest and Natan the prophet and Benayahu ben Yehoyada.' They came before the king ³³and the king said to them, 'Take with you your lord's servants and have Shelomoh my son ride on the mule that belongs to me and have him go down to Gihon. ³⁴Tsadoq the priest is to anoint him there, with Natan the prophet, as king over Yisra'el. You're to blow on a horn and say, "Long live King Shelomoh!" ³⁵And go up after him so he comes and sits on my throne. He will reign in place of me. Him I have ordered to be chief over Yisra'el and over Yehudah.' ³⁶Benayahu ben Yehoyada answered the king, 'Yes, so may Yahweh the God of my lord king say it! ³⁷As Yahweh has been with my lord king, so may he be with Shelomoh. May he make his throne greater than the throne of my lord king David!'

³⁸So Tsadoq the priest went down, with Natan the prophet and Benayahu ben Yehoyada, and the Keretites and the Peletites, and they had Shelomoh ride on King David's mule and had him go to Gihon. ³⁹Tsadoq the priest got the horn of oil from the tent and anointed Shelomoh. They blew on the horn and the entire company said, 'Long live King Shelomoh!' ⁴⁰The entire company went up after him. The company were playing on pipes and rejoicing greatly. The earth split with the sound of them.

## The danger when a coup fails

⁴¹Adoniyyah heard, he and all the people who had been called who were with him, as they had finished eating. Yo'ab heard the sound of the horn and said, 'Why the sound of the township in turmoil?' ⁴²While he was still speaking, there, Yonatan ben Ebyatar the priest came. Adoniyyah said, 'Come in, because you're a reliable man, and you announce good news.'

⁴³But Yonatan answered Adoniyyah, 'Well, our lord King David has made Shelomoh king!

⁴⁴The king has sent with him Tsadoq the priest and Natan the prophet and Benayahu ben Yehoyada, and the Keretites and the Peletites, and they've had him ride on the king's mule. ⁴⁵Tsadoq the priest and Natan the prophet have anointed him as king at Gihon, and they went up from there rejoicing and the township was in an uproar. That was the sound that you heard. ⁴⁶Also Shelomoh has sat on the royal throne. ⁴⁷And also, the king's servants came to bless our lord King David, saying "May your God make Shelomoh's name better than your name and make his throne greater than your throne." And the king has bowed low on his bed. ⁴⁸And also the king said this: "Blessed be Yahweh the God of Yisra'el who has today given someone sitting on my throne, and my eyes are seeing it.'"

⁴⁹All the people who had been called who were for Adoniyyah trembled, got up and went each one his way, ⁵⁰while Adoniyyah was afraid of Shelomoh and got up and went and took strong hold of the altar horns. ⁵¹It was told Shelomoh, 'There, Adoniyyah is afraid of King Shelomoh. There, he's grasped the altar horns, saying "King Shelomoh must swear to me this very day: if he puts his servant to death with the sword . . ."'

⁵²Shelomoh said, 'If he becomes a reliable man, not one of his hairs will fall to the ground, but if something bad is found in him, he will die.' ⁵³So King Shelomoh sent and they got him to come down from the altar. He came and bowed low to King Shelomoh, and Shelomoh said to him, 'Go to your house.'

## David's last will and testament

**2** The days for David to die drew near, and he ordered Shelomoh his son: ²'I am going the way of all the earth. You're to be strong and be a man, ³and to keep the charge of Yahweh your God by walking in his ways, by keeping his decrees, his orders, his rulings and his affirmations as written in Mosheh's [Moses'] instruction, in order that you may thrive in everything you do and everywhere you turn your face, ⁴in order that Yahweh may implement his word which he spoke to me: "If your sons keep watch over their way by walking before me in truthfulness with their entire mind and with their entire being, there will not be cut off for you someone on Yisra'el's throne."

⁵Further, you yourself know what Yo'ab ben Tseruyah did to me, what he did to the two officers of Yisra'el's armies, to Abner ben Ner and to Amasa ben Yeter. He killed them, and put the bloodshed of battle into peacetime. He put the bloodshed of battle on his belt that's round his hips and on his boot that's on his feet. ⁶Act in accordance with your smartness but don't let his white hair go down to She'ol in peace.

⁷The sons of Barzillay the Gil'adite: act with commitment to them so that they are among the people who eat at your table, because they approached me when I took flight from before Abshalom your brother. ⁸But here, Shim'i ben Gera the Binyaminite [Benjaminite] from Bahurim is with you. He uttered a grievous slight of me on the day I went to Mahanayim, but when he came down to meet me at the Yarden [Jordan] I swore to him by Yahweh, "If I put you to death by the sword . . ."

⁹But now, don't treat him as free of guilt, because you're a smart man and you'll know how you should act towards him and have his white hair go down to She'ol in blood.'

## A not-very subtle request

¹⁰So David lay down with his ancestors and was buried in David's Town. ¹¹The time that David reigned over Yisra'el was forty years. In Hebron he reigned seven years; in Yerushalaim he reigned thirty-three years. ¹²Shelomoh sat on David his father's throne and his kingship was well established.

¹³Adoniyyah ben Haggit came to Bat-sheba, Shelomoh's mother. She said, 'Is your coming in peace?' He said, 'In peace', ¹⁴and said, 'I have a word for you.' She said, 'Speak.' ¹⁵He said, 'You yourself know that the kingship was mine. All Yisra'el had set their faces towards me reigning. But the kingship turned round and became my brother's, because it was his from Yahweh. ¹⁶But now I'm making one request from you yourself. Don't turn my face back.' She said to him, 'Speak.' ¹⁷He said, 'Please say to Shelomoh the king (because he won't turn your face back) that he should give me

Abishag the Shunammite as wife.' ¹⁸Bat-sheba said, 'Very well, I myself will speak to the king about you.'

¹⁹Bat-sheba came to King Shelomoh to speak to him about Adoniyyah. The king got up to meet her and bowed low to her. He sat on his throne and placed a throne for the king's mother, and she sat at his right. ²⁰She said, 'I'm going to make one small request from you yourself. Don't turn back my face.' The king said to her, 'Ask, mother, because I shall not turn your face back.' ²¹She said, 'Abishag the Shunammite should be given to Adoniyyah your brother as wife.'

²²King Shelomoh answered his mother, 'Why are you asking for Abishag the Shunammite for Adoniyyah? Ask for the kingship for him, because he's my brother who's older than me – for him and for Ebyatar the priest and for Yo'ab ben Tseruyah.' ²³King Shelomoh swore by Yahweh: 'May God act in this way to me, and do more in this way, because Adoniyyah has spoken this word at the cost of his life. ²⁴So now, as Yahweh lives, who has established me and made me sit on the throne of David my father, and made me a household, as he spoke: today Adoniyyah will indeed be put to death.'

## The penalty for backing the wrong horse

²⁵So King Shelomoh sent by the hand of Benayahu ben Yehoyada, and he came upon him and he died. ²⁶And to Ebyatar the priest, the king said 'Go to Anatot to your fields, because you deserve death, but on this day I shall not put you to death, because you carried my Lord Yahweh's chest before David my father and because you let yourself be humbled in all that my father let himself be humbled.' ²⁷So Shelomoh drove Ebyatar out from being Yahweh's priest, fulfilling Yahweh's word which he spoke about the household of Eli in Shiloh.

²⁸When the report came to Yo'ab (because Yo'ab had turned away to follow Adoniyyah, though he had not turned away to follow Abshalom), Yo'ab fled to Yahweh's tent and took strong hold of the altar horns. ²⁹It was told King Shelomoh that Yo'ab had fled to Yahweh's tent. There, he was beside the altar. Shelomoh sent Benayahu ben Yehoyada, saying 'Go, come upon him.'

³⁰Benayahu came to Yahweh's tent and said to him, 'The king has said this: "Out!"' He said, 'No! Rather I shall die here.' Benayahu took word back to the king, 'Yo'ab spoke like this; he answered me like this.' ³¹The king said to him, 'Do as he spoke, and come upon him and bury him and remove the blood shed for nothing that Yo'ab poured out, from upon me and from upon my father's household. ³²Yahweh will bring back his blood on his head, because he came upon two men more faithful and better than him and killed them with the sword, when my father David didn't know, Abner ben Ner, Yisra'el's army officer, and Amasa ben Yeter, Yehudah's army officer. ³³Their shed blood is to come back on Yo'ab's head and on the head of his offspring permanently. But for David, for his offspring, for his household and for his throne, may things be well from Yahweh permanently.'

³⁴So Benayahu ben Yehoyada went up and came upon him and put him to death. He was buried in his house in the wilderness. ³⁵The king made Benayahu ben Yehoyada in charge of the army in place of him, while the king made Tsadoq the priest in place of Ebyatar.

### The man who might have thought twice

³⁶The king sent and called for Shim'i, and said to him, 'Build yourself a house in Yerushalaim and live there. You will not go out from there anywhere. ³⁷On the day you go out and cross Wadi Qidron, acknowledge clearly that you will definitely die; your blood will be on your own head.' ³⁸Shim'i said to the king, 'The word is good. As my lord king spoke, so your servant will do.' So Shim'i lived in Yerushalaim for a long time.

³⁹But at the end of three years two of Shim'i's servants took flight to Akish ben Ma'akah king of Gat. People told Shim'i, 'There, your servants are in Gat.' ⁴⁰So Shim'i set off, saddled his donkey and went to Gat to Akish to look for his servants.

So Shim'i went, and brought his servants from Gat, ⁴¹but it was told Shelomoh that Shim'i had gone from Yerushalaim to Gat and had come back. ⁴²The king sent and called for Shim'i. He said to him, 'I got you to swear by Yahweh and I testified to you, didn't I, "On the day you go out and go anywhere, you're to acknowledge clearly that you will definitely die", and you said to me, "The word is good. I've listened." ⁴³So why didn't you keep the oath before Yahweh and the order that I gave you?' ⁴⁴The king said to Shim'i, 'You yourself know all the bad dealing (which you acknowledge in your heart) that you undertook towards David my father. Yahweh will bring back your bad dealing on your head, ⁴⁵whereas King Shelomoh will be blessed and David's throne will be established before Yahweh permanently.' ⁴⁶And the king gave orders to Benayahu ben Yehoyada, and he went out and came upon him and put him to death.

So the kingship was established in Shelomoh's hand.

**3** Shelomoh made a marriage relationship with Par'oh king of Misrayim [Pharaoh king of Egypt]; he took Par'oh's daughter and brought her to David's Town until he had finished building his house and Yahweh's house and the wall of Yerushalaim all round. ²Only, the people were sacrificing at the shrines because the house for Yahweh's name was not yet built up to that time, ³but Shelomoh was loyal to Yahweh in walking by the decrees of David his father; only, he was sacrificing and burning incense at the shrines.

### What do you most want?

⁴The king went to Gib'on to sacrifice there, because it was the biggest shrine; Shelomoh would offer up a thousand burnt offerings on that altar. ⁵At Gib'on Yahweh appeared to Shelomoh in a dream by night. God said, 'Ask for what I should give you.' ⁶Shelomoh said, 'You yourself acted in great commitment with your servant David my father as he walked before you in truthfulness and faithfulness and in uprightness of mind with you. You have kept this great commitment for him and given him a son sitting on his throne this very day.

⁷Now, Yahweh my God, you yourself have made your servant king in place of my father David, when I am a small boy who doesn't know how to go out and come in. ⁸Your servant is among your people that you chose, a numerous people that can't be measured or counted because of the large number. ⁹So you should

give your servant a listening mind to decide
cases for your people, to discern between good
and bad, because who can exercise authority for
this substantial people of yours?'

¹⁰The thing was good in the Lord's eyes, that
Shelomoh had asked for this thing. ¹¹God said
to him, 'Since you've asked for this thing and
you haven't asked for a long life for yourself
and haven't asked for wealth for yourself and
haven't asked for the life of your enemies, but
asked for yourself to be discerning in hearing
a case: ¹²there, I'm acting in accordance with
your words. Here, I am giving you a smart and
discerning mind such that there has not been
anyone like you before you and there will not
arise anyone like you after you. ¹³What you did
not ask I am also giving you, both wealth and
splendour for all your days, such that there has
not been anyone like you among the kings. ¹⁴If
you walk in my ways by keeping my decrees
and my orders as your father David walked,
I will make your days long.'

¹⁵Shelomoh woke up. There, a dream.
He came to Yerushalaim and stood before
the Lord's pact chest, and offered up whole
offerings and made well-being sacrifices, and
made a banquet for all his servants.

## Two mothers, one baby

¹⁶Then two women who were prostitutes
came to the king and stood before him. ¹⁷The
one woman said, 'Pardon me, my lord, I and
this woman are living in one house. I gave
birth with her in the house. ¹⁸On the third day
after I gave birth, this woman also gave birth.
We were together. There was no outsider in the
house with us, only the two of us in the house.
¹⁹This woman's son died in the night because
she lay on it, ²⁰and she got up in the middle
of the night and took my son from beside me
while your handmaid was asleep, laid him in
her arms and laid her dead son in my arms.
²¹So I got up in the morning to nurse my son
and there – he was dead. But I considered him
closely in the morning, and there – it was not
my son, whom I had given birth to.' ²²The other
woman said, 'No, because the live one is my
son and the dead one is your son', while the
first woman was saying, 'No, because the dead
one is your son and the live one is my son.'

So they spoke before the king, ²³and the king
said, 'The one woman is saying "This is my
son, the live one, and the dead one is your son",
while the other one is saying, "No, because the
dead one is your son, and the live one is mine."'
²⁴The king said, 'Get me a sword.' They brought
a sword before the king. ²⁵The king said,
'Divide the live child in two and give half to
one and half to the other.' ²⁶The woman whose
son was the live one said to the king (because
her insides burned for her son) – she said,
'Pardon me, my lord, give her the live baby, my
lord. Don't actually put it to death', whereas the
other was saying, 'It won't be either mine or
yours – divide it.' ²⁷The king answered, 'Give
her the live baby. Don't actually put it to death.
She's its mother.'

²⁸When all Yisra'el heard the decision that
the king had made, they were in awe before the
king, because they saw that there was divine
smartness within him for exercising authority.

## Shelomoh's administration

**4** So King Shelomoh was king over all Yisra'el.
²These were the officials that he had:

Azaryahu ben Tsadoq (the priest);
³Elihoreph and Ahiyyahu, sons of Shisha
    (secretaries);
Yehoshaphat ben Ahilud (the recorder);
⁴Benayahu ben Yehoyada (in charge of the
    army);
Tsadoq and Ebyatar (priests);
⁵Azaryahu ben Natan (in charge of the
    prefects);
Zabud ben Natan the priest (the king's
    friend);
⁶Ahishar (in charge of the household);
Adoniram ben Abda (in charge of the
    workforce).

⁷Shelomoh had twelve prefects over all
Yisra'el; they would provide for the king and his
household. There would be a month per year for
each for provisioning. ⁸These were their names:
the son of Hur, in the highland of Ephrayim;
⁹the son of Deqer, in Maqats, in Sha'albim,
    Bet Shemesh and Bet Hanan Oak;
¹⁰the son of Hesed, in Arubot: Sokoh and the
    entire region of Hepher was his;

<sup>11</sup>the son of Abinadab: all Do'r Height (Taphat, Shelomoh's daughter, was his wife);

<sup>12</sup>Ba'ana ben Ahilud: Ta'anak, Megiddo, and all Bet She'an, which is beside Tsaratan, below Yizre'e'l, from Bet She'an as far as Meholah Meadow, as far as across from Yoqmo'am;

<sup>13</sup>the son of Geber: in Heights-in-Gil'ad, the Villages of Ya'ir ben Menashsheh which are in Gil'ad, were his; the district of Argob, which is in Bashan, sixty big towns with a wall and a copper bar, were his;

<sup>14</sup>Ahinadab ben Iddo: Mahanayim;

<sup>15</sup>Ahima'ats: in Napthali (also he took Basemat, Shelomoh's daughter, as wife);

<sup>16</sup>Ba'ana ben Hushay: in Asher and in Alot;

<sup>17</sup>Yehoshaphat ben Paruah: in Yissakar [Issachar];

<sup>18</sup>Shim'i ben Ela: in Binyamin;

<sup>19</sup>Geber ben Uri: in the region of Gil'ad (the country of Sihon king of the Amorites and Og the king of Bashan), and the one prefect who was in the region.

<sup>20</sup>Yehudah and Yisra'el were as many as the sand that's by the sea in large number, eating, drinking and rejoicing.

## Shelomoh's prosperity and his smartness

<sup>21</sup>Shelomoh was ruling over all the kingdoms from the River to the country of the Pelishtites [Philistines], as far as the border of Misrayim, bringing offerings and serving Shelomoh all the days of his life. <sup>22</sup>Shelomoh's food for one day was thirty ten-gallon measures of fine flour, sixty ten-gallon measures of ordinary flour, <sup>23</sup>ten sturdy cattle, twenty pasture cattle and a hundred sheep, apart from deer, gazelle, roebuck and fattened geese, <sup>24</sup>because he was holding sway over all of Beyond the River, from Tiphsah as far as Azzah [Gaza], over all the kings of Beyond the River, and he had peace on all his borders, all round.

<sup>25</sup>Yehudah and Yisra'el lived in confidence, each person under his vine and under his fig tree, from Dan as far as Be'er-sheba, all Shelomoh's days. <sup>26</sup>Shelomoh had 40,000 stalls of horses for his chariotry and 12,000 cavalry. <sup>27</sup>These prefects would provide for King Shelomoh and for everyone who approached King Shelomoh's table, each for his month. They did not let anything

be lacking. <sup>28</sup>As for the barley and the straw for the horses and for the steeds, they would bring it to the place where he would be, each person according to the ruling for him.

<sup>29</sup>God gave Shelomoh smartness and understanding in very great measure and width of mind like the sand that's on the seashore. <sup>30</sup>Shelomoh's smartness was greater than the smartness of all the Qedemites and all the smartness of the Misrayimites. <sup>31</sup>He was smarter than all humanity, than Etan the Ezrahite, and Heman, Kalkol and Darda, the sons of Mahol. His name was among all the nations around. <sup>32</sup>He spoke 3,000 aphorisms and his songs were 1,005. <sup>33</sup>He spoke about trees from the cedar that's in the Lebanon as far as the hyssop that comes out on the wall. He spoke about animals, about birds, about moving things and about fish. <sup>34</sup>They came from all the peoples to listen to Shelomoh's smartness, from all the kings of the earth who had heard of his smartness.

## The chance to build a house for Yahweh

**5** Hiram king of Tsor [Tyre] sent his servants to Shelomoh because he had heard that they had anointed him as king in place of his father, because Hiram had always been loyal to David. <sup>2</sup>Shelomoh sent to Hiram to say, <sup>3</sup>'You yourself know of David my father, that he was not able to build a house for the name of Yahweh his God because of the battle that surrounded him until Yahweh put them beneath the soles of his feet. <sup>4</sup>But now Yahweh my God has made things settle for me all round. There's no adversary and there's nothing bad happening.

<sup>5</sup>So here I'm saying to build a house for the name of Yahweh my God, as Yahweh spoke to David my father: "Your son, whom I will put on your throne in place of you, he will build the house for my name." <sup>6</sup>So now, order that they cut down cedars for me from the Lebanon. My servants will be with your servants, and your servants' wages – I will give it to you in accordance with anything that you say, because you yourself know that there is no one among us who knows about cutting down trees like the Tsidonites.'

<sup>7</sup>When Hiram heard Shelomoh's words, he rejoiced greatly. He said, 'Yahweh be blessed

today, who has given David a smart son over this numerous people.' ⁸Hiram sent to Shelomoh: 'I've heard what you sent me. I myself will do all you want in cedar trees and in juniper trees. ⁹My servants will get them down from the Lebanon to the sea. It'll be me who makes them into rafts at the sea for the place that you send to me, and I'll split them up there. It'll be you who carries them, and you who'll do what I want in giving bread to my household.'

## The labourers for the building

¹⁰So Hiram was giving Shelomoh cedar wood and juniper wood, all that he wanted, ¹¹while Shelomoh gave Hiram 20,000 ten-gallon measures of wheat as provision for his household and 20,[000] ten-gallon measures of pressed oil. Thus Shelomoh would give Hiram year by year. ¹²Because Yahweh gave Shelomoh smartness, as he had spoken to him, there was peace between Hiram and Shelomoh. The two of them solemnized a pact.

¹³King Shelomoh raised a workforce from all Yisra'el; the workforce came to 30,000 men. ¹⁴He sent them to the Lebanon 10,000 per month in shifts. They would be a month in the Lebanon, two months at home. Adoniram was in charge of the workforce.

¹⁵Shelomoh had 70,000 load-carriers and 80,000 stonecutters in the highland, ¹⁶apart from Shelomoh's prefect officers who were in charge of the work, 3,300 holding sway over the company who were doing the work. ¹⁷The king gave them orders and they transported big stones, fine stones, so as to found the house with hewn stones. ¹⁸Shelomoh's builders, Hiram's builders and men from Byblos shaped them, and prepared the wood and the stones for building the house.

**6** In the four hundred and eightieth year of the Yisra'elites' getting out of the country of Misrayim, in the fourth year in the month Ziv (i.e. the second month) of Shelomoh's reign over Yisra'el, he built the house for Yahweh. ²The house that King Shelomoh built for Yahweh:

> its length was thirty metres;
> its width ten metres;
> its height fifteen metres.

³The porch on the front of the hall of the house:

> its length was ten metres (along the width of the house);
> its width five metres (along the front of the house).

⁴He made recessed latticed windows for the house, ⁵against the wall of the house he built an extension all round (the walls of the house round the hall and the inner sanctuary), and he made side rooms all round.

> ⁶The lowest extension: its width was two and a half metres;
> the middle: its width was three metres;
> the third: its width was three and a half metres;

because he put supports for the house all round outside so as not to fasten them to the walls of the house.

## If you walk

⁷When the house was built, it was built of whole quarry stone. Hammers or chisel, any iron tool, did not make itself heard in the house when it was built. ⁸The entrance to the middle side room was on the right side of the house, and winding stairs went up to the middle one and from the middle one to the third.

⁹So he built the house and finished it, and panelled the house with beams and planks of cedar. ¹⁰He built the extension against the entire house, two and a half metres its height, and secured the house with cedar wood.

¹¹Yahweh's word came to Shelomoh: ¹²'This house that you're building: if you walk by my decrees and act by my rulings and keep all my orders, walking by them, I will implement with you my word that I spoke to David your father. ¹³I will dwell among the Yisra'elites and I will not abandon my people Yisra'el.'

¹⁴So Shelomoh built the house and finished it. ¹⁵He built the walls of the house on the inside with cedar planks from the floor of the house up to the ceiling walls. He overlaid it with wood on the inside and overlaid the floor

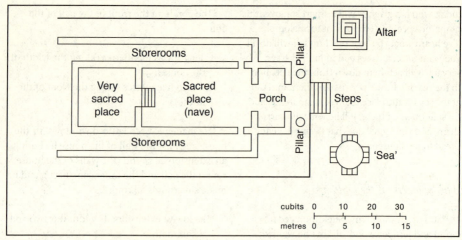

*1 Kings 6: The temple of Shelomoh (Solomon)*

of the house with juniper planks. ¹⁶He built with cedar boards ten metres from the sides of the house, from the floor as far as the walls, and built for it inside an inner room as the very sacred place. ¹⁷The house (i.e. the hall, in front) was twenty metres. ¹⁸The cedar for the house within: carving of melons and open flowers, everything cedar. No stone was visible.

¹⁹He prepared an inner room inside the house, within, to put Yahweh's pact chest there. ²⁰In front of the inner room it was ten metres in length, ten metres in width and ten metres in its height. He overlaid it with beaten gold and overlaid the altar with cedar.

## The inner room

²¹Shelomoh overlaid the house inside with beaten gold, and passed gold chains in front of the inner room and overlaid it with gold. ²²So the entire house he overlaid with gold until the entire house was complete, and the entire altar belonging to the inner room he overlaid with gold. ²³In the inner room he made two sphinxes of oil wood; its height was five metres. ²⁴One sphinx's wing was two and a half metres and the second sphinx's wing was two and a half metres. From the ends of its wings to the other ends of its wings was five metres, ²⁵and the second sphinx was five metres: one measure and one profile for the two sphinxes. ²⁶The height of one sphinx was five metres, and so the second sphinx.

²⁷He put the sphinxes in the middle of the inner house. They spread the sphinxes' wings so that the wing of the one touched the wall and the wing of the second sphinx was touching the second wall, with their wings towards the middle of the house, wing touching wing. ²⁸He overlaid the sphinxes with gold, ²⁹and all the walls of the house, all round, he carved with carved engravings of sphinxes, palms and open flowers, inside and outside. ³⁰The floor of the house he overlaid with gold, inside and outside.

³¹As the entrance of the inner room he made doors of oil wood, the upright (the doorposts) fivefold, ³²the two doors of oil wood. He carved on them carvings of sphinxes, palms and open flowers, and overlaid them with gold. He hammered the gold on to the sphinxes and on to the palms. ³³In this way he made for the entrance to the hall doorposts of oil wood, out of a quarter, ³⁴and two doors of juniper wood, one door of two leaves folding and the other door of two leaves folding. ³⁵He carved sphinxes, palms and open flowers and overlaid them with gold, fitted on to the chiselling. ³⁶He built the inner courtyard with three rows of hewn stone and a row of cedar timbers.

## The forest-like meeting house

³⁷In the fourth year Yahweh's house was founded, in the month of Ziv, ³⁸and in the

eleventh year in the month of Bul (i.e. the eighth month) the house got finished in keeping with all his words and with all his rulings. He built it over seven years.

**7** His own house Shelomoh built over thirteen years. He finished his entire house ²and built the Lebanon Forest house:
its length fifty metres, its width twenty-five metres and its height fifteen metres;
on four rows of cedar pillars, with cedar timbers on the pillars;
³it was panelled with cedar above, on top of the planks that were on the forty-five pillars (fifteen per row);
⁴frames, three rows, face to face, three times;
⁵all the entrances and the doorposts, square in frame, in front, face to face, three times;
⁶the porch of pillars he made, twenty-five metres its length and fifteen metres its width;
a porch in front of them and pillars and a canopy in front.

⁷He made the porch for the throne where he would exercise authority (the authority porch). It was covered in cedar from floor to floor. ⁸His house where he would live (the other courtyard within the porch) was of this same making. He would make a house for Par'oh's daughter, whom Shelomoh took, like this porch. ⁹All these things:
fine stone, hewn according to measure, trimmed with a trimmer, inside and outside, from foundation to coping, from outside as far as the big courtyard;
¹⁰the foundation: fine stones, big stones, five-metre stones and four-metre stones;
¹¹on top: fine stones, hewn according to measure, and cedar;
¹²the big courtyard all round: three rows of hewn stone and a row of cedar timbers, both for the inner courtyard of Yahweh's house and for the house's porch.

### The other Hiram

¹³King Shelomoh sent and got Hiram from Tsor. ¹⁴He was the son of a woman who was a widow from the clan of Naphtali, but his father had been a Tsorite, a coppersmith. He was full of smartness, of understanding and of knowledge for doing all work in copper. So he came to King Shelomoh and did all his work. ¹⁵He shaped the two pillars, of copper.
The height of one pillar was nine metres.
A line of six metres would go round the second pillar.
¹⁶Two capitals he made to put on the tops of the pillars, cast in copper; the height of one capital was two and a half metres and the height of the second capital was two and a half metres.
¹⁷Nets of netted work, twists of chainwork, for the capitals that were on the top of the pillars, seven for one capital, seven for the second capital.
¹⁸He made the pillars with two rows all round on each net, to cover the capitals that were on the top of the pomegranates, and in this way he made it for the second capital.
¹⁹The capitals that were on the top of the pillars made of lotuses, in the porch, two metres.
²⁰The capitals on the two pillars also above, next to the bulge that was across from the net.
The 200 pomegranates in rows all round on the second capital.
²¹He set up the pillars for the porch of the hall: he set up the right pillar and named it 'He-Establishes' and set up the left pillar and named it 'In-Him-Is-Strength'.
²²On the top of the pillars: lotus work.
So the work on the pillars was complete.

### The 'sea' and its stands

²³He made the sea, cast:
five metres from its lip to its lip, circular all round, two and a half metres its height;
a line of fifteen metres would go round it all round;
²⁴melons under its lip going round it, all round, five metres, encircling the sea all round; two rows of melons cast with its casting;
²⁵standing on twelve cattle, three facing north, three facing west, three facing south, three facing east, with the sea on them, above, and all their rears inwards;
²⁶its thickness a handbreadth;
its lip like the making of the lip of a cup, a lotus petal;

it could contain 2,000 five-gallon measures.
²⁷He made the ten stands, copper:
the length of one stand two metres, two
　metres its width, and one and a half metres
　its height;
²⁸this was the making of a stand: they had
　rims, and rims between the frames;
²⁹on the rims that were between the frames,
　lions, cattle and sphinxes;
on the frames a stand;
on top and below the lions and the cattle,
　spirals of hammered making;
³⁰four copper wheels for each stand, and
　copper axles;
its four legs had shoulder-pieces under the
　basin;
the shoulder-pieces, cast, with spirals across
　from each;
³¹its mouth inside the capital and half a
　metre above;
its mouth circular, the making of a stand,
　three quarters of a metre;
also on the mouth, carvings;
their rims square, not circular;
³²the four wheels below the rims;
the wheels' supports in the stand;
the height of a wheel three quarters of a
　metre;
³³the making of the wheels like the making
　of a chariot wheel;
their supports, their backs, their spokes and
　their hubs, all cast;
³⁴four shoulder-pieces at the four corners of
　each stand; from the stand its shoulder-
　pieces;
³⁵at the top of the stand a circular band all
　round, the height a quarter of a metre;
on the top of the stand, its handles and its
　rims coming from it.

## The engraved sphinxes

³⁶He engraved on the panels of its handles
and on its rims sphinxes, lions and palms,
according to the space on each, with spirals all
round. ³⁷Like this he made the ten stands, each
cast, one measure, one shape for all of them.
³⁸He made ten copper basins. Each basin would
contain 45-gallon measures, each basin two
metres, each on its stand, for the ten stands.
³⁹He put the stands five at the right shoulder

of the house and five at the left shoulder of
the house. The sea he put at the right shoulder
of the house to the east, towards the south.
⁴⁰Hiram made the basins, the shovels and the
bowls.
　So Hiram finished doing all the work that he
did for King Shelomoh at Yahweh's house:
⁴¹two pillars;
two globes for the capitals that were on the
　top of the pillars;
two nets to cover the two globes for the
　capitals that were on the top of the pillars;
⁴²the 400 pomegranates for the two nets,
　two rows of pomegranates for each net, to
　cover the two globes for the capitals that
　were on the face of the pillars;
⁴³the ten stands and the ten basins on the
　stands;
⁴⁴the one sea and the twelve cattle beneath
　the sea;
⁴⁵the buckets, the shovels, the basins, all
　these articles that Hiram made for King
　Shelomoh for Yahweh's house, polished
　copper.
⁴⁶The king cast them in the Yarden Plain,
in the earthen compactness between Sukkot
and Tsaretan. ⁴⁷Shelomoh left all the articles
alone [unweighed], because of the very, very
large number; the weight of the copper was not
searched out.
⁴⁸Shelomoh made all the articles that were
for Yahweh's house:
　the gold altar;
　the table on which was the presence bread,
　　gold;
⁴⁹the lights (five on the right and five on the
　left) in front of the inner room, beaten
　gold;
the flowers, the lamps and the tongs, gold;
⁵⁰the basins, the snuffers, the sprinklers, the
　ladles and the pans, beaten gold;
the hinges for the doors of the inner house,
　for the very sacred place, for the doors of
　the house, for the hall, gold.

## The work completed

⁵¹So all the work that King Shelomoh had
done for Yahweh's house was complete, and
Shelomoh brought in the sacred things from
David his father; the silver, the gold and the

articles he put in the treasuries of Yahweh's house.

**8** Then Shelomoh congregated Yisra'el's elders (all the heads of the clans, the Yisra'elites' ancestral leaders) to King Shelomoh in Yerushalaim, to take up Yahweh's pact chest from David's Town (i.e. Tsiyyon [Zion]). ²All the Yisra'elites congregated to King Shelomoh in the month of Etanim at the festival (i.e. the seventh month). ³All Yisra'el's elders came and the priests carried the chest. ⁴They took up Yahweh's chest, the appointment tent and all the sacred articles that were in the tent. The priests and the Levites took them up ⁵while King Shelomoh and the entire assembly of Yisra'el who had assembled to him were with him before the chest, sacrificing sheep and cattle that could not be numbered and could not be counted because of the large number.

⁶The priests brought Yahweh's pact chest to its place, to the inner room of the house, to the very sacred place, under the sphinxes' wings, ⁷because the sphinxes were spreading their wings to the chest's place; the sphinxes screened the chest and its poles from above. ⁸The poles extended and the heads of the poles could be seen from the sacred place in front of the inner room, but they could not be seen outside. They have been there until this day. ⁹There was nothing in the chest, only the two stone tablets that Mosheh had set down there at Horeb, when Yahweh solemnized things with the Yisra'elites, when they got out from the country of Misrayim.

¹⁰When the priests went out from the sacred place and the cloud was filling Yahweh's house, ¹¹the priests were not able to stand to minister before the cloud, because Yahweh's splendour was filling Yahweh's house.

### The God who dwells in the cloud

¹²Then Shelomoh said:

Yahweh has said he would dwell in a
    thundercloud.
¹³I have indeed built a stately house for you, an
    established place for you to live in to the ages.

¹⁴The king turned his face round and blessed Yisra'el's entire congregation, as Yisra'el's entire congregation was standing. ¹⁵He said, 'Blessed be Yahweh the God of Yisra'el who spoke by his own mouth with David my father, and by his own hand has fulfilled it: ¹⁶"From the day that I got my people Yisra'el out of Misrayim I didn't choose a town from all Yisra'el's clans to build a house for my name to be there, but I chose David to be in charge of my people Yisra'el."

¹⁷It was in David my father's mind to build a house for the name of Yahweh the God of Yisra'el, ¹⁸but Yahweh said to David my father, "In that it was in your mind to build a house for my name, you did well that it was in your mind. ¹⁹Only you yourself will not build the house. Rather, your son, who is going to come out from your insides, he will build the house for my name."

²⁰Yahweh has implemented his word that he spoke. I have arisen in place of David my father, I have sat on Yisra'el's throne as Yahweh spoke and I have built the house for the name of Yahweh the God of Yisra'el. ²¹I have set a place there for the chest where Yahweh's pact is, which he solemnized with our ancestors when he got them out of the country of Misrayim.'

²²Shelomoh stood before Yahweh's altar in front of the entire congregation of Yisra'el and spread out his palms to the heavens.

### Will God really live on earth?

²³He said, 'Yahweh, God of Yisra'el, there is no god like you in the heavens above or on the earth beneath, keeping pact and commitment for your servants who walk before you with their entire mind, ²⁴who has kept for your servant David my father what you spoke to him. You spoke with your own mouth and with your own hand you have fulfilled it, this very day. ²⁵So now, Yahweh, God of Yisra'el, keep for your servant David my father what you spoke to him: "There will not be cut off for you someone before me sitting on Yisra'el's throne, if only your sons keep watch over their way in walking before me as you have walked before me." ²⁶So now, God of Yisra'el, may your word please prove trustworthy that you spoke to your servant David my father.

²⁷Because will God truly live on the earth? There – the heavens, even the highest heavens, could not contain you, certainly not this house that I have built. ²⁸But turn your face towards your servant's plea and towards his prayer for grace, Yahweh my God, so as to listen to the resounding cry and to the plea that your servant is making before you today, ²⁹so that your eyes are opened towards this house night and day, towards the place of which you've said, "My name will be there", so as to listen to the plea that your servant makes towards this place. ³⁰May you listen to the prayer for grace by your servant and your people Yisra'el, which they make towards this place. May you yourself listen towards the place where you live, towards the heavens, listen and pardon.

## Some things to pray for

³¹Someone who does wrong, an individual to his neighbour, and he takes up an oath against him to get him to swear, and the oath comes before your altar in this house, ³²may you yourself listen in the heavens, and act, and exercise authority for your servants, so as to show the person in the wrong to be in the wrong, bringing his conduct on his head, and to show the person in the right to be in the right, bringing to him in accordance with his being in the right.

³³When your people Yisra'el take a beating before an enemy because they do wrong in relation to you, but they turn back to you and confess your name and plead and pray for grace towards you in this house, ³⁴may you yourself listen in the heavens and pardon your people Yisra'el's wrongdoing and take them back to the land that you gave to their ancestors.

³⁵When the heavens hold back and there's no rain because they do wrong in relation to you, but they plead towards this place and confess your name, and turn back from their wrongdoing because you humble them, ³⁶may you yourself listen in the heavens and pardon the wrongdoing of your servants, of your people Yisra'el, when you instruct them in the good way that they should walk in, and give rain on your country that you gave your people as a domain.

## More things to pray for

³⁷When famine happens in the country, when an epidemic happens, blight, mildew, locust, caterpillar, when it happens; when its enemy besieges it in the region of its settlements; any affliction, any illness; ³⁸any plea, any prayer for grace that any human being belonging to your entire people Yisra'el may have, who acknowledge, each one, the affliction of his heart and spreads out his palms towards this house, ³⁹may you yourself listen in the heavens, the established place where you live, and pardon, and act, and give to the individual in accordance with all his ways, in that you know his mind (because you alone know the mind of all human beings), ⁴⁰in order that they may live in awe of you all the days that they are alive on the face of the ground that you gave to our ancestors.

⁴¹Further, to the foreigner who is not of your people Yisra'el but comes from a distant country for the sake of your name (⁴²because they hear of your big name, your strong hand and your extended arm) and comes and pleads towards this house, ⁴³may you yourself listen in the heavens, in the established place where you live, and act in accordance with everything for which the foreigner calls to you, in order that all earth's peoples may acknowledge your name so as to live in awe of you like your people Yisra'el and to acknowledge that your name is called out over this house that I have built.

⁴⁴When your people goes out to battle against its enemy by the way that you send them and they plead to Yahweh in the direction of the town that you have chosen and the house that I have built for your name, ⁴⁵may you listen in the heavens to their plea and to their prayer for grace, and decide for them.

## One more

⁴⁶When they do wrong in relation to you (because there is no human being who doesn't do wrong) and you're angry with them and you give them up before an enemy, and their captors take them off captive to the enemy's country, far or near, ⁴⁷and they turn their mind back in the country where they are captive,

and turn back and pray towards you for grace in their captors' country, saying "We've done wrong, we've been wayward, we've been faithless", <sup>48</sup>and they turn back to you with their entire mind and with their entire being in the country of their enemies who have taken them off captive, and make their plea to you in the direction of their country that you gave their ancestors, the town that you've chosen and the house that I've built for your name, <sup>49</sup>may you listen in the heavens, in the established place where you live, to their plea, their prayer for grace, and decide for them, <sup>50</sup>and pardon your people who've done wrong in relation to you, for all their acts of rebellion that they have committed against you, and give them compassion before their captors so they may have compassion on them, <sup>51</sup>because they are your people, your domain, which you got out of Misrayim, from inside the iron furnace, <sup>52</sup>so that your eyes are opened to your servant's prayer for grace and to your people Yisra'el's prayer for grace, so that you listen to them every time they call to you, <sup>53</sup>because you yourself made them distinct for yourself as a domain from all the peoples of the earth, as you spoke by means of Mosheh your servant when you got our ancestors out of Misrayim, Lord Yahweh.'

## Blessings

<sup>54</sup>When Shelomoh had finished making to Yahweh all this plea and prayer for grace, he got up from before Yahweh's altar, from bending down on his knees with his palms spread out to the heavens, <sup>55</sup>and stood and blessed the entire congregation of Yisra'el, in a loud voice: <sup>56</sup>'Blessed be Yahweh, who has given his people Yisra'el a place to settle down in accordance with all that he spoke. Not one word has fallen down of all his good word that he spoke by means of Mosheh his servant. <sup>57</sup>May Yahweh our God be with us as he was with our ancestors and may he not abandon us, may he not leave us, <sup>58</sup>by inclining our mind to him so that we walk in all his ways and keep his orders, his decrees and his rulings that he ordered our ancestors. <sup>59</sup>May these words of mine that I have made as a plea before Yahweh be near to Yahweh our God day and night so

that he may decide for his servant and decide for his people Yisra'el, each day's requirement in its day, <sup>60</sup>in order that all the peoples of the earth may acknowledge that Yahweh is God; there is no other. <sup>61</sup>And may your mind be perfect with Yahweh your God so as to walk in his decrees and keep his orders this very day.'

<sup>62</sup>The king and all Yisra'el with him were making sacrifice before Yahweh. <sup>63</sup>Shelomoh made as well-being sacrifices, which he made for Yahweh, 22,000 cattle and 120,000 sheep. So the king and all the Yisra'elites dedicated Yahweh's house. <sup>64</sup>That day the king made the middle part of the court sacred, which was in front of Yahweh's house, because he made the burnt offering, the grain offering and the fat parts of the well-being sacrifices there, because the copper altar that was before Yahweh was too small to contain the burnt offering, the grain offering and the fat parts of the well-being sacrifices.

## Yahweh appears again, with a warning

<sup>65</sup>Shelomoh made the festival at that time, he and all Yisra'el with him (a big congregation from Lebo Hamat as far as the Misrayimite Wadi) before Yahweh our God for seven days, then seven days, fourteen days. <sup>66</sup>On the eighth day he sent the people off and they blessed the king. They went to their tents, rejoicing and good-hearted because of all the good things that Yahweh had done for David his servant and for Yisra'el his people.

**9** When Shelomoh had finished building Yahweh's house and the king's house and everything that drew Shelomoh's attraction that he wanted to do, <sup>2</sup>Yahweh appeared to Shelomoh a second time, as he had appeared to him at Gib'on. <sup>3</sup>Yahweh said to him, 'I've listened to your plea and your prayer for grace which you've made before me. I've made this house that you have built sacred, so as to put my name there permanently. My eyes and my mind will be there for all time. <sup>4</sup>You yourself, if you walk before me as David your father walked, with wholeness of mind and with uprightness, acting in accordance with all that I've ordered you, you will keep my decrees and my rulings, <sup>5</sup>and I will set up your kingly throne over Yisra'el permanently, as I spoke to David your father: "There will not be cut off for you someone on Yisra'el's throne." ⁶If you all and your sons actually turn back from following me and don't keep my orders, my decrees that I've put before you, and you go and serve other gods and bow low to them, ⁷I will cut off Yisra'el from on the face of the land that I gave them, and the house that I have made sacred for my name I will send off from before my face. Yisra'el will become an object lesson and a taunt among all the peoples. ⁸Whereas this house is high, anyone who passes by it will be desolate and will whistle. They will say, "Why did Yahweh act in that way to this country and to this house?" ⁹And people will say, "On account of the fact that they abandoned Yahweh their God who got their ancestors out of the country of Misrayim, and took strong hold of other gods and bowed low to them and served them. That's why Yahweh brought upon them all this bad experience.'"

## Building projects

¹⁰At the end of the twenty years while Shelomoh built the two houses, Yahweh's house and the king's house, ¹¹when Hiram king of Tsor had supported Shelomoh with cedar wood and with juniper wood and with gold, all he wanted, King Shelomoh then gave Hiram twenty towns in the region of Galilee. ¹²Hiram went out from Tsor to see the towns that Shelomoh had given him, but they were not right in his eyes. ¹³He said, 'What are these towns that you've given me, brother?' He called them the Region of Kabul ['Like-Nothing'], until this day. ¹⁴(Hiram had sent the king 120 talents of gold.)

¹⁵This is the account of the workforce that King Shelomoh raised to build Yahweh's house, his own house, the Fill, the Yerushalaim wall, and Hatsor, Megiddo and Gezer, ¹⁶when Par'oh king of Misrayim had gone up and taken Gezer, burned it with fire, killed the Kena'anites who lived in the town and given it as a dowry to his daughter, Shelomoh's wife. ¹⁷Shelomoh built up Gezer, Lower Bet Horon, ¹⁸Ba'alat and Tadmor in the wilderness, within the country, ¹⁹and all the supply towns that Shelomoh had, the chariot towns, the cavalry towns and the things Shelomoh felt an attraction for building

in Yerushalaim, in the Lebanon and in all the country that he ruled.

²⁰The entire people that was left of the Amorite, the Hittite, the Perizzite, the Hivvite and the Yebusite, who were not born of the Yisra'elites (²¹their descendants who were left after them in the country, whom the Yisra'elites were not able to devote), Shelomoh raised as a serf workforce until this day. ²²Of the Yisra'elites Shelomoh did not make anyone a serf; rather they were men of battle, his servants, his officers, his adjutants, his chariot officers and his cavalry; ²³these were the prefect officers who were in charge of the work for Shelomoh, 550, holding sway over the company doing the work. ²⁴Yet Par'oh's daughter went up from David's Town to her house which he built for her. Then he built the Fill.

## Enter the queen of Sheba

²⁵Three times a year Shelomoh used to offer up burnt offerings and well-being sacrifices on the altar that he built for Yahweh, and burn incense with it (the one that was before Yahweh). So he completed the house.

²⁶King Shelomoh made a fleet at Etsyon-geber, which is by Elot on the shore of the Reed Sea in the country of Edom. ²⁷In the fleet Hiram sent his servants, shipmen who knew the sea, with Shelomoh's servants. ²⁸They came to Ophir and got gold from there, 420 talents, and brought it to King Shelomoh.

**10** Since the queen of Sheba had been hearing report of Shelomoh in connection with Yahweh's name, she came to test him with conundrums. ²She came to Yerushalaim with a very substantial force, camels carrying spices, very much gold and precious stones. She came to Shelomoh and spoke to him of everything that was in her mind, ³and Shelomoh told her about all the things she said. Nothing was concealed from the king that he didn't tell her.

⁴The queen of Sheba saw all Shelomoh's smartness, the house that he had built, ⁵the food on his table, the seating of his servants, the standing of his ministers and their dress, his wine waiters, and his burnt offering that he would offer up at Yahweh's house, and there was no longer any breath left in her.

*Far more impressive than I had been told*

⁶She said to the king, 'The thing was true that I heard in my country about your words and about your smartness. ⁷I didn't trust in the words until I came and my eyes saw. But here, the half had not been told me. You have more smartness and good things than the report that I heard. ⁸The blessings of your people, the blessings of these servants of yours who are standing continually before you, listening to your smartness! ⁹May Yahweh your God be blessed, who delighted in you so as to put you on Yisra'el's throne in Yahweh's loyalty to Yisra'el, permanently. He made you king to exercise authority with faithfulness.'

¹⁰She gave the king 120 talents of gold, very many spices and precious stones. There never again came spices in the quantity that the queen of Sheba gave King Shelomoh. ¹¹Hiram's fleet, which carried gold from Ophir, also brought very much almug wood and precious stones. ¹²The king made the almug wood into supports for Yahweh's house and for the king's house and into guitars and mandolins for the singers. Such almug wood has not come and has not been seen until this day. ¹³King Shelomoh himself gave the queen of Sheba all that she wanted, that she asked for, beyond what he gave her in accordance with what King Shelomoh possessed. Then she turned her face and went to her country, she and her servants.

¹⁴The weight of the gold that came to Shelomoh in one year was 666 talents of gold, ¹⁵apart from what came from the traders, from the merchants' business, and all the kings of Arabia and the governors of the region. ¹⁶King Shelomoh made 200 body-shields of hammered gold (he would raise 600 gold pieces for each shield) ¹⁷and 300 hand-shields of hammered gold (he would raise three pounds of gold for each shield). The king put them in the Lebanon Forest house.

*Throne, fleet, trade*

¹⁸The king made a big ivory throne and overlaid it with refined gold, ¹⁹with six steps to the throne, and a circular top for the throne at the back of it, and arms on this side and on that side of the place where one sat, and two lions standing beside the arms, ²⁰and twelve lions standing there on the six steps on this side and on that side. None was made like this for any kingdom.

²¹All King Solomon's drinking vessels were of gold and all the vessels in the Lebanon Forest house were beaten gold, none silver – it was not thought of for anything in Shelomoh's days, ²²because the king had a Tarshish fleet at sea with Hiram's fleet. Once in three years the Tarshish fleet would come carrying gold and silver, tusks, monkeys and peacocks.

²³King Shelomoh was bigger than all the kings of the earth in wealth and in smartness. ²⁴All the earth was seeking audience with Shelomoh to listen to his smartness, which God had put into his mind, ²⁵and they were bringing each his offering: silver objects and gold objects, robes, weaponry and spices, horses and mules, each year's requirement in its year. ²⁶Shelomoh gathered chariotry and cavalry, and had 1,400 chariotry and 12,000 cavalry. He settled them in chariot towns, and with the king in Yerushalaim.

²⁷The king made the silver in Yerushalaim like the stones, and made the cedars like the wild fig trees that are in the foothills in the large number. ²⁸The origin of the horses that Shelomoh had was from Misrayim and from Qewe. The king's dealers would get them from Qewe at a price; ²⁹a chariot went up (it came out from Misrayim) for 600 silver pieces, a horse for 150. In this way they would get them out by their own hand to all the kings of the Hittites and to the kings of Aram.

*Diplomatic marriages*

**11** Now King Shelomoh loved many foreign women (and Par'oh's daughter), Mo'abites, Ammonites, Edomites, Tsidonites and Hittites, ²from the nations of which Yahweh had said to the Yisra'elites, 'You will not have sex with them and they will not have sex with you. They will surely turn away your mind after their gods.' To them Shelomoh attached himself in love. ³He had 700 consorts and 300 secondary wives, and his wives did turn away his mind.

⁴So in Shelomoh's old age, his wives did turn his mind away after other gods. His mind

became not perfect with Yahweh his God like the mind of David his father. ⁵Shelomoh followed Shameful Ashtar the god of the Tsidonites and Milkom the abomination of the Ammonites. ⁶Shelomoh did what was bad in Yahweh's eyes and did not fully follow Yahweh like David his father. ⁷Shelomoh built a shrine for Kemosh the abomination of Mo'ab on the mountain that's facing Yerushalaim, and for the Shameful King, the abomination of the Ammonites. ⁸He did so for all his foreign wives who were burning incense and sacrificing to their gods.

⁹Yahweh showed himself angry with Shelomoh because his mind turned away from Yahweh the God of Yisra'el who had appeared to him twice ¹⁰and had given him orders about this thing, not to follow other gods. He didn't keep what Yahweh ordered. ¹¹Yahweh said to Shelomoh, 'Since this has been with you, and you haven't kept my pact and my decrees which I ordered you, I will tear the kingdom right away from you and give it to your servant. ¹²Yet in your days I won't do it, for the sake of David your father; from the hand of your son I will tear it away. ¹³Only, the entire kingdom I will not tear away; one clan I will give to your son, for the sake of David my servant and for the sake of Yerushalaim, which I chose.'

## Adversaries

¹⁴Yahweh made rise as an adversary for Shelomoh Hadad the Edomite. He was from the royal offspring in Edom. ¹⁵When David had been with Edom, Yo'ab went up to bury the people who had been run through, and he had struck down every male in Edom, ¹⁶because for six months Yo'ab and all Yisra'el stayed there until he had cut down every male in Edom. ¹⁷But Adad took flight, he and some Edomite men, some of his father's servants, with him, so as to come to Misrayim; Hadad was a small boy. ¹⁸They set off from Midyan and came to Pa'ran, took some men with them from Pa'ran and came to Misrayim, to Par'oh king of Misrayim. He gave him a house, said there would be bread for him and gave him land.

¹⁹Hadad found grace greatly in Par'oh's eyes and he gave him his wife's sister, the sister of Tahpenes, the queen, as wife. ²⁰Tahpenes'

sister gave birth to Genubat, his son, for him. Tahpenes weaned him within Par'oh's household, and Genubat was in Par'oh's household among Par'oh's sons.

²¹When Hadad heard in Misrayim that David had lain down with his ancestors and that Yo'ab the army officer was dead, Hadad said to Par'oh, 'Send me off, so I may go to my country.' ²²Par'oh said to him, 'What do you lack with me, that here, you're seeking to go to your country?' He said, 'No, but do send me off.' ²³And God made rise for him as an adversary Retson ben Elyada, who had taken flight from Hadad'ezer king of Tsobah, his lord. ²⁴He collected men round him and became officer over a raiding gang (when David was killing them); they went to Dammeseq [Damascus] and lived there, and reigned in Dammeseq. ²⁵He was an adversary to Yisra'el all Shelomoh's days, along with the bad thing that Hadad was. He harassed Yisra'el. He reigned over Aram.

## Yarob'am (Jeroboam)

²⁶Now Yarob'am ben Nebat, an Ephraite from Tseredah (his mother's name was Tseru'ah, a woman who was a widow), a servant of Shelomoh, raised a hand against the king. ²⁷This was the thing in connection with which he raised a hand against the king. When Shelomoh built the Fill, he secured the breach in David his father's town. ²⁸This individual Yarob'am was a forceful strong man, and Shelomoh saw the boy when he was doing work and appointed him over the entire labour force in the household of Yoseph.

²⁹At that time, when Yarob'am went out of Yerushalaim, Ahiyyah the Shilonite, the prophet, found him on the road. He was covering himself with a new coat and the two of them were alone in the open country. ³⁰Ahiyyah seized the new coat that was on him and tore it into twelve pieces. ³¹He said to Yarob'am, 'Take yourself ten pieces, because Yahweh the God of Yisra'el has said this: "Here am I, tearing the kingdom from Shelomoh's hand and giving you the ten clans. ³²One clan will be his, for the sake of my servant David and for the sake of Yerushalaim, the town that I chose from all Yisra'el's clans. ³³Because they've

abandoned me and bowed low to Shameful
Ashtar the god of the Tsidonites, to Kemosh
the god of Mo'ab and to Milkom the god of the
Ammonites, and have not walked in my ways
by doing what is upright in my eyes, my
decrees and my rulings, like David his father.

<sup>34</sup>I shall not take the entire kingdom from his
hand and I shall make him leader all the days
of his life for the sake of David my servant,
whom I chose, who kept my orders and my
decrees. <sup>35</sup>But I shall take the kingdom from
his son's hand and give it to you (the ten clans).
<sup>36</sup>To his son I will give one clan for the sake of
there always being hegemony for David my
servant before me in Yerushalaim, the town
that I chose for myself to put my name there.
<sup>37</sup>But you I shall take, and you will reign over
all that your appetite longs for. You will be
king over Yisra'el. <sup>38</sup>If you listen to all that I
command you, walk in my ways and do what is
upright in my eyes by keeping my decrees and
my orders as David my servant did, I will be
with you and I will build for you a trustworthy
household as I built for David, and I will give
Yisra'el to you. <sup>39</sup>I will humble David's offspring
on account of this (yet not for all time)."'

## Rehab'am (Rehoboam)

<sup>40</sup>Shelomoh sought to put Yarob'am to death,
but Yarob'am set off and took flight to Misrayim
to Shishaq king of Misrayim, and he was in
Misrayim until Shelomoh's death. <sup>41</sup>The rest
of the things about Shelomoh, all that he did
and his smartness, they're written on the
document about things regarding Shelomoh,
aren't they. <sup>42</sup>The time that Shelomoh reigned
in Yerushalaim over all Yisra'el was forty years.
<sup>43</sup>Then Shelomoh lay down with his ancestors
and was buried in David his father's town, and
Rehab'am his son began to reign in place of him.

**12** Rehab'am went to Shekem, because
all Yisra'el had come to Shekem to
make him king. <sup>2</sup>When Yarob'am ben Nebat
heard while he was still in Misrayim, where he
had taken flight from before King Shelomoh
(so Yarob'am lived in Misrayim), <sup>3</sup>they sent
and called for him. Yarob'am came with the
entire congregation of Yisra'el and they spoke
to Rehab'am: <sup>4</sup>'Your father – he made our yoke
tough. So you, now, lighten something of your

father's tough servitude and of his heavy yoke
that he put on us, and we'll serve you.'
<sup>5</sup>He said to them, 'Go for three more days,
and come back to me.' The people went, <sup>6</sup>and
King Rehab'am took counsel with the elders
who had been standing before Shelomoh his
father when he was alive: 'How do you counsel
me to give back word to this people?' <sup>7</sup>They
spoke to him, 'If today you'll be a servant to
this people, and serve them, and answer them
and speak good words to them, they'll be your
servants for all time.'

## Declining the chance to be a servant leader

<sup>8</sup>But he abandoned the elders' counsel
which they gave him and took counsel with
the young men who grew up with him, who
were standing before him. <sup>9</sup>He said to them,
'What are you going to counsel, so that we may
give back word to this people who spoke to
me, "Lighten something of the yoke that your
father put on us"?' <sup>10</sup>The young men who grew
up with him spoke with him: 'You should say
this to this people who spoke to you, "Whereas
your father made our yoke heavy, you, lighten
it from on us" – you should speak like this
to them: "My little finger is thicker than my
father's hips. <sup>11</sup>So now, whereas my father
imposed a heavy yoke on you, I myself will add
to your yoke. Whereas my father disciplined
you with whips, I myself will discipline you
with scorpions."'

<sup>12</sup>Yarob'am and the entire people came to
Rehab'am on the third day as the king had
spoken, 'Come back to me on the third day',
<sup>13</sup>and the king answered the people toughly.
He abandoned the counsel of the elders that
they had given him <sup>14</sup>and spoke to them in
accordance with the counsel of the young men:
'Whereas my father made your yoke heavy,
I myself will add to your yoke. Whereas my
father disciplined you with whips, I myself will
discipline you with scorpions.' <sup>15</sup>The king didn't
listen to the people, because it was a turn of
affairs from Yahweh in order to implement his
word, which Yahweh had spoken by means of
Ahiyyah the Shilonite to Yarob'am ben Nebat.

<sup>16</sup>All Yisra'el saw that the king had not
listened to them, and the people gave word
back to the king:

What share do we have in David?
– we have no domain in ben Yishay
[Jesse].
To your tents, Yisra'el;
now see to your own household, David.

So Yisra'el went to its tents, ¹⁷though the
Yisra'elites who were living in the towns of
Yehudah – Rehab'am reigned over them. ¹⁸King
Rehab'am sent Adoram, who was in charge of
the workforce, but all Yisra'el pelted him with
stones and he died, while King Rehab'am got
himself together to get up into the chariot to
flee to Yerushalaim.

¹⁹So Yisra'el has rebelled against David's
household until this day.

### Yahweh confronts Rehab'am

²⁰When all Yisra'el heard that Yarob'am had
come back, they sent and called him to the

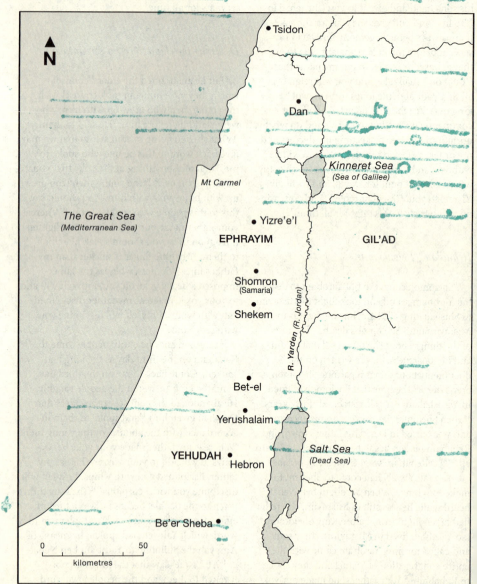

*1 Kings 12: The two nations – Ephrayim and Yehudah (Ephraim and Judah)*

assembly and made him king over all Yisra'el. No one followed David's household except the clan of Yehudah alone.

²¹Rehab'am came to Yerushalaim and congregated Yehudah's entire household and the clan of Binyamin, 180,000 picked men doing battle, to go to battle with the household of Yisra'el, to get the kingship back for Rehab'am son of Shelomoh. ²²But God's word came to Shema'yah, the supernatural man: ²³'Say to Rehab'am son of Shelomoh king of Yehudah, and to the entire household of Yehudah and Binyamin and the rest of the people: ²⁴"Yahweh has said this: 'You will not go up, you will not go to battle with your Yisra'elite brothers. Go back each one to his house, because this thing has come about from me.'" They listened to Yahweh's word and turned back to go, in accordance with Yahweh's word.

²⁵Yarob'am built up Shekem in the highland of Ephrayim and lived there; then he went out from there and built up Penu'el. ²⁶Yarob'am said to himself, 'The kingship will now go back to the household of David: ²⁷if this people go up to make sacrifices in Yahweh's house in Yerushalaim, this people's mind will turn back to their lord, to Rehab'am king of Yehudah. They'll kill me and turn back to Rehab'am king of Yehudah.' ²⁸So the king took counsel and made two gold bullocks. He said to them, 'It's too much for you to go up to Yerushalaim. Yisra'el, here are your gods who brought you up from the country of Misrayim.' ²⁹He placed the one in Bet-el and the other he put in Dan, ³⁰and this thing became a wrongdoing; the people went before the one as far as Dan. ³¹And he made the house at the shrines and made priests from the sections of the people who were not from the Levites.

## The destiny of Yarob'am's altar

³²Yarob'am made a festival in the eighth month, on the fifteenth day of the month, like the festival that was in Yehudah, and went up on to the altar. He acted in this way at Bet-el, sacrificing to the bullocks that he had made. So he put in place at Bet El the priests of the shrines that he had made ³³and went up on the altar that he had made at Bet-el on the fifteenth

day of the eighth month, which he devised out of his own mind, and made a festival for the Yisra'elites. He went up on to the altar to burn an offering,

**13** and there, a supernatural man came from Yehudah by Yahweh's word to Bet-el, when Yarob'am was standing on the altar to burn an offering. ²He called out against the altar by Yahweh's word: 'Altar, altar, Yahweh has said this: "Here, a son is going to be born to David's household (Yo'shiyyahu [Josiah] his name). He will sacrifice on you the priests of the shrines who burn offerings on you. People will burn human bones on you."' ³He gave a sign that day: 'This is the sign that Yahweh has spoken: "There, the altar is going to split apart and the waste that's on it will pour out."'

⁴When the king heard the word of the supernatural man which he called out against the altar at Bet-el, Yarob'am put out his hand from above the altar, saying, 'Seize him!' But his hand which he put out against him dried up and he couldn't take it back to himself, ⁵while the altar split apart and the waste from the altar poured out in accordance with the sign that the supernatural man had given by Yahweh's word. ⁶The king avowed to the supernatural man, 'Please seek the goodwill of Yahweh your God and plead for me so that my hand comes back to me.' The supernatural man sought Yahweh's goodwill and the king's hand came back to him, and became as it was previously.

## Another prophet in Bet-el

⁷The king spoke to the supernatural man: 'Do come with me to the house and have some sustenance, and I'll give you a gift.' ⁸The supernatural man said to the king, 'If you give me half your household I won't come with you; I won't eat bread or drink water in this place, ⁹because that's how he ordered me, by Yahweh's word: "You will not eat bread and you will not drink water, and you will not go back by the way that you went".' ¹⁰So he went by another way and didn't go back by the way that he came to Bet-el.

¹¹Now an old prophet was living in Bet-el. His son came and recounted to him everything that the supernatural man had done this day

in Bet-el, the words that he had spoken to the king. They recounted them to their father ¹²and their father spoke to them: 'Where exactly is the way he went?' His sons had seen the way that the supernatural man had gone, who had come from Yehudah. ¹³He said to his sons, 'Saddle the donkey for me.' They saddled the donkey for him and he mounted it ¹⁴and went after the supernatural man. He found him sitting under an oak. He said to him, 'Are you the supernatural man who came from Yehudah?' He said, 'I am.' ¹⁵He said to him, 'Go with me to my house and eat some bread.' ¹⁶He said, 'I can't go back with you or come with you. I won't eat bread and I won't drink water with you in this place, ¹⁷because a thing came to me by Yahweh's word, "You will not eat bread and you will not drink water there; you will not go back by going the way that you went."'

### Prophets, and when to ignore them

¹⁸He said to him, 'I am also a prophet, like you, and an envoy spoke to me by Yahweh's word: "Get him to go back with you to your house so he can eat bread and drink water."' He was lying to him. ¹⁹But he went back with him and ate bread in his house and drank water.

²⁰As they were sitting at the table, Yahweh's word came to the prophet who had got him to go back, ²¹and he called out to the supernatural man who had come from Yehudah, 'Yahweh has said this: "Since you have rebelled against Yahweh's bidding and not kept the order that Yahweh your God gave you, ²²but have gone back and eaten bread and drunk water in the place of which he spoke to you, 'You're not to eat bread and you're not to drink water', your corpse will not come to your ancestors' grave."'

²³After he had eaten bread and after he had drunk, he saddled for him the donkey belonging to the prophet whom he had got to go back, ²⁴and he went, but a lion met him on the way and put him to death. His corpse was thrown on the way. The donkey was standing beside it and the lion was standing beside the corpse, ²⁵and there, some men were passing and they saw the corpse thrown on the way with the lion standing beside the corpse. They came and spoke of it in the town where the old

prophet was living. ²⁶The prophet who had got him to go back from the way heard and said, 'It's the supernatural man who rebelled against Yahweh's bidding. Yahweh has given him over to the lion and it's mauled him and put him to death in accordance with Yahweh's word, which he spoke to him.'

²⁷He spoke to his sons: 'Saddle the donkey for me', and they saddled it. ²⁸He went and found his corpse thrown on the way, with the donkey and the lion standing beside the corpse. The lion had not eaten the corpse and it had not mauled the donkey.

²⁹The prophet took up the supernatural man's corpse, laid it on the donkey and took it back. So it came to the old prophet's town for lamenting and burying it. ³⁰He laid his corpse in his own grave and they lamented over it, 'Oh, my brother!' ³¹After burying him he said to his sons, 'When I die, bury me in the grave where the supernatural man is buried; lay my bones beside his bones, ³²because the word that he called out by Yahweh's word against the altar that's in Bet-el and against all the houses at the shrines that are in the towns of Shomron [Samaria] will definitely come about.'

³³After this thing Yarob'am did not turn back from his bad ways but again made priests for the shrines from all sections of the people. Anyone who wanted commissioned himself and became priests of the shrines. ³⁴This thing was the wrongdoing of Yarob'am's household both to efface and to annihilate it from upon the face of the ground.

### When the apostate king's son gets ill

**14** At that time Abiyyah ben Yarob'am got ill. ²Yarob'am said to his wife, 'Set off, please, make yourself look different so people won't know that you're Yarob'am's wife, and go to Shiloh. There, the prophet Ahiyyah is there. It was he who spoke of me that I would be king over this people. ³Take ten loaves of bread in your hand, and some crackers and a jar of syrup, and come to him. It's he who will tell you what will happen to the boy.' ⁴Yarob'am's wife did so. She set off and went to Shiloh and came to the house of Ahiyyah. Ahiyyahu couldn't see, because his eyes had set, through his old age, ⁵but Yahweh himself had said to Ahiyyahu, 'Here, Yarob'am's wife is coming to enquire for a word from you concerning her son, because he's ill. You're to speak such and such things to her. But when she comes she'll be acting like a stranger.'

## Tough prophet, tough message

[6]So when Ahiyyahu heard the sound of her feet as she came through the entrance, he said 'Come in, wife of Yarob'am. Why is it you're acting like a stranger?

I'm sent to you with something tough. [7]Go say to Yarob'am, "Yahweh the God of Yisra'el has said this: 'Since I raised you from among the people and made you chief over my people Yisra'el [8]and tore the kingship from David's household and gave it to you, but you have not been like my servant David who kept my orders and followed me with all his mind by doing only what was upright in my eyes, [9]and you've dealt more badly in what you've done than all who were before you, and gone and made yourself other gods and cast images, so as to provoke me, and me you've thrown behind your back, [10]therefore here I am bringing bad fortune to Yarob'am's household. I shall cut off for Yarob'am the one who pisses against a wall (bound or freed) in Yisra'el. I shall burn away after Yarob'am's household, as one burns away dung, until it's finished. [11]The person who belongs to Yarob'am who dies in the town the dogs will eat; the person who dies in the open country the birds of the heavens will eat. Because Yahweh has spoken.'"

[12]So you, set off, go to your house. When your foot comes to the town, the child will die. [13]All Yisra'el will lament for him and bury him, because this person alone who belongs to Yarob'am will come into a grave since in him something good has been found in relation to Yahweh the God of Yisra'el, in the household of Yarob'am. [14]But Yahweh will set up for himself a king over Yisra'el who will cut off the household of Yarob'am. This is the day, and what even now? [15]Yahweh will strike Yisra'el down as a reed sways in the water and he will uproot Yisra'el from upon this good ground that he gave to their ancestors, and scatter them beyond the River, since they've made their totem poles that provoke Yahweh. [16]He

will give Yisra'el over on account of Yarob'am's wrongdoings that he committed and that he caused Yisra'el to commit.'

[17]Yarob'am's wife set off and went, and came to Tirtsah. She was coming through the threshold of the house as the boy died. [18]They buried him, and all Yisra'el lamented for him in accordance with Yahweh's word which he had spoken by means of his servant Ahiyyahu the prophet.

[19]The rest of the things about Yarob'am, how he did battle and how he reigned: there, they're written on the document about things of the time regarding the kings of Yisra'el. [20]The time that Yarob'am reigned was twenty-two years; then he lay down with his ancestors, and Nadab his son began to reign in place of him.

## In Yehudah: Rehab'am

[21]Rehab'am son of Shelomoh reigned in Yehudah. Rehab'am was a man of forty-one years when he began to reign and he reigned seventeen years in Yerushalaim, the town where Yahweh chose to put his name out of all the clans of Yisra'el. His mother's name was Na'amah the Ammonite. [22]Yehudah did what was bad in Yahweh's eyes and aroused greater passion in him than anything that their ancestors had done by the wrongdoings that they did. [23]They too built for themselves shrines, columns and totem poles on every lofty hill and under every verdant tree. [24]There were also hierodules in the country. They acted in accordance with all the offensive practices of the nations that Yahweh dispossessed before the Yisra'elites.

[25]In the fifth year of King Rehab'am, Shishaq king of Misrayim went up against Yerushalaim [26]and took the treasures of Yahweh's house and the treasures of the king's house. He took everything. He took the gold shields that Shelomoh had made; [27]King Rehab'am made copper shields in place of them and appointed them to the control of the officers in charge of the runners who kept watch over the entrance to the king's house. [28]Whenever the king came to Yahweh's house the runners would carry them, then take them back to the runners' chamber.

[29]The rest of the things about Rehab'am and all that he did are written on the document about things of the time regarding the kings

of Yehudah, aren't they. ³⁰There was battle between Rehab'am and Yarob'am all the time.

## Abiyyam, Asa

³¹Rehab'am lay down with his ancestors and was buried with his ancestors in David's Town. His mother's name was Na'amah the Ammonite. Abiyyam his son began to reign in place of him.

**15** It was in the eighteenth year of King Yarob'am ben Nebat that Abiyyam began to reign over Yehudah. ²He reigned three years in Yerushalaim. His mother's name was Ma'akah bat Abishalom. ³He walked in all the wrongdoings of his father, which he did before him. His mind was not perfect with Yahweh his God like the mind of David his father. ⁴Because it was for David's sake that Yahweh his God gave him hegemony in Yerushalaim by setting up his son after him and by having Yerushalaim stand, ⁵because David did what was upright in Yahweh's eyes and did not turn aside from anything that he ordered him all the days of his life, except in the thing about Uriyyah the Hittite. ⁶There was battle between Rehab'am and Yarob'am all the days of his life.

⁷The rest of the things about Abiyyam and all that he did are written on the document about things of the time regarding the kings of Yehudah, aren't they. There was battle between Abiyyam and Yarob'am. ⁸Abiyyam lay down with his ancestors and they buried him in David's Town. Asa his son began to reign in place of him.

⁹It was in the twentieth year of Yarob'am king of Yisra'el that Asa began to reign as king of Yehudah. ¹⁰He reigned forty-one years in Yerushalaim. His mother's name was Ma'akah bat Abishalom. ¹¹Asa did what was upright in Yahweh's eyes, like David his ancestor. ¹²He put away the hierodules from the country and removed all the idols that his ancestors had made. ¹³In addition, Ma'akah his mother he removed from being queen mother, because she had made a monstrosity for Asherah. Asa cut down her monstrosity and burned it in Wadi Qidron, ¹⁴though the shrines did not disappear. Yet Asa's mind was perfect with Yahweh all his days. ¹⁵He brought into Yahweh's house the sacred things belonging to his father and his own sacred things, silver, gold and articles.

## Asa and Ben-hadad

¹⁶There was battle between Asa and Ba'sha king of Yisra'el all their days. ¹⁷Ba'sha king of Yisra'el went up against Yehudah and built up The Height, so as not to grant Asa king of Yehudah anyone going out or coming in. ¹⁸Asa got all the silver and gold that was left in the treasuries of Yahweh's house and the treasuries of the king's house and gave them into the hand of his servants, and King Asa sent them to Ben-hadad ben-Tabrimmon son of Hezyon king of Aram, who lived in Dammeseq, saying ¹⁹'A pact between me and you, between my father and your father: here, I have sent you a bribe of silver and gold. Go contravene your pact with Ba'sha king of Yisra'el so he may go up from me.'

²⁰Ben-hadad listened to King Asa and sent the officers of the forces that he had against Yisra'el's towns. He struck down Iyyon, Dan, Bet-ma'akah Meadow and all Kinnerot, on top of all the region of Naphtali. ²¹When Ba'sha heard, he left off building up The Height and stayed in Tirtsah, ²²while King Asa got all Yehudah to listen (there was no one free of obligation) and they carried the stones from The Height and its timber with which Ba'sha had built, and with them King Asa built up Geba in Binyamin and The Watchtower.

²³The rest of all the things about Asa, all his strength, all that he did and the towns that he built up, are written on the document about things of the time regarding the kings of Yehudah. Only, at the time when he was old he had an illness in his feet. ²⁴Asa lay down with his ancestors and was buried with his ancestors in David his father's town. Yehoshaphat his son began to reign in place of him.

## In Ephrayim: Nadab, Ba'sha

²⁵Now Nadab ben Yarob'am had become king over Yisra'el in the second year of Asa king of Yehudah. He reigned over Yisra'el two years. ²⁶He did what was bad in Yahweh's eyes; he walked in the way of his father and in his wrongdoing, which he caused Yisra'el to commit. ²⁷Ba'sha ben Ahiyyah, of the household of Yissakar, conspired against him. Ba'sha struck him down at Gibbeton, which

belonged to the Pelishtites, while Nadab and all Yisra'el were besieging Gibbeton. ²⁸Ba'sha put him to death in the third year of Asa king of Yehudah and became king in place of him. ²⁹When he began to reign he struck down Yarob'am's entire household and did not allow anyone breathing to remain to Yarob'am until he had annihilated it, in accordance with Yahweh's word which he spoke by means of his servant Ahiyyah the Shilonite ³⁰because of the wrongs that Yarob'am committed and that he caused Yisra'el to commit, with his provocation that he offered to Yahweh the God of Yisra'el.

³¹The rest of the things about Nadab and all that he did are written on the document about things of the time regarding the kings of Yisra'el, aren't they.

³²There was battle between Asa and Ba'sha king of Yisra'el all their days. ³³It was in the third year of Asa king of Yehudah that Ba'sha ben Ahiyyah began to reign over all Yisra'el in Tirtsah, for twenty-four years. ³⁴He did what was bad in Yahweh's eyes. He walked in the way of Yarob'am and in his wrongdoing that he caused Yisra'el to commit.

**16** Yahweh's word came to Yehu ben Hanani, against Ba'sha: ²'Since I raised you from the ground and made you chief over my people Yisra'el, but you have walked in the way of Yarob'am and caused my people Yisra'el to do wrong, so as to provoke me with their wrongdoings, ³here, I'm going to burn away after Ba'sha and after his household. I shall make your household like the household of Yarob'am ben Nebat. ⁴The person belonging to Ba'sha who dies in the town, the dogs will eat; and the person belonging to him who dies in the open country, the birds of the heavens will eat.'

### The devastating word

⁵The rest of the things about Ba'sha, what he did and his strength, are written on the document about things of the time regarding the kings of Yisra'el, aren't they. ⁶Ba'sha lay down with his ancestors and was buried in Tirtsah, and Elah his son began to reign in place of him. ⁷But by means of Yehu ben Hanani the prophet, Yahweh's word had come regarding Ba'sha and regarding his household

also, because of all that was bad that he did in Yahweh's eyes, so as to provoke him by the action of his hands, in being like Yarob'am's household, and because he had struck it down.

⁸It was in the twenty-sixth year of Asa king of Yehudah that Elah ben Ba'sha began to reign over Yisra'el in Tirtsah, for two years. ⁹His servant Zimri, officer in charge of half the chariotry, conspired against him. When he was in Tirtsah getting drunk in the house of Artsa who was in charge of the household at Tirtsah, ¹⁰Zimri came in, struck him down and put him to death, in the twenty-seventh year of Asa king of Yehudah. He began to reign in place of him, ¹¹and when he began to reign, as soon as he sat on his throne, he struck down Ba'sha's entire household. He did not let anyone who pisses against a wall remain to him, either a restorer of his or a friend of his.

¹²So Zimri annihilated Ba'sha's entire household, in accordance with Yahweh's word that he spoke regarding Ba'sha by means of Yehu the prophet ¹³and regarding all Ba'sha's wrongdoings and Elah his son's wrongdoings that they had committed and that they had caused Yisra'el to commit, so as to provoke Yahweh the God of Yisra'el with their hollow things. ¹⁴The rest of the things about Elah and all that he did are written on the document about things of the time regarding the kings of Yisra'el, aren't they.

### King for a week

¹⁵It was in the twenty-seventh year of Asa king of Yehudah that Zimri reigned seven days in Tirtsah, when the company was encamped at Gibbeton which belonged to the Pelishtites. ¹⁶The company encamped heard, 'Zimri has conspired, and he has actually struck down the king', and all Yisra'el made Omri the army officer king over Yisra'el that day in the camp. ¹⁷Omri went up, and all Yisra'el with him, from Gibbeton, and they besieged Tirtsah. ¹⁸When Zimri saw that the town was taken, he came into the citadel in the king's house and burned the king's house with fire over himself. So he died ¹⁹because of his wrongdoings that he committed by doing what was bad in Yahweh's eyes by walking in the way of Yarob'am, and through his wrongdoing that he committed

by causing Yisra'el to do wrong. <sup>20</sup>The rest of the things about Zimri and his conspiracy which he formed are written on the document about things of the time regarding the kings of Yisra'el, aren't they.

<sup>21</sup>Then the people of Yisra'el split in half. Half the people followed Tibni ben Ginat to make him king, and half followed Omri. <sup>22</sup>The company that followed Omri was stronger than the company of those who followed Tibni ben Ginat, but Tibni died and Omri began to reign.

<sup>23</sup>It was in the thirty-first year of Asa king of Yehudah that Omri began to reign over Yisra'el, for twelve years. In Tirtsah he reigned six years, <sup>24</sup>then he acquired the Shomron Mountain from Shemer for two talents of silver, built up the mountain, and called the town he built by the name of Shemer, the lord of the Shomron Mountain.

<sup>25</sup>Omri did what was bad in Yahweh's eyes; he dealt badly more than all who were before him. <sup>26</sup>He walked in all the way of Yarob'am ben Nebat and in his wrongdoing that he caused Yisra'el to commit so as to provoke Yahweh the God of Yisra'el with their hollow things. <sup>27</sup>The rest of the things about Omri, what he did and his strength that he showed, are written on the document about things regarding the kings of Yisra'el, aren't they.

## Ah'ab and Izebel (Jezebel)

<sup>28</sup>Omri lay down with his ancestors and was buried in Shomron, and Ah'ab his son began to reign in place of him. <sup>29</sup>Ah'ab ben Omri began to reign over Yisra'el in the thirty-eighth year of Asa king of Yehudah. Ah'ab ben Omri reigned over Yisra'el in Shomron twenty-two years. <sup>30</sup>Ah'ab ben Omri did what was bad in Yahweh's eyes, more than all who were before him. <sup>31</sup>Was it a slight thing, his walking in the wrongdoings of Yarob'am ben Nebat, that he took as wife Izebel bat Etba'al, king of the Tsidonites, and went and served the Master? He bowed low to him <sup>32</sup>and set up an altar for the Master at the Master's house which he built in Shomron, <sup>33</sup>and Ah'ab made a totem pole. Ah'ab continued to act so as to provoke Yahweh the God of Yisra'el more than all the kings of Yisra'el who were before him.

<sup>34</sup>In his time Hi'el the Bet Elite built up Yeriho [Jericho]. With Abiram his firstborn he founded it and with Segub his youngest he put up its doors, in accordance with Yahweh's word which he spoke by means of Yehoshua ben Nun.

**17** Eliyyahu [Elijah] the Tishbite from the inhabitants of Gil'ad said to Ah'ab, 'As Yahweh lives, the God of Yisra'el before whom I have stood, if during these years there will be dew or rain except at the bidding of my word . . .'

<sup>2</sup>Yahweh's word came to him: <sup>3</sup>'Go from here. Turn your face east and hide in Wadi Kerit, which faces the Yarden. <sup>4</sup>You will drink from the wadi and I have ordered the ravens to provide for you there.' <sup>5</sup>He went and acted in accordance with Yahweh's word. He went and stayed in Wadi Kerit, which faces the Yarden, <sup>6</sup>while the ravens were bringing him bread and meat in the morning and bread and meat in the evening, and he drank from the wadi.

## The ravens and the widow

<sup>7</sup>After a time the wadi dried up because there was no rain in the country. <sup>8</sup>Yahweh's word came to him: <sup>9</sup>'Set off, go to Tsarephat which belongs to Tsidon and stay there. Here, I have ordered a woman there who is a widow to provide for you.'

<sup>10</sup>He set off and went to Tsarephat, and came to the entrance to the town. There, a woman who was a widow was gathering wood there. He called to her, 'Please get me a little water in a container so I can drink', <sup>11</sup>and she went to get it. He called to her, 'Please get me a bit of bread in your hand.' <sup>12</sup>She said, 'As Yahweh your God lives, if I have anything baked, only a fistful of flour in a jar and a little oil in a jug . . . So here I am, collecting a couple of pieces of wood and I shall come and make it for me and for my son, and we'll eat it and die.' <sup>13</sup>Eliyyahu said to her, 'Don't be afraid. Come, act in accordance with your word, only make me a small loaf from there first and bring it out to me, and make one for you and for your son afterwards. <sup>14</sup>Because Yahweh the God of Yisra'el has said this: "The jar of flour will not be finished and the jug of oil will not lack until the day Yahweh gives rain on the

face of the ground.'" **15**She went and acted in accordance with Eliyyahu's word, and she ate, she and he and her household for some time. **16**The jar of flour was not finished and the jug of oil did not lack, in accordance with Yahweh's word which he spoke by means of Eliyyahu.

## Back from the dead

**17**After these things, the son of the woman who was mistress of the household got ill. His illness grew very severe, until no breath remained in him. **18**She said to Eliyyahu, 'What is between you and me, supernatural man? You've come to me to bring my waywardness to mind and put my son to death.' **19**He said to her, 'Give me your son.' He took him out of her arms and brought him up to the upper floor where he was staying, laid him on his bed **20**and called to Yahweh: 'Yahweh my God, the woman with whom I am residing, are you really going to deal badly with her by putting her son to death?' **21**He measured himself out over the child three times and called to Yahweh, 'Yahweh my God, please may this child's breath come back inside him!' **22**Yahweh listened to the voice of Eliyyahu. The child's breath came back inside him and he came alive. **23**Eliyyahu got the child and took him down from the upper floor into the house, and gave him to his mother. Eliyyahu said, 'Look, your son is alive.' **24**The woman said to Eliyyahu, 'Now I do acknowledge that you are a supernatural man and Yahweh's word in your mouth is truthful.'

**18** After much time, Yahweh's word came to Eliyyahu, in the third year: 'Go appear to Ah'ab, and I will give rain on the face of the ground.' **2**So Eliyyahu went to appear to Ah'ab. Now the famine was severe in Shomron, **3**and Ah'ab had called for Obadyah, who was in charge of the household. Obadyah was someone who lived greatly in awe of Yahweh. **4**When Izebel cut off Yahweh's prophets, Obadyah had got a hundred prophets and hidden them, fifty individuals to a cave, and provided them with bread and water. **5**Ah'ab said to Obadyah, 'Go through the country, to all the water springs and to all the wadis. Perhaps we'll find grass so we can keep horse and mule alive so we don't cut off some of the animals.'

## The man who served God and king

**6**They split the country for themselves so as to pass through it. While Ah'ab went one way alone and Obadyah went the other way alone, **7**and Obadyah was on the way, there, Eliyyahu met him. He recognized him and fell on his face, and said, 'Is this you, my lord Eliyyahu?' **8**He said to him, 'It's me. Go say to your lord, "There's Eliyyahu."' **9**He said, 'What wrong have I done that you're giving your servant into the hand of Ah'ab, to put me to death? **10**As Yahweh your God lives, if there's a nation or kingdom to which my lord has not sent to seek you out . . . They say, "He's not here", and he makes the kingdom or the nation swear that it can't find you. **11**And now you're saying, "Go say to your lord, 'There's Eliyyahu'", **12**and I myself will go from being with you and Yahweh's spirit will carry you to where I don't know, and I'll come to tell Ah'ab and he won't find you and he'll kill me, when your servant has lived in awe of Yahweh from my youth. **13**It's been told my lord, hasn't it, what I did when Izebel killed Yahweh's prophets and I hid a hundred of Yahweh's prophets, fifty individuals to a cave, and fed them bread and water. **14**And now you're saying, "Go say to your lord, 'There's Eliyyahu'", and he'll kill me.' **15**Eliyyahu said, 'As Yahweh of Armies lives, before whom I have stood, I will indeed appear to him today.' **16**So Obadyah went to meet Ah'ab and told him, and Ah'ab went to meet Eliyyahu. **17**When Ah'ab saw Eliyyahu, Ah'ab said to him, 'Is this you, troubler of Yisra'el?' **18**He said, 'I haven't troubled Yisra'el. Rather, you and your father's household have, by abandoning Yahweh's orders and following the Masters. **19**So now, send to gather all Yisra'el to me to Mount Carmel, with the 450 prophets of the Master and the 400 prophets of Asherah who eat at Izebel's table.'

## There are times when you have to choose

**20**So Ah'ab sent among all the Yisra'elites and gathered the prophets to Mount Carmel. **21**Eliyyahu came up to the entire people and said, 'How long are you going to dither between two positions? If Yahweh is God, follow him. If it's the Master, follow him.' The people didn't answer him a word.

²²Then Eliyyahu said to the people, 'I alone am left as a prophet of Yahweh. The Master's prophets are 450 individuals. ²³They're to give us two bulls, and they're to choose one bull for themselves, divide it up and put it on the wood, but not set fire. I shall prepare the other bull and put it on the wood, but not set fire. ²⁴You will call in your god's name; I'll call in Yahweh's name. The God who answers by fire – he is God.' The entire people answered, 'What you say is good.'

²⁵So Eliyyahu said to the Master's prophets, 'Choose one bull for yourselves and prepare it first, because you're the majority. Call on your god's name but don't set fire.' ²⁶They took the bull that someone gave them, prepared it and called on the Master's name from morning until midday, saying 'Master, answer us', but there was no sound, no one answering. They jumped round the altar that people had made.

²⁷At midday Eliyyahu played about with them: 'Call in a loud voice, because he's a god, but it's because he's talking or he's moving or he's on a journey. Perhaps he's asleep and he'll wake up.' ²⁸So they called in a loud voice and slashed themselves in accordance with their ruling with swords and with spears until blood flowed over them. ²⁹After midday passed they prophesied until the time for presenting the offering, but there was no sound, no one answering, no heeding.

## Yahweh, he is God

³⁰Then Eliyyahu said to the entire people, 'Come up to me.' The entire people came up to him and he mended Yahweh's altar that was torn down. ³¹Eliyyahu got twelve stones, in accordance with the number of the twelve clans of the sons of Ya'aqob [Jacob] (to whom Yahweh's word had come, 'Yisra'el will be your name'). ³²He built the stones into an altar in Yahweh's name and made a trench, like a receptacle for a two-measure barrel of seed, round the altar. ³³He laid out the wood and divided the bull and put it on the wood.

³⁴He said, 'Fill four jars with water and pour it over the burnt offering and over the wood.' He said, 'Do it a second time.' They did it a second time. He said, 'Do it a third time.' They did it a third time. ³⁵The water went round the altar and he also filled the trench with water.

³⁶At the time for presenting the offering, Eliyyahu the prophet came up and said, 'Yahweh, God of Abraham, Yitshaq [Isaac] and Yisra'el, today may it be acknowledged that you are God in Yisra'el and that I am your servant, and that by your word I have done all these things. ³⁷Answer me, Yahweh, answer me, so that this people may acknowledge that you Yahweh are God and that you yourself have turned their mind round.'

³⁸Yahweh's fire fell and consumed the burnt offering, the wood, the stones and the earth, and the water that was in the trench it licked up. ³⁹The entire people saw and fell on their faces and said, 'Yahweh, he is God; Yahweh, he is God.' ⁴⁰Eliyyahu said to them, 'Capture the Master's prophets. None of them must escape.' They captured them, and Eliyyahu took them down to Wadi Qishon and slaughtered them there.

## The prophet takes flight

⁴¹Eliyyahu said to Ah'ab, 'Go up, eat and drink, because there's a rumbling sound of rain.' ⁴²Ah'ab went up to eat and to drink, while Eliyyahu went up to the top of Carmel, crouched to the ground and put his face between his knees. ⁴³He said to his boy, 'Please go up and look in the direction of the sea.' He went up and looked and said, 'There isn't anything.' He said 'Go back,' seven times. ⁴⁴On the seventh he said, 'There, a small cloud, like a person's fist, going up from the west.' He said, 'Go up, say to Ah'ab, "Hitch up, and get down, so that the rain won't hold you back."' ⁴⁵Right then, right then, when the heavens grew black with clouds and wind, there was a great downpour.

Ah'ab got into his chariot and went to Yizre'e'l. ⁴⁶Yahweh's hand came on Eliyyahu, he hitched things round his hips, and he ran before Ah'ab as far as when you come to Yizre'e'l.

**19** Ah'ab told Izebel all that Eliyyahu had done and all about how he had killed all the prophets with the sword, ²and Izebel sent an envoy to Eliyyahu saying, 'May the gods do like this and may they do more, because this very time tomorrow I shall make your life like the life of one of them.'

[3]He was afraid, and he set off and went for his life. He came to Be'er Sheba which belongs to Yehudah, left his boy behind there, [4]and he himself went a day's journey into the wilderness. He came and sat under a broom bush and asked for his life, that he might die: 'It's too much. Take my life now, Yahweh, because I'm no better than my ancestors.'

### The low murmuring sound

[5]He lay down and slept under a broom bush. And there, an envoy touching him. He said to him, 'Get up, eat.' [6]He looked, and there, by his head a loaf baked on coals and a jar of water. He ate and drank, and lay down again. [7]Yahweh's envoy came back a second time and touched him and said, 'Get up, eat, because the journey is too much for you.' [8]He got up and ate and drank, and went in the energy of that food for forty days and forty nights as far as God's mountain, Horeb.

[9]He came to a cave there and stayed the night there. And there, Yahweh's word came to him. He said to him, 'What is there for you here, Eliyyahu?' [10]He said, 'I've been very passionate for Yahweh, the God of Armies, because the Yisra'elites have abandoned your pact. Your altars they've torn down; your prophets they've killed with the sword. I alone am left, and they've been seeking my life, to take it.' [11]He said, 'Go out and stand on the mountain before Yahweh.' There was Yahweh passing, and a great, strong wind, splitting mountains and breaking up cliffs before Yahweh (Yahweh was not in the wind), after the wind an earthquake (Yahweh was not in the earthquake), [12]after the earthquake a fire (Yahweh was not in the fire) and after the fire a low murmuring sound.

[13]When Eliyyahu heard it, he wrapped his face in his coat, went out and stood at the cave's entrance. And there, a voice came to him and said, 'What is there for you here, Eliyyahu?' [14]He said, 'I've been very passionate for Yahweh, the God of Armies, because the Yisra'elites have abandoned your pact. Your altars they've torn down, your prophets they've

killed with the sword. I alone am left, and they've been seeking my life, to take it.'

### The chilling commission

[15]Yahweh said to him, 'Go, turn back on your way, to the Dammeseq wilderness. You're to come and anoint Haza'el as king over Aram. [16]And Yehu ben Nimshi you're to anoint as king over Yisra'el, and Elisha ben Shaphat, from Meholah Meadow, you're to anoint as prophet in place of you. [17]The person who escapes from Haza'el's sword, Yehu will put to death. The person who escapes from Yehu's sword, Elisha will put to death. [18]But I will leave in Yisra'el 7,000, all the knees that have not bent down to the Master and every mouth that has not kissed him.'

[19]So he went from there and found Elisha ben Shaphat. He was ploughing with twelve pairs in front of him; he was with the twelfth. Eliyyahu crossed over to him and threw his coat towards him. [20]He abandoned the cattle, ran after Eliyyahu and said, 'I shall kiss my father and my mother, please, and follow you.' He said to him, 'Go, turn back, because what have I done to you?' [21]He went back from following him, took a pair of cattle and sacrificed it. With the cattle's equipment he cooked them (the meat) and gave it to the people, and they ate. Then he set off and followed Eliyyahu, and ministered to him.

**20** Now Ben-hadad king of Aram had collected his entire force, thirty-two kings with him, and horse and chariotry. He went up and besieged Shomron. He did battle against it [2]and sent envoys to the town to Ah'ab king of Yisra'el, [3]and said to him, 'Ben-hadad has said this: "Your silver and your gold are mine; your good wives and children are mine."' [4]The king of Yisra'el answered, 'In accordance with your word, my lord king, I and all that I have are yours.'

### The point to say no

[5]The envoys went back and said, 'Ben-hadad has said this: "When I sent to you saying 'You're to give me your silver and your gold, your wives and your children': [6]rather at this

very time tomorrow I shall send my servants to you and they will search your house and your servants' houses, and everything that's desirable in your eyes they will put into their own hand and take.' "

[7]The king of Yisra'el called for all the country's elders and said, 'Please acknowledge and see how this man is seeking something bad, because he sent to me for my wives and for my children, for my silver and for my gold, and I didn't hold them back from him.' [8]All the elders and the entire people said to him, 'Don't listen. You will not agree.' [9]So he said to Ben-hadad's envoys, 'Say to my lord the king, "Everything about which you sent to your servant at first, I will do, but this thing I cannot do."' The envoys went and took back word. [10]Ben-hadad sent to him: 'May the gods do like this and may they do more if the earth of Shomron suffices for handfuls for the entire company that's behind me.' [11]The king of Yisra'el answered, 'Speak: "The one who buckles on should not take pride like the one who loosens."'

[12]When he heard this word (he was drinking, he and the kings, at Sukkot), he said to his servants, 'Get set', and they got set against the town'. [13]But there, a prophet came up to Ah'ab king of Yisra'el and said, 'Yahweh has said this: "You've seen all of this big horde? Here, I'm giving it into your hand today, and you will acknowledge that I am Yahweh."' [14]Ah'ab said, 'Through whom?' He said, 'Yahweh has said this: "Through the provincial officials' boys".' He said, 'Who will hitch up for the battle?' He said, 'You.'

## The boys lead the way to victory

[15]So he registered the provincial officers' boys (they were 232) and after them registered the entire company, all the Yisra'elites (7,000), [16]and they went out at midday. Ben-hadad was getting drunk at Sukkot, he and the thirty-two kings helping him. [17]The provincial officials' boys went out first. Ben-hadad sent, and they told him, 'Some men have gone out from Shomron.' [18]He said, 'If they've gone out for peace, capture them alive – and if they've gone out for battle, capture them alive.' [19]But these men went out from the town, the provincial officials' boys with the force that was behind

them, [20]and they struck down each his man. So the Aramites fled, and the Yisra'elites pursued them. Ben-hadad king of Aram escaped on a horse, with cavalry.

[21]The king of Yisra'el went out and struck down the horse and the chariotry. He struck the Aramites down in a great rout. [22]But the prophet came up to the king of Yisra'el and said to him, 'Go, assert your strength, acknowledge and see what you're to do, because at the turn of the year the king of Aram is going to go up against you.'

[23]Now the king of Aram's servants said to him, 'Their God is a mountain God. That's why they were stronger than us. However, we should do battle with them in the flatland. If we will not be stronger than them . . .

[24]This is the thing you should do. Remove the kings, each from his place, and put governors in their places. [25]You should count for yourself a force like the force that fell away from being with you, horse for horse, chariot for chariot, so we can battle with them in the flatland, if we will not be stronger than them . . .'

He listened to their voice and did so.

## Ben-hadad tries again

[26]At the turn of the year Ben-hadad registered the Aramites and went up to Apheq for battle with Yisra'el. [27]When the Yisra'elites had been registered and provided for, they went to meet them. The Yisra'elites camped opposite them like two bare flocks of goats, while the Aramites filled the region. [28]A supernatural man came up and said to the king of Yisra'el, 'Yahweh has said this: "Since the Aramites have said, 'Yahweh is a mountain God, he's not a vale God', I shall give all of this big horde into your hand, and you will acknowledge that I am Yahweh."'

[29]One side camped opposite the other side for seven days. On the seventh day the battle began, and the Yisra'elites struck down the Aramites, 100,000 men on foot on one day. [30]The ones who were left fled to Apheq, into the town, but the wall fell on the 27,000 men who were left.

Now Ben-hadad had fled and come into the town, to an inner room. [31]His servants said to him, 'Here, please, we've heard that the kings of the household of Yisra'el – that they are kings

who show commitment. Please let's put sack on
our hips and ropes on our head and go out to
the king of Yisra'el. Perhaps he will let you live.'
³²So they wrapped sack on their hips and
ropes on their heads, came to the king of
Yisra'el and said, 'Your servant Ben-hadad has
said, "Please let me live."' He said, 'Is he still
alive? He's my brother.' ³³Now the men could
divine and they speedily caught it from him,
and said, 'Ben-hadad is your brother.' He said,
'Go on, get him.'

## A prophet puts on a disguise

Ben-hadad went out to him and he got him
up into the chariot. ³⁴He said to him, 'The
towns that my father got from your father, I'll
give back, and you may put street markets for
yourself in Dammeseq as my father put them
in Shomron.'
[Ahab said,] 'And I myself in pact will send
you off.' He solemnized a pact towards him and
sent him off.
³⁵Now a certain man from among the people
who prophesied said to his neighbour, 'By
Yahweh's word, please strike me down.' But the
man refused to strike him down. ³⁶He said to
him, 'Since you haven't listened to Yahweh's
voice, there, you will be going from being with
me and a lion will strike you down.' He went
from beside him and a lion found him and
struck him down.
³⁷He found another man and said, 'Please
strike me down', and the man struck him down
and wounded him. ³⁸Then the prophet went and
stood for the king by the road and disguised
himself with a bandage over his eyes. ³⁹As the
king was passing, he cried out to the king, 'Your
servant went out in the middle of the battle and
there, a man turned aside and brought a man to
me and said, "Keep watch over this man! If he's
actually counted missing, it will be your life in
place of his life, or you'll weigh out a talent of
silver." ⁴⁰But your servant was doing things here
and there and he – he wasn't there.' The king
of Yisra'el said to him, 'Thus you yourself have
determined the decision about you.'
⁴¹He speedily removed the bandage from
on his eyes and the king of Yisra'el recognized
him, that he was one of the prophets. ⁴²He said
to him, 'Yahweh has said this: "Since you sent

off from your hand the man who was to be
devoted to me, it will be your life in place of
his life and your people in place of his people."'
⁴³The king of Yisra'el went to his house ill-
disposed and vexed, and came to Shomron.

## Nabot and the family land

**21** After these things, as Nabot the
Yizre'e'lite had a vineyard that was
in Yizre'e'l beside the palace of Ah'ab king of
Shomron, ²Ah'ab spoke to Nabot: 'Give me
your vineyard so it can be a vegetable garden
for me, because it's right beside my house. In
place of it I'll give you a better vineyard than
it. If it's good in your eyes, I'll give you silver as
the price for this one.' ³But Nabot said to Ah'ab,
'Far be it from me by Yahweh that I give you
my ancestors' domain.'
⁴Ah'ab came to his house ill-disposed and
vexed because of the word that Nabot the
Yizre'e'lite had spoken to him when he said 'I
won't give you my ancestors' domain.' He lay on
his bed and turned his face round, and didn't eat
bread. ⁵Izebel his wife came to him and spoke
to him: 'Why is it that your spirit's ill-disposed
and you're not eating bread?' ⁶He spoke to her:
'I spoke to Nabot the Yizre'e'lite and said to
him, "Give me your vineyard for silver, or if you
want I'll give you a vineyard in place of it", but
he said, "I won't give you my vineyard."' ⁷Izebel
his wife said to him, 'You should now exercise
kingship over Yisra'el. Get up, eat bread so you
may be in good heart. I myself will give you the
vineyard of Nabot the Yizre'e'lite.'
⁸She wrote documents in Ah'ab's name,
sealed them with his seal, and sent the
documents to the elders and to the important
people who were living in the town with
Nabot. ⁹She wrote in the documents: 'Call a
fast and sit Nabot at the head of the people,
¹⁰and sit two scoundrels in front of him. They
are to testify against him: "You have 'blessed'
God and the king", and take him out and stone
him so that he dies.'

## The capital of corruption

¹¹The men of the town, the elders and the
important people who were living in his town,

did as Izebel sent to them, as was written in the documents that she sent to them. ¹²They called a fast and sat Nabot at the head of the people. ¹³The two scoundrels came and sat in front of him. The two scoundrels testified against Nabot in front of the people, 'Nabot "blessed" God and the king', and they took him outside the town and pelted him with stones, and he died.

¹⁴They sent to Izebel: 'Nabot has been stoned. He has died.' ¹⁵When Izebel heard that Nabot had been stoned and had died, Izebel said to Ah'ab, 'Set off, take possession of the vineyard of Nabot the Yizre'e'lite, which he refused to give you for silver, because Nabot is not alive. Rather he's dead.' ¹⁶When Ah'ab heard that Nabot was dead, Ah'ab set off to go down to the vineyard of Nabot the Yizre'e'lite to take possession of it.

¹⁷But Yahweh's word came to Eliyyahu the Tishbite: ¹⁸'Set off, go down to meet Ah'ab king of Yisra'el who is in Shomron: there, in Nabot's vineyard, where he's gone down to take possession of it. ¹⁹You're to speak to him: "Yahweh has said this: 'Have you murdered and also taken possession?'" You're to speak to him: "Yahweh has said this: 'In the place where dogs lapped up Nabot's blood, dogs will lap up your blood, yours too.'"'

## The dogs will eat Izebel

²⁰Ah'ab said to Eliyyahu, 'Have you found me, my enemy?' He said, 'I've found you, since you sold yourself to do what is bad in Yahweh's eyes. ²¹"Here am I: I'm going to deal badly with you. I'm going to burn away after you and cut off for Ah'ab the one who pisses against a wall (bound or freed) in Yisra'el. ²²I will make your household like the household of Yarob'am ben Nebat and like the household of Ba'sha ben Ahiyyah, for the provocation that you have offered, and you caused Yisra'el to do wrong."

²³Yahweh has also spoken about Izebel: "The dogs will eat Izebel on the rampart of Yizre'e'l. ²⁴The person who belongs to Ah'ab who dies in the town the dogs will eat; the person who dies in the open country the birds of the heavens will eat.'" (²⁵Indeed there was no one like Ah'ab who sold himself to do what was bad in Yahweh's eyes, whom Izebel his wife incited.

²⁶He acted most offensively in following idols, in accordance with everything that the Amorites did, whom Yahweh dispossessed from before the Yisra'elites.)

²⁷When Ah'ab heard these words, he tore his clothes and put sack on his body, and fasted. He lay down in sack and went about quietly. ²⁸And Yahweh's word came to Eliyyahu the Tishbite: ²⁹'Have you seen that Ah'ab has bowed down before me? Since he has bowed down before me, I will not bring the bad fortune in his days. In the days of his son I will bring the bad fortune on his household.'

## The prophet with ten horns

**22** They stayed three years while there was no battle between Aram and Yisra'el. ²In the third year Yehoshaphat king of Yehudah went down to the king of Yisra'el. ³The king of Yisra'el had said to his servants, 'Do you acknowledge that Heights-in-Gil'ad belongs to us but we are sitting still instead of taking it from the hand of the king of Aram?' ⁴So he said to Yehoshaphat, 'Will you go with me for battle at Heights-in-Gil'ad?' Yehoshaphat said to the king of Yisra'el, 'I'll be the same as you, my company the same as your company, my horses the same as your horses.' ⁵But Yehoshaphat said to the king of Yisra'el, 'Please enquire for Yahweh's word today.'

⁶So the king of Yisra'el collected the prophets, some 400 individuals, and said to them, 'Shall I go up against Heights-in-Gil'ad for the battle, or leave off?' They said, 'Go up, and the Lord will give it into the king's hand.' ⁷But Yehoshaphat said, 'Is there no further prophet of Yahweh here, so we can enquire of him?' ⁸The king of Yisra'el said to Yehoshaphat, 'There's one further individual to enquire of Yahweh from, but I myself dislike him because he doesn't prophesy good for me, but bad: Mikayehu ben Yimlah.' Yehoshaphat said, 'The king shouldn't say that.' ⁹So the king of Yisra'el called to a courtier and said, 'Do hurry Mikayehu ben Imlah.'

¹⁰As the king of Yisra'el and Yehoshaphat king of Yehudah were sitting, each on his throne, dressed in robes, at the threshing floor at the entrance to the gateway at Shomron, and all the prophets were prophesying before them,

[11]Tsidqiyyah ben Kena'anah had made himself iron horns, and he said, 'Yahweh has said this: "With these you will gore the Aramites until you have finished them off."' [12]All the prophets were prophesying in this way: 'Go up to Heights-in-Gil'ad and succeed. Yahweh will give it into the king's hand.'

[13]Now the envoy who went to call for Mikayehu spoke to him: 'Here, please, the prophets' words are good for the king as one bidding. Your word should please be like the word of one of them. You should speak of something good.' [14]Mikayehu said, 'As Yahweh lives, what Yahweh says to me – I will speak it.'

## Who will entice Ah'ab?

[15]He came to the king and the king said to him, 'Mikayehu, shall we go up to Heights-in-Gil'ad for battle, or shall we leave off?' He said to him, 'Go up and succeed. Yahweh will give it into the king's hand.' [16]The king said to him, 'How many times am I going to get you to swear that you won't speak to me anything but truth in Yahweh's name?'

[17]So he said, 'I saw all Yisra'el scattering towards the mountains like a flock that have no shepherd. Yahweh said, "These people have no lords. They should go back, each to his house, with things being well."' [18]The king of Yisra'el said to Yehoshaphat, 'I said to you, "He won't prophesy good fortune for me, but only bad", didn't I.'

[19]He said, 'Therefore listen to Yahweh's word. I saw Yahweh sitting on his throne, with the entire heavenly army standing by him on his right and on his left. [20]Yahweh said, "Who will entice Ah'ab so he'll go up but fall at Heights-in-Gil'ad?" One said "In this way" and another said "In this way". [21]Then a spirit went out and stood before Yahweh and said, "I'm the one who'll entice him." Yahweh said to him, "How?" [22]He said, "I'll go out and become a false spirit in the mouth of all his prophets." He said, "You're to entice. Yes, you'll be able to. Go out and do it." [23]So now, there, Yahweh put a spirit of falsehood in the mouth of all these prophets, in that Yahweh has spoken of something bad for you.'

[24]Tsidqiyyahu ben Kena'anah went up and struck Mikayehu on the jaw, and said, 'Which way did Yahweh's spirit pass from being with me to speak with you?' [25]Mikayehu said, 'There, you're going to see, on that day when you come to an innermost room to hide.'

## You can disguise but you can't hide

[26]The king of Yisra'el said, 'Get Mikayehu and take him back to Amon the town official and to Yo'ash the king's son, [27]and say "The king has said this: 'Put this man in the cells and give him slave bread and slave water until I come with things being well.'"' [28]Mikayehu said, 'If you really do come back with things being well, Yahweh did not speak through me.' (And he said, 'Listen, you peoples, all of them.')

[29]So the king of Yisra'el went up with Yehoshaphat king of Yehudah to Heights-in-Gil'ad. [30]The king of Yisra'el said to Yehoshaphat, 'I'm putting on disguise and coming into battle, but you, dress in your robes.' So the king of Yisra'el put on disguise and came into battle.

[31]Now the king of Aram had ordered the thirty-two chariot officers that he had, 'You will not battle anyone small or great except the king of Yisra'el alone.' [32]When the chariot officers saw Yehoshaphat and said, 'Yes, he's the king of Yisra'el', they turned aside to him to do battle. But Yehoshaphat cried out, [33]and when the chariot officers saw that he was not the king of Yisra'el, they turned back from following him. [34]But a man drew his bow innocently, and struck the king of Yisra'el between the links and the armour. He said to his charioteer, 'Turn your hand, get me out from the camp, because I'm wounded.'

[35]The battle mounted that day, while the king was kept standing in his chariot opposite the Aramites. But he died in the evening. The blood from the wound poured down into the base of the chariot. [36]A shout passed through the camp as the sun set: 'Each man to his town, each man to his land.'

[37]So the king died and came to Shomron, and they buried the king in Shomron. [38]They washed off the chariot by the pool in Shomron, and the dogs licked up his blood as the prostitutes bathed, in accordance with the word of Yahweh that he had spoken.

*The fleet that sank*

[39] The rest of the things about Ah'ab, all that he did, the ivory house that he built and all the towns that he built up, are written on the document about things of the time regarding the kings of Yisra'el, aren't they. [40] Ah'ab lay down with his ancestors, and Ahazyahu, his son, began to reign in place of him.

[41] Yehoshaphat ben Asa had become king over Yehudah in the fourth year of Ah'ab king of Yisra'el. [42] Yehoshaphat was a man of thirty-five years when he began to reign and he reigned in Yerushalaim twenty-five years. His mother's name was Azubah bat Shilhi. [43] He walked in all the way of Asa his father. He did not turn aside from it, in doing what was upright in Yahweh's eyes. Yet the shrines did not disappear; the people were still sacrificing and burning incense at the shrines. [44] Yehoshaphat made peace with the king of Yisra'el. [45] The rest of the things about Yehoshaphat, and his strength with which he acted and with which he battled, are written on the document about things of the time regarding the kings of Yehudah, aren't they. [46] The rest of the hierodules who were left in the time of Asa his father he burned away from the country.

[47] There being no king in Edom, a prefect was king, [48] and Yehoshaphat made Tarshish ships to go to Ophir for gold, but he didn't go because the ships broke up at Etsyon Geber. [49] It was then that Ahazyahu ben Ah'ab said to Yehoshaphat, 'My servants should go on the ships with your servants', but Yehoshaphat was not willing.

[50] Yehoshaphat lay down with his ancestors and was buried with his ancestors in David his ancestor's town, and Yehoram his son began to reign in place of him.

[51] Now Ahazyahu ben Ah'ab had become king over Yisra'el in Shomron in the seventeenth year of Yehoshaphat king of Yehudah. He reigned over Yisra'el two years. [52] He did what was bad in Yahweh's eyes; he walked in the way of his father and in the way of his mother, and in the way of Yarob'am ben Nebat, who had caused Yisra'el to do wrong. [53] He served the Master and bowed low to him, and provoked Yahweh the God of Yisra'el in accordance with all that his father did.

# 2 KINGS

The division of the books of Kings into two is arbitrary; the narrative continues seamlessly. The first two thirds of 2 Kings continue the interwoven account of Israel and Judah, with the involvement of prophets such as Elijah and Elisha. While the background of the book's opening chapters is tension between Israel (and Judah) and Syria (Aram), on the horizon is the bigger power of Assyria, the first great Middle Eastern empire to have an impact on Israel and Judah. The middle of the book relates how the Assyrians invade Israel and attempt to require them to function as Assyria's underlings, but Israel resists and in due course the Assyrians invade again, conquer the Israelite capital, Samaria, transport its people and replace them with people from other parts of their empire. Subsequently, the Assyrians did take action to enable these immigrants to know how they should properly worship Yahweh in this land of his, and in some respects they do, but many people continue to worship the gods they had followed in the countries they came from. The aftermath of this forced migration forms background to relations between Judah and Samaria about which we read in Ezra.

The second book of Kings pauses at this point to explain what has happened, not politically but religiously (see 2 Kings 17). The fall of Samaria happened because of its people's false worship of Yahweh and its worship of other deities, its resistance to its prophets, to its covenant and to the rules of that covenant, and its practices such as human sacrifice. The interwovenness of the political and the religious in the story supports the suggestion that one of the key themes in 2 Kings is the interwovennness of divine sovereignty and human sovereignty in politics. Sometimes human leaders do things they wish to do, and it can form part of positive things God wishes to achieve. Sometimes human leaders do things they want to do, and it can form part of negative things God wishes to do. Sometimes human leaders do things they want to do, and it works against God's purpose, and he then frustrates their aims.

The last part of 2 Kings tells more briefly the less complicated story of the last generations of Judah when it has become the rump embodiment of Israel. The story begins with the great King Hezekiah. He also experiences invasion by Assyria, but he is faithful to Yahweh and he has on his side the temple in Jerusalem and the promise to David, not to say the prophet Isaiah. The Assyrians wreak havoc in Judah but fail to take Jerusalem, which constitutes Yahweh's great act of deliverance.

Sadly, Hezekiah's son is the renegade Manasseh, who experiences more Assyrian pressure, adopts much of northern Israel's apostate ways, but reigns much longer than he therefore should. His grandson Josiah is both motivated and politically able to revert to Hezekiah's commitments. In the course of cleaning up the temple, his envoys discover a scroll of Moses' Torah there which causes panic when people read of the consequences that follow practices like the ones Manasseh sponsored. The discovery thereby encourages further reform. Overlaps with what Josiah does suggest that the Torah scroll may have been a version of what we call Deuteronomy.

Alas, it seems that the policies Manassah implemented are too deeply ingrained to be eliminated, and after Josiah's untimely death things revert to the way they were, which results in Jerusalem and Judah going through the same experience that northern Israel and Samaria had had. The account of the fall of Jerusalem and associated events has a pained atmosphere that conveys something of the grief of the people who went through the experience.

The book of 2 Kings comprises the last part the gargantuan work that began in Genesis and it takes the story down to the time of the people who will have heard the story read when it was first compiled. It thus helps them understand who they are and how they need to look at themselves. As is often the case with stories or histories, reading it from the end is illuminating.

One of the factors that has influenced God in keeping the state of Judah in being is the promise he had made that he would never let David's line of kings disappear, and the last event related by 2 Kings is the release of a deposed and exiled king of Judah. It is a hint that God has indeed not abandoned his promises.

## The lord of the flies

**1** Mo'ab rebelled against Yisra'el [Israel] after Ah'ab's death.

[2] Ahazyah fell through the lattice in his upper quarters, which were in Shomron [Samaria], and he was ill. He sent envoys and said to them, 'Go enquire of the Fly Master, the god of Eqron, whether I will live on after this illness.' [3] But Yahweh's envoy – he spoke to Eliyyahu [Elijah] the Tishbite: 'Set off, go up to meet the king of Shomron's envoys and speak to them: "Is it for lack of a God in Yisra'el that you're going to enquire of the Fly Master, the god of Eqron? [4] So, therefore, Yahweh has said this: 'The bed that you have climbed into, you won't get down from, because you will actually die.'"' And Eliyyahu went.

[5] The envoys went back to him, and he said to them, 'Why is it that you've come back?' [6] They said to him, 'There was a man came up to meet us and he said to us, "Go, turn back to the king who sent you, and speak to him: 'Yahweh has said this: "Is it for lack of a God in Yisra'el that you are sending to enquire of the Fly Master, the god of Eqron? Therefore the bed that you have climbed into, you won't get down from, because you will actually die."'"' [7] He spoke to them, 'What was the manner of the man who came up to meet you and spoke these words to you?' [8] They said to him, 'A man with lots of hair and a leather wrap belted round his hips.' He said, 'It was Eliyyahu the Tishbite.'

[9] He sent to him an officer over fifty and his fifty men, and he went up to him. There, he was sitting on the top of a mountain. He spoke to him: 'Supernatural man, the king himself has spoken: come down.' [10] Eliyyahu answered the officer over fifty, 'If I'm a supernatural man, may fire come down from the heavens and consume you and your fifty men!' And fire came down from the heavens and consumed him and his fifty men.

## Fire from the heavens again

[11] He again sent to him another officer over 50 and his 50 men. He went up and spoke to him, 'Supernatural man, the king himself has said this: "Come down speedily!"' [12] Eliyyahu answered them, 'If I'm a supernatural man,

may fire come down from the heavens and consume you and your 50 men!' And supernatural fire came down from the heavens and consumed him and his 50 men.

[13] He again sent a third officer over 50 and his 50 men. The third officer over 50 went up, and came and bent down on his knees in front of Eliyyahu and asked him for grace. He spoke to him: 'Supernatural man, please may my life and the life of these 50 servants of yours be valuable in your eyes! [14] Here, fire fell from the heavens and consumed the previous two officers over 50 and their 50 men. But now, may my life be valuable in your eyes.'

[15] Yahweh's envoy spoke to Eliyyahu: 'Go down with him. Don't be afraid of him.' So he set off and went down with him to the king, [16] and spoke to him: 'Yahweh has said this: "Since you sent envoys to enquire of the Fly Master, the god of Eqron: is it for lack of a God in Yisra'el to enquire of his word? Therefore the bed that you have climbed into, you will not get down from, because you will actually die."'

[17] He died in accordance with Yahweh's word which Eliyyahu spoke. Yehoram began to reign in place of him, in the second year of Yehoram ben Yehoshaphat king of Yehudah [Judah], because he had no son. [18] The rest of the things about Ahazyahu, what he did, are written on the document about things of the time regarding the kings of Yisra'el, aren't they.

## Eliyyahu's cloak

**2** When Yahweh took Eliyyahu up to the heavens in a hurricane, Eliyyahu had gone with Elisha from Gilgal. [2] Eliyyahu said to Elisha, 'Stay here, please, because Yahweh has sent me as far as Bet-el.' Elisha said, 'As Yahweh lives and as you yourself live, if I abandon you . . .' So they went down to Bet-el. [3] The people who prophesied who were at Bet-el went out to Elisha and said to him, 'Do you know that today Yahweh is going to take your lord from being your head?' He said, 'Yes, I myself know. Be quiet.'

[4] Eliyyahu said to him, 'Elisha, stay here, please, because Yahweh has sent me to Yeriho [Jericho].' He said, 'As Yahweh lives and as you yourself live, if I abandon you . . .' So they came

to Yeriho. ⁵The people who prophesied who were at Yeriho went up to Elisha and said to him, 'Do you know that today Yahweh is going to take your lord from being your head?' He said, 'Yes, I myself know. Be quiet.'

⁶Eliyyahu said to him, 'Stay here, please, because Yahweh has sent me to the Yarden [Jordan].' He said, 'As Yahweh lives and as you yourself live, if I abandon you . . .' So the two of them went, ⁷while fifty men from among the people who prophesied went and stood at a distance, far off, and the two of them stood at the Yarden.

⁸Eliyyahu got his cape, rolled it up and struck the water. It divided in both directions and the two of them crossed on dry ground.

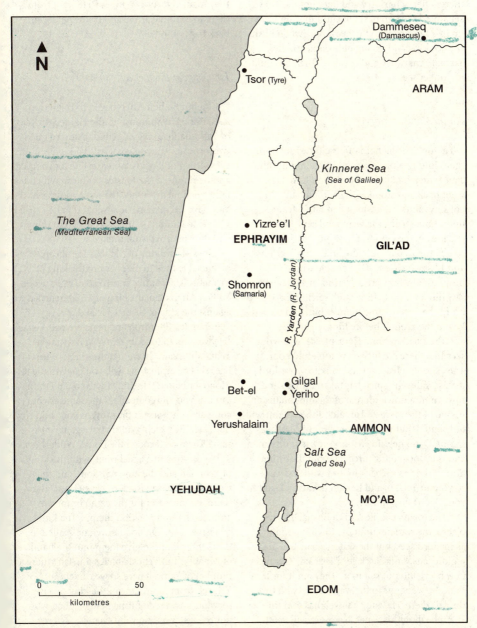

*2 Kings 2: Eliyyahu (Elijah) and Elisha*

⁹As they crossed, Eliyyahu said to Elisha, 'Ask what I should do for you before I'm taken from being with you.' Elisha said, 'A double share in your spirit should please come to me.' ¹⁰He said, 'You've been tough in asking. If you see me taken from being with you, so it will happen for you. If not, it won't happen.'

¹¹As they were continuing to walk and speak, there – fiery chariotry and fiery horses. They separated the two of them and Eliyyahu went up in a hurricane to the heavens, ¹²while Elisha was looking and crying out, 'Father, father, Yisra'el's chariotry and cavalry!' Then he could no longer see.

### No more miscarriage

He took strong hold of his clothes and tore them into two pieces, ¹³and lifted up Eliyyahu's cape which had fallen from upon him. He went back and stood at the Yarden bank. ¹⁴He got Eliyyahu's cape which had fallen from upon him, struck the water and said, 'Where is Yahweh, the God of Eliyyahu? Yes, him?' He struck the water, it divided in both directions and Elisha crossed. ¹⁵The people who prophesied who were at Yeriho, at a distance, saw him and said, 'Eliyyahu's spirit has alighted on Elisha!' They came to meet him and bowed low to the ground before him.

¹⁶They said to him, 'Here, please, with your servants there are fifty men, forceful people. They should please go and look for your lord in case Yahweh's spirit has taken him up and thrown him down on one of the mountains or in one of the ravines.' He said to them, 'You will not send.' ¹⁷But they pressed him until he was shamed, and he said, 'Send.' They sent fifty men and they looked for three days but didn't find him. ¹⁸They came back to him while he was staying in Yeriho, and he said to them, 'I said to you, "Don't go", didn't I.'

¹⁹The town's people said to Elisha, 'Here, please, the settlement in the town is good, as my lord sees, but the water is bad and the region causes miscarriage.' ²⁰He said, 'Get me a new bowl and put salt in it.' They got it for him ²¹and he went out to the water outlet and threw the salt there. He said, 'Yahweh has said this: "I am healing this water. No more will death and miscarriage come from there."' ²²The water

became healthy, until this day, in accordance with the word of Elisha which he spoke.

²³He went up from there to Bet-el. He was going up the road and small boys came out of the town and mocked him: 'Go up, baldy, go up, baldy!' ²⁴He turned his face behind him and saw them and slighted them in Yahweh's name, and two bears came out of the forest. Of them they mauled forty-two boys. ²⁵He went from there to Mount Carmel and from there went back to Shomron.

### Isn't there a prophet we can ask?

3 Yehoram ben Ah'ab began to reign over Yisra'el in Shomron in the eighteenth year of Yehoshaphat king of Yehudah and reigned twelve years. ²He did what was bad in Yahweh's eyes, only not like his father or like his mother, and he removed the Master's column which his father had made. ³Only, the wrongdoings of Yarob'am [Jeroboam] ben Nebat that he caused Yisra'el to commit – he was attached to them and didn't depart from them.

⁴Now Mesha king of Mo'ab was a sheep breeder. He used to give back to the king of Yisra'el 100,000 lambs and 100,000 rams' wool. ⁵When Ah'ab died, the king of Mo'ab rebelled against the king of Yisra'el. ⁶That day King Yehoram left Shomron and registered all Yisra'el. ⁷He went on to send to Yehoshaphat king of Yehudah to say, 'Given that the king of Mo'ab has rebelled against me, will you go with me to Mo'ab for battle?' He said, 'I will go up; I'm the same as you, my company is the same as your company, my horse is the same as your horse.' ⁸He said, 'By which road shall we go up?' He said, 'The road through the Edom Wilderness.'

⁹So the king of Yisra'el went, with the king of Yehudah and the king of Edom, and they went round on the road for seven days. Then there was no water for the camp or for the animals that were behind them. ¹⁰The king of Yisra'el said, 'Oh no! Yahweh has called for these three kings to give them into the hand of Mo'ab!' ¹¹But Yehoshaphat said, 'Isn't there a prophet of Yahweh here so we can enquire of Yahweh from him?' One of the king of Yisra'el's servants answered, 'Elisha ben Shaphat, who poured water on Eliyyahu's hands, is here.' ¹²Yehoshaphat said, 'Yahweh's word is with

him.' So the king of Yisra'el and Yehoshaphat and the king of Edom went down to him,

## The water that looked like blood

¹³Elisha said to the king of Yisra'el, 'What do you and I have in common? Go to your father's prophets and to your mother's prophets.' The king of Yisra'el said to him, 'No, because Yahweh has called for these three kings to give them into the hand of Mo'ab.' ¹⁴Elisha said, 'As Yahweh of Armies lives, before whom I stand, if I did not have regard for Yehoshaphat king of Yehudah, I would not look to you or see you. ¹⁵But now, get me a musician' (when the musician played, Yahweh's hand would come on him).

¹⁶Then he said, 'Yahweh has said this: "This wadi is going to make pools, pools." ¹⁷Because Yahweh has said this: "You will not see wind, you will not see rain, but that wadi – it will fill with water. Both you and your cattle and your livestock will drink." ¹⁸This is a slight thing in Yahweh's eyes: and he will give the Mo'abites into your hand. ¹⁹You will strike down every fortified town and every choice town. Every good tree you will fell, all springs of water you will stop up and every good plot you will make suffer with stones.' ²⁰And in the morning at the time for making the offering – there, water was coming from the direction of Edom. The region filled with water.

²¹Now all the Mo'abites had heard that the kings had gone up to battle against them. They had themselves called out, from everyone who could fasten a belt and upwards, and they stood at the border. ²²In the morning they started early, and when the sun rose over the water, from a distance the Mo'abites saw the water red like blood. ²³They said, 'This is blood! The kings have actually been put to the sword. Each man has struck down his neighbour. Now, to the plunder, Mo'abites!' ²⁴They came to the Yisra'elite camp, but the Yisra'elites set to and struck down the Mo'abites, and they fled from before them.

## An ultimate sacrifice

So they came into it and struck down Mo'ab. ²⁵The towns they tore down, on every good plot they threw each man his stone and covered it, every water spring they stopped up and every good tree they would fell, until what was left remaining in Qir Hareset was its stones. The slingers surrounded it and struck it down.

²⁶The king of Mo'ab saw that the battle was too hard for him and he got with him 700 men drawing a sword to break through to the king of Edom, but they couldn't. ²⁷So he got his eldest son who was to reign in place of him, and offered him up as a burnt offering on the wall. A great fury came on Yisra'el, and they moved on from there and went back to the land.

**4** Now a woman, one of the wives of the people who prophesied, cried out to Elisha, 'Your servant, my husband, is dead, and you yourself acknowledge that your servant was someone who has lived in awe of Yahweh, and a creditor is coming to take my two children for himself as servants.' ²Elisha said to her, 'What am I to do for you? Tell me what you have in the house.' She said, 'Your maidservant has nothing at all in the house except a jug of oil.' ³He said, 'Go and ask for containers for yourself from outside, from all the people who live near you, empty containers. Don't make it a few. ⁴Come in, shut the door behind you and behind your sons, and pour into all these containers. The full one, remove.'

⁵She went from being with him and shut the door behind her and behind her sons. People were bringing them up to her and she was pouring. ⁶When the containers were full, she said to her son, 'Bring up another container to me', but he said to her, 'There isn't another container'; and the oil halted. ⁷She came and told the supernatural man. He said, 'Go sell the oil and make good your debt, and you and your children can live on what's left.'

## The woman who had almost everything

⁸One day Elisha passed through to Shunem. A big woman was there and she took strong hold of him so he would eat bread. Whenever he passed through, he would turn aside there to eat bread. ⁹She said to her husband, 'Here, please, I know that it's a sacred supernatural man who passes by us regularly. ¹⁰Please let's make a little upstairs room with a wall and put a bed for him there and a table and a chair

and a lamp. When he comes to us he can turn aside there.'

¹¹One day he came there and turned aside to the upstairs room and lay down there, ¹²and said to Gehazi, his boy, 'Call this Shunammite woman.' He called her and she stood before him. ¹³He said to him, 'Please say to her, "Here, you've acted towards us with all this concern. What is there to do for you? Is there something to speak to the king for you, or to the army officer?"' She said, 'I'm living among my own people.' ¹⁴He said, 'So what is there to do for her?' Gehazi said, 'Well, she doesn't have a son, and her husband is old.' ¹⁵He said, 'Call her.' He called her and she stood in the entrance. ¹⁶He said, 'At this season, at [nature's] reviving time, you're going to embrace a son.' She said, 'Don't, my lord, supernatural man, don't lie to your maidservant.' ¹⁷But the woman got pregnant and gave birth to a son at this season at reviving time, as Elisha spoke to her.

¹⁸The child grew up, but one day he went out to his father, to the reapers, ¹⁹and he said to his father, 'My head, my head!' He said to a boy, 'Carry him to his mother.' ²⁰He carried him and brought him to his mother, and he sat on her knees until noon, and died. ²¹She took him up, laid him down on the supernatural man's bed, closed up behind him and went out.

## Did I ask for a son?

²²She called her husband and said, 'Please send me one of the boys and one of the she-donkeys so I can run to the supernatural man, and come back.' ²³He said, 'Why are you going to him today? It's not new month or sabbath.' She said, 'Things will be well.' ²⁴She saddled the donkey and said to her boy, 'Drive, go, don't hold back from riding unless I say it to you.'

²⁵So she went, and came to the supernatural man at Mount Carmel. When the supernatural man saw her from a distance, he said to Gehazi his boy, 'There's that Shunammite woman. ²⁶Now please run to meet her and say to her, "Are things well with you? Are things well with your husband? Are things well with the child?"' She said, 'Things are well.' ²⁷She came to the supernatural man at the mountain and took strong hold of his feet. Gehazi came up to push her away, but the

supernatural man said, 'Let go of her, because her entire being is bitter to her, whereas Yahweh has hidden it from me and not told me.'

²⁸She said, 'Did I ask for a son from my lord? I said, "Don't deceive me", didn't I.' ²⁹He said to Gehazi, 'Wrap things round your hips, take my staff in your hand and go. When you meet someone, you will not bless him, and when someone blesses you, you will not answer him. Place my staff on the boy's face.' ³⁰But the boy's mother said, 'As Yahweh lives and as you yourself live, if I abandon you . . .'

So he set off and followed her. ³¹Now Gehazi passed on before them and placed the staff on the boy's face. But there was no sound and no heeding. He went back to meet him and told him, 'The boy has not woken up.' ³²Elisha came to the house and there – the boy was dead, laid on his bed. ³³He came in and shut the door behind the two of them and pleaded with Yahweh.

## Death and life

³⁴He climbed up and lay on the child, put his mouth on his mouth, his eyes on his eyes, his palms on his palms, and crouched over him. And the child's flesh warmed up. ³⁵He went back and went into the house here and there, then climbed up and crouched over him, and the boy sneezed seven times. Then the boy opened his eyes. ³⁶He called Gehazi and said, 'Call this Shunammite woman.' He called her and she came to him. He said, 'Take up your son.' ³⁷She came, and fell at his feet and bowed low to the earth, and took up her son and went out.

³⁸When Elisha went back to Gilgal and there was a famine in the region, and the people who prophesied were sitting before him, he said to his boy, 'Put the big pot on and cook stew for the people who prophesy.' ³⁹One went out into the wild to gather herbs, found a vine of the wild and gathered gourds of the wild from it, enough to fill his garment. He came and sliced them into the pot of stew, because they didn't know them. ⁴⁰They poured it out for the people to eat, but as they ate some of the stew and they cried out, they said, 'There's death in the pot, supernatural man.' They couldn't eat it. ⁴¹He said, 'So get some flour', and he threw it into the pot and said, 'Pour it out for the company

so that they eat.' And there was nothing bad in the pot.

⁴²Now a man came from Ba'al Shalishah and brought the supernatural man some first-products bread, twenty barley loaves and some plantation growth on the stalk. He said, 'Give it to the company so they can eat.' ⁴³His minister said, 'How can I put this before a hundred individuals?' He said, 'Give it to the company so they can eat. Because Yahweh has said this: "Eat and have some left."' ⁴⁴So he put it before them, they ate and they had some left, in accordance with Yahweh's word.

## The little girl who knows

5 Now Na'aman, army officer of the king of Aram, was a big man before his lord, and held in high regard, because through him Yahweh had given deliverance to Aram. Now the man was a forceful strong man, with scaliness. ²The Aramites had gone out as raiding gangs and had taken captive a little girl from the country of Yisra'el. She was before Na'aman's wife ³and she said to her mistress, 'If only my lord were before the prophet who's in Shomron. Then he would restore him from his scaliness.' ⁴He came and told his lord, 'The girl who's from the country of Yisra'el has spoken such and such', ⁵and the king of Aram said, 'Come on, go, I'll send a document to the king of Yisra'el.' So he went, took in his hand ten talents of silver, 6,000 gold pieces and ten changes of clothes, ⁶and brought the document to the king of Yisra'el, saying: 'Now, when this document comes to you: here, I've sent Na'aman my servant to you so you may restore him from his scaliness.'

⁷When the king of Yisra'el read the document, he tore his clothes and said, 'Am I God, to put to death and make alive, that this man is sending to me to restore someone from his scaliness? Rather, please acknowledge for sure and see, that he is seeking a confrontation with me.'

⁸When Elisha the supernatural man heard that the king of Yisra'el had torn his clothes, he sent to the king: 'Why have you torn your clothes? He should please come to me, so he may acknowledge that there is a prophet in Yisra'el.'

⁹Na'aman came with his horses and with his chariotry and halted at the entrance of Elisha's house. ¹⁰Elisha sent an envoy to him to say, 'Go and wash seven times in the Yarden so your flesh may come back for you, and be pure.'

## A skin disorder removed

¹¹Na'aman was furious and went. He said, 'Here, I said to myself, "He'll definitely come out and stand and call in the name of Yahweh his God and wave his hand at the place and restore the scaliness. ¹²Amanah and Pharpar, the rivers in Dammeseq [Damascus], are better than all the water in Yisra'el, aren't they. I could wash in them and be pure, couldn't I.' So he turned his face and went in wrath. ¹³But his servants came up and spoke to him: 'Father, had the prophet spoken to you of a big thing, wouldn't you do it? How much more when he said to you, "Wash, and be pure"?'

¹⁴So he went down and dipped in the Yarden seven times in accordance with the word of the supernatural man, and his flesh came back like a little boy's. He was pure. ¹⁵He went back to the supernatural man, he and all his camp, and came and stood before him, and said, 'Here, please, I acknowledge that there is no God in all the earth except in Yisra'el. So now please take a blessing from your servant.' ¹⁶He said, 'As Yahweh lives, before whom I stand, if I take anything . . .'

He pressed him to take it, but he refused. ¹⁷Na'aman said, 'Then please may there not be given to your servant a mule pair's load of earth, because your servant will no longer make a burnt offering or a sacrifice to any other god but Yahweh. ¹⁸With regard to this thing, may Yahweh pardon your servant: when my lord comes into Rimmon's house to bow down there and he leans on my hand and I bow down there in Rimmon's house – when I bow down in Rimmon's house, may Yahweh pardon your servant in this thing.' ¹⁹He said to him, 'Go, and things will be well.'

He went a distance in the region from him, ²⁰and Gehazi, Elisha the supernatural man's boy, said, 'Here, my lord has held back Na'aman this Aramite from taking from his hand what he brought. As Yahweh lives, I shall run after him and take something from him.'

## A skin disorder imposed

[21]So Gehazi pursued after Na'aman. Na'aman saw him running after him, fell from his chariot to meet him and said, 'Are things well?' [22]He said, 'Things are well. My lord has sent me to say, "Here, just now two boys have come to me from the highland of Ephrayim, from among the people who prophesy. Please give them a talent of silver and two changes of clothes."' [23]Na'aman said, 'Resolve to take two talents!' He pressed him, and tied up two talents of silver in two bags and two changes of clothes and gave them to two of his boys. They carried them before him. [24]He came to the acropolis, took them from their hand, deposited them in the house and sent the men off.

So they went, [25]while he came and stood with his lord. Elisha said to him, 'Where have you come from, Gehazi?' He said, 'Your servant hasn't gone here or there.' [26]He said to him, 'My mind didn't go along as the man turned from his chariot to meet you? Is it time to take silver or to take clothes or olive trees or vineyards or sheep or cattle or servants or maidservants? [27]Na'aman's scaliness will attach itself to you and to your offspring permanently.' He went out from before him, made scaly like snow.

**6** The people who prophesied said to Elisha, 'Here, please, the place where we're living before you is too confined for us. [2]Please let's go as far as the Yarden and get a beam each from there and make ourselves a place there to live in.' He said, 'Go.' [3]One said, 'Please resolve to go with your servants.' He said, 'I'll go.' [4]He went with them and they came to the Yarden. They cut down trees, [5]but one was felling a beam and the iron fell into the water. He cried out, 'Oh, my lord, and it was borrowed!' [6]The supernatural man said, 'Where did it fall?' He let him see the place, and he cut down a stick and threw it there, and it made the iron float. [7]He said, 'Take it up for yourself', and he put out his hand and got it.

## Horses and chariots of fire round Elisha

[8]Now the king of Aram was battling against Yisra'el, and he took counsel with his servants, saying, 'My camp will be at such and such a place', [9]but the supernatural man sent to the king of Yisra'el saying, 'Keep watch not to pass by this place, because the Aramites are going down there.' [10]So the king of Yisra'el sent to the place that the supernatural man had said to him and warned him, and kept watch there more than once or twice.

[11]The mind of the king of Aram was agitated about this thing. He called his servants and said to them, 'Won't you tell me who of us is on the king of Yisra'el's side?' [12]One of his servants said, 'No, my lord king, rather it's Elisha, the prophet who's in Yisra'el, who tells the king of Yisra'el the things that you speak in your bedroom.' [13]He said, 'Go and see where he is so I can send and get him.'

It was told him, 'There, in Dotan', [14]and he sent horses and chariotry there, with a substantial force. They came by night and encircled the town. [15]The supernatural man's minister started early and got up and went out, and there, a force was surrounding the town, with horses and chariotry. His boy said to him, 'Oh no, my lord, what shall we do?' [16]He said, 'Don't be afraid, because there are more with us than with them.' [17]Elisha pleaded, 'Yahweh, please open his eyes so he sees.' Yahweh opened the boy's eyes and he saw: there, the highland was full of fiery horses and chariotry surrounding Elisha.

## The depths to which people can be driven

[18]They came down against him, and Elisha pleaded with Yahweh, 'Please strike down this nation with dazzling.' He struck them down with dazzling in accordance with Elisha's word. [19]Elisha said to them, 'This isn't the way, and this isn't the town. Follow me and I'll enable you to go to the man that you're looking for', and he enabled them to go to Shomron.

[20]When they came to Shomron, Elisha said, 'Yahweh, open these people's eyes so they can see.' Yahweh opened their eyes and they saw: there, they were inside Shomron. [21]The king of Yisra'el said to Elisha, on seeing them, 'Shall I strike them down, strike them down, father?' [22]He said, 'You will not strike them down. Do you strike down people whom you took captive with your sword and with your bow? Put bread and water before them so they can eat and drink, and go to their lords.' [23]He made a great

banquet for them, and they ate and drank. Then he sent them off and they went to their lords, and the Aramite raiding gangs no longer came into Yisraʼel.

²⁴Subsequently, Ben-hadad king of Aram collected his entire camp and went up and besieged Shomron, ²⁵and there was a big famine in Shomron. There, they were besieging it until a donkey's head was eighty silver pieces and a quarter of a litre of pigeon dung was five silver pieces. ²⁶The king of Yisraʼel was passing by on the wall when a woman cried out to him: 'Deliver me, my lord king!' ²⁷He said, 'Don't. Yahweh must deliver you. From where am I to deliver you – from the threshing floor or from the winepress?' ²⁸But the king said to her, 'What's the matter?' She said, 'This woman said to me, "Give up your son and we'll eat him today, and we'll eat my son tomorrow", ²⁹and we cooked my son and ate him. The next day I said to her, "Give up your son and we'll eat him", but she hid her son.'

## The men who gave up

³⁰When the king heard the woman's words, he tore his clothes, and as he passed by on the wall, the people saw: there, sack on his flesh, inside. ³¹He said, 'May God do this to me and may he do more if the head of Elisha ben Shaphat stays on him today.'

³²While Elisha was sitting in his house and the elders were sitting with him, he sent a man from before him. Before the envoy came to him, he himself said to the elders, 'Do you see that this murderous man has sent to remove my head? See, when the envoy comes, shut the door and press him against the door. The sound of his lord's feet will be behind him, won't it.'

³³While he was still speaking with them, there, the envoy was coming down to him. He said, 'Here, this is the bad fate coming from Yahweh. How can I wait for Yahweh any more?'

**7** Elisha said, 'Listen to Yahweh's word. Yahweh has said this: "This very time tomorrow: a measure of fine flour will be for a sheqel, two measures of barley for a sheqel, at the gateway of Shomron."' ²The adjutant on whose hand the king leaned answered the supernatural man, "There, were Yahweh

making apertures in the heavens, would this thing happen?' He said, 'There, you're going to see it with your eyes, but you won't eat of it.'

³Now there were four men with scaliness at the entrance to the gateway. They said, one to his neighbour, 'Why are we sitting here until we die? ⁴If we say, "Let's go into the town", there's famine in the town and we'll die there, and if we sit here, we'll die. So now, come on, let's surrender to the Aramite camp. If they let us live, we'll live. If they put us to death, we'll die.' ⁵ᵃSo they set off at dusk to come to the Aramite camp.

## The mysterious panicked flight

⁵ᵇThey came to the edge of the Aramite camp, and there – no one was there. ⁶The Lord had made the Aramite camp hear the sound of chariotry, the sound of horse, the sound of a big force, and they had said to one another, 'Here, the king of Yisraʼel has hired against us the kings of the Hittites and the kings of Misrayim [Egypt], to come against us.' ⁷They had set off and fled at dusk. They had abandoned their tents and their horses and their donkeys, the camp as it was, and fled for their life.

⁸So these men with scaliness came to the edge of the camp and came into a tent and ate and drank and carried silver and gold and clothes from there and went and buried it, and went back and came into another tent and carried silver and gold and clothes from there and went and buried it. ⁹But they said each to his neighbour, 'We're not doing right. This day is a day of good news. We're keeping quiet. And should we wait until morning light, waywardness will find us out. Now, come on, let's go and tell the king's household.' ¹⁰So they came and called to the town gateman. They told them, 'We came to the Aramite camp and there, no one and no human sound was there, but horse tied up and donkey tied up and tents as they were.'

¹¹The gatemen called, and they told the king's household, within. ¹²The king got up in the night and said to his servants, 'May I please tell you what the Aramites have done to us? They know that we're starving, and they've gone out of the camp to hide in the fields, saying "When they go out from the town we'll capture them alive and come into the town."'

## Was it just a coincidence? (1)

[13]One of his servants answered, 'People should please take five of the remaining horses, the ones that have remained here. There, they are like the entire horde of Yisra'el that have remained here: there they are, like the entire horde of Yisra'el that have come to an end. So let's send them and see.'

[14]They got two chariots of horses and the king sent them after the Aramite camp, saying 'Go and see.' [15]They followed them as far as the Yarden and there, the entire road was full of clothes and articles that the Aramites had thrown away in their haste. The envoys came back and told the king. [16]So the people went out and plundered the Aramite camp, and it was a measure of fine flour for a sheqel and two measures of barley for a sheqel, in accordance with Yahweh's word.

[17]Now in charge of the gateway the king had appointed the adjutant on whose hand he leaned, and the people trampled on him in the gateway and he died, as the supernatural man had spoken when the king went down to him, [18]when the supernatural man said to the king, 'Two measures of barley for a sheqel and a measure of fine flour for a sheqel, it will be at this very time tomorrow at the gateway of Shomron.' [19]The adjutant had answered the supernatural man, 'There, were Yahweh making apertures in the heavens, would something such as this happen?' And he had said, 'There, you're going to see it with your eyes, but you won't eat of it.' [20]It happened to him. The people trampled him in the gateway and he died.

## Was it just a coincidence? (2)

**8** Now Elisha had spoken to the woman whose son he brought to life: 'Set off and go, you and your household, and reside wherever you can reside, because Yahweh has called for a famine and it is indeed going to come on the country for seven years.' [2]The woman set off and acted in accordance with the word of the supernatural man. She went, she and her household, and resided in the Pelishtites' [Philistines'] country seven years.

[3]At the end of the seven years the woman came back from the Pelishtites' country and went out to cry out to the king about her house and about her fields. [4]The king was speaking with Gehazi, the supernatural man's boy, saying, 'Please tell me all the big things that Elisha has done.' [5]He was recounting to the king how he had brought the dead person to life, and there, the woman whose son he had brought to life was crying out to the king about her house and about her fields. Gehazi said, 'My lord king, this is the woman and this is her son whom Elisha brought to life.' [6]The king asked the woman and she recounted it to him, and the king gave her a courtier, saying, 'Get back all that belongs to her and all the yield from her fields from the day she abandoned the country until now.'

[7]Elisha came to Dammeseq, when Ben-hadad king of Aram was ill. It had been told him, 'The supernatural man is coming here.' [8]The king said to Haza'el, 'Take an offering in your hand and go to meet the supernatural man and enquire of Yahweh from him, "Will I live on after this illness?"'

## The assassination

[9]Haza'el went to meet him and took an offering in his hand, all the good things of Dammeseq, forty camel loads. He came and stood before him and said, 'Your son, Ben-hadad king of Aram, sent me to you, saying "Will I live on after this illness?"' [10]Elisha said to him, 'Go say to him: "You will definitely live on." But Yahweh has let me see that he will definitely die.' [11]He made his face stay firm, until he was shamed. But the supernatural man cried, [12]and Haza'el said, 'Why is my lord crying?' He said, 'Because I know the bad things that you will do to the Yisra'elites. Their fortifications you will set on fire. Their young men you will slay with the sword. Their little ones you will tear to pieces. Their pregnant women you will rip open.' [13]Haza'el said, 'What is your servant, a dog, that he should do this big thing?' Elisha said, 'Yahweh has let me see you as king over Aram.'

[14]He went from Elisha and came to his lord. He said to him 'What did Elisha say to you?' He said, 'He said to me, "You will definitely live on."' [15]But next day he got a cloth, dipped it in water and spread it over his

face, and he died. So Haza'el began to reign in place of him.

¹⁶In the fifth year of Yoram ben Ah'ab king of Yisra'el, whereas Yehoshaphat had been king of Yehudah, Yehoram ben Yehoshaphat began to reign as king of Yehudah. ¹⁷He was a man of thirty-two years when he began to reign and he reigned eight years in Yerushalaim.

¹⁸He walked in the way of the kings of Yisra'el, as Ah'ab's household had done, because he had Ah'ab's daughter as wife. He did what was bad in Yahweh's eyes. ¹⁹But Yahweh was not willing to devastate Yehudah, for the sake of Dayid his servant, as he had said to him that he would give him hegemony for his sons for all time.

## Two kings called Yoram/Yehoram

²⁰In his days Edom rebelled from under Yehudah's hand, and they made a king reign over themselves. ²¹Yoram crossed to Tsa'ir, he and all the chariotry with him. He set off by night and struck down the Edomites (who were surrounding him) and the chariotry officers, and the company fled to their tents. ²²But Edom has rebelled from under Yehudah's hand until this day. Then Libnah rebelled at this time.

²³The rest of the things about Yoram and all that he did are written on the document about things of the time regarding the kings of Yehudah, aren't they. ²⁴Yoram lay down with his ancestors and was buried with his ancestors in David's Town, and Ahazyahu his son began to reign in place of him.

²⁵It was in the twelfth year of Yoram ben Ah'ab king of Yisra'el that Ahazyahu ben Yehoram began to reign in Yehudah. ²⁶Ahazyahu was a man of twenty-two years when he began to reign and he reigned one year in Yerushalaim. His mother's name was Atalyahu bat Omri, king of Yisra'el. ²⁷He walked in the way of the household of Ah'ab and did what was bad in Yahweh's eyes like Ah'ab's household, because he was an in-law of Ah'ab's household. ²⁸He went with Yoram ben Ah'ab for battle with Haza'el king of Aram at Heights-in-Gil'ad. The Aramites struck down Yoram, ²⁹and King Yoram went back to heal in Yizr'e'el from the wounds with

which the Aramites had struck him down at The Height when he was battling with Haza'el king of Aram, while Ahazyahu ben Yehoram king of Yehudah went down to see Yoram ben Ah'ab because he was ill.

## The anointing of another assassin

**9** Now Elisha the prophet had called one of the people who prophesied and said to him, 'Wrap things round your hips, take this flask of oil in your hand and go to Heights-in-Gil'ad. ²When you come there, look for Yehu ben Yehoshaphat son of Nimshi, there. You're to come and get him up from among his brothers and bring him to an inner room. ³Take the flask of oil, pour it on his head and say, "Yahweh has said this: 'I anoint you king over Yisra'el'", and open the door and flee; don't wait.'

⁴So the boy (the prophet's boy) went to Heights-in-Gil'ad. ⁵When he came, there, the officers of the force were sitting. He said, 'I have a word for you, officer.' Yehu said, 'For whom out of all of us?' He said, 'For you, officer.'

⁶He got up and came into the house, and he poured the oil on his head and said to him, 'Yahweh, the God of Yisra'el, has said this: "I anoint you king for Yahweh's people, for Yisra'el. ⁷You're to strike down the household of Ah'ab, your lord, and I will take redress from the hand of Izebel [Jezebel] for the shed blood of my servants the prophets and the shed blood of all Yahweh's servants. ⁸The entire household of Ah'ab will perish, and I shall cut off for Ah'ab the one who pisses against a wall (bond or freed) in Yisra'el. ⁹I shall make Ah'ab's household like the household of Yarob'am ben Nebat and like the household of Ba'sha ben Ahiyyah. ¹⁰And Izebel: the dogs will eat her in a Yizre'e'l plot and there will be no one burying her.' And he opened the door and fled.

## The man who drives like a madman

¹¹When Yehu went out to his lord's servants, they said to him, 'Are things well? Why did this madman come to you?' He said to them, 'You know the man and his talk.' ¹²They said, 'Lies! Tell us, please.' He said, 'This and that

very thing he said to me: "Yahweh has said this: 'I anoint you king for Yisra'el.'"" [13]They made speed and got each person his coat and put it under him on the top step, and blew on a horn and said, 'Yehu has become king!' [14]So Yehu ben Yehoshaphat son of Nimshi conspired against Yoram.

Now Yoram had been keeping watch at Heights-in-Gil'ad, he and all Yisra'el, from before Haza'el king of Aram, [15]but King Yehoram had gone back to heal in Yizre'e'l from the wounds with which the Aramites had struck him down when he was battling with Haza'el king of Aram.

So Yehu said, 'If it's your desire, no one is to escape and go out of the town to go to tell of it in Yizre'e'l.' [16]Yehu got into his chariot and went to Yizre'e'l, because Yoram was lying there, and Ahazyah king of Yehudah had come down to see Yehoram. [17]The lookout was standing on the tower in Yizre'e'l and saw Yehu's pack as it was coming. He said, 'I see a pack!' Yehoram said, 'Get a rider and send him to meet them. He's to say, "Are things well?"' [18]The horse rider went to meet him and said, 'The king has said this: "Are things well?"' Yehu said, 'What do you and "Are things well" have in common? Turn round after me.' The lookout told them, 'The envoy came right to them, but he didn't come back.'

[19]He sent a second horse rider. He came to them and said, 'The king has said this: "Are things well?"' And Yehu said, 'What do you and "Are things well" have in common? Turn round after me.' [20]The lookout told them, 'The envoy came right to them, but he didn't come back. The driving is like the driving of Yehu ben Nimshi, because he drives like a madman.'

## The whorings of Izebel

[21]Yehoram said, 'Hitch up!', and they hitched up his chariot. Yehoram king of Yisra'el went out, with Ahazyahu king of Yehudah, each in his chariot. They went out to meet Yehu, and found him on the plot of Nabot the Yizre'e'lite. [22]When Yehoram saw Yehu he said, 'Are things well, Yehu?' He said, 'What can be well while the whorings of Izebel your mother and her sorceries are so many?' [23]Yehoram turned his hands round and fled, and said to Ahazyahu,

'Guile, Ahazyah!', [24]as Yehu put his hand to his bow and struck down Yehoram between the shoulders. The arrow went out through his heart and he bowed down on his knees in his chariot.

[25]He said to Bidqar his adjutant, 'Take him up, throw him into the plot of field belonging to Nabot the Yezre'e'lite, because remember me and you riding as a pair behind Ah'ab his father when Yahweh took up this oracle about him: [26]"If I did not see Nabot's shed blood and his sons' shed blood yesterday (Yahweh's proclamation) . . . And I will make it good to you on this plot (Yahweh's proclamation)." So now take him up, throw him on the plot in accordance with Yahweh's word.'

[27]When Ahazyah king of Yehudah saw it, he fled by the Bet Haggan road. Yehu pursued after him and said, 'Him as well, strike him down' – in his chariot at the Gur Ascent, which is by Yible'am. He fled to Megiddo and died there. [28]His servants took him in a chariot to Yerushalaim and buried him in his grave with his ancestors in David's Town. [29]It had been in the eleventh year of Yoram ben Ah'ab that Ahazyah began to reign over Yehudah.

## Izebel puts on her make-up

[30]Yehu came to Yizre'e'l, and when Izebel heard, she put mascara on her eyes and made her hair look good and watched through the window. [31]When Yehu came through the gateway, she said 'Are things well, Zimri, slayer of his lord?' [32]He lifted his face to the window and said, 'Who is with me? Who?' Two or three courtiers looked towards him. [33]He said, 'Drop her down!' They dropped her down, and some of her blood spattered on the wall and on the horses, and they trampled her.

[34]He came in and ate and drank, and said 'Please attend to this accursed woman and bury her, because she's the daughter of a king.' [35]They went to bury her, but they couldn't find anything of her, only the skull and the feet and the palms of her hands. [36]They came back and told him, and he said, 'It's Yahweh's word that he spoke by means of his servant Eliyyahu the Tishbite: "On a Yizre'e'l plot the dogs will eat Izebel's flesh. [37]Izebel's carcase will be like manure on the face of the fields on a Yizre'e'l plot, so that people cannot say, 'This is Izebel.'"'

# 10

Now Ah'ab had seventy sons in Shomron. Yehu wrote documents and sent them to Shomron, to the officials in Yizre'e'l, the elders, and to Ah'ab's guardians, saying, ²'Now, when this document comes to you, and your lord's sons are with you, and chariotry and horses are with you, and a fortified city, and weaponry, ³see who is the best and most upright of your lord's sons, put him on his father's throne and do battle for your lord's household.' ⁴But they were very, very fearful, and said, 'Here, two kings didn't stand before him; how can we stand?' ⁵So the one in charge of the household, the one in charge of the town, the elders and the guardians sent to Yehu saying, 'We are your servants. Everything that you say to us we will do. We will not make anyone king. Do what is good in your eyes.'

## Seventy heads fall

⁶So he wrote them a second document: 'If you're on my side and you're going to listen to my voice, take the heads of the men (your lord's sons) and come to me this very time tomorrow in Yizre'e'l.' The king's sons, seventy of them, were with the big people in the town, who were bringing them up. ⁷When the document came to them, they got the king's sons, slaughtered the seventy, put their heads in baskets and sent them to him in Yizre'e'l. ⁸An envoy came and told him, 'They've brought the heads of the king's sons.' He said, 'Put them in two heaps at the entrance to the town gateway until morning.' ⁹In the morning he went out and stood and said to the entire people, 'You are in the right. There, I myself conspired against my lord and killed him, but who struck down all these? ¹⁰Acknowledge how nothing will fall to the earth of Yahweh's word, which Yahweh spoke concerning the household of Ah'ab, since Yahweh has done what he spoke by means of his servant Eliyyahu.' ¹¹Yehu struck down all that remained of the household of Ah'ab in Yizre'e'l, and all his big people, his friends and his priests, until he let no survivor remain to him.

¹²Then he set off; he came, and went to Shomron; he was at the shepherds' binding house on the way, ¹³and when Yehu found brothers of Ahazyahu king of Yehudah, he said, 'Who are you?' They said, 'We are brothers of Ahazyahu. We've come down regarding whether things are well with the king's sons and the queen's sons.' ¹⁴He said, 'Capture them alive.' They captured them alive but slew them at the binding house cistern, forty-two individuals. He didn't let one of them remain.

## The great festival for Ba'al

¹⁵He went from there and found Yehonadab ben Rekab, coming to meet him. He blessed him and said to him, 'Is your mind upright, as my mind is with your mind?' Yehonadab said, 'It is.' 'Since it is, give me your hand.' He gave him his hand and took him up to him into the chariot. ¹⁶He said, 'Go with me and see my passion for Yahweh.' So he got him to ride in his chariot. ¹⁷He came to Shomron and struck down all the people who remained to Ah'ab in Shomron until he had annihilated them, in accordance with Yahweh's word that he spoke to Eliyyahu.

¹⁸Yehu collected all the people and said to them, 'Whereas Ah'ab served the Master a little, Yehu will serve him much. ¹⁹So now, all the Master's prophets, all his servants and all his priests – call them to me. Not one is to be counted missing, because I have a big sacrifice for the Master. No one who is counted missing will live.' Yehu was acting with guile in order that he might obliterate the Master's servants.

²⁰So Yehu said, 'Make a sacred assembly for the Master', and they called it. ²¹Yehu sent through all Yisra'el, and all the Master's servants came. Not one remained who didn't come. They came to the Master's house; the Master's house filled, end to end. ²²He said to the person in charge of the wardrobe, 'Get out apparel for all the Master's servants.' He got the apparel out for them. ²³Yehu came with Yehonadab ben Rekab into the Master's house and said to the Master's servants, 'Search, and see that there are none of Yahweh's servants here with you, but rather the Master's servants alone.' ²⁴They came to make sacrifices and burnt offerings, while Yehu had placed for himself eighty people outside and had said, 'The individual who escapes from the people that I am bringing into your hands: his life in place of his life.'

## The sacrifice

²⁵When he'd finished making the burnt offering, Yehu said to the runners and to the adjutants, 'Come, strike them down. No one is to get out.' The runners and the adjutants struck them down with the edge of the sword and threw them down. They went right to the town in the Master's house, ²⁶got out the columns in the Master's house and burned them. ²⁷They demolished the Master's columns and demolished the Master's house and turned it into latrines, until this day.

²⁸So Yehu annihilated the Master from Yisra'el; ²⁹only, the wrongdoings of Yarob'am ben Nebat that he caused Yisra'el to commit – Yehu did not depart from them (the gold bullocks that were at Bet-el and that were at Dan). ³⁰But Yahweh said to Yehu, 'Since you've done what is good, in doing what was upright in my eyes (in accordance with all that was in my mind you have acted towards the household of Ah'ab), sons to the fourth [generation] will sit on Yisra'el's throne for you.' ³¹But Yehu did not keep watch to walk by the instruction of Yahweh the God of Yisra'el with his entire mind. He did not depart from the wrongdoings of Yarob'am that he caused Yisra'el to commit.

³²In those days Yahweh began to reduce Yisra'el, and Haza'el struck them down through Yisra'el's entire territory ³³from the Yarden eastward, the entire region of Gil'ad (the Gadites, the Re'ubenites and the Menashshites), from Aro'er, which is by Wadi Arnon, both Gil'ad and Bashan.

³⁴The rest of the things about Yehu, all that he did and all his strength, are written on the document about things of the time regarding the kings of Yisra'el, aren't they. ³⁵Yehu lay down with his ancestors and they buried him in Shomron, and Yeho'az his son began to reign in place of him. ³⁶The time that Yehu reigned over Yisra'el was twenty-eight years in Shomron.

## The boy king-in-waiting

**11** When Atalyah, Ahazyahu's mother, saw that her son was dead, she set to and obliterated all the royal offspring. ²But Yehosheba the daughter of King Yoram, sister of Ahazyahu, got Yo'ash ben Ahazyah and stole him away from among the king's sons who were being put to death, him and his nanny, in a bedroom. They concealed him from Atalyahu and he wasn't put to death.

³He was with her in Yahweh's house hiding six years, while Atalyah was reigning over the country. ⁴In the seventh year, Yehoyada sent and got the centurions of the Karites and of the runners and brought them to him into Yahweh's house. He solemnized a pact with them and made them swear in Yahweh's house, and let them see the king's son.

⁵He ordered them, 'This is the thing that you're to do: a third of you who are coming in on the sabbath and keeping watch over the king's house, ⁶a third at the Sur Gate and a third at the gateway behind the runners: you're to keep watch over the house, as a defence. ⁷The two sections among you, all who are going out on the sabbath, will keep watch over Yahweh's house for the king. ⁸You're to encircle the king all round, each man with his equipment in his hand. Anyone who comes against the ranks is to be put to death. Be with the king when he goes out and when he comes in.'

⁹The centurions acted in accordance with all that Yehoyada the priest ordered. They took each his men who were coming in on the sabbath with those who were going out on the sabbath, and came to Yehoyada the priest. ¹⁰The priest gave the centurions the lance and the bows that belonged to King David, which were in Yahweh's house. ¹¹The runners stood, each with his equipment in his hand, from the shoulder of the house on the right to the shoulder of the house on the left, at the altar and at the house, in charge of the king all round.

## An unusual covenant

¹²Then he got the king's son out and put the diadem and the affirmation on him, and they made him king and anointed him. They clapped the palms of their hands and said 'Long live the king.'

¹³Atalyah heard the sound of the runners, the people, and came to the people at Yahweh's

house. ¹⁴She saw, there, the king was standing by the pillar in accordance with the ruling, the officials with the trumpets by the king, and the entire people of the country rejoicing and blowing on trumpets. Atalyah tore her clothes and called, 'Conspiracy, conspiracy!'

¹⁵Yehoyada the priest ordered the centurions appointed over the force, 'Take her out between the rows. The person who follows her, put to death with the sword' (because the priest said she should not be put to death in Yahweh's house). ¹⁶They laid hands on her and she came by way of the Horses' Entrance to the king's house, and she was put to death there.

¹⁷Yehoyada solemnized a pact between Yahweh, the king and the people, that they would be a people for Yahweh, and between the king and the people. ¹⁸The entire people of the country came to the Master's house and tore it down. Its altars and its images they broke up, doing it well, and Mattan, the Master's priest, they killed before the altars.

The priest set appointees over Yahweh's house. ¹⁹He got the centurions, the Karites, the runners and the entire people of the country, and they took the king down from Yahweh's house. They came by way of the Runners' Gate to the king's house, and he sat on the kings' throne.

²⁰The entire people of the country rejoiced, while the town was calm, when they had put Atalyahu to death with the sword at the king's house. ²¹Yeho'ash was seven years of age when he began to reign.

## A plan to restore the temple

**12** It was in the seventh year of Yehu that Yeho'ash began to reign and he reigned forty years in Yerushalaim. His mother's name was Tsibyah from Be'er-sheba. ²Yeho'ash did what was upright in Yahweh's eyes all his days that Yehoyada the priest taught him. ³Only, the shrines did not disappear; the people were still sacrificing and burning incense at the shrines.

⁴Yeho'ash said to the priests, 'All the silver from the sacred offerings that's brought into Yahweh's house, the silver that's current for an individual (the silver for persons), his evaluation, all the silver that it comes into an individual's mind to bring to Yahweh's house, ⁵the priests are to take for themselves, each from his assessor, and they themselves are to strengthen the defects in the house, everywhere a defect is found.'

⁶But in the twenty-third year of King Yeho'ash the priests had not strengthened the defects in the house. ⁷So King Yeho'ash called Yehoyada the priest, with the priests, and said to them, 'Why are you not strengthening the defects in the house? So now don't take the silver from your assessors but give it for the defects in the house.'

⁸The priests consented not to take silver from the people and not to strengthen the defects in the house. ⁹Yehoyada the priest got a chest, bored a hole in its lid and put it by the altar, on the right when one comes into Yahweh's house. The priests who were keeping watch over the threshold would put there all the silver that was brought to Yahweh's house. ¹⁰When they saw that the amount of silver in the chest was great, the royal scribe went up with the big priest and they tied up and counted the silver that was found in Yahweh's house.

## Not the fate he deserved

¹¹So they would put the silver that had been quantified into the hands of the men doing the work, who had been appointed to Yahweh's house. They would have it go out to the carpenters and to the builders who were doing things in Yahweh's house, ¹²and to the masons and to the stonecutters, and for acquiring wood and dressed stones to strengthen the defects in Yahweh's house, and for all that would need to go out in connection with Yahweh's house. ¹³Yet silver basins, snuffers, bowls, trumpets, all gold articles and silver articles, were not made for Yahweh's house from the silver brought into Yahweh's house, ¹⁴because they would give it to the people doing the work so they would strengthen Yahweh's house.

¹⁵They didn't keep a reckoning of the men into whose hand they would give the silver to give to the people doing the work, because they were acting with trustworthiness. ¹⁶Reparation silver and decontamination silver would not be brought into Yahweh's house; it would be the priests'.

<sup>17</sup>Then Haza'el king of Aram went up and battled against Gat, and captured it, and Haza'el set his face to go up to Yerushalaim. <sup>18</sup>Yeho'ash king of Yehudah got all the sacred things that Yehoshaphat, Yehoram and Ahazyahu, his ancestors, kings of Yehudah, had made sacred, and his own sacred things, and all the gold that could be found in the treasuries of Yahweh's house and the king's house, and sent them to Haza'el king of Aram, and he went up from Yerushalaim.

<sup>19</sup>The rest of the things about Yo'ash, and all that he did, are written on the document about things of the time regarding the kings of Yehudah, aren't they. <sup>20</sup>His servants arose and formed a conspiracy, and struck down Yo'ash at Fill House, which goes down to Silla. <sup>21</sup>Yozabad ben Shim'at and Yehozabad ben Shomer, of his servants – they struck him down and he died. They buried him with his ancestors in David's Town, and Amatsyah his son began to reign in place of him.

## God sees Yisra'el's affliction

**13** In the twenty-third year of Yo'ash ben Ahazyahu king of Yehudah, Yeho'ahaz ben Yehu began to reign over Yisra'el in Shomron, for seventeen years. <sup>2</sup>He did what was bad in Yahweh's eyes and followed the wrongdoings of Yarob'am ben Nebat that he caused Yisra'el to commit. He did not depart from it.

<sup>3</sup>So Yahweh's anger raged against Yisra'el and he gave them into the hand of Haza'el king of Aram and into the hand of Ben-hadad ben Haza'el, all the time. <sup>4</sup>Yeho'ahaz sought to gain Yahweh's goodwill and Yahweh listened to him, because he saw Yisra'el's affliction, how the king of Aram afflicted them. <sup>5</sup>Yahweh gave Yisra'el a deliverer and they got out from under the hand of Aram, and the Yisra'elites lived in their tents as they had in previous days. <sup>6</sup>Yet they didn't depart from the wrongdoings of Yarob'am's household that it caused Yisra'el to commit. They walked in them, and further, the totem pole stood in Shomron. (<sup>7</sup>Because he didn't leave a company to Yeho'ahaz, except 50 cavalry, 10 chariotry and 10,000 men on foot, because the king of Aram had obliterated them and made them like earth for trampling.)

<sup>8</sup>The rest of the things about Yeho'ahaz and all that he did, and his strength, are written on the document about things of the time regarding the kings of Yisra'el, aren't they. <sup>9</sup>Yeho'ahaz lay down with his ancestors and they buried him in Shomron. Yo'ash his son began to reign in place of him. <sup>10</sup>It was in the thirty-seventh year of Yo'ash king of Yehudah that Yeho'ash ben Yeho'ahaz began to reign over Yisra'el in Shomron, for sixteen years. <sup>11</sup>He did what was bad in Yahweh's eyes. He didn't depart from all the wrongdoings of Yarob'am ben Nebat that he caused Yisra'el to commit. He walked in them.

<sup>12</sup>The rest of the things about Yo'ash, all that he did, and his strength in that he battled with Amatsyah king of Yehudah, are written on the document about things of the time regarding the kings of Yisra'el, aren't they. <sup>13</sup>Yo'ash lay down with his ancestors, and Yarob'am sat on his throne. Yo'ash was buried in Shomron with the kings of Yisra'el.

## The God who has to be merciful

<sup>14</sup>Now Elisha was ill with the illness of which he died, and Yo'ash king of Yisra'el went down to him. He wept upon his face and said, 'Father, father, the chariotry of Yisra'el and its cavalry!' <sup>15</sup>Elisha said to him, 'Get a bow and arrows.' He got himself a bow and arrows. <sup>16</sup>He said to the king of Yisra'el, 'Mount your hand on the bow.' He mounted his hand. Elisha put his hands on the king's hands <sup>17</sup>and said, 'Open the window to the east.' He opened it. Elisha said, 'Shoot', and he shot. He said, 'Yahweh's deliverance arrow! A deliverance arrow against Aram! You will strike down Aram at Apheq so as to finish it off!'

<sup>18</sup>He said, 'Get the arrows', and he got them. He said to the king of Yisra'el, 'Strike the ground.' He struck three times, and stopped. <sup>19</sup>The supernatural man was furious with him and said, 'Striking five or six times! Then you would have struck Aram so as to finish it off, but now it will be three times that you strike Aram.'

<sup>20</sup>Elisha died and they buried him. Now raiding gangs from Mo'ab would come into the country at the coming of the new year. <sup>21</sup>People were burying someone and there – they saw a raiding band, and they threw the man into

Elisha's grave. He went, and touched Elisha's bones, and came to life and stood on his feet.

²²Now Haza'el king of Aram afflicted Yisra'el all the days of Yeho'ahaz, ²³but Yahweh was gracious to them and had compassion on them. He turned his face to them for the sake of his pact with Abraham, Yitshaq [Isaac] and Ya'aqob [Jacob]. He was not willing to devastate them, and he has not thrown them out from before his face until now.

²⁴Haza'el king of Aram died, and Ben-hadad his son began to reign in place of him. ²⁵Yeho'ash ben Yeho'ahaz took back again from the hand of Ben-hadad ben Haza'el the towns that he had taken from the hand of his father Yeho'ahaz in battle. Three times Yo'ash struck him down and got back the Yisra'elite towns.

## Individuals are put to death for their own wrongdoing

**14** In the second year of Yo'ash ben Yo'ahaz king of Yisra'el, Amatsyahu ben Yo'ash king of Yehudah began to reign. ²He was a man of twenty-five years when he began to reign and he reigned twenty-nine years in Yerushalaim. His mother's name was Yeho'addan from Yerushalaim. ³He did what was upright in Yahweh's eyes, only not like David his ancestor; in accordance with all that Yo'ash his father did, he did. ⁴Only, the shrines did not disappear; the people were still sacrificing and burning incense at the shrines.

⁵When the kingship was strong in his control, he struck down his servants who had struck down the king, his father. ⁶But the sons of the people who had struck him down, he did not put to death, as it is written in Mosheh's [Moses'] instruction document where Yahweh ordered: 'Parents will not be put to death for children and children will not be put to death for parents. Rather, an individual will be put to death for his own wrongdoing.' ⁷It was he who struck down Edom in Salt Ravine, 10,000, and captured The Cliff in the battle. He named it Yoqte'el, until now.

⁸Then Amatsyah sent envoys to Yeho'ash ben Yeho'ahaz son of Yehu, king of Yisra'el, saying, 'Come on, let's face each other.' ⁹Yeho'ash king of Yisra'el sent to Amatsyahu king of Yehudah, saying, 'A thistle that was in the Lebanon sent to a cedar that was in the Lebanon, saying "Give your daughter to my son as wife." But an animal of the wild that was in the Lebanon passed by and trampled the thistle. ¹⁰You have indeed struck down Edom and your mind has lifted you up. Enjoy your splendour but stay in your house. Why engage with bad fortune and fall, you and Yehudah with you?'

## The king who didn't listen

¹¹Amatsyahu didn't listen. So Yeho'ash king of Yisra'el went up and they faced each other, he and Amatsyahu king of Yehudah at Bet-shemesh, which belongs to Yehudah. ¹²Yehudah took a beating before Yisra'el and they fled each man to his tents. ¹³Amatsyahu king of Yehudah, son of Yeho'ash ben Ahazyahu – Yeho'ash king of Yisra'el captured him at Bet-shemesh, came to Yerushalaim and broke down the Yerushalaim wall at the Ephrayim Gate as far as the Corner Gate, 200 metres. ¹⁴He took all the gold and the silver and all the articles that were to be found in Yahweh's house and in the treasuries of the king's house, and pledges, and went back to Shomron.

¹⁵The rest of the things about Yeho'ash, what he did, and his strength and how he battled with Amatsyahu king of Yehudah, are written on the document about things of the time regarding the kings of Yisra'el, aren't they. ¹⁶Yeho'ash lay down with his ancestors and was buried in Shomron with the kings of Yisra'el, and Yarob'am his son began to reign in place of him.

¹⁷Amatsyahu ben Yo'ash king of Yehudah lived after the death of Yeho'ash ben Yeho'ahaz king of Yisra'el fifteen years. ¹⁸The rest of the things about Amatsyahu are written on the document about things of the time regarding the kings of Yehudah, aren't they. ¹⁹People formed a conspiracy against him in Yerushalaim and he fled to Lakish, but they sent after him to Lakish and put him to death there. ²⁰But they carried him on horses and he was buried in Yerushalaim with his ancestors in David's Town. ²¹All the people of Yehudah got Azaryah (he was sixteen years of age) and made him king in place of his father Amatsyahu. ²²It was he who built up Elat. He had got it back for Yehudah after the king lay down with his ancestors.

## The king who heard from Yonah [Jonah]

²³In the fifteenth year of Amatsyahu ben Yo'ash king of Yehudah, Yarob'am ben Yo'ash king of Yisra'el began to reign in Shomron, for forty-one years. ²⁴He did what was bad in Yahweh's eyes; he didn't depart from all the wrongdoings of Yarob'am ben Nebat that he caused Yisra'el to commit. ²⁵It was he who got Yisra'el's territory back from Lebo Hamat as far as the Steppe Sea, in accordance with the word of Yahweh the God of Yisra'el which he spoke by means of his servant Yonah ben Amittay the prophet, who was from Gat-hepher. ²⁶Because Yahweh saw Yisra'el's very bitter humbling (neither bound nor freed) and there was no helper for Yisra'el. ²⁷Yahweh had not spoken of wiping out Yisra'el's name from under the heavens, and he delivered them by the hand of Yarob'am ben Yo'ash.

²⁸The rest of the things about Yarob'am, all that he did, and his strength, how he battled and how he got back Dammeseq and Hamat belonging to Yehudah in Yisra'el, are written on the document about things of the time regarding the kings of Yisra'el, aren't they. ²⁹Yarob'am lay down with his ancestors, with the kings of Yisra'el, and Zekaryah his son began to reign in place of him.

**15** It was in the twenty-seventh year of Yarob'am king of Yisra'el that Azaryah ben Amatsyah king of Yehudah began to reign. ²He was sixteen years of age when he began to reign and he reigned fifty-two years in Yerushalaim. His mother's name was Yekolyahu from Yerushalaim. ³He did what was upright in Yahweh's eyes in accordance with all that Amatsyahu his father did. ⁴Only, the shrines did not disappear; the people were still sacrificing and burning incense at the shrines. ⁵Yahweh touched the king and he was made scaly until the day of his death. He lived in a house apart, while Yotam the king's son was in charge of the household, exercising authority over the people in the country.

## A war crime

⁶The rest of the things about Azaryahu and all that he did are written on the document about things of the time regarding the kings of

Yehudah, aren't they. ⁷Azaryah lay down with his ancestors and they buried him with his ancestors in David's Town, and Yotam his son began to reign in place of him.

⁸It was in the thirty-eighth year of Azaryahu king of Yehudah that Zekaryahu ben Yarob'am began to reign over Yisra'el in Shomron, for six months. ⁹He did what was bad in Yahweh's eyes as his ancestors had done. He didn't depart from the wrongdoings of Yarob'am ben Nebat that he caused Yisra'el to commit. ¹⁰Shallum ben Yabesh conspired against him; he struck him down before the people, put him to death and began to reign in place of him. ¹¹The rest of the things about Zekaryah, there they are, written on the document about things of the time regarding the kings of Yisra'el. ¹²That was Yahweh's word which he spoke to Yehu: 'Sons to the fourth [generation] will sit on Yisra'el's throne for you.' So it came about.

¹³Shallum ben Yabesh began to reign in the thirty-ninth year of Uzziyah king of Yehudah, and reigned for a full month in Shomron. ¹⁴Menahem ben Gadi went up from Tirtsah, came to Shomron, and struck down Shallum ben Yabesh in Shomron and put him to death. He began to reign in place of him. ¹⁵The rest of the things about Shallum and his conspiracy that he formed, there they are, written on the document about things of the time regarding the kings of Yisra'el.

¹⁶Then Menahem struck down Tiphsah and everyone who was in it and its territories, from Tirtsah, because it didn't open up, so he struck it down. He split open all its pregnant women.

## The Assyrians start to cause trouble

¹⁷It was in the thirty-ninth year of Azaryah king of Yehudah that Menahem ben Gadi began to reign over Yisra'el, for ten years. ¹⁸He did what was bad in Yahweh's eyes; he didn't depart from the wrongdoings of Yarob'am ben Nebat that he caused Yisra'el to commit, all his days. ¹⁹Pul king of Ashshur [Assyria] came against the country, and Menahem gave Pul a thousand talents of silver so that his hands would be with him to strengthen the kingship in his hand. ²⁰Menahem put the silver out on Yisra'el, on all the forceful strong men, to give to the king of Ashshur, fifty sheqels of silver for

each man, and the king of Ashshur went back and did not stop there in the country.

²¹The rest of the things about Menahem and all that he did are written on the document about things of the time regarding the kings of Yisra'el, aren't they. ²²Menahem lay down with his ancestors, and Peqahyah his son began to reign in place of him.

²³It was in the fiftieth year of Azaryah king of Yehudah that Peqahyah ben Menahem began to reign over Yisra'el in Shomron, for two years. ²⁴He did what was bad in Yahweh's eyes; he didn't depart from the the wrongdoings that Yarob'am ben Nebat caused Yisra'el to commit. ²⁵Peqah ben Remalyahu, his adjutant, conspired against him and struck him down in Shomron in the citadel of the king's house (with Argob and with Aryeh, so along with him were fifty men from the Gil'adites). He put him to death and began to reign in place of him.

²⁶The rest of the things about Peqahyah, all that he did, there they are, written on the document about things of the time regarding the kings of Yisra'el.

## Land begins to be lost

²⁷It was in the fifty-second year of Azaryah king of Yehudah that Peqah ben Remalyahu began to reign over Yisra'el in Shomron, for twenty years. ²⁸He did what was bad in Yahweh's eyes; he didn't depart from the wrongdoings that Yarob'am ben Nebat caused Yisra'el to commit. ²⁹In the days of Peqah king of Yisra'el, Tiglat-pil'eser king of Ashshur came and took Iyyon, Bet-ma'akah Meadow, Yanoah, Qedesh, Hatsor, Gil'ad, and the Galilee, the entire region of Naphtali, and exiled them to Ashshur.

³⁰Hoshea ben Elah formed a conspiracy against Peqah ben Remalyahu, and struck him down. He put him to death and began to reign in place of him, in the twentieth year of Yotam ben Uzziyyah. ³¹The rest of the things about Peqah and all that he did, there they are, written on the document about things of the time regarding the kings of Yisra'el.

³²It was in the second year of Peqah ben Remalyahu king of Yisra'el that Yotam ben Uzziyyahu king of Yehudah began to reign. ³³He was a man of twenty-five years when he began to reign and he reigned sixteen years in

Yerushalaim. His mother's name was Yerusha bat Tsadoq. ³⁴He did what was upright in Yahweh's eyes; in accordance with all that Uzziyyahu his father had done, he did. ³⁵Only, the shrines did not disappear; the people were still sacrificing and burning incense at the shrines. It was he who built up the Upper Gate of Yahweh's house.

³⁶The rest of the things about Yotam that he did are written on the document about things of the time regarding the kings of Yehudah, aren't they. ³⁷During that time Yahweh began to send Retsin king of Aram and Peqah ben Remalyahu against Yehudah. ³⁸Yotam lay down with his ancestors and was buried with his ancestors in David his ancestor's town, and Ahaz his son began to reign in place of him.

## How not to render to Caesar

**16** It was in the seventeenth year of Peqah ben Remalyahu that Ahaz ben Yotam king of Yehudah began to reign. ²Ahaz was a man of twenty years when he began to reign and he reigned sixteen years in Yerushalaim. He did not do what was upright in the eyes of Yahweh his God like David his ancestor ³but walked in the way of the kings of Yisra'el. Further, his own son he passed through the fire in accordance with the offensive practices of the nations that Yahweh dispossessed from before the Yisra'elites. ⁴He sacrificed and burned incense at the shrines, on the hills and under every verdant tree.

⁵Then Retsin king of Aram and Peqah ben Remalyahu king of Yisra'el went up to Yerushalaim for battle. They besieged Ahaz but couldn't win the battle. ⁶At that time Retsin king of Aram took back Elat for Aram. He cleared out the Yehudahites from Elot, and Edomites came to Elat and have lived there until this day.

⁷Ahaz sent envoys to Tiglat-pileser king of Ashshur saying, 'I am your servant and your son. Go up and deliver me from the fist of the king of Aram and from the fist of the king of Yisra'el, who are rising up against me.' ⁸Ahaz got the silver and the gold that could be found in Yahweh's house and in the treasuries of the king's house and sent them to the king of Ashshur as a bribe, ⁹and the king of Ashshur

listened to him. The king of Ashshur went up to Dammeseq, captured it, exiled it to Qir and put Retsin to death.

¹⁰King Ahaz went to meet Tiglat-pileser king of Ashshur at Dammeseq, and saw the altar at Dammeseq. King Ahaz sent Uriyyah the priest a picture of the altar and a plan of it, for every aspect of making it, ¹¹and Uriyyah the priest built the altar. In accordance with all that King Ahaz had sent from Dammeseq, so Uriyyah the priest did, before King Ahaz came from Dammeseq.

## A new altar

¹²The king came from Dammeseq and the king saw the altar. The king drew near the altar, went up on it, ¹³and turned into smoke his burnt offering and his grain offering, poured his libation, and tossed the blood of the well-being offerings that he had, on the altar. ¹⁴The copper altar that was before Yahweh, he brought near from the front of the house (between his altar and Yahweh's house) and put it by the side of his altar, to the north. ¹⁵King Ahaz ordered Uriyyah the priest, 'On the big altar, turn into smoke the morning burnt offering and the evening grain offering, the king's burnt offering and his grain offering, the burnt offering of the entire people of the country, their grain offering and their libations. All the blood of the burnt offering and all the blood of the sacrifice you're to toss on it. The copper altar will be for me to consult at.' ¹⁶Uriyyah the priest acted in accordance with all that King Ahaz ordered.

¹⁷King Ahaz cut off the stands' rims and removed the basin from on them, took down the sea from on the copper cattle that were beneath it and put it on a pavement of stones, ¹⁸and the sabbath-covered-way that they had built in the house and the king's outside entrance he moved round to Yahweh's house, on account of the king of Ashshur.

¹⁹The rest of the things about Ahaz that he did are written on the document about things of the time regarding the kings of Yehudah, aren't they. ²⁰Ahaz lay down with his ancestors and was buried with his ancestors in David's Town, and Hizqiyyahu [Hezekiah] his son began to reign in place of him.

## The fall of the northern kingdom

**17** It was in the twelfth year of Ahaz king of Yehudah that Hoshea ben Elah began to reign over Yisra'el in Shomron, for nine years. ²He did what was bad in Yahweh's eyes, only not like the kings of Yisra'el who were before him.

³Shalman'eser king of Ashshur went up against him, and Hoshea became his servant and gave back an offering to him. ⁴But the king of Ashshur found a conspiracy in Hoshea, when he sent envoys to So king of Misrayim and did not take up an offering to the king of Ashshur, as he did year by year. So the king of Ashshur detained him, and confined him in the cells.

⁵Then the king of Ashshur went up against the entire country. He went up to Shomron and besieged it for three years. ⁶In the third year of Hoshea, the king of Ashshur took Shomron. He exiled Yisra'el to Ashshur and made them live at Halah and at Habor, the River Gozan and the towns of Maday [Media].

⁷It happened because the Yisra'elites did wrong in relation to Yahweh their God who had got them up from the country of Misrayim, from under the hand of Par'oh king of Misrayim [Pharaoh king of Egypt]. They had lived in awe of other gods ⁸and had walked by the decrees of the nations that Yahweh had dispossessed from before the Yisra'elites, and the kings of Yisra'el that they made.

⁹The Yisra'elites had imputed things that were not so to Yahweh their God and built for themselves shrines in all their towns, from a keepers' tower to a fortified town. ¹⁰They put up columns and totem poles for themselves on every lofty hill and under every verdant tree. ¹¹They burned incense there in all the shrines, like the nations that Yahweh exiled from before them. They undertook bad things so as to provoke Yahweh. ¹²They served idols, of which Yahweh had said to them, 'You will not do this thing.'

## By means of every prophet

¹³Yahweh had testified against Yisra'el (and against Yehudah) by means of every prophet of his, every seer, saying, 'Turn back from your

bad ways, keep my orders and my decrees in accordance with the entire instruction that I ordered your ancestors and that I sent to you by means of my servants the prophets.' [14]They didn't listen. They toughened their neck, like the neck of their ancestors who didn't trust in Yahweh their God. [15]They rejected his decrees, his pact which he solemnized with their ancestors, and his affirmations which he testified against them. They followed hollowness and became hollow, followed the nations that were round them, ones that Yahweh had ordered them not to act like them.

[16]They abandoned all the orders of Yahweh their God, and made a cast image (two bullocks) for themselves, made a totem pole, bowed low to the entire heavenly army and served the Master. [17]They made their sons and their daughters pass through fire, engaged in divination and practised augury, and sold themselves to do what was bad in Yahweh's eyes so as to provoke him.

[18]Yahweh showed himself very angry with Yisra'el and he removed them from before his face; only the clan of Yehudah remained, alone, [19]though Yehudah, too, did not keep the orders of Yahweh their God but walked by the decrees of Yisra'el that they made.

[20]So Yahweh rejected all Yisra'el's offspring and humbled them. He gave them into the hand of pillagers until he threw them out from his presence. [21]When he tore Yisra'el from David's household, they made Yarob'am ben Nabat king, and Yarob'am drove Yisra'el away from following Yahweh and caused them to commit great wrong. [22]The Yisra'elites walked in all the wrongdoings of Yarob'am that he committed; they did not depart from them, [23]until Yahweh turned Yisra'el aside from his presence, as he spoke by means of all his servants the prophets. So Yisra'el went into exile from upon its soil to Ashshur, until this day.

## The forced immigrants

[24]The king of Ashshur brought people from Babel, from Kutah, from Avva, and from Hamat and Sepharvayim, and made them live in the towns of Shomron in place of the Yisra'elites. They took possession of Shomron and lived in its towns. [25]When they first lived there, they didn't live in awe of Yahweh, and Yahweh sent lions against them; they became killers among them. [26]They said to the king of Ashshur, 'The nations that you exiled and made to live in the towns of Shomron don't know the ruling of the country's god, and he's sent lions against them, and there, they are putting them to death, because they don't know the ruling of the country's god.'

[27]So the king of Ashshur ordered, 'Make one of the priests go there that you exiled from there. They're to go and live there and instruct them in the ruling of the god of the land.' [28]So one of the priests that they exiled from

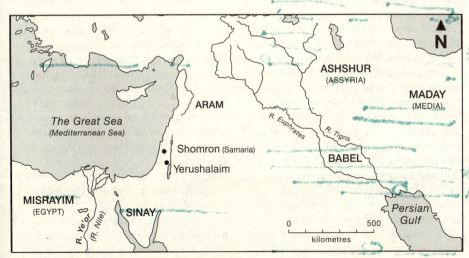

*2 Kings 17: The fall of Ephrayim and Yehudah (Ephraim and Judah)*

Shomron came and lived in Bet-el and was instructing them in how they were to live in awe of Yahweh. <sup>29</sup>But they were making nation by nation its own god, and they set them down in the house at the shrines that the Shomronites had made, nation by nation in their towns where they were living. <sup>30</sup>The people from Babel made Sukkot-benot, the people from Kut made Nergal, the people from Hamat made Ashima, <sup>31</sup>the Avvites made Nibhaz and Tartaq, the Sepharvites were burning their children in fire for Adrammelek and Anammelek, the gods of Sepharvayim. <sup>32</sup>They were living in awe of Yahweh, but they made themselves shrine priests from their sections. They were acting for them in the houses at the shrines.

<sup>33</sup>So they were living in awe of Yahweh and they were serving their gods in accordance with the ruling of the nations from which they had exiled them. <sup>34</sup>Until this day they are acting in accordance with the previous rulings. They are not living in awe of Yahweh and they are not acting in accordance with their decrees, with their rulings, with the instruction and with the order that Yahweh gave the sons of Ya'aqob, whose name he made into Yisra'el.

## The copper snake

<sup>35</sup>Yahweh had solemnized a pact with them and ordered them, 'You will not live in awe of other gods; you will not bow low to them, you will not serve them and you will not sacrifice to them. <sup>36</sup>Rather, Yahweh who got you up from the country of Misrayim by great energy and by an outstretched arm: you are to live in awe of him, bow low to him and sacrifice to him. <sup>37</sup>The decrees, the rulings, the instruction and the order that he wrote for you, you're to keep by acting on it, always. You will not live in awe of other gods. <sup>38</sup>The pact that I've solemnized with you, you will not put out of mind. You will not live in awe of other gods. <sup>39</sup>Rather you will live in awe of Yahweh your God, and it's he who will rescue you from the hand of all your enemies.' <sup>40</sup>But they hadn't listened. Rather they'd been acting in accordance with their previous ruling.

<sup>41</sup>And these nations became people who were in awe of Yahweh but were also serving their sculptures. Their children and grandchildren

are also acting as their ancestors acted, until this day.

# 18

It was in the third year of Hoshea ben Elah king of Yisra'el that Hizqiyyah ben Ahaz began to reign as king of Yehudah. <sup>2</sup>He was a man of twenty-five years when he began to reign and he reigned twenty-nine years in Yerushalaim. His mother's name was Abi bat Zekaryah. <sup>3</sup>He did what was upright in Yahweh's eyes in accordance with all that David his ancestor did. <sup>4</sup>It was he who removed the shrines, broke up the columns, cut down the totem pole, and crushed the copper snake that Mosheh had made, because until that time the Yisra'elites had been burning incense to it (it was called 'The Copper').

## The faithfulness and the rebellion of Hizqiyyahu

<sup>5</sup>It was on Yahweh the God of Yisra'el that he relied. After him there was no one like him among all the kings of Yehudah, or that were before him. <sup>6</sup>He stuck to Yahweh. He did not depart from following him but kept his orders, which Yahweh had given Mosheh, <sup>7</sup>and Yahweh was with him. Wherever he went out, he thrived. But he rebelled against the king of Ashshur and didn't serve him, <sup>8</sup>and he himself struck down the Pelishtites as far as Azzah [Gaza] and its borders, from the keepers' tower to the fortified town.

<sup>9</sup>In the fourth year of King Hizqiyyahu (i.e. the seventh year of Hoshea ben Elah king of Yisra'el) Shalman'eser king of Ashshur went up against Shomron and besieged it. <sup>10</sup>They captured it at the end of three years; in the sixth year of Hizqiyyah (i.e. the ninth year of Hoshea king of Yisra'el) Shomron was captured, <sup>11</sup>and the king of Ashshur exiled the Yisra'elites to Ashshur and settled them in Halah and in Habor, the River Gozan and the towns of Maday, <sup>12</sup>because of the fact that they didn't listen to the voice of Yahweh their God but transgressed his pact, all that Mosheh Yahweh's servant had ordered. They didn't listen and they didn't act.

<sup>13</sup>In the fourteenth year of King Hizqiyyahu, Sanherib [Sennacherib] king of Ashshur went up against all the fortified towns of Yehudah and captured them. <sup>14</sup>Hizqiyyah king of

Yehudah sent to the king of Ashshur at Lakish saying, 'I have done wrong. Turn back from me. What you put upon me, I will carry.' The king of Ashshur placed on Hizqiyyah king of Yehudah 300 talents of silver and thirty talents of gold. ¹⁵Hizqiyyah gave him all the silver that could be found in Yahweh's house and in the treasuries of the king's house. ¹⁶At that time Hizqiyyah cut down the doors of Yahweh's palace and the posts that Hizqiyyah king of Yehudah had overlaid, and gave them to the king of Ashshur.

## Shut up like a bird in a cage (as Sanherib put it)

¹⁷The king of Ashshur sent the Tartan, the Rab-saris and the Rab-shaqeh from Lakish to King Hizqiyyahu in Yerushalaim with a heavy force. They went up, and came to Yerushalaim and stood at the Upper Pool channel, which is by the Washer's Field causeway. ¹⁸They called to the king, and Elyaqim ben Hilqiyyahu who was in charge of the household, Shebna the secretary and Yo'ah ben Asaph the recorder went out to them.

¹⁹The Rab-shaqeh said to them, 'Say to Hizqiyyahu, please, "The Great King, the king of Ashshur, has said this: 'What is this reliance that you have? ²⁰You've said, "Just the word on some lips are counsel and strength for the battle." Now, on whom have you relied, that you've rebelled against me? ²¹Now, there, you've relied for yourself on the support of this broken reed, on Misrayim, which when someone leans on it, comes into his palm and pierces it. Such is Par'oh king of Misrayim to all the people who rely on him. ²²But when you say to me, "On Yahweh our God – we've relied on him", he's the one whose shrines and whose altars Hizqiyyahu has removed, isn't he, and who's said to Yehudah and to Yerushalaim, "Before this altar you're to bow low in Yerushalaim."

²³But now, please make a wager with my lord the king of Ashshur. I'll give you 2,000 horses if you can put riders on them for yourself. ²⁴So how could you turn back the face of the governor of one of my lord's lesser servants and rely on Misrayim for chariotry and for cavalry for yourself? ²⁵Is it now without Yahweh that I've gone up to this place to devastate it? It was

Yahweh who said to me, "Go up to this country and devastate it."''''

## Don't speak in their language

²⁶Elyaqim ben Hilqiyyahu, Shebna and Yo'ah said to the Rab-shaqeh, 'Please speak to your servants in Aramaic, because we're listening. Don't speak to us in Yehudahite in the ears of the people, which is on the wall.' ²⁷The Rab-shaqeh said to them, 'Was it to your lord and to you that my lord sent me to speak these words? Wasn't it to the individuals who are sitting on the wall, to eat their faeces and to drink the water between their legs with you?'

²⁸The Rab-shaqeh stood and called in a loud voice in Yehudahite, and spoke: 'Listen to the word of the Great King, the king of Ashshur. ²⁹The king has said this: "Hizqiyyahu must not deceive you", because he won't be able to rescue you from his hand. ³⁰And Hizqiyyahu must not get you to rely on Yahweh, saying "Yahweh will definitely rescue us; this town won't be given into the hand of the king of Ashshur." ³¹Don't listen to Hizqiyyahu.

Because the king of Ashshur has said this: "Make a blessing [agreement]with me. Go out to me, and eat each one his vine and each one his fig tree, and drink each one the water from his cistern, ³²until I come and take you to a country like your country, a country of grain and new wine, a country of bread and vineyards, a country of fresh olive oil and syrup, and you will live and not die. Don't listen to Hizqiyyahu when he incites you, saying, 'Yahweh will rescue us.' ³³Have the gods of the nations actually rescued, one of them, his country from the hand of the king of Ashshur? ³⁴Where were the gods of Hamat and Arpad? Where were the gods of Sepharvayim, Hena and Ivvah? Indeed did they rescue Shomron from my hand? ³⁵Who was it among all the gods of the countries that rescued their country from my hand, that Yahweh should rescue Yerushalaim from my hand?"'

## Perhaps Yahweh will listen

³⁶They were silent. They didn't answer him a word, because it was the king's order, 'Don't

answer him.' [37]But Elyaqim ben Hilqiyyah who was in charge of the household, Shebna the secretary and Yo'ah ben Asaph the recorder came to Hizqiyyahu, their clothes torn, and told him the Rab-shaqeh's words.

**19** When King Hizqiyyahu heard, he tore his clothes and covered himself in sack. He came into Yahweh's house [2]but he sent Elyaqim, who was in charge of the household, Shebna the secretary and the priestly elders, covering themselves in sack, to Yesha'yahu [Isaiah] ben Amots the prophet. [3]They said to him, 'Hizqiyyahu has said this: "This is a day of pressure, reproof and disdain, because 'children have come to breaking but there's no energy to give birth'. [4]Perhaps Yahweh your God will listen to all the words of the Rab-shaqeh, whom the king of Ashshur his lord sent to revile the living God, and will issue a reproof for the words that Yahweh your God heard, and you will lift up a plea on behalf of the remains that are to be found here."'

[5]King Hizqiyyahu's servants came to Yesha'yahu, [6]and Yesha'yahu said to them, 'You're to say this to your lord: "Yahweh has said this: 'Don't be afraid before the words you've heard with which the king of Ashshur's boys have insulted me. [7]Here, I'm going to put a spirit in him, and he'll hear a report and go back to his country, and I shall cause him to fall by the sword in his country.'"'

[8]The Rab-shaqeh went back and found the king of Ashshur battling against Libnah, because he heard that he had moved on from Lakish, [9a]and he heard about Tirhaqah king of Kush [Sudan], 'There, he's gone out to battle with you.'

## What to do with tricky mail

[9b]He again sent envoys to Hizqiyyahu, saying [10]'You're to say this to Hizqiyyahu king of Yehudah: "Your God on whom you're relying mustn't deceive you, saying, 'Yerushalaim won't be given into the hand of the king of Ashshur.' [11]Here, you yourself have heard what the kings of Ashshur have done to all the countries, devoting them, and are you the one who'll be rescued? [12]Did the gods of the nations that my ancestors devastated rescue them – Gozan, Harran, Retseph, and the Edenites who were in Tela'ssar? [13]Where is the king of Hamat, the king of Arpad, the king of La'ir, Sepharvayim, Hena and Yivvah?"'

[14]Hizqiyyahu took the documents from the envoys' hand, read them out and went up to Yahweh's house. Hizqiyyahu spread it before Yahweh, [15]and Hizqiyyahu pleaded before Yahweh: 'Yahweh, Yisra'el's God, sitting above the sphinxes: you are God, you alone, for all the kingdoms of the earth. You are the one who made the heavens and the earth. [16]Yahweh, bend your ear and listen. Yahweh, open your eyes and see. Listen to the words of Sanherib that he has sent to revile the living God.

[17]Truly, Yahweh, the kings of Ashshur have put to the sword the nations, and their own country, [18]and put their gods into the fire, because they were not gods but rather the making of human hands, wood and stone, and they obliterated them. [19]But now, Yahweh our God, please deliver us from his hand, so that all the kingdoms of the earth may acknowledge that you alone are Yahweh God.'

[20]Yesha'yahu ben Amots sent to Hizqiyyahu saying, 'Yahweh, Yisra'el's God, with whom you pleaded concerning Sanherib king of Ashshur, has said this: "I have heard." [21a]This is the word that Yahweh has spoken about him.

## Yahweh's own ridicule

[21b]Maiden Miss Tsiyyon
    despises you, she ridicules you.
Behind you Miss Yerushalaim
    has shaken her head.
[22]Whom have you reviled and insulted,
    against whom have you lifted your voice?
You've raised your eyes on high
    against Yisra'el's sacred one.
[23]By the hand of your envoys
    you've reviled the Lord, and said:
'With the large number of my chariotry
    I'm the one who's gone up
to the mountains' height,
    Lebanon's farthest parts.
I've cut down the highest of its cedars,
    the choicest of its junipers.
I've come to its ultimate lodge,
    its forest of farmland.

²⁴I'm the one who's dug
    and drunk foreign water.
I've dried with the sole of my feet
    all Misrayim's streams.

²⁵Haven't you heard?
    – long ago I did it.
In days of old I formed it;
    now I've made it come about.
It's happened, crashing fortified towns
    into wasted heaps.
²⁶Their inhabitants, short of ability,
    are scared and shamed.
They were vegetation of the fields,
    green herbage,
Grass on the roofs,
    blasted before it grows up.
²⁷Your staying, your going out, and your
    coming I know,
    and your raging at me.
²⁸Since you raged at me,
    and your din came up into my ears,
I shall put my hook in your nose,
    my bit in your mouth,
I shall make you go back
    by the way that you came.

## The promise for Hizqiyyahu

²⁹This will be the sign for you:

This year, eat the natural growth;
    in the second year, the secondary
      growth.
In the third year sow and reap,
    plant vineyards and eat their fruit.
³⁰An escape group from Yehudah's household
    that remains
    will add root downwards and produce fruit
      above.
³¹Because a remainder will go out from
    Yerushalaim,
    and an escape group from Mount Tsiyyon.
The passion of Yahweh of Armies
    will do this.

³²Therefore Yahweh has said this concerning
the king of Ashshur:

He will not come into this town;
    he will not shoot an arrow there.

He will not approach it with a shield;
    he will not heap up a ramp against it.
³³By the way that he comes he will go back;
    into this city he will not come
    (Yahweh's declaration).
³⁴I will shield this town so as to deliver it,
    for my sake and for the sake of David my
      servant.

³⁵That night Yahweh's envoy went out and struck down 185,000 in the Ashshurites' camp. People started early in the morning – there, all of them were dead corpses.

³⁶Sanherib king of Ashshur moved on and went, and returned and lived in Nineveh. ³⁷He was bowing low in the house of Nisrok his god when Adrammelek and Sar'etser his sons struck him down with the sword. While they escaped to the country of Ararat, Esar-haddon his son began to reign in place of him.

## How to gain God's sympathy

**20** In those days Hizqiyyahu became deathly ill. Yesha'yahu ben Amots the prophet came to him and said to him, 'Yahweh has said this: "Give orders to your household, because you're dying. You won't live on."' ²He turned his face round to the wall and pleaded with Yahweh, ³'Oh, Yahweh, please be mindful of how I've walked about before you in truth and with a perfect mind, and done what is good in your eyes.' Hizqiyyahu cried and cried much.

⁴Yesha'yahu had not gone out of the middle courtyard when Yahweh's word came to him: ⁵'Go back and say to Hizqiyyahu, the chief of my people, "Yahweh, the God of David your ancestor, has said this: 'I have listened to your plea, I've seen your tears. Here, I'm going to heal you. On the third day you'll go up to Yahweh's house. ⁶I shall add fifteen years to your time. From the fist of the king of Ashshur I shall rescue you and this town, and I shall shield this town for my sake and for David my servant's sake.'"' ⁷Yesha'yahu said, 'Get a block of figs.' They got one and put it on the inflammation and he lived on.

⁸Hizqiyyahu had said to Yesha'yahu, 'What will be the sign that Yahweh will heal me and I shall go up to Yahweh's house on the third day?' ⁹Yesha'yahu said, 'This will be the sign for you

from Yahweh that Yahweh will do the thing that he has spoken of. The shadow has gone ten steps. Can it go back ten steps?' [10]Yehizqiyyahu said, 'It's a slight thing for the shadow to extend ten steps, not that the shadow should turn back ten steps.' [11]So Yesha'yahu the prophet called to Yahweh and he made the shadow go back ten steps on the steps where it had gone down, on the steps of Ahaz.

## How to lose God's sympathy

[12]At that time Ber'odak Bal'adan ben Bal'adan king of Babel sent documents and an offering to Hizqiyyahu because he had heard that Hizqiyyahu was ill. [13]Hizqiyyahu heard about them and let them see his entire repository house, the silver, the gold, the spices and the fine oil, and his equipment house and everything that was to be found in his storehouses. There was not a thing that Hizqiyyahu didn't let them see in his house and in his entire realm.

[14]Yesha'yahu the prophet came to King Hizqiyyahu and said to him, 'What did these men say? Where did they come from to you?' Hizqiyyahu said, 'From a far country; they came from Babel.' [15]He said, 'What did they see in your house?' Hizqiyyahu said, 'They saw everything that's in my house. There wasn't a thing that I didn't let them see in my storehouses.'

[16]Yesha'yahu said to Hizqiyyahu, 'Listen to Yahweh's word: [17]"There, days are going to come when everything that's in your house, and that your ancestors have stored up until this day, will be carried to Babel. Not a thing will be left", Yahweh has said. [18]"Some of your descendants who will issue from you, whom you will father, will be taken and will become courtiers in the palace of the king of Babel."'

[19]Hizqiyyahu said to Yesha'yahu, 'The word of Yahweh that you have spoken is good.' He said, 'Isn't it so, if there'll be well-being and truthfulness in my days?'

[20]The rest of the things about Hizqiyyahu and all his strength, and how he made the pool and the channel and brought the water into the town, are written on the document about things of the time regarding the kings of Yehudah. [21]Hizqiyyahu lay down with his ancestors and Menashsheh his son began to reign in place of him.

## How to be the bad guy

**21** Menashsheh was twelve years of age when he began to reign and he reigned fifty-five years in Yerushalaim. His mother's name was Hephtsibah. [2]He did what was bad in Yahweh's eyes in accordance with the offensive practices of the nations that Yahweh dispossessed from before the Yisra'elites. [3]He rebuilt the shrines that Hizqiyyahu his father obliterated, and set up altars for the Master and made a totem pole, as Ah'ab king of Yisra'el had done. He bowed low to all the heavenly army and served them. [4]He built altars in Yahweh's house of which Yahweh had said, 'In Yerushalaim I will put my name.' [5]He built altars for all the heavenly army in the two courtyards of Yahweh's house. [6]He made his son pass through fire and practised augury and divination and dealt with ghosts and spirits. He did much that was bad in Yahweh's eyes, so as to provoke him.

[7]He put a sculpture of Asherah that he made in the house of which Yahweh said to David and to Shelomoh [Solomon] his son, 'In this house and in Yerushalaim, which I chose from all Yisra'el's clans, I will put my name permanently. [8]And I shall not continue to make Yisra'el's foot wander from the land that I gave their ancestors, only if they keep watch to act in accordance with all that I ordered them, and regarding the entire instruction that my servant Mosheh ordered them.' [9]But they didn't listen, and Menashsheh got them to wander so as to deal badly more than the nations that Yahweh annihilated from before the Yisra'elites.

[10]Yahweh spoke by means of his servants the prophets: [11]'Since Menashsheh king of Yehudah has done these offensive things (he has dealt badly more than all that the Amorites did who were before him) and has also caused Yehudah to do wrong with his idols, [12]therefore Yahweh the God of Yisra'el has said this: "Here, I am going to bring bad fortune on Yerushalaim and Yehudah such that everyone who hears it – both his ears will screech.

## Wiping the dish clean

[13]Over Yerushalaim I will stretch Shomron's measuring line and the household of Ah'ab's

scale. I will wipe Yerushalaim clean as one wipes a dish clean, wipe it and turn it on its face. <sup>14</sup>I will leave the remains of my domain and give them into the hand of their enemies. They will be plunder and spoil for all their enemies, <sup>15</sup>since they've done what is bad in my eyes and they've been provoking me from the day that I got their ancestors out of Misrayim until this day.'"

<sup>16</sup>Further, Menashsheh poured out very much blood of people who were free of guilt, until he filled Yerushalaim end to end, beside the wrong that he caused Yehudah to commit in doing what was bad in Yahweh's eyes. <sup>17</sup>The rest of the things about Menashsheh, all that he did and the wrongdoing that he committed, are written on the document about things of the time regarding the kings of Yehudah, aren't they. <sup>18</sup>Menashsheh lay down with his ancestors and was buried in the garden of his house, in Uzza's Garden, and Amon his son began to reign in place of him.

<sup>19</sup>Amon was a man of twenty-two years when he began to reign and he reigned two years in Yerushalaim. His mother's name was Meshullemet bat Haruts, from Yotbah. <sup>20</sup>He did what was bad in Yahweh's eyes, as Menashsheh his father did. <sup>21</sup>He walked in all the way that his father walked, and served the idols that his father served and bowed low to them. <sup>22</sup>He abandoned Yahweh, his ancestors' God, and did not walk in Yahweh's way. <sup>23</sup>Amon's servants conspired against him and put the king to death in his house, <sup>24</sup>but the people of the country struck down all those who had conspired against King Amon. The people of the country made Yo'shiyyahu [Josiah] king in place of him.

<sup>25</sup>The rest of the things about Amon that he did are written on the document about things of the time regarding the kings of Yehudah, aren't they. <sup>26</sup>They buried him in his grave in Uzza's Garden, and his son Yo'shiyyahu began to reign in place of him.

## Last chance to take the Torah and the Prophets seriously

**22** Yo'shiyyahu was eight years of age when he began to reign and he reigned thirty-one years in Yerushalaim. His mother's name was Yedidah bat Adayah, from Botsqat. <sup>2</sup>He did what was upright in Yahweh's eyes and walked in the entire way of David his ancestor. He did not depart right or left.

<sup>3</sup>In the eighteenth year of King Yo'shiyyahu, the king sent Shaphan ben Atsalyahu son of Meshullam to Yahweh's house, saying <sup>4</sup>'Go up to Hilqiyyahu the big priest so he may weigh the silver that's been brought to Yahweh's house, which the people keeping watch over the threshold have gathered from the people. <sup>5</sup>They're to put it into the hand of the people doing the work who were appointed to Yahweh's house, so they may give it to the people doing the work who are in Yahweh's house, to strengthen the defects in the house, <sup>6</sup>to the craftsmen, to the builders, to the masons, and for the acquiring of wood and hewn stones to strengthen the house. <sup>7</sup>Only there will be no reckoning made with them of the silver given into their hand, because they're acting with trustworthiness.'

<sup>8</sup>Hilqiyyahu, the big priest, said to Shaphan, the secretary, 'I've found an instruction document in Yahweh's house.' Hilqiyyahu gave the document to Shaphan and he read it out. <sup>9</sup>Shaphan the secretary came to the king and took back word to the king: 'Your servants have melted down the silver that was found in the house and they've given it into the hand of the people doing the work who were appointed to Yahweh's house.' <sup>10</sup>And Shaphan the secretary told the king, 'Hilqiyyah the priest gave me a document.' Shaphan read it out before the king.

## The tough and gentle prophetess

<sup>11</sup>When the king heard the words in the instruction document, he tore his clothes. <sup>12</sup>The king ordered Hilqiyyah the priest, Ahiqam ben Shaphan, Akbor ben Mikayah, Shaphan the secretary and Asayah the king's servant, <sup>13</sup>'Go enquire of Yahweh on my behalf and on behalf of the people and on behalf of all Yehudah about the words in this document that's been found, because great is Yahweh's wrath that has set on fire against us because our ancestors didn't listen to the words in this document by acting in accordance with everything that's written for us.'

<sup>14</sup>Hilqiyyahu the priest went, with Ahiqam, Akbor, Shaphan and Asayah, to Huldah the prophetess, wife of Shallum ben Tikvah son of Harhas, keeper of the robes; she was living in Yerushalaim in the Second Quarter. They spoke to her.

<sup>15</sup>She said to them, 'Yahweh the God of Yisra'el has said this: "Say to the man who sent you to me: <sup>16</sup>'Yahweh has said this: "Here, I'm going to bring bad fortune to this place and to its inhabitants, all the things in the document that the king of Yehudah read out, <sup>17</sup>because of the fact that they abandoned me and burned incense to other gods in order to provoke me with all the actions of their hands. My wrath will set on fire against this place and it will not douse.""'

<sup>18</sup>But to the king of Yehudah who sent you to enquire of Yahweh, you're to say this to him: "Yahweh the God of Yisra'el has said this: 'The words that you have heard: <sup>19</sup>since your mind softened and you bowed down before Yahweh when you heard what I had spoken against this place and against its inhabitants (becoming a desolation and a slighting) and you tore your clothes and cried before me, I for my part have also listened (Yahweh's declaration). <sup>20</sup>Therefore, here, I am going to gather you to your ancestors and you will gather yourself to your great grave with things being well. Your eyes will not see all the bad fortune that I am going to bring on this place.""' They took the word back to the king.

## The covenant and the clean-up

**23** The king sent and gathered to him all the elders of Yehudah and Yerushalaim, <sup>2</sup>and the king went up to Yahweh's house, with everyone in Yehudah and all the inhabitants of Yerushalaim with him, and the priests and the prophets, and the entire people, young and old. He read out in their ears all the words in the pact document found in Yahweh's house. <sup>3</sup>The king stood by the pillar and solemnized a pact before Yahweh, to follow Yahweh and keep his orders, his affirmations and his decrees with their entire mind and with their entire being, by setting up the words of this pact that were written on this document. The entire people stood by the pact.

<sup>4</sup>The king ordered Hilqiyyahu the big priest, the priests of the second order, and the people keeping watch over the threshold to take out from Yahweh's palace all the articles made for the Master and for Asherah and for the entire heavenly army, and he burned them outside Yerushalaim in the Qidron Fields, and carried their dust to Bet-el. <sup>5</sup>He did away with the clergy whom the kings of Yehudah had made to burn incense in the shrines in the towns of Yehudah and the areas round Yerushalaim, and the people who burned incense for the Master, for the sun, for the moon, for the constellations and for the entire heavenly army. <sup>6</sup>He took the totem pole out of Yahweh's house, outside of Yerushalaim, to Wadi Qidron, and burned it in Wadi Qidron, crushed it to dust and threw its dust over the grave of the ordinary people. <sup>7</sup>He demolished the houses of the hierodules that were in Yahweh's house, where the women were weaving 'houses' for the totem pole.

<sup>8</sup>He brought all the priests from the towns of Yehudah and defiled the shrines where the priests burned incense, from Geba as far as Be'er-sheba. He demolished the shrines at the gateways, which were at the entrance of the gateway of Yehoshua, the official over the town, which were on one's left at the town gateway. <sup>9</sup>Yet the priests of the shrines did not go up to Yahweh's altar in Yerushalaim; rather, they ate flatbread among their brothers.

## Honouring the long-ago prophets

<sup>10</sup>He defiled the Hearth which is in the Ben-hinnom Ravine so that no one would make his son or his daughter pass through fire to the Shameful King. <sup>11</sup>He did away with the horses that the kings of Yehudah gave for the sun, from the entrance of Yahweh's house, near the hall of Natan-melek the courtier, which was in the precincts. He burned the sun chariots in fire. <sup>12</sup>The altars that were on the roof of Ahaz's upper quarters, which the kings of Yehudah had made, and the altars that Menashsheh had made in the two courtyards of Yahweh's house, the king demolished. He ran from there and threw their dust into Wadi Qidron.

<sup>13</sup>The shrines that were facing Yerushalaim, which were south of Destroyer Mountain, which

Shelomoh king of Yisra'el had built for Shameful Ashtar the abomination of the Tsidonites, for Kemosh the abomination of Mo'ab and for Milkom the offence of the Ammonites, the king defiled. [14]He broke up the columns and cut up the totem poles and filled their site with human bones.

[15]Also the altar which was at Bet-el (the shrine that Yarob'am ben Nebat, who caused Yisra'el to do wrong, made) – also that altar and the shrine, he demolished. He burned the shrine and beat it to dust, and burned the totem pole.

[16]Yo'shiyyahu turned his face and saw the graves that were there on the mountain. He sent and got the bones from the graves and burned them on the altar, and defiled it in accordance with Yahweh's word that the supernatural man called out, who called out these things. [17]He said, 'What's that sign that I'm looking at?' The people of the town said to him, 'The grave of the supernatural man who came from Yehudah and called out these things that you have done to the Bet-el altar.' [18]He said, 'Let him be. No one is to disturb his bones.' So they saved his bones, and the bones of the prophet who came from Shomron.

### The incomparable reformer

[19]All the houses at the shrines that were in the towns of Shomron, which the kings of Yisra'el had made so as to provoke, Yo'shiyyahu also removed. He acted towards them in accordance with the actions that he undertook at Bet'el. [20]He sacrificed all the priests of the shrines who were there, on the altars, and burned human bones on them, and went back to Yerushalaim.

[21]The king ordered the entire people: 'Make Pesah [Passover] for Yahweh your God as is written on this pact document.' [22]Because it had not been made like this Pesah since the days of the leaders who had led Yisra'el or all the days of the kings of Yisra'el and the kings of Yehudah. [23]Rather, in the eighteenth year of King Yo'shiyyahu this Pesah was made for Yahweh in Yerushalaim.

[24]The ghosts, the spirits, the effigies, the idols and all the abominations that were to be seen in the country of Yehudah and in Yerushalaim, Yo'shiyyahu also burned away, in order to implement the things in the instruction that were written on the document that Hilqiyyahu the priest had found in Yahweh's house.

[25]Before him there was no king like him who turned back to Yahweh with his entire mind, with his entire being and with his entire might in accordance with Mosheh's entire instruction, and after him none rose up like him. [26]Yet Yahweh did not turn back from the great angry rage with which his anger raged against Yehudah because of all the provocative acts with which Menashsheh had provoked him. [27]Yahweh said, 'Yehudah, too, I shall remove from before my face, as I removed Yisra'el. I shall reject this town that I chose, Yerushalaim, and the house of which I said, "My name will be there."'

### The loss of Yo'shiyyahu

[28]The rest of the things about Yo'shiyyahu and all that he did are written on the document about things of the time regarding the kings of Yehudah, aren't they. [29]In his days Par'oh Neko king of Misrayim went up against the king of Ashshur at the River Euphrates. King Yo'shiyyahu went to meet him, but he put him to death at Megiddo when he saw him. [30]His servants transported him dead from Megiddo and brought him to Yerushalaim, and buried him in his grave.

The people of the country got Yeho'ahaz ben Yo'shiyyahu, and anointed him and made him king in place of his father. [31]Yeho'ahaz was a man of twenty-three years when he began to reign and he reigned three months in Yerushalaim. His mother's name was Hamutal bat Yirmeyahu, from Libnah. [32]He did what was bad in Yahweh's eyes in accordance with all that his ancestors had done. [33]Par'oh Neko confined him at Riblah in the region of Hamat to stop him reigning in Yerushalaim, and put a levy on the country of a hundred talents of silver and a talent of gold.

[34]Par'oh Neko made Elyaqim ben Yo'shiyyahu king in place of his father, but turned his name into Yehoyaqim. He took Yeho'ahaz, and he came to Misrayim and died there. [35]The silver and the gold Yehoyaqim gave to Par'oh, only

he assessed the country so as to give the silver in accordance with Par'oh's bidding. Each person according to his assessment, he exacted the silver and the gold from the people of the country so as to give it to Par'oh Neko.

³⁶Yehoyaqim was a man of twenty-five years when he began to reign and he reigned eleven years in Yerushalaim. His mother's name was Zebudah bat Pedayah, from Rumah. ³⁷He did what was bad in Yahweh's eyes, in accordance with all that his ancestors did.

## How things start to collapse

**24** In his days Nebukadne'tstsar king of Babel went up and Yehoyaqim became his servant for three years, but he turned back and rebelled against him. ²Yahweh sent against him raiding gangs of the Kasdites [Babylonians], raiding gangs from Aram, raiding gangs from Mo'ab and raiding gangs of the Ammonites. He sent them against Yehudah to obliterate it, in accordance with Yahweh's word which he spoke by means of his servants the prophets. ³Indeed, it was at Yahweh's bidding that it happened to Yehudah, to remove them from before his face because of Menashsheh's wrongdoings, in accordance with all that he did, ⁴and also the blood of people who were free of guilt that he had shed. He had filled Yerushalaim with the blood of people free of guilt, and Yahweh was not willing to pardon.

⁵The rest of the things about Yehoyaqim and all that he did are written on the document about things of the time regarding the kings of Yehudah, aren't they. ⁶Yehoyaqim lay down with his ancestors and his son Yehoyakin began to reign in place of him. ⁷The king of Misrayim did not go out of his country again, because the king of Babel had taken all that had belonged to the king of Misrayim from the Misrayimite Wadi as far as the River Euphrates.

⁸Yehoyakin was eighteen years of age when he began to reign and he reigned three months in Yerushalaim. His mother's name was Nehushta bat Elnatan, from Yerushalaim. ⁹He did what was bad in Yahweh's eyes, in accordance with all that his father did. ¹⁰At that time the servants of Nebukadne'tstsar king of Babel went up to Yerushalaim and the town came under siege. ¹¹Nebukadne'tstsar king of Babel came against the town while his servants were besieging it, ¹²and Yehoyakin king of Yehudah went out to the king of Babel, he, his mother, his servants, his officials and his courtiers. The king of Babel took him in the eighth year of his reign.

## The first Yehudahite exile and the final siege

¹³He took away from there the treasures of Yahweh's house and the treasures of the king's house, and cut off all the gold objects that Shelomoh had made in Yahweh's palace, as Yahweh had said. ¹⁴He exiled all Yerushalaim, all the officials and all the forceful strong men, 10,000 exiles, and every craftsman and smith. No one remained apart from the poorest element of the people in the country. ¹⁵He exiled Yehoyakin to Babel, and the king's mother, the king's wives, his courtiers and the country's leaders he made go as exiles from Yerushalaim to Babel, ¹⁶with all the forceful men, 7,000 (and craftsman and smith, 1,000), all of them the strong men doing battle. The king of Babel made them come as exiles to Babel.

¹⁷The king of Babel made Mattanyah, his uncle, king in place of him, and turned his name to Tsidqiyyahu [Zedekiah]. ¹⁸Tsidqiyyahu was twenty-one years of age when he began to reign and he reigned eleven years in Yerushalaim. His mother's name was Hamutal bat Yirmeyahu, from Libnah. ¹⁹He did what was bad in Yahweh's eyes in accordance with all that Yehoyaqim had done, ²⁰because of the fact that Yahweh's anger was against Yerushalaim and against Yehudah until he threw them out of his presence.

Tsidqiyyahu rebelled against the king of Babel,

**25** and in the ninth year of his reign, in the tenth month, on the tenth of the month, Nebukadne'tstsar king of Babel came against Yerushalaim, he and his entire force. He camped against it and built blockades all round. ²The town came under siege until the eleventh year of King Tsidqiyyahu. ³On the ninth of the month the famine had become overwhelming in the town and there was no bread for the people of the country. <sup>4a</sup>The town broke open, and all the men of battle [left] in the night by way of the gateway between the double wall which was by the king's garden, while the Kasdites were all round the town.

### The destruction and the second Yehudahite exile

<sup>4b</sup>He went by the steppe road, <sup>5</sup>but the Kasdite force pursued after the king. They overtook him in the Yeriho steppes when his entire force had scattered from him. <sup>6</sup>They captured the king and took him up to the king of Babel at Riblah, and he pronounced a decision about him. <sup>7</sup>Tsidqiyyahu's sons they slaughtered before his eyes, Tsidqiyyahu's eyes he gouged out, and he bound him with copper chains and brought him to Babel.

<sup>8</sup>In the fifth month, on the seventh of the month (i.e. the nineteenth year of King Nebukadne'tstsar king of Babel), Nebuzar'adan the chief of the guards, servant of the king of Babel, came to Yerushalaim <sup>9</sup>and burned Yahweh's house, the king's house and all the houses in Yerushalaim. Every house of a big person he burned in fire. <sup>10</sup>The walls round Yerushalaim, the entire Kasdite force that was with the chief of the guards demolished. <sup>11</sup>The rest of the people who remained in the town and the people who had submitted (who had submitted to the king of Babel) and the rest of the horde, Nebuzar'adan the chief of the guards took into exile, <sup>12</sup>but some of the poorest elements in the country the chief of the guards let remain as vinedressers and farm workers.

<sup>13</sup>The copper pillars that were in Yahweh's house, and the stands and the copper sea that were in Yahweh's house, the Kasdites broke up and carried their copper to Babel. <sup>14</sup>The buckets, the shovels, the snuffers, the ladles and all the copper articles with which they ministered, they took. <sup>15</sup>The pans and the sprinklers, whatever was of gold and whatever was of silver, the chief of the guards took. <sup>16</sup>The two pillars, the one sea and the stands that Shelomoh made for Yahweh's house – there was no weighing the copper in all these articles. <sup>17</sup>The height of the one pillar was nine metres, with a copper capital on it; the height of the capital was one and a half metres, with a net with pomegranates on the capital all round, all of it copper, and like these was the second pillar with the net.

### Is it the end or is there hope?

<sup>18</sup>The chief of the guards took Serayah the head priest, Tsephanyahu the number two priest and the three keepers of the threshold, <sup>19</sup>and from the town he took a courtier who was appointee over the men of battle, and five people from the heads who were before the king, who were found in the town, the secretary of the army officer who mustered the people of the country, and sixty individuals from the people of the country who were found in the town. <sup>20</sup>Nebuzar'adan the chief of the guards took them and made them go to the king of Babel at Riblah. <sup>21</sup>The king of Babel struck them down and put them to death at Riblah, in the region of Hamat.

So Yehudah went into exile from upon its land, <sup>22</sup>while the people that remained in the country of Yehudah whom Nebukadne'tstsar king of Babel allowed to remain – he appointed over them Gedalyahu ben Ahiqam son of Shaphan. <sup>23</sup>All the officers of the forces, they and their men, heard that the king of Babel had appointed Gedalyahu, and they came to Gedalyahu at The Watchtower, with Yishma'e'l ben Netanyah, Yohanan ben Qareah, Serayah ben Tanhumet the Netophatite and Ya'azanyahu son of the Ma'akatite, and their men. <sup>24</sup>Gedalyahu swore to them and to their men, and said, 'Don't be afraid of the Kasdites' servants. Stay in the country. Serve the king of Babel. Things will be good for you.'

<sup>25</sup>But in the seventh month Yishma'e'l ben Netanyah son of Elishama, of royal descent, came with ten men with him, and struck down Gedalyahu and put him to death, him and the Yehudahites and the Kasdites who were with him at The Watchtower. <sup>26</sup>And all the people, young and old, and the officers over the forces, set off and came to Misrayim, because they were afraid of the Kasdites.

<sup>27</sup>But in the thirty-seventh year of the exile of Yehoyakin king of Yehudah, in the twelfth month, on the twenty-seventh of the month, Ewil-merodak king of Babel, in the year he

began to reign, lifted up the head of Yehoyakin king of Yehudah from the cells. <sup>28</sup>He spoke of good things with him, gave him a seat above the seat of the kings who were with him in Babel <sup>29</sup>and changed his prison clothes. He ate bread before him regularly for his entire life. <sup>30</sup>His provision was given him as a regular provision from the king, a day's allocation on its day, for his entire life.

# I CHRONICLES

The first book of Chronicles retells the entire story from Adam to David which is told in Genesis to Samuel. Why does it do so, and why does the Bible include two versions of the story? One could compare the fact that the New Testament includes four versions of the Jesus story. It would be less confusing to have just one. But a good story can be told from different angles, and the more you tell it, the more illuminating it becomes. You get a different take on it, you get a different author's angle on what it means and you look at it from the perspective of a different audience.

The first thing that strikes you when you start reading Chronicles is that the opening third is just lists of names. In part, that's the way it summarizes the entire story from Adam to David. It's a bit like the opening frames of an episode in a TV serial that provide a lightning reminder of the story so far. This 'series' as a whole is going to focus on David, but the audience needs to see David in his context in the entire story of Israel – indeed, the entire story of the world. This entire story leads up to him. But the chapters also preserve lots of other information that helps the readers know where they came from. The coverage is uneven; perhaps it simply preserves what was available.

The lists of names include references to people living much later than David's day, and Book One of Chronicles as a whole leads into Book Two which takes the story on through another five centuries after David, up to the time when people from Judah are taken off into exile and are then encouraged to return to Jerusalem to rebuild the temple. So Chronicles was not written in David's day, which makes that focus striking. Chronicles is a version of Israel's story told by someone living in Jerusalem in the time of the Second Temple and told for people living in that context. The books of Ezra and Nehemiah and the visions in Daniel give us some insight into events during those times.

Why does Chronicles focus on David? The answer emerges when we consider the book's angle on its hero. Its interest lies not in the great warrior or the smart operator of 1 and 2 Samuel, nor is he the intriguing human being with clay feet that those books also portray. Those books also relate how David set going the process whereby the first temple was built, and it's this aspect of David's achievement that interests Chronicles.

Its angle would be significant for people living in Second Temple times. They were hard times. The community in Judah that centred on Jerusalem was a shadow of its former self. Geographically it was the size of a county, not a country. Politically it was a colony of the Persian Empire. Its faith and its life were often under pressure from neighbouring peoples. When things are like that, how do you hold on?

The First Testament gives people several complementary answers. The prophets' answer is that you look to the future and tell yourself that things are going to get better. Judah was not just whistling in the wind when it lived by such hopes. God had made a commitment to David that God could not get out of, and people could live in the light of promises that God would one day send them a new David.

A complementary answer is that you look to the past, to what God has done in the past, and it is this answer that attracts Chronicles. Its interest in the past doesn't focus on creation, Abraham, the exodus, or Joshua, but on David. It does so from this angle, David as founder of the temple worship. Telling that story encourages people in Jerusalem to live in the present, because for all the limitations of present experience, one great privilege they do have is the daily round of temple worship. Some of the lists in the first third of the book, and the lists in the last third, relate to the actual arrangements for worship and other aspects of community life in David's day, and in the time of the book's readers.

That daily worship is also significant for people who don't live in Jerusalem. The priest in an English church used to ring the church bell before going into church morning and evening. People who could not respond to the summons could know that the priest was conducting the prayers and could join in at a distance. Elsewhere in Judah, people could know that temple worship was being offered and could associate themselves with it. They could even do so from many miles away, as Daniel did.

*In the beginning*

**1** Adam, Seth, Enosh, <sup>2</sup>Kenan, Mahalalel, Yared, <sup>3</sup>Hanok [Enoch], Methuselah, Lamek, <sup>4</sup>Noah, Shem, Ham and Yaphet. <sup>5</sup>Yaphet's sons: Gomer, Magog, Maday, Yavan [Greece], Tubal, Meshek and Tiras.
<sup>6</sup>Gomer's sons: Ashkenaz, Diphat and Togarmah.
<sup>7</sup>Yavan's sons: Elishah, Tarshish, Kittites and Rodanites.
<sup>8</sup>Ham's sons: Kush [Sudan], Misrayim [Egypt], Put and Kena'an [Canaan].
<sup>9</sup>Kush's sons: Seba, Havilah, Sabta, Ra'ama and Sabteka.
Ra'ama's sons: Sheba and Dedan.
<sup>10</sup>Kush fathered Nimrod; he was the first to be a strong man on the earth.
<sup>11</sup>Misrayim fathered Ludites, Anamites, Lehabites, Naphtuhites, <sup>12</sup>Patrusites, Kasluhites (Pelishtites [Philistines] came out from there) and Kaphtorites.
<sup>13</sup>Kena'an fathered Tsidon (his firstborn), Het, <sup>14</sup>the Yebusite, the Amorite, the Girgashite, <sup>15</sup>the Hivvite, the Arkite, the Sinite, <sup>16</sup>the Arvadite, the Tsemarite and the Hamatite.
<sup>17</sup>Shem's sons: Elam, Ashshur, Arpakshad, Lud, Aram, Uts, Hul, Geter and Meshek.
<sup>18</sup>Arpakshad fathered Shelah and Shelah fathered Eber.
<sup>19</sup>To Eber two sons were born:
The name of the one was Peleg ['Division'] because in his days the earth divided.
His brother's name was Yoktan.
<sup>20</sup>Yoktan fathered Almodad, Sheleph, Hatsarmavet, Yerah, <sup>21</sup>Hadoram, Uzal, Diklah, <sup>22</sup>Ebal, Abima'el, Sheba, <sup>23</sup>Ophir, Havilah and Yobab; all these were Yoktan's sons.
<sup>24</sup>Shem, Arpakshad, Shelah, <sup>25</sup>Eber, Peleg, Re'u, <sup>26</sup>Serug, Nahor, Terah, <sup>27</sup>Abram (i.e. Abraham).
<sup>28</sup>Abraham's sons: Yitshaq [Isaac] and Yishma'e'l; <sup>29</sup>these are their lines of descent:
Yishma'e'l's firstborn, Nebayot, Qedar, Adbe'el, Mibsam, <sup>30</sup>Mishma, Dumah, Massa, <sup>31</sup>Hadad, Tema, Yetur, Naphish and Qedemah; these are Yishma'e'l's sons.
<sup>32</sup>The sons of Qeturah, Abraham's secondary wife: she gave birth to Zimran, Yoqshan, Medan, Midyan, Yishbaq and Shuah.
Yoqshan's sons: Sheba and Dedan.
<sup>33</sup>Midyan's sons: Ephah, Epher, Hanok, Abida and Elda'ah; all these were Qeturah's sons.

*Esaw's line*

<sup>34</sup>Abraham fathered Yitshaq.
Yitshaq's sons: Esaw and Yisra'el.
<sup>35</sup>Esaw's sons: Eliphaz, Re'u'el, Ye'ush, Ya'lam and Qorah.
<sup>36</sup>Eliphaz's sons: Teman, Omar, Tsephi, Ga'tam, Qenaz, Timna, and Amaleq;
<sup>37</sup>Re'u'el's sons: Nahat, Zerah, Shammah and Mizzah;
<sup>38</sup>Se'ir's sons: Lotan, Shobal, Tsib'on, Anah, Dishon, Etser and Dishan;
<sup>39</sup>Lotan's sons: Hori and Homam; and Timna was Lotan's sister;
<sup>40</sup>Shobal's sons: Alyan, Manahat, Ebal, Shephi and Onam;
Tsib'on's sons: Ayyah and Anah;
<sup>41</sup>Anah's sons: Dishon;
Dishon's sons: Hamran, Eshban, Yitran and Keran;
<sup>42</sup>Etser's sons: Bilhan, Za'avan, Ya'aqan;
Dishan's sons: Uts and Aran.
<sup>43</sup>These are the kings who reigned in the country of Edom before a king reigned among the Yisra'elites:
Bela ben Be'or; his town's name was Dinhabah.
<sup>44</sup>Bela died, and Yobab ben Zerah from Botsrah began to reign in place of him.
<sup>45</sup>Yobab died, and Husham from the Temanites' country began to reign in place of him.
<sup>46</sup>Husham died, and Hadad ben Bedad, who struck down Midyan in Mo'ab's area, began to reign in place of him; his town's name was Avit.
<sup>47</sup>Hadad died, and Samlah from Masrekah began to reign in place of him.
<sup>48</sup>Samlah died, and Sha'ul from Broads-on-the-River began to reign in place of him.
<sup>49</sup>Sha'ul died, and Ba'al Hanan ben Akbor began to reign in place of him.
<sup>50</sup>Ba'al Hanan died, and Hadad began to reign in place of him; his town's name was

Pa'i, and his wife's name was Mehetabel bat Matred, the daughter of Gold Water. <sup>51</sup>Hadad died.

The Edomite clans were:
the Timna clan;
the Alvah clan;
the Yetet clan;
<sup>52</sup>the Oholibamah clan;
the Elah clan;
the Pinon clan;
<sup>53</sup>the Qenaz clan;
the Teman clan;
the Mibtsar clan;
<sup>54</sup>the Magdi'el clan;
the Iram clan.
These were the Edomite clans.

## The beginning of Yehudah's line

**2** These are Yisra'el's sons:
Re'uben, Shim'on, Levi, Yehudah, Yissakar, Zebulun, <sup>2</sup>Dan, Yoseph, Binyamin, Naphtali, Gad, and Asher.
<sup>3</sup>Yehudah's sons: Er, Onan and Shelah (the three were born to him from Bat-shua the Kena'anite); Er, Yehudah's firstborn, was bad in Yahweh's eyes, and he put him to death; <sup>4</sup>since Tamar his daughter-in-law gave birth to Perets and Zerah for him, altogether Yehudah's sons were five.
<sup>5</sup>Perets's sons: Hezron and Hamul;
<sup>6</sup>Zerah's sons: Zimri, Etan, Heman, Kalkol and Dara – five altogether;
<sup>7</sup>Karmi's sons: Akar ['Trouble'], the troubler of Yisra'el, who trespassed on something devoted;
<sup>8</sup>Etan's sons: Azaryah;
<sup>9</sup>Hezron's sons, who were born to him: Yerahme'el, Ram and Kelubay;
<sup>10</sup>Ram fathered Amminadab, Amminadab fathered Nahshon, a leader of the Yehudahites, <sup>11</sup>Nahshon fathered Salma, Salma fathered Bo'az, <sup>12</sup>Bo'az fathered Obed, and Obed fathered Yishay.
<sup>13</sup>Yishay fathered Eli'ab as his firstborn, Abinadab the second, Shim'a the third, <sup>14</sup>Netan'el the fourth, Radday the fifth, <sup>15</sup>Otsem the sixth, David the seventh.
<sup>16</sup>Their sisters were Tseruyah and Abigayil. Tseruyah's sons: Abshay, Yo'ab and Asah'el – three.

<sup>17</sup>Abigayil gave birth to Amasa; Amasa's father was Yeter the Yishma'e'lite.
<sup>18</sup>Kaleb ben Hezron fathered children with Azubah his wife, and with Yeri'ot; these were her sons: Yesher, Shobab and Ardon.
<sup>19</sup>Azubah died and Kaleb took himself Ephrat, who gave birth to Hur for him.
<sup>20</sup>Hur fathered Uri and Uri fathered Betsal'el.
<sup>21</sup>Afterwards, Hezron had sex with a daughter of Makir, father of Gil'ad; he had taken her when he was a man of sixty years and she gave birth to Segub for him.
<sup>22</sup>Segub fathered Ya'ir; he had twenty-three towns in the region of Gil'ad, <sup>23</sup>but Geshur and Aram took from them the Villages of Ya'ir, Qenat and its daughter-towns, sixty towns; all these were sons of Makir, father of Gil'ad.
<sup>24</sup>After Hezron's death in Kaleb Ephratah, Hezron's wife Abiyyah gave birth to Ashhur, father of Teqoa, for him.

## Yehudah's line

<sup>25</sup>The sons of Yerahme'el, Hezron's firstborn, were: the firstborn Ram, Bunah, Oren, Ozem and Ahiyyah.
<sup>26</sup>Yerahme'el had another wife and her name was Atarah; she was the mother of Onam.
<sup>27</sup>The sons of Ram, Yerahme'el's firstborn, were: Ma'ats, Yamin and Eqer.
<sup>28</sup>Onam's sons were: Shammay and Yada. Shammay's sons: Nadab and Abishur.
<sup>29</sup>The name of Abishur's wife was Abihayil; she gave birth to Ahban and Molid for him.
<sup>30</sup>Nadab's sons: Seled and Appayim. Seled died without sons.
<sup>31</sup>Appayim's sons: Yish'i;
Yish'i's sons: Sheshan;
Sheshan's sons: Ahlay.
<sup>32</sup>The sons of Yada, Shammay's brother: Yeter and Yonatan.
Yeter died without sons.
<sup>33</sup>Yonatan's sons: Pelet and Zaza.
These were Yerahme'el's sons.
<sup>34</sup>Sheshan did not have sons, but rather daughters, but Sheshan had a Misrayimite servant and his name was Yarha; <sup>35</sup>Sheshan

gave his daughter to Yarha his servant as wife, and she gave birth to Attay for him. ³⁶Attay fathered Natan, Natan fathered Zabad, ³⁷Zabad fathered Ephlal, Ephlal fathered Obed, ³⁸Obed fathered Yehu, Yehu fathered Azaryah, ³⁹Azaryah fathered Helets, Helets fathered El'asah, ⁴⁰El'asah fathered Sismay, Sismay fathered Shallum, ⁴¹Shallum fathered Yeqamyah and Yeqamyah fathered Elishama.

## Kaleb's line

⁴²The sons of Kaleb, Yerahme'el's brother:
Mesha his firstborn; he was the father of Ziph.
The sons of Mareshah, father of Hebron.
    ⁴³Hebron's sons: Qorah, Tappuah, Reqem, and Shema.
    ⁴⁴Shema fathered Raham the father of Yorqo'am.
Reqem fathered Shammay.
    ⁴⁵Shammay's son was Ma'on; Ma'on was the father of Bet-tsur.
    ⁴⁶Ephah, Kaleb's secondary wife, gave birth to Haran, Motsa and Gazez.
Haran fathered Gazez.
    ⁴⁷Yahday's sons: Regem, Yotam, Geshan, Pelet, Ephah and Sha'aph.
⁴⁸Kaleb's secondary wife Ma'akah gave birth to Sheber and Tirhanah, ⁴⁹she gave birth to Sha'aph the father of Madmannah, Sheva the father of Makbenah, and the father of Gib'a, and Kaleb's daughter was Aksah; ⁵⁰these were Kaleb's children.
    The son of Hur, Ephratah's firstborn: Shobal father of Ye'arim Township, ⁵¹Salma father of Bet-lehem, Hareph father of Bet-gader.
    ⁵²Shobal father of Ye'arim Township had sons, Haro'eh, half of the Menuhot, ⁵³and the kin-groups of Ye'arim Township: the Itrites, the Putites, the Shumatites and the Mishra'ites (from these the Tsor'atites and the Eshta'olites came).
    ⁵⁴Salma's sons: Bet Lehem, Netophatites, Atrot Bet Yo'ab, half the Manahatites (the Tsor'ites), ⁵⁵and the kin-groups of the secretaries living in Ya'bets, Tir'atites, Shim'atites, Sukatites; these are the Qenites who come from Hamat, father of Rekab's household.

## David's line

**3** These were David's sons who were born to him in Hebron:
the firstborn Amnon, by Ahino'am the Yizre'e'lite;
the second Daniyye'l, by Abigayil the Carmelite;
²the third Abshalom, the son of Ma'akah the daughter of Talmay king of Geshur;
the fourth Adoniyyah, the son of Haggit;
³the fifth Shephatyah, by Abital;
the sixth Yitre'am, by Eglah his wife.
⁴Six were born to him in Hebron; he reigned there seven years and six months, in Yerushalaim he reigned thirty-three years, ⁵and these were born to him in Yerushalaim:
Shim'a, Shobab, Natan and Shelomoh [Solomon] – four by Bat-shua bat Ammi'el;
⁶Yibhar, Elishama, Eliphelet, ⁷Nogah, Nepheg, Yaphia, ⁸Elishama, Elyada and Eliphelet – nine.
⁹All were David's sons, besides the secondary wives' sons; and Tamar was their sister.

¹⁰Shelomoh's son: Rehab'am [Rehoboam]; his son Abiyyah; his son Asa; his son Yehoshaphat; ¹¹his son Yoram; his son Ahazyahu; his son Yo'ash; ¹²his son Amatsyahu; his son Azaryah; his son Yotam; ¹³his son Ahaz; his son Hizqiyyahu; his son Menashsheh; ¹⁴his son Amon; his son Yo'shiyyahu.

¹⁵Yo'shiyyahu 's sons: the first-born Yohanan, the second Yehoyaqim, the third Tsidqiyyahu, the fourth Shallum.
¹⁶Yehoyaqim's sons: his son Yekonyah, his son Tsidqiyyahu.
¹⁷The sons of Yekonyah, the captive: She'alti'el his son, ¹⁸Malkiram, Pedayah, Shen'atstsar, Yeqamyah, Hoshama and Nedabyah.
¹⁹Pedayah's sons: Zerubbabel and Shim'i. Zerubbabel's sons: Meshullam and Hananyah; and Shelomit was their sister.
²⁰Hashubah, Ohel, Berekyah, Hasadyah, Yushab Hesed – five;
²¹Hananyah's son: Pelatyah and Yesha'yah; Rephayah's sons, Arnan's sons, Obadyah's sons, Shekanyah's sons;
²²Shekanyah's sons: Shemayah;

Shemayah's sons: Hattush, Yig'al, Bariah, Ne'aryah and Shaphat – six;

<sup>23</sup>Ne'aryah's son: Elyo'enay, Hizqiyyah and Azriqam – three;

<sup>24</sup>Elyo'enay's sons: Hodavyah, Elyashib, Pelayah, Aqqub, Yohanan, Delayah and Anani – seven.

## The prayer of Ya'bets

**4** Yehudah's sons: Perets, Hezron, Karmi, Hur and Shobal. <sup>2</sup>Re'ayah ben Shobal fathered Yahat; Yahat fathered Ahumay and Lahad; these were the kin-groups of the Tsor'atites. <sup>3</sup>The father of Etam, these: Yizre'e'l, Yishma and Yidbash, and their sister's name was Hatslelponi. <sup>4</sup>Penu'el was the father of Gedor and Ezer was the father of Hushah.

These were the sons of Hur, the firstborn of Ephratah, the father of Bet Lehem. <sup>5</sup>Asshur the father of Teqoa had two wives, Hel'ah and Na'arah. <sup>6</sup>Na'arah gave birth to Ahuzzam, Hepher, Temeni and Ha'ahashtari for him; these were Na'arah's sons. <sup>7</sup>Helah's sons: Tseret, Tsohar and Etnan. <sup>8</sup>Qots fathered Anub, Hatstsobebah and the kin-groups of Aharhel ben Harum. <sup>9</sup>Ya'bets was more honourable than his brothers. His mother had named him Ya'bets 'Because I gave birth to him in suffering pain [otseb]'. <sup>10</sup>Ya'bets called to the God of Yisra'el, 'If only you will really bless me and enlarge my territory and your hand will be with me and you will act against bad fortune so that I don't suffer pain'. God brought about what he asked. <sup>11</sup>Kelub, Shuhah's brother, fathered Mehir; he was father of Eshton. <sup>12</sup>Eshton fathered Bet Rapha, Paseah, and Tehinnah, father of Ir Nahash; these were the people of Rekah.

## More Yehudahites

<sup>13</sup>Qenaz's sons: Otni'el and Seryah; Otni'el's sons: Hatat <sup>14</sup>and Me'onotay; he fathered Ophrah.

Seryah fathered Yo'ab, father of Craftsmen's Ravine (because they were craftsmen). <sup>15</sup>The sons of Kaleb ben Yephunneh: Iru, Elah and Na'am, the sons of Elah, and Qenaz. <sup>16</sup>Yehallel'el's sons: Ziph, Ziphah, Tirya and Asar'el. <sup>17</sup>Ezrah's sons: Yeter, Mered, Epher and Yalon. She got pregnant with Miryam, Shammay and Yishbah father of Eshtemoa; <sup>18</sup>his Yehudahite wife gave birth to Yered father of Gedor, Heber father of Soko, and Yequti'el father of Zanoah; these were the sons of Bityah, daughter of Par'oh [Pharaoh], whom Mered took. <sup>19</sup>The sons of Hodiyyah's wife, Naham's sister: the father of Qe'ilah the Garmite and Eshtemoa the Ma'akatite. <sup>20</sup>Shimon's sons: Amnon, Rinnah, Ben-hanan and Tilon.

Yishi's sons: Zohat and Ben-zohet. <sup>21</sup>The sons of Shelah son of Yehudah: Er father of Lekah, La'addah father of Mareshah, the kin-groups of the linen service household at Bet Ashbea, <sup>22</sup>Yoqim, the people of Kozeba, Yo'ash and Saraph who ruled in Mo'ab, and Yashubi Lehem (the words are ancient). <sup>23</sup>They were the potters and the people who lived at Neta'im and Gederah; they lived there with the king, in working for him.

## Descendants of Shim'on

<sup>24</sup>Shim'on's sons: Nemu'el, Yamin, Yarib, Zerah, Sha'ul; <sup>25</sup>Shallum his son, Mibsam his son, Mishma his son; <sup>26</sup>Mishma's sons: Hammu'el his son, Zakkur his son, Shim'i his son; <sup>27</sup>Shim'i had sixteen sons and six daughters, but his brothers didn't have many sons. Their entire kin-group did not produce as many as the Yehudahites. <sup>28</sup>They lived

in Be'er-sheba
in Moladah
in Hatsar Shu'a,
<sup>29</sup>in Bilhah
in Etsem
in Tolad
<sup>30</sup>in Betu'el

in Hormah
in Tsiqlag,
<sup>31</sup>in Bet Markabot
in Hatsar Susim
in Bet Bir'i
and in Sha'arayim.

These were their towns until David began to reign; [32]and their villages, Etam, Ayin, Rimmon, Token and Ashan (five towns), [33]and all their villages that were round these towns as far as Ba'al. These were their settlements.

They had their enrolment by genealogy:

| | |
|---|---|
| [34]Meshobab | Yeshohayah |
| Yamlek | Asayah |
| Yoshah ben | Adi'el |
| Amatsyah | Yesimi'el |
| [35]Yo'el | Benayah |
| Yehu ben Yoshibyah | [37]Ziza ben Shiph'i |
| son of Serayah | son of Allon son |
| son of Asi'el | of Yedayah son |
| [36]Elyo'enay | of Shimri son of |
| Ya'aqobah | Shema'yah |

[38]These who come by name were leaders in their kin-groups.

Their ancestral households broke out so as to become a large number [39]and went to the approaches to Gedor on the east of the ravine to look for pasture for their flock. [40]They found rich, good pasture and the region was wide on both sides, calm and peaceful, because the people who lived there before had been from Ham, [41]but these people who are written down by name came in the days of Hizqiyyahu king of Yehudah and struck down their tents, and the Me'unites who were found there devoted them until this day, and settled in place of them, because there was pasture for their flock there. [42]Of them, some of the Shim'onites went to Mount Se'ir – 500 people, with Pelatyah, Ne'aryah, Rephayah and Uzzi'el, the sons of Yishi, at their head. [43]They struck down the remaining escapees of Amaleq, and they have lived there until this day.

## Re'uben

**5** The sons of Re'uben, Yisra'el's firstborn (because he was the firstborn, but when he defiled his father's bed, his birthright was given to the sons of Yoseph, the son of Yisra'el, and he was not for enrolment by genealogy on the basis of the birthright, [2]because Yehudah was strong among his brothers and a chief came from him, but the birthright belonged to Yoseph) – [3]the sons of Re'uben, Yisra'el's firstborn: Hanok, Pallu, Hezron and Karmi.

[4]The sons of Yo'el: Shema'yah his son, Gog his son, Shim'i his son, [5]Mikah his son, Re'ayah his son, Ba'al his son, [6]and Be'erah his son, whom Tillegat Pilne'eser king of Ashshur exiled; he was leader of the Re'ubenites.

[7]His brothers by his kin-groups according to the enrolment by genealogy, by their lines of descent: the head, Ye'i'el, Zekaryahu [8]and Bela ben Azaz son of Shema son of Yo'el. He lived in Aro'er and as far as Nebo and Ba'al Me'on, [9]and to the east he lived as far as when you come to the wilderness this side of the River Euphrates, because their cattle became many in Gil'ad. [10]In the days of Sha'ul [Saul] they did battle with the Hagri'tes, and they fell by their hand. So they lived in their tents over the entire face of east of Gil'ad.

[11]Gad's sons lived opposite them in the region of Bashan as far as Salkah: [12]Yo'el the head, Shapham the second, Ya'nay and Shaphat, in Bashan. [13]Their brothers by their ancestral households: Mika'el, Meshullam, Sheba, Yoray, Ya'akan, Zia and Eber – seven. [14]These were the sons of Abihayil ben Huri son of Gil'ad son of Mika'el son of Yeshishay son of Yahdo son of Buz. [15]Ahi ben Abdi'el son of Guni was head of their ancestral household. [16]They lived in Gil'ad, in Bashan, in its daughter-towns, and in all the Sharon pasturelands, to their farthest extent. [17]All of them were enrolled by genealogy in the days of Yotam king of Yehudah and in the days of Yarob'am [Jeroboam] king of Yisra'el.

## The warriors

[18]Re'uben's sons, the Gadites and the half-clan of Menashsheh: of the forceful men carrying shield and sword, drawing the bow and trained in battle, 44,760 able to go out in the army, [19]did battle with the Hagri'tes, Yetur, Naphish and Nodab, [20]and sought help against them. The Hagri'tes and all the people who were with them were given into their hand, because they cried out to God in the battle and he let himself be entreated by them because they relied on him. [21]They captured

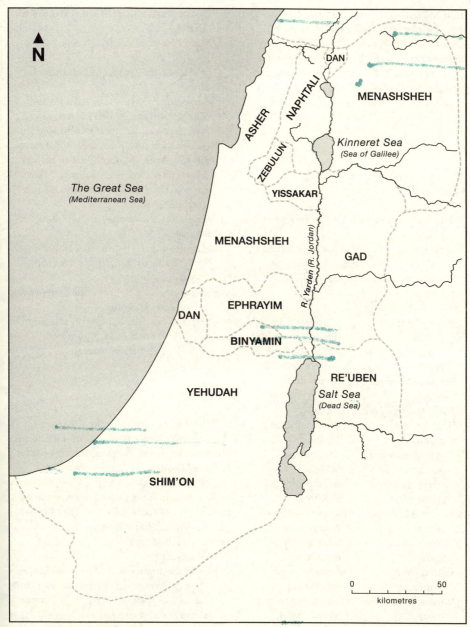

*1 Chronicles 5: The twelve clans*

their livestock, 50,000 camels, 250,000 sheep, 2,000 donkeys and 100,000 people, <sup>22</sup>because many fell, run through, because the battle was God's. They lived in place of them until the exile.

<sup>23</sup>The people in the half-clan of Menashsheh lived in the region. They were numerous from Bashan as far as Ba'al Hermon, Senir and Mount Hermon. <sup>24</sup>These were the heads of their ancestral households: Epher, Yish'i, Eli'el, Azri'el, Yirmeyah, Hodavyah and Yahdi'el, forceful strong men, men with names, heads of their ancestral households.

<sup>25</sup>But they trespassed against their ancestors' God and whored after the gods of the peoples of the country, whom God had annihilated

from before them. ²⁶And the God of Yisra'el stirred the spirit of Pul king of Ashshur (the spirit of Tillegat Pilneser king of Ashshur) and he took them into exile – the Re'ubenites, the Gadites and the half-clan of Menashsheh. He brought them to Halah, Habor, and the River Gozan, until this day.

## Levi's sons

**6** Levi's sons: Gershon, Qehat and Merari.

²Qehat's sons: Amram, Yitshar, Hezron and Uzzi'el;

³Amram's sons: Aharon [Aaron], Mosheh [Moses] and Miryam;

Aharon's sons: Nadab and Abihu, El'azar and It'amar.

⁴El'azar fathered Pinhas

Pinhas fathered Abishua

⁵Abishua fathered Buqqi

Buqqi fathered Uzzi

⁶Uzzi fathered Zerahyah

Zerahyah fathered Merayot

⁷Merayot fathered Amaryah

Amaryah fathered Ahitub

⁸Ahitub fathered Tsadoq

Tsadoq fathered Ahima'ats

⁹Ahima'ats fathered Azaryah

Azaryah fathered Yohanan

¹⁰Yohanan fathered Azaryah (it was he who acted as priest in the house that Shelomoh built in Yerushalaim)

¹¹Azaryah fathered Amaryah

Amaryah fathered Ahitub

¹²Ahitub fathered Tsadoq

Tsadoq fathered Shallum

¹³Shallum fathered Hilqiyyah

Hilqiyyah fathered Azaryah

¹⁴Azaryah fathered Serayah

Serayah fathered Yehotsadaq

¹⁵Yehotsadaq went when Yahweh exiled Yehudah and Yerushalaim by the hand of Nebukadne'tstsar

¹⁶Levi's sons: Gershom, Qehat and Merari.

¹⁷These are the names of Gershom's sons: Libni and Shim'i.

¹⁸Qehat's sons: Amram, Yitshar, Hebron and Uzzi'el.

¹⁹Merari's sons: Mahli and Mushi.

These are the kin-groups of Levi by their ancestors:

²⁰Gershom's: Libni his son, Yahat his son, Zimmah his son, ²¹Yo'ah his son, Iddo his son, Zerah his son, Ye'ateray his son;

²²Qehat's sons: Amminadab his son, Qorah his son, Assir his son, ²³Elqanah his son, Ebyasaph his son, Assir his son, ²⁴Tahat his son, Uri'el his son, Uzziyyah his son and Sha'ul his son;

²⁵Elqanah's sons: Amasay and Ahimot;

²⁶Elqanah;

Elqanah's sons: Tsopay his son, Nahat his son, ²⁷Eli'ab his son, Yeroham his son, Elqanah his son;

²⁸Shemu'el's [Samuel's] sons: the firstborn and the second (Abiyyah);

²⁹Merari's sons: Mahli, Libni his son, Shim'i his son, Uzzah his son, ³⁰Shim'a his son, Haggiah his son, Asayah his son.

## The singers

³¹These whom David put in place over the singing in Yahweh's house, from when the chest was set down, ³²were ministering before the dwelling, the appointment tent, with singing, until Shelomoh built Yahweh's house in Yerushalaim. They stood in connection with their service in accordance with the ruling given to them. ³³These were the people who stood, with their sons:

Of the Qehatites:

Heman the singer, son of Yo'el son of Shemu'el ³⁴son of Elqanah son of Yeroham son of Eli'el son of Toah ³⁵son of Tsuph son of Elqanah son of Mahat son of Amasay ³⁶son of Elqanah son of Yo'el son of Azaryah son of Tsephanyah ³⁷son of Tahat son of Assir son of Ebyasaph son of Qorah ³⁸son of Yitshar son of Qehat son of Levi son of Yisra'el.

³⁹His brother Asaph who stood at his right – Asaph ben Berekyahu son of Shim'a ⁴⁰son of Mika'el son of Ba'aseyah son of Malkiyyah ⁴¹son of Etni son of Zerah of Adayah ⁴²son of Etan son of Zimmah son of Shim'i ⁴³son of Yahat son of

Gershom son of Levi.

⁴⁴The Merarites, their brothers, were on
the left: Etan ben Qishi son of Abdi son
of Malluk ⁴⁵son of Hashabyah son of
Amatsyah son of Hilqiyyah ⁴⁶son of Amtsi
son of Bani son of Shemer ⁴⁷son of Mahli
son of Mushi son of Merari son of Levi.

⁴⁸Their brother Levites were given to all the
service at the dwelling, God's house, ⁴⁹while
Aharon and his sons were burning incense
on the burnt-offering altar and on the incense
altar in connection with all the work in the
very sacred place and in connection with
making expiation for Yisra'el in accordance
with all that Mosheh, God's servant, ordered.

### Aharon's family's settlements

⁵⁰These are the sons of Aharon: El'azar
his son, Pinhas his son, Abishua his son,
⁵¹Buqqi his son, Uzzi his son, Zerahyah his
son, ⁵²Merayot his son, Amaryah his son,
Ahitub his son, ⁵³Tsadoq his son, Ahima'ats
his son. ⁵⁴These are their settlements, by their
enclosures, in their territory:
   To Aharon's sons, the Qehatite kin-group
   (because theirs was the lot), ⁵⁵they gave
   them Hebron in the region of Yehudah
   and its surrounding pasturelands, ⁵⁶but
   the town's fields and its villages they
   gave to Kaleb ben Yephunneh. ⁵⁷To
   Aharon's sons they gave the asylum towns,
   Hebron, Libnah and its pasturelands,
   Yattir, Eshtemoa and its pasturelands,
   ⁵⁸Hilen and its pasturelands, Debir
   and its pasturelands, ⁵⁹Ashan and its
   pasturelands, and Bet Shemesh and
   its pasturelands. ⁶⁰From the clan of
   Binyamin, Geba and its pasturelands,
   Alemet and its pasturelands, and Anatot
   and its pasturelands. All their towns
   thirteen among their kin-groups.
⁶¹To the remaining sons of Qehat from the
   clan kin-group, from the half-clan,
   the half of Menashsheh by lot, ten towns.
⁶²To the sons of Gershom by their kin-
   groups, from the clan of Yissakar, from the
   clan of Asher, from the clan of Naphtali
   and from the clan of Menashsheh in
   Bashan, thirteen towns.
⁶³To the sons of Merari by their kin-groups,

from the clan of Re'uben, from the clan of
Gad and from the clan of Zebulun, by lot
twelve towns.

⁶⁴So the Yisra'elites gave the Levites the
towns and their pasturelands. ⁶⁵They gave them
by lot from the clan of the Yehudahites and
from the clan of the Shim'onites and from the
clan of the Binyaminites these towns that they
call by their names.

### The Qehatites, the Gershomites and the Merarites

⁶⁶Some of the kin-groups of the Qehatites:
there were towns in their territory from the
clan of Ephrayim. ⁶⁷They gave them
   the asylum towns;
   Shekem and its pasturelands in the highland
      of Ephrayim;
   Gezer and its pasturelands;
   ⁶⁸Yoqme'am and its pasturelands;
   Bet Horon and its pasturelands;
   ⁶⁹Ayyalon and its pasturelands;
   Gat-rimmon and its pasturelands;
   ⁷⁰and from the half-clan of Menashsheh
      Aner and its pasturelands;
   Bil'am and its pasturelands for the remaining
      kin-group of the Qehatites who remained.
⁷¹To the Gershomites:
from the half-clan of Menashsheh, Golan in
   Bashan and its pasturelands and Ashtarot
   and its pasturelands;
⁷²from the clan of Yissakar, Qedesh and its
   pasturelands, Dobrat and its pasturelands,
⁷³Heights and its pasturelands, Anem and
   its pasturelands;
⁷⁴from the clan of Asher, Mashal and its
   pasturelands, Abdon and its pasturelands,
⁷⁵Huqoq and its pasturelands, and Rehob
   and its pasturelands;
⁷⁶from the clan of Naphtali, Qedesh-in-
   Galilee and its pasturelands, Hammon and
   its pasturelands, and Qiryatayim and its
   pasturelands.
⁷⁷To the Merarites, those who remain:
from the clan of Zebulun, Rimmono and its
   pasturelands, Tabor and its pasturelands;
⁷⁸across the Yarden [Jordan] at Yeriho
   [Jericho], on the east of the Yarden:
   from the clan of Re'uben, Betser in the
   wilderness and its pasturelands, Yahtsah

and its pasturelands, [79]Qedemot and its pasturelands, and Mepha'at and its pasturelands;

[80]and from the clan of Gad, Heights-in-Gil'ad and its pasturelands, Mahanayim and its pasturelands, [81]Heshbon and its pasturelands, and Ya'zer and its pasturelands.

## Down to our own day: Yissakar, Binyamin, Naphtali, Menashsheh

7 Yissakar's sons: Tola, Pu'ah, Yashub and Shimron – four. [2]Tola's sons: Uzzi, Rephayah, Yeri'el, Yahmay, Yibsam and Shemu'el, heads of their ancestral households belonging to Tola, forceful strong men; by their lines of descent, their number in David's days, 22,600.

[3]Uzzi's sons: Yizrahyah; Yizrahyah's sons: Mika'el, Obadyah, Yo'el and Yishshiyyah – five, all of them heads; [4]with them, by their lines of descent, by their kin-groups, army raiding gangs ready for battle, 36,000, because they had many wives and children. [5]Their brothers in all the kin-groups of Yissakar, forceful strong men, their enrolment by genealogy, 87,000, all of them.

[6]Binyamin: Bela, Beker and Yedi'a'el – three. [7]Bela's sons: Etsbon, Uzzi, Uzzi'el, Yerimot and Iri – five, heads of ancestral households, forceful strong men, their enrolment by genealogy, 22,034. [8]Beker's sons: Zemirah, Yo'ash, El'ezer, Eli'onay, Omri, Yeremot, Abiyyah, Anatot, and Alemet, all these sons of Beker, [9]their enrolment by genealogy by their lines of descent, heads of their ancestral households, forceful strong men, 20,200. [10]Yedi'a'el's sons: Bilhan; Bilhan's sons: Ye'ush, Binyamin, Ehud, Kena'anah, Zetan, Tarshish and Ahishahar, [11]all these sons of Yedi'a'el, ancestral heads, forceful strong men, 17,200 able to go out in the army to battle.

([12]And Shuppim and Huppim, Ir's sons; Hushim; Aher's sons.)

[13]Naphtali's sons: Yahtsi'el, Guni, Yetser and Shallum, sons of Bilhah.

[14]Menashsheh's sons: Asri'el, to whom his Aramite secondary wife gave birth; she gave birth to Makir, father of Gil'ad. [15]Makir took a wife for Huppim and for Shuppim; his sister's name was Ma'akah. The name of the second was Tselophhad; Tselophhad had daughters. [16]Ma'akah, Makir's wife, gave birth to a son and named him Peresh; his brother's name: Sheresh; his sons: Ulam and Reqem. [17]Ulam's sons: Bedan. These were the sons of Gil'ad ben Makir son of Menashsheh; [18]his sister Hammoleket gave birth to Ishhod, Abi'ezer and Mahlah. [19]Shemida's sons were Ahyan, Shekem, Liqhi and Ani'am.

## Down to our own day: Ephrayim, Asher

[20]Ephrayim's sons: Shutelah, Bered his son, Tahat his son, Ele'adah his son, Tahat his son, [21]Zabad his son, Shutelah his son, and Ezer and Ele'ad. The men of Gat who were born in the region killed them, because they went down to take their cattle. [22]Ephrayim their father grieved for many days, and his brothers came to comfort him. [23]He had sex with his wife and she got pregnant and gave birth to a son. He named him Beri'ah because there had been actual bad fortune [bera'ah] in his household. [24]His daughter was She'erah. She built up Bet-horon (Lower and Upper) and Uzzen She'erah.

[25]Rephah his son, Resheph, Telah his son, Tahan his son, [26]La'dan his son, Ammihud his son, Elishama his son, [27]Non his son, Yehoshua his son: [28]their holding and their settlements were Bet-el and its daughter-towns, and on the east Na'aran, and on the west Gezer and its daughter-towns, Shekem and its daughter-towns, as far as Ayyah and its daughter-towns, [29]and alongside the Menashshites Bet-she'an and its daughter-towns, Ta'anak and its daughter-towns, Megiddo and its daughter-towns, Do'r and its daughter-towns. The sons of Yoseph the son of Yisra'el lived in these.

[30]Asher's sons: Yimnah, Yishvah, Yishvi and Beri'ah, and Serah their sister. [31]Beriah's sons: Heber and Malki'el.

He was Birzayit's father. ^32Heber fathered Yaphlet, Shomer, Hotam and Shua their sister. ^33Yaphlet's sons: Pasak, Bimhal and Ashvat; these were Yaphlet's sons. ^34Shemer's sons: Ahi, Rohgah, Hubbah and Aram. ^35The son of Helem his brother: Tsophah, Yimna, Shelesh and Amal. ^36Tsophah's sons: Suah, Harnepher, Shu'al, Beri, Yimrah, ^37Betser, Hod, Shamma, Shilshah, Yitran and Be'era. ^38Yeter's sons: Yephunneh, Pispah and Ara. ^39Ulla's sons: Arah, Hanni'el and Ritsya. ^40All these sons of Asher, heads of the ancestral households, proven men, forceful strong men, heads among the leaders. Their enrolment by genealogy in the army in battle: their number, 26,000 men.

## Down to our own day: Binyamin

**8** Binyamin fathered Bela his firstborn, Ashbel the second, Aharah the third, ^2Nohah the fourth and Rapha the fifth. ^3Bela had sons: Addar, Gera, Abihud, ^4Abishua, Na'aman, Ahoah, ^5Gera, Shephupham and Huram. ^6These are Ehud's sons, ancestral heads of the inhabitants of Geba, but they exiled them to Manahat: ^7Na'aman, Ahiyyah and Gera; he exiled them and fathered Uzza and Ahihud. ^8Shaharayim fathered sons in the open country in Mo'ab after he had sent them away (Husham and Ba'ara were his wives); ^9by Hodesh his wife he fathered Yobab, Tsibya, Mesha, Malkam, ^10Ye'uts, Sakeyah and Mirmah; these were his sons, ancestral heads; ^11by Hushim he fathered Ahitub and Elpa'al. ^12The sons of Elpa'al: Eber, Misham, Shemed (he built Ono and Lod and its daughter-towns), ^13Beri'ah and Shema (they were ancestral heads of the inhabitants of Ayyalon – they put to flight the inhabitants of Gat), ^14Ahyo, Shashaq and Yeremot. ^15Zebadyah, Arad, Eder, ^16Mika'el, Yishpah and Yoha were Beri'ah's sons. ^17Zebadyah, Meshullam, Hizqi, Heber,

^18Yishmeray, Yizliah and Yobab were Elpa'al's sons. ^19Yaqim, Zikri, Zabdi, ^20Eli'enay, Zilletay, Eli'el, ^21Adayah, Bera'yah and Shimrat were Shim'i's sons. ^22Yishpan, Eber, Eli'el, ^23Abdon, Zikri, Hanan, ^24Hananyah, Elam, Antotiyyah, ^25Yiphdeyah and Penu'el were Shashaq's sons. ^26Shamsheray, Sheharyah, Atalyah, ^27Ya'areshyah, Eliyyah and Zikri were Yeroham's sons. ^28These were the ancestral heads by their lines of descent. These heads lived in Yerushalaim.

## Sha'ul's family

^29Gib'on's father lived in Gib'on. His wife's name was Ma'akah. ^30His firstborn son Abdon, Tsur, Qish, Ba'al, Nadab, ^31Gedor, Ahyo and Zeker. ^32Miklot fathered Shim'ah. They also lived opposite their brothers in Yerushalaim, with their brothers. ^33Ner fathered Qish, Qish fathered Sha'ul, and Sha'ul fathered Yehonatan, Malki-shua, Abinadab and Eshba'al. ^34Yehonatan's son was Merib Ba'al. Merib Ba'al fathered Mikah. ^35Mikah's sons: Piton, Melek, Ta'area and Ahaz. ^36Ahaz fathered Yeho'addah; Yeho'addah fathered Alemet, Azmavet and Zimri. Zimri fathered Motsa. ^37Motsa fathered Bin'a, Rapha his son, El'asah his son, Atsel his son. ^38Atsel had six sons; these are their names: Azriqam, Bokeru, Yishma'e'l, She'aryah, Obadyah and Hanan; all these were Atsel's sons. ^39The sons of Esheq his brother: Ulam his firstborn, Ye'ush the second and Eliphelet the third. ^40Ulam's sons were forceful strong men, drawing the bow, and they produced a large number of children and grandchildren, 150, all these Binyaminites.

**9** All Yisra'el was enrolled by genealogy: there, they are written down on the document about the kings of Yisra'el. But Yehudah was taken into exile to Babel because of their trespass.

## The returners

²The first people settling who were on their holding in their towns were Yisra'el, priests, Levites and assistants, ³while some Yehudahites, some Binyaminites, some Ephrayimites and some Menashshehites settled in Yerushalaim:

⁴Utay ben Ammihud son of Omri son of Imri son of Bani, from the sons of Perets son of Yehudah.

⁵Of the Shilonites: Asayah the firstborn and his sons.

⁶Of the sons of Zerah: Ye'u'el and his brothers – 690.

⁷Of the Binyaminites: Sallu ben Meshullam son of Hodavyah son of Hassenu'ah, ⁸Yibneyah ben Yeroham, Elah ben Uzzi son of Mikri, and Meshullam ben Shephatyah son of Re'u'el son of Yibneyah, ⁹and their brothers, by their lines of descent – 956. All these people were ancestral heads of their ancestral households.

¹⁰Of the priests: Yedayah, Yehoyarib, Yakin, ¹¹and Azaryah ben Hilqiyyah son of Meshullam son of Tsadoq son of Merayot son of Ahitub, chief over God's house, ¹²and Adayah ben Yeroham son of Pashhur son of Malkiyyah, and Ma'asay ben Adi'el son of Yahzerah son of Meshullam son of Meshillemit son of Immer, ¹³and their brothers, heads of their ancestral households – 1,760, forceful strong men for the work in the service of God's house.

¹⁴Of the Levites: Shema'yah ben Hashshub son of Azriqam son of Hashabyah, of the Merarites; ¹⁵and Baqbaqqer, Heresh, Galal, and Mattanyah ben Mika son of Zikri son of Asaph; ¹⁶and Obadyah ben Shemayah son of Galal son of Yedutun; and Berekyah ben Asa son of Elqanah who lived in the villages of the Netophatites.

## The gatemen

¹⁷The gatemen: Shallum, Aqqub, Talmon, Ahiman, with their brother Shallum the head. ¹⁸Until now they have been at the King's Gate on the east, gatemen for the Levites' camp. ¹⁹Shallum ben Qore son of Ebyasaph son of Qorah and his brothers belonging to his ancestral household, the Qorahites, were in charge of the work involved in the service, keeping watch over the tent thresholds; their ancestors had been in charge of Yahweh's camp as people keeping watch over the entrance. ²⁰Pinhas ben El'azar was chief over them before; Yahweh was with him. ²¹Zekaryah ben Meshelemyah was gateman at the door of the appointment tent. ²²All of them, people proven as gatemen at the thresholds – 212. They were in their villages enrolled by genealogy. David and Shemu'el the seer had established them in their position of trust.

²³They and their sons were in charge of the gateways of Yahweh's house (of the tent house) by watches. ²⁴The gatemen were on the four sides, east, west, north and south. ²⁵Their brothers in the villages were to come every seven days on a schedule, with these men, ²⁶because the four strongest gatemen (they were Levites) were in the position of trust; they were in charge of the halls and of the treasuries in God's house. ²⁷They stayed the night round God's house because the watch was their responsibility and they were in charge of the opening morning by morning.

## Sha'ul's family background

²⁸Some of them were in charge of the articles used in the service, because they would bring them in with a count and take them out with a count. ²⁹Some of them were put in charge of the articles, both all the sacred articles and the flour, the wine, the oil, the incense and the spices ³⁰(some of the priests were the people who made the blend of the spices). ³¹Mattityah of the Levites (he was the firstborn of Shallum the Qorahite) was in the position of trust in charge of the making of the griddle cakes. ³²Some of the Qehatites from among their brothers were in charge of the row bread, to prepare it sabbath by sabbath.

³³These are the singers, the ancestral heads of the Levites, in the halls, free, because responsibility was upon them day and night in the work. ³⁴These were the ancestral heads of the Levites by their lines of descent. These heads lived in Yerushalaim.

³⁵Gib'on's father Ye'i'el lived in Gib'on (his wife's name was Ma'akah) ³⁶with his firstborn

son Abdon, Tsur, Qish, Ba'al, Ner, Nadab,
³⁷Gedor, Ahyo, Zekaryah and Miklot.

³⁸Miklot fathered Shim'am, and they too
  lived in Yerushalaim opposite their
  brothers, with their brothers.
³⁹Ner fathered Qish, Qish fathered Sha'ul,
  Sha'ul fathered Yehonatan, Malki-shua,
  Abinadab and Eshba'al; ⁴⁰Yehonatan's son
  was Merib Ba'al; Meri-ba'al fathered Mikah.
⁴¹Mikah's sons: Piton, Melek and Ta'area.
⁴²Ahaz fathered Yarah; Yarah fathered
  Alemet, Azmavet and Zimri; Zimri
  fathered Motsa.
⁴³Motsa fathered Bin'a, Raphayah his son,
  El'asah his son, Atsel his son.
⁴⁴Atsel had six sons; these are their names:
  Azriqam, Bokeru, Yishma'e'l, She'aryah,
  Obadyah and Hanan; these were Atsel's
  sons.

## The end of Sha'ul

**10** Now the Pelishtites battled against
Yisra'el. The Yisra'elites fled from
before the Pelishtites and fell, run through, on
Mount Gilboa, ²and the Pelishtites caught up
with Sha'ul and with his sons. The Pelishtites
struck down Yonatan, Abinadab and Malki-
shua, Sha'ul's sons. ³The battle was hard against
Sha'ul, and the archers found him with an
arrow; he was run through by the archers.
⁴Sha'ul said to his equipment-bearer, 'Draw
your sword and thrust me through with it, so
these foreskinned men don't come and deal
abusively with me.' But his equipment-bearer
wasn't willing, because he was very fearful.
So Sha'ul took the sword and fell on it. ⁵His
equipment-bearer saw that Sha'ul was dead
and he too fell on his sword and died. ⁶So
Sha'ul died, with his three sons; his entire
household died, all together. ⁷All the Yisra'elites
who were in the vale saw that people had fled
and that Sha'ul and his sons were dead, and
they abandoned their towns and fled (the
Pelishtites came and lived in them).
⁸Next day the Pelishtites came to strip the
people who had been run through. They
found Sha'ul and his sons fallen on Mount
Gilboa, ⁹stripped him, took up his head and
his equipment, and sent them off through the
Pelishtites' country all round, to announce

the news to their idols and their people. ¹⁰They
put his equipment in the house of their gods, and
his skull they fastened to the house of Dagan.
¹¹All Yabesh-in-Gil'ad heard all that the
Pelishtites had done to Sha'ul, ¹²and they set
off, every forceful man, took up the corpse of
Sha'ul and the corpses of his sons, and brought
them to Yabesh. They buried their bones under
the oak at Yabesh and fasted for seven days.
¹³Sha'ul died because of his trespass, which
he committed against Yahweh in regard to
Yahweh's word which he had not kept, and also
in asking something of a spirit, so as to make
enquiry;¹⁴he didn't enquire of Yahweh. So he
put him to death and turned the kingship over
to David ben Yishay.

## David anointed

**11** All Yisra'el collected to David at
Hebron, saying, 'Here, we are your
flesh and blood. ²Further, in previous days,
even when Sha'ul was king, you were the one
who took Yisra'el out and brought Yisra'el in.
Yahweh your God said to you, "You're the one
who'll shepherd my people Yisra'el. You're the
one who'll be chief over my people Yisra'el."'
³So all Yisra'el's elders came to the king at
Hebron, David solemnized a pact towards them
at Hebron before Yahweh, and they anointed
David as king over Yisra'el in accordance with
Yahweh's word by means of Shemu'el.
⁴David and all Yisra'el went to Yerushalaim
(i.e. Yebus); the Yebusites were there as
inhabitants of the region. ⁵The inhabitants
of Yebus said to David, 'You won't come in
here', but David captured the Zion stronghold
(i.e. David's Town). ⁶David said, 'Anyone
striking down the Yebusites first will be
head and officer.' Yo'ab ben Tseruyah went
up first and became head.
⁷David lived in the stronghold; that's why
they named it 'David's Town'. ⁸He built up the
town all round, from the Fill all round, while
Yo'ab brought to life the remainder of the town.
⁹David went on getting bigger and bigger,
as Yahweh of Armies was with him.
¹⁰These are the heads of the strong men
that David had, the people who asserted their
strength with him in his kingship, with all
Yisra'el, in making him king in accordance

with Yahweh's word concerning Yisra'el, ¹¹and these are the number of the strong men that David had.

Yashob'am the Hakmonite was head of the adjutants. He was wielding his lance against 300, run through on one occasion. ¹²After him was El'azar ben Dodo, the Ahohite; he was one of the Three Strong Men, ¹³and he was with David at Pas Dammim when the Pelishtites gathered there for battle. A plot of field was full of barley. Whereas the company fled from before the Pelishtites ¹⁴they made a stand in the middle of the plot, defended it and struck down the Pelishtites. Yahweh brought about a great deliverance.

## Some spectacular exploits

¹⁵Three of the Thirty Heads went down to the crag to David at the Adullam Cave. The Pelishtite camp was camped in Repha'ites Vale. ¹⁶David was then in the stronghold, and an outpost of Pelishtites was then at Bet Lehem. ¹⁷David had a longing and said, 'If only someone could give me a drink of water from the Bet-lehem cistern that's at the gateway!' ¹⁸The Three broke through the Pelishtites' camp, drew water from the Bet-lehem cistern that's at the gateway, and carried it and brought it to David. But David was unwilling to drink it. He poured it out for Yahweh ¹⁹and said, 'Far be it from me by God that I should do this. Am I to drink the blood of these men, at the cost of their lives?' – because they had brought it at the cost of their lives. So he was unwilling to drink it. These are things that the Three Strong Men did.

²⁰Abshay, the brother of Yo'ab, was head of a Three. He was wielding his lance against 300, run through. He had a name among the Three. ²¹Of the Three, he was doubly honoured, and he became officer for them, but he didn't come to the [other] Three.

²²Benayah ben Yehoyada was a forceful man, prolific in deeds, from Qabtse'el. He struck down the two of Ari'el from Mo'ab. It was he who went down and struck down a lion inside a cistern on a snowy day, ²³and it was he who struck down a Misrayimite man, a huge man of two metres. In the Misrayimite's hand there was a lance like a weavers' rod, but he went down to him with a club, seized the lance from the Misrayimite's hand and killed him with his lance. ²⁴These things Benayah ben Yehoyada did, and he had a name among the Three Strong Men. ²⁵Of the Thirty, there he is, most honoured, but he didn't come to the Three. David put him in charge of his guard.

## The forceful strong men

²⁶The forceful strong men:

Asah-el, Yo'ab's brother
Elhanan ben Dodo from Bet Lehem
²⁷Shammot the Harorite
Helets the Palonite
²⁸Ira ben Iqqesh the Teqo'ite
Abi'ezer the Anatotite
²⁹Sibbekay the Hushatite
Ilay the Ahohite
³⁰Mahray the Netophatite
Heled ben Ba'anah the Netophatite
³¹Ittay ben Ribay from Gib'ah-of-the-Binyaminites
Benayah the Pir'atonite
³²Huray from the Ga'ash Wadis
Abi'el the Arbatite
³³Azmavet the Bahrumite
Elyahba the Sha'albonite
³⁴The sons of Hashem the Gizonite
Yonatan ben Shageh the Hararite
³⁵Ahi'am ben Sakar the Hararite
Eliphal ben Ur
³⁶Hepher the Mekeratite
Ahiyyah the Pelonite
³⁷Hetsro the Carmelite
Na'aray ben Ezbay
³⁸Yo'el, Natan's brother
Mibhar ben Hagri
³⁹Tseleq the Ammonite
Nahray the Berotite, equipment-bearer for Yo'ab ben Tseruyah
⁴⁰Ira the Yitrite
Gareb the Yitrite
⁴¹Uriyyah the Hittite
Zabad ben Ahlay
⁴²Adina ben Shiza, the Re'ubenite, head of the Re'ubenites, and thirty with him
⁴³Hanan ben Ma'akah
Yoshaphat the Mitnite
⁴⁴Uzziyya the Ashteratite
Shama and Ye'i'el sons of Hotam the Aro'erite
⁴⁵Yedi'a'el ben Shimri and Yoha his brother the Titsite
⁴⁶Eli'el the Mahavite
Yeribay and Yoshavyah sons of Elna'am
Yitmah the Mo'abite
⁴⁷Eli'el, Obed and Ya'asi'el the Metsobayite

## A time of encouragement

**12** These are the people who came to David at Tsiqlag when he was still held back because of Sha'ul ben Qish. They were among the strong men helping in battle, ²able to wield the bow, right-handed and left-handed with stones and with arrows from the bow, from among Sha'ul's brothers from Binyamin.

³The head, Ahi'ezer, and Yo'ash, the sons of Shema'ah the Gib'atite Yezi'el and Pelet, the sons of Azmavet Berakah Yehu the Anatotite ⁴Yishma'yah the Gib'onite, a strong man among the Thirty, and in charge of the Thirty Yirmeyah Yahazi'el

Yohanan Yozabad the Gederatite ⁵Eluzay Yerimot Be'alyah Shemaryahu Shephatyahu the Haruphite ⁶Elqanah, Yishsheyahu, Azar'el, Yo'ezer and Yashob'am, the Qorahites ⁷Yo'e'lah and Zebahyah, sons of Yeroham from Gedor

⁸Forceful strong men from the Gadites made themselves distinct to join David at the stronghold in the wilderness, forceful strong men in the army, ready for battle, able to wield shield and spear, with their face the face of a lion, and making speed like gazelles on the mountains:

⁹Ezer the head Obadyah the second Eli'ab the third ¹⁰Mishmannah the fourth Yirmeyah the fifth ¹¹Attay the sixth

Eli'el the seventh ¹²Yohanan the eighth Elzabad the ninth ¹³Yirmeyahu the tenth Makbannay the eleventh

¹⁴These of the Gadites were army heads, the smallest for a hundred, the biggest for a thousand. ¹⁵These were those people who crossed the Yarden in the first month when it was filling up over all its banks, and put to flight all the vale people to the east and to the west.

## A time for caution

¹⁶Some Binyaminites and Yehudahites came as far as the stronghold to David, ¹⁷and David went out before them. He avowed to them, 'If you've come to me so that things may go well, to help me, my mind will be one with you, but if it's to beguile me in relation to my attackers when there is no violence in my fists, may our ancestors' God see and reprove.' ¹⁸And a spirit put on Amasay, head of the Thirty:

For you, David, and with you, ben Yishay, may things be well;
May things be well for you, and things be well for the person who helps you,
Because your God has helped you.

So David received them and made them into the heads of his raiding gangs.

¹⁹Some of Menashsheh submitted to David when he came with the Pelishtites for battle against Sha'ul, but they didn't help them because the Pelishtites' lords in council sent him off, saying, 'He'll submit to his lord, Sha'ul, at the cost of our heads.' ²⁰When he went to Tsiqlag, some Menashshites submitted to him, Adnah, Yozabad, Yedi'a'el, Mika'el, Yozabad, Elihu and Tsillethay, chiliarchs belonging to Menashsheh. ²¹It was those people who helped David against the raiding gang, because all of them were forceful strong men. They became officers in the army, ²²because day by day people were coming to David to help him, until the camp was as big as God's camp.

## Time for celebration

²³These are the numbers of the heads of the people equipped for the army who came to David at Hebron to turn over Sha'ul's kingship to him in accordance with Yahweh's bidding:
²⁴Yehudahites carrying shield and spear – 6,800 equipped for the army.
²⁵Of the Shim'onites, forceful strong men for the army – 7,100.
²⁶Of the Levites – 4,600; ²⁷Yehoyada, the chief of Aharon, and with him 3,700; ²⁸and Tsadoq, a boy, a forceful strong man, and his ancestral household, 22 officers.
²⁹Of the Binyaminites, Sha'ul's brothers, 3,000 (until now the majority of them were keeping watch for Sha'ul's household).
³⁰Of the Ephrayimites, 20,800 forceful strong men, people with names in their ancestral household.

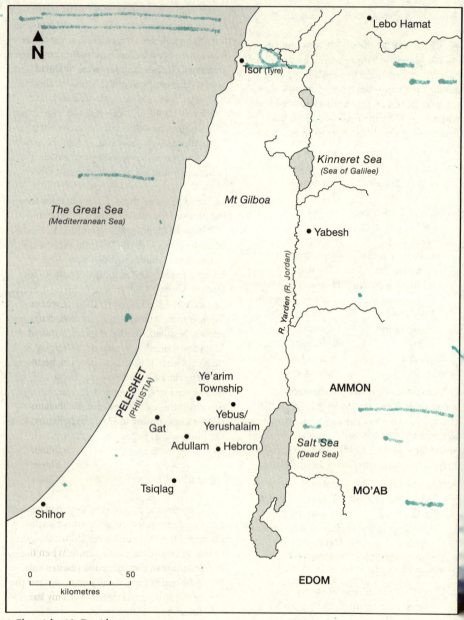

N

Lebo Hamat

Tsor (Tyre)

Kinneret Sea
(Sea of Galilee)

*Mt Gilboa*

The Great Sea
(Mediterranean Sea)

Yabesh

R. Yarden (R. Jordan)

PELESHET
(PHILISTIA)

Ye'arim
Township

AMMON

Gat

Yebus/
Yerushalaim

Adullam  Hebron

Salt Sea
(Dead Sea)

Tsiqlag

MO'AB

Shihor

0       50
kilometres

EDOM

*1 Chronicles 12: David*

³¹Of the half-clan of Menashsheh, 18,000, who were designated by their names to come to make David king. ³²Of the Yissakarites, people who had understanding of the times so as to know what Yisra'el should do – their heads 200, and all their brothers at their bidding.

³³Of Zebulun, people able to go out in the army, lining up for battle with all battle equipment – 50,000 to help, without a double mind. ³⁴From Naphtali, 1,000 officers, and with them, with shield and lance – 37,000. ³⁵From the Danites, people lining up for battle – 28,600.

³⁶From Asher, people able to go out in the
　army to line up for battle – 40,000.
³⁷From across the Yarden, from the
　Re'ubenites, the Gadites and the half-
　clan of Menashsheh, with all battle army
　equipment – 120,000.
³⁸All these men of battle, assisting the
line-up, with a perfect mind, came to Hebron
to make David king over all Yisra'el, while
all the remainder of Yisra'el also were of one
mind in making David king. ³⁹They were
there with David for three days eating and
drinking, because their brothers had prepared
it for them. ⁴⁰People who were near to them
as far as Yissakar, Zebulun and Naphtali were
also bringing food on donkeys, on camels,
on mules and on cattle, edibles of flour, fig
blocks, raisin blocks, wine, oil, cattle and
sheep in quantity, because there was rejoicing
in Yisra'el.

## A frightening outburst

**13** David took counsel with the
chiliarchs and centurions, every
chief, ²and David said to the entire Yisra'elite
congregation, 'If it seems good to you and it's
from Yahweh our God, let's break out and send
to our remaining brothers in all the regions
of Yisra'el, and with them the priests and the
Levites in their pastureland towns, so they may
collect to us ³and we may turn our God's chest
over to us, because we didn't enquire of him in
Sha'ul's days.' ⁴The entire congregation said to
do so, because the thing was upright in the eyes
of the entire people.

⁵So David congregated all Yisra'el from
Shihor in Misrayim as far as Lebo Hamat,
to bring God's chest from Ye'arim Township.
⁶David and all Yisra'el went up to Ba'alah (to
Ye'arim Township which belongs to Yehudah)
to take up from there the chest of God, Yahweh
who sits above the sphinxes, which is called
by the name. ⁷They transported God's chest
on a new wagon from Abinadab's house, with
Uzza and Ahyo driving the wagon ⁸and David
and all Yisra'el making fun before God with
all their vigour, with songs, with guitars, with
mandolins, with tambourines, with cymbals
and with trumpets. ⁹But they came as far as
Kidon's threshing floor and Uzza put out his

hand to grasp the chest, because the cattle had
stumbled. ¹⁰Yahweh's anger raged at Uzza and
he struck him down on account of the fact
that he had put out his hand to the chest. He
died there before God. ¹¹It enraged David that
Yahweh had broken out at Uzza. He called that
place Perets Uzza ['Breakout at Uzza'], until
this day.

¹²David was afraid of God that day, saying,
'How can I bring God's chest to me?' ¹³So David
did not move the chest to him, to David's Town.
He got it to turn aside to the house of Obed-
edom the Gittite. ¹⁴God's chest stayed with
Obed Edom's household in his house for three
months, and Yahweh blessed the household of
Obed-edom and everything he had.

## When you need to know what to do

**14** Hiram king of Tsor [Tyre] sent envoys
to David, with cedar wood, craftsmen
in walls and craftsmen in wood, to build him a
house. ²David acknowledged that Yahweh had
established him as king over Yisra'el, because
his kingship had been exalted exceptionally
high for the sake of his people Yisra'el.

³David took more wives in Yerushalaim
and David fathered more sons and daughters.
⁴These are the names of the ones born, who
were his in Yerushalaim: Shammua, Shobab,
Natan, Shelomoh, ⁵Yibhar, Elishua, Elpelet,
⁶Nogah, Nepheg, Yaphia, ⁷Elishama, Be'elyada
and Eliphelet.

⁸The Pelishtites heard that David had been
anointed as king over all Yisra'el, and all the
Pelishtites went up to look for David. David
heard, and went out before them. ⁹When the
Pelishtites came, they raided Repha'ites Vale.
¹⁰David asked of God, 'Shall I go up against the
Pelishtites? Will you give them into my hand?'
Yahweh said to him, 'Go up, and I shall give
them into your hand.' ¹¹So they went up to Ba'al
Peratsim, and David struck them down there.
David said, 'God has broken out on my enemies
by my hand like a breakout of water.' That's why
they named that place Ba'al Peratsim ['Master of
Breakouts']. ¹²They abandoned their gods there.
David said it, and they were burned in fire.

¹³The Pelishtites again raided the vale.
¹⁴David again asked of God, but God said to
him, 'You will not go up after them. Make a

turn away from them and come to them from the direction of the weeper trees. ¹⁵When you hear the sound of marching in the tops of the weeper trees, then you're to go out in battle, because God will have gone out before you to strike down the Pelishtite camp,' ¹⁶David did as God ordered him, and they struck down the Pelishtite camp from Gib'on as far as Gezer.

¹⁷David's name went out through all the countries as Yahweh put a dread of him on all the nations.

## Preparations for taking the chest

**15** He made houses for himself in David's Town, and prepared a place for God's chest and pitched a tent for it. ²Then David said no one was to carry God's chest but only the Levites, because Yahweh chose them to carry Yahweh's chest and to minister to him permanently. ³David congregated all Yisra'el to Yerushalaim to take up Yahweh's chest to its place which he had prepared for it. ⁴David gathered the Aharonites and the Levites:

⁵of the Qehatites, Uri'el the official and his brothers – 120;
⁶of the Merarites, Asayah the official and his brothers – 220;
⁷of the Gershomites, Yo'el the official and his brothers – 130;
⁸of the Elitsaphanites, Shemayah the official and his brothers – 200;
⁹of the Hebronites, Eli'el the official and his brothers – 80;
¹⁰of the Uzzi'elites, Amminadab the official and his brothers – 112.

¹¹David called for Tsadoq and for Ebyatar the priests, and of the Levites for Uri'el, for Asayah, for Yo'el, for Shemayah, for Eli'el and for Amminadab. ¹²He said to them, 'You are the Levites' ancestral heads. Make yourselves sacred, you and your brothers, so that you may take up the chest of Yahweh, the God of Yisra'el, to where I have prepared for it. ¹³Because you were not there the first time, Yahweh our God broke out on us, because we did not enquire of him in accordance with the ruling.'

¹⁴The priests and the Levites made themselves sacred for taking up the chest of

Yahweh, the God of Yisra'el. ¹⁵The Levites carried God's chest as Mosheh had ordered in accordance with Yahweh's word, on their shoulder, with poles on them. ¹⁶David said to the Levites' officials to get their brothers, the singers, with musical instruments, guitars, mandolins and cymbals, to stand, making things heard by raising their voice in rejoicing.

## The great celebration

¹⁷So the Levites got to stand:
Heman ben Yo'el;
of his brothers Asaph ben Berekyahu;
of the Merarites, their brothers, Etan ben Qushayahu;
¹⁸with them their brothers as number two Zekaryahu, son, Ya'azi'el, Shemiramot, Yehi'el, Unni, Eli'ab, Benayahu, Ma'aseyahu, Mattityahu, Eliphalehu, Miqneyahu, Obed Edom and Ye'i'el, the gatemen;
¹⁹the singers Heman, Asaph and Etan making things heard on copper cymbals;
²⁰Zekaryah, Azi'el, Shemiramot, Yehi'el, Unni, Eli'ab, Ma'aseyahu and Benayah with guitars, on 'Eternal Things';
²¹Mattityahu, Eliphelehu, Miqneyahu, Obed Edom, Ye'i'el and Azazyahu with mandolins, on 'The Eighth';
²²Kenanyahu, the Levites' official, with prophecy, to exercise discipline with prophecy because he was discerning;
²³Berekyah and Elqanah, the chest's gatemen;
²⁴Shebanyahu, Yoshaphat, Netan'el, Amasay, Zekaryahu, Benayah and Eli'ezer the priests, sounding on the trumpets before God's chest;
Obed Edom and Yehiyyah the chest's gatemen.
²⁵David, Yisra'el's elders and the chiliarchs went to take up Yahweh's pact chest from Obed-edom's house with rejoicing. ²⁶As God helped the Levites carrying Yahweh's pact chest, they sacrificed seven bulls and seven rams, ²⁷with David clad in a robe of Misrayimite linen, and all the Levites who were carrying the chest, and the singers, and Kenanyah the singers' prophetic officer, and on David a linen chasuble, ²⁸as all Yisra'el were taking up Yahweh's pact chest with a shout, with the sound of a horn, with trumpets and

with cymbals, making things heard with guitars and mandolins.

²⁹Yahweh's pact chest was coming into David's Town as Mikal, Sha'ul's daughter, was looking out through the window. She saw King David jumping and having fun, and she despised him inside.

**16** They brought in God's chest and put it inside the tent that David had pitched for it, and presented burnt offerings and well-being sacrifices before God. ²David finished offering up the burnt offering and the well-being sacrifices, blessed the people in Yahweh's name, ³and shared out to each person in Yisra'el, man and woman, to each individual a round of bread, a date block and a raisin block.

## Sing to Yahweh, all the earth!

⁴He put some of the Levites before Yahweh's chest as ministers, to make mention, to confess and to praise Yahweh the God of Yisra'el:
⁵Asaph the head;
number two to him, Zekaryah;
Ye'i'el, Shemiramot, Yehi'el, Mattityah,
Eli'ab, Benayahu, Obed Edom and Ye'i'el,
with guitars as instruments and with
mandolins;
Asaph making things heard with the cymbals;
⁶Benayahu and Yahazi'el the priests with
trumpets regularly before God's pact chest.
⁷Then on that day David first put confession of Yahweh into the hand of Asaph and his brothers:

⁸Confess Yahweh, call out in his name,
get his deeds acknowledged among the
peoples.
⁹Sing for him, make music for him,
talk of all his extraordinary deeds.
¹⁰Take pride in his sacred name;
the heart of those who seek Yahweh should
rejoice.
¹¹Enquire of Yahweh and his vigour;
seek his face continually.
¹²Be mindful of his extraordinary deeds, which
he has done,
his signs and the rulings of his mouth,
¹³Offspring of Yisra'el his servant,
descendants of Ya'aqob [Jacob], his chosen
ones.

¹⁴He is Yahweh our God;
his rulings are in all the earth,
¹⁵Be mindful of his pact permanently,
the word he ordered for a thousand
generations,
¹⁶Which he solemnized with Abraham,
his oath to Yitshaq,
¹⁷Made to stand for Ya'aqob as a decree,
for Yisra'el as a lasting pact,
¹⁸Saying, 'To you I will give the country of
Kena'an
as an allocation and as your domain.'
¹⁹When you were few in number,
a tiny group, and sojourning in it,
²⁰And they went about from nation to nation,
from a kingdom to another people.
²¹He didn't leave be anyone to oppress them,
but reproved kings on account of them:
²²'Don't touch my anointed ones,
don't deal badly towards my prophets.'

## All the people said, 'Yes!'

²³Sing for Yahweh all the earth,
announce the news of his deliverance, from
day to day.
²⁴Recount his splendour among the nations,
among all the peoples his extraordinary
deeds.
²⁵Because Yahweh is great and much to be
praised;
he is to be held in awe above all gods.
²⁶Because all the gods of the peoples are non-
entities,
whereas Yahweh made the heavens.
²⁷Grandeur and magnificence are before him,
vigour and glory at his site.
²⁸Kin-groups of the peoples, give Yahweh,
give Yahweh splendour and vigour.
²⁹Give Yahweh the splendour due to his name,
take up an offering and come before him.
Bow low to Yahweh in his sacred glory;
³⁰tremble before him, all the earth.
Yes, the world stands firm, it does not slip;
³¹the heavens should rejoice, the earth be
glad.
They should say among the nations,
'Yahweh has become king.'
³²The sea should roar and everything that fills it,
the open country should triumph and all
that's in it.

<sup>33</sup>Then the trees in the forest should resound
   before Yahweh,
     because he is coming to exercise authority
     over the earth.
<sup>34</sup>Confess Yahweh, because he is good,
   because his commitment lasts permanently.
<sup>35</sup>Say, 'Deliver us, our God who delivers,
   collect us and rescue us from the nations,
To confess your sacred name,
   to glory in your praise.'
<sup>36</sup>Blessed be Yahweh the God of Yisra'el
   from age to age.

All the people said 'Yes' and 'Praise Yahweh.'
<sup>37</sup>And he abandoned before Yahweh's pact chest
there:
   Asaph and his brothers to minister before
    the chest regularly in connection with
    each day's requirement in its day;
<sup>38</sup>Obed Edom and their brothers – sixty-eight;
Obed Edom ben Yeditun and Hosah as
   gatemen;
<sup>39</sup>Tsadoq the priest and his brothers, the
   priests, before Yahweh's dwelling at the
   shrine which was at Gib'on, <sup>40</sup>to offer
   up burnt offerings for Yahweh on the
   burnt-offering altar regularly, morning
   and evening, in connection with all that
   is written in Yahweh's instruction with
   which he ordered Yisra'el;
<sup>41</sup>with them Heman, Yedutun and the
   remainder of the proven men who were
   designated by their names to confess
   Yahweh 'because his commitment is
   permanent';
<sup>42</sup>with them (Heman and Yedutun) trumpets
   and cymbals for the people who make
   things heard, and instruments for a song
   to God;
the sons of Yedutun at the gateway.
<sup>43</sup>The entire people went each one to his house
and David turned to bless his household.

## Who builds a house, and what kind?

# 17

When David had gone to live in
his house, David said to Natan the
prophet, 'Here am I living in a cedar house and
Yahweh's pact chest is under tent cloths.' <sup>2</sup>Natan
said to David, 'Do everything that's in your
mind, because God is with you.'

<sup>3</sup>But that night God's word came to Natan:
<sup>4</sup>'Go and say to David my servant, "Yahweh
has said this: 'It's not you who will build me a
house to live in. <sup>5</sup>Because I haven't lived in a
house from the day that I brought Yisra'el up,
until this day. I've been from tent to tent, and
from a dwelling. <sup>6</sup>Everywhere I went about
in all Yisra'el, did I speak a word to one of the
people exercising authority in Yisra'el whom I
ordered to shepherd my people, saying "Why
have you not built me a cedar house?"'"

<sup>7</sup>So now you're to say this to my servant,
to David: "Yahweh of Armies has said this:
'I myself took you from the pasture, from
following the flock, to be chief over my people
Yisra'el, <sup>8</sup>and I've been with you everywhere
you've gone. I've cut off all your enemies from
before you and I shall make for you a name like
the name of the big people who are on the earth.
<sup>9</sup>I shall make a place for my people Yisra'el and
plant it. It will dwell in its place and not tremble
again. Evil people will not wear it down again
as they did previously, <sup>10</sup>from the days when I
ordered leaders over my people Yisra'el. I shall
make all your enemies bow down.

And I tell you: Yahweh will build a
house(hold) for you. <sup>11</sup>When your days are
full for going to be with your ancestors, I
shall set up your offspring after you, who
will be one of your sons, and I shall establish
his kingship. <sup>12</sup>He is the one who will build
me a house. I shall establish his throne
permanently. <sup>13</sup>I myself will become a father
to him and he will become a son to me. I shall
not remove my commitment from him as I
removed it from the one who was before you.
<sup>14</sup>I shall let him stand in my house and in my
kingship permanently. His throne will become
established permanently."'

## There is no one like Yahweh

<sup>15</sup>In accordance with all these words and in
accordance with this entire vision, so Natan
spoke to David.

<sup>16</sup>King David came and sat before Yahweh
and said, 'Who am I, Yahweh God, and who
are my household, that you have brought me
as far as this? <sup>17</sup>And this has been small in your
eyes, God. You've spoken about your servant's
household for the distant future. You've seen

me as one of lofty human form, Yahweh God. [18]What more can David add regarding your servant's honour? You yourself have acknowledged your servant. [19]Yahweh, for your servant's sake and in accordance with your own mind you are doing this entire big thing, making known all the big things.

[20]Yahweh, there is no one like you, no God except you, in all that we've heard with our ears. [21]And who is like your people Yisra'el, a nation on the earth that God went to redeem for himself as a people, to make yourself a name for big and awe-inspiring deeds, in driving nations out from before your people that you redeemed from Misrayim. [22]You made your people Yisra'el into a people for yourself permanently, and you Yahweh became God for them.

[23]Now, Yahweh, the word that you have spoken about your servant and about his household – may it be trustworthy permanently. Do as you have spoken. [24]May it be trustworthy so that your name may be great permanently: "Yahweh of Armies, the God of Yisra'el, is God for Yisra'el". May your servant David's household be established before you. [25]Because you, my God, have opened your servant's ear about building him a household. That's why your servant has found it to plead before you.

[26]Now, Yahweh, you are God. You've spoken this good thing about your servant. [27]Now you've resolved to bless your servant's household so it will be before you permanently, because you, Yahweh, have blessed, and it is blessed permanently.'

## Wars and rumours of wars

**18** Subsequently, David struck down the Pelishtites and made them bow down; David took Gat and its daughter-towns from the hand of the Pelishtites. [2]He struck down the Mo'abites, and the Mo'abites became David's servants, bringing offerings. [3]David struck down Hadad'ezer king of Tsobah Hamat, when he was going to put up his monument at the River Euphrates. [4]David captured from him 1,000 chariotry, 7,000 cavalry and 20,000 men on foot. David hamstrung all the chariotry, but of them left 100 chariotry.

[5]Aramites from Dammeseq [Damascus] came to help Hadad'ezer king of Tsobah, and David struck down the Aramites, 22,000 men. [6]David put men in Aram of Dammeseq, and the Aramites became David's servants, bringing offerings. Yahweh delivered David in every place where he went. [7]David took the gold quivers that were with Hadad'ezer's servants and brought them to Yerushalaim, [8]and from Tibhat and from Kun, Hadad'ezer's towns, David took very much copper with which Shelomoh made the copper sea, the columns and the copper articles.

[9]To'u king of Hamat heard that David had struck down the entire force of Hadad'ezer king of Tsobah, [10]and he sent Hadoram his son to King David to ask him about whether things were well and to bless him, on account of the fact that he had battled against Hadad'ezer and had struck him down, on account of the fact that Hadad'ezer had been involved in battles with To'u.

All the gold, silver and copper objects – [11]David also made them sacred for Yahweh, with the silver and the gold that he took up from all the nations, from Edom, from Mo'ab, from the Ammonites, from the Pelishtites and from Amaleq. [12]When Abishay ben Tseruyah struck down Edom in Salt Ravine, 18,000, [13a]he put outposts in Edom; all Edom became David's servants.

## Suspicion and humiliation

[13b]Yahweh delivered David wherever he went. [14]David reigned over all Yisra'el, and he was exercising authority in a faithful way for his entire people.

[15]Yo'ab ben Tseruyah was over the army. Yehoshaphat ben Ahihud was recorder. [16]Tsadoq ben Ahitub and Abimelek ben Ebyatar were priests. Shavsha was secretary. [17]Benayah ben Yehoyada was over the Keretites and the Peletites. David's sons were the first people at the king's right hand.

**19** Subsequently, Nahash king of the Ammonites died, and his son began to reign in place of him. ²David said, 'I will act in commitment with Hanun ben Nahash, because his father acted in commitment with me.' So David sent envoys to console him about his father. David's servants came to the Ammonites' country to Hanun, to console him, ³but the Ammonites' officials said to Hanun, 'Is David honouring your father, in your eyes, because he sent you people offering consolation? It's for the sake of searching out and overthrowing, investigating the country, that his servants have come to you, isn't it.'

⁴So Hanun got David's servants, clipped them and cut their clothes in half up to their behinds, and sent them off. ⁵People went and told David about the men and he sent to meet them, because the men were very ashamed. The king said, 'Stay in Yeriho until your beard grows and you can come back.' ⁶The Ammonites saw that they stank with David. So Hanun and the Ammonites sent a thousand silver talents to hire themselves chariotry and cavalry from Aram-of-the-Two-Rivers, Aram Ma'akah and Tsobah. ⁷They hired themselves 32,000 chariotry, the king of Ma'akah and his company, and came and camped before Medeba, while the Ammonites gathered from their towns and came for battle. ⁸David heard and sent Yo'ab and the entire army, the strong men.

## Be strong and show yourself strong

⁹The Ammonites went out and lined up for battle at the entrance to the town, with the kings who came in the open country on their own. ¹⁰Yo'ab saw that the face of the battle was against him in front and behind. He picked some of all the picked men in Yisra'el and lined them up to meet the Aramites, ¹¹while he gave the rest of the company into the hand of Abshay his brother and they lined up to meet the Ammonites. ¹²He said, 'If the Aramites are too strong for me, you'll be my deliverance, and if the Ammonites are too strong for you, I'll deliver you. ¹³Be strong, and let's assert our strength on behalf of our people and on behalf of our God's towns, as Yahweh does what is good in his eyes.'

¹⁴So Yo'ab went up before the Aramites for the battle, he and his company who were with

him, and they fled from before him. ¹⁵When the Ammonites saw that the Aramites had fled, they too fled from before Abishay his brother and came into the town. So Yo'ab came to Yerushalaim.

¹⁶The Aramites saw that they had taken a beating before Yisra'el, and they sent envoys and got the Aramites who were from across the River to go out, with Shophak, Hadad'ezer's army officer, at their head. ¹⁷It was told David, and he gathered all Yisra'el, crossed the Yarden, came to them and lined up against them. So David lined up to meet the Aramites in battle, and they did battle with him. ¹⁸The Aramites fled from before Yisra'el and David killed 7,000 of the Aramite chariotry and 40,000 men on foot, and put to death Shophak the army officer. ¹⁹The servants of Hadad'ezer saw that they had taken a beating before Yisra'el and they made peace with David and served him. The Aramites were not willing to deliver the Ammonites any more.

## Giants of men

**20** At the time of the turn of the year, at the time when the kings go out, Yo'ab led out the army force, devastated the Ammonites' country, and came and besieged Rabbah, while David was staying in Yerushalaim. Yo'ab struck down Rabbah and tore it down. ²David got their king's crown from on his head and found its weight a talent of gold, with precious stones in it. It came on to David's head, as he took out very much spoil from the town. ³The people that was in it he took out and submitted to saws, iron harrows and axes. So David would do to all the towns of the Ammonites. Then David and the entire company went back to Yerushalaim.

⁴Subsequently, a battle started at Gezer with the Pelishtites. Then Sibbekay the Hushatite struck down Sippay, one of the descendants of the Repha'ites. So they bowed down. ⁵There was again a battle with the Pelishtites. Elhanan ben Ya'ir struck down Lahmi, brother of Golyat [Goliath] the Gittite; the wood of his lance was like a weavers' rod. ⁶There was again a battle at Gat, and there was a man of stature with twenty-four fingers and toes, six on each. ⁷He

reviled Yisra'el, and Yehonatan ben Shim'a, David's brother, struck him down. ⁸These had descended from the Healer in Gat. They fell by the hand of David and by the hand of his servants.

## Temptation and fall

**21** An adversary stood up against Yisra'el and incited David to count Yisra'el. ²So David said to Yo'ab and to the company's officers, 'Go number Yisra'el, from Be'er Sheba as far as Dan, and bring it to me so I may know their number.' ³Yo'ab said, 'May Yahweh add to his people a hundred times as many as they are. My lord king, all of them are my lord's servants, aren't they. Why does my lord seek this? Why should it bring liability on Yisra'el?' ⁴But when the king's word was strong over Yo'ab, Yo'ab went out and went about in all Yisra'el, then came to Yerushalaim. ⁵Yo'ab gave David the number for the registration of the people. All Yisra'el was 1,100,000 men drawing the sword; Yehudah was 470,000 men drawing the sword; ⁶Levi and Binyamin he did not register among them because the king's word was offensive to Yo'ab.

⁷This thing was bad in God's eyes, and he struck Yisra'el down. ⁸David said to God, 'I've acted very wrongly in that I have done this thing. But now, please make your servant's waywardness pass away, because I've been very idiotic.'

⁹Yahweh spoke to Gad, David's seer: ¹⁰'Go and speak to David: "Yahweh has said this: 'I'm holding out three things to you. Choose one of these for yourself and I shall do it for you.'"' ¹¹Gad came to David and said to him, 'Yahweh has said this: "Accept for yourself ¹²either three years of famine, or three months of being swept away before your adversaries, with your enemies' sword overtaking, or three days of Yahweh's sword and epidemic in the country and Yahweh's envoy causing devastation in the entire territory of Yisra'el." So now see what word I am to take back to the one who sent me.'

¹³David said to Gad, 'It's very pressurizing for me. I shall fall into Yahweh's hand, please, because his compassion is very great. Into a human hand I will not fall.'

## No cost-free offerings

¹⁴So Yahweh put an epidemic on Yisra'el and 70,000 individuals from Yisra'el fell. ¹⁵God sent an envoy to Yerushalaim to devastate it, but as he was devastating it, Yahweh saw and relented over the bad thing and said to the devastating envoy, 'So much! Now slacken your hand.' Yahweh's envoy was standing by the threshing floor of Ornan the Yebusite. ¹⁶David lifted his eyes and saw Yahweh's envoy standing between the earth and the heavens with his drawn sword in his hand extended over Yerushalaim. David and the elders, covered in sack, fell on their faces. ¹⁷David said to God, 'I'm the one who said to number the people, aren't I. I'm the one who did wrong and did what was definitely bad. These people are the flock; what did they do? Yahweh my God, your hand should please be against me and against my ancestral household, not as an epidemic against your people.'

¹⁸Now Yahweh's envoy said to Gad to say to David that David should go up to set up an altar for Yahweh at the threshing floor of Ornan the Yebusite. ¹⁹David went up at Gad's word which he spoke in Yahweh's name. ²⁰Ornan came back and saw the envoy (his four sons with him were hiding; Ornan was threshing wheat). ²¹David came to Ornan and Ornan looked and saw David, went out of the threshing floor and bowed low to David, face to the ground.

²²David said to Ornan, 'Give me the threshing-floor site so I can build an altar for Yahweh on it. Give it to me at the full price so that the epidemic may hold back from the people.' ²³Ornan said to David, 'Take it for yourself. My lord the king may do what is good in his eyes. See, I'm giving the cattle as the burnt offerings and the threshing boards as wood and the wheat as the grain offering. All of it, I'm giving.' ²⁴But King David said to Ornan, 'No, because I will definitely acquire them at the full price, because I won't lift up to Yahweh what belongs to you. I won't offer up a burnt offering that cost nothing.'

## Preparations begin

²⁵So David gave Ornan 600 gold sheqels in weight for the site. ²⁶David built an altar there

for Yahweh and offered up burnt offerings and well-being sacrifices. He called to Yahweh, and he answered him with fire from the heavens on the burnt-offering altar. <sup>27</sup>Yahweh said it to the envoy and he put his sword back into its sheath.

<sup>28</sup>At that time, when David saw that Yahweh had answered him at the threshing floor of Ornan the Yebusite, he sacrificed there. <sup>29</sup>Yahweh's dwelling which Mosheh made in the wilderness, and the burnt-offering altar, were at the shrine at Gibon at that time, <sup>30</sup>and David could not go before it to enquire of God because he was terrified before the sword of Yahweh's envoy.

**22** David said, 'This is the house of Yahweh God. This is the burnt-offering altar for Yisra'el.'

<sup>2</sup>David said to assemble the resident aliens who were in the country of Yisra'el, and he got them to stand as hewers to hew dressed stones for building God's house. <sup>3</sup>David prepared iron in quantity for the nails for the doors of the gateways and for the clasps, copper in quantity, beyond weighing, <sup>4</sup>and cedar logs beyond numbering (because the Tsidonites and the Tsorites brought cedar logs in quantity to David). <sup>5</sup>David said, 'Shelomoh my son is a boy and green, and the house to build for Yahweh is to be exceptionally big so as to have a name and glory in all the countries. I should please prepare for him.' So David prepared in quantity before he died.

<sup>6</sup>He called Shelomoh his son, and ordered him to build a house for Yahweh the God of Yisra'el.

### The man of peace for a time of peace and a place of peace

<sup>7</sup>David said to Shelomoh his son, 'I myself – it was in my mind to build a house for the name of Yahweh my God, <sup>8</sup>but Yahweh's word came to me: "You've shed blood in quantity and fought big battles. You will not build a house for my name, because you've shed much blood on the earth before me. <sup>9</sup>Here, a son has been born to you. He'll be a settled man. I'll enable him to settle down from all his enemies all round, because his name will be Shelomoh and I'll give peace [*shalom*] and calm upon

Yisra'el in his days. <sup>10</sup>It's he who will build a house for my name. He'll become a son to me and I'll become a father to him. I'll establish his kingly throne over Yisra'el permanently."

<sup>11</sup>Now, son, may Yahweh be with you, and may you succeed and build the house of Yahweh your God, as he spoke concerning you. <sup>12</sup>Yet may Yahweh give you insight and understanding and may he order you over Yisra'el, and so that you keep the instruction of Yahweh your God. <sup>13</sup>Then you will succeed, if you keep watch over acting on the decrees and the rulings that Yahweh ordered Mosheh for Yisra'el.

Be strong and stand firm. Don't be afraid, don't be scared. <sup>14</sup>Here, by my restraint I've prepared for Yahweh's house 100,000 talents of gold, 1,000,000 talents of silver, and copper and iron beyond weighing (because it was in quantity). I've prepared logs and stones, but you can add to them. <sup>15</sup>With you in large numbers are workmen (hewers, craftsmen in stone and wood, and every kind of smart person in all work), <sup>16</sup>the gold, the silver, the copper and the iron, beyond numbering. Set to and do it. May Yahweh be with you.'

<sup>17</sup>David ordered all Yisra'el's officials to help Shelomoh his son: <sup>18</sup>'Yahweh your God is with you, isn't he, and he's enabled you to settle all round, because he's given into my hand the inhabitants of the country, and the country is in subjection before Yahweh and before his people. <sup>19</sup>Now give your mind and your being to enquiring of Yahweh your God, and set to and build Yahweh your God's sanctuary so as to bring Yahweh's pact chest and God's sacred articles to the house that's built for Yahweh's name.'

### The Levites' divisions

**23** When David was old and full of years, he made Shelomoh his son king over Yisra'el. <sup>2</sup>David gathered all the officials of Yisra'el, and the priests and the Levites. <sup>3</sup>The Levites were numbered, from age thirty and upwards; their head count for the males was 38,000. <sup>4</sup>Of these, in charge of the work in Yahweh's house were 24,000; overseers and authorities, 6,000; <sup>5</sup>4,000 gatemen; and 4,000 praising Yahweh 'with instruments that I made for praising'. ⁶David allocated them to divisions:

The sons of Levi: Gershon, Qehat and Merari. ⁷The Gershonites: La'dan and Shim'i.

⁸La'dan's sons: the head Yehi'el, Zetam and Yo'el – three.
⁹Shim'i's sons: Shelomit, Hazi'el and Haran – three.
These were La'dan's ancestral heads.
¹⁰Shim'i's sons: Yahat, Zina, Ye'ush and Beri'ah; these were Shim'i's sons – four.
¹¹Yahat was the head, Zina the second, and Ye'ush and Beri'ah did not have many sons so they became an ancestral household with one appointment.
¹²Qehat's sons: Amram, Yitshar, Hebron and Uzzi'el – four.
¹³Amram's sons: Aharon and Mosheh. Aharon was distinguished to make sacred the very sacred things, he and his sons permanently, to burn incense before Yahweh, to minister to him and to bless in his name, permanently.
¹⁴Mosheh, the supernatural man: his sons were named after the clan of Levi.
¹⁵Mosheh's sons: Gershom and Eli'ezer.
¹⁶Gershom's sons: Shebu'el the head.
¹⁷Eli'ezer's sons were Rehabyah the head; Eli'ezer didn't have other sons but Rehabyah's sons were exceptionally numerous.
¹⁸Yitshar's sons: Shelomit the head.
¹⁹Hebron's sons: Yeriyyahu the head, Amaryah the second, Yahazi'el the third and Yeqam'am the fourth.
²⁰Uzzi'el's sons: Mikah the head and Yishshiyyah the second.
²¹Merari's sons: Mahli and Mushi. Mahli's sons: El'azar and Qish.
²²El'azar died and didn't have sons, but rather daughters, and the sons of Qish, their brothers, took them.
²³Mushi's sons: Mahli, Eder and Yeremot – three.

## The Levites' roles

²⁴These are the Levites by their ancestral households – the ancestral heads as they were registered by a headcount of names, the people doing the work in connection with the service of Yahweh's house, from age twenty and upwards. ²⁵Because David said, 'Yahweh the God of Yisra'el has settled his people down and come to dwell in Yerushalaim permanently, ²⁶so also for the Levites there's no carrying the dwelling and all its articles, for its service.' ²⁷Because by the last words of David, those are the number of the Levites from the age of twenty and upwards. ²⁸Because their standing was at the side of the Aharonites for the service of Yahweh's house:
over the courtyards and over the halls;
over the purity of everything that was sacred, and the work involved in the service of God's house;
²⁹the row bread, the fine flour for a grain offering, the flatbread wafers, the griddle loaves, the mixed loaves, and every weight and measure;
³⁰standing morning by morning to confess and praise Yahweh, and similarly in the evening;
³¹all offering up of burnt offerings for Yahweh for the sabbaths, for the new months and for the appointed festivals by number, in accordance with the ruling for them, regularly, before Yahweh.
³²So they would keep watch over the appointment tent, over what was sacred, and over the Aharonites, their brothers, for the service of Yahweh's house.

**24** The divisions of the Aharonites. Aharon's sons: Nadab and Abihu, El'azar and Itamar. ²Nadab and Abihu died before their father and they had no sons, so El'azar and Itamar acted as priests. ³David, Tsadoq of the sons of El'azar, and Ahimelek of the sons of Itamar allocated them to their appointment by their service. ⁴El'azar's sons were found to be more numerous by male heads than Itamar's sons, so they allocated El'azar's sons as sixteen heads of ancestral households and Itamar's sons as eight heads of ancestral households. ⁵They allocated them by lots, both of them, because they were the sacred place's officials and God's officials, from El'azar's sons and from Itamar's sons.

## The Aharonites' divisions

⁶Shema'yah ben Netan'el the secretary, of the Levites, wrote them down before the king, the officials, Tsadoq the priest, Ahimelek ben Ebyatar, and the ancestral heads of the priests

and of the Levites – an ancestral household taken for El'azar, then one taken for Itamar.

<sup>7</sup>The first lot came out for Yehoyarib
the second for Yeda'yah
<sup>8</sup>the third for Harim
the fourth for Se'orim
<sup>9</sup>the fifth for Malkiyyah
the sixth for Miyyamin
<sup>10</sup>the seventh for Haqqots
the eighth for Abiyyah
<sup>11</sup>the ninth for Yeshua
the tenth for Shekanyahu
<sup>12</sup>the eleventh for Eliyashib
the twelfth for Yaqim
<sup>13</sup>the thirteenth for Huppah
the fourteenth for Yeshebe'ab
<sup>14</sup>the fifteenth for Bilgah
the sixteenth for Immer
<sup>15</sup>the seventeenth for Hezir
the eighteenth for Happitstsets
<sup>16</sup>the nineteenth for Petahyah
the twentieth for Yehezqe'l
<sup>17</sup>the twenty-first for Yakin
the twenty-second for Gamul
<sup>18</sup>the twenty-third for Delayahu
the twenty-fourth for Ma'azyahu

<sup>19</sup>These were their appointment, in relation to their service, for coming into Yahweh's house in accordance with the ruling for them by means of Aharon their father, as Yahweh the God of Yisra'el had ordered him. <sup>20</sup>Of the Levites who were left:

Of Amram's sons: Shuba'el;
Shuba'el's sons: Yehdeyahu;
<sup>21</sup>of Rehabyahu – of Rehabyahu's sons: the head Yishshiyyah.
<sup>22</sup>Of the Yitsharites: Shelomot; of Shelomot's sons: Yahat.
<sup>23</sup>Yeriyyahu's sons: Amaryahu the second, Yahazi'el the third, Yeqam'am the fourth.
<sup>24</sup>Uzzi'el's sons: Mikah; of Mikah's sons: Shamir;
<sup>25</sup>Mikah's brother: Yishshiyyah; of Yishshiyyah's sons: Zekaryahu.
<sup>26</sup>Merari's sons: Mahli and Mushi; the sons of Ya'aziyyahu, his son (<sup>27</sup>Merari's sons by Ya'aziyyahu, his son): Shoham, Zakkur, and Ibri;
<sup>28</sup>of Mahli: El'azar (he did not have sons);
<sup>29</sup>of Qish – Qish's sons: Yerahme'el;
<sup>30</sup>Mushi's sons: Mahli, Eder and Yerimot.

These were the sons of the Levites by the ancestral households.

<sup>31</sup>They also let lots fall, along with their Aharonite brothers, before David the king, Tsadoq, Ahimelek, and the ancestral heads of the priests and the Levites, the ancestral head along with his younger brother.

**25** And David and the army officers made distinct for the service the sons of Asaph, Heman and Yedutun, who prophesied with guitars, mandolins and tambourines.

## The watches

The number of them (the people fulfilling the work in connection with their service) was: <sup>2</sup>Asaph's sons: Zakkur, Yoseph, Netanyah and Asar'elah, Asaph's sons at the side of Asaph, who prophesied at the side of the king; <sup>3</sup>Yedutun – Yedutun's sons: Gedalyah, Tseri, Yeshayahu, Hashabyahu, Mattityahu, six, at the side of Yedutun their father with the mandolin, who prophesied in confessing and praising Yahweh; <sup>4</sup>Heman – Heman's sons: Buqqiyyahu, Mattanyahu, Uzzi'el, Shebu'el, Yerimot, Hananyah, Hanani, Eli'atah, Giddalti, Romamti Ezer, Yoshbeqashah, Malloti, Hotir and Mahazi'ot. <sup>5</sup>All these sons of Heman the king's seer with God's words, to lift up his horn. God gave Heman fourteen sons and three daughters, <sup>6</sup>all these by their father's side in singing in Yahweh's house with cymbals, mandolins and guitars, for the service of God's house. Asaph, Yedutun and Heman were by the king's side. <sup>7</sup>Their number with their brothers, trained in singing for Yahweh, every one discerning, 288. <sup>8</sup>They let lots fall for the watch, the big man along with the young man, discerning man with learner.

<sup>9</sup>The first lot (Asaph's) came out for Yoseph; Gedalyah, the second, he, his brothers and his sons – 12;
<sup>10</sup>the third Zakkur, his sons and his brothers – 12;
<sup>11</sup>the fourth for Yitsri, his sons and his brothers – 12;
<sup>12</sup>the fifth Netanyah, his sons and his brothers – 12;

<sup>13</sup>the sixth Buqqiyyah, his sons and his
brothers – 12;
<sup>14</sup>the seventh Yesar'elah, his sons and his
brothers – 12;
<sup>15</sup>the eighth Yesha'yahu, his sons and his
brothers – 12;
<sup>16</sup>the ninth Mattanyahu, his sons and his
brothers – 12;
<sup>17</sup>the tenth Shim'i, his sons and his brothers – 12;
<sup>18</sup>eleventh Azar'el, his sons and his brothers – 12;
<sup>19</sup>the twelfth for Hashabyah, his sons and his
brothers – 12;
<sup>20</sup>for the thirteenth Shuba'el, his sons and his
brothers – 12;
<sup>21</sup>for the fourteenth Mattityahu, his sons and
his brothers – 12;
<sup>22</sup>for the fifteenth for Yeremot, his sons and
his brothers – 12;
<sup>23</sup>for the sixteenth for Hananyahu, his sons
and his brothers – 12;
<sup>24</sup>for the seventeenth for Yoshbeqashah, his
sons and his brothers – 12;
<sup>25</sup>for the eighteenth for Hanani, his sons and
his brothers – 12;
<sup>26</sup>for the nineteenth for Malloti, his sons and
his brothers – 12;
<sup>27</sup>for the twentieth for Eli'atah, his sons and
his brothers – 12;
<sup>28</sup>for the twenty-first for Hotir, his sons and
his brothers – 12;
<sup>29</sup>for the twenty-second for Giddalti, his sons
and his brothers – 12;
<sup>30</sup>for the twenty-third for Mahazi'ot, his sons
and his brothers – 12;
<sup>31</sup>for the twenty-fourth for Romamti Ezer,
his sons and his brothers – 12.

## The gatemen

# 26

The divisions of the gatemen:

Qorahites: Meshelemeyahu ben Qore of the
sons of Asaph;
<sup>2</sup>of Meshelemeyahu, sons: Zekaryahu the
firstborn, Yedi'a'el the second, Zebadyahu
the third, Yatni'el the fourth, <sup>3</sup>Elam the
fifth, Yehohanan the sixth, Elyeho'enay
the seventh.
<sup>4</sup>Of Obed Edom, sons: Shema'yah the firstborn,
Yehozabad the second, Yo'ah the third, Sakar
the fourth, Netan'el the fifth, <sup>5</sup>Ammi'el the

sixth, Yissakar the seventh, Pe'ulletay the
eighth (because God blessed him);
<sup>6</sup>to Shema'yah his son sons were born
who ruled for their ancestral households
because they were forceful strong men;
<sup>7</sup>Shema'yah's sons: Otni, Repha'el, Obed,
Elzabad;
his brothers, forceful men: Elihu and
Semakyahu;
<sup>8</sup>all these of the sons of Obed Edom, they,
their sons and their brothers, people
forceful in their energy for the service – of
Obed Edom, sixty-two.
<sup>9</sup>Meshelemeyahu had sons and brothers,
forceful men – eighteen.
<sup>10</sup>Hosah of the Merarites had sons: Shimri
the head (because he was not the firstborn
but his father made him head), <sup>11</sup>Hilqiyyahu
the second, Tebalyahu the third, Zekaryahu
the fourth; all sons and brothers of Hoseh –
thirteen.

<sup>12</sup>These are the gatemen's divisions by the
strong men who were the heads, in watches
along with their brothers, to minister in
Yahweh's house. <sup>13</sup>They let lots fall, small and
big alike, gateway by gateway:
<sup>14</sup>the lots to the east fell to Shelemyahu;
Zekaryahu his son, a counsellor with insight:
they let lots fall and his lot came out to the
north;
<sup>15</sup>for Obed Edom, to the south, and for his
sons, the stores;
<sup>16</sup>for Suppim and for Hosah, to the west, with
the Shalleket Gate on the upper causeway.
Watch along with watch:
<sup>17</sup>to the east, six Levites;
to the north, four daily;
to the south, four daily;
for the stores, two by two;
<sup>18</sup>at the colonnade to the west, four at the
causeway, two at the colonnade.
<sup>19</sup>These are the divisions of the gatemen
belonging to the Qorahites and the Merarites.

## The Levites' responsibilities

<sup>20</sup>The Levites:
Ahiyyah in charge of the treasuries of God's
house and the treasuries of the sacred
things.

²¹La'dan's sons, the sons of the Gershonites belonging to La'dan, the ancestral heads of La'dan the Gershonite: Yehi'eli. ²²Yehi'eli's sons: Zetam and Yo'el his brother, in charge of the treasuries of Yahweh's house; ²³of the Amramites, the Yitsharites, the Hebronites and the Uzzi'elites: ²⁴Shebu'el ben Gershom, the son of Mosheh, chief over the treasuries. ²⁵His brothers by Eli'azar: Rehabyahu his son, Yesha'yahu his son, Yoram his son, Zikri his son and Shelomit his son. ²⁶That Shelomit and his brothers were in charge of all the treasuries of the sacred things that David the king made sacred, with the ancestral heads, for the chiliarchs, the centurions and the army officers; ²⁷some of the spoil from battles they made sacred for strengthening Yahweh's house; ²⁸everything that Shemu'el the seer, Sha'ul ben Qish, Abner ben Ner and Yo'ab ben Tseruyah made sacred (anyone who made something sacred) was in the control of Shelomit and his brothers. ²⁹Of the Yitsharites: Kenanyahu and his sons – in connection with work outside, in charge of Yisra'el as overseers and authorities. ³⁰Of the Hebronites: Hashabyahu and his brothers, forceful men, 1,700, with an appointment over Yisra'el across the Yarden westward regarding all Yahweh's work and regarding the king's service. ³¹Of the Hebronites, Yeriyyah the head of the Hebronites by his lines of descent, by his ancestors: in the fortieth year of David's reign they were enquired after, and forceful strong men were found among them in Ya'zir-in-Gil'ad; ³²his brothers, forceful men, 2,700, ancestral heads – David the king appointed them in charge of the Re'ubenites, the Gadites and the half-clan of Menashsheh in connection with everything of God's and everything of the king's.

## The army roster

**27** The Yisra'elites by their number (the ancestral heads, the chiliarchs, the centurions and their overseers who ministered to the king in everything concerning the divisions that came in and went out month by month, all the months of the year); each division was 24,000: ²in charge of the first division, for the first month: Yashob'am ben Zabdi'el, in charge of his division of 24,000 – ³of the sons of Perets, the head over all the army officers, for the first month; ⁴in charge of the second month's division: Doday the Ahohite in charge of his division with Miqlot the chief, in charge of his division of 24,000; ⁵the third army officer, for the third month: Benayah ben Yehoyada, the head priest, in charge of his division of 24,000; ⁶that was Benayah the strongest man among the Thirty and in charge of the Thirty and his division, Ammizabad his son; ⁷the fourth, for the fourth month: Asah-el, Yo'ab's brother, and Zebadyah his son after him, in charge of his division of 24,000; ⁸the fifth, for the fifth month: the officer Shamhut the Yizrahite, in charge of his division of 24,000; ⁹the sixth, for the sixth month: Ira ben Iqqesh, the Teqo'ite, in charge of his division, 24,000; ¹⁰the seventh, for the seventh month: Helets the Pelonite, from the Ephrayimites, in charge of his division of 24,000; ¹¹the eighth, for the eighth month: Sibbekay, the Hushatite of the Zerahites, in charge of his division of 24,000; ¹²the ninth, for the ninth month: Abi'ezer, the Anatotite of Binyamin, in charge of his division of 24,000; ¹³the tenth, for the tenth month: Mahray, the Netophatite of the Zerahites, in charge of his division of 24,000; ¹⁴the eleventh, for the eleventh month: Benayah, the Peratonite from the Ephrayimites, in charge of his division of 24,000; ¹⁵the twelfth, for the twelfth month: Helday the Netophatite of Otni'el, in charge of his division of 24,000.

## The administration

¹⁶In charge of the Yisra'elite clans:

for the Re'ubenites: chief, Eli'ezer ben Zikri; for the Shim'onites: Shephatyahu ben Ma'akah;

¹⁷for the Levites: Hashabyah ben Qemu'el;
for Aharon: Tsadoq;
¹⁸for Yehudah: Elihu, from David's brothers;
for Yissakar: Omri ben Mika'el;
¹⁹for Zebulun: Yishma'yahu ben Obadyahu;
for Naphtali: Yerimot ben Azri'el;
²⁰for the Ephrayimites: Hoshea ben Azizyahu;
for the half-clan of Menashsheh: Yo'el ben
    Pedayah;
²¹for the half of Menashsheh in Gil'ad: Yiddo
    ben Zekaryahu;
for Binyamin: Ya'asi'el ben Abner;
²²for Dan: Azar'el ben Yeroham.

These were the officers of the Yisra'elite clans.
²³David did not take their number for the
people of twenty years or less, because Yahweh
had said he would make Yisra'el as numerous
as the stars in the heavens, ²⁴though Yo'ab ben
Tseruyyah began to count, but he did
not finish; at this, fury came on Yisra'el and
the number did not go into the number of the
things concerning King David.

²⁵In charge of the king's treasuries: Azmavet
    ben Adi'el;
in charge of the treasuries in the open
    country (in the towns, in the hamlets and
    in the towers): Yehonatan ben Uzziyyahu;
²⁶in charge of the people doing work in the
    open country, in the service of the ground:
    Ezri ben Kelub;
²⁷in charge of the vineyards: Shim'i the
    Ramatite;
in charge of what was in the vineyards for
    the wine treasuries: Zabdi the Shiphmite;
²⁸in charge of the olive trees and the wild fig
    trees that were in the foothills: Ba'al Hanan
    the Gederite;
in charge of the oil treasuries: Yo'ash;
²⁹in charge of the cattle pasturing in Sharon:
    Shirtay the Sharonite;
in charge of the cattle in the vales: Shaphat
    ben Adlay;
³⁰in charge of the camels: Obil the Ishma'elite;
in charge of the she-donkeys: Yehdeyahu the
    Meronotite;
³¹in charge of the flocks: Yaziz the Hagrite.
All these were officials over the property that
belonged to King David.
³²Yehonatan, David's uncle, was a counsellor;
    he was a discerning person and a
    secretary.

Yehi'el ben Hackmoni was with the king's sons.
³³Ahitophel was counsellor to the king.
Hushay the Arkite was the king's friend.
³⁴After Ahitophel were Yehoyada ben
    Benayah and Ebyatar.
Yo'ab was the king's army officer.

## David's commission

**28** David congregated in Yerushalaim all
Yisra'el's officials, the clan officials, the
divisional officials who ministered to the king,
the chiliarchs, the centurions, and the officials
over all the property and cattle belonging
to the king and to his sons, with the courtiers
and the strong men, every forceful strong man.
²David the king rose to his feet and said, 'Listen
to me, my brothers, my people. I – it was in
my mind to build a place to settle down for
Yahweh's pact chest, for our God's footstool,
and I have prepared for building it. ³But God
said to me, "You aren't the one to build a house
for my name because you're a man of battles;
you've shed blood."

⁴Yahweh the God of Yisra'el chose me from
my father's entire household to be king over
Yisra'el permanently, because he chose Yehudah
as chief, and in Yehudah's household, my
father's household and from my father's sons he
accepted me to make me king over all Yisra'el.
⁵And from all my sons (because Yahweh has
given me many sons) he chose Shelomoh my
son to sit on Yahweh's kingly throne over Yisra'el.
⁶He said to me, "Shelomoh your son – he will
build my house and my courtyards, because I've
chosen him as a son to me, and I myself will
become a father to him. ⁷I will establish his reign
permanently if he is strong in acting on my
orders and my rulings this very day."

⁸So now before the eyes of all Yisra'el,
Yahweh's congregation, and in the ears of our
God: keep and enquire of all the orders of
Yahweh our God in order that you may possess
the good country and give it to your children
as their domain after you permanently.
⁹And you, Shelomoh my son: acknowledge
your father's God and serve him with a perfect
mind and with a willing being, because Yahweh
enquires of all minds and discerns every
inclination in people's intentions. If
you enquire of him, he will be found by you,

but if you abandon him, he will spurn you permanently. ¹⁰See, now, that Yahweh has chosen you to build a house for the sanctuary. Be strong and act!'

## The plan and the charge

¹¹David gave Shelomoh his son the plan for the porch, its houses, its storerooms, its upper quarters, its inside rooms, the house for the expiation cover, ¹²the plan for all that was with him by the spirit for the courtyards of Yahweh's house and for all the halls around, for the treasuries in God's house and for the treasuries for sacred things, ¹³for the divisions of the priests and the Levites and all the work involved in the service of Yahweh's house, for all the articles involved in the service of Yahweh's house, ¹⁴for the gold with the weight (for the gold for all the articles used service by service), for the silver vessels with the weight (for all the articles used service by service), ¹⁵the weight for the gold candelabra and the gold lamps, with the weight candelabrum by candelabrum and its lamps, and for the silver candelabra, with the weight for the candelabrum and its lamps in accordance with the service of candelabrum by candelabrum, ¹⁶the weighed gold for the tables for the row [of bread] table by table, and silver for the silver tables, ¹⁷the forks, the basins and the pitchers, pure gold, for the gold vessels, with the weight vessel by vessel, and the silver vessels, with the weight vessel by vessel, ¹⁸for the incense altar refined gold, with the weight, and for the plan for the chariot, the gold sphinxes spreading and shielding Yahweh's pact chest, ¹⁹all of it in writing, through Yahweh's hand upon me. He has given me insight into all the plan's workings.'

²⁰David said to Shelomoh his son, 'Be strong and stand firm, and act. Don't be afraid, don't be scared, because Yahweh God, my God, is with you. He won't let go of you, he won't abandon you, until the finishing of all the work in connection with the service of Yahweh's house. ²¹Here are the divisions of the priests and the Levites for the service of God's house, and with you in all the work everyone who is free with smartness for every service, and the officials and all the people in connection with all your words.'

## David's provision

**29** David the king said to the entire congregation, 'Shelomoh my son, the one God chose, is a boy and green, though the work is big, because the castle is not for a human being but for Yahweh God. ²With all my energy I have prepared for my God's house the gold for the gold things, the silver for the silver, the copper for the copper, the iron for the iron, the logs for the logs, onyx stones and settings, stones of antimony and colour, every precious stone, and alabaster stones, in quantity. ³And further, through my acceptance in my God's house, I have gold and silver as personal treasure that I'm giving for my God's house on top of all I have prepared for the sacred house: ⁴3,000 talents of gold (Ophir gold), 7,000 talents of refined silver to overlay the houses' walls (⁵the gold for the gold, the silver for the silver), and for all the work in the hand of the craftsmen. So who is going to give freely, commissioning himself to Yahweh today?'

⁶The ancestral officials, the Yisra'elite clans' officials, the chiliarchs, the centurions and the officials over the king's work gave freely. ⁷They gave for the service of God's house 5,000 talents of gold, 10,000 darics, 10,000 talents of silver, 18,000 talents of copper and 100,000 talents of iron. ⁸The person who had stones to be found with him – they gave them to the treasury of Yahweh's house, into the hand of Yehi'el the Gershonite. ⁹The people rejoiced over their free giving because it was with a perfect mind that they had given freely for Yahweh. David the king, too, rejoiced greatly.

## Who am I and who is my people?

¹⁰David blessed Yahweh before the eyes of the entire congregation. David said, 'You are to be blessed, Yahweh, God of Yisra'el our father, from age to age. ¹¹Yours, Yahweh, is greatness, strength, glory, honour and grandeur, because everything in the heavens and on the earth is yours, Yahweh – the kingship and pre-eminence in relation to everything, as head. ¹²Wealth and splendour come from before you. You rule over everything. In your hand are energy and strength. It's in your hand to make

anyone big or strong. [13]So now, our God, we confess you and praise your glorious name.

[14]But who am I and who is my people that we hold on to the energy to give freely like this, because everything comes from you, and it's from your hand that we've given you. [15]Because we are resident aliens before you, transients like all our ancestors. Our days are like a shadow on the earth, and without hope. [16]Yahweh our God, all this mass that we have prepared to build a house for you, for your sacred name, is from your hand. Everything is yours.

[17]My God, I acknowledge that you test the mind and that integrity is what you accept. I myself with my integrity of mind have freely given all these things, and now your people who have presented themselves here – I have seen them giving freely to you with rejoicing. [18]Yahweh, God of Abraham, Yitshaq and Yisra'el, our ancestors, keep this permanently as the inclination of the intentions in your people's mind, and establish their mind in relation to you. [19]To Shelomoh my son give a perfect mind to keep your orders, your affirmations and your decrees, and to do it all, and to build the castle for which I have prepared.'

## Full of years

[20]David said to the entire congregation, 'Bless Yahweh your God, please.' The entire congregation blessed Yahweh, their ancestors'

God. They knelt and bent their heads to Yahweh and to the king [21]and made sacrifices for Yahweh and offered up burnt offerings for Yahweh the next day after that day: 1,000 bulls, 1,000 rams, 1,000 lambs, with their libations, sacrifices in large numbers for all Yisra'el. [22]They ate and drank before Yahweh that day with great rejoicing.

They again made Shelomoh ben David king and anointed him for Yahweh as chief, and Tsadoq as priest. [23]Shelomoh sat on Yahweh's throne as king in place of his father. He was successful and all Yisra'el listened to him. [24]All the officials, the strong men, and also all King David's sons, gave their support to Shelomoh the king. [25]Yahweh made Shelomoh exceptionally big before the eyes of all Yisra'el and gave him a royal grandeur that had not been on any king over Yisra'el before him.

[26]When David ben Yishay reigned over all Yisra'el, [27]the time that he reigned over Yisra'el was forty years. In Hebron he reigned seven years and in Yerushalaim he reigned thirty-three. [28]He died in a good old age full of years, of wealth and of honour, and Shelomoh his son began to reign in place of him. [29]The things about David the king, early and late, there they are, written down in the things of Shemu'el the seer, in the things of Natan the prophet and in the things of Gad the seer, [30]with his entire reign and his might, and the times that passed for him, for Yisra'el and for the kingdoms of the earth.

# 2 CHRONICLES

Like 1 Chronicles, 2 Chronicles is a history of Israel that focuses on the history of the temple and its worship. The first part (chapters 1—9) retells the story of Solomon's reign with a focus on his activity in building the temple, on the basis of the preparation and provision that David completed.

The middle part (chapters 10—28) retells the story of the two centuries when Judah and Ephraim were divided into two nations, but it does so by focusing almost entirely on Judah. By setting up its independent state, Ephraim has cut itself off from Jerusalem and cut itself off from the household of David. In effect it has cut itself off from the real people of God, so its story does not really belong in that story. The book makes clear that it comes from the Second Temple period, when the Persian king has made it possible for Judahites to rebuild the temple but when Judah is merely a Persian colony and an embattled little community whose relationships with surrounding Persian colonies are difficult. The stories of Ezra and Nehemiah open a window into some of that trickiness. One of the most difficult is with the people of Samaria, who are the people now living in the area of what was once Ephraim. The second book of Chronicles encourages Judah to trust in its special relationship with God and not be threatened by or tempted into compromise with Samaria/Ephraim.

One way its stories offer encouragement is the way they relate monumental victories that Judah won over those two centuries when Ephraim and Judah were separate peoples. The battles are told larger than life in a way that enhances their excitement and their encouragement. The numbers are way out of line with the actual size of the peoples of the day, and even more out of line with the size of the peoples for whom Chronicles' version of the stories was written. The stories underline the way that trust in God, not the size of your army, is the key to survival and to success.

The last part of the book (chapters 29—36) returns to giving more focused attention to the temple. It covers the period after the downfall of Ephraim to the Assyrians, though it ignores that event because Ephrayim's story is not really part of the story of Israel. (The use of the word 'Israel' is often confusing in the First Testament, but especially in 2 Chronicles. On one hand, 'Israel' was the usual political name of the northern kingdom, and it is then set over against 'Judah'. On the other hand, 'Israel' denotes the people that God chose, the people of Abraham and Moses and David. In this sense Chronicles can refer to Judah as 'Israel'. Let the reader beware! I myself refer to the northern kingdom by its other name, Ephraim, to try to reduce the confusion.)

This last part of the book has two heroes, Hezekiah and Josiah, who were both involved in reforming the temple's worship. The odd thing about Josiah is that having acted with great faithfulness to Yahweh, he died quite young. His story contrasts with that of his grandfather, Manasseh, an apostate king who nevertheless reigned for fifty-five years. Chronicles offers implicit explanations of those disparities by describing how Manasseh repented of his wrongdoing while Josiah ignored a word from God in taking on the battle in which he died. Chronicles is thus able to affirm the truth of one of its important themes, that God is faithful and responsive to the people who are faithful and responsive to him but that failing in your faithfulness and responsiveness leads to trouble.

The book almost closes with Judah's own undoing of the reforms of Hezekiah and Josiah and with the temple's destruction by the Babylonians. But finally the Persian emperor declares that he has a commission from Yahweh (!) to rebuild the temple, and he encourages Judahites in exile throughout his empire to go back to Jerusalem to do it. That last little paragraph is also the first paragraph in the story in Ezra and Nehemiah, and the order of the books in the English Bible encourages us to read them in this sequence. But in most Hebrew Bibles these books come at the very end, in the order Ezra–Nehemiah–Chronicles, which points to the possibility that Ezra and Nehemiah are not the sequel to Chronicles; Chronicles is the prequel to Ezra–Nehemiah. That overlap between Chronicles and Ezra is the way Chronicles encourages its readers to see it as such a prequel. It offers further encouragement to see the book as speaking to the needs and pressures and questions of the Second Temple period.

## What would you like me to give you?

**1** Shelomoh [Solomon] ben David showed himself strong over his kingdom; Yahweh his God was with him and made him exceptionally big.

²Shelomoh spoke to all Yisra'el (to the chiliarchs and the centurions, to the authorities and to every leader in all Yisra'el, the ancestral heads), ³and Shelomoh and the entire congregation with him went to the shrine which was at Gib'on, because God's appointment tent, which Mosheh [Moses], Yahweh's servant, made in the wilderness, was there, ⁴though God's chest David had taken up from Ye'arim Township when David had prepared for it, because he had pitched a tent for it in Yerushalaim. ⁵But the copper altar, which Betsal'el ben Uri the son of Hur made, was there before Yahweh's dwelling. So Shelomoh and the congregation enquired of it. ⁶There Shelomoh went up on the copper altar before Yahweh, which was at the appointment tent, and offered up a thousand burnt offerings on it.

⁷That night God appeared to Shelomoh and said to him, 'Ask for what I should give you.' ⁸Shelomoh said to God, 'You yourself acted in great commitment with David my father and you have made me king in place of him. ⁹Now, Yahweh God, may your word with David my father prove trustworthy, because you have made me king over a people as numerous as the earth on the ground. ¹⁰Now give me smartness and knowledge so that I may go out and come in before this people. Because who can exercise authority for this great people of yours?'

¹¹God said to Shelomoh, 'Since this was in your mind, and you haven't asked for wealth and possessions and honour, or the life of the people hostile to you, nor was it even long life that you asked for, but you've asked for smartness and knowledge so you can exercise authority for my people over which I've made you king, ¹²smartness and knowledge are going to be given to you, and wealth and possessions and honour I will give to you, which have not belonged in this way to the kings who have been before you, nor will belong in this way to those after you.'

## Shelomoh's flourishing

¹³Shelomoh came, apropos the shrine which was at Gib'on, to Yerushalaim from before the appointment tent, and reigned over Yisra'el.

¹⁴Shelomoh gathered chariotry and cavalry; he had 1,400 chariotry and 12,000 cavalry. He settled them in chariot towns and with the king in Yerushalaim. ¹⁵The king made the silver and the gold in Yerushalaim like the stones, and made the cedars like the wild fig trees that are in the foothills, in the large number. ¹⁶The origin of the horses that Shelomoh had was from Misrayim [Egypt] and from Qewe. The king's dealers would get them from Qewe at a price; ¹⁷they took up a chariot (they brought it out from Misrayim) for 600 silver pieces, a horse for 150. In this way they would get them out by their own hand to all the kings of the Hittites, and to the kings of Aram.

**2** Shelomoh said to build a house for Yahweh's name and a house for himself as king. ²Shelomoh numbered 70,000 carriers, 80,000 hewers in the highland and 3,600 supervisors over them.

³Shelomoh sent to Huram king of Tsor [Tyre], saying, 'As you did with David my father when you sent him cedars to build himself a house to live in: ⁴here, I'm going to build a house for the name of Yahweh my God, to make sacred for him for burning spiced incense before him, and the regular row [of bread], and burnt offerings morning and evening, for the sabbaths, for the new months and for the appointed occasions of Yahweh our God. This is laid upon Yisra'el permanently. ⁵The house that I'm going to build will be big, because our God is bigger than all gods. ⁶But who can hold on to the energy to build him a house, because the heavens, even the highest heavens cannot contain him, so who am I that I should build him a house except for burning incense before him?

## What's needed for the house of God

⁷But now send me someone who's smart at working in gold, in silver, in copper, in iron, in purple, scarlet and blue, and who knows how to do engraving, with the smart people

who're with me in Yehudah and in Yerushalaim whom David my father prepared. [8]And send me cedar, juniper and algum logs from the Lebanon, because I acknowledge that your servants know about cutting Lebanese logs. And there, my servants will be with your servants [9]to prepare logs in large number for me, because the house that I'm going to build will be big, extraordinary. [10]Here, for the choppers, the people who cut the logs, I'm giving: crushed wheat for your servants, 20,000 ten-gallon measures; barley, 20,000 ten-gallon measures; wine, 20,000 five-gallon measures; and oil, 20,000 five-gallon measures.'

[11]Huram king of Tsor said in a written message, and sent to Shelomoh, 'In Yahweh's loyalty to his people he has made you king over them.' [12]Huram said, 'Blessed be Yahweh the God of Yisra'el who made the heavens and the earth, who gave David the king a smart son, who knows about insight and understanding, who will build a house for Yahweh and a house for himself as king. [13]So now I'm sending someone smart who knows about understanding, Huram Abi, [14]the son of one of the Danite women and his father a Tsorite man, who knows about working in gold, in silver, in copper, in iron, in stones, in wood, in purple, in blue, in fine linen and in scarlet, and how to do all engraving and to do any designing that will be given him, with your smart people and the smart people of my lord David your father. [15]And now the wheat, the barley, the oil and the wine that my lord said, he should send them to his servants. [16]We ourselves will cut down trees from the Lebanon in accordance with all your need and we will bring them to you as rafts by sea to Yafo, and you can take them up to Yerushalaim.'

## The work begins

[17]Shelomoh numbered all the people who were resident aliens who were in the country of Yisra'el, following on the numbering of them by David his father. They were found to be 153,600. [18]Of them he made 70,000 carriers, 80,000 hewers in the highland and 3,600 supervisors to get the company to serve.

**3** And Shelomoh began building Yahweh's house in Yerushalaim on Mount Moriyyah

where he had appeared to David his father, at David's site which he had prepared, at the threshing floor of Ornan the Yebusite. [2]He began to build in the second month, on the second, in the fourth year of his reign. [3]These were Shelomoh's foundation for building God's house:

the length 30 metres (by the former measure);
the width 10 metres;
[4]the porch corresponding to the length, corresponding to the width of the house, 10 metres;
the height 60 metres.

He overlaid it on the inside with pure gold. [5]The big house he covered with juniper wood, and he covered it with fine gold. He put on top of it palms and chains. [6]He decorated the house with precious stones for glory; the gold was Parvayim gold. [7]He covered the house (the beams, the thresholds, and its walls and its doors) with gold, and engraved sphinxes on the walls.

[8]He made the very sacred house: its length corresponding to the house's width, ten metres, and its width ten metres. He covered it with fine gold, 600 talents, [9]the weight of the nails fifty sheqels of gold. The upper quarters he covered in gold.

[10]In the very sacred house he made two sphinxes, sculptured work, and they overlaid them with gold. [11]The sphinxes' wings: their length ten metres – the wing of the first two-and-a-half metres touching the wall of the house and the other wing two-and-a-half metres touching the other sphinx's wing, [12]the other sphinx's wing two-and-a-half metres touching the wall of the house and the other wing two-and-a-half metres attaching to the first sphinx's wing, [13]these sphinxes' wings spreading ten metres; they were standing on their feet with their faces to the house.

## The features of the house

[14]He made the expiation cover of purple, blue, scarlet and fine linen, and made sphinxes on it. [15]Before the house he made two pillars sixteen metres in length; the capital that was on top of it was two and a half metres. [16]He made chains in the inner room and put them on top of the pillars, and he made a hundred

pomegranates and put them into the chains.
¹⁷He set up the pillars in front of the palace,
one on the right and one on the left. He named
the right 'He-Establishes' and the left 'In-Him-
Is-Strength'.

**4** He made a copper altar, ten metres its
length, ten metres its width, five metres
its height. ²He made the sea, cast:

five metres from its lip to its lip, circular all
  round, two and a half metres its height;
a line of fifteen metres would go round it all
  round;
³figures of cattle under it round it, all round,
  ten metres, encircling the sea all round;
two rows of the cattle, cast along with its
  casting;
⁴standing on twelve cattle, three facing
  north, three facing west, three facing
  south, three facing east, with the sea on
  them, above, and all their rears inwards;
⁵its thickness a handbreadth;
its lip like the making of the lip of a cup, a
  lotus petal;
taking strong hold of 10,000 gallons, which it
  would hold.

⁶He made ten basins and put them five
on the right and five on the left, for washing
in them. In them they would rinse the work
for the burnt offering, while the sea was for
the priests' washing in. ⁷He made the ten gold
candelabra in accordance with the ruling for
them and put them in the palace, five on the
right and five on the left. ⁸He made ten tables
and set them in the palace, five on the right and
five on the left. He made a hundred gold
sprinklers. ⁹He made the priests' courtyard and
the big enclosure and doors for the enclosure,
and their doors he overlaid with copper. ¹⁰He
put the sea at the right shoulder, to the east,
towards the south.

### The work completed

¹¹Huram made the basins, the shovels and the
bowls. So Huram finished doing all the work
that he did for King Shelomoh in God's house:
¹²two pillars;
the two globes and capitals on the top of the
  pillars;
two nets to cover the two globes for the
  capitals that were on the top of the pillars;

¹³the 400 pomegranates for the two nets,
  two rows of pomegranates for each net, to
  cover the two globes for the capitals that
  were on the face of the pillars;
¹⁴he made the stands and he made the basins
  on the stands;
¹⁵the one sea and the twelve cattle under it;
¹⁶the buckets, the shovels, the basins and all
  their articles that Huram his father made
  for King Shelomoh for Yahweh's house,
  polished copper.
¹⁷The king cast them in the Yarden [Jordan]
Plain, in the earthen compactness between
Sukkot and Tsaretan. ¹⁸Shelomoh made all
these articles, a large number, so that the
weight of the copper was not searched out.
¹⁹Shelomoh made all the articles that were in
God's house:
the gold altar;
the table on which was the presence bread;
²⁰the candelabra and their lamps for burning
  in accordance with the ruling, before the
  inner room, beaten gold;
²¹the flowers, the lamps and the tongs, gold
  (i.e. solid gold);
²²the snuffers, the sprinklers, the ladles
  and the pans, beaten gold;
the entrance for the house, its doors, the
  inside parts for the very sacred place, and
  the doors of the house for the palace, gold.

**5** So all the work that Shelomoh did for
Yahweh's house was complete, and
Shelomoh brought in the sacred things from
David his father; the silver, the gold and all the
articles he put in the treasuries of God's house.

### When you can tell God is present

²Then Shelomoh congregated Yisra'el's elders
(all the heads of the clans, the Yisra'elites'
ancestral leaders) to Yerushalaim, to take
up Yahweh's pact chest from David's Town
(i.e. Zion). ³Every individual in Yisra'el
congregated to the king at the festival (i.e. the
seventh month). ⁴All Yisra'el's elders came
and the Levites carried the chest. ⁵They took
up the chest, the appointment tent and all
the sacred articles that were in the tent. The
priests, the Levites, took them up ⁶while King
Shelomoh and the entire assembly of Yisra'el
who had assembled to him before the chest

were sacrificing sheep and cattle that could not be numbered and could not be counted because of the large number.

⁷The priests brought Yahweh's pact chest to its place, to the inner room of the house, to the very sacred place, under the sphinxes' wings. ⁸The sphinxes were spreading their wings over the chest's place; the sphinxes covered the chest and its poles from above. ⁹The poles extended and the heads of the poles coming from the chest could be seen in front of the inner room, but they could not be seen outside. It has been there until this day. ¹⁰There was nothing in the chest, only the two tablets that Mosheh put in at Horeb, when Yahweh solemnized things with the Yisraelites when they got out from Misrayim.

¹¹When the priests went out of the sacred place (because all the priests who were to be found had made themselves sacred – there was no keeping to the divisions), ¹²the Levite singers, all of them, Asaph, Heman and Yedutun, and their sons and their brothers, dressed in linen, with tambourines and with guitars and mandolins, were standing east of the altar, and with them were 120 priests blowing trumpets. ¹³When the trumpeters and the singers as one made one sound to be heard to praise and confess Yahweh and raised a sound on trumpets, on tambourines and on musical instruments, and praised Yahweh 'Because he is good, because his commitment is permanent', the house filled with a cloud – Yahweh's house. ¹⁴The priests could not stand ministering before the cloud because Yahweh's splendour filled God's house.

### A thick cloud and a stately house

**6** Then Shelomoh said:

Yahweh has said he would dwell in a
    thundercloud,
²but I myself have built you a stately house,
    an established place for you to live in to the ages.

³The king turned his face round and blessed Yisrael's entire congregation, as Yisrael's entire congregation was standing. ⁴He said, 'Blessed be Yahweh the God of Yisrael who spoke by his own mouth with David my father, and

by his own hand has fulfilled it: ⁵"From the day when I got my people out of the country of Misrayim I didn't choose a town from all Yisrael's clans to build a house for my name to be there and I didn't choose anyone to be chief over my people Yisrael. ⁶But I have chosen Yerushalaim for my name to be there, and I have chosen David to be in charge of my people Yisrael."

⁷It was in David my father's mind to build a house for the name of Yahweh the God of Yisrael, ⁸but Yahweh said to David my father, "In that it was in your mind to build a house for my name, you did well that it was in your mind. ⁹Only you yourself will not build the house. Rather your son, who is going to come out from your insides, he will build the house for my name."

¹⁰Yahweh has implemented his word that he spoke. I have arisen in place of David my father, I have sat on Yisrael's throne as Yahweh spoke and I have built the house for the name of Yahweh the God of Yisrael. ¹¹I have set there the chest where Yahweh's pact is, which he solemnized with the Yisraelites.'

### God dwells with humanity on earth!

¹²He stood before Yahweh's altar in front of the entire congregation of Yisrael and spread out his palms ¹³(because Shelomoh had made a copper platform and put it in the middle of the enclosure, its length two and a half metres, its width two and a half metres and its height one and a half metres; so he stood on it, and knelt on his knees in front of the entire congregation of Yisrael, and spread out his palms to the heavens).

¹⁴He said, 'Yahweh, God of Yisrael, there is no god like you in the heavens or on the earth, keeping pact and commitment to your servants who walk before you with their entire mind, ¹⁵who has kept for your servant David my father what you spoke to him. You spoke with your own mouth and with your own hand you have fulfilled it, this very day. ¹⁶So now, Yahweh, God of Yisrael, keep for your servant David my father what you spoke to him: "There will not be cut off for you someone before me sitting on Yisrael's throne, if only your sons keep watch over their way in

walking by my instruction, as you have walked before me." [17]So now, Yahweh, God of Yisra'el, may your word prove trustworthy that you spoke to your servant David.

[18]Because will God truly live with humanity on the earth? There, the heavens, even the highest heavens, could not contain you, certainly not this house that I've built. [19]But turn your face towards your servant's plea and towards his prayer for grace, Yahweh my God, so as to listen to the resounding cry and the plea that your servant's uttering before you, [20]so that your eyes are opened towards this house day and night, towards the place of which you said you would put your name there, so as to listen to the plea that your servant makes towards this place. [21]May you listen to the prayers for grace by your servant and your people Yisra'el, which they make towards this place. May you yourself listen from the place where you live, from the heavens, listen and pardon.'

## Be one who listens to us

[22]If someone does wrong to his neighbour, and he takes up an oath against him to get him to swear, and the oath comes before your altar in this house, [23]may you yourself listen from the heavens and act and exercise authority for your servants, so as to turn it back on the one who is in the wrong, bringing his conduct on his head, and to show the person in the right to be in the right, giving to him in accordance with his being in the right.

[24]If your people Yisra'el take a beating before an enemy because they do wrong in relation to you, but they turn back and confess your name and plead and pray for grace before you in this house, [25]may you yourself listen from the heavens and pardon your people Yisra'el's wrongdoing and take them back to the land that you gave to them and to their ancestors.

[26]When the heavens hold back and there's no rain because they do wrong in relation to you, but they plead towards this place and confess your name, when they turn back from their wrongdoing because you humble them, [27]may you yourself listen in the heavens and pardon the wrongdoing of your servants, your people Yisra'el, when you instruct them in the good

way that they should walk in, and give rain on your country that you gave your people as a domain.

[28]When famine happens in the country, when an epidemic happens, blight, mildew, locust or caterpillar, when it happens; when its enemies besiege it in the region of their settlements; any affliction or any illness; [29]any plea, any prayer for grace that any human being may have or your entire people Yisra'el may have, who acknowledge each one his affliction or illness, and he spreads out his palms towards this house, [30]may you yourself listen from the heavens, the established place where you live, and pardon, and give to the individual in accordance with all his ways (in that you know his mind because you alone know the mind of human beings), [31]in order that that they may live in awe of you by walking in your ways all the days that they are alive on the face of the ground that you gave to our ancestors.

## No ethnic limits to Yahweh

[32]Further, to the foreigner who is not of your people Yisra'el but comes from a distant country for the sake of your big name, your strong hand and your extended arm, and comes and pleads towards this house, [33]may you yourself listen from the heavens, from the established place where you live, and act in accordance with everything for which the foreigner calls to you, in order that all earth's peoples may acknowledge your name, and so as to live in awe of you like your people Yisra'el and to acknowledge that your name is called out over this house that I have built.

[34]When your people goes out to battle against its enemies by the way that you send them and they plead to you in the direction of this town that you have chosen and the house that I have built for your name, [35]may you listen from the heavens to their plea and to their prayer for grace, and decide for them.

[36]When they do wrong in relation to you (because there is no human being who doesn't do wrong) and you're angry with them and you give them up before an enemy, and their captors take them off captive to a country far or near, [37]and they turn their mind back in the country where they are captive, and turn back

and pray towards you for grace in the country
of their captivity, saying, "We've done wrong,
we've been wayward, we've been faithless",
<sup>38</sup>and they turn back to you with their entire
mind and with their entire being in the
country of their captivity where people have
taken them off captive, and make their plea
in the direction of their country that you gave
their ancestors, the town that you've chosen,
and to the house that I've built for your name,
<sup>39</sup>may you listen from the heavens, from the
established place where you live, to their plea,
their prayers for grace, and decide for them,
and pardon your people who have done wrong
in relation to you.
<sup>40</sup>Now, my God, may your eyes please be
opened and your ears be heeding to a plea
from this place.

### A committed people can rejoice

<sup>41</sup>So now,

Yahweh God, rise to your settled place,
   you and your powerful chest.
May your priests, Yahweh God,
   clothe themselves in deliverance.
May your committed people rejoice in good
   things,
  <sup>42</sup>Yahweh God.
Don't turn back the face of your anointed ones;
   be mindful of your servant David's acts of
   commitment.'

**7** When Shelomoh had finished pleading,
and the fire had come down from the
heavens and consumed the burnt offering and
the sacrifices, and Yahweh's splendour had
filled the house, <sup>2</sup>the priests couldn't come into
Yahweh's house because Yahweh's splendour
filled Yahweh's house. <sup>3</sup>When all the Yisraelites
saw the fire and Yahweh's splendour on the
house, they bent down, face to the ground, on
the pavement. They bowed low and confessed
Yahweh, 'Because he is good, because his
commitment lasts permanently'.
<sup>4</sup>When the king and all the people
made sacrifice before Yahweh, <sup>5</sup>King Shelomoh
sacrificed 22,000 cattle and 120,000 sheep, and
the king and the entire people dedicated God's
house, <sup>6</sup>while the priests were standing at their

watches, the Levites with the instruments for
singing to Yahweh, which David the king had
made for confessing Yahweh, 'Because his
commitment lasts permanently', with David's
praise in their hand, and the priests blowing
trumpets in front of them, and all Yisrael
standing.
<sup>7</sup>Shelomoh made sacred the middle of the
courtyard which was before Yahweh's house,
because he made the burnt offerings and the fat
parts of the well-being sacrifices there, because
the copper altar that Shelomoh had made
couldn't contain the burnt offering, the grain
offering and the fat parts. <sup>8</sup>Shelomoh made
the festival at that time for seven days, and all
Yisrael with him, a very big congregation, from
Lebo Hamat as far as the Misrayimite Wadi.
<sup>9</sup>On the eighth day they made an assembly,
because they made the dedication of the altar
for seven days and the festival for seven days.
<sup>10</sup>On the twenty-third day of the seventh
month he sent the people off to their tents,
rejoicing and good-hearted because of the
good things that Yahweh had done for David,
for Shelomoh and for Yisrael his people.

### If my people

<sup>11</sup>Shelomoh had finished Yahweh's house
and the king's house. Everything that had
come into Shelomoh's mind to do in Yahweh's
house and in his own house he succeeded in
doing. <sup>12</sup>And Yahweh appeared to Shelomoh
at night and said to him, 'I've listened to your
plea and chosen this place for myself as a
house for sacrifice. <sup>13</sup>If I hold back the heavens
and there's no rain, or if I order the locust
to consume the country, or if I send off an
epidemic against my people, <sup>14</sup>and my people
over whom my name is called out bow down
and plead and seek my face, and turn back
from their bad ways, I myself will listen from
the heavens and pardon their wrongdoing,
and heal their country. <sup>15</sup>My eyes will now
be opened and my ears be heeding to this
place's plea. <sup>16</sup>So now I've chosen and made
sacred this house for my name to be there
permanently. My eyes and my mind will be
there for all time.
<sup>17</sup>You yourself, if you walk before me as
David your father walked, acting in accordance

with all that I've ordered you, and you keep my decrees and my rulings, <sup>18</sup>I will set up your kingly throne as I solemnized it to David your father, saying "There will not be cut off for you someone ruling in Yisra'el."

<sup>19</sup>But if you people turn back and abandon my decrees and my orders that I've put before you, and you go and serve other gods and bow low to them, <sup>20</sup>I will uproot them from upon my land that I gave them, and this house that I've made sacred for my name I will throw out from before my face and make it into an object lesson and a taunt among all the peoples.

<sup>21</sup>This house, which has been high – everyone who passes by it will be desolate and will say, "Why did Yahweh act in that way to this country and to this house?" <sup>22</sup>And people will say, "On account of the fact that they abandoned Yahweh their ancestors' God who got them out of the country of Misrayim, and took strong hold of other gods and bowed low to them and served them. That's why he brought upon them all this bad fate."

## Shelomoh's other projects

**8** At the end of the twenty years while Shelomoh built Yahweh's house and his own house <sup>2</sup>(and the towns that Huram gave Shelomoh – he built them up and got Yisra'elites to live there), <sup>3</sup>Shelomoh went to Hamat Tsobah and overpowered it, <sup>4</sup>and built Tadmor in the wilderness, and all the supply towns that he built in Hamat. <sup>5</sup>He built Upper Bet Horon and Lower Bet Horon as fortified towns (walls, gateways and a bar), <sup>6</sup>Ba'alat and the supply towns that belonged to Shelomoh, all the chariotry towns and the cavalry towns – every attraction that Shelomoh had for building in Yerushalaim, in the Lebanon and in all the country he ruled.

<sup>7</sup>The entire people that were left of the Hittite, the Amorite, the Perizzite, the Hivvite and the Yebusite, who were not of Yisra'elite birth (<sup>8</sup>of their descendants who were left after them in the country, whom the Yisra'elites had not finished off), Shelomoh raised them as a workforce until this day. <sup>9</sup>Of the Yisra'elites, whom Shelomoh did not make into servants for his work; rather they were men of battle, adjutant officers, and officers over his chariotry

and his cavalry, <sup>10</sup>and these were King Shelomoh's prefect officers, 250, holding sway over the people.

<sup>11</sup>Par'oh's [Pharaoh's] daughter Shelomoh took up from David's Town to the house that he built for her, because (he said), 'My wife will not live in the house of David king of Yisra'el, because those places where Yahweh's chest has come are sacred.'

<sup>12</sup>Shelomoh then offered up burnt offerings for Yahweh on Yahweh's altar which he built before the porch, <sup>13</sup>offering up each day's requirement in its day in accordance with Mosheh's order for the sabbaths, the new months and the three appointed occasions in the year, on the Flatbread Festival, on the Shabu'ot Festival and on the Sukkot Festival.

<sup>14</sup>In accordance with the ruling of David his father, he put in place the priests' divisions for their service, the Levites for their watches to praise and to minister in front of the priests, each day's requirement in its day, and the gatemen by their divisions, gateway by gateway, because this was the order of David, the supernatural man. <sup>15</sup>They did not depart from the king's order regarding the priests or the Levites in connection with anything, or in connection with the treasuries.

## There had been nothing like it

<sup>16</sup>So all Shelomoh's work was established from the day Yahweh's house was founded and until Yahweh's house was finished, complete.

<sup>17</sup>Shelomoh then went to Etsyon-geber and to Elot on the sea coast in the country of Edom. <sup>18</sup>Huram sent ships to him by the hand of his servants; his servants knew the sea. They came with Shelomoh's servants to Ophir and got gold from there, 450 talents, and brought it to King Shelomoh.

**9** Since the queen of Sheba heard report of Shelomoh, she came to test Shelomoh in Yerushalaim with conundrums, with a very substantial force, both camels carrying spices, and gold in quantity, and precious stones. She came to Shelomoh and spoke with him of everything that was in her mind, <sup>2</sup>and Shelomoh told her about all the things she said. Nothing was concealed from Shelomoh that he didn't tell her.

³The queen of Sheba saw Shelomoh's smartness, the house that he had built, ⁴the food on his table, the seating of his servants, the standing of his ministers and their dress, his wine waiters and their dress, and his stairway by which he would go up to Yahweh's house, and there was no longer any breath in her. ⁵She said to the king, 'The thing is true that I heard in my country about your words and about your smartness. ⁶I didn't believe their words until I came, and my eyes saw, but here, half of the extent of your smartness had not been told me; you exceed the report that I heard. ⁷The blessings of your people, the blessings of these servants of yours who are standing continually before you and listening to your smartness! ⁸May Yahweh your God be blessed, who delighted in you so as to put you on his throne as king for Yahweh your God, in your God's loyalty to Yisra'el in enabling them to stand, permanently, and made you king over them to exercise authority with faithfulness.'

## All that she wanted

⁹She gave the king 120 talents of gold, spices in very large quantity and precious stones. There never again came spice like that spice that the queen of Sheba gave King Shelomoh. ¹⁰Huram's servants and Shelomoh's servants, who brought gold from Ophir, also brought algum wood and precious stones. ¹¹The king made the algum logs into causeways for Yahweh's house and for the king's house and into guitars and mandolins for the singers. Ones like these had not been seen before in the country of Yehudah. ¹²King Shelomoh himself gave the queen of Sheba all that she wanted, that she asked for, beyond what she brought to the king. Then she turned round and went to her country, she and her servants.

¹³The weight of the gold that came to Shelomoh in one year was 666 talents of gold, ¹⁴apart from what the traders and the merchants were bringing; and all the kings of Arabia and the governors of the region were bringing gold and silver to Shelomoh. ¹⁵King Shelomoh made 200 body-shields of hammered gold (he would raise 600 gold pieces for each shield) ¹⁶and 300 hand-shields

of hammered gold (he would raise 300 pieces of gold for each shield). The king put them in the Lebanon Forest house.

¹⁷The king made a big ivory throne and overlaid it with refined gold, ¹⁸with six steps to the throne, and a gold footstool for the throne attached, and arms on this side and on that side of the place where one sat, and two lions standing beside the arms, ¹⁹and twelve lions standing there on the six steps on this side and on that side; none was made like this for any kingdom.

## Tusks, monkeys and peacocks

²⁰All King Shelomoh's drinking vessels were gold and all the vessels in the Lebanon Forest house were beaten gold – silver was not thought of for anything in Shelomoh's days, ²¹because the king had a fleet going to Tarshish with Huram's servants. Once in three years the Tarshish fleet would come carrying gold and silver, tusks, monkeys and peacocks. ²²King Shelomoh was bigger than all the kings of the earth in wealth and in smartness. ²³All the kings of the earth were seeking audience with Shelomoh to listen to his smartness, which God had put into his mind, ²⁴and they were bringing each his offering: silver objects and gold objects, robes, weaponry and spices, horses and mules, each year's requirement in its year. ²⁵Shelomoh had 4,000 stalls for horses and chariots and 12,000 cavalry. He settled them in chariot towns, and with the king in Yerushalaim.

²⁶He was ruling over all the kings from the River as far as the Pelishtites' [Philistines'] country and as far as the Misrayimite border. ²⁷The king made the silver in Yerushalaim like the stones, and made the cedars like the wild fig trees that are in the foothills in the large number. ²⁸They were getting horses out of Misrayim for Shelomoh, and out of all the countries.

²⁹The rest of the things about Shelomoh, early and late, are written in the words of Natan the prophet, in the prophecy of Ahiyyah the Shilonite and in the visions of Ye'do the seer concerning Yarob'am [Jeroboam] ben Nebat, aren't they. ³⁰Shelomoh reigned in Yerushalaim over all Yisra'el forty years. ³¹Shelomoh lay down with his ancestors and they buried him

in the town of David his father. Rehab'am [Rehoboam] his son began to reign in place of him.

## How Rehab'am could win people's allegiance

**10** Rehab'am went to Shekem, because all Yisra'el had come to Shekem to make him king. ²But when Yarob'am ben Nebat heard while he was in Misrayim, where he had taken flight from before Shelomoh the king, Yarob'am came back from Misrayim, ³and they sent and called for him. Yarob'am and all Yisra'el came and spoke to Rehab'am: ⁴'Your father – he made our yoke tough. So now, lighten something of your father's tough servitude and of his heavy yoke that he put on us, and we'll serve you.'

⁵He said to them, 'In three more days, come back to me.' The people went, and ⁶King Rehab'am took counsel with the elders who had been standing before Shelomoh his father when he was alive: 'How do you counsel me to give back word to this people?' ⁷They spoke to him: 'If you're good to this people and accept them and speak good words to them, they'll be servants to you for all time.'

⁸But he abandoned the elders' counsel which they gave him and took counsel with the young men who grew up with him, who were standing before him. ⁹He said to them, 'What are you going to counsel, so that we may give back word to this people who spoke to me: "Lighten something of the yoke that your father put upon us"?' ¹⁰The young men who grew up with him spoke with him: 'You should say this to the people who spoke to you: "Whereas your father made our yoke heavy, you, lighten it from on us" – you should say this to them: "My little finger is thicker than my father's hips. ¹¹So now, whereas my father imposed a heavy yoke on you, I myself will add to your yoke. Whereas my father disciplined you with whips, I myself will with scorpions."'

## How to forfeit people's allegiance

¹²Yarob'am and all the people came to Rehab'am on the third day as the king had spoken, "Come back to me on the third day", ¹³and the king answered them toughly. So King Rehab'am abandoned the elders' counsel ¹⁴and spoke to them in accordance with the young men's counsel: 'I shall make your yoke heavy. I myself shall add to it. Whereas my father disciplined you with whips, I myself will with scorpions.' ¹⁵The king didn't listen to the people, because the turn of affairs came from God in order that Yahweh might implement his word, which he had spoken by means of Ahiyyahu the Shilonite to Yarob'am ben Nebat.

¹⁶All Yisra'el [saw] that the king had not listened to them, and the people said back to the king:

What share do we have in David? –
we have no domain in ben Yishay.
Each one to your tents, Yisra'el;
now see to your own household, David.

So all Yisra'el went to their tents, ¹⁷though the Yisra'elites who were living in the towns of Yehudah – Rehab'am reigned over them. ¹⁸King Rehab'am sent Hadoram, who was in charge of the workforce, but the Yisra'elites pelted him with stones and he died, though King Rehab'am got himself together to climb up into the chariot to flee to Yerushalaim. ¹⁹So Yisra'el rebelled against David's household, until this day.

**11** Rehab'am came to Yerushalaim and congregated the household of Yehudah and Binyamin, 180,000 picked men doing battle, to go to battle with Yisra'el and get the kingship back for Rehab'am. ²But Yahweh's word came to Shema'yahu, the supernatural man: ³'Say to Rehab'am son of Shelomoh king of Yehudah, and to all Yisra'el in Yehudah and in Binyamin: ⁴'Yahweh has said this: 'You will not go up, you will not go to battle with your brothers. Go back each one to his home, because this thing has come about from me.''' They listened to Yahweh's words and turned back from going against Yarob'am.

## People from Ephrayim join Rehab'am

⁵Rehab'am lived in Yerushalaim but built up towns as a fortress in Yehudah. ⁶He built up Bet-lehem, Etam, Teqoa, ⁷Bet-tsur, Soko, Adullam, ⁸Gat, Mareshah, Ziph, ⁹Adorayim, Lakish, Azeqah, ¹⁰Tsorah, Ayyalon and Hebron,

which are in Yehudah and in Binyamin, as fortress towns. [11]He strengthened the fortresses and put chiefs in them, and treasuries of food, oil and wine, [12]and in each and every town shields and spears. He strengthened them very greatly.

So Yehudah and Binyamin were his, [13]while the priests and the Levites who were in all Yisra'el took their stand with him, from all their territory, [14]because the Levites abandoned their pasturelands and their holding and went to Yehudah and to Yerushalaim (because Yarob'am and his sons rejected them from acting as priests for Yahweh [15]and put in place priests for himself for the shrines for the goats and for the calves that he made). [16]Following them from all the Yisra'elite clans, the people who were giving their mind to seek Yahweh the God of Yisra'el came to Yerushalaim to sacrifice for Yahweh, their ancestors' God. [17]They strengthened the kingdom of Yehudah and enabled Rehab'am to be firm for three years, because they walked in the way of David and Shelomoh for three years.

[18]Rehab'am took Mahalat bat Yerimot, the son of David, and Abihayil bat Eli'ab, the son of Yishay. [19]She gave birth to sons for him, Ye'ush, Shemaryah and Zaham. [20]After her he took Ma'akah bat Abshalom. She gave birth for him to Abiyyah, Attay, Ziza and Shelomit. [21]Rehab'am loved Ma'akah bat Abshalom more than all his wives and his secondary wives (because he had 18 wives and 60 secondary wives, and fathered 28 sons and 60 daughters). [22]Rehab'am put in place Abiyyah son of Ma'akah as head, as chief among his brothers, because it was to make him king. [23]He was discerning and he got some of all his sons to break out to all the regions of Yehudah and Binyamin, to all the fortified towns, gave them provisions in quantity and asked for a horde of wives.

## You abandon me; I abandon you

**12** When Rehab'am had established his kingship and he was strong, he abandoned Yahweh's instruction, he and all Yisra'el with him, [2]and in the fifth year of King Rehab'am, Shishaq king of Misrayim went up against Yerushalaim because they had trespassed against Yahweh, [3]with 1,200 chariotry and 60,000 cavalry; there was no numbering of the company that came with him from Misrayim (Lubites, Sukkiyyites and Kushites). [4]He captured the fortified towns that belonged to Yehudah and came as far as Yerushalaim.

[5]Shema'yah the prophet came to Rehab'am and the Yehudahite officers who had gathered in Yerushalaim in face of Shishaq, and said to them, 'Yahweh has said this: "You people have abandoned me, so I myself have also abandoned you into the hand of Shishaq."' [6]The Yisra'elite officers and the king bowed down and said, 'Yahweh is in the right.' [7]When Yahweh saw that they had bowed down, Yahweh's word came to Shema'yah: 'They have bowed down. I will not devastate them, but in a little while will give them an escape group. My wrath will not pour out on Yerushalaim by means of Shishaq, [8]but rather they will be servants to him and will acknowledge [the difference between] serving me and serving the kingships of the earth.'

[9]Shishaq king of Misrayim went up against Yerushalaim and took the treasures of Yahweh's house and the treasures of the king's house. He took everything. He took the gold shields that Shelomoh had made; [10]King Rehab'am made copper shields in place of them and appointed them to the control of the officers in charge of the runners who kept watch over the entrance to the king's house. [11]Whenever the king came to Yahweh's house the runners came and they would carry them, then take them back to the runners' chamber.

[12]So when he bowed down, Yahweh's anger turned back from him and did not completely devastate him; and in Yehudah there were good things, too.

## A salt covenant

[13]King Rehab'am showed himself strong in Yerushalaim and reigned, in that he was a man of forty-one years when he began to reign and he reigned seventeeen years in Yerushalaim, the town that Yahweh chose to put his name there out of all Yisra'el's clans. His mother's name was Na'amah the Ammonite. [14]But he did

what was bad, because he didn't establish his mind to enquire of Yahweh.

¹⁵The things about Rehab'am, early and late, are written in the words of Shema'yah the prophet and Iddo the seer regarding enrolment by genealogy, aren't they. There were battles between Rehab'am and Yarob'am all the time. ¹⁶Rehab'am lay down with his ancestors and was buried in David's Town, and Abiyyah his son began to reign in place of him.

**13** In the eighteenth year of King Yarob'am, Abiyyah began to reign over Yehudah. ²Three years he reigned in Yerushalaim. His mother's name was Mikayahu bat Uri'el, from Gib'ah. There was a battle between Abiyyah and Yarob'am, ³and Abiyyah hitched up for the battle with a force of strong men of battle, 400,000 picked men, while Yarob'am lined up with him for battle with 800,000 picked men – strong, forceful.

⁴Abiyyah got up on Mount Tsemarayim, which is in the highland of Ephrayim, and said, 'Listen to me, Yarob'am and all Yisra'el. ⁵It's for you to acknowledge, isn't it, that Yahweh the God of Yisra'el gave kingship over Yisra'el to David permanently, to him and to his sons, by a salt pact. ⁶Yarob'am ben Nebat, a servant of Shelomoh ben David, rose up and rebelled against his lord. ⁷There collected to him empty-headed scoundrels, and they took a firm stand against Rehab'am son of Shelomoh when Rehab'am was a boy and green in mind, and he didn't assert his strength before them. ⁸Now you're saying you'll assert your strength before Yahweh's kingship in the hand of David's sons. Whereas you're a numerous horde and you have with you the gold calves that Yarob'am made for you as gods, ⁹you drove out Yahweh's priests, the Aharonites and the Levites, didn't you, and made priests for yourselves, like the peoples of the countries. Anyone who comes to commission himself, with a bull from the herd and seven rams, becomes a priest, for no-gods.

### Don't do battle with Yahweh

¹⁰But for us, Yahweh is our God. We haven't abandoned him. The priests ministering to Yahweh are Aharonites, with the Levites at work, ¹¹burning up whole offerings for Yahweh morning by morning and evening by evening, with spiced incense and the row of bread on the pure table, and the gold candelabrum and its lamps to burn evening by evening, because we are keeping the charge of Yahweh our God, but you people have abandoned it. ¹²So here, God is with us, at the head, and his priests with resounding trumpets to sound against you. Yisra'elites, don't battle with Yahweh, your ancestors' God, because you won't succeed.'

¹³Now Yarob'am had sent an ambush round to come from behind them, so they were before Yehudah, and the ambush was behind them. ¹⁴Yehudah turned their face, and there – the battle was in front and behind for them. They cried out to Yahweh, with the priests blowing on the trumpets, ¹⁵and the men of Yehudah shouted. When the men of Yehudah shouted, God himself hit Yarob'am and all Yisra'el before Abiyyah and Yehudah. ¹⁶The Yisra'elites fled from before Yehudah and God gave them into their hand. ¹⁷Abiyyah and his company struck them down in a great rout. There fell of Yisra'el, run through, 500,000 picked men.

¹⁸So the Yisra'elites bowed down at that time and the Yehudahites stood firm because they relied on Yahweh, their ancestors' God. ¹⁹Abiyyah pursued after Yarob'am and captured some towns from him, Bet-el and its daughter-towns, Yeshanah and its daughter-towns, and Ephrayin and its daughter-towns. ²⁰Yarob'am did not retain energy any more in the days of Abiyyahu, and Yahweh struck him and he died, ²¹but Abiyyahu showed himself strong. He got himself 14 wives and fathered 22 sons and 16 daughters. ²²The rest of the things about Abiyyah, his ways and his words, are written in the commentary of the prophet Iddo.

### We rest on thee

**14** Abiyyah lay down with his ancestors and they buried him in David's Town, and Asa his son began to reign in place of him. In his days the country was calm ten years. ²Asa did what was good and upright in the eyes of Yahweh his God. ³He removed the alien altars and the shrines, broke up the columns and cut down the totem poles. ⁴He said to Yehudah that they were to look to Yahweh, their ancestors' God, and to act on the instruction and the order. ⁵From all the towns in Yehudah he removed the shrines and the incense stands. The kingdom was calm before him, ⁶and he built up fortified towns in Yehudah because the country was calm and there was no battle made with him in those years, because Yahweh enabled him to settle down. ⁷He said to Yehudah, 'Let's build up these towns and surround them with a wall and towers, gateways and bars, while the country is before us, because we've enquired of Yahweh our God. We've enquired of him and he has enabled us to settle down all round.' So they built and they were successful.

⁸Asa had a force carrying body-shield and spear from Yehudah, 300,000 men, and from Binyamin 280,000 men carrying hand-shield and drawing a bow. All these were forceful strong men. ⁹Zerah the Kushite went out against them with a force of 1,000,000 and 300 chariots, and came as far as Mareshah. ¹⁰Asa went out before him and lined up for battle in the Tsephat Ravine near Mareshah. ¹¹Asa called to Yahweh his God: 'Yahweh, there is no one compared with you to help, between the numerous and the powerless. Help us, Yahweh our God, because we lean on you and in your name we've come against this horde. You are Yahweh our God. A mere human being is not to hold on with you.'

## God's spirit comes

¹²Yahweh hit the Kushites before Asa and before Yehudah, and the Kushites fled. ¹³Asa and the company that was with him pursued them as far as Gerar, and some of the Kushites fell. There was no saving of life for them, because they broke up before Yahweh and before his camp.

They took up very much spoil ¹⁴and struck down all the towns round Gerar, because a dread of Yahweh was on them. They plundered all the towns because there was much plunder in them. ¹⁵They also struck down the cattle tents and captured sheep in large number and camels, then went back to Yerushalaim.

**15** Azaryahu ben Oded – God's spirit came on him ²and he went out before Asa and said to him, 'Listen to me, Asa and all Yehudah and Binyamin. Yahweh is with you when you are with him. If you enquire of him

he will be found by you, but if you abandon him, he will abandon you. ³For a long time Yisra'el had no true God, no priest instructing and no instruction, ⁴but in the pressure upon it, it turned back to Yahweh the God of Yisra'el. They sought him, and he let himself be found by them.

⁵In those times there was no well-being for the person who went out or for the person who came in, because there was much turmoil among all the inhabitants of the countries. ⁶Nation was crushed by nation, town by town, because God put them into a turmoil with every kind of pressure. ⁷But you: be strong. Your hands are not to slacken, because there will be wages for your work.'

⁸When Asa heard these words, the prophecy of Oded the prophet, he showed himself strong and got rid of the abominations from the entire country of Yehudah and Binyamin and from the towns that he had captured from the highland of Ephrayim, and he renovated Yahweh's altar which was before Yahweh's porch.

## Taking the initiative in covenant

⁹He collected all Yehudah and Binyamin and the resident aliens with them from Ephrayim and Menashsheh and from Shim'on, because people from Yisra'el in great number had submitted to him when they saw that Yahweh his God was with him. ¹⁰They collected in Yerushalaim in the third month of the fifteenth year of Asa's reign. ¹¹They sacrificed for Yahweh that day some of the spoil; they brought 700 cattle and 7,000 sheep ¹²and came into a pact to enquire of Yahweh their ancestors' God, with their entire mind and with their entire being. ¹³Anyone who would not enquire of Yahweh the God of Yisra'el would be put to death, whether small or great, man or woman. ¹⁴They swore to Yahweh with a loud voice, with a shout, with trumpets and with horns. ¹⁵All Yehudah rejoiced over the oath because they swore with their entire mind and sought him with their entire heart, and he let himself be found by them. Yahweh enabled them to be settled all round.

¹⁶In addition, Ma'akah mother of Asa the king he removed as queen mother, because she had made a monstrosity for Asherah. Asa cut

down her monstrosity, turned it to dust and burned it in Wadi Qidron, [17]though the shrines did not disappear from Yisra'el. Yet Asa's mind was perfect all his days. [18]He brought into God's house the sacred things belonging to his father and to him, silver, gold and articles, [19]while no battle happened until the thirty-fifth year of Asa's reign.

# 16

In the thirty-sixth year of Asa's reign, Ba'sha king of Yisra'el went up against Yehudah and built up The Height so as not to grant Asa king of Yehudah anyone going out or coming. [2]Asa got silver and gold out from the treasuries of Yahweh's house and the king's house and sent to Ben-hadad king of Aram who lived in Dammeseq [Damascus], saying, [3]'A pact between me and you and between my father and your father: here, I've sent you silver and gold; go contravene your pact with Ba'sha king of Yisra'el so that he may go up from me.'

## God's eyes are ranging through the earth

[4]Ben-hadad listened to King Asa and sent the officers of the forces that he had against Yisra'el's towns. He struck down Iyyon, Dan, Water Meadow and all the supply places, the towns in Naphtali. [5]When Ba'sha heard, he left off building up The Height and stopped his work, [6]while Asa the king got all Yehudah and they carried the stones from The Height and its timber with which Ba'sha had built, and with them he built up Geba and The Watchtower.

[7]But at that time Hanani the seer came to Asa king of Yehudah and said to him, 'For your leaning on the king of Aram and not leaning on Yahweh your God, because of this the king of Aram's force has escaped from your hand. [8]The Kushites and the Lubites were a force in large numbers, of chariotry and cavalry, very many, weren't they, but when you leaned on Yahweh, he gave them into your hand. [9]Because Yahweh – his eyes are ranging through the entire earth, to show himself strong with people whose mind is perfect towards him. You've been very idiotic in connection with this, because from now on there will be battles with you.' [10]Asa was provoked by the seer, and he put him into the stocks because he was in a rage with him on account of this, and Asa oppressed some of the people at that time.

[11]There, the things about Asa, early and late – there they are, written on the document about the kings of Yehudah and Yisra'el. [12]In the thirty-ninth year of his reign Asa had an ailment in his feet, until his ailment was exceptionally serious, and further, in his ailment he did not enquire of Yahweh but with physicians. [13]Asa lay down with his ancestors and died in the forty-first year of his reign. [14]They buried him in the graveyard that he had cut for himself in David's Town. They laid him in his bed, which they filled with spices and perfumes blended by blending work, and they made for him a very great fire.

## A teaching mission

# 17

Yehoshaphat his son began to reign in place of him and showed himself strong over Yisra'el. [2]He put a force in all the fortified towns of Yehudah and put outposts in the country of Yehudah and in the towns of Ephrayim that Asa his father had captured.

[3]Yahweh was with Yehoshaphat because he walked in the earlier ways of David his ancestor and did not enquire of the Masters. [4]He enquired of the God of his father and walked by his orders, not in accordance with the practice of Yisra'el. [5]Yahweh established the kingship in his hand and all Yehudah gave offerings to Yehoshaphat, so that he had wealth and splendour in quantity. [6]His mind was lofty in Yahweh's ways, and further he removed the shrines and the totem poles from Yehudah.

[7]In the third year of his reign he sent his officials Ben-hayil, Obadyah, Zekaryah, Netan'el and Mikayahu to teach in the towns of Yehudah, [8]and with them the Levites Shema'yahu, Netanyahu, Zebadyahu, Asah'el, Shemiramot, Yehonatan, Adoniyyah, Tobiyyahu and Tob Adoniyyah, the Levites, and with them Elishama and Yehoram, the priests. [9]They taught in Yehudah, Yahweh's instruction document being with them. They went round through all the towns of Yehudah and taught among the people.

[10]A dread of Yahweh was on all the kingships of the countries that were round Yehudah and they didn't battle with Yehoshaphat. [11]Some Pelishtites were bringing Yehoshaphat offerings

and silver as a levy; also the Arabs were bringing him flocks: 7,700 rams and 7,700 goats.

[12]So Yehoshaphat was getting bigger and bigger. He built castles and supply towns in Yehudah; [13]he had much work in the towns of Yehudah, and men of battle, forceful strong men, in Yerushalaim. [14]These, their registering by their ancestral households was:

for Yehudah as chiliarchs –
Adnah the officer, and with him 300,000 forceful strong men;
[15]next to him Yehohanan the officer, and with him 280,000;
[16]next to him Amasyah ben Zikri, who gave freely for Yahweh, and with him 200,00 forceful strong men;
[17]and from Binyamin –
a forceful strong man, Elyada, and with him 200,000 men able to wield bow and shield;
[18]next to him Yehozabad, and with him 180,000 men equipped for the army.

[19]These were the people ministering to the king, apart from the people that the king put in the fortified towns in all Yehudah.

## The prophet whom Ah'ab didn't like

**18** Yehoshaphat had wealth and splendour in quantity. He made a marriage alliance with Ah'ab, [2]and at the end of some years went down to Ah'ab in Shomron [Samaria]. Ah'ab sacrificed sheep and cattle in quantity for him and for the company that was with him, and incited him into going up to Heights-in-Gil'ad.

[3]Ah'ab king of Yisra'el said to Yehoshaphat king of Yehudah, 'Will you go with me to Heights-in-Gil'ad?' He said to him, 'I'll be the same as you, my company the same as yours, with you in the battle.' [4]But Yehoshaphat said to the king of Yisra'el, 'Please enquire for Yahweh's word today.'

[5]So the king of Yisra'el collected the prophets, 400 individuals, and said to them, 'Shall we go to Heights-in-Gil'ad for battle, or shall I leave off?' They said, 'Go up, and God will give it into the king's hand.' [6]But Yehoshaphat said, 'There isn't any further

prophet of Yahweh here, is there, so we may enquire of him?' [7]The king of Yisra'el said to Yehoshaphat, 'There is one further individual to enquire of Yahweh from, but I myself dislike him because he doesn't prophesy good for me but always bad. He's Mikayehu ben Yimlah.' Yehoshaphat said, 'The king shouldn't say that.' [8]So the king of Yisra'el called to a courtier and said, 'Hurry Mikayehu ben Yimlah.'

[9]As the king of Yisra'el and Yehoshaphat king of Yehudah were sitting, each on his throne, dressed in robes, sitting at the threshing-floor at the entrance to the gateway of Shomron, and all the prophets were prophesying before them, [10]Tsidqiyyahu ben Kena'anah had made himself iron horns, and he said, 'Yahweh has said this: "With these you will gore the Aramites until you have finished them off."' [11]All the prophets were prophesying in this way: 'Go up to Heights-in-Gil'ad and succeed! Yahweh will give it into the king's hand.'

## The lying spirit

[12]Now the envoy who went to call for Mikayehu spoke to him: 'Here, the prophets' words are good for the king, as one bidding. Your word should please be like one of them. You should speak of something good.' [13]Mikayehu said, 'As Yahweh lives, what my God says to me – I will speak it.'

[14]He came to the king and the king said to him, 'Mikah, shall we go up to Heights-in-Gil'ad for battle, or should I leave off?' He said, 'Go up, and succeed! They will be given into your hand.' [15]The king said to him, 'How many times am I going to get you to swear that you won't speak to me anything but truth in Yahweh's name?'

[16]So he said, 'I saw all Yisra'el scattered on the mountains like a flock that have no shepherd. Yahweh said, "These people have no lords. They should go back, each to his house, with things being well."' [17]The king of Yisra'el said to Yehoshaphat, 'I said to you, "He won't prophesy something good for me, but rather something bad", didn't I.'

[18]He said, 'Therefore, listen to Yahweh's word. I saw Yahweh sitting on his throne, with the entire heavenly army standing to his right and his left. [19]Yahweh said, "Who'll entice

Ah'ab king of Yisra'el so he'll go up but fall at Heights-in-Gil'ad?" One spoke, saying "Like this", and another saying "Like this". ²⁰Then a spirit went out and stood before Yahweh and said, "I'm the one who'll entice him." Yahweh said to him, "How?" ²¹He said, "I'll go out and become a false spirit in the mouth of all his prophets." He said, "You are to entice him. Yes, you'll be able to. Go out and do it." ²²So now, there, Yahweh put a false spirit in the mouth of these prophets of yours, in that Yahweh has spoken of something bad for you.'

## The power of chance

²³Tsidqiyyahu ben Kena'anah went up and struck Mikayehu on the jaw, and said, 'Which way did Yahweh's spirit pass from being with me to speak with you?' ²⁴Mikayehu said, 'Here, you are going to see, on that day when you come to an innermost room to hide.' ²⁵The king of Yisra'el said, 'Get Mikeyahu and take him back to Amon the town official and to Yo'ash the king's son ²⁶and say, "The king has said this: 'Put this man in the cells and give him slave bread and slave water until I come back with things being well.''' ²⁷Mikayehu said, 'If you really do come back with things being well, Yahweh did not speak through me.' (And he said, 'Listen, you peoples, all of them.')

²⁸So the king of Yisra'el went up with Yehoshaphat king of Yehudah to Heights-in-Gil'ad. ²⁹The king of Yisra'el said to Yehoshaphat, 'I'm putting on disguise and coming into battle, but you, dress in your robes.' So the king of Yisra'el put on disguise and they came into battle.

³⁰Now the king of Aram had ordered his chariot officers, 'You will not battle anyone small or great except the king of Yisra'el alone.' ³¹When the chariot officers saw Yehoshaphat and said 'He's the king of Yisra'el', they turned round to him to do battle. But Yehoshaphat cried out and Yahweh helped him. God incited them away from him, ³²and when the chariot officers saw that it was not the king of Yisra'el, they turned back from following him. ³³But a man drew his bow innocently and struck the king of Yisra'el between the links and the armour. He said to his charioteer, 'Turn your hand, get me out from the camp, because I'm wounded.'

³⁴The battle mounted that day, while the king of Yisra'el was keeping himself standing in the chariot opposite the Aramites until the evening. But he died towards the time of the sun's setting.

## Proper exercise of authority

**19** Yehoshaphat king of Yehudah went back to Yerushalaim to his house with things being well, ²but Yehu ben Hanani the seer went out before him. He said to King Yehoshaphat, 'Do you help the faithless, are you loyal to the people hostile to Yahweh? For this, there is fury upon you from before Yahweh. ³Yet good things are found with you, because you burned away the totem poles in the country and set your mind on enquiring of God.'

⁴Yehoshaphat lived in Yerushalaim, but he again went out among the people from Be'er Sheba as far as the highland of Ephrayim and got them to come back to Yahweh, their ancestors' God. ⁵He put in place authorities in the country in all the fortified towns in Yehudah, town by town. ⁶He said to the authorities, 'Watch what you're doing, because it's not for a human being that you exercise authority but for Yahweh, who is with you when you speak an authoritative word. ⁷So now, a dread of Yahweh is to be upon you. Keep watch and act, because with Yahweh our God there is no evil or honouring of the face or taking of a bribe.' ⁸(Also in Yerushalaim Yehoshaphat put in place some of the Levites and the priests and some of the ancestral heads of Yisra'el for the exercise of Yahweh's authority and for arguments.)

They came back to Yerushalaim ⁹and he ordered them, 'You're to act like this: with awe for Yahweh, with truthfulness and with a perfect mind. ¹⁰Every argument that comes to you from your brothers who are living in their towns, between blood and blood, between instruction and order, decrees or rulings, you're to warn them so that they don't become liable before Yahweh and fury come on you and on your brothers. So you will do, and you won't become liable. ¹¹Here, Amaryahu the head priest is over you in everything to do with Yahweh, and Zebadyahu ben Yishma'el is the chief of Yehudah's household in everything to do with the king. The Levite overseers are before you. Be strong when you act. Yahweh be with the good.'

## How to pray in a political crisis

**20** Subsequently the Mo'abites and the Ammonites, and some of the Me'unites, came against Yehoshaphat for battle. [2]People came and told Yehoshaphat, 'A great horde is coming against you from across the sea, from Aram. There, they're at Hatsetson Tamar (i.e. Gedi Spring).' [3]Yehoshaphat was afraid and gave himself to enquiring of Yahweh, and he called a fast for all Yehudah. [4]Yehudah collected to seek help from Yahweh; from all the towns in Yehudah, too, people came to seek Yahweh.

[5]Yehoshaphat stood in the congregation of Yehudah and Yerushalaim in Yahweh's house before the new court. [6]He said, 'Yahweh, our ancestors' God: you are God in the heavens and one who rules all the kingships of the nations, are you not. In your hand are energy and strength. There's no one able to take a stand with you. [7]It was you, our God, wasn't it, who dispossessed the inhabitants of this country from before your people Yisra'el and gave it to the offspring of Abraham your friend permanently. [8]They lived in it and built you a sanctuary in it for your name, saying [9]"If bad fortune comes upon us (the sword exercising authority, or epidemic, or famine), we will stand before this house and before you, because your name is in this house, and we will cry out to you because of the pressure on us, and you will listen and deliver."

[10]Now, there, people from Ammon and Mo'ab and Mount Se'ir, into which you did not let Yisra'el come when they came from the country of Misrayim (rather they departed from being against them and did not annihilate them), [11]here – they are dealing to us by coming to drive us out from your possession which you let us possess. [12]Our God, you will exercise authority over them, won't you, because there's no energy in us before this great horde that's coming against us. We don't know what we'll do, but our eyes are on you.' [13]All Yehudah was standing before Yahweh,

also their little ones, their wives and their children.

## The two stages whereby we see answers to prayer

[14]Then Yahazi'el ben Zekaryahu son of Benayah son of Ye'i'el son of Mattanyah, the Levite, one of the sons of Asaph – Yahweh's spirit came on him in the middle of the congregation, [15]and he said, 'Heed, all Yehudah, inhabitants of Yerushalaim and King Yehoshaphat. Yahweh has said this to you: "Don't be afraid, don't be scared before this great horde, because the battle is not yours but God's.

[16]Tomorrow, go down against them. There they'll be, going up by the Tsits Ascent. You'll find them at the end of the wadi, before the Yeru'el Wilderness. [17]It's not for you to battle on this occasion. Take your position, stand and see Yahweh's deliverance of you, Yehudah and Yerushalaim. Don't be afraid, don't be scared. Tomorrow, go out before them. Yahweh will be with you."'

[18]Yehoshaphat bowed his head, face to the ground, and all Yehudah and the inhabitants of Yerushalaim fell before Yahweh to bow low to Yahweh. [19]The Levites from the Qehatites and from the Qorahites stood up to praise Yahweh the God of Yisra'el with an exceptionally loud voice.

[20]They started early in the morning and went out to the Teqoa Wilderness. When they went out, Yehoshaphat stood and said, 'Listen to me, Yehudah and inhabitants of Yerushalaim. Stand firm in faith in Yahweh your God and you will stand firm; stand firm in faith in his prophets and you will succeed.' [21]He took counsel with the people and put in place people singing for Yahweh and praising his sacred glory as they went out before the armed company, and saying, 'Confess Yahweh, because his commitment is permanent.'

[22]At the time when they began resounding and praising, Yahweh set ambushes against the people of Ammon, Mo'ab and Mount Se'ir who were coming to Yehudah, and they took a beating. [23]The people of Ammon and Mo'ab stood against the inhabitants of Mount Se'ir to devote and annihilate them. When they'd

finished off the inhabitants of Se'ir, they helped, each individual, to devastate his neighbour.

## Relief and thanksgiving

²⁴When Yehudah came to a watchtower towards the wilderness and they turned their faces towards the horde – there, they were corpses fallen to the ground. There was no escape group. ²⁵Yehoshaphat came with his company to plunder their spoil and they found among them, in quantity, both property and corpses and desirable articles. They rescued things for themselves until they couldn't carry anything. They were plundering the spoil for three days because there was so much.

²⁶On the fourth day they congregated in Blessing Vale (because they blessed Yahweh there, that's why people have called the place Blessing Vale until this day). ²⁷Everyone from Yehudah and Yerushalaim went back with Yehoshaphat at their head, going back to Yerushalaim with rejoicing, because Yahweh had let them rejoice over their enemies. ²⁸They came to Yerushalaim with mandolins, with guitars and with trumpets, to Yahweh's house. ²⁹Dread of God came over all the kingships in the countries when they heard that Yahweh had battled with Yisra'el's enemies. ³⁰So Yehoshaphat's kingship was calm; his God enabled him to settle down all round.

³¹Yehoshaphat began to reign over Yehudah as a man of thirty-five years, when he began to reign, and he reigned twenty-five years in Yerushalaim. His mother's name was Azubah bat Shilhi. ³²He walked in the way of his father Asa and did not turn aside from it in doing what was upright in Yahweh's eyes. ³³Yet the shrines did not disappear and the people did not set their minds on their ancestors' God.

³⁴The rest of the things about Yehoshaphat, early and late – there they are, written in the words of Yehu ben Hanani, which were entered into the document about the kings of Yisra'el. ³⁵But subsequently, Yehoshaphat king of Yehudah joined with Ahazyah king of Yisra'el; he was faithless in so doing. ³⁶He joined with him in making ships to go to Tarshish. They made the ships at Etsyon Geber. ³⁷Eli'ezer ben Dodavahu from Mareshah prophesied against Yehoshaphat: 'As you've joined with Ahazyahu,

Yahweh is breaking out on your work.' And the ships broke up and had to hold back from going to Tarshish.

## The son who killed his brothers

**21** Yehoshaphat lay down with his ancestors and was buried with his ancestors in David's Town, and his son Yehoram began to reign in place of him. ²He had brothers, Yehoshaphat's sons: Azaryah, Yehi'el, Zekaryahu, Azaryahu, Mika'el and Shephatyahu. All these were sons of Yehoshaphat king of Yisra'el. ³Their father gave them many gifts of silver and of gold, and of choice things, with fortified towns in Yehudah, but the kingship he gave to Yehoram, because he was the firstborn.

⁴Yehoram rose up over his father's kingship and showed himself strong, and killed all his brothers with the sword, and also some Yisra'elite ministers. ⁵Yehoram was a man of thirty-two years when he began to reign and he reigned eight years in Yerushalaim. ⁶He walked in the way of the kings of Yisra'el, as Ah'ab's household had done, because he had Ah'ab's daughter as wife. He did what was bad in Yahweh's eyes. ⁷But Yahweh was not willing to devastate David's household, for the sake of the pact that he solemnized towards David, and as he had said he would give him and his sons hegemony for all time.

⁸In his days Edom rebelled from under Yehudah's hand and got a king to reign over them. ⁹Yehoram went across with his officers and all his chariotry with him. He rose by night and struck down the Edomites, who were surrounding him and the chariot officers. ¹⁰But Edom has rebelled from under Yehudah's hand until this day. Then Libnah rebelled from under his hand at that time, because he had abandoned Yahweh, his ancestors' God. ¹¹He also made shrines in the highland of Yehudah, and got the inhabitants of Yerushalaim to whore, and drove Yehudah away.

## How to be really unpopular

¹²A document from Eliyyahu [Elijah] the prophet came to him, saying 'Yahweh the

God of David your ancestor has said this: "Since you have not walked in the ways of Yehoshaphat your father and in the ways of Asa king of Yehudah [13]but have walked in the way of the kings of Yisra'el, and got Yehudah and the inhabitants of Yerushalaim to whore, as the household of Ah'ab got them to whore, and your brothers, your father's household, who were better men than you, you have also killed – [14]here, Yahweh is going to inflict a great beating on your people, on your sons, on your wives and on all your property, [15]and you yourself with a great illness, with an illness of the insides, until your insides come out because of the illness, days upon days.'"

[16]Yahweh made the spirit of the Pelishtites and the Arabs who were near the Kushites rise against Yehoram. [17]They went up against Yehudah, broke into it and took captive all the property that could be found belonging to the king's house, and also his sons and his wives. No son remained to him except Yeho'ahaz, the youngest of his sons.

[18]After all this, Yahweh hit him in his insides with an illness without healing. [19]After days upon days, as the end of two years came, his insides came out with his illness, and he died because of the bad illness. His people did not make a fire for him like the fire for his ancestors. [20]He was a man of thirty-two years when he began to reign and he reigned eight years in Yerushalaim but went without people caring. They buried him in David's Town but not in the kings' graves.

## 22
The inhabitants of Yerushalaim made Ahazyahu, his youngest son, king in place of him, because the raiding gang which came into the camp with Arabs had killed all the older ones. So Ahazyahu ben Yehoram began to reign as king of Yehudah.

### Two forceful women

[2]Ahazyahu was a man of twenty-two years when he began to reign and he reigned one year in Yerushalaim. His mother's name was Atalyahu bat Omri. [3]He too walked in the ways of Ah'ab's household, because his mother was his counsellor in acting faithlessly. [4]He did what was bad in Yahweh's eyes, like Ah'ab's household, because they became his

counsellors after his father's death, to his devastation. [5]He also went by their counsel when he went to battle with Yehoram ben Ah'ab king of Yisra'el, against Haza'el king of Aram at Heights-in-Gil'ad. The Aramites struck Yoram down, [6]so he went back to heal in Yizr'e'el because they had been striking him down (the people who struck him down at The Height when he was battling with Haza'el king of Aram).

Now Azaryahu ben Yehoram king of Yehudah went down to see Yehoram ben Ah'ab in Yizr'e'el because he was ill. [7]But from God came the treading down of Ahazyahu for coming to Yoram. When he came, he went out with Yehoram to Yehu ben Nimshi whom Yahweh had anointed to cut down Ah'ab's household. [8]When Yehu entered into judgement with Ah'ab's household, he found the Yehudahite officers and Ahazyahu's nephews, Ahazyahu's ministers, and killed them. [9]He looked for Ahazyahu and took him captive; he was hiding in Shomron. They brought him to Yehu and put him to death. They buried him, because (they said), 'He's the son of Yehoshaphat, who enquired of Yahweh with his entire mind.'

Ahazyahu's household could not retain energy for reigning. [10]When Atalyahu, Ahazyahu's mother, saw that her son was dead, she set to and obliterated all the royal offspring of Yehudah's household. [11]But Yehoshab'at, the king's daughter, got Yo'ash ben Ahazyahu and stole him away from among the king's sons who were being put to death and put him and his nanny in a bedroom. Yehoshab'at bat Yehoram, the wife of Yehoyada the priest, concealed him (because she was Ahazyahu's sister) from Atalyahu, and she didn't put him to death. [12]He was with them in God's house hiding for six years, while Atalyah was reigning over the country.

### Two covenants among people

## 23
In the seventh year, Yehoyada showed himself strong and got the centurions, Azaryahu ben Yeroham, Yishma'e'l ben Yehohanan, Azaryahu ben Obed, Ma'aseyahu ben Adayahu and Elishaphat ben Zikri, into a pact with him. [2]They went round in Yehudah

and collected the Levites from all the towns in Yehudah, and the ancestral heads of Yisra'el. They came to Yerushalaim ³and the entire congregation solemnized a pact in God's house with the king.

He said to them, 'Here, the king's son will reign, as Yahweh spoke concerning David's sons. ⁴This is the thing that you're to do: a third of you who are coming in on the sabbath as priests and as Levites are to be gatemen on the thresholds, ⁵a third in the king's house, a third at the Foundation Gate, the entire people in the courts of Yahweh's house. ⁶No one is to come into Yahweh's house except the priests and the ministering Levites; they may come in because they are sacred, but the entire people is to keep Yahweh's charge. ⁷The Levites are to encircle the king all round, each with his equipment in his hand. Anyone who comes into the house is to be put to death. They are to be with the king when he comes in and when he goes out.'

⁸The Levites and all Yehudah acted in accordance with all that Yehoyada the priest ordered. They took each his men who were coming in on the sabbath with those who were going out on the sabbath (because Yehoyada the priest did not free the divisions).

⁹Yehoyada the priest gave the centurions the lances, the hand-shields and the body-shields that belonged to King David, which were in God's house. ¹⁰He put in place the entire people, each with his weapon in his hand, from the shoulder of the house on the right as far as the shoulder of the house on the left, at the altar and at the house, in charge of the king all round. ¹¹Then they got the king's son out, put the diadem and the affirmation on him, and made him king. Yehoyada and his sons anointed him and said, 'Long live the king!'

## A new covenant with God

¹²Atalyahu heard the sound of the people running and praising the king and came to the people at Yahweh's house. ¹³She saw, there, the king was standing by his pillar at the entrance, and the officials with their trumpets by the king, and the entire people of the country rejoicing and blowing on trumpets, and the singers with musical instruments, who were helping them to know how to give praise.

Atalyahu tore her clothes and said, 'Conspiracy, conspiracy!'

¹⁴Yehoyada the priest sent out the centurions who were appointed over the force and said to them, 'Take her out between the rows. The person who follows her is to be put to death with the sword' (because the priest said, 'You will not put her to death in Yahweh's house'). ¹⁵They laid hands on her and she came to the Horse Gate entrance to the king's house, and they put her to death there.

¹⁶Yehoyada solemnized a pact between himself and the entire people and the king, that they would be a people for Yahweh. ¹⁷The entire people came to the Master's house and tore it down. Its altars and its images they broke down, and Mattan, the Master's priest, they killed before the altars. ¹⁸Yehoyada put the appointments in Yahweh's house in the hand of the Levite priests to whom David had given a share over Yahweh's house in offering up Yahweh's burnt offerings in accordance with what is written in Mosheh's instruction, with rejoicing and with song on the basis of David's directions. ¹⁹He put in place the gatemen at the gateways of Yahweh's house so that anyone who was defiled in any way should not come in. ²⁰He got the centurions, the august people, the people's rulers and all the people of the country, and took the king down from Yahweh's house. They brought him through the Upper Gate to the king's house and seated the king on the royal throne. ²¹The entire people of the country rejoiced, while the town was quiet, when they had put Atalyahu to death by the sword.

## Boy king, insistent young man

**24** Yo'ash was seven years of age when he began to reign and he reigned forty years in Yerushalaim. His mother's name was Tsibyah, from Be'er Sheba. ²Yo'ash did what was upright in Yahweh's eyes all the days of Yehoyada the priest. ³Yehoyada got him two wives, and sons and daughters were born to him.

⁴Subsequently, it came into Yo'ash's mind to renovate Yahweh's house. ⁵He collected the priests and the Levites and said to them, 'Go out to the towns of Yehudah and collect silver from all Yisra'el to strengthen your God's

house, each year's requirement in its year. You're to make speed about the thing.' But the Levites didn't make speed. [6]So the king called for Yehoyada the head and said to him, 'Why have you not required of the Levites to bring from Yehudah and from Yerushalaim the levy of Mosheh, Yahweh's servant, and the congregation of Yisra'el, to the affirmation tent?' [7]Because the faithless Atalyahu – her sons had broken into God's house, and further had made all the sacred things in Yahweh's house for the Masters.

[8]So the king said, and they made a chest and put it at the gateway of Yahweh's house, outside, [9]and they gave voice in Yehudah and in Yerushalaim to bring to Yahweh the levy of Mosheh, Yahweh's servant, made on Yisra'el in the wilderness. [10]All the officials and the entire people rejoiced and brought it, and threw it into the chest until they'd filled it. [11]At the time when they would bring the chest to the king's appointees by the hand of the Levites, when they saw that the silver was much, the king's secretary and the head priest's appointee would come and empty the chest and carry it and take it back to its place. So they did day by day, and they gathered silver in quantity.

[12]The king and Yehoyada gave it to the people doing the work, the service for Yahweh's house, and they were hiring masons and craftsmen to renovate Yahweh's house, and also craftsmen in iron and copper to strengthen Yahweh's house.

## But when the mentor's gone . . . .

[13]The people doing the work did it, and restoration progressed by the work at their hand. They set up God's house in accordance with its design and made it stand firm. [14]When they'd finished, they brought before the king and Yehoyada the remainder of the silver and they made articles for Yahweh's house, articles for ministry and the burnt offerings, ladles, and gold and silver articles. They were offering up burnt offerings in Yahweh's house regularly all the days of Yehoyada.

[15]But Yehoyada grew old and became full of years and died, a man of 130 years when he died. [16]They buried him in David's Town with the kings, because he had done good things

in Yisra'el with God and God's house. [17]But after Yehoyada's death the officials of Yehudah came and bowed low to the king. Then the king listened to them [18]and they abandoned the house of Yahweh, their ancestors' God, and served the totem poles and the idols, and fury came on Yehudah and Yerushalaim because of this liability of theirs.

[19]Yahweh sent prophets among them to turn them back to Yahweh, and they testified against them, but they didn't give ear. [20]God's spirit clothed Zekaryahu ben Yehoyada, the priest, and he stood above the people and said to them: 'God has said this: "Why are you transgressing Yahweh's orders? You will not succeed. Because you have abandoned Yahweh, he has abandoned you."' [21]But they conspired against him and pelted him with stones, by the king's order, in the court of Yahweh's house. [22]So Yo'ash the king was not mindful of the commitment with which Yehoyada his father had acted with him, and he killed his son. As he died he said, 'May Yahweh see and require.'

[23]At the turn of the year, a force from Aram went up against him. They came to Yehudah and Yerushalaim and eliminated all the people's officers from the people. All their plunder they sent off to the king of Dammeseq, [24a]because the Aramite force had come with a few men but Yahweh gave into their hand a force of a very large number because they had abandoned Yahweh, their ancestors' God.

## Boy king, insistent young man, apostate adult

[24b]So they executed acts of authority upon Yo'ash, [25]and when they went from him (because they abandoned him with many wounds), his servants conspired against him because of the shedding of the blood of the sons of Yehoyada the priest, and they killed him on his bed. So he died and they buried him in David's Town, but they didn't bury him in the kings' graves. [26]These were the people who conspired against him: Zabad ben Shim'at (the Ammonite woman) and Yehozabad ben Shimrit (the Mo'abite woman). [27]His sons, the quantity of prophecy against him, and the founding of God's house – there, they are written in the exposition in the document about the kings.

His son Amatsyahu began to reign in place of him.

**25** Amatsyahu began to reign as a man of twenty-five years and he reigned twenty-nine years in Yerushalaim. His mother's name was Yeho'addan, from Yerushalaim. ²He did what was upright in Yahweh's eyes, only not with a perfect mind. ³When the kingship was strongly in his control, he killed his servants who had struck down the king, his father, ⁴but the children he didn't put to death, because it was in accordance with what is written in the instruction in Mosheh's document where Yahweh ordered, 'Parents will not die because of children and children will not die because of parents. Rather, it is as an individual for his own wrongdoing that people are to die.'

⁵Amatsyahu collected the Yehudahites and set them by ancestral households under chiliarchs and centurions, for all Yehudah and Binyamin. He registered them from the age of twenty upwards and found them to be 300,000 picked men able to go out in the army, able to grasp spear and shield. ⁶He hired from Yisra'el 100,000 forceful strong men for a hundred talents of silver. ⁷But a supernatural man came to him saying, 'Your Majesty, the army of Yisra'el is not to come with you, because Yahweh is not with Yisra'el (all the Ephrayimites). ⁸Rather, come, you act, be strong for battle. God could make you collapse before an enemy, because there's energy in God to help and to make collapse.'

## A war crime

⁹Amatsyahu said to the supernatural man, 'But what am I to do about the hundred talents that I gave to the Yisra'elite raiding gang?' The supernatural man said, 'Yahweh has the means to give you much more than this.' ¹⁰So Amatsyahu made them distinct (the raiding gang that had come to him from Ephrayim) for them to go to their own place. Their anger raged greatly against Yehudah, and they went back to their place in angry fury.

¹¹But Amatsyahu showed himself strong and drove his company, and went to Salt Ravine. He struck down the men of Se'ir, 10,000, ¹²and the Yehudahites captured 10,000 alive, brought them to the top of The Cliff, and threw them down from the top of The Cliff; all of them tore

apart. ¹³But the men in the raiding gang that Amatsyahu sent back from going with him to the battle made a raid against the Yehudahite towns from Shomron as far as Bet Horon, struck down 3,000 of them and took much plunder.

¹⁴After Amatsyahu came from striking down the Edomites, he brought the gods of the people of Se'ir and set them up for himself as gods, and he would bow low before them and burn incense for them. ¹⁵Yahweh's anger raged at Amatsyahu and he sent a prophet to him. He said to him, 'Why have you enquired of the gods of the people who did not rescue their people from your hand?' ¹⁶When he spoke to him, he said to him, 'Have we made you a counsellor to the king? Leave off for yourself! Why should they strike you down.' The prophet left off, and said, 'I know that God has counselled to devastate you, because you have done this and not listened to my counsel.'

## What counts as effective counsel

¹⁷Amatsyahu king of Yehudah took counsel and sent to Yo'ash ben Yeho'ahaz son of Yehu, king of Yisra'el, saying 'Come on, let's face each other.' ¹⁸Yo'ash king of Yisra'el sent to Amatsyahu king of Yehudah, saying, 'A thistle that was in the Lebanon sent to a cedar that was in the Lebanon, saying "Give your daughter to my son as wife." But an animal of the wild that was in the Lebanon passed by and trampled the thistle. ¹⁹You've said, "There, you've struck down Edom", and your mind has lifted you up, so that you behave with splendour. Stay in your house now. Why stir up something bad? You'll fall, you and Yehudah with you.'

²⁰Amatsyahu didn't listen, because it was from God, in order that he might give them into his hand, because he'd enquired of the Edomite gods. ²¹So Yo'ash king of Yisra'el went up, and he and Amatsyahu king of Yehudah faced each other at Bet Shemesh, which belongs to Yehudah. ²²Yehudah took a beating before Yisra'el and they fled each man to his tents. ²³Amatsyahu king of Yehudah, son of Yo'ash son of Yeho'ahaz – Yo'ash king of Yisra'el captured him at Bet Shemesh, brought him to Yerushalaim and broke down the Yerushalaim

wall from the Ephrayim Gate as far as the Corner Gate, 200 metres. [24]He took all the gold and the silver and all the articles that were to be found in God's house with Obed Edom, and the treasuries of the king's house, and hostages, and went back to Shomron.

[25]Amatsyahu ben Yo'ash king of Yehudah lived after the death of Yo'ash ben Yeho'ahaz king of Yisra'el fifteen years. [26]The rest of the things about Amatsyahu, early and late, there, they are written on the document about the kings of Yehudah and Yisra'el, aren't they. [27]After the time when Amatsyahu departed from following Yahweh, people formed a conspiracy against him in Yerushalaim and he fled to Lakish, but they sent after him to Lakish and put him to death there. [28]They carried him on horses and buried him in Yerushalaim with his ancestors in the Town of Yehudah.

## A young man's achievements

**26** All the people of Yehudah got Uzziyyahu (he was sixteen years of age) and made him king in place of his father Amatsyahu. [2]It was he who built up Elot. He had got it back for Yehudah after the king lay down with his ancestors.

[3]Uzziyyahu was sixteen years of age when he began to reign and he reigned fifty-two years in Yerushalaim. His mother's name was Yekolyah, from Yerushalaim. [4]He did what was upright in Yahweh's eyes in accordance with all that Amatsyahu his father did. [5]He came to enquire of God in the days of Zekaryahu, who enabled him to understand awe for God, and in the days when he enquired of Yahweh, God enabled him to be successful.

[6]He went out and battled against the Pelishtites and broke through the wall of Gat, the wall of Yabneh and the wall of Ashdod, and built up towns in Ashdod and among the Pelishtites. [7]God helped him against the Pelishtites, against the Arabs who lived in Gur-ba'al, and the Me'unites. [8]The Ammonites gave offerings to Uzziyyahu, and his name went as far as the entry point to Misrayim, because he became exceptionally strong. [9]Uzziyyahu built towers in Yerushalaim on the Corner Gate, on the Ravine Gate and on the Angle, and made them strong. [10]He built towers in the wilderness and hewed many cisterns, because he had much livestock, and in the foothills and in the flatland – ploughmen and vinedressers in the mountains and in the farmland, because he loved the ground.

## On the separation of church and state, First Testament style

[11]Uzziyyahu had a battle force, men able to go out in the army as a raiding gang by the number of their registering by the hand of Ye'i'el the secretary and Ma'aseyahu the overseer, in the control of Hananyahu from the king's officials. [12]The total number of the ancestral heads of the forceful strong men was 2,600, [13]and in their control an army force of 307,500 able to do battle with forceful energy to help the king against the enemy.

[14]Uzziyyahu prepared for them, for the entire army, shields, spears, helmets, coats of armour, bows and slingstones. [15]He made in Yerushalaim contrivances, an inventor's invention, to be on the towers and on the corners, for shooting arrows and big stones. His name went out far, because he did extraordinarily in acquiring help, until he was strong.

[16]But when he became strong, his mind became lofty, until he acted devastatingly. He trespassed against Yahweh his God, and came into Yahweh's palace to burn incense on the incense altar. [17]Azaryahu the priest followed him; with him were eighty priests of Yahweh, forceful men. [18]They stood against Uzziyyahu the king and said to him, 'It's not for you, Uzziyyahu, to burn incense for Yahweh, but for the priests, the Aharonites, who have been made sacred, to burn incense. Get out of the sanctuary, because you've trespassed. It will not mean splendour for you from Yahweh God.'

[19]Uzziyyahu was furious, the censer for burning incense in his hand. When he got furious with the priests, scaliness broke out on his forehead before the priests in Yahweh's house, by the incense altar. [20]Azaryahu the head priest turned his face to him, with all the priests: there, he was scaly on his forehead. They hurried him from there, and he himself hastened to get out, because Yahweh had touched him. [21]Uzziyyahu the king was made

scaly until the day of his death. He lived in a house apart as a person who was scaly, because he was cut off from Yahweh's house, while Yotam his son was in charge of the king's house, exercising authority over the people in the country.

## The son who had learned a lesson

[22]The rest of the things about Uzziyyahu, early and late, Yesha'yahu [Isaiah] ben Amots the prophet wrote. [23]Uzziyyahu lay down with his ancestors, but they buried him with his ancestors in the burial field that belonged to the kings because (they said), 'He was made scaly.' Yotam his son began to reign in place of him.

**27** Yotam was a man of twenty-five years when he began to reign and he reigned sixteen years in Yerushalaim. His mother's name was Yerushah bat Tsadoq. [2]He did what was upright in Yahweh's eyes in accordance with all that his father Uzziyyahu had done, only he did not come into Yahweh's palace. But the people acted devastatingly.

[3]It was he who built up the Upper Gate of Yahweh's House, and built on a large scale on the Ophel Wall. [4]He built up towns in the highland of Yehudah, and in the forests he built castles and towers. [5]When he battled with the king of the Ammonites he was stronger than them; the Ammonites gave him that year 100 talents of silver, 10,000 ten-gallon measures of wheat and 10,000 of barley. This the Ammonites gave back to him – and in the second and third year. [6]Yotam showed himself strong because he established his ways before Yahweh his God. [7]The rest of the things about Yotam, and all his battles and his ways – there they are, written on the document about the kings of Yisra'el and Yehudah. [8]He was a man of twenty-five years when he began to reign and he reigned sixteen years in Yerushalaim. [9]Yotam lay down with his ancestors and they buried him in David's Town, and Ahaz his son began to reign in place of him.

**28** Ahaz was a man of twenty years when he began to reign and he reigned sixteen years in Yerushalaim. He did not do what was upright in Yahweh's eyes like David his ancestor, [2]but walked in the ways of the kings of Yisra'el. He even made cast images

for the Masters. [3]He was the one who burned incense in the Ben-himmon Ravine and burned up his sons in fire in accordance with the offensive practices of the nations that Yahweh dispossessed from before the Yisra'elites. [4]He sacrificed and burned incense at the shrines, on the hills and under every verdant tree.

## The warning to the victors

[5]So Yahweh his God gave him into the hand of the king of Aram, and they struck him down, took captive a large group of his and brought them to Dammeseq. He was also given into the hand of the king of Yisra'el; he struck him down in a great rout. [6]Peqah ben Remalyahu killed 120,000 in Yehudah on one day, all forceful men, because of their abandoning Yahweh, their ancestors' God. [7]Zikri, the Ephrayimite strong man, killed Ma'aseyahu the king's son, Azriqam the chief over the house, and Elqanah, number two to the king, [8]and the Yisra'elites took captive 200,000 of their brothers, wives, sons and daughters, and also plundered much spoil from them and brought the plunder to Shomron. [9]There was a prophet of Yahweh there, Oded by name. He went out before the army which was coming to Shomron and said to them, 'Here, because of the wrath of Yahweh your ancestors' God with Yehudah, he gave them into your hand and you killed them in a fury that reached as far as the heavens. [10]And now you are saying that you'll subjugate the people of Yehudah and Yerushalaim as your servants and maidservants, while you yourselves – with you there are only liabilities in relation to Yahweh your God, aren't there. [11]So now listen to me. Give back the captives that you've taken from your brothers, because the angry rage of Yahweh is on you.' [12]People from among the heads of the Ephrayimites, Azaryahu ben Yehohanan, Berekyahu ben Meshillemot, Yehizqiyyahu ben Shallum and Amasa ben Hadlay, rose up against the people coming from the army. [13]They said to them, 'You will not bring the captives here, because it will be a liability upon us in relation to Yahweh; you're saying you'll add to our wrongdoings and to our liabilities, because our liability is great and there's angry

rage against Yisraèl.' ¹⁴So the armed men abandoned the captives and the plunder before the officers and the entire congregation.

## The administrators with compassion

¹⁵The people who were designated by their names set to, took strong hold of the captives and clothed all the naked with the spoil. They both clothed them and gave them boots and food and drink, and bathed them and led them (everyone who was collapsing) on donkeys, and brought them to Yeriho (Palms Town) beside their brothers, and went back to Shomron.

¹⁶At that time King Ahaz sent to the kings of Ashshur for help for himself. ¹⁷The Edomites had again come and struck down Yehudah and taken captives, ¹⁸and the Pelishtites had raided the towns in the foothills and in the Negeb belonging to Yehudah. They had taken Bet-shemesh, Ayyalon, Gederot, Soko and its daughter-townships, Timnah and its daughter-townships, and Gimzo and its daughter-townships, and gone to live there, ¹⁹because Yahweh made Yehudah bow down on account of Ahaz king of Yisraèl, because he had been lax in Yehudah and had trespassed against Yahweh.

²⁰Tillegat Pilnèeser king of Ashshur came out against him and put him under pressure; he did not strengthen him, ²¹because Ahaz had divided up Yahweh's house and the house of the king and the officers and given it to the king of Ashshur, but it was no help to him.

²²In his time of pressure he added to his trespassing against Yahweh, that King Ahaz, ²³and sacrificed to the gods of Dammeseq who had struck him down; he had said, 'Because the gods of the king of Aram help them, I will sacrifice to them so that they may help me.' So those became the cause of his collapsing, and that of all Yisraèl. ²⁴Ahaz gathered the articles from God's house and cut up the articles from God's house. He shut the doors of God's house and made himself altars in every corner of Yerushalaim. ²⁵In each and every town in Yehudah, he made shrines to burn incense for other gods, and provoked Yahweh, his ancestors' God.

²⁶The rest of the things about him and all his ways, early and late – there they are, written on the document about the kings of Yehudah and Yisraèl. ²⁷Ahaz lay down with his ancestors and they buried him in the town, in Yerushalaim, because they didn't bring him into the graves of the kings of Yisraèl. His son Yehizqiyyahu [Hezekiah] began to reign in place of him.

## The new David

**29** Yehizqiyyahu began to reign as a man of twenty-five years and reigned twenty-nine years in Yerushalaim. His mother's name was Abiyyah bat Zekaryahu. ²He did what was upright in Yahweh's eyes in accordance with all that David his ancestor did. ³He, in the first year of his reign, in the first month, opened the doors of Yahweh's house and strengthened them.

⁴He brought the priests and the Levites and gathered them in the eastern square, ⁵and said to them, 'Listen to me, Levites. Make yourselves sacred now and make sacred the house of Yahweh, your ancestors' God. Take out the defilement from the sacred place. ⁶Because our fathers trespassed and did what was bad in the eyes of Yahweh our God, and abandoned him. They turned their faces from Yahweh's dwelling. They turned their back. ⁷They also shut the porch's doors and put out the lamps. They didn't burn incense and they didn't offer up a burnt offering in the sacred place for the God of Yisraèl. ⁸So Yahweh's fury came on Yehudah and Yerushalaim. He made them a thing of horror and desolation and a thing to whistle at, as you see with your own eyes. ⁹There, our fathers have died by the sword and our sons and daughters and wives have been in captivity on account of this.

¹⁰It's now in my mind to solemnize a pact towards Yahweh the God of Yisraèl so that his angry rage may turn back from us. ¹¹My sons, don't be negligent now, because you're the ones Yahweh chose to stand before him to minister for him, to be people who minister and burn incense for him.'

¹²So the Levites set to:

Mahat ben Amasay and Yoèl ben Azaryahu, of the Qehatites;
of the sons of Merari, Qish ben Abdi and Azaryahu ben Yehallelèl;

of the Gershonites, Yo'ah ben Zimmah and
   Eden ben Yo'ah;
[13]of the sons of Elitsaphan, Shimri and Ye'i'el;
   of the sons of Asaph, Zekaryahu and
   Mattanyahu;
[14]of the sons of Heman, Yehi'el and Shim'i;
and of the sons of Yedutun, Shema'yah and
   Uzzi'el.

## The great purification

[15]They gathered their brothers and made
themselves sacred, and came in accordance
with the king's order, by Yahweh's words, to
purify Yahweh's house. [16]The priests came into
the inside of Yahweh's house to purify it, and
took out all that was defiled that they found
in Yahweh's palace into the court of Yahweh's
house. The Levites received it to take it outside
to Wadi Qidron. [17]They began to make it
sacred on the first of the first month, and on
the eighth of the month they came to Yahweh's
porch. They made Yahweh's house sacred in
eight days, and on the sixteenth day of the first
month they finished.

[18]Then they came inside to Hizqiyyahu the
king and said, 'We've purified Yahweh's entire
house, the burnt-offering altar and all its
implements, and the table for the row [of bread]
and all its implements. [19]All the implements
that King Ahaz spurned when he was king,
when he trespassed, we've prepared and made
sacred. There they are, before Yahweh's altar.'

[20]Yehizqiyyahu the king started early,
gathered the town officials and went up to
Yahweh's house. [21]They brought seven bulls,
seven rams, seven lambs and seven goats as a
purification offering for the kingship, for the
sanctuary and for Yehudah. He said to the
Aharonites, the priests, to offer them up on
Yahweh's altar. [22]They slaughtered the cattle,
and the priests received the blood and tossed
it against the altar. They slaughtered the rams
and tossed the blood against the altar. They
slaughtered the lambs and tossed the blood
against the altar. [23]They took up the goats for
the purification offering before the king
and the congregation, and they leaned their
hands on them. [24]The priests slaughtered them
and made the purification with their blood
to make expiation for all Yisra'el, because the

king had said that the burnt offering and
the purification offering were for all Yisra'el.
[25]He put the Levites in place in Yahweh's
house with cymbals, with mandolins and with
guitars, by the order of David, Gad the king's
seer and Natan the prophet, because the order
was through Yahweh through his prophets.

## What God has made possible

[26]So the Levites stood with David's
instruments and the priests with the trumpets,
[27]and Hizqiyyahu said to offer up the burnt
offering at the altar. At the time when the burnt
offering began, Yahweh's song and the trumpets
began, along with the instruments of David king
of Yisra'el, [28]with the entire congregation bowing
low, the singers singing and the trumpeters
trumpeting, all of it until they finished the burnt
offering. [29]When they'd finished offering it up,
the king and all who were to be found with him
bent down and bowed low. [30]Yehizqiyyahu the
king with the officers said to the Levites to praise
Yahweh in the words of David and of Asaph the
seer, and they praised with rejoicing and bent
their heads and bowed low.

[31]Yehizqiyyahu avowed, 'You have now
commissioned yourselves to Yahweh. Come
up and bring sacrifices and thank offerings
to Yahweh's house.' The congregation brought
sacrifices and thank offerings, and everyone
who was free in heart, a burnt offering. [32]The
number of burnt offerings that the congregation
brought was 70 cattle, 100 rams, 200 lambs as
a burnt offering for Yahweh, all these. [33]The
sacred things were 600 cattle and 3,000 from
the flocks. [34]Only the priests were few and they
could not skin all the burnt offerings, so their
brothers, the Levites, added to their strength
until the finishing of the work and until the
priests had made themselves sacred (because
the Levites were more upright in mind in
making themselves sacred than the priests).
[35]Also there were burnt offerings in quantity
with the fat parts of the well-being sacrifices
and with the libations for the burnt offering.

So the service of Yahweh's house was
established, [36]and Yehizqiyyahu rejoiced, with
all the people, over what God had established
for the people, because the thing had happened
so rapidly.

## One nation

### 30
Yehizqiyyahu sent to all Yisra'el and Yehudah and also wrote communiqués to Ephrayim and Menashsheh to come to Yahweh's house in Yerushalaim to make Pesah [Passover] for Yahweh, the God of Yisra'el. ²The king took counsel, he and his officials and the entire congregation in Yerushalaim, about making the Pesah in the second month, ³because they couldn't do it at that time because the priests had not made themselves sacred in sufficiency, and the people had not assembled to Yerushalaim.

⁴The thing was upright in the king's eyes and in the congregation's eyes. ⁵So they put in place a word to pass an announcement through all Yisra'el from Be'er-sheba as far as Dan about coming to make Pesah for Yahweh, the God of Yisra'el, in Yerushalaim, because they hadn't done it in large numbers as it is written.

⁶The runners went out with the communiqués from the hand of the king and his officials, through all Yisra'el and Yehudah, in accordance with the king's order, saying 'Yisra'elites, turn back to Yahweh the God of Abraham, Yitshaq and Yisra'el, and he will turn back to the escape group that remains to you from the fist of the kings of Ashshur. ⁷Don't be like your fathers and like your brothers who trespassed against Yahweh, their ancestors' God, and he made them into a desolation, as you see. ⁸Don't toughen your neck now like your ancestors. Give your hand to Yahweh, come to his sanctuary which he made sacred permanently, serve Yahweh your God, so that his angry rage may turn back from you. ⁹When you turn back to Yahweh, your brothers and your children will find compassion before their captors and they will come back to this country, because Yahweh your God is gracious and compassionate, and he will not turn aside his face from you if you turn back to him.'

## Laughter and response

¹⁰The runners were passing from town to town in the region of Ephrayim and Menashsheh and as far as Zebulun, but they were making fun of them and ridiculing them. ¹¹Yet people from Asher, Menashsheh and Zebulun bowed down and came to Yerushalaim. ¹²God's hand was on Yehudah, too, to give them one mind to act on the order of the king and the officials by Yahweh's word.

¹³So a numerous people gathered to Yerushalaim to make the Flatbread Festival in the second month, a congregation in very large numbers. ¹⁴They set to and removed the altars that were in Yerushalaim and removed all the incense stands and threw them into Wadi Qidron.

¹⁵They slaughtered the Pesah on the fourteenth of the second month, while the priests and the Levites were ashamed, and made themselves sacred and brought burnt offerings to Yahweh's house. ¹⁶They stood in their position in accordance with the ruling for them, in accordance with the instruction of Mosheh the supernatural man, the priests tossing the blood from the Levites' hand. ¹⁷Because much of the congregation had not made themselves sacred, the Levites were in charge of the slaughter of the Pesah animals for everyone who was not pure, to make them sacred for Yahweh, ¹⁸because most of the people (much of the group from Ephrayim and Menashsheh, Yissakar and Zebulun) had not purified themselves, but they ate the Pesah not in accordance with what is written, because Yehizqiyyahu had pleaded for them: 'May the good Yahweh expiate on behalf of ¹⁹everyone who has set his mind on enquiring of God, Yahweh his ancestors' God, though not in accordance with purification in the sacred place.' ²⁰Yahweh listened to Yehizqiyyahu and healed the people.

## The great rejoicing

²¹The Yisra'elites who were to be found in Yerushalaim made the Flatbread Festival for seven days with great rejoicing and the Levites and the priests praising Yahweh daily with powerful instruments for Yahweh. ²²Yehizqiyyahu spoke to encourage all the Levites who showed good insight for Yahweh, and they ate what was appointed for the seven days, making well-being sacrifices and confessing Yahweh, their ancestors' God. ²³The entire congregation took counsel to make another seven days, and made seven

days with rejoicing, [24]because Hizqiyyahu king of Yehudah raised for the congregation 1,000 bulls and 7,000 from the flock, while the officials raised for the congregation 1,000 bulls and 10,000 from the flock, and the priests made themselves sacred in large numbers.

[25]The entire congregation of Yehudah rejoiced, with the priests and the Levites, the entire congregation that came from Yisra'el, and the resident aliens who had come from the country of Yisra'el but who lived in Yehudah. [26]So there was great rejoicing in Yerushalaim, because from the days of Shelomoh ben David king of Yisra'el there had not been something like this in Yerushalaim. [27]The Levite priests rose and blessed the people. And there was listening to their voice; their plea came to his sacred abode, to the heavens.

**31** When they had finished all this, all Yisra'el who were to be found went out to the towns of Yehudah and broke up the columns, cut down the totem poles and demolished the shrines and the altars from all Yehudah and Binyamin, and in Ephrayim and Menashsheh, until they had finished. Then all the Yisra'elites went back each to his holding, to their towns.

## Embarras de richesse

[2]Yehizqiyyahu put in place the divisions of the priests and the Levites, by their divisions, each in accordance with his service (with regard to the priests and the Levites), for the burnt offering and the well-being offerings, to minister and to confess and to praise in the gateways of Yahweh's camps; [3]and the king's share, from his property, for the burnt offerings – the morning and the evening burnt offerings and the burnt offerings for sabbaths, for beginning of months and for set times, as it is written in Yahweh's instruction. [4]He said to the people, the inhabitants of Yerushalaim, to give the priests' and Levites' share, in order that they might hold fast to Yahweh's instruction.

[5]When the word broke out, the Yisra'elites produced much of the very first of grain, new wine, fresh oil, syrup and all the yield of the field. They brought a tenth of everything, in quantity. [6]The people of Yisra'el and Yehudah who lived in the towns of Yehudah – they too brought a tenth of cattle and flock and a tenth of sacred things that had been made sacred for Yahweh their God, and put them in heaps upon heaps. [7]In the third month they began to found the heaps and in the seventh month they finished.

[8]Yehizqiyyahu and the officials came and saw the heaps, and blessed Yahweh and his people Yisra'el. [9]Yehizqiyyahu enquired of the priests and the Levites about the heaps [10]and Azaryahu the head priest, of the household of Tsadoq, said to him, 'From when they began bringing the contribution into Yahweh's house, there's been eating and being full and having a quantity remain, because Yahweh has blessed his people, and this horde remains over.' [11]So Yehizqiyyahu said to prepare halls in Yahweh's house, and they prepared them, [12a]and brought in the contribution, the tenth and the sacred things, truthfully.

## The trustworthy administrators

[12b]The chief over them was Kananyahu the Levite; Shim'i his brother was number two. [13]Yehi'el, Azazyahu, Nahat, Asah'el, Yerimot, Yozabad, Eli'el, Yismakyahu, Mahat and Benayah were appointees under the control of Kananyahu and Shim'i his brother, by the appointment of Yehizqiyyahu the king and Azaryahu the chief over God's house. [14]Qore ben Yimnah the Levite, gateman on the east, was in charge of the free offerings to God, to give out the contribution for Yahweh and the very sacred things. [15]In his control were Eden, Minyamin, Yeshua, Shema'yahu, Amaryahu and Shekanyahu, in the priests' towns in their trustworthy position, to give out to their brothers by their divisions, old and young alike:

[16]apart from their enrolment by genealogy,
   to males from three years and upwards;
   to everyone who came into Yahweh's house,
   each day's requirement in its day, for their
   service in their watches, by their divisions;
[17]the priests' enrolment by genealogy, by
   their ancestral households;
   the Levites from twenty years and upwards
   in their watches, by their divisions,
[18]and (in line with the enrolment by
   genealogy of all their little ones, their

wives, their sons and their daughters) to the entire congregation, because in their trustworthy position they would make themselves very sacred.

[19]And to the Aharonites, the priests, in their towns' pastureland fields, everywhere town by town: men who were designated by their names were to give portions to every male among the priests, and to the entire enrolment by genealogy among the Levites.

[20]Yehizqiyyahu acted like this in all Yehudah. He did what was good, upright and trustworthy before Yahweh his God. [21]In all the work that he began in the service of God's house and in the instruction and in the order, by enquiring of his God with his entire mind, he acted and succeeded.

## The Assyrian crisis

**32** After these things with their trustworthiness, Sanherib [Sennacherib] king of Ashshur came. He came against Yehudah, camped against the fortified towns and said he would break into them for himself. [2]Yehizqiyyahu saw that Sanherib had come with his face directed to battle against Yerushalaim [3]and took counsel with his officials and his strong men about blocking the water in the springs that were outside the town. They helped him, [4]and a large company collected and blocked all the springs and the stream flowing through the middle of the country, saying 'Why should the kings of Ashshur come and find much water?' [5]He showed himself strong and built up all the wall that had been broken through, and raised the towers on it, and outside it another wall. He strengthened the Fill in David's Town and made weaponry in quantity, and shields, [6]and put battle officers over the people.

He collected them to him in the square at the town gateway and spoke to encourage them: [7]'Be strong and stand firm. Don't be afraid, don't be scared in face of the king of Ashshur and in face of the entire horde that's with him, because with us is one greater than with him. [8]With him is an arm of flesh, but with us is Yahweh our God to help us and to fight our battles.' The people leaned on the words of Yehizqiyyahu king of Yehudah.

[9]Subsequently, Sanherib king of Ashshur sent his servants to Yerushalaim (he was at Lakish, and his command with him) to Yehizqiyyahu king of Yehudah and to all Yehudah who were in Yerushalaim, saying, [10]Sanherib king of Ashshur has said this: "On what are you relying, living in a siege in Yerushalaim? [11]Yehizqiyyahu is inciting you to give yourselves over to dying by hunger and by thirst, isn't he, in saying, 'Yahweh our God will rescue us from the fist of the king of Ashshur.' [12]He, Yehizqiyyahu, removed his shrines and his altars, didn't he, and said to Yehudah and to Yerushalaim, 'Before one altar you are to bow low, and on it burn incense.'

## The superpower's boast

[13]You acknowledge what I and my ancestors have done to all the peoples of the countries, don't you. Were the gods of the countries' nations at all able to rescue their country from my hand? [14]Which among all the gods of these nations that my ancestors devoted was able to rescue his people from my hand, that your God should be able to rescue you from my hand? [15]Hizqiyyahu should not now deceive you. He should not incite you like this. Don't trust him. Because no god of any nation or kingdom has been able to rescue his people from my hand or from the hand of my ancestors. Certainly your gods will not rescue you from my hand.'"

[16]His servants spoke further against Yahweh God and against Yehizqiyyahu his servant, [17]and he wrote documents to revile Yahweh the God of Yisra'el and to say about him, 'Like the gods of the countries' nations that did not rescue their people from my hand, so Yehizqiyyahu's God will not rescue his people from my hand.' [18]They called in a loud voice in Yehudahite to the people of Yerushalaim who were on the wall, to make them afraid and fearful, in order that they might take the town. [19]They spoke of Yerushalaim's God as they spoke about the gods of the peoples of the earth, the making of human hands.

[20]Yehizqiyyahu the king and Yesha'yahu ben Amots the prophet pleaded about this and cried out to the heavens, [21]and Yahweh sent an envoy and he effaced every forceful strong man, chief and officer in the camp of the king of Ashshur. He went back in shame to his

country. He came into his god's house, and there some of the people who had come out from inside him made him fall by the sword.

## Even Yehizqiyyahu can stumble

²²Yahweh delivered Yehizqiyyahu and Yerushalaim's inhabitants from the hand of Sanherib king of Ashshur and from the hand of everyone. He led them all round ²³and many were bringing offerings for Yahweh to Yerushalaim and choice things for Yehizqiyyahu king of Yehudah. He rose high in the eyes of all the nations from then on.

²⁴In those days Yehizqiyyahu became deathly ill, but he pleaded to Yahweh, and he spoke to him and gave him a sign, ²⁵but Yehizqiyyahu did not give back in accordance with the dealing done to him, because his mind became lofty. So there was fury on him and on Yehudah and Yerushalaim. ²⁶But Yehizqiyyahu bowed down, when his mind had become lofty, he and the inhabitants of Yerushalaim, and Yahweh's fury didn't come on them in Yehizqiyyahu's days.

²⁷Yehizqiyyahu had wealth and splendour, very great. He made himself treasuries for silver, for gold, for precious stone, for spices, for shields and for all desirable objects, ²⁸supplies of the yield of grain, new wine and fresh oil, and stalls for each and every cattle, and flocks for folds. ²⁹He made himself towns and livestock, flocks and cattle, in large numbers, because God gave him very much property. ³⁰He, Yehizqiyyahu, blocked the Upper Gihon water outlet and directed it down on the west of David's Town. Yehizqiyyahu succeeded in all his action. ³¹And so with the spokesmen of the officials from Babel who sent to him to enquire about the sign that happened in the country, when God abandoned him to test him so as to know everything in his mind.

³²The rest of the things about Yehizqiyyahu and his acts of commitment – there they are, written in the vision of Yesha'yahu ben Amots the prophet, on the document regarding the kings of Yehudah and Yisra'el. ³³Yehizqiyyahu lay down with his ancestors and they buried him in the upper floor of the graves of David's sons, and all Yehudah and the inhabitants of Yerushalaim did him honour when he died. Menashsheh his son began to reign in place of him.

## The possibility of repentance

**33** Menashsheh was twelve years of age when he began to reign and he reigned fifty-five years in Yerushalaim. ²He did what was bad in Yahweh's eyes in accordance with the offensive practices of the nations that Yahweh dispossessed from before the Yisra'elites. ³He rebuilt the shrines that Yehizqiyyahu his father had demolished, set up altars for the Masters and made totem poles, and bowed low to all the heavenly army and served them. ⁴He built altars in Yahweh's house, of which Yahweh had said, 'In Yerushalaim my name will be permanently.' ⁵He built altars for all the heavenly army in the two courtyards of Yahweh's house. ⁶He himself made his sons pass through fire in Ben-hinnom Ravine. He practised augury, divined, acted as a medium, and dealt with ghosts and spirits. He did much that was bad in Yahweh's eyes, so as to provoke him.

⁷He put the image sculpture that he made in God's house, of which God had said to David and to Shelomoh his son, 'In this house and in Yerushalaim, which I chose from all Yisra'el's clans, I will put my name permanently. ⁸And I will never again remove Yisra'el's foot from upon the land that I put in place for their ancestors, only if they keep watch to act on all that I ordered them – the entire instruction, the decrees and the rulings by means of Mosheh.' ⁹Menashsheh made Yehudah and Yerushalaim and the inhabitants of Yerushalaim wander so as to deal badly, more than the nations that Yahweh annihilated from before the Yisra'elites.

¹⁰Yahweh spoke to Menashsheh and to his people but they didn't heed, ¹¹so Yahweh brought against them the officers of the army belonging to the king of Ashshur. They took Menashsheh captive in hooks, bound him with copper shackles and made him go to Babel. ¹²But when he was under pressure, he sought the goodwill of Yahweh his God. He bowed right down before his ancestors' God ¹³and pleaded to him. He let himself be entreated by him and listened to his prayer for grace, and let him go back to Yerushalaim to his kingship. So Menashsheh acknowledged that Yahweh was God.

## Menashsheh and Amon

[14]Subsequently he built an outer wall for David's Town, west of Gihon, in the wadi and as you come through the Fish Gate. It went round the Ophel. He made it very lofty. He put forceful officers in all the fortified towns in Yehudah. [15]He removed the foreign gods and the image from Yahweh's house and all the altars that he had built on the mountain of Yahweh's house and in Yerushalaim, and threw them outside the town. [16]He built up Yahweh's altar and made on it well-being sacrifices and thank offerings. He said to Yehudah to serve Yahweh the God of Yisra'el, [17]though the people were still sacrificing at the shrines, only for Yahweh their God.

[18]The rest of the things about Menashsheh, his plea to his God, and the words of the seers who spoke to him in the name of Yahweh his God – there they are, on the things of the kings of Yisra'el. [19]His plea and his being entreated by him, and all his wrongdoing and his trespass, and the sites in which he built shrines and put in place totem poles and sculptures, before he bowed down – there, they're written in the words of his seers. [20]Menashsheh lay down with his ancestors and they buried him in his house, and Amon his son began to reign in place of him.

[21]Amon was a man of twenty-two years when he began to reign and he reigned two years in Yerushalaim. [22]He did what was bad in Yahweh's eyes, as Menashsheh his father had done. To all the sculptures that Menashsheh his father had made, Amon sacrificed and served them. [23]He did not bow down before Yahweh as Menashsheh his father bowed down, but rather he, Amon, made his liability great. [24]His servants conspired against him and put him to death in his house, [25]but the people of the country struck down those who had conspired against King Amon. The people of the country made Yo'shiyyahu his son king in place of him.

## The great reformer

# 34
Yo'shiyyahu [Josiah] was eight years of age when he began to reign and he reigned thirty-one years in Yerushalaim. [2]He did what was upright in the eyes of Yahweh and walked in the ways of David his ancestor. He did not depart right or left.

[3]In the eighth year of his reign when he was still a boy he began to enquire of the God of David his ancestor, and in the twelfth year began to purify Yehudah and Yerushalaim of the shrines, the totem poles, the sculptures and the cast images. [4]They demolished the Masters' altars before him, and the incense stands that were above, over them, he cut down. The totem poles, the sculptures and the cast images he broke up, made dust of them and threw it over the face of the graves of the people who had sacrificed to them. [5]The priests' bones he burned on their altars. He purified Yehudah and Yerushalaim, [6]and in the towns of Menashsheh, Ephrayim and Shim'on, and as far as Naphtali, and in their ruins all round, [7]he demolished the altars and the totem poles, crushed the sculptures to dust and cut down the incense stands in the entire country of Yisra'el, and went back to Yerushalaim.

[8]In the eighteenth year of his reign, when he had purified the country and the house, he sent Shaphan ben Atsalyahu, Ma'aseyahu the town official and Yo'ah ben Yo'ahaz the recorder to strengthen the house of Yahweh his God. [9]They came to Hilqiyyahu the big priest and gave him the silver that had been brought to God's house, which the Levites who keep watch over the threshold had gathered from the hand of Menashsheh and Ephrayim, from the entire remainder of Yisra'el and from all Yehudah and Binyamin and the inhabitants of Yerushalaim. [10]They gave it into the hand of the one doing the work, the people appointed in Yahweh's house. The ones doing the work who were doing it in Yahweh's house gave it for dealing with the defects and for strengthening the house. [11]They gave it to craftsmen and masons for acquiring hewn stones and logs for the clasps and for roofing the houses that the kings of Yehudah had let become devastated.

## The worrying discovery

[12]The men were acting with trustworthiness in the work:

appointed in charge of them: Yahat and Obadyahu, Levites from the Mararites, and Zekaryah and Meshullam from the Qehatites, to supervise;

the Levites, everyone with understanding of musical instruments, ¹³both in charge of the carriers and supervising everyone doing the work, service by service; some of the Levites: secretaries, overseers and gatemen.

¹⁴When they were taking out the silver that had been brought to Yahweh's house, Hilqiyyahu the priest found a document of Yahweh's instruction by means of Mosheh. ¹⁵Hilqiyyahu avowed to Shaphan the secretary, 'I've found an instruction document in Yahweh's house.' Hilqiyyahu gave the document to Shaphan, ¹⁶and Shaphan brought the document to the king. He also took word back to the king: 'All that was given into your servants' hands, they're doing. ¹⁷They've melted down the silver that was found in Yahweh's house and given it into the hand of the appointees and into the hand of the people doing the work.' ¹⁸And Shaphan the secretary told the king, 'Hilqiyyahu the priest gave me a document', and he read it out before the king.

¹⁹When the king heard the words in the instruction, he tore his clothes. ²⁰The king ordered Hilqiyyahu, Ahiqam ben Shaphan, Abdon ben Mikah, Shaphan the secretary and Asayah the king's servant, ²¹'Go enquire of Yahweh on my behalf and on behalf of the remainder in Yisra'el and Yehudah about the words in the document that's been found, because great is Yahweh's wrath that's poured upon us because our ancestors didn't keep Yahweh's word by acting in accordance with everything that's written on this document.'

²²Hilqiyyahu and those whom the king [had said] went to Huldah the prophetess, wife of Shallum ben Toqhat son of Hasrah, keeper of the robes; she was living in Yerushalaim in the Second Quarter. They spoke to her in this way.

### The prophetess speaks straight

²³She said to them, 'Yahweh the God of Yisra'el has said this: "Say to the man who sent you to me: ²⁴Yahweh has said this: "Here, I'm going to bring bad fortune on this place and its inhabitants, all the curses written on the document that they read out before the king

of Yehudah, ²⁵because of the fact that they abandoned me and burned incense to other gods, in order to provoke me with all the actions of their hands, so that my wrath will pour out on this place and will not go out."'"

²⁶But to the king of Yehudah who sent you to enquire of Yahweh, you're to say to him, "Yahweh the God of Yisra'el has said this: 'The words that you have heard: ²⁷since your mind softened and you bowed down before God when you heard his words about this place and about its inhabitants, and you bowed down before me and tore your clothes and cried before me, I for my part have also listened (Yahweh's declaration). ²⁸Here, I'm going to gather you to your ancestors, and you'll gather yourself to your great grave with things being well. Your eyes will not see all the bad fortune that I'm going to bring on this place and on its inhabitants.'"

They took word back to the king ²⁹and the king sent and gathered all the elders of Yehudah and Yerushalaim. ³⁰The king went up to Yahweh's house, with everyone in Yehudah, the inhabitants of Yerushalaim, the priests, the Levites, and all the people, old and young. He read out in their ears all the words of the pact document found in Yahweh's house. ³¹The king stood in his position and solemnized a pact before Yahweh to follow Yahweh and to keep his orders, his affirmations and his decrees with his entire mind and with his entire being, by acting on the words of the pact that were written on this document. ³²He got everyone who was to be found in Yerushalaim and Binyamin to stand, and the inhabitants of Yerushalaim acted in accordance with the pact of God, their ancestors' God.

### Preparations for a great celebration

³³Yo'shiyyahu removed all the offensive things from all the regions that belonged to the Yisra'elites and got everyone who was to be found in Yisra'el to give their service to Yahweh their God. All his days they did not depart from following Yahweh, their ancestors' God.

**35** Yo'shiyyahu made Pesah for Yahweh in Yerushalaim; they slaughtered the Pesah on the fourteenth of the first month. ²He put in place the priests at their watches and he strengthened them for the service of Yahweh's house. [3]He said to the Levites, who helped all Yisra'el understand, who were sacred for Yahweh, 'Put the sacred chest in the house that Shelomoh ben David, king of Yisra'el, built. There's no carrying it on the shoulder for you now; serve Yahweh your God and his people Yisra'el now.

[4]Establish yourselves by your ancestral households according to your divisions, by the writing of David king of Yisra'el and by the writing of Shelomoh his son. [5]Stand in the sacred place by the ancestral household groupings of your brothers (the members of the people) and the ancestral household divisions of the Levites, [6]and slaughter the Pesah. Make yourselves sacred and prepare it for your brothers, acting in accordance with Yahweh's word by means of Mosheh.'

[7]Yo'shiyyahu raised for the members of the people flocks, lambs and goats (all of it for the Pesah occasions for everyone who was to be found) to the number of 30,000, and cattle 3,000, these from the king's property. [8]His officials raised a free offering for the people, for the priests and for the Levites; Hilqiyyah, Zekaryahu and Yehi'el, the chiefs over God's house, gave for the Pesah occasions 2,600, and 300 cattle. [9]Kananyahu, Shema'yahu and Netan'el his brothers, and Hashabyahu, Ye'i'el and Yozabad, the Levites' officials, raised for the Levites for the Pesah occasions 5,000, and 500 cattle.

## No Pesah (Passover) like this for centuries

[10]So the service was prepared. The priests stood in their position, with the Levites by their divisions in accordance with the king's order. [11]They slaughtered the Pesah and the priests tossed some of the blood they had while the Levites were doing the skinning. [12]They removed the burnt offering to give them to the groups by ancestral households, to the members of the people, to present to Yahweh in accordance with what is written in Mosheh's document, and so for the cattle. [13]They cooked the Pesah in fire in accordance with the ruling, and the sacred things they cooked in pots, in cauldrons and in pans, and ran them to all the members of the people.

[14]After, they prepared things for themselves and for the priests, because the priests, the Aharonites, were involved in offering up the burnt offering and the fat parts until evening, while the Levites prepared for themselves and for the priests, the Aharonites. [15]The singers, the Asaphites, were in their place in accordance with the order of David, Asaph, Heman and Yedutun the king's seer, and the gatemen were at gateway by gateway: there was no departing from their service for them, because their Levite brothers prepared for them.

[16]The entire service of Yahweh was prepared that day, making the Pesah and offering up burnt offerings on Yahweh's altar in accordance with the order of King Yo'shiyyahu. [17]The Yisra'elites who were to be found made the Pesah at that time, and the Flatbread Festival, for seven days. [18]Pesah had not been made like this in Yisra'el since the days of Shemu'el [Samuel] the prophet. No kings of Yisra'el had made one like the Pesah that Yo'shiyyahu made, with the priests, the Levites, all Yehudah and Yisra'el to be found, and the inhabitants of Yerushalaim. [19]This Pesah was made in the eighteenth year of Yo'shiyyahu 's reign.

## One fatal mistake

[20]After all this, when Yo'shiyyahu had established the house, Neko king of Misrayim went up to do battle at Karkemish on the Euphrates, and Yo'shiyyahu went out to meet him. [21]He sent envoys to him saying, 'What is there between you and me, king of Yehudah? You're not the one I'm against today, but against the household that's doing battle with me. God said I should hurry. Hold yourself back from God, who's with me, so he doesn't devastate you.' [22]But Yo'shiyyahu didn't turn his face round from him but disguised himself to do battle against him. He didn't listen to the words of Neko from the mouth of God but came to battle in the Megiddo Valley, [23]and the archers shot King Yo'shiyyahu. The king said to his servants, 'Get me out, because I'm badly hurt.' [24]His servants got him out of the chariot, put him on the second-in-command's chariot and took him to Yerushalaim, but he died. He was buried

in his ancestors' graves, and all Yehudah and Yerushalaim was mourning over Yo'shiyyahu.

²⁵Yirmeyahu [Jeremiah] lamented over Yo'shiyyahu, and all the singers (male and female) have spoken of Yo'shiyyahu in their laments until this day. They made them a decree in Yisra'el. There, they're written in the laments. ²⁶The rest of the things about Yo'shiyyahu and his acts of commitment in accordance with what is written in Yahweh's instruction, ²⁷his words early and late: there, they are written on the document about the kings of Yisra'el and Yehudah.

**36** The people of the country got Yeho'ahaz ben Yo'shiyyahu and made him king in place of his father in Yerushalaim.

## The rebellious end

²Yeho'ahaz was a man of twenty-three years when he began to reign and he reigned three months in Yerushalaim, ³but the king of Misrayim removed him in Yerushalaim and levied the country for a hundred talents of silver and a talent of gold. ⁴The king of Misrayim made Elyaqim his brother king over Yehudah and Yerushalaim and changed his name to Yehoyaqim. Neko took Yo'ahaz his brother and brought him to Misrayim.

⁵Yehoyaqim was a man of twenty-five years when he began to reign and he reigned eleven years in Yerushalaim. He did what was bad in the eyes of Yahweh his God. ⁶Nebukadne'tstsar king of Babel went up against him and bound him with copper shackles to make him go to Babel. ⁷Nebukadne'tstsar brought some of the articles from Yahweh's house and put them in his palace in Babel. ⁸The rest of the things about Yehoyaqim and the offensive things that he did, and what was found against him – there, they are written on the document about the kings of Yisra'el and Yehudah. His son Yehoyakin began to reign in place of him.

⁹Yehoyakin was eighteen years of age when he began to reign and he reigned three months and ten days in Yerushalaim. He did what was bad in Yahweh's eyes. ¹⁰At the turn of the year King Nebukadne'tstsar sent and brought him to Babel with desirable articles from Yahweh's house. He made Tsidqiyyahu, his brother, king over Yehudah and Yerushalaim.

¹¹Tsidqiyyahu was twenty-one years of age when he began to reign and he reigned eleven years in Yerushalaim. ¹²He did what was bad in the eyes of Yahweh his God and did not bow down before Yirmeyahu the prophet from Yahweh's mouth. ¹³Further, he rebelled against Nebukadne'tstsar, who had made him swear by God. He toughened his neck and firmed up his mind from turning back to Yahweh the God of Yisra'el. ¹⁴Further, all the officials of the priests and the people committed many acts of trespass, in accordance with the offensive practices of the nations, and defiled Yahweh's house which he had made sacred in Yerushalaim.

## The land fulfils its sabbaths

¹⁵Yahweh, their ancestors' God, sent to them by means of his envoys, starting early and sending, because he had pity on his people and on his abode. ¹⁶But they were mocking God's envoys, despising his words and scoffing at his prophets, until Yahweh's wrath against his people rose, until there was no healing.

¹⁷So he brought up the king of the Kasdites [Babylonians] against them. They killed their young men by the sword in their sacred house. He did not have pity on young man or young girl, elder or greybeard. He gave everything into his hand. ¹⁸All the articles in God's house, big and small, the treasures of Yahweh's house, and the treasures of the king and his officers – he brought everything to Babel. ¹⁹They burned God's house and demolished the wall of Yerushalaim. They burned all its citadels with fire and devastated all its desirable objects.

²⁰He exiled to Babel the people who remained from the sword and they became his and his sons' servants until Parsite [Persian] kingship reigned, ²¹to fulfil Yahweh's word by the mouth of Yirmeyahu, until the country made amends for its sabbaths. All the days of its desolation it stopped [*shabat*], to fill up seventy years.

²²But in the first year of Koresh king of Paras [Cyrus king of Persia], fulfilling Yahweh's word by the mouth of Yirmeyahu, Yahweh stirred the spirit of Koresh king of Paras, and he made an announcement pass through his entire

kingdom, and also in writing: <sup>23</sup>'Koresh king of Paras has said this:

Yahweh the God of the heavens has given me all the kingdoms of the earth, and

he himself has appointed me to build him a house in Yerushalaim, which is in Yehudah. Whoever among you from all his people: may Yahweh his God be with him, and he is to go up.

# EZRA

Ezra and Nehemiah were originally one book; they were divided into two some time after Christ's day. They tell the story of the community in Judah over the first hundred years after the moment when Judahites who had been taken off into exile (or whose parents had been taken off into exile) were allowed to return to Judah to rebuild the temple, in about 539 BC. The books thus continue the story told in Kings and in Chronicles. But whereas those books relate a fairly continuous story, Ezra-Nehemiah is episodic.

- First, Ezra 1—6 tells of the actual return of some of those Judahites, by the commission of the Persian emperor and in fulfilment of the promise of Jeremiah, and of their rebuilding of the temple. In relating this story, Ezra 1—6 emphasizes the problem of opposition from the other little peoples that surrounded Judah, all of them provinces of the Persian Empire. The prophets Haggai and Zechariah were allies of Zerubbabel the governor and Joshua the priest in getting the community to complete the work. But the work does get completed, and the achievement is reason for a great celebration.

- Without warning Ezra 7—10 then jumps forward half a century to the mission of Ezra himself. The opening date indicates that he came from Babylon to Jerusalem in 458 BC. (That fact in itself makes evident that by no means all Judahites had accepted the chance to join in the move to Jerusalem described in Ezra 1—6.) He comes as a theologian who is an expert in the Torah of Moses, and he brings a copy of the Torah with him in order to campaign for people in Jerusalem to implement what it says. It wouldn't be surprising if this mission marks the moment when the 'Books of Moses' (Genesis to Deuteronomy) have reached the form in which we know them. Ezra comes to Jerusalem with the support of the Persian emperor, who will have seen the advantage to him of having a good administrative order in the province, of a kind that the people themselves would accept. A key feature of Ezra's work is his persuading Judahites to terminate their marriages with people from the other communities around, which imperilled the distinctiveness of Israel as God's people.

- Next the story moves to the mission of Nehemiah (Nehemiah 1—7). Nehemiah came from Susa in Persia to Jerusalem in 445 BC. He has heard in Susa of the broken-down state of things in Jerusalem. He first prays, then he too gets the support of the emperor (whose butler he is) for him to go to Jerusalem to do something about it. His signature achievement is the rebuilding of the city's walls, again despite opposition from neighbouring communities. But he also campaigns for the community to be generous rather than self-serving as it lives with the economic pressures of the times.

- Finally the two books give some account of Ezra and Nehemiah working together, and of some further events (Nehemiah 8—13). This last section of the story involves the community reading the Torah and accepting a commitment to aspects of the way of life that marks them out that were apparently neglected, such as proper observance of the sabbath and support for the temple and its worship. The story also speaks of action to get more people to come and live in Jerusalem, which will have been discouraged by the city's broken-down state. The books close with further action by Nehemiah to deal with offensive practices such as trading on the sabbath (again) and intermarrying with people from other communities that could lead them into unfaithfulness (again). It is an important initiative in seeing that the people of God stayed in being and did not cease to exist through assimilation.

So if one was going to subdivide Ezra-Nehemiah, it might have been more illuminating to divide it into four parts, not just two.

## *Yahweh stirs the emperor and the people*

**1** In the first year of Koresh king of Paras [Cyrus king of Persia], fulfilling Yahweh's word from the mouth of Yirmeyah [Jeremiah], Yahweh stirred the spirit of Koresh king of Paras, and he made an announcement pass through his entire kingdom, and also in writing: ²Koresh king of Paras has said this:

Yahweh the God of the heavens has given me all the kingdoms of the earth, and he himself has appointed me to build him a house in Yerushalaim, which is in Yehudah. ³Whoever among you from all his people: may his God be with him, and may he go up to Yerushalaim which is in Yehudah and build the house of Yahweh the God of Yisra'el; he is the God who is in Yerushalaim. ⁴Anyone who remains, from all the places where he is a resident – the people of his place are to support him with silver, with gold, with property and with cattle, along with the free offering for the house of God which is in Yerushalaim.

⁵So the ancestral heads of Yehudah and Binyamin, and the priests and the Levites, everyone whose spirit God stirred, set to so as to go up to build up Yahweh's house which is in Yerushalaim. ⁶All the people who were round about them strengthened their hands with silver articles, with gold, with property, with cattle and with choice things,

apart from every free offering. ⁷Koresh the king took out the articles belonging to Yahweh's house that Nebukadne'tstsar had taken out from Yerushalaim and put in his god's house. ⁸Koresh king of Paras took them out by the hand of Mitredat the treasurer, and counted them out to Sheshbatstsar, the Yehudahite leader. ⁹These are their count:

gold bowls: 30;
silver bowls: 1,000;
knives: 29;
¹⁰gold dishes: 30;
double silver bowls: 410;
other articles: 1,000.
¹¹All the articles of gold and of silver: 5,400.

All these Sheshbatstsar took up when the exiles were taken up from Babel to Yerushalaim.

## *Who we were*

**2** These are the people of the province, who went up from among the captives in exile whom Nebukadne'tstsar king of Babel had exiled to Babel and who went back to Yerushalaim and Yehudah, each to his town, ²who came with Zerubbabel, Yeshua, Nehemyah, Serayah, Re'elayah, Mordokay, Bilshan, Mispar, Bigvay, Rehum, Ba'anah.
The number of the men belonging to the Yisra'elite people:

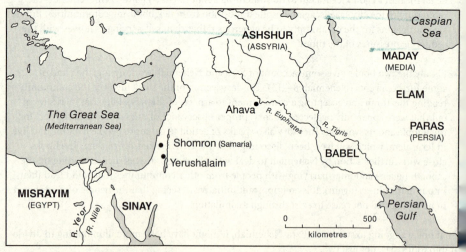

*Ancient Near East at the time of Ezra*

³sons of Par'osh 2,172
⁴sons of Shephatyah 372
⁵sons of Arah 775
⁶sons of Pahat Mo'ab (by the sons of Yeshua, Yo'ab) 2,812
⁷sons of Elam 1,254
⁸sons of Zattu 945
⁹sons of Zakkay 760
¹⁰sons of Bani 642
¹¹sons of Bebay 623
¹²sons of Azgad 1,222
¹³sons of Adoniqam 666
¹⁴sons of Bigvay 2,056
¹⁵sons of Adin 454
¹⁶sons of Ater (by Yehizqiyyah) 98
¹⁷sons of Betsay 323
¹⁸sons of Yorah 112
¹⁹sons of Hashum 223
²⁰sons of Gibbar 95
²¹sons of Bet-lehem 123
²²people of Netophah 56
²³people of Anatot 128
²⁴sons of Azmavet 42

²⁵sons of Arim Township, Kephirah and Be'erot 743
²⁶sons of The Height and Geba 621
²⁷people of Mikmas 122
²⁸people of Bet-el and Ha'ay 223
²⁹sons of Nebo 52
³⁰sons of Magbish 156
³¹sons of the other Elam 1,254
³²sons of Harim 320
³³sons of Lod, Hadid and Ono 725
³⁴sons of Yereho 345
³⁵sons of Sena'ah 3,630

³⁶The priests:
sons of Yeda'yah (by the household of Yeshua) 973
³⁷sons of Immer 1,052
³⁸sons of Pashhur 1,247
³⁹sons of Harim 1,017

⁴⁰The Levites:
sons of Yeshua and Qadmi'el (by the sons of Hodavyah) 74
⁴¹The singers:
sons of Asaph 128

## Gatemen, assistants and undocumented people

⁴²The sons of the gatemen:
sons of Shallum
sons of Ater
sons of Talmon
sons of Aqqub
sons of Hatita
sons of Shobay
altogether 139

⁴³The assistants:
sons of Tsiha
sons of Hasupha
sons of Tabba'ot
⁴⁴sons of Qeros
sons of Si'aha
sons of Padon
⁴⁵sons of Lebanah
sons of Hagabah
sons of Aqqub
⁴⁶sons of Hagab
sons of Shalmay
sons of Hanan
⁴⁷sons of Giddel
sons of Gahar
sons of Re'ayah

⁴⁸sons of Retsin
sons of Neqodah
sons of Gazzam
⁴⁹sons of Uzza
sons of Paseah
sons of Besay
⁵⁰sons of Asnah
sons of Me'unim
sons of Nephusim
⁵¹sons of Baqbuq
sons of Haqupha
sons of Harhur
⁵²sons of Batslut
sons of Mehida
sons of Harsha
⁵³sons of Barqos
sons of Sisera
sons of Temah
⁵⁴sons of Netsiah
sons of Hatipha

⁵⁵The sons of Shelomoh's [Solomon's] servants:
sons of Sotay
sons of Hassopheret
sons of Peruda
⁵⁶sons of Ya'alah
sons of Darqon
sons of Giddel
⁵⁷sons of Shephatyah
sons of Hattil
sons of Pokeret Hatstsebayim
sons of Ami

⁵⁸All the assistants and the sons of Shelomoh's servants 392.

⁵⁹These are the people who came up from Tel Melah, Tel Harsha, Kerub, Addan, Immer, but who could not tell their ancestral household and their origin, whether they were from Yisra'el:

⁶⁰sons of Delayah
sons of Tobiyyah
sons of Neqoda 652
sons of Haqqots
sons of Barzillay (who had taken a wife from the daughters of Barzillay the Gil'adite and was called by their name):
⁶¹Of the sons of the priests:
sons of Habayah

⁶²these looked for their record in the enrolment by genealogy but they couldn't be found, and they were deconsecrated from the priesthood. ⁶³The administrator said to them that they should not eat of the very sacred things until there was a priest standing with Urim and Tummim.

⁶⁴The entire congregation altogether 42,360; ⁶⁵apart from their servants and handmaids: these were 7,337; and they had 200 male and female singers; ⁶⁶their horses 736; their mules 245; ⁶⁷their camels 435; their donkeys 6,720.

## New beginnings

⁶⁸Some of the ancestral heads, when they came to Yahweh's house in Yerushalaim, gave

a free offering for God's house, to put it in its place on its established site. <sup>69</sup>In accordance with their energy, to the treasury for the work they gave gold, 61,000 drakmas; silver, 5,000 minas; and priests' robes, 100. <sup>70</sup>The priests, the Levites, some of the people, the singers, the gatemen and the assistants went to live in their towns, and all Yisra'el in their towns.

**3** When the seventh month arrived, with the Yisra'elites in their towns, the people gathered as one person in Yerushalaim. <sup>2</sup>Yeshua ben Yotsadaq and his brother priests, and Zerubbabel ben She'alti'el and his brothers, set to and built the altar of the God of Yisra'el, to offer up burnt offerings on it as is written in the instruction of Mosheh [Moses] the supernatural man. <sup>3</sup>They established the altar on its established site because they were in dread of the peoples of the countries, and they offered up burnt offerings on it for Yahweh, the burnt offerings for morning and for evening. <sup>4</sup>They made the Sukkot Festival as it is written, and the burnt offering day by day, by the number in accordance with the ruling, each day's requirement in its day, <sup>5</sup>and afterwards the regular burnt offering and the ones for the new months and for all the occasions set by Yahweh that were made sacred, and for anyone making a free offering for Yahweh.

<sup>6</sup>From the first day of the seventh month they began to offer up burnt offerings for Yahweh, though Yahweh's palace had not been started. <sup>7</sup>They gave silver to the hewers and to the craftsmen, and food, drink and oil to the Tsidonites and to the Tsorites, to bring cedar logs from the Lebanon by sea to Yafo, in accordance with the authorization to them by Koresh king of Paras.

## Shouts of joy and the sound of crying

<sup>8</sup>In the second year of their coming to the house of God at Yerushalaim, in the second month, Zerubbabel ben She'alti'el and Yeshua ben Yotsadaq, and the rest of their brothers (the priests, the Levites and all the people who had come from the captivity to Yerushalaim) began, and put in place the Levites from people of twenty years and upwards to supervise the work on Yahweh's house. <sup>9</sup>Yeshua,

his sons and his brothers, and Qadmi'el and his sons (descendants of Yehudah) stood up together to oversee the one doing the work on God's house (the sons of Henadad, their sons and their brothers, the Levites).

<sup>10</sup>When the builders started Yahweh's palace, they put in place the priests in their vestments with trumpets, and the Levites, the sons of Asaph, with cymbals, to praise Yahweh in accordance with the directions of David king of Yisra'el. <sup>11</sup>They sang responsively in praise and confession to Yahweh, 'Because he is good, because his commitment stands permanently for Yisra'el', and the entire people gave a big shout in praise of Yahweh, because Yahweh's house had been started. <sup>12</sup>While many of the priests and the Levites and the ancestral heads, the old men who had seen the first house, at the start on this house before their eyes were crying with a loud voice, many were raising their voice in a shout of rejoicing. <sup>13</sup>The people couldn't recognize the sound of the shout of rejoicing from the sound of the people's crying, because the people were giving a big shout. The sound was audible from afar.

**4** The adversaries of Yehudah and Binyamin heard that the people from the exile were building a palace for Yahweh the God of Yisra'el, <sup>2</sup>and they came up to Zerubbabel and to the ancestral heads and said to them, 'We'll build with you, because we enquire of your God like you, and we've been sacrificing for him since the days of Esar Haddon king of Ashshur, who got us up here.'

## Offers of help refused

<sup>3</sup>Zerubbabel, Yeshua and the remainder of the ancestral heads of Yisra'el said to them, 'It's not for you and for us to build a house for our God, because we as one will build for Yahweh the God of Yisra'el, as Koresh king of Paras ordered us.'

<sup>4</sup>Then the people of the country were making the hands of the people of Yehudah slacken and making them fearful to build. <sup>5</sup>They were bribing counsellors against them so as to contravene their counsel all the days of Koresh king of Paras and until the reign of Doryavesh [Darius] king of Paras, <sup>6</sup>and in the reign of Ahashverosh [Xerxes], at the beginning of his

reign, they wrote an accusation against the inhabitants of Yehudah and Yerushalaim.

[7]Then in the days of Artahshasta [Artaxerxes], Bishlam, Mitredat, Tabe'el and the remainder of his associates wrote to Artahshasta king of Paras. The writing of the document was in Aramaic and translated.

(Aramaic.) [8]Rehum the administrator and Shimshay the secretary wrote a communiqué about Yerushalaim to King Artahshasta as follows.

[9]Rehum the administrator, Shimsay the secretary and the remainder of their associates, the authorities and officials, of Tarpel, Paras, Erek, Babel, Shushan (i.e. the Elamites) [10]and the remainder of the peoples that the great and glorious Osnapper [Ashurbanipal] exiled and made live in the town of Shomrayin [Samaria] and the remainder of Beyond-the-River province (so now [11]this is a copy of the communiqué they sent him) to Artahshasta the king.

Your servants, men of Beyond-the-River province:

So now [12]be it known to the king that the Yehudahites who came up from you to us have come to Yerushalaim. They are building up the rebellious and wicked town. They have completed the walls and strengthened the foundations. [13]Now be it known to the king that if this town is built up and its walls are completed, they will not give tribute, taxes or tolls, so the kings' interests will suffer harm.

## A pattern of tension running through the story

[14]Now since we share the salt of the palace and it's not right for us to see the king's dishonour, therefore we have sent and made it known to the king [15]so that they may search in the document with your ancestors' records. You will find in the records document and acknowledge that this town is a rebellious town, harmful to kings and provinces. People have been making mutiny in it from days of old. Because of that this town was destroyed. [16]We make it known to the king that if this town is built up and its walls are completed, as a result of that you will not have a share in Beyond-the-River.

[17]The king sent a message:

To Rehum the administrator, Shimshay the secretary, the remainder of their associates who live in Shomrayin, and the remainder of Beyond-the-River, good wishes.

So now [18]the letter that you sent to us was explained, read out before me. [19]A decree was made by me, and they searched and found that this town from days of old has risen against kings. Rebellion and mutiny have been made in it. [20]There have been powerful kings over Yerushalaim and they have exercised authority over the whole of Beyond-the-River. Tribute, taxes and tolls were rendered to them. [21]Now make a decree to stop these men. That town will not be built up until the order is made by me. [22]Be careful about acting negligently in this. Why should damage grow so as to harm kings?

[23]When a copy of the letter from Artahshasta the king was read out before Rehum, Shimshay the secretary and their associates, they went with speed to Yerushalaim to the Yehudahites and stopped them with compelling force.

## To return to the time of the temple building . . .

[24]So work stopped on God's house in Yerushalaim. It stopped until the second year of the reign of Doryavesh king of Paras, **5** and Haggay the prophet and Zekaryah ben Iddo prophesied to the Yehudahites who were in Yehudah and in Yerushalaim in the name of the God of Yisra'el, over them. [2]Then Zerubbabel ben She'alti'el and Yeshua ben Yotsadaq set to and began to build God's house in Yerushalaim, God's prophets being with them, supporting them.

³At that time Tattenay the governor of Beyond-the-River, Shetar Bozenay and their associates came to them and said this to them: 'Who made you a decree to build this house and finish these supplies?' ⁴Then we said to them, 'What are the names of the men who are constructing this building?' ⁵But God's eye was on the Yehudahite elders, and they didn't stop them while an account could go to Doryavesh, and then they would bring back a letter about this.

⁶A copy of the communiqué that Tattenay governor of Beyond-the-River, Shetar Bozenay and his associates, the officials of Beyond-the-River, sent to Doryavesh the king. ⁷They sent a message to him, and in it was written as follows:

To Doryavesh the king, all good wishes. ⁸Be it known to the king that we went to Yehudah province to the house of the great God. It's being built up of dressed stone, and wood is being set in the walls. This work is being done punctiliously and it is succeeding in their hand. ⁹Then we asked of these elders as follows: 'Who made you a decree to build this house and finish these supplies?' ¹⁰We also asked for their names to make them known to you, so that we could write down the name of the men who are at their head.

## A defence

¹¹They sent back a message like this to us: 'We are the servants of the God of the heavens and the earth. We are building up the house that was built many years before this, when a great king of Yisra'el built it and completed it. ¹²Yet because our ancestors angered the God of the heavens, he gave them into the hand of Nebukadne'tstsar king of Babel, the Kasdite. He destroyed this house and exiled the people to Babel. ¹³However, in the first year of Koresh king of Babel, Koresh the king made a decree to build up this house of God. ¹⁴The articles belonging to the house of God, of gold and silver, which Nebukadne'tstsar took out of the palace in Yerushalaim and brought to the palace in Babel, Koresh the king also took

out of the palace in Babel and they gave them to someone named Sheshbatstsar whom he made governor. ¹⁵He said to him, "Take up these articles, go off, put them in the palace in Yerushalaim. And the house of God is to be built up on its place." ¹⁶This Sheshbatstsar then came and made a start on the house of God in Yerushalaim. From then until now it's been being built, but it's not complete.'

¹⁷Now, if it seems good to the king, there should be a search in the king's treasure-house there in Babel, if it's the case that a decree was made by Koresh the king for building up that house of God in Yerushalaim. And may the king send us his wish concerning this.

**6** Then a decree was made by Doryavesh the king and they searched in the documents house where treasures were kept in Babel.

## An astounding result

²But a scroll was found in the fortress at Ahmeta in Maday [Media] province. In it was written as follows:

Memorandum. ³In the first year of Koresh the king, Koresh the king made a decree: 'The house of God in Yerushalaim. The house is to be built up, a place where people make sacrifices, with its foundations buttressed, its height 30 metres, its width 30 metres, ⁴three courses of dressed stone and a course of new wood. The expense will be paid by the king's house. ⁵Also the articles belonging to the house of God, of gold and silver, which Nebukadne'tstsar took out of the palace in Yerushalaim and brought to Babel are to be given back. It is to go to the palace in Yerushalaim to its place. You are to deposit it in God's house.'

⁶'Now Tattenay governor of Beyond-the-River, Shetar Bozenay and their associates, officials of Beyond-the-River, stay away from there. ⁷Leave the work on this house of God alone. The governor of the Yehudahites and the elders of the Yehudahites are to build up

this house of God on its place, [8]and a decree is made by me about what you're to do with these elders of the Yehudahites, to build up this house of God. The expense is to be paid punctiliously to these men out of the assets of the king, out of the tribute from Beyond-the-River, so as not to cause a stop. [9]Whatever they need, both young bulls, rams and lambs for burnt offerings for the God of the heavens, wheat, salt, wine and oil, in accordance with the word of the priests in Yerushalaim – it's to be given them day by day without fail, [10]so that they may present pleasing sacrifices to the God of the heavens and pray for the life of the king and his sons.

[11]And a decree is made by me that anyone who defies this message, wood will be removed from his house and he will be lifted up and beaten upon it, and his house will be made forfeit, because of this. [12]And may the God who had his name dwell there overthrow any king or people who puts out a hand to defy – to damage this house of God in Yerushalaim. I, Doryavesh, have made a decree. It's to be put into effect scrupulously.'

## Success and celebration

[13]Then Tattenay governor of Beyond-the-River, Shetar Bozenay and their associates, in keeping with what Doryavesh the king sent, accordingly acted punctiliously. [14]The elders of the Yehudahites built, and succeeded through the prophesying of Haggay the prophet and Zekaryah ben Iddo. They built and finished by the decree of the God of Yisra'el and by the decree of Koresh, Doryavesh and Artahshasta king of Paras. [15]This house was completed on the third day of the month of Adar; it was in the sixth year of the reign of Doryavesh the king.

[16]The Yisra'elites, the priests, the Levites and the remainder of the exiles made the dedication of this house of God with celebration. [17]For the dedication of this house of God they presented 100 bulls, 200 rams, 400 lambs and twelve goats as a purification offering for all Yisra'el, according to the number of the clans of Yisra'el. [18]They set up the priests in their divisions and the Levites in their groups for the service of God in Yerushalaim, in accordance with what is written in Mosheh's document.

[19]The people from the exile made the Pesah [Passover] on the fourteenth of the first month, [20]because the priests had purified themselves, and the Levites altogether were pure, all of them. They slaughtered the Pesah for all the people from the exile, for their brother priests and for themselves. [21]The Yisra'elites who had come back from the exile ate, with everyone who had made himself distinct from the defilement of the nation in the country, to join them to enquire of Yahweh the God of Yisra'el. [22]They made the Flatbread Festival for seven days with rejoicing, because Yahweh had made them rejoice when he turned round the mind of the king of Ashshur to them so as to strengthen their hands in the work on the house of God, the God of Yisra'el.

## Enter the priest-theologian

7 After these things, in the reign of Artahshasta king of Paras, Ezra ben Serayah, son of Azaryah son of Hilqiyyah [2]son of Shallum son of Tsadoq son of Ahitub [3]son of Amaryah son of Azaryah son of Merayot [4]son of Zerahyah son of Uzzi son of Buqqi [5]son of Abishua son of Pinhas son of El'azar son of Aharon the head priest – [6]that Ezra went up from Babel. He was a smart scholar in the instruction of Mosheh which Yahweh the God of Yisra'el had given. In accordance with the hand of Yahweh his God upon him, the king had given him everything that he sought.

[7]Some Yisra'elites, some priests, Levites, singers, gatemen and assistants went up to Yerushalaim in the seventh year of Artahshasta the king, [8]and he came to Yerushalaim in the fifth month (it was the king's seventh year), [9]because on the first of the first month it was the start of the journey up from Babel, and on the first of the fifth month he came to Yerushalaim in accordance with the good hand of his God upon him, [10]because Ezra had set his mind to enquire of Yahweh's instruction so as both to keep and to teach decree and ruling in Yisra'el.

[11]This is a copy of the letter that King Artahshasta gave Ezra the priest-scholar, scholar in things concerning Yahweh's orders and his decrees for Yisra'el:

¹²Artahshasta, king of kings, to Ezra the priest-scholar in the instruction of the God of the heavens (and so on). Now: ¹³a decree is made by me that anyone in my kingdom from the people of Yisra'el and its priests and Levites who freely offers to go to Yerushalaim with you may go. ¹⁴Because you are sent by the king and his seven counsellors to enquire about Yehudah and Yerushalaim on the basis of the instruction of your God which is in your hand, ¹⁵and to take silver and gold that the king and his counsellors have made as a free offering for the God of Yisra'el whose dwelling is in Yerushalaim, ¹⁶and any silver and gold that you find in all Babel province, with the free offering of the people and the priests that they make for the house of their God in Yerushalaim.

## What we owe, and what we give because we want to

¹⁷Therefore with this money acquire punctiliously bulls, rams and lambs, and their grain offerings and their drink offerings, and present them on the altar in the house of your God in Yerushalaim. ¹⁸And what seems good to you and to your brothers to do with the remainder of the silver and the gold, in accordance with the will of your God, you may do. ¹⁹The articles given to you for the service of your God's house, deliver before God in Yerushalaim. ²⁰The remainder of the needs of your God's house that it falls to you to give, you may give from the king's treasure-house.

²¹I, Artahshasta the king – by me a decree is made to all the treasurers in Beyond-the-River, that anything Ezra the priest-scholar in the instruction of the God of the heavens asks of you is punctiliously to be done, ²²up to 100 talents of silver, to 100 ten-gallon measures of wheat, to 100 five-gallon measures of wine, to 100 five-gallon measures of oil, and salt without prescribed limit. ²³Anything that is by the decree of the God of the heavens is to be done scrupulously for the house of the God of the heavens, so that fury does not come on the realm of the king and his sons. ²⁴And to you we make it known that all priests, Levites, musicians, gatemen, assistants and workers in this house of God – it's not permitted to impose tribute, taxes and tolls on them.

²⁵You, Ezra, in accordance with your God's smartness which is in your possession, appoint authorities and judges who will give judgement for all the people in Beyond-the-River, for all who acknowledge your God's instructions, and make them known to anyone who does not acknowledge them. ²⁶Anyone who does not observe the instruction of your God and the instruction of the king, judgement will be done to him punctiliously, whether by death, by banishment, by confiscation of property or by imprisonment.

## God working through the king

²⁷Blessed be Yahweh, our ancestors' God, who put into the king's mind in this way to glorify Yahweh's house which is in Yerushalaim ²⁸and extended commitment to me before the king and his counsellors and all the king's officials, the powerful men.

I myself showed myself strong in accordance with the hand of Yahweh my God upon me, and collected heads from Yisra'el to go up with me.

**8** These are the ancestral heads and the enrolment by genealogy of the people who went up with me in the reign of Artahshasta the king from Babel:
²of the sons of Pinhas, Gershom;
of the sons of Itamar, Daniyy'el;
of the sons of David, Hattush, ³of the sons of Shekanyah;
of the sons of Parosh, Zekaryah, and with him were enrolled by genealogy 150 males;
⁴of the sons of Pahat Mo'ab, Elyeho'enay ben Zerahyah, and with him 200 males;
⁵of the sons of Shekanyah, ben Yahazi'el, and with him 300 males;
⁶and of the sons of Adin, Ebed ben Yonatan, and with him 50 males;
⁷and of the sons of Elam, Yesha'yah ben

Atalyah, and with him 70 males;
[8]and of the sons of Shephatyah, Zebadyah
ben Mika'el, and with him 80 males;
[9]of the sons of Yo'ab, Obadyah ben Yehi'el,
and with him 218 males;
[10]and of the sons of Shelomit, ben Yosiphyah,
and with him 160 males;
[11]and of the sons of Bebay, Zekaryah ben
Bebay, and with him 28 males;
[12]and of the sons of Azgad, Yohanan ben
Haqqatan, and with him 110 males;
[13]and of the sons of Adoniqam, the last ones –
these are their names: Eliphelet, Ye'i'el and
Shemayah, and with them 60 males;
[14]and of the sons of Bigvay, Utay and Zakkur,
and with him 70 males.

## God's good hand

[15]I collected them at the river that comes
to Ahava and we camped there for three
days. I considered the people and the priests,
and didn't find any of the Levites there. [16]So
I sent for Eli'ezer, for Ari'el, for Shema'yah,
for Elnatan, for Yarib, for Elnatan, for Natan,
for Zekaryah and for Meshullam as heads,
and for Yoyarib and for Elnatan as people of
understanding, [17]and ordered them to Iddo,
the head at Kasiphaya, the [worship] site, and
put words in their mouth to speak to Iddo, his
brother, the assistants at Kasiphaya, the site, to
bring us ministers for the house of our God.

[18]In accordance with the good hand of
our God upon us they brought us a man of
insight from the sons of Mahli ben Levi, son of
Yisra'el, namely Sherebyah, and his sons and his
brothers, eighteen people, [19]and Hashabyah and
with him Yesha'yah of the sons of Merari, his
brothers and their sons, twenty people, [20]and
of the assistants that David and the officials
had given for the service of the Levites, 220
assistants; all of them were recorded by name.

[21]I called a fast there at the River Ahava to
humble ourselves before our God so as to seek
from him a straightforward journey for us
and for our little ones and for all our property,
[22]because I was ashamed to ask the king for a
force and cavalry to help us against an enemy
on the way, because we'd said to the king, 'The
hand of our God is upon all who seek him, for
good, but his vigour and his anger are on all

who abandon him.' [23]So we fasted and sought
God about this, and he let himself be entreated
by us.

## The journey and the arrival

[24]I distinguished twelve of the priestly
officials, Sherebyah and Hashabyah and with
them ten of their brothers, [25]and weighed out
to them the silver, the gold and the articles, the
contribution for our God's house that the king,
his counsellors, his officials, and all Yisra'el who
were to be found, had raised. [26]I weighed out
into their hand the silver, 650 talents; the silver
articles, 100 talents, the gold, 100 talents;
[27]the gold bowls, twenty, worth 100 darics;
and two articles of good, shining copper, as
precious as gold.

[28]I said to them, 'You are sacred for Yahweh,
and the articles are sacred, and the silver and
the gold are a free offering for Yahweh, your
ancestors' God. [29]Be watchful and keep them
until you weigh them out before the priestly
officials, the Levites and the ancestral officials
of Yisra'el in Yerushalaim in the halls of
Yahweh's house.'

[30]The priests and the Levites received the
weighed-out silver and gold and the articles to
bring to Yerushalaim to our God's house. [31]We
moved on from the River Ahava on the twelfth
of the first month to go to Yerushalaim. The
hand of our God was upon us and he rescued
us from an enemy's fist and ambush on the way.

[32]We came to Yerushalaim, stayed there
three days, [33]and on the fourth day the silver
and the gold and the articles were weighed
out in our God's house into the hand of
Meremot ben Uriyyah the priest and with him
El'azar ben Pinhas, and with them Yozabad
ben Yeshua and No'adyah ben Binnuy, the
Levites, [34]everything by number/by weight.
The entire weight was written down at that
time. [35]The people who had come from the
captivity, the people from the exile, presented
burnt offerings for the God of Yisra'el, 12 bulls
for all Yisra'el, 96 rams, 77 lambs and 12 goats
as a purification offering. The whole was a
burnt offering for Yahweh. [36]They gave the
king's instructions to the king's satraps and
the governors of Beyond-the-River, and they
supported the people and the house of God.

## The importance of keeping distinct

**9** When these things finished, the officials came up to me to say, 'The people of Yisra'el and the priests and the Levites have not made themselves distinct from the peoples of the countries in light of their offensive practices (of the Kena'anite [Canaanite], the Hittite, the Perizzite, the Yebusite, the Ammonite, the Mo'abite, the Misrayimite [Egyptian] and the Amorite), ²because they've got some of their daughters for themselves and for their sons, and the sacred seed has mixed with the peoples of the countries, while the hand of the officials and the overseers has been first in this trespass.'

³When I heard this thing, I tore my garment and my coat, pulled hair from my head and from my beard, and sat desolate. ⁴Anyone who trembled at the words of the God of Yisra'el was gathering to me because of the exiles' trespass. I was sitting desolate until the evening offering.

⁵At the evening offering I got up from my self-affliction but bent down on my knees in my torn garment and coat and spread out my palms to Yahweh my God, ⁶and said, 'My God, I'm disgraced and ashamed to lift up my face to you, my God, because our wayward acts have grown above our head, and our liability is great, as far as the heavens. ⁷From the days of our ancestors until this day we've been in great liability, and through our wayward acts we've been given into the hand of the kings of the countries, we, our kings, our priests, with sword, with captivity, with plunder and with shame of face, this very day.

⁸Now for a little while there's been grace from Yahweh our God, in letting an escape group remain for us and giving us a stake in his sacred place, in our God's brightening our eyes and giving us a little life in our servitude. ⁹Because we're serfs, but in our serfdom our God hasn't abandoned us but has extended commitment to us before the kings of Paras so as to give us life, to raise up our God's house and make its wastes stand, and to give us a fence in Yehudah and in Yerushalaim.

## How to make your people's confession

¹⁰But now what can we say, our God, after this? Because we've abandoned your orders ¹¹that you issued by means of your servants the prophets, saying, "The country into which you're going to take possession of it is a country polluted by the pollution of the peoples of the countries, through their offensive practices with which they've filled it from end to end in their defilement. ¹²So now don't give your daughters to their sons or get their daughters for your sons. You will not enquire after their well-being or benefit, ever, so that you may be strong and eat the good of the country and enable your children to possess it permanently."

¹³After all that's come upon us because of our bad ways and our great liabilities, when you, our God, have held back [in punishing] below our waywardness, and given us an escape group like this, ¹⁴shall we go back to contravening your orders and intermarrying with the peoples who are characterized by these offensive practices? You will be angry with us so as to finish us off, so that there's no people remaining, no escape group, won't you. ¹⁵Yahweh, God of Yisra'el, you're in the right, because we remain as an escape group this very day. Here we are before you with our liability, but there's no standing before you on account of this.'

**10** While Ezra was pleading and making confession, crying and falling down before God's house, a very great congregation from Yisra'el, men, women and children, collected to him, because the people were crying bitterly. ²Shekanyah ben Yehi'el of the sons of Elam answered Ezra, 'We've trespassed against our God and got foreign women come to live from the peoples of the country. But now there's hope for Yisra'el over this, ³so now let's solemnize a pact towards our God to get all the women and those born from them to go away, by the counsel of my lord and of those who tremble at our God's order. It should be done in accordance with the instruction. ⁴Set to, because the thing rests on you, and we're with you. Be strong and act.'

## Where there's commitment there's hope

⁵Ezra set to and swore the priestly officials, the Levites and all Yisra'el to act in accordance with this word, and they swore. ⁶Ezra got up

from his place before God's house and went into the hall of Yehohanan ben Elyashib. When he went there, he didn't eat food and he didn't drink water, because he was grieving over the exiles' trespass.

⁷They passed an announcement through Yehudah and Yerushalaim to all the people from the exile, that they should collect in Yerushalaim. ⁸Anyone who didn't come in three days, in accordance with the counsel of the officials and the elders – all his property would be devoted and he himself would be distinguished from the exile congregation.

⁹So all the men of Yehudah and Binyamin collected in Yerushalaim in three days; it was the ninth month, the twentieth of the month. All the people sat in the square at God's house, trembling about the thing and because of the rains.

¹⁰Ezra the priest got up and said to them, 'You've trespassed. You've got foreign women come to live, adding to Yisra'el's liability. ¹¹But now, make confession to Yahweh, your ancestors' God, and do what is acceptable to him. Make yourselves distinct from the peoples of the country and from the foreign women.'

¹²The entire congregation answered with a loud voice, 'Yes, it's for us to act in accordance with your word. ¹³Nevertheless the company is large and the time is the rains. We don't have the energy to stand outside, and it's not the work of one day or of two, because we've become greatly rebellious in this thing. ¹⁴Our officials should please stand [here] for the entire congregation, and anyone in our towns who's got foreign women come to live should come at set times, and with them the elders town by town, and its authorities, until we turn back the angry rage of our God from us over this thing.' ¹⁵Only Yonatan ben Asah'el and Yahzeyah ben Tiqvah stood against this, but Meshullam and Shabbatay the Levites helped them.

## The tough action

¹⁶The people from the exile acted in this way. Ezra the priest, the men who were the ancestral heads, for their ancestral family, and all of them by their names, made themselves distinct and sat on the first day of the tenth month to enquire into the thing. ¹⁷They finished with all the men who'd got foreign women to come to live, by the first day of the first month.

¹⁸There were found among the sons of the priests who'd got foreign women to come to live:

Yeshua ben Yotsadaq and his brothers
  Ma'aseyah, Eli'ezer, Yarib and Gedalyah;
    ¹⁹they gave their hand that they would
    send away their wives and, being liable, a
    ram from the flock, for their liability;
²⁰of the sons of Immer, Hanani and
  Zebadyah;
²¹of the sons of Harim, Ma'aseyah, Eliyyah,
  Shema'yah, Yehi'el and Uzziyyah;
²²of the sons of Pashhur, Elyo'enay,
  Ma'aseyah, Yishma'e'l, Netan'el, Yozabad,
  and El'asah;

²³of the Levites:
Yozabad, Shim'i, Qelayah (i.e. Qelita),
  Petahyah, Yehudah and Eli'ezer;

²⁴of the singers:
Eliyashib;

of the gatemen:
Shallum, Telem and Uri.
²⁵Of the Yisra'elites:
of the sons of Parosh, Ramyah, Yizzeyah,
  Malkiyyah, Miyyamin, El'azar, Malkiyyah
  and Benayah;
²⁶of the sons of Elam, Mattanyah, Zekaryah,
  Yehi'el, Abdi, Yeremot and Eliyyah;
²⁷of the sons of Zattu, Elyo'enay, Elyashib,
  Mattanyah, Yeremot, Zabad and Aziza;
²⁸of the sons of Bebay, Yehohanan,
  Hananyah, Zabbay, Atlay;
²⁹of the sons of Bani, Meshullam, Malluk,
  Adayah, Yashub, She'al and Ramot;
³⁰of the sons of Patah Mo'ab, Adna, Kelal,
  Benayah, Ma'aseyah, Mattanyah, Betsal'el,
  Binnuy and Menashsheh;
³¹of the sons of Harim, Eli'ezer, Ishshiyyah,
  Malkiyyah, Shema'yah, Shim'on,
³²Binyamin, Malluk, Shemaryah;
³³of the sons of Hashum, Mattenay, Mattattah,
  Zabad, Eliphelet, Yeremay, Menashsheh,
  Shim'i;
³⁴of the sons of Bani, Ma'aday, Amram
  and U'el, ³⁵Benayah, Bedeyah,
  Keluhu, ³⁶Vanyah, Meremot, Elyashib,

³⁷Mattanyah, Mattenay, Ya'asay, ³⁸Bani, Binnuy, Shim'i, ³⁹Shelemyah, Natan, Adayah, ⁴⁰Maknadebay, Shashay, Sharay, ⁴¹Azar'el, Shelemyahu, Shemaryah, ⁴²Shallum, Amaryah, Yoseph;

⁴³of the sons of Nebo, Ye'i'el, Mattityah, Zabad, Zebina, Yadday and Yo'el, Benayah. ⁴⁴All these had got foreign wives, and there were some of them who were women who had had children.

# NEHEMIAH

For an introduction, see the introduction to Ezra.

## Survivors troubled and disgraced

**1** The words of Nehemyah ben Hakalyah.

In the month of Kislev in the twentieth year, when I was in Shushan, the fortress, [2]Hanani, one of my brothers, came, he and some men from Yehudah, and I asked them about the Yehudahites, the escape group that remained from the captivity, and about Yerushalaim. [3]They said to me, "The remaining people, who remain from the captivity there in the province, are in a very bad way and are subject to reviling there in the province, with Yerushalaim's wall broken down and its gateways set on fire." [4]When I heard these things I sat and cried and grieved for days. I was fasting and pleading before the God of the heavens.

[5]I said, 'Oh! Yahweh, God of the heavens, great and awe-inspiring God, keeping pact and commitment for people who are loyal to him and keep his orders! [6]Please may your ear become heeding and your eyes opened to listen to the plea of your servant that I'm making before you today, day and night, for the Yisra'elites [Israelites] your servants, making confession concerning the wrongdoings of the Yisra'elites that we have committed in relation to you. I and my ancestral household have done wrong. [7]We've acted very ruinously in relation to you. We haven't kept the orders, the decrees and the rulings with which you ordered Mosheh [Moses] your servant.

[8]Be mindful, please, of the word with which you ordered Mosheh your servant: "Should you people trespass, I for my part will scatter you among the peoples, [9]but should you turn back to me and keep my orders and do them, if the people who've been driven away are at the end of the heavens, from there I will collect them and bring them to the place where I chose to have my name dwell." [10]And they are your servants and your people whom you redeemed by your great energy and your strong hand. [11a]Oh! Lord, please may your ear become heeding to your servant's plea and to the plea of your servants who want to live in awe of your name. Please enable your servant to succeed today and give him compassion before this man.'

## Boldness (and discretion) as a king's servant

**2** [11b]Now I was the king's butler, and in the month of Nisan in the twentieth year of Artahshasta [Artaxerxes] the king, when wine was before him, I carried the wine and gave it to the king. I hadn't been in a bad way before him, [2]so the king said to me, 'Why is your face looking bad when you're not ill? This is nothing but something bad on your mind.' I became very much afraid, [3]but I said to the king, 'Long live the king! Why should my face not look bad when the town where my ancestors' graves are lies waste and its gateways have been consumed by fire?'

[4]The king said to me, 'What are you asking for?' I pleaded with the God of the heavens [5]and said to the king, 'If it seems good to the king and if your servant seems good before you, that you send me to Yehudah to the town of my ancestors' graves so that I may build it up.' [6]The king said to me, with the consort sitting beside him, 'How long will your journey be? When will you come back?' So it seemed good before the king and he sent me, and I gave him a date.

[7]I said to the king, 'If it seems good to the king, may they give me communiqués for the governors of Beyond-the-River so that they may let me pass until I come to Yehudah, [8]and a communiqué to Asaph the keeper of the park which belongs to the king so that he may give me logs for roofing the gateways of the fortress that belongs to the house, for the town wall and for the house to which I shall come.' The king gave them to me in accordance with the good hand of my God upon me. [9]I came to the governors of Beyond-the-River and gave them the king's communiqués. The king sent with me officers of a force and cavalry. [10]But Sanballat the Horonite and Tobiyyah the Ammonite servant heard, and it seemed very bad to them that someone had come to seek something good for the Yisra'elites.

## A secret survey

[11]I came to Yerushalaim and I was there for three days, [12]then I set to by night, I and

a few men with me. I didn't tell anyone what my God had put into my mind to do for Yerushalaim, and there was no animal with me except the animal that I was riding on. [13]I went out through the Ravine Gate by night, to the Jackals Spring and to the Rubbish Gate. I was examining the Yerushalaim walls that had been broken down and its gateways that had been consumed by fire. [14]I passed on to the Spring Gate and to the King's Pool, but there was no room for the animal under me to pass. [15]So I was going up through the wadi by night and I was examining the wall, then I went back and came in through the Ravine Gate.

Thus I went back, [16]while the overseers didn't know where I'd gone or what I was doing, and I hadn't until now told the Yehudahites, the priests, the important people, the overseers and the rest of the people who were going to be doing the work. [17]I said to them, 'You see the bad situation that we're in, that Yerushalaim lies waste and its gateways have been set on fire. Come, let's build up the Yerushalaim wall and no longer be subject to reviling.' [18]I told them of my God's hand, that it was good upon me, and also of the king's words that he said to me, and they said, 'Let's set to and build.' So they strengthened their hands for the good work.

[19]Sanballat the Horonite, Tobiyyah the Ammonite servant and Geshem the Arab heard, and they ridiculed us and despised us. They said, 'What's this thing that you're doing? Are you rebelling against the king?' [20]I sent back word to them: 'The God of the heavens – he'll enable us to succeed. We, his servants – we'll set to and build. You have no share or right or record in Yerushalaim.'

## Everyone played their part (1)

**3** So Elyashib the big priest and his brother priests set to and built up the Sheep Gate. They made it sacred and put in place its doors, and as far as the Hundred Tower they made it sacred, as far as Hanan'el's Tower;
[2]next to him the men of Yereho [Jericho] built;
next to him Zakkur ben Imri built;

[3]the Fish Gate, the sons of Hassena'ah built up; they roofed it and put in place its doors, its bolts and its bars;
[4]next to them Meremot ben Uriyyah son of Haqqots did the strengthening;
next to them Meshullam ben Berekyah son of Meshezab'el did the strengthening;
next to them Tsadoq ben Ba'ana did the strengthening;
[5]next to them the Teqo'ites did the strengthening, but their august people didn't give their neck to the service of their lord;
[6]the Yeshanah Gate, Yoyada ben Paseah and Meshullam ben Besodeyah did the strengthening of; they roofed it and put in place its doors, its bolts and its bars;
[7]next to them Melatyah the Gib'onite and Yadon the Meronotite did the strengthening (people of Gib'on and The Watchtower, the seat of the Beyond-the-River governor);
[8]next to him Uzzi'el ben Harhayah (goldsmiths) did the strengthening;
next to him Hananyah of the perfumers did the strengthening, but they abandoned Yerushalaim as far as the wide wall;
[9]next to them Rephayah ben Hur, official over half the district of Yerushalaim, did the strengthening;
[10]next to them Yedayah ben Harumaph did the strengthening, in front of his house;
next to him Hattush ben Hashabneyah did the strengthening;
[11]a second section Malkiyyah ben Harim and Hashshub ben Paha Mo'ab did the strengthening, and the Ovens Tower.

## Everyone played their part (2)

[12]Next to him Shallum ben Hallohesh, official over half the district of Yerushalaim, did the strengthening, he and his daughters;
[13]the Ravine Gate, Hanun and the inhabitants of Zanoah did the strengthening; they built it up and put in place its doors, its bolts and its bars, and 500 metres in the wall as far as the Rubbish Gate;

¹⁴the Rubbish Gate, Malkiyyah ben Rekab, official over the district of Bet-hakkerem, did the strengthening; he built it up and put in place its doors, its bolts and its bars;

¹⁵the Spring Gate, Shallun ben-Kol-hozeh the official over the district of The Watchtower did the strengthening; he built it up, covered it, and put in place its doors, its bolts and its bars, and the wall of the Shelah Pool belonging to the King's Garden, and as far as the steps going down from David's Town;

¹⁶after him Nehemyah ben Azbuq, official over half the district of Bet-tsur, did the strengthening as far as opposite David's graves, as far as the man-made pool and as far as the Strong Men's House;

¹⁷after him the Levites did the strengthening: Rehum ben Bani;

next to him Hashabyah, official over half the district of Qe'ilah, did the strengthening for his district;

¹⁸after him their brothers did the strengthening: Bavvay ben Henadad, official over half the district of Qe'ilah;

¹⁹next to him Ezer ben Yeshua, official over The Watchtower, did the strengthening of a second section, from opposite the ascent to the armoury at the corner;

²⁰after him Baruk ben Zakkay burned [with zeal]; he did the strengthening of a second section, from the corner as far as the entrance of the house of Elyashib the big priest.

## Everyone played their part (3)

²¹After him Meremot ben Uriyyah son of Haqqots did the strengthening of a second section, from the entrance of Elyashib's house and as far as the end of Elyashib's house;

²²after him the priests who were the people of the plain did the strengthening;

²³after him Binyamin and Hashshub did the strengthening opposite their house;

after him Azaryah ben Ma'aseyah son of Ananyah did the strengthening beside his house;

²⁴after him Binnuy ben Henadad did the strengthening of a second section, from the house of Azaryah to the corner, to the angle;

²⁵Palal ben Uzzay: from opposite the corner and the tower going out from the king's upper house which belongs to the court of the guard;

after him Pedayah ben Parosh ²⁶(the assistants were living on the Ophel as far as opposite the Water Gate to the east and the projecting tower);

²⁷after him the Teqo'ites did the strengthening of a second section from opposite the big projecting tower as far the Ophel wall;

²⁸above the Horses Gate, the priests did the strengthening, each one opposite his house;

²⁹after him Tsadoq ben Immer did the strengthening opposite his house;

after him Shema'yah ben Shekanyah, keeper of the East Gate, did the strengthening;

³⁰after him Hananyah ben Shelemyah and Hanun ben Tsalaph (the sixth) did the strengthening of a second section;

after him Meshullam ben Berekyah did the strengthening opposite his room;

³¹after him Malkiyyah of the goldsmiths did the strengthening as far as the house of the assistants and the merchants, opposite the Registration Gate and as far as the upper floor at the angle;

³²between the upper floor of the angle to the Sheep Gate the goldsmiths and the merchants did the strengthening.

## Reasons for discouragement

**4** When Sanballat heard that we were building up the wall, it enraged him. He was greatly provoked. He ridiculed the Yehudahites ²and said before his brothers and the Shomron [Samaria] force, 'What are the feeble Yehudahites doing? Will they abandon it for themselves? Will they sacrifice? Will they finish in the day? Will they bring to life the stones from the heaps of earth, when they're burnt?' ³Tobiyyah the Ammonite, being beside him, said, 'What they're building, if a fox went up, he'd breach their wall of stones.'

⁴'Listen, our God, because we've become an object of contempt. May their reviling turn

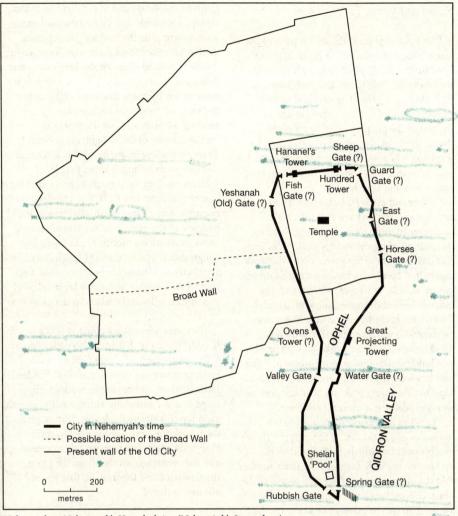

*Nehemiah 4: Nehemyah's Yerushalaim (Nehemiah's Jerusalem)*

back on their own head. Make them into spoil in a land of captivity. **5**Don't cover over their waywardness. Their wrongdoing should not be blotted out from before you, because they've uttered provocation in front of the builders.'

**6**So we built up the wall, and the entire wall joined up until it was half done. The mind of the people was on doing it. **7**But when Sanballat, Tobiyyah, the Arabs, the Ammonites and the Ashdodites heard that restoration of the Yerushalaim walls had progressed in that the broken parts had begun to close up, it enraged them very much, **8**and all of them conspired together to come to battle against Yerushalaim and cause confusion in it. **9**We

pleaded with our God and put in place a watch over them day and night in the face of them.
**10**But Yehudah said,

The carrier's energy has collapsed,
    and there is much earth.
We ourselves are not able
    to build up the wall.

**11**And our adversaries said, 'They won't know and they won't see when we come in among them and kill them, and stop the work.' **12**And when the Yehudahites who lived beside them came, they said to us ten times from all the places, 'You should come back to us.'

## Sword and trowel, faith and hope

[13]So I put in place at the lowest parts of the space behind the wall at the exposed points – I put the people in place by kin-groups with their swords, their lances and their bows. [14]I looked, and I stood up and said to the important people, to the overseers and to the rest of the people, 'Don't be afraid of them. The Lord, the one who is great and awe-inspiring – be mindful of him and do battle for your brothers, your sons and your daughters, your wives and your homes.'

[15]When our enemies heard that it had become known to us and that God had contravened their counsel, we went back to the wall, all of us, each to his work. [16]But from that day, half of my boys were doing the work and half of them were holding strongly on to lances, shields, bows and armour, with the officials behind the entire house of Yehudah [17]who were building up the wall. The basket-carriers who were transporting: with one hand he was doing the work and with one he was holding strongly on to the weapon. [18]The builders were fixed each with his sword on his hips, but they were building. And the person who sounded the horn was beside me.

[19]I said to the important people, to the overseers and to the rest of the people, 'There's much work, and widely spread, and we're divided on the wall, far away one from another. [20]At the place where you hear the sound of the horn, collect there to us. Our God – he'll battle for us.' [21]So we were doing the work with half of them holding strongly on to lances, from when dawn came up until the stars came out. [22]Further, at that time I said to the people, 'Each man and his boy should stay the night within Yerushalaim; they'll be a watch for us at night and they'll work by day.' [23]I, my brothers, my boys and the men in the watch behind me – we didn't take off our clothes, each one, with his weapon at the water.

## The community's moral challenge

**5** But there was a great outcry by the people and their wives towards their Yehudahite brothers. [2]There were some saying, 'Our sons and our daughters, we are many. We must get grain so we can eat and live.' [3]There were some saying, 'Our fields, our vineyards, our homes – we're mortgaging them so we can get grain during a famine.' [4]And there were some saying, 'We've borrowed silver for the king's tax – our fields and our vineyards. [5]Now, our flesh is the same as our brothers' flesh, our children are the same as their children, but here – we're binding our sons and our daughters as servants. Some of our daughters are bound. There's no power in our hand; our fields and our vineyards belong to other people.'

[6]It enraged me very much when I heard their outcry and these words. [7]When my mind had counselled me, I argued with the important people and the overseers: 'Are you advancing loans, one with his brother?', and I set a big congregation against them. [8]I said to them, 'We acquired our Yehudahite brothers who'd been sold to the Gentiles, as far as it lay in us. Will you indeed sell your brothers so that they may be sold to us?'

They were silent. They couldn't find a word. [9]I said, 'The thing that you're doing isn't good. Will you not walk in awe of God to avoid reviling before our Gentile enemies? [10]Indeed, I, my brothers and my boys are advancing loans of silver and grain with them. Please let's abandon this advancing loans. [11]Please give them back this very day their fields, their vineyards, their olive trees and their houses, and the percentage on the silver, the grain, the new wine and the fresh oil that you're advancing them.'

## Putting your money where your mouth is

[12]They said, 'We'll give them back, and we won't seek anything from them. We'll act in this way, as you're saying.' So I called for the priests and swore them to act in accordance with this word. [13]I also shook out my pocket and said, 'May God shake out like this anyone who does not implement this word, from his house and from his labour. May he become shaken out like this and empty.' The entire congregation said 'Yes', and praised Yahweh, and the people acted in accordance with this word.

[14]Further, from the day I was ordered to become governor in the country of Yehudah, from the twentieth year until the thirty-second

year of Artahshasta the king, twelve years, I
with my brothers didn't eat the governor's food.
¹⁵The previous governors who were before
me made things heavy for the people, and for
food and wine for one day took from them
forty sheqels of silver (further, their boys had
power over the people). I didn't do so, out of
awe for God.

¹⁶And further, I strengthened the work on
this wall; we didn't acquire fields, and all my
boys were collected there for the work. ¹⁷The
Yehudahites and the overseers, 150 individuals,
and the people who came to us from the
nations that were round us, were at my table.
¹⁸What was being prepared for one day, an ox,
six choice sheep, and birds, they were prepared
for me with all kinds of wine in quantity at an
interval of ten days, but with this I didn't seek
the governor's food, because the service was
heavy on this people.

¹⁹Be mindful for me of all that I've done for
this people, my God, for good.

## Don't trust anybody

**6** When it came to be heard by Sanballat,
Tobiyyah, by Geshem the Arab and by the
rest of our enemies, that we had built up the
wall and that no breach was left in it (though
up to that time I hadn't put in place doors in
the gateways), ²Sanballat and Geshem sent to
me: 'Come, let's meet together at Kephirim in
Ono Valley.' But these men were thinking to do
something bad to me, ³so I sent envoys to them
saying, 'I'm doing some big work and I can't
come down. Why should the work stop when
I slacken hold of it and come down to you?'
⁴They sent me this same message four times,
and I sent this same message back to them.
⁵Sanballat sent me this same message with his
boy a fifth time, with an open communiqué in
his hand, ⁶written in it: 'Among the nations it's
come to be heard (and Gashmu says): you and
the Yehudahites are thinking to rebel. That's
why you're building up the wall. You're going
to be their king, according to these words.
⁷You've also put prophets in place to call out in
Yerushalaim about you, "A king in Yehudah".
It will now make itself heard to the king,
these very words. So now go, and let's take
counsel together.'

⁸I sent to him: 'Nothing like these things
that you're saying has happened; rather
you're devising things out of your own mind',
⁹because they were all of them making us
afraid, saying 'Their hands will slacken from
the work and it won't be done.'

So now strengthen my hands.

## The work completed

¹⁰I myself came to the house of Shema'yah
ben Delayah son of Mehetab'el, when he was
confined. He had said,

Let's meet in God's house,
    inside the palace.
Let's shut the doors of the palace,
    because they're coming to kill you,
    by night they're coming to kill you.

¹¹I said, 'Will a person like me take flight?
And who is there like me who may go into the
palace and live? I won't come.' ¹²I realized: there,
God had not sent him, because he'd spoken
the prophecy about me when Obiyyah and
Sanballat had hired him. ¹³It was to this end that
he'd been hired, to the end that I'd be afraid and
I'd act in this way and do wrong, and they'd have
a bad name, in order that they could revile me.
¹⁴Be mindful, my God, of Tobiyyah, and of
Sanballat in accordance with these acts of his,
and also of Noadyah the prophetess and of the
rest of the prophets who were making me afraid.
¹⁵The wall was complete on the twenty-fifth
of Elul, after fifty-two days. ¹⁶When all our
enemies heard, all the nations that were round
us were afraid, and they fell greatly in their
own eyes because they acknowledged that this
work had been done by our God.

¹⁷Also in those days, the important people
among the Yehudahites were having many
communiqués go to Tobiyyah, and ones
that were Tobiyyah's were coming to them,
¹⁸because many people in Yehudah were under
oath to him, because he was a son-in-law of
Shekanyah ben Arah, and Yehohanan his son
had taken the daughter of Meshullam ben
Berekyah. ¹⁹Further, they were saying good
things about him before me, and they were
letting my words go out to him when Tobiyyah
sent communiqués to make me afraid.

## The need for a new population

**7** When the wall was built and I'd put in place the doors, they appointed the gatemen, the singers and the Levites. ²I ordered in charge of Yerushalaim Hanani my brother and Hananyah the fortress officer, because he was truly a trustworthy man and one who lived in awe of God more than many. ³I said to them, 'The Yerushalaim gateways will not open until the sun is hot; until those men are standing in position they must shut the doors and hold them fast. And put in place the inhabitants of Yerushalaim as watches, one individual at his watch and another individual opposite his own house.'

⁴Now the town was wide on both sides and big, but the people within it was small, and there were no houses built up. ⁵My God put it into my mind and I collected the important people, the overseers and the people, for enrolment by genealogy. I found the document with the roll of the people who went up at the first, and found written in it:

⁶These are the people of the province who went up from among the captives in exile whom Nebukadne'tstsar king of Babel had exiled and who went back to Yerushalaim and to Yehudah, each to his town, ⁷who came with Zerubbabel, Yeshua, Nehemyah, Azaryah, Ra'amyah, Nahamani, Mordecay, Bilshan, Misperet, Bigvay, Nehum, Ba'anah.

The number of the men belonging to the Yisra'elite people:

⁸sons of Par'osh 2,172
⁹sons of Shephatyah 372
¹⁰sons of Arah 652
¹¹sons of Pahat Mo'ab (by the sons of Yeshua and Yo'ab) 2,818
¹²sons of Elam 1,254
¹³sons of Zattu 845
¹⁴sons of Zakkay 760
¹⁵sons of Binnuy 648
¹⁶sons of Bebay 628
¹⁷sons of Azgad 2,322
¹⁸sons of Adoniqam 667
¹⁹sons of Bigvay 2,067
²⁰sons of Adin 655
²¹sons of Ater (by Hizqiyyah) 98
²²sons of Hashum 328
²³sons of Bezay 324
²⁴sons of Hariph 112
²⁵sons of Gib'on 95
²⁶people of Bet-lehem and Netophah 188
²⁷people of Anatot 128
²⁸people of Bet-azmavet 42
²⁹sons of Ye'arim Township, Kephirah and Be'erot 743
³⁰sons of The Height and Geba 621
³¹people of Mikmas 122
³²people of Bet-el and Ha'ay 123
³³people of the other Nebo 52
³⁴people of the other Elam 1,254
³⁵sons of Harim 320
³⁶sons of Yereho 345
³⁷sons of Lod, Hadid and Ono 721
³⁸sons of Sena'ah 3,930

## Ministers on the roll

³⁹The priests:
sons of Yeda'yah (by the household of Yeshua) 973
⁴⁰sons of Immer 1,052
⁴¹sons of Pashhur 1,247
⁴²sons of Harim 1,017

⁴³The Levites:
sons of Yeshua (by Qadmi'el, by the sons of Hodavyah) 74

⁴⁴The singers:
sons of Asaph 148

⁴⁵The gatemen:
sons of Shallum
sons of Ater
sons of Talmon
sons of Aqqub
sons of Hatita
sons of Shobay altogether 138

⁴⁶The assistants:
sons of Tsiha
sons of Hasupha
sons of Tabba'ot
⁴⁷sons of Qeros
sons of Si'ah
sons of Padon
⁴⁸sons of Lebanah
sons of Hagabah
sons of Shalmay
⁴⁹sons of Hanan
sons of Giddel
sons of Gahar
⁵⁰sons of Re'ayah
sons of Retsin
sons of Neqodah
⁵¹sons of Gazzam
sons of Uzza
sons of Paseah
⁵²sons of Besay
sons of Me'unim
sons of Nephishesim
⁵³sons of Baqbuq
sons of Haqupha
sons of Harhur
⁵⁴sons of Batslit
sons of Mehida
sons of Harsha
⁵⁵sons of Barqos
sons of Sisera
sons of Temah
⁵⁶sons of Netsiah
sons of Hatipha

⁵⁷The sons of Shelomoh's [Solomon's] servants:
sons of Sotay
sons of Sopheret
sons of Perida
⁵⁸sons of Ya'ela
sons of Darqon
sons of Giddel
⁵⁹sons of Shephatyah
sons of Hattil
sons of Pokeret Hatstsebayim
sons of Amon

<sup>60</sup>All the assistants and the sons of Shelomoh's servants 392.

<sup>61</sup>These are the people who came up from Tel Melah, Tel Harsha, Kerub, Addan and Immer, but who could not tell their ancestral household and their origin, whether they were from Yisra'el:

<sup>62</sup>sons of Delayah sons of Haqqots
sons of Tobiyyah sons of Barzillay (who
sons of Neqoda had taken a wife
642 from the daughters of
 Barzillay the Gil'adite
<sup>63</sup>Of the priests: and was called by
sons of Habayah their name):

<sup>64</sup>these looked for their record in the enrolment by genealogy but it was not found, and they were deconsecrated from the priesthood. <sup>65</sup>The administrator said to them that they should not eat of the very sacred things until there was a priest standing with Urim and Tummim.

## The need for a new community

<sup>66</sup>The entire congregation altogether 42,360; <sup>67</sup>apart from their servants and handmaids: these were 7,337; and they had 245 male and female singers; <sup>68</sup>their horses 736; their mules 245; <sup>69</sup>camels 435; donkeys 6,720.

<sup>70</sup>Some of the ancestral heads gave to the work. The administrator gave to the treasury gold (1,000 drakmas), basins (50), priests' robes (530). <sup>71</sup>Some of the ancestral heads gave to the work treasury gold (20,000 drakmas) and silver (2,200 minas). <sup>72</sup>What the remainder of the people gave: gold (20,000 drakmas), silver (2,000) and priests' robes (67).

<sup>73</sup>The priests, the Levites, the gatemen, the singers, some of the people, the assistants and all Yisra'el went to live in their towns. The seventh month arrived, with the Yisra'elites in their towns,

**8** and the entire people gathered as one person to the square that's before the Water Gate, and said to Ezra the scholar to bring Mosheh's instruction document with

which Yahweh had ordered Yisra'el. <sup>2</sup>Ezra the priest brought the instruction before the congregation (men and women and all who could understand when they listened) on the first day of the seventh month. <sup>3</sup>He read out in it before the square which is before the Water Gate from dawn until midday, in front of the men and the women and the people who could understand, with the ears of the entire people towards the instruction document.

<sup>4</sup>Ezra the scholar stood on a wooden tower that they made for the thing. There stood beside him Mattityah, Shema, Anayah, Uriyyah, Hilqiyyah and Ma'aseyah on his right, and at his left Pedayah, Misha'el, Malkiyyah, Hashum, Hashbaddanah, Zekaryah, Meshullam. <sup>5</sup>Ezra opened the document before the eyes of the entire people, because he was above the entire people, and as he opened it, the entire people stood. <sup>6</sup>Ezra blessed Yahweh, the great God, and the entire people answered, 'Yes, yes', with a raising of their hands, then bent their heads and bowed low to Yahweh, faces on the ground. <sup>7</sup>Yeshua, Bani, Sherebyah, Yamin, Aqqub, Shabbetay, Hodiyyah, Ma'aseyah, Qelita, Azaryah, Yozabad, Hanan, Pela'yah, and the Levites, helped the people understand the instruction, with the people in their place. <sup>8</sup>They read out in the document, in God's instruction, explaining and giving insight so they understood the reading.

## Mourning or celebration?

<sup>9</sup>Nehemyah (he was the administrator), Ezra the priest-scholar and the Levites who were helping the people understand said to the entire people, 'Today is sacred for Yahweh your God. Don't mourn, don't cry', because the entire people were crying as they heard the words of the instruction. <sup>10</sup>He said to them, 'Go, eat rich food, drink sweet drinks and send off portions to anyone who has nothing prepared, because today is sacred for our Lord. Don't be in pain, because joy in Yahweh is your protection.' <sup>11</sup>The Levites were silencing the entire people, saying 'Hush, because today is sacred, don't be in pain.' <sup>12</sup>So the entire people went to eat and drink and send off portions and make great rejoicing, because

they understood the things that they had made known to them.

[13]On the second day, the ancestral heads of the entire people, the priests and the Levites gathered to Ezra the scholar, to get insight into the words of the instruction. [14]They found written in the instruction that Yahweh had ordered by means of Mosheh that the Yisra'elites should live in bivouacs [sukkot] in the festival in the seventh month [15]and that they should make heard and should pass on an announcement in all their towns and in Yerushalaim: 'Go out into the mountains and bring olive branches, pine-tree branches, myrtle branches, palm branches and leafy tree branches to make bivouacs, as it is written.'

[16]So the people went out and brought them, and made themselves bivouacs, each person on his roof, or in their courtyards, in the courtyards of God's house, in the square at the Water Gate or in the square at the Ephrayim Gate. [17]The entire congregation of people who had come back from the captivity made bivouacs and lived in the bivouacs, because the Yisra'elites had not done so since the days of Yehoshua [Joshua] ben Nun until that day, and there was very great rejoicing.

[18]So he read out in the document of God's instruction day by day, from the first day until the last day. They made festival for seven days and an assembly on the eighth day, in accordance with the ruling.

## How to make your confession

**9** On the twenty-fourth day of this month the Yisra'elites assembled with fasting and with sack, and earth on themselves. [2]The offspring of Yisra'el distinguished themselves from all foreigners and stood and confessed their wrongdoings and their ancestors' wayward acts. [3]They got up in their position and read out in Yahweh their God's instruction document for a quarter of the day, and for a quarter they were confessing and bowing low to Yahweh their God.

[4]On the Levites' stairway Yeshua and Bani (Qadmi'el, Shebanyah, Bunni, Sherebyah, Bani, Kenani) got up and cried out in a loud voice to Yahweh their God. [5]The Levites Yeshua

and Qadmi'el (Bani, Hashabneyah, Sherebyah, Hodiyyah, Petahyah) said, 'Get up, bless Yahweh your God from age to age:

May people bless your glorious name,
    though exalted above all blessing and praise.
[6]You are Yahweh, you alone;
    you made the heavens,
The highest heavens and all their army,
    the earth and all that's on it,
    the seas and all that's in them.
You give life to all of them,
    and the army in the heavens bow low to you.

[7]You are Yahweh, the God who chose Abram and got him to go out from Ur of the Kasdites, and made his name Abraham. [8]You found his mind trustworthy before you and you solemnized the pact with him to give the country of the Kena'anite [Canaanite], the Hittite, the Amorite, the Perizzite, the Yebusite and the Girgashite – to give [it] to his offspring. You implemented your words, because you're faithful.

[9]You saw our ancestors' humbling in Misrayim [Egypt] and you heard their cry at the Reed Sea. [10]You performed signs and proofs against Par'oh [Pharaoh] and against all his servants and against all the people of his country because you acknowledged that they asserted themselves over them, and you made a name for yourself this very day.

## Self-assertion and pardon

[11]You split the sea before them and they passed through the middle of the sea on dry ground, but you threw their pursuers into the depths, like a stone into vigorous water. [12]With a cloud column you led them by day, and with a fire column by night, to give light for them on the way in which they were to go. [13]On Mount Sinai you came down and spoke with them from the heavens. You gave them upright rulings and truthful instructions, good decrees and orders. [14]Your sacred sabbath you caused to be acknowledged by them, and you ordained for them orders, decrees and instruction by means of Mosheh your servant. [15]Bread from the heavens you gave them for their hunger, and you made water go out from

a cliff for them, for their thirst. You said to them to go and take possession of the country that you had raised your hand [to swear] to give them.

¹⁶But they, our ancestors, asserted themselves, toughened their neck and didn't listen to your orders. ¹⁷They refused to listen and were not mindful of your extraordinary deeds, which you'd done with them. They toughened their neck and appointed a head so as to go back to their serfdom, in their rebelliousness.

But you are a pardoning God, gracious and compassionate, long-tempered and big in commitment, and you didn't abandon them, ¹⁸even when they made themselves a calf figurine and said, "This is your God who got you up from Misrayim." They committed great acts of disdain. ¹⁹But you in your great compassion – you didn't abandon them in the wilderness. The cloud column didn't depart from them by day to lead them on the way, nor the fire column by night to give light to them and on the way in which they were to go.

## Provision and rebellion

²⁰You gave them your good spirit to enable them to succeed. You didn't withhold your *maan* [manna] from their mouth and you gave them water for their thirst. ²¹When for forty years you provided for them in the wilderness, they didn't lack, their clothes didn't wear out and their feet didn't swell. ²²You gave them kingdoms and peoples, and allocated these as a border. They took possession of the country of Sihon, which was the country of the king of Heshbon, and the country of Og king of Bashan.

²³You made their children as many as the stars in the heavens and brought them to the country that you said to their parents to go in to possess. ²⁴The children came and took possession of the country. You made the inhabitants of the country, the Kena'anites, bow down before them, and you gave them into their hand, both their kings and the peoples of the country, to do with them in accordance with what was acceptable to them. ²⁵They took fortified towns and rich land and took possession of houses full of every good thing: hewn cisterns, vineyards, olives and fruit trees,

in large number. They ate, were full, grew stocky and revelled in your great goodness.

²⁶But they defied and rebelled against you and threw your instruction behind their back. They killed your prophets who testified against them to get them to come back to you, and they committed great acts of disdain. ²⁷You gave them into the hand of their adversaries and they oppressed them. In their time of pressure they cried out to you and from the heavens you yourself would listen. In accordance with your great compassion you gave them deliverers and they delivered them from the hand of their adversaries.

## Servants or serfs

²⁸But when things settled down for them, they again dealt badly before you. You abandoned them into the hand of their enemies and they held sway over them. They again cried out to you, and from the heavens you yourself would listen and rescue them in accordance with your great compassion, time after time. ²⁹You testified against them to get them to come back to your instruction, but they themselves asserted themselves and didn't listen to your orders. They did wrong by your rulings, which a person should act on and live by. They presented a defiant shoulder, they toughened their neck and they didn't listen. ³⁰You prolonged things for them for many years and testified against them by your spirit by means of your prophets, but they didn't give ear, so you gave them into the hand of the peoples of the countries. ³¹But in your great compassion you didn't make an end of them and you didn't abandon them, because you are a God gracious and compassionate.

³²So now, our great God, strong and awe-inspiring, keeping pact and commitment, may all the suffering not seem small before you that has found us, our kings, our officials, our priests, our prophets, our ancestors and all your people, from the days of the kings of Ashshur until this day. ³³You are in the right over everything that has come upon us, because you've acted truthfully, but we've acted faithlessly. ³⁴Our kings, our officials, our priests and our ancestors – they didn't act on your instruction and they didn't heed your orders and your affirmations that you

testified against them. [35]Despite their kingship and despite your great goodness that you gave them and despite the wide and rich country that you gave before them, they didn't serve you and they didn't turn back from their bad ways.

[36]Here we are, serfs today. The country you gave our ancestors to eat its fruit and its goodness, here we are, serfs on it. [37]Its great yield belongs to the kings that you've put over us because of our wrongdoings. They're ruling over our bodies and among our animals in accordance with what is acceptable to them. We're under great pressure.

## Putting your life where your mouth is

[38]Because of all this, we are confirming a pledge and putting it in writing, and on the sealed document are our officials, our Levites and our priests.'

**10** So on the sealed documents are Nehemyah ben Hakalyah, the administrator and

| | |
|---|---|
| Tsidqiyyah | Meremot |
| [2]Serayah | Obadyah |
| Azaryah | [6]Daniyye'l |
| Yirmeyah | Ginneton |
| [3]Pashhur | Baruk |
| Amaryah | [7]Meshullam |
| Malkiyyah | Abiyyah |
| [4]Hattush | Miyyamin |
| Shebanyah | [8]Ma'azyah |
| Malluk | Bilgay |
| [5]Harim | Shema'yah |

These were the priests. [9]The Levites:

Yeshua ben Azanyah, Binnuy of the sons of Henadad, Qadmi'el; [10]their brothers Shebanyah, Hodiyyah, Qelita, Pela'yah, Hanan, [11]Mika, Rehob, Hashabyah, [12]Zakkur, Sherebyah, Shebanyah, [13]Hodiyyah, Bani, Beninu.

[14]The heads of the people:

| | |
|---|---|
| Par'osh | Bani |
| Pahat Mo'ab | [15]Bunni |
| Elam | Azgad |
| Zattu | Bebay |

| | |
|---|---|
| [16]Adoniyyah | [22]Pelatyah |
| Bigvay | Hanan |
| Adin | Anayah |
| [17]Ater | [23]Hoshea |
| Hizqiyyah | Hananyah |
| Azzur | Hashshub |
| [18]Hodiyyah | [24]Hallohesh |
| Hashum | Pilha |
| Betsay | Shobeq |
| [19]Hariph | [25]Rehum |
| Anatot | Hashabnah |
| Nebay | Ma'aseyah |
| [20]Magpi'ash | [26]and Ahiyyah |
| Meshullam | Hanan |
| Hezir | Anan |
| [21]Meshezab'el | [27]Malluk |
| Tsadoq | Harim |
| Yaddua | Ba'anah |

[28]The remainder of the people, the priests, the Levites, the gatemen, the singers, the assistants and everyone who made themselves distinct from the peoples of the countries to God's instruction, their wives, their sons and their daughters, everyone who knows, having understanding, [29]were taking strong hold of their brothers, the august ones among them, and coming into a curse and into an oath to walk by God's instruction that was given by means of Mosheh, God's servant, and to keep and act on all the orders of Yahweh our Lord, and his rulings and his decrees.

## On being specific

[30]Namely:

We will not give our daughters to the peoples of the country and we will not take their daughters for our sons. [31]The peoples of the country who bring items of merchandise or any grain on the sabbath day to sell, we will not get from them on the sabbath, or on a sacred day. We will leave alone the seventh year and the loan linked to any pledge. [32]We have put in place for ourselves orders to impose on ourselves one third of a sheqel per year for the service of our God's house, [33]for the bread in the row, the regular grain offering and for the regular burnt offering, that of the sabbaths, of the

new months, for the appointed occasions,
for sacred things and for purification
offerings to make expiation for Yisra'el,
and all the work in our God's house.
³⁴We have let lots fall for the wood offering
(the priests, the Levites and the people)
to bring it to our God's house by ancestral
households at designated times year by
year to burn up on the altar of Yahweh our
God, as it is written in the instruction.
³⁵And to bring the first fruits of our ground
and the first fruits of every fruit of every
tree year by year for Yahweh's house,
³⁶and the firstborn of our sons and of our
animals, as it is written in the instruction,
and to bring the firstborn of our cattle and
of our flocks to our God's house to the
priests who minister in our God's house.
³⁷We will bring the first of our dough, our
contributions, and the fruit of every tree,
new wine and fresh oil, to the priests to the
halls in our God's house, and the tenth of
our ground to the Levites; the Levites are
the ones who collect the tenths in all the
towns where we serve. ³⁸The priest, the son
of Aaron, is to be with the Levites during the
tenthing by the Levites, and the Levites are
to take up a tenth of the tenth to our God's
house, to the halls of the treasure-house,
³⁹because the Yisra'elites and the Levites
are to bring to the halls the contribution of
grain, new wine and fresh oil. The sanctuary
articles, the priests who minister, the
gatemen and the singers are there. We will
not abandon our God's house.

## The sacred town (1)

**11** The people's officials lived in
Yerushalaim, while the remainder of
the people let lots fall to get one out of ten to
come to live in Yerushalaim, the sacred town,
while nine tenths were in the towns. ²The
people blessed all the individuals who decided
freely to live in Yerushalaim.
    ³These are the heads of the province who
lived in Yerushalaim; while in the towns of
Yehudah people lived in their towns, each
individual on his holding, Yisra'el, the priests,
the Levites, the assistants and the descendants
of Shelomoh's servants, ⁴and some of the

Yehudahites and some of the Binyaminites
[Benjaminites] lived in Yerushalaim.

    Of the Yehudahites:
    Atayah ben Uzziyyah son of Zekaryah son
    of Amaryah son of Shephatyah son
    of Mahalal'el of the descendants of Perets;
    ⁵and Ma'aseyah ben Baruk son of Kol-
    hozeh son of Hazayah son of Adayah son
    of Yoyarib son of Zekaryah son of the
    Shilonite.
    ⁶All the descendants of Perets who were
    living in Yerushalaim: 468 forceful men.
    ⁷These are the Binyaminites:
    Sallu ben Meshullam son of Yo'ed son of
    Pedayah son of Qolayah son of Ma'aseyah
    son of Iti'el son of Yesha'yah;
    ⁸and after him Gabbay, Sallay: 928.
    ⁹Yo'el ben Zikri was appointee in charge
    of them;
    and Yehudah ben Hassenu'ah was second-
    in-command over the town.
    ¹⁰Of the priests:
    Yeda'yah ben Yoyarib, Yakin, ¹¹Serayah ben
    Hilqiyyah son of Meshullam son of Tsadoq
    son of Merayot son of Ahitub, chief over
    God's house, ¹²and their brothers doing
    the work for the house: 822;
    Adayah ben Yeroham son of Pelalyah son
    of Amtsi son of Zekaryah son of Pashhur
    son of Malkiyyah, ¹³and his brothers,
    ancestral heads: 242;
    and Amashsay ben Azar'el son of Ahzai
    son of Meshillemot son of Immer, ¹⁴and
    their brothers, forceful strong men: 128;
    Zabdi'el ben Haggedolim was appointee in
    charge of them.

## The sacred town (2)

    ¹⁵Of the Levites:
    Shema'yah ben Hashshub, son of Azriqam
    son of Hashabyah son of Bunni;
    ¹⁶and Shabbetay and Yozabad in charge of
    the outside work for God's house, of the
    heads of the Levites;
    ¹⁷Mattanyah ben Mikah son of Zabdi son
    of Asaph, head; at prayer, the one who
    began the confession;
    Baqbuqyah, second-in-command, one of
    his brothers;

and Abda ben Shammua son of Galal son
of Yedutun.
[18]All the Levites in the sacred town: 284.
[19]The gatemen:
Aqqub, Talmon and their brothers who
watched at the gateways: 172.
[20]The remainder of Yisra'el, the priests, the
Levites in all the towns of Yehudah, each on
his property.
[21]The assistants were living on the Ophel;
Tsipha and Gishpa were in charge of the
assistants.
[22]The Levites' appointee in Yerushalaim
was Uzzi ben Bani son of Hashabyah son
of Mattanyah son of Mika, of the Asaphite
singers, in charge of the work in God's
house, [23]because there was an order from
the king concerning them, a pledge about
the singers, each day's requirement in its day.
[24]Petahyah ben Meshezab'el, of the
descendants of Zerah son of Yehudah,
was at the king's hand in connection with
everything regarding the people.
[25]As for the villages, with their fields:
some of the Yehudahites lived in Arba's
Township and its daughter-towns,
in Dibon and its daughter-towns, and in
Yeqabtse'el and its villages, [26]in Yeshua,
in Moladah, in Bet Pelet, [27]in Hatsar
Shu'al, in Be'er Sheba and its daughter-
towns, [28]in Tsiqlag, in Mekonah and its
daughter-towns, [29]in En Rimmon, in
Tsorah, in Yarmut, [30]Zanoah, Adullam
and their villages, Lakish and its
fields, and Azeqah and its daughter-
towns. So they camped from Be'er-sheba
to the Hinnom Ravine.
[31]The Binyaminites:
from Geba, Mikmash, Ayyah, and Bet-el
and its daughter-towns; [32]Anatot, Nob,
Ananyah, [33]Hatsor, Ramah, Gittayim,
[34]Hadid, Tsebo'im, Neballat, [35]Lod and
Ono, Craftsmen's Ravine. [36]Some of the
Levites who were Yehudah's allocations
belonged to Binyamin.

*Priests and Levites in the community*

**12** These are the priests and the Levites
who went up with Zerubbabel ben
She'alti'el and Yeshua:

| | |
|---|---|
| Serayah | Abiyyah |
| Yirmeyah | [5]Miyyamin |
| Ezra | Ma'adyah |
| [2]Amaryah | Bilgah |
| Malluka | [6]Shema'yah |
| Hattush | Yoyarib |
| [3]Shekanyah | Yeda'yah |
| Rehum | [7]Sallu |
| Meramot | Amoq |
| [4]Iddo | Hilqiyyah |
| Ginnetoy | Yeda'yah |

These were the heads of the priests and their
brothers in the time of Yeshua. [8]The Levites:
Yeshua, Binnuy, Qadmi'el, Sherebyah, and
Yehudah;
Mattanyah, in charge of confession songs, he
and his brothers;
[9]Baqbuqyah and Unni, their brothers, were
opposite them for the watches.
[10]Yeshua fathered Yoyaqim, Yoyaqim
fathered Elyashib, Elyashib fathered
Yoyada, [11]Yoyada fathered Yonatan,
Yonatan fathered Yaddua.
[12]In the time of Yoyaqim, priests who were
the ancestral heads were:

| | |
|---|---|
| for Serayah, Merayah | [17]for Abiyyah, Zikri |
| for Yirmeyah, | for Minyamin |
| Hananyah | for Mo'adyah, Piltay |
| [13]for Ezra, | [18]for Bilgah, Shammua |
| Meshullam | for Shema'yah, |
| for Amaryah, | Yehonatan |
| Yehohanan | [19]and for Yoyarib, |
| [14]for Meliku, Yonatan | Mattenay |
| for Shebanyah, | for Yeda'yah, Uzzi |
| Yoseph | [20]for Sallay, Qallay |
| [15]for Harim, Adna | for Amoq, Eber |
| for Merayot, Helqay | [21]for Hilqiyyah, |
| [16]for Iddo, Zekaryah | Hashabyah |
| for Ginneton, | for Yeda'yah, Netan'el |
| Meshullam | |

[22]The Levites in the time of Elyashib, Yoyada
and Yohanan, and Yaddua, written down as
ancestral heads (and the priests in the reign
of Doryavesh the Parsite); [23]the Levites as
ancestral heads written down on the document
about things of the time right up to the time
of Yohanan ben Elyashib; [24]so the Levites' heads:
Hashabyah, Sherebyah, Yeshua ben Qadmi'el
and their brothers opposite them, for

praising, for confessing, by the order
of David the supernatural man, watch
responding to watch;
<sup>25</sup>Mattanyah, Baqbuqyah, Obadyah,
Meshullam, Talmon, Aqqub, keeping
watch as gatemen at the storerooms by the
gateways.
<sup>26</sup>These were in the time of Yoyaqim ben
Yeshua son of Yotsadaq, and in the time of
Nehemyah the governor and Ezra the priest-
scholar.

## Dedication choirs

<sup>27</sup>At the dedication of the Yerushalaim wall,
they looked for the Levites from all their places
to get them to come to Yerushalaim to make
a dedication with rejoicing, with confessions
and with song, cymbals, mandolins and with
guitars. <sup>28</sup>The singers gathered both from the
plain round Yerushalaim and from the villages
of the Netophatites, <sup>29</sup>from Bet Hagilgal, and
from the fields of Geba and Azmavet, because
the singers had built themselves villages round
Yerushalaim. <sup>30</sup>The priests and the Levites
purified themselves and purified the people,
the gateways and the wall.

<sup>31</sup>I got the officials of Yehudah to go up on to
the wall and I put in place two big confessions
and processions:

To the right on the wall to the Rubbish
Gate. <sup>32</sup>Hosha'yah and half the
officials of Yehudah followed them,
<sup>33</sup>with Azaryah, Ezra and Meshullam,
<sup>34</sup>Yehudah, Binyamin, Shema'yah,
Yirmeyah, <sup>35</sup>some of the priests' sons
with trumpets, Zekaryah ben Yonatan
son of Shema'yah son of Mattanyah son
of Mikayah son of Zakkur son of Asaph,
<sup>36</sup>his brothers Shema'yah and Azar'el,
Milalay, Gilalay, Ma'ay, Netan'el, Yehudah,
Hanani, with the musical instruments
of David the supernatural man, and
Ezra the scholar before them. <sup>37</sup>Above
the Spring Gate, straight ahead of them
they went up the ascent to David's Town
by the ascent to the wall, above David's
house, and as far as the Water Gate on
the east.
<sup>38</sup>The second confession which went the
opposite way with me behind it and half

the people, on the wall above the Ovens
Tower as far as the wide wall, <sup>39</sup>and above
the Ephrayim Gate, by the Yeshanah Gate,
by the Fish Gate, Hananel's Tower, the
Hundred Tower and as far as the Sheep
Gate. They halted at the Guard Gate.
<sup>40</sup>The two confessions halted at God's
house, as did I and half the overseers
with me, <sup>41</sup>and the priests Elyaqim,
Ma'aseyah, Minyamin, Mikayah, Elyo'enay,
Zekaryah, Hananyah, with trumpets,
<sup>42</sup>and Ma'aseyah, Shema'yah, El'azar, Uzzi,
Yehohanan, Malkiyyah, Elam and Ezer.
The singers made themselves heard, with
Yizrahyah the appointee. <sup>43</sup>They made big
sacrifices that day and rejoiced, because
God had enabled them to rejoice greatly.
The women and the children also rejoiced.
The rejoicing in Yerushalaim was heard
from afar.

## Intermarriage again

<sup>44</sup>On that day they appointed people over
the treasury rooms for the contributions, for
first fruits and for the tenths, to collect in
them (for the fields belonging to the towns)
the portions mentioned by the instruction
for the priests and for the Levites, because
there was rejoicing in Yehudah over the priests
and over the Levites who stood <sup>45</sup>and kept
their God's watch and the purity watch, and
the singers and the gatemen, in accordance
with the order of David, Shelomoh his son
<sup>46</sup>(because in the days of David and Asaph
of old, there were heads of the singers and
a song of praise and confession to God).
<sup>47</sup>In the days of Zerubbabel and in the days
of Nehemyah all Yisra'el were giving the
singers and the gatemen's portions, each day's
requirement in its day, and making things
sacred for the Levites, while the Levites were
making things sacred for the Aaronites.

**13** On that day there was a reading out
in Mosheh's document in the ears of
the people and it was found written in it that
an Ammonite or Mo'abite should not come
into God's congregation, permanently,
<sup>2</sup>because they did not meet the Yisra'elites
with bread and with water but hired Bil'am
[Balaam] to slight them (but our God turned

the slighting into blessing). ³When they heard the instruction, they distinguished the entire mixed crowd from Yisra'el.

⁴Before this, Elyashib the priest had been put in a hall in our God's house. Being near to Tobiyyah, ⁵he had made for him a big hall where before they had been putting the grain offering, the incense, the articles, the tenth of grain, new wine and fresh oil, the order for the Levites, the singers and the gatemen, and the contribution for the priests.

## More frustrations

⁶During all this time I was not in Yerushalaim because in the thirty-second year of Artahshasta king of Babel I came to the king, but at the end of a period of time I asked of the king ⁷and came to Yerushalaim. I considered the bad thing that Elyashib had done for Tobiyyah in making a room for him in the courtyards of God's house. ⁸It seemed very bad to me. I threw all the articles of Tobiyyah's household outside from the hall ⁹and said they should purify the halls, and I put back there the articles from God's house, the grain offering and the incense.

¹⁰I got to know that the Levites' portions had not been given, so that the Levites and the singers doing the work had taken flight each to his field. ¹¹I argued with the overseers and said, 'Why has God's house been abandoned?' I collected them and put them in place at their position, ¹²and all Yehudah brought the tenth of the grain, the new wine and the fresh oil into the treasuries. ¹³I made as treasurers in charge of the treasuries Shelemyah the priest, Tsadoq the secretary, Pedayah from the Levites, and next to them Hanan ben Zakkur son of Mattanyah, because they were reckoned trustworthy, and it was up to them to make allocations to their brothers.

¹⁴Be mindful of me, my God, because of this. Don't blot out my acts of commitment, which I have performed in God's house and in its duties.

¹⁵In those days I saw people in Yehudah treading winepresses on the sabbath, and bringing grain heaps and stacking them on donkeys, and also wine, grapes, figs and every load, and bringing them into Yerushalaim on the sabbath day. I testified on the day when

they sold provisions ¹⁶and when the Tsorites who lived there were bringing fish and all merchandise and selling on the sabbath to Yehudahites and in Yerushalaim, ¹⁷and I argued with the important people in Yehudah: 'What is this bad thing that you're doing, and profaning the sabbath day? ¹⁸Our ancestors acted like this, didn't they, and our God brought on us all this bad fortune, and on this town. You're bringing more rage against Yisra'el by profaning the sabbath.'

## Desecration and trespass

¹⁹When the gateways of Yerushalaim grew dark before the sabbath, I said that the doors should shut, and I said that they should not open them until after the sabbath. Given that I put in place some of my boys at the gateways, no load would come in on the sabbath day. ²⁰The merchants and the people selling all merchandise stayed the night outside Yerushalaim once or twice, ²¹but I testified against them: 'Why are you staying the night opposite the wall? If you do it again, I'll lay hands on you'; from that time they didn't come on the sabbath. ²²I said to the Levites that they should purify themselves and come keep watch over the gateways to make the sabbath day sacred.

Be mindful of this for me as well, my God, and have pity on me in accordance with the abundance of your commitment.

²³In those days I also saw the Yehudahites had got Ashdodite, Ammonite and Mo'abite women to come to live. ²⁴Their children were speaking half in Ashdodite, and none of them knew how to speak Yehudahite, but in accordance with the tongue of one people or the other. ²⁵I argued with them and slighted them, and struck some of them down and pulled out their hair, and made them swear by God: 'If you give your daughters to their sons or if you get some of their daughters for your sons or for yourselves . . . ²⁶It was in these things that Shelomoh king of Yisra'el did wrong, wasn't it. Among the many nations there was no king like him. He was loved by God, and God made him king over all Yisra'el; foreign women caused even him to do wrong. ²⁷Are we to listen to you doing this great bad thing, trespassing against our God by getting foreign women come to live?'

²⁸One of the sons of Yoyada, the son of Elyashib the big priest, was son-in-law to Sanballat the Horonite. I made him take flight from me. ²⁹Be mindful with regard to them, my God, because they polluted the priesthood, the pact of the priesthood and the Levites.

³⁰I purified them of everything foreign and put the watches in place for the priests and for the Levites, each one in his work, ³¹and for the wood offering at designated times and for the first fruits. My God, be mindful for me for good.

# ESTHER

In the 1930s, the Nazi regime in Germany formulated a 'final solution to the Jewish question' that involved the killing of all the Jews in Germany and in the areas of Europe it controlled. The book of Esther tells the story of the first great attempt at such a 'final solution' formulated by a Persian state official, Haman, in the fifth century BC. It is the same period as Ezra and Nehemiah and another reminder that by no means did all Judahites return to Jerusalem after the exile.

Haman's plan is frustrated as a result of some coincidences and some brave acceptance of responsibility by a young woman called Hadassah whose Persian name was Esther. As it happens, the king has dismissed his queen because she wouldn't be put on display at a party; and as it happens, Esther wins a beauty contest and becomes the next queen. She is therefore in a position to get the king to reverse his decision to have Haman's plan implemented and to give the Judahites permission to kill any Persians who are foolish enough to attack them anyway (which a large number are).

The story is full of irony, humour and exaggeration, such as the twelve-month beauty preparation and Haman's twenty-five-metre-high gallows on which he ends up being hanged himself. It makes no reference to God or prayer or the Torah and it thus puts the emphasis on Judahites taking responsibility for their destiny and on coincidences. It therefore both contrasts with and compares with the exodus story. It testifies to God's involvement in ensuring that his people are preserved, but it keeps that involvement operative behind the scenes – in the way we usually experience it.

## The woman who won't play ball

**1** In the days of Ahashverosh [Xerxes], that Ahashverosh who reigned from Hoddu [India] as far as Kush [Sudan] over 127 provinces – ²in those days, when King Ahashverosh sat on his royal throne which was in the Shushan fortress, ³in the third year of his reign, he made a banquet for all his officials and his servants. The force of Paras and Maday [Persia and Media], the nobles and the officials of the provinces were before him, ⁴while he let them see the wealth of his royal splendour and the glorious dignity of his greatness for many days – 180 days.

⁵At the fulfilment of these days the king made a banquet for the entire people to be found in the Shushan fortress, great to small, for seven days, in the courtyard of the king's palace garden:

⁶white cloth, cotton and blue cloth, held by bands of fine linen and purple to silver rods and alabaster pillars; couches of gold and silver on a pavement of porphyry, alabaster, marble and mosaic; ⁷giving of drinks in gold vessels (vessels differing from one another); much royal wine in accordance with the king's liberality; ⁸drinking in accordance with the rule 'There's no one restraining', because the king had laid it down in this way with every senior person in his household, to act in accordance with what was acceptable, individual by individual.

⁹Queen Vashti also made a women's banquet at the royal house of King Ahashverosh.

¹⁰On the seventh day, when the king was in good heart because of the wine, he said to Mehuman, Bizzeta, Harbona, Bigta, Abagta, Zetar and Karkas, the seven eunuchs who ministered to the presence of King Ahashverosh, ¹¹to get Vashti the queen to come before the king in her royal diadem, to let the peoples and the officials see her beauty, because she was good-looking. ¹²ᵃQueen Vashti refused to come at the king's word by means of the eunuchs.

## The men who are afraid

¹²ᵇThe king was quite furious. His wrath burned up in him. ¹³The king said to the

experts who knew the times (because this was the thing with the king in relation to all the people who knew law and judgement; ¹⁴near to him were Karshena, Shetar, Admata, Tarshish, Meres, Marsena and Memukan, the seven officials of Paras and Maday who could see the king and sat in first place in the realm), ¹⁵'According to law, what should be done with Queen Vashti because she has not acted on the word of King Ahashverosh by means of the eunuchs?'

¹⁶Memukan said before the king and the officials, 'It's not against the king alone that Vashti the queen has gone astray, but against all the officials and against all the peoples that are in all King Ahashverosh's provinces. ¹⁷Because the thing about the queen will get out to all the women, so as to make them despise their masters in their eyes, when they say, "King Ahashverosh said to get Vashti the queen to come before him, and she didn't come." ¹⁸This day the leading women of Paras and Maday who have heard the thing about the queen will say it to all the king's officials, with quite enough despising and fury.

¹⁹If it seems good to Your Majesty, a royal word should issue from his presence and it should be written in the laws of Paras and Maday, and not pass away, that Vashti will not come before King Ahashverosh. The king should give her royal position to another woman who is better than her. ²⁰The king's proclamation that he makes will make itself heard in all his realm (because it's great), and all the women will give dignity to their masters, great to small.'

²¹The thing seemed good in the eyes of the king and the officials, and the king acted in accordance with Memukan's word. ²²He sent documents to all the king's provinces, to each province in accordance with its script and to each people in accordance with its language, for every man to be ruling in his household and to be speaking in accordance with the language of his own people.

## The beauty contest

**2** Subsequently, when King Ahashverosh's wrath had subsided, he was mindful of Vashti and what she had done and what had been determined against her. [2]The king's boys ministering to him said, 'They should seek for the king young, good-looking girls. [3]The king should appoint people in all the provinces of his realm so they can collect every young, good-looking girl to the Shushan fortress, to the women's household, into the control of Hege, the king's eunuch who keeps watch over the women, and their cleansing treatments should be given them. [4]The girl who seems good in the king's eyes should reign in place of Vashti.' The thing seemed good in the king's eyes, and he did so.

[5]Now there was a Yehudahite [Judahite] man in the Shushan fortress named Mordokay ben Ya'ir son of Shim'i son of Qish, a Binyaminite [Benjaminite], [6]who had been taken into exile from Yerushalaim with the group of exiles that had been exiled with Yekonyah [Jehoiachin] king of Yehudah, which Nebukadne'tstsar king of Babel took into exile. [7]He was guardian of Hadassah (i.e. Esther), his uncle's daughter, because she had no father or mother. The girl was lovely of figure and good-looking. When her father and mother died, Mordokay took her as a daughter to him.

[8]When the king's word, his law, made itself heard and many girls collected to the Shushan fortress into the control of Hegay, Esther was taken into the king's household into the control of Hegay, who kept watch over the women. [9]The girl seemed good in his eyes and she gained commitment before him. He hastened to give to her her cleansing treatments and her portions, and the seven girls who had been looked out to give to her from the king's household. He changed her and her girls to the best part of the women's household. [10]Esther did not tell of her people or her family, because Mordokay had ordered her not to tell of it.

## The girl who pays a price

[11]Each and every day Mordokay used to walk about before the courtyard of the women's household so as to know about Esther's welfare and what was being done with her.

[12]When a turn arrived, girl by girl, for coming to King Ahashverosh, at the end of things happening to her in accordance with the law for the women, for twelve months (because

their cleansing days were fulfilled like this, six months with oil of myrrh and six months with perfumes and women's cleansing treatments), [13]in this way the girl came to the king: everything that she would say would be given her, so as to come with her from the women's household to the king's household. [14]Whereas she came in the evening, in the morning she went back to the second women's household, into the control of Sha'ashgaz, the king's eunuch who kept watch over the secondary wives. She would not come again to the king unless the king wanted her and she was called for by name.

[15]When the turn arrived for Esther bat Abihayil (uncle of Mordokay, who had taken her as daughter to him) to come to the king, she did not seek anything except what Hegay the king's eunuch who kept watch over the women said. Esther would gain grace in the eyes of everyone who saw her.

[16]Esther was taken to King Ahashverosh in his royal household in the tenth month (i.e. the month of Tebet) in the seventh year of his reign. [17]The king liked Esther more than all the women and she gained grace and commitment before him more than all the young girls, and he put a royal diadem on her head and made her queen in place of Vashti. [18]The king made a great banquet for all his officials and his servants, 'Esther's Banquet'. He made a holiday for the provinces and gave gifts in accordance with the capacity of the king.

## Amaleq redivivus

[19]When the young girls collected a second time, Mordokay was sitting at the king's gateway. [20]Esther had not told of her family or her people, as Mordokay had ordered her; Esther did as Mordokay said, as when she was in guardianship with him.

[21]During that time, when Mordokay was sitting at the king's gateway, Bigtan and Teresh, two of the king's eunuchs who kept watch over the threshold, became furious and sought to lay hand on King Ahashverosh. [22]The thing became known to Mordokay, he told Esther the queen, and Esther told the king in Mordokay's name. [23]The thing was enquired into and found to be so, and the two of them were hanged on

a pole. It was written in the document about things of the time, before the king.

**3** Subsequently, King Ahashverosh promoted Haman ben Hammedata the Agagite. He elevated him and put his seat above all the officials who were with him. ²All the king's servants who were at the king's gateway would kneel and bow low to Haman, because the king had ordered this regarding him. But Mordokay didn't kneel and didn't bow low. ³The king's servants who were at the king's gateway said to Mordokay, 'Why are you transgressing the king's order?' ⁴But when they said it to him day by day, he didn't listen to them.

They told Haman, to see whether Mordokay's words would stand, because he had told them that he was a Yehudahite. ⁵Haman saw that Mordokay was not kneeling or bowing low to him, and Haman filled with wrath, ⁶but in his eyes he despised laying hand on Mordokay alone, because they had told him Mordokay's people, and Haman sought to annihilate all the Yehudahites who were in Ahashverosh's entire kingdom – Mordokay's people.

### The lottery that meant death

⁷In the first month (i.e. the month of Nisan) in King Ahashverosh's twelfth year, they made *pur* (i.e. the lot) fall before Haman, from day to day and from month to month: [it fell on] the twelfth (i.e. the month of Adar). ⁸Haman said to King Ahashverosh, 'There is a people, spread about and divided among the peoples in all the provinces in your kingdom, and their laws are different from every people. They don't act on the king's laws, and it's not advantageous for the king to let them be. ⁹If it seems good to Your Majesty, it should be written down to obliterate them. I will weigh out 10,000 talents of silver into the hands of those who do the work, to bring into the king's treasuries.'

¹⁰The king removed his ring from on his hand and gave it to Haman ben Hammedata the Agagite, the Yehudahites' adversary. ¹¹The king said to Haman, 'The silver is given to you, and the people, to do with it as seems good in your eyes.'

¹²So the king's secretaries were called for in the first month, on the thirteenth day of it, and it was written down in accordance with all that Haman had ordered, to the king's satraps and to the governors who were over each and every province and to the officials people by people, province by province, in accordance with its script, and people by people in accordance with its language, written in the name of King Ahashverosh and sealed with the king's ring. ¹³Documents were sent by means of the runners to all the king's provinces regarding annihilating, killing and eliminating all the Yehudahites, from young to old, little ones and women, on one day, on the thirteenth of the twelfth month (i.e. Adar), and for despoiling them as plunder. ¹⁴A copy of the document was to be given out as a law in each and every province, shown to all the peoples so that they would be ready for this day.

¹⁵The runners went out, driven by the king's word, and the law was given out in the Shushan fortress. While the king and Haman sat down to a banquet, the town of Shushan was perplexed.

### The risk that needs taking

**4** When Mordokay got to know of all that had been done, Mordokay tore his clothes and put on sack and earth. He went out into the middle of the town and cried out with a loud and bitter cry. ²He came as far as before the king's gateway, because there was no coming into the king's gateway in sack clothing. ³In each and every province, the place where the king's word and his law arrived, there was great mourning on the part of the Yehudahites, fasting, weeping and lamenting; sack and earth were laid down for most people.

⁴Esther's girls and her eunuchs came and told her, and the queen went all-a-tremble. She sent Mordokay clothes to put on so he could remove the sack from on him, but he didn't accept them. ⁵Esther called for Hatak, one of the king's eunuchs whom he had put in place before her, and ordered him to Mordokay to get to know what this was and why this was happening.

⁶Hatak went out to Mordokay in the town square which was before the king's gateway ⁷and Mordokay told him everything that had happened to him and the details about the silver that Haman said he would weigh out to the king's treasuries for the Yehudahites, to

obliterate them. [8]He gave him a copy of the document containing the law that had been given out in Shushan for their annihilation, to let Esther see and to tell her, and to order her to come to the king and seek grace with him and enquire before him concerning her people.

[9]Hatak came and told Esther Mordokay's words, [10]but Esther said to Hatak and ordered him to Mordokay, [11]'All the king's servants and the people of the king's provinces know that any man or woman who comes to the king in the inner courtyard who has not been called for – he has one law, to put them to death, unless the king extends to him the gold sceptre, and he lives. And I haven't been called for to come to the king these thirty days.'

### The possibility of a non-miraculous miracle

[12]They told Mordokay Esther's words, [13]and Mordokay said to take back word to Esther: 'Don't imagine within yourself that you'll escape in the king's household better than all the Yehudahites, [14]because if you stay quite silent at this time, relief and rescue will arise for the Yehudahites from a place, but you and your father's household will perish. Who knows if it was for a time like this that you arrived at the royal position?'

[15]Esther said to take back word to Mordokay: [16]'Go assemble all the Yehudahites to be found in Shushan and fast for me. Don't eat or drink for three days, night or day. I, too, will fast with my girls in this way, and in this way I'll come to the king, which is not in accordance with the law. And as I perish, I perish.' [17]Mordokay passed it on and acted in accordance with everything that Esther ordered him.

5 On the third day, Esther put on royal dress and stood in the inner courtyard of the king's house, opposite the king's house, while the king was sitting on his royal throne in the royal house opposite the entrance to the house. [2]When the king saw Esther the queen standing in the courtyard, she gained grace in his eyes. The king extended to Esther the gold sceptre that was in his hand and Esther drew near and touched the head of the sceptre.

[3]The king said to her, 'What do you have, Esther, queen? What's your request? Up to half the kingdom, it will be given you.' [4]Esther said, 'If it seems good to the king, may the king and Haman come today to the banquet that I have made for him.' [5]The king said, 'Hurry Haman to act on Esther's word.' So the king and Haman came to the banquet that Esther had made.

### The girl who knows how to work her man

[6]The king said to Esther at the wine banquet, 'What's your petition? It will be given you. What's your request? Up to half the kingdom, it will be done.' [7]Esther answered, 'My petition, my request: [8]if I have found grace in the king's eyes and if it seems good to the king to grant my petition, to act on my request, may the king and Haman come to the banquet that I will make for them, and tomorrow I will act in accordance with the king's word.'

[9]Haman went out that day rejoicing and good-hearted, but when Haman saw Mordokay at the king's gateway and he didn't get up and didn't tremble because of him, Haman filled with wrath at Mordokay. [10]But Haman controlled himself and came to his house. He sent and got his friends and Zeresh his wife to come. [11]Haman recounted to them the splendour of his wealth and the large number of his sons and all the way that the king had promoted him and that he had elevated him above the officials and the king's servants. [12]And Haman said, 'Indeed, Esther the queen did not get anyone to come to the banquet with the king that she made, except me. Tomorrow, too, I am called to her with the king. [13]But all this does not seem advantageous to me every time that I see Mordokay the Yehudahite sitting at the king's gateway.'

[14]Zeresh his wife with all his friends said to him, 'They should make a pole twenty-five metres high, and in the morning you should say to the king that they should hang Mordokay on it; and go with the king to the banquet rejoicing.' The thing seemed good to Haman and he made the pole.

6 That night the king's sleep took flight and he said to bring the records document (the things about the time). They were being read out before the king [2]and it was found written that Mordokay had told of Bigtana and Teresh, two of the king's eunuchs among

the guards of the threshold, who had sought to lay a hand on King Ahashverosh. ³The king said, 'What dignity or promotion was done for Mordokay for this?' The king's boys, his ministers, said, 'Nothing was done with him.'

## Haman comes unstuck

⁴The king said, 'Who's in the courtyard?' Now Haman had come into the outer courtyard of the king's house to say to the king to hang Mordokay on the pole that he had prepared for him. ⁵The king's boys said to him, 'There's Haman standing in the courtyard.' The king said, 'He's to come in.' ⁶Haman came in, and the king said to him, 'What's to do with a man whose dignity the king wants?' Haman said to himself, 'For whom would the king want dignity more than me?'

⁷So Haman said to the king, 'A man whose dignity the king wants: ⁸they should bring royal apparel that the king has worn and a horse on which the king has ridden and on whose head a royal diadem has been put, ⁹and put the apparel and the horse into the hand of one of the king's noble officials. They should clothe the man whose dignity the king wants, have him ride on the horse through the town square and call out before him, 'This is what is done for the man whose dignity the king wants!'

¹⁰The king said to Haman, 'Hurry, get the apparel and the horse, as you've spoken, and do that for Mordokay the Yehudahite, who sits in the king's gateway. No word of all that you have spoken should fall.' ¹¹Haman got the apparel and the horse, clothed Mordokay, had him ride through the town square and called out before him, 'This is what is done for the man whose dignity the king wants.'

¹²Mordokay went back to the king's gateway while Haman hastened to his house, mourning and head covered. ¹³Haman recounted to Zeresh his wife and to all his friends everything that had happened to him. His smart people and Zeresh his wife said to him, 'If Mordokay, before whom you have begun to fall, is of Yehudahite origin, you will not overcome him, because you will surely fall before him.'

## Fates reversed

¹⁴While they were still speaking with him, the king's eunuchs arrived and hastened to bring Haman to the banquet that Esther had made. **7** So the king and Haman came to drink with Esther the queen, ²and the king said to Esther again on the second day at the wine banquet, 'What's your petition, Queen Esther? It will be given you. What's your request, up to half the kingdom? It will be done.' ³Esther answered, 'If I've found grace in your eyes, Your Majesty, and if it seems good to Your Majesty, may my life be given me as my petition, and my people as my request, ⁴because I and my people have been sold for annihilating, killing and obliterating. Had we been sold as servants and as maidservants, I would have kept silent, because the adversity would not be commensurate to the damage to the king.'

⁵King Ahashverosh said – he said to Esther the queen, 'Who's this? Where's this man who is so full of himself to act like this?' ⁶Esther said, 'The man who's an adversary and an enemy is this bad man Haman.' As Haman was terrified before the king and the queen, ⁷in his wrath the king set off from the wine banquet for the palace garden, while Haman stayed to seek for his life with Esther the queen, because he saw that a bad fate was certain for him from the king. ⁸When the king came back from the palace garden into the wine banquet house, Haman was falling on the couch where Esther was. The king said, 'Is he also to violate the queen with me, in the house?' As the word went out from the king's mouth, they covered Haman's face. ⁹Harbonah, one of the eunuchs before the king, said, 'In addition, there's the pole that Haman made for Mordokay, who spoke something good for the king, standing in Haman's house, twenty-five metres high.' The king said, 'Hang him on it.'

## The right to self-defence

¹⁰So they hanged Haman on the pole that he had set up for Mordokay, and the king's wrath subsided. **8** That day King Ahashverosh gave over the household of Haman, the Yehudahites'

adversary, to Esther the queen, while Mordokay came before the king because Esther had told of what he was to her. [2]The king removed his ring, which he had taken away from Haman, and gave it to Mordokay, and Esther put Mordokay in charge of Haman's household.

[3]Esther again spoke before the king, and fell before his feet and cried. She sought grace from him to take away the bad action of Haman the Agagite, the intention that he had thought up against the Yehudahites. [4]The king extended to Esther the gold sceptre and Esther got up and stood before the king. [5]She said, 'If it seems good to the king, if I have found grace before him, if the thing seems proper before the king and I seem good in his eyes, may things be written to turn back the documents, the intention of Haman ben Hammedata the Agagite, which he wrote so as to obliterate the Yehudahites who are in all the king's provinces, [6]because how can I look upon the bad fate that will befall my people? How can I look upon my family's obliteration?'

[7]King Ahashverosh said to Esther the queen and to Mordokay the Yehudahite, 'Here, I have given Esther the household of Haman and they have hanged him on the pole because he put out his hand against the Yehudahites. [8]You yourselves – write as it seems good in your eyes concerning the Yehudahites in the king's name and seal it with the king's ring' (because a document that's been written in the king's name and sealed with the king's ring can't be turned back).

## Rejoicing with relief

[9]So the king's secretaries were called at that time, in the third month (i.e. the month of Sivan) on the twenty-third of it, and it was written in accordance with all that Mordokay ordered, to the Yehudahites and to the satraps, the governors and the officials of the provinces that are from Hoddu as far as Kush, 127 provinces, province by province in accordance with its script, and people by people in accordance with its language, and to the Yehudahites in accordance with their script and in accordance with their language.

[10]He wrote in King Ahashverosh's name, sealed it with the king's seal, and sent documents by the hand of the runners on horses, riding royal relay steeds, the offspring of racehorses, [11]that the king permitted the Yehudahites who were in each and every town to congregate and stand up for themselves, so as to annihilate, to kill and to obliterate the entire force of a people or province attacking them, little ones and women, and to plunder their spoil [12]on one day, in all King Ahashverosh's provinces, on the thirteenth of the twelfth month (i.e. the month of Adar), [13]a copy of the document to be given out as a law in each and every province, shown to all the peoples, so that the Yehudahites would be ready for this day to take redress from their enemies. [14]The runners went out riding royal relay steeds, hastening and driven by the king's word, and the law was given out in the Shushan fortress.

[15]When Mordokay went out from before the king in royal apparel, blue and white, a big gold crown, and a robe of fine linen and purple, the town of Shushan shouted and rejoiced. [16]For the Yehudahites there was light and rejoicing, joy and dignity. [17]In each and every province and in each and every town, in a place where the king's word and his law arrived, there was rejoicing and joy for the Yehudahites, a banquet and a good time. Many of the peoples of the country professed to be Yehudahites, because dread of the Yehudahites had fallen upon them.

## The slaughter

**9** So in the twelfth month (i.e. the month of Adar), on the thirteenth, the day when the king's word and his law were due to be acted on, on the day when the Yehudahites' enemies expected to be in power over them, that was turned round, so that the Yehudahites – they were in power over the people hostile to them. [2]The Yehudahites in their towns in all King Ahashverosh's provinces congregated to lay a hand on people who sought something bad for them, but no one stood up before them, because dread of them had fallen on all the peoples. [3]All the king's provincial officials, satraps, governors and people doing work were elevating the Yehudahites, because dread of Mordokay had fallen on them, [4]because

Mordokay was big in the king's house and report of him was going through all the provinces, because the man Mordokay was getting bigger and bigger.

⁵So the Yehudahites struck down all their adversaries with a stroke of the sword, with killing and obliteration, and acted against the people hostile to them in accordance with what was acceptable to them. ⁶In the Shushan fortress the Yehudahites killed and obliterated 500 people, ⁷and killed Parshandata, Dalphon, Aspata, ⁸Porata, Adalya, Aridata, ⁹Parmashta, Arisay, Ariday and Vayzata, ¹⁰the ten sons of Haman ben Hammedata, the Yehudahites' adversary, but they did not lay their hand on the plunder.

¹¹That day the number of the people killed in the Shushan fortress came before the king, ¹²and the king said to Esther the queen, 'Given that in the Shushan fortress the Yehudahites have slaughtered and obliterated 500 people, and Haman's ten sons, in the remainder of the king's provinces what have they done? But what's your petition? It will be given you. What else is your request? It will be done.' ¹³Esther said, 'If it seems good to the king, may it be given to the Yehudahites who are in Shushan tomorrow also to act in accordance with today's law, and may they hang Haman's ten sons on the pole.' ¹⁴The king said this was to be done, and a law was given out in Shushan and they hanged Haman's ten sons.

## The commemoration

¹⁵So the Yehudahites who were in Shushan congregated again on the fourteenth day of the month of Adar and killed 300 people in Shushan, but did not lay their hand on the plunder. ¹⁶The remainder of the Yehudahites, who were in the king's provinces, congregated and stood up for themselves and got relief from their enemies. They killed 75,000 of the people hostile to them, but did not lay their hand on the plunder, ¹⁷on the thirteenth day of the month of Adar. They let be on its fourteenth and made it a day of banquet and rejoicing, ¹⁸while the Yehudahites who were in Shushan congregated on its thirteenth and on its fourteenth, but let be on its fifteenth and made it a day of banquet and rejoicing. ¹⁹That's why

the rural Yehudahites, who live in the rural towns, make the fourteenth day of the month of Adar into rejoicing and banquet, a good time and one of sending portions one to his neighbour.

²⁰Mordokay wrote down these things and sent documents to all the Yehudahites who were in all King Ahashverosh's provinces, near and far, ²¹to lay upon them to make the fourteenth day of the month of Adar, and its fifteenth day, each and every year, ²²as the days when the Yehudahites got relief for themselves from their enemies and the month that turned for them from sadness to rejoicing and from grief to a good time – to make them days of banquet and celebration, and sending portions one to his neighbour and gifts to the needy.

²³The Yehudahites accepted what they had begun to do and what Mordokay had written to them, ²⁴because Haman ben Hammedata the Agagite, the adversary of all the Yehudahites, had thought to obliterate the Yehudahites and had caused the *pur* to fall (i.e. the lot) so as to crush them and obliterate them. ²⁵But when it came before the king, he said with the document: his bad intention, which he had thought up against the Yehudahites, should come back on to his own head, and they should hang him and his sons on the pole. ²⁶ᵃOn account of this they called these days Purim, after the word *pur*.

## A law that will last

²⁶ᵇOn account of this, on account of all the words in this communiqué and what they had seen – on account of such things and what had come to them, ²⁷the Yehudahites implemented and accepted for themselves and for their offspring and for all who would join them, so that it should not pass away, to make these two days, in accordance with the document about them and in accordance with their time, each and every year, ²⁸these days being commemorated and made in each and every generation, family, province and town. These days of Purim will not pass away from among the Yehudahites, and their commemoration will not cease from their offspring.

²⁹Esther the queen, daughter of Abihayil, and Mordokay the Yehudahite wrote with all

force to implement this second communiqué about Purim. ³⁰He sent documents to all the Yehudahites in the 127 provinces in Ahashverosh's realm, words about well-being and truthfulness, ³¹to implement these days of Purim at their times as Mordokay the Yehudahite and Esther the queen implemented them for themselves, and as they had implemented for themselves and for their offspring words about the fasts and their outcry. ³²Esther's word implemented these statements about Purim and it was written down in the document.

# 10

King Ahashverosh put a workforce on the country and the shores across the sea. ²All his forceful and strong action, and the detail about the importance of Mordokay which the king conferred on him, are written down on the document with the things of the time regarding the kings of Maday and Paras, aren't they, ³because Mordokay the Yehudahite was second-in-command to King Ahashverosh, important to the Yehudahites and accepted by the large number of his brothers, enquiring after what was good for his people and speaking of well-being for all its offspring.

# JOB

The book of Job is something like the script for a play – there's no indication that it was performed, but it could have been. The main part of the book is an argument between Job, three of his friends, an angry young man who appears later, and then Yahweh himself, who eventually responds to Job. The framework for the argument is the story of how Job, someone exemplary in his commitment to Yahweh and someone who has done really well in life, loses everything in a series of calamities, and how Yahweh eventually restores him. The argument happens in poetry, which puts us on the track of the fact that this isn't simply the transcript of something that happened, though the basic story line reflects things that happen often enough, and in this sense I imagine it is based on fact.

But the book's point isn't dependent on its being factual. The point about the book is to discuss various approaches to handling the way that people do experience the kind of horrifying tragedy that comes to Job. In this work, discussing the issue doesn't mean trying to explain why people suffer. It's not about the problem of evil, or theodicy, in this sense. It's more about how one lives with an experience like Job's. And it presupposes that the experience of tragedy raises even bigger questions about the very nature of our relationship with God and the basis of that relationship.

Making these questions the basis of an argument between the participants enables the book to look at the questions from different angles. All these angles have some truth to them, though they are not all very relevant to Job.

1. The book's starting point is that there is a relationship of deep mutual commitment between Job and God. But that starting point raises the question whether Job is committed to God because it means God blesses him. The story therefore imagines God agreeing that Job should be tested by taking away his blessings, to see how he reacts; and Job passes the test. So the first insight about the relationship between God and us is that it's based on the free trust and commitment between God and us, not on what we get out of it; and that tragedy can be a means of testing us. (In this introduction to the book, a key role is played by 'The Adversary', who is a member of God's staff whose job it is to make sure that people don't get away with things that they shouldn't get away with. He is a safeguard against God being too soft. In English translations, he is often referred to as Satan, but this is misleading.)

2. The second insight about the relationship is that Job can have an exceptional freedom in expressing his grief, anguish and puzzlement, and in expressing to God his anger, frustration and sense of betrayal (see chapters 3—27).

3. A third insight is expressed time and time again by Job's three friends (interwoven in chapters 3—27), who know that tragedy often issues from our disobedience. The problem is that often it does not. But often it does, so their insight is a real one, though it's irrelevant to Job.

4. The poem about wisdom in Job 28 reminds readers that awe and thus obedience in relation to God is the key to being smart.

5. The insight expressed by the angry young man (chapters 32—37) is that tragedy can be something through which God speaks to you and through which he draws you nearer to himself. It too is a real insight, but not very relevant to Job.

6. When God appears (chapters 38—41) he reminds Job that he is God and Job isn't, and that the world doesn't circulate round Job. If Job thinks he can run the world better than God, he should try. Tragedy drives one to recognize that one must and can trust God and submit to God.

7. The close of the story affirms that in the end God is faithful. The fact that most people's stories don't end as comfortingly as Job's makes it all the more important to affirm this truth about God.

## The man of integrity

**1** There was a man in the country of Uz named Iyyob [Job]. That man was a person of integrity and upright, in awe of God and turning aside from what is bad. ²There had been born to him seven sons and three daughters. ³His acquisitions comprised 7,000 sheep, 3,000 camels, 500 yoke of cattle, 500 she-donkeys and a very large servant body. That man was bigger than all eastern people.

⁴His sons used to make a feast at the house of an individual on his day, and send and call for their three sisters to eat and to drink with them. ⁵When the days of the feast had made their round, Iyyob would send and make them sacred. He would start early in the morning and offer up burnt offerings for the number of them all, because (Iyyob said) 'Perhaps my children have done wrong and "blessed" God inside.' In this way Iyyob would act continually.

⁶There was a day when the divine beings came to take their stand with Yahweh. The adversary, too, came among them. ⁷Yahweh said to the adversary, 'From where do you come?' The adversary answered Yahweh, 'From roaming on the earth and from walking about on it.' ⁸Yahweh said to the adversary, 'Have you applied your mind to my servant Iyyob, because there's no one like him on the earth, a person of integrity and upright, in awe of God and turning aside from what is bad?' ⁹The adversary answered Yahweh, 'Is it for nothing that Iyyob lives in awe of God? ¹⁰Have you yourself not hedged about him and about his household and about everything that he has, all round? You've blessed the action of his hands, and his acquisitions have spread through the earth. ¹¹However, put out your hand, please, and touch everything that he has. If he doesn't "bless" you to your face . . .'

¹²Yahweh said to the adversary, 'There, everything that he has is in your hand. Only against him you may not put out your hand.' So the adversary went out from being in Yahweh's presence.

## When life falls apart

¹³There was a day when his sons and his daughters were eating and drinking wine in the house of their oldest brother ¹⁴when an envoy came to Iyyob and said, 'The cattle were ploughing and the she-donkeys were pasturing next to them, ¹⁵and Sabeans fell and took them, and struck down the boys with the edge of the sword. I alone am the only one who has escaped to tell you.'

¹⁶While this man was still speaking, another came and said, 'Fire from God fell from the heavens and burned up the flocks and the boys, and consumed them. I alone am the only one who has escaped to tell you.'

¹⁷While this one was still speaking, another came and said, 'Kasdites made three columns and made a dash on the camels and took them, and struck down the boys with the edge of the sword. I alone am the only one who has escaped to tell you.'

¹⁸While this one was still speaking, another came and said, 'Your sons and your daughters were eating and drinking wine in the house of their oldest brother, ¹⁹and there – a big wind came from across the wilderness and touched the four corners of the house. It fell on the young people and they died. I alone am the only one who has escaped to tell you.'

²⁰Iyyob got up, tore his coat and shaved his head, fell to the ground and bowed low, ²¹and said, 'Naked I came out of my mother's womb, and naked I will go back there. Yahweh gave and Yahweh has taken. Yahweh's name be blessed.'

²²In all this Iyyob did not do wrong. He did not ascribe corruptness to God.

## The wise silence of friends

**2** There was a day when the divine beings came to take their stand with Yahweh. The adversary, too, came among them to take his stand with Yahweh. ²Yahweh said to the adversary, 'From where do you come?' The adversary answered Yahweh, 'From roaming on the earth and from walking about on it.' ³Yahweh said to the adversary, 'Have you applied your mind to my servant Iyyob, because there's no one like him on the earth, a person of integrity and upright, in awe of God and turning aside from what is bad? He's still holding strongly to his integrity whereas you incited me against him to swallow him up for nothing.'

⁴The adversary answered Yahweh, 'Skin for skin! All that a man has he will give for the sake of his life. ⁵However, put out your hand, please, and touch his bones and his flesh. If he doesn't "bless" you to your face . . .'

⁶Yahweh said to the adversary, 'There he is, in your hand. Only keep his life.' ⁷So the adversary went out from Yahweh's presence and struck Iyyob down with a bad inflammation from the sole of his foot as far as the crown of his head, ⁸and he got himself a piece of pot to scratch himself with as he was sitting among ashes.

⁹His wife said to him, 'Are you still holding strongly to your integrity? "Bless" God and die.' ¹⁰He said to her, 'Like the speaking of one of the villainous women, you too speak. We accept good fortune from Yahweh. Do we not accept bad fortune?' In all this Iyyob didn't do wrong with his lips.

¹¹Three friends of Iyyob heard about all these bad things that had come upon him, and they came each one from his place: Eliphaz the Temanite, Bildad the Shuhite and Tsophar the Na'amatite. They met together by agreement to come to express their sorrow to him and to comfort him, ¹²but they raised their eyes from afar and didn't recognize him. They raised their voice and cried. They ripped, each one, his coat and they threw earth over their heads, to the heavens.

¹³They sat with him on the ground seven days and seven nights with no one speaking a word to him because they saw that his suffering was very great.

## Iyyob: Perish the day I was born

**3** Subsequently, Iyyob opened his mouth and slighted his day. ²Iyyob avowed:

³Perish the day on which I was born,
  and the night that said 'A male has been
    conceived!'
⁴That day should be darkness,
  God above should not enquire about it,
  and light should not shine on it.
⁵Darkness and deathly shadow should reclaim it,
  cloud should dwell over it.
Blackness by day should terrify it,
  ⁶that night – shadow should take it.

It should not be one with the days of the year,
  it should not come in the number of months.
⁷There, that night should be barren,
  no resounding should come in it.
⁸The people who curse a day should damn it,
  the people ready to rouse Livyatan [Leviathan].
⁹Its dusk stars should be dark,
  it should hope for light when there is none.
It should not see the eyelids of dawn,
  ¹⁰because it did not shut the doors of my
    womb,
  and conceal oppression from my eyes.

## Iyyob: Life means turmoil, death means rest

¹¹Why did I not die at birth,
  go out from the womb and breathe my last?
¹²Why did knees meet me,
  or why breasts that I would suck?
¹³Because now I would be lying and calm,
  I would have slept then and would rest myself,
¹⁴With kings and the counsellors of the earth,
  who build up ruins for themselves,
¹⁵Or with officials who have gold,
  who fill their houses with silver.
¹⁶Or why was I not like a buried stillborn,
  like babies that have not seen the light?
¹⁷There the faithless leave off causing turmoil;
  there people wearied of energy rest.
¹⁸All at once prisoners relax;
  they don't hear the boss's voice.
¹⁹Small and big are there;
  the servant is free of his master.

²⁰Why does he give light to the oppressed,
  life to the bitter in spirit,
²¹People who wait for death but there is none,
  who search for it more than hidden treasures,
²²Who rejoice with gladness,
  who are joyful, because they find a grave,
²³To the man whose way has concealed itself,
  and whom God has hedged about?
²⁴Because my sighing comes before my food,
  my groans pour out like water.
²⁵Because I dreaded something and it happened
    to me,
  what I was terrified of comes to me.
²⁶I was not at ease, I was not calm,
  I did not rest, and turmoil came.

*Eliphaz: Can a mere human being be in the right in God's eyes?*

**4** Eliphas the Temanite answered:

²Should one venture a word to you, will you be
  distraught?
 but holding back utterances: who could?
³Here, you have disciplined many,
 you would strengthen weak hands.
⁴Your utterances would enable one who was
  collapsing to get up,
 you would firm up bending knees.
⁵Yet now it comes to you, and you are
  distraught;
 it touches you, and you are fearful.
⁶Is your awe not your assurance,
 and the integrity of your ways your hope?
⁷Be mindful, please: who is that person free of
  guilt who has perished,
 where did the upright people disappear?
⁸As I have seen, the people who plough trouble,
 and sow oppression, reap them.
⁹By God's breath they perish,
 by his angry blast they come to a finish.
¹⁰The lion's roar, the cub's sound,
 the teeth of the whelps – they crumple;
¹¹The tiger perishes for lack of prey,
 the cougar's children scatter.

¹²A word stole to me,
 my ear got a whisper of it.
¹³In uneases from visions of the night,
 when deep sleep falls on human beings,
¹⁴Dread befell me, and trembling,
 and brought dread to the mass of my bones.
¹⁵A wind was sweeping over my face,
 it was bristling the hair on my flesh.
¹⁶It was halting, but I didn't recognize its
  appearance,
 the form in front of my eyes.
I heard a murmur, a voice:
 ¹⁷'Can a mere human being be in the right
  before God,
 can a man be pure before his maker?'
¹⁸If he does not trust his servants,
 and attributes folly to his envoys,
¹⁹How much more people who dwell in mud
  houses,
 whose foundation is in the dirt,
 so that people crush them before [they crush]
  a moth.

²⁰Between morning and evening they are struck
  down;
 without anyone noticing they perish
  permanently.
²¹Is it not that, when their tent cord is pulled up
  from them,
 they die, and without smartness?

*Eliphaz: God frustrates the intentions of the shrewd*

**5** Please call – is anyone going to answer you,
  and to which of the sacred ones will you turn
  your face?
²Because provocation kills the dense person,
 passion puts the simple-minded to death.
³I myself have seen a dense person who was
  taking root,
 but I have immediately declared his home
  cursed,
⁴His children will be far from deliverance;
 they will collapse in the gateway and with no
  one to rescue.
⁵A hungry person will eat his harvest, will take it
  into baskets,
 and thirsty people will pant after their
  resources.
⁶Because trouble does not grow out from dirt,
 oppression does not spring up from the
  ground.
⁷Because a human being may be born for
  oppression
 and plagues go flying lofty.

⁸However, I myself enquire of God,
 and before God I set my words,
⁹One who does big things of which there is no
  searching out,
 extraordinary deeds until there is no
  numbering,
¹⁰The one who gives rain on the face of the earth,
 sends water on the face of the countryside,
¹¹Setting the lowly on high,
 so that mourners soar to deliverance,
¹²Contravening the intentions of the shrewd,
 so that their hands don't achieve adeptness,
¹³Capturing smart people through their
  shrewdness,
 so that the counsel of the clever sweeps away.
¹⁴By day they meet with darkness,
 at noon they grope as in the night.

<sup>15</sup>But he delivers the needy person from the sword
    of their mouth,
  from the hand of the strong;
<sup>16</sup>So there is hope for the poor person,
  and evil shuts its mouth.

## Eliphaz: God wounds but binds up

<sup>17</sup>There – the good fortune of the man God
    reproves;
  so don't reject Shadday's correction.
<sup>18</sup>Because he is the one who wounds but binds up,
  he hits but his hands heal.
<sup>19</sup>During six attacks he will rescue you;
  during seven, bad things will not affect you.
<sup>20</sup>In famine he redeems you from dying;
  in battle – from the hands of the sword.
<sup>21</sup>During the scourge of the tongue, you will hide,
  you will not be afraid of destruction when it
    comes.
<sup>22</sup>Of destruction and of blight you will make fun;
  you will not be afraid of the animals of the
    country.
<sup>23</sup>Because your pact is with the stones of the field,
  and the animals of the wild are made at peace
    with you.
<sup>24</sup>You will acknowledge that there is well-being
    in your tent;
  you will attend to your home and not miss
    anything.
<sup>25</sup>You will acknowledge that your offspring are many,
  your descendants like the grass of the earth.
<sup>26</sup>You will come to the grave in fullness,
  as a sheaf comes up at its time.
<sup>27</sup>There – we have searched this out and it is so;
  listen to it, acknowledge it for yourself.

## Iyyob: There's no help for me

**6** Iyyob answered:

<sup>2</sup>If only my provocation could be truly weighed,
  and people could lift on the scales the malice
    shown to me, altogether.
<sup>3</sup>Because it would now be heavier than the sand
    of the seas;
  that is why my words have been wild.
<sup>4</sup>Because Shadday's arrows are in me,
  their poison my spirit drinks up,
  God's terrors line up against me.

<sup>5</sup>Does a wild donkey bray over grass,
  does an ox bellow over its fodder?
<sup>6</sup>Is something insipid eaten without salt,
  is there taste in the juice of a mallow?
<sup>7</sup>My appetite refuses to touch;
  those things are like food for when I am ill.
<sup>8</sup>If only my request would come about,
  and God would grant my hope,
<sup>9</sup>That God would show willing and crush me,
  let loose his hand and cut me off.
<sup>10</sup>It would still be my consolation
  (though I would contort with writhing that
    wouldn't spare),
  because I have not disowned the things said by
    the Sacred One.

<sup>11</sup>What energy do I have that I should wait,
  what end do I have that I should prolong my
    life?
<sup>12</sup>Is my energy the energy of stones,
  or is my flesh copper?
<sup>13</sup>Surely there is no help for me in myself,
  and adeptness has driven itself away from me.

## Iyyob: You call this friendship?

<sup>14</sup>As for one who refuses commitment to his
    friend,
  he abandons awe for Shadday,
<sup>15</sup>My brothers have broken faith like a wadi,
  like the canyons with wadis that pass away,
<sup>16</sup>That are dark with ice,
  when snow piles over them.
<sup>17</sup>At the time when they flow, they've expired;
  in the heat, they've disappeared from their
    place.
<sup>18</sup>Caravans divert their path;
  they go up into the wasteland and perish.
<sup>19</sup>Caravans from Tema have looked to them,
  travelling groups from Sheba have hoped in
    them.
<sup>20</sup>They're confounded, because they had
    trusted;
  they came right to it and they're shamed.

<sup>21</sup>Because now you've become nothing;
  you see something fearful and you're afraid.
<sup>22</sup>Did I say to you, 'Give me –
  out of your energy pay a bribe on my behalf?
<sup>23</sup>Save me from the hand of my adversary,
  from the hand of violent people redeem me'?

²⁴Instruct me, and I myself will be quiet;
   enable me to understand how I've erred.
²⁵How painful are upright things that have been
      said –
   but how does reproof from you reprove?
²⁶Do you think up utterances for reproof,
   and are the sayings of a despairing man for the
      wind?
²⁷Would you also make the lot fall for an orphan,
   and barter over your friend?
²⁸But now, show willing, turn your face to me;
   if I lie to your face . . .
²⁹Please turn back, there should not be evil;
   turn back, my right standing is still intact.
³⁰Is there evil on my tongue,
   or can my palate not discern malice?

### Iyyob to God: A human being has hard service on earth

**7** A mere human being has hard service on
      earth, doesn't he,
   and his days are like the days of an employee,
²Like a servant who longs for shadow,
   and like an employee who hopes for his
      wages.
³Thus I have been given months of emptiness as
      my domain,
   nights of oppression have been counted out
      for me.
⁴If I lie down, I say
   'When shall I get up?'
But evening drags on,
   and I am full of tossings until morning
      twilight.
⁵My flesh is clothed in maggots,
   and clods of earth,
   my skin has become broken and oozing.
⁶My days have been swifter than a weaver's
      shuttle,
   and they've come to a finish in an absence of
      thread.
⁷Be mindful that my life is wind;
   my eye will not again see good things.
⁸The eye that sees me will not behold me;
   your eye will be on me, but I will be no more.
⁹A cloud comes to a finish and goes;
   so the person who goes down to She'ol does not
      come up.
¹⁰He does not go back to his home again;
   his place does not recognize him again.

### Iyyob: What are human beings that you pay them so much attention?

¹¹Indeed I will not hold back my mouth;
   I will speak in the pressure of my spirit,
   I will talk in the bitterness of my entire being.
¹²Am I the Sea or the Dragon,
   that you set a watch over me?
¹³When I've said, 'My bed will comfort me,
   my mattress will carry part of my talk',
¹⁴You scare me with dreams,
   and terrify me with visions.
¹⁵My entire being would choose strangling,
   death, away from my bones.
¹⁶I've rejected it, I shall not live permanently;
   leave off from me, because my days are hollow.
¹⁷What is a mere human being that you make him
      great,
   and that you set your mind on him,
¹⁸That you attend to him each morning
   and test him every moment?
¹⁹How long will you not look away from me,
   not slacken hold of me until I swallow my spit?
²⁰If I've done wrong, what do I do to you,
   you who preserve humanity?
Why have you made me into a target for yourself
   so that I've become a burden to myself?
²¹Why do you not carry my rebellion
   and let my waywardness pass?
Because I shall now lie down in the earth,
   and when you look urgently for me, I will be
      no more.

### Bildad: On learning from the past

**8** Bildad the Shuhite answered:

²How long will you utter these things?
   – the sayings of your mouth are a massive wind.
³Does God twist the exercise of authority,
   does Shadday twist what is right?
⁴If your sons did wrong in relation to him,
   he sent them into the hand of their rebellion.
⁵If you yourself look urgently for God,
   and seek for grace with Shadday,
⁶If you're clean and upright,
   surely he will now arise for you
   and he will make good your faithful estate:
⁷your beginning may have been small,
   but your end will grow very great.

⁸Because ask the former generation, please,
  set your mind to what their ancestors searched
    out,
⁹Because we are of yesterday and we don't know,
  because our days on earth are a shadow.
¹⁰They can instruct you, can't they, and say to you,
  and get utterances out from their mind?
¹¹Can papyrus get tall where there's no marsh,
  can reed grow without water?
¹²While still in its shoot form when it's not cut,
  it would wither before any grass does.
¹³So are the paths of all who put God out of
    mind;
  the hope of the impious man perishes.
¹⁴His assurance breaks off,
  his trust is a spider's house.
¹⁵He relies on his house but it doesn't stand;
  he takes strong hold of it but it does not hold.
¹⁶While he may be moist before the sun,
  and his shoot may go out over his garden,
¹⁷His roots may interweave over a heap,
  may behold a house among stones,
¹⁸If they swallow him up from his place,
  it denies him: 'I didn't see you.'
¹⁹There, that's the joy of his way;
  and from the earth another springs.
²⁰On the other hand, God does not reject the man
    of integrity,
  and does not take strong hold of the hand of
    the person who acts badly.
²¹He will fill your mouth with laughter again,
  and your lips will shout.
²²The people hostile to you will clothe themselves
    in disgrace;
  the tent of the faithless will be no more.

*Iyyob: God does not answer*

# 9

Iyyob answered:

²Truly I acknowledge that it is so;
  but how can a mere human being be in the
    right with God?
³If he wants to argue with him,
  he doesn't answer him once in a thousand.
⁴Smart in mind and firm in energy –
  who has been tough with him and been at
    peace? –
⁵The one who moves mountains though they don't
    acknowledge him,
  who overturns them in his anger,

⁶Who shakes the earth from its place
  so that its pillars shudder,
⁷Who says to the sun that it should not shine
  and seals over the stars,
⁸Who spread out the heavens by himself
  and trod on the back of the sea,
⁹Who is the maker of the Bear, Orion,
  Pleiades and the rooms of the South,
¹⁰Who does big things, beyond searching out,
  extraordinary deeds, beyond numbering.
¹¹If he were to pass by me, I would not see,
  were he to sweep past, I would not discern
    him.
¹²If he were to snatch away, who could make him
    turn back,
  who could say to him, 'What are you
    doing?'
¹³God – he doesn't turn back his anger;
  under him Rahab's helpers bow low.
¹⁴How much less can I be one to answer him,
  to choose words against him?
¹⁵Though I am in the right, I would not answer
    him;
  I would ask for grace from the one who
    exercises authority for me.
¹⁶If I called and he answered me,
  I would not trust that he would give ear to my
    voice,
¹⁷He who crushes me for a trifle,
  and multiplies my wounds for nothing.
¹⁸He doesn't let me get my breath back,
  but fills me with bitterness.
¹⁹If it's about energy – there, he is firm;
  if it's about exercising authority – who can
    enable me to meet him?
²⁰Though I were in the right, my mouth would
    declare me in the wrong;
  I am a man of integrity, but it could declare me
    crooked.

*Iyyob: There is no arbiter between us*

²¹Whereas I am a man of integrity, I don't
    acknowledge myself,
  I reject my life.
²²It's all the same, that's why I say
  'He finishes off the person of integrity and the
    faithless.'
²³If a scourge suddenly puts to death,
  he ridicules the plight of people who are free
    of guilt.

²⁴When the earth is given into the hand of the
  faithless,
he covers the face of the people who exercise
  authority in it –
if not he, then who is it?

²⁵My days have been swifter than a runner;
  as they've taken flight, they haven't seen good
    things.
²⁶They've swept by like boats of reed,
  as an eagle that swoops on prey.
²⁷If my saying is, 'I'll put my talk out of mind,
  I'll abandon my look and be cheerful',
²⁸I'm terrified of all my pains,
  I know that you won't hold me free of guilt.
²⁹I am the one who'll be declared in the wrong;
  why then should I get weary in vain?
³⁰If I wash with soap,
  and cleanse the palms of my hands with caustic,
³¹You would then dip me in a pit,
  so that my clothes would take offence at me.
³²Because he isn't a man like me so I could answer
    him,
  should we come to make a ruling together.
³³No, there's no arbiter between us
  who might lay his hand on the two of us.
³⁴Were he to remove his club from upon me,
  so that dread of him might not terrify me,
³⁵I would speak and not be afraid of him,
  because I am not like this in myself.

**10** With my entire being I loathe my life;
  I shall let loose my talk for myself,
  I shall speak in the bitterness of my being.
²I will say to God, 'Don't declare me in the
    wrong;
  let me know what it is you argue with me
    about.
³Does it seem good to you that you oppress,
  that you reject the labour of your fists
  and smile on the counsel of faithless people?

*Iyyob: Do you have eyes of flesh?*

⁴Do you have eyes of flesh,
  do you see as a mere human being sees?
⁵Are your days like the days of a mere human
    being,
  are your years like the years of a man,
⁶That you seek for my waywardness,
  enquire after my wrongdoings?

⁷Although you know that I'm not in the wrong,
  and there's no one who rescues from your
    hand.
⁸Whereas your hands shaped me and made me,
  altogether, all round, you've swallowed me up.
⁹Be mindful, please, that you made me like mud:
  but you turn me back to earth.
¹⁰Did you not pour me out like milk,
  set me like cheese?
¹¹You clothed me with skin and flesh,
  wove me with bones and sinews.
¹²You showed me life and commitment,
  your attention watched over my spirit.
¹³But these things you hid in your mind,
  I know that this was in your thinking:
¹⁴If I did wrong, you would watch me,
  and not hold me free of the guilt of my
    waywardness.
¹⁵If I'm in the wrong, alas for me:
  but if I am in the right, I can't lift my head,
Full of being slighted,
  drenched with my humbling.
¹⁶Should [my head] stand high, you'd hunt me like
    a cub,
  and again show extraordinary power against me.
¹⁷You bring new witnesses in front of me,
  increase your vexation towards me,
  changes of hard service with me.

¹⁸So why did you get me out of the womb?
  – I could have breathed my last, and eye not
    seen me.
¹⁹I could have been as if I never was,
  I could have been carried from the womb to
    the grave.
²⁰My days are few, aren't they, so leave off,
  get away from me so I may look cheerful for a
    moment,
²¹Before I go (and I will not come back)
  to a country of darkness and deathly shadow,
²²A land of gloom like darkness,
  deathly shadow without order,
  so that it shines like dark.

*Tsophar: Can you plumb God's depth?*

**11** Tsophar the Na'amatite answered:

²Should an abundance of words not be answered,
  or should a man with lip be treated as in the
    right?

³Your prattle may silence human beings,
 you may ridicule and there may be no one to
  rebuke,
⁴You may say 'My grasp of things is clean,
 and I have been pure in your eyes',
⁵However, would that God might speak
 and open his lips with you,
⁶And tell you the secrets of being smart,
 because there are two sides to adeptness and
  you should acknowledge
 that God lets some of your waywardness be
  forgotten for you.

⁷Could you find God's reaches,
 or find Shadday's completeness?
⁸The loftiness of the heavens – what can you do,
 deeper than She'ol – what can you know?
⁹Its measure is longer than the earth,
 wider than the sea.
¹⁰If he sweeps by and takes captive and
  congregates,
 who can turn him back?
¹¹Because he knows empty men;
 when he sees trouble, does he not discern?
¹²A hollow man will get a mind
 when a wild donkey is born a human being.
¹³If you direct your mind
 and spread your palms towards him,
¹⁴If there is trouble in your hand, put it far
  away,
 and don't let evil dwell in your tents,
¹⁵Because then you will lift your face, free of
  blemish,
 and you will be constrained, but you won't be
  afraid.
¹⁶Because you yourself will put trouble out of
  mind,
 you'll remember it as water that has passed
  by.
¹⁷Your life span will rise brighter than
  noonday;
 though it be gloomy, it will become like
  morning.
¹⁸You'll be confident, because there'll be hope;
 when you search, you'll take your rest in
  confidence.
¹⁹You'll lie down and there'll be no one to
  disturb,
 and many will seek your goodwill.
²⁰But the eyes of the faithless will fail,
 retreat vanishes from them,
  their hope is a dying breath.

*Iyyob: You're so smart*

**12** Iyyob answered:

²Truly you are the people
 and smartness will die with you.
³I too have a mind like you, I don't fall lower than
  you,
 and in whose thinking are there not things like
  these?
⁴I shall become one who is a laughing stock to his
  friend,
 who calls to God and he answers;
 one in the right, a man of integrity, is a
  laughing stock.
⁵While there is contempt for calamity in the
  thought of the person who is secure,
 it is prepared for people whose foot slips.
⁶Tents stay at ease for robbers
 and people who provoke God have
  confidence,
 as people whom God has brought into his
  hand.

⁷However, please ask the animals so they can
  instruct you,
 and the birds of the heavens so they can tell
  you,
⁸Or talk to the earth so it may instruct you,
 and so the fish of the sea can recount it to
  you.
⁹Who does not acknowledge, among all these,
 that Yahweh's hand has done this,
¹⁰The one in whose hand is the life of every living
  thing,
 and the spirit of all human flesh?
¹¹The ear tests utterances, doesn't it,
 as the palate tastes food for itself.
¹²Among the aged lies smartness,
 in length of days lies discernment.

¹³With him are smartness and strength,
 to him belong counsel and discernment.
¹⁴On one hand, he tears down and it is not built
  up,
 he locks up a man and he is not released.
¹⁵On the other, he holds back the water and it
  dries up,
 he sends it off and it overwhelms the country.
¹⁶With him are vigour and adeptness,
 to him belong the person who goes astray and
  the one who leads astray.

## Iyyob: Just listen, will you?

17He makes counsellors go stripped,
  makes people who exercise authority go crazy.
18He loosens the bond put on by kings,
  ties a belt round their hips.
19He makes priests go stripped,
  overthrows the enduring.
20He removes speech from trustworthy men,
  takes the discretion of elders.
21He pours contempt on leaders,
  slackens the belt of the strong.
22He reveals mysteries from the darkness,
  gets deathly shadow out into the light.
23He lifts up nations and obliterates them,
  expands nations and leads them.
24He removes the mind from the heads of a
    country's people,
  and makes them wander in a wasteland where
    there's no way.
25They grope in the darkness where there is no
    light,
  and he makes them wander like a drunk.

**13** There, my eye has seen all this,
  my ear has heard and understood it.
2Corresponding to your knowledge, I too know;
  I don't fall lower than you.
3However, I myself will speak to Shadday,
  I want to reprove God.
4However, you are smearers of falsehood,
  non-entity physicians, all of you.
5If only you would simply be quiet;
  it would be smartness for you.
6Please listen to my reproof,
  heed the arguments from my lips.
7Is it for God that you speak evil,
  or for him that you speak deceitfully?
8Is it for him that you show regard,
  or for God that you argue?
9Would it be good if he searched you out,
  would you play about with him as one plays
    about with a mere human being?
10He would reprove you strongly,
  even if you covertly show regard.
11His dignity would terrify you, wouldn't it,
  and dread of him would fall on you.
12Your reminders are aphorisms made of ash,
  your responses are responses made of mud.

13Be quiet for me and I myself will speak;
  there will befall me whatever may.

14Why do I lift my flesh between my teeth,
  put my life into the palms of my hands?
15There, though he may slay me, I will not wait,
  yet I will defend my ways to his face.
16That, too, will be deliverance for me,
  that an impious person does not come before
    him.
17Listen attentively to my utterances,
  to my declaration in your ears.

## Iyyob: God, why do you conceal your face?

18Here, please, I have lined up a case;
  I know that I am the one who will prove to be
    in the right.
19Who is the one who will argue with me?
  – because now I would be quiet and breathe
    my last.
20Yet don't do two things with me,
  then I need not conceal myself from
    your face:
21Take the palm of your hand far from me;
  may dread of you not scare me.
22Call and I will be the one who answers,
  or I will speak and you speak back to me.
23How many are my acts of waywardness and my
    wrongdoings?
  – make known to me my rebellion and my
    wrongdoing.

24Why do you conceal your face,
  and think of me as an enemy to you?
25Do you frighten a leaf that's being blown away,
  do you pursue dried-up chaff,
26That you should write down bitter things
    for me
  and make me own the wayward acts of my
    youth,
27Put my feet in the stocks,
  keep watch on all my paths,
  put a mark on the roots of my feet?
28And that is one who wears out like something
    rotten,
  like a garment moth has eaten.

**14** A human being, born of a woman,
  is short in days and full of turmoil.
2Like a flower, he comes up but withers,
  takes flight like a shadow and does not stand.
3Yes, at this person you open your eye,
  and bring me into making a ruling with you.

⁴Who can bring clean from defiled?
  – not one person.
⁵If his days are determined, the number of his
      months is with you,
  you have set his limits and he cannot pass them,
⁶Turn away from him so that he may leave off,
  until he's happy with his day, like an employee.

## Iyyob: If only you would hide me in She'ol

⁷Because there is hope for a tree;
  if it is cut down, it can renew itself again,
  and its sucker will not leave off.
⁸If its root grows old in the earth,
  and its stump dies in the earth,
⁹At the scent of water it will bud,
  and make a shoot like a plant.
¹⁰But a man – he dies and is prostrate;
  a human being breathes his last, and where is he?
¹¹The water goes from a sea,
  a river becomes parched and dry,
¹²And a man lies down and does not get up,
  until the heavens are no longer.
They don't wake up,
  they don't rise from their sleep.

¹³If only you would hide me in She'ol,
  conceal me until your anger turns back,
Set a limit for me and be mindful of me:
      ¹⁴if a man were to die, could he come to life?
All the days of my hard service
  I would wait until my renewal came.
¹⁵You would call and I myself would answer you;
  for the making of your hands you would long.
¹⁶Because now when you counted my steps,
  you would not keep watch for my wrongdoings.
¹⁷My rebellion would be sealed up in a pouch;
  you would coat over my waywardness.

¹⁸However, a falling mountain crumbles,
  and a crag dislodges from its place,
¹⁹Water wears away stones,
  its torrents wash away the earth from the
      ground:
And you obliterate a mere human being's hope;
      ²⁰you overpower him permanently and he goes;
  you alter his face and send him off.
²¹His sons find honour but he doesn't know,
  or they are insignificant and he doesn't discern it.
²²Only, his flesh hurts him
  and his own self grieves for him.

## Eliphaz: Are you really so smart?

**15** Eliphaz the Temanite answered:

²Would a smart man answer with windy
      knowledge,
  fill his belly with the east wind,
³Argue with talk that's no use,
  and utterances by which he cannot profit?
⁴Indeed you – you contravene awe,
  you restrain talk before God.
⁵Because your waywardness teaches your mouth,
  you choose the tongue of shrewd people.
⁶Your mouth declares you in the wrong, not I;
  your lips testify against you.

⁷Are you the first human being who was born,
  or were you birthed before the hills?
⁸Do you listen in God's cabinet,
  or do you restrain smartness to yourself?
⁹What do you know and we don't know it,
  or understand and it is not in our possession?
¹⁰Among us are a grey-haired man, an old man,
  mightier in days than your father.
¹¹Are God's comforts too small for you,
  a word in gentleness with you?
¹²Why does your mind capture you,
  why do your eyes flash,
¹³That you turn back your spirit on God
  and let out your utterances from your mouth?
¹⁴What is a human being that he should be clean,
  one born of woman that he should be in the
      right?
¹⁵There, in his sacred ones he does not trust,
  and the heavens are not clean in his eyes.
¹⁶How much less one offensive and foul,
  a man drinking evil like water.
¹⁷I will explain, listen to me,
  and what I have beheld I will recount,
¹⁸Things that smart people tell,
  and have not concealed, from their ancestors.
¹⁹To them alone the land was given,
  when no stranger passed among them.

## Eliphaz: What happens to the faithless

²⁰All the days of the faithless man, he writhes,
  the number of years that are hidden for the
      violent man.
²¹Dreadful sounds are in his ears;
  when he is doing well, a robber comes upon him.

²²He is not sure of coming back from darkness;
   he is spied over for the sword.
²³He wanders about for bread, where is it?
   – he knows that the day of darkness is
     prepared, at his hand.
²⁴Pressure terrifies him, anguish overwhelms him,
   like a king ready to attack.
²⁵Because he stretched out his hand against God,
   acted the strong man against Shadday.
²⁶He runs against him head down
   with the thickness of his shields' backs,
²⁷Because he has covered his face with fat
   and put brawn on his thighs.
²⁸But he will dwell in ruined towns,
   houses that people don't live in,
   that have prepared to be heaps.
²⁹He will not be wealthy, his resources will not
     rise up;
   their gains will not extend over the land.
³⁰He will not depart from darkness,
   flame will wither his shoot;
   he will depart by the wind from his mouth.

³¹He should not trust in emptiness, leading
     himself astray,
   because emptiness will be his recompense.
³²Before his time he will wither;
   his branches will not be verdant.
³³He will do violence to his unripe grapes like a
     vine,
   he will throw off his blossom like an olive tree.
³⁴Because the impious man's assembly is barren,
   and fire consumes the tents of one who gives
     bribes.
³⁵He conceives oppression and gives birth to
     trouble;
   their womb prepares guile.

### Iyyob: Comforters? More like troublemakers

**16** Iyyob answered:

²I have heard many things like these;
   all of you are oppressive comforters.
³Is there a limit to windy words –
   what ails you that you answer?
⁴I too could speak like you
   if you yourselves were in my own place.
I could sound out against you in utterances
   and shake my head over you.
⁵I could firm you up with my speech;

   the moving of my lips could hold things back.

⁶If I speak, my hurt does not hold back;
   but if I leave off, what goes from me?
⁷Indeed he has now worn me out;
   you have desolated my whole assembly.
⁸You have shrivelled me, it's become a witness;
   my gauntness rises up against me, it testifies
     against me.
⁹His anger has torn and been hostile to me,
   he's gnashed his teeth at me.
My adversary sharpens his eyes towards me;
   ¹⁰people have gaped at me with their mouth.
With reviling they've struck me on the cheek,
   they mass together against me.
¹¹God has delivered me up to an evildoer,
   thrown me into the hands of the faithless.
¹²I was at ease, but he's shattered me,
   he's grasped me by the neck and smashed me,
He's set me up for himself as a target,
   ¹³his archers surround me.
He pierces my kidneys and doesn't spare;
   he pours my bile on the earth.
¹⁴He assaults me, with assault on top of assault;
   he runs at me like a strong man.

¹⁵I've sewn sack over my skin
   and buried my horn in the earth.
¹⁶My face is red from crying
   and over my eyelids is deathly shadow,
¹⁷Although there was no violence in my fists
   and my plea was clean.

### Iyyob: A witness in the heavens?

¹⁸Earth, don't cover my blood;
   there must not be a place for my cry.
¹⁹Even now, there – my witness is in the heavens,
   my advocate is on high.
²⁰Though my friends are people who scorn me,
   my eye pours out to God.
²¹He will issue reproof for a man with God
   [as] a human being does for his friend.
²²Because numbered years will come
   and I will go the path on which I shall not
     come back.

**17** My spirit is broken, my days are
   extinguished,
   the graves are for me.
²If it's not the case that mockeries are with me,

and on their recalcitrance my eye lodges . . .
³Please put my pledge by you –
  who is the one who will clap my hand?
⁴Because you've hidden their mind from insight;
  therefore you will not be exalted.
⁵'For a meal he tells on friends,
  and his children's eyes fail':
⁶He has made me a proverb for peoples,
  I shall become something at which to spit in
    the face.
⁷My eye has grown dim from provocation,
  my limbs are like a shadow, all of them.

⁸The upright are desolate at this,
  the one who is free of guilt arises against the
    impious.
⁹The faithful person grasps his way;
  the man who is pure of hands grows firmer.
¹⁰However, all of you, please come back again –
  but I will not find a smart man among you.
¹¹My days have passed, my strategies have snapped,
  the desires of my heart.
¹²They make night into day;
  light is nearer than darkness.
¹³If I hope for She'ol as my home,
  lay out my bed in the darkness,
¹⁴I call out to the Pit, 'You are my father',
  to the worm, 'My mother', 'My sister'.
¹⁵Where then is my hope,
  who can behold my hope?
¹⁶Will they go down to the poles of She'ol,
  will we descend together to the earth?

## Bildad: Reaffirming the moral foundation of the world

# 18
² Bildad the Shuhite answered:

²How long until you put an end to utterances?
  – consider, and afterwards we will speak.
³Why are we thought of as cattle,
  stupid in your eyes?
⁴One who tears himself apart with his anger –
  for your sake will the earth be abandoned,
  will a crag dislodge from its place?

⁵Yes, the light of the faithless goes out,
  the flame of his fire doesn't shine.
⁶Light darkens in his tent,
  his lamp above him goes out.
⁷His vigorous steps become short,

his own counsel throws him down,
⁸Because he's thrust into a net by his own feet;
  he walks about on to the mesh.
⁹A trap grasps him by the heel,
  clamps get strong hold of him.
¹⁰A rope for him is hidden in the earth,
  a trap for him on the trail.
¹¹All around, terrors terrify him,
  shatter him at his feet.
¹²Trouble is hungry for him,
  disaster has prepared for his stumbling.
¹³It consumes his skin-covered limbs;
  death's firstborn consumes his limbs.
¹⁴His confidence tears away from his tent,
  and it marches him to the king of terrors.
¹⁵Fire dwells in his tent,
  sulphur scatters over his home.
¹⁶Below, his roots dry up;
  above, his foliage withers.
¹⁷Commemoration of him perishes from the
    country,
  and he has no name in the outside world.
¹⁸They thrust him out from light to darkness,
  drive him out of the world.
¹⁹He has no posterity, no offspring, among his
    people,
  and he has no survivor in his place where he
    resided.
²⁰At his day people in the west are desolate,
  people in the east grasp horror.
²¹Indeed, these are the dwellings of the evildoer,
  this is the place of the one who did not
    acknowledge God.

## Iyyob: Ten times you've shamed me

# 19
² Iyyob answered:

²How long will you torment my entire being,
  crush me with utterances?
³These ten times you have shamed me;
  you feel no disgrace when you abuse me.
⁴Yet truly, should I have erred,
  my error lodges with me.
⁵If you truly magnify yourselves above me,
  and argue with me on the basis of my
    reviling,
⁶Acknowledge here that God has put me in the
    wrong,
  has put siege works round me.
⁷If I cry out 'Violence', I don't get an answer;

if I call for help, there's no exercise of authority.
⁸He's barred my path and I can't pass,
   and he sets darkness over my trails.
⁹He's stripped my splendour from me,
   removed the crown on my head.
¹⁰He tears me down all round, and I am gone;
   he uproots my hope like a tree.
¹¹He makes his anger rage against me;
   he thinks of me as like his adversaries for him.
¹²His raiding gangs come on all together,
   they've built up their way against me,
   they've camped at my tent all round.

## Iyyob: I know that my restorer lives, but . . .

¹³He's put my brothers far from me;
   my acquaintances have indeed become
     strangers to me.
¹⁴The people near to me and the people I knew
   have left off,
   the people residing in my house have put me
     out of mind.
¹⁵My servant girls think of me as a stranger;
   I've become a foreigner in their eyes.
¹⁶I've called to my servant but he doesn't answer,
   when with my own mouth I ask him for
     grace.
¹⁷My breath is strange to my wife,
   I'm loathsome to my siblings.
¹⁸Even little children have rejected me;
   when I get up, they speak against me.
¹⁹All my confidential friends have taken offence
   at me,
   and those I've been loyal to have turned against
     me.
²⁰My bone sticks to my skin and my flesh,
   and I've escaped by the skin of my teeth.

²¹Be gracious to me, be gracious to me, you're my
     friends,
   because God's hand has touched me.
²²Why do you pursue me like God,
   and why aren't you full of my flesh?
²³If only here my utterances were written down,
   if only they were inscribed in a document,
²⁴With an iron pen and lead,
   engraved on a crag permanently.
²⁵But I myself know that my restorer is alive,
   and as the last will get up on the earth.
²⁶After my skin has thus been stripped,
   away from my flesh I will behold God,

²⁷Whom I will behold for myself;
   my eyes will have seen him, and not a
     stranger.
My inner being within my chest fails,
   ²⁸when you say, 'How have we pursued him?'
The root of the thing is found in me;
   ²⁹be terrified of the sword for yourselves.
Because your wrath is wayward acts that deserve
   the sword,
   in order that you may acknowledge that there
     is judgement.

## Tsophar: My uneases

# 20 Tsophar the Na'amatite answered:

²This is why my uneases make me speak back,
   because of my feelings within me.
³When I hear correction that shames me,
   a spirit from my understanding makes me
     answer.

⁴Do you acknowledge this: from of old,
   from the placing of humanity on the earth,
⁵That the resounding of faithless people is of the
     briefest,
   the rejoicing of the impious is for a moment?
⁶If his exaltation climbs to the heavens
   and his head touches the clouds,
⁷Like his dung he perishes permanently;
   people who saw him say, 'Where is he?'
⁸Like a dream he flies away and people cannot
     find him;
   he is driven away like a night vision.
⁹Though an eye looked on him, it does not do so
     again;
   his place beholds him no more.
¹⁰His children seek the grace of poor people,
   his hands give back his vigour.
¹¹His bones were full of his youthfulness,
   but with him it lies down in the earth.
¹²If something bad is sweet in his mouth
   as he hides it under his tongue,
¹³As he spares it and does not abandon it,
   but holds it back inside his palate,
¹⁴His food in his stomach turns
   into the venom of asps within him.
¹⁵The resources he has swallowed he vomits,
   as God discharges it from his insides.

## Tsophar: How wickedness gets its reward

<sup>16</sup>He sucks the poison of asps,
  the viper's tongue kills him.
<sup>17</sup>He is not to see the streams,
  the rivers, the wadis of syrup and cream.
<sup>18</sup>He gives back the gains and doesn't swallow,
  he doesn't exult in the very resources from his
    trading.
<sup>19</sup>Because he crushed, abandoned poor people,
  seized a house when he was not building it,
<sup>20</sup>Because he doesn't know ease inside him,
  he doesn't let any of what he desired escape.
<sup>21</sup>There'll be no survivor to eat it;
  therefore his good things will not endure.
<sup>22</sup>When his abundance is full, pressure will
    overtake him;
  every hand of the oppressor will come upon
    him.
<sup>23</sup>May he be for the filling of his belly,
  may he send off on him his angry rage,
  and rain it upon him as his food.

<sup>24</sup>When he takes flight from an iron weapon,
  a copper arrow will pass through him.
<sup>25</sup>When he pulls it out and it comes out of his body,
  the shining thing out of his gall bladder,
Dreads come upon him,
  <sup>26</sup>all darkness is hidden up for his treasures.
Fire will consume him, unfanned;
  may it pasture on the survivor in his tent.
<sup>27</sup>The heavens will reveal his waywardness,
  the earth is going to rise up for him.
<sup>28</sup>May a flood exile his household,
  torrents on the day of his anger.
<sup>29</sup>This is the faithless person's share from God,
  the domain spoken of by God.

## Iyyob: If only wickedness did get its reward!

# 21  Iyyob answered:

<sup>2</sup>Listen properly to my utterance;
  may this be the comfort you offer.
<sup>3</sup>Bear with me while I myself speak,
  and after I have spoken, you may ridicule.
<sup>4</sup>Am I: is my talk towards a human being,
  so why should my spirit not be short?
<sup>5</sup>Turn your face to me and be desolated,
  put your hand on your mouth.

<sup>6</sup>If I am mindful, I am terrified;
  trembling grasps my flesh.
<sup>7</sup>Why do faithless people live on,
  as they grow older, also get stronger in
    resources?
<sup>8</sup>Their offspring are established before them, with
    them,
  their descendants are before their eyes.
<sup>9</sup>Their households are doing well, without fear;
  with no club of God on them.
<sup>10</sup>His bull breeds and does not fail;
  his cow delivers and does not miscarry.
<sup>11</sup>They send off their little ones like sheep,
  their children skip about.
<sup>12</sup>They lift their voice to tambourine and guitar,
  rejoice to the sound of the pipe.
<sup>13</sup>They finish their days with good things,
  and in peace go down to She'ol.
<sup>14</sup>They say to God, 'Depart from us,
  we don't want to acknowledge your ways.
<sup>15</sup>What is Shadday that we should serve him,
  and how do we profit when we pray to him?'
<sup>16</sup>There, are their good things not in their own
    hand,
  though the counsel of faithless people is far
    away from me.

## Iyyob: Your words of comfort are hollow

<sup>17</sup>How often does the lamp of faithless people go
    out,
  and the disaster due to them come upon them,
  the destiny he shares out in his anger.
<sup>18</sup>They should be like straw before wind,
  like chaff that a tempest seizes.
<sup>19</sup>Whereas God may hide up his trouble for his
    children,
  he should make it good to him, so that he
    acknowledges it.
<sup>20</sup>His eyes should see his destruction;
  he should drink Shadday's wrath.
<sup>21</sup>Because what will he want for his household
    after him,
  when the number of his months has been
    curtailed?

<sup>22</sup>Can one teach God knowledge,
  when he is the one who exercises authority over
    people on high?
<sup>23</sup>One person dies in his full strength,
  all peaceable and at ease.

²⁴His pails are full of milk
  and the marrow in his bones is juicy.
²⁵Another person dies bitter in himself;
  he has not tasted good things.
²⁶All together they lie down in the earth
  and worms cover over them.

²⁷There, I know your intentions,
  the strategies with which you will do violence
    against me,
²⁸That you will say, 'Where is the leader's house,
  where is the tent that was the dwelling of the
    faithless people?'
²⁹Have you not asked people who pass by on the
    way,
  not recognized their evidences,
³⁰That on the day of disaster a bad person is held
    back,
  on the day when outbursts are carried along.
³¹Who tells of his conduct to his face;
  when he has acted, who makes good to him?
³²When he is carried along to the graves,
  and someone watches over his tomb,
³³The clods in the wadi are sweet to him;
  behind him everyone follows,
  and there is no numbering those before him.
³⁴So how can you comfort me with hollowness?
  – the things that you say back: trespass
    remains.

## Eliphaz rewrites Iyyob's life

# 22
  Eliphaz answered:

²Is a man useful to God,
  that a person of insight should be of benefit
    to him?
³Is it a delight to Shadday when you are in the right,
  or is there profit when you show integrity in
    your ways?
⁴Is it because of your awe that he reproves you,
  comes to make a ruling with you?
⁵Are your bad ways not great,
  and is there no end to your acts of waywardness?
⁶Because you take pledges from your brothers for
    nothing,
  you strip the clothes of the naked.
⁷You don't give water to the weary person,
  you hold back bread from the hungry,
⁸As a strong man to whom the land belongs,
  a man held in high regard who lives on it.

⁹Widows you've sent off empty,
  the strength of orphans is crushed.
¹⁰That's why traps are all round you,
  and sudden dread frightens you,
¹¹Or darkness when you cannot see,
  and a flood of water that covers you.

¹²God is lofty in the heavens, isn't he;
  see the peak of the stars, how high!
¹³You've said, 'What does God know,
  can he exercise authority through the
    thundercloud?
¹⁴The clouds are a screen for him and he doesn't see,
  as he goes about the circuit of the heavens.'

## Eliphaz: Come back!

¹⁵Do you keep watch on the age-old path
  that men of trouble have trod,
¹⁶Who were shrivelled up when it was not time,
  whose foundation was washed away in a river,
¹⁷People who said to God, 'Depart from us',
  and 'What will Shadday do for them?'
¹⁸But he was the one who filled their houses with
    good things;
  the counsel of faithless people is far away
    from me.
¹⁹Faithful people see and celebrate,
  the one who is free of guilt ridicules them:
²⁰'Is it not the case that those who rose against us
    have disappeared,
  and what was left of them the fire has
    consumed?'

²¹Please be of benefit to him and be at peace;
  by these things good will come to you.
²²Please take instruction from his mouth
  and lay up in your mind the things he said.
²³If you come back to Shadday you'll be built up,
  when you move evil far from your tent.
²⁴You'll regard precious metal as earth,
  Ophir gold as a crag in the wadis.
²⁵Shadday will be your precious metal,
  choice silver for you,
²⁶When you then revel in Shadday,
  and lift your face to God.
²⁷You'll pray to him and he will listen to you,
  and you'll make good your pledges.
²⁸You'll determine something and it will arise
    for you,
  and on your ways light will shine.

²⁹When people make others fall, you'll say 'Lift
    them up',
    and he'll deliver the downcast of eyes.
³⁰He'll rescue one who is not free of guilt –
    he'll find rescue through the cleanness of your
    palms.

## Iyyob: Who moved?

# 23

Iyyob answered:

²My talk is indeed rebellious today,
    though my hand is heavy with my groaning.
³If only I knew how I could find him,
    could come as far as his established place.
⁴I'd lay out my case before him,
    fill my mouth with reproofs.
⁵I'd get to know the utterances he would answer
    me,
    I'd understand what he'd say to me.
⁶Would he argue with me with abundance of
    energy?
    – no, surely he'd set his mind on me.
⁷There it would be an upright man who would
    enter into reproof with him,
    and I would survive permanently from the one
    who exercises authority over me.

⁸If I go east, he is not there,
    and west, I don't discern him,
⁹North where he acts, I don't behold him;
    he may turn south, but I don't see him.
¹⁰But he knows the way that is mine;
    if he tests me, I'll come out as gold.
¹¹My foot has grasped his track,
    I've kept his way and not turned aside.
¹²From the order of his lips I haven't moved away,
    I've hidden up the sayings of his mouth more
    than my portion of food.
¹³He is one; who can turn him back?
    – what he himself desires, he does,
¹⁴Because he'll bring to completion what was
    decreed regarding me,
    and there are many things like these in his
    mind.
¹⁵Therefore I'm fearful of his presence;
    when I consider, I'm in dread of him.
¹⁶God has made my mind soft;
    Shadday has made me fearful,
¹⁷But I haven't expired before the darkness;
    from before me he has covered the gloom.

## Iyyob: Why are times not kept by Shadday?

# 24

Why are times not hidden up by
    Shadday?
    – those who acknowledge him do not behold
    his days.
²People remove boundary stones,
    seize a flock and pasture it,
³Drive away the orphans' donkey,
    take the widow's bull as a pledge,
⁴Turn aside the needy from the road:
    the humble in the land have been made to hide
    together.
⁵There, they're wild donkeys in the wilderness,
    who go out in the course of their work.
Looking urgently for prey, the steppe belongs
    to it,
    food for the boys.
⁶In the open country they harvest its fodder,
    and glean the vineyard of the faithless.
⁷They stay the night naked, without clothing;
    there's no covering against the cold.
⁸They get wet from the mountain rain,
    and without a shelter they embrace a crag.
⁹People seize the orphan from the breast,
    take the baby of a humble person as a
    pledge.
¹⁰They go about naked, without clothing,
    and hungry, though they carry sheaves.
¹¹Between their terraces they press oil,
    and they tread the winepresses, but they are
    thirsty.
¹²From the town men groan,
    the entire being of people run through cries
    for help,
    but God does not lay a charge of corruptness.

## Iyyob: Who can prove me a liar?

¹³Those people – they are among those who are
    rebels against the light,
    they don't recognize its ways,
    they don't live in its trails.
¹⁴At first light the murderer gets up
    so he may slay the humble and needy,
    And in the evening become like a thief,
    ¹⁵while the eye of the adulterer watches for
    dusk,
    Saying 'No eye will behold me',
    and he puts a cover on his face.

¹⁶He breaks into houses in the dark,
  by day they shut themselves in; they don't
    acknowledge light.
¹⁷Because for them, all together, morning is
    deathly shadow,
  because he recognizes deathly shadow's
    terrors.

¹⁸He should be a slight thing on the face of the
    water,
  their domain in the land should be slighted;
  no one should turn his face by way of their
    vineyards.
¹⁹Both drought and heat seize snow water,
  and She'ol, people who have done wrong.
²⁰The womb should put him out of mind,
  the worm should find him sweet.
No longer should he be kept in mind;
  evil should break like a tree.
²¹He deals badly with the infertile woman, who
    does not give birth,
  he does no good to the widow.
²²He drags off the sturdy by means of his
    energy;
  he rises up, and he should not trust in his life.
²³He gives himself confidence and leans on it,
  and his eyes are on their ways.

²⁴They are on high for a while, then there is
    nothing of them;
  they are brought low, like a mallow they
    shrivel,
  like a head of grain they wither.
²⁵If it is not so, who can prove me a liar,
  make my utterance into nothing?

## Bildad: Even the stars are not clean

**25** Bildad the Shuhite answered:

²Rule and dread are with him;
  he brings about well-being in his heights.
³Is there any numbering of his raiding gangs,
  or on whom does his light not rise?
⁴And how can a mere human being be right with
    God,
  how can someone born of a woman be clean?
⁵There, even the moon is not bright
  and the stars are not clean in his eyes.
⁶How much less a mere human being, a worm,
  or a man, a maggot.

## Iyyob: The edges of his ways

**26** Iyyob answered:

²How you have helped someone without
    energy,
  delivered an arm without vigour!
³How you have counselled someone without
    smartness,
  and made known adeptness in abundance!
⁴With whom have you told utterances,
  and whose breath came out from you?

⁵The ghosts are made to writhe
  beneath the water, with those who dwell in it.
⁶She'ol is naked in front of him,
  there is no cover for Abaddon.
⁷The one who stretched out the north over the
    waste,
  suspended earth over nothingness,
⁸Wrapped the water in his clouds
  (and the thundercloud did not break beneath
    them),
⁹Enclosed the view of his throne,
  spread his thundercloud over it.
¹⁰He drew a borderline on the face of the water
  at light's boundary with darkness.
¹¹The heavens' pillars quake,
  they are aghast at his reprimand.
¹²By his energy he stirred up the sea,
  by his understanding he hit Rahab.
¹³By his wind the heavens became clear;
  his hand ran through the twisting snake.
¹⁴There, these are the edges of his ways,
  and what a whisper is the word that we hear
    of him,
  so who understands the thunder of his
    strength?

## Iyyob: I do identify with the people of integrity

**27** Iyyob again took up his poem:

²By the life of God who has dismissed the exercise
    of authority for me,
  Shadday who has made my life bitter,
³All the while there is breath in me,
  and God's spirit is in my nostrils,
⁴If my lips speak evil,
  or my tongue – if it murmurs deceit . . .

⁵Far be it from me that I should say you are right;
    until I breathe my last I will not dismiss my
      integrity from me.
⁶I hold strongly to my being in the right and I will
    not slacken hold of it;
    my conscience does not revile me for any of
      my days.

⁷May my enemy be like the faithless,
    may the one who rises against me be like the
      evildoer.
⁸Because what is the hope of the impious man
    when he is cut down,
    when God requires his life?
⁹Will God listen to his cry,
    when pressure comes upon him,
¹⁰Or will he revel in Shadday,
    call God at any time?
¹¹I will instruct you in God's hand,
    what is with Shadday I will not hide.
¹²There, you have beheld, all of you,
    so why this total hollowness you manifest?

### Iyyob: And I do affirm that wicked people get their deserts

¹³This is the share of the person who is faithless
    with God,
    the domain that violent people get from
      Shadday.
¹⁴If his children are many – it is for the sword,
    and his descendants will not be full of bread.
¹⁵The people who survive him will be buried by
    death,
    and their widows will not cry.
¹⁶If he heaps up silver like earth,
    and prepares clothing like mud,
¹⁷He may prepare, but a faithful person will wear,
    and a person free of guilt will share out the
      silver.
¹⁸He has built a house like a nest,
    like the bivouac a watchman makes,
¹⁹He may lie down a wealthy man but he will not
    do so again;
    when he opens his eyes, there is none of it.
²⁰Terrors overtake him like water;
    by night a tempest has seized him.
²¹The east wind lifts him and he has gone;
    it sweeps him from his place.
²²It throws itself at him and does not spare,
    though he takes flight urgently from its hand.

²³It claps the palms of its hands at him
    and whistles at him from its place.

### Interlude: There is a mine for silver . . .

**28** Indeed there is a source for silver,
    a place for gold that people will refine.
²Iron is taken from the earth,
    stone that someone pours as copper.
³He has put an end to darkness,
    and to every limit, he was searching out.
Stone in darkness and deathly shadow
    ⁴has been broken open by a wadi, away from
      any resident.
Forgotten people, away from anyone's foot, have
    dangled,
    away from a human being they've swayed.
⁵Earth from which food comes forth
    has been changed like fire below it.
⁶Its stones were the place of sapphire,
    and it had gold dust.
⁷The bird of prey did not know the trail,
    the falcon's eye has not gazed on it.
⁸Majestic beasts have not made a way to it,
    the cub has not advanced on it.
⁹Someone has put out his hand against the flint,
    overturned the mountains by the root,
¹⁰He has split channels through the crags
    and his eye has seen every precious thing.
¹¹He has dammed up the sources of the rivers
    so that he might bring hidden things out into
      the light.

### . . . but where can wisdom be found?

¹²But smartness: from where can it be found,
    where is understanding's place?
¹³No human being can know its comparative
    value,
    and it's not found in the country of the living.
¹⁴The deep says, 'It's not in me';
    the sea says, 'It's not with me.'
¹⁵Fine gold can't be given in its place;
    silver can't be weighed out as its price.
¹⁶It can't be balanced against Ophir gold,
    against precious onyx or sapphire.
¹⁷Gold or crystal can't compare with it,
    or containers of fine gold be its exchange.
¹⁸Coral and jasper can't be brought to mind;
    a pouch of smartness is more than rubies.

¹⁹Topaz from Kush cannot compare with
    it;
  it can't be balanced against pure gold.

²⁰So smartness: from where does it come,
  where is understanding's place?
²¹It hides from the eyes of every living thing;
  from the birds in the heavens it conceals itself.
²²Abaddon and death say,
  'With our ears we've heard report of it.'

²³God understands the way to it;
  he's the one who knows its place.
²⁴Because he's the one who looks to the ends of
    the earth,
  sees beneath all the heavens.
²⁵In setting a weight for the wind,
  and establishing the water by measure,
²⁶When setting a decree for the rain
  and a way for the bolt of thunder,
²⁷Then he saw it and took account of it,
  established it and also searched it out.

²⁸And he said to humanity:
  'There, smartness is awe for the Lord,
  understanding is departing from evil.'

## Iyyob: The way things were (1)

# 29 Iyyob again took up his poem:

²If only it was like the months of the past,
  like the days when God was keeping watch over
    me,
³When his lamp was shining over my head,
  when I was walking through the darkness with
    his light,
⁴As I was in my days early in the year,
  when God's confidences were at my tent,
⁵When Shadday was still with me,
  my boys were round me,
⁶When my steps bathed in cream,
  and the crag poured streams of oil for me,
⁷When I went out of the township gateway,
  set my seat in the square,
⁸Boys saw me and withdrew,
  old men got up, stood.
⁹Officials held back utterances,
  put the palm of their hand to their mouth.
¹⁰The voices of rulers were quiet,
  their tongue stuck to their palate.

¹¹When the ear heard, it wished me good fortune;
  when the eye saw, it testified to me.

## Iyyob: The way things were (2)

¹²Because I rescued the humble person crying for
    deliverance,
  the orphan and the one who had no one to
    help.
¹³The blessing of the person who was perishing
    would come upon me;
  I made the heart of the widow resound.
¹⁴I clothed myself in faithfulness so that it clothed
    itself in me;
  the [proper] exercise of authority by me was
    coat and turban.
¹⁵I was eyes to the blind person,
  I was feet to the lame.
¹⁶I was father to the needy;
  I sought out the argument of the person I did
    not know.
¹⁷I broke the jaws of the evildoer
  and threw the prey from his teeth.

¹⁸I said, 'I shall breathe my last with my nest,
  I shall make my days as many as the phoenix,
¹⁹My root opened to the water,
  dew lodging in my branches,
²⁰My splendour fresh with me,
  my bow renewing itself in my hand.'

²¹People listened to me and waited,
  they kept themselves quiet for my counsel.
²²After my utterance they would not speak again;
  upon them my word would drop.
²³They would wait for me as for rain,
  they would open their mouth as for the late rain.
²⁴When I would make fun with them, they would
    not believe it;
  the light of my face they would not discount.
²⁵I would choose the way for them and sit as head,
  I would dwell like a king among his troops,
  like one who comforts mourners.

## Iyyob: The way things are (1)

# 30 But now people make fun of me,
    people younger than me in days,
People whose fathers I would have rejected
  from putting with my sheep dogs.

²Indeed, what use would the energy of their hands
        be to me,
    when their vigour has perished from them,
³People who in want and desolate hunger flee,
    to the arid ground, the edge of devastating
        devastation,
⁴Who pick the saltwort on bushes;
    the root of broom is their food.
⁵They are driven out from society,
    people shout at them like a thief,
⁶So they dwell in the gully of wadis,
    holes in the earth and rocks.
⁷They bray among the bushes,
    huddle under the thistles,
⁸Villains, yes, nameless people,
    they are struck down from the country.
⁹And now I've become their song,
    I've become something to talk about for them.

¹⁰People take offence at me, they stay far from me,
    but they don't hold back spit from my face.
¹¹Because someone has loosened my bow and
        humbled me,
    before me they've let loose restraint.
¹²When a brood arises at my right,
    they let my feet loose,
    and build up their paths to disaster against me.
¹³They break down my trail to express malice to me;
    they profit though they have no helper.
¹⁴They come as through a wide breach,
    beneath the devastation they roll in.
¹⁵Terrors are turned upon me;
    like the wind it pursues my honour.
My deliverance passes on like a cloud,
    ¹⁶so now my life pours out for me.
Days of humbling grasp me,
    ¹⁷night pierces my bones for me,
    and the things that gnaw at me don't rest.

## Iyyob: The way things are (2)

¹⁸With abundance of energy he grasps my
        clothing,
    belts me like the neck of my garment.
¹⁹He has thrown me into the mud,
    and I've come to resemble earth and ashes.

²⁰I cry for help to you but you don't answer me,
    though I stood, and you considered me.
²¹You turn into someone cruel to me;
    with the might of your hand you're hostile to me.

²²You lift me to the wind, make me ride on it,
    and dissolve me with a crash.
²³Indeed I know you'll take me back to death,
    to the appointed home for every living
        person.
²⁴Surely no one puts out his hand against a ruin,
    if in his calamity there is a cry for help
        regarding these things.
²⁵If I did not cry for one whose day was tough –
    my entire being grieved for the needy.
²⁶Indeed I hoped for good things, but bad things
        came;
    I waited for light, but darkness came.
²⁷My insides churn and don't stop,
    my days of humbling meet me.
²⁸I walk about dark, without warmth;
    when I get up in the congregation I cry for
        help.
²⁹I've become a brother to jackals,
    a friend to ostriches.
³⁰My skin turns black on me,
    my bones burn with heat.
³¹My guitar has become for mourning,
    my pipe for the sound of people crying.

## Iyyob: The way I have walked (1)

**31** I sealed a pact for my eyes,
        so how could I consider a girl?
²What is the share that God gives from above,
    the domain that Shadday gives from the
        heights?
³It's disaster for the evildoer, isn't it,
    ruin for the people who devise trouble.
⁴He himself sees my ways, doesn't he,
    takes account of all my steps.
⁵Have I walked with emptiness,
    has my foot hastened after guile?
⁶He should weigh me on faithful scales,
    so that God may acknowledge my integrity.

⁷If my step turns aside from the way,
    or my mind has gone after my eyes,
    or a blemish has stuck to my palms,
⁸May I sow but another eat,
    may my descendants be uprooted.

⁹If my mind has been enticed by a woman
    or I have lain in wait at my neighbour's door,
¹⁰May my wife grind for another,
    and over her may other men kneel,

¹¹Because this would have been a deliberate
     wickedness;
   it would be waywardness for the mediators to
     deal with,
¹²Because it is a fire that consumes to Abaddon,
   and it would uproot my entire yield.

## Iyyob: The way I have walked (2)

¹³If I've rejected the case of my servant or my
     maidservant
   when they argued with me,
¹⁴What will I do when God arises;
   when he pays attention, what will I say back?
¹⁵Didn't my maker make him inside his mother,
   didn't one person prepare us in the womb?

¹⁶If I hold back from the want of poor people,
   or let a widow's eyes fail,
¹⁷And eat my bit of food alone,
   so that the orphan has not eaten of it,
¹⁸Because from my youth he has grown up with
     me like a father,
   and I have guided her from my mother's
     womb;
¹⁹If I see someone perishing for lack of clothing,
   and a needy person has no covering,
²⁰If his insides have not blessed me
   when he would get warm from the shearing of
     my sheep;
²¹If I have shaken my hand against the orphan
   because I could see that I had help at the
     gateway;
²²My shoulder blade should fall from the
     shoulder,
   my forearm break from the joint,
²³Because disaster from God would be dread to
     me
   and I could not endure his dignity.

## Iyyob: The way I have walked (3)

²⁴If I've made gold my assurance
   or said to fine gold, 'My confidence',
²⁵If I rejoice because my resources are great,
   because my hand has found a massive amount,
²⁶If I see light when it shines,
   or the bright moon going,
²⁷And my mind was enticed in secret
   and my hand kissed my mouth,

²⁸That, too, would be waywardness calling for
     mediation,
   because I would have been deceiving God
     above.

²⁹If I rejoice in the calamity of someone hostile
     to me
   or thrill when bad fortune found him –
³⁰But I haven't given my mouth to wrongdoing,
   to asking for his life by a curse.
³¹If the men in my tent have not said,
   'If only there was someone who had not been
     full of his meat!'
³²No stranger lodges in the street;
   I open my doors to the path.
³³If I covered my rebellion like Adam,
   hiding my waywardness in my heart,
³⁴Because I fear the great horde,
   and the contempt of kin-groups would terrify
     me,
   so that I would keep quiet and not go out of my
     entrance . . .

³⁵If only I had someone listening to me:
   here is my mark – Shadday should answer
     me,
   the one who argues with me should write a
     document.
³⁶If I did not carry it on my shoulder,
   bind it on me as my crown.
³⁷I would tell him the number of my steps,
   present it as to a ruler.

³⁸If my land cries out against me
   and its furrows weep together,
³⁹If I have consumed its energy without silver
   and made its owners sigh,
⁴⁰In place of wheat may thistle come up,
   in place of barley, stinkweed.

The words of Iyyob have come to an end.

## Elihu: The angry young man

**32** These three men stopped answering
Iyyob, because he was in the right in
his eyes. ²But anger raged in Elihu ben Barak'el
the Buzite, of the family of Ram. His anger
raged at Iyyob because he thought himself
more in the right than God, ³and his anger
raged at his three friends because they didn't

find an answer although they declared him in the wrong. ⁴While Elihu had waited for Iyyob with his words because they were older than him in years, ⁵Elihu saw that there was no answer in the mouth of the three men, and his anger raged. ⁶So Elihu ben Barak'el the Buzite answered:

I am young in years
    and you are old.
For this reason I hesitated and was afraid
    of explaining what I know to you.
⁷I said, 'Age should speak,
    abundance of years should make smartness
      known.'
⁸Nevertheless it is the spirit in a human being,
    the breath of Shadday, that gives
      understanding.
⁹It's not the advanced people who are smart
    or the elders who understand the exercise of
      authority.
¹⁰Therefore I say, 'Listen to me,
    I myself will explain what I know, I as well.'
¹¹There, I've waited for your words,
    I've given ear to your understanding.
While you searched out utterances,
    ¹²I was giving consideration to you.
But there, there is no one who has reproved Iyyob,
    none of you has answered the things he said.
¹³Beware that you say, 'We've found smartness;
    God must blow him away, not a human being.'
¹⁴He did not line up utterances for me,
    and I shall not give back reply to him with the
      things you said.

¹⁵Because they are fearful, they haven't answered
    any more;
    utterances have moved on from them.
¹⁶I waited when they didn't speak,
    when they halted, they didn't answer any more.
¹⁷I myself will answer, I too, with my share,
    I will declare what I know, I too.
¹⁸Because I am full of utterances;
    the spirit in my insides constrains me.
¹⁹There, my insides are like wine that isn't open,
    like skins of new wine that burst.
²⁰I must speak so it will relieve me,
    I shall open my lips and answer.
²¹Please, I will not show regard for anyone
    or give titles to any person.
²²Because I don't know how to give titles;
    my maker would soon carry me off.

## Elihu: Don't argue with God

**33** However, please listen to my utterances,
    Iyyob,
    give ear to all I have to say.
²Here, please, I'm opening my lips,
    my tongue is speaking in my palate.
³The things I say are the uprightness of my
      mind,
    my lips utter knowledge, purified.
⁴God's spirit made me;
    Shadday's breath keeps me alive.
⁵If you can, speak back to me;
    lay it out before me, take your stand.
⁶Here am I, the same as you to God;
    I was nipped from clay, I too.
⁷There, dread of me should not terrify you;
    pressure from me should not be heavy on you.

⁸You indeed have said in my ears,
    I could hear the sound of the utterances:
⁹'I am clean, without rebellion;
    I am pure and there's no waywardness in me.
¹⁰There, he finds occasions for opposition to me,
    he thinks of me as his enemy.
¹¹He puts my feet in the stocks,
    he watches all my paths.'
¹²There, in this you're not in the right;
    I shall answer to you, that God is greater than a
      mere human being.
¹³Why do you argue with him,
    because he doesn't answer any of someone's
      words?
¹⁴Because God speaks once,
    and twice, though he does not behold it.

## Elihu: How God tries to win us back

¹⁵In a dream, a vision in the night,
    when deep sleep falls on people,
    during slumbers in bed,
¹⁶Then he opens the ear of people,
    and in disciplining them perturbs them,
¹⁷To turn a person away from an action
    and cover a man's majesty from him.
¹⁸He holds his life back from the Pit,
    his existence from crossing the River.
¹⁹He is reproved by pains on his bed,
    constant argument in his bones.
²⁰His existence makes him loathe bread,
    his life desirable food.

²¹His flesh fails so that it cannot be seen,
  his bones that could not be seen are laid bare.
²²His life draws near to the Pit,
  his existence to the bringers of death.
²³If there is an envoy by him,
  one spokesperson from the thousand,
To tell of the person's uprightness,
  ²⁴and be gracious to him and say,
'Redeem him from going down to the Pit,
  I have found a ransom':
²⁵His flesh healthier than his youth,
  he will go back to his young days.
²⁶He will pray to God and he will accept him;
  he will see his face with a shout.
So he will give back his right standing to the
    person;
²⁷he will sing to people and say,
'I did wrong and twisted what was upright,
  and it was not advantageous for me.
²⁸He redeemed my life from passing into the Pit;
  my existence will see light.'
²⁹There, God does all these things,
  twice, three times with a man,
³⁰To bring him back from the Pit
  so that he may be alight with the light of life.

³¹Heed, Iyyob, listen to me;
  be quiet, and I will speak.
³²If there are things to say, speak back;
  speak, because I want you to be in the right.
³³If there are not, you listen to me;
  be quiet, and I will teach you smartness.

## Elihu: Drinking ridicule like water

# 34

Elihu answered:

²Listen to my utterances, you smart people;
  give ear to me, you who have knowledge.
³Because the ear tests utterances,
  as the palate tastes something to eat.
⁴Let's choose a ruling for ourselves,
  let's acknowledge between ourselves what is
    good.
⁵Because Iyyob has said, 'I'm in the right;
  God has turned aside the case about me.
⁶Regarding the case about me, I declare it a lie,
  my arrow-wound grave, without having
    rebelled.'
⁷What man is like Iyyob,
  who drinks ridicule like water?

⁸He travels in company with people who devise
    trouble,
  and he walks with faithless people,
⁹Because he's said, 'There's no benefit to a man,
  in his being accepted with God.'

¹⁰Therefore, you sensible people,
  listen to me.
Far be it for God to act in faithlessness,
  for Shadday to do evil.
¹¹Because he makes good for a person's action to
    him,
  and in accordance with an individual's path he
    makes him meet with things.
¹²Indeed, in truth God does not act faithlessly;
  Shadday does not twist the exercise of
    authority.
¹³Who appointed the earth to him,
  who set the world [to him], all of it?
¹⁴If he sets his mind to it,
  he can gather his spirit and his breath to him.
¹⁵All flesh would breathe their last together
  and humanity go back to earth.
¹⁶So if there is to be understanding, listen to this,
  give ear to the sound of my utterances.
¹⁷Is someone indeed in control who is hostile to
    the [proper] exercise of authority
  do you declare the faithful, strong one to be
    in the wrong?
¹⁸He is the one who says to a king, 'Scoundrel',
  to rulers, 'Faithless',
¹⁹ᵃWho does not show regard to officials
  and does not recognize the important person
    before the poor.

## Elihu: Tested to the limit

¹⁹ᵇBecause all of them are the making of his
    hands;
  ²⁰suddenly they die, in the middle of the night.
A people is in turmoil and they pass away;
  a sturdy person is removed, not by human
    hand.
²¹Because his eyes are on an individual's ways;
  he sees all his steps.
²²There is no darkness, there is no deathly
    shadow,
  for people who devise trouble to hide there.
²³Because he doesn't lay down a set time for an
    individual
  to go to God for a ruling.

<sup>24</sup>He shatters strong people without searching out,
and puts others in place instead of them.
<sup>25</sup>Thus he recognizes their deeds;
he overturns them in the night and they
collapse.
<sup>26</sup>He pummels them among the faithless
in a place where people see.
<sup>27</sup>Because of the fact that they have departed from
following him;
they have not had insight into any of his ways,
<sup>28</sup>So as to cause the cry of the poor to come to
him,
so that he listens to the cry of the humble.
<sup>29</sup>Should he be calm, who can call him faithless,
should he hide his face, who can behold him?
He is over nation and over individual together,
<sup>30</sup>to stop the impious person reigning,
to stop a people's traps.
<sup>31</sup>Because has someone said to God,
'I will carry it, I will not act ruinously.'
<sup>32</sup>What I cannot behold, instruct me in yourself;
if I have done evil, I will not do so again'?
<sup>33</sup>Is he to make good in the way you think, when
you've rejected him?
– because you should choose, not I;
speak what you know.
<sup>34</sup>People with sense say to me,
a smart man listening to me:
<sup>35</sup>'Iyyob doesn't speak with knowledge,
his words are not with insight.
<sup>36</sup>Would that Iyyob were tested to the limit,
about replies befitting people who devise
trouble.
<sup>37</sup>Because he adds to his wrongdoing:
he abounds in rebellion among us,
and multiplies the things he says to God.'

### Elihu: What difference do you make to God?

## 35 Elihu answered:

<sup>2</sup>Do you think this is a good ruling,
when you say, 'I am more in the right than
God'?
<sup>3</sup>When you say, how does it benefit you –
'How do I profit more than from wrongdoing?'
<sup>4</sup>I myself will make utterances back to you,
and your friends with you.
<sup>5</sup>Look to the heavens and see,
behold the skies that are lofty above you.

<sup>6</sup>If you have done wrong, what do you do to him,
and if your rebellions have been many, what do
you do to him?
<sup>7</sup>If you are in the right, what do you give him,
or what does he get from your hand?
<sup>8</sup>Your faithlessness affects a person like yourself,
your being in the right affects a human being.
<sup>9</sup>Because of the multitude of the oppressed, people
cry out;
they cry for help because of the power
exercised against so many,
<sup>10</sup>But no one says, 'Where is God my maker,
who gives melodies in the night,
<sup>11</sup>Who teaches us more than the animals of the
earth,
makes us smarter than the birds in the
heavens?'
<sup>12</sup>They cry out there but he does not answer
before the majesty of bad people.
<sup>13</sup>Indeed God does not listen to emptiness,
Shadday does not behold it.
<sup>14</sup>How much less when you say you don't behold
him,
your case is before him, and you wait for him,
<sup>15</sup>And now that his anger has given no attention,
and he has not given much acknowledgement
to rebellion.
<sup>16</sup>Iyyob opens his mouth with hollowness,
multiplies words that are without knowledge.

### Elihu: The God who opens our ear

## 36 Elihu again spoke:

<sup>2</sup>Wait for me a little and I will explain to you,
because there are yet utterances to be said for
God.
<sup>3</sup>I will carry my knowledge from far away,
and I will ascribe faithfulness to my maker.
<sup>4</sup>Because truly my utterances are not false;
one with integrity in knowledge is with you.

<sup>5</sup>There, God is strong but he doesn't reject –
strong in energy of mind.
<sup>6</sup>He doesn't let the faithless person live,
and he gives a ruling for the humble people.
<sup>7</sup>He doesn't hold back his eyes from faithful
people,
but seats them with kings on a throne,
permanently, and they are lofty.

⁸If people are bound in chains,
  caught in humbling bonds,
⁹He tells them what they've done,
  and their acts of rebellion, that they acted big.
¹⁰He opens their ear to correction
  and says how they should turn back from
    trouble.
¹¹If they listen and serve,
  they'll finish their days with good things,
  their years in happiness.
¹²But if they don't listen, they'll cross the River,
  they'll breathe their last without knowledge.
¹³But the impious of mind lay up anger,
  they don't cry for help when he binds them.
¹⁴They die in youth,
  their existence among the hierodules.
¹⁵He pulls the humble person out through his
    humbling,
  and opens their ear through affliction.

## Elihu: God is great, and we cannot know

¹⁶Indeed, he has drawn you away from the brink
    of pressure,
  to a broad place where there is no constraint,
    instead of it,
  and what is laid on your table is full of richness.
¹⁷But you're full of the judgement due to the
    faithless person;
  judgement and the exercise of authority take
    hold.
¹⁸Because wrath mustn't draw you away through
    wealth;
  a large amount of ransom money must not turn
    you aside.
¹⁹Would your wealth line up, without pressure,
  and all your energetic efforts?
²⁰Don't long for the night,
  to take up peoples where they are.
²¹Keep watch, don't turn your face to trouble,
  because you've chosen this rather than
    humbling.
²²There, God towers in his energy;
  who is an instructor like him?
²³Who has appointed his way for him,
  who has said, 'You've done evil'?
²⁴Be mindful that you should exalt what he does,
  which people have sung about.

²⁵All humanity has beheld it;
  a human being looks at it from afar.

²⁶There, God is great, and we cannot know –
  of the number of his years there is no searching
    out.
²⁷Because he draws up the drops of water
  that distil as rain in his mist,
²⁸Which the skies pour down,
  dispense upon humanity as a shower.
²⁹Indeed, can one understand the spreading of
    cloud,
  the thunders from his bivouac?
³⁰There, he spreads his lightning over it,
  he uncovers the roots of the sea.
³¹Because by these things he governs peoples,
  gives food in abundance.
³²He covers over the palms of his hands with
    lightning,
  and orders it against its mark.
³³His thunder tells of him,
  his angry passion against evil.

## Elihu: The awe-inspiring Creator

**37** Indeed at this my heart trembles
  and leaps from its place.
²Listen, listen to the raging of his voice,
  the murmur that comes out from his mouth.
³Beneath the entire heavens he lets it loose,
  and his lightning over the corners of the earth.
⁴After it, a voice roars;
  he thunders with his majestic voice.
He doesn't hold them back
  when his voice makes itself heard;
⁵God thunders with his voice in extraordinary
    ways,
  does great things that we cannot know,
⁶When he says to the snow,
  'Fall on the earth',
And the downpour of rain,
  his vigorous downpour of the rains.
⁷On every human being's hand he imposes a seal,
  so that everyone may acknowledge what he
    does.
⁸Living things come into the lair,
  lie down in their den.
⁹The tempest comes out of its room,
  the cold from the driving winds.
¹⁰By God's breath he makes ice,
  and the expanse of water into something
    frozen.
¹¹He also loads the cloud with moisture,
  scatters his lightning thundercloud,

¹²And it turns round and round at his directions,
  so that they do all that he commands them.
Over the face of the earthly world,
  ¹³either for the exercise of his club, or for the
    sake of his earth,
  or for the sake of his commitment – he makes
    them happen.

¹⁴Give ear to this, Iyyob;
  stand and consider God's extraordinary deeds.
¹⁵Do you know how God lays things upon them,
  how the lightning from his thundercloud
    shines out?
¹⁶Do you know about the balancing of the
    clouds,
  the extraordinary deeds of the one who is
    perfect in knowledge,
¹⁷You whose clothes become hot,
  when the earth is calm because of the south
    wind?
¹⁸Could you spread the skies with him,
  hard like a mirror of cast metal?
¹⁹Help us know what we're to say to him;
  we can't lay it out, from before darkness.
²⁰Will it be announced to him that I shall speak,
  has someone said that he is confused?
²¹But now, people cannot look at the light,
  when it is bright in the skies.
And the wind has passed and cleared them,
  ²²when gold comes from the north.
God On High, awe-inspiring in grandeur,
  ²³Shadday: we couldn't find him.
Great in energy and in the exercise of authority,
  but with abundance of faithfulness, he doesn't
    humble.
²⁴Therefore people live in awe of him,
  though he doesn't look at any of the smart-
    minded.

## Yahweh: You need to accept your limits

**38** Yahweh answered Iyyob from a
hurricane:

²Who is this who darkens counsel
  by utterances without knowledge?
³Belt up your thighs like a man, please,
  so I can ask you and you can let me know.

⁴Where were you when I founded the earth?
  – tell, if you know and understand.

⁵Who set its dimensions, since you will know,
  or who stretched a line over it?
⁶On what were its bases sunk,
  or who threw its cornerstone,
⁷When the morning stars resounded together
  and all the divine beings shouted?

⁸And who shut the sea in with doors,
  when it gushed from the womb it came out of,
⁹When I made cloud its clothing,
  thundercloud its blanket,
¹⁰Decreed my limit for it,
  set a bar and doors,
¹¹And said, 'You may come as far as this,
  but not go further;
  here it's set, at the majesty of your waves'?

¹²Since your days began, have you ordered
    morning,
  let the dawn know its place,
¹³For it to grasp the earth by the corners,
  so that faithless people shake out of it?
¹⁴It turns like clay under a seal,
  so that they stand out like a garment.
¹⁵From faithless people their light holds back,
  and their high arm breaks.

¹⁶Have you come to the springs of the sea,
  or walked about through the reaches of the deep?
¹⁷Have the gateways of death opened to you,
  or can you see the gateways of deathly shadow?
¹⁸Have you considered the expanses of the earth?
  – tell, if you know it all.

## Yahweh: What do you really know?

¹⁹Where is the way to where light dwells,
  and darkness – where is its place,
²⁰That you may take it to its territory,
  and understand the trails to its home?
²¹You know, because you were coming to birth
    then,
  and the number of your years is many.

²²Have you come to the storehouses of snow,
  or can you see the storehouses of hail,
²³Which I have held back for the time of pressure,
  for the day of drawing near and of battle?
²⁴Where then is the way to where lightning is
    shared out,
  where the east wind is scattered over the earth?

²⁵Who cut a channel for the torrent,
and a way for the bolt of thunder,
²⁶To rain on land with no people,
wilderness with no one in it,
²⁷To satisfy the devastated devastation,
and make a crop of grass flourish?
²⁸Does the rain have a father,
or who fathered the drops of dew?
²⁹From whose womb did the ice come out,
the frost from the heavens, who fathered it,
³⁰When water hardens like stone,
and the surface of the deep freezes?

³¹Can you tie Pleiades' bonds,
or loose Orion's belt?
³²Can you lead out Mazzarot at its time,
or lead out the Bear with its children?
³³Do you know the decrees of the heavens,
or can you implement its authority on earth?

³⁴Can you lift up your voice to the cloud,
so that a flood of water may cover you?
³⁵Can you send off shafts of lightning so that they
go,
and say to you, 'Here we are!'
³⁶Who put smartness in the ibis,
or who gave understanding to the cockerel?
³⁷Who can give an account of the skies with
smartness,
and tilt the water skins in the heavens,
³⁸When earth pours into a mass,
and clods are made to stick together?

## Yahweh: Could you care for nature?

³⁹Can you hunt prey for a lion,
and fill the appetite of whelps,
⁴⁰When they crouch in dens,
lie in wait in a bivouac?
⁴¹Who prepares its provision for the raven
when its young cry for help to God
and wander without food?

# 39
Do you know the time for the mountain
goats to give birth,
keep watch as the deer goes into labour?
²Do you count the months they complete,
or know the time for their giving birth?
³They crouch so that they may deliver their
young,
as they send off their pains.

⁴Their offspring become strong, they grow up in
the open,
they go out and don't come back to them.

⁵Who sends off the wild donkey, free,
and who looses the ropes of the wild mule,
⁶Whose home I made the steppe,
its dwellings the salty land?
⁷It makes fun of the uproar of the township;
it doesn't listen to the shouts of a driver.
⁸It ranges mountains as its pasture,
and searches after any green thing.

⁹Is an oryx willing to serve you,
will it lodge by your feeding trough?
¹⁰Can you hold an oryx with a harness to the
furrow,
will it till the vales behind you?
¹¹Can you rely on it because its energy is great,
and abandon your toil to it?
¹²Can you trust it that it will bring back your seed,
and gather it to your threshing floor?

¹³The wing of the screechers exults:
is it a stork's wing and plumage?
¹⁴Because she abandons her eggs on the earth,
lets them get warm on the earth,
¹⁵And puts out of mind that a foot may crush it,
or a creature of the wild trample it.
¹⁶She's tough with her offspring so that they are
not hers,
her toil is in vain, without dread.
¹⁷Because God made her forget smartness,
didn't give a share of understanding to her.
¹⁸At the time when she flaps on high,
she makes fun of the horse and its rider.

## Yahweh: So many extraordinary creatures!

¹⁹Do you give the horse its strength,
do you clothe its neck with a mane?
²⁰Do you make it quiver like a locust?
– the grandeur of its snort is a dread.
²¹They paw with force; it rejoices in its energy,
as it goes out to meet the weapons.
²²It makes fun of dread, doesn't frighten,
doesn't turn back from the face of the sword.
²³By it a quiver resounds,
a flash of lance and javelin.
²⁴With shaking and raging it swallows the earth,
and it can't stand firm when there's the sound
of the horn.

²⁵At the blast of the horn it says, 'Ah',
  and from far away it smells battle,
  the thunder of the officers, and the shout.

²⁶Is it by your understanding that the hawk takes
    flight,
  spreads its wings to the south?
²⁷Is it at your bidding that the eagle is lofty,
  and that it puts its nest high?
²⁸It dwells on the cliff,
  and lodges on an outcrop of the cliff, a
    stronghold.
²⁹From there it searches for food,
  from far away its eyes look out,
³⁰So its young drink blood;
  where there are people who have been run
    through, there it is.

# 40   Yahweh answered Iyyob:

²Does the person who argues with Shadday
    correct him?
  – the one who reproves God must answer it.

³Iyyob answered Yahweh:

⁴There, I am slight, what could I say back?
  – I put my hand to my mouth.
⁵I have spoken once, and I will not answer –
  twice, and I will not do so again.

## Yahweh: Think about the Great Creature

⁶But Yahweh answered Iyyob from a hurricane:

⁷Belt up your thighs like a man, please,
  so I can ask you and you can let me know.
⁸Would you indeed contravene my exercise of
    authority,
  declare me in the wrong in order that you may
    be in the right?
⁹Do you have an arm like God,
  or can you thunder with a voice like his?
¹⁰Adorn yourself with majesty and loftiness,
    please,
  clothe yourself in splendour and grandeur.
¹¹Scatter your angry outbursts about,
  see every majestic person and bring him low.
¹²See every majestic person and make him bow
    down,
  throw down the faithless where they stand.

¹³Bury them in the earth all together,
  conceal their faces in the hidden place.
¹⁴And I too will confess you,
  that your right hand can bring deliverance to you.

¹⁵There, please, is the Great Creature, which I
    made along with you,
  which eats grass like cattle.
¹⁶There, please, its energy is in its insides,
  its vigour in the muscles of its stomach.
¹⁷It hangs its tail like a cedar,
  the sinews of its thighs are intertwined.
¹⁸Its bones are tubes of copper,
  its limbs like a bar of iron.
¹⁹It is the first of God's ways;
  its maker can draw near with his sword.

²⁰Because the mountains carry produce for it,
  and all the animals of the wild have fun there,
²¹It lies down underneath the lotuses,
  in the cover of the reeds and in the marsh.
²²The lotuses screen it as its shade,
  the willows of the wadi surround it.
²³There – when the river gushes, it doesn't make
    haste;
  it's confident that Yarden [Jordan] bursts forth
    at its bidding.
²⁴Can someone take it by its eyes
  or pierce its nose, in traps?

## Yahweh: Think about Livyatan

# 41   Can you pull in Livyatan with a
        fishhook
  or tie down its tongue with a rope?
²Can you put a reed in its nose
  or pierce its jaw with a hook?
³Will it make many prayers for grace to you,
  will it speak smooth words to you?
⁴Will it seal a pact with you
  that it will be taken as a lifelong servant?
⁵Will you have fun with it like a bird
  or put it on a leash for your girls?
⁶Will partners barter over it,
  will they divide it up among the dealers?
⁷Can you fill its skin with harpoons
  or its head with fish spears?
⁸Lay your fist on it,
  be mindful of the battle, don't do it again.
⁹There, hope for [capturing] it tells a lie
  – isn't one even overwhelmed at the sight of it?

¹⁰No one is so cruel that he gets it to rise;
 so who is the one who takes a stand before me?
¹¹Who confronts me so that I make good?
 – under the entire heavens, things are mine.

¹²I will not be silent about its limbs or its strong
 word,
 or the grace of its frame.
¹³Who has stripped off the surface of its garment,
 who can come with a double bridle for it?
¹⁴Who has opened the doors of its face?
 – its teeth all round are a dread.
¹⁵Its back is rows of shields,
 shut up with a tight seal.
¹⁶One comes up to the other;
 a breath could not come between them.
¹⁷They stick each one to its brother;
 they clasp each other and cannot separate.
¹⁸Its sneezes flash lightning,
 its eyes are like the eyelids of dawn.
¹⁹From its mouth go torches,
 sparks of fire escape.
²⁰From its nostrils smoke goes out,
 like a pot heated, with rushes.
²¹Its breath sets coals on fire;
 flame goes out from its mouth.

## Iyyob relents

²²In its neck vigour lodges;
 dismay leaps before it.
²³The folds of its flesh stick;
 it is cast on it, it doesn't slip.
²⁴Its heart is cast like stone,
 cast like a bottom millstone.
²⁵At its rising up, divine beings are in dread;
 at its crashes, they fail.
²⁶The sword that reaches it does not prevail –
 spear, dart or lance.
²⁷It thinks of iron as straw,
 of copper as rotten wood.
²⁸Arrow doesn't make it take flight;
 sling stones turn into chaff for it.
²⁹A club is thought of as chaff;
 it makes fun of the shaking of a javelin.
³⁰Its underparts are sharp bits of pot;
 it spreads a threshing sledge on mud.
³¹It makes the deep boil like a pot,
 it makes the sea like a pot of ointment.
³²Behind it, it lightens a trail;
 one would think the deep to be white hair.

³³There is no one on the earth to rule it,
 made without fright.
³⁴It sees everything lofty;
 it is king over all noble creatures.

# 42 Iyyob answered Yahweh:

²I acknowledge that you can do anything;
 no strategy is impracticable for you.
³'Who is this who darkens counsel without
 knowledge?'
 – thus I told of things that I did not understand,
 things too extraordinary for me, that I did not
 know.
⁴'Listen, please, and I myself will speak;
 I will ask and you can let me know.'
⁵I have listened to you with the listening of an ear,
 and now my eye has seen you.
⁶Therefore I reject and find consolation
 about earth and ashes.

## So they all lived happily ever after

⁷After Yahweh had spoken these words to
Iyyob, Yahweh said to Eliphaz the Temanite,
'My anger rages against you and against your
two friends, because you haven't spoken to
me what is established truth, like my servant
Iyyob. ⁸So now get yourselves seven bulls and
seven rams, go to my servant Iyyob and offer
up a burnt offering on your behalf. Iyyob my
servant can plead for you, because I will show
regard to him so as not to act with you in
the light of your villainy, because you haven't
spoken to me what is established truth, like my
servant Iyyob.' ⁹Eliphaz the Temanite, Bildad
the Shuhite and Tsophar the Na'amatite went
and did as Yahweh spoke to them.
 Yahweh showed regard to Iyyob. ¹⁰When
Yahweh restored Iyyob's fortunes after he
pleaded on behalf of his friends, Yahweh
increased all that Iyyob had to double. ¹¹All his
brothers and all his sisters and all his former
acquaintances came and ate a meal with him at
his house. They consoled and comforted him
for all the bad things that Yahweh had brought
on him, and they gave him a piece of silver
each and a gold ring each.
 ¹²When Yahweh blessed the latter part of
Iyyob's life more than the former, he had 14,000
sheep, 6,000 camels, 1,000 yoke of cattle and

1,000 donkeys. ¹³He had seven sons and three daughters. ¹⁴He named the first Yemimah, the second Ketsiyah and the third Qeren Happuk. ¹⁵There could not be found women as beautiful as Iyyob's daughters in the entire country. And their father gave them a domain among their brothers.

¹⁶Afterwards, Iyyob lived 140 years, and saw his sons and his grandsons, four generations. ¹⁷Iyyob died old and full of years.

# PSALMS

The book of Psalms is a collection of 150 things that we can say to God. In putting it that way, I oversimplify slightly, as a few psalms have God speaking to us, but the vast majority are prayers and praises addressed to God. You could say that they are Israel's hymn book and prayer book.

They are divided into five books – English translations make that point explicit with the headings 'Book One' (at the beginning), 'Book Two' (at Psalm 42), and so on. The five books of Psalms thus parallel the five books of the Torah. The Torah comprises teaching on what God has done for Israel and on the life God expects of Israel. The Psalms comprise teaching on the nature of praise and prayer. But they teach not by giving instructions but by giving examples. The examples divide into a few main types.

1. There are hymns of praise for who God is and for the great things God has done in creation and for his people. They refer to the exodus and to God's involvement in Israel's subsequent story. But they also emphasize how all the nations should therefore come to acknowledge this God.
2. There are prayers of protest about the way things are now working out, which contrasts with the affirmations appearing in the praise hymns. There are protests that belong on the lips of the people as a whole, of their leader and of individuals. They describe how Israel itself has been defeated, how its leader is under attack, and how an individual is overwhelmed by people's attacks or accusations. One noteworthy feature is the amount of space they give to description of the plight and suffering of the people who are praying; they are much less specific about what they expect God to do beyond acting to rescue. While formulating this description no doubt offers release for them, its more direct point is to get God to notice and take action. And sometimes before these psalms end, they already express the conviction that God has heard the pleas, so that the person praying can look forward to the act of God that will follow.
3. There are some prayers that presuppose the reality of that kind of experience but are more dominated by a note of trust and hope.
4. There are songs of praise that testify to the way God has responded to a prayer of this kind and has delivered the people or the leader or the individual. A noteworthy feature of them is the way they mingle addressing God in thanksgiving and addressing other people in testimony. They are designed both to glorify God and to build up the faith and trust of people who have not had this experience of deliverance.

A few psalms don't fit into these categories. Some speak from God or from a human teacher to the community rather than from human beings to God. The first two psalms are examples, Psalm 1 being a challenge to faithful living, Psalm 2 a declaration about God's faithfulness to the Davidic king. Such psalms remind worshippers that they can't be involved in praise or prayer unless they are people living faithful lives. And they remind them that the God of whom the psalms speak is one involved in the political affairs of the nation and committed to fulfilling his purpose in the world. The fact that there was no Davidic king after the fall of Jerusalem meant that the psalms' references to the king became promises and declarations of hope about the Davidic king that God would surely enthrone again one day, and this development is part of the background to references to them in the New Testament.

The Davidic king is an important figure in the Psalms, though the references to David in the introductions to the psalms don't imply that he wrote them. The introductions relate to ways in which the Psalms were used in worship (e.g. tunes), and we don't understand many of the terms they use. However many psalms David may have written, his position as the patron of the Temple means that they all appear under his sponsorship. The key to using the Psalms is the realization that they are designed for ongoing use by the people of God and by individuals, so that who wrote them is not very important.

## Psalm 1 *You have a choice*

¹The blessings of someone who has not walked
  by the counsel of the faithless,
Or stood on the way of wrongdoers,
  or lived in the settlement of the arrogant!
²Rather, his delight is in Yahweh's instruction,
  and he murmurs about his instruction day and
    night.
³He's like a tree planted by channels of water,
  which gives its fruit in its time,
And its foliage doesn't fade;
  all that he does succeeds.
⁴Not so the faithless people;
  rather, they're like the chaff that the wind blows
    away.
⁵Therefore the faithless don't rise up when a ruling
    is given,
  nor wrongdoers in the assembly of the faithful.
⁶Because Yahweh acknowledges the way of the
    faithful,
  but the way of the faithless perishes.

## Psalm 2 *God laughs on his people's behalf*

¹Why have nations crowded together,
  and peoples murmur about something empty,
²Earth's kings take a stand,
  leaders made plans together,
  against Yahweh and against his anointed –
³'We'll break off their means of discipline,
  throw off their ropes from us'?
⁴The one who sits in the heavens makes fun;
  the Lord ridicules them.
⁵Then he speaks to them in his anger,
  terrifies them with his rage.
⁶'But I myself installed my king on Tsiyyon [Zion],
  my sacred mountain!'
⁷I shall recount Yahweh's decree:
  he said to me,
'You're my son;
  today I myself have fathered you.
⁸Ask of me and I'll make nations your domain,
  earth's ends your holding.
⁹You'll smash them with an iron club,
  shatter them like an object made by a potter.'
¹⁰So now, show some insight, you kings,
  accept discipline, you people who exercise
    authority in the earth.
¹¹Serve Yahweh with awe,
  rejoice with trembling, surrender sincerely,

¹²So that he doesn't get angry
  and you perish as regards the way,
Because his anger will soon burn up;
  the blessings of all who take shelter with him!

## Psalm 3 *You're not alone*

A composition. For David when he took flight
from Abshalom his son.

¹Yahweh, how many are my adversaries;
  many people are rising up against me.
²Many people are saying of me,
  'There's no deliverance in God for him!' *(Rise)*
³But you are Yahweh, a shield about me,
  my splendour, the one who lifts my head
    high.
⁴With my voice I would call to Yahweh,
  and he's answered me from his sacred
    mountain. *(Rise)*
⁵I myself have lain down and slept;
  I've woken up, because Yahweh sustains me.
⁶I'm not afraid of a company of myriads
  that has set itself against me all round.

⁷Rise up, Yahweh,
  deliver me, my God,
Because you've struck all my enemies on the jaw;
  you've smashed the teeth of the faithless.
⁸Deliverance belongs to Yahweh,
  your blessing is on your people. *(Rise)*

## Psalm 4 *Who can I turn to?*

The leader's. With strings. A composition.
David's.

¹When I call, answer me,
  my faithful God!
Under pressure you widened me;
  be gracious to me and listen to my plea!

²You people, how long will the one I honour be
    for shaming,
  will you be loyal to something empty, will you
    seek a lie? *(Rise)*
³So acknowledge that Yahweh has distinguished
    the committed person for himself;
  Yahweh is the one who listens when I call to
    him.

⁴Tremble and don't do wrong;
    say it in your heart on your bed and be quiet.
    *(Rise)*
⁵Offer faithful sacrifices,
    and put your confidence in Yahweh.
⁶Increased numbers of people are saying,
    'Who will enable us to see good fortune?
    – the light of your face has fled from upon us,
    Yahweh.'
⁷You've put rejoicing in my heart
    from the time when their grain and their new
    wine has increased.
⁸In well-being I will lie down and sleep, all at
    once,
    because you alone are Yahweh;
    you enable me to live in confidence.

## Psalm 5 *Pleading with the King*

The leader's. To flutes. A composition.
David's.

¹Give ear to the things I say, Yahweh,
    consider my murmur.
²Heed the sound of my cry for help,
    my King and my God, because it's with you I
    plead.
³Yahweh, at morning may you listen to my
    voice,
    at morning I lay it out to you and wait.
⁴Because you're not a God who delights in
    faithlessness;
    that which is bad can't reside with you.
⁵Wild people can't take their stand in front of your
    eyes;
    you're hostile to all who devise trouble.
⁶You obliterate people who speak a lie;
    at someone of blood and guile, Yahweh takes
    offence.

⁷But I myself will come to your house through the
    abundance of your commitment;
    I will bow low to your sacred palace in awe of
    you.
⁸Yahweh, lead me in your faithfulness
    for the sake of the people who are watching
    for me;
    make your way direct before me.
⁹Because there's no established truth in their
    mouth;
    their inner being is malice.

Their throat is an opened grave,
    they're slippery with their tongue.
¹⁰Have them make restitution, God;
    they should fall by means of their own
    counsels.
Because of the abundance of their rebellions drive
    them out,
    because they've defied you.
¹¹But may all the people who take shelter with you
    rejoice,
    may they resound permanently.
As you protect them,
    may the people who are loyal to your name
    triumph in you.
¹²Because you yourself bless the faithful person,
    Yahweh;
    you surround him with acceptance like a body-
    shield.

## Psalm 6 *The way prayer makes a difference*

The leader's. With strings. On the eighth
[tone]. A composition. David's.

¹Yahweh, don't reprove me in your anger,
    don't discipline me with your wrath.
²Be gracious to me, Yahweh, because I'm faint;
    heal me, Yahweh, because my bones shake in
    fearfulness.
³My entire being shakes in great fearfulness,
    and you, Yahweh – how long?
⁴Turn back, Yahweh, pull me out,
    deliver me for the sake of your commitment!
⁵Because there's no commemoration of you in
    death;
    in She'ol who confesses you?
⁶I'm weary of my groaning, I make my bed swim
    every night,
    I melt my mattress with my tears.
⁷My eye has wasted away through provocation,
    grown old because of all my adversaries.

⁸Depart from me, all you who devise trouble,
    because Yahweh has heard the sound of my
    crying.
⁹Yahweh has heard my prayer for grace;
    Yahweh receives my plea.
¹⁰All my enemies will be shamed and be very
    fearful;
    they will turn back and be shamed instantly.

## Psalm 7 *The Judge is on your side*

Lament. David's, which he sang for Yahweh concerning the Kushite [Sudanese] words. The Binyaminite.

[1]Yahweh my God, in you I take shelter
  – deliver me from all the people who are
    pursuing me, rescue me,
[2]So that one doesn't tear me apart like a lion,
  ripping me to pieces when there's no one to
    rescue.
[3]Yahweh my God, if I did this,
  if there's evil in the palms of my hands,
[4]If I have dealt something bad to my friend,
  but pulled out my adversary without reason,
[5]May the enemy pursue me and overtake me,
  may he trample my life to the ground,
  may he lay down my splendour in the dirt.
    *(Rise)*

[6]Rise up, Yahweh, in your anger;
  lift yourself up at the great outburst of my
    adversaries.
Awake, my God, you must order the exercise of
    authority;
  [7]the assembly of the nations should come
    round you.
Take your seat over it on high;
  [8]Yahweh must rule the peoples.
Exercise authority for me, Yahweh,
  in accordance with my faithfulness and with
    my integrity, over me.
[9]The bad ways of faithless people must please
    come to an end,
  and you must establish the faithful person.

The faithful God
  is one who tests minds and inner being.
[10]God is my shield on high,
  one who delivers people who are upright in
    mind.
[11]God exercises authority for the faithful person;
  God condemns each day.
[12]If someone doesn't turn back, he whets his
    sword;
  he's directed his bow and fixed it.
[13]He's fixed deadly weapons for himself,
  he makes his arrows into flames.
[14]There, someone twists with trouble,
  he's pregnant with oppression, he gives birth to
    falsehood.

[15]He's dug a cistern and made it deep,
  but he's fallen into the hole he makes.
[16]His act of oppression comes back on to his own
    head,
  his violence comes down on his own skull.

[17]I will confess Yahweh in accordance with his
    faithfulness
  and make music to the name of Yahweh, the
    One on High.

## Psalm 8 *Thus far and no further*

The leader's. On the Gittite. A composition. David's.

[1]Yahweh our God,
  how august is your name in all the earth,
You who put your grandeur above the heavens
  [2]by the mouth of babies and sucklings.
You founded something vigorous to deal with
    your adversaries,
  to stop the enemy and the person taking
    redress.
[3]When I see the heavens, the things that your
    fingers made,
  moon and stars that you established,
[4]What are people that you are mindful of them,
  human beings that you attend to them?
[5]But you made them fall short of God by a little,
  and you crown them with honour and
    magnificence.
[6]You let them rule over the things that your hands
    made;
  you put everything under their feet –
[7]Sheep and cattle, all of them,
  and the animals of the wild, too,
[8]The birds of the heavens, the fish of the sea,
  what passes over the paths in the seas.
[9]Yahweh our God,
  how mighty is your name in all the earth!

## Psalm 9 *Praise and thanksgiving as a key to prayer*

The leader's. Secrets. The son's. A composition. David's.

[1]I will confess you, Yahweh, with my whole mind,
  I will recount all your extraordinary deeds.

²I will rejoice and exult in you,
  I will commemorate your name, the One on
    High.
³When my enemies turn back,
  they collapse and perish before you,
⁴Because you exercised authority for me and
    made a judgement for me;
  you sat on your throne as one who exercises
    authority in faithfulness.
⁵You reprimanded nations, you obliterated the
    faithless person,
  you wiped out their name for ever and ever.
⁶The enemy is finished, ruins permanently;
  you uprooted towns, their commemoration
    perished.
Them! ⁷But Yahweh sits for ever;
  he established his throne for exercising
    authority.
⁸He's the one who exercises authority for the
    world with faithfulness,
  he gives judgement for the peoples with
    uprightness.
⁹Yahweh became a turret for the downtrodden
    person,
  a turret for times of pressure,
¹⁰So that people who acknowledge your name will
    rely on you,
  because you didn't abandon people who
    enquired of you, Yahweh.

¹¹Make music for Yahweh who sits in Tsiyyon,
  tell among the peoples of his deeds,
¹²Because the one who enquires about bloodshed
    was mindful of them,
  he didn't put out of mind the cry of the
    humble.
¹³Be gracious to me, Yahweh,
  see my humbling at the hand of the people
    hostile to me,
  you who lift me up from death's gateways,
¹⁴In order that I may recount all your
    praiseworthy acts;
  in the gateways of Miss Tsiyyon I will rejoice in
    your deliverance.
¹⁵Nations plunged into the pit they made;
  in the net that they hid, their foot caught.
¹⁶Yahweh caused himself to be acknowledged, he
    made an authoritative decision;
  by the act of his own fists the faithless person
    trapped himself. *(Recitation. Rise)*
¹⁷Faithless people should turn back to She'ol,
  all the nations that put Yahweh out of mind,

¹⁸Because the needy person will not be out of
    mind without end,
  or the hope of the humble perish permanently.
¹⁹Rise up, Yahweh, a human being should not
    exercise power,
  nations should enter into judgement in your
    presence.
²⁰Appoint something fearful for them, Yahweh;
  nations should acknowledge that they are
    human beings. *(Rise)*

## Psalm 10 *The wretched of the earth*

¹Why do you stand far off, Yahweh,
  hide in times of pressure?
²When the faithless person in his position of
    majesty hounds the humble,
  they should catch themselves by the strategies
    that they have thought up.
³Because the faithless person has praised the
    longing of his appetite
  and blessed the greedy person.
The faithless person has disdained Yahweh,
  ⁴in accordance with the loftiness of his look.
'God won't enquire, he's not here';
  in all his strategies ⁵his ways are profane.
All the time your acts of authority are high up, at
    a distance from him;
  all his adversaries – he snorts at them.
⁶He's said to himself, 'I shall not slip, generation
    after generation';
  'I shall not be in bad circumstances,' ⁷he's
    sworn.
His mouth is full of acts of guile and repression;
  under his tongue are oppression and trouble.
⁸He lives in a hiding place in the villages,
  so that in complete secret he can kill someone
    free of guilt.
His eyes watch for the wretched person;
  ⁹he waits in secret like a lion in its lair.
He waits to catch the humble;
  he catches the humble by dragging him in his
    net.
¹⁰The wretched, collapsing, sinks down,
  and falls because he is so numerous.
¹¹He's said to himself, 'God has put it out of
    mind,
  he's hidden his face, he's never looked.'
¹²Rise up, Yahweh;
  God, lift your hand,
  don't put the humble out of mind.

¹³Why has the faithless person disdained God,
    said to himself, 'He does not enquire'?
¹⁴You've seen, because you yourself
    look out at oppression and vexation.
Giving it into your hand, the wretched abandons
    it to you;
    the orphan – you're the one who has been a
        helper.
¹⁵Break the arm of the faithless and the bad
        person,
    so that when you enquire after his faithlessness,
    you will not find it.

¹⁶Yahweh will be king for ever and ever;
    the nations will have perished from his
        country.
¹⁷When you've heard the longing of the humble,
        Yahweh,
    you establish their mind, you bend your ear,
¹⁸To exercise authority for orphan and
        downtrodden;
    no one from the earth will frighten ever again.

## Psalm 11 Flee or stay?

The leader's. David's.

¹With Yahweh I take shelter;
    how can you say to me,
'Flit to your mountain, bird,
    ²because there – the faithless direct a bow.
They've set their arrow on a string,
    to shoot in the shadow at the people who're
        upright in mind.
³When the foundations are torn down,
    the faithful person – what can he do?'

⁴Yahweh is in his sacred palace,
    Yahweh whose throne is in the heavens.
His eyes behold,
    his eyelids examine human beings.
⁵Yahweh examines the faithful person,
    and the faithless, and the ones who love
        violence –
    his entire being is hostile to them.
⁶He rains coals of fire and sulphur on the faithless
        people;
    a scorching wind is the portion in their cup.
⁷Because Yahweh is faithful, he loves faithful
        deeds;
    the upright person – his face beholds him.

## Psalm 12 Sometimes God speaks

The leader's. On the eighth [tone]. A
composition. David's.

¹Deliver, Yahweh, because the committed person
    has come to an end,
    because the people who are true have vanished
        from among humankind.
²An individual speaks emptiness to his
        neighbours;
    with smooth lip through a double mind they
        speak.
³Yahweh should cut off all the smooth lips,
    the tongue that speaks big things,
⁴The people who've said, 'With our tongues we
        will be strong:
    our lips will be with us – who will be lord over
        us?'

⁵'Because of the destruction of the humble,
    because of the cry of the needy,
    now I will rise up,' Yahweh says.
'I will set myself up as deliverance,'
    he testifies to him.

⁶Yahweh's words are pure words,
    silver purified in a furnace on the ground,
    refined seven times.
⁷Yahweh, you will keep them;
    you will preserve us from the generation that
        lasts permanently.
⁸All round, the faithless walk about,
    as flimsiness stands high for humankind.

## Psalm 13 How long, how long, how long, how long?

The leader's. A composition. David's.

¹How long, Yahweh: will you put me out of mind
        permanently,
    how long will you hide your face from me?
²How long must I lay up [people's] plans in my
        entire being,
    sadness in my heart day by day,
    – how long will my enemy stand high over
        me?
³Look out, answer me, Yahweh my God;
    give light to my eyes, so that I don't sleep in
        death,

⁴So that my enemy doesn't say, 'I've finished him
off',
  my adversaries celebrate because I slip.
⁵But I myself trust in your commitment;
  my heart will celebrate your deliverance.
I will sing to Yahweh,
  because he has dealt to me.

## Psalm 14 What a rogue says to himself

The leader's. David's.

¹A villain has said to himself,
  'There's no God here.
People have become devastating, offensive, in
  their action;
  there's no one doing good here.'
²From the heavens Yahweh has looked out
  at humankind,
To see if there is someone insightful,
  enquiring of God.
³Everyone has departed, altogether they're
  foul;
  there's no one doing good here, there isn't even
  one.
⁴They don't acknowledge him, do they, all the
  people devising trouble,
  who eat my people.
They've eaten food;
  they haven't called Yahweh.

⁵They're experiencing dreadful terror there,
  because God is among the faithful circle.
⁶You people may shame the humble person's
  counsel,
  but Yahweh is his shelter.

⁷If only there were deliverance for Yisra'el from
  Tsiyyon,
  when Yahweh turns back his people's
  fortunes.
Ya'aqob [Jacob] will celebrate,
  Yisra'el will rejoice!

## Psalm 15 How to dwell with God

A composition. David's.

¹Yahweh, who may reside in your tent,
  who may dwell on your sacred mountain?

²One who walks with integrity, acts with
  faithfulness,
  and speaks truth inside.
³He has not gone about talking,
  has not done wrong to his neighbour,
  has not taken up reviling against someone near
  him.
⁴In his eyes a contemptible person is to be
  rejected,
  but he honours people who live in awe of
  Yahweh;
  he has sworn to bring about something bad and
  not changed it.
⁵He has not given his silver on interest,
  and not taken a bribe against someone free of
  guilt;
  one who does these things, who does not slip
  ever.

## Psalm 16 I've set Yahweh in front of me

An inscription. David's.

¹Keep me, God,
  because I take shelter with you.
²I've said of Yahweh,
  'My Lord, you are my good, none above you',
³To the sacred ones who are in the country,
  and the august ones in whom is all my delight.
⁴Their pains will be many,
  the people who attend to another [god].
I will not pour their blood libations;
  I will not take up their names on my lips.
⁵Yahweh, my allocated share, my cup,
  you're the one who takes hold of my lot.
⁶Apportionments have fallen to me in lovely
  places;
  yes, a perfect domain for me.
⁷I will bless Yahweh who has counselled me;
  yes, by night my inner being disciplines me.
⁸I have set Yahweh in front of me continually;
  because he's at my right hand, I shall not slip.
⁹Therefore my entire being rejoices,
  my spirit celebrates,
  yes, my flesh will dwell in confidence.
¹⁰Because you won't abandon my life to She'ol,
  you won't give over someone committed to you
  to see the Abyss.
¹¹You will let me know the path to life,
  joyful fulfilment with your face,
  lovely things at your right hand permanently.

## Psalm 17 *Go on, look into my heart*

A plea. David's.

¹Listen in faithfulness, Yahweh,
  heed my resounding cry.
Give ear to my plea,
  on lips that are without guile.
²May an authoritative ruling for me go out from
  your presence;
  may your eyes behold what is upright.
³Were you to test my mind, visit me by night,
  try me, you wouldn't have found [anything]
  – I had determined that my mouth would not
    transgress.
⁴As for human actions, in accord with the word of
  your lips,
  I myself have kept watch on the paths of the
    robber.
⁵My steps have taken hold of your tracks,
  my feet have not slipped.
⁶I myself call you, because you will answer me,
  God;
  bend your ear to me, listen to my word.
⁷Act in an extraordinary way with deeds of
  commitment,
  you who deliver those who take shelter with
    you
  from the people who rise up against them, by
    your right hand.
⁸Keep me like the apple of your eye,
  in the shadow of your wings hide me,
⁹From the faithless who've destroyed me,
  the enemies of my life who surround me.
¹⁰They've closed their minds,
  with their mouth they have spoken with
    majesty.
¹¹Our steps – they've now surrounded us;
  their eyes – they set them to extend through
    the country.
¹²His appearance is like a lion that's eager to tear,
  like a whelp that sits in ambush.
¹³Rise up, Yahweh,
  meet him face to face, bring him down!
Enable me to survive from the faithless with your
  sword,
    ¹⁴from human beings with your hand,
  Yahweh.
From human beings – in their lifetime will you fill
  their belly,
  with their share in life and with what you have
    stored up.

Their children are to be full,
  and they are to leave what they have over to
    their own young.
¹⁵When I behold your face in faithfulness,
  I will be full with your form when I awake.

## Psalm 18.1–24 *Rescued from death*

The leader's. Yahweh's servant's. David's, who
spoke to Yahweh the words of this song on the
day Yahweh rescued him from the fist of all his
enemies and from the hand of Sha'ul [Saul].
He said:

¹I dedicate myself to you, Yahweh, my strength,
  ²Yahweh my cliff, my fortress, the one who
    enables me to survive,
My God, my crag in which I take shelter,
  my shield, the horn that delivers me, my turret.
³As one to be praised, I called Yahweh,
  and from my enemies I found deliverance.
⁴Death's ropes have overwhelmed me,
  Beliyya'al's wadis terrified me,
⁵She'ol's ropes have surrounded me,
  death's snares have confronted me.
⁶In my pressure I called on Yahweh,
  I cried for help to my God.

⁷And the earth has quaked and rocked,
  the mountains' foundations shook.
They've quaked because it enraged him;
  ⁸smoke has gone up in his anger.
Fire from his mouth consumed,
  coals have burned up from him.
⁹He's spread the heavens and come down,
  with thundercloud beneath his feet.
¹⁰He's ridden on a sphinx and flown,
  swooped on the wings of the wind.
¹¹He's made darkness his hiding place round
    him,
  his bivouac water cloud, masses of mist.
¹²From the brightness in front of him, through his
    masses there have passed
  hail and fiery coals.
¹³Yahweh has thundered in the heavens,
  the One on High gave out his voice.
Hail and fiery coals:
  ¹⁴he's sent off his arrows and scattered them,
  shot lightning and routed them.
¹⁵Canyons of water have appeared,
  the world's foundations have come into sight,

At your reprimand, Yahweh,
    at the breath of your angry wind.

[16]He sent from on high, he got me,
    he drew me out of much water.
[17]He rescued me from my vigorous enemy,
    from people hostile to me, because they stood
        too firm for me.
[18]They met me on the day of my disaster,
    but Yahweh has become a support for me.
[19]He's brought me out into a roomy place;
    he's pulled me out because he delighted in me.
[20]Yahweh has dealt to me in accordance with my
        faithfulness;
    in accordance with the purity of my hands he
        gave back to me,
[21]Because I have kept Yahweh's ways
    and not been faithless to my God.
[22]Because all his rulings have been in front of
        me;
    his decrees I didn't let depart from me.
[23]I've been a person of integrity with him;
    I've kept myself from waywardness I might
        have done.
[24]So Yahweh has given back to me in accordance
    with my faithfulness,
    in accordance with the purity of my hands
        before his eyes.

### Psalm 18.25–50 The one who keeps my lamp alight

[25]With the committed person you show
        commitment;
    with the man of integrity you show integrity.
[26]With the pure you show yourself pure;
    with the crooked you show yourself
        refractory.
[27]Because you're one who delivers a humble
        people
    but puts down exalted eyes.
[28]Because you're the one who keeps my lamp
        alight;
    it's Yahweh my God who illumines my
        darkness.
[29]Because with you I can rush at a barricade;
    with my God I can scale a wall.
[30]God: his way has integrity;
    Yahweh's word is proven.
He is a shield
    to all who take shelter with him.

[31]Because who is God apart from Yahweh,
    who is a crag except our God?
[32]God is the one who belts me with forcefulness,
    and makes my way one that has integrity,
[33]Who fashions my feet like a deer,
    enables me to stand on the heights,
[34]Who trains my hands for battle,
    so that my arms could bend a copper bow.

[35]You've given me your shield that delivered;
    your right hand sustained me, your avowal
        made me great.
[36]You widened my step beneath me;
    my ankles have not slipped.
[37]I pursued my enemies so that I could overtake
        them;
    I didn't turn back until I finished them off.
[38]I hit them and they couldn't get up;
    they fell beneath my feet.
[39]You've belted me with forcefulness for battle;
    you bent down beneath me the people who
        rose up against me.
[40]My enemies you've made turn tail for me;
    the people who were hostile to me – I wiped
        them out.
[41]They cried for deliverance, but there was no
        deliverer –
    [cried] to Yahweh, but he has not answered
        them.
[42]I ground them fine like earth before the wind,
    flattened them like mud in the streets.
[43]You enabled me to survive from arguments with
        the people,
    you set me as head of nations.
A people I did not acknowledge serve me;
    [44]on hearing with the ear, they listened to me.
Foreigners wither before me,
    [45]foreigners wilt and come quaking out of their
        strongholds.

[46]Yahweh lives, my crag be blessed,
    may my God who delivers be exalted,
[47]The God who gives me total redress,
    and subjects peoples under me,
[48]Who enabled me to escape from my enemies,
    yes, exalts me above the people who rise up
        against me,
    rescues me from the violent man!

[49]Therefore I will confess you, Yahweh, among the
        nations,
    and make music for your name,

⁵⁰The one who gives great acts of deliverance to
    his king,
    acting with commitment to his anointed,
    to David and to his offspring permanently!

## Psalm 19 *The mystery of sin*

The leader's. A composition. David's.

¹The heavens are recounting God's splendour,
    the sky is telling of what his hands made.
²Day by day it pours out speech,
    night by night it proclaims knowledge.
³There's no speech, there are no words,
    whose voice does not make itself heard.
⁴In all the earth their noise has gone out,
    at the end of the world their utterances.
For the sun he put a tent in them;
    ⁵it's like a groom going out of his dressing
        room.
It rejoices to run the path, like a strong man,
    ⁶as its going out is from the end of the
        heavens.
Its completed circuit is at their [other] end,
    and there's nothing hidden from its heat.

⁷Yahweh's instruction has integrity,
    bringing life back.
Yahweh's affirmation is trustworthy,
    making the naïve smart.
⁸The things Yahweh has determined are upright,
    rejoicing the mind.
Yahweh's order is clean,
    enlightening the eyes.
⁹Awe for Yahweh is pure,
    standing permanently.
Yahweh's rulings are true;
    they're faithful altogether.
¹⁰They're more desirable than gold,
    than much pure gold,
Sweeter than syrup,
    than the juice of honeycombs.
¹¹Yes, your servant takes warning through them,
    and in keeping them there are great results.

¹²Who can understand mistakes?
    – free me from things that are hidden;
    ¹³yes, hold your servant back from assertive
        deeds.
May they not rule over me, then I'll be whole,
    and free of great rebellion.

¹⁴May the sayings of my mouth be acceptable to
    you,
    and the murmur of my mind before you,
    Yahweh, my crag and my restorer.

## Psalm 20 *Chariotry, horses, Yahweh*

The leader's. A composition. David's.

¹May Yahweh answer you on the day of pressure,
    the name of Ya'aqob's God set you on high.
²May he send your help from the sacred place,
    support you from Tsiyyon.
³May he be mindful of all your offerings,
    enrich your burnt sacrifice. *(Rise)*
⁴May he give to you what is in accordance with
        your mind,
    fulfil every counsel of yours.
⁵May we resound at your deliverance,
    in the name of our God we'll lift our banners:
    may Yahweh fulfil all your requests.

⁶Now I acknowledge
    that Yahweh has delivered his anointed.
He answers him from his sacred heavens,
    with the mighty acts of deliverance of his right
        hand.
⁷These people [make mention] of chariotry, those
        people of horses,
    but as for us – we make mention of the name of
        Yahweh our God.
⁸Those people have bent down and fallen,
    but as for us – we've risen up and taken our
        stand.
⁹'Yahweh, deliver the king!'
    – may he answer us on the day we call.

## Psalm 21 *An embodiment of blessing*

The leader's. A composition. David's.

¹Yahweh, the king rejoices in your vigour,
    how greatly he takes joy in your deliverance!
²You gave him the longing of his heart;
    the request of his lips you didn't deny.
³Because you meet him with blessings of good,
    set on his head a crown of pure gold.
⁴When he asked for life from you, you gave
        him,
    length of days for ever and ever.

⁵Great is his splendour through your deliverance,
  grandeur and magnificence you bestow on
  him.
⁶Because you make him [an embodiment of]
  blessing permanently,
  you gladden him with rejoicing at your
  presence.
⁷Because the king trusts in Yahweh
  and by the commitment of the One on High he
  doesn't slip.

⁸Your hand finds all your enemies,
  your right hand finds the people hostile to you.
⁹You make them like a blazing furnace
  at the time of your appearing.
Yahweh in anger swallows them up;
  fire consumes them.
¹⁰Their posterity you destroy from the earth,
  their offspring from among humanity.
¹¹When they've directed something bad against
  you,
  thought up a strategy, they don't succeed.
¹²Because you set them back
  when you aim at their faces with your bows.
¹³Be on high, Yahweh, in your vigour
  – we will sing and make music about your
  strength.

## Psalm 22.1–18 My God, my God, why?

The leader's. On Dawn Help. A composition.
David's.

¹My God, my God, why have you abandoned me,
  far away from delivering me, from the word I
  yell?
²My God, I call by day but you don't answer,
  and by night – there's no quietness for me.

³But you sit as the sacred one,
  the great praise of Yisra'el.
⁴In you our ancestors trusted;
  they trusted and you enabled them to
  survive.
⁵To you they cried out and they escaped;
  in you they trusted and they were not
  shamed.

⁶But I'm a worm, not a person,
  an object of reviling for human beings, an
  object of contempt for the people.

⁷All who see me ridicule me,
  open their mouth, shake their head.
⁸'He should commit it to Yahweh, he must enable
  him to survive,
  he must rescue him, because he delights in
  him.'

⁹Because you're the one who enabled me to break
  out of the womb,
  enabled me to trust at my mother's breast.
¹⁰On you I was thrown from birth;
  from my mother's womb you were my God.

¹¹Don't be far away from me,
  because pressure is near, and there's no one to
  help.
¹²Many bulls have surrounded me,
  sturdy Bashan steers have encircled me.
¹³Tearing and roaring lions
  have opened their mouth at me.
¹⁴I've spilled out like water,
  all my bones have become loose.
My mind's become like wax;
  it's melted inside me.
¹⁵My energy's withered like a piece of pot,
  my tongue sticks to my palate.
You've put me into death's earth,
  ¹⁶because dogs have surrounded me.
An assembly of bad people has hemmed me in;
  my hands and feet have shrivelled.
¹⁷I can count all my bones,
  while those people look out and see me.
¹⁸They divide my clothes for themselves;
  for my garments they let lots fall.

## Psalm 22.19–31 When you know that God has heard

¹⁹But you, Yahweh, don't be far away
  – my strength, come quickly as my help.
²⁰Rescue my life from the sword,
  my very self from the dog's power.
²¹Deliver me from the lion's mouth;
  may you have answered me from the oryxes'
  horns.

²²I will recount your name to my brothers;
  in the middle of the congregation I will praise
  you.
²³You who live in awe of Yahweh, praise him,
  all Ya'aqob's offspring, honour him!

Revere him,
    all Yisra'el's offspring!
²⁴Because he hasn't despised, he hasn't treated as
    abominable,
    the lament of the humble.
He hasn't hidden his face from him
    but listened to his cry for help to him.
²⁵From you will be my praise in the great
    congregation;
    my pledges I will make good in front of the
    people who live in awe of him.
²⁶Humble people will eat and be full;
    people who enquire of Yahweh will praise
    him
    – may your heart live permanently.
²⁷All the ends of the earth will be mindful and
    turn back to Yahweh;
    all the kin-groups of the nations will bow low
    before you.
²⁸Because kingship belongs to Yahweh;
    he rules over the nations.
²⁹All the enriched of the earth have eaten, and
    bowed low;
    before him all the people who are going down
    into the earth will kneel,
    and the person who hasn't been able to keep
    himself alive.
³⁰Offspring will serve him;
    a generation to come will be told of my
    Lord.
³¹They will recount his faithfulness to a people to
    be born,
    because he has acted.

## Psalm 23 *In the dark of the canyon*

A composition. David's.

¹My shepherd being Yahweh, I don't lack;
    ²he enables me to lie down in grassy pastures.
He leads me to settled water;
    ³he turns my life back.
He guides me in faithful tracks
    for the sake of his name.
⁴Even when I walk in a deathly dark ravine,
    I'm not afraid of bad fortune,
Because you're with me;
    your club and your cane – they comfort me.

⁵You spread a table before me
    in front of my adversaries.

You've enriched my head with oil;
    my cup fills me up.
⁶Yes, goodness and commitment pursue me
    all the days of my life.
I shall go back to Yahweh's house
    for long days.

## Psalm 24 *Will God let you in? Will you let God in?*

David's. A composition.

¹The earth and what fills it are Yahweh's,
    the world and the people who live in it.
²Because he founded it on the seas,
    set it on the rivers.

³Who goes up on to Yahweh's mountain,
    who gets up in his sacred place?
⁴One clean as to the palms of his hands and pure
    in mind,
    who has not lifted up himself to emptiness
    and not sworn so as to beguile.
⁵He lifts a blessing from Yahweh
    and faithfulness from his God who delivers.
⁶This is the circle of people who enquire of him,
    Ya'aqob who seek your face. *(Rise)*

⁷Lift your heads, gateways;
    lift yourself up, age-old doors,
    so that the glorious King may come in.
⁸'Who is he, then, the glorious King?'
    – Yahweh the vigorous one and the strong
    man,
    Yahweh the strong man in battle.
⁹Lift up your heads, gateways;
    lift up, age-old doors,
    so that the glorious King may come in.
¹⁰'Who is that, then, the glorious King?'
    – the glorious King is Yahweh of Armies.
    *(Rise)*

## Psalm 25 *I can't wait*

David's.

¹To you, Yahweh,
    I lift my entire being, ²my God.
I've trusted in you – I must not be shamed;
    my enemies must not exult about me.

³Yes, all the people who hope in you will not be
    shamed;
  the people who break faith without reason will
    be shamed.
⁴Enable me to acknowledge your ways, Yahweh,
    teach me your paths.
⁵Direct me in your truthfulness and teach me,
  because you're my God who delivers;
  in you I have hoped all day.
⁶Be mindful of your compassion, Yahweh, and
    your commitment,
  because they are age-old.
⁷Don't be mindful of the wrongs of my youth
  and my acts of rebellion.
In accordance with your commitment be mindful
    of me yourself,
  for the sake of your goodness, Yahweh.
⁸Yahweh is good and upright;
  therefore he instructs wrongdoers in the way.
⁹He directs the humble by his authority,
  teaches the humble his way.
¹⁰All Yahweh's paths are commitment and
    truthfulness
  to people who keep his pact, his affirmations.
¹¹For the sake of your name, Yahweh,
  pardon my waywardness, because it's great.
¹²Who, then, is the individual who lives in awe of
    Yahweh?
  – he instructs him in the way he should
    choose.
¹³His life lodges in goodness,
  and his offspring possess the country.
¹⁴Yahweh's confidences are with people who live
    in awe of him,
  and his pact, in enabling them to acknowledge
    him.
¹⁵My eyes are continually towards Yahweh,
  because he's the one who gets my feet out of
    the net.
¹⁶Turn your face to me and be gracious to me,
  because I'm alone and humble.
¹⁷The pressures in my mind have widened;
  get me out from my straits.
¹⁸Look at my humbling and oppression;
  carry all my wrongdoings.
¹⁹Look at my enemies, how they are many,
  and at the violent hostility they show to me.
²⁰Keep my life, rescue me;
  I must not be shamed, because I've taken
    shelter with you.
²¹Integrity and uprightness must preserve me,
  because I've hoped in you.

²²God, redeem Yisra'el
  from all its pressures.

## Psalm 26 I wash my hands in innocence

David's.

¹Exercise authority for me, Yahweh,
  because I – I have walked in integrity.
In Yahweh I've trusted;
  I don't slip.
²Probe me, Yahweh, try me,
  test my inner being and my mind.
³Because your commitment is in front of my eyes;
  I walk about by your truthfulness.
⁴I haven't sat with empty men;
  I don't come with deceitful people.
⁵I'm hostile to the congregation of people who
    deal badly;
  I don't sit with the faithless.
⁶I wash the palms of my hands with freedom from
    guilt
  so that I may go about your altar, Yahweh,
⁷To let people hear the sound of confession,
  to recount all your extraordinary deeds.
⁸Yahweh, I'm loyal to the abode that is your house,
  the dwelling place of your splendour.
⁹Don't gather me up with wrongdoers,
  my life with men of bloodshed,
¹⁰In whose hand is deliberate wickedness,
  and whose right hand is full of bribes.
¹¹But I'm one who walks in my integrity;
  redeem me, be gracious to me!
¹²My foot has stood on level ground;
  in the great congregation I will bless Yahweh.

## Psalm 27 One thing

David's.

¹Yahweh is my light, my deliverance:
  of whom should I be afraid?
Yahweh is the stronghold of my life:
  of whom should I be in dread?
²When people who deal badly drew near me,
  to devour my flesh,
My adversaries and my enemies:
  those people collapsed, fell.
³If an army camps against me,
  my heart will not be afraid.

If battle arises against me,
   during this I trust.

[4]One thing I've asked from Yahweh,
   it's what I seek,
For me to live in Yahweh's house,
   all the days of my life,
To behold Yahweh's loveliness,
   and to consult each morning in his palace.
[5]Because he keeps me safe in his shelter
   on the day of bad fortune.
He hides me in his tent as a hiding place;
   he lifts me high on a crag.
[6]So now my head is high,
   above my enemies round me.
In his tent I will offer noisy sacrifices;
   I will sing and make music for Yahweh.

[7]Listen, Yahweh, to my voice when I call;
   be gracious to me, answer me.
[8]For you my mind said,
   'Seek my face!'
Your face I seek, Yahweh:
   [9]don't hide your face from me.
Don't turn aside your servant in anger;
   you've been my help.
Don't leave me, don't abandon me,
   my God who delivers.
[10]When my father and my mother have
      abandoned me,
   then Yahweh will take me in.
[11]Instruct me in your way, Yahweh,
   lead me on a level path.
In view of the people watching for me,
   [12]don't give me over to the will of my
      adversaries.
Because there have arisen against me false
      witnesses,
   a person who testifies violence.
[13]Unless I trusted to see good things from
      Yahweh
   in the country of the living . . .
[14]Hope in Yahweh, be strong,
   may your mind stand firm, hope in Yahweh!

## Psalm 28 Our vigour and God's

David's.

[1]To you, Yahweh, I call;
   my crag, don't be deaf towards me,

So that you aren't silent in relation to me,
   and I become like the people who go down into
      the Cistern.
[2]Listen to the sound of my prayers for grace,
   when I cry for help to you,
When I lift up my hands
   to your sacred inner room.
[3]Don't drag me off with faithless people,
   with people who devise trouble,
People who speak of well-being with their
      neighbours,
   when there is bad dealing in their mind.
[4]Give to them in accordance with their doings,
   in accordance with the badness of their deeds.
In accordance with the action of their hands give
      to them,
   give back their dealing to them.
[5]Because they don't consider Yahweh's acts,
   the work of his hands;
   may he tear them down and not build them up.

[6]Yahweh be blessed,
   because he's heard the sound of my prayers for
      grace.
[7]Yahweh is my vigour and my shield;
   in him my mind has trusted, and I will find help.
My mind has exulted,
   and I will glorify him with my song.
[8]Yahweh is vigour for him and stronghold;
   he is the great deliverance of his anointed.
[9]Deliver your people, bless your domain,
   shepherd them and carry them permanently.

## Psalm 29 Yahweh's voice produces convulsions

A composition. David's.

[1]Give Yahweh, you divine beings,
   give Yahweh splendour and vigour.
[2]Give Yahweh the glory of his name,
   bow low to Yahweh in sacred array.
[3]Yahweh's voice was over the water,
   the glorious God thundered,
   Yahweh over mighty water.
[4]Yahweh's voice was with energy;
   Yahweh's voice was with magnificence.
[5]Yahweh's voice breaks cedars;
   Yahweh breaks off cedars of Lebanon.
[6]He makes them jump like a calf,
   Lebanon and Siryon like a young oryx.

[7]Yahweh's voice splits flames of fire,
  [8]Yahweh's voice convulses the wilderness,
  Yahweh convulses the Qadesh Wilderness.
[9]Yahweh's voice convulses oaks,
  strips forests.
In his palace everyone in it says,
  'In splendour [10]Yahweh sat on high;
  Yahweh sat as king permanently.'
[11]Yahweh gives vigour to his people;
  Yahweh blesses his people with well-being.

## Psalm 30 I prayed, Yahweh answered, Yahweh acted

A composition. A song at the dedication of the house. David's.

[1]I will exalt you, Yahweh, because you put me down,
  but did not let my enemies rejoice about me.
[2]Yahweh my God,
  I cried for help to you, and you healed me.
[3]Yahweh, you got my life up from She'ol,
  you kept me alive from going down into the Cistern.
[4]Make music for Yahweh, you who are committed to him,
  confess his sacred commemoration,
[5]Because there's a moment in his anger,
  a life in his acceptance.
In the evening crying lodges,
  but at morning there's resounding.

[6]I – I had said when I was at ease,
  'I shall not slip ever.'
[7]Yahweh, in your acceptance
  you'd put in place vigour for my mountain.
You hid your face;
  I became fearful.
[8]To you, Yahweh, I would call,
  to my Lord I would pray for grace.
[9]'What would be the gain in my blood being shed,
  in my going down to She'ol?
Can the earth confess you,
  can it tell of your truthfulness?
[10]Listen, Yahweh, be gracious to me;
  Yahweh, be a helper for me.'

[11]You turned my lament into dancing for me,
  you undid my sack and belted me with rejoicing,

[12]so that my heart might make music and not stop;
  Yahweh my God, I will confess you permanently.

## Psalm 31 My times are in your hand

The leader's. A composition. David's.

[1]Since I've taken shelter with you, Yahweh,
  may I never be shamed;
  enable me to survive by your faithfulness.
[2]Bend your ear to me,
  hurry and rescue me.
Be for me a crag, a stronghold,
  a fortress to deliver me.
[3]Because you're my cliff, my stronghold;
  for your name's sake lead me and guide me.
[4]Do get me out of the net that they concealed for me,
  because you're my stronghold.
[5]Into your hand I assign my spirit;
  you've redeemed me, Yahweh, truthful God.
[6]I'm hostile to people who keep things that are empty and hollow;
  I myself trust in Yahweh.
[7]I shall celebrate and rejoice in your commitment,
  you who've seen my humbling;
  you've acknowledged the pressures on me.
[8]You haven't delivered me into the hand of the enemy;
  you've stood my feet in a wide place.

[9]Be gracious to me, Yahweh,
  because there's pressure on me.
My eye wastes away because of vexation;
  my entire being and my body.
[10]Because my life comes to a finish in sadness,
  my years in groaning.
My energy has collapsed because of my waywardness,
  my bones waste away.
[11]Before all my adversaries I've become an object of reviling,
  and very much so for my neighbours,
A dread to my acquaintances;
  people who see me in the street flee away from me.
[12]I'm put out of mind like someone who's died;
  I've become like a container perishing.
[13]Because I've heard the smears of many people,
  alarm all round,

As they scheme together against me;
  they've conspired to take my life.
[14]But I – I've trusted in you, Yahweh;
  I've said, 'You are my God.'
[15]My times are in your hand;
  rescue me from the hand of my enemies, from
    my pursuers.
[16]May your face shine upon your servant;
  deliver me, in your commitment.
[17]Yahweh, may I not be shamed, because I have
    called you;
  may the faithless people be shamed.
As they go silent to She'ol,
  [18]may false lips be quiet,
Which speak arrogantly against the faithful,
  with majesty and contempt.
[19]How much good you have,
  which you've stored up for those who live in
    awe of you,
With which you've acted towards those who take
    shelter with you,
  in front of people.
[20]You hide them in a hiding place in your presence
  from human plots.
You conceal them in a bivouac
  from arguing tongues.

[21]Yahweh be blessed,
  because he has been extraordinary in his
    commitment to me,
  as a town besieged.
[22]I myself had said in my haste,
  'I'm cut off at a distance from your eyes.'
On the contrary, you heard my voice praying for
    grace,
  when I cried out for help to you.
[23]Be loyal to Yahweh, all you who are committed
    to him;
  Yahweh preserves the people who are true,
  but makes good plentifully to the person who
    acts with majesty.
[24]Be strong; your mind should stand firm,
  all you who wait for Yahweh.

## Psalm 32 *Love covers a multitude of sins*

  David's. An instruction.

[1]The blessings of the one whose rebellion is
    carried,
  whose wrongdoing is covered!

[2]The blessings of the person
  whose waywardness Yahweh does not think
    about,
  in whose spirit there is no deceit!
[3]When I was silent,
  my bones wasted away with my anguish all day.
[4]Because day and night your hand was heavy on me;
  my strength was sapped [as] in summer
    drought. *(Rise)*
[5]I acknowledged my wrongdoing to you;
  I didn't cover my waywardness.
I said, 'I shall confess my rebellions to Yahweh',
  and you yourself carried the waywardness of
    my wrongdoing. *(Rise)*
[6]Because of this everyone who is committed
    should plead with you,
  at the time when he is found out.
Yes, when much water overwhelms,
  it will not reach him.
[7]You're a hiding place for me, you preserve me
    from trouble,
  you surround me with survival shouts.

[8]'I shall give you insight, instruct you in the way
    you should go;
  I shall offer counsel, my eye on you,
[9]Don't be like a horse,
  like a mule that has no understanding,
Whose advance requires curbing with bit and
    bridle,
  or there is no coming near you.'

[10]Many are the pains of the faithless,
  but the person who trusts in Yahweh –
    commitment surrounds him.
[11]Rejoice in Yahweh, celebrate, you faithful;
  shout, all you upright of mind.

## Psalm 33 *God's commitment fills the earth*

[1]Resound, faithful people, in Yahweh;
  praise is fitting for the upright.
[2]Confess Yahweh with the mandolin;
  make music for him with the ten-stringed
    guitar.
[3]Sing him a new song;
  do well in playing, with a shout.
[4]Because Yahweh's word is upright,
  and every act of his is done in truthfulness.
[5]He's loyal to faithfulness in exercising authority;
  Yahweh's commitment fills the earth.

⁶By Yahweh's word the heavens were made,
by the breath of his mouth all their army,
⁷Gathering the sea's water as in a dam,
putting the deeps in treasuries.

⁸All the earth is to live in awe of Yahweh;
all the world's inhabitants are to revere him.
⁹Because he's the one who spoke, and it happened;
he's the one who ordered, and it stood up.
¹⁰Yahweh has contravened the nations' counsel,
frustrated the peoples' intentions.
¹¹Yahweh's counsel stands permanently,
the intentions of his mind for generation after
generation.
¹²The blessings of the nation for which Yahweh is
its God,
the people he chose as a domain for himself!
¹³From the heavens Yahweh has looked,
seen all humanity.
¹⁴From the established place where he lives he's
gazed
at all the people who live on the earth,
¹⁵The one who shapes their mind, all together,
who considers all their actions.

¹⁶There is no king who delivers himself by the
abundance of his resources;
a strong man doesn't rescue himself by the
abundance of his energy.
¹⁷The horse is a falsehood for deliverance,
and by the abundance of its forcefulness it
doesn't provide escape.
¹⁸There, it's Yahweh's eye that's on people who live
in awe of him,
people who wait for his commitment,
¹⁹To rescue their life from death,
and keep them alive in famine.
²⁰Our entire being hopes for Yahweh;
he is our help and our shield.
²¹Because in him our heart rejoices;
because in his sacred name we've trusted.
²²May your commitment be over us, Yahweh,
as we've waited for you.

*Psalm 34 Look to him and become bright*

David's. When he concealed his sanity before
Abimelek so that he drove him out, and he went.

¹I will bless Yahweh all the time;
his praise will be in my mouth continually.

²In Yahweh my entire being takes pride;
the humble should listen and rejoice.
³Magnify Yahweh with me;
we'll exalt his name together.
⁴I enquired of Yahweh and he answered me,
and rescued me from all my terrors.
⁵People look to him and become bright;
their faces need not be confounded.
⁶This humble man called and Yahweh himself
listened,
and delivered him from all his pressures.
⁷Yahweh's envoy camps round the people who live
in awe of him
and pulls them out.
⁸Taste and see that Yahweh is good;
the blessings of the man who takes shelter with
him!
⁹Live in awe of Yahweh, you who are his sacred
ones,
because there's no lack for people who live in
awe of him.
¹⁰Lions are destitute and starve,
but people who enquire of Yahweh don't lack
any good thing.
¹¹Come, children, listen to me;
I'll teach you about awe for Yahweh.
¹²Who's the individual who delights in life,
who loves days for seeing good fortune?
¹³Preserve your tongue from what is bad,
your lips from speaking a lie.
¹⁴Depart from what's bad and do what's good;
seek well-being, pursue it.
¹⁵Yahweh's eyes are on the faithful,
his ears are to their cry for help.
¹⁶Yahweh's face is against people who do what's bad,
to cut off their commemoration from the
country.
¹⁷People cry out, and Yahweh listens,
and rescues them from all their pressures.
¹⁸Yahweh is near to the people who are breaking
inside,
and delivers the people who are crushed in
spirit.
¹⁹When the bad things that come to the faithful
person are many,
Yahweh rescues him from them all.
²⁰He keeps all his bones;
not one of them breaks.
²¹Bad fortune brings the death of the faithless
person,
and the people who are hostile to the faithful
incur liability.

<sup>22</sup>Yahweh redeems the life of his servants,
    and none who take shelter with him incur
        liability.

## Psalm 35.1–16 Argue for me

David's.

<sup>1</sup>Argue with the people who argue with me,
    Yahweh,
        battle with the people who battle me.
<sup>2</sup>Take strong hold of hand-shield and body-shield,
    and arise as my help.
<sup>3</sup>Draw lance and pike
    to meet my pursuers.
Say to me,
    'I am your deliverance.'
<sup>4</sup>They must be shamed and disgraced,
    the people seeking my life.
They must turn backwards and be confounded,
    the people thinking up something bad for me.
<sup>5</sup>They must be like chaff before the wind,
    with Yahweh's envoy chasing.
<sup>6</sup>Their way must be darkness and slipperiness,
    with Yahweh's envoy pursuing them.
<sup>7</sup>Because for nothing they've hidden their net's pit
        for me,
    for nothing they dug it for my life.
<sup>8</sup>Devastation must come that he doesn't know,
    his own net that he hid must catch him,
    as devastation may he fall into it.
<sup>9</sup>But my entire being will rejoice in Yahweh,
    it shall be glad at his deliverance.
<sup>10</sup>All my bones will say,
    'Yahweh, who is like you,
One who rescues the humble person from the one
        stronger than him,
    the humble and needy person from the robber?'

<sup>11</sup>Violent witnesses arise,
    people who ask me about what I don't
        acknowledge.
<sup>12</sup>They make good to me with bad for good,
    mourning for my entire being.
<sup>13</sup>But I – when they were ill,
    my clothing was sack.
I humbled myself with fasting,
    and my plea would turn back to my heart.
<sup>14</sup>I walked about as if it was my friend, as if it was
        a brother;
    as if I were a mother grieving, mourning, gloomy.

<sup>15</sup>But at my stumbling they've rejoiced and
        gathered,
    gathered against me as assailants.
People I didn't know
    have torn at me and not stopped.
<sup>16</sup>As the most profane twisted people who
        ridicule,
    they have ground their teeth against me.

## Psalm 35.17–28 'We've swallowed him up!'

<sup>17</sup>Lord, how long until you see?
    – bring back my life from their devastation,
    my dear life from the lions.
<sup>18</sup>I shall confess you in the great congregation,
    among a numerous people I shall praise you.
<sup>19</sup>My lying enemies must not rejoice at me,
    the people hostile to me for nothing, who glint
        their eyes.
<sup>20</sup>Because they don't speak of peace;
    they're against the quiet people in the
        country.
They think up false statements,
    <sup>21</sup>and they've widened their mouth against me.
They have said,
    'Ah, ah, our eye has seen it!'
<sup>22</sup>You've seen, Yahweh, don't be silent;
    Lord, don't be far away from me!
<sup>23</sup>Stir yourself, wake up, to exercise authority for
        me,
    to argue for me, my God and Lord!
<sup>24</sup>Exercise authority for me in accordance with
        your faithfulness,
    Yahweh my God; they mustn't rejoice over me.
<sup>25</sup>They must not say inside, 'Ah, our desire!'
    – they must not say, 'We've swallowed him up!'
<sup>26</sup>They must be shamed and confounded
        altogether,
    the people who rejoice at bad fortune coming
        to me.
They must be clothed in disgrace and shame,
    the people who act big over me.
<sup>27</sup>They must resound and rejoice,
    the people who delight in the faithfulness
        shown me,
So that they will say continually, 'Yahweh is
        great,
    the one who delights in the well-being of his
        servant.'
<sup>28</sup>And my tongue will tell of your faithfulness,
    of your praise all day.

## Psalm 36 *Your truthfulness reaches to the skies*

The leader's. Yahweh's servant's. David's.

¹A rebellious utterance by a faithless person
   is in my mind.
There is no reverence for God
   in front of his eyes.
²Because he flatters himself in his own eyes,
   about being found out for his waywardness,
      about meeting hostility.
³The words of his mouth are trouble and deceit;
   he's left off having insight, doing good.
⁴He thinks up trouble on his bed,
   he takes his stand on a no-good way, he doesn't
   reject what is bad.

⁵Yahweh, your commitment is in the heavens,
   your truthfulness reaches as far as the skies.
⁶Your faithfulness is like supernatural mountains,
   your authority is like the great deep.
Human being and animal you deliver, Yahweh;
   ⁷how valuable is your commitment.
Divine beings and human beings
   take shelter in the shadow of your wings.
⁸They feast on the richness of your house,
   you let them drink from your lovely wadi.
⁹Because with you there is a living spring;
   in your light we see light.

¹⁰Draw out your commitment to the people who
      acknowledge you,
   your faithfulness to the upright in mind.
¹¹The majestic foot must not come on me,
   the hand of faithless people must not make me
   flee.
¹²The people who devise trouble have fallen there,
   they have been thrown down, they can't get up.

## Psalm 37.1–20 *The humble will enter into possession of the land*

David's.

¹Don't get into a rage because of people who deal
      badly,
   don't get passionate because of people who do
   evil.
²Because like grass they fade quickly,
   like green plants they wither.

³Trust in Yahweh and do good,
   dwell in the country and pasture on
      truthfulness.
⁴Revel in Yahweh,
   and he'll give you the requests of your heart.
⁵Commit your way to Yahweh;
   trust in him and he'll act,
⁶He'll bring out faithfulness for you like light,
   exercise of authority for you like midday.
⁷Be still before Yahweh,
   and wait patiently for him.
Don't get into a rage with the person who makes
      his way successful,
   with the individual who acts on his strategies.
⁸Let go of anger, abandon wrath;
   don't get into a rage, only to do something
   bad.
⁹Because people who deal badly will be cut off,
   but those who hope in Yahweh – they'll enter
      into possession of the country.
¹⁰Yet a little while and there'll be no faithless
      person;
   you'll consider his place, and there'll be no one.
¹¹The humble – they'll enter into possession of the
      country
   and revel in abundance of well-being.
¹²The faithless person schemes against the faithful
   and grinds his teeth against him.
¹³The Lord makes fun of him,
   because he's seen that his day will come.
¹⁴Faithless people have drawn the sword,
   and directed their bow,
To make the humble and needy fall,
   to slaughter people who are upright in their
   way.
¹⁵Their sword will come into their own heart,
   their bows will break.
¹⁶Better is the little of the faithful
   than the great mass of the faithless.
¹⁷Because the arms of the faithless will break,
   but Yahweh upholds the faithful.
¹⁸Yahweh will acknowledge the days of people of
      integrity,
   and their domain will last permanently.
¹⁹They won't be shamed at a time when things are
      bad,
   and in days of famine they'll be full.
²⁰Because faithless people will perish,
   Yahweh's enemies.
They'll come to a finish like the most valuable of
      pastures,
   come to a finish in smoke.

## Psalm 37.21–40 What I've seen and not seen

<sup>21</sup>The faithless person borrows and cannot make good,
  but the faithful person is gracious and gives.
<sup>22</sup>Because the people blessed by him will enter
    into possession of the country,
  but the people slighted by him will be cut off.
<sup>23</sup>A man's steps are established by Yahweh,
  when he delights in his way.
<sup>24</sup>When he falls he's not thrown headlong,
  because Yahweh supports with his hand.
<sup>25</sup>I was young and yes, I'm old,
  but I haven't seen a faithful person abandoned,
  or his offspring seeking bread.
<sup>26</sup>All day he's gracious and lends,
  and his offspring are a blessing.
<sup>27</sup>Depart from what's bad and do good,
  and dwell permanently.
<sup>28</sup>Because Yahweh is loyal to the exercise of authority,
  and doesn't abandon people committed to him.
They are kept watch over permanently,
  but the offspring of the faithless are cut off.
<sup>29</sup>Faithful people will enter into possession of the
    country,
  and dwell for ever and ever.
<sup>30</sup>The mouth of the faithful person murmurs
    smartness,
  and his tongue speaks with authority.
<sup>31</sup>His God's instruction is in his mind;
  his steps don't slip.
<sup>32</sup>The faithless person watches for the faithful,
  and seeks to put him to death.
<sup>33</sup>Yahweh doesn't abandon him into his hand,
  and doesn't declare him in the wrong when
    entering into judgement about him.
<sup>34</sup>Hope in Yahweh,
  and keep his way.
He'll raise you up so that you enter into
    possession of the country;
  when the faithless are cut off, you'll see.
<sup>35</sup>I've seen a faithless man, violent,
  arousing himself like a verdant native tree,
<sup>36</sup>But he passed on – there, he was gone;
  I sought him and he couldn't be found.
<sup>37</sup>Keep watch on the person of integrity, see the
    upright person,
  because there is a future for the man of peace.
<sup>38</sup>But rebels are annihilated all at once;
  the future of the faithless is cut off.

<sup>39</sup>The deliverance of the faithful comes from
    Yahweh,
  their stronghold in time of pressure.
<sup>40</sup>Yahweh helps them and enables them to survive,
  he enables them to survive from the faithless
    and delivers them,
  because they take shelter with him.

## Psalm 38 Suffering can sometimes link to sin

A composition. David's. For commemoration.

<sup>1</sup>Yahweh, don't reprove me in your fury,
  or discipline me in your wrath.
<sup>2</sup>Because your arrows have descended on me,
  your hand has descended upon me.
<sup>3</sup>There's no integrity in my body by reason of your
    condemnation;
  there's no well-being in my bones by reason of
    my wrongdoings.
<sup>4</sup>Because my wayward acts have passed over my
    head;
  like a heavy burden, they're too heavy for me.
<sup>5</sup>My wounds have smelled and festered
  by reason of my denseness.
<sup>6</sup>Because I went astray, I'm utterly bowed down;
  all day I've gone about gloomy.
<sup>7</sup>Because my thighs are full of burning,
  and there is no integrity in my body.
<sup>8</sup>I've become numb, utterly crushed;
  I howl because of the rumbling in my heart.
<sup>9</sup>Lord, all my longing is in front of you;
  my groaning has not hidden from you.
<sup>10</sup>My heart has taken flight, my energy has
    abandoned me;
  the light in my eyes – they, too, are not with
    me.
<sup>11</sup>My friends and my neighbours
  stand back at a distance from my affliction.
The people near me have stood far off,
  <sup>12</sup>and people who seek my life have laid traps.
People who enquire about something bad for me
    have spoken malice;
  all day they murmur lies.
<sup>13</sup>But I myself am like a deaf person, I cannot hear,
  like a dumb person who cannot open his
    mouth.
<sup>14</sup>I've become like someone who doesn't hear;
  there's no reproof in my mouth.

¹⁵Because I've waited for you, Yahweh;
  you – you will answer, Lord my God.
¹⁶Because I said, 'They must not rejoice about me;
  when my foot slipped, they acted big over me.'
¹⁷Because I am set for stumbling;
  my pain is in front of me continually.
¹⁸Because I tell of my waywardness,
  I'm anxious because of my wrongdoings.
¹⁹My mortal enemies are numerous,
  the people hostile to me with falsehood are many.
²⁰The people who make good with something bad
    for something good
  attack me on account of my pursuing what is
    good.
²¹Don't abandon me, Yahweh;
  my God, don't be far from me.
²²Hurry to my help,
  Lord my deliverance.

## Psalm 39 *Just a breath*

The leader's. Yedutun's. A composition.
David's.

¹I said, 'I shall keep watch on my ways,
  so that I don't do wrong with my tongue.
I shall keep a muzzle on my mouth,
  as long as a faithless person is in front of me.'
²I was dumb, in silence;
  I was quiet, more than it was good.
And as my pain stirred,
  ³my mind became heated inside me.
As I murmured, fire burned up;
  I spoke out with my tongue.

⁴Get me to acknowledge my end, Yahweh,
  the number of my days, what it is.
⁵There, you made my days handbreadths;
  my span is as nothing in front of you.
Yes, every human being, standing firm, is simply a
    breath; *(Rise)*
  ⁶yes, it's as a shadow that a person walks about.
Yes, it's for a breath that people are in turmoil;
  someone may heap up, but not know who's
    going to gather them in.

⁷So now, what have I hoped for, Lord?
  – my waiting is for you.
⁸Rescue me from all my acts of rebellion,
  don't make me an object of reviling to the
    villain.

⁹I was dumb, I didn't open my mouth,
  because you were the one who acted.
¹⁰Turn away your affliction from me;
  because of the blow of your hand I – I am
    finished.
¹¹With reproofs for waywardness you've
    disciplined someone,
  and consumed like a moth what he desires;
  yes, every human being is a breath. *(Rise)*

¹²Listen to my plea, Yahweh, give ear to my cry
    for help,
  don't be silent at my crying.
Because I'm a sojourner with you,
  a transient like all my ancestors.
¹³Look away from me so that I may smile,
  before I go and there is nothing of me.

## Psalm 40 *I didn't hide your faithfulness within my heart*

The leader's. David's. A composition.

¹I hoped and hoped in Yahweh,
  and he bent to me and listened to my cry for help.
²He got me up from a roaring cistern,
  from the overflowing mud.
He set up my feet on a cliff,
  he established my steps.
³He put a new song in my mouth,
  an act of praise to our God.
Many could see it and live in awe,
  and trust in Yahweh.

⁴The blessings of the man
  who makes Yahweh his trust
And has not turned his face to the arrogant
  or to people who follow a lie!
⁵You, Yahweh, my God,
  have done many things.
Your extraordinary deeds and your intentions
    for us
  – there is no one to set alongside you.
Were I to tell and speak,
  they are too numerous to recount.
⁶Sacrifice and offering you didn't want
  – you dug ears for me;
  burnt offering and purification offering you
    didn't ask for.
⁷Then I said, 'Here, I've come;
  in a written scroll it is inscribed for me.'

8I wanted to do what's acceptable to you, my God;
   your instruction was within my inmost self.
9I announced the news of your faithfulness in the
      great congregation;
   there – I wouldn't close my lips,
   as, Yahweh, you yourself know.
10I didn't hide your faithfulness within my heart;
   I told of your truthfulness and your
      deliverance.
I didn't conceal your true commitment
   before the great congregation.

11You, Yahweh,
   may you not close up your compassion from
      me;
   may your true commitment preserve me
      continually.
12Because bad experiences have surrounded me,
   beyond numbering.
My wayward acts have caught up with me;
   I haven't been able to see.
They're more numerous than the hairs on my
      head;
   my mind has abandoned me.
13Show acceptance, Yahweh, by rescuing me;
   Yahweh, hurry to my help.
14May they be shamed and reviled altogether,
   the people who seek my life, to destroy it.
May they turn backwards and be confounded,
   the people who want what is bad for me.
15May they be desolate on account of their shame,
   the people who say to me 'Ah, ah!'
16May they celebrate and rejoice in you, all the
      people who seek you;
   may they say continually 'Yahweh is great',
   the people loyal to your deliverance.

17But I'm humble and needy;
   may my Lord take thought for me.
You're my help and the one who enables me to
      survive;
   my God, don't delay!

## Psalm 41.1–12 Learning from the poor

The leader's. A composition. David's.

1The blessings of the one who has insight into the
      poor person,
   whom Yahweh saves on the day when bad
      things happen!

2Yahweh keeps watch over him and keeps him
      alive,
   and blesses him in the country,
   and you won't give him to the appetite of his
      enemies.
3Yahweh sustains him on his sickbed;
   his entire bed you've transformed, in his
      illness.

4I myself said, 'Yahweh, be gracious to me;
   heal me, because I have done wrong in relation
      to you.'
5My enemies speak of bad fortune for me:
   'When will he die, and his name perish?
6If he comes to see [someone],
   he speaks emptiness.
His mind collects trouble for himself,
   which he speaks when he goes outside.'
7All the people hostile to me whisper together
      against me;
   they think up bad things for me.
8'A lethal pestilence besets him;
   in that he has lain down, he won't get up again.'
9Even my friend whom I trusted,
   one who eats bread with me,
   has acted big against me as a cheat.
10But you, Yahweh, be gracious to me,
   raise me up, and I'll make good to them.

11Through this I have acknowledged that you
      delighted in me,
   because my enemy does not shout over me,
12And I – in my integrity you've taken hold of me,
   and stood me up before you permanently.

## Psalm 41.13 An interim closing act of praise

13Yahweh the God of Yisra'el be blessed,
   from age to age,
Amen, amen.

## Psalm 42 Where is your God?

The leader's. An instruction. The Qorahites'.

1Like a deer that strains towards water canyons,
   so my entire being strains towards you, God.
2My entire being is thirsty for God,
   for the living God;

When will I come
and appear before God?
³My crying has become my food,
day and night,
While people say to me all day,
'Where is your God?'
⁴These things I shall bring to mind,
as I pour out my entire being within me:
That I shall pass along in the shelter,
lead people right to God's house,
With a voice of resounding and confession,
the festive crowd.
⁵Why do you bow low, my entire being,
[why] are you in turmoil within me?
Wait for God, because I shall yet confess him
for the deliverance that comes from his face.

⁶My God, my entire being bows low within me;
therefore I bring you to mind,
From the Yarden [Jordan] region and the Hermons,
from Little Mountain.
⁷Deep is calling to deep,
in the sound of your waterfalls.
All your breakers and your waves
have passed over me.
⁸By day may Yahweh order his commitment,
and by night may his song be with me.
A plea to my living God:
⁹I will say to God, my cliff,
'Why have you put me out of mind,
why do I go about gloomy,
With affliction from an enemy,
¹⁰with murder in my bones?
My adversaries have reviled me,
while they say to me all day,
'Where is your God?'
¹¹Why do you bow low, my entire being,
and why are you in turmoil within me?
Wait for God, because I shall yet confess him,
as the deliverance of my face and my God.

## Psalm 43 *God's light and truthfulness to lead me*

¹Exercise authority for me, God,
argue for my cause.
From a nation that is not committed,
from a deceitful and evil individual, enable me
to survive.
²Because you are God my stronghold;
why have you rejected me?

Why do I go about gloomy,
through an enemy's affliction?
³Send your light and your truthfulness, they will
lead me;
they will bring me to your sacred mountain, to
your great dwelling,
⁴So that I can come to God's altar,
to the God in whom I rejoice joyfully,
And confess you with the guitar,
God my God.
⁵Why do you bow low, my entire being,
and why are you in turmoil within me?
Wait for God, because I shall yet confess him
as the deliverance of my face and my God.

## Psalm 44.1–16 *It's not in my bow that I trust*

The leader's. The Qorahites.' An instruction.

¹God, we've heard with our ears,
our ancestors have recounted to us,
The deed you did in their days, in past days,
²you yourself with your own hand.
You dispossessed nations and planted them;
you brought bad fortune on peoples and sent
them off.
³Because it was not by their sword that they
entered into possession of the country,
it was not their arm that delivered them,
But your hand and your arm, and the light of your
face,
because you accepted them.
⁴You are my king, God;
order Ya'aqob's deliverance!
⁵Through you we charge at our adversaries,
by your name we tread down our attackers.
⁶Because it's not in my bow that I trust;
my sword doesn't deliver me.
⁷Because you've delivered us from our adversaries,
and shamed the people hostile to us.
⁸God is the one whom we praise all day;
your name we shall confess permanently. *(Rise)*

⁹Yet you've rejected and disgraced us,
and you don't go out with our armies.
¹⁰You turn us back from the adversary,
and the people hostile to us have plundered us
at will.
¹¹You make us like sheep for food,
and you've scattered us among the nations.

¹²You sell your people without profit;
    you didn't go high in their price.
¹³You make us an object of reviling to our
      neighbours,
    an object of ridicule and derision to the people
      round us.
¹⁴You make us an object lesson among the
      nations,
    something to shake the head at among the
      peoples.
¹⁵All day my disgrace is in front of me;
    the shame of my face has covered me,
¹⁶At the voice of the person reviling and insulting,
    at the presence of the enemy exacting redress.

## Psalm 44.17–26 Wake up, God!

¹⁷All this has come upon us and we haven't put
      you out of mind;
    we haven't been false to your pact.
¹⁸Our mind has not turned backwards;
    our steps have not deviated from your path,
¹⁹That you should have crushed us into the place
      of jackals,
    covered us over with deathly darkness.
²⁰If we'd put our God's name out of mind,
    and spread our palms to a foreign god,
²¹God would search this out, wouldn't he,
    because he knows the mind's secrets.
²²Rather, it's because of you that we've been run
      through all day;
    we have been thought of as sheep for slaughter.

²³Rise up, why do you sleep, Lord?
    – wake up, don't reject permanently!
²⁴Why do you hide your face,
    put our humbling and affliction out of mind?
²⁵Because our being bows down in the earth,
    our heart clings to the ground.
²⁶Get up as our help,
    redeem us for the sake of your commitment!

## Psalm 45 The marriage challenge

The leader's. On Lotuses. The Qorahites'. An
instruction. A love song.

¹My mind stirs with a fine message;
    I'm speaking my work to a king,
    my tongue is the pen of a speedy secretary.

²You're the most handsome of human beings;
    grace is poured on to your lips
    – therefore God has blessed you permanently.
³Wrap your sword on to your side,
    strong man, with your grandeur and
      magnificence,
⁴and in your magnificence win.
Ride in the cause of truthfulness and faithful
    lowliness,
    so that your right hand directs you to awe-
      inspiring deeds.
⁵Your arrows are sharpened;
    peoples are beneath you.
They fall in the heart of the king's enemies;
    ⁶your throne, God's, is lasting and permanent.
Your royal club is an upright club;
    ⁷you're loyal to faithfulness and you're hostile to
      faithlessness.
Therefore God, your God,
    has anointed you with celebratory oil beyond
      your companions.
⁸All your clothes are myrrh, aloes and cassia;
    from your great ivory palace strings entertain
      you.
⁹The great princess stands in your jewels,
    the queen at your right hand in gold of Ophir.

¹⁰Listen, young lady, look, bend your ear;
    put out of mind your people, your father's
      household.
¹¹The king will desire your beauty;
    because he's your lord, bow low to him.
¹²The daughter-town of Tsor [Tyre] will seek your
      goodwill with a gift,
    the wealthiest of the people ¹³with all splendour.

To the inside, the princess, with her gold
      embroidery,
    her dress ¹⁴of coloured cloth, will be taken to
      the king,
The girls behind her, her friends,
    will be brought to you.
¹⁵They'll be taken with joyful celebration;
    they'll come into the king's palace.
¹⁶In place of your ancestors will be your sons;
    you will appoint them as officials throughout
      the country.

¹⁷I shall make mention of your name in every
      generation after generation;
    therefore peoples will confess you lastingly,
      permanently.

*Psalm 46 Be still and know that I am God*

The leader's. The Qorahites'. On Secrets. A song.

¹God is for us shelter and vigour,
   a help in pressures, readily to be found.
²Therefore we're not afraid when the earth moves,
   when mountains slip into the middle of the
   seas.
³Its water may be in turmoil and foam,
   the mountains may quake when it lifts up high.
   *(Rise)*

⁴A river with its streams rejoices God's town,
   the sacred place where the great dwelling of the
   One on High is.
⁵God being in the middle of it, it will not slip;
   God helps it as morning turns its face.
⁶Nations are in turmoil, kingdoms slip;
   when he gives his voice, earth dissolves.
⁷Yahweh of Armies is with us;
   Ya'aqob's God is a turret for us. *(Rise)*

⁸Go behold the deeds of Yahweh,
   who is causing great destruction in the earth,
⁹Stopping battles
   as far as the end of the earth,
When he breaks up the bow and snaps the lance,
   burns chariots in the fire.
¹⁰'Relax, and acknowledge that I am God;
   I will be high among the nations, I will be high
   in the earth.'
¹¹Yahweh of Armies is with us;
   Ya'aqob's God is a turret for us. *(Rise)*

*Psalm 47 The outrageous confession*

The leader's. The Qorahites'. A composition.

¹All you peoples, clap the palms of your hands,
   shout to God with a resounding voice.
²Because Yahweh, the One on High, is awe-
   inspiring,
   the great king over all the earth.
³He subdues peoples under us,
   nations under our feet.
⁴He chooses our domain for us,
   the majesty of Ya'aqob to whom he is loyal. *(Rise)*
⁵God has gone up with a shout,
   Yahweh with the sound of a horn.

⁶Make music for God, make music;
   make music for our king, make music.
⁷Because God is king of all the earth;
   make music with insight.
⁸God has become king over the nations;
   God has sat on his sacred throne.
⁹The leaders of the peoples have gathered,
   the people of Abraham's God.
Because the shields of the earth belong to God;
   he has gone up very high.

*Psalm 48 Our town*

A song. A composition. The Qorahites'.

¹Yahweh is great, and much to be praised,
   in our God's town.
His sacred mountain ²is a beauty of a height,
   the greatest joy in all the earth.
The heights of Tsaphon are Mount Tsiyyon,
   the great king's town.
³In its citadels God
   has caused himself to be acknowledged as a
   turret.
⁴Because there – the kings assembled,
   passed along together.
⁵When those men saw, they were stunned,
   they were frightened, they made haste.
⁶Trembling grasped them there,
   writhing like a woman in labour.
⁷With an east wind
   you break up Tarshish ships.
⁸As we've heard, so we've seen,
   in Yahweh of Armies' town,
In our God's town,
   which God will establish permanently. *(Rise)*
⁹God, we have reflected on your commitment,
   within your palace.
¹⁰God, like your name,
   so your praise reaches to the ends of the
   earth.
Your right hand is full of faithfulness;
   ¹¹Mount Tsiyyon will rejoice.
Yehudah's towns will celebrate
   on account of your rulings.
¹²Go round Tsiyyon, circle it,
   count its towers.
¹³Set your mind on its rampart,
   tour its citadels,
So that you can recount to a future age
   ¹⁴that this is God,

Our God lastingly and permanently
 – he will direct us against death.

## Psalm 49 *You can't take it with you*

The leader's. The Qorahites'. A composition.

¹Listen to this, all you peoples;
 give ear, all you inhabitants of the world,
²Both ordinary people and important people,
 wealthy and needy together.
³My mouth will speak smartness,
 the murmur from my mind will be
 understanding.
⁴I shall bend my ear to a poem,
 resolve my conundrum with the guitar.

⁵Why should I be afraid in bad days,
 when the waywardness of people cheating me
 surrounds me,
⁶People who trust in their resources,
 and take pride in the abundance of their
 wealth?
⁷Huh; it definitely can't redeem someone;
 it can't give God his ransom.
⁸The redemption of his life would be expensive;
 it would be insufficient permanently,
⁹So that he should live on permanently,
 not see the Pit.
¹⁰Because one can see that smart people die,
 the dimwit and stupid person perish together.
They abandon their resources to others,
 ¹¹whereas their inward thought is that their
 home will be permanent,
Their dwelling to generation after generation
 – they had called lands by their names.
¹²A human being does not lodge in honour;
 he is like cattle that are terminated.
¹³This is the way things are for them, the people
 characterized by dim-wittedness,
 and after them the people who accept their
 talk. *(Rise)*
¹⁴Like sheep they've headed for She'ol;
 death shepherds them.
The upright hold sway over them at morning,
 and their form is for wasting in She'ol,
 away from its lofty home.

¹⁵Yet God will redeem my life from the hand of
 She'ol,
 because he will take me. *(Rise)*

¹⁶Don't be afraid when someone becomes wealthy,
 when the splendour of his house becomes
 great,
¹⁷Because when he dies he doesn't take it all;
 his splendour doesn't go down after him.
¹⁸If he blesses himself in his lifetime,
 and people confess you, that you do well for
 yourself,
¹⁹He comes to the circle of his ancestors;
 never does he see the light.
²⁰A human being in honour but who does not
 have understanding
 is like cattle that are terminated.

## Psalm 50 *Keep it simple*

A composition. Asaph's.

¹God, Yahweh God, has spoken,
 and called the earth from the rising of the sun
 as far as its going down.
²From Tsiyyon, the fullness of beauty,
 God has shone out; ³our God comes and
 cannot be silent.
Fire devours before him,
 and round him it has stormed greatly.
⁴He calls to the heavens above,
 and to the earth for a judgement about his
 people.
⁵'Gather to me the people committed to me,
 the people who sealed a pact with me over a
 sacrifice.'
⁶The heavens have told of his faithfulness,
 because he is a God who exercises authority.
 *(Rise)*

⁷Listen, my people, and I will speak;
 Yisra'el, and I will testify against you –
 I am God, your God.

⁸About your sacrifices I don't reprove you,
 and your burnt offerings are continually in
 front of me.
⁹I would not take a bull from your house,
 goats from your pens.
¹⁰Because every animal in the forest is mine,
 the cattle on a thousand mountains.
¹¹I know every bird in the mountains,
 and every creature of the wild is with me.
¹²If I were hungry, I would not say so to you,
 because the world and what fills it is mine.

¹³Do I eat the flesh of the sturdy
  or drink the blood of goats?
¹⁴Sacrifice a thank-offering to God,
  and make good your pledges to the One on High.
¹⁵Call me on the day of pressure;
  I'll pull you out, then you'll honour me.

¹⁶But to the faithless person, God has said:
  What's your business, recounting my decrees,
  and taking my pact on to your mouth,
¹⁷When you're one hostile to discipline,
  and you throw my words behind you?
¹⁸If you've seen a thief, you've accepted him,
  and your lot has been with adulterers.
¹⁹You've given your mouth to bad dealing;
  you harness your tongue to deceit.
²⁰As you sit you speak against your brother,
  with your mother's son you find fault.
²¹These things you've done and I have been silent;
  you've thought I really was like you.
I reprove you and lay it out before your eyes;
  ²²please consider this, you who put God out of
  mind,
  so that I don't tear you apart and there's no one
  to rescue.

²³The person who sacrifices a thank-offering
  honours me,
  and the person who directs his way
  – I let him see God's deliverance.

## Psalm 51 *Teach me to repent*

The leader's. A composition. David's. When
Natan the prophet came to him as he had come
to Bat-sheba.

¹Be gracious to me, God, in accordance with your
  commitment.
  in accordance with the abundance of your
  compassion wipe away my rebellions.
²Wash me thoroughly from my waywardness,
  cleanse me from my wrongdoing.
³Because I myself acknowledge my rebellions;
  my wrongdoing is in front of me continually.
⁴In relation to you alone have I acted wrongly,
  and done what is bad in your eyes,
In order that you are faithful in your speaking,
  clean in your exercise of authority.
⁵On one hand, in waywardness I was birthed,
  in wrongdoing my mother conceived me.

⁶On the other, you delight in truthfulness in
  hidden places;
  in the secret place you make me acknowledge
  smartness.
⁷Remove my wrongdoing with hyssop so I'm pure,
  wash me so I'm whiter than snow.
⁸Let me listen to joy and rejoicing;
  may the bones you've crushed celebrate.
⁹Hide your face from my wrongdoings,
  wipe away all my wayward acts.
¹⁰Create for me a pure mind, God;
  renew an established spirit within me.
¹¹Don't throw me out of your presence;
  don't take your sacred spirit from me.
¹²Give back to me the joy of being delivered by
  you;
  may your generous spirit sustain me.

¹³I will teach rebels your ways,
  and wrongdoers will turn back to you.
¹⁴Rescue me from shed blood, God,
  the God who delivers me;
  my tongue will resound concerning your
  faithfulness.
¹⁵Lord, open my lips,
  and my mouth will tell of your praise.
¹⁶Because you wouldn't delight in a sacrifice, were
  I to give it;
  you wouldn't accept a burnt offering.
¹⁷Godly sacrifices are a broken spirit;
  a broken, crushed mind. God, you would not
  despise.

¹⁸Do good to Tsiyyon through your acceptance;
  build up Yerushalaim's walls.
¹⁹Then you will delight in faithful sacrifices,
  burnt offering and whole offering;
  then people will take bulls up on to your altar.

## Psalm 52 *How to stand tall*

The leader's. An instruction. David's. When
Do'eg the Edomite came and told Sha'ul, 'David
came to Ahimelek's house.'

¹Why do you take pride in what is bad, strong
  man,
  when God's commitment holds all day?
²Your tongue thinks up malice,
  like a sharpened razor, you who're acting with
  deceit.

³You're loyal to what is bad rather than what is
    good,
    to falsehood rather than faithful words. *(Rise)*
⁴You're loyal to all devouring words,
    you deceitful tongue.
⁵God will indeed tear you down permanently,
    break you and pull you from your tent,
    uproot you from the land of the living. *(Rise)*

⁶Faithful people will see and be in awe,
    and make fun of him:
⁷'There's the man
    who didn't make God his stronghold,
But trusted in the abundance of his wealth,
    found vigour in his malice.'
⁸But I'm like a verdant olive tree
    in God's house.
I have trusted in God's commitment lastingly and
        permanently;
⁹I will confess you permanently, because you've
    acted.
And I will hope in your name, because it's good,
    in front of the people committed to you.

## Psalm 53 There's no God here

The leader's. On Pipe. An instruction. David's.

¹A villain has said to himself,
    'There's no God here.'
People have been devastating and offensive in evil;
    there's no one doing good here.
²From the heavens God has looked out
    at human beings,
To see if there is someone insightful,
    enquiring of God.
³The whole of it has turned backwards, altogether
        they're foul;
    there's no one doing good, there isn't even one.
⁴They don't acknowledge, do they, the people
        devising trouble,
    who eat my people?
They've eaten food;
    they haven't called God.

⁵They're experiencing dreadful terror there,
    when there had been no terror.
Because God is scattering the bones of the one
    camping against you;
    you've shamed them, because God has rejected
    them.

⁶If only there were deliverance for Yisra'el from
        Tsiyyon,
    when God turns back his people's fortunes.
Ya'aqob will celebrate,
    Yisra'el will rejoice!

## Psalm 54 With a free offering I will sacrifice to you

The leader's. With strings. An instruction.
David's. When the Ziphites came and told
Sha'ul, 'David's hiding with us, isn't he.'

¹God, deliver me by your name,
    by your strength give judgement for me.
²God, listen to my plea,
    heed the sayings of my mouth.
³Because aliens have risen up against me,
    frightening people have sought my life,
    people who haven't put God in front of them.
⁴Here – God is my helper,
    my Lord is the very sustainer of my life.
⁵May he make the bad experience come back to
        the people who are watching for me;
    in your truthfulness wipe them out.
⁶With a free offering I will sacrifice to you,
    I will confess your name, Yahweh, because it's
        good.
⁷Because it has rescued me from every pressure,
    and my eye has looked at my enemies.

## Psalm 55 Throwing things on to God

The leader's. With strings. An instruction.
David's.

¹God, give ear to my plea,
    don't hide from my prayer for grace.
²Heed me and answer me;
    I'm frantic in my talking and I reel,
³At the voice of the enemy,
    in the face of the oppression of the faithless.
Because they make trouble fall down on me,
    and in anger they harass me.
⁴My mind whirls within me,
    deathly dreads have fallen upon me.
⁵Fear and trembling come into me,
    horror has covered me.
⁶I said, 'If only I had wings;
    like a pigeon I could fly and dwell somewhere.'

⁷There, I would go far away in flight,
  I would lodge in the wilderness. *(Rise)*
⁸I would hurry to a place where I could survive,
  from the sweeping wind, from the
    hurricane.

⁹Lord, swallow up, divide their speech,
  because I've seen violence and argument in the
    town.
¹⁰Day and night they go round it on its walls,
  while trouble and oppression are inside it.
¹¹Malice is within it;
  repression and deceit don't move away from its
    square.
¹²Because it's not an enemy that reviles me, which
    I could bear,
  or someone hostile to me that has acted big
    over me,
  from whom I could hide,
¹³But you, a person of my kind,
  my companion, someone I knew,
¹⁴Together we would enjoy confidences
  as we walked about in the throng into God's
    house.

¹⁵Great desolation on them,
  they should go down to She'ol alive,
  because there are bad dealings in their
    residence, among them.
¹⁶I am one who calls to God;
  Yahweh will deliver me.
¹⁷Evening and morning and noon I talk,
  and I am in turmoil, but he has listened to my
    voice.
¹⁸He has redeemed my life in well-being from my
    encounter,
  because many indeed were with me.
¹⁹God listens and puts them down,
  the one who sits of old, *(Rise)*
The one in whom there are no changes;
  but they had no awe of God.
²⁰He put out his hand against his friends,
  he violated his pact.
²¹The butter in his mouth was smooth,
  but encounter was in his mind.
His words were softer than oil,
  but they – they were unsheathed swords.

²²Throw on to Yahweh what is given you,
  and he himself will sustain you.
He will never let
  the faithful person fall down.

²³God, you yourself will bring them down,
  to the deepest pit,
The people of bloodshed and deceit
  will not have half their days,
  but I – I will trust in you.

## *Psalm 56 I am afraid, I'm not afraid*

The leader's. On the Silent Pigeon of Far-off
Places. David's. An inscription. When the
Pelishtites [Philistines] seized him in Gat.

¹Be gracious to me, God, because a man has
    hounded me;
  all day a man of battle afflicts me.
²The people watching for me have hounded me
    all day,
  because those battling me from a lofty position
    are many.
³On the day I am afraid,
  I do trust in you.
⁴In God whose word I praise,
  in God I've trusted.
I'm not afraid:
  what can flesh do to me?
⁵All day they pervert my words;
  all their intentions to deal badly are against me.
⁶They stir up strife, they lie in ambush, those people,
  they keep watch on my steps,
  as if they're hoping for my life.
⁷For the trouble they devise, reduce them to
    survivors, vs. thriven
  in anger put the peoples down, God.

⁸You've recorded my lamenting,
  you yourself have put my tears into your flask;
  they're in your record, aren't they.
⁹Then my enemies will turn back
  on the day I call;
  I know this, because God is mine.
¹⁰In God whose word I praise,
  in Yahweh whose word I praise,
¹¹In God I've trusted, I'm not afraid:
  what can a human being do to me?
¹²Given that pledges to you are binding upon me,
    God,
  I shall make good my thank-offerings to you,
¹³Because you've rescued my life from death,
  my foot from tripping up, haven't you,
So that I might walk about before God,
  in the light of life.

## Psalm 57 *My mind is set*

The leader's. Do Not Destroy. David's. An
inscription. When he fled from before Sha'ul
into the cave.

¹Be gracious to me, God, be gracious to me,
　　because my life has taken shelter with you,
And in the shadow of your wings I shall take
　　　shelter
　　until malice passes.
²I will call to God, the One on High,
　　to God who is going to bring it to an end for me.
³May he send from the heavens and deliver me,
　　as he reviles the one who hounds me. *(Rise)*
May God send his commitment
　　and his truthfulness ⁴to my life.
I shall lie down among lions,
　　devouring human beings,
Their teeth a pike and arrows,
　　their tongue a sharp sword.
⁵Rise above the heavens, God,
　　your splendour above all the earth.

⁶People set a net for my feet;
　　my life was bowing down.
They dug a pit before me;
　　they fell right into it. *(Rise)*
⁷My mind is set, God,
　　my mind is set.
I shall sing and make music;
　　⁸wake up, my heart.
Wake up, mandolin and guitar;
　　I shall wake up the dawn.
⁹I will confess you among the peoples, Lord,
　　I will make music for you among the nations.
¹⁰Because your commitment is big, as far as the
　　　heavens,
　　your truthfulness as far as the skies.
¹¹Rise above the heavens, God,
　　your splendour above all the earth.

## Psalm 58 *A challenge to the principalities and powers*

The leader's. Do Not Destroy. David's. An
instruction.

¹You gods, do you truly speak with faithfulness,
　　exercise authority for human beings with
　　　uprightness?

²Actually, with your mind you devise acts of evil
　　in the country;
　　with your hands you deal out violence.
³Faithless people go astray from the womb;
　　people who speak lies are wayward from birth.
⁴Their poison is like snake poison,
　　like a deaf viper that blocks its ear,
⁵That does not listen to the voice of the charmers,
　　the expert weaver of spells.
⁶God, smash their teeth in their mouth;
　　break the fangs of the lions, Yahweh.
⁷They should vanish like water when it goes away;
　　when one aims his arrows, so should they dry
　　　up.
⁸Like a snail that vanishes as it goes,
　　like a woman's stillbirth, they should not
　　　behold the sun.
⁹Before your pots sense the thorn,
　　as a living person, so should rage whirl them off.
¹⁰The faithful person will rejoice when he beholds
　　　redress,
　　when he bathes his feet in the blood of the
　　　faithless.
¹¹Someone will say, 'Yes, there is fruit for the
　　　faithful,
　　yes, there are gods exercising authority in the
　　　country.'

## Psalm 59 *My turret*

The leader's. Do Not Destroy. David's. An
instruction. When Sha'ul sent and watched his
house so as to put him to death.

¹Rescue me from my enemies, my God;
　　do set me on high above the people who rise up
　　　against me.
²Rescue me from those who devise trouble,
　　deliver me from people of bloodshed.
³Because there, they lie in wait for my life;
　　vigorous people stir up strife against me.
Not for my rebellion, not for my wrongdoing,
　　Yahweh,
　　⁴nor for my waywardness, do they run and set
　　　themselves up.
Stir yourself to meet me, and look,
　　⁵yes, you, Yahweh God Armies,
　　God of Yisra'el.
Wake up to attend to all the nations;
　　don't show grace to any of the people who
　　　break faith, who devise trouble. *(Rise)*

⁶They come back at evening,
    they howl like a dog and go round the town.
⁷There, they bellow with their mouth,
    swords on their lips, because who is listening?
⁸But you, Yahweh, make fun of them,
    you ridicule all the nations.
⁹My vigour, I keep watch for you,
    because God is my turret.
¹⁰The God committed to me will meet me,
    God will enable me to look at the people who
        are watching for me.
¹¹Don't kill them, in case my people are
        unmindful;
    by your resources, make them wander.
Put them down, Lord our shield,
    ¹²for the wrongdoing of their mouth, the word
        of their lips.
So that they are caught by their majesty
    and by the oath and by the lie they recount.
¹³Finish them off in wrath,
    finish them off so they are no more,
So that people may acknowledge that God rules
        in Ya'aqob,
    to the ends of the earth. *(Rise)*
¹⁴They come back at evening,
    they howl like a dog and go round the town.
¹⁵Those people – they wander about for food;
    if they are not full they stay the night.
¹⁶But I – I will sing about your vigour,
    I will resound at morning about your
        commitment.
Because you've become my turret,
    a retreat on the day when I was under
        pressure.
¹⁷My vigour, to you I will make music,
    because God is my turret,
        the God committed to me.

## Psalm 60 *How to deal with unfulfilled promises*

The leader's. On The Lotus of Testimony. An
inscription. David's. For teaching. When he
fought Aram-of-the-Two-Rivers and Aram
Tsobah, and Yo'ab went back and struck down
Edom in Salt Ravine, 12,000 men.

¹God, you've rejected us, broken us,
    been angry – turn back to us!
²You've shaken the country, torn it open
    – mend its splits, because it's slipped.

³You've made your people see tough things,
    you've made us drink wine that caused us to
        stagger.
⁴You have given people who live in awe of you a
        banner to flee to
    because of the bow. *(Rise)*
⁵In order that your beloved people may pull out,
    deliver with your right hand, answer me.

⁶God had spoken by his sacredness:

'I will exult as I allocate Shekem
    and measure out Sukkot Vale.
⁷Gil'ad will be mine,
    Menashsheh will be mine,
Ephrayim will be a stronghold for my head,
    Yehudah my sceptre,
⁸Mo'ab will be my washbasin,
    against Edom I will throw my boot,
    raise a shout against me, Peleshet [Philistia]!
⁹Who will conduct me to the fortified town,
    who would lead me to Edom?'

¹⁰You yourself have rejected us, God, haven't you,
    you don't go out with our armies, God.
¹¹Grant us help against the adversary,
    given that human deliverance is empty.
¹²Through God we will act with forcefulness;
    he's the one who will trample on our
        adversaries.

## Psalm 61 *How to pray with your leader*

The leader's. On a stringed instrument.
David's.

¹Listen to my resounding noise, God,
    heed my plea.
²From the end of the earth I call to you,
    while my heart flags.
To a crag that rises high above me may you lead
        me,
    ³because you've been a shelter for me,
    a vigorous tower before the enemy.

⁴I shall reside in your tent permanently,
    I shall shelter in the hiding place of your wings.
        *(Rise)*
⁵Because you, God, have listened to my pledges;
    you gave their possession to the people who
        hold your name in awe.

⁶You will add days to the king's days;
 his years will be like generation after generation.
⁷He will live permanently before God;
 appoint commitment and truthfulness so they
  may preserve him.
⁸Thus I shall make music to your name
  permanently,
 in making good my pledges day by day.

## Psalm 62 Silence towards God

The leader's. On Yedutun. A composition.
David's.

¹Indeed, towards God my entire being is silent;
 from him my deliverance comes.
²Indeed, he is my crag and my deliverance,
 my turret – I shall not slip far.
³How long will you attack someone,
 commit murder, all of you?
Like a bent wall, a fence that's been pulled down
 – ⁴indeed, they have taken counsel so as to pull
  him down from his dignity.
They accept lying;
 they bless with their mouth, but inside they
  slight. *(Rise)*

⁵Indeed, be silent towards God, my entire being,
 because from him my hope comes.
⁶Indeed, he's my crag, my deliverance,
 my turret – I shall not slip.
⁷On God rests my deliverance and my splendour;
 my strong rock, my shelter, is God in person.
⁸Trust in him at all times, you people,
 pour out your heart before him;
 God is our shelter. *(Rise)*

⁹Indeed, human beings are hollow,
 people are a lie.
Going up on scales,
 they're less than hollow, altogether.
¹⁰Don't trust in fraud, don't put hollow hopes in
  robbery;
 resources – when they bear fruit, don't set your
  mind on them.
¹¹God spoke of one thing,
 two things that I heard:
That God has vigour ¹²and you, Lord, have
  commitment,
 that you yourself make good for someone in
  accordance with his action.

## Psalm 63 I am mindful of you on my bed

A composition. David's. When he was in the
Wilderness of Yehudah.

¹God, you are my God, I look urgently for you,
 my whole person thirsts for you.
My body aches for you,
 in a dry, faint country without water.
²Yes, in the sacred place I've beheld you,
 seeing your vigour and your splendour.
³Because your commitment is better than life;
 my lips will extol you.
⁴Yes, I shall bless you throughout my life;
 in your name I shall lift up the palms of my
  hands.
⁵As with juiciness and richness my appetite will
  be full,
 and with resounding lips my mouth will give
  praise,
⁶If I am mindful of you on my bed,
 murmur about you during the watches.
⁷Because you've been my help,
 and in the shade of your wings I shall resound.
⁸My whole person has clung after you;
 your right hand has taken hold of me.

⁹But those people, who seek devastation for my
  life,
 will come into the depths of the earth.
¹⁰The people who hurl someone on to the edges of
  the sword
 will be the prey of jackals.
¹¹But the king – he will rejoice in God;
 everyone who swears by him will take pride,
 because the mouth of people who speak
  falsehood is stopped up.

## Psalm 64 The failure of the well-plotted plot

The leader's. A composition. David's.

¹Listen to my voice, God, as I talk,
 may you preserve my life from the enemy's
  terror.
²May you hide me from the council of people
  dealing badly,
 from the crowd of people devising trouble,
³Who have whetted their tongue like a sword,
 who have directed their bitter word like arrows,

4To shoot from hiding at the person of integrity
– they shoot at him suddenly and they're not
afraid.
5They take strong hold for themselves of a word
about bad dealing,
they recount it, in hiding traps.
They've said 'Who will see them?'
6as they plot evil.
'We have completed a plot that's well plotted;
the inner thinking of a person and his mind
are deep.'

7But God has shot them with an arrow;
suddenly the blows that strike them down have
come.
8They've made it collapse on themselves with their
tongue;
all who look at them shake their head.
9Everyone was in awe; they've told of God's act,
they've gained insight into his deed.
10The faithful person rejoices in Yahweh
and takes shelter with him;
all the upright in mind take pride.

## Psalm 65 *The God of atonement and the God of the harvest*

The leader's. A composition. David's. A song.

1To you silence is praise,
God in Tsiyyon.
To you a pledge is made good,
2the one who listens to a plea.
All flesh come right to you
3with wayward words.
Whereas our rebellions would have been too
strong for me,
you yourself expiate them.
4The blessings of the person you choose and bring
near,
so that he dwells in your courtyards!
May we be full with the good things of your house,
your sacred palace.
5Answer us with awe-inspiring deeds in
faithfulness,
God who delivers us!

Object of trust for all the ends of the earth
and the far-off sea,
6Who established the mountains by his energy,
who is belted with strength,

7Who stills the din of the seas,
the din of their waves, yes, the tumult of the
peoples.
8The people who live at the ends are in awe at
your signs;
you make the entry points of morning and
evening resound.

9You've attended to the earth and watered it;
you greatly enrich it.
God's channel is full of water;
you prepare their grain.
Because in this way you prepare it:
10saturating its furrows, smoothing its ridges,
You soften it with rains,
you bless its growth.
11You've crowned the year with your good things;
your cart tracks flow with richness.
12The pastures of the wilderness flow,
the hills wrap on celebration.
13The meadows put on flocks,
the vales envelop themselves in wheat,
they shout, and sing too.

## Psalm 66 *I shall make good my pledges*

The leader's. A song. A composition.

1Shout for God, all the earth,
2make music for the splendour of his name!
Make his praise splendour,
3say to God, 'How awe-inspiring are your acts!
At the abundance of your vigour
your enemies wither before you.
4All the earth bow low to you,
they make music to you, make music to your
name!' *(Rise)*

5Come and see the deeds of God,
the one who is awe-inspiring for his activity in
relation to human beings.
6He turned sea into dry land,
so they could cross the river on foot.
There let us rejoice in him,
7the one who rules permanently by his strength!
His eyes watch the nations;
the defiant – they should not rise up against
him. *(Rise)*

8Peoples, bless our God,
let the sound of his praise be heard,

⁹The one who places us in life,
   and doesn't give our foot to slipping.
¹⁰Because you've tried us, God;
   you've refined us like someone refining silver.
¹¹You let us come into a net,
   put a constraint on our hips.
¹²You let someone ride at our head,
   we've come into fire and into water,
   but you've got us out into flourishing.

¹³I shall come into your house with burnt
     offerings,
   I shall make good my pledges to you,
¹⁴The ones that my lips uttered,
   that my mouth spoke when I was under
     pressure.
¹⁵As burnt offerings I will offer up fatlings to you,
   with the aroma of rams;
   I'll make ready bulls with goats. *(Rise)*
¹⁶Come listen and I'll recount,
   all you who live in awe of God,
   what he's done for me.
¹⁷To him with my mouth I called;
   he was exalted by my tongue.
¹⁸If I could have seen trouble in my heart,
   my Lord would not listen.
¹⁹In fact God listened,
   heeded the sound of my plea.
²⁰God be blessed,
   the one who didn't turn aside my plea
   or his commitment from me!

## Psalm 67 Bless us, and let other peoples acknowledge it

The leader's. With strings. A composition.
A song.

¹May God be gracious to us and bless us,
   may he shine his face with us, *(Rise)*
²For the acknowledging of your way in the
     earth,
   your deliverance in all the nations.
³May peoples confess you, God,
   may peoples confess you, all of them.
⁴May countries rejoice and resound,
   because you exercise authority over peoples
     with uprightness,
   you guide nations in the earth. *(Rise)*
⁵May peoples confess you, God,
   may peoples confess you, all of them.

⁶As earth has given its produce,
   may God, our God, bless us.
⁷May God bless us,
   may all the ends of earth live in awe of him.

## Psalm 68.1–18 Father of the orphan, protector of the widow

The leader's. David's. A composition. A song.

¹When God arises, his enemies scatter,
   the people hostile to him flee before him.
²You blow them away like smoke blowing away,
   like wax melting before fire.
The faithless perish before God,
   ³but the faithful rejoice.
They exult before God,
   they celebrate with rejoicing.

⁴Sing to God,
   make music to his name.
Lift up the one who rides on the clouds,
   whose name is Yah, and exult before him.
⁵Father for orphans, judge for widows,
   is God in his sacred abode.
⁶God enables people who are alone to live at home,
   brings out prisoners in chains,
   yet the defiant dwell in parched land.

⁷God, when you went out before your people,
   when you marched through the wilderness,
     *(Rise)*
⁸Earth shook, yes, heavens poured,
   before God, the one of Sinay,
   before God, the God of Yisra'el.
⁹You shed generous rain, God;
   your own domain, when it was languishing –
     you yourself provided for it.
¹⁰Your dwelling – they've lived in it;
   you provide for the humble with your
     goodness, God.
¹¹The Lord gives a word;
   the women announcing the news are a great
     army.
¹²Kings of armies flee, flee;
   the young girls of the house share the spoil,
    ¹³though they stay among the sheepfolds,
The wings of a dove covered in silver,
   its pinions in pale gold,
¹⁴When Shadday scatters kings there,
   it snows on Tsalmon.

<sup>15</sup>Mount Bashan is a supernatural mountain,
Mount Bashan is a many-peaked mountain.
<sup>16</sup>Why do you keep watch, mountains, peaks,
on the mountain that God desired as his place
to live?
– yes, Yahweh will dwell there permanently.
<sup>17</sup>God's chariotry were myriads, thousands
doubled;
the Lord was among them at Sinay in
sacredness.
<sup>18</sup>You went up on high, you took captives,
to get gifts among people,
Yes, defiant ones,
to dwell as Yah God.

## Psalm 68.19–35 Kingdoms of the earth, sing to God

<sup>19</sup>The Lord be blessed day by day;
the God who is our deliverance supports us.
(Rise)
<sup>20</sup>God is for us a God of deliverance;
to Yahweh God belong departures to death.
<sup>21</sup>Yes, God hits his enemies' head,
the hairy crown of the one who walks about in
his great liability.
<sup>22</sup>The Lord said, 'I'll bring them back from
Bashan,
I'll bring them back from the depths of the
sea,
<sup>23</sup>In order that your foot may hit in blood;
your dogs' tongue – its share may be from your
enemies.'

<sup>24</sup>People saw your journeyings, God,
the journeyings of my God, my king, into the
sacred place.
<sup>25</sup>Singers came first, then string-players,
amid girls playing tambourines.
<sup>26</sup>In the great congregation that bless God,
Yahweh, you [who issued] from Yisra'el's
fountain.
<sup>27</sup>There was little Binyamin, holding sway over
them,
Yehudah's officials, their noisy crowd,
Zebulun's officials, Naphtali's officials:
<sup>28</sup>your God ordered vigour for you.
Be vigorous, God,
you who acted for us <sup>29</sup>from your palace;
Right up to Yerushalaim to you
kings will bring tribute.

<sup>30</sup>Reprimand the creature in the reeds,
the assembly of sturdy among the bullocks, the
peoples.
Trampling on those who accept silver,
you scattered peoples who delight in
confrontations.
<sup>31</sup>Envoys will come from Misrayim [Egypt],
Kush will run with its hands to God.

<sup>32</sup>Kingdoms of the earth, sing to God,
make music to the Lord, (Rise)
<sup>33</sup>To the one who rides on the highest heavens of old
– there, he gives out his voice, a vigorous voice.
<sup>34</sup>Give vigour to God, whose majesty is over
Yisra'el,
his vigour in the skies.
<sup>35</sup>God, you are to be held in awe in your most
sacred place,
the one who is God of Yisra'el.
He gives vigour and great might to his people;
God be blessed.

## Psalm 69.1–18 Passion means persecution

The leader's. On Lotuses. David's.

<sup>1</sup>Deliver me, God,
because the water has come up to my neck.
<sup>2</sup>I've sunk in a deep flood;
there's no foothold.
I've come into torrents of water;
a deluge has overwhelmed me.
<sup>3</sup>I've become weary with calling,
my throat has become dry.
My eyes fail,
waiting for my God.
<sup>4</sup>They are more numerous than the hairs on my
head,
the people hostile to me for nothing.
Numerous are the people who are trying to put an
end to me,
my enemies, with falsehood.
What I haven't stolen,
then I must give back.
<sup>5</sup>God, you yourself know my denseness;
the things for which I'm liable are not hidden
from you.

<sup>6</sup>The people who hope in you must not be shamed
through me,
Lord Yahweh of Armies.

The people who seek you must not be disgraced
    through me,
    God of Yisra'el.
⁷Because it's on account of you that I've carried
    reviling,
    that disgrace has covered my face.
⁸I've become a stranger to my brothers,
    an alien to my mother's children.
⁹Because passion for your house has consumed
    me;
    the words of reviling with which people have
    reviled you have fallen on me.
¹⁰I cried with fasting, with my entire being,
    and it became words of reviling for me.
¹¹I made sack my clothing,
    and I became an object lesson for them.
¹²The people who sit at the gateway talk about me;
    the drinkers' song.
¹³But I: my plea to you, Yahweh,
    is a time of acceptance.
God, in the abundance of your commitment
    answer me,
    in the truthfulness of your deliverance.
¹⁴Rescue me from the mud; I must not sink;
    may I be rescued from the people hostile to me,
        from the torrents of water.
¹⁵The deluge of water must not overwhelm me,
    the flood must not swallow me,
    the pit must not close its mouth over me.
¹⁶Answer me, Yahweh, because your commitment
    is good;
    in accordance with the abundance of your
        compassion turn your face to me.
¹⁷Don't hide your face from your servant,
    because I'm under pressure, hurry, answer me.
¹⁸Draw near to me, restore me;
    because of my enemies, redeem me.

## Psalm 69.19–36 Trusting God with your anger

¹⁹You yourself know my reviling,
    my shame, my disgrace.
All the people watching for me are in front of
    you;
    ²⁰reviling has broken my spirit, and I'm ailing.
I've hoped for someone to sympathize but there's
    no one,
    for comforters but I haven't found any.
²¹People have put poison in my food,
    for my thirst they've given me vinegar to drink.

²²May their table become a trap before them,
    a snare for their allies.
²³May their eyes go dark so they can't see,
    may their hips shudder continually.
²⁴Pour out your condemnation on them;
    may your angry rage overtake them.
²⁵May their encampment become desolate,
    may there be no one living in their tents.
²⁶Because you – the person you struck down,
    they've pursued,
    and the suffering of the people run through by
    you, they've heralded.
²⁷Put waywardness on top of their waywardness;
    may they not come to your faithfulness.
²⁸May they be erased from the document of living
    people;
    may they not be written down with the faithful.
²⁹When I'm humble and suffering,
    may your deliverance set me on high, God.

³⁰I shall praise God's name with a song,
    I shall magnify it with confession.
³¹It will seem good to Yahweh more than an ox,
    a bull with horns and divided hoofs.
³²Humble people have seen and rejoiced;
    you who enquire of God – may your spirit
        revive.
³³Because Yahweh is going to listen to the needy,
    and not despise his captives.
³⁴May heavens and earth praise him,
    seas and everything that moves in them.
³⁵Because God will deliver Tsiyyon
    and build Yehudah's towns.
People will live there and possess it,
    ³⁶the offspring of his servants will hold it as
        their domain,
    people who are loyal to his name will dwell in it.

## Psalm 70 Telling God what to do

The leader's. David's. For commemoration.

¹God, to rescue me,
    Yahweh, to my help, hurry!
²They should be shamed and reviled,
    the people who seek my life.
They should turn backwards and be confounded,
    the people who want what is bad for me.
³They should turn back on account of their
    disgrace,
    the people who say, 'Ah, ah!'

⁴They should celebrate and rejoice in you, all the
  people who seek you;
    they should say continually, 'God is great',
    the people loyal to your deliverance.
⁵But I am humble and needy –
    God, hurry to me.
  You're my help and the one who enables me to
    survive;
    Yahweh, don't delay!

## Psalm 71.1–16 *From birth through to old age*

¹I have taken shelter with you, Yahweh;
  I must not be shamed ever.
²In your faithfulness rescue me, enable me to
    survive,
  bend your ear to me, deliver me.
³Be for me a crag,
  an abode for coming to continually,
Which you've ordered to deliver me,
  because you're my cliff, my fastness.
⁴My God, enable me to survive from the fist of the
    faithless,
  from the grip of the evildoer and robber.
⁵Because you have been my hope, Lord Yahweh,
  the one whom I've trusted from my youth.
⁶On you I have leaned from birth,
  from my mother's womb.
You've been my support;
  my praise has continually been of you.
⁷I've been a true sign for many people,
  as you have been my strong shelter.
⁸My mouth is full of your praise,
  of your glory all day.

⁹Don't cast me off for my old age,
  when my energy is finished, don't abandon me.
¹⁰Because my enemies have said of me,
  and people who keep watch for my life have
    taken counsel together:
¹¹'Since God has abandoned him, pursue him,
  seize him, because there's no one to rescue
    him.'
¹²God, don't be far from me;
  my God, hurry to my help.
¹³They should be shamed and finished,
  the people who attack my life.
They should dress themselves in reviling and
    disgrace,
  the people who seek something bad for me.

¹⁴But I – I will wait continually,
  and add to all your praise.
¹⁵My mouth – it will recount your faithfulness,
  your deliverance all day.
Because I don't know how to write,
  ¹⁶I'll come with the mighty acts of my Lord
    Yahweh,
  I'll make mention of your faithfulness, yours
    alone.

## Psalm 71.17–24 *You've taught me and I will tell of it*

¹⁷God, you have taught me from my youth,
  and until now I tell of your extraordinary
    deeds.
¹⁸So even until my old age and grey hair,
  God, don't abandon me,
Until I tell of your strength to a generation,
  [tell] to everyone who is to come your strength,
    ¹⁹and your faithfulness, God, on high.
You who have done big things, God
  – who is like you?
²⁰You who have let me see pressures,
  many and bad,
Will give me life again,
  and from the depths of the earth bring me up
    again.
²¹You will grant me much greatness
  and turn round to comfort me.
²²And I myself will confess you with a mandolin
  for your truthfulness, God.
I will make music for you with the guitar,
  sacred one of Yisra'el.
²³My lips will resound when I make music for
    you,
  and my entire being, which you've redeemed.
²⁴Yes, my tongue will talk of your faithfulness all
    day,
  because they have been shamed, because they
    have been confounded,
  the people who sought something bad for me.

## Psalm 72.1–17 *How to pray for the government*

Shelomoh's [Solomon's].

¹God, give the king your rulings,
  the royal son your faithfulness.

²May he give judgement for your people with
    faithfulness,
    your humble ones with authority.
³May the mountains bear well-being for the
    people,
    and the hills, in faithfulness.
⁴May he exercise authority for the humble among
    the people,
    deliver the needy, crush the fraud.
⁵May they live in awe of you while the sun
    shines,
    and before the moon, generation after
    generation.
⁶May he come down like rain on mown grass,
    like downpours, an overflowing on the
    earth.
⁷May the faithful person flourish in his days,
    and abundance of well-being, until the moon
    is no more.
⁸May he hold sway from sea to sea,
    from the river to the ends of the earth.
⁹May wildcats kneel before him,
    may his enemies lick the dust.
¹⁰May the kings of Tarshish and foreign shores
    bring back an offering.
May the kings of Sheba and Seba
    present a gift.
¹¹May all kings bow low to him,
    all nations serve him.
¹²Because he rescues the needy person crying for
    deliverance
    and the humble person who has no helper.
¹³May he have pity on poor and needy,
    so that he delivers the lives of needy people.
¹⁴From repression and from violence may he
    restore their life,
    and may their blood be valuable in his eyes.
¹⁵May he live and be given
    gold from Sheba.
May pleas be said on his behalf continually;
    all day may people pray for blessing for him.
¹⁶May there be an abundance of grain in the
    country,
    on the top of the mountains.
May his fruit shake like Lebanon,
    may people thrive from the town like the grass
    in the country.
¹⁷May his name be permanent,
    before the sun may his name have offspring,
So that people may pray to be blessed through
    him;
    may all nations count him fortunate.

## Psalm 72.18–20 Another interim closing act of praise

¹⁸Yahweh God,
    the God of Yisra'el be blessed,
    the one who alone does extraordinary things.
¹⁹His splendid name be blessed permanently;
    may the entire earth fill with his splendour.
Amen, amen.

²⁰The pleas of David ben Yishay [Jesse] end.

## Psalm 73.1–14 I had nearly tripped

Composition. Asaph's.

¹Indeed, God is good to Yisra'el,
    to the pure in heart.
²But I – my feet all but turned away,
    my steps were nearly tipped out.
³Because I was passionate about the wild
    people,
    the well-being of the faithless that I can see.
⁴Because there are no stresses threatening their
    death,
    and their chest is portly.
⁵In oppression from people they have no part;
    they are not afflicted like other people.
⁶Therefore majesty is round their neck;
    a coat of violence wraps round them.
⁷Their eye bulges because of hardness;
    the schemes in their mind have overflowed.
⁸They scoff and speak of dealing badly,
    from their position on high they speak of
    fraud.
⁹They've set their mouth in the heavens,
    and their tongue walks about on the earth.
¹⁰Thus hammering comes back to his people,
    and full waters are drained by them.

¹¹And they say, 'How does God know,
    is there knowledge with the One on High?'
¹²There – these are the faithless people, at ease
    permanently,
    as they have amassed resources.
¹³Indeed, it was with empty results that I had kept
    my heart clean
    and washed the palms of my hands in freedom
    from guilt,
¹⁴I've come to be afflicted all day,
    and my reproof happens each morning.

## Psalm 73.15–28 God redeems now

<sup>15</sup>If I had said I would recount it thus,
  there, I would have broken faith with the circle
    of your children.
<sup>16</sup>But when I thought about how to know about this,
  it was oppressive in my eyes,
<sup>17</sup>Until I came to God's great sanctuary,
  so that I might consider their end.
<sup>18</sup>Indeed, you will set them among deceptions;
  you're making them fall to lies.
<sup>19</sup>How they're coming to desolation suddenly;
  they've come to an end, they're finished,
    through terrors.
<sup>20</sup>Like a dream on waking, Lord,
  on stirring, you will despise their shadow.

<sup>21</sup>When my mind is embittered,
  and in my inner being I'm cut through,
<sup>22</sup>Then I'm stupid and I don't know things;
  I became an animal with you.
<sup>23</sup>But I've been with you continually;
  you've grasped my right hand.
<sup>24</sup>By your counsel you lead me,
  and afterwards you will take me to splendour.
<sup>25</sup>Whom do I have in the heavens?
  – and with you, I haven't wanted anyone on the
    earth.
<sup>26</sup>Though my flesh and my mind are finished,
  God is my mind's crag and my share
    permanently.
<sup>27</sup>Because there – the people who are far from you
    perish;
  you're terminating everyone who whores in
    relation to you.
<sup>28</sup>But I – nearness to God is good for me;
  I've made my Lord Yahweh my shelter,
  so as to recount all your deeds.

## Psalm 74 Destruction, blasphemy, villainy

An instruction. Asaph's.

<sup>1</sup>God, why have you rejected us permanently,
  [why] does your anger smoke at the flock you
    pasture?
<sup>2</sup>Be mindful of your assembly,
  which you acquired long ago,
Which you restored as the clan that was your
    domain,
  Mount Tsiyyon, where you dwelt.

<sup>3</sup>Lift up your steps to the perpetual desolations,
  every bad action that the enemy undertook in
    the sacred place.
<sup>4</sup>Your adversaries roared inside your appointed
    places,
  they made their own signs into signs.
<sup>5</sup>It could be recognized as like someone bringing up
  axes against a thicket of trees.
<sup>6</sup>And now its engravings altogether
  they were smashing with hatchet and cleavers.
<sup>7</sup>They sent off your sanctuary in fire, down to the
    ground;
  they defiled the dwelling of your name.
<sup>8</sup>They said to themselves, 'We'll put them down
    altogether';
  they burned all God's appointed places in the
    country.
<sup>9</sup>We couldn't see our signs, there was no longer a
    prophet,
  there was no one with us who knew how long.
<sup>10</sup>Until when, God, will the adversary blaspheme,
  will the enemy revile your name permanently?
<sup>11</sup>Why do you turn back your hand,
  withhold your right hand in the fold of your
    coat?

<sup>12</sup>But God, my king of old,
  the one who effects acts of deliverance in the
    middle of the earth:
<sup>13</sup>You're the one who parted the sea by your vigour,
  you smashed the dragons' heads on the water.
<sup>14</sup>You're the one who crushed Livyatan's heads,
  so you could make it food for a company of
    wildcats.
<sup>15</sup>You're the one who split spring and wadi,
  you're the one who dried up perennial rivers.
<sup>16</sup>Day is yours, night is also yours;
  you're the one who established the light, the
    sun.
<sup>17</sup>You're the one who set all earth's boundaries;
  summer and winter – you're the one who
    shaped them.

<sup>18</sup>Be mindful of this: an enemy has blasphemed,
    Yahweh,
  a villainous people has reviled your name.
<sup>19</sup>Don't give the life of your dove to an animal,
  don't put out of mind permanently the life of
    your humble ones.
<sup>20</sup>Look at the pact,
  because the dark places in the country are full
    of pastures of violence.

²¹The broken must not turn back shamed;
  the humble and needy should praise your name.
²²Rise, God, argue for your judgement,
  be mindful of your reviling by villains all day.
²³Don't put out of mind the voice of your
      adversaries,
  the din of the people who rise against you,
      going up continually.

## Psalm 75 *The promise of an intoxicating chalice*

The leader's. Do Not Destroy. A composition.
Asaph's. A song.

¹We have confessed you, God, we have confessed,
  and when your name drew near, people have
      recounted your extraordinary deeds.
²'Indeed I will take the set time,
  when I myself will exercise authority with
      uprightness.
³Whereas earth and all its inhabitants are
      trembling,
  I am the one who ordered its pillars. *(Rise)*
⁴I have said to the wild people, 'Don't be wild',
  and to the faithless, 'Don't lift your horn.
⁵Don't lift your horn high,
  [or] speak with forward neck.'

⁶Because it's not from the east or from the west,
  not from the mountains' pasturage,
⁷But God exercises authority;
  this person he puts down, that person he lifts up.
⁸Because there is a chalice in Yahweh's hand,
  with fermented wine, full of spices.
He's pouring from it, they will indeed drain its
      dregs;
  all the faithless on the earth will drink.
⁹But I – I will tell of it permanently,
  I will make music for Ya'aqob's God.
¹⁰'Whereas I will cut all the horns of the faithless,
  the horns of the faithful person I will lift up.'

## Psalm 76 *To be held in awe by earth's kings*

The leader's. With strings. A composition.
Asaph's. A song.

¹God made himself be acknowledged in Yehudah,
  in Yisra'el his name is great.

²His shelter came to be in Shalem,
  his abode in Tsiyyon.
³There he shattered the bow's flames,
  shield, sword and battle. *(Rise)*
⁴You were resplendent,
  august on the mountains of prey.
⁵The sturdy-hearted let themselves be plundered,
  they fell into a deep sleep,
None of the forceful men could lift their hands
  ⁶at your reprimand, God of Ya'aqob.
Both chariot and horse lay stunned;
  ⁷you – you were to be held in awe.
Who can stand before you
  in the time of your anger?
⁸From the heavens you let your judgement be
      heard;
  the earth was in awe and was still,
⁹When God rose to exercise authority,
  to deliver all the humble in the land. *(Rise)*
¹⁰Because human wrath confesses you;
  you wrap on the remainder of your wrath.

¹¹Give pledges and make them good, to Yahweh
      your God;
  all those round him bring tribute to the one
      who is to be held in awe.
¹²He curbs the spirit of leaders;
  he is to be held in awe by earth's kings.

## Psalm 77 *Has God changed?*

The leader's. On Yedutun. Asaph's. A
composition.

¹With my voice to God, yes, I will cry out;
  with my voice to God, yes, so that he may give
      ear to me.
²On the day when I was under pressure,
  I have enquired of my Lord.
My hand has reached out by night and does not
      grow numb;
  my entire being refuses to find comfort.
³I shall be mindful of God and be in turmoil,
  I shall talk as my spirit faints. *(Rise)*
⁴You've grasped the guards on my eyes;
  I've been constrained and I can't speak.
⁵I've thought of days of old,
  years of ages past.
⁶I shall be mindful of my song by night,
  as I murmur in my heart, and my spirit has
      sought hard.

⁷Will it be permanently that my Lord rejects,
  and never again shows acceptance?
⁸Has his commitment ceased to exist
    permanently,
  his word come to an end for generation after
    generation?
⁹Has God put out of mind the showing of grace,
  or shut off his compassion in anger? *(Rise)*

¹⁰I said, 'That has distressed me:
  the change in the right hand of the One on
    High.'
¹¹I shall be mindful of Yah's deeds;
  yes, I shall be mindful of your extraordinary
    deeds of old.
¹²I shall murmur about your every act,
  I shall talk of your deeds.
¹³God, your way is characterized by sacredness;
  who is a god as great as God?
¹⁴You are the God who performs extraordinary
    deeds;
  you caused your vigour to be acknowledged
    among the peoples.
¹⁵You restored your people with your arm,
  the descendants of Ya'aqob and Yoseph. *(Rise)*
¹⁶Water saw you, God;
  when water saw you, it would convulse.
Yes, deeps would tremble;
  ¹⁷clouds poured down water.
Skies gave voice;
  yes, your arrows would go about.
¹⁸The sound of your thunder was in the whirlwind,
  lightning lit up the world.
The earth trembled and shook;
  ¹⁹your way was in the sea.
Your paths were in mighty water,
  though your steps were not acknowledged.
²⁰You led your people like a flock
  by the hand of Mosheh [Moses] and Aharon
    [Aaron].

## *Psalm 78.1–11 Pass on the story*

An instruction. Asaph's.

¹Give ear to my instruction, my people;
  bend your ear to the sayings of my mouth.
²I shall open my mouth with a poem,
  pour out conundrums from of old.
³Things that we have heard and acknowledged,
  that our ancestors have recounted to us,

⁴We will not hide from their descendants,
  recounting to the next generation,
The praises of Yahweh and his vigour,
  the extraordinary things that he did.

⁵He implemented an affirmation in Ya'aqob,
  put instruction in Yisra'el,
Which he ordered our ancestors
  to get their descendants to acknowledge,
⁶In order that the next generation might
    acknowledge them,
  descendants who would be born,
So they might rise up and recount them to their
    descendants,
  ⁷so they might put their assurance in God,
And not put out of mind God's acts,
  but observe his orders,
⁸And not become like their ancestors,
  a defiant and rebellious generation,
A generation that did not set its mind,
  and whose spirit was not true to God.

⁹The Ephrayimites, equipped as archers,
  turned back on the day of meeting [in
    battle].
¹⁰They didn't keep God's pact
  but refused to walk by his instruction.
¹¹They put out of mind his deeds,
  the extraordinary things that he had let them
    see.

## *Psalm 78.12–31 God's generosity and people's response*

¹²In the sight of their ancestors he had done
    something extraordinary,
  in the country of Misrayim, in the region of
    Tso'an.
¹³He divided the sea and enabled them to pass
    through it,
  he made the water stand like a mound.
¹⁴He led them by means of a cloud by day,
  and all night by means of a fiery light.
¹⁵He divided crags in the wilderness,
  and enabled them to drink like the deeps,
    abundantly.
¹⁶He got streams out from a cliff,
  and made water flow down like rivers.
¹⁷But they went on repeatedly doing wrong in
    relation to him,
  and defying the One on High in the desert.

<sup>18</sup>They tested God with [deliberation of] their
   mind,
   in asking food for themselves.
<sup>19</sup>They spoke against God:
   'Can God lay a table in the wilderness?
<sup>20</sup>Yes, he struck a crag and water flowed,
   wadis gushed.
Can he also give bread,
   or provide meat for his people?'
<sup>21</sup>Therefore Yahweh listened and raged;
   fire broke out against Ya'aqob,
   and also anger arose against Yisra'el,
<sup>22</sup>Because they didn't trust in God,
   they didn't rely on his deliverance.
<sup>23</sup>So he ordered the skies above,
   opened the doors of the heavens.
<sup>24</sup>He rained *maan* [manna] on them to eat,
   gave them grain from the heavens.
<sup>25</sup>Each one ate food fit for the sturdy;
   he sent them provisions to fill them.
<sup>26</sup>He would make the east wind move in the
   heavens,
   he drove the south wind by his vigour.
<sup>27</sup>He rained meat on them like earth,
   winged birds like the sand at the seas.
<sup>28</sup>He made them fall inside his camp,
   round his great dwelling.
<sup>29</sup>They ate, and they were very full;
   he would bring them their longing.
<sup>30</sup>They hadn't turned aside from their longing,
   their food was still in their mouth,
<sup>31</sup>When God's anger rose against them,
   and he killed some of their beefiest,
   put down Yisra'el's youth.

## Psalm 78.32–55 Responsiveness is short-lived, but so is wrath

<sup>32</sup>For all this they did wrong again,
   and didn't trust in all his extraordinary
   deeds.
<sup>33</sup>He made their days end in hollowness,
   their years in terror.
<sup>34</sup>If he killed them, they would enquire of him,
   turn back and look urgently for God.
<sup>35</sup>They were mindful that God was their crag,
   God on High their restorer.
<sup>36</sup>But they deceived him with their mouth,
   with their tongue they would lie to him.
<sup>37</sup>Their mind was not set with him;
   they didn't stay true to his pact.

<sup>38</sup>But because he was compassionate,
   he would expiate waywardness and not
   devastate.
He repeatedly turned his anger back;
   he didn't stir all his wrath.
<sup>39</sup>He was mindful that they were flesh,
   a passing wind that doesn't come back.
<sup>40</sup>How much they would defy him in the
   wilderness,
   pain him in the wasteland.
<sup>41</sup>Repeatedly they tested God,
   upset Yisra'el's Sacred One.
<sup>42</sup>They weren't mindful of his hand,
   the day when he redeemed them from the
   adversary,
<sup>43</sup>When he put his signs in Misrayim,
   his portents in the region of Tso'an.
<sup>44</sup>He turned their great river into blood;
   people couldn't drink from their streams.
<sup>45</sup>He would send off a swarm against them and it
   ate them,
   frogs and they devastated them.
<sup>46</sup>He gave their produce to the caterpillar,
   their crop to the locust.
<sup>47</sup>He killed their vine with hail,
   their wild figs with flood.
<sup>48</sup>He surrendered their animals to hail,
   their livestock to lightning flashes.
<sup>49</sup>He would send off among them his angry rage,
   outburst, condemnation and pressure,
A delegation of bad envoys,
   <sup>50</sup>that would clear a trail for his anger.
He didn't hold back their life from death
   but surrendered their existence to epidemic.
<sup>51</sup>He struck down every firstborn in Misrayim,
   the first issue of vigour in the tents of Ham.
<sup>52</sup>He got his people on the move like sheep,
   drove them like a flock in the wilderness.
<sup>53</sup>He led them in confidence and they were not
   fearful,
   but their enemies – the sea covered them.
<sup>54</sup>He brought them to his sacred territory,
   the mountain that his right hand acquired.
<sup>55</sup>He dispossessed nations before them,
   allotted them a share as their domain;
   he enabled Yisra'el's clans to dwell in their tents.

## Psalm 78.56–72 When God woke up

<sup>56</sup>But they tested and defied God On High;
   they didn't keep his affirmations.

⁵⁷They turned backwards and broke faith like their
  ancestors;
  they turned like a deceitful bow.
⁵⁸They vexed him with their shrines,
  aroused his passion with their images.
⁵⁹God listened and raged,
  and quite rejected Yisra'el.
⁶⁰He left the dwelling at Shiloh,
  the tent where he had dwelt among humanity.
⁶¹He gave his vigour to captivity,
  his glory to the hand of the adversary.
⁶²He surrendered his people to the sword;
  he raged at his own domain.
⁶³Fire consumed its young men,
  and its girls were not lamented.
⁶⁴Its priests fell by the sword;
  its widows could not cry.

⁶⁵But my Lord woke up like someone asleep,
  like a strong man shouting because of wine.
⁶⁶He beat back his adversaries,
  gave them permanent reviling.
⁶⁷He rejected Yoseph's tent,
  didn't choose the clan of Ephrayim.
⁶⁸He chose the clan of Yehudah,
  Mount Tsiyyon, to which he was loyal.
⁶⁹He built his sanctuary like the heights,
  like the earth that he founded permanently.
⁷⁰He chose David as his servant
  and took him from the sheep pens.
⁷¹He brought him from following the ewes
  to shepherd Ya'aqob his people,
  Yisra'el his domain.
⁷²He shepherded them in accordance with the
  integrity of his mind;
  he would lead them by the skilful acts of his fists.

*Psalm 79 How long will your
passion burn?*

A composition. Asaph's.

¹God, nations came into your domain,
  defiled your sacred palace,
  made Yerushalaim into ruins.
²They gave your servants' corpses
  as food to the birds of the heavens,
  the flesh of the people committed to you to the
  creatures of the earth.
³They poured out their blood like water
  round Yerushalaim with no one to bury them.

⁴We became an object of reviling to our
  neighbours,
  of ridicule and derision to the people round us.
⁵How long, Yahweh – will you be angry
  permanently,
  will your passion burn up like fire?
⁶Pour out your wrath on the nations
  which have not acknowledged you,
On the kingdoms
  which have not called on your name.
⁷Because they have consumed Ya'aqob,
  and desolated his home.
⁸Don't keep in mind the wayward acts of the past
  for us;
  may your compassion meet us quickly,
  because we've got very low.
⁹Help us, our God who delivers,
  for the sake of the splendour of your name.
Rescue us, make expiation for our wrongdoings,
  for the sake of your name.
¹⁰Why should the nations say,
  'Where is their God?'
May redress for your servants' blood that was
  poured out
  be acknowledged among the nations before
  our eyes.
¹¹May the captive's groan come before you;
  in accordance with the greatness of your
  might
  preserve the people about to die.
¹²Give back to our neighbours sevenfold, into
  their heart,
  their reviling with which they've reviled you,
  Lord.
¹³But we are your people,
  the flock you shepherd.
We will confess you permanently;
  to generation after generation we will recount
  your praise.

*Psalm 80 Bring back! Come back!*

The leader's. For Lotuses. An affirmation.
Asaph's. A composition.

¹You who shepherd Yisra'el, give ear,
  you who drive Yoseph like a flock.
You who sit above the sphinxes, shine out
  ²before Ephrayim, Binyamin and Menashsheh.
Stir your might,
  come as deliverance for us.

³God, bring us back,
  shine your face so we may find deliverance.

⁴Yahweh, God Armies,
  how long have you fumed at your people's plea?
⁵You've fed them weeping as food,
  made them drink tears by measure.
⁶You've set us at contention with our neighbours;
  our enemies ridicule us at will.

⁷God Armies, bring us back,
  shine your face so we may find deliverance.

⁸You moved a vine from Misrayim,
  dispossessed nations and planted it.
⁹You cleared a way before it,
  it put its roots down and filled the country.
¹⁰Mountains were covered by its shade,
  supernatural cedars by its branches.
¹¹It put out its boughs as far as the sea,
  its shoots to the river.
¹²Why have you broken open its walls,
  so that all the people who pass by the way pluck
    it?
¹³The boar from the forest tears at it,
  the creature of the wild feeds on it.

¹⁴God Armies, please come back,
  look from the heavens and see,
Attend to this vine,
  ¹⁵the stock that your right hand planted,
And over the offspring you took firm hold of for
    yourself.
¹⁶Burned in fire, cut;
  at the reprimand from your face they perish.
¹⁷May your hand be upon the one at your right hand,
  upon the man you took firm hold of for yourself.
¹⁸We will not turn backwards from you;
  give us life, and we will call on your name.
¹⁹Yahweh, God Armies, bring us back,
  shine your face so that we may find deliverance.

## Psalm 81 Praising and listening

The leader's. On the Gittite. Asaph's.

¹Resound for God our vigour,
  shout for Ya'aqob's God.
²Raise the music, strike the tambourine,
  the melodious guitar with the mandolin.
³Blow the horn at the new month,
  at the full moon for our festival day.

⁴Because it's a decree of Yisra'el,
  a ruling of Ya'aqob's God,
⁵An affirmation he laid on Yoseph,
  when he went out over the country of Misrayim.

I listen to a lip I had not acknowledged:
  ⁶'I removed his shoulder from the burden;
  his fists passed on from the basket.
⁷Under pressure you called and I pulled you out,
  I answered you in the secret place of thunder.
I tested you at Argument Water:
  ⁸'Listen, my people, and I will testify to you;
  Yisra'el, if you listen to me . . .
⁹There will not be for you a foreign god,
  you will not bow low to an alien god.
¹⁰I Yahweh am your God,
  the one who brought you up from the country
    of Misrayim;
  widen your mouth and I will fill it."
¹¹But my people didn't listen to my voice;
  Yisra'el was unwilling in relation to me.
¹²So I sent them off in the determination of their
    mind,
  so that they might walk by their own counsels.
¹³If only my people were listening to me,
  [if only] Yisra'el would walk about in my ways.
¹⁴In a little while I would put down their enemies,
  turn my hand against their adversaries.'
¹⁵The people hostile to Yahweh would wither at him,
  and their fate would be permanent.
¹⁶He let them eat of the best of wheat;
  'From the crag I filled you with syrup.'

## Psalm 82 Challenging the gods and God

A composition. Asaph's.

¹God is standing in the divine assembly;
  among the gods he exercises authority.
²How long will you [gods] exercise authority for
    evil,
  show regard to faithless people? (Rise)
³Exercise authority for the poor and the orphan,
  show faithfulness to the humble and the
    destitute.
⁴Enable the poor and the needy to survive,
  rescue them from the hand of the faithless.
⁵They don't acknowledge,
  they don't consider.
As they walk about in darkness,
  all earth's foundations slip.

<sup>6</sup>I myself said, 'You're gods,
offspring of the One on High, all of you.
<sup>7</sup>Therefore you will die like a human being,
fall like one of the officials.'
<sup>8</sup>Arise, God, exercise authority for the earth,
because you possess all the nations as your
domain.

## Psalm 83 Don't be calm, God

A song. A composition. Asaph's.

<sup>1</sup>God, don't keep your silence, don't be mute,
don't be calm, God.
<sup>2</sup>Because there – your enemies are in turmoil,
the people who are hostile to you have reared
their head.
<sup>3</sup>They formulate shrewd confidences against your
people,
they take counsel with one another against the
people you cherish.
<sup>4</sup>They've said, 'Come on, let's wipe them out from
being a nation,
so that Yisra'el's name will be brought to mind
no more.'
<sup>5</sup>Because they've taken counsel together with one
mind;
against you they seal a pact –
<sup>6</sup>The tents of Edom and the Yishma'e'lites
[Ishmaelites],
Mo'ab and the Hagrites,
<sup>7</sup>Gebal, Ammon and Amaleq,
Peleshet with the inhabitants of Tsor.
<sup>8</sup>Ashshur, too, has joined with them;
they've become a source of strength for Lot's
descendants. *(Rise)*

<sup>9</sup>Act towards them like Midyan,
like Sisera, like Yabin, at the Qishon Wadi.
<sup>10</sup>They were destroyed at Dor Spring;
they became manure for the ground.
<sup>11</sup>Treat them – their leaders like Oreb and like Ze'eb,
all their chiefs like Zebah and Tsalmunna,
<sup>12</sup>People who said, 'Let's take possession
of God's pastures for ourselves.'
<sup>13</sup>My God, make them like a whirl,
like stubble before the wind.
<sup>14</sup>Like fire that burns up a forest,
like a flame that sets mountains on fire,
<sup>15</sup>So may you chase them with your hurricane,
terrify them with your tempest.

<sup>16</sup>Fill their faces with slighting,
so that they seek your name, Yahweh.
<sup>17</sup>May they be shamed and terrified permanently,
may they be confounded and may they perish.
<sup>18</sup>May they acknowledge that you, whose name is
Yahweh,
you alone are the One on High over all the earth.

## Psalm 84 The one day and the thousand days

The leader's. On the Gittite. The Qorahites'. A
composition.

<sup>1</sup>How much loved is your fine dwelling,
Yahweh of Armies.
<sup>2</sup>My entire being yearned, yes it failed,
for Yahweh's courtyards,
So that my mind and my body
might resound for the living God.
<sup>3</sup>Yes, a bird – it found a home,
a pigeon a nest for itself,
Where it put its young – your great altar,
Yahweh of Armies, my King and my God.
<sup>4</sup>The blessings of the people who live in your house,
who can still praise you! *(Rise)*
<sup>5</sup>The blessings of the person whose vigour comes
through you,
the causeways in their mind!
<sup>6</sup>The people who pass through Balsam Vale
make it a spring.
Yes, the first rain will cover it with blessings;
<sup>7</sup>they will go from rampart to rampart.
The God of gods will appear in Tsiyyon,
<sup>8</sup>Yahweh God Armies.

Listen to my plea, give ear,
God of Ya'aqob. *(Rise)*
<sup>9</sup>See our shield, God,
look to the face of your anointed.
<sup>10</sup>Because a day in your courtyards is better than
a thousand,
I would choose being at the threshold of my
God's house,
Rather than dwelling in the tents of the faithless
person,
<sup>11</sup>because Yahweh God is sun and shield.
Yahweh gives grace and splendour;
he does not withhold good for people who walk
with integrity.
<sup>12</sup>Yahweh of Armies,
the blessings of the person who trusts in you!

## Psalm 85 Faithfulness and well-being have embraced

The leader's. The Qorahites'. A composition.

[1]Yahweh, you accepted your country,
  you turned back Ya'aqob's fortunes.
[2]You carried your people's waywardness,
  you covered all their wrongdoings.
[3]You withdrew all your outburst,
  you turned from your angry burning.
[4]Turn us back, God who delivers us,
  contravene your vexation with us.
[5]Will you be angry at us permanently,
  prolong your anger to generation after
    generation?
[6]Will you yourself not again bring us to life,
  so that your people may rejoice in you?
[7]Yahweh, let us see your commitment,
  give us your deliverance.

[8]I will listen to what the God Yahweh will speak,
  because he will speak of well-being.
To his people and to those committed to him,
  those who do not turn back to dim-wittedness.
[9]Indeed his deliverance is near for people who live
    in awe of him,
  so that his splendour may settle in our
    country.
[10]Commitment and truthfulness – they've met;
  faithfulness and well-being – they've
    embraced.
[11]Truthfulness – it springs up from the earth;
  faithfulness – it has looked down from the
    heavens.
[12]Yes, Yahweh – he will give good things;
  our land – it will give its produce.
[13]Faithfulness – it will walk about before him
  as he sets his feet on the way.

## Psalm 86 A servant leans on his master

A plea. David's.

[1]Bend your ear, Yahweh, answer,
  because I'm humble and needy.
[2]Keep watch over my life, because I'm committed;
  deliver your servant – you are my God.
As one who trusts in you, [3]be gracious to me, my
    Lord,
  because to you I call all day.

[4]Make your servant's entire being rejoice,
  because to you, my Lord, I lift up my being.
[5]Because you, my Lord, are good and
    pardoning,
  big in commitment to everyone who calls you.
[6]Give ear to my plea, Yahweh,
  heed the sound of my prayers for grace.
[7]On the day when I'm under pressure I call you,
  because you answer me.
[8]There is no one like you among the gods, my
    Lord,
  and there are no acts like yours.
[9]All the nations that you've made will come
  and bow low before you, my Lord.
They will honour your name,
  [10]because you're great, one who does
    extraordinary things.
You are God, you alone;
  [11]instruct me in your way, Yahweh.
I will walk about by your truthfulness;
  may my mind be one, in awe at your name.
[12]I will confess you, my Lord, my God, with all
    my mind;
  I will honour your name permanently.
[13]Because your commitment is great over me;
  you will rescue my life from deepest She'ol.
[14]God, assertive people have arisen against me,
  an assembly of terrifying people has sought
    my life.
Whereas they haven't put you in front of them,
  [15]you are my Lord,
The compassionate and gracious God,
  long-tempered and big in commitment and
    truthfulness.
[16]Turn your face to me and be gracious to me,
  give your vigour to your servant.
Deliver the son of your handmaid,
  [17]show me a sign for good,
So that the people who are hostile to me may see
    and be shamed,
  because you, Yahweh, have helped me and
    comforted me.

## Psalm 87 Glorious things of thee are spoken, Tsiyyon

The Qorahites'. A composition. A song.

[1]Founded by him among the sacred mountains,
  [2]Yahweh is loyal to Tsiyyon's gates
    more than all Ya'aqob's dwellings.

3Honourable things are spoken in you,
  God's town. *(Rise)*
4I will make mention of Rahab and Babel
  to the people who acknowledge me.
There are Peleshet, Tsor, with Kush
  – each was born there.
5To Tsiyyon it will be said,
  'Each and every one was born in it.'
He is the one who will establish it, the One on
  High;
6Yahweh will record, in writing down the
  peoples,
  'Each was born there.' *(Rise)*
7They sing as they dance,
  'All my fountains are in you.'

## Psalm 88 *A cry from the grave*

A song. A composition. The Qorahites'. The
leader's. On Pipe. For affliction. An instruction.
Heman the Ezrahite's.

1Yahweh, my God who delivers,
  by day I have cried out, by night in front of
  you.
2May my plea come before you;
  bend your ear to my resounding noise.
3Because my whole person is full of bad
  experiences;
  my life has arrived at She'ol.
4I am thought of with the people who go down
  into the Cistern,
  I've become like a man without strength,
5An outcast among the dead, like people run
  through,
  lying in the grave,
Of whom you've been mindful no more,
  when they are cut off from your hand.
6You've put me in the deepest Cistern,
  in dark places, in the depths.
7Upon me your wrath has pressed down;
  with all your breakers you've humbled me.
  *(Rise)*
8You've taken my acquaintances far from me,
  made me a great offence to them.
I'm confined so that I cannot go out,
  9my eye has become dim through humbling.
I've called you, Yahweh, each day,
  I've stretched out my palms to you.
10Do you do extraordinary things for the dead,
  do ghosts rise to confess you? *(Rise)*

11Is your commitment recounted in the grave,
  your truthfulness in Abaddon?
12Are your extraordinary deeds made known in
  the darkness,
  your faithfulness in the land of forgetting?
13But I, Yahweh, I've cried to you for help,
  in the morning my plea meets you.
14Yahweh, why do you reject me,
  hide your face from me?
15I'm afflicted, breathing my last since youth;
  I've borne your dreads, I despair.
16Your acts of rage have passed over me,
  your acts of terror have destroyed me.
17They are round me like water all day,
  they've encircled me altogether.
18You've taken friend and neighbour far from me,
  my acquaintances – darkness.

## Psalm 89.1–18 *The stable world*

An instruction. Ethan the Ezrahite's.

1Of Yahweh's acts of commitment I will sing
  permanently,
  for generation after generation I will cause his
  truthfulness to be acknowledged with my
  mouth.
2Because I've said, 'Your commitment is built up
  permanently;
  the heavens – you establish your truthfulness
  in them.'

3'I sealed a pact for my chosen,
  I swore to David my servant:
4"I will establish your offspring permanently,
  I will build your throne for generation after
  generation."'

5In the heavens they confess your extraordinary
  deeds, Yahweh,
  yes, your truthfulness in the congregation of
  the sacred ones.
6Because who in the sky can equal Yahweh,
  can compare with Yahweh among the divine
  beings,
7The God inspiring great reverence in the council
  of the sacred ones,
  inspiring awe above all those round him?
8Yahweh, God of Armies, who is like you,
  mighty Yah, with your truthfulness
  surrounding you?

⁹You rule over the majesty of the sea;
  when it lifts its waves, you're the one who can
    still them.
¹⁰You're the one who crushed Rahab, like
  someone run through;
  with your vigorous arm you scattered your
    enemies.
¹¹The heavens are yours, yes, the earth is yours,
  the world and what fills it: you're the one who
    founded them.
¹²North and south – you're the one who created
    them;
  Tabor and Hermon – they resound at your
    name.
¹³To you belongs an arm with strength;
  your hand is vigorous, your right hand stands
    high.
¹⁴Faithfulness in the exercise of authority is the
  establishment of your throne;
  commitment and truthfulness come to meet
    your face.
¹⁵The blessings of the people that acknowledges
    the shout,
  that walks about in the light of your face,
    Yahweh!
¹⁶In your name they celebrate all day,
  in your faithfulness they stand high.
¹⁷Because you're their vigorous glory;
  through your acceptance our horn stands high.
¹⁸Because our shield belongs to Yahweh,
  our king to Yisra'el's Sacred One.

## Psalm 89.19–37 The stable promise

¹⁹Then you spoke in a vision to the people
  committed to you:
  'I put help on a strong man,
  I raised high one chosen from the people.
²⁰I found David, my servant,
  with my sacred oil I anointed him,
²¹The one with whom my hand will be established;
  yes, my arm will enable him to stand firm.
²²No enemy will extort from him,
  or evil person humble him.
²³I will crush his adversaries before him,
  beat down the people hostile to him.
²⁴My truthfulness and commitment will be with
    him,
  and in my name his horn will stand high.
²⁵I will set his hand on the sea,
  his right hand on the great river.

²⁶That man will call me, 'You're my father,
  my God, the crag that delivers me.'
²⁷Yes, I myself will make him my firstborn,
  on high in relation to earth's kings.
²⁸Permanently will I keep my commitment to
    him;
  my pact will be true for him.
²⁹I will set his offspring evermore,
  his throne like the days of the heavens.
³⁰If his sons abandon my instruction,
  don't walk by my rulings,
³¹If they profane my decrees
  don't keep my orders,
³²I will attend to their rebellion with a club,
  their waywardness with blows,
³³But my commitment I will not contravene from
    him;
  I will not be false to my truthfulness.
³⁴I will not profane my pact;
  what's come out of my lips I will not change.
³⁵Once and for all I've sworn by my sacredness:
  'If I lie to David ...'
³⁶His offspring will be there permanently,
  his throne like the sun in front of me,
³⁷Like the moon, which is established
    permanently,
  a witness in the sky that's truthful.' *(Rise)*

## Psalm 89.38–51 But is the promise stable?

³⁸But you yourself have rejected, spurned,
  burst out with your anointed.
³⁹You've renounced your servant's pact,
  profaned his diadem to the earth.
⁴⁰You've broken through all his walls,
  made his fortifications a ruin.
⁴¹All the people who pass his way have plundered
    him;
  he's become an object of reviling to his
    neighbours.
⁴²You've lifted high his adversaries' right hand,
  you've made all his enemies rejoice.
⁴³Yes, you've turned back his sword's blade,
  not enabled him to rise up in the battle.
⁴⁴You've made his purity cease;
  his throne you've hurled to the earth.
⁴⁵You've cut short the days of his youth,
  clothed him in shame. *(Rise)*

⁴⁶How long, Yahweh – will you hide permanently,
  will your wrath burn up like fire?

⁴⁷Be mindful – I, what a short span,
 for what emptiness you created all human
  beings.
⁴⁸Who is the man who can live on and not see
  death,
 can enable himself to escape from She'ol's hand?
 (Rise)
⁴⁹Where are your former acts of commitment, my
  Lord,
 which you swore to David in your truthfulness?
⁵⁰Be mindful, my Lord, of your servant's reviling,
 which I've carried in my heart,
Of all the many peoples
 ⁵¹who have reviled,
Of your enemies, Yahweh,
 those who have reviled the steps of your
  anointed.

## Psalm 89.52 Amen anyway

⁵²Yahweh be blessed permanently.
 Amen, amen.

## Psalm 90 God's time and our time

A plea. Mosheh's, supernatural man.

¹Lord, you were an abode for us,
 generation after generation.
²Before mountains were birthed
 and you laboured with the earth and the
  world,
From age to age,
 you were God.
³You would turn back mere human beings, right
  to being crushed;
 you said, 'Turn back, people!'
⁴Because a thousand years
 in your eyes were like a day,
Yesterday when it passes,
 or a watch in the night.
⁵You swept them away in sleep,
 though in the morning they would be like grass
  that grows fresh.
⁶In the morning it can flourish and grow fresh;
 by evening it dries up and withers.
⁷Because we are finished through your anger,
 through your wrath we have been fearful.
⁸You've set our wayward acts in front of you,
 our youthful deeds in the light of your face.

⁹Because all our days have turned their face
 through your outburst;
 we've finished up our years as murmuring.
¹⁰The days of our years in themselves are seventy
 years, or with strength eighty years.
But their drive has been oppression and trouble,
 because it's passed by speedily and we've flown
  away.
¹¹Who acknowledges the vigour of your anger,
 and your outburst, in accordance with awe for
  you?
¹²In counting our days, so make us acknowledge
  it,
 in order that we may bring home a smart mind.

¹³Turn back, Yahweh, how long?
 – relent about your servants.
¹⁴Fill us in the morning with your commitment,
 and we will resound and rejoice all our days.
¹⁵Enable us to rejoice in accordance with the days
 of your humbling us,
 the years we've seen bad fortune.
¹⁶May your deed appear to your servants,
 your magnificence for their descendants.
¹⁷May the Lord's loveliness come about,
 our God for us.
Establish the deed of our hands for us;
 yes, the deed of our hands – establish it.

## Psalm 91 Shadow of the Almighty

¹As someone who lives in the hiding place of the
 One on High,
 who lodges in the shade of Shadday,
²I say of Yahweh, 'My shelter,
 my stronghold, my God in whom I trust.'
³Because he's the one who will rescue you from
 the hunter's trap,
 from the malicious epidemic.
⁴With his pinion he'll cover you,
 and under his wings you'll find shelter;
 his truthfulness will be a body-shield, a
  rampart.
⁵You needn't be afraid of something dreadful by
  night,
 of an arrow that flies by day,
⁶Of an epidemic that walks in the dark,
 of a scourge that destroys at noon.
⁷A thousand may fall at your side,
 ten thousand at your right hand
 – it will not reach to you.

⁸You'll only look with your eyes
  and see a making good to the faithless.
⁹Because you're one who has made Yahweh
    'My abode',
  the One on High your shelter.
¹⁰Nothing bad will be given access to you,
  no harm will approach your tent.
¹¹Because he'll order his envoys to you,
  to keep you in all your ways.
¹²They'll carry you on the palms of their hands
  so you don't hit your foot on a stone.
¹³You'll tread on cub and viper,
  you'll trample on lion and serpent.
¹⁴'Because he's attracted to me, I shall enable him
    to survive;
  I shall set him on high, because he's
    acknowledged my name.
¹⁵He will call me and I'll answer, I'll be with him
    when he is under pressure,
  I'll pull him out and honour him.
¹⁶I'll fill him with long days,
  and show him my deliverance.'

## Psalm 92 A psalm used on the sabbath

A composition. A song. For the sabbath day.

¹It's good to confess Yahweh,
    to make music for your name, you who are the
    One on High,
²To tell of your commitment in the morning,
  and of your truthfulness at night,
³With ten-string and with mandolin,
  with recitation, on the guitar.
⁴Because you've made me rejoice, Yahweh, by
    your act;
  at the deeds of your hands I resound.
⁵How great your deeds have been, Yahweh;
  your intentions were very deep.
⁶The stupid person – he doesn't acknowledge,
  the dimwit – he doesn't understand this:
⁷When the faithless flourish like grass,
  and all the people who devise trouble thrive,
It's to be annihilated for all time,
    ⁸whereas you are up on high permanently,
    Yahweh.
⁹Because there – your enemies, Yahweh,
  because there – your enemies perish;
  all the people who devise trouble scatter.
¹⁰But you've raised up my horn like an oryx,
  my exhaustion with refreshing oil.

¹¹My eye has looked at the people who're watching
    for me;
  the people who rise against me, dealing badly
  – my ears can hear them.
¹²The faithful person is like a date palm that
    flourishes,
  like a Lebanese cedar that grows great,
¹³Planted in Yahweh's house,
  which flourish in our God's courtyards.
¹⁴They still fruit in old age,
  they become verdant and fresh,
¹⁵Telling that Yahweh is upright,
  my crag in whom there is no evil.

## Psalm 93 Is the earth vulnerable?

¹Yahweh began to reign,
  he put on majesty;
  Yahweh put on, belted on vigour.
Yes, the world is established, it doesn't slip;
    ²your throne is established since long ago,
  you are from of old.
³Rivers lifted up, Yahweh,
  rivers lifted up their voice,
  rivers lift up their crushing.
⁴Above the voices of much water,
  august, the sea's breakers,
  Yahweh was august on high.
⁵Your affirmations have been very truthful,
  your sacredness has adorned your house,
  Yahweh, for long days.

## Psalm 94 The God of redress

¹God of total redress, Yahweh,
  God of total redress, shine out.
²Rise up as the one who exercises authority over
    the earth,
  give back their dealing to the majestic people.
³How long will the faithless, Yahweh,
  how long will the faithless exult,
⁴Will they pour out, speak assertively,
  will all the people who devise trouble hold
    forth?
⁵They crush your people, Yahweh,
  they humble your domain.
⁶They kill the widow and alien,
  they murder the orphan.
⁷And they say, 'Yah does not see,
  Ya'aqob's God does not consider it.'

⁸Consider, you stupid among the people,
    you dimwits, when will you show some insight?
⁹The one who plants the ear – he listens, doesn't he;
    the one who shapes the eye – he looks, doesn't
    he.
¹⁰The one who disciplines nations – he reproves,
    doesn't he,
    the one who teaches humanity about
    knowledge.
¹¹Yahweh knows about humanity's intentions,
    that they are hollow.
¹²The blessings of the man whom you discipline,
    Yah,
    and teach from your instruction,
¹³To give him calm from bad times,
    until a pit is dug for the faithless person!
¹⁴Because Yahweh does not leave his people,
    does not abandon his domain.
¹⁵Because authority will come right back to
    faithfulness,
    and all those who are upright in mind will
    follow it.

¹⁶Who rises up for me with the people dealing
    badly,
    who takes a stand for me with the people
    devising trouble?
¹⁷Were Yahweh not a help for me,
    soon I myself would have dwelt in silence.
¹⁸If I said, 'My foot is slipping',
    your commitment, Yahweh, sustains me.
¹⁹When anxieties multiply inside me,
    your comforts give me pleasure.
²⁰Can a malicious throne ally with you,
    someone who shapes oppression by means of
    a decree?
²¹They gang up against the life of the faithful
    person,
    they condemn to death the person who's free
    of guilt.
²²But Yahweh has been a turret for me,
    my God a crag that's a shelter.
²³He has turned back their troublemaking on them,
    he will put an end to them through their bad
    ways;
    Yahweh our God will put an end to them.

## Psalm 95 Will you just shut up and listen?

¹Come, let's resound for Yahweh,
    let's shout for our crag who delivers us.

²Let's draw near to his face with confession;
    we'll shout for him with melodies.
³Because Yahweh is the great God,
    the great king over all gods,
⁴The one in whose hand are the far reaches of the
    earth,
    and to whom the mountain peaks belong,
⁵The one to whom the sea belongs (he made it)
    and the dry land (his hands shaped it).

⁶Come, let's bow low, let's bend down,
    let's bow the knee before Yahweh our maker.
⁷Because he's our God
    and we're the people he pastures,
    the sheep in his hand.

Today, if you listen to his voice,
⁸don't toughen your mind as you did at
    Meribah ['Argument'],
As on the day at Massah ['Testing'] in the
    wilderness,
⁹when your ancestors tested me.
They tried me, though they'd seen my action;
    ¹⁰for forty years I loathed the generation.
I said, 'They're a people who go astray in mind,
    and they – they have not acknowledged my ways,
¹¹Of whom I swore in my anger,
    "If they come to my place to settle down . . ."'

## Psalm 96 Yes, Yahweh has begun to reign

¹Sing for Yahweh a new song,
    sing for Yahweh all the earth!
²Sing for Yahweh, bless his name,
    announce the news day after day of his
    deliverance!
³Recount his splendour among the nations,
    his extraordinary deeds among all the peoples!
⁴Because Yahweh is great and much to be praised;
    he's to be held in awe above all gods.
⁵Because all the nations' gods are non-entities,
    whereas Yahweh made the heavens.
⁶Grandeur and magnificence are before him,
    vigour and glory in his sanctuary.

⁷Bestow on Yahweh, you kin-groups of the
    peoples,
    bestow on Yahweh splendour and vigour.
⁸Bestow on Yahweh the splendour due to his
    name,
    carry an offering and come into his courtyards.

⁹Bow low to Yahweh in his sacred splendour;
  tremble before him, all the earth.
¹⁰Say among the nations, 'Yahweh has begun to
  reign!'
  – yes, the world will stand firm, it will not slip.
He will give judgement for the peoples with
  uprightness;
  ¹¹the heavens may rejoice and the earth
  celebrate.
The sea and what fills it may thunder,
  ¹²the field and all that is in it exult.
Then all the trees in the forest may resound
  ¹³before Yahweh, because he is coming.
Because he is coming to exercise authority over
  the earth;
  he will exercise authority over the world with
  faithfulness,
  over the peoples with truthfulness.

## Psalm 97 *The real King of kings*

¹Yahweh has begun to reign, earth should
  celebrate,
  many foreign shores should rejoice!
²Cloud and darkness are round him,
  faithfulness in exercising authority is the
  establishment of his throne.
³Fire goes before him
  and has set on fire his adversaries all round.
⁴His lightning flashes have lit up the world;
  the earth has seen and convulsed.
⁵Mountains like wax have melted before Yahweh,
  before the Lord of all the earth.
⁶The heavens have told of his faithfulness,
  and all the peoples will see his splendour.
⁷They will be shamed, all those who serve an
  image,
  those who take pride in non-entities;
  all the gods have bowed low to him.

⁸Tsiyyon has listened and rejoiced,
  the daughter-towns of Yehudah have celebrated,
  on account of your authoritative rulings, Yahweh.
⁹Because you, Yahweh, are the One on High over
  all the earth,
  you have ascended very high over all the gods.
¹⁰You who are loyal to Yahweh, be hostile to what
  is bad;
  he keeps watch on the lives of people
  committed to him,
  he rescues them from the hand of the faithless.

¹¹Light has been sown for the faithful person,
  rejoicing for those who are upright in mind.
¹²Rejoice in Yahweh, you faithful,
  confess the commemoration of his sacredness!

## Psalm 98 *Revealed to the eyes of the nations*

A composition.

¹Sing for Yahweh a new song,
  because he has performed extraordinary deeds!
His right hand has wrought deliverance for him,
  yes, his sacred arm.
²Yahweh has caused his deliverance to be
  acknowledged;
  to the eyes of the nations he has revealed his
  faithfulness.
³He has been mindful of his commitment and his
  truthfulness
  to the household of Yisra'el.
All the ends of the earth have seen
  the deliverance of our God.

⁴Shout for Yahweh, all the earth,
  break out and resound and make music!
⁵Make music for Yahweh with the guitar,
  with the guitar and the sound of music!
⁶With trumpets and the sound of the horn,
  shout before the King, Yahweh!
⁷The sea and what fills it should thunder,
  the world and the people who live in it.
⁸Rivers should clap the palms of their hands,
  mountains should resound together,
⁹Before Yahweh, because he has come
  to exercise authority over the earth.
He exercises authority over the world with
  faithfulness,
  over the peoples with uprightness.

## Psalm 99 *The one who carries things*

¹Yahweh has begun to reign – peoples should
  tremble;
  the one who sits above the sphinxes – the earth
  should shake.
²In Tsiyyon Yahweh is great,
  and he is on high over all the peoples.
³They should confess your name, great and awe-
  inspiring
  – he is sacred.

⁴With the vigour of a king, loyal to the exercise of
　authority,
　　you are the one who established uprightness.
Authority and faithfulness in Ya'aqob:
　　you are the one who implemented them.
⁵Lift Yahweh our God high
　and bow low to his footstool
　　– he's sacred.

⁶Mosheh, and Aharon among his priests,
　and Shemu'el [Samuel] among the people who
　　call his name,
They were people calling to Yahweh, and he
　himself would answer them,
⁷in the pillar of cloud he would speak to them.
They kept his affirmations, the decree he gave
　them;
　⁸Yahweh our God, you answered them.
You became a God who carried things for them,
　but one who exacted redress for their actions.
⁹Lift Yahweh our God high and bow low to his
　sacred mountain
　　– because Yahweh our God is sacred.

## Psalm 100 *Shout for Yahweh, all the earth*

A composition. For the thank-offering.

¹Shout for Yahweh, all the earth,
　²serve Yahweh with rejoicing,
　come before him with resounding.
³Acknowledge that Yahweh is God,
　he is the one who made us and we are his,
　his people and the sheep he pastures.
⁴Come into his gateways with confession,
　his courtyards with praise,
　confess him, bless his name.
⁵Because Yahweh is good,
　his commitment is permanent,
　his truthfulness to generation after generation.

## Psalm 101 *The leadership challenge*

David's. A composition.

¹I will sing of commitment and the exercise of
　authority,
　for you Yahweh I will make music.
²I will show insight in the way that has integrity;
　when will you come to me?

I will go about with integrity in my mind
　within my household.
³I will not set in front of my eyes anything of
　Beliyya'al;
　I'm hostile to the action of deviant people
　– it will not stick to me.
⁴A crooked mind will depart from me;
　I will not acknowledge bad ways.
⁵The person who speaks against his neighbour in
　secret
　– I will put an end to him.
The person lofty in his own eyes and wide of
　mind
　– I will not tolerate him.
⁶My eyes will be on the person who is trustworthy
　in the country,
　to live with me.
The person who walks on the way of integrity
　– he will minister to me.
⁷The person who practises deceit
　will not live within my household.
The person who speaks lies
　will not be established in front of my eyes.
⁸Each morning I will put an end to all the people
　who are faithless in the country,
　so as to cut off from Yahweh's town all who
　devise trouble.

## Psalm 102.1–11 *My heart's withered*

A plea. For a humble person when he is faint
and pours out his talk before Yahweh.

¹Yahweh, listen to my plea;
　may my cry for help come to you.
²Don't hide your face from me
　on a day when there is pressure for me.
Bend your ear to me;
　on the day when I call, be quick, answer me.
³Because my days are finished in smoke,
　my bones have burned as in a fireplace.
⁴My heart's been stricken like grass and it's
　withered,
　because I've put out of mind eating my food.
⁵Because of the sound of my groaning,
　my bone sticks to my flesh.
⁶I've come to resemble a tawny owl of the
　wilderness,
　I've become like a screech owl of the ruins.
⁷I've been awake and I've become like a bird,
　alone on a roof.

8 All day my enemies have reviled me;
   people whom I call crazy have sworn oaths by
      me.
9 Because I've eaten ashes like bread
   and mixed my drink with tears,
10 In the face of your condemnation and your fury,
   because you picked me up and threw me out.
11 My days are like an extended shadow,
   and I – I wither like grass.

*Psalm 102.12–28 I have hope for
Tsiyyon, but is there hope for me?*

12 But you, Yahweh – you will sit permanently,
   your commemoration will continue for
      generation after generation.
13 You – you will arise, you will have compassion
      on Tsiyyon,
   because it's time to be gracious to it, because
      the set time has come.
14 Because your servants have accepted its stones,
   and been gracious to its earth.
15 Nations will live in awe of Yahweh's name,
   all earth's kings of your splendour.
16 Because Yahweh has built up Tsiyyon,
   has appeared in his splendour.
17 He has turned his face to the plea of the naked
      person
   and not despised their plea.
18 May this be written down for the next
      generation,
   so that a people to be created may praise Yah,
19 Because he has looked down from his sacred
      height,
   from the heavens Yahweh has looked at the
      earth,
20 To listen to the prisoner's cry,
   to release people doomed to death,
21 For the recounting of Yahweh's name in
      Tsiyyon,
   his praise in Yerushalaim,
22 When peoples collect together,
   yes, kingdoms, to serve Yahweh.

23 He has humbled my energy on my way,
   he has cut my days.
24 I will say, 'My God, don't take me up
   in the middle of my days.
Your years continue generation after generation;
   25 before, you founded the earth,
   and the heavens are the making of your hands.

26 Whereas they may perish,
   you will stand.
All of them could wear out like a coat;
   like clothing you could pass them on.
They would pass on, 27 but you are the one,
   and your years will not come to an end.
28 May your servants' children dwell,
   and their offspring endure, before you.'

*Psalm 103 He has distanced our
rebellions from us*

David's.

1 Bless Yahweh, my entire being;
   all my being, [bless] his sacred name.
2 Bless Yahweh, my entire being;
   don't put out of mind all his dealings.
3 He's the one who pardons all your
      waywardness,
   who heals all your illnesses,
4 Who restores your life from the Pit,
   who garlands you with commitment and
      compassion,
5 Who fills you in your finery with goodness,
   so that your youth renews like an eagle.
6 Yahweh performs faithful deeds,
   acts of authority for all the oppressed.
7 He would make his ways known to Mosheh,
   his deeds to the Yisra'elites.
8 Yahweh is compassionate and gracious,
   long-tempered and big in commitment.
9 He doesn't argue permanently,
   he doesn't hold on to it for a long time.
10 He hasn't acted towards us in accordance with
      our wrongdoings;
   he hasn't dealt to us in accordance with our
      wayward acts.
11 Because in accordance with the loftiness of the
      heavens over the earth,
   his commitment has been strong over people
      who hold him in awe.
12 In accordance with the distance of east from
      west,
   he has distanced our rebellions from us.
13 In accordance with a father's compassion for his
      children,
   Yahweh has had compassion for people who
      hold him in awe.
14 Because he himself knows our frame;
   he is mindful that we are earth.

¹⁵A mere human being: his days are like grass;
  like a flower in the fields – that's how he
    blooms.
¹⁶When the wind passes by it, it is no more;
  its place doesn't recognize it any more.
¹⁷But Yahweh's commitment lasts from age to age
  for people who hold him in awe, and his
    faithfulness to their grandchildren,
¹⁸For people who keep his pact
  and are mindful of the things he has
    determined, so that they perform them.
¹⁹Yahweh established his throne in the heavens;
  his reign rules over everything.
²⁰Bless Yahweh, his envoys,
  energetic strong men performing his word,
  listening to the sound of his word.
²¹Bless Yahweh, all his armies,
  his ministers doing what is acceptable to him.
²²Bless Yahweh, all his works,
  in all the places where he rules.
  Bless Yahweh, my entire being.

## Psalm 104.1–23 Provision for human beings and donkeys

¹Bless Yahweh, my entire being!
  – Yahweh my God, you became very great.
You put on grandeur and magnificence,
    ²wrapping on light like a coat,
Stretching the heavens like a tent,
    ³one fixing his lofts in the water,
One making clouds his transport,
  one going about on the wings of the wind,
⁴Making his envoys of winds,
  his ministers of flaming fire.
⁵He founded the earth on its establishments,
  so that it would never slip, ever.
⁶You covered it with the deep like a garment,
  so that the water would stand above the
    mountains.
⁷At your reprimand they would flee;
  at the sound of your thunder they would make
    haste.
⁸They would go up mountains, they would go
    down valleys,
  to the place that you founded for them.
⁹You set a boundary they were not to pass;
  they would not again cover the earth.

¹⁰You're the one who sends out springs in wadis,
  so that they go about between the mountains.

¹¹They water every animal of the field;
  donkeys break their thirst.
¹²By them the birds of the heavens dwell;
  from among the branches they give voice.
¹³You're one who waters mountains from his lofts
  – from the fruit of your deeds the earth has its
    fill.
¹⁴You are one who grows grass for the cattle,
  and plants for the service of human beings,
To make bread go out from the earth,
    ¹⁵and wine that rejoices a person's heart,
To make the face shine with oil,
  and bread that sustains a person's heart.
¹⁶Yahweh's trees get their fill,
  the cedars of Lebanon that he planted,
¹⁷Where birds nest,
  the stork – the junipers are its home.
¹⁸The lofty mountains belong to the ibex,
  the cliffs are a shelter for the rock badgers.
¹⁹He made the moon for set times;
  the sun knows its setting.
²⁰You bring darkness so that it becomes night:
  in it every creature of the forest moves about.
²¹The lions roar for prey,
  yes, in seeking their food from God.
²²When the sun rises, they gather,
  and crouch in their abodes.
²³Human beings go out to their work,
  and to their service until evening.

## Psalm 104.24–35 Withdrawing breath, giving breath

²⁴How the things you made multiplied, Yahweh;
  you made them all with smartness;
  the earth is full of your possessions.
²⁵That's the sea, great,
  and wide in reach.
There are moving things without number,
  living things small and great.
²⁶There ships go about,
  Livyatan that you shaped to have fun in it.
²⁷All of them look to you,
  to give their food at its time.
²⁸You give them, they gather;
  you open your hand, they have their fill of good
    things.
²⁹You hide your face, they're fearful;
  you gather up their breath, they breathe their
    last,
  and go back to their earth.

³⁰You send out your breath, they are created,
   and you renew the face of the ground.

³¹May Yahweh's splendour be permanent;
   may Yahweh rejoice in his deeds,
³²The one who looks on the earth and it trembles;
   he touches the mountains and they smoke.
³³I will sing for Yahweh while I live,
   I will make music for my God while I'm still here.
³⁴May my talk be pleasant to him;
   I myself will rejoice in Yahweh.
³⁵May wrongdoers come to an end from the
     earth;
   faithless people – may there be none of them
     any more.
Bless Yahweh, my entire being;
   praise Yah.

## Psalm 105.1–22 Tell your story

¹Confess Yahweh, call in his name,
   make known his deeds among the peoples.
²Sing for him, make music for him,
   talk about all his extraordinary deeds.
³Take pride in his sacred name;
   the heart of all who seek Yahweh should rejoice.
⁴Enquire of Yahweh and his vigour;
   seek his face continually.
⁵Be mindful of his extraordinary deeds, those
     which he has done,
   his portents and the rulings of his mouth,
⁶You offspring of Abraham his servant,
   descendants of Ya'aqob, his chosen ones.

⁷He is Yahweh our God;
   his rulings are in all the earth.
⁸He has been mindful permanently of his pact,
   the word he ordered to a thousand generations,
⁹That which he sealed to Abraham,
   and swore to Yitshaq [Isaac].
¹⁰He established it as a decree to Ya'aqob,
   to Yisra'el as a lasting pact,
¹¹saying, 'I will give the country of Kena'an
     [Canaan] to you,
   as a share, your domain.'
¹²When they were few in number,
   little and resident aliens in it,
¹³And they went about from nation to nation,
   from one kingdom to another people,
¹⁴He did not allow anyone to oppress them,
   but reproved kings on account of them:

¹⁵'Don't touch my anointed ones,
   don't do wrong to my prophets.'

¹⁶He called for hunger on the country;
   every staff of bread he broke.
¹⁷He sent before them an individual
   who was sold as a servant, Yoseph.
¹⁸They subjected his foot to the fetter;
   iron came on to his person.
¹⁹Until the time his word came about,
   Yahweh's saying refined him.
²⁰A king sent and freed him,
   a ruler of peoples, and released him.
²¹He made him lord of his household,
   ruler over all his possessions,
²²To constrain his officials according to his will,
   and to make his elders smart.

## Psalm 105.23–45 In order that they might keep his decrees

²³Yisra'el came to Misrayim;
   Ya'aqob resided in the country of Ham.
²⁴He made his people very fruitful,
   made them more numerous than their
     adversaries.
²⁵He turned their mind against his people,
   to scheme against his servants.
²⁶He sent Mosheh his servant,
   Aharon whom he had chosen.
²⁷They placed among them words about his
     signs,
   his portents in the country of Ham.
²⁸He sent darkness, and it became dark;
   they did not defy his word.
²⁹He turned their water into blood,
   and put their fish to death.
³⁰Their country teemed with frogs,
   in their kings' rooms.
³¹He spoke, and a swarm came,
   mosquitoes in all their territory.
³²He made their rain hail,
   flaming fire in their country.
³³He struck down their vine and their fig tree,
   broke down the trees in their territory.
³⁴He spoke, and the locust came,
   the grasshopper without number.
³⁵It ate all the vegetation in their country,
   ate the fruit of their land.
³⁶He struck down every firstborn in their country,
   the first of all their vigour.

³⁷He got them out, with silver and gold;
  none among their clans collapsed.
³⁸Misrayim rejoiced when they got out,
  because dread of them had fallen on them.
³⁹He spread a cloud for covering,
  and a fire to light the night.
⁴⁰They asked and he brought quail,
  and he would fill them with bread from the
    heavens.
⁴¹He opened a crag and water flowed,
  went in dry places as a river.
⁴²Because he was mindful of his sacred word
  with Abraham his servant,
⁴³He got his people out with joy,
  his chosen ones with resounding.
⁴⁴He gave them the nations' countries,
  and they took possession of the labour of the
    peoples,
⁴⁵In order that they might keep his decrees
  and observe his instructions.
Praise Yah!

## Psalm 106.1–22 He gave them what they asked

¹Praise Yah! –
  confess Yahweh, because he is good,
  because his commitment is permanent.
²Who can utter Yahweh's mighty acts,
  get people to listen to all his praises?
³The blessings of people who keep watch over the
    exercise of authority,
  of the person who does what is faithful at all
    times!
⁴Be mindful of me, Yahweh, when you act with
    acceptance towards your people,
  attend to me when you deliver them,
⁵So that I may see the good things that come to
    your chosen,
  rejoice in the rejoicing of your nation,
  take pride with your domain.

⁶We've done wrong with our ancestors,
  we've been wayward, we've been faithless.
⁷Our ancestors in Misrayim did not have insight
    into your extraordinary deeds,
  they were not mindful of the magnitude of
    your acts of commitment.
⁸But he delivered them for the sake of his
    name,
  so that his might would be acknowledged.

⁹He reprimanded the Reed Sea and it dried up,
  and he enabled them to go through the deeps
    like a wilderness.
¹⁰He delivered them from the hand of the one
    who was hostile to them,
  restored them from the hand of the enemy.
¹¹Water covered their adversaries;
  not one of them was left.
¹²They trusted in his words,
  and sang his praise.
¹³They quickly put his deeds out of mind;
  they did not wait for his counsel.
¹⁴They felt a deep longing in the wilderness,
  they tested God in the wasteland.
¹⁵He gave them what they asked,
  but sent a wasting in their entire being.
¹⁶They were jealous of Mosheh in the camp,
  of Aharon, Yahweh's sacred one.
¹⁷The earth opened and swallowed Datan,
  closed over Abiram's assembly.
¹⁸Fire burned up among their assembly,
  a flame that set on fire the faithless.
¹⁹They made a bullock at Horeb,
  bowed low to an image.
²⁰They exchanged their splendour
  for the representation of an ox eating grass.
²¹They put out of mind their deliverer,
  the one who had done great things in
    Misrayim,
²²Extraordinary deeds in the country of Ham,
  awe-inspiring deeds at the Reed Sea.

## Psalm 106.23–47 Deliver us in the same way!

²³He said he would annihilate them,
  except that Mosheh, his chosen,
Stood in the breach before him,
  to turn back his wrath from devastating.
²⁴They rejected the beautiful country,
  and didn't trust in his word.
²⁵They muttered in their tents,
  and didn't listen to Yahweh's voice.
²⁶So he raised his hand [to swear] to them,
  that he would make them fall in the wilderness,
²⁷Make their offspring fall among the nations,
  and scatter them among the countries.
²⁸They joined the Master-of-Pe'or,
  and ate sacrifices offered for the dead.
²⁹They provoked by their deeds,
  and an epidemic broke out among them.

³⁰But Pinhas stood and intervened,
　　and the epidemic held back.
³¹It was thought of for him as a faithful deed,
　　generation after generation permanently.
³²They angered at Meribah Water;
　　it was bad for Mosheh because of them.
³³Because they rebelled against his spirit,
　　he was rash with his tongue.

³⁴They didn't devastate the peoples,
　　as Yahweh had said to them.
³⁵They mixed with the nations,
　　and learned what they did.
³⁶They served their images;
　　they became a snare for them.
³⁷They sacrificed their sons
　　and their daughters to demons.
³⁸They shed the blood of someone free of guilt,
　　the blood of their sons and their daughters,
Whom they sacrificed to the images of Kena'an,
　　so that the land became ungodly through the
　　　bloodshed.
³⁹They became defiled through their deeds;
　　they whored in their actions.
⁴⁰Yahweh's anger burned against his people,
　　he loathed his domain.
⁴¹He gave them into the hand of the nations;
　　people hostile to them ruled over them.
⁴²Their enemies afflicted them,
　　and they bowed down under their hand.
⁴³Many times he would rescue them,
　　but those people – they were rebellious in their
　　　counsel.
They sank low because of their waywardness,
　　⁴⁴and he saw the pressure that came to them.
When he heard their resounding shout,
　　⁴⁵he was mindful of his pact to them.
He relented in accordance with the magnitude of
　　his acts of commitment,
　　⁴⁶and made them objects of compassion
　　before all their captors.

⁴⁷Deliver us, Yahweh our God,
　　collect us from the nations,
To confess your sacred name,
　　to glory in your praise.

## Psalm 106.48 Another amen

Yahweh, the God of Yisra'el, be blessed,
　　from age to lasting age!

All the people is to say,
　　'Amen'; praise Yah!

## Psalm 107.1–22 Let the redeemed of the Lord say so

¹Confess Yahweh, because he is good,
　　because his commitment is permanent.
²The people restored by Yahweh are to say it,
　　those whom he restored from the hand of the
　　　adversary,
³And collected from the countries,
　　from the north and from the west.

⁴They wandered in the wilderness, in the
　　wasteland;
　　they didn't find the way to a settled town.
⁵Hungry, thirsty too,
　　their entire being within them fainted.
⁶But they cried out to Yahweh in the pressure that
　　came to them,
　　and he rescued them from their straits.
⁷He directed them by a straight way,
　　so as to go to a settled town.
⁸They are to confess to Yahweh his commitment,
　　his extraordinary deeds for human beings,
⁹Because he has sated the person who is scurrying
　　about,
　　and filled the hungry person with good things.

¹⁰People living in darkness and deathly gloom,
　　prisoners of humbling and iron,
¹¹Because they had defied the things God said,
　　despised the counsel of the One on High:
¹²He humbled their heart with oppression;
　　they collapsed without a helper.
¹³But they cried out to Yahweh in the pressure
　　that came to them,
　　and he delivered them from their straits.
¹⁴He got them out of darkness and deathly gloom,
　　and would break their bonds.
¹⁵They are to confess to Yahweh his commitment,
　　his extraordinary deeds for human beings.
¹⁶Because he has broken up copper doors,
　　shattered iron bars.

¹⁷Dense people, because of their rebellious way,
　　and through their acts of waywardness,
　　experienced humbling.
¹⁸Their appetite loathed all food;
　　they reached death's gateways.

¹⁹But they cried out to Yahweh in the pressure
    that came to them,
  and he delivered them from their straits.
²⁰He sent his word and healed them;
  he released them from their deep pit.
²¹They are to confess to Yahweh his commitment,
  his extraordinary deeds for human beings.
²²They are to offer thanksgiving sacrifices,
  and tell of his deeds with resounding noise.

## Psalm 107.23–43 Consider Yahweh's acts of commitment

²³People who go down to the sea in ships,
  doing work in extensive waters,
²⁴These people – they saw Yahweh's deeds,
  and his extraordinary deeds in the deep.
²⁵He spoke and set a hurricane in place,
  and it lifted its waves.
²⁶They went up to the heavens, they went down to
    the depths;
  their entire being melted away in their trouble.
²⁷They reeled and staggered like a drunk,
  and all their smartness swallowed itself up.
²⁸But they cried out to Yahweh in the pressure
    that came to them,
  and he delivered them from their straits.
²⁹He turned the hurricane into stillness;
  their waves went quiet.
³⁰They rejoiced when they became silent,
  and he led them to the haven they wanted.
³¹They are to confess to Yahweh his commitment,
  his extraordinary deeds for human beings.
³²They are to exalt him in the congregation of the
    people,
  and praise him in the session of the elders.

³³He turns rivers into wilderness,
  water outlets into thirsty land,
³⁴Fruitful land into salt marsh,
  because of the bad ways of the people who live
    in it.
³⁵He turns wilderness into a pool of water,
  dry land into water outlets.
³⁶He has let hungry people live there;
  they have established a settled town.
³⁷They've sown fields and planted vineyards,
  and they have produced fruit, a yield.
³⁸He's blessed them and they've increased
    greatly,
  and he doesn't let their cattle decrease.

³⁹But they have decreased and become low
  through oppression, bad fortune and sadness.
⁴⁰He pours contempt on leaders,
  and makes them wander in a waste where there
    is no way.
⁴¹But he sets the needy person on high out of
    humbling,
  and makes their kin-groups like a flock.

⁴²The upright will see and rejoice;
  all evil has stopped its mouth.
⁴³Who is the smart person who will keep watch
    on these things?
  – they will consider Yahweh's acts of
    commitment.

## Psalm 108 Urging God to act in the light of his promises

A song. A composition. David's.

¹My mind is established, God,
  I will sing and make music, yes, my entire being.
²Wake up, mandolin and guitar;
  I will wake the dawn.
³I will confess you among the peoples, Yahweh,
  I will make music for you among the nations.
⁴Because your commitment is great, over the
    heavens,
  your truthfulness up to the skies.
⁵Be high over the heavens, God,
  over all the earth your splendour.
⁶In order that the people you love may be pulled
    out,
  deliver me by your right hand and answer me.

⁷God had spoken by his sacredness:
  'I will exult as I allocate Shekem
  and measure out Sukkot Vale.
⁸Gil'ad will be mine,
  Menashsheh will be mine.
Ephrayim will be a stronghold for my head,
  Yehudah my sceptre.
⁹Mo'ab will be my washbasin,
  over Edom I will throw my boot,
  over Peleshet I will shout out.
¹⁰Who will conduct me to the fortified town,
  who would lead me to Edom?

¹¹You've rejected us, haven't you, God;
  you don't go out with our armies, God.

<sup>12</sup>Grant us help against the adversary,
   given that human deliverance is empty.
<sup>13</sup>Through God we will act with forcefulness;
   he is the one who will trample on our
      adversaries.

## Psalm 109.1–19 *How to deal with being swindled*

The leader's. David's. A composition.

<sup>1</sup>God, my praise, don't be silent,
   <sup>2</sup>because it's a faithless mouth,
And a deceitful mouth, that people have opened
      against me;
   they have spoken with me by means of a lying
      tongue.
<sup>3</sup>With hostile words they've surrounded me,
   and battled against me for nothing.
<sup>4</sup>In return for my friendliness they accuse me;
   so I [am making] a plea.
<sup>5</sup>They've brought on me bad in return for good,
   hostility in return for my friendliness.

<sup>6</sup>'Appoint a faithless person over him,
   an accuser who will stand at his right hand.
<sup>7</sup>When he enters into judgement, may he come
      out as faithless;
   may his plea lead to condemnation.
<sup>8</sup>May his days be few;
   may another person take his appointment.
<sup>9</sup>May his children become orphans,
   his wife a widow.
<sup>10</sup>May his children wander about,
   ask and enquire from their ruins.
<sup>11</sup>May the creditor strike at all that he has,
   may strangers plunder his earnings.
<sup>12</sup>May he have no one showing commitment,
   may there be no one being gracious to his
      orphans.
<sup>13</sup>May his succession be for cutting off,
   in the next generation may their name be
      blotted out.
<sup>14</sup>May the waywardness of his ancestors stay in
      mind for Yahweh,
   may his mother's wrongdoings not be blotted out.
<sup>15</sup>May they be in front of Yahweh continually;
   may he cut off their commemoration from the
      earth.
<sup>16</sup>Because of the fact that he was not mindful
   to keep commitment,

But pursued the person who was humble and
      needy,
   and the one crushed in spirit, to put him to
      death.
<sup>17</sup>He liked slighting, and it came about for him;
   he didn't want blessing, and it was far from
      him.
<sup>18</sup>He put on slighting like a coat,
   it came into his insides like water,
   into his bones like oil.
<sup>19</sup>May it be for him like clothing in which he
      covers himself,
   and as a belt that he wraps round continually.'

## Psalm 109.20–31 *Wages for accusers*

<sup>20</sup>May this be the wages of my accusers
   from Yahweh,
   the people who speak what is bad against me.
<sup>21</sup>So you, Yahweh, Lord,
   deal with me for the sake of your name;
   because your commitment is good, rescue me.
<sup>22</sup>Because I am humble and needy,
   and my heart is run through within me.
<sup>23</sup>Like a shadow as it lengthens, I am gone;
   I am shaken off like a locust.
<sup>24</sup>My knees have collapsed from hunger;
   my body has wasted, away from fatness.
<sup>25</sup>I – I have become an object of reviling to them;
   when they see me, they shake their head.
<sup>26</sup>Help me, Yahweh my God,
   deliver me in accordance with your
      commitment,
<sup>27</sup>So that people may acknowledge that this is
      your hand,
   that you, Yahweh, you have done it.
<sup>28</sup>Those people may slight me, but you – may you
      bless;
   they will have arisen and been disgraced, but
      your servant will rejoice.
<sup>29</sup>May my accusers put on shame,
   may they wrap round their disgrace like a
      coat.

<sup>30</sup>I will confess Yahweh greatly with my mouth,
   in the middle of many people I will praise
      him,
<sup>31</sup>Because he stands at the right hand of the needy
      person,
   to deliver him from the people who exercise
      authority over him.

## Psalm 110 Enemies become footstool

David's. A psalm.

¹Yahweh's proclamation to my lord:
  'Sit at my right
    until I make your enemies your footstool.'
²Yahweh will send your vigorous sceptre out from
    Tsiyyon;
  hold sway among your enemies.
³Your people are willing offerings
  on the day you deploy your forces.
In sacred magnificence from the womb of dawn
  the dew of your youths is yours.
⁴Yahweh has sworn,
  and will not relent:
'You are a priest permanently
  after the manner of Melkitsedeq.'
⁵The Lord is at your right;
  he has hit kings on the day of his anger.
⁶He judges among the nations, filling them with
    bodies;
  he has hit heads over the earth, far and wide.
⁷From the wadi by the way he drinks;
  therefore he can raise his head.

## Psalm 111 The lasting pact

¹Praise Yah! –
  I will confess Yahweh with my whole mind
  in the council of the upright, the assembly.
²Yahweh's doings are great,
  enquired about for all their delights.
³His action is grandeur and magnificence,
  his faithfulness stands permanently.
⁴He achieved commemoration for his
    extraordinary deeds;
  Yahweh is gracious and compassionate.
⁵He has given meat to people who live in awe of him;
  he is mindful of his pact permanently.
⁶He told his people of the energy of his doings
  in giving them the domain of the nations.
⁷The doings of his hands are true and
    authoritative;
  all the things he has determined are truthful,
⁸Established lastingly and permanently,
  done in truth and uprightness.
⁹He sent redemption to his people,
  he ordered his pact permanently.
His name is sacred and to be held in awe;
  ¹⁰awe for Yahweh is the essence of smartness.

Good insight belongs to all who do them;
  his praise stands permanently.

## Psalm 112 Blessed so as to bless

¹Praise Yah! –
  the blessings of the person who lives in awe of
    Yahweh,
  who delights much in his orders!
²His offspring will become a strong man in the
    country;
  the generation of the upright will be blessed.
³Riches and wealth are in his house,
  and his faithfulness stands permanently.
⁴He rises in the darkness as light for the
    upright,
  gracious, compassionate and faithful.
⁵Good is the person who is gracious and lends,
  as he fulfils his words with the [proper] exercise
  of authority.
⁶Because he will not slip, ever;
  the faithful person will become an object of
  commemoration permanently.
⁷He is not afraid of bad news;
  his mind is established, reliant on Yahweh.
⁸His mind is held firm so that he is not afraid,
  until he looks on his adversaries.
⁹He spreads abroad as he gives to the needy;
  his faithfulness stands permanently.
His horn will stand high in splendour;
  ¹⁰the faithless person will see and be vexed.
He will grind his teeth and waste away;
  the longing of faithless people will perish.

## Psalm 113 The one who gets down low to look

¹Praise Yah! –
  praise, Yahweh's servants,
  praise Yahweh's name!
²May Yahweh's name be blessed,
  now and permanently!
³From the rising of the sun to its setting,
  Yahweh's name be praised!
⁴Yahweh is on high over all nations,
  his splendour is over the heavens!
⁵Who is like Yahweh our God,
  the one who goes on high to sit,
⁶Who gets down low to look,
  in the heavens and the earth,

⁷Who lifts up the poor person from the earth,
    raises the needy person from the rubbish heap,
⁸To enable them to sit with leaders,
    with the leaders of the people,
⁹Who enables the childless woman to sit in the
      household,
    the mother of children, rejoicing?
Praise Yah!

## Psalm 114 The sacred place

¹When Yisra'el got out from Misrayim,
    Ya'aqob's household from a jabbering people,
²Yehudah became its sacred place,
    Yisra'el its realm.
³When the sea saw, it fled;
    the Yarden – it was turning back.
⁴The mountains – they jumped like rams,
    the hills like the children of the flock.
⁵What was it with you, sea, that you were fleeing,
    Yarden, that you were turning back,
⁶Mountains that you were jumping like rams,
    hills like the children of the flock?
⁷Tremble, before the Lord, earth,
    before Ya'aqob's God,
⁸Who turned the crag into a pool of water,
    basalt into a spring of water.

## Psalm 115 The gods with bodies that don't work

¹Not to us, Yahweh,
    not to us,
But to your name give splendour,
    for your commitment, for your truthfulness.
²Why should the nations say,
    'Where is their God, please?'
³Whereas our God is in the heavens;
    everything that he wants he has done.
⁴Their images are silver and gold,
    the making of human hands.
⁵They have a mouth but they don't speak,
    they have eyes but they don't see,
⁶They have ears but they don't hear,
    they have a nose but they don't smell,
⁷Their hands but they don't feel, their feet but they
    don't walk about;
    they don't murmur with their throat.
⁸Their makers become like them,
    everyone who relies on them.

⁹Yisra'el, rely on Yahweh!
    – he is their help and their shield.
¹⁰Household of Aharon, rely on Yahweh!
    – he is their help and their shield.
¹¹People who live in awe of Yahweh, rely on
    Yahweh!
    – he is their help and their shield.
¹²In that Yahweh has been mindful of us, he will
    bless us;
    he will bless Yisra'el's household,
    he will bless Aharon's household.
¹³He will bless the people who live in awe of
    Yahweh,
    the small along with the great.
¹⁴May Yahweh add to you,
    to you and to your children.
¹⁵May you be blessed by Yahweh,
    maker of heavens and earth.
¹⁶The heavens are heavens belonging to
    Yahweh,
    but the earth he gave to human beings.
¹⁷Whereas the dead do not praise Yah,
    nor any who go down to silence,
¹⁸We – we will bless Yah,
    now and permanently.
Praise Yah!

## Psalm 116 I will make good my pledges

¹I am loyal, because Yahweh listens
    to my voice, my prayers for grace.
²Because he has bent his ear to me,
    and through my days I will call.

³Death's ropes encompassed me,
    She'ol's restraints found me.
When I find pressure and sadness,
    ⁴I call out in Yahweh's name:
'Oh now, Yahweh,
    save my life!'
⁵Yahweh is gracious and faithful;
    our God is compassionate.
⁶Yahweh keeps watch over simple people;
    I sank low, and he delivered me.
⁷Turn back, my entire being, to your rest,
    because Yahweh – he has dealt to you.
⁸Because you pulled out my life from death,
    my eye from tears, my foot from being pushed
      down,
⁹I can walk about before Yahweh
    in the land of the living.

¹⁰I trust, because I could say,
  'I – I have become very low.'
¹¹I – I said in my haste,
  'Every human being lies.'
¹²What shall I give back to Yahweh,
  for all his dealings with me?
¹³I will lift the deliverance cup,
  and call out in Yahweh's name.
¹⁴I will make good my pledges to Yahweh,
  right in front of all his people, please.
¹⁵Valuable in Yahweh's eyes
  is the death of people who are committed to
  him.
¹⁶Oh, Yahweh,
  because I am your servant,
I am your servant, the son of your handmaid;
  you loosed my bonds.
¹⁷I will make a thanksgiving sacrifice to you,
  I will call in Yahweh's name.
¹⁸I will make good my pledges to Yahweh,
  right in front of all his people, please,
¹⁹in the courtyards of Yahweh's house,
  in the middle of Yerushalaim.
Praise Yah!

## Psalm 117 *A lot in a few words*

¹Praise Yahweh, all you nations,
  extol him all you peoples.
²Because his commitment to us has been strong;
  Yahweh's truthfulness is permanent.
Praise Yah.

## Psalm 118 *This is the day that the Lord has made*

¹Confess Yahweh, because he is good,
  because his commitment is permanent.
²Yisra'el is please to say,
  'His commitment is permanent.'
³Aharon's household is please to say,
  'His commitment is permanent.'
⁴The people who live in awe of Yahweh are please
    to say,
  'His commitment is permanent.'

⁵Out of constraint I called Yah;
  Yah answered me with roominess.
⁶Because Yahweh is mine, I will not be afraid;
  what can a human being do to me?

⁷Yahweh is mine as my helper,
  and I shall look on the people who are hostile
    to me.
⁸It's better to take shelter with Yahweh
  than to rely on human beings.
⁹It's better to take shelter with Yahweh
  than to rely on leaders.
¹⁰All nations surrounded me;
  in Yahweh's name I can indeed wither them.
¹¹They surrounded me, yes, surrounded me;
  in Yahweh's name I can indeed wither them.
¹²They surrounded me like bees;
  they've been extinguished like a fire of thorns
  – in Yahweh's name I can indeed wither them.
¹³You pushed me hard, so as to fall,
  but Yahweh – he helped me.
¹⁴Yah was my vigour and protection,
  and he became my deliverance.
¹⁵The noise of resounding and deliverance
  was in the tents of the faithful.
Yahweh's right hand acts with forcefulness,
  ¹⁶Yahweh's right hand lifts up high,
  Yahweh's right hand acts with forcefulness.
¹⁷I shall not die, but live,
  and recount Yah's deeds.
¹⁸Yahweh severely disciplined me,
  but didn't give me over to death.

¹⁹Open the faithful gateways to me;
  when I come through them, I shall confess
    Yahweh.
²⁰This is Yahweh's gateway;
  faithful people come through it.
²¹I will confess you, because you answered me
  and became deliverance for me.
²²'The stone that the builders spurned
  became the head cornerstone.'
²³This came about from Yahweh;
  it's been extraordinary in our eyes.
²⁴This was the day that Yahweh made;
  so that we would celebrate and rejoice in it.

²⁵Oh, Yahweh, will you deliver us, please?
  – oh, Yahweh, enable us to succeed, please.
²⁶Blessed be the one who comes in Yahweh's
    name;
  we are blessing you from Yahweh's house.
²⁷Yahweh is God; he has shone light to us
  – tie the festal offering with cords to the horns
    of the altar.
²⁸You are my God and I will confess you;
  my God, I will exalt you.

²⁹Confess Yahweh, because he is good,
  because his commitment is permanent.

## Psalm 119.1–24 God's laws as the way to blessing

¹The blessings of people who have integrity in
      their way,
  who walk by Yahweh's instruction!
²The blessings of people who observe his
      affirmations,
  who enquire of him with their entire mind!
³Indeed, they have not done evil;
  they have walked in his ways.
⁴You yourself have given the order that the things
      you have determined
  are to be well kept.
⁵Oh that my ways may be firm
  in keeping your decrees!
⁶Then I shall not be shamed
  when I look to all your orders.
⁷I will confess you with uprightness of mind
  as I learn of your faithful rulings.
⁸I will keep your decrees;
  don't totally abandon me.

⁹How can a youth keep his path clean?
  – by keeping watch in accordance with your
      word.
¹⁰I've enquired of you with my whole mind;
  don't let me stray from your orders.
¹¹I've treasured your words in my mind
  in order that I may not do wrong in relation
      to you.
¹²Blessed are you, Yahweh;
  teach me your decrees.
¹³With my lips I've recounted
  all the rulings of your mouth.
¹⁴In the way of your affirmations
  I've rejoiced as over all riches.
¹⁵I shall talk about the things you have determined
  and look to your paths.
¹⁶In your decrees I will take pleasure;
  I will not put out of mind your words.

¹⁷Deal to your servant
  so that I may live, and keep your word.
¹⁸Open my eyes so that I may look
  to extraordinary things from your instruction.
¹⁹I'm a sojourner on the earth;
  don't hide your orders from me.

²⁰My entire being has failed with longing
  for your rulings all the time.
²¹You've reprimanded the assertive;
  cursed are the people who stray from your orders.
²²Roll away from me reviling and shame,
  because I've observed your affirmations.
²³Although officials have sat, have spoken against
      me,
  your servant talks about your decrees.
²⁴Yes, your affirmations are my pleasure,
  my counsellors.

## Psalm 119.25–48 Standing on the promises

²⁵My entire being is stuck in the earth:
  bring me to life in accordance with your word.
²⁶I recounted my ways and you answered me;
  teach me your decrees.
²⁷Help me understand the way of the things you
      have determined,
  so that I may talk about your extraordinary
      deeds.
²⁸My entire being has wept itself away through
      sorrow;
  set me up in accordance with your word.
²⁹Remove the way of falsehood from me;
  grace me with your instruction.
³⁰I've chosen the way of truthfulness;
  I've set out your rulings.
³¹I've stuck to your affirmations;
  Yahweh, don't shame me.
³²I run the way of your orders,
  because you widen my mind.

³³Teach me the way of your decrees, Yahweh,
  so that I may preserve it to the utmost.
³⁴Help me understand, so that I may observe your
      instruction,
  and keep it with all my mind.
³⁵Direct me on the trail of your orders,
  because I delight in it.
³⁶Bend my mind to your affirmations
  and not to profit.
³⁷Help my eyes pass from seeing emptiness;
  bring me to life by your way.
³⁸Implement for your servant what you've said,
  that which was for people who live in awe of you.
³⁹Make my reviling, which I dread, pass,
  because your rulings are good.
⁴⁰There, I long for the things you've determined;
  in your faithfulness bring me to life.

⁴¹So may your commitment come to me, Yahweh,
  your deliverance in accordance with what
    you've said.
⁴²And I shall answer the person who reviles me
    with a word,
  because I've relied on your word.
⁴³So don't snatch right away from my mouth your
    truthful word,
  because I've waited for your rulings.
⁴⁴And I will keep your instruction continually,
    lastingly and permanently.
⁴⁵So I will walk about in wideness,
  because I've enquired of the things you've
    determined.
⁴⁶And I will speak of your affirmations in front of
    kings,
  and not be shamed.
⁴⁷So I will take pleasure in your orders,
  to which I am loyal.
⁴⁸And I will lift the palms of my hands to your
    orders, to which I am loyal,
  and I will talk about your decrees.

## Psalm 119.49–72 Teach me

⁴⁹Be mindful of your word to your servant,
  upon which you've caused me to wait.
⁵⁰This is my comfort in my humbling,
  that what you've said has brought me to life.
⁵¹Though the assertive have mocked me greatly,
  I haven't turned away from your instruction.
⁵²I've been mindful of your rulings from of old,
  Yahweh, and found comfort.
⁵³Rage has grasped me because of the faithless
    people,
  who abandon your instruction.
⁵⁴Your decrees have been my protection
  in the house where I reside.
⁵⁵I've been mindful by night of your name,
    Yahweh,
  and I've kept your instruction.
⁵⁶This is how it's been for me,
  because I've observed the things you've
    determined.
⁵⁷Yahweh being my share,
  I've said I would keep your words.
⁵⁸I've sought your goodwill with all my heart;
  be gracious to me in accordance with what
    you've said.
⁵⁹I've thought about my ways
  and turned back my feet to your affirmations.

⁶⁰I've hurried and not delayed
  to keep your orders.
⁶¹Though the ropes of the faithless were round
    me,
  I haven't put out of mind your instruction.
⁶²In the middle of the night I get up
  to confess you for your faithful rulings.
⁶³I'm a friend to all who live in awe of you
  and to the people who keep the things you've
    determined.
⁶⁴The earth is full of your commitment, Yahweh;
  teach me your decrees.

⁶⁵You've done good things with your servant,
  Yahweh, in accordance with your word.
⁶⁶Teach me goodness of discretion and
    acknowledgement,
  because I've trusted in your orders.
⁶⁷Before I became low I was going astray,
  but now I've kept what you said.
⁶⁸You're good and you do good;
  teach me your decrees.
⁶⁹The assertive have smeared falsehood over me,
  whereas I observe the things you've determined
    with my whole mind.
⁷⁰Their mind is thick like fat,
  whereas I've taken pleasure in your instruction.
⁷¹It was good for me that I was humbled,
  in order that I might learn your decrees.
⁷²The instruction that comes from your mouth is
    better for me
  than thousands of gold and silver pieces.

## Psalm 119.73–96 Waiting

⁷³Given that your hands made me, established me,
  help me understand so that I may learn your
    orders.
⁷⁴People who live in awe of you will see and
    rejoice,
  because I've waited for your word.
⁷⁵I've acknowledged, Yahweh, that your rulings
    are faithful,
  and in truthfulness you've humbled me.
⁷⁶May your commitment become my comfort,
    please,
  in accordance with what you've said to your
    servant.
⁷⁷May your compassion come to me so that I may
    live,
  because your instruction is my pleasure.

<sup>78</sup>May the assertive be shamed, because they have
    put me in the wrong by means of falsehood,
  whereas I talk about the things you've
    determined.
<sup>79</sup>May the people who live in awe of you turn back
    to me,
  the people who acknowledge your
    affirmations.
<sup>80</sup>May my mind be of integrity in your decrees
  in order that I may not be shamed.

<sup>81</sup>My entire being fails [in looking] for your
    deliverance;
  for your word I've waited.
<sup>82</sup>My eyes fail regarding what you've said,
  in saying 'When will you comfort me?'
<sup>83</sup>When I've become like a water-skin in smoke,
  I haven't put out of mind your decrees.
<sup>84</sup>How many are your servant's days:
  when will you act with authority against my
    pursuers?
<sup>85</sup>The assertive have dug pits for me,
  which is not in accordance with your
    instruction.
<sup>86</sup>All your orders are truthful;
  when people pursue me with falsehood, help
    me.
<sup>87</sup>They've almost finished me off in the country,
  but I haven't abandoned the things you've
    determined.
<sup>88</sup>In accordance with your commitment bring me
    to life,
  so that I may keep the affirmations of your
    mouth.

<sup>89</sup>Your word is permanent, Yahweh,
  standing in the heavens.
<sup>90</sup>Your truthfulness lasts generation after
    generation;
  you established the earth and it has stood firm.
<sup>91</sup>As for your rulings, they've stood firm today,
  because all are your servants.
<sup>92</sup>Were not your instruction my pleasure,
  I would then have perished through my
    humbling.
<sup>93</sup>Never will I put out of mind the things you've
    determined,
  because by means of them you've brought me
    to life.
<sup>94</sup>I am yours, deliver me,
  because I've enquired of the things you've
    determined.

<sup>95</sup>Whereas faithless people have hoped to make
    me perish,
  I show understanding of your affirmations.
<sup>96</sup>As for every finish, I've seen an end,
  but your order is very wide.

## Psalm 119.97–120 I can be smarter than my professor

<sup>97</sup>How loyal I am to your instruction!
  – all day it is my talk.
<sup>98</sup>Your orders make me smarter than my enemies,
  because they are mine permanently.
<sup>99</sup>I've gained more insight than all my teachers,
  because your affirmations are my talk.
<sup>100</sup>I show more understanding than the elders,
  because I've observed the things you've
    determined.
<sup>101</sup>I've kept back my foot from every bad path,
  in order that I might keep your word.
<sup>102</sup>I haven't departed from your rulings,
  because you've instructed me.
<sup>103</sup>How smooth the things you say have been to
    my palate,
  more than syrup to my mouth.
<sup>104</sup>Through the things you've determined I show
    understanding;
  therefore I oppose every false path.

<sup>105</sup>Your word is a lamp to my foot,
  a light to my trail.
<sup>106</sup>I swore and set it up,
  that I would keep your faithful rulings.
<sup>107</sup>I am low, very low, Yahweh;
  bring me to life in accordance with your word.
<sup>108</sup>Please accept the free offerings of my mouth,
    Yahweh,
  and teach me your rulings.
<sup>109</sup>My life is in the palm of my hand continually,
  but I haven't put out of mind your instruction.
<sup>110</sup>Faithless people have placed a trap for me,
  but I haven't strayed from the things you've
    determined.
<sup>111</sup>I've made your affirmations my own
    permanently,
  because they are the joy of my heart.
<sup>112</sup>I've bent my mind to act on your decrees,
  permanently, to the utmost.

<sup>113</sup>I'm hostile to divided people,
  and I'm loyal to your instruction.

114Since you've been my shelter and shield,
  I've waited for your word.
115Depart from me, you who deal badly,
  so that I may observe my God's orders.
116Hold me up in accordance with what you said,
    so that I may live;
  don't let me be ashamed of my expectation.
117Sustain me so that I may find deliverance,
  and have regard to your decrees continually.
118You've thrown out everyone who wanders from
    your decrees,
  because their deceptiveness is false.
119As dross, you've made all the faithless people in
    the country cease;
  therefore I'm loyal to your affirmations.
120My flesh shivers in reverence for you;
  I live in awe of your rulings.

*Psalm 119.121–144 The opening up of
your words gives light*

121I've made faithful rulings;
  don't leave me to oppressors.
122Make a pledge to your servant for good things;
  the assertive must not oppress me.
123My eyes fail [in looking] for your deliverance,
  for what you said about your faithfulness.
124Act with your servant in accordance with your
    commitment,
  and teach me your decrees.
125As I am your servant, help me understand,
  so that I may acknowledge your affirmations.
126It's a time for Yahweh to act;
  people have violated your instruction.
127Therefore I'm loyal to your orders,
  more than to gold and silver.
128Therefore I've treated as upright everything that
    you've determined about everything;
  I've been hostile to every false path.

129Your affirmations are extraordinary things;
  therefore my entire being has observed them.
130The opening up of your words gives light,
  helping the simple to understand.
131I opened wide my mouth and panted,
  because I longed for your orders.
132Turn your face to me and be gracious to me,
  in accordance with your ruling for people who
    are loyal to your name.
133Establish my feet by what you say,
  so that no evil may have power over me.

134Redeem me from human oppression,
  so that I may keep the things you've
    determined.
135Shine your face on your servant,
  and teach me your decrees.
136My eyes have run down streams of water,
  because people have not kept your instruction.

137You're faithful, Yahweh,
  and upright in your rulings.
138You've ordered the faithfulness of your
    affirmations,
  and the truthfulness, exceedingly.
139My passion has devoured me,
  because my adversaries have put your words
    out of mind.
140What you say has been much proven,
  and your servant is loyal to it.
141Although I am small and despised,
  I haven't put out of mind the things you've
    determined.
142Your faithfulness is a faithfulness that is
    permanent,
  and your instruction is truth.
143Although pressure and straits have found me,
  your orders are my pleasure.
144The faithfulness of your affirmations is
    permanent;
  help me understand so that I may live.

*Psalm 119.145–160 My eyes have
anticipated the watches*

145I've called with all my heart; answer me,
    Yahweh,
  so that I may observe your decrees.
146I've called you – deliver me,
  so that I may keep your affirmations.
147I've anticipated the twilight and cried for help,
  as I waited for your word.
148My eyes have anticipated the watches,
  to talk about what you've said.
149Listen to my voice in accordance with your
    commitment;
  Yahweh, bring me to life in accordance with
    your ruling.
150People who pursue deliberate wickedness are
    near;
  they are far from your instruction.
151You are near, Yahweh,
  and all your orders are true.

[152]Of old I've acknowledged from your
    affirmations
    that you founded them permanently.

[153]See my humbling, pull me out,
    because I haven't put out of mind your
    instruction.
[154]Argue my cause and restore me;
    in the light of what you've said, bring me
    to life.
[155]Deliverance is far from the faithless,
    because they haven't enquired of your decrees.
[156]Your compassion is great, Yahweh;
    bring me to life in accordance with your
    rulings.
[157]Although my pursuers and adversaries are
    many,
    I haven't turned away from your affirmations.
[158]I've seen people who break faith and loathed
    them,
    people who didn't keep what you said.
[159]See that I've been loyal to the things you've
    determined;
    Yahweh, bring me to life in accordance with
    your commitment.
[160]Truthfulness is the first principle of your
    word,
    and every faithful ruling of yours is
    permanent.

## Psalm 119.161–176 *The appeal of the lost sheep*

[161]Officials have pursued me for nothing,
    but my heart has revered your word.
[162]I rejoice over what you've said,
    like someone who finds much plunder.
[163]Whereas I'm hostile to and take offence at
    falsehood,
    I'm loyal to your instruction.
[164]I've praised you seven times a day
    for your faithful rulings.
[165]There is much well-being for people who are
    loyal to your instruction,
    and there isn't anything that can make them
    collapse.
[166]I've looked for your deliverance, Yahweh,
    and acted on your orders.
[167]I've kept your affirmations with my entire
    being;
    I am totally loyal to them.

[168]I've kept the things you've determined and your
    affirmations,
    because all my ways are in front of you.
[169]May my resounding come near your presence,
    Yahweh;
    in accordance with your word, help me
    understand.
[170]May my prayer for grace come before you;
    in accordance with what you've said, rescue me.
[171]May my lips pour forth praise,
    because you teach me your decrees.
[172]May my tongue chant of what you've said,
    because all your orders are faithful.
[173]May your hand come to my help,
    because I've chosen the things you've
    determined.
[174]I've longed for your deliverance, Yahweh,
    and your instruction is my pleasure.
[175]May my entire being live and praise you,
    and may your rulings help me.
[176]I've wandered like a lost sheep:
    look for your servant,
    because I haven't put your orders out of mind.

## Psalm 120 *Peaceableness*

A song of the ascents.

[1]To Yahweh, when I was under pressure,
    I called and he answered me.
[2]Yahweh, rescue my life from false lips,
    from a deceitful tongue.
[3]What will it give you, what will it add to you,
    deceitful tongue?
[4]The arrows of a strong man, sharpened,
    with coals of broom shrubs.
[5]Oh for me, that I've resided with Meshek,
    dwelt with Qedar's tents.
[6]A long time I've been dwelling
    with someone hostile to peace.
[7]I am for peace, but when I speak,
    they are for battle.

## Psalm 121 *Peacefulness*

A song for the ascents.

[1]I raise my eyes to the mountains:
    from where does my help come?

²My help comes from Yahweh,
  maker of heavens and earth.
³He doesn't give your foot to slipping;
  your keeper doesn't doze.
⁴There, he doesn't doze and he doesn't sleep,
  Yisra'el's keeper.
⁵Yahweh is your keeper, Yahweh is your shade,
  at your right hand.
⁶By day the sun will not strike you down,
  or the moon by night.
⁷Yahweh will keep you from everything bad;
  he will keep your life.
⁸Yahweh will keep your going out and your
    coming in,
  from now and permanently.

## Psalm 122 Praying for Yerushalaim

A song of the ascents. David's.

¹I rejoiced when people said to me,
  'We'll go to Yahweh's house.'
²Our feet have been standing
  in your gates, Yerushalaim,
³Yerushalaim, which is built
  as a town that is joined together to itself,
⁴Where the clans went up, Yah's clans,
  (an affirmation for Yisra'el),
  to confess Yahweh's name.
⁵Because thrones for exercising authority sat there,
  thrones for David's household.
⁶Ask for the well-being of Yerushalaim;
  may people who are loyal to it be secure.
⁷May there be well-being in your rampart,
  ease in your citadels.
⁸For the sake of my brothers and my friends
  I shall please speak of well-being for you.
⁹For the sake of the house of Yahweh our God
  I will seek good things for you.

## Psalm 123 Praying for grace

A song of the ascents.

¹To you I raise my eyes,
  you who sit in the heavens.
²There, like the eyes of servants
  towards the hand of their masters,
Like the eyes of a maidservant
  towards the hand of her mistress,

So are our eyes towards Yahweh our God,
  until he is gracious to us.
³Be gracious to us, Yahweh, be gracious,
  because we've become very full of contempt.
⁴Our entire being has become very full for itself
  of the ridicule of complacent people,
  of the contempt of majestic people.

## Psalm 124 Our help is the name of the Lord

A song of the ascents. David's.

¹Were it not Yahweh who was ours,
  Yisra'el is please to say,
²Were it not Yahweh who was ours
  when people arose against us,
³Then they would have swallowed us alive
  in their angry burning against us.
⁴Then the water – it would have carried us off;
  the torrent – it would have passed right over us.
⁵Then it would have passed right over us,
  the seething water.
⁶Yahweh be blessed,
  who did not give us as prey to their teeth.
⁷Our life is like a bird
  that has escaped from the hunters' trap.
The trap – it broke;
  and we – we escaped.
⁸Our help is the very name of Yahweh,
  maker of heavens and earth.

## Psalm 125 Mountains round Yerushalaim, Yahweh round his people

A song of the ascents.

¹The people who rely on Yahweh are like Mount
    Tsiyyon,
  which will not slip – it will sit permanently.
²Yerushalaim – mountains are round it;
  Yahweh – he is round his people,
  now and permanently.
³Because the faithless club will not rest
  over the allocation of the faithful,
In order that the faithful do not put
  their hands to evil.

⁴Do good, Yahweh, to the people who are good,
  yes, to the people who are upright in their mind.
⁵But the people who bend their crooked ways,

may Yahweh make them go, the people who
    devise trouble;
well-being [be] on Yisra'el!


## Psalm 126 Dreaming, crying, resounding

A song of the ascents.

¹When Yahweh turned back Tsiyyon's fortunes,
    we became like people dreaming.
²Then our mouth would fill with laughter,
    our tongue with resounding.
Then they would say among the nations,
    'Yahweh has shown greatness in acting with
        them.'
³Yahweh has shown greatness in acting with us;
    we became people celebrating.

⁴Turn back our fortunes, Yahweh,
    like canyons in the Negev.
⁵May people who sow with crying
    reap with resounding.
⁶The person who goes, but goes crying,
    carrying the seed bag –
As he comes, may he come with resounding,
    carrying his sheaves.


## Psalm 127 Insomnia

A song of the ascents. Shelomoh's.

¹If Yahweh doesn't build a house,
    in vain the builders have laboured on it.
If Yahweh doesn't keep a town,
    in vain the one who keeps watch has been
        wakeful.
²It is in vain for you, being people early to get up,
    people late to sit down,
People who eat bread of toil
    – yes, he gives sleep to his beloved.

³There, sons are your domain from Yahweh;
    the fruit of the womb is a reward.
⁴Like arrows in a strong man's hand
    – so are the sons of youth.
⁵The blessings of the man
    who has filled his quiver!
Of them he will not be shamed
    when they speak with enemies in the gateway.


## Psalm 128 Blessings and good things

A song of the ascents.

¹The blessings of anyone who lives in awe of Yahweh,
    who walks in his ways!
²Because you will eat the fruit of the palms of
        your hands,
    your blessings and good things of yours.
³Your wife like a fruitful vine
    in the inner rooms of your house,
Your children like the slips of olive trees
    round your table.
⁴There, surely thus will he be blessed,
    a man who lives in awe of Yahweh.
⁵May Yahweh bless you from Tsiyyon;
    you can look at the good things of Yerushalaim,
All the days of your life,
    ⁶and look at your grandchildren;
    well-being [be] on Yisra'el!


## Psalm 129 Atrocities

A song of the ascents.

¹People have attacked me much since my youth,
    Yisra'el is please to say,
²People have attacked me much,
    though not prevailed over me.
³Over my back ploughmen have ploughed;
    they made long furrows.
⁴Yahweh is faithful;
    he cut through the ropes of the faithless people.
⁵May they be shamed and may they turn
        backwards,
    all the people who are hostile to Tsiyyon.
⁶May they become like the grass on roofs
    that withers before someone has plucked it,
⁷With which a reaper has not filled his fist,
    or a gatherer his arm,
⁸And passers-by have not said,
    'Yahweh's blessing on you;
    we bless you in Yahweh's name.'


## Psalm 130 From the depths

A song of the ascents.

¹From the depths I have called you, Yahweh:
    ²Lord, listen to my voice.

May your ears become attentive
    to the sound of my prayers for grace.
³If you keep watch on wayward acts, Yah:
    Lord, who can stand?
⁴Because with you there is pardon,
    in order that you may be held in awe.
⁵I have hoped for Yahweh,
    my entire being has hoped.
For his word I have waited,
    ⁶my entire being for the Lord,
More than people keeping watch for the morning,
    people keeping watch for the morning.
⁷Yisra'el, wait for Yahweh,
    because with Yahweh there is commitment.
With him the redemption will be great,
    ⁸when he himself redeems Yisra'el from all its
        wayward acts.

## Psalm 131 *No big ideas*

A song of the ascents. David's.

¹Yahweh, my mind has not been lofty,
    my eyes have not looked high.
I haven't gone about with big ideas
    or extraordinary deeds beyond me.
²If I haven't conformed
    and quietened my entire being . . .
Like someone nursed with its mother,
    so my entire being is nursed with me.
³Yisra'el, wait for Yahweh,
    now and for evermore.

## Psalm 132 *If you build it, he will come*

A song of the ascents.

¹Yahweh, be mindful for David
    of all his being humbled,
²In that he swore to Yahweh,
    pledged to Ya'aqob's Champion,
³'If I come into my tent, my house,
    if I climb into my bed, my couch,
⁴If I give sleep to my eyes,
    slumber to my eyelids,
⁵Until I find the place belonging to Yahweh,
    the dwelling belonging to Ya'aqob's Champion . . .'

⁶There, we heard of it at Ephrata,
    we found it in the Ya'ar fields.

⁷Let's come to his dwelling,
    let's bow low to his footstool.
⁸Rise, Yahweh, to your place, to settle down,
    you and your powerful chest.
⁹Your priests put on faithfulness,
    the people who are committed to you resound.
¹⁰For the sake of David your servant,
    don't turn back the face of your anointed one.

¹¹Yahweh swore to David in truthfulness,
    he will not turn back from it:
'One from the fruit of your body
    I will put on your throne.
¹²If your sons keep my pact,
    my affirmations that I will teach them,
For all time their sons
    also will sit on your throne.
¹³Because Yahweh chose Tsiyyon,
    which he wanted as a seat for himself.
¹⁴For all time this is my place to settle down,
    where I will sit, because I wanted it.
¹⁵Its supplies I will greatly bless;
    its needy people I will fill with bread.
¹⁶Its priests I will clothe with deliverance,
    its committed people will resound loudly.
¹⁷There I will make David's horn flourish;
    I am setting up a lamp for my anointed one.
¹⁸Its enemies I will clothe in shame,
    but on him his crown will sparkle.'

## Psalm 133 *Brothers living as one*

A song of the ascents. David's.

¹There, how good and how lovely
    is brothers living as one,
²Like good oil on the head,
    going down on to the beard,
Aharon's beard,
    which goes down on the collar of his clothes,
³Like the dew of Hermon,
    which goes down on the mountains of Tsiyyon.
Because there Yahweh ordered blessing,
    life for evermore.

## Psalm 134 *How to end the day*

A song of the ascents.

¹There, bless Yahweh, all you servants of Yahweh,
    you who stand in Yahweh's house at night.

²Raise your hands to the sacred place
 and bless Yahweh.
³May Yahweh bless you from Tsiyyon
 – the one who is maker of heavens and earth.

## Psalm 135 Anything that Yahweh has wished, he has done

¹Praise Yah! –
 praise Yahweh's name;
 praise, servants of Yahweh,
²You who stand in Yahweh's house,
 in the courtyards of the house of our God.
³Praise Yah, because Yahweh is good;
 make music for his name, because it's lovely.
⁴Because Yah chose Ya'aqob for himself,
 Yisra'el as his personal treasure.

⁵Because I myself acknowledge that Yahweh is
 great;
 our Lord above all gods.
⁶Anything that Yahweh has wished,
 he has done in the heavens and on the earth,
In the seas and all the depths,
 ⁷making clouds rise from the end of the earth.
He has made flashes of lightning for the rain,
 getting wind out from his storehouses,
⁸The one who struck down the firstborn of
 Misrayim,
 both human beings and cattle.
⁹He sent signs and portents
 in the middle of Misrayim
 against Par'oh [Pharaoh] and against all his
 servants,
¹⁰The one who struck down many nations
 and killed numerous kings,
¹¹Sihon king of the Amorites,
 Og king of Bashan,
And all the kingdoms of Kena'an,
 ¹²and gave their country as a domain,
 a domain for Yisra'el his people.

¹³Yahweh, your name is permanent;
 Yahweh, your commemoration is through
 generation after generation.
¹⁴Because Yahweh acts in judgement for his
 people
 and gets relief in connection with his servants.

¹⁵The nations' images are silver and gold,
 the making of human hands.

¹⁶They have a mouth but they don't speak,
 they have eyes but they don't see.
¹⁷They have ears but they don't hear;
 no, there's no breath in their mouths.
¹⁸Their makers will become like them,
 anyone who relies on them.

¹⁹Household of Yisra'el, bless Yahweh;
 household of Aharon, bless Yahweh.
²⁰Household of Levi, bless Yahweh;
 you who live in awe of Yahweh, bless Yahweh.
²¹Yahweh be blessed from Tsiyyon,
 the one who dwells in Yerushalaim.
Praise Yah!

## Psalm 136 His commitment is permanent

¹Confess Yahweh, because he is good
 (because his commitment is permanent).
²Confess the God of gods
 (because his commitment is permanent).
³Confess the Lord of lords
 (because his commitment is permanent).
⁴The one who did big, extraordinary things alone
 (because his commitment is permanent),
⁵Who made the heavens with understanding
 (because his commitment is permanent),
⁶Who spread the earth over the water
 (because his commitment is permanent),
⁷Who made the big lights
 (because his commitment is permanent),
⁸The sun to rule the day
 (because his commitment is permanent),
⁹The moon and the stars to rule the night
 (because his commitment is permanent),
¹⁰Who struck down Misrayim through their
 firstborn
 (because his commitment is permanent),
¹¹And got Yisra'el out from the middle of them
 (because his commitment is permanent),
¹²With a strong hand and an extended arm
 (because his commitment is permanent),
¹³The divider of the Reed Sea into two divisions
 (because his commitment is permanent),
¹⁴Who let Yisra'el pass through the middle of it
 (because his commitment is permanent),
¹⁵But shook Par'oh and his force into the Reed Sea
 (because his commitment is permanent),
¹⁶The one who enabled his people to go through
 the wilderness
 (because his commitment is permanent),

¹⁷The one who struck down great kings
  (because his commitment is permanent),
¹⁸Who killed august kings
  (because his commitment is permanent),
¹⁹Sihon king of the Amorites
  (because his commitment is permanent),
²⁰Og king of Bashan
  (because his commitment is permanent),
²¹And gave their country as a domain
  (because his commitment is permanent),
²²A domain for Yisra'el his servant
  (because his commitment is permanent),
²³Who was mindful of us in our lowliness
  (because his commitment is permanent),
²⁴And tore us away from our adversaries
  (because his commitment is permanent),
²⁵Giver of food to all flesh
  (because his commitment is permanent).
²⁶Confess the God of the heavens
  (because his commitment is permanent).

## Psalm 137 Mindfulness, God's and ours

¹By the rivers of Babel,
  there we sat, yes, we cried
  as we were mindful of Tsiyyon.
²On the poplars in the middle of it
  we hung our guitars.
³Because there they asked,
  our captors, for the words of a song,
The people who play about with us, for rejoicing:
  'Sing us one of the Tsiyyon songs!'
⁴How can we sing Yahweh's song
  on foreign soil?
⁵If I put you out of mind, Yerushalaim,
  may my right hand put out of mind.
⁶May my tongue stick to my palate
  if I am not mindful of you,
If I do not exalt Yerushalaim
  above the pinnacle of my rejoicing.

⁷Yahweh, be mindful for the Edomites
  of Yerushalaim's day,
The people who were saying, 'Strip it,
  strip it, to its foundation.'
⁸Ms Babel, you who are to be destroyed:
  the blessings of the person who makes good
    to you
  for the thing that you dealt to us.
⁹The blessings of the person who grasps your babies
  and dashes them on the cliff.

## Psalm 138 How to be defiant in spirit

David's.

¹I will confess you with all my heart,
  in front of the gods I will make music for you.
²I will bow low to your sacred palace,
  and confess your name for your commitment
    and for your truthfulness,
Because you have made great above everything
  your name, your word.
³On the day I called, you answered me;
  you make me defiant in my being, with vigour.
⁴All earth's kings will confess you, Yahweh,
  because they will have heard the sayings of
    your mouth.
⁵They will sing of Yahweh's ways,
  because Yahweh's splendour will be great.v
⁶Because Yahweh is on high, but he sees the lowly;
  lofty, he acknowledges from afar.
⁷If I walk in the middle of pressure you will give
    me life;
  on account of my enemies' anger you will put
    out your hand.
  Your right hand will deliver me;
⁸Yahweh will bring it to an end for me.
  Yahweh, your commitment is permanent;
  don't slacken your hold of the things your
    hands made.

## Psalm 139 Openness

The leader's. David's. A composition.

¹Yahweh, you've searched me out and got to know
    me:
  ²you yourself have got to know my sitting and
    my rising,
  you've understood my intention, from far
    away.
³My walking and my reclining you've measured;
  with all my ways you've become familiar.
⁴Because there's not an utterance on my tongue
  – there, Yahweh, you've got to know it all.
⁵Behind and in front you've bound me,
  and put the palm of your hand on me.
⁶Your knowledge is too extraordinary for me;
  it's towered high, I can't prevail over it.

⁷Where could I go from your spirit,
  where could I take flight from your face?

⁸If I were to go up to the heavens, you would be
    there;
    if I were to make She'ol my bed – there you
        would be.
⁹Were I to take dawn's wings,
    dwell on the far side of the sea,
¹⁰There, too, your hand could lead me away,
    your right hand could grasp me.
¹¹Were I to say, 'The darkness can certainly seize
    me,
    light can be night round me',
¹²Darkness, too, would not be too dark for you,
    and night would be light like day;
    darkness and light are the same.

¹³Because you are the one who created my inner
    being,
    when you wove me in my mother's womb.
¹⁴I will confess you, on account of the fact that I
    was made distinct in an awe-inspiring way;
    the things you made were extraordinary.
I myself acknowledge you fully;
    ¹⁵my frame was not concealed from you,
When I was made in secret,
    when I was embroidered in earth's depths.
¹⁶Your eyes saw me as an embryo,
    and on your document were written, all of
        them,
The days that were shaped,
    when there was not one of them.
¹⁷So for me, how valuable were your intentions,
    God,
    how numerous was the sum of them!
¹⁸If I could count them, they would be more than
    the sand;
    when I've come to an end, I will still be with you.

¹⁹If you would only slay the faithless person, God,
    and people of bloodshed would depart from
        me,
²⁰People who speak of you in connection with a
    strategy,
    your adversaries who have lifted you up for
        emptiness.
²¹I'm hostile to people who are hostile to you,
    Yahweh, am I not,
    and I loathe people who rise up against you.
²²With complete hostility I'm hostile to them;
    they've become enemies for me.

²³Search me out, God, and acknowledge my mind;
    test me and acknowledge my concerns.

²⁴See if there is an idolatrous way in me
    and lead me in the ancient way.

## Psalm 140 *The shield*

The leader's. A composition. David's.

¹Pull me out, Yahweh, from the bad person,
    preserve me from the individual of great
        violence,
²People who've thought up bad things in their
    mind,
    who stir up battles every day.
³They've sharpened their tongue like a snake;
    a spider's poison is under their lips. *(Rise)*
⁴Keep me from the hand of the faithless person,
    Yahweh,
    preserve me from the individual of great
        violence,
People who've thought up how to trip my steps;
    ⁵majestic people have hidden a trap for me, and
        ropes.
They've spread a net by the side of the track,
    they've set snares for me. *(Rise)*

⁶I've said to Yahweh, 'You are my God';
    give ear, Yahweh, to the sound of my prayer for
        grace.
⁷Yahweh, my Lord, the [one with the] vigour that
    delivers me,
    you've shielded my head on the day of
        weaponry.
⁸Yahweh, don't grant the wishes of the faithless
    person;
    don't let his plan succeed so that they are
        exalted. *(Rise)*
⁹The head of the people who surround me
    – may the oppression caused by their lips cover
        them.
¹⁰May burning coals tumble on them with fire;
    may it make them fall into pits so that they
        don't get up.
¹¹May the person with a [violent] tongue not be
    established in the country;
    the violent person – may bad fortune hunt him
        into pens.
¹²I've come to acknowledge that Yahweh makes a
    judgement for the humble,
    a ruling for the needy.
¹³Yes, the faithful will confess your name;
    the upright will live in your presence.

## Psalm 141 *On keeping one's mouth shut*

A composition. David's.

¹Yahweh, when I call you, hurry to me,
  give ear to my voice when I call to you.
²May my plea be established as incense before
    you,
  the lifting of the palms of my hands as the
    evening offering.
³Set a watch at my mouth, Yahweh,
  keep guard at the door of my lips.
⁴Don't let my mind turn away to something bad,
  to have dealings in faithlessness
  with people who devise trouble.
So I shall not feed on their delights;
  ⁵the faithful person may hit me with
    commitment and reprove me.
May choice oil not adorn my head,
  because my plea is still against their bad ways.
⁶When their authorities have fallen at the sides of
    the cliff,
  they will listen to the things I say, because they
    are lovely.

⁷Like someone cleaving and splitting the earth,
  our bones have been scattered at the mouth of
    She'ol.
⁸Because my eyes are towards you, Yahweh my
    Lord,
  with you I have taken shelter, don't expose my
    life.
⁹Keep me from the sides of the trap that they have
    laid for me,
  and from the snares of people who devise
    trouble.
¹⁰May the faithless fall into their own nets all at
    once,
  while I myself pass through.

## Psalm 142 *A prisoner's plea*

An instruction. David's. When he was in the
cave. A plea.

¹With my voice I will cry out to Yahweh,
  with my voice I will pray for grace to Yahweh.
²I will pour out my talk before him;
  the pressure on me I will declare before him.
³When my spirit faints away within me,
  you're the one who knows my trail.

On the way that I walk about,
  they've hidden a trap for me.
⁴Look at my right hand and see
  – there's no one who recognizes me.
Retreat has failed for me;
  there's no one who enquires about my life.
⁵I've cried out to you, Yahweh;
  I've said, 'You're my shelter,
  my share in the land of the living.'
⁶Heed my resounding shout,
  because I've been brought very low.
Rescue me from my pursuers,
  because they stand too firm for me.
⁷Get me out of my prison,
  to confess your name.
Round me faithful people will gather,
  because you've dealt to me.

## Psalm 143 *God's faithfulness, not mine*

A composition. David's.

¹Yahweh, listen to my plea,
  give ear to my prayer for grace, in your
    truthfulness,
  answer me in your faithfulness.
²Don't come into the exercise of authority with
    your servant,
  because no living person counts as faithful
    before you.
³Because my enemy has pursued my life,
  crushed my existence to the earth,
Made me live in darkness,
  like people long dead.
⁴My spirit has fainted away within me;
  my mind is desolate inside me.
⁵I have been mindful of the days of old,
  I've murmured about all you had done,
  I would talk about the action of your hands.
⁶I've spread out my hands to you,
  my entire being has been like dry earth in
    relation to you. *(Rise)*

⁷Be quick, answer me, Yahweh;
  my spirit is finished.
Don't hide your face from me,
  so that I shall be like the people who go down
    into the Cistern.
⁸Let me hear of your commitment in the
    morning,
  because it's on you that I've relied.

Let me know the way that I should walk,
   because it is to you that I've lifted up my soul.
⁹Rescue me from my enemies, Yahweh;
   with you I've found cover.
¹⁰Teach me to do what's acceptable to you,
   because you are my God.
May your good spirit lead me
   on level ground.
¹¹For the sake of your name, Yahweh, give me
   life;
   in your faithfulness will you get me out of the
    pressure on me.
¹²In your commitment will you put an end to my
   enemies,
   obliterate all the people who are attacking me,
   because I'm your servant.

## Psalm 144 *The God who snatches away*

David's.

¹Yahweh, my crag, be blessed,
   the one who trains my hands for encounter,
   my fingers for battle,
²The one committed to me, my fastness,
   my turret, the one who enables me to survive,
My shield, the one with whom I take shelter,
   who subdues my people under me.

³Yahweh, what is a human person that you should
   acknowledge him,
   a mere human being that you should think
    about him?
⁴A human person is like a breath,
   his days like a passing shadow.
⁵Yahweh, spread your heavens and come down,
   touch the mountains so that they smoke.
⁶Make lightning flash and scatter them,
   send your arrows and rout them.
⁷Send your hands from on high,
   snatch me away, rescue me,
From the great water,
   from the hand of foreigners,
⁸Whose mouth has spoken emptiness,
   and whose right hand is a right hand of
    falsehood.

⁹God, I will sing
   a new song for you,
   on a ten-stringed mandolin I will make music
    for you.

¹⁰As the one who gives deliverance to kings,
   who snatches away David his servant,
From the deadly sword ¹¹snatch me away,
   rescue me from the hand of foreigners,
Whose mouth has spoken emptiness,
   and whose right hand is a right hand of
    falsehood.

¹²In that our sons are like saplings,
   nourished in their youth,
Our daughters are like a corner pillar,
   carved in the pattern of a palace,
¹³Our storehouses are full
   of provisions of this kind and that kind,
Our flocks number thousands, myriads in our
   fields,
   ¹⁴our cattle are laden,
There is no breach and no going out
   and no cry in our squares:
¹⁵The blessings of the people that has it like this,
   the blessings of the people whose God is
    Yahweh!

## Psalm 145 *Thine is the kingdom, the power and the glory*

An act of praise. David's.

¹I will exalt you, my God, King;
   I will bless your name lastingly and
    permanently.
²Every day I will bless you;
   I will praise your name lastingly and
    permanently.
³Yahweh is great and much to be praised;
   of his greatness there is no searching out.
⁴One generation will extol your works to another
   generation,
   and tell of your mighty acts.
⁵Of the glorious magnificence of your grandeur,
   and your extraordinary deeds, I will talk.
⁶People will speak of the might of your awe-
   inspiring acts;
   your greatness – I will recount it.
⁷They will pour forth commemoration of your
   great goodness,
   and resound at your faithfulness.
⁸Yahweh is gracious and compassionate,
   long-tempered and big in commitment.
⁹Yahweh is good to all;
   his compassion is over all the things he made.

<sup>10</sup>All the things you made will confess you,
Yahweh;
the people committed to you will bless you.
<sup>11</sup>They will talk of the splendour of your reign,
they will speak of your might,
<sup>12</sup>To get his mighty acts acknowledged by human
beings,
the splendour and magnificence of his reign.
<sup>13</sup>Your reign is a reign over all ages,
your rule over generation after generation.

<sup>14</sup>Yahweh supports all who are falling,
and lifts upright all who are bent down.
<sup>15</sup>The eyes of all look to you,
and you give them their food at its time.
<sup>16</sup>You open your hand,
and fill every living thing with your
acceptance.
<sup>17</sup>Yahweh is faithful in all his ways,
committed in all his actions.
<sup>18</sup>Yahweh is near to all who call him,
to all who call him in truth.
<sup>19</sup>He acts with acceptance to the people who live
in awe of him;
he listens to their cry for help and delivers
them.
<sup>20</sup>Yahweh keeps watch over all who are loyal to
him,
but he devastates all the faithless.
<sup>21</sup>My mouth will speak Yahweh's praise;
all flesh will bless his sacred name,
lastingly and permanently.

## Psalm 146 Don't rely on leaders

<sup>1</sup>Praise Yah! –
praise Yahweh, my entire being.
<sup>2</sup>I will praise Yahweh through my life,
I will make music for my God while I exist.
<sup>3</sup>Don't rely on leaders,
on a human being with whom there is no
deliverance.
<sup>4</sup>His breath leaves, he goes back to his ground;
on that day, his deliberations have perished.
<sup>5</sup>The blessings of the one who has Ya'aqob's God
as his help,
whose expectation is of Yahweh his God,
<sup>6</sup>Maker of heavens and earth,
the sea and all that is in them!
The one who keeps faith permanently,
<sup>7</sup>exercising authority for the oppressed,

Giving food to the hungry
– Yahweh frees captives.
<sup>8</sup>Yahweh opens the blind;
Yahweh lifts upright the people who are bent
down.
Yahweh is loyal to the faithful;
<sup>9</sup>Yahweh keeps watch over the resident aliens.
He relieves orphan and widow,
but subverts the way of the faithless.
<sup>10</sup>Yahweh will reign permanently
– your God, Tsiyyon, for generation after
generation.
Praise Yah!

## Psalm 147 Reasons for hope

<sup>1</sup>Praise Yah! –
because making music for our God is good,
because glorifying the one who is our praise is
beautiful.
<sup>2</sup>Yahweh is the builder of Yerushalaim,
he gathers those of Yisra'el who were driven
out.
<sup>3</sup>He's the one who heals the broken in heart,
and bandages their wounds.
<sup>4</sup>He calculates the number of the stars
and pronounces the names of them all,
<sup>5</sup>Our Lord is great and mighty in energy;
of his understanding there is no reckoning.
<sup>6</sup>Yahweh restores the humble,
brings down the faithless to the earth.

<sup>7</sup>Chant for Yahweh with confession,
make music for our God with the guitar.
<sup>8</sup>He's the one who covers the heavens with
clouds,
provides rain for the earth,
makes the mountains grow grass.
<sup>9</sup>He gives their food to cattle,
to the offspring of the raven when they call.
<sup>10</sup>He doesn't delight in the strength of a horse;
he doesn't value the thighs of a person.
<sup>11</sup>Yahweh values people who live in awe of him,
people who put their expectation in his
commitment.

<sup>12</sup>Yerushalaim, extol Yahweh,
praise your God, Tsiyyon,
<sup>13</sup>Because he's made strong the bars of your
gateways,
blessed your children within you.

<sup>14</sup>He gives your territory well-being,
  fills you with the finest of wheat.
<sup>15</sup>He sends his utterance to the earth;
  his word runs quickly.
<sup>16</sup>He gives snow like wool;
  he scatters frost like ash.
<sup>17</sup>He throws his hail like bits of bread;
  who can stand before his ice?
<sup>18</sup>He sends his word and melts them;
  when he blows his breath, water flows.
<sup>19</sup>He tells his words to Ya'aqob,
  his decrees and his rulings to Yisra'el.
<sup>20</sup>He has not done so for any nation;
  his rulings – they don't know them.
  Praise Yah!

## Psalm 148 Reasons for praise

<sup>1</sup>Praise Yah! –
  praise Yahweh from the heavens,
  praise him in the heights.
<sup>2</sup>Praise him, all his envoys,
  praise him all his armies.
<sup>3</sup>Praise him, sun and moon,
  praise him, all bright stars.
<sup>4</sup>Praise him, highest heavens,
  and you water that is above the heavens.
<sup>5</sup>They should praise Yahweh's name,
  because it was he who gave the order so they
    were created.
<sup>6</sup>He set them in place lastingly and
    permanently,
  he gave a decree and it will not pass.

<sup>7</sup>Praise Yahweh from the earth,
  sea monsters and all depths,
<sup>8</sup>Fire and hail, snow and fog,
  hurricane doing his word,
<sup>9</sup>Mountains and all hills,
  fruit trees and all cedars,
<sup>10</sup>Creatures and all cattle,
  things that move and winged birds,
<sup>11</sup>Kings of the earth and all peoples,
  officials and all authorities in the earth,
<sup>12</sup>Young men and young women too,
  old and young too.
<sup>13</sup>They should praise Yahweh's name,
  because his name alone is on high.
His grandeur is over the earth and the heavens,
  <sup>14</sup>but he has lifted up a horn for his people,

A reason for praise for all who are committed to
    him,
  for the Yisra'elites, the people who come near
    him.
  Praise Yah!

## Psalm 149 Dance and slaughter

<sup>1</sup>Praise Yah! –
  sing for Yahweh a new song,
  his praise in the congregation of the committed
    people.
<sup>2</sup>Yisra'el is to rejoice in its maker,
  the children of Tsiyyon are to celebrate their King.
<sup>3</sup>They are to praise his name in dancing;
  tambourine and guitar are to make music for him.
<sup>4</sup>Because Yahweh accepts his people;
  he adorns the humble with deliverance.
<sup>5</sup>The committed people are to exult in their
    splendour,
  they are to resound on their beds,
<sup>6</sup>Acclamations of God in their throat
  and a two-edged sword in their hand,
<sup>7</sup>To execute redress on the nations,
  reproofs on the peoples,
<sup>8</sup>To bind their kings with shackles,
  their nobles with iron chains,
<sup>9</sup>To execute on them the ruling that is written
  – it will be magnificence for all the people
    committed to him.
  Praise Yah!

## Psalm 150 The praise of God, the eternal Creator, is finished and completed

<sup>1</sup>Praise Yah! –
  praise God in his sacred place,
  praise him in his strong firmament.
<sup>2</sup>Praise him in his acts of strength,
  praise him in accordance with his immense
    greatness.
<sup>3</sup>Praise him with the blast of the horn,
  praise him with mandolin and guitar.
<sup>4</sup>Praise him with tambourine and dancing;
  praise him with strings and pipe.
<sup>5</sup>Praise him with cymbals that can be heard,
  praise him with noisy cymbals.
<sup>6</sup>Every breath should praise Yah:
  praise Yah!

# PROVERBS

The book called 'Proverbs' is indeed dominated by one-liners that express a truth, often vividly and concretely, but it is the middle third of the book (chapters 10—22) that is most characterized by these sayings. The first third (chapters 1—9) is a collection of something more like sermonettes that may occupy half a chapter. The last third is a mixture of the two.

They all have in common that they are teaching about life that bases itself on how life itself works out in practice – or at least on how it's supposed to work out. Proverbs doesn't appeal to the exodus or the covenant and it doesn't refer to the Torah or to the Prophets. It does presuppose that the God of Israel is the real God (it uses the name Yahweh) and it presupposes that life must always be lived within the framework of faithfulness and uprightness. But while it takes that framework for granted, it then works empirically. It fits with this feature of Proverbs that it is a part of the First Testament that has close parallels with works we know from other Middle Eastern cultures (the 'Thirty Sayings' in chapters 22—24 parallel an Egyptian set of Thirty Sayings). Proverbs thus recognizes that God has not left the world as a whole without any awareness of his ways, of right and wrong, and of how life works. Such awarenesses are hardwired into humanity.

The proverbs are 'Solomon's', though the implication is not that he wrote them. Indeed, you could almost say that nobody 'writes' proverbs – at least the one-liners. They just happen. Solomon is the patron of the worldly wisdom that appears in Proverbs (and in Ecclesiastes and the Song of Songs) as David is the patron of psalmody. If we wonder about the background of the material in Proverbs, then three contexts are worth bearing in mind.

First, much of the material presents itself as the teaching that parents offer their children. While this image may have become a figure of speech, the family is indeed the natural first context in which people are encouraged to grow up from naïvety to smartness. Such teaching in Proverbs would ultimately go back to way before Solomon's day. One can imagine its teaching in the context of the life of the clan in Genesis. And the story of Joseph illustrates a number of the themes of Proverbs.

Second, scattered through the book are a number of observations about kings and how to relate to them, and that material suggests another context in which the material could naturally be used: the training of young men and women for the administration. Beyond the explicit references to the king there are many other references to wise speech, the dynamics of decision-making, and self-control that would be important for people involved in the administration.

Third, the opening part of the book also includes some reflection on the nature of creation, of God's involvement in creation and of the way creation reflects something of God. That reflection makes one think in terms of the syllabus for theological education in Israel. By New Testament times the 'scribes' were certainly people who had been involved in theological education. We don't know how it developed in Israel, but it wouldn't be surprising if Proverbs was a set text in theological schools when they came into being.

The opening chapters speak of Smartness as a woman who is its embodiment, and the last verses of the book comprise a description of the resourceful woman. It occupies 22 lines, one line for each letter of the Hebrew alphabet, so that it describes the resourceful woman from A to Z. The poem shows how extensive were the opportunities for a woman in Israel – in this case, a woman who is the mistress of a household, but she is active outside the house and not just inside. Alongside the metaphor of Ms Smartness and the picture of the resourceful woman is the metaphor of Ms Stupidity and the picture of the woman who can lead a man astray. In the Torah, the point would be that sexual dallying and adultery are wrong. In Proverbs, the point is that they are also really stupid.

*Knowledge, ethics and spirituality*

**1** Aphorisms of Shelomoh [Solomon] ben David king of Yisra'el:

²So as to know smartness and discipline,
  to understand words that express understanding,
³To get discipline so as to act with insight,
  faithfulness, the exercise of authority, and
    uprightness,
⁴To give shrewdness to the naïve,
  knowledge and strategy to the youth,
⁵So that the smart person may listen and increase
  in his grasp,
  the understanding may acquire skill,
⁶So as to understand an aphorism and a parable,
  the words of the smart and their conundrums:
⁷The first principle of knowledge is awe for
  Yahweh;
  dense people despise smartness and discipline.

⁸Listen to your father's discipline, son,
  don't leave your mother's instruction,
⁹Because they're a graceful garland for your head,
  a chain for your neck.
¹⁰Son, if wrongdoers entice you, don't be willing,
  ¹¹if they say 'Go with us.
Let's lie in wait for blood,
  let's ambush someone free of guilt, for nothing.
¹²Let's swallow them alive, like She'ol –
  whole, like people going down to the Cistern.
¹³We'll find every sort of valuable riches,
  we'll fill our houses with spoil.
¹⁴Let your lot fall among us;
  there'll be one purse for us all.'
¹⁵Son, don't go on the way with them;
  keep your foot from their trail.
¹⁶Because their feet run to bad dealing,
  they hurry to shed blood.
¹⁷Because it's for nothing that a net is spread
  before the eyes of any owner of wings.
¹⁸But those people lie in wait for their own blood,
  they ambush their own lives.
¹⁹Such are the paths of everyone who gets
  wrongful gain;
  it takes the life of its owners.

*The naïve, the arrogant, the dimwit*

²⁰Smartness resounds in the open streets,
  in the squares she gives her voice.

²¹At the head of the noisy places,
  at the entrances of the gateways,
  in the town she says her words.

²²'How long will you naïve people be loyal to
  naïvety?
  – arrogant people desire arrogance for
    themselves.
Dimwits are hostile to knowledge;
  ²³do turn back at my rebuke.
Here, I will pour out my spirit to you,
  I will let you know my words.
²⁴Since I called but you refused me,
  I stretched out my hand but there was no one
    heeding,
²⁵You've spurned all my counsel,
  and you weren't willing for my rebuke,
²⁶I myself too will make fun of your disaster;
  I shall ridicule when what you dread comes,
²⁷When what you dread comes like devastation,
  and your calamity arrives like a tempest,
  when trouble and disaster come upon you.
²⁸Then they'll call me but I won't answer,
  they'll look urgently for me but they won't find
    me,
²⁹Because of the fact that they were hostile to
  acknowledgement,
  didn't choose awe for Yahweh.
³⁰They weren't willing for my counsel,
  they spurned every rebuke of mine.
³¹They'll eat the fruit of their way,
  they'll have their fill of their own counsels.
³²Because the turning back of the naïve will kill
  them,
  and the ease of dimwits will obliterate them.
³³But the person who listens to me will dwell in
  confidence,
  safe from the dread of bad fortune.'

*The household that goes down to death*

**2** Son, if you take the things I say,
  hide up my orders with you,
²Getting your ear to heed smartness,
  inclining your mind to understanding,
³If you indeed call to understanding,
  give your voice to understanding,
⁴If you seek it like silver,
  search for it like treasure,
⁵Then you'll understand awe for Yahweh,
  you'll find acknowledgement of God.

⁶Because Yahweh gives smartness;
  from his mouth come acknowledgement and
  understanding.
⁷He hides up adeptness for the upright,
  being a shield for people who walk with
  integrity,
⁸Preserving the paths of authority,
  he keeps watch on the way of people
  committed to him.
⁹Then you'll understand faithfulness and
  authority,
  and uprightness, every good track.
¹⁰Because smartness will come into your mind,
  acknowledgement be lovely to your entire
  being.
¹¹Strategy will keep watch over you,
  understanding will preserve you,
¹²Rescuing you from the way of the bad person,
  from the one speaking things that are crooked,
¹³People who abandon upright paths,
  going in the ways of darkness,
¹⁴Who rejoice to deal badly,
  celebrate the crooked actions of the bad
  person,
¹⁵People whose paths are crooked,
  who are deviant in their tracks;
¹⁶Rescuing you from the other woman,
  from the alien woman who is slippery in the
  things she says,
¹⁷Who abandons the partner of her youth,
  puts out of mind her pact with God.
¹⁸Because her household goes down to death,
  her tracks to the ghosts.
¹⁹Anyone who comes to her doesn't come back;
  he doesn't reach the paths of life;
²⁰In order that you may walk in the way of good
  people,
  keep the paths of the faithful.
²¹Because the upright will dwell in the country,
  the people of integrity will be left in it.
²²But the faithless will be cut off from the
  country,
  the people who break faith will be ripped up
  from it.

## Commitment, truthfulness, trust

**3** Son, don't put my instruction out of mind;
    your mind is to observe my orders,
²Because length of days and years of life
  and well-being is what they will add to you.

³Commitment and truthfulness must not
  abandon you;
  bind them on your neck, write them on the
  tablet of your mind.
⁴Thus find grace and good insight,
  in the eyes of God and of human beings.
⁵Rely on Yahweh with all your mind,
  don't lean on your own understanding.
⁶In all your ways acknowledge him,
  and he himself will keep your paths straight.
⁷Don't become smart in your own eyes;
  live in awe of Yahweh and depart from what's
  bad.
⁸It will be health for your body,
  a tonic for your bones.
⁹Honour Yahweh with your riches,
  with the first of all your yield.
¹⁰Your barns will fill with plenty,
  your vats will overflow with new wine.
¹¹Don't reject Yahweh's discipline, son,
  don't be dismayed at his reproof.
¹²Because the one Yahweh is loyal to, he reproves,
  just like a father the son he accepts.

## The tree of life

¹³The blessings of the person who finds
  smartness,
  the person who obtains understanding!
¹⁴Because her profit is better than the profit of
  silver,
  her yield than pale gold.
¹⁵She's more valuable than rubies;
  nothing you delight in equals her.
¹⁶Length of days is in her right hand;
  in her left hand wealth and splendour.
¹⁷Her ways are lovely ones;
  all her trails are well-being.
¹⁸She's a tree of life to people who take strong hold
  of her;
  one who gets hold of her is blessed.
¹⁹It was by smartness that Yahweh founded the
  earth;
  he established the heavens by understanding.
²⁰By his knowledge the deeps split,
  and the skies would drop dew.

²¹Son, they must not deviate from your eyes;
  preserve adeptness and strategy.
²²They will be life for your whole person,
  and grace for your neck.

<sup>23</sup>Then you'll go your way with confidence,
  and you won't hit your foot.
<sup>24</sup>If you lie down, you won't be fearful;
  you'll lie down and your sleep will be pleasant.
<sup>25</sup>You won't be afraid of a sudden terror
  or of the devastation of the faithless when it
    comes,
<sup>26</sup>Because Yahweh will be your assurance,
  and will keep your foot from being caught.

<sup>27</sup>Don't withhold good from the one to whom it's
    due
  when it's in your hand to act.
<sup>28</sup>Don't say to your neighbour, 'Go, and come back,
  I'll give it tomorrow', when it's with you.
<sup>29</sup>Don't devise something bad against your
    neighbour,
  when he's living with a feeling of security with
    you.
<sup>30</sup>Don't argue with someone for nothing,
  if he hasn't dealt you something bad.
<sup>31</sup>Don't be jealous of a violent individual,
  and don't choose any of his ways.
<sup>32</sup>Because a deviant person is offensive to Yahweh;
  his confidences are with upright people.
<sup>33</sup>Yahweh's curse is on the household of the
    faithless person,
  but he blesses the home of faithful people.
<sup>34</sup>If he himself behaves arrogantly to the arrogant,
  to the humble he gives grace.
<sup>35</sup>Smart people will have splendour as their
    domain,
  but dimwits take up slighting.

## On discipline

**4** Listen to a father's discipline, sons,
  heed, so as to acknowledge understanding.
<sup>2</sup>Because I give you a good grasp;
  don't abandon my instruction.
<sup>3</sup>Because I was a son to my father,
  tender and the only one before my mother.
<sup>4</sup>He instructed me and said to me,
  'Your mind is to take hold of my words;
  keep my orders and you'll live.'

<sup>5</sup>Acquire smartness, acquire understanding;
  don't put it out of mind and don't turn away
    from the sayings of my mouth.
<sup>6</sup>Don't abandon her and she'll keep you;
  be loyal to her and she'll protect you.

<sup>7</sup>The first principle of smartness is, acquire
    smartness,
  and among all the things you acquire, acquire
    understanding.
<sup>8</sup>Exalt her and she'll elevate you;
  she'll honour you when you embrace her.
<sup>9</sup>She'll give your head a graceful garland,
  she'll present you with a glorious diadem.
<sup>10</sup>Listen, son, and take my sayings,
  and the years of your life will be many.
<sup>11</sup>I instruct you in the way of smartness,
  I direct you in upright tracks.
<sup>12</sup>As you go, your step will not be in straits;
  if you run, you won't collapse.
<sup>13</sup>Take a strong hold of discipline, don't slacken
    hold,
  preserve it, because it's your life.
<sup>14</sup>Don't come on to the path of faithless people,
  don't walk in the way of people who deal
    badly.
<sup>15</sup>Avoid it, don't pass through it;
  turn from it and pass by.
<sup>16</sup>Because they won't sleep if they don't act badly;
  they're robbed of their sleep if they don't make
    someone collapse.
<sup>17</sup>Because they eat bread that comes from
    faithlessness
  and drink wine that comes from violent acts.
<sup>18</sup>But the path of the faithful is like dawn light,
  getting more light until the establishing of the
    day.
<sup>19</sup>The way of faithless people is very darkness;
  they don't acknowledge how they will
    collapse.

## On resisting temptation

<sup>20</sup>Son, heed my words,
  bend your ear to the things I say.
<sup>21</sup>They must not deviate from your eyes;
  keep them within your mind.
<sup>22</sup>Because they are life to the people who find
    them,
  health for one's whole body.
<sup>23</sup>Above everything that you keep watch over,
    preserve your mind,
  because from it things go out into life.
<sup>24</sup>Keep away from you crookedness of mouth;
  put deviousness of lips far away.
<sup>25</sup>Your eyes must turn forward,
  your eyelids be straight ahead of you.

²⁶Weigh the track for your foot;
all your ways must be firm.
²⁷Don't turn right or left;
keep your foot away from evil.

5 Heed my smartness, son,
bend your ear to my understanding,
²So as to keep strategy,
and so that your lips may protect knowledge.
³Because the lips of an alien woman drip honey,
her mouth is smoother than oil.
⁴But her end is as bitter as gall,
sharp as a two-edged sword.
⁵Her feet go down to death,
her steps take hold of She'ol.
⁶So that she doesn't weigh the path to life,
her tracks wander, though she doesn't
acknowledge it.
⁷So now, sons, listen to me,
and don't depart from the sayings of my
mouth.
⁸Keep your way far from her,
don't go near the entrance to her house,
⁹So that you don't give your wealth to other
people,
your years to someone cruel,
¹⁰So that strangers don't eat their fill of your
energy,
and [the fruit of] your pains are in the house of
a foreigner.
¹¹You'll groan at your end,
when your flesh and body are finished.
¹²You'll say, 'How I was hostile to discipline,
and my mind spurned rebuke.
¹³I didn't listen to my instructors' voice,
I did not bend my ear to my teachers.
¹⁴I was soon in every kind of bad situation
in the middle of the assembled congregation.'

## Crazy for love

¹⁵Drink water from your cistern,
running water from within your well.
¹⁶Should your fountains gush outside,
your streams of water in the squares?
¹⁷They should be for you alone,
so that there's none for strangers with you.
¹⁸May your spring be blessed,
may you rejoice in the wife of your youth,
¹⁹She's a doe to love,
a graceful deer.

Her breasts should drench you all the time;
be crazy on her love continually.
²⁰Why be crazy on a stranger, son,
and embrace the arms of a foreigner?
²¹Because an individual's ways are in front of
Yahweh's eyes;
he weighs all his tracks.
²²His wayward acts capture the faithless person;
he gets taken hold of by the ropes of his
wrongdoing.
²³That person dies for lack of discipline;
he's crazy on the abundance of his denseness.

6 Son, if you've given a guarantee for your
neighbour,
clapped the palms of your hands for a stranger,
²Trapped yourself by the sayings of your mouth,
caught yourself by the sayings of your mouth:
³Do this then,
son, and rescue yourself.
When you've come into the palm of your
neighbour's hand,
go, lower yourself, press your neighbour.
⁴Don't give sleep to your eyes
or slumber to your eyelids.
⁵Rescue yourself like a gazelle from the hand,
like a bird from the hand, of a hunter.

⁶Go to the ant, you sloth,
look at its ways and get smart.
⁷One that has no commander,
overseer, or ruler,
⁸Prepares its bread in summer,
gathers its food at harvest.
⁹How long will you lie down, you sloth,
when will you get up from your sleep?
¹⁰A little sleep, a little slumber,
a little folding of the hands to lie down,
¹¹And your destitution will come like someone
walking about,
your want like someone with a shield.

¹²Someone who is a scoundrel, an evil individual,
going with a crooked mouth,
¹³Winking his eyes, speaking with his feet,
pointing with his fingers,
¹⁴Crooked actions in his mind, devising
something bad;
all the time he lets loose disputes.
¹⁵Therefore suddenly his disaster will come on
him,
in an instant he'll break, with no healing.

## *Jealousy and wrath*

¹⁶These are six things Yahweh is hostile to,
  seven offensive to his entire being:
¹⁷Haughty eyes, a false tongue,
  and hands shedding the blood of someone free
    of guilt,
¹⁸A mind devising troublesome intentions,
  feet hurrying to run to something bad,
¹⁹Someone who breathes out lies as a false
    witness,
  and someone who lets loose disputes between
    brothers.

²⁰Son, observe your father's order,
  don't leave your mother's instruction.
²¹Fasten them into your mind continually,
  bind them on to your neck.
²²When you're going about, it will lead you,
  when you lie down it will keep watch over you,
  when you wake up, it will talk to you.
²³Because an order is a lamp and instruction is a
    light,
  and the rebuke that disciplines is a way to life,
²⁴To keep you from the woman who is bad,
  from the smoothness of the tongue of an alien
    woman.
²⁵Don't desire her beauty in your heart;
  she must not take you with her eyelids.
²⁶Because for a woman who's a whore,
  [the cost is] as much as a loaf of bread.
But a man's wife,
  she'll capture your dear life.
²⁷Can someone scoop up fire into the fold of his
    coat,
  and his clothes will not burn?
²⁸If someone walks about on coals,
  will his feet not burn?
²⁹So it is with one who has sex with his
    neighbour's wife;
  no one who touches her will go free.
³⁰People don't despise a thief when he steals
  to fill his appetite, when he's hungry.
³¹But if he's found out, he'll make good sevenfold;
  he'll give all the riches of his household.
³²One who commits adultery with a woman is
    lacking in sense;
  one who does it is devastating himself.
³³He'll find injury and slighting;
  his reviling will not wipe away.
³⁴Because jealousy means a man's wrath;
  he won't spare on the day of redress.

³⁵He won't show regard for any compensation;
  he won't agree, even when you offer a big bribe.

## *Let me tell you a story*

**7** Son, keep my words,
  store up my orders with you.
²Keep my orders and live,
  and my instruction as the apple of your eye.
³Fasten them on your fingers,
  write them on the tablet of your mind.
⁴Say to smartness, 'You're my sister',
  and call understanding 'Friend',
⁵To keep you from the alien woman,
  the foreign woman who is smooth in the things
    she says.

⁶Because through the window of my house,
  by way of my lattice, I looked out,
⁷And I saw among the naïve, I considered among
    the young men,
  a youth lacking in sense.
⁸He was passing along the street by her corner,
  he was walking the way to her house,
⁹At dusk, in the evening of the day,
  at the approach of night and darkness.
¹⁰There, a woman to meet him,
  dressed as a whore, restrained in heart.
¹¹She's noisy and defiant;
  her feet don't stay in her house.
¹²Now in the street, now in the squares,
  and by every corner, she lies in wait.
¹³She takes strong hold of him and kisses him,
  makes her face forceful and says to him,
¹⁴'Though well-being sacrifices were incumbent
    on me,
  today I've made good my pledges.
¹⁵Therefore I've come out to meet you,
  to look urgently for your face, and I've found
    you.
¹⁶I've spread my couch with coverlets,
  coloured Egyptian linens.
¹⁷I've perfumed my bed,
  with myrrh, aloes and cinnamon.
¹⁸Come on, let's drench ourselves in love until
    morning,
  let's exult in lovemaking.
¹⁹Because the man isn't here in his house,
  he's gone on a journey a long way.
²⁰He's taken a bag of silver in his hand;
  he'll come home at the middle of the month.'

## The story has a solemn end

²¹She's turned him away with the abundance of
   her grasp of things,
   with the smoothness of her lips she drives him.
²²All at once he's going after her,
   like an ox that comes to the slaughter,
Like a dense person bounding into constraint,
   ²³until an arrow pierces his liver,
Like a bird rushing into a trap,
   when it doesn't know it will be at the cost of
      its life.

²⁴So now listen to me, sons,
   heed the sayings of my mouth.
²⁵Your mind isn't to turn into her ways;
   don't wander into her trails.
²⁶Because she's made many fall, run through;
   numerous are all the ones killed by her.
²⁷Her house is a major road to She'ol,
   going down to death's rooms.

**8** Smartness calls, doesn't she;
   understanding gives her voice.
²At the highest point along the trail,
   at the crossroads, she takes her stand.
³At the side of the gateways at the township entrance,
   at the way in to the entrances, she resounds.
⁴"People, I call to you,
   my voice is to humankind.
⁵Understand shrewdness, you naïve;
   understand sense, you dimwits.
⁶Listen, because I speak honourable things;
   the opening of my lips, upright things.
⁷Because my palate murmurs truth;
   faithlessness is offensive to my lips.
⁸All the sayings of my mouth are characterized by
      faithfulness;
   there's nothing crooked or twisted in them.
⁹All of them are straight to someone of
      understanding,
   upright to people who have found knowledge.
¹⁰Take my discipline and not silver,
   knowledge more than choice pale gold.
¹¹Because smartness is better than rubies,
   and no delights can compare with her.

## Let me tell you my story

¹²I, smartness, dwell with shrewdness;
   I find knowledge of strategies.

¹³Awe for God
   is hostility to what is bad.
Majesty and majesticness and the bad way,
   and a crooked mouth, I am hostile to.
¹⁴Mine are counsel and adeptness;
   I am understanding, I have strength.
¹⁵By me kings reign
   and rulers decree what is faithful;
¹⁶By me officials govern,
   leaders, all who exercise authority faithfully.
¹⁷I am loyal to people who are loyal to me;
   people who look urgently for me find me.
¹⁸Wealth and splendour are with me,
   enduring riches and faithfulness.
¹⁹My fruit is better than pale gold, even than fine
      gold,
   my yield than choice silver.
²⁰I walk about in the way of faithfulness,
   among the trails of authority,
²¹Giving a domain to people who are loyal with
      substance,
   and I fill their treasuries.

²²Yahweh acquired me at the beginning of his
      way,
   before his actions of old.
²³Long ago I was formed,
   at the beginning, at earth's origins.
²⁴When there were no deeps I was birthed,
   when there were no springs heavy with water.
²⁵Before the mountains were settled,
   before the hills I was birthed,
²⁶While he had not yet made the earth and
      fields,
   and the first of the world's lumps of earth.
²⁷When he established the heavens, I was there,
   when he marked out the horizon on the face of
      the deep,
²⁸When he made the skies above firm,
   when the deep's fountains were vigorous,
²⁹When he set its limit for the sea,
   so that its water might not transgress his
      bidding.
When he marked out earth's foundations,
   ³⁰I was a child by his side.
I was full of pleasure day by day,
   having fun before him all the time,
³¹Having fun in his world, in his earth,
   and full of pleasure in humanity.

³²So now, sons, listen to me:
   the blessings of people who keep my ways!

<sup>33</sup>Listen to discipline and become smart, don't put
    it out of mind;
    <sup>34</sup>the blessings of the person who listens to me,
Seeking my gateways keenly day by day,
    keeping watch at the posts of my entrances!
<sup>35</sup>Because one who finds me finds life,
    and obtains acceptance from Yahweh.
<sup>36</sup>But one who wrongs me does violence to his
    life;
    all who are hostile to me are loyal to death.'

## The two voices

**9** Smartness has built her house;
    she's hewn her seven pillars.
<sup>2</sup>She's slaughtered her animals, mixed her wine,
    indeed set her table.
<sup>3</sup>She's sent her girls so she can call,
    on the township's high elevations,
<sup>4</sup>'Whoever is naïve should turn aside here';
    one who is lacking in sense, she says to him,
<sup>5</sup>'Come, eat my bread,
    drink of the wine I've mixed.
<sup>6</sup>Abandon naïvety and live,
    walk in the way of understanding.'

<sup>7</sup>One who disciplines an arrogant person gets
    slighting for himself;
    one who reproves someone faithless, a hurt for
    himself.
<sup>8</sup>Don't reprove an arrogant person or he'll be
    hostile to you;
    reprove someone smart and he'll be loyal to
    you.
<sup>9</sup>Give something to someone smart and he'll get
    yet smarter;
    make something known to a faithful person
    and he'll increase in his grasp.
<sup>10</sup>Awe for Yahweh is the beginning of smartness;
    understanding lies in acknowledgement of the
    Sacred One.
<sup>11</sup>Because through me your days will be many
    and the years of your life will increase.
<sup>12</sup>If you're smart, you're smart for your benefit;
    if you're arrogant, you'll carry it alone.

<sup>13</sup>The Dimwit Woman is noisy;
    naïvety, and she doesn't acknowledge
    anything.
<sup>14</sup>She sits at the entrance of her house,
    on a seat at the township's heights,

<sup>15</sup>Calling to passers-by, people making their paths
    straight:
    <sup>16</sup>'Whoever is naïve should turn aside here.'
The person who is lacking in sense, she says to
    him,
    <sup>17</sup>'Stolen water is sweet, a secret meal is lovely.'
<sup>18</sup>He doesn't acknowledge that the ghosts are
    there;
    the people she calls are in the depths of She'ol.

## The mouth of the faithful is fruitful

**10** Shelomoh's aphorisms.
A smart son rejoices a father,
    but a dimwit son is a mother's sorrow.
<sup>2</sup>Treasures that come from faithlessness don't
    profit,
    but faithfulness rescues from death.
<sup>3</sup>Yahweh doesn't let the faithful person go
    hungry,
    but he thwarts the malice of faithless people.
<sup>4</sup>A lazy fist makes destitute,
    but the hand of determined people makes
    wealthy.
<sup>5</sup>One who gathers in summer is an insightful son;
    one who sleeps in harvest is a disgraceful son.
<sup>6</sup>There are blessings on the head of the faithful
    person,
    but the mouth of faithless people conceals
    violence.
<sup>7</sup>The commemoration of the faithful person
    becomes a blessing,
    but the name of faithless people rots.
<sup>8</sup>One who is smart of mind accepts orders,
    but one dense of lips comes to ruin.
<sup>9</sup>One who walks in integrity walks in confidence,
    but one who makes his ways crooked gets
    known.
<sup>10</sup>One who winks an eye gives hurt,
    and one dense of lips comes to ruin.
<sup>11</sup>The mouth of a faithful person is a fountain of
    life,
    but the mouth of faithless people conceals
    violence.
<sup>12</sup>Hostility stirs up disputes,
    but loyalty covers over all acts of rebellion.
<sup>13</sup>Smartness is found on the lips of the person of
    understanding,
    but there's a club on the back of one who is
    lacking in sense.

<sup>14</sup>Smart people store up knowledge,
 but the mouth of a dense person is ruin
  drawing near.
<sup>15</sup>The riches of the wealthy person are his strong
 township;
 their destitution is the ruin of the poor.
<sup>16</sup>The earnings of the faithful person make for
 life;
 the yield of the faithless person makes for
  wrongdoing.

## The dimwit's real fun

<sup>17</sup>One who keeps correction is on the path to
 life,
 one who abandons reproof goes astray.
<sup>18</sup>Someone who conceals hostility with false
 lips,
 and the one who issues charges, he's a dimwit.
<sup>19</sup>Where there's an abundance of words, rebellion
 doesn't leave off,
 but one who holds back his lips is insightful.
<sup>20</sup>The tongue of a faithful person is choice silver;
 the mind of faithless people is worth little.
<sup>21</sup>The lips of a faithful person pasture many,
 but dense people die for lack of sense.
<sup>22</sup>Yahweh's blessing – it makes wealthy,
 and painful toil doesn't add to it.
<sup>23</sup>Real fun for a dimwit is implementing a
 deliberate wickedness,
 but for someone of understanding, it's
  smartness.
<sup>24</sup>The dread of a faithless person – it comes to
 him,
 but the longing of faithful people is granted.
<sup>25</sup>When a tempest passes, the faithless person isn't
 there,
 but the faithful person is a lasting foundation.
<sup>26</sup>Like vinegar to the teeth, like smoke to the
 eyes,
 so is the lazy person to the people who sent
  him.
<sup>27</sup>Awe for Yahweh prolongs days,
 but the years of the faithless shorten.
<sup>28</sup>The waiting of faithful people will be rejoicing,
 but the hope of faithless people will perish.
<sup>29</sup>Yahweh is a stronghold for someone of integrity
 in his way,
 but the ruin of people who devise trouble.
<sup>30</sup>The faithful person will never slip,
 but the faithless will not dwell in the country.

<sup>31</sup>The mouth of the faithful person is fruitful with
 smartness,
 but the crooked tongue will be cut off.
<sup>32</sup>The lips of the faithful person know what finds
 acceptance,
 but the mouth of the faithless, things that are
  crooked.

## On lying scales

**11** Lying scales are an offence to Yahweh,
 and a perfect weight is what he accepts.
<sup>2</sup>Assertiveness comes, and slighting comes,
 but with modest people there is smartness.
<sup>3</sup>The integrity of the upright guides them,
 but the deviousness of people who break faith
  destroys them.
<sup>4</sup>Riches don't avail on the day of an outburst [of
 wrath],
 but faithfulness rescues from death.
<sup>5</sup>The faithfulness of a man of integrity makes his
 way straight,
 but the faithless person falls by his faithlessness.
<sup>6</sup>The faithfulness of the upright rescues them,
 but people who break faith are captured
  through malice.
<sup>7</sup>At the death of a faithless person hope perishes,
 and waiting for riches perishes.
<sup>8</sup>The faithful person pulls out from pressure,
 and the faithless person comes in in place of
  him.
<sup>9</sup>With the mouth the impious person devastates
 his neighbour,
 but through the knowledge of the faithful,
  people pull out [from trouble].
<sup>10</sup>When things are good for the faithful, the
 township exults;
 when the faithless perish, there is resounding.
<sup>11</sup>By the blessing of the upright a township rises
 up,
 but by the mouth of the faithless it's torn
  down.
<sup>12</sup>One who despises his neighbour lacks sense,
 and a person of understanding keeps quiet.
<sup>13</sup>Someone who goes about as a slanderer reveals
 a confidence,
 but someone trustworthy of spirit conceals a
  thing.
<sup>14</sup>When there's no steering, a people falls,
 but deliverance comes with an abundance of
  counsellors.

¹⁵A bad person will do badly when he stands
  surety for a stranger,
  but someone hostile to people clapping hands
  will be secure.

## The gold ring in a pig's nose

¹⁶A woman of grace takes hold of splendour,
  and violent men take hold of wealth.
¹⁷A person of commitment deals to himself;
  someone cruel troubles his own self.
¹⁸One who is faithless makes a false profit,
  but someone who sows faithfulness,
  a trustworthy wage.
¹⁹One established in faithfulness goes to life,
  but one who pursues what is bad, to his
  death.
²⁰The crooked in mind are an offence to Yahweh,
  but people of integrity in their way are the ones
  he accepts.
²¹Hand to hand, the bad person will not go free
  of guilt,
  but the offspring of the faithful will escape.
²²A gold ring in a pig's nose
  is a beautiful woman turning aside from
  discretion.
²³The longing of the faithful is only good;
  the hope of the faithless is for an outburst
  [of wrath].
²⁴There is one who scatters and gets still more,
  and one who holds back beyond what is
  upright, only to be in want.
²⁵A person of blessing will be enriched,
  and someone who drenches – he'll also be
  drenched.
²⁶One who withholds grain – the people will curse
  him,
  but blessing will be on the head of one who
  sells.
²⁷Someone who urgently looks for what is good
  seeks acceptance,
  but the one who looks for what is bad, it comes
  on him.
²⁸One who relies on his wealth – he falls,
  but the faithful flourish like foliage.
²⁹Someone who troubles his household gets wind
  as his domain,
  and someone dense is a servant to one who is
  smart of mind.
³⁰The fruit of a faithful person is a tree of life,
  but a smart person takes lives.

³¹If someone who is faithful on earth is made good,
  how much more the faithless person and the
  wrongdoer.

## The one who knows his animal's appetite

**12** One who befriends correction befriends
     knowledge,
  but one who is hostile to reproof is stupid.
²One who is good obtains acceptance from
  Yahweh,
  but he regards a man of strategies as faithless.
³A person cannot be established through
  faithlessness,
  but the root of the faithful will not slip.
⁴A resourceful woman is her husband's crown,
  but a shameful one is like decay in his bones.
⁵The intentions of the faithful are the [proper]
  exercise of authority;
  the steering of the faithless is deceit.
⁶The words of the faithless are a deadly ambush,
  but the mouth of the upright rescues them.
⁷Overturn the faithless and they're not there,
  but the household of the faithful stands.
⁸On the basis of his insight an individual is praised,
  but one who's crooked in mind comes to
  contempt.
⁹Better one who is slighted but is his own servant
  than one who looks honourable but lacks
  bread.
¹⁰A faithful person knows his animal's appetite,
  but the compassion of the faithless is cruel.
¹¹One who serves his land will have his fill of
  bread,
  but one who pursues empty things lacks sense.
¹²The faithless person desires what is a trap for
  bad people,
  but the root of the faithful gives.
¹³In the rebellion of lips is a snare for a bad
  person,
  but a faithful person gets out of pressure.
¹⁴From the fruit of an individual's mouth he has
  his fill of good things,
  and the dealing of someone's hands comes back
  to him.

## Silence, words and smartness

¹⁵The way of a dense person is upright in his eyes,
  but the smart person listens to counsel.

¹⁶A dense person – his vexation makes itself
   known at the time,
   but a shrewd person conceals a slighting.
¹⁷Someone who testifies truthfully tells things
   with faithfulness,
   but a false witness with deceit.
¹⁸There is one who rants like sword-thrusts,
   but the tongue of smart people is a healing.
¹⁹A truthful lip is established permanently,
   but a false tongue lasts for the blink of an eye.
²⁰Deceit is in the mind of people who devise
   something bad,
   but for people who counsel well-being, there is
   rejoicing.
²¹No trouble befalls the faithful person,
   but the faithless are full of bad fortune.
²²False lips are an offence to Yahweh;
   people who act truthfully are the ones he accepts.
²³A shrewd person conceals knowledge,
   but the mind of dimwits calls out denseness.
²⁴The hand of determined people rules,
   but [someone characterized by] laziness will
   belong to a workforce.
²⁵Anxiety in someone's mind weighs it down,
   but a good word makes it rejoice.
²⁶A faithful person shows his neighbour the path,
   but the way of the faithless leads them astray.
²⁷Laziness will not roast game,
   but the riches of a person are valuable –
   determined.
²⁸On the path of faithfulness there is life,
   and on the way of its trail, no death.

## Hope deferred sickens the heart

**13** A smart son [listens] to a father's
   discipline,
   but someone arrogant doesn't listen to a
   reprimand.
²From the fruit of his mouth a person eats what
   is good,
   but the appetite of the people who break faith is
   for violence.
³One who preserves his mouth preserves his life,
   but one who opens his lips wide – ruin is his.
⁴The lazy person – his appetite desires, but there
   is nothing;
   the appetite of the determined is enriched.
⁵A faithful person is hostile to a lying word,
   but a faithless person stinks and comes to
   confounding.

⁶Faithfulness preserves [the person of] integrity
   in the way,
   but faithlessness overturns a wrong[doer].
⁷There is one who acts wealthy but there's
   nothing,
   one who acts destitute but there's much riches.
⁸The ransom for someone's life is his wealth,
   but one who is destitute doesn't listen to a
   reprimand.
⁹The light of the faithful rejoices,
   but the lamp of the faithless goes out.
¹⁰Only by means of assertiveness does someone
   produce strife;
   smartness is with people who take counsel.
¹¹Riches gained from emptiness diminish,
   but someone who gathers by hand makes it
   grow.
¹²Hope deferred sickens the heart,
   but longing that comes about is a tree of life.

## The company you keep

¹³One who despises a word, it will be ruinous for
   him,
   but one who lives in awe of an order, he'll be
   made good.
¹⁴The instruction of a smart person is a fountain
   of life,
   for departing from deadly snares.
¹⁵Good insight gives grace,
   but the way of people who break faith is
   strong.
¹⁶Every shrewd person acts with knowledge,
   but a dimwit spreads denseness.
¹⁷A faithless envoy falls into bad fortune,
   but a trustworthy emissary – healing.
¹⁸Destitution and slighting – one who rejects
   discipline,
   but one who keeps watch on correction is
   honoured.
¹⁹Longing that comes about is pleasant to the
   appetite,
   but departing from bad ways is an offence to
   the dimwit.
²⁰One who walks with smart people gets smart,
   but the friend of dimwits does badly.
²¹Bad fortune pursues wrongdoers,
   but good fortune makes good to the faithful.
²²A good man gives a domain to grandchildren,
   but the resources of the wrongdoer are stored
   up for the faithful person.

²³The fallow ground of the destitute – abundance of food,
  but it's swept away for want of the exercise of authority.
²⁴Someone who holds back his club is hostile to his son,
  but one who loves him gets him up early with discipline.
²⁵The faithful person eats to fill his appetite,
  but the stomach of the faithless lacks.

## Even in laughter a heart may hurt

**14** The smartest of women builds her house,
  but denseness tears it down with her own hands.
²One who lives in awe of Yahweh walks in uprightness,
  but one who despises him is deviant in his ways.
³In the mouth of the dense person there is a shoot of majesty,
  but the lips of smart people keep watch over them.
⁴When there are no oxen the stall is clean,
  but there's abundance of yield through the energy of a bull.
⁵A trustworthy witness doesn't lie,
  but a false witness testifies lies.
⁶Someone arrogant seeks smartness and there is none,
  but knowledge is easy for the person of understanding.
⁷Go at a distance from the dimwit;
  you won't have known knowledgeable lips.
⁸The smartness of someone shrewd means understanding his way,
  but the denseness of dimwits is deception.
⁹Dense people are arrogant about reparation,
  but between upright people there is acceptance.
¹⁰The heart knows its own bitterness,
  and in its rejoicing a stranger doesn't share.
¹¹The house of the faithless will be devastated,
  but the tent of the upright will flourish.
¹²There is a way that is upright before someone,
  but its end is the ways of death.
¹³Even in laughter a heart may hurt,
  and rejoicing – its end may be grief.
¹⁴Someone who turns backwards in heart will be full from his ways,
  and a good person from his deeds.

¹⁵A naïve person trusts in anything,
  but someone shrewd understands his step.
¹⁶A smart person is afraid and turns aside from what is bad,
  but a dimwit rages and is confident.

## Oppressing the poor reviles their maker

¹⁷One who is short-tempered will do dense things,
  and a person of strategies will meet with hostility.
¹⁸The naïve get denseness as their domain,
  but the shrewd wear a crown of knowledge.
¹⁹Bad people bow down before good people,
  and the faithless at the gateways of someone faithful.
²⁰Even with his neighbour someone destitute meets with hostility,
  but the friends of a wealthy person are many.
²¹One who despises his neighbour is a wrongdoer,
  but one who is gracious to the humble: his blessings!
²²People who devise bad things go astray, don't they,
  but people who devise good things: commitment and truthfulness.
²³In all painful toil there will be profit,
  but the word of lips: only being in want.
²⁴Their wealth is the crown of the smart,
  but the denseness of dimwits is denseness.
²⁵A truthful witness saves lives,
  but one who testifies lies, deceit.
²⁶In awe for Yahweh, vigorous security,
  and for one's children it will be a shelter.
²⁷Awe for Yahweh is a fountain of life,
  to depart from deadly snares.
²⁸The glory of a king lies in the abundance of a people,
  and in the absence of a nation lies the ruin of a ruler.
²⁹Long-temperedness is abundant in understanding,
  but shortness of spirit exalts denseness.
³⁰A healthy mind is life for the flesh,
  but passion is rot for the bones.
³¹One who oppresses a poor person reviles his maker,
  but one who is gracious to a needy person honours him.

³²In his bad fortune a faithless person is thrown
down,
but a faithful person finds shelter when he's
dying.
³³In the mind of a person of understanding
smartness settles,
and in the middle of dimwits it makes itself
known.
³⁴Faithfulness exalts a nation,
but wrongdoing is a reproach to peoples.
³⁵The acceptance of a king [will be] towards an
insightful servant,
but his outburst will be [towards] a shameful
one.

## A gentle response turns back wrath

**15** A gentle answer turns back wrath,
but a painful word arouses anger.
²The tongue of the smart makes knowledge
good,
but the mouth of dimwits pours out denseness.
³Yahweh's eyes are in every place,
observing the bad and the good people.
⁴A healing tongue is a tree of life,
but deviation in it is brokenness in spirit.
⁵A dense person spurns his father's discipline,
but one who keeps watch on reproof shows
shrewdness.
⁶The house of the faithful person: much riches,
but in the yield of the faithless, trouble.
⁷The lips of the smart spread knowledge,
but the mind of dimwits – not so.
⁸The sacrifice of the faithless is an offence to
Yahweh,
but the plea of the upright is acceptable to him.
⁹The way of the faithless person is an offence to
Yahweh,
but he is loyal to one who pursues faithfulness.
¹⁰Discipline is bad to one who abandons the path,
but one who is hostile to reproof dies.
¹¹She'ol and Abaddon are in front of Yahweh;
how much more the minds of human beings.
¹²Someone arrogant doesn't befriend one who
reproves him;
he doesn't go to the smart.
¹³A rejoicing heart makes the face good,
but by hurt in the heart the spirit is crushed.
¹⁴The mind of a person of understanding seeks
knowledge,
but the mouth of dimwits feeds on denseness.

¹⁵All the days of a humble person are bad,
but a good heart is a continual feast.
¹⁶Better a little with awe for Yahweh,
than much treasure and turmoil with it.

## Better a helping of greens when love is there

¹⁷Better a helping of greens when love is there,
than a fattened bull when hostility is with it.
¹⁸A wrathful man stirs up a dispute,
but one who is long-tempered calms an
argument.
¹⁹The way of a lazy person is like a hedge of thorn,
but the path of the upright is cleared.
²⁰A smart son rejoices his father,
but a dim-witted man despises his mother.
²¹Denseness is a joy to one who lacks sense,
but a person of understanding makes his going
upright.
²²Intentions get contravened when there is no
counsel,
but with an abundance of counsellors they get
implemented.
²³In the answer of his mouth there is rejoicing for
a person,
and a word at its time – how good!
²⁴The path of life is upwards for someone
insightful,
in order to depart from She'ol below.
²⁵Yahweh tears down the house of the majestic,
but establishes the boundary of the widow.
²⁶Bad intentions are an offence to Yahweh,
but lovely sayings are pure.
²⁷One who gets dishonest gain troubles his
household,
but one who is hostile to a gift will live.
²⁸The mind of a faithful person murmurs so as to
answer,
but the mouth of faithless people pours out bad
things.
²⁹Yahweh is far away from the faithless,
but listens to the plea of the faithful.
³⁰The lamp of the eyes rejoices the heart;
good news enriches the bones.
³¹The ear that listens to life-giving reproof
lodges among the smart.
³²One who leaves go of discipline despises himself,
but one who listens to reproof acquires sense.
³³Awe for Yahweh is smartness's discipline;
lowliness is before splendour.

*31) Grey hair*

## Yahweh weighs spirits

**16** The ordering of the mind belongs to a
human being,
but the answer of the tongue comes from Yahweh.
²All an individual's ways are clean in his eyes,
but Yahweh weighs spirits.
³Roll your actions on to Yahweh,
and your intentions will be established.
⁴Every deed of Yahweh is for what it answers,
even the faithless person for a bad day.
⁵Anyone lofty of mind is an offence to Yahweh;
hand to hand he won't go free of guilt.
⁶By commitment and truthfulness waywardness
is expiated,
and with awe for Yahweh there's a departing
from anything bad.
⁷When Yahweh accepts an individual's ways,
he causes even his enemies to be at peace with
him.
⁸Better is a little with faithfulness
than abundance of yield without judgement.
⁹The mind of a person thinks out his course,
but Yahweh establishes his step.
¹⁰There is divination on a king's lips;
in giving judgement, one doesn't trespass
against his bidding.
¹¹Balance and scales for judgement belong to
Yahweh;
all the stones in the bag are his making.
¹²Acting with faithlessness is an offence to kings,
because the throne stands on faithfulness.
¹³Faithful lips are what kings accept;
he's loyal to one who speaks upright things.
¹⁴The king's wrath is death's envoy,
but someone smart will expiate it.
¹⁵There is life in the light of the king's face,
and his acceptance is like a cloud with spring
rain.
¹⁶Acquiring smartness – how much better than
pale gold,
and acquiring understanding is to be chosen
rather than silver.

## Majesty, loftiness; brokenness, collapsing

¹⁷The causeway of the upright: departing from
anything bad;
one who preserves his way keeps his life.
¹⁸Majesty goes before brokenness,
loftiness of spirit before collapsing.

¹⁹Lowliness of spirit with the humble
is better than sharing plunder with the
majestic.
²⁰One who is insightful about a thing will find
good fortune,
and one who relies on Yahweh, his blessings.
²¹One who is smart of mind is called
understanding,
and sweetness of lips increases people's grasp.
²²The insight of people who possess it is a fountain
of life,
but denseness is the discipline of dense
people.
²³The mind of someone smart makes his speech
insightful,
and on his lips it increases people's grasp.
²⁴Lovely sayings are a honeycomb,
sweet to the entire being and healing for the
body.
²⁵There is a road that is right before someone,
but its end is roads that lead to death.
²⁶The appetite of a labourer labours for him,
because his mouth is pressing on him.
²⁷A scoundrel digs for bad things,
and on his lip is a veritable scorching fire.
²⁸A crooked person lets loose a dispute,
and a gossip separates a friend.
²⁹A violent person misleads his neighbour,
and makes him go in a way that isn't good.
³⁰A person winks his eyes in thinking up crooked
things;
he purses his lips when he's finished something
bad.
³¹Grey hair is a glorious crown;
it's found by way of faithfulness.
³²Better to be long-tempered than a strong man,
and one ruling over his spirit than one taking
a town.
³³The lot is cast in the fold of the coat,
but every ruling it makes is from Yahweh.

## Yahweh tests minds

**17** Better a dry bit of bread and ease with it,
than a house full of sacrifices with
arguments.
²An insightful servant will rule over a disgraceful
son,
and share in the domain among the brothers.
³The crucible for silver, the furnace for gold,
and Yahweh tests minds.

⁴Someone who deals badly heeds a lip that brings
    trouble;
  falsehood gives ear to a malicious tongue.
⁵One who ridicules a destitute person reviles his
    maker;
  one who rejoices at disaster will not go free of
    guilt.
⁶Grandchildren are the crown of elders,
  and their parents are the glory of children.
⁷A plentiful tongue isn't fitting for a villain,
  much less a false tongue for a leader.
⁸A bribe is a gracious stone in its owner's eyes;
  wherever he turns his face, he'll thrive.
⁹One who seeks loyalty covers over rebellion,
  but one who repeats a thing separates a friend.
¹⁰A reprimand gets down into a person of
    understanding,
  more than lashes into a dimwit – a hundred.
¹¹A bad person seeks only rebellion,
  but a cruel envoy will be sent off against him.
¹²Let a bereaved bear meet with someone,
  but not a dimwit in his denseness.
¹³Someone who gives back something bad for
    something good –
  bad fortune will not move away from his
    household.
¹⁴The beginning of a dispute releases water,
  so before contention breaks out, abandon it.

## A rejoicing heart enhances healing

¹⁵One who declares a faithless person faithful or
    declares a faithful person faithless,
  both of them are an offence to Yahweh.
¹⁶Why is the price in a dimwit's hand
  for acquiring smartness, when he has no
    sense?
¹⁷A neighbour is a friend at any time;
  a brother is born for pressure.
¹⁸Someone lacking in sense claps the palm of his
    hand,
  standing surety before his neighbour.
¹⁹One who likes rebellion likes strife;
  one who makes his entrance lofty seeks
    breaking down.
²⁰Someone crooked of mind doesn't find good
    fortune,
  and someone who twists with his tongue falls
    into bad fortune.
²¹One begets a dimwit to one's grief,
  and the father of a villain doesn't rejoice.

²²A rejoicing heart enhances healing,
  but a crushed spirit dries up bones.
²³A faithless person takes a bribe from the fold of
    his coat,
  to bend the paths of the exercise of authority.
²⁴Smartness is before someone of understanding,
  but the eyes of the dimwit are at the end of the
    earth.
²⁵A dimwit son is a vexation to his father,
  and bitterness to the one who gave birth to
    him.
²⁶Surely penalizing a faithful person is not good –
  striking down leaders for uprightness.
²⁷One who has knowledge holds back his words;
  a person of understanding is cool of spirit.
²⁸Even a dense person, keeping silence, is thought
    smart;
  one who keeps his lips closed, understanding.

## Yahweh's name is a refuge

**18** One who isolates himself seeks what he
    longs for;
  he breaks out against all adeptness.
²The dimwit doesn't delight in understanding,
  but rather in disclosing his thinking.
³When a faithless person comes, contempt also
    comes,
  and with slighting comes reviling.
⁴The words from someone's mouth are deep
    water;
  a fountain of smartness is a flowing wadi.
⁵Showing regard to the faithless person is not
    good,
  by turning away the faithful person when
    exercising authority.
⁶The lips of a dimwit come into an argument,
  and his mouth calls to blows.
⁷The mouth of a dimwit is his ruin,
  and his lips are a snare for his life.
⁸The words of a gossip are like bites of food,
  and they go down into the inner rooms of the
    stomach.
⁹Really, one who slackens in his work –
  he is brother to a master of devastation.
¹⁰Yahweh's name is a strong tower,
  into which the faithful person runs and is high
    up.
¹¹A wealthy person's riches are his strong
    township,
  and like a high wall, in his thinking.

¹²Before being broken, someone's mind is lofty,
  but before splendour comes lowliness.

## A crushed spirit – who can bear it?

¹³One who gives word back before he listens –
  it's his denseness and shame.
¹⁴A person's spirit sustains his illness,
  but a crushed spirit – who can bear it?
¹⁵An understanding mind acquires knowledge,
  and the ear of smart people seeks knowledge.
¹⁶A person's gift widens the way for him,
  and conducts him before big people.
¹⁷The first person in a dispute seems in the
    right,
  then his neighbour comes and examines him.
¹⁸The lot stops disputes,
  and separates numerous people.
¹⁹A brother acting rebelliously is stronger than a
    strong township,
  and disputes are like the barrier of a citadel.
²⁰From the fruit of someone's mouth his stomach
    gets full;
  from the yield of his lips he gets full.
²¹Death and life are in the hand of the tongue;
  those who love it eat its fruit.
²²When someone finds a wife, he finds something
    good,
  and obtains acceptance from Yahweh.
²³The destitute person speaks prayers for grace,
  but the wealthy person answers fierce things.
²⁴There are neighbours to act like neighbours,
  and there's one who's loyal, sticking firmer than
    a brother.

## Riches make many friends

**19** Better one who's destitute who walks
       with integrity
  than one who's crooked with his lips and he's a
    dimwit.
²Surely without knowledge appetite isn't good,
  and one who's hasty on his feet goes wrong.
³A person's denseness overturns his way,
  but his mind rages against Yahweh.
⁴Riches make many friends,
  and a poor person becomes separate from his
    friend.
⁵A false witness will not go free of guilt,
  one who testifies lies will not escape.

⁶Many seek the goodwill of a leader,
  and everyone befriends the person with a gift.
⁷All the brothers of a destitute person are hostile
    to him –
  how much more do his neighbours keep their
    distance from him;
  someone who pursues things to say – he
    doesn't have them.
⁸One who acquires sense befriends himself;
  one who keeps understanding finds good
    fortune.
⁹A false witness will not go free of guilt,
  and one who testifies lies will perish.
¹⁰Luxury isn't fitting for a dimwit,
  certainly not for a servant to rule over officials.
¹¹A person's insight lengthens his anger,
  and his glory is to pass over an act of rebellion.
¹²The king's rage is a growl like a lion's,
  and his acceptance is like dew on grass.
¹³A dimwit son is malicious to his father,
  but a woman's disputes are a continuing drip.
¹⁴House and riches are a domain from parents,
  but a woman of insight comes from Yahweh.

## The peril of laziness

¹⁵Laziness makes deep sleep fall,
  and a slack person gets hungry.
¹⁶One who keeps an order keeps his life;
  one who despises his ways will die.
¹⁷One who's gracious to a poor person lends to
    Yahweh,
  and he'll make good to him for his dealing.
¹⁸Discipline your son when there's hope,
  and don't apply yourself to putting him to
    death.
¹⁹One who's big in wrath carries a penalty;
  if you rescue him, you'll do it again.
²⁰Listen to counsel and accept discipline,
  in order that you may be smart when you come
    to the end.
²¹Many intentions may be in a person's mind,
  but Yahweh's counsel is the one that gets
    implemented.
²²A person's longing is his reproach,
  but a destitute person is better than a liar.
²³Awe for Yahweh leads to life;
  one eats one's fill, spends the night, doesn't fear
    bad fortune.
²⁴The lazy person buries his hand in the bowl;
  he can't even bring it back to his mouth.

²⁵Strike down someone arrogant and the naïve
　　person will become shrewd;
　reprove someone of understanding – he'll
　　understand knowledge.
²⁶One who destroys a father, puts a mother to
　　flight,
　is a son who brings shame and confounding.
²⁷Son, leave off listening to discipline,
　and you'll stray from words of knowledge.
²⁸A witness who's a scoundrel is arrogant towards
　　the exercise of authority,
　and the mouth of faithless people swallows
　　trouble.
²⁹Acts of authority are prepared for the arrogant,
　and blows for the back of dimwits.

## Drink is noisy

**20** Wine is arrogant, drink is noisy,
　　and anyone who goes astray through
　　them isn't smart.
²The king's dreadfulness is a growl like a lion's;
　one who infuriates him wrongs himself.
³Ceasing from an argument is splendour for a
　　person,
　but every dense person breaks out.
⁴After autumn the lazy person doesn't plough,
　and he asks at harvest, and there's nothing.
⁵The counsel in someone's mind is deep water,
　but someone understanding can draw it up.
⁶An abundance of people may call out, 'a person
　　of commitment',
　but a person of truthfulness who can find?
⁷A faithful person walks about with integrity –
　the blessings of his children after him!
⁸A king sitting on a throne of judgement
　winnows all that's bad with his eyes.
⁹Who can say, 'I've kept my mind clean,
　I'm pure from my offence'?
¹⁰Different stones, different measures,
　both of them are an offence to Yahweh.
¹¹It is indeed by his deeds that a youth lets himself
　　be recognized,
　whether his action is clean and whether it's
　　upright.
¹²The ear listens, the eye sees;
　Yahweh made both of them.
¹³Don't love sleep, so that you don't become poor;
　open your eyes, be full of bread.
¹⁴'Bad, bad', says the buyer,
　and goes off, then takes pride.

¹⁵There is gold and abundance of jewels,
　but lips with knowledge are a valuable object.

## Don't say, 'I'll recompense a bad deed'

¹⁶Take his garment, because he made a pledge to
　　a stranger;
　bind him, on account of a foreign woman.
¹⁷Dishonest bread is pleasant to someone,
　but afterwards his mouth will fill with gravel.
¹⁸Intentions are established through counsel;
　do battle with steering.
¹⁹One who reveals a confidence goes about as a
　　slanderer;
　don't share with someone who has his lips
　　open.
²⁰One who slights his father and his mother,
　his lamp will go out at the approach of
　　darkness.
²¹A domain hastened at the beginning,
　at the end of it will not be blessed.
²²Don't say, 'I'll make good for a bad deed';
　hope in Yahweh and he'll deliver you.
²³Different stones are an offence to Yahweh;
　deceptive scales are not good.
²⁴A man's steps come from Yahweh;
　how can someone understand his way?
²⁵It's a snare when someone is wild regarding
　　making something sacred,
　and consults after vows.
²⁶A smart king winnows faithless people,
　and turns back the wheel over them.
²⁷The breath of a person is Yahweh's lamp,
　revealing all the rooms in your insides.
²⁸Commitment and truthfulness protect a king;
　he maintains his throne by commitment.
²⁹The glory of youths is their energy;
　the magnificence of elders is their grey hair.
³⁰Blows that wound scour things that are bad,
　and beatings, the rooms of one's insides.

## The way of a man can be strange

**21** The king's mind is a water channel in
　　Yahweh's hand,
　which he bends wherever he wants.
²Someone's entire way is upright in his own eyes,
　but Yahweh weighs minds.
³Exercising authority in a faithful way
　is to be chosen for Yahweh over a sacrifice.

⁴Exaltedness of eyes and wideness of mind:
  the fallow ground of the faithless is
    wrongdoing.
⁵The intentions of the determined person do end
    up in gain,
  but anyone who's hasty does end up in want.
⁶Working for treasures by means of a false
    tongue
  is a breath driven away, people seeking death.
⁷The destructiveness of the faithless sweeps them
    off,
  because they refuse to exercise [proper]
    authority.
⁸The way of a man: twisting, and strange,
  but his action: clean and upright.
⁹Living on a corner of the roof is better
  than a disputatious woman and a shared house.
¹⁰The appetite of the faithless person desires what
    is bad;
  his neighbour isn't graced in his eyes.
¹¹Through the punishing of someone arrogant a
    naïve person gets smart,
  and through gaining insight into someone
    smart he gets knowledge.
¹²One who is faithful gains insight into the
    household of the faithless person,
  turning over the faithless to their bad fortune.
¹³One who shuts his ear to the cry of the poor
    person –
  he too will call and not be answered.
¹⁴A gift in secret calms anger,
  a bribe in the fold of the coat, vigorous wrath.
¹⁵Exercising authority means rejoicing for the
    faithful
  but ruin to one who brings trouble.
¹⁶Someone who wanders from the way of insight
  will settle down in the congregation of ghosts.

## The sacrifice of the faithless is an offence

¹⁷One who loves rejoicing: a person in want;
  one who loves wine and oil will not get wealthy.
¹⁸The faithless person is a ransom for someone
    faithful,
  and one who breaks faith, in place of upright
    people.
¹⁹Living in a wilderness region is better
  than a disputatious and vexatious woman.
²⁰Desirable treasure and oil are in the home of
    someone smart,
  but a dimwit of a person will swallow them up.

²¹One who pursues faithfulness and commitment
  finds life, faithfulness and splendour.
²²Someone smart went up to a town of strong
    men
  and brought down the stronghold in which it
    was confident.
²³One who keeps his mouth and his tongue
  keeps his life from pressures.
²⁴The assertive, presumptuous person – arrogant
    his name –
  acts in an outburst of assertiveness.
²⁵The longing of the lazy person puts him to
    death,
  because his hands have refused to act.
²⁶All day someone may feel longing,
  but the faithful gives and doesn't hold back.
²⁷The sacrifice of the faithless is an offence,
  yes, because he brings it with a deliberate
    wickedness.
²⁸A lying witness will perish,
  but someone who listens to the end will speak.
²⁹A faithless person looks forceful in his face,
  but one who is upright – he understands his
    way.
³⁰There's no smartness, there's no understanding,
  there's no counsel in front of Yahweh.
³¹The horse is prepared for the day of battle
  but the deliverance belongs to Yahweh.

## Rich and poor meet

**22** A name is to be chosen rather than
        much wealth;
  grace is better than silver and than gold.
²Wealthy and destitute meet;
  Yahweh makes all of them.
³Someone shrewd sees something bad and hides;
  naïve people pass on and pay the penalty.
⁴The effect of lowliness is awe for Yahweh,
  wealth, splendour and life.
⁵Thorns (traps) are in the way of the crook;
  one who keeps watch on his life stays far from
    them.
⁶Initiate a youth with regard to his way;
  even when he gets old, he won't depart from it.
⁷The wealthy person rules over the destitute,
  and the borrower is a servant to the one who
    lends.
⁸One who sows evil will reap trouble;
  the club with which he expresses his outburst
    will be finished off.

⁹One who is good of eye will be blessed,
because he gives of his bread to the poor person.
¹⁰Drive out the arrogant person and dispute will
depart;
judgement and slighting will cease.
¹¹One who is loyal to being pure in mind,
grace on his lips, the king is his friend.
¹²Yahweh's eyes preserve knowledge,
but he overturns the words of one who breaks
faith.
¹³Someone lazy says, 'A lion in the street,
in the middle of the square I shall be
murdered!'
¹⁴The mouth of alien women is a deep pit;
one condemned by Yahweh falls there.
¹⁵Denseness is bound up in a youth's mind;
the club of discipline will take it far away from
him.
¹⁶One who oppresses the poor person: it's to make
much for himself;
one who gives to the wealthy person: it's only to
come to want.

*Thirty sayings: from 1 to 5*

¹⁷Bend your ear, listen to smart people's words,
and apply your mind to my knowledge.
¹⁸Because it will be lovely when you keep them
inside you;
they will be prepared all at once on your lips.
¹⁹So that your reliance may be on Yahweh,
I enable you to know them today – yes, you.
²⁰I've written for you thirty, haven't I,
with counsels and knowledge,
²¹To enable you to know the truest of truthful
sayings,
so as to take back sayings in truthfulness to the
people who send you.

²²[1] Don't rob the poor person because he's poor,
and don't crush the humble person at the
gateway.
²³Because Yahweh will argue their cause,
and despoil the people who despoil them of life.

²⁴[2] Don't befriend someone characterized by
anger,
and you will not come with someone of
frequent wrath,
²⁵So that you don't learn his paths,
and get a snare for your life.

²⁶[3] Don't be among the people who clap the
palm of the hand,
among the people who stand surety for debts.
²⁷If you have nothing to make good with,
why should someone take your bed from under
you?

²⁸[4] Don't remove an age-old boundary mark,
one that your ancestors made.

²⁹[5] You've beheld someone quick at his work?
– he'll stand before kings,
he won't stand before people who are in the
dark.

*Thirty sayings: from 6 to 14*

**23** [6] When you sit to dine with a ruler,
understand well who is before you.
²Put a knife to your throat
if you're someone with an appetite.
³Don't long for his titbits,
given that it's a lying meal.

⁴[7] Don't get weary in order to become
wealthy;
out of your understanding, leave off.
⁵Should your eyes flit upon it, it's gone,
because it definitely makes itself wings;
like an eagle, it flies to the heavens.

⁶[8] Don't eat the meal of someone who is bad of
eye,
and don't be desirous of his titbits.
⁷Because like a hair in the throat, so is he;
he says to you, 'Eat and drink',
but his heart isn't with you.
⁸The bit you've eaten you'll throw up,
and ruin your lovely words.

⁹[9] In the ears of a dimwit don't speak,
because he'll despise the insight of your
utterances.

¹⁰[10] Don't remove an age-old boundary mark,
and don't come into the fields of orphans.
¹¹Because their restorer is strong;
he'll argue their cause with you.

¹²[11] Bring your mind to discipline,
and your ear to knowledgeable sayings.

<sup>13</sup>[12] Don't withhold discipline from a youth;
  if you strike him down with a club, he won't die.
<sup>14</sup>You may strike him down with a club,
  and rescue his life from She'ol.

<sup>15</sup>[13] Son, if your mind is smart,
  my mind will rejoice, mine too.
<sup>16</sup>My inner being will exult,
  when your lips speak with uprightness.

<sup>17</sup>[14] Your mind must not be jealous of wrongdoers,
  but rather of [people who live in] awe for
    Yahweh all day.
<sup>18</sup>Rather there will be a future,
  and your hope will not cut off.

*Thirty sayings: from 15 to 18*

<sup>19</sup>[15] You, my son, listen, and be smart,
  and direct your mind on the way.
<sup>20</sup>Don't become among the people who toss down
    wine,
  among those who gorge themselves on meat.
<sup>21</sup>Because one who tosses down and gorges will
    lose his possession,
  and slumbering will clothe him in rags.

<sup>22</sup>[16] Listen to your father who begot you,
  and don't despise your mother when she's old.
<sup>23</sup>Acquire truth, don't sell it –
  smartness, discipline and understanding.
<sup>24</sup>The father of someone faithful will truly celebrate,
  the one who begets someone smart will rejoice
    in him.
<sup>25</sup>May your father and your mother rejoice,
  the one who gave birth to you celebrate.

<sup>26</sup>[17] Give your mind to me, son,
  may your eyes preserve my ways.
<sup>27</sup>Because a whore is a deep pit,
  a foreign woman is a narrow well.
<sup>28</sup>Indeed, she lies in wait as if for prey,
  and multiplies the people who break faith
    among humanity.

<sup>29</sup>[18] Who has 'Oh', who has 'Aagh',
  who has disputes, who has talk,
Who has wounds for nothing,
  who has bleary eyes?
<sup>30</sup>People who linger over wine,
  who come to investigate mixed wine.

<sup>31</sup>Don't look at wine because it's red,
  because it gives its eye in the chalice,
  goes about smoothly.
<sup>32</sup>At its finish it bites like a snake,
  poisons like a viper.
<sup>33</sup>Your eyes will see strange things,
  your mind will speak twisted things.
<sup>34</sup>You'll become like someone lying down in the
    middle of the sea,
  like someone lying down on the top of the rigging.
<sup>35</sup>'Though they struck me down, I didn't hurt,
  though they beat me, I didn't know.
When will I wake up? –
  I'll seek it once again!'

*Thirty sayings: from 19 to 30*

**24** [19] Don't be jealous of bad people,
  don't desire to be with them.
<sup>2</sup>Because their mind mutters destruction,
  and their lips speak of oppression.

<sup>3</sup>[20] By smartness a house gets built,
  and by understanding it gets established.
<sup>4</sup>By knowledge its rooms get filled
  with all valuable and lovely riches.

<sup>5</sup>[21] A smart man is vigour itself,
  someone knowledgeable firms his energy.
<sup>6</sup>Because by steering you do battle to your
    advantage,
  and deliverance comes through an abundance
    of counsellors.

<sup>7</sup>[22] Smartness is too high for a dense person;
  at the gateway he doesn't open his mouth.

<sup>8</sup>[23] While they may call one who intends to deal
    badly
  'a master of strategies',
<sup>9</sup>Dense deliberate wickedness, an expression of
    denseness, is wrongdoing,
  and an arrogant person is an offence to people.

<sup>10</sup>[24] Should you slacken on a day of constraint,
  your energy will be constrained.

<sup>11</sup>[25] Rescue people who are being taken off to
    death,
  who are slipping towards slaughter; if you hold
    back . . .

¹²When you say, 'There, we didn't know this',
   the one who weighs minds will discern, won't
      he.
The one who preserves your life, he will know,
   and will give back to a person in accordance
      with his deed.

¹³[26] Eat syrup, son, because it's good,
   liquid honey, sweet to your palate.
¹⁴In this way acknowledge smartness for your
      appetite;
   if you find it, there's a future,
   and your hope will not be cut off.

¹⁵[27] Don't lie in wait, faithless one, at the home
      of a faithful person,
   don't destroy his dwelling.
¹⁶Because seven times a faithful person may fall,
      and rise,
   but the faithless will collapse through one bad
      fortune.

¹⁷[28] When your enemy falls, don't rejoice,
   and when he collapses, your heart should not
      celebrate,
¹⁸So that Yahweh doesn't see and it's bad in his
      eyes,
   and he turns back his anger from him.

¹⁹[29] Don't get heated at people who do bad
      things,
   don't get jealous of the faithless,
²⁰Because there's no future for the bad person;
   the lamp of the faithless goes out.

²¹[30] Live in awe of Yahweh, son, and of the
      king,
   and don't share with people who are changing,
²²Because suddenly disaster may arise for them,
   and ruin from both of them: who can know?

*Another set of sayings*

²³These also belong to the sages.

Recognizing the person in exercising authority
      isn't good:
   ²⁴someone saying to the faithless person 'You're
      in the right.'
Peoples curse him,
   nations condemn him.

²⁵But for people who issue reproof, things will be
      lovely,
   and upon them will come the blessing of good
      things.
²⁶He kisses with the lips,
   the one who speaks back with straight words.

²⁷Prepare your work outside,
   get it ready in the fields for yourself;
   afterwards build your house.
²⁸Don't become a witness against your neighbour
      for nothing;
   will you mislead with your lips?
²⁹Don't say, 'As he did to me,
   so I'll do to him,
   I'll give back to the man in accordance with his
      deed.'

³⁰I passed by the field of someone lazy,
   and by the vineyard of one lacking sense.
³¹There, it had all come up in weeds,
   chickpeas covered its surface,
   its stone wall was torn down.
³²When I myself beheld, I applied my mind;
   when I saw, I grasped some discipline.
³³A little sleep, a little slumber,
   a little folding of the hands to lie down,
³⁴And your destitution comes walking about,
   your want like someone with a shield.

*Golden apricots in silver settings*

**25** These, too, are aphorisms of
      Shelomoh, which the men of
Hizqiyyahu [Hezekiah] king of Yehudah
compiled.

²It's God's splendour to conceal a thing,
   but kings' splendour to explore a thing.
³The heavens regarding height, the earth
      regarding depth,
   and the mind of kings – there's no exploring.
⁴Remove dross from silver,
   and an article comes out for the smith;
⁵Remove the faithless person before a king,
   and his throne is established in faithfulness.
⁶Don't magnify yourself before a king,
   and don't stand in the place of big people,
⁷Because it's better for someone to say to you 'Go
      up there',
   than move you down before a leader.

What your eyes have seen
    [8]should not go out into an argument quickly,
In case – what will you do at the end of it,
    when your neighbour puts you to shame?
[9]Argue for your cause with your neighbour,
    but don't reveal someone else's confidence,
[10]In case someone who hears it reproaches you
    and the charge against you doesn't turn back.
[11]Golden apricots in silver settings
    is a word appropriately spoken.
[12]A gold earring or an ornament of fine gold
    is someone smart reproving into a listening
        ear.
[13]Like the cold of snow at harvest time
    is a trustworthy envoy to the people who sent
        him;
    he brings back his lord's soul.
[14]Clouds and wind but no rain
    is someone who takes pride in a false gift.

## A gentle tongue can break a bone

[15]Through being long-tempered a commander
        can be enticed;
    a gentle tongue can break a bone.
[16]When you find syrup, eat enough for yourself,
    so that you don't get your fill of it and throw up.
[17]Make your foot rare at your neighbour's house,
    so that he doesn't get his fill of you and become
        hostile to you.
[18]A hammer, a sword, a sharpened arrow,
    is someone who testifies against his neighbour
        as a false witness.
[19]A bad tooth and a wobbly foot,
    is confidence in someone who breaks faith on a
        day of pressure.
[20]One who takes off a coat on a cold day,
    vinegar on a wound,
    and a singer of songs to a bad heart.
[21]If someone hostile to you is hungry, give him
        bread to eat;
    if he's thirsty, give him water to drink,
[22]Because you're heaping coals on his head,
    and Yahweh will make good to you.
[23]A north wind may give birth to rain,
    and a secretive tongue a condemning face.
[24]Living on a corner of the roof is better
    than a disputatious woman and a shared
        house.
[25]Cold water to a dry throat
    is good news from a far-off land.

[26]A muddied spring, a ruined fountain,
    is a faithful person slipping before a faithless
        person.
[27]Eating much syrup isn't good,
    nor is it splendid to investigate people's
        splendour.
[28]A town that's been opened up, where there's no
        wall,
    is someone for whose spirit there's no restraint.

## The dimwit

# 26
Like snow during summer and like rain
    during harvest,
    so splendour is not fitting for a dimwit.
[2]Like a sparrow flitting and like a swallow flying,
    so being slighted for nothing will not come
        about.
[3]A whip for a horse, a bridle for a donkey,
    and a club for the back of dimwits.
[4]Don't answer a dimwit in accordance to his
        denseness,
    so that you don't become like him, you too.
[5]Answer a dimwit in accordance with his
        denseness,
    so he doesn't become smart in his own eyes.
[6]Someone cutting off his feet, drinking violence,
    sending words by means of a dimwit.
[7]Legs hang down from someone disabled,
    and an aphorism in the mouth of dimwits.
[8]Like binding a stone in a sling,
    so is one who gives splendour to a dimwit.
[9]A thorn grows up into the hand of a drunk
    and an aphorism in the mouth of dimwits.
[10]An archer running through everyone
    and one who hires a dimwit or hires people
        passing through.
[11]As a dog goes back to its vomit,
    a dimwit repeats his denseness.
[12]I've seen someone smart in his own eyes;
    there's hope for a dimwit more than for him.
[13]A lazy person says, 'There's a lion cub on the
        road,
    a lion among the squares.'
[14]The door turns on its hinge,
    the lazy person on his bed.
[15]The lazy person buries his hand in the bowl;
    he's too weary to bring it back to his mouth.
[16]The lazy person is smarter in his own eyes
    than seven people speaking back with
        discretion.

### When there's no gossip, disputes go quiet

<sup>17</sup>One who takes strong hold of the ears of a
passing dog
is one who bursts out in an argument that isn't
his.
<sup>18</sup>Like a madman who is shooting
fiery arrows of death,
<sup>19</sup>So is someone who beguiles his neighbour
and says, 'I was having fun, wasn't I.'
<sup>20</sup>In the absence of wood a fire goes out,
and when there's no gossip, disputes go quiet.
<sup>21</sup>Charcoal for embers and wood for a fire,
and a disputatious person for heating up an
argument.
<sup>22</sup>The words of a gossip are like bites of food,
and they go down into the rooms of the
stomach.
<sup>23</sup>Silver dross laid over a pot,
burning lips but a bad mind.
<sup>24</sup>With his lips a hostile person disguises himself;
inside him, he puts deceit.
<sup>25</sup>When he makes his voice gracious, don't trust
him;
because seven offences are in his mind.
<sup>26</sup>His hostility will be concealed by deception;
his bad action will reveal itself in a
congregation.
<sup>27</sup>One who digs a pit will fall into it;
one who rolls a stone, it will come back on to
him.
<sup>28</sup>A false tongue is hostile to the people crushed
by it;
a smooth mouth works a pushing down.

### Trustworthy are the wounds of a friend

# 27
Don't take pride in tomorrow,
because you don't know what a day will
give birth to.
<sup>2</sup>A stranger should praise you and not your mouth,
a foreigner and not your lips.
<sup>3</sup>A stone is weighty and sand is heavy,
but a dense person's vexation is heavier than
both of them.
<sup>4</sup>The cruelty of wrath and the flooding of anger:
but who can stand before jealousy?
<sup>5</sup>Reproof openly expressed is better
than friendship concealed.
<sup>6</sup>The wounds of a friend are trustworthy;
the kisses of someone hostile are importunate.

<sup>7</sup>Someone full despises honey,
but someone hungry: anything bitter is sweet.
<sup>8</sup>Like a sparrow flitting from its nest,
so is someone flitting from his place.
<sup>9</sup>Oil and incense rejoice the heart,
and the sweetness of one's friend, more than
one's own counsel.
<sup>10</sup>Don't abandon your friend or your father's
friend,
and don't come to your brother's house on your
day of disaster.
Better one who dwells near
than a brother far away.
<sup>11</sup>Be smart, son, and rejoice my heart,
so I may speak back to one who reviles me with
a word.
<sup>12</sup>When someone shrewd sees something bad, he
hides;
naïve people pass on and pay the penalty.
<sup>13</sup>Take his garment, because he made a pledge to
a stranger;
bind him, on account of a foreign woman.

### The crucible of praise

<sup>14</sup>One who blesses his neighbour in a loud voice
in the morning, early:
it will be thought of for him as a slighting.
<sup>15</sup>A continuing drip on a rainy day,
and a disputatious woman, are similar.
<sup>16</sup>People who hide her could hide the wind,
or he could grasp oil in his right hand.
<sup>17</sup>Iron sharpens iron,
and a person sharpens the face of his friend.
<sup>18</sup>One who guards a fig tree will eat its fruit,
and one who keeps watch on his lord will be
honoured.
<sup>19</sup>Like water, face to face,
so the heart of a person to a person.
<sup>20</sup>She'ol and Abaddon don't get full,
and the eyes of a human being don't get full.
<sup>21</sup>A crucible for silver, a furnace for gold,
and an individual for a mouth praising him.
<sup>22</sup>If you grind the dense person in a mortar,
in the middle of the grain in a pestle,
his denseness will not depart from him.
<sup>23</sup>You should really know the faces of your
flock,
apply your mind to your herds,
<sup>24</sup>Because riches aren't permanent
or a crown for generation after generation.

²⁵Hay goes away and new grass appears
　　and the growth of the mountains is gathered.
²⁶Lambs are for your clothing,
　　goats for the price of a field,
²⁷Enough goats' milk for your meal,
　　for a meal for your household and life for your
　　young girls.

## Interest and profiteering

**28** The faithless flee when there's no one
　　pursuing,
　　but faithful people are as confident as a lion.
²When there's rebellion in the country,
　　its rulers are many.
But when there's someone who understands,
　　someone who knows, established order will
　　last long.
³A man who is destitute and who oppresses the
　　poor:
　　rain beating down and there's no bread.
⁴People who abandon instruction praise the
　　faithless person;
　　people who keep instruction fight against them.
⁵Bad people don't understand the exercise of
　　authority,
　　but people who seek Yahweh understand
　　everything.
⁶Better someone destitute walking in integrity,
　　than someone crooked in his ways, but he's
　　wealthy.
⁷An understanding son observes instruction,
　　but one who befriends gluttons disgraces his
　　father.
⁸Someone who increases his riches through
　　interest and profiteering
　　amasses it for someone who will be gracious to
　　the poor.
⁹One who turns his ear aside from listening to
　　instruction:
　　even his plea is an offence.
¹⁰One who misleads the upright into a bad way,
　　he'll fall into his own pit, but people of integrity
　　get good things as their domain.
¹¹A wealthy person is smart in his own eyes,
　　but a poor person of understanding can search
　　him out.
¹²At the exulting of the faithful there's much
　　glorying,
　　but at the rise of the faithless, people have to be
　　searched for.

¹³One who covers his rebellions will not succeed,
　　but one who confesses and abandons will be
　　shown compassion.
¹⁴The blessings of the person who continually
　　reveres,
　　whereas one who toughens his mind falls to
　　bad fortune.

## The peril of shutting the eyes

¹⁵A roaring lion or an advancing bear:
　　a faithless ruler over a poor people.
¹⁶A leader lacking understanding and abundant in
　　acts of oppression;
　　one hostile to dishonest gain will extend his days.
¹⁷When one oppressed by shedding someone's
　　blood
　　flees to a cistern, people should not take hold
　　of him.
¹⁸A person who walks in integrity will find
　　deliverance,
　　but one who's crooked in his ways will fall at
　　once.
¹⁹One who serves his land will be full of bread,
　　but one who pursues empty things will be full
　　of destitution.
²⁰A person of trustworthy deeds will be abundant
　　in blessings,
　　but one hasty to get wealthy will not go free of
　　guilt.
²¹Recognizing a person isn't good,
　　but a man may rebel for a bit of bread.
²²One who is bad in eye hurries for riches,
　　and doesn't acknowledge that lack will come
　　to him.
²³One who reproves a person in the end
　　will find more grace than one who makes his
　　tongue smooth.
²⁴One who robs his father and his mother
　　and says 'It's not an act of rebellion' –
　　he is a companion of one who devastates.
²⁵One wide of appetite provokes dispute,
　　but one who relies on Yahweh will be enriched.
²⁶One who relies on his own mind – he's a
　　dimwit,
　　but one who walks in smartness – he'll escape.
²⁷One who gives to a destitute person – there's no
　　lack,
　　but one who shuts his eyes – many are the curses.
²⁸When the faithless rise up, people hide,
　　and when they perish, the faithful become many.

*You could suddenly break and there could be no healing*

# 29
A person of many reproofs who toughens his neck

will suddenly break, and there will be no healing.

2 When the faithful increase, the people rejoice,
  but when a faithless person rules, the people groan.

3 Someone who loves smartness rejoices his father,
  but one who befriends whores obliterates riches.

4 A king enables a country to stand by the exercise of authority,
  but a man of great deceit tears it down.

5 A man who flatters his neighbour
  spreads a net for his steps.

6 In the rebellion of someone bad there's a snare,
  but a faithful person resounds and rejoices.

7 A faithful person acknowledges the cause of the poor;
  a faithless person doesn't understand acknowledgement.

8 Arrogant people stir up a township,
  but the smart turn back anger.

9 Someone smart may enter into judgement with a dense person,
  but he'll rage and have fun and there'll be no settlement.

10 People inclined to bloodshed may be hostile to someone of integrity,
  but the upright will seek the person out.

11 A dimwit lets all his spirit out;
  someone smart holds it back.

12 A ruler who gives heed to a false word:
  all his ministers will be faithless.

13 A destitute man and a man given to deceit meet:
  Yahweh enlightens the eyes of them both.

## How the throne will stand firm

14 A king who exercises authority for the poor in truth:
  his throne will be established permanently.

15 Club and reproof give smartness,
  but a youth sent off shames his mother.

16 When the faithless increase, rebellion increases,
  but the faithful will see their downfall.

17 Discipline your son and he'll enable you to settle down,
  and give much delight to your entire being.

18 When there's no vision, the people throw off restraint,
  but someone who keeps instruction – his blessings!

19 By words a servant will not be disciplined,
  when he understands but there's no answer.

20 If you behold someone hasty with his words,
  there's hope for a dimwit more than for him.

21 Someone who indulges his servant from youth:
  at the end he'll become his offspring.

22 Someone angry provokes a dispute,
  and someone given to wrath rebels much.

23 A person's majesty will make him fall,
  but one lowly of spirit will take hold of splendour.

24 Someone who shares with a thief is hostile to himself;
  he hears the oath and doesn't tell.

25 A person's trembling sets a snare,
  but one who relies on Yahweh will be set on high.

26 Many seek the regard of a ruler,
  but the ruling about a person comes from Yahweh.

27 An evildoer is an offence to the faithful,
  and someone upright in his way is an offence to the faithless person.

*I'm just a weary sojourner but I have some words from God*

# 30
Words of Agur ben Yaqeh. The oracle. The man's pronouncement to Iti'el, to Iti'el and Ukal.

2 Truly I'm a brute more than a person,
  and I don't have human understanding.

3 I haven't learned smartness
  and I don't possess the knowledge of the sacred ones.

4 Who has gone up to the heavens and come down,
  who has gathered the wind in his open hands?
Who has confined the water in a cloak,
  who has set all earth's ends?
What is his name and what is his son's name,
  if you know?

5 Everything God says is tested;
  he's a shield to those who take shelter with him.

6 Don't add to his words,
  so that he doesn't reprove you and you prove a liar.

⁷Two things I ask of you;
   don't hold back from me before I die.
⁸Emptiness and a lying word keep far from me,
   destitution and wealth don't give me,
   let me grab the bread that is my due,
⁹So that I don't get full and renounce
   and say, 'Who is Yahweh?'
Or so that I don't get poor and rob,
   and take the name of my God.

¹⁰Don't mention a servant to his lord,
   in case he slight you, and you're liable.

¹¹A generation that slights its father,
   and doesn't bless its mother!
¹²A generation that's pure in its own eyes,
   but its filth isn't washed off!
¹³A generation – how its eyes are high,
   and its eyelids rise!
¹⁴A generation whose teeth are swords,
   and their jaws knives,
To consume the humble from the earth,
   the needy from humanity!

## Creation and numbers

¹⁵The leech has two daughters,
   'Give, give!'
These are three things that don't get full,
   four that don't say 'Plenty!' –
¹⁶She'ol, a barren womb,
   a country that isn't full of water,
   and fire that doesn't say 'Plenty!'

¹⁷The eye that ridicules a father
   and despises obedience to a mother:
The ravens in the wadi will gouge it out,
   and young eagles will eat it.

¹⁸Those are three things too extraordinary for me,
   four that I don't know:
¹⁹An eagle's way in the heavens,
   a snake's way on a crag,
A ship's way in the heart of the sea,
   and a man's way with a girl.

²⁰Such is the way of an adulterous woman:
   she eats and wipes her mouth,
   and says, 'I haven't brought trouble.'

²¹Under three things the earth shudders,
   and under four that it cannot bear:

²²Under a servant when he becomes king,
   and villain when he's full of bread,
²³Under a woman who has met with hostility
      when she marries,
   and a maidservant when she dispossesses her
      mistress.

²⁴Those are four smallest things on earth,
   but they are the smartest of the smart:
²⁵Ants are a people not strong,
   but they prepare their bread in summer;
²⁶Hyraxes are a people not numerous,
   but they make their home in a cliff;
²⁷Locusts have no king,
   but they go out organized, all of them;
²⁸You can take hold of a lizard in your hands,
   but it's in a king's palaces.

²⁹Those are three things good in their stride,
   four that are good in moving:
³⁰The lion is the strong man among animals,
   it doesn't turn back from before anyone;
³¹One belted round the hips; or a goat;
   and a king – no rising against him.

³²If you've been villainous in exalting yourself,
   and if you've schemed – hand on your
      mouth!
³³Because pressing milk issues in butter,
   pressing the nose issues in blood,
   and pressing anger issues in an argument.

## The demon drink

**31** The words of King Lemu'el. A
pronouncement with which his
mother disciplined him.

²What, my son, what, son of my womb,
   what, son of my pledges?
³Don't give your resources to women,
   your ways to women who wipe out kings.
⁴It's not for kings, Lemuel,
   not for kings to drink wine,
   and for rulers, or liquor.
⁵In case they drink and put out of mind what has
      been decreed,
   and are hostile to the cause of all humble
      people.
⁶Give liquor to someone who is perishing,
   wine to one who is bitter inside.

[7]He can drink and put out of mind his destitution,
  and his oppression he won't keep in mind any
    more.
[8]Open your mouth for the dumb,
  for the cause of all the people who are passing
    away.
[9]Open your mouth, exercise authority faithfully,
  give judgement for the humble and needy
    person.

## The resourceful woman

[10]Who can find a resourceful woman?
  – her value is far above rubies.
[11]Her husband's mind relies on her,
  and he lacks no spoil.
[12]She deals him good, not bad,
  all the days of her life.
[13]She looks for wool and flax,
  and works with delight with the palms of her
    hands.
[14]She becomes like a trader's ships,
  when she brings her bread from far away.
[15]She rises while it's still night,
  and gives a bite to her household,
  and an allocation to her girls.
[16]She schemes about a field and gets it;
  from the fruit of the palms of her hands she
    plants a vineyard.
[17]She wraps her hips in vigour,
  and firms up her arms.

[18]She checks that her trading is good;
  her lamp doesn't go out at night.
[19]She puts out her hands to the spindle,
  and her palms take hold of the wheel.
[20]She opens her palm to the humble person,
  puts out her hands to the needy person.
[21]She isn't afraid for her household because of
    snow,
  because her entire household is dressed in
    crimson.
[22]She makes coverlets for herself;
  her clothing is linen and purple.
[23]Her husband is acknowledged at the gateways,
  as he sits with the country's elders.
[24]She makes fabric and sells it,
  and gives a sash to the merchant.
[25]Vigour and magnificence are her clothing;
  she can make fun of a future day.
[26]She opens her mouth with smartness;
  committed instruction is on her tongue.
[27]She watches over the goings of her household;
  she doesn't eat the bread of laziness.
[28]Her children rise up and declare her blessed;
  her husband praises her:
[29]'Many women produce resources,
  but you surpass all of them.'
[30]Grace is false, beauty is hollow,
  but a woman who lives in awe of Yahweh –
    she is to take pride.
[31]Give to her from the fruit of her hand;
  her deeds should praise her at the
    gateways.

# ECCLESIASTES : "Yes, But"

Ecclesiastes is one of the most reassuring books in the Bible in the way it encourages us to face facts about how life is. Whereas Proverbs majors on positive aspects to the way life works out, Ecclesiastes acknowledges that things are more complicated than a first, surface reading of Proverbs might seem to imply. Often Ecclesiastes proceeds by quoting the kind of observation that appears in Proverbs and saying 'Yes, but . . .'

A substantial chunk of the beginning of the book takes Solomon as a test case for looking at life, though the book never mentions Solomon by name. It refers to the author as Qohelet, which is related to the Hebrew word for 'congregation'. I translate it as 'congregant'. An implication of using this name is that this book is proper 'congregational teaching', proper teaching for the people of God. It refers to its 'hero' as 'David's son', which probably suggests Solomon, though there are many other people to whom the phrase applies. But Solomon was the man who had everything – women, wisdom, achievement, power, pleasure. So he provides a test case for whether these things can make life worthwhile. And his answer is, they don't.

It's not that these things are totally useless. They are all worthwhile. But they are not ultimately significant. They don't provide the ultimate answers. In the absence of such ultimate answers, really everything is 'hollow'. This declaration forms a bracket round the book as a whole. When one looks empirically at life in the world, one can see ways in which things make sense and ways in which life is worthwhile, but also ways in which they don't make sense and in which the things that people tell themselves make life worthwhile are not really of ultimate significance. Qohelet encourages us to remember that they are nevertheless things that 'God gives' – that phrase recurs in the book. There's some value in seeking to live a faithful life and in enjoying life with one's family, work, and food and drink. It's not enough, but it's not nothing.

## Everything is hollow

**1** The words of Congregant, son of David, king in Yerushalaim.

[2]Utter hollowness, said Congregant,
    utter hollowness, everything is hollow.
[3]What value is there for a person
    in all the labour that he undertakes under
        the sun?

[4]A generation goes, a generation comes;
    the earth stands permanently.
[5]The sun rises and the sun sets
    and rushes to its place where it rises.
[6]The wind goes to the south and turns round to
        the north,
    it turns, turns as it goes,
    and on its turnings the wind goes back.
[7]All the wadis go to the sea, but the sea isn't full;
    to the place where the wadis go,
    there they go again.
[8]All the things are laborious;
    no one could speak of it.
The eye isn't replete as regards looking,
    the ear isn't full as regards listening.
[9]What has happened is what will happen;
    what has occurred is what will occur;
    there's nothing new under the sun.
[10]Where there is a thing that someone says,
    'See this, it's new',
Already it has happened
    for ages that were before us.
[11]There is no commemoration for the earlier
        people,
    and also for future people who are to come.
For them there will be no commemoration,
    with the people who will be in the future.

## A king's achievement

[12]I, Congregant, began to reign over
Yisra'el in Yerushalaim. [13]I gave my mind to
looking into and exploring with smartness
everything that occurs under the heavens. It's
a bad business God gave human beings to be
busy with. [14]I saw all the actions that occur
under the sun. There, everything is hollow,
a shepherding of wind.

[15]Something crooked cannot become straight,
    and something lacking cannot be counted.

[16]I myself spoke inside myself: 'Here, I've got
big and increased in smartness above everyone
who has been over Yerushalaim before
me. My mind has seen much of smartness
and knowledge. [17]I've given my mind to a
knowledge of smartness and a knowledge of
madness and apparent insight. I've come to
acknowledge that this, too, was a shepherding
of wind.

[18]Because with abundance of smartness there's
        much vexation,
    and one who increases knowledge increases
        pain.

**2** I myself said inside myself, 'Come on,
please, I'll test you with rejoicing. Look
into what's good.' There, that is also hollow.

[2]Of having fun, I said, 'It's mad',
    and of rejoicing, 'What does this do?'

[3]I explored inside myself, stretching my flesh
with wine while directing my mind with
smartness and taking hold of idiocy, until
I could see which one was good for human
beings, which they should practise under the
heavens for the number of the days of their
life. [4]I made my achievements big. I built
houses for myself, I planted vineyards for
myself, [5]I made gardens and parks for myself
and planted in them trees with every fruit. [6]I
made pools of water for myself, to water from
them a forest flourishing with trees. [7]I acquired
servants and maidservants and ones born in
my household. I also had livestock, herd and
flock; I had more than all who were before me
in Yerushalaim.

## Wealth and learning

[8]I also amassed for myself silver and
gold and the personal treasure of kings
and provinces. I made for myself male and
female singers, and the pleasures of human
beings, many women. [9]I got big and increased
more than anyone who was before me in
Yerushalaim; also my smartness stood with
me. [10]Nothing that my eyes asked for did I
keep from them. I didn't hold my mind back
from any rejoicing; rather, my mind rejoiced in

all my labour. This was my share from all my labour.

¹¹But I myself turned my face to all the things that my hands had done and to the labour that I had put into doing it. There, everything was hollow, a shepherding of wind. There was no value under the sun.

¹²I turned my face to see smartness, madness and idiocy. Because what will the person do who comes after the king? That which people have already done. ¹³I myself saw that

There is value to smartness over idiocy,
   like the value of light over darkness.
¹⁴The smart person – his eyes are in his head,
   but the dimwit walks in darkness.

But I myself also acknowledged that one experience happens to each of them. ¹⁵So I myself said inside myself: like the experience of the dimwit, so it will happen to me, too. So why have I myself then been exceedingly smart? I spoke inside myself: 'This is hollow, too.' ¹⁶Because there's no commemoration permanently of the smart person, just like the dimwit, in that already in the coming days each will have gone out of mind. But how can the smart man die just like the dimwit? ¹⁷So I was hostile to life, because the action that occurs under the sun is bad with me, because everything is hollow, a shepherding of wind. ¹⁸So I myself was hostile to all the labour that I myself have expended under the sun, which I shall leave to the person who will be after me. ¹⁹Who knows whether he'll be a smart person or an idiot? But he'll hold power over all the labour that I've expended and the smartness that I've exercised under the sun. This too is hollow.

### Everything has its time

²⁰So I myself turned round to letting myself despair about all the labour that I've expended under the sun. ²¹Because there's a person whose labour was with smartness, with knowledge and with skill, and he gives his share from it to a person who didn't labour for it. This is also hollow, something very bad. ²²Because what does the person have for all his labour and for his mind's shepherding, with

which he's laboured under the sun? ²³Because all his days, his busyness is pain and vexation. By night, too, his mind doesn't lie down. This is also hollow.

²⁴There's nothing better with a person than that he eats and drinks and lets himself see good things through his labour. I myself have also seen that this is from God's hand. ²⁵Because who eats and who hastens apart from me? ²⁶Because to the person who is good before him he gives smartness, knowledge and rejoicing, and to the wrongdoer he gives the busyness of gathering and collecting – to give to someone who is good before God.

This too is hollow, a shepherding of wind.

**3** Everything has a moment,
   every purpose under the sun has a time:
²A time of birthing, a time of dying,
   a time of planting, a time of uprooting what
     is planted,
³A time of killing, a time of healing,
   a time of demolishing, a time of building,
⁴A time of crying, a time of having fun,
   a time of wailing, a time of dancing,
⁵A time of throwing stones, a time of collecting
     stones,
   a time of embracing, a time of staying far
     from embracing,
⁶A time of searching, a time of obliterating,
   a time of keeping, a time of throwing out,
⁷A time of tearing, a time of mending,
   a time of being silent, a time of speaking,
⁸A time of being loyal, a time of being hostile,
   a time of battle and a time of peace.

⁹What's the value for the person who acts, in what he labours over? ¹⁰I've seen the busyness that God has given human beings to be busy with. ¹¹He's made everything beautiful in its time; he's also put permanence into their mind, but not so that humanity can find out what God has done from the beginning until the end.

### There's no justice

¹²I acknowledged that there is nothing good with them except to rejoice and do what's good in their lifetime. ¹³Also, everyone who eats and drinks and sees good things through all his labour – it's God's gift. ¹⁴I acknowledged that

Everything that God does,
  it will be permanent.
To it there is nothing to add,
  and from it, there's nothing to take away.

God has acted so that people live in awe
before him.

¹⁵What has happened already is,
  and that which is to happen has already
    happened.

And God seeks out what has been driven
away. ¹⁶Further, I've seen under the sun:

In the place for the [proper] exercise of
  authority, faithlessness was there,
in the place for faithfulness, faithlessness was
  there.

¹⁷I myself said inside myself,

Over the faithful person and the faithless
  God will exercise authority.
Because there will be a time for every purpose
  and for every activity there.

¹⁸I myself said inside myself with regard
to human beings, it's for God to purify them
and for them to see that they are animals.
¹⁹Because the experience of human beings and
the experience of animals is a single experience
for them. Like the dying of the one, so is the
dying of the other. Each has the same spirit.
The advantage of humanity over animals –
there is none, because each is hollow. ²⁰Each
goes to the same place. Each came into being
from earth and each goes back to earth. ²¹Who
knows if the spirit of human beings goes up
and the spirit of animals goes down beneath
the ground?
²²So I saw that there is nothing better than
that a person enjoys his activities, because
this is his share, because who can give him
discernment to see what will happen after him?

**4** I again saw all the oppressed people
that are appearing under the sun. There,
the tears of the oppressed, and there is no
comforter for them; yes, from the hand of
their oppressors is the energy, and there is no
comforter for them. ²I myself extolled the dead
people, who had already died, more than the

living people, who were still alive. ³Better than
both of them is the one who hasn't yet come
into being, who hasn't seen the bad activity that
occurs under the sun.

*Two people who lie together can be warm*

⁴I myself saw all labour and all skill in activity:
it's the jealousy of a person by his neighbour.
This too is hollow, a shepherding of wind.

⁵The dimwit folds his hands,
  and eats his own flesh.

⁶Better a palmful with settlement than two
fistfuls with labour, and a shepherding of wind.
⁷I again saw hollowness under the sun.
⁸There's one person, and he has no second
person, either son or brother. And there's
no end to all his labour; nor is his eye full of
wealth. 'But for whom am I labouring and
depriving myself of good things?' This too is
hollow, a bad business. ⁹Two are better than
one, in that they have better reward for their
labour. ¹⁰Because if they fall, one can lift up his
companion; but alas for the single person who
falls and has no second person to lift him up.
¹¹Further, if two people lie down together, they
are warm, but for one – how can he be warm?
¹²And if someone overpowers him (the one
person), the two can stand up in front of him.
And a triple cord doesn't break quickly.
¹³Better a young man who's poor but smart
than a king who's old but a dimwit, who
doesn't know how to heed a warning any more,
¹⁴because from the prison house he can get
out to become king, even when he was born
destitute in the kingdom. ¹⁵I saw all the living
who walk about under the sun with the youth,
the second [king], who stands in place of him.
¹⁶There was no end to all the people, to all
before whom he stood; also those who are after
him will not rejoice in him. Because this too is
hollow, a shepherding of wind.

*Sell your tongue and buy a thousand ears*

**5** Keep watch on your feet as you go to
God's house. Drawing near to listen is
better than the giving of a sacrifice by dimwits,

because they don't acknowledge that they are doing something bad. ²Don't be hasty with your mouth; your mind shouldn't be quick to let out a word before God, because God is in the heavens and you're on the earth. Thus your words should be few. ³Because

A dream comes with an abundance of busyness,
     and the voice of a dimwit with an abundance
          of words.

⁴When you make a pledge to God, don't delay making it good, because there's no delight in dimwits. What you pledge, make it good. ⁵It's better that you don't make a pledge than that you make a pledge and don't make it good. ⁶Don't give your mouth to causing your flesh to do wrong. Don't say before the envoy, 'It was a mistake.' Why should God be furious at your voice and destroy what your hands have made? ⁷Because in an abundance of dreams is much hollowness, and many words. Rather, live in awe of God.

⁸If you see oppression of the destitute person and violation of the faithful exercise of authority in the province, don't marvel at the matter, because one who is lofty keeps watch over one who is lofty, and ones who are lofty over them. ⁹The value for the land in every way is this: a king for the field that's worked.

## It's not enough but it's not nothing

¹⁰Someone who loves silver doesn't have his fill of silver, nor whoever loves riches of his yield. This too is hollow. ¹¹With the increase of his goods, the people who consume them increase, so what's the profit of their owners except his eyes seeing them? ¹²The sleep of someone who serves is sweet whether he eats little or much, but the richness of the wealthy person doesn't leave him to sleep. ¹³There is a sick bad fortune I saw under the sun: wealth kept by its owner to his bad fortune, ¹⁴or that wealth perishes through a bad business; and he fathers a son but there's nothing in his hand. ¹⁵As he got out from his mother's womb, naked he again goes, as he came; he carries nothing of his labour in his hand when he goes. ¹⁶This too is a sick bad fortune. Corresponding to the way he comes, so he goes, and what's the value

to him that he labours for the wind? ¹⁷Further, all his days he eats in darkness with much vexation, illness and fury.

¹⁸Here's what I myself saw as good, that it's beautiful to eat and to drink and to see what's good in all his labour that he expends under the sun for the number of the days of his life that God gives him, because this is his share. ¹⁹Further, each person to whom God gives wealth and possessions and whom he empowers to consume some of them, to take up his share and to rejoice in his labour – this is God's gift. ²⁰Because he won't be very mindful of the days of his life, because God busies him with his mind's rejoicing.

## Everyone is going to the same place

**6** There's something bad that I saw under the sun, and there's much of it with human beings: ²a person to whom God gives wealth, possessions and splendour, and who has no lack regarding his appetite for anything that he desires, but God doesn't empower him to consume any of it, and a stranger consumes it. This is hollow and a bad sickness. ³If a man fathers a hundred children and lives many years, and however many are the days of his years, his appetite can't be full from the good things: then even if it was not buried, I say the stillbirth is better off than him. ⁴Because it comes in hollowness and it goes in darkness, and its name is covered in darkness; ⁵though it doesn't see or know the sun, that one is more settled than the other one.

⁶Even if he lives a thousand years twice over but doesn't see the good things, each is going to one place, isn't he. ⁷All a person's labour is for his mouth, but his appetite doesn't get full. ⁸Because what's the value for the smart person over the dimwit? What does the humble person have, who knows how to walk in front of the living? ⁹The eyes seeing is better than the appetite journeying. This too is hollow, a shepherding of wind.

¹⁰What happens has already been named, and what a person is has become known. He cannot contend with one who is stronger than him, ¹¹because the more the words are, the more is the hollowness. What's the value for a person? ¹²Because who knows what is good for

a person in life for the number of the days of
his hollow life? He spends them like a shadow,
so who can tell the person what will happen
under the sun after him?

## Better the house of mourning than the house of feasting

**7** A good name is better than good oil,
and the day of death than the day of birth.
[2] Going to a house of mourning
is better than going to a house of feasting,
Inasmuch as that is the end of everyone
and the living person should put it into his
mind.
[3] Vexation is better than fun,
because despite a bad look in the face,
the mind will be good.
[4] The mind of smart people is in a house of
mourning,
the mind of dimwits in a house of rejoicing.

[5] It's better to listen to the reprimand of a smart
person
than be listening to the song of dimwits,
[6] Because the fun of a dimwit
is like the sound of thistles under a pot.
But this too is hollow,
[7] because fraud can make a fool out of a
smart person,
and a gift can obliterate the mind.
[8] The end of something is better than its
beginning,
endurance of spirit is better than loftiness of
spirit.
[9] Don't be quick to feel vexed in your spirit,
because vexation settles in the heart of dimwits.
[10] Don't say, 'How did it happen
that the former days were better than these?',
because it's not out of smartness that you ask
about this.
[11] Smartness is good, like a domain,
and something valuable to people who see
the sun.
[12] Because as smartness is a veritable shelter,
silver is a veritable shelter.
But the value of knowledge
is that smartness keeps its masters alive.

[13] Look at God's activity,
because who can straighten
what he has twisted?

[14] In the day when things are good, be with what
is good,
and in the day when things are bad, see:
God made both this one as well as that one,
with the result that a person cannot find out
anything after him.

## I haven't found a woman

[15] I've seen everything in my hollow days.

There's a faithful person who perishes in his
faithfulness
and there's a faithless person who endures in
his faithlessness.
[16] Don't be exceedingly faithful
and don't act excessively smart: why should
you be devastated?
[17] Don't be exceedingly faithless and don't be
idiotic:
why should you die when it's not your time?
[18] It's good that you take hold of the one
but also not let go of your grasp of the other,
because someone in awe of God will go out
with all of them.
[19] Smartness strengthens a smart person
more than ten people holding power who
were there in a town.

[20] Because there's no faithful human being on
earth who does good and doesn't do wrong.
[21] Further, don't give your mind to all the things
that people speak, so that you don't hear your
servant slighting you, [22] because many times
your mind also knows that you too have
slighted other people.
[23] When I tested all this with smartness, I said 'I
shall be smart', but it's far away from me. [24] What
happens is far away and deep, deep; who can find
it out? [25] I myself turned round with my mind
to know and to explore, and to seek smartness
and thought, and to know faithlessness as dim-
wittedness and idiocy as madness.
[26] I myself find more bitter than death the
woman who is a great trap, whose mind is a
great snare, whose hands are a great chain.
One who is good before God escapes from her,
but a wrongdoer is caught by her. [27] Look, this
is what I've found, Congregant said, adding
one thing to another to find some thinking,
[28] which I myself sought further but didn't find.

I found one human being among a thousand, but a woman among these I didn't find. [29]Only, look at this, I found that God made humanity upright, but they have sought many thoughts.

*For every purpose there's a time to make a decision*

**8** Who is like the smart person,
and who knows the meaning of a saying:
'A person's smartness lightens up his face,
and the strength of his face is changed.'
[2]I [say]: keep the king's bidding,
and on account of the oath to God [3]don't be fearful.
You should go out from before him;
don't stand against something bad.
Because he can do anything that he purposes,
[4]in that the king's word has power,
And who can say to him, 'What are you doing?';
[5]one who keeps an order will not know something bad.
And the time to exercise authority
the mind of a smart person will know.
[6]Because for every purpose there's a time to exercise authority,
when what is bad for a person is great for him.
[7]Because he doesn't know what will happen,
because who can tell him when it will happen?
[8]There's no one who has power over the spirit,
to restrain the spirit,
And there's no one who has power
over the day of death.
There's no discharge during a battle,
and faithlessness cannot rescue the people
who are masters of it.

[9]All this I saw as I gave my mind to every action that occurs under the sun, the time when a human being held power over a human being, with bad results for him. [10]And then I saw faithless people buried, when they came from the sacred place. They went about and they were put out of mind in the town where they had so acted. This too is hollow.

*To eat and to drink and to rejoice*

[11]When the edict regarding something bad isn't enacted quickly, consequently the mind

of people inside them is full of dealing badly, [12]when a wrongdoer does something bad a hundred times, and it is extended for him. Because I do know that

It will be good for people who live in awe of God,
because they live in awe of him,
[13]And it will not be good for the faithless person
and he won't extend his days, like a shadow,
because he doesn't live in awe of God.

[14]There's a hollowness that occurs on the earth, that there are faithful people to whom things befall in accordance with the action of the faithless, and there are faithless people to whom things befall in accordance with the action of the faithful. I said, 'This too is hollow.' [15]So I myself extolled rejoicing, because there's no good for a person under the sun except to eat and to drink and to rejoice. That can accompany him in his labour for the days of his life that God has given him under the sun. [16]When I gave my mind to knowing smartness and looking at the busyness that is fulfilled on the earth (because even day and night one does not see sleep with one's eyes), [17]and I looked at all the action of God: a human being cannot find out about the action that is undertaken under the sun. When a human being persists in seeking, he doesn't find. Even if a smart person says he'll know, he cannot find out.

*Remember you're going to die . . .*

**9** Because all this I put into my mind, and I sifted all this, that faithful and smart people and their acts of service are in God's hands. Both love and hostility: a person doesn't know anything beforehand. [2]Everything is as it is for everyone. One experience comes to the faithful person and to the faithless, to the good and to the pure and to the polluted, to the person who sacrifices and to the person who doesn't sacrifice. As the good person so is the wrongdoer. The person who swears is like the person who is afraid of an oath. [3]This is something bad about everything that occurs under the sun, that there is one experience for everyone.

Further, the mind of human beings is full of bad things and there is madness in their mind during their life, and afterwards – to the dead. [4]Because whoever is joined to all the living – there is confidence, because a living dog is better than a dead lion. [5]Because the living know that they will die, but the dead don't know anything. There is no more reward for them, because their commemoration has gone out of mind. [6]Both their love and their hostility and their passion has already perished. They have no more share permanently in all that occurs under the sun.

[7]Go, eat your bread with rejoicing, drink your wine with a good mind, because God has already approved your actions. [8]At all times your clothes should be white and oil should not be lacking on your head. [9]See life with the woman that you love all the days of your hollow life that you've been given under the sun, all your hollow days, because that is your share in life and in your labour that you expend under the sun. [10]Everything that your hand finds to do, do with all your energy, because there is no action, thought, knowledge or smartness in Sheol, where you're going.

*. . . and it may be sooner than you think*

[11]I again saw under the sun that

The race doesn't belong to the swift people,
  the battle doesn't belong to the strong people,
Nor bread to the smart people,
  nor wealth to the discerning people,
Nor grace to the knowledgeable people,
  because time and chance happen to all of them.

[12]Rather, a person cannot know his time.

Like fish that are taken in a bad net
  and like birds that are taken by a trap,

like them, human beings are snared by a bad time when it falls on them suddenly. [13]This too I've seen as smartness under the sun, and it seemed big to me. [14]There was a small town and the people in it were few. A big king came to it, surrounded it and built big strongholds against it. [15]There was found in it a poor man who was smart, and he saved the town by his smartness, but no one was mindful of that poor man. [16]I myself said,

Smartness is better than strength,
  but the poor man's smartness is despised
  and his words are not listened to.
[17]The words of smart people with calmness
  are listened to more than the crying out of a
  ruler among dimwits.
[18]Smartness is better than implements of
  engagement,
  but one wrongdoer can obliterate much good.

**10** When dead flies make a stink,
  they ferment the perfumer's oil.
Outweighing smartness, splendour,
  is a little idiocy.
[2]The mind of a smart person goes to his right,
  the mind of a dimwit goes to his left.
[3]Further, on a journey, as an idiot goes, his
    sense is lacking,
  and he tells everyone that he's an idiot.
[4]If the spirit of the ruler arises against you,
  don't let go of your place,
  because calmness can let go of great
    wrongdoings.

## The distressing dynamics of smartness and power

[5]There's something bad I've seen under the sun,
  the very error that comes from someone
    holding power:
[6]Idiocy has been put in many high positions,
  and wealthy people sit in a lowly place.
[7]I've seen servants on horses,
  and officials walking on the ground like
    servants.
[8]The person who digs a pit falls into it;
  the person who breaks down a wall – a snake
    bites him.
[9]The person who quarries stones is hurt by them;
  the person who splits logs is endangered by
    them.
[10]If the iron has become dull,
  and he hasn't sharpened it before,
He must exert more force,
  so smartness is a value for giving success.
[11]If the snake bites when there's no spell,
  there's no value in a master of the tongue.
[12]The words from the smart person's mouth
    mean grace,
  but the lips of a dimwit swallow him.
[13]The beginning of the words from his mouth
    is idiocy

and the end of his mouth is bad madness,

[14]But the idiot multiplies words,
though a person doesn't know what will
happen.
And what will happen after him,
who can tell him?

[15]The labour of dimwits wearies him,
because he doesn't know how to go to a town.

[16]Alas for you, country whose king is a youth
and whose ministers eat in the morning.

[17]Your blessings, country whose king is one
born of important people
and whose officials eat at the proper time,
for strength and not drinking.

[18]Through laziness the roof sags,
through drooping hands the house drips.

[19]For fun people make a meal,
wine rejoices life;
silver answers everything.

[20]Even in your thinking don't slight the king,
and in your bedroom don't slight a wealthy
person,
Because a bird of the heavens may make the
sound travel,
an owner of wings may tell of the thing.

## Enjoy your life . . .

**11** Send off your bread on the surface of
the water,
because in an abundance of days you will find it.

[2]Give a share to seven or even to eight,
because you don't know what bad thing may
happen on the earth.

[3]If the clouds fill,
they will pour down rain on the earth;
If a tree falls
on the south or on the north,
In the place where the tree falls,
there it will be.

[4]Someone who keeps watch on the wind will not
sow,
and someone who sees the clouds will not
reap.

[5]As you don't know the way of the wind,
like the limbs in the womb of a pregnant
woman,
So you don't know the action of God
who does everything.

[6]In the morning sow your seed
and at evening don't let your hand relax,

Because you don't know
which one will succeed,
This one or the other,
or if both of them will be equally good.

[7]The light is sweet
and it's good for the eyes to see the sun.

[8]Because if a person lives many years,
he should rejoice in all of them.
But be mindful of the days of darkness,
because they will be many; everything that
will come is hollow.

[9]Rejoice, young man, during your youth;
your mind should make you feel good in the
days of your youth.
Walk about in the ways of your mind
and in the sights of your eyes.
But acknowledge that for all these things
God will bring you to account.

## Mindful of your creator

[10]So remove vexation from your mind
and make what is bad pass from your body
Because youth and vigour are hollow.

**12** So be mindful of your creator in the
days of your youth,
Before the bad days come,
and the years arrive of which you'll say,
'There's no purpose for me in them',
[2]before it goes dark,
The sun, the light, the moon and the stars,
and the clouds come back after the rain,

[3]On the day when the keepers of the house
tremble,
and the strong men stoop.
The women who grind stop because they are few,
and the women who look through the
windows get dark.

[4]The gateways to the street are shut,
as the sound of the mill becomes low.
One gets up at the sound of a bird,
but all the songs get weak.

[5]Further, people are afraid of a height
and there are terrors on the road.
The almond blossoms, the grasshopper carries
itself along,
and the caperberry bears fruit.
But the human being is going to his eternal home
and the mourners are coming round in the
street –

⁶Before the silver cord snaps,
  and the gold bowl breaks,
The jar shatters at the spring,
  and the wheel breaks at the cistern,
⁷The earth goes back to the ground as it was,
  and the spirit goes back to the God who
    gave it.
⁸Utter hollowness, said Congregant,
  utter hollowness, everything is hollow.

⁹But further: because Congregant was smart, he still taught the people knowledge. He weighed and examined, set in order many aphorisms. ¹⁰Congregant sought to find purposeful words, and what is written was upright. Truthful words, ¹¹smart words, are like goads; the masters of collections are like fixed nails. They were given by one shepherd.

¹²But further, beyond these, son, beware. Of the making of many books there is no end, and much study is a wearying of the body. ¹³The end of the thing; everything has been heard. Live in awe of God and keep his orders, because this is for everyone. ¹⁴Because God brings every action to account, including everything hidden, whether good or bad.

# THE SONG OF SONGS

The expression 'song of songs' means it's 'the best song'. It's a series of poems about the relationship between two people who are in love. They are poems that describe in an imaginative way moments in a relationship. They may all refer to the same relationship or they may be separate imaginative compositions; there are no indications that they are poems that tell one couple's story. The relationship between the two people is evidently exclusive and it implies a commitment that will surely be lifelong, but the two are not living together, so they are apparently not married. Further, they speak of tensions and conflicts in the community over their relationship, so their relationship is apparently not yet 'official' in the community. They are not betrothed, though in their own minds and hearts they are evidently committed.

The opening description of the songs as Solomonic marks them as expressions of wisdom or smartness in the same way as Proverbs and Ecclesiastes. They are the kind of smart teaching of which Solomon was the patron. The description need not imply that he composed the poems, and what we know of him from his story in Kings and Chronicles doesn't suggest he would have had the kind of experience or would think the kind of way that the poems do. Indeed, he would have a lot to learn from them. (In the imaginative picture in chapter 3, the emphasis lies on his opulence and might rather than on his love.)

There are expressions in the poems that can also describe something about relationships between God and his people: 'I belong to my love and he belongs to me.' But there are no indications that the poems were written to illustrate that relationship or that they were included in the Scriptures on that basis. Indeed, while the Scriptures do use marriage as an image for the relationship between God and his people, the kind of marriage they have in mind in that connection is one where the husband is master and the wife is submissive. The relationship portrayed in the Song of Songs is egalitarian rather than hierarchical, so that most of it does not correspond to the way relationships between God and his people work.

Like Proverbs and Ecclesiastes, the poems issue from reflection on how life actually works out, and what they do is invite people to live in the light of the reality that they describe. They would thus have things to say to young couples and also to the wider community. They have things to say about the wonder of the relationship between two people, and also about its frustrations, fears and pressures.

The way Hebrew works often indicates whether a male or a female is the speaker, and in these poems it is therefore generally possible to know when the man is speaking and when the woman is speaking.

## ❧ *Alone together* ❧

**1** The Song of Songs, which is Shelomoh's [Solomon's].

Woman  ²May he kiss me with some of the
        kisses of his mouth! –
      because your love is better than wine.
³The fragrance – your oils are good,
    your name is oil poured out.
Therefore girls love you;
    ⁴pull me after you, let's run.
The king has brought me into his
      rooms;
    let's celebrate and rejoice in you.
Let's make mention of your love more
      than wine;
    rightly they love you.

⁵I am dark but lovely,
    Yerushalaim daughters,
Like the tents of Qedar,
    like Shelomoh's curtains.
⁶Don't look at me because I'm dark-
      skinned,
    because the sun has stared at me.
My mother's sons were enraged with
      me,
    they made me someone who guards
      the vineyards.
My vineyard, the one I had,
    I didn't guard.
⁷Tell me, you whom my entire being
      loves,
    where do you pasture,
    where do you rest them at midday?
Why should I be like someone
      covering herself
    by the flocks of your companions?

Man  ⁸If you don't know for yourself,
    loveliest of women,
Get yourself out in the tracks of the
      flock,
    pasture your goats
    by the shepherds' dwellings.
⁹To a mare among Par'oh's [Pharaoh's]
      chariots
    I have compared you, my dear.
¹⁰Lovely are your cheeks with earrings,
    your neck with necklaces;
¹¹We will make gold earrings for you,
    with studs of silver.

Woman  ¹²While the king was on his couch,
    my nard gave its fragrance.
¹³My love to me is a bag of myrrh
    that lodges between my breasts.
¹⁴My love to me is a cluster of henna
    in the vineyards of Gedi Spring.

Man  ¹⁵There you are, so lovely, my dear;
    there you are, so lovely, your eyes
      doves.

## *The crocus and the apricot*

Woman  ¹⁶There you are so lovely, my love,
    yes beautiful, yes our couch is
      verdant.
¹⁷Cedars are the beams of our house,
    junipers our rafters.

**2** I am a crocus of Sharon,
    a lotus of the vales.

Man  ²Like a lotus among thorns,
    so is my dear among the daughters.

Woman  ³Like an apricot among the trees of the
      forest,
    so is my love among the sons.
In its shade I desired to sit,
    and its fruit was sweet to my palate.
⁴He brought me into the house of wine,
    and love was his standard over me.
⁵Refresh me with raisins, revive me
      with apricots,
    because I'm ill with love.
⁶His left arm under my head,
    his right arm would embrace me.
⁷I want you to swear, Yerushalaim
      daughters,
    by the gazelles or by the deer in the
      fields:
If you awaken, if you arouse love,
    before it wishes . . .

⁸The sound of my love! – there, he's
      coming;
    leaping over the mountains,
    bounding over the hills.
⁹My love is like a gazelle,
    or a young stag.
There, he's standing, behind our wall,
    gazing from the window, peering
      from the lattice.

¹⁰My love affirmed and said to me:
  'Get yourself up, my dear,
  my lovely one, and get yourself going!
¹¹Because there – the winter has passed,
  the rain has stopped and taken itself
  off.
¹²The blossoms have appeared in the
  country,
  the time of music has arrived,
The voice of the dove
  has made itself heard in our country.
¹³The fig tree has ripened its green fruit,
  the blossoming vines have given
  their fragrance.
Get yourself up, my dear,
  my lovely one, and get yourself
  going!
¹⁴My dove, in the clefts of the crag,
  in the hiddenness of the cliff,
Let me see your appearance,
  let me hear your voice.
Because your voice is pleasing,
  your appearance is alluring.'

¹⁵Catch the foxes for us, the little foxes,
  ruining the vineyards, when our
  vineyards are in blossom.

## My love is mine and I am his

Woman  ¹⁶My love belongs to me and I belong
  to him,
  the one who pastures among the
  lotuses.
¹⁷While the day breathes and the
  shadows flee,
  turn round, be like a gazelle, my love,
  or a young stag on the Beter
  Mountains.

**3** On my bed by night, I searched
  for the one my entire being loves;
I searched for him but didn't find
  him.
²'I'll get up, please, and go round the
  town,
  through the streets and through the
  squares.
I'll search for the one my entire being
  loves;
  I've searched for him but not found
  him.'

³The watchmen found me as they went
  round the town:
  'Have you seen the one my entire
  being loves?'
⁴Scarcely had I passed them,
  when I found the one my entire
  being loves.
I took hold of him and wouldn't
  slacken hold of him,
  until I'd brought him to my mother's
  house,
  to the room of the one who
  conceived me.
⁵I want you to swear, Yerushalaim
  daughters,
  by the gazelles or by the deer in the
  fields:
If you awaken, if you arouse love,
  before it wishes . . .

Man  ⁶Who is this coming up from the
  wilderness,
  like columns of smoke,
Perfumed with myrrh and incense,
  from every powder of a merchant?
⁷There, Shelomoh's bed,
  sixty strong men round it,
  of the strong men of Israel.
⁸All of them are girded with a sword,
  trained in battle,
Each with his sword on his side,
  because of the terror of the night.
⁹King Shelomoh had made himself a
  sedan,
  of wood from the Lebanon.
¹⁰He had made its posts of silver,
  its base of gold, its seat of purple.
Its inside was inlaid with love
  by the Yerushalaim daughters.
¹¹Go out and look, Tsiyyon [Zion]
  daughters,
  at King Shelomoh in the crown
With which his mother has crowned him
  on his wedding day,
  on the day of his heartfelt rejoicing.

## Crazy for love

Man  **4** There you are, so lovely, my dear,
  there you are, so lovely.
Your eyes are doves
  behind your veil.

Your hair is like a flock of goats
  that stream from Mount Gil'ad.
²Your teeth are like a flock of shorn ewes
  that climb up from the washing,
Which are all of them twinning,
  and there's none bereaved among
    them.
³Like a crimson ribbon are your lips;
  your mouth is lovely.
Like the splitting of a pomegranate
  is your brow behind your veil.
⁴Like David's Tower is your neck,
  built in courses,
Hung with a thousand shields on it,
  all the bows of strong men.
⁵Your two breasts are like two fawns,
  the twins of a gazelle pasturing
    among the lotuses.
⁶While the day breathes,
  and the shadows flee,
I'll get myself to the mountain of myrrh,
  to the hill of incense.
⁷Every part of you is lovely, my dear;
  there's no flaw in you.
⁸With me from Lebanon, my bride,
  with me from Lebanon, you should
    come!
You should gaze from the top of
    Amana,
  from the top of Senir and Hermon,
From the abodes of lions,
  from the mountains of leopards.

⁹You've captured my heart, my sister, my
    bride, you've captured my heart,
  with one of your eyes,
  with one strand of your necklace.
¹⁰How beautiful is your love,
  my sister, my bride!
How much better is your love than
    wine,
  the fragrance of your oils than all
    perfumes!
¹¹Your lips drop honey, my bride;
  syrup and milk are under your
    tongue.
The fragrance of your robes
  is like the fragrance of Lebanon.
¹²A locked garden, my sister, my bride,
  a locked fountain, a sealed fountain:
¹³Your shoots are an orchard of
    pomegranates,
  with choice fruit,

Henna with much spikenard,
  ¹⁴spikenard and saffron,
Cane and cinnamon,
  with all the incense woods,
Myrrh and aloes,
  with all the top perfumes:
¹⁵A garden spring,
  a well of living water,
    flowing from Lebanon.

## Nightmares and dreams

Woman   ¹⁶Awake, north wind, and come, south
    wind,
  breathe on my garden so its
    perfumes may spread.
May my love come to his garden,
  and eat its choice fruit!

Man   **5** I've come to my garden, my sister,
    my bride.
I've plucked my myrrh with its
    perfume.

Girls   Eat, friends, drink,
  get drunk on love.

Woman   ²I was sleeping, but my mind was
    awake;
  the sound of my love, knocking!
'Open for me, my sister, my dear,
  my dove, my perfect one.
My head is full of dew,
  my hair with the moisture of night.'
³'I've taken off my robe; how can I get
    dressed?
  I've washed my feet, how can I get
    them dirty?'
⁴My love put out his hand through the
    hole;
  my heart was in turmoil for him.
⁵I myself got up to open to my love;
  my hands dripped with myrrh.
So my fingers were flowing myrrh
  on the hollows of the bolt.
⁶I myself opened the door for my love,
  but my love had turned, passed on.
My entire being had gone out at his
    speaking;
  I looked for him but I didn't find
    him,
  I called him, but he didn't answer me.

⁷The watchmen found me as they went
        round the town;
    they struck me down, injured me.
They took my shawl from upon me,
    the watchmen on the walls.
⁸I want you to swear, Yerushalaim
        daughters,
    if you find my love:
What are you to tell him?
    – that I am ill with love.

## How is your love more than another love?

Girls        ⁹How is your love more than another
                love,
            most beautiful among women?
        How is your love more than another
            love,
            that you want us to swear in that
                way?

Woman    ¹⁰My love is radiant and ruddy,
                outstanding among ten thousand.
        ¹¹His head is gold, fine gold;
            his hair curly, black as a raven.
        ¹²His eyes are like doves by water
                canyons,
            bathing in milk, sitting by a full pool.
        ¹³His cheeks like a bed of spice,
            towers of perfumes.
        His lips are lotuses,
            dripping flowing myrrh.
        ¹⁴His hands are gold rods,
            covered in Tarshish-stone.
        His stomach is an ivory plate,
            overlaid with sapphires.
        ¹⁵His legs are alabaster pillars,
            founded on sockets of fine gold.
        His appearance is like the Lebanon,
            choice as the cedars.
        ¹⁶His palate is total sweetness;
            all of him is desirable.
        This is my love, this is my dear,
            Yerushalaim daughters!

Girls     **6** Where has your love gone,
            loveliest among women?
        Where has your love turned his face,
            so we may search for him with you?

Woman    ²My love has gone down to his garden,
            to the beds of spice,

To pasture in the gardens,
    and to pick lotuses.
³I belong to my love and my love
    belongs to me,
    the one who pastures among the
        lotuses.

Man    ⁴You're beautiful, my dear, as Tirtsah,
            lovely as Yerushalaim, awe-inspiring
            as bannered armies.
        ⁵Turn your eyes round from in front
            of me;
            they – they overwhelm me.
        Your hair is like a flock of goats
            that stream from Mount Gil'ad.
        ⁶Your teeth are like a flock of shorn
            ewes
            that climb up from the washing,
        Which are all of them twinning,
            and there's none bereaved among
                them.
        ⁷Like the splitting of a pomegranate
            is your brow behind your veil.
        ⁸There are sixty queens,
            eighty secondary wives,
        Girls without number;
            ⁹my dove, my perfect one, is
                unique.
        She's unique to her mother,
            she's special to the one who gave
                birth to her.
        Daughters have seen her and called her
            blessed;
            queens and secondary wives have
                praised her.

## His desire is toward me

Girls        ¹⁰Who is this who looks out like the
                dawn,
            beautiful as the moon,
        Special like the sun,
            awe-inspiring as bannered armies?

Woman    ¹¹I went down to the garden of nut-
                trees
            to see the blossoms in the wadi,
        To see the budding of the vine,
            whether the pomegranates had
                bloomed.
        ¹²Though I didn't know,
            my entire being set me with the
                chariots of my generous people.

Girls  ¹³Turn back, turn back, Shulammite;
Turn back, turn back, so we may
behold you!

Man  Why will you behold the Shulammite,
like the Mahanayim dance?

# 7

How beautiful are your feet
in sandals, noble daughter!
The curves of your hips are like rings,
the work of a craftsman's hands.
²Your navel is a round bowl;
mixed wine will not be lacking.
Your waist is a heap of wheat,
encircled by lotuses.
³Your two breasts are like two fawns,
the twins of a gazelle.
⁴Your neck is like an ivory tower,
your eyes are pools at Heshbon,
By the gate of Bat-rabbim,
your nose like the Lebanon tower,
Watching towards Damascus,
⁵your head upon you like Carmel,
The locks on your head like purple;
a king is captivated by your tresses.
⁶How beautiful you are, how lovely
you are,
love with delights;
⁷This, your stature, is like a palm,
your breasts are clusters.
⁸I've said, I shall climb the palm,
I'll take hold of its stems.
May your breasts please be like the
clusters of the vine,
the fragrance of your breath like
apricots,
⁹your palate like good wine.

Woman  It goes straight to my love,
gliding over the lips of sleepers.
¹⁰I belong to my love
and his desire is towards me.
¹¹Come, my love, let's go out to the
fields,
let's lodge in the hamlets.
¹²Let's start early for the vineyards,
let's see if the vine has budded,
The blossom has opened, the
pomegranates have bloomed;
there I'll give my love to you.
¹³The mandrakes have given fragrance,
and at our doors are all choice
things.

Fresh and also old things, my love,
I've stored for you.

## Love is as fierce as death

Woman  # 8

If only you could be made like a
brother to me,
one who was nursing at my mother's
breasts.
When I found you in the street I could
kiss you;
people would not despise me,
either.
²I would lead you, I would bring you,
to the house of my mother, the one
who taught me.
I would get you to drink some spiced
wine,
some of my pomegranate juice.
³His left hand would be under my
head,
his right hand would hold me.
⁴I want you to swear, Yerushalaim
daughters, don't awaken,
don't arouse love, before it wishes.

Girls  ⁵Who is this coming up from the
wilderness,
leaning on her love?

Woman  Under the apricot tree I aroused you;
there your mother conceived you,
there the one who gave birth to
you conceived you.
⁶Make me like a seal on your heart,
like a seal on your arm.
Because love is as fierce as death,
passion as tough as She'ol.
Its darts are darts of fire,
a supernatural flame.
⁷Much water could not quench love,
nor rivers overflow it.
If someone gave all his household's
resources for love,
people would totally despise him.

Boys  ⁸We have a little sister;
she doesn't have breasts.
What shall we do for our sister
on the day when she's spoken for?
⁹If she's a wall,
we'll build on it a silver battlement.

If she's a door,
    we'll enclose it with cedar
      panelling.

Woman  [10]I am a wall
    and my breasts are like towers;
Then I've become in his eyes
    like one who finds well-being.
[11]Shelomoh had a vineyard
    in Ba'al Hamon;
He gave the vineyard to guards;
    someone would give for its fruit
  a thousand silver pieces.

[12]My vineyard is before me;
    the thousand are yours, Shelomoh,
    and 200 for the people who guard
      the fruit.

Man  [13]You who live in the gardens, with
    friends listening:
    let me hear your voice.

Woman  [14]Take flight, my love,
    be like a gazelle,
Or like a young stag,
    on the mountains of spices.

# ISAIAH

The book of Isaiah [Yesha'yahu] is a collection of prophecies addressed to the people of Judah. Isaiah lived in the eighth century BC, a time of crisis for Judah associated with the expansion of the Assyrian Empire into the region. A major focus of Isaiah's prophecies concerns how Judah needs to deal with different aspects of the challenge this crisis brings.

- Chapters 1—12 give dates in the time of King Ahaz, the 730s, when Ephraim and Syria are leaning on Judah to resist Assyria, and Isaiah urges Judah to trust God for its future.
- Chapters 13—23 speak of what God intends to do in relation to the other peoples around Judah, so as to urge Judah not to be afraid of them but not to trust them either.
- Chapters 24—27 widen the horizon to speak of God's purpose for the world as a whole.
- Chapters 28—39 return to focus directly on Judah, but now in the time of King Hezekiah, the 700s, when Ephraim and Syria have fallen and Judah is seeking help from Egypt in order to resist Assyria.

Isaiah's prophecies are thus quite coherently organized on a large scale, though readers are often bemused about the train of thought within these major collections of chapters. The chapters collect short prophecies delivered on different occasions. So any given chapter probably brings together several separate prophecies that did not originally belong together.

Isaiah wants Judah and its king to live by trust in the commitment Yahweh made to David and his successors and to Jerusalem as the place where he himself deigned to dwell. The promises that work out God's commitment to David are ones that help us understand Jesus. But in origin they brought God's word to his people in Isaiah's day. So Christians need to read them as indications of the way God was speaking to his people in that context and as promises that can help us understand Jesus, and understand what God still intends to do.

The first 39 chapters of Isaiah close with a declaration that members of Hezekiah's family are going to end up in exile in Babylon. It happened a century or so later. When we then turn over the page into Isaiah 40 we read a message of comfort to those exiles: the time of their restoration from exile has arrived. Babylon is about to fall to the Persians, which happened in 539 BC.

These prophecies are not couched as promises that one day Yahweh will restore his people. They are declarations that Yahweh is taking that action now. The implication is that they were given in the sixth century, not the eighth century. In the chapters that follow Isaiah 40 we can see links with earlier prophecies in the book. They continue to use Isaiah's favourite title for Yahweh, that he is 'Israel's Holy One' or 'Sacred One'. So in these chapters a prophet or a series of prophets is taking up Isaiah's message and proclaiming what he would say if he were here now. He had spoken of how Yahweh's being Israel's Holy One had been bad news – it meant Yahweh was going to discipline Judah for its rebellion against him. These chapters declare that Yahweh's being Israel's Holy One is now good news for Judah – it is this Holy One who is their restorer. Once again there are prophecies that helped the New Testament understand the significance of Jesus, particularly Isaiah 52.13—53.12. It describes a servant of God who has been persecuted but will be restored. This description will have applied to someone in the prophet's day, but it helped Jesus and people who believed in Jesus to understand him.

When we turn over the page again after Isaiah 40—55, we discover that the situation has again moved on. Isaiah 56—66 relates to the situation of Judah when people have been free to return there after their exile but where things are not as wonderful as they might have expected, and they bring together messages designed to enable the community to live in that context and keep being hopeful and committed. In Isaiah 61 there is a testimony by a prophet called to bring that message, and it is another chapter that Jesus took up and applied to himself.

*Haven't you had enough?*

**1** The vision of Yesha'yahu ben Amots which he beheld concerning Yehudah and Yerushalaim in the days of Uzziyyahu, Yotam, Ahaz and Yehizqiyyahu [Uzziah, Jotham, Ahaz and Hezekiah], kings of Yehudah.

²Listen, heavens, give ear, earth,
  because Yahweh has spoken.
I reared children, I raised them,
  but they – they rebelled against me.
³An ox acknowledges its owner,
  a donkey its master's manger.
Yisra'el doesn't acknowledge,
  my people doesn't show any discernment.
⁴Hey, wrongdoing nation,
  a people heavy with waywardness!
Offspring of people who deal badly, devastating
  children,
    they've abandoned Yahweh.
They've disdained Yisra'el's sacred one,
  they've become estranged, backwards.

⁵Why will you be struck down more,
  continue being defiant?
The whole head has come to sickness,
  the whole mind is faint.
⁶From the sole of the foot to the head,
  there's no integrity in it.
Bruise, blotch, fresh wound –
  they haven't been pressed out.
They haven't been bandaged,
  it hasn't been softened with oil.
⁷Your country's a desolation,
  your towns burned with fire.
Your land – in front of you,
  foreigners are consuming it,
A desolation, quite overthrown by foreigners,
  ⁸and Miss Tsiyyon [Zion] is left like a shelter in
    a vineyard,
Like a place to stay the night in a melon field,
  like a town besieged.
⁹Had Yahweh of Armies
  not left us survivors, a few,
We'd have been like Sedom [Sodom],
  we'd have resembled Amorah [Gomorrah].

*I'm fed up to the teeth with your worship*

¹⁰Listen to Yahweh's word,
  rulers of Sedom!

Give ear to our God's instruction,
  people of Amorah!
¹¹What use to me is the large number of your sacrifices?
  (Yahweh says).
I'm full of burnt offerings of rams
  and the fat of fatlings.
In the blood of bulls and lambs and goats
  I do not delight.
¹²When you come to appear to my face,
  who sought this from your hand?
Trampling my courtyards – ¹³you will do it no more,
  bringing an empty offering.
Incense is an offence to me,
  new month and sabbath, the calling of a
    convocation.
I cannot bear trouble and assembly;
  ¹⁴your new moons and your appointed times
    my entire being dislikes.
They've become a burden to me
  that I'm weary of carrying.
¹⁵And when you spread the palms of your hands,
  I shall lift up my eyes from you.
Even when you offer many a plea,
  there will be no listening on my part.
Your hands are full of bloodshed –
  ¹⁶wash, get clean.
Remove the badness of your practices
  from in front of my eyes.
Stop dealing badly,
  ¹⁷learn doing good.
Require the exercise of authority, put the
    oppressor right,
  exercise authority for the orphan, argue for the
    widow.

¹⁸Come on, please, let's argue it out
  (Yahweh says).
If your wrongdoings are like scarlet,
  they're to be white like snow.
If they're red like crimson,
  they're to be like wool.
¹⁹If you're willing and you listen,
  you will consume the good things of the country.
²⁰But if you refuse and rebel,
  you'll be consumed by the sword;
  because Yahweh's mouth has spoken.

*Second-degree manslaughter*

²¹Aagh, she's become a whore,
  the trustworthy township, full of the exercise of
    authority.

Faithfulness was lodging in it,
  but now murderers.
<sup>22</sup>Your silver has become slag,
  your drink is diluted with water.
<sup>23</sup>Your officers are defiant, the associates of thieves;
  every one of them loves a bribe, chases gifts.
They don't exercise authority for the orphan;
  the widow's cause doesn't come to them.

<sup>24</sup>Therefore the declaration of the Lord,
  Yahweh of Armies, Yisra'el's champion, is:
'Hey, I shall get relief from my adversaries,
  take redress from my enemies,
<sup>25</sup>turn back my hand against you.

But I shall smelt your slag as with lye,
  remove all your contamination.
<sup>26</sup>I shall restore your leaders as of old,
  your counsellors as at the beginning.
Afterwards you will be called faithful town,
  trustworthy township.'

<sup>27</sup>Tsiyyon will find redemption through the
  exercise of authority,
  and the people in it who turn back, through
  faithfulness.
<sup>28</sup>But there will be a breaking of rebels and
  wrongdoers, all together,
  and the people who abandon Yahweh will be
  finished.
<sup>29</sup>Because they'll be shamed on account of the
  oaks that you desired;
  you will be confounded on account of the
  gardens that you chose.
<sup>30</sup>Because you'll be like an oak wilting of foliage,
  like a garden for which there's no water.
<sup>31</sup>The strong person will become tinder,
  his work a spark.
The two of them will burn all together,
  and there will be no one quenching.

**2** The word that Yesha'yahu ben Amots
beheld concerning Yehudah and
Yerushalaim.

*Study war no more*

<sup>2</sup>It will come about at the end of the time:

The mountain of Yahweh's house will have
  become established

at the head of the mountains, and it will lift up
  higher than the hills.
All the nations will stream to it;
  <sup>3</sup>many peoples will come and say,
'Come on, let's go up to Yahweh's mountain,
  to the house of Ya'aqob's [Jacob's] God,
So he may instruct us in his ways,
  and we may walk in his paths.'
Because instruction will go out from Tsiyyon,
  Yahweh's word from Yerushalaim.
<sup>4</sup>He will exercise authority among the nations,
  and issue reproof to many peoples.
They'll beat their swords into hoes,
  their spears into pruning hooks.
Nation will not carry sword against nation;
  they will no more learn about battle.
<sup>5</sup>Ya'aqob's household, come on,
  let's walk by Yahweh's light.

<sup>6</sup>Because you have left your people alone,
  Ya'aqob's household.
Because they are full from the east,
  yes, of diviners like the Pelishtites [Philistines],
  and they abound in children of foreigners.
<sup>7</sup>Its country's full of silver and gold;
  there's no end to its treasures.
Its country's full of horses;
  there's no end to its chariots.
<sup>8</sup>Its country's full of non-entities;
  they bow low to the making of their hands,
  to what their fingers made.
<sup>9</sup>So humanity bows down, the individual falls
  down
  (may you not carry them).

<sup>10</sup>Come into the crag,
  bury yourself in the earth,
Before the fearfulness of Yahweh,
  from the dreadfulness of his majesty.
<sup>11</sup>Lofty human eyes have fallen down,
  the exaltedness of individuals has bowed down.
Yahweh alone will be on high
  on that day.

*The destiny of all that is humanly
impressive*

<sup>12</sup>Because Yahweh of Armies has a day
  against all majesty and exaltedness,
Against all that is high –
  and it will fall down,

<sup>13</sup>Against all the cedars of the Lebanon, exalted
  and high,
  against all the oaks of the Bashan,
<sup>14</sup>Against all the exalted mountains,
  against all the high hills,
<sup>15</sup>Against every lofty tower,
  against every fortified wall,
<sup>16</sup>Against every Tarshish ship,
  against all the impressive vessels.
<sup>17</sup>Human loftiness will bow down,
  people's exaltedness will fall down.
Yahweh alone will be on high on that day;
  <sup>18</sup>non-entities – they will completely vanish.
<sup>19</sup>People will go into caves in the crags,
  into holes in the earth,
From before the fearfulness of Yahweh,
  from the dreadfulness of his majesty,
  when he arises to terrify the country.
<sup>20</sup>On that day humanity will throw away
  its silver non-entities and its gold non-
    entities,
Which they made for it to bow down to,
  to the moles and to the bats,
<sup>21</sup>To come into the clefts in the crags,
  into the crevices in the cliffs,
Before the fearfulness of Yahweh,
  from the dreadfulness of his majesty,
  when he arises to terrify the earth.
<sup>22</sup>Get yourselves away from humanity,
  that has breath in its nostrils,
  because what is it to count for?

*You have a coat, you can be a leader*

**3** Because there,
  the Lord Yahweh of Armies
Is removing from Yerushalaim and from
    Yehudah
  supply and support:
All supply of bread
  and all supply of water,
<sup>2</sup>Strong man and man of battle,
  leader and prophet, diviner and elder,
<sup>3</sup>Officer over fifty, person held in high regard,
    counsellor,
  person smart with charms and understanding
    chants.
<sup>4</sup>I will make youths their officials;
  infants will rule over them.
<sup>5</sup>The people will oppress one another,
  each his neighbour.

The youth will be arrogant towards the elder,
  one who is slighted towards someone
    honourable.
<sup>6</sup>Because a man will seize one of his brothers,
  his father's household:
'You have a coat, you will be a leader for us,
  this ruin will be under your hand.'
<sup>7</sup>On that day he will shout,
  'I won't be one to bind up.
In my house there's no bread and no coat –
  you won't make me leader of the people.'

<sup>8</sup>Because Yerushalaim has collapsed,
  Yehudah has fallen.
Because their tongue and their practices have
    been towards Yahweh
  to be rebellious against his glorious eyes.
<sup>9</sup>The look on their face testifies against them;
  they declare their wrongdoing like Sedom and
    don't hide it.
Aagh, for their lives,
  because they have dealt themselves bad fortune.
<sup>10</sup>Say of the faithful person, 'It will be good',
  because they will eat the fruit of their practices.
<sup>11</sup>Aagh, for the faithless person, 'It will be bad',
  because the dealing of his hands will be done
    to him.
<sup>12</sup>My people – infants are their bosses,
  women rule over them.
My people – your guides make you wander;
  they've swallowed up the course of your paths.

<sup>13</sup>Yahweh is taking his stand to argue,
  he's rising to give judgement for peoples.
<sup>14</sup>Yahweh will come in the exercise of authority
  with his people's elders and its officials.
'You – you've burned up the vineyard,
  the humble person's plunder is in your houses.
<sup>15</sup>What do you mean that you crush my people,
  grind the faces of humble ones?
  (a declaration of the Lord Yahweh of Armies).'

*Dresses, shawls and purses*

  <sup>16</sup>Yahweh has said:

Since Tsiyyon's daughters are lofty,
  and walk outstretched with their neck,
Flirting with their eyes,
  walking and mincing as they walk,
  and they jingle with their feet,

<sup>17</sup>The Lord will bare the crown of Tsiyyon's
  daughters,
    Yahweh will expose their forehead.

<sup>18</sup>On that day the Lord will remove the
splendour of the anklets, the bands and
the necklaces, <sup>19</sup>the earrings, the bracelets
and the veils, <sup>20</sup>the hats, the armlets, the
scarves, the amulets and the charms, <sup>21</sup>the rings
and the nose rings, <sup>22</sup>the dresses, the capes, the
shawls, the purses, <sup>23</sup>the gowns, the blouses,
the tiaras, the veils and the sashes.

<sup>24</sup>Instead of perfume there will be a stench;
  instead of a wrap, a rope;
Instead of a hairdo, a shorn head;
  instead of a robe, a wrapping of sack;
    branding instead of beauty.
<sup>25</sup>Your men [Tsiyyon] will fall by the sword,
  your strength by battle.
<sup>26</sup>Her gateways will lament and mourn;
  she'll be empty, she'll sit on the ground.

**4** Seven women will take strong hold of one
      man
  on that day,
Saying, 'We'll eat our bread,
  we'll wear our clothes,
Only may your name be called out over us –
  gather up our reviling.'

<sup>2</sup>On that day, Yahweh's shoot will be
  for beauty and for splendour,
And the country's fruit
  for majesty and for glory for Yisra'el's escape
    group.
<sup>3</sup>What remains in Tsiyyon,
  what is left in Yerushalaim –
'Sacred' will be said of it,
  everyone who's been written down for life in
    Yerushalaim.

<sup>4</sup>If the Lord has washed away
  the filth of Tsiyyon's daughters,
And cleanses from within it
  the shed blood of Yerushalaim,
By a spirit of the exercise of authority
  and by a spirit of burning away,
<sup>5</sup>Yahweh will create
  over the entire establishment of Mount Tsiyyon,
  and over its meeting place,
A cloud by day, and smoke,
  and a brightness of flaming fire by night.

Because over all the splendour will be a canopy,
  <sup>6</sup>and it will be a bivouac,
For shade by day from the heat,
  and for shelter and for a hiding place from
    storm and from rain.

## A singer-songwriter's strange song

**5** I want to sing a song for my friend,
    my love song about his vineyard.
My friend had a vineyard
  on a fertile ridge.
<sup>2</sup>He dug it and de-stoned it,
  and planted it with choice vine.
He built a tower in the middle of it,
  and also hewed a press in it.
He hoped it would make grapes,
  but it made rotten grapes.
<sup>3</sup>So now, population of Yerushalaim,
  people of Yehudah,
  decide, please, between me and my vineyard.
<sup>4</sup>What more was there to do for my vineyard,
  and I didn't do in it?
Why, when I hoped for it to make grapes,
  did it make rotten grapes?
<sup>5</sup>So now I want to let you know, please,
  what I'm doing about my vineyard:
Remove its hedge, so it will be for burning up,
  break down its wall so it will be for
    trampling,
  <sup>6</sup>so that I make an end of it.
It won't be pruned and it won't be hoed;
  briar and thorn will grow.
I shall order the clouds
  not to send rain on it.
<sup>7</sup>Because the vineyard of Yahweh of Armies
  is the household of Yisra'el.
The people of Yehudah
  are the planting in which he took pleasure.
He hoped for the exercise of authority, but there –
  blood pouring out;
  for faithfulness, but there – a cry.

## She'ol has broadened its appetite

<sup>8</sup>Hey, people adding house to house,
  who join field to field,
Until there's no room,
  and you're made to live alone in the middle of
    the country.

[9]In my ears Yahweh of Armies [has said]:

If many houses do not become desolation,
  big and good ones without inhabitant . . .
[10]Because ten acres of vineyard
  will make five gallons.
Ten barrels of seed
  will make a barrel.

[11]Hey, people who start early in the morning
  so they can chase liquor,
Stay late in the dusk
  so wine can inflame them.
[12]There'll be guitar and mandolin,
  tambourine and pipe and wine at their
    banquets.
But Yahweh's deed they don't look to,
  the action of his hands they haven't watched.
[13]Therefore my people are going into exile
  because of not acknowledging.
Its splendour – hungry people,
  its horde – parched with thirst.
[14]Therefore She'ol has broadened its appetite,
  opened its mouth without limit.
Its magnificence will go down,
  its horde and its din and the one who exults
    in it.
[15]Human beings bow down, individuals fall down,
  the eyes of the lofty fall down.
[16]And Yahweh of Armies is lofty in exercising
    authority;
  the sacred God shows himself sacred in
    faithfulness.
[17]Lambs will pasture as in their meadow,
  aliens will eat the fatlings' wastes.

[18]Hey, people who haul waywardness
  with cords of emptiness,
  and wrongdoing as with cart ropes,
[19]Who say, 'He should hurry,
  he should speed up his action, in order that we
    may see.
It should draw near and come about,
  the counsel of Yisra'el's sacred one, so we may
    acknowledge.'

[20]Hey, people who say about what is bad, 'Good',
  and about what is good, 'Bad',
Who make darkness into light,
  and light into darkness,
Who make bitter into sweet,
  and sweet into bitter.

## Yahweh will whistle

[21]Hey, people who are smart in their eyes,
  who in their view are understanding.
[22]Hey, strong men at drinking wine,
  forceful people at mixing a drink,
[23]Who declare a faithless person to be in the
    right
  in return for a bribe,
And the faithfulness of the faithful people
  they remove from them.
[24]Therefore: like the consuming of straw in a
    tongue of fire,
  when hay sinks down in the flame,
Their root will become veritable rot,
  and their blossom will go up like dust,
Because they've rejected the instruction of
    Yahweh of Armies,
  spurned the word of Yisra'el's sacred one.

[25]On account of this Yahweh's anger flared against
    his people;
  he stretched out his hand against it and struck
    it down.
Mountains shook, and their corpses became
  like refuse in the middle of the streets.
For all this his anger did not turn back;
  his hand was still stretched out.

[26]He will lift a signal to the nations from afar,
  he will whistle to one from the end of the
    earth,
  and there – with speed, quick, it will come.
[27]There's none weary, there's none collapsing,
    in it;
  it doesn't slumber, it doesn't sleep.
The belt on its waist doesn't come loose,
  the thong on its boots doesn't break.
[28]Its arrows are sharpened,
  all its bows are directed.
Its horses' hoofs are thought of like flint,
  its wheels like a whirlwind.
[29]Its roar is like a cougar's;
  it roars like lions.
It growls and seizes prey,
  and carries it off and there's no one rescuing.
[30]It will growl over it on that day, like the growling
    of the sea;
  and he will look to the land,
And there, darkness, pressure,
  and the light will have gone dark with its
    thunderclouds.

## A commission to frighten people into repentance

**6** In the year King Uzziyyahu died, I saw the Lord sitting on a throne, high and lofty, with his train filling the palace. ²Seraphs were standing above him; each had six wings. With two it would cover its face, with two it would cover its feet, with two it would fly. ³One would call to another, 'Sacred, sacred, sacred, Yahweh of Armies, his splendour is the filling of the entire earth.' ⁴The doorposts on the sills shook at the sound of the one who called, while the house was filling with smoke.

⁵I said, 'Aagh me, because I'm ruined, because I'm a man polluted of lips, and I live among a people polluted of lips, because my eyes have seen the King, Yahweh of Armies.' ⁶But one of the seraphs flew to me, in his hand a coal that he had taken with tongs from on the altar. ⁷He made it touch my mouth, and he said, 'There, this has touched your lips, and your waywardness will depart, your wrongdoing will be expiated.'

⁸I heard the Lord's voice saying, 'Whom shall I send, who will go for us?' I said, 'Here I am, send me.' ⁹He said,

Go, and say to this people:
  'Keep listening, but don't understand,
  keep looking, but don't acknowledge.'
¹⁰Fatten this people's mind,
  make its ears heavy, smear its eyes,
So it doesn't see with its eyes and listen with its
     ears,
  and its mind understands and it turns and
     there is healing for it.

¹¹I said, 'For how long, Lord?' He said,

'Until towns have crashed into ruins,
  so that there is no inhabitant,
And houses so that there are no people,
  and the land crashes into ruins, a desolation.'
¹²Yahweh will send the people away;
  vast will be the abandonment in the middle of
     the country.
¹³When there is still a tenth in it,
  it will again be for burning up.'
But like a terebinth or like an oak
  of which there's a stump after their felling,
  the sacred seed will be its stump.

## Stand firm in faith, or you won't stand at all

**7** In the days of Ahaz ben Yotam son of Uzziyyahu king of Yehudah, Retsin king of Aram and Peqah ben Remalyahu king of Yisra'el went up to Yerushalaim for a battle against it, but they couldn't do battle against it.

²It had been told David's household, 'Aram has set down on Ephrayim', and his mind and his people's mind shook like the trees in a forest shaking before wind. ³Yahweh said to Yesha'yahu, 'Go out, please, to meet Ahaz, you and "A Remainder Will Go Back" your son, at the end of the Upper Pool channel at the Washer's Field causeway. ⁴You're to say to him, "Keep watch over yourself, be calm. Don't be afraid; your mind is not to go soft on account of these two stumps of smoking firewood, because of the angry burning of Retsin and Aram and ben Remalyahu. ⁵Since Aram has counselled something bad against you (Ephrayim and ben Remalyahu), saying ⁶'We'll go up against Yehudah and dismay it and break it open for ourselves and enthrone as king within it ben Tabe'el', ⁷the Lord Yahweh has said this:

It won't arise,
  it won't happen.
⁸Because the head of Aram is Dammeseq
     [Damascus],
  and the head of Aram is Retsin.
Within yet sixty-five years
  Ephrayim will shatter from being a people.
⁹The head of Ephrayim is Shomron [Samaria],
  and the head of Shomron is ben Remalyahu.
If you don't stand firm in trust,
  indeed you won't stand firm at all.'"

¹⁰Yahweh again spoke to Ahaz: ¹¹'Ask for yourself a sign from Yahweh your God. Make it deep, to She'ol, or make it lofty, to the heights.' ¹²Ahaz said, 'I won't ask, I won't test Yahweh.'

¹³He said, 'Listen, please, household of David. Is it too small for you, wearying human beings, that you weary my God as well? ¹⁴Therefore the Lord – he will give you a sign. There – a girl is pregnant and she's going to give birth to a son, and she'll name him Immanu El ['God Is with Us']. ¹⁵He will

eat yoghurt and syrup in knowing how to
reject the bad and choose the good. [16]Because
before the boy knows how to reject the bad
and choose the good, the land whose two kings
you're dismayed at will be abandoned.'

## Plunder Hurries Loot Rushes

[17]Yahweh will bring on you and on your
people and on your father's household days
that have not come since the day Ephrayim
departed from Yehudah (the king of
Ashshur).
[18]On that day Yahweh will whistle to the fly
that's at the end of the streams of Misrayim
[Egypt] and to the bee that's in the country of
Ashshur. [19]They'll come and settle down, all of
them, in the steep wadis, in the craggy cliffs,
in all the thorn bushes and in all the watering
holes.
[20]On that day the Lord will shave with a
razor hired beyond the River (with the king of
Ashshur) the head and the hair on the feet, and
it will also sweep away the beard.
[21]On that day someone will keep alive a
heifer from the cattle and two from the flock,
[22]but from the quantity of the milk they make
he will eat yoghurt, because everyone who's
left within the country will eat yoghurt and
syrup.
[23]On that day every place where there used
to be a thousand vines worth a thousand
sheqels of silver will be for briar and for thorn.
[24]With arrows and a bow someone will come
there, because the entire country will be briar
and thorn. [25]But all the hills that are hoed with
a hoe – the fear of briar and thorn won't come
there; it will be for the roaming of oxen and for
the trampling of sheep.

**8** Yahweh said to me, 'Get yourself a big
panel and write on it with an ordinary
stylus, "For Plunder Hurries Loot Rushes".
[2]I invoked as trustworthy witnesses for me
Uriyyahu the priest and Zekaryahu ben
Yeberekyahu. [3]I had sex with the prophetess
and she got pregnant and gave birth to a son.
Yahweh said to me, 'Call him Plunder Hurries
Loot Rushes', [4]because before the boy knows
how to call "father" and "mother", someone will
carry off Dammeseq's wealth and Shomron's
plunder before the king of Ashshur.'

## Where to look for guidance

[5]Yahweh spoke to me yet further:

[6]Since this people has rejected
    the water of Shiloah, which goes gently
    (and been glad about Retsin and ben
       Remalyahu),
[7]Therefore: there, the Lord is bringing up against
       them
    the water of the River, substantial, vast
    (the king of Ashshur and all his splendour).
It will rise up over all its canyons
    and go up over its banks.
[8]It will sweep through Yehudah, flood as it passes
       over,
    reach as far as its neck.
Its wings spread out will be
    the filling of the breadth of your country.

God is with us:
    [9]do what is bad, peoples, and shatter.
Give ear, all you distant parts of the earth;
    belt yourselves and shatter,
Belt yourselves and shatter;
    [10]take counsel, but it will be contravened.
Speak a word, but it won't arise,
    because God is with us.

[11]Because Yahweh said this to me as he
took strong hold of my hand so that he might
discipline me out of walking in the way of this
people:

[12]You shall not say 'conspiracy'
    about everything that this people says
       'conspiracy' about.
What they're in awe of, you shall not be in awe of,
    and not dread.
[13]Yahweh of Armies – regard him as sacred;
    he's to be the object of your awe, he your dread.
[14]He's to be a sacred place, but a stone to trip on,
    a crag to collapse on,
For the two households of Yisra'el –
    a trap and a snare for Yerushalaim's inhabitants.
[15]Many people will collapse on them,
    they'll fall and break, be snared and caught.

[16]Bind up the testimony, seal the instruction
among my disciples. [17]I shall wait for Yahweh,
who's hiding his face from Ya'aqob's household,
and I shall hope for him. [18]Here am I and the

children Yahweh has given me as signs and portents in Yisra'el from Yahweh of Armies who dwells on Mount Tsiyyon. ¹⁹So when they say to you, 'Enquire of the ghosts and the spirits who chirp and whisper. A people is to enquire of its gods, isn't it, of the dead on behalf of the living, ²⁰for instruction and testimony': if they do not speak in accordance with this word, for which there will be no dawn . . .

## Darkness and dawning

²¹It will pass through it wretched and hungry. When it is hungry it will rage and slight its king and its gods. It will turn its face upwards ²²and look to the earth, but there, pressure and darkness, oppressive gloom, driven murkiness,

**9** because there will be no dawn for the one that experiences oppression.

As the earlier time has slighted
    the region of Zebulun and the region of
       Naphtali,
The later one is bringing splendour to the Sea
      Way,
    the other side of the Yarden [Jordan], Galilee of
      the nations.
²The people walking in darkness
    has seen big light.
Those living in deathly gloom –
    light has shone on them.
³You've made the nation many,
    you've given it great rejoicing.
They've rejoiced before you like the rejoicing at
      harvest,
    like people who celebrate at the dividing of
      spoil.
⁴Because the yoke that burdened it,
    the rod on its shoulder,
The boss's club over it,
    you've shattered as on the day at Midyan.
⁵Because every shoe of someone trampling, with
      shaking,
    and the coat rolled in shed blood,
Have been for burning,
    consumed by fire.
⁶Because a child has been born to us,
    a son has been given to us,
    and government has come on to his shoulder.

People have called him
    'An Extraordinary Counsellor Is the Strong
      Man God,
    the Everlasting Father Is an Official for Well-
      being'.
⁷Of the growing of government and of well-being
    there will be no end, on David's throne and on
      his kingship,
To establish it and support it,
    with authority and faithfulness,
From now and permanently;
    the passion of Yahweh of Armies will do this.

## For all this, his anger did not turn back

⁸The Lord has sent out a word against Ya'aqob,
    and it has fallen on Yisra'el.
⁹But the people, all of it, acknowledge it
    (Ephrayim and the inhabitants of Shomron)
    with loftiness and big-headedness:
¹⁰'Bricks have fallen, but we'll build with dressed
      stone;
    sycamore-figs have been cut down, but we'll
      substitute cedars.'
¹¹But Yahweh has lifted high the adversaries of
      Retsin over it,
    and spurred on its enemies,
¹²Aram from the east, the Pelishtites from the west,
    and they've devoured Yisra'el with their entire
      mouth.
For all this, his anger did not turn back;
    his hand was still stretched out.

¹³The people didn't turn back to the one who hit it;
    they haven't enquired of Yahweh of Armies.
¹⁴So Yahweh cut off from Yisra'el head and tail,
    palm branch and reed, in one day.
¹⁵The elder and the person held in high regard, he
    is the head,
    and the prophet who instructs in falsehood, he
      is the tail.
¹⁶The guides of this people became ones who
    make them wander;
    the ones who were guided were people who
      were swallowed up.
¹⁷Therefore the Lord does not rejoice over its
    young men,
    and does not show compassion for its widows
      and orphans,
Because all of it is impious and deals badly,
    and every mouth speaks villainy.

For all this, his anger did not turn back;
　　his hand was still stretched out.

[18]Because faithlessness has burned up like fire,
　　which consumes briar and thorn.
It set light to the forest thickets,
　　and they swirled as a column of smoke.
[19]By the fury of Yahweh of Armies
　　the country was scorched.
The people became like a fire consuming;
　　one person would not spare his brother.
[20]He carved to the right but was hungry,
　　and ate to the left but was not full;
An individual eats the flesh of his offspring,
　　[21]Menashsheh, Ephrayim, Ephrayim,
　　Menashsheh,
　　all together they were against Yehudah.
For all this, his anger did not turn back;
　　his hand was still stretched out.

## My officers are kings, aren't they

10 Hey, you who make decrees that bring
　　trouble,
　　who write documents that bring oppression,
[2]To subvert the case of poor people,
　　and steal the rights of the humble among my
　　　people,
So that widows become their spoil,
　　and orphans their plunder.
[3]What will you do on the day when attention is
　　　given,
　　when devastation comes from afar?
To whom will you flee for help,
　　and where will you abandon your splendour?
[4]Except bend beneath a prisoner,
　　fall beneath the slain?
For all this, his anger did not turn back;
　　his hand was still stretched out.

[5]Hey, Ashshur, my angry club –
　　and the mace in their hand is my
　　　condemnation.
[6]Against an impious nation I send it;
　　I order it against a people towards which I am
　　　wrathful,
To seize spoil and to take plunder,
　　and to make it into something trampled, like
　　　mud in the streets.
[7]But it doesn't picture it this way;
　　its mind doesn't think this way.

Because in its mind is to annihilate,
　　to cut off nations not a few.
[8]Because it says,
　　'My officers are kings, altogether, aren't they.
[9]Kalno's like Karkemish, isn't it, or Hamat like
　　　Arpad –
　　or Shomron like Dammeseq.
[10]As my hand found the non-entity kingdoms
　　(and their images were more than Shomron
　　　and Yerushalaim) –
[11]As I did to Shomron and to its non-entities,
　　so I will do to Yerushalaim and to its idols,
　　　won't I.'

[12]But when the Lord finishes all his action
　　against Mount Tsiyyon and against Yerushalaim:
'I will attend to the fruit of the king of Ashshur's
　　big-headedness
　　and to the lofty splendour of his eyes.
[13]Because he said, "By the energy of my hand I've
　　　acted,
　　by my smartness, because I have understanding.
I've removed peoples' borders,
　　I've plundered their treasures,
　　as a champion I've subdued inhabitants.
[14]My hand found, as in a nest,
　　the resources of peoples.
Like one gathering abandoned eggs,
　　I myself gathered the entire earth.
There was not one flapping a wing,
　　or opening its mouth and chirping."'

## The remainder of Yisra'el

[15]Does the axe glorify itself over the one who
　　chops with it,
　　or the saw magnify itself over the one who
　　wields it,
As if the club wields the one who lifts it up,
　　as if the mace lifted up the one who is not made
　　　of wood?
[16]Therefore the Lord Yahweh of Armies will send
　　off
　　a wasting disease against his beefy ones.
Beneath its splendour it will burn,
　　with a burning like the burning of fire.
[17]Yisra'el's light will become fire,
　　its sacred one a flame.
It will burn up and consume its thorn and its
　　thistle,
　　in one day.

<sup>18</sup>The splendour of its forest and its farmland
  it will finish off, soul and body.
It will be like the fading away of a sick person;
  <sup>19</sup>the remainder of the trees in its forest will be
    so few,
  a boy could write them down.

<sup>20</sup>But on that day,
  no more will the remainder of Yisra'el,
The escape group from Ya'aqob's household,
  lean on the one that struck them down.
They will lean on Yahweh,
  Yisra'el's sacred one, in truth.
<sup>21</sup>The remainder will turn back, the remainder of
    Ya'aqob,
  to God, the God who is a strong man.
<sup>22</sup>Though your people, Yisra'el,
  were like the sand of the sea,
It will be a remainder of it that will turn back;
  a finishing is determined, overwhelming
    faithfulness.
<sup>23</sup>Because a finish, a thing determined –
  the Lord Yahweh of Armies is going to do it,
  within the entire country.

<sup>24</sup>Therefore the Lord Yahweh of Armies has
said this:

Don't be afraid, my people,
  who dwell on Tsiyyon, of Ashshur,
Which strikes you down with a club
  and raises its mace against you in the manner
    of the Misrayimites.
<sup>25</sup>Because in a very little while more,
  my condemnation will finish,
  and my anger will be towards their destruction.
<sup>26</sup>Yahweh of Armies is lifting up a whip against it
  like the striking down of Midyan at the Oreb
    Crag,
Like his mace over the sea,
  and he will raise it in the manner of Misrayim.
<sup>27</sup>And on that day
  its burden will depart from your shoulder,
Its yoke from upon your neck;
  the yoke will be destroyed in the face of your
    beefiness.

## Visions of threat and promise

<sup>28</sup>He has gone against Ayat, he has passed by Migron,
  at Mikmas he put his equipment in place.

<sup>29</sup>They crossed at the pass;
  'Geba will be lodging for us.'
The Height trembles,
  Gib'ah of Sha'ul [Saul] has fled.
<sup>30</sup>Bellow loudly, Bat-gallim, heed, Layshah,
  answer, Anatot!
<sup>31</sup>Madmenah has run away,
  the inhabitants of Gebim have taken refuge.
<sup>32</sup>More, today at Nob,
  standing, he will wave his hand
At the mount of Miss Tsiyyon,
  the hill of Yerushalaim.

<sup>33</sup>There is the Lord Yahweh of Armies,
  lopping off boughs with a crash.
The loftiest in height are being felled,
  the tall ones fall down.
<sup>34</sup>The forest thickets will be cut down with iron,
  the Lebanon will fall by the august one.
**11** But a shoot will go out from Yishay's
  [Jesse's] stump,
  a branch will fruit from his roots.
<sup>2</sup>Yahweh's breath will alight on him,
  a breath with smartness and understanding,
A breath with counsel and strength,
  a breath with acknowledgement and awe for
    Yahweh;
<sup>3</sup>his scent will be awe for Yahweh.
He will not exercise authority by the seeing of his
    eyes,
  he will not reprove by the hearing of his ears.
<sup>4</sup>He will exercise authority with faithfulness for
    the poor,
  and reprove with uprightness for the humble
    people in the country.
He will strike the country down with the club in
    his mouth,
  with the breath from his lips he will put the
    faithless person to death.
<sup>5</sup>Faithfulness will be the belt round his hips,
  truthfulness the belt round his thighs.
<sup>6</sup>Wolf will reside with lamb,
  leopard will lie down with goat,
Calf, lion and fatling together,
  with a little boy driving them.
<sup>7</sup>Cow and bear will pasture,
  their young will lie down together.
Cougar, like cattle,
  will eat straw.
<sup>8</sup>A baby will play over the cobra's burrow;
  an infant will hold its hand over the viper's
    hole.

⁹People will not deal badly, they will not devastate,
   in all my sacred mountain.
Because the country will be full of the
     acknowledgement of Yahweh
   like the water covering the sea.
¹⁰On that day,
   Yishay's root which will be standing
   as a signal for peoples,
Nations will enquire of him,
   and where he settles down will be [a place of]
   splendour.

*A day when there will be a song to sing*

¹¹On that day,
   the Lord will again act, a second time,
   with his hand to acquire the remainder of his
     people,
That remain from Ashshur, from Misrayim, from
     Patros,
   from Kush [Sudan], from Elam, from Shin'ar,
   from Hamat and from the shores across the
     Sea.
¹²He will lift up a signal to the nations,
   and gather the men of Yisra'el who were driven
     out,
And the women of Yehudah who were scattered
     he will collect
   from the four corners of the earth.
¹³Ephrayim's jealousy will go away,
   and the people putting pressure on Yehudah
     will be cut off.
Ephrayim won't be jealous of Yehudah,
   and Yehudah won't put pressure on Ephrayim.
¹⁴They will fly against the back of the Pelishtites
     to the west;
   together they will plunder the easterners,
The putting out of their hand: Edom and Mo'ab;
   the people obeying them: the Ammonites.
¹⁵Yahweh will dry up the tongue of the
     Misrayimite sea,
   and wave his hand over the River
   with the heat of his breath.
He will strike it down into seven wadis,
   and let people make their way in boots.
¹⁶There will be a causeway for the remainder of
     his people
   that remain from Ashshur,
As there was for Yisra'el
   on the day it went up from the country of
   Misrayim.

## 12

You will say on that day,

I will confess you Yahweh, because whereas you
     were angry with me,
   your anger turned back and you comforted me.
²There is God, my deliverance,
   I will be confident and not be fearful,
Because Yah, Yahweh, is my vigour and might,
   and he has been my deliverance.

³You will draw water with joy
   from the deliverance fountains.

⁴And you will say on that day,

Confess Yahweh,
   call out in his name.
Make his deeds known among the peoples,
   make mention that his name is on high.
⁵Make music for Yahweh, because he has acted in
     majesty;
   this is to be acknowledged in the entire earth.
⁶Bellow and resound, inhabitants of Tsiyyon,
   because great among you is Yisra'el's sacred one.

*The downfall of the superpower*

## 13

A pronouncement about Babel, which
Yesha'yahu ben Amots beheld.

²On a bare mountain lift up a banner,
   raise your voice to them.
Wave your hand,
   so they'll come through the leaders' entrances.
³I myself have ordered the people I made sacred,
   yes, I've called my strong men in connection
     with my anger,
   the people who exult in my majesty.
⁴The sound of a horde on the mountains,
   the semblance of a great company,
The sound of the din of kingdoms,
   nations gathering:
Yahweh of Armies is numbering
   an army for war.
⁵They're coming from a distant country,
   from the end of the heavens,
Yahweh and the instruments of his
     condemnation,
   to destroy the entire earth.
⁶Howl, because Yahweh's day is near;
   like destruction from the Destroyer it comes.

⁷Therefore all hands go limp,
    every human mind melts.
⁸They're terrified, spasms and throes grasp them,
    they writhe like a birthing woman.
An individual looks aghast at his neighbour;
    their faces are faces aflame.

⁹There, Yahweh's day is coming, ruthless,
    with fury and angry blazing,
To turn the earth into a desolation,
    so it can annihilate its wrongdoers from it.
¹⁰Because the stars in the heavens and their
        constellations
    will not flash their light.
The sun will have gone dark when it comes out,
    the moon will not shine its light.
¹¹I will attend to the world for its bad dealing,
    to the faithless for their waywardness.
I will put a stop to the majesty of the arrogant,
    and make the dignity of the violent fall down.
¹²I will make people scarcer than pure gold,
    human beings than Ophir gold.
¹³Therefore I will make the heavens quake,
    and the earth will shake out of its place,
At the fury of Yahweh of Armies,
    on the day of his angry blazing.
¹⁴Like a hunted gazelle,
    like sheep with no one collecting them,
Each person will turn his face to his people,
    each will flee to his country.
¹⁵Everyone who is found will be thrust through,
    everyone who is swept up will fall by the sword.
¹⁶Their little ones will be smashed before their eyes,
    their homes will be despoiled, their wives
        bedded.

## Deliverance and compassion

¹⁷Here am I, stirring up Maday [the Medes]
        against them,
    who don't think about silver,
Gold – they don't want it,
    ¹⁸but their bows will smash the young,
They won't have compassion on the fruit of the
        womb,
    their eye won't spare children.
¹⁹So Babel, the most splendid of kingdoms,
    the majestic glory of the Kasdites
        [Babylonians],
    will become like God's overturning of Sedom
        and Amorah.

²⁰It will not be inhabited ever,
    it will not be dwelt in for generation after
        generation,
Arab will not camp there,
    shepherds will not make flocks lie down there.
²¹Wild creatures will lie down there;
    their houses will be full of owls.
Ostriches will dwell there,
    wild goats will leap about there.
²²Hyenas will live in its citadels,
    dragons in its luxurious palaces.
Its time is near coming,
    its days will not draw on.

**14** Because Yahweh will have compassion
    on Ya'aqob
    and will again choose Yisra'el.
He will settle them down on their land and the
        alien will join them,
    and attach themselves to Ya'aqob's household.
²Peoples will get them
    and bring them to their place.
The household of Yisra'el will have them as their
        domain on Yahweh's land
    as servants and maidservants.
They will be captors to their captors
    and will rule over their bosses.

## A greeting from the ghosts

³On the day Yahweh settles you down after
your suffering, after your turmoil and after the
tough service that was imposed on you, ⁴you
will take up this poem about the king of Babel:

Ah, the boss has stopped,
    the storm has stopped.
⁵Yahweh has broken the mace of the faithless,
    the club of the rulers,
⁶That strikes down peoples with fury,
    a striking down without turning aside,
Subdues nations in anger,
    a persecution without holding back.
⁷The entire earth has settled down, it's calm;
    people have broken out in resounding.
⁸The juniper trees have also rejoiced over you,
    the cedars of Lebanon:
'Now you've lain down,
    no one will go up who will cut us down.'
⁹She'ol below has been astir for you,
    to meet your coming,

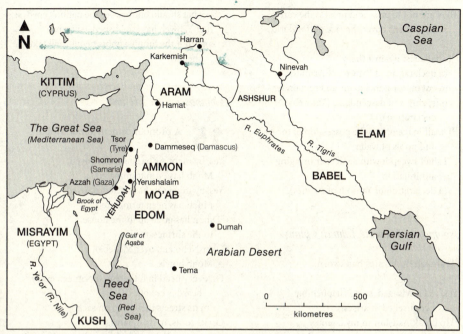

*Isaiah 14: Ancient Near East at the time of Yesha'yahu (Isaiah)*

Rousing the ghosts for you,
  all earth's big guys,
Raising from their thrones
  all the nations' kings.
¹⁰All of them answer
  and say to you,
'You too have been made weak as we are,
  you have become like us!'
¹¹Your majesty has been taken down to She'ol,
  the sound of your mandolins.
Beneath you worm is spread out,
  maggot is your covering.

### Thus you have fallen from the heavens

¹²Ah, you've fallen from the heavens,
  bright one, son of dawn!
You've been felled to the earth,
  enfeebler of nations!
¹³But you yourself said within yourself,
  'I shall go up to the heavens.
Above the supernatural stars
  I shall raise my throne.
I shall sit on the mountain for the appointed
    meeting,
  on the extremities of Tsaphon.

¹⁴I shall go up on cloud tops,
  I will be like the One on High.'
¹⁵Yet you're taken down to She'ol,
  to the extremities of the Pit.
¹⁶The people who see you stare,
  they consider you.
'Is this the man who shook the earth,
  who made kingdoms tremble,
¹⁷Who made the world a veritable wilderness
  and tore down its towns?
Its prisoners he did not release for home,
  ¹⁸all the nations' kings.'
All of them lay down in splendour,
  each in his 'house'.
¹⁹But you've been thrown away from your tomb,
  like offensive carrion,
Clothed in the slain,
  pierced by the sword,
People who go down to the stones of the Pit
  like a trampled corpse.
²⁰You won't be one with them in burial,
  because you devastated your country, you
    killed your people.
The offspring of people who deal badly
  will not be named permanently.
²¹Prepare a place of slaughter for his children
  because of the waywardness of their ancestors.

They are not to arise and possess the earth,
    so that towns cover the face of the world.

22I shall arise against them
    (a declaration of Yahweh of Armies),
And cut off for Babel name and remainder,
    offspring and descendants (Yahweh's
    declaration).
23I shall make it into the possession of the owl,
    and pools of water;
I shall sweep it with a sweeper bringing
    annihilation
    (a declaration of Yahweh of Armies).

## No one can frustrate Yahweh's plans

24Yahweh of Armies has sworn:

Yes, as I envisaged, so it is happening;
    as I counselled, it arises,
25To break Ashshur in my country –
    I will crush it upon my mountains.
Its yoke will depart from upon them,
    its burden will depart from upon his shoulder.
26This is the counsel that has been formulated for
    the entire earth,
    this is the hand that is stretched out over all the
    nations.
27Because Yahweh of Armies has taken counsel,
    and who can contravene it?
His hand is stretched out,
    and who can turn it back?

28In the year King Ahaz died, this
pronouncement came:

29Don't rejoice, all you Pelishtites,
    because the club of the one who struck you
    down has broken.
Because from the snake's root a viper will come
    out,
    its fruit a flying seraph.
30The firstborn of poor people will pasture,
    the needy will lie down in confidence.
But I will put your root to death with hunger,
    I will slay the remainder of you.
31Howl, gateway; cry out, town;
    melt, all you Pelishtites.
Because a cloud is coming from the north,
    and there's no one straggling in its appointed
    ranks.

32So what should one answer the nation's envoys? –
    that Yahweh has established Tsiyyon,
    and in it the humble of his people will take
    shelter.

## Compassion for Mo'ab

**15** A pronouncement about Mo'ab.

Yes, by night Ar has been destroyed,
    Mo'ab has been terminated.
Yes, by night Qir has been destroyed,
    Mo'ab has been terminated.
2Dibon has gone up to the house,
    to the shrines, to cry.
Over Nebo and over Medeba
    Mo'ab howls.
On every head in it there is shornness, every
    beard is cut off,
    3in its streets they wrap on sack.
On its roofs, in its squares,
    everyone in it howls, falling down with crying.
4Heshbon and Ele'aleh cry out,
    their voice makes itself heard in Yahats.
Therefore the equipped men of Mo'ab shout,
    its entire being trembles for it.
5My heart cries out for Mo'ab –
    its fugitives as far as So'ar, Eglat Shelishiyyah.
Because the ascent of Luhit – with crying they
    climb it;
    because the road to Horonayim – they raise a
    broken cry.
6Because the water of Nimrim
    becomes a great desolation.
Because the grass is dry, the vegetation is finished,
    there is no greenery.
7Therefore the gains they've made and what they
    have in their charge –
    they carry them across the Willows Wadi.
8Because the cry has surrounded Mo'ab's border,
    as far as Eglayim its howl, and in Be'er Elim its
    howl.
9Because Dimon's water is full of blood,
    because I put more on Dimon –
A lion for Mo'ab's escape group,
    for the remainder of the land.

**16** Send a ram belonging to the country's
ruler,
    from Sela in the wilderness to the mountain of
    Miss Tsiyyon.

²Like a bird flitting, a nest thrown out,
   are the Mo'abite women at the fords of the
     Arnon.
³'Bring counsel,
   make a decision.
Make your shadow like night
   in the middle of the day.
Hide the banished, don't betray the fugitive;
    ⁴the people banished from Mo'ab should reside
     with you.
Be a hiding place for them
   from the face of the destroyer.'

When the oppressor is no more, when destruction
    finishes,
   when the devastator has come to an end from
    the country,
⁵A throne will be established with commitment,
   there will sit on it in truthfulness
In David's tent one who exercises authority,
   enquiring after judgement, and quick with
    faithfulness.

## Mo'ab open to learning

⁶We have heard of Mo'ab's majesty,
   very majestic,
Its majesty, its loftiness and its arrogance –
   its empty talk is not like that.
⁷Therefore Mo'ab should howl,
   everyone in it should howl for Mo'ab,
For the raisin blocks from Qir-hareset you should
    moan,
   utterly stricken.
⁸Because the terraces of Heshbon languish,
   the vines of Sibmah.
The nations' lords have struck down their clusters
   that had reached as far as Ya'zer,
That wandered into the wilderness;
   when its shoots spread, they crossed to the sea.
⁹Therefore I cry with Ya'zer's crying for Ya'zer,
   for Sibmah's vines.
I drench you with my tears,
   Heshbon and Ele'aleh.
Because over your summer fruit and over your
    harvest
   the cheering has fallen still.
¹⁰Rejoicing and gladness have gathered up from
    the farmland,
   in the vineyards no one resounds, no one
    shouts.

Wine in the presses – the treader doesn't tread;
   I have made the cheering stop.
¹¹Therefore my heart murmurs for Mo'ab like a
    guitar,
   my inner being for Qir Heres.
¹²When Mo'ab appears, when it wearies itself,
   at the shrine,
Comes to its sanctuary to plead,
   it won't prevail.

¹³This is the word that Yahweh spoke for
Mo'ab then. ¹⁴But now Yahweh has spoken:
'In three years in accordance with the years
of an employee, Mo'ab's splendour with all its
great horde will be slighted. The remainder will
be a small thing, tiny, not much.'

## Don't worry about the Aramites

# 17   A pronouncement about Dammeseq.

There is Dammeseq, removed from being a town;
   it will become a fallen ruin.
²The towns of Aro'er will be abandoned,
   they will be for flocks,
   and they will lie down with no one disturbing.
³Fortress will cease from Ephrayim,
   kingship from Dammeseq.
The remainder of Aram
   will become like the Yisra'elites' splendour
   (a declaration of Yahweh of Armies).

⁴On that day
Ya'aqob's splendour will become poor,
   the beefiness of his body will become thin.
⁵It will be like the gathering of the standing
    harvest,
   when someone harvests the ears in his arm.
It will be like someone gleaning ears
   in Repha'ites Vale.
⁶There will remain garnerings in it,
   like the beating of an olive tree:
Two, three berries on the top (the height);
   four, five on a fruitful bough
   (a declaration of Yahweh, the God of Yisra'el).
⁷On that day a person will pay regard to his maker,
   and his eyes will look to Yisra'el's sacred one.
⁸He won't pay regard to the altars that are the
    making of his hands,
   he won't look to what his fingers made,
   both the totem poles and the incense stands.

⁹On that day,
  his strong towns will be
  like an abandoned piece of woodland and height
That people abandoned from before the
      Yisra'elites,
  and it will be a desolation.
¹⁰Yes, you have put out of mind the God who
      delivers you;
  your strong crag you have not kept in mind.
Therefore you may plant the plants of the Lovely
      One
  and sow the cutting of an alien god.
¹¹On the day you plant, you may get them to grow,
  and in the morning you sow, get it to blossom,
Though the harvest disappears
  on the day of sickness and grave pain.

## Who would want to be a superpower?

¹²Hey, the horde of many peoples
  that roar like the seas' roar,
The din of nations
  that make a din like the din of mighty water!
¹³Nations make a din like the din of much water,
  but he reprimands it and it flees far away,
Driven like the chaff on the mountains before the
      wind,
  like tumbleweed before a storm.
¹⁴Towards evening time there – terror;
  before morning, it is no more.
This is the share of the people who despoil us,
  the lot of the people who plunder us.

**18** Hey, country of the buzzing of wings,
      which is beyond the rivers of Kush,
²Which sends envoys by sea
  in papyrus boats on the face of the water.
Go, swift envoys,
  to a nation towering and smooth,
To a people feared far and near,
  a nation of gibberish and aggressiveness,
  whose country rivers divide.
³All you inhabitants of the world,
  people who dwell in the earth:
At the raising of a signal on the mountains, you
      should look,
  and at the sounding of the horn, you should
      listen.
⁴Because Yahweh has said this to me:
  'I shall be calm and I shall look to my
      established place,

Like glowing heat in daylight,
  like a dew cloud in the heat of harvest.'
⁵Because before harvest, when the blossom is
      complete,
  and the flower becomes a ripening grape,
He will cut the shoots with pruning knives,
  and the tendrils he has removed he will have
      taken away.
⁶They will be abandoned, altogether, to the birds
  of prey of the mountains,
  and to the animals of the earth.
The birds of prey will summer on them
  and all the animals of the earth will winter on
      them.
⁷At that time
  tribute will be brought to Yahweh of Armies,
(A people towering and smooth,
  a people feared far and near,
A nation of gibberish and aggressiveness,
  whose country rivers divide)
To the place of the name of Yahweh of Armies,
  Mount Tsiyyon.

## Misrayim at a loss

**19** A pronouncement about Misrayim.

There is Yahweh, riding on a swift cloud,
  coming to Misrayim.
Misrayim's non-entities will tremble from before
      him,
  and Misrayim's mind will melt within it.
²I will stir up Misrayimites against Misrayimites,
  and one will do battle against his brother,
One against his neighbour, town against town,
  kingdom against kingdom.
³Misrayim's spirit will drain away within it,
  and I will swallow up its counsel.
They will enquire of the non-entities and of the
      ghosts,
  of the mediums and of the spirits.
⁴But I will put Misrayim
  into the hand of a tough master.
A vigorous king will rule over them
  (a declaration of the Lord Yahweh of
      Armies).

⁵Water will dry up from the sea,
  the river will wither and parch.
⁶Rivers will stink as they get low,
  the channels of Misrayim will dry up.

Reed and rush will wither,
  <sup>7</sup>the plants by the Ye'or [Nile], by the mouth of
    the Ye'or.
Everything sown at the Ye'or will wither,
  blow away, and there will be none of it.
<sup>8</sup>The fishermen will lament and mourn,
  all the people who throw a hook into the
    Ye'or.
The people who spread a net
  on the face of the water will have languished.
<sup>9</sup>The workers with combed flax will be shamed,
  and the weavers of linen.
<sup>10</sup>Its textile workers will become crushed,
  all the wage-earners troubled in their entire
    being.
<sup>11</sup>The officials at Tso'an are simply dense,
Par'oh's [Pharaoh's] smart counsellors – stupid
    counsel.
How can you say to Par'oh,
  'I'm a son of experts, a son of the kings of
    Qedem?' –
<sup>12</sup>Where on earth are your experts,
  so they may please tell you, may acknowledge
  what Yahweh of Armies has planned against
    Misrayim.

<sup>13</sup>The officials at Tso'an have become fools,
  the officials at Noph have deceived themselves.
They've made Misrayim wander –
  they, the cornerstone of its clans.
<sup>14</sup>Yahweh has mixed within it
  a spirit of distortion.
They'll make Misrayim wander in all it does,
  like the wandering of a drunk in his vomit.
<sup>15</sup>There'll be no action by Misrayim
  that head or tail can take,
  palm branch or reed.

## Misrayim my people

<sup>16</sup>On that day, Misrayim will be like women,
and will be trembling and in dread before the
shaking of the hand of Yahweh of Armies,
which he is shaking against it. <sup>17</sup>The land of
Yehudah will be a terror to the Misrayimites.
Everyone to whom someone makes mention
of it will be fearful in the face of the counsel
of Yahweh of Armies, which he is formulating
against it.

<sup>18</sup>On that day, there will be five towns in
the country of Misrayim speaking the tongue

of Kena'an [Canaan] and taking oaths to
Yahweh of Armies. 'Sun Town', one will be
called.

<sup>19</sup>On that day there will be an altar for
Yahweh in the middle of the country of
Misrayim and a column for Yahweh at its
border. <sup>20</sup>It will be a sign and a testimony
for Yahweh of Armies in the country of
Misrayim; when they cry out to Yahweh
before oppressors, he will send them
someone to deliver and argue, and he will
rescue them.

<sup>21</sup>Yahweh will cause himself to be
acknowledged by the Misrayimites, and the
Misrayimites will acknowledge Yahweh on that
day. They will serve with sacrifice and offering,
and make pledges to Yahweh and make good
on them. <sup>22</sup>Yahweh will strike Misrayim,
striking but healing, and they will turn back to
Yahweh and he will let himself be entreated by
them and will heal them.

<sup>23</sup>On that day there will be a causeway from
Misrayim to Ashshur. Ashshur will come to
Misrayim and Misrayim to Ashshur. Misrayim
will serve with Ashshur.

<sup>24</sup>On that day Yisra'el will be the third for
Misrayim and for Ashshur, a blessing in the
middle of the earth, <sup>25</sup>because Yahweh of
Armies has blessed it, saying 'Blessed be my
people Misrayim, my handiwork Ashshur and
my domain Yisra'el.'

## Prophet as crazy man

**20** In the year the commander-in-chief
came to Ashdod when Sargon king
of Ashshur sent him, and battled against
Ashdod and took it, <sup>2</sup>at that time Yahweh
spoke by means of Yesha'yahu ben Amots:
'Go, loose the sack from on your hips and
unfasten the boot from on your feet.' He did
so, going stripped and barefoot. <sup>3</sup>Yahweh
said, 'As my servant Yesha'yahu has gone
stripped and barefoot three years as a sign
and portent for Misrayim and Kush, <sup>4</sup>so the
king of Ashshur will drive off the captives
of Misrayim and the exiles of Kush, young
and old, stripped and barefoot, bare of
behind, Misrayim's nakedness. <sup>5</sup>People will
be shattered and shamed because of Kush
their confidence and Misrayim their glory.

⁶The one who lives on this foreign shore will say on that day, "There, such is the state of the one on whom we had confidence, where we fled for help, to find rescue from before the king of Ashshur. How can we ourselves escape?'"

## What is there of the night?

**21** A pronouncement about the Sea Wilderness.

Like storms in the Negeb passing through,
     from the wilderness it comes, from a fearful
          country.
²A tough vision has been told me:
     'The betrayer is betraying, the destroyer is
          destroying.
Go up, Elam, lay siege, Maday [Media] –
     I have stopped all its groaning.'
³Therefore my hips are full of convulsing,
     pains have grasped me, like the pains of
          someone giving birth.
I'm too struck down to listen, I'm too terrified to
          look;
     ⁴my mind wanders, shuddering has
          overwhelmed me.
The dusk to which I was attracted
     he has turned to horror for me.
⁵Setting the table, spreading the rug,
     eating, drinking . . .
'Get up, officers,
     oil the shield.'

⁶Because the Lord said this to me:

Go, set a watch,
     so he may tell what he sees.
⁷He will see a rider, a cavalry pair,
     a donkey chariot, a camel chariot.
He is to heed, with heeding,
     great heeding.

⁸The lookout called:

On the watchtower, my lord, I've been
          standing,
     continually by day,
And on my watch I have been taking my
          position,
     every night.

⁹And there, a chariot with men is coming,
     a cavalry pair.

He avowed:

Babel has fallen, fallen,
     all its gods' images.
He has smashed to the ground ¹⁰my crushed
          one,
     my son on the threshing-floor.
What I heard from Yahweh of Armies,
     Yisra'el's God, I have told you.

¹¹A pronouncement about Dumah.

Someone is calling to me from Se'ir:
     'Watchman, what is there of the night,
     Watchman, what is there of the night?'
¹²The watchman said,
     'Morning came, and night, too;
     if you enquire, enquire; come back again.'

¹³A pronouncement in the steppe.

In the forest, in the steppe, you lodge,
     caravans of Dedanites.
¹⁴Meet the thirsty one, bring water,
     you who inhabit the country of Tema,
     present the fugitive with his bread.
¹⁵Because they've fled from before swords,
     from before the drawn sword,
From before the directed bow,
     from before the weight of battle.

¹⁶Because the Lord has said this to me:

Yet a year according to the years of an employee,
     all the splendour of Qedar will be finished.
¹⁷The remainder of the number of the bows,
     the strong men of the Qedarites, will be few,
     because Yahweh, Yisra'el's God, has spoken.

## Yerushalaim (aka Vision Ravine)

**22** A pronouncement about Vision Ravine.

What are you doing here, then,
     that you have gone up, all of you, on to the roofs,
²You, full of din, tumultuous town,
     exultant township?

Those of you who were run through were not run
    through by the sword,
  they were not dead in battle.
[3]All your leaders fled together,
  without the bow they were captured.
All those of you who were found were captured
    together,
  they took flight far away.
[4]Therefore I have said, 'Look away from me,
  I will express bitterness in crying.
Don't try to comfort me
  over the destruction of the daughter of my
    people.'
[5]Because the Lord Yahweh of Armies
  had a day of tumult, trampling and confusion,
In Vision Ravine someone tearing down the
    wall,
  and a cry for help to the mountain.
[6]Elam carried the quiver,
  in chariotry with men, cavalry;
  Qir bared the shield.
[7]Your choicest vales became full
  of chariotry and cavalry.
They took their stand at the gateway
    [8]and it exposed Yehudah's covering.

You'd looked that day
  to the armoury in the Forest House.
[9]The breaches in David's Town –
  you'd seen them, that there were many.
You'd collected the water of the Lower Pool
    [10]and counted the houses in Yerushalaim.
You'd torn down the houses to strengthen the
    wall
    [11]and made a basin between the two walls
  for the water from the old pool.
But you didn't look to the one who made it,
  you didn't consider the one who formed it long
    before.

[12]The Lord Yahweh of Armies called
  on that day
To crying and to lamenting,
  to shaving the head and to wrapping on sack.
[13]But here – celebration and rejoicing,
  killing cattle and slaughtering sheep,
Eating meat and drinking wine:
  'Eat and drink, because tomorrow we die!'
[14]Yahweh of Armies revealed himself in my ears:
  'If this waywardness of yours is to be expiated
    before you die . . .'
  (the Lord Yahweh of Armies has said).

## The administrator who fancied himself

[15]The Lord Yahweh of Armies said this:
'Come, go to this administrator, to Shebna,
who is in charge of the house.

[16]What are you doing here,
  and whom do you have here,
  that you have hewn a tomb for yourself here,
You who have hewn his tomb on high,
  who has carved a dwelling for himself in the
    cliff?
[17]There: Yahweh is going to hurl you far;
  strong man, he's going to grasp you firmly.
[18]He's going to roll you up tight, rolling you up
    like a ball,
  to a country broad on both sides.
There you'll die;
  there will be your splendid chariots,
  a slight for your master's house.
[19]I shall thrust you out from your position;
  you'll be torn down from your office.

[20]On that day I shall call my servant
Elyaqim ben Hilqiyyahu. [21]I shall clothe him
in your coat and fasten him with your belt,
and put your ruling power in his hand. He
will become a father to the inhabitants of
Yerushalaim and to the household of Yehudah.
[22]I shall put the key of David's household on his
shoulder; he will open and no one will shut, he
will shut and no one will open. [23]I shall fix
him as a peg in a trustworthy place; he will
be a throne of splendour for his father's
household. [24]All the splendour of his
father's household will hang on him, offspring
and shoots, all the little articles, from the
bowls to all the jars.'
    [25]On that day (a declaration of Yahweh of
Armies) the peg fixed in a trustworthy place
will move away. It will be hacked off and it will
fall, and the load that's on it will be cut down.
Yahweh has indeed spoken.

## The great sea power broken

**23** A pronouncement about Tsor [Tyre].

Howl, Tarshish ships,
  because it has been destroyed so that there is
    not a house.

After they came from the country of Kittim [Cyprus],
   it was revealed to them.
²Be still, inhabitants of the foreign shore,
   merchants of Tsidon.
Seafarers filled you;
   ³by mighty waters came the seed of Shihor.
The harvest of the Ye'or was its yield,
   and it became the marketplace of the nations.
⁴Be shamed, Tsidon, because the sea has said,
   the stronghold of the sea,
'I haven't laboured, I haven't given birth,
   I haven't brought up young men or raised girls.'
⁵When the report came to Misrayim, they were in
     anguish,
   when the report came about Tsor.

⁶Cross over to Tarshish;
   howl, inhabitants of the foreign shore.
⁷Is this your exultant one,
   whose antiquity is from ancient days,
Whose feet carried it
   to reside far away?
⁸Who counselled this for Tsor,
   the giver of crowns,
Whose merchants were officials,
   its traders the most honoured in the earth?
⁹Yahweh of Armies counselled it,
   to defile all its splendid majesty,
   to slight all the most honoured in the earth.
¹⁰Pass through your country like the Ye'or, Miss
     Tarshish;
   there's a harbour no more.
¹¹He stretched out his hand over the sea,
   shook kingdoms.
It was Yahweh gave an order regarding Kena'an,
   to annihilate its strongholds.
¹²He said, 'You will no more exult,
   afflicted maiden, Miss Tsidon.
Get up, cross over to Kittim;
   there will be no settling for you, even there.'
¹³There, the country of the Kasdites –
   this is the people that is no longer.
Ashshur founded it for ships;
   they set up its citadels.
They've stripped its strongholds,
   they've made it into a ruin.

## What to do with a whore's fee

¹⁴Howl, ships of Tarshish,
   because your stronghold has been destroyed.

¹⁵On that day,
   Tsor will be put out of mind for seventy years,
   like the days of a king.
At the end of seventy years
   it will be for Tsor like the song about the whore:
¹⁶'Get a guitar, go about the town,
   whore who is put out of mind.
Be good, play, sing many a song,
   in order that you may be brought to mind.'
¹⁷At the end of seventy years
   Yahweh will attend to Tsor.
It will go back to its 'gift' and its whoring
   with all the world's kingdoms on the face of the
     earth.
¹⁸But its profits and its 'gifts' will be sacred to
     Yahweh;
   it won't be treasured, it won't be stored,
Because its profit will be for the people who live
     before Yahweh,
   for eating till they are full, and for fine clothes.

## The broken world covenant

# 24   There:

Yahweh is laying waste to the earth and making it
     desolate,
   twisting its surface and scattering its
     inhabitants.
²It will be: as people, so priest;
   as servant, so his lord;
As maidservant, so her mistress;
   as buyer, so seller;
As creditor, so borrower;
   as lender, so the one to whom he lends.
³The earth will be totally wasted,
   it will be totally plundered,
   (because it is Yahweh who has spoken this
     word).

⁴The earth dries up, withers;
   the world languishes, withers;
   the height languishes with the earth.
⁵The earth was impious under its inhabitants,
   because they transgressed instructions.
They violated statute,
   contravened an age-old pact.
⁶That's why a vow has consumed the earth;
   the people who live in it incurred liability.
That's why earth's inhabitants have been ablaze,
   and few people remain.

7The new wine dries up, the vine has languished,
    all the people who were rejoicing in heart
        groan.
8The joy of tambourines has stopped,
    the din of the exultant has left off,
    the joy of the mandolin has stopped.
9They do not drink wine with a song,
    liquor is bitter to the one who drinks it.
10The empty township is broken up,
    every house is closed against entering.
11There's a cry over the wine in the streets,
    all rejoicing has reached evening,
    earth's joy has gone into exile.
12Desolation is what remains in the town;
    the gateway is struck down, a ruin.
13Because so it will be within the earth,
    among the peoples,
Like the beating of an olive tree,
    like gleanings if the harvest finishes.

14Those people lift their voice, resound,
    because of Yahweh's majesty they've bellowed
        from the west.
15Therefore honour Yahweh in the east,
    in shores across the sea,
    the name of Yahweh, Yisra'el's God.

16From a corner of the earth we've heard melodies,
    'Splendour belongs to the Faithful One.'
But I said, I waste away,
    I waste away! Oh, me!
People have broken faith,
    in broken faith people have broken faith.

## Heavenly powers shamed

17Dread and pit and trap
    for you who inhabit the earth!
18The one who flees at the dreadful sound
    will fall into the pit.
The one who climbs up from the pit
    will be caught in the trap.
Because sluices have opened on high,
    and earth's foundations have shaken.
19The earth has quite broken up;
    earth has quite split up;
    earth has quite slipped.
20The earth quite reels like a drunk,
    it sways about like an overnight shelter.
Its rebellion weighs heavy upon it;
    it will fall, and not get up again.

21On that day Yahweh will attend
    to the army of the height, in the height,
    and to the kings of the earth, on the earth.
22They will be gathered as a gathering,
    as captives in a pit.
They will be imprisoned in a prison,
    but after many days will get attention.
23The moon will be confounded,
    the sun will be disgraced.
Because Yahweh of Armies will have begun to
        reign
    in Mount Tsiyyon and in Yerushalaim,
    with his splendour in front of his elders.

# 25 Yahweh, you are my God, I will exalt
        you,
    I will confess your name,
Because you have done something extraordinary,
    plans from a distant time, truthfulness, truth.
2Because you've made out of a town a heap,
    a fortified township into a ruin.
The citadel of foreigners is no longer a town;
    it won't be built up ever.
3Therefore a vigorous people will honour you,
    a township of violent nations will revere you.
4Because you've been a stronghold for the poor
        person,
    a stronghold for the needy person in his
        pressures,
A shelter from rain,
    a shade from heat,
When the spirit of the violent was like winter rain,
    5the din of aliens like heat in the desert.
You subdue the heat with a cloud shade;
    the music of the violent succumbs.

## Grief brought to an end

6And Yahweh of Armies will make
    for all peoples on this mountain
A banquet with rich foods, a banquet with aged
        wines,
    juicy rich foods, refined aged wines.
7He will swallow up on this mountain the layer of
        wrapping,
    the wrapping over all the peoples,
The covering that is spread out over all the
        nations;
8he will have swallowed up death permanently.
The Lord Yahweh will wipe the tears
    from on all faces.

*! ♀ Resurrection!*

The reviling of his people
    he will take away from on all the earth;
    because Yahweh is the one who has spoken.

⁹On that day one will say:

There, this is our God,
    we hoped for him and he delivered us.
This is Yahweh, we hoped for him;
    let's celebrate and rejoice in his deliverance.
¹⁰Because Yahweh's hand will alight
    on this mountain.
Mo'ab will be trodden down in its place
    like the treading of straw at Madmenah.
¹¹It will spread out its hands within it,
    as a swimmer spreads his hands to swim.
He will bring down its majesty
    with the spoils of its hands.
¹²The towering fortification of its walls
    he will have laid low, taken down,
    knocked down to the ground, right to the earth.

**26** On that day this song will be sung in
the country of Yehudah:

We have a strong town;
    he makes walls and rampart into deliverance.
²Open the gateways so that the faithful nation
    may come in,
    one that keeps truthfulness.
³A mind that is sustained, you preserve in well-
    being,
    in well-being because it's filled with reliance
    on you.
⁴Rely on Yahweh permanently, because in Yah –
    Yahweh is crag for the ages.
⁵Because he has laid low the people who live in
    the height;
    the towering township he brings down.
He brings it down right to the ground,
    knocks it down right to the earth.
⁶The foot treads it down, the feet of the humble
    person,
    the soles of the poor people.

*Your dead will live*

⁷The path is clear for the faithful person,
    when you level the faithful person's track clear.
⁸Yes, on the path determined by your rulings,
    Yahweh, we have hoped for you.

The longing of our entire being
    has been for your name and your renown.
⁹With my entire being I've longed for you by
    night;
    yes, my spirit within me seeks urgently for you.
Because when your rulings are in the earth,
    the inhabitants of the world learn faithfulness.
¹⁰Were the faithless person shown grace,
    he wouldn't learn faithfulness.
In a country characterized by straightness he does
    what's evil,
    and doesn't live in awe of Yahweh's majesty.
¹¹Yahweh, they don't behold your hand raised;
    they should behold and be shamed.
Your passion for the people,
    yes, your fire for your adversaries, should
    consume them.
¹²Yahweh, may you institute well-being for us,
    because all the things we've done, you did for
    us.
¹³Yahweh our God,
    lords apart from you have been masters over us,
    but of you alone we will make mention, of your
    name.
¹⁴Dead people don't live,
    ghosts don't rise.
That's why you attended to them and annihilated
    them,
    and obliterated any mention of them.
¹⁵You added to the nation, Yahweh;
    when you added to the nation you were
    honoured,
    you furthered all the country's boundaries.
¹⁶Yahweh, under pressure they attended to you,
    a whispered prayer during your correction of
    them.

¹⁷Like a pregnant woman who draws near to
    giving birth,
    who writhes, cries out in her pain,
So have we become,
    because of you, Yahweh.
¹⁸We were pregnant, we writhed,
    it is as if we gave birth to wind.
We don't achieve deliverance in the earth;
    the inhabitants of the world don't fall.

¹⁹Your dead will live, my corpse will rise;
    wake up and resound, you who dwell in the
    earth!
Because your dew is the dew of the lights,
    and you make the country of ghosts fall.

²⁰Go, my people, come into your rooms,
  and shut your door after you.
Hide for a little moment,
  until condemnation passes.
²¹Because there, Yahweh is going to come out
    from his place,
  to attend to the waywardness of the earth's
    inhabitants upon them.
The earth will uncover its shed blood,
  and will no more cover over its slain.

## Livyatan (Leviathan) meets its end

**27** On that day Yahweh will attend with his
       sword,
  tough and big and strong,
To Livyatan the fleeing serpent,
  to Livyatan the twisting serpent;
  he will slay the dragon that's in the sea.

²On that day,
  a delightful vineyard, chant of it!
³I Yahweh am going to preserve it;
  moment by moment I will water it.
In case someone attends to it,
  night and day I will preserve it.
⁴I have no wrath;
  if only someone gives me briar and thorn!
In battle I will march against it,
  and set fire to them altogether.
⁵Or he can take hold of my stronghold,
  he can make peace with me,
  peace he can make with me.

⁶Coming days: Ya'aqob will root,
  Yisra'el will bud and blossom,
  and the face of the world will be full of
    produce.

⁷Did he strike it down like the striking of the one
    who struck it down,
  was it slain like the slaying of the ones slain by
    him?
⁸By driving away, by sending off, you argue with
    it;
  he removed it by a tough blast on a day of east
    wind.
⁹Therefore by this Ya'aqob's waywardness will be
    expiated;
  this is the entire fruit of the removing of its
    wrongdoing.

Through his making all the altar stones
  like shattered blocks of limestone,
  totem poles and incense altars won't stand.
¹⁰Because the fortified town is desolate,
  the abode sent off and abandoned like the
    wilderness.
There a calf pastures,
  there it lies down and consumes its boughs.
¹¹When its branches wither, they break;
  women come, set light to them.
Because it is not a people of understanding;
  therefore its maker will not have compassion
    on it,
  its former will not be gracious to it.

¹²On that day
  Yahweh will thresh from the channel of the
    River [Euphrates]
  to the Misrayimite Wadi,
And you will be gleaned
  one by one, Yisra'elites.
¹³On that day
  there will be a sound on a great horn.
The people will come who are perishing in the
    country of Ashshur,
  and who are scattered in the country of
    Misrayim.
They will bow low to Yahweh
  on the sacred mountain, in Yerushalaim.

## The drunks of Ephrayim and Yehudah

**28** Hey, majestic crown of Ephrayim's
       drunks,
  and its splendid beauty, a fading flower,
One that's on the majestic head of beefy
    people,
  struck down by wine!
²Here, the Lord has someone strong and
    powerful,
  like a storm of hail, a destructive tempest.
Like a storm of water, forceful, rushing,
  he has set it down on the earth by his power.
³It will be trampled underfoot,
  the majestic crown of Ephrayim's drunks.
⁴The fading flower, its splendid beauty,
  that's on the majestic head of beefy people,
Will be like a fig before harvest
  that someone sees.
The one who sees it –
  while it's still in his palm, he swallows it.

⁵On that day,
    Yahweh of Armies will become
A splendid crown and a glorious diadem
    for the remainder of his people,
⁶An authoritative spirit
    for the one who sits over the exercise of
        authority,
    and the strength of the people who turn back
        the battle at the gateway.

⁷But these also wander because of wine,
    stagger because of liquor:
Priest and prophet wander because of liquor,
    they're swallowed up by wine, they stagger
        because of liquor.
They wander when they are seeing,
    they go astray in giving judgement.
⁸Because all the tables are full of vomit, filth –
    there's no place.

⁹'Whom does he instruct in knowledge,
    whom does he help to understand a report?
People weaned from milk,
    moving on from the breast?
¹⁰Because order upon order,
    order upon order,
Rule upon rule, rule upon rule,
    a little there, a little there.
¹¹Because with mockings of lip and in another
        tongue
    he speaks to this people,
¹²The one who has said to them,
    "This is the place to settle down,
Settle the weary person down,
    yes, this is the place of repose."'

But they have not been willing to listen,
    ¹³so to them Yahweh's word will be
Order upon order,
    order upon order,
Rule upon rule, rule upon rule,
    a little there, a little there,
In order that they may go, but fall back,
    and be broken and snared and captured.

## God's strange work

¹⁴Therefore listen to Yahweh's word,
    you arrogant,
Who rule this people,
    which is in Yerushalaim.

¹⁵Because you've said:

'We have solemnized a pact with death,
    with She'ol we've made an agreement.
The sweeping flood, when it passes,
    won't come to us,
Because we've made a lie our shelter,
    we have hidden in falsehood.'

¹⁶Therefore the Lord Yahweh has said this:

Here am I founding in Tsiyyon a stone,
    a testing stone, a valuable cornerstone,
A well-founded foundation;
    the one who stands firm in faith will not be
        hasty.
¹⁷I will make authority the rule,
    faithfulness the weight.
Hail will sweep away the lying shelter;
    water will flood the hiding place.
¹⁸Your pact with death will be covered over,
    your agreement with She'ol won't stand up.
The sweeping flood, when it passes –
    you will be for trampling by it.
¹⁹The times when it passes, it will get you,
    because it will pass morning after morning,
By day and by night,
    and understanding the report will be simply a
        horror.
²⁰Because the bed will be too short for stretching
        out,
    the blanket too narrow for gathering round
        oneself.
²¹Because Yahweh will arise as on Mount Peritsim,
    he will be astir as in Gib'on Vale,
To do his deed – strange is his deed,
    to perform his service – foreign is his service.
²²So now, don't be arrogant,
    or your chains will get strong.
Because I've heard of a finish, a thing determined,
    by the Lord Yahweh of Armies,
    against the entire country.

²³Give ear, listen to my voice,
    heed, listen to what I say.
²⁴Is it all the time that the ploughman ploughs to
        sow,
    opens up and harrows his ground?
²⁵When he's levelled its surface,
    he scatters caraway and sprinkles cumin,
Sets wheat (millet) and barley in its place,
    and spelt in its border, doesn't he.

*Saffron*

²⁶One disciplines him for acting with judgement:
  his God instructs him.
²⁷Because caraway isn't threshed with a sled,
  and the wheel of a cart isn't rolled over
    cumin.
Because caraway is beaten with a rod,
  and cumin with a club.
²⁸Cereal is crushed,
  because the thresher doesn't thresh
    permanently.
The wheel of his cart may rumble,
  but he doesn't crush it with his horse riders.
²⁹This too comes from Yahweh of Armies;
  he formulates extraordinary plans,
  he shows great skill.

## Like a ghost from the earth

**29** Hey, God's Hearth, God's Hearth,
    township where David camped!
Add year to year;
  the festivals may come round.
²But I will oppress God's Hearth,
  and there'll be sorrow and sighing.
It will be to me God's very hearth;
  ³I shall camp against you with a very
    encircling.
I shall lay siege against you with a rampart,
  set up siege works against you.
⁴You'll be lower than the ground when you
    speak,
  your words will be lower than the earth.
Your voice will be like a ghost from the ground,
  your words will chirp from the earth.
⁵But like fine dust will be the horde of your
    adversaries,
  like passing chaff the horde of the violent.
In an instant, suddenly,
  ⁶by Yahweh of Armies you will be attended,
With thunder and with shaking, and a loud
    voice,
  storm and hurricane and a flame of consuming
    fire.
⁷It will be like a dream, a vision in the night:
  the horde of all the nations,
Which are making war against God's Hearth,
  and all its besiegers and its stronghold and its
    oppressors.
⁸It will be like when someone hungry dreams,
  and there, he's eating, but he wakes up,
  and his throat is empty,

Or like when someone thirsty dreams,
  and there, he's drinking, but he wakes up,
  and there, he's faint, and his throat is craving.
So will the horde of all the nations be
  that are making war against Mount Tsiyyon.

⁹Wait about and be stupefied,
  blind yourselves and be blind.
They are drunk but not from wine,
  they totter but not from liquor.
¹⁰Because Yahweh has poured over you
  a spirit of coma.
He has closed your eyes, the prophets,
  and covered your heads, the seers.
¹¹The vision of anything has become for you
  like the words of a sealed scroll,
Which they give to someone who knows
    writing,
  saying 'Read this out, please',
And he says, 'I can't,
  because it's sealed.'
¹²So the scroll is given to someone who doesn't
    know writing,
  saying 'Read this out, please',
  but he says, 'I don't know writing.'

## Who sees us?

¹³The Lord has said,

'Since this people has come near with its mouth,
  and with its lips has honoured me,
But has kept its mind far from me,
  and their awe for me has been a learned human
    order:
¹⁴Therefore here I am,
  once more doing something extraordinary with
    this people,
  acting in an extraordinary way, something
    extraordinary.
The smartness of its smart people will perish,
  the understanding of its people of
    understanding will hide.'
¹⁵Hey, you who go deeper than Yahweh
  to hide your counsel,
Whose action is in the dark and who say,
  'Who sees us, who knows about us?'
¹⁶Your overturning of things! – if the potter is
  thought of as like the clay,
  or the thing that's made says of its maker, 'He
    didn't make me',

Or the pot says of its potter,
  'He didn't understand.'

<sup>17</sup>In yet a little while,
  Lebanon will turn back into farmland, won't it,
  and the farmland be thought of as forest.
<sup>18</sup>Deaf people will listen on that day to the words
    of a document,
  and out of murk and darkness the eyes of blind
    people will see.
<sup>19</sup>The humble will regain rejoicing in Yahweh,
  and the neediest of people will celebrate
    Yisra'el's Sacred One.
<sup>20</sup>Because the violent person will not exist, the
    arrogant person will be finished,
  and all the people who are wakeful over trouble
    will be cut off,
<sup>21</sup>The people who make someone into a
    wrongdoer with a statement they make,
  who trap the judge at the gateway,
  and who turn aside the one in the right with
    empty words.

<sup>22</sup>Therefore, Yahweh has said this to Ya'aqob's
household, the one who redeemed Abraham:

Ya'aqob won't now be shamed;
  his face won't now be pale.
<sup>23</sup>Because when he (his descendants) sees
  the action of my hands within him,
  he'll make my name sacred.
People will make Ya'aqob's Sacred One sacred,
  and be in dread of Yisra'el's God.
<sup>24</sup>The people who wander in spirit will
  acknowledge understanding,
  and the people who complain will learn a grasp
    of things.

## God is our refuge and strength, really?

**30** Hey, defiant sons (Yahweh's declaration),
  in forming counsel but not from me,
In pouring a drink offering but not from my
    spirit,
  in order to heap wrong on wrong,
<sup>2</sup>You who go to descend to Misrayim,
  but have not asked my bidding,
In protecting yourselves by Par'oh's protection
  and in taking shelter in Misrayim's shade.
<sup>3</sup>But Par'oh's protection will become shame for you,
  and shelter in Misrayim's shade, disgrace.

<sup>4</sup>Because his officials have been at Tso'an,
  his envoys reach Hanes:
<sup>5</sup>Everyone will have come to shame
  because of a people that's no use to them,
No help and no use,
  but rather shame and yes, reviling.

<sup>6</sup>A pronouncement about The Animals of the
Negeb.

In a country of pressure and distress,
  lion and cougar among them,
  viper and flying serpent,
They carry their resources on the back of
    donkeys,
  their treasures on the hump of camels,
To a people that's no use,
  <sup>7</sup>Misrayim which helps with a breath,
    emptiness.
Therefore I call this
  'They are Rahab sitting.'

<sup>8</sup>Now, come,
  write it on a tablet with them,
  inscribe it on a scroll,
So that it may be for a future day
  a witness permanently.
<sup>9</sup>Because it's a rebellious people,
  deceitful children,
Children who didn't wish to listen
  to Yahweh's instruction,
<sup>10</sup>People who've said to seers,
  'Don't see',
And to visionaries,
  'Don't give us visions of straightness.
Speak nice things to us,
  give us visions that are deceptions.
<sup>11</sup>Depart from the way, turn away from the path,
  make Yisra'el's Sacred One cease from before us.'

<sup>12</sup>Therefore Yisra'el's Sacred One has said this:

Since you've rejected this word,
  and relied on fraud and crookedness,
  and leaned on it,
<sup>13</sup>Therefore this waywardness will be for you
  like a breach falling,
Swelling out in a high wall,
  whose breaking comes suddenly, in an instant.
<sup>14</sup>Its breaking is like the breaking of a potters'
    jug,
  smashed so he doesn't spare:

Through its smashing there won't be found a
    fragment
    for picking up fire from a hearth
    or for skimming water from a pool.

## Yahweh waits

[15]Because the Lord Yahweh, Yisra'el's Sacred
One, has said this:

By turning back and settling down you'll find
    deliverance;
    in calm and reliance will be your strength.
But you were unwilling,
    [16]and you said 'No,
Rather we'll flee on a horse' –
    therefore you'll flee.
'We'll ride on a swift one' –
    therefore your pursuers will be swift.
[17]A thousand from before the reprimand of one,
    from before the reprimand of five, you'll flee,
Until you're left like a beacon on the top of a
    mountain,
    like a banner on a hill.

[18]Therefore Yahweh waits to be gracious to you;
    but therefore he will arise to show compassion
    to you.
Because Yahweh is a God with authority –
    the blessings of all who wait for him!
[19]Because, people in Tsiyyon, which dwells in
    Yerushalaim,
    you really will not weep.
He really will be gracious to you at the sound of
    your cry;
    as he hears it, he'll have answered you.
[20]The Lord will give you pressure bread
    and affliction water.
But your instructors will no longer be marginalized;
    your eyes will be seeing your instructors.
[21]Your ears will listen to a word from behind you,
    saying, 'This is the way, walk in it',
    when you go right and when you go left.
[22]You'll defile the plating of your silver images,
    and the sheath of your gold idol.
You'll scatter them like something sick;
    'Get out', you'll say to it.
[23]And he'll give the rain for your seed
    with which you sow your ground,
And the bread that's the yield of your ground,
    and it will be rich and fat.

Your livestock will pasture on that day
    in a broad pasture.
[24]The oxen and the donkeys that serve the ground
    will eat seasoned fodder
    that's been winnowed with shovel and fork.

## The Hearth prepared for the King

[25]There will be, on every high mountain
    and on every lofty hill,
    streams running with water,
On the day of great slaughter,
    when towers fall.
[26]But the moon's light will be like the sun's light,
    and the sun's light will be sevenfold,
    like the light of seven days,
On the day when Yahweh bandages his people's
    wound,
    and heals the wound from his striking down.

[27]There, Yahweh's name is coming from afar,
    his anger burning, his load a weight.
His lips are full of condemnation,
    his tongue is like a consuming fire.
[28]His breath is like a rushing wadi
    that comes halfway to the neck,
To shake the nations in an empty shaker,
    with a halter that makes them wander on the
    peoples' jaws.
[29]The song will be for you
    like the night when a festival gets made sacred,
The rejoicing of heart like someone going with a
    pipe,
    to come on Yahweh's mountain, to Yisra'el's
    crag.
[30]Yahweh will make the majesty of his voice heard,
    and show the alighting of his arm,
In angry wrath and consuming fiery flame,
    cloudburst, storm and hailstone.
[31]Because at Yahweh's voice
    Ashshur that strikes down with a club will be
    shattered.
[32]Every passing of the appointed mace,
    which Yahweh causes to alight on him,
Will be with tambourines and guitars,
    and with battles involving its shaking he will
    battle against them.
[33]Because the Hearth is laid out already;
    yes, it's prepared for the King.
He's made its firepit deep and wide,
    fire and wood a-plenty,

Yahweh's breath
  like a sulphur wadi burning up in it.

## The hawks hovering over the town

**31** Hey, you who are going down to
Misrayim for help,
  who lean on horses,
Who've relied on chariotry because it's vast,
  and on cavalry because they're very numerous,
And not turned to Yisra'el's Sacred One,
  and not enquired of Yahweh.
²But he too is smart, and he has brought bad
    fortune,
  and not made his words turn away.
He will arise against the household of people who
    deal badly,
  and against the help of people who bring
    trouble.
³The Misrayimites are human, not God,
  their horses are flesh and not spirit.
When Yahweh stretches out his hand,
  helper will collapse and the one who is helped
    will fall;
  all of them will be finished together.

⁴Because Yahweh has said this to me:

As a lion murmurs,
  or a cougar over its prey
(When a whole group of shepherds
  is called against it,
At their voice it isn't shattered,
  at the horde of them it doesn't succumb),
So Yahweh of Armies will go down
  to fight on Mount Tsiyyon and on its hill.
⁵Like birds flying,
  so Yahweh of Armies will shield Yerushalaim,
Shielding and rescuing,
  passing over and saving.
⁶Turn back to the one whom you have deeply
    defied,
  Yisra'elites.
⁷Because on that day they will reject, each one,
  his silver non-entities and his gold non-entities,
  which your hands made for you, a wrongdoing.
⁸Ashshur will fall by a sword not human;
  a sword that doesn't belong to a human being
    will consume it.
It will flee for its life from before the sword;
  its young men will become a workforce.

⁹Its cliff will pass away because of the terror,
  its officers will be shattered because of the
    ensign
(a declaration of Yahweh, whose fire is in Tsiyyon,
  his furnace in Yerushalaim).

**32** There, a king will reign to promote
faithfulness;
  as for officials, they'll govern to promote the
    exercise of authority.
²Each will be a veritable hiding place from wind,
  a place of concealment from rain,
Like channels of water in the desert,
  like the shade of a heavy cliff in a weary
    country.
³The eyes of people who see won't be blind,
  the ears of people who listen will heed.
⁴The mind of the quick will understand
    knowledge,
  the tongue of the hesitant will be quick
  to speak dazzling words.
⁵No more will a villain be called a leader,
  or a rogue called a deliverer.
⁶Because a villain speaks villainy,
  and his mind brings trouble,
Acting impiously,
  and speaking of wandering in regard to
    Yahweh,
Leaving the hungry person empty,
  and letting the drink of the thirsty fail.
⁷The rogue: his tools are bad,
  he's one who counsels schemes,
To destroy the humble by false words,
  and when the needy person speaks his case.
⁸But a leader will counsel acts of leadership,
  and that man will rise up with acts of
    leadership.

## When the spirit empties itself

⁹Carefree women, get up, listen to my voice;
  confident daughters, give ear to what I say.
¹⁰Some days over a year
  you confident ones will shake,
Because the harvest will be finished,
  the ingathering won't come.
¹¹Tremble, you carefree; shake, you confident,
  strip, be bare, a skirt round your waist,
¹²Lamenting upon your breasts for the lovely
    fields,
  for the fruitful vine,

¹³For my people's soil,
   which will produce thorn and briar,
Indeed, for all the joyful households,
   the exultant township.
¹⁴Because the fortress will have been deserted,
   the uproar of the town will have been
      abandoned.
Citadel and tower will have become
   empty spaces permanently,
Enjoyment for donkeys,
   pasture for flocks:
¹⁵Until spirit empties on us from on high,
   and wilderness becomes farmland,
   and farmland is thought of as forest.
¹⁶Authority will dwell in the wilderness,
   faithfulness will live in the farmland.
¹⁷The effect of faithfulness will be well-being,
   the service of faithfulness will be calm and
      confidence permanently.
¹⁸My people will live in an abode characterized by
      well-being,
   in secure dwellings, in carefree places to settle
      down.

¹⁹Though it hails when the forest flattens,
   and the town falls utterly down,
²⁰The blessings you will have as you sow by all
      water,
   as you let loose the foot of ox and donkey!

## The offensive hope of the city of God

**33** Hey, destroyer, and you're not
      destroyed,
   one who breaks faith, and people have not
      broken faith with you!
When you finish destroying you will be destroyed,
   when you stop breaking faith, they'll break
      faith with you.
²Yahweh, be gracious to us,
   we have hoped in you.
Be people's arm every morning,
   yes, our deliverance in time of pressure.
³Before the sound of uproar peoples fled,
   before your rising nations scattered.
⁴Your spoil was gathered like the gathering of
      locusts;
   like the rushing of grasshoppers someone
      rushes on it.
⁵Yahweh is lofty, because he dwells on high;
   he filled Tsiyyon with authority and faithfulness.

⁶He will become the truthfulness of your times;
   smartness and knowledge are the wealth that
      brings deliverance,
   awe for Yahweh – that is its treasure.

⁷There – the people in God's Hearth have cried
      out aloud in the streets,
   the envoys of Shalom cry bitterly.
⁸Causeways have become desolate,
   people passing on the road have ceased.
He has contravened the pact, rejected the towns,
   not taken account of anyone.
⁹The country has withered, wasted away;
   Lebanon is confounded, it has shrivelled.
The Sharon has become like the steppe,
   Bashan and Carmel are shaking things off.
¹⁰'Now I will arise,' Yahweh says,
   'now I will exalt myself, now I will lift myself.
¹¹You will conceive hay, give birth to straw;
   your breath a fire that consumes you.
¹²Peoples will be burnings of lime,
   thorns cut off that are set on fire.
¹³Listen, you far off, to what I have done;
   acknowledge, you that are near, my strength.'

## Your eyes will behold the King in his beauty

¹⁴Wrongdoers in Tsiyyon are frightened,
   trembling grasps the impious.
Who of us can reside with consuming fire,
   who of us can reside with the permanent blaze?
¹⁵One who walks in faithfulness,
   speaks uprightly,
Rejects profit from fraud,
   waves the palms of his hands rather than
      grasping a bribe,
Stops his ear rather than listening to talk of
      bloodshed,
   closes his eyes rather than look at what is bad –
¹⁶That person can dwell on the heights,
   with fortresses in the cliffs as his high tower.
His food will be given,
   his water reliable.

¹⁷Your eyes will behold the King in his beauty,
   they'll see the country stretching far.
¹⁸Your mind will murmur about what you dreaded –
   where's the person counting, where's the person
      weighing?
Where's the person counting the towers? –
   ¹⁹when you don't see the barbarous people,

The people too way-out of speech to listen,
   so stammering of tongue that there's no
      understanding.
²⁰Behold Tsiyyon, the township of our appointed
      festivals;
   your eyes will see Yerushalaim,
A carefree abode,
   a tent that will not move about,
Whose pegs one will never pull up,
   none of whose ropes will break.
²¹Rather, there the august one, Yahweh, will be
      for us
   a place of rivers, streams, broad on both sides.
No rowing vessel can go in it,
   no august ship can pass through it.
²²Because Yahweh is the one exercising authority
      for us,
   Yahweh is the one who makes decrees for us.
Yahweh is our King, he is the one who will deliver
      us,
   ²³when your ropes are loose.
They cannot take strong hold on the base of their
      mast,
   they cannot spread a sail.
Then much spoil is divided,
   lame people take plunder.
²⁴No dweller will say, 'I'm ill';
   the people that lives in it – its waywardness is
      carried.

## Putting down Edom

**34** Come near to listen, nations,
      heed, peoples.
The earth and what fills it should listen,
   the world and all who come out from it.
²Because Yahweh has fury for all the nations,
   wrath for all their army.
He's devoting them, giving them to slaughter,
   ³and those of them who are run through will be
      thrown out.
Their corpses – their stench will go up,
   and the mountains will dissolve with their
      blood.
⁴All the army of the heavens will rot,
   and the heavens will roll up like a document.
All their army will droop
   like the droop of foliage from a vine,
And the droop from a fig tree,
⁵because my sword will have drunk its fill in the
      heavens.

There, on Edom it goes down,
   and on a people I am devoting, so as to exercise
      authority.
⁶Yahweh's sword is full of blood,
   soaked in fat,
In the blood of lambs and goats,
   in fat from the kidneys of rams.
Because Yahweh has a sacrifice in Botsrah,
   a big slaughter in the country of Edom.
⁷Oryxes will go down with them,
   bullocks with sturdy steers.
Their country will be full of blood,
   their earth will be soaked in fat.
⁸Because it's a day of redress for Yahweh,
   a year of making good for Tsiyyon's
      argument.
⁹Its wadis will turn to pitch,
   its earth to sulphur.
Its country will become pitch burning up;
   ¹⁰day and night it won't go out.
Its smoke will go up permanently;
   from generation to generation it will lie waste.
Lastingly and permanently
   there will be no one passing through it.
¹¹Hawk and hedgehog will possess it,
   owl and raven will dwell in it.
He'll stretch out over it the measuring line of
      emptiness,
   and the weights of the void ¹²over its nobles.
People will call it 'There's No Kingship There';
   all its officials will be nothing.
¹³Thorns will grow up in its citadels,
   briar and thistle in its fortresses.
It will become an abode of jackals,
   a dwelling for ostriches.
¹⁴Wildcats will meet hyenas,
   a wild goat will call to its neighbour.
Indeed, the night creature is resting there,
   finding herself a place of repose.
¹⁵There the snake is nesting and laying eggs,
   sitting and hatching in its shade.
Yes, there buzzards are gathering,
   each with her mate.

## Giving the mute their voice

   ¹⁶Enquire from in Yahweh's document, and
read out:

Not one of these is lacking,
   they do not miss, any of them, her mate,

Because by my mouth he ordered,
and with his spirit he collected them.
[17]He's the one who made the lot fall for them,
his hand shared it out for them with the line.
They will possess it for all time,
to generation after generation they will dwell
there.

## 35

The wilderness and the dry land will be
glad,
the steppe will celebrate and bloom like a
crocus.
[2]It will bloom abundantly and celebrate,
indeed with celebration and resounding.
The Lebanon's splendour will be given it,
the Carmel and the Sharon's glory.
Those people will see Yahweh's splendour,
our God's glory.

[3]Strengthen slackening hands,
firm up collapsing knees.
[4]Say to the hesitant of mind,
'Be strong, don't be afraid, there is your God.
Redress will come, God's dealing,
he will come and deliver you.'

[5]Then the eyes of the blind will open,
the ears of the deaf will unfasten.
[6]Then the handicapped person will jump like a
deer,
the mute's tongue will resound.
Because water will burst out in the wilderness,
wadis in the steppe.
[7]The burning sand will become a pool,
the thirsty ground fountains of water.
In the abode of jackals, its resting place,
the dwelling will be reed and rush.

[8]There will be a highway there, a way,
the sacred way it will be called;
an unclean person won't pass along it.
It will be for them, the one who walks the way;
stupid people won't wander there.
[9]There'll be no lion there;
violent beast won't go up on it,
It won't be found there;
the restored people will go.
[10]The people redeemed by Yahweh will go back,
they will come to Tsiyyon with resounding,
With eternal rejoicing on their head,
as joy and rejoicing overtake them
and sorrow and sighing flee.

## What are you relying on?

## 36

In the fourteenth year of King
Hizqiyyahu, Sanherib [Sennacherib]
king of Ashshur went up against all the
fortified towns of Yehudah and captured
them.
[2]The king of Ashshur sent the Rab-
shaqeh from Lakish to Yerushalaim to King
Hizqiyyahu with a heavy force, and he stood at
the Upper Pool channel at the Washer's Field
causeway. [3]Elyaqim ben Hilqiyyahu who was in
charge of the household, Shebna the secretary
and Yo'ah ben Asaph the recorder went out
to him.
[4]The Rab-shaqeh said to them, 'Say to
Hizqiyyahu, please, "The Great King, the king
of Ashshur, has said this: 'What is this reliance
that you have: [5]"I've said, 'Just the word on some
lips are counsel and strength for battle'"? Now,
on whom have you relied, that you've rebelled
against me? [6]There, you've relied on the support
of this broken reed, on Misrayim, which when
someone leans on it, comes into his palm and
pierces it. Such is Par'oh king of Misrayim to
all the people who rely on him. [7]But when you
say to me, "On Yahweh our God – we've relied
on him", he's the one whose shrines and whose
altars Hizqiyyahu removed, isn't he, and who's
said to Yehudah and to Yerushalaim, "Before
this altar you're to bow low."
[8]But now, please make a wager with my lord
the king of Ashshur. I'll give you 2,000 horses
if you can put riders on them for yourself.
[9]So how could you turn back the face of the
governor of one of my lord's lesser servants and
rely on Misrayim for chariotry and for cavalry
for yourself? [10]And now, is it without Yahweh
that I've gone up to this country to devastate it?
It was Yahweh who said to me, "Go up to this
country and devastate it."'"

## Don't rely on Yahweh

[11]Elyaqim, Shebna and Yo'ah said to the
Rab-shaqeh, 'Please speak to your servants in
Aramaic, because we're listening. Don't speak to
us in Yehudahite in the ears of the people, which
is on the wall.' [12]The Rab-shaqeh said, 'Was it
to your lord and to you that my lord sent me to
speak these words? Wasn't it to the individuals

who are sitting on the wall, to eat their faeces and drink the water between their legs with you?'

¹³The Rab-shaqeh stood and said and called in a loud voice in Yehudahite: 'Listen to the words of the Great King, the king of Ashshur. ¹⁴The king has said this: "Hizqiyyahu must not deceive you", because he won't be able to rescue you. ¹⁵And Hizqiyyahu must not get you to rely on Yahweh, saying, "Yahweh will definitely rescue us, this town won't be given into the hand of the king of Ashshur." ¹⁶Don't listen to Hizqiyyahu.

Because the king of Ashshur has said this: "Make a blessing [agreement] with me. Go out to me, and eat each one his vine and each one his fig tree, and drink each one the water from his cistern, ¹⁷until I come and take you to a country like your country, a country of grain and new wine, a country of bread and vineyards. ¹⁸Don't let Hizqiyyahu incite you, saying 'Yahweh will rescue us.' Have the gods of the nations, any of them, rescued his country from the hand of the king of Ashshur? ¹⁹Where were the gods of Hamat and Arpad? Where were the gods of Sepharvayim? And indeed did they rescue Shomron from my hand? ²⁰Who was it among all the gods of these countries that rescued their country from my hand?"'

²¹They were silent. They didn't answer him a word, because it was the king's order, 'Don't answer him.' ²²But Elyaqim ben Hilqiyyahu who was in charge of the household, Shebna the secretary and Yo'ah ben Asaph the recorder came to Hizqiyyahu, their clothes torn, and told him the Rab-shaqeh's words.

## A politician's one fatal mistake

**37** When King Hizqiyyahu heard, he tore his clothes and covered himself in sack. He came into Yahweh's house, ²but he sent Elyaqim, who was in charge of the household, Shebna the secretary and the priestly elders, covered in sack, to Yesha'yahu ben Amots. ³They said to him, 'Hizqiyyahu has said this: "This day is a day of pressure, reproof and disdain, when 'children have come to breaking but there's no energy to give birth'. ⁴Perhaps Yahweh your God will listen to the words of the Rab-shaqeh, whom the king of Ashshur his lord sent to revile the living God,

and will issue a reproof for the words that Yahweh your God has heard, and you will lift up a plea on behalf of the remainder that are to be found here."'

⁵King Hizqiyyahu's servants came to Yesha'yahu, ⁶and Yesha'yahu said to them, 'You're to say this to your lord: "Yahweh has said this: 'Don't be afraid before the words you've heard with which the king of Ashshur's boys have insulted me. ⁷Here – I'm going to put a spirit in him, and he'll hear a report and go back to his country, and I shall cause him to fall by the sword in his country.'"'

⁸The Rab-shaqeh went back and found the king of Ashshur battling against Libnah, because he heard that he had moved on from Lakish, ⁹and he heard about Tirhaqah king of Kush, 'He's gone out to do battle with you.' So he heard and sent envoys to Hizqiyyahu, saying, ¹⁰'You're to say this to Hizqiyyahu king of Yehudah: "Your God on whom you're relying mustn't deceive you, saying 'Yerushalaim won't be given into the hand of the king of Ashshur.' ¹¹Here, you yourself have heard what the kings of Ashshur have done to all the countries, devoting them, and are you the one who'll be rescued? ¹²Did the gods of the nations that my ancestors devastated rescue them – Gozan, Harran, Reseph, and the Edenites who were in Tela'ssar? ¹³Where is the king of Hamat, king of Arpad, the king of La'ir, Sepharvayim, Hena and Yivvah?"'

## Dealing with tricky mail

¹⁴Hizqiyyahu took the documents from the envoys' hand, read it out and went up to Yahweh's house. Hizqiyyahu spread it before Yahweh, ¹⁵and Hizqiyyahu pleaded with Yahweh: ¹⁶'Yahweh of Armies, Yisra'el's God, sitting above the sphinxes: you are God, you alone, for all the kingdoms of the earth. You are the one who made the heavens and the earth. ¹⁷Yahweh, bend your ear and listen. Yahweh, open your eye and see. Listen to all the words of Sanherib that he has sent to revile the living God.

¹⁸Truly, Yahweh, the kings of Ashshur have put to the sword all the countries, and their own country, ¹⁹and put their gods into the fire, because they were not gods but rather

the making of human hands, wood and stone, and they obliterated them. ²⁰But now, Yahweh our God, deliver us from his hand, so that all the kingdoms of the earth may acknowledge that you alone are Yahweh.'

²¹Yesha'yahu ben Amots sent to Hizqiyyahu saying, 'Yahweh, Yisra'el's God, with whom you pleaded concerning Sanherib king of Ashshur, has said this. ²²This is the word that Yahweh has spoken about him:

Maiden Miss Tsiyyon
    despises you, she ridicules you.
Behind you Miss Yerushalaim
    has shaken her head.
²³Whom have you reviled and insulted,
    against whom have you lifted your voice?
You've raised your eyes on high
    towards Yisra'el's sacred one.
²⁴By the hand of your servants
    you've reviled the Lord, and said,
"With the large number of my chariotry I'm the
        one who has gone up
    to the mountains' height, Lebanon's farthest
        parts.
I've cut down the highest of its cedars,
    the choicest of its junipers.
I've come to its ultimate height,
    its forest of farmland.
²⁵I'm the one who has dug
    and drunk water,
I've dried with the sole of my feet
    all Misrayim's streams."

### Reminder to Sanherib, promise to Hizqiyyahu

²⁶Haven't you heard?
    – long ago I did it.
From days of old I formed it;
    now I've made it come about.
It's happened, crashing fortified towns
    into wasted heaps.
²⁷Their inhabitants, short of ability,
    are scared and shamed.
They were vegetation of the fields,
    green herbage,
Grass on the roofs,
    blasted before it grows up.
²⁸Your sitting, your going out and your coming I
    know,
    and your raging at me.

²⁹Since you raged at me,
    and your din came up into my ears,
I shall put my hook in your nose,
    my bit in your mouth,
I shall make you go back
    by the way that you came.'

³⁰This will be the sign for you:

This year, eat the natural growth;
    in the second year, the secondary growth.
In the third year, sow and reap,
    plant vineyards and eat their fruit.
³¹An escape group from Yehudah's household that
        remains
    will add root downwards and produce fruit
        above.
³²Because a remainder will go out from
        Yerushalaim,
    and an escape group from Mount Tsiyyon.
The passion of Yahweh of Armies
    will do this.'

³³Therefore Yahweh has said this concerning the king of Ashshur:

'He will not come into this town;
    he will not shoot an arrow there.
He will not meet it with a shield;
    he will not heap up a ramp against it.
³⁴By the way that he came he will go back;
    into this town he will not come
    (Yahweh's declaration).
³⁵I will shield this town so as to deliver it,
    for my sake and for the sake of David my
        servant.'

### The praying Hizqiyyahu

³⁶Yahweh's envoy went out and struck down 185,000 in the Ashshurites' camp. People started early in the morning – there, all of them were dead corpses.
³⁷Sanherib the king of Ashshur moved on and went, and returned and lived in Nineveh.
³⁸He was bowing low in the house of Nisrok his god when Adrammelek and Sar'etser his sons struck him with the sword. While they escaped to the country of Ararat, Esar-haddon his son began to reign in place of him.

# 38

In those days Hizqiyyahu became deathly ill. Yesha'yahu ben Amots the prophet came to him and said to him, 'Yahweh has said this: "Give orders to your household, because you're dying. You won't live on."' ²Hizqiyyahu turned his face round to the wall and pleaded with Yahweh, ³'Oh, Yahweh, please be mindful of how I've walked before you in truth and with a perfect mind, and done what is good in your eyes.' Hizqiyyahu cried and cried much.

⁴Yahweh's word came to Yesha'yahu: ⁵'Go and say to Hizqiyyahu: "Yahweh, the God of David your ancestor, has said this: 'I have listened to your plea, I've seen your tears. Here, I am going to add to your time fifteen years. ⁶From the fist of the king of Ashshur I shall rescue you and this town, and I shall shield this town."' ⁷This will be the sign for you from Yahweh that Yahweh will do this thing that he has spoken of. ⁸"Here, I'm going to make the shadow go back on the steps, which has gone down on the steps of Ahaz with the sun, back ten steps."' And the sun went back ten steps by the steps that it had gone down.

## The prayer

⁹Something written for Hizqiyyahu king of Yehudah, when he was ill and came back to life from his sickness.

¹⁰I myself said,
  'In the middle of my days I shall go.
I've been appointed to She'ol's gateways
  for the rest of my years.'
¹¹I said, 'I shall not see Yah;
  Yah is in the land of the living.
I shall not look to humanity again,
  with the inhabitants of the world.
¹²My dwelling has moved on and gone into exile
    from me,
  like a shepherd's tent.
I've rolled up my life like a weaver,
  as he cuts me from the loom.
While from day until night you make an end of me,
  ¹³I have composed myself until morning.
Like a lion that thus breaks up all my bones,
  from day until night you make an end of me.
¹⁴Like a swift, a swallow, so I chirp;
  I murmur like a dove.'

My eyes have looked to the height:
'Lord, it's oppression to me, make a pledge to
    me.
¹⁵What shall I speak of when he has said it to
    me,
  and he himself has acted?
I shall walk all my years
  in the bitterness of my heart.
¹⁶Lord, in such things people live,
  and in all of them is the life of my spirit;
  may you restore me and let me live.'

¹⁷There – as regards well-being,
  it was bitter for me, bitter.
But you yourself delighted in me,
  out of the pit of nothingness,
Because you threw all my wrongdoings
  behind your back.
¹⁸Because She'ol does not confess you,
  death praise you.
People who go down to the Pit
  don't expect your truthfulness.
¹⁹The living person, the living person, that one
    confesses you,
  this very day.
A father makes known to his children
  your truthfulness.
²⁰Yahweh will deliver me,
  and we will make music,
All the days of our lives
  at Yahweh's house.

(²¹Yesha'yahu had said, 'They are to get a block of figs and apply it to the infection, and he will live on', and Hizqiyyahu had said, 'What will be the sign that I shall go up to Yahweh's house?')

## How to lose God's sympathy

# 39

At that time Merodak Bal'adan ben Bal'adan king of Babel sent documents and an offering to Hizqiyyahu; he had heard that he had been ill and had regained strength. ²Hizqiyyahu rejoiced about them and let them see his repository house, the silver, the gold, the spices and the fine oil, and his entire equipment house, and everything that was to be found in his storehouses. There was not a thing that Hizqiyyahu didn't let them see in his house and his entire kingdom.

9) Human perception of "good"

³Yesha'yahu the prophet came to King Hizqiyyahu and said to him, 'What did these men say? Where did they come from to you?' Hizqiyyahu said, 'From a far country, they came to me from Babel.' ⁴He said, 'What did they see in your house?' Hizqiyyahu said, 'They saw everything that's in my house. There wasn't a thing that I didn't let them see in my storehouses.'

⁵Yesha'yahu said to Hizqiyyahu, 'Listen to the word of Yahweh of Armies. ⁶"There, days are going to come when everything that's in your house, and that your ancestors have stored up until this day, will be carried to Babel. Not a thing will be left," Yahweh has said. ⁷"Some of your descendants who will issue from you, whom you will father, will be taken and will become courtiers in the palace of the king of Babel."' ⁸Hizqiyyahu said to Yesha'yahu, 'The word from Yahweh that you have spoken is good.' He said, 'Because there'll be well-being and truthfulness in my days.'

## Comfort my people

**40** 'Comfort, comfort my people',
    says your God.
²'Speak to Yerushalaim's heart,
    call to it
That its tour of duty is fulfilled,
    that its waywardness is paid for,
That it has taken from Yahweh's hand
    double for all its wrongdoings.'

³A voice is calling:

'In the wilderness clear Yahweh's way,
    make straight in the steppe a causeway for our
        God.
⁴Every ravine is to rise up,
    every mountain and hill is to fall down.
The ridge is to become level,
    the cliffs a valley.
⁵Yahweh's splendour will appear,
    and all flesh will see it together,
    because Yahweh's mouth has spoken.'

⁶A voice is saying, 'Call',
    but someone says, 'Call what?'
All flesh is grass,
    and all its commitment is like a wild flower's.

⁷Grass withers, a flower fades,
    when Yahweh's wind blows on it.'
'Yes, the people is grass;
    ⁸grass withers, a flower fades –
but our God's word rises up permanently.'

⁹Get yourself up on to a high mountain
    as a bringer of news to Tsiyyon.
Raise your voice with energy
    as a bringer of news to Yerushalaim.
Raise it, don't be afraid,
    say to Yehudah's towns,
'Here is your God,
    ¹⁰here is the Lord Yahweh.'
He comes as the strong one,
    his arm is going to rule for him.
Here, his reward is with him,
    his earnings before him.
¹¹Like a shepherd who pastures his flock,
    he collects lambs in his arm.
He carries them in his embrace,
    guides the nursing ones.

¹²Who gauged the water in his palm,
    surveyed the heavens with his span,
Measured the world's earth by the gallon,
    weighed the mountains with a balance,
    the hills with scales?
¹³Who directed Yahweh's spirit,
    or as the person to give him counsel made it
        known to him?
¹⁴With whom did he take counsel, so that he
        helped him understand,
    taught him the way to exercise authority,
Taught him knowledge,
    made known to him the way of understanding?
¹⁵There, nations count like a drop from a pan,
    like a cloud on scales;
    there, foreign shores are like a fine cloud that
        rises.
¹⁶Lebanon – there's not enough to burn up,
    its animals – there aren't enough as a burnt
        offering.
¹⁷All the nations are like nothing over against him;
    they count as less than naught, emptiness, to
        him.

## Hope means energy

¹⁸So to whom would you compare God,
    or what comparison would you line up for him?

¹⁹The image, which a craftworker casts? –
  a smith beats it out with gold,
  and a smith with silver chains.
²⁰Is it sissoo fit for tribute,
  wood that doesn't rot, that someone chooses?
He seeks for himself a smart craftworker
  to set up an image so it doesn't slip.

²¹You acknowledge, don't you,
  you listen, don't you?
It's been told you from the beginning, hasn't it,
  you've understood earth's foundations, haven't
    you?
²²There's one who sits above earth's horizon,
  with its inhabitants like grasshoppers,
One who stretched out the heavens like net,
  spread them like a tent for sitting in,
²³One who turns sovereigns into nothing,
  makes earth's authorities pure emptiness.
²⁴They're really not planted, really not sown,
  their stem is really not rooting in the earth,
Then he blows on them and they shrivel,
  and a hurricane carries them off like straw.

²⁵So to whom would you compare me,
  so I could be similar (says the Sacred One)?
²⁶Lift your eyes on high and see –
  who created these?
The one who takes out their army by number
  calls to all of them by name.
Because of the greatness of his power,
  and as one firm in energy, not one lags behind.

²⁷Why do you say, Ya'aqob,
  and speak, Yisra'el,
'My way has hidden from Yahweh,
  a ruling for me passes away from my God'?
²⁸Haven't you acknowledged,
  or haven't you listened?
Yahweh is God of the ages,
  creator of earth's ends.
He doesn't get faint or weary;
  there's no searching out of his understanding.
²⁹He gives energy to the faint,
  and to the one who has no resources he gives
    much strength.
³⁰Youths may get faint and weary,
  young men may totally collapse.
³¹But people who hope in Yahweh get new energy,
  they grow pinions like eagles.
They run and don't get weary,
  they walk and don't faint.

## Don't be afraid

**41** Be silent for me, foreign shores;
  peoples must renew their energy.
They must come up, then speak;
  together let us draw near for making a ruling.
²Who aroused someone from the east
  whom faithfulness calls to its heel?
He gives up nations before him,
  enables him to put down kings.
He makes them like earth with his sword,
  like driven straw with his bow.
³As he pursues them, he passes on with things
    being well
  by a path on which he doesn't come straight.
⁴Who acted and did it,
  calling the generations from the beginning?
I am Yahweh, the first,
  and I myself am with the last.
⁵Foreign shores have seen and become afraid,
  earth's ends tremble,
  they've drawn near and come.
⁶An individual helps his neighbour,
  and says to his brother, 'Be strong!'
⁷Craftworker bids smith be strong,
  one who flattens with a hammer [bids] one
    who strikes with a mallet.
One who says of the joint, 'It's good',
  strengthens it with fastenings so it doesn't slip.

⁸But you as Yisra'el are my servant,
  as Ya'aqob you're the one that I chose.
As the offspring of Abraham you're my friend,
  ⁹the one of whom I took strong hold from
    earth's ends,
Called from its corners, and said to you,
  'You're my servant, I chose you, and didn't
    spurn you.'
¹⁰Don't be afraid, because I'm with you;
  don't be frightened, because I'm your God.
I'm making you firm, yes, helping you,
  yes, supporting you with my faithful right hand.
¹¹There, they'll be shamed and disgraced,
  all who rage at you.
They'll become absolutely nothing, they'll perish,
  the people who argue with you.
¹²You will seek them and not find them,
  the people who attack you.
They'll become absolutely nothing, zero,
  the people who do battle against you.
¹³Because I am Yahweh your God,
  who takes strong hold of your right hand,

Who says to you, 'Don't be afraid,
   I myself am helping you.'

[14]Don't be afraid, worm Ya'aqob,
   relics Yisra'el.
I'm helping you (Yahweh's declaration),
   Yisra'el's sacred one is your restorer.
[15]There, I'm making you into a harrow,
   a new thresher fitted with points.
You'll trample mountains and crush them,
   and make hills like chaff.
[16]You'll winnow them and the wind will carry them,
   the hurricane will scatter them.
And you yourselves will rejoice in Yahweh;
   in Yisra'el's sacred one you'll exult.

## Do anything!

[17]When the humble and the needy are seeking
   water,
   but there is none, their tongue is parched with
     thirst.
I Yahweh will answer them;
   the God of Yisra'el will not abandon them.
[18]I will open up rivers on the bare places,
   springs in the middle of the valleys.
I will make the wilderness into a pool of water,
   dry land into water courses.
[19]In the wilderness I will put cedar,
   acacia, myrtle and oil tree.
In the steppe I will set juniper,
   maple and cypress, together,
[20]In order that people may see and acknowledge,
   consider and discern together,
That Yahweh's hand did this,
   Yisra'el's sacred one created it.

[21]'Present your argument,'
   Yahweh says.
'Bring up your strong points,'
   says Ya'aqob's King.
[22]They should bring them up
   and tell us what will happen.
The previous events – tell us what they were,
   so we may apply our mind and acknowledge
     their outcome.
Or let us hear about the coming events,
   [23]tell us things that will arrive after,
   so we may acknowledge that you are gods.
Yes, do something good or do something bad,
   so we may bow low and see together.

[24]Here, you're less than nothing,
   your action is less than a sigh;
   it's an offence that someone chooses in you.

[25]I aroused one from the north and he arrived,
   from the rising of the sun one who would call
     on my name.
He came on viceroys as if they were mire,
   as if he was a potter who treads clay.
[26]Who told of it from the beginning so we might
     acknowledge him,
   beforehand so we might say 'He was right'?
No, there was no one telling of it;
   no, there was no one letting us hear about it;
   no, there was no one hearing your words.
[27]The first for Tsiyyon ('Here, here they are'),
   for Yerushalaim, I give a bringer of news.
[28]Were I to look, there was no one;
   of them, there was no counsellor,
   who could speak a word back if I asked them.
[29]There, they are all a bane, their acts are zero,
   their images are a breath, emptiness.

## There is my servant

**42** There is my servant whom I support,
   my chosen whom I myself accept.
I'm putting my breath on him;
   he will see that my exercise of authority gets
     out to the nations.
[2]He won't cry out and he won't raise
   or make his voice heard, in the streets.
[3]A broken cane he won't snap,
   a flickering lamp he won't snuff.
For the sake of truthfulness he'll see the exercise
     of authority gets out,
   [4]he won't flicker or break,
Until he sets the exercise of authority in the earth,
   as foreign shores wait for his instruction.

[5]The God Yahweh has said this,
   the one who created the heavens and stretched
     them,
   beating out the earth and its produce,
Giving air to the people on it,
   breath to those who walk on it:
[6]'I am Yahweh, I called you in faithfulness,
   took strong hold of your hand.
I formed you and gave you as a pact for the
     people,
   a light for the nations,

⁷In opening blind eyes,
    in getting the captive out from the dungeon,
    from the prison people who are living in the
      dark.
⁸I am Yahweh, that is my name;
    my splendour I do not give to another,
    or my praise to images.
⁹The previous events – here, they came about;
    and I'm telling of new events –
    before they grow, I let you hear.'

¹⁰Sing Yahweh a new song,
    his praise from the end of the earth,
You who go down to the sea, and what fills it,
    foreign shores and those who live in them.
¹¹The wilderness and its towns are to raise their
      voice,
    the villages where Qedar lives.
The people who live in Sela are to resound,
    they are to yell from the top of the
      mountains.
¹²They are to ascribe splendour to Yahweh,
    to tell of his praise on foreign shores.

## What will we do when God's servant is deaf and blind?

¹³Yahweh goes out like a strong man,
    like a man of battle he arouses his passion.
He shouts, yes roars,
    acts as a strong man against his enemies.
¹⁴'I've been quiet from of old;
    I've been being still and restraining myself.
Like a woman giving birth I shall shriek,
    I shall devastate and crush together.
¹⁵I shall waste mountains and hills,
    wither all their growth.
I shall turn rivers into shores,
    wither wetland.
¹⁶I shall enable blind people to go by a way they
      haven't known,
    lead them on paths they haven't known.
I shall make the darkness in front of them into
      light,
    rough places into level ground.
These are the words I am acting on,
    and I will not abandon them.'
¹⁷They're turning back, they're utterly shamed,
    the people who trust in an image,
Who say to an idol,
    'You're our god.'

¹⁸Listen, you deaf people;
    you blind people, look and see!
¹⁹Who is blind except my servant,
    as deaf as my envoy I send?
Who is as blind as the one made good to,
    as blind as Yahweh's servant?
²⁰While seeing many things, you don't heed;
    while opening ears, he doesn't listen.
²¹Yahweh wants, for the sake of his faithfulness,
    that he should magnify the instruction, glorify
      it.
²²But that is a people plundered and spoiled,
    trapped in holes, all of them,
    and they're confined in jails.
They've become plunder with no rescuer,
    spoil with no one saying, 'Give it back!'
²³Who among you will give ear to this,
    will heed and listen for the future?
²⁴Who gave Ya'aqob as spoil, Yisra'el to
      plunderers? –
    it was Yahweh, against whom we had done
      wrong, wasn't it.
They were not willing to walk in his ways,
    they didn't listen to his instruction.
²⁵So he poured wrath upon it,
    his anger and battling vigour.
It blazed upon it all round, but it didn't
      acknowledge;
    it burned it up, but it doesn't take it into its
      mind.

## You'll still be my witnesses

**43** But now Yahweh has said this,
    your creator, Ya'aqob, your former,
    Yisra'el:
'Don't be afraid, because I'm restoring you;
    I call you by name, you're mine.
²When you pass through water, I'll be with you,
    and through rivers, they won't overwhelm you.
When you go in the middle of fire you won't burn,
    and into flames, they won't consume you.
³Because I am Yahweh your God,
    Yisra'el's Sacred One, your deliverer.
I gave Misrayim as your ransom,
    Kush and Seba in place of you.
⁴Because you were valuable in my eyes;
    you were honoured and I myself was loyal to
      you,
So that I would give people in place of you,
    nations in place of your life.

⁵Don't be afraid,
　　because I'll be with you.
From the east I shall bring your offspring,
　　from the west I shall gather you.
⁶I shall say to the north, "Give",
　　and to the south, "Don't restrain.
Bring my sons from far away,
　　my daughters from the end of the earth,
⁷Everyone called in my name and for my
　　　splendour,
　　whom I created, formed, yes made."'

⁸Take out the people that is blind though it has
　　　eyes,
　　those who are deaf though they have ears.
⁹All the nations must collect together,
　　the peoples must gather.
Who among them could tell of this,
　　could let us hear of the earlier events?
They must give their witnesses so they may prove
　　　right,
　　so people may listen and say, 'It's true.'
¹⁰You're my witnesses (Yahweh's declaration),
　　and my servant whom I chose,
In order that you may acknowledge and trust in
　　　me,
　　and understand that I am the one.
Before me no god was formed,
　　and after me there will be none.
¹¹I myself, I am Yahweh,
　　and apart from me there's no deliverer.
¹²I'm the one who told of it and delivered;
　　I let you hear, and there was no stranger among
　　　you.
And you're my witnesses (Yahweh's declaration);
　　I am God.
¹³Yes, from this day I'm the one,
　　and there is no one rescues from my hand;
　　I act, and who can make it go back?

## I'm sending to Babel

¹⁴Yahweh has said this,
　　your restorer, Yisra'el's sacred one:
'For your sake I am sending to Babel,
　　and I shall take down all of them as fugitives,
　　the Kasdites into their boats with a shout.
¹⁵I am Yahweh, your Sacred One,
　　Yisra'el's creator, your King.'
¹⁶Yahweh has said this,
　　the one who made a way in the sea,

A path in vigorous water,
　　¹⁷who took out chariot and horse,
　　force and vigorous one, altogether.
(They lie down, they don't get up;
　　they were extinguished, they went out like a wick):
¹⁸Don't be mindful of the earlier events,
　　don't consider previous events.
¹⁹Here am I, doing something new;
　　now it is to grow – you will acknowledge it,
　　　won't you.
Yes, I shall make a way in the wilderness,
　　rivers in the desert.
²⁰The animals of the wild will honour me,
　　jackals and ostriches,
Because I'm giving water in the wilderness,
　　rivers in the desert,
To give drink to my people, my chosen,
　　²¹the people that I formed for myself:
　　they will recount my praise.

²²But it's not me you've called on, Ya'aqob,
　　because you've been weary of me, Yisra'el.
²³You haven't brought me sheep as your whole
　　　offerings,
　　nor honoured me with your sacrifices.
I haven't made you serve me with an offering,
　　nor made you weary with incense.
²⁴You haven't gained me cane with silver,
　　nor soaked me with the fat of your sacrifices.
Actually you have made me serve with your
　　　wrongdoings,
　　wearied me with your wayward acts.
²⁵I, I'm the one,
　　who wipes away your rebellions for my sake,
　　and your wrongdoings I will not keep in mind.
²⁶Remind me; let's enter into judgement together –
　　you give an account, so you may prove to be in
　　　the right.
²⁷Your first ancestor – he did wrong,
　　and your interpreters – they rebelled against me.
²⁸So I treated the sacred officials as ordinary,
　　give Ya'aqob to being devoted, Yisra'el to taunts.

## People will say, 'I am Yahweh's'

**44** But now listen, Ya'aqob my servant,
　　　Yisra'el whom I chose.
²Yahweh your maker has said this,
　　your former from the womb, who will help you:
Don't be afraid, my servant Ya'aqob,
　　Yeshurun whom I chose.

³Because I shall pour water on the thirsty,
  streams on the dry ground.
I shall pour my spirit on your offspring,
  my blessing on those who go out from you.
⁴They'll grow like a grassy tamarisk,
  like willows by water channels.
⁵One will say, 'I am Yahweh's',
  one will call out in Yahweh's name.
One will write on his hand 'Yahweh's',
  take as his name 'Yisra'el'.

⁶Yahweh, Yisra'el's King, has said this,
  your restorer, Yahweh of Armies:
'I am first and I am last;
  apart from me there is no God.
⁷Who is like me? – he must call out,
  tell and lay it out for me.
Who let people hear of coming events from of
      old? –
  they must tell us what will happen.
⁸Don't fear or take fright,
  I let you hear of it in time past, and told of it,
      didn't I.
And you're my witnesses:
  is there a God apart from me? –
  but there is no crag, I don't acknowledge one.'

## The stupidity of images

⁹People who form an image – all of them are
      emptiness,
  and the objects of their delight are no use.
They are their witnesses – they don't see and they
      don't acknowledge,
  in order that they may be shamed.
¹⁰Who forms a god or casts an image
  so that it may be of no use?
¹¹There, all his associates will be shamed;
  craftworkers are but human.
If all of them collect together and stand up,
  they'll be afraid, shamed, together.
¹²A craftworker in metal with a cutter
  works in the fire.
He forms it with hammers,
  works it with his energetic arm.
Should he get hungry, he'd have no energy;
  should he not drink water, he'd be faint.
¹³A craftworker in wood stretches a line,
  outlines it with a chalk.
He makes it with squares,
  outlines it with a compass.

He makes it in the image of a person,
  with the majesty of a human being, to live at
      home.
¹⁴In cutting himself cedars,
  getting ilex or oak,
He secures it for himself among the trees of the
      forest,
  plants a pine so the rain may make it grow,
¹⁵So it may be fuel for someone,
  and he takes some of them and gets warm.
He both lights it and bakes bread,
  and also makes a god and bows down to it.
He makes an image and prostrates himself to it,
  ¹⁶while half of it he burns in the middle of the
      fire.
Over the half of it he eats meat,
  he makes a roast and is full.
He also gets warm and says,
  'Ah, I'm warm, I see a flame.'
¹⁷The remainder of it he makes into a god, into
      his image,
  to which he will kneel down and bow low.
He will plead with it and say,
  'Rescue me, because you're my god.'
¹⁸They don't acknowledge,
  they don't understand,
Because their eyes are smeared so they don't see,
  their minds so they don't discern.
¹⁹He doesn't bring back to his mind,
  there's no knowledge nor understanding to say,
'Half of it I burned in the middle of the fire,
  also I baked bread on the coals.
I roasted meat and ate,
  and the rest of it I'll make into an offence.
I'll kneel down to a lump of wood' –
  ²⁰feeder on earth!
A deluded mind has directed him,
  and he can't rescue himself.
He can't say,
  'Isn't it a falsehood in my hand?'

## No forgetting

²¹Be mindful of these things, Ya'aqob,
  Yisra'el, because you're my servant.
I formed you as a servant, you're mine;
  Yisra'el, there is to be no forgetting.
²²I'm wiping away your rebellions like a cloud,
  your wrongdoings like a thundercloud.
Turn back to me,
  because I'm restoring you.

²³Resound, heavens, because Yahweh has
    acted;
    shout, depths of the earth.
Break out in sound, mountains,
    forest and every tree in it.
Because Yahweh is restoring Ya'aqob,
    and will show his majesty in Yisra'el.

²⁴Yahweh, your restorer, has said this –
    your former from the womb:
'I am Yahweh,
    maker of everything,
Who stretched out the heavens on my own,
    spread out the earth of myself,
²⁵Who contravenes the signs of soothsayers,
    makes fools of diviners,
Turns the smart back,
    makes idiocy of their knowledge,
²⁶Implements his servant's word,
    fulfils his envoys' plan –
Who says of Yerushalaim, "It will be
    inhabited",
    and of Yehudah's towns, "They'll be built up",
    and "I will raise its wastes",
²⁷Who says to the deep,
    "Be wasted – I shall dry up your rivers",
²⁸Who says to Koresh [Cyrus], "My shepherd,
    he'll fulfil my every want",
By saying of Yerushalaim, "It will be built up",
    and to the palace, "Be founded."'

## Creator of good and bad things

**45** Yahweh has said this to his anointed, to
    Koresh,
    'The one whom I took by the right hand,
Putting down nations before him,
    undoing the hips of kings,
Opening doors before him,
    so that gateways might not shut:
²I will go before you and level walls;
    I will break up copper doors,
    cut up iron bars.
³I will give you dark treasuries
    and hidden hoards,
In order that you may acknowledge that I am
    Yahweh;
    Yisra'el's God is the one who calls you by
    your name.
⁴For the sake of my servant Ya'aqob,
    Yisra'el my chosen,

I called you by your name,
    I designate you though you haven't
    acknowledged me.
⁵I am Yahweh and there is no other;
    apart from me there is no God.
I put the belt on you, though you have not
    acknowledged me,
⁶in order that people may acknowledge,
    from the rise of the sun and from the setting,
That there is none apart from me,
    I am Yahweh and there is no other,
⁷Forming light and creating dark,
    making well-being and creating bad fortune.
I am Yahweh,
    doing all these things.'

⁸Rain, heavens above;
    skies are to pour down faithfulness.
Earth is to open so that deliverance may fruit,
    faithfulness is to burst out all at once;
    I Yahweh have created it.

⁹Hey, you who argue with the one who forms him,
    a pot with earthen pots.
Can clay say to the one who forms it, 'What do
    you do',
    or can the thing you make say, 'It has no handles'?
¹⁰Hey, you who say to a father, 'What do you beget?'
    or to a woman, 'What do you give birth to?'
¹¹Yahweh has said this –
    Yisra'el's Sacred One and the one who forms it:
'Ask me about things to come for my children –
    you can give me orders about the work of my
    hands.
¹²I'm the one who made the earth
    and created humanity upon it.
I – my hands stretched out the heavens,
    I ordered their entire army.
¹³I'm the one who aroused him in faithfulness
    and level all his ways.
He's the one who will build up my town
    and send off my exiles,
Not for payment, not for a bribe,'
    Yahweh of Armies has said.

## Every knee will bend

¹⁴Yahweh has said this:

'Misrayim's toil, Kush's profit,
    the Seba'ites, people of stature,

Will pass over to you and be yours;
  they'll follow behind you.
They'll pass over in fetters and bow low to you,
  to you they'll make their plea:
"God is in you only,
  and there's no other, no God.
¹⁵Certainly you're the God who hides,
  God of Yisra'el who delivers."
¹⁶They are shamed, yes, they are disgraced, all of
    them at once,
  they have gone in disgrace, the people who
    craft forms.
¹⁷Yisra'el has found deliverance in Yahweh,
  everlasting deliverance.
You will not be shamed, you will not be disgraced,
  to everlasting ages.'

¹⁸Because Yahweh has said this,
  the creator of the heavens, he is God,
the former of the earth and its maker –
  he established it, he did not create it an
    emptiness,
  he formed it for inhabiting:

'I am Yahweh
  and there is no other.
¹⁹It was not in hiddenness that I spoke,
  in a place in a dark country.
I didn't say to Ya'aqob's offspring,
  "Enquire of me in emptiness."
I am Yahweh, speaking of faithfulness,
  telling of what is right.
²⁰Gather, come, draw near together,
  escapees of the nations.
The people who carry their wooden images have
    not acknowledged,
  the people who plead with a god who does not
    deliver.
²¹Tell out, bring near,
  yes, consult together.
Who let people hear of this beforehand,
  told about it of old?
Was it not I, Yahweh? –
  and there was no other God apart from me,
The faithful God and deliverer;
  there's none except me.
²²Turn your faces to me and find deliverance, all
    the ends of the earth,
  because I am God and there's no other.
²³By myself I've sworn,
  faithfulness has gone out from my mouth,
  a word that will not turn back:

To me every knee will bend,
  every tongue swear.
²⁴"Only in Yahweh (of me it is said)
  are faithful acts and vigour.'"
To him they will come and be shamed,
  all who rage at him.
²⁵In Yahweh all Yisra'el's offspring
  will be faithful and will exult.

*Gods you have to carry and the God
who carries you*

**46** Bel has bent down, Nebo is stooping;
  their images have come to belong to
  creatures, to animals.
The things carried by you are loaded as a burden
    for weary ones;
  ²they've stooped, they've bent down together.
They couldn't save the burden;
  they themselves have gone into captivity.
³Listen to me, Ya'aqob's household,
  all the remainder of Yisra'el's household,
Who've been loaded from birth,
  who've been carried from the womb.
⁴Even until old age I will be the one;
  even until grey-headedness I will be the one
    who will bear.
I'm the one who made, I'm the one who carries;
  I'm the one who bears, and I will save.
⁵To whom can you compare me so I should be
    similar,
  or liken me so we are comparable?
⁶People who lavish gold from a purse,
  or weigh out silver by the rod,
Hire a smith so he may make it into a god
  to which they may fall down, bow low.
⁷They carry it on their shoulder, bear it,
  so they can set it down in its position and it can
    stand;
  from its place it won't move away.
Yes, someone can cry out to it, but it doesn't answer;
  it doesn't deliver him from the pressure on him.

⁸Keep this in mind, be strong,
  bring it back to mind, you rebels,
⁹Keep in mind earlier events of old,
  because I am God and there is no other.
I am God and there is none like me,
  ¹⁰telling of the outcome from the beginning,
And from beforehand things that haven't been done,
  saying 'My counsel will arise, all I want I shall do',

¹¹Calling from the east a shriek,
    from a far country the person in my counsel.
I both spoke and will also bring it about;
    I formed and will also do it.
¹²Listen to me, you sturdy of mind,
    you who are far away from faithfulness.
¹³I have brought faithfulness near; it's not far away,
    and my deliverance won't delay.
I shall put deliverance in Tsiyyon,
    my magnificence for Yisra'el.

## The unexpected fall of the superpower

**47** Get down, sit in the earth, young Miss Babel,

sit on the ground without a throne, Miss Kasdim.
Because you will not again have people call you
    sensitive and delightful.
²Get the millstones and grind meal,
    expose your hair.
Uncover your tresses, expose your leg,
    cross rivers.
³Your nakedness will be exposed,
    yes, your reviling will be visible.
I shall take redress,
    no one will intervene.
⁴(Our restorer: Yahweh of Armies is his name,
    Yisra'el's Sacred One.)

⁵Sit in silence, enter into darkness,
    Miss Kasdim.
Because you will not again have them call you
    mistress of kingdoms.
⁶I was angry with my people, I treated my domain
    as ordinary,
    I gave them into your hand.
You didn't show compassion to them;
    upon the aged you made your yoke very heavy.
⁷You said, 'I shall be here permanently,
    mistress always.'
You didn't receive these things into your mind;
    you were not mindful of its outcome.

⁸So now listen to this, charming one,
    who sits in confidence,
Who says to herself,
    'I and none else am still here,
I shall not sit as a widow,
    I shall not know the loss of children.'
⁹The two of these will come to you,
    in a moment, on one day.

The loss of children and widowhood
    in full measure will have come upon you.
In the multiplying of your chants
    and in the great abounding of your charms,
¹⁰You've been confident in your bad dealing;
    you said, 'There's no one looking at me.'
Your smartness, your knowledge,
    it turned you back.
You said to yourself,
    'I and none else am still here.'
¹¹But bad fortune is going to come upon you
    whose countercharm you won't know.
Disaster will fall upon you
    that you won't be able to expiate.
There will come upon you suddenly
    devastation that you won't know about.
¹²Stand, please, in your charms and in the
    multiplying of your chants,
in which you've laboured from your youth.
Perhaps you'll be able to succeed,
    perhaps you will terrify.

## I knew you were tough-minded

¹³You're collapsing in the multiplying of your plans;
    they should indeed stand up and deliver you,
The people who observe the heavens,
    who look at the stars,
Who make known for the months
    some of what will come upon you.
¹⁴There, they've become like straw
    that fire burns up.
They can't rescue themselves
    from the power of the blaze.
It's not a coal for warming,
    a flame for sitting before.
¹⁵Such have they been for you,
    those with whom you have laboured,
    your charmers from your youth.
They've wandered, each of them his own way;
    there's no one delivering you.

**48** Listen to this, Ya'aqob's household,
    you who call yourselves by Yisra'el's name,
You who came out of Yehudah's water,
    who swear by Yahweh's name,
Who make mention of Yisra'el's God –
    not in truthfulness, not in faithfulness –
²Because they call themselves by the sacred town,
    lean on Yisra'el's God,
    whose name is Yahweh of Armies.

³The earlier events I told about of old,
　from my mouth they came out so I could make
　　them heard.
Suddenly I acted and they came about,
　⁴because of my knowing that you're tough.
Your neck is an iron sinew,
　your forehead copper.
⁵I told you about them of old,
　before they came about I let you hear,
So you couldn't say, 'My icon did them;
　my image, my idol ordered them.'

⁶You've heard – look at all of it;
　will you yourselves not tell of it?
I'm letting you hear of new events right now,
　secrets that you didn't know.
⁷Now they're created, not of old,
　or before today, and you haven't heard of
　　them,
　so you could say, 'There, I knew about them.'
⁸No, you haven't heard; no, you haven't known;
　no, of old your ear didn't open up.
Because I knew you would utterly break faith;
　rebel from birth, you were called.

⁹For the sake of my name I delay my anger,
　for the sake of my praise I muzzle it for you
　so that I don't cut you off.
¹⁰There, I smelted you, and not in the silver
　　[furnace];
　I chose you in the affliction furnace.
¹¹For my sake, for my sake, I act,
　because how can my splendour be treated as
　　ordinary? –
　I will not give it to someone else.

## If only . . .

¹²Listen to me, Ya'aqob,
　Yisra'el whom I called.
I'm the one, I'm the first,
　yes, I'm the last.
¹³Yes, it was my hand formed earth;
　my right hand spanned the heavens.
I'm going to call them
　so they stand together.
¹⁴Collect together, all of you, and listen –
　who among them told of these things?
One to whom Yahweh is loyal will do what he
　　wants to Babel,
　and his arm to the Kasdites.

¹⁵I, I'm the one who spoke,
　yes, I called him,
　I brought him and he will succeed in his
　　journey.
¹⁶Draw near to me,
　listen to this.
Not from the first did I speak in hiddenness;
　from the time it came to be, I was there.

Now the Lord Yahweh
　has sent me, with his spirit.
¹⁷Yahweh has said this – your restorer,
　Yisra'el's Sacred One.
'I am Yahweh your God,
　the one who teaches you to succeed,
Who directs you in the way you should go –
　¹⁸if only you had heeded my orders.
Your well-being would have been like a river,
　your faithfulness like the waves of the sea.
¹⁹Your offspring would have been like the sand,
　the people who went out from you like its grains.
Your name would not be cut off,
　not be annihilated, from before me.'

²⁰Go out from Babel,
　flee from the Kasdites!
Tell it with resounding voice,
　make it heard.
Send it out to the end of the earth,
　say, 'Yahweh is restoring his servant Yisra'el.'
²¹They were not thirsty
　as he made them go through wastes.
He made water flow from the crag for them,
　he split the crag and water gushed out.

²²There's no well-being
　(Yahweh has said) for faithless people.

## The servant's servant

# 49
Listen, foreign shores, to me;
　heed, peoples far away.
Yahweh called me from the womb,
　from my mother's insides he made mention of
　　my name.
²He made my mouth like a sharp sword,
　in the shadow of his hand he hid me.
He made me into a burnished arrow,
　in his quiver he concealed me.
³He said to me, 'You're my servant, Yisra'el;
　in you I will show my majesty.'

⁴But I myself said, 'It was to empty results that I
        toiled,
    for futility and hollowness that I used up my
        energy.'
Yet a ruling for me is with Yahweh,
    my earnings are with my God.
⁵Now Yahweh has said –
    the one who formed me from the womb as a
        servant for him,
By bringing Ya'aqob back to him,
    so that Yisra'el might not withdraw;
And I have found honour in Yahweh's eyes,
    and my God has become my vigour –
⁶He has said, 'It's slight, your being a servant for
        me
    to raise Ya'aqob's clans and bring back Yisra'el's
        shoots.
I shall make you into a light of nations,
    to be my deliverance to the end of the earth.'

⁷Yahweh has said this –
    Yisra'el's restorer, its Sacred One –
To one despised in spirit, offensive to nations,
    to a servant of rulers:

Kings will see and rise,
    leaders, and they will fall low,
For the sake of Yahweh, who is trustworthy,
    Yisra'el's Sacred One – he chose you.

⁸Yahweh has said this:

In a time of acceptance I'm answering you,
    on a day of deliverance I'm helping you.
I'll guard you and make you
    into a pact for people,
By raising up the country,
    by giving out the desolate domains,
⁹By saying to captives, 'Go out',
    to people in darkness, 'Appear.'
Along the roads they will pasture,
    on all the bare places will be their pasture.
¹⁰They will not hunger and not thirst;
    khamsin and sun won't strike them down.
Because the one who has compassion on them
        will lead them,
    and guide them by springs of water.
¹¹I'll make all my mountains into a road;
    my causeways will rise up.
¹²There – these will come from afar;
    there – these from the north and the west,
    and these from the country of Sinim.

## Can a mother forget?

¹³Resound, heavens, celebrate, earth,
    break into sound, mountains.
Because Yahweh is comforting his people;
    he will have compassion on his humble ones.

¹⁴But Tsiyyon says, 'Yahweh has abandoned me,
    the Lord has put me out of mind.'
¹⁵Can a woman put her baby out of mind,
    so as not to have compassion on the child of
        her womb?
Yes, these may put out of mind,
    but I – I cannot put you out of mind.
¹⁶There, on my palms I engraved you;
    your walls are in front of me continually.
¹⁷Your children are hurrying the people who tore
        you down,
    your devastators will go out from you.
¹⁸Lift your eyes round and look,
    they're all collecting, they're coming to you.
As I am alive (Yahweh's declaration),
    you will indeed put on all of them like
        jewellery,
    bind them on like a bride.
¹⁹Because your wastes, your devastations,
    your country that was torn down –
Because now you'll be too confined for your
        population,
    while the people who swallowed you up go
        away.
²⁰The children of your bereavement
    will yet say in your ears,
'The place is too narrow for me,
    move over for me so I can settle down.'
²¹You'll say to yourself,
    'Who fathered these for me,
When I was bereaved and barren,
    gone into exile and passing away?
These, who reared them,
    there, when I remained alone,
    these – where were they?'

## Can prey be taken from a strong man?

²²The Lord Yahweh said this:

Here, I shall raise my hand to the nations,
    to the peoples I will lift up my signal.
They will bring your sons in their embrace,
    carry your daughters on their shoulder.

23Kings will be your foster fathers,
   their queens your nursing mothers.
Face to the ground they'll bow low to you,
   they'll lick up the earth under your feet.
And you will acknowledge that I am Yahweh;
   those who hope in me will not be shamed.

24Can prey be taken from a strong man
   or the captives of a faithful one escape?

25Because Yahweh has said this:

Yes, the strong man's captives may be taken,
   the prey of the violent may escape.
I myself will argue with the one arguing with
   you,
   and your children I will deliver.
26I'll feed your oppressors with their own flesh;
   they'll be drunk on their own blood as on
      grape juice.
And all flesh will acknowledge
   that I am Yahweh your deliverer,
   Ya'aqob's strong one, your restorer.

# 50 Yahweh has said this:

Where now is the divorce document
   belonging to your mother whom I sent off?
Or who among my creditors was it
   to whom I sold you?
There – you were sold for your wayward acts,
   and for your rebellions your mother was sent
      off.
2Why did I come and there was no one there,
   did I call and there was no one answering?
Has my hand become far too short for
      redeeming,
   or is there no energy in me to rescue?
There, with my reprimand I can dry up the sea,
   I can make rivers into wilderness.
Their fish will smell because there's no water;
   they'll die of thirst.
3I can clothe the heavens in black,
   make sack their covering.

## Will you follow?

4The Lord Yahweh gave me a disciples' tongue,
   so as to know how to aid someone faint.
With a word he wakens, morning by morning,
   wakens my ear so as to hear like the disciples.

5The Lord Yahweh opened my ear,
   and I didn't rebel, I didn't turn away.
6I gave my back to people striking me,
   my cheeks to people pulling out my beard.
I didn't hide my face
   from deep disgrace and spit.
7The Lord Yahweh helps me;
   therefore I haven't been disgraced.
Therefore I set my face like flint,
   and I knew I wouldn't be shamed.
8The one who shows that I'm in the right is
      near;
   who will argue with me? – let us stand up
      together.
Who's the person with a case against me? –
   he should come forward to me.
9There, the Lord Yahweh will help me –
   who's the one who will show that I'm in the
      wrong?
There, all of them will wear out like clothing;
   moth will consume them.

10Who among you lives in awe of Yahweh,
   listens to his servant's voice?
One who has walked in darkness
   and has no illumination
Must rely on Yahweh's name
   and lean on his God.
11There, all of you who kindle fire,
   who belted on firebrands:
Walk into your fiery flame,
   into the firebrands you've lit.
This is coming about from my hand for you;
   you'll lie down in pain.

## Wake up, Yahweh

# 51 Listen to me, you who pursue
      faithfulness,
   who seek help from Yahweh.
Look to the crag from which you were hewn,
   to the cavity, the hole, from which you were
      dug.
2Look to Abraham your ancestor,
   and Sarah who was labouring with you.
Because he was one when I called him,
   so I might bless him and make him many.
3Because Yahweh is comforting Tsiyyon,
   he's comforting all its wastes.
He's making its wilderness like Eden,
   its steppe like Yahweh's garden.

Gladness and rejoicing will be found there,
    thanksgiving and the sound of music.
[4]Heed me, my people;
    give ear to me, my nation.
Because instruction goes out from me,
    my exercise of authority for the light of
      peoples.
In a flash [5]my faithfulness is near,
    my deliverance is going out,
    my arm will exercise authority for peoples.
Foreign shores will hope in me,
    they will wait for my arm.
[6]Lift up your eyes to the heavens,
    look to the earth below.
Because the heavens are shredding like smoke,
    the earth will wear out like clothing,
    its inhabitants will die in like manner.
But my deliverance will be permanent,
    my faithfulness will not shatter.

[7]Listen to me, you who acknowledge my
    faithfulness,
    a people with my instruction in its mind.
Don't be afraid of human reviling,
    don't shatter at their taunting.
[8]Because moth will consume them like clothing,
    grub will consume them like wool.
But my faithfulness will be permanent,
    my deliverance to all generations.

[9]Wake up, wake up, put on vigour,
    Yahweh's arm.
Wake up as in days of old,
    generations long ago.
You're the one who split Rahab,
    pierced the dragon, aren't you.
[10]You're the one who dried up the sea,
    the water of the great deep,
Who made the depths of the sea
    a way for the restored people to pass, aren't
      you.
[11]The people redeemed by Yahweh will go back,
    they will come to Tsiyyon with resounding.
With eternal rejoicing on their head,
    as joy and rejoicing overtake them,
    and sorrow and sighing flee.

*Wake up, Yerushalaim*

[12]I, I am the one who's comforting you –
    who are you to be afraid

Of a mortal who dies,
    of a human being who is treated like grass?
[13]You've put Yahweh your maker out of mind,
    the one who stretched out the heavens and
      founded the earth.
You're fearful constantly, all day,
    of the fury of the oppressor,
    as he is preparing to devastate.
But where is the fury of the oppressor? –
    [14]the one stooping is hastening to be released.
He won't die in the pit,
    he won't lack his bread.
[15]I am Yahweh your God,
    one who stills the sea when its waves roar –
    Yahweh of Armies is his name.
[16]I've put my words in your mouth,
    and covered you with the shade of my hand,
In planting the heavens and founding the earth,
    in saying to Tsiyyon 'You're my people.'

[17]Wake yourself up, wake yourself up,
    get up, Yerushalaim,
You who drank from Yahweh's hand
    his fury cup.
The chalice, the shaking cup,
    you drank, you drained.
[18]There was no one guiding her,
    of all the children to whom she gave birth.
There was no one taking her by the hand,
    of all the children she brought up.
[19]There were two things befalling you
    (who was to mourn for you?),
Destruction and breaking, famine and sword
    (who was I to comfort you?).
[20]Your children were overcome,
    they lay down at the entrance to all the streets
    like a snared oryx,
The people full of Yahweh's fury,
    of your God's reprimand.
[21]Therefore please listen to this, humble one,
    drunk but not with wine.
[22]Your Lord Yahweh has said this,
    your God who argues for his people:
'There, I'm taking from your hand
    the shaking cup,
My chalice, the fury cup,
    which you will never drink again.
[23]I'll put it into the hand of your tormentors,
    the people who said to your neck,
    "Bow down so we may pass over."
And you made your back like the earth,
    like the street for them to pass over.'

*Beautiful feet*

# 52
Wake up, wake up,
　put on your vigour, Tsiyyon!
Put on your majestic clothes,
　Yerushalaim, sacred town!
Because the foreskinned or taboo person
　will never again come into you.
²Shake yourself from the earth,
　get up, sit down, Yerushalaim!
They are loosening the bonds from on your neck,
　captive Miss Tsiyyon.

³Because Yahweh has said this:

For nothing you were sold,
　without silver you will be restored.

⁴Because the Lord Yahweh has said this:

My people went down to Misrayim at the
　　beginning
　to reside there.
But Ashshur oppressed them to no purpose,
　⁵so now what was there for me here (Yahweh's
　　declaration)?
Because my people was taken to no end,
　while its rulers boast (Yahweh's declaration).
And constantly, all day,
　my name stands reviled.
⁶Therefore my people will acknowledge my
　　name,
　therefore on that day [it will acknowledge]
　that I'm the one who speaks – here I am.

⁷How lovely on the mountains are the feet of one
　　who brings news,
　one who lets people hear 'All is well',
One who brings good news, lets people hear of
　　deliverance,
　who says to Tsiyyon, 'Your God has begun to
　　reign.'
⁸A voice! – lookouts are lifting voice,
　together they resound.
Because with both eyes
　they see Yahweh going back to Tsiyyon.
⁹Break out, resound together,
　wastes of Yerushalaim.
Because Yahweh is comforting his people;
　he's restoring Yerushalaim.
¹⁰Yahweh is baring his sacred arm
　before the nations' eyes.

All the ends of the earth
　will see our God's deliverance.

¹¹Depart, depart, get out from there,
　don't touch what is taboo.
Get out from within it, purify yourselves,
　you who carry Yahweh's things.
¹²Because you won't get out in haste,
　you won't go in flight.
Because Yahweh is going before you,
　and Yisra'el's God is bringing up your rear.

*Who could have believed it?*

¹³There, my servant will thrive,
　he'll rise and lift up and be very high.
¹⁴As many people were appalled at you,
　so his appearance is anointed beyond anyone,
　his look beyond that of human beings.
¹⁵So he'll spatter many nations;
　at him kings will shut their mouths.
Because what hadn't been told them they will
　　have seen,
　and what they hadn't heard they will have
　　understood.

# 53
Who believed what we heard,
　and upon whom did Yahweh's arm
　　appear?
²He grew before him like a sucker
　or a root out of dry ground.
He had no look and no majesty so we should look
　　at him,
　no appearance so we should want him.
³He was despised and the most frail of human
　　beings,
　a man of great suffering and acquainted with
　　weakness.
As when people hide their face from someone,
　he was despised and we didn't count him.
⁴Yet it was our weaknesses that he carried,
　our great suffering that he bore.
But we ourselves had counted him touched,
　struck down, by God, and afflicted.
⁵But he was the one who was wounded through
　　our rebellions,
　crushed through our wayward acts.
Chastisement to bring us well-being was on him,
　and by means of his being hurt there was
　　healing for us.
⁶All of us like sheep had wandered,
　each had turned his face to his own way.

Yahweh – he let fall on him
    the waywardness of all of us.

### The man who kept his mouth shut

⁷He was put down, but he was one who let himself
    be afflicted,
    and he wouldn't open his mouth.
Like a sheep that's led to slaughter
    or like a ewe that's silent before its shearers,
    he wouldn't open his mouth.
⁸By the restraint of authority he was taken;
    who would complain at his generation?
Because he was cut off from the land of the living;
    because of my people's rebellion the touch
      came to him.
⁹He was given his tomb with the faithless,
    his burial mound with the rich person,
Because he'd done no violence,
    and no deceit with his mouth.
¹⁰While Yahweh desired the crushing of the one
    he weakened,
    if with his whole person he lays down a
      reparation offering,
He'll see offspring, he'll prolong his life,
    and Yahweh's desire will succeed in his hand.
¹¹Out of his personal trouble, when he sees he will
    be sated;
    by his acknowledgement my servant will show
      many that he is indeed in the right,
    when he bears their wayward acts.

¹²Therefore I'll give him a share with the many;
    he'll share out the numerous as spoil,
In return for the fact that he exposed his person
    to death,
    when he let himself be numbered with the rebels,
When he was the one who carried the
      wrongdoing of many people,
    and was appealing for the rebels.

### A time to cry and a time to whoop

**54** Resound, infertile one, you who haven't
    given birth;
    break out into sound and bellow, you who
      haven't laboured.
Because the children of the desolate are many,
    more than the married woman's children
      (Yahweh has said).

²Enlarge your tent space;
    people must stretch your dwelling curtains,
      don't hold back.
Lengthen your ropes, strengthen your pegs,
    ³because you'll spread out right and left.
Your offspring will dispossess the nations,
    they'll inhabit the desolate towns.
⁴Don't be afraid, because you will not be shamed;
    don't be disgraced, because you will not be
      confounded.
Because you will put out of mind the shame of
      your youth,
    you will no more be mindful of the reviling of
      your widowhood.
⁵Because your maker will be the one who marries
    you;
    Yahweh of Armies is his name.
Yisra'el's Sacred One is your restorer;
    he calls himself 'God of all the earth'.
⁶Because it's as a wife abandoned
    and distressed in spirit that Yahweh is calling
      you,
The wife of his youth when she's been spurned,
    your God has said.
⁷For a short moment I abandoned you,
    but with great compassion I'll gather you.
⁸In a burst of anger
    I hid my face from you for a moment,
But with permanent commitment I'm having
      compassion for you
    (your restorer, Yahweh, has said),
    ⁹because this is Noah's water to me.
In that I swore that Noah's water
    would not pass over the earth again,
So I'm swearing
    not to be angry with you or to reprimand you.
¹⁰Because mountains may move away, hills slip,
    but my commitment will not move away from
      you.
My pact of well-being will not slip,
    the one who has compassion for you, Yahweh,
      has said.

### David's covenant will become yours

¹¹Humble, tossing, not comforted –
    here I am, resting your stones in antimony.
I'll found you with sapphires,
    ¹²make chalcedony your pinnacles,
Your gateways into sparkling stones,
    your entire border into delightful stones.

¹³All your children will be Yahweh's disciples;
　　great will be your children's well-being.
¹⁴In faithfulness you'll establish yourself;
　　you can be far from oppression,
Because you will not be afraid,
　　and from shattering, because it will not come
　　　near you.
¹⁵There, someone need be in dread
　　of nothing from me.
Who quarrels with you? –
　　he'll fall to you.
¹⁶There, I'm the one who created the smith
　　who blows into the fire of coals,
And who brings out a tool for his work,
　　and I'm the one who created the destroyer to
　　　ravage.
¹⁷Any tool formed against you will not succeed;
　　you will show to be in the wrong every tongue
　　that arises with you for a judgement.

This is the domain of Yahweh's servants,
　　their faithfulness from me (Yahweh's declaration).

**55** Hey, anyone who's thirsty,
　　come for water.
Whoever has no silver, come,
　　buy and eat.
Come, buy without silver,
　　wine and milk without cost.
²Why weigh out silver for what isn't bread,
　　and your labour for what isn't filling?
Listen hard to me and eat what's good;
　　you can delight your appetite with rich food.
³Bend your ear, come to me;
　　listen, so you may come to life.
I will solemnize for you a permanent pact,
　　the trustworthy commitments to David.
⁴Here, I made him a witness for peoples,
　　a leader and commander for peoples.
⁵Here, you'll call a nation that you don't
　　acknowledge,
　　and a nation that doesn't acknowledge you will
　　　run to you,
For the sake of Yahweh your God,
　　and for Yisra'el's Sacred One, because he's
　　glorifying you.

## Our ideas and plans, and God's

⁶Enquire of Yahweh while he is letting himself be
　　found,
　　call him while he's near.

⁷The faithless person must abandon his way,
　　the person who brings trouble [must abandon]
　　his intentions.
He must turn back to Yahweh so he may have
　　compassion on him,
　　to our God because he does much pardoning.
⁸Because my intentions are not your intentions,
　　your ways are not my ways (Yahweh's
　　declaration).
⁹Because the heavens are higher than the earth;
　　so are my ways higher than your ways,
　　my intentions than your intentions.

¹⁰Because as the rain or snow
　　falls from the heavens,
And doesn't go back there
　　but rather soaks the earth,
And makes it bear and produce,
　　and give seed to the sower and bread to the
　　　eater,
¹¹So will my word be
　　that goes out from my mouth.
It will not come back to me empty,
　　but rather do that which I wanted,
　　achieve that for which I sent it.

¹²Because you'll go out with joy,
　　and be brought in with well-being.
The mountains and the hills
　　will break out before you in resounding.
All the trees in the open country
　　will clap the palms of their hands.
¹³Instead of the thorn a juniper will come up,
　　instead of the briar a myrtle will come up.
It will be a memorial for Yahweh,
　　a permanent sign that will not be cut down.

## An ambiguous 'Because'

**56** Yahweh has said this:

Keep the exercise of authority,
　　act in faithfulness,
Because my deliverance is near to coming,
　　my faithfulness to appearing.
²The blessings of the person who does this,
　　the individual who holds on to it,
Keeping the sabbath rather than treating it as
　　ordinary,
　　and keeping his hand from doing anything
　　bad.

³So the foreigner who attaches himself to Yahweh
  is not to say,
'Yahweh will quite separate me
  from among his people.'
The eunuch is not to say,
  'Here am I, a dry tree.'

⁴Because Yahweh has said this:

'To the eunuchs who keep my sabbaths,
  and choose what I want, and hold on to my
    pact –
⁵I will give to them,
  within my house and within my walls,
A memorial and name
  better than sons and daughters.
I will give him a permanent name,
  one that will not be cut off.
⁶And the foreign people
  who attach themselves to Yahweh, to minister
    to him
And to give themselves to Yahweh's name,
  to be servants to him,
Anyone who keeps the sabbath rather than
    treating it as ordinary,
  and holds strongly to my pact,
⁷I will bring them to my sacred mountain,
  and let them rejoice in my prayer house.
Their burnt offerings and their sacrifices
  will be for acceptance on my altar.
Because my house will be called
  a prayer house for all the peoples.'
⁸A declaration of the Lord Yahweh,
  the one gathering the scattered people of Yisraël:
  'I will gather yet more towards it, to its gathered
    ones.'

*Slaughter in the wadis*

⁹All you animals of the wild, come and eat –
  all you animals in the forest.
¹⁰Its lookouts are blind,
  all of them; they don't know.
All of them are dumb dogs, they can't bark;
  they're lying snoozing, loving to doze.
¹¹But the dogs are vigorous of appetite;
  they don't know about being full.
And these people – they are shepherds
  that don't know how to discern.
All of them have turned their face to their own way,
  each to his loot, every last bit of it.

¹²'Come on, I'll get wine,
  we'll swill liquor.
Tomorrow will be like this,
  exceedingly, very great!'

**57** The faithful person has perished,
  and there was no one taking it into their
    mind.
Committed people are gathered up
  without anyone discerning
That it is from before a bad situation
  that the faithful person has been gathered up.
²He goes while things are well (while they rest on
    their beds),
  the one who walks straight.

³But you people, draw near here,
  children of a diviner.
Offspring of an adulterer and a woman who acts
    the whore,
⁴in whom do you revel?
At whom do you open your mouth wide,
  put out your tongue?
Are you not rebellious children,
  the offspring of falsehood,
⁵You who inflame yourselves among the oaks,
  under any verdant tree,
Who slaughter children in the wadis,
  under the clefts in the cliffs?
⁶Among the deceptions in the wadi is your share;
  they are your allocation.
Yes, to them you've poured a libation,
  you've lifted up an offering:
  in view of these things, should I relent?
⁷On a high and lofty mountain
  you've put your bed.
Yes, you've gone up there
  to offer a sacrifice.
⁸Behind the door and the doorpost
  you've set your memorial.
Because from me you've gone away, you've gone
    up,
  you've opened wide your bed.
You've solemnized things for yourself from them,
  you've been loyal to their bed, you've beheld
    their love.

*High and holy, but present with
the crushed*

⁹You've appeared to the King in your oils,
  you've multiplied your perfumes.

You've sent off your envoys afar,
  you've got them to go down to She'ol.
¹⁰When you grew weary with the length of your
    way,
  you didn't say, 'It's futile.'
You found life for your capacity;
  therefore you haven't weakened.
¹¹For whom have you felt reverence and awe,
  that you lie?
You haven't been mindful of me;
  you haven't received me into your mind.
I've been still, yes from of old, haven't I,
  but you're not in awe of me.
¹²I myself will tell of your 'faithfulness',
  and your acts – they won't avail you.
¹³When you cry out, your abominable gatherings
    can rescue you;
  but a wind will carry them all off, a breath will
    take them.
But the person who takes shelter with me will
    receive the country as his domain,
  will possess my sacred mountain.

¹⁴Someone has said, 'Build up, build up, clear a
    way,
  lift high the obstacles from my people's way.'
¹⁵Because the one who is high and lofty
    has said this,
The one who dwells permanently,
  whose name is 'Sacred One':
'I dwell on high and sacred,
  but with the crushed and low in spirit,
Bringing life to the spirit of people who are low,
  bringing life to the heart of the crushed.
¹⁶Because I will not argue permanently,
  I will not be perpetually irate.
Because before me the spirit would faint,
  the breathing beings I made.
¹⁷At the waywardness of its looting I was irate;
  I hit it, hiding – I was irate.
It lived turning back to the way of its own mind;
  ¹⁸I've seen its ways, but I will heal it.
I'll lead it and make good all comfort to it;
  for its mourners ¹⁹creating as the fruit of lips
    well-being,
Well-being for one far away and one near
  (Yahweh has said), and I'll heal it.
²⁰But the faithless – they are like the sea tossing,
  because it cannot be calm.
Its waters toss muck and mud;
  ²¹there's no well-being (my God has said) for
    faithless people.'

## (Un)spiritual practices

**58** Call with full throat, don't hold back,
    lift your voice like the horn.
Tell my people about their rebellion,
  Ya'aqob's household about their wrongdoings.
²They enquire of me day by day
  and want to acknowledge my ways,
Like a nation that has acted in faithfulness,
  and not abandoned its God's ruling.
They ask me for faithful rulings,
  they want to draw near to God.
³'Why have we fasted and you haven't seen,
  we've humbled ourselves and you haven't
    acknowledged?'
There – on your fast day you find what you want,
  but you oppress the people who toil for you.
⁴There – you fast for argument and strife,
  and for hitting with faithless fist.
You don't fast this very day
  in such a way as to make your voice heard on
    high.
⁵Will the fast that I choose be of this very kind,
  a day for a person to humble himself?
Will it be for bowing one's head like a bulrush,
  and spreading sack and ash?
Is it this that you call a fast,
  a day accepted by Yahweh?
⁶This will be the fast I choose, won't it:
  loosing faithless chains,
Untying the cords of the yoke,
  letting the oppressed go free,
  and tearing apart every yoke.
⁷It will be dividing your food with the hungry
    person, won't it,
  and bringing home the humble, downtrodden.
When you see the naked, you'll cover him,
  and not hide from your fellow flesh and
    blood.
⁸Then your light will break out like dawn,
  and your restoration will flourish speedily.
Your faithfulness will go before you;
  Yahweh's splendour will gather you.
⁹Then you'll call and Yahweh will answer;
  you'll cry for help and he'll say, 'I'm here.'
If you do away with the yoke from within you,
  the pointing of the finger and the troublesome
    word,
¹⁰And offer yourself to the hungry person,
  and fill the need of the humble person,
Your light will shine in the darkness,
  your gloom will be like midday.

¹¹Yahweh will guide you continually,
  and fill your appetite in scorched places.
He'll renew your frame
  and you will be like a watered garden,
Like a spring of water
  whose water does not deceive.
¹²People of yours will build up the ruins of old;
  you'll raise the foundations from past
    generations.
You'll be called 'Repairer of a Breach,
  Restorer of Paths for Living On'.

## Honouring the sabbath

¹³If you take back your foot from the sabbath,
  doing the things you want on my sacred day,
Call the sabbath 'Revelling',
  and Yahweh's sacred thing 'Honourable',
And honour it rather than acting in your ways,
  or finding what you want, and speaking your
    word,
¹⁴Then you'll revel in Yahweh
  and I'll let you ride over the heights of the
    earth.
I'll let you eat the domain of Ya'aqob your father;
  because Yahweh's mouth has spoken.

**59** Here – Yahweh's hand hasn't become too
    short to deliver,
  his ear hasn't become too heavy to listen.
²Rather, your wayward acts have become
    separators
  between you and your God.
Your wrongdoings have hidden his face
  so as not to listen to you.
³Because your fists – they've become polluted
    with blood,
  your fingers – with waywardness.
Your lips – they've spoken falsehood,
  your tongue – it talks of evil.
⁴There's no one calling in faithfulness,
  there's no one entering into judgement with
    trustworthiness.
Relying on nothingness and speaking emptiness,
  conceiving trouble and giving birth to
    wickedness.
⁵They've broken open a serpent's eggs,
  they spin a spider's webs.
Someone who eats of their eggs – he will die,
  and one that is smashed – an adder breaks
    out.

⁶Their webs won't become a garment,
  they won't cover themselves in the things they
    make.
The things they make are things that bring trouble;
  the doing of violence is in their fists.
⁷Their feet run to what is bad,
  they hurry to shed the blood of one free of guilt.
Their intentions are troublesome intentions,
  destruction and breaking is on their causeways.
⁸The way of well-being they haven't
    acknowledged,
  and there's no exercise of authority on their
    tracks.
They've made their paths crooked for themselves;
  no one who walks on it acknowledges well-
    being.

## That's why there's no restoration

⁹That's why the exercise of authority is far from us,
  faithfulness doesn't reach us.
We look for light but there, darkness;
  for brightness, whereas we walk in gloom.
¹⁰We grope like blind people along a wall;
  like people without eyes we grope.
We've fallen over at midday as if it was dusk,
  among sturdy people as if we were dead.
¹¹We rumble like bears, all of us,
  and murmur on like doves.
We look for the exercise of authority but there is
    none,
  for deliverance that's far from us.

¹²Because our rebellions are many in your sight,
  and our wrongdoings have testified against us.
Because our rebellions are with us,
  and our wayward acts – we acknowledge them.
¹³Rebelling, breaking faith with Yahweh,
  and turning back from following our God,
Speaking of fraud, conceiving defiance,
  and talking words of falsehood inside us.
¹⁴So the exercise of authority has turned away,
  faithfulness stands far off.
Because truthfulness has fallen over in the square,
  and straightness can't come in.
¹⁵Truthfulness has gone missing;
  the one who turns from dealing badly is
    despoiled.

Yahweh saw and it was bad in his eyes
  that there was no exercise of authority.

<sup>16</sup>He saw that there was no one,
he was devastated that there was no one
intervening.
But his arm brought deliverance for him;
his faithfulness – it sustained him.
<sup>17</sup>He put on faithfulness like a coat of mail,
and a deliverance helmet on his head.
He put on redress clothes as clothing,
he wrapped on passion as a coat.
<sup>18</sup>In accordance with their dealings,
as the One on High he will make good with
fury to his adversaries,
With dealings to his enemies,
dealings to foreign shores, he will make good.
<sup>19</sup>They will be in awe of Yahweh's name from the
west,
and of his splendour from the sunrise.
When an adversary comes like the river,
Yahweh's wind raises a banner against him.
<sup>20</sup>He will come to Tsiyyon as restorer,
to the people who turn from rebellion in Ya'aqob
(Yahweh's declaration).

<sup>21</sup>'And me – this is my pact with them
(Yahweh has said). My breath that is on you,
and my words that I've put in your mouth, will
not move away from your mouth, from the
mouth of your offspring and from the mouth
of your offspring's offspring (Yahweh has said)
from now and permanently.'

## An invitation to imagination

# 60
Get up, be alight, because your light is
coming,
Yahweh's splendour has shone on you.
<sup>2</sup>Because there – darkness covers the earth,
gloom the peoples.
But on you Yahweh will shine;
his splendour will appear over you.
<sup>3</sup>Nations will come to your light,
kings to your shining brightness.
<sup>4</sup>Lift your eyes round and look,
all of them are collecting, they're coming to you.
Your sons will come from afar,
your daughters will support themselves on the
hip.
<sup>5</sup>Then you'll see and glow,
your mind will be in awe and will swell.
Because the sea's horde will turn to you,
the resources of nations will come to you.

<sup>6</sup>A mass of camels will cover you,
dromedaries from Midyan and Ephah;
all of them will come from Sheba.
They will carry gold and frankincense,
and bring news of Yahweh's great praise.
<sup>7</sup>All the sheep of Qedar will collect to you,
rams of Nebayot will minister to you.
They will go up with acceptance on my altar,
and I will add majesty to my majestic house.
<sup>8</sup>Who are these that fly like a cloud,
and like doves to their hatches?
<sup>9</sup>Because foreign shores will look for me,
Tarshish ships at the first,
To bring your sons from afar,
their silver and their gold with them,
For the name of Yahweh your God, for Yisra'el's
Sacred One,
because he has made you majestic.
<sup>10</sup>Foreigners will build your walls,
kings will minister to you.
Because in wrath I struck you,
but with acceptance I'm having compassion
on you.
<sup>11</sup>Your gateways will open continuously,
day and night they will not shut,
To bring you the nations' resources,
with their kings being led along.
<sup>12</sup>Because the nation or kingdom that doesn't
serve you –
they will perish, and the nations will become a
total waste.

## An invitation to hope

<sup>13</sup>The Lebanon's splendour will come to you,
juniper, fir and cypress together,
To add majesty to my sacred place,
so I may honour the place for my feet.
<sup>14</sup>They'll walk to you bending down,
the children of the people who humbled you.
They'll bow low at the soles of your feet,
all the people who despised you.
They'll call you 'Yahweh's Town,
the Tsiyyon of Yisra'el's Sacred One'.
<sup>15</sup>Instead of being abandoned,
treated hostilely with no one passing
through,
I'll make you an object of permanent pride,
a joy generation after generation.
<sup>16</sup>You'll suck the nations' milk,
suck the kings' breast.

And you will acknowledge that I am Yahweh;
    Ya'aqob's champion is your deliverer and your
      restorer.
<sup>17</sup>Instead of copper I'll bring gold,
    instead of iron I'll bring silver,
Instead of wood, copper;
    instead of stone, iron.
I'll make well-being your oversight,
    faithfulness your bosses.
<sup>18</sup>Violence will not make itself heard any more in
      your country,
    destruction and breaking in your borders.
You will call deliverance your walls,
    praise your gateways.
<sup>19</sup>The sun will no longer be light for you by day,
    and as brightness the moon will not be light
      for you.
Because Yahweh will be light for you
    permanently;
    your God will be your majesty.
<sup>20</sup>Your sun will not set any more,
    your moon will not withdraw.
Because Yahweh will be light for you
    permanently;
    your mourning days will be complete.
<sup>21</sup>Your people, all of them, will be faithful ones,
    who will possess the country permanently.
They will be the shoot that I plant,
    the work of my hands, to demonstrate majesty.
<sup>22</sup>The smallest will become a clan,
    the least a numerous nation.
I am Yahweh;
    I will speed it in its time.

## Blown over and anointed

**61** The Lord Yahweh's breath is on me,
    because Yahweh has anointed me.
He's sent me to bring news to the humble,
    to bind up the people broken in mind,
To call for release for captives,
    the opening of eyes for prisoners,
<sup>2</sup>To call for a year of Yahweh's acceptance,
    our God's day of redress,
To comfort all the mourners,
    <sup>3</sup>to provide for the people who mourn
      Tsiyyon –
To give them majesty instead of ash,
    festive oil instead of mourning,
A praise garment
    instead of a flickering spirit.

They'll be called faithful oaks,
    Yahweh's planting, to demonstrate majesty.
<sup>4</sup>People will build up permanent ruins,
    raise up the ancestors' desolations.
They'll renew ruined towns,
    desolations from generation after generation.
<sup>5</sup>Strangers will stand and pasture your sheep,
    foreigners will be your farmworkers and
      vinedressers.
<sup>6</sup>You yourselves will be called 'Yahweh's priests',
    you'll be termed 'our God's ministers'.
You'll eat the nations' resources
    and thrive on their splendour.
<sup>7</sup>Instead of your shame, double;
    [instead of] disgrace, people will resound at the
      share you have.

Therefore in their country they'll possess double;
    permanent joy will be theirs.
<sup>8</sup>Because I am Yahweh, one loyal to exercising
      authority,
    hostile to robbery in evil.
I'll give them their earnings in truthfulness;
    a permanent pact I'll solemnize for them.
<sup>9</sup>Their offspring will gain acknowledgement with
      the nations,
    their descendants among the peoples.
All who see them will recognize them,
    that they are offspring Yahweh has blessed.

## People who won't let Yahweh rest

<sup>10</sup>I shall be ardently glad in Yahweh,
    my entire being will joy in my God.
Because he's clothing me in deliverance clothes,
    wrapping me in a faithfulness coat,
Like a groom who behaves priestly in majesty,
    or like a bride who adorns herself in her things.
<sup>11</sup>Because as the earth brings out its growth
    and as a garden makes its seed grow,
So the Lord Yahweh will make faithfulness and
    praise grow
    before all the nations.

**62** For the sake of Tsiyyon I will not be
    silent,
    for Yerushalaim's sake I will not be calm,
Until its faithfulness goes out like brightness,
    its deliverance like a torch that blazes.
<sup>2</sup>The nations will see your faithfulness,
    all the kings your splendour.

You'll be called by a new name,
 which Yahweh's mouth will determine.
³You'll be a majestic crown in Yahweh's hand,
 a royal diadem in your God's palm.
⁴You'll no longer be termed 'Abandoned',
 your country will no longer be termed
   'Desolate'.
Rather, you'll be called 'My Delight Is in Her',
 and your country 'Married'.
Because Yahweh delights in you,
 and your country will be married.
⁵Because a young man marries a girl;
 your sons will marry you.
With a groom's gladness over a bride,
 your God will be glad over you.

⁶Upon your walls, Yerushalaim,
 I'm appointing guards.
All day and all night
 they will never be silent.
You who remind Yahweh,
 there's no stopping for you.
⁷Don't give him stopping, until he establishes,
 until he makes Yerushalaim an object of praise
   in the earth.

*I had to do it myself*

⁸Yahweh has sworn by his right hand,
 by his vigorous arm:

If I give your grain again
 as food for your enemies,
If foreigners drink your new wine,
 for which you've laboured . . .
⁹Because the people who harvest it will eat it,
 and praise Yahweh.
The people who collect it will drink it
 in my sacred courtyards.

¹⁰Pass through, pass through the gateways,
 clear the people's way!
Build up, build up the causeway,
 clear it of stones!
Raise a banner over the peoples –
 ¹¹there, Yahweh has let it be heard to the end of
   the earth.
Say to Miss Tsiyyon,
 'There, your deliverance is coming.
There, his reward is with him,
 his earnings before him.'

¹²People will call them
 'The Sacred People, Ones Restored by Yahweh'.
You'll be called
 'Sought Out, a Town Not Abandoned'.

**63** Who's this coming from Edom,
 marked in clothes from Botsrah,
This person majestic in attire,
 stooping in his mighty energy?
'I'm the one speaking in faithfulness,
 mighty to deliver.'
²Why is your attire red,
 your clothes like someone treading in a wine
   trough?
³'I trod a press alone;
 from the peoples there was no one with me.
I tread them in my anger,
 trample them in my fury.
Their spray spatters on my clothes;
 I've stained all my attire.
⁴Because a day of redress has been in my mind,
 my year of restoration has arrived.
⁵But I look, and there's no helper;
 I stare, and there's no support.
So my arm has effected deliverance for me;
 my fury – it's supported me.
⁶I trample peoples in my anger,
 make them drunk in my fury,
 bring down their eminence to the earth.'

*On hurting God's sacred spirit*

⁷I shall recount Yahweh's acts of commitment,
 Yahweh's praises,
In accordance with all that Yahweh dealt to us,
 the great goodness to Yisra'el's household,
That which he dealt to them in accordance with
   his compassion
 and the greatness of his acts of commitment.
⁸He said, 'Yes, they're my people,
 children who won't be false.'
He became their deliverer;
⁹in all their trouble it became troublesome to him.
His personal envoy –
 he delivered them, in his love and pity.
He was the one who restored them, lifted them up,
 carried them all the days of old.
¹⁰But they – they rebelled
 and hurt his sacred spirit.
So he turned into their enemy;
 he himself battled against them.

11But he was mindful of the days of long ago,
    of Mosheh [Moses], of his people.

Where is the one who brought them up from the
    sea,
    the shepherds of his flock?
Where is the one who put within it
    his sacred spirit,
12The one who made his majestic arm go
    at Mosheh's right hand,
Dividing the water in front of them
    to make himself a name permanently,
13Enabling them to go through the depths like a
    horse in the wilderness,
    so they wouldn't collapse,
14Like a beast in the valley that goes down,
    so that Yahweh's spirit would enable them to
    settle down?
In that way you drove your people,
    to make a majestic name for yourself.

15Look out from the heavens,
    see from your sacred and majestic height!
Where are your passion and your acts of strength,
    the roar from inside you and your compassion?
In relation to me they have withheld themselves,
    16when you are our Father.
When Abraham wouldn't acknowledge us,
    Yisra'el wouldn't recognize us,
You Yahweh are our Father;
    'Our Restorer from Forever' is your name.
17Why do you let us wander from your ways,
    Yahweh,
    let our mind be tough so as not to be in awe of
    you?
Turn for the sake of your servants,
    the clans that are your domain.
18As something small they dispossessed your
    sacred people;
    our adversaries trampled your sanctuary.
19Permanently we have become people over
    whom you haven't ruled,
    who haven't been called by your name.

## But you're our Father

**64** Oh that you'd torn apart the heavens
        and gone down,
    that mountains had quaked before you,
2Like fire lighting brushwood,
    so that the fire boils water,

To cause your name to be acknowledged by your
    adversaries,
    so that the nations might tremble before you.
3When you did wonders that we didn't hope for,
    you went down and mountains quaked before
    you.
4Never had people heard or given ear,
    eye had not seen,
A God apart from you,
    who acts for one who waits for him.
5You met with the one who was joyful and doing
    what was faithful,
    the people who were mindful of you in your
    ways.
There, you yourself got furious,
    and of old we did wrong in relation to them,
    but we were delivered.
6We became like something taboo, all of us,
    and all our faithful deeds like menstrual
    clothing.
We withered like leaves, all of us,
    and our wayward acts carry us off like the wind.
7There's no one calling on your name,
    stirring himself to take hold of you.
Because you've hidden your face from us,
    and made us fade away at the hand of our
    wayward acts.

8But now, Yahweh, you're our Father;
    we're the clay, you're our potter –
    the work of your hand, all of us.
9Don't be so very furious, Yahweh,
    don't be mindful of waywardness.
There, please do look at your people, all of us:
    10your sacred towns became a wilderness,
Tsiyyon became a wilderness,
    Yerushalaim a devastation.
11Our sacred and majestic house,
    where our ancestors praised you,
Became something consumed by fire,
    and all that we valued became a ruin.
12At these things do you restrain yourself, Yahweh,
    do you remain still and let us be humbled so
    much?

## Straight-talking meets straight-talking

**65** I could be enquired of people who didn't
        ask,
    I could be found by people who didn't seek help
    from me.

I said, 'I'm here, I'm here',
  to a nation that wasn't calling on my name.
²I spread my hands all day
  to a defiant people,
Who walk in a way that is not good,
  following their own intentions.
³The people are ones who provoke me,
  to my face, continually,
Sacrificing in the gardens,
  burning incense on the bricks,
⁴Ones who sit in tombs,
  who spend the night in secret places,
Who eat swine's flesh,
  with a broth of desecrating things in their
    bowls,
⁵Who say, 'Keep to yourself, don't come near me,
  because I'm too sacred for you.'
These people are smoke in my nostrils,
  a fire burning all day.
⁶There, it's written before me,
  I will not be still, rather I am making good,
I'll make good into their lap ⁷your waywardness
  and your ancestors' waywardness together
  (Yahweh has said).
The people who burned incense on the mountains,
  who reviled me on the hills:
I'm counting out their earnings
  first of all into their lap.

  ⁸Yahweh has said this:

As the new wine can be found in the cluster,
  and someone will say 'Don't destroy it,
  because there's a blessing in it',
So I will act for my servants' sake,
  so as not to destroy everything.
⁹I shall bring out offspring from Ya'aqob,
  and from Yehudah one who's going to possess
    my mountains.
My chosen ones will possess it,
  my servants will dwell there.
¹⁰The Sharon will become an abode for sheep,
  Disaster Vale a resting-place for cattle,
  for my people who've enquired of me.
¹¹But you who abandon Yahweh,
  who put out of mind my sacred mountain,
Who set a table for Luck,
  who fill a mixing chalice for Destiny:
¹²I shall destine you to the sword,
  all of you will bend down for slaughter.
Because I called but you didn't answer,
  I spoke but you didn't listen.

You did what was bad in my eyes,
  and what I didn't want, you chose.

## The renewed Yerushalaim

  ¹³Therefore the Lord Yahweh has said this:

There, my servants will eat,
  but you'll be hungry.
There, my servants will drink,
  but you'll be thirsty.
There, my servants will rejoice,
  but you'll be shamed.
¹⁴There, my servants will resound
  from happiness of heart,
But you'll cry out from pain of heart,
  from brokenness of spirit you'll howl.
¹⁵You'll leave your name
  as an oath for my chosen ones,
'So may the Lord Yahweh kill you',
  but for his servants he will call out another
    name,
¹⁶So that the person who prays for blessing in the
    country
  will pray for blessing by the God who says
    'Amen'.
Because the earlier pressures will have been put
    out of mind,
  and because they'll have been hidden from my
    eyes.

¹⁷Because here I am, creating
  new heavens and a new earth.
The earlier ones won't be recollected;
  they won't come into mind.
¹⁸Rather, be glad and celebrate permanently
  what I am creating.
Because here I am, creating Yerushalaim as reason
    for celebration
  and its people as reason for gladness.
¹⁹I will celebrate Yerushalaim
  and be glad in my people.
There will not make itself heard in it any more
  the sound of weeping or the sound of a cry.
²⁰There will no longer be from there any more
  a baby of [few] days
  or an old person who doesn't fulfil his days.
Because the youth will die as a person of a
    hundred years,
  and the wrongdoer will be slighted as a person
    of a hundred years.

21They'll build houses and dwell [in them],
    they'll plant vineyards and eat their fruit.
22They won't build and another dwell;
    they won't plant and another eat.
The days of my people will be like a tree's days;
    my chosen ones will use up the work of their
       hands.
23They won't toil with empty result;
    they won't give birth with fearful outcome.
Because they'll be offspring blessed by Yahweh,
    they and their descendants with them.
24Before they call, I myself will answer;
    while they're still speaking, I myself will
      listen.
25The wolf and the lamb will pasture together,
    the cougar, like cattle, will eat straw,
    but the snake – earth will be its food.
People won't deal badly, they won't devastate,
    in all my sacred mountain (Yahweh has said).

## Trembling at Yahweh's word

**66** Yahweh has said this:

The heavens are my throne,
    the earth is my footstool.
Wherever would be the house that you would
      build for me,
    wherever would be the place that would be for
      me to settle down?
2All these things my hand made (Yahweh's
      declaration),
    and to this person I look:
To the humble, to the broken in spirit,
    one who trembles at my word.

3One who slaughters an ox is one who strikes a
      person down;
    one who sacrifices a lamb is one who strangles
      a dog.
One who lifts up an offering – it's pig's blood;
    one who makes a memorial of incense – he
      worships a bane.
They for their part have chosen their ways,
    their soul delights in their abominations.
4I for my part will choose caprices for them,
    and bring upon them what they dread.
Because I called and there was no one answering,
    I spoke and they didn't listen.
They did what was bad in my eyes,
    and what I didn't delight in, they chose.

5Listen to Yahweh's word,
    you who tremble at his word.
'Your brothers have said, people who are hostile
      to you,
    who exclude you for the sake of my name,
"May Yahweh be severe, so that we may see your
      celebration" –
    they will be shamed.'
6The sound of a din from the town,
    a sound from the palace,
The sound of Yahweh
    making good with his dealings to his
      enemies.

7Before she labours she's given birth,
    before pain comes to her she delivers a boy.
8Who has heard something like this,
    who has seen things like these?
Can a country be brought through labour in one
      day,
    or a nation be born in one moment?
Because Tsiyyon is labouring
    and also giving birth to her children.
9'Will I myself make a breach
    and not bring to birth? (Yahweh says).
Or will I myself bring to birth
    and close [the womb]? (your God says).'

10Rejoice with Yerushalaim,
    be glad in her, all you who love her.
Be glad with her in joy,
    all you who mourned over her,
11In order that you may nurse and be full
    from her comforting breast,
In order that you may drink deeply and delight
      yourself
    from her splendid bosom.

## Choose your ending

12Because Yahweh has said this:

Here I am, stretching out to her
    well-being like a river,
Like a flooding wadi
    the splendour of the nations,
So you may drink of it as you're carried on her
      side
    and dandled on her knees.
13Like someone whom his mother comforts,
    so I myself will comfort you.

You'll be comforted in Yerushalaim,
¹⁴you'll see, and your heart will be glad,
    and your limbs will flourish like grass.

Yahweh's hand will cause itself to be
        acknowledged among his servants,
    and he will condemn his enemies.
¹⁵Because there – Yahweh will come in fire,
    his chariots like a whirlwind,
To give back his anger in wrath,
    his reprimand in fiery flame.
¹⁶Because Yahweh is going to enter into
        judgement with fire,
    with his sword, among all flesh;
    the people run through by Yahweh will be many.
¹⁷'The people who make themselves sacred and
        purify themselves for the gardens,
    following after one in the middle,
People who eat the flesh of pig, reptile and mouse
    will come to an end together (Yahweh's
        declaration).'

¹⁸But as for me, on the basis of their deeds
and their intentions, the gathering of all
the nations and tongues is coming. They'll
come and see my splendour. ¹⁹I shall set a
sign among them and send off from them
survivors to the nations – Tarshish, Pul and
Lud, the people who draw the bow, Tubal,
Yavan [Greece], the distant shores, which
haven't heard report of me and haven't seen
my splendour. They will tell of my splendour
among the nations.

²⁰They will bring all your kin-group
members from all the nations as an offering
to Yahweh, by means of horses, chariotry,
coaches, mules and dromedaries, to my sacred
mountain, Yerushalaim (Yahweh has said),
as the Yisra'elites bring the offering in a pure
vessel to Yahweh's house. ²¹Also from them I
will take people as priests and Levites (Yahweh
has said).

²²Because as the new heavens and the new
earth that I'm going to make are going to stand
before me (Yahweh's declaration), so will your
offspring and your name stand. ²³New moon
by new moon, sabbath by sabbath, all flesh will
come to bow low before me (Yahweh has said).
²⁴But they will go out and look at the corpses
of the people who rebel against me. Because
their worm will not die and their fire will not
go out. They will be a horror to all flesh.

# JEREMIAH

Jeremiah [Yirmeyahu] lived a century later than Isaiah. He was summoned to be a prophet in 626 BC and he continued prophesying until after the fall of Jerusalem to the Babylonians forty years later. He thus lived through tumultuous years and changing fortunes in Judah. His summons came as King Josiah was involved in a reformation of religious life in Judah and a cleaning up of forms of worship that accepted other Middle Eastern peoples' practices (including sacrificing children) instead of Israel's own. After Josiah's death the nation reverted to those habits, which led to Yahweh's abandoning Jerusalem to the Babylonians. Jeremiah speaks positively of Josiah but spent most of his life confronting kings and people about their faithlessness to Yahweh and to one another.

That confrontation involves him in issuing repeated warnings that this continuing faithlessness will issue in disaster, which makes him a deeply unpopular figure, especially with Judah's leadership. From their perspective he is simply a troublemaker. Slightly illogically, they do not become more tolerant of Jeremiah as a result of the fact that Yahweh keeps not fulfilling his threats. One might have inferred that Jeremiah looked like a prophet who could safely be ignored. Instead they persecute him, imprison him and threaten to kill him. Naturally this has an effect on Jeremiah himself, who doesn't appreciate the fact that he has to keep issuing warnings that don't come true. He expresses his resentment frankly to Yahweh. His book includes many stories about him, presumably written by people such as Baruk who do support him. More surprisingly, his book also incorporates a number of the prayers he prayed, which have a place there not because of an assumption that his readers will be interested in the nature of his relationship with God but because (like the stories) they give readers another angle on his persecution. It is an expression of the attitude the community takes to the God whom he serves.

The book of Jeremiah is not clearly organized like Isaiah and Ezekiel, but we can say that the first half is dominated by his prophecies and by those prayers, while the second half is dominated by stories about him and then by prophecies about other nations.

Some stand-out chapters in his book are:

1. his account of his summons to be a prophet (Jer. 1), which later inspired the prophet who speaks in Isaiah 49 and still later inspired Paul (Gal. 1.15) in their accounts of their summons;
2. his grief over Judah's failure of memory (Jer. 2);
3. his reminder about the fate of Shiloh (Jer. 7);
4. his ridicule of the making of images (Jer. 10);
5. his accepting a command not to marry (Jer. 16);
6. his emphasis on the way God can have a change of mind over his threats and over his promises in the light of the response they receive (Jer. 18);
7. his wrestling with the question of how to tell a false prophet from a true one (Jer. 23);
8. his declaration that the Babylonian king is Yahweh's servant (Jer. 25);
9. his declaration that the exile will last seventy years – both a warning and a promise (also Jer. 25);
10. his confrontation with the prophet Hananiah (Jer. 28);
11. his exhortation to people already exiled in 597 to settle down and not think they are coming back soon (Jer. 29);
12. his promise that after the exile God will make a new covenant with Judah (Jer. 31);
13. his willingness to invest in land at an inauspicious moment (Jer. 32);
14. the account of how he puts his prophecies into writing and enlarges the collection when the king burns his scroll (Jer. 36);
15. the account of his continuing struggle with people resisting Yahweh's expectations after the fall of Jerusalem and their forcing him to flee with them to Egypt (Jer. 39—44);
16. the closing narrative that shows how he was proved right after all (Jer. 52).

*Yahweh's summons*

**1** The words of Yirmeyahu ben Hilqiyyahu, one of the priests of Anatot in the Binyamin [Benjamin] region, ²to whom Yahweh's word came in the days of Yoshiyyahu [Josiah] ben Amon king of Yehudah in the thirteenth year of his reign, ³and came in the days of Yehoyaqim ben Yoshiyyahu king of Yehudah, until the end of the eleventh year of Tsidqiyyahu [Zedekiah] ben Yoshiyyahu king of Yehudah, until Yerushalaim's exile in the fifth month.

⁴Yahweh's word came to me:

⁵Before I formed you in the womb I
      acknowledged you,
   before you went out from the womb I made
      you sacred.
   I made you a prophet concerning the
      nations.

⁶I said:

Oh, Lord Yahweh –
   here, I don't know how to speak,
   because I'm a boy.

⁷But Yahweh said to me:

Don't say, 'I'm a boy,'
   because you're to go out to anyone to whom I
      send you,
   and speak anything that I order you.
⁸Don't be afraid of their faces,
   because I'll be with you to rescue you (Yahweh's
      declaration).

⁹Yahweh put out his hand and touched my mouth, and Yahweh said to me:

Here, I'm putting my words into your mouth:
   ¹⁰see, I'm appointing you this day
   over the nations, over the kingdoms,
To uproot and to pull down, to obliterate and to
      tear down,
   to build and to plant.

¹¹Yahweh's word came to me:

What are you looking at, Yirmeyahu?

I said:

I'm looking at the branch of a watcher tree.

¹²Yahweh said to me:

You've done good in looking,
   because I'm watching, over my word, to put it
      into effect.

*The iron pillar*

¹³Yahweh's word came to me a second time:

What are you looking at?

I said:

I'm looking at a boiling pot,
   with its face facing from the north.

¹⁴Yahweh said to me:

From the north bad things will open out
   on all the inhabitants of the country.
¹⁵Because here am I calling
   all the kin-groups of the northern kingdoms
      (Yahweh's declaration).
They'll come and put each one his throne
   at the opening of Yerushalaim's gateways,
Against all its walls round,
   and against all Yehudah's towns.
¹⁶I shall speak my rulings to them,
   for all their bad dealing, in that they've
      abandoned me.
They've burned incense to other gods,
   bowed low to things their hands made.
¹⁷You, you're to put your belt round your hips,
   and get up and speak to them
   anything that I myself order you.
Don't shatter before them,
   in case I shatter you before them.
¹⁸I – here I am, making you
   into a fortified town today,
Into an iron pillar
   and copper walls against the entire country,
For Yehudah's kings and its officers,
   for its priests and the people of the country.
¹⁹They'll battle against you but they won't prevail
      over you,
   because I'm with you (Yahweh's declaration) to
      rescue you.

## Digging cisterns that leak

**2** Yahweh's word came to me: ²Go, call out
in Yerushalaim's ears,
Yahweh has said this:

I have kept in mind for you the commitment of
your youth,
your loyalty as a bride,
Your following me through the wilderness,
through a country not sown.
³Yisra'el was sacred to Yahweh,
the first fruits of his yield.
All the people who ate of it would incur liability;
bad fortune would come upon them (Yahweh's
declaration).

⁴Listen to Yahweh's word, Ya'aqob's [Jacob's]
household,
all the kin-groups of Yisra'el's household.

⁵Yahweh has said this:

What did your ancestors find that was evil in me,
that they went far away from me,
Followed something hollow and became hollow,
⁶and didn't say 'Where is Yahweh,
The one who got us up from the country of
Misrayim [Egypt]
and enabled us to go through the wilderness,
Through a country of steppe and pit,
through a country of drought and deep
darkness,
Through a country through which no one
passed
and where no human being lived?'
⁷I enabled you to come into a country of
farmland,
to eat its fruit and its good things.
But you came and defiled my country;
you made my domain something offensive.
⁸The priests didn't say 'Where is Yahweh?',
the people controlling the instruction didn't
acknowledge me.
The shepherds rebelled against me,
the prophets prophesied by the Master,
and followed beings that couldn't prevail in
anything.

⁹Therefore I'll argue with you more (Yahweh's
declaration)
and I'll argue with your grandchildren.

¹⁰Because cross over to the shores of Kittim
[Cyprus] and see,
send off to Qedar and consider well,
see if something like this has happened.
¹¹Has a nation changed its gods,
when those are not gods?
But my people have changed my splendour
for what doesn't prevail in anything.
¹²Be devastated at this, heavens,
shudder, be utterly desolate (Yahweh's
declaration).
¹³Because my people have done two bad things:
they've abandoned me, the fountain of living
water,
To dig themselves cisterns, breakable cisterns,
that don't prevail over water.

## 'I haven't become defiled'

¹⁴Was Yisra'el a servant, or someone born in a
household –
why has he become plunder?
¹⁵Lions roar over him,
they've given their voice.
They've made his country a devastation;
his towns are burned, without inhabitant.
¹⁶The people of Memphis and Tahpanhes
will also break your skull [Yerushalaim].
¹⁷It's this that does it to you, isn't it –
your abandoning of Yahweh your God
at the time when he was enabling you to go on
your journey?
¹⁸So now what is there for you in a journey to
Misrayim
to drink the Ye'or's [the Nile's] water?
What is there for you in a journey to Ashshur
to drink the River's water?
¹⁹Your bad dealing should discipline you,
your turning back should reprove you.
Acknowledge and see how bad and bitter it is,
your abandoning Yahweh your God,
And you have no dread towards me
(a declaration of the Lord Yahweh of Armies).

²⁰Because of old you broke your yoke,
you tore off your straps, and said, 'I won't serve.'
Because on every high hill and under every
verdant tree
you're lying down as a whore.
²¹I – I planted you as a top-class vine,
all of it trustworthy seed.

So how have you changed for me
  into the turnings of a foreign vine?
²²Because if you wash with soap
  and use much detergent for yourself,
Your waywardness is inscribed before me
  (a declaration of the Lord Yahweh).

²³How can you say, 'I haven't become defiled,
  I haven't followed the Masters'?
Look at your journey into the Ravine,
  acknowledge what you've done,
A swift camel twisting her journeys,
  ²⁴a wild donkey taught about the wilderness,
Sniffing the wind in the desire of her appetite –
  who can turn back her craving?
None who seek her get tired;
  in her season they find her.

## Why do you gad about?

²⁵Hold your foot back from being shoeless
  and your throat from being dry.
But you say, 'It's desperate,
  because I'm loyal to strangers, I shall follow
    them.'
²⁶Like a thief's shame when he's found out,
  so Yisra'el's household was shamed.
They, their kings, their officials,
  their priests, their prophets,
²⁷Were saying to a piece of wood, 'You're our
    father',
  to some stone, 'You gave me birth.'
Because they turned their back to me,
  not their face.
At the time when something bad happened to
    them
  they'd say, 'Arise, deliver us.'
²⁸But where are your gods
  that you made for yourself?
They should arise if they can deliver you,
  at the time when something bad happens to you.
Because your gods have become
  more than the number of your towns, Yehudah.
²⁹Why do you argue with me
  when all of you have rebelled against me?
    (Yahweh's declaration).

³⁰With empty results I struck down your children;
  they didn't accept discipline.
Your sword consumed your prophets
  like a destroying lion.

³¹This generation,
  look at Yahweh's word.
Did I become a wilderness to Yisra'el,
  or a country of deep darkness?
Why did my people say, 'We've wandered off,
  we won't come to you any more'?
³²Can a girl put her jewellery out of mind,
  a bride her adornments?
But my people have put me out of mind,
  days without number.

³³How good you've made your journey in seeking
    love [Yerushalaim];
  therefore you've even taught bad women your
    journeys.
³⁴Further, on your garments is found
  the blood of the lives of needy people who are
    free of guilt
  (you didn't find them breaking in).
Because despite all these things,
  ³⁵you've said, 'I'm free of guilt,
  his anger has surely turned back from me.'
Here I am, entering into judgement with you,
  because of your saying 'I haven't done wrong.'

³⁶Why do you go about so much,
  changing your journey?
Through Misrayim you'll be shamed again,
  as you were shamed through Ashshur.
³⁷Through this you'll again come out
  with your hands on your head.
Because Yahweh has rejected the ones you rely
    on,
  and you won't succeed through them.

## Is it possible to come back?

**3** Saying: 'If someone sends off his wife, she
goes from him, and she comes to belong
to another man, can he come back to her
again?' That country will be totally profaned,
won't it. And you [Yerushalaim] have been
whoring with many lovers. Would you come
back to me? (Yahweh's declaration).

²Raise your eyes to the bare places and look –
  where have you not been laid?
By the roads you sat for them,
  like a Bedouin in the wilderness.
You profaned the country
  with your whoring and your bad dealing.

³Showers held back,
  there was no rain,
But you had the brazenness of a whore;
  you refused to be shamed.
⁴Now you've called to me, haven't you,
  'Father, you're the partner of my youth.'
⁵'Does he hold on to things permanently
  or keep watch for all time?'
There – you've spoken;
  you've done what was bad, and prevailed.

⁶Yahweh said to me in the days of King Yoshiyyahu, 'Have you seen what Yisraʾel did, she who turned back? She was going on to every high mountain and under every verdant tree and whoring there. ⁷I said, "After she's done all these things, she'll come back to me." But she didn't come back. And her faith-breaking sister Yehudah saw. ⁸I saw that because of the acts of adultery that Yisraʾel committed, she who turned back, I sent her off and gave her divorce document to her. But her sister Yehudah, she who broke faith, wasn't afraid. She went and acted as a whore, too. ⁹It came about that because of the frivolity of her whoring she profaned the country; she committed adultery with stone and wood. ¹⁰But even in all this, her sister, faith-breaking Yehudah, didn't come back to me with her whole mind but rather with falsehood (Yahweh's declaration).'

## Breaking faith

¹¹Yahweh said to me, 'Yisraʾel who turned back has shown herself more faithful than Yehudah who broke faith. ¹²Go and call out these words to the north. Say, "Come back, Yisraʾel who turned back (Yahweh's declaration); I shall not make my face fall against you, because I am committed (Yahweh's declaration), I don't hold on to things permanently. ¹³Only acknowledge your waywardness, that you've rebelled against Yahweh your God and scattered your journeys to strangers under every verdant tree, and not listened to my voice (Yahweh's declaration).

¹⁴Come back, children who are turning back (Yahweh's declaration), because I'm your master. I'll take you, one from a town, two from a kin-group, and bring you to Tsiyyon

[Zion]. ¹⁵I'll give you shepherds in accordance with my will and they'll shepherd you with knowledge and insight.

¹⁶When you increase and are fruitful in the country in those days (Yahweh's declaration), people will no longer say 'Yahweh's pact chest'. It won't come to mind, they won't be mindful of it or give attention; it won't be made again. ¹⁷At that time they'll call Yerushalaim 'Yahweh's Throne', and all the nations will gather to it, to Yahweh's name, to Yerushalaim. People will no more follow the bad determination of their mind.

¹⁸In those days Yehudah's household will go to Yisraʾel's household, and they'll come together from the northern country to the country that I gave your ancestors as a domain.

¹⁹I myself had said, 'How gladly I'll put you among my children and give you a desirable country, the most splendid domain of the nations.' I said you'd call me 'Father', and not turn back from following me. ²⁰Actually, as a woman breaks faith with her lover, so you broke faith with me, Yisraʾel's household (Yahweh's declaration).'"

## I'll heal their turnings

²¹A sound makes itself heard on the bare places,
  the Yisraʾelites' crying that pleads for grace.
Because they've misdirected their way,
  they've put Yahweh their God out of mind.
²²Come back, children who are turning back;
  I'll heal your turnings.
'Here we are, we're coming to you,
  because you are Yahweh our God.
²³Yes, what comes from the hills belongs to
    falsehood,
  the uproar from the mountains.
Yes, in Yahweh our God
  is the deliverance of Yisraʾel.
²⁴But the Shame has consumed
  our ancestors' labour from our youth,
Their flock and their cattle,
  their sons and their daughters.
²⁵We must lie down in our shame,
  our disgrace should cover us.
Because we've done wrong to Yahweh our God,
  we and our ancestors from our youth until this
    day.

We haven't listened
    to the voice of Yahweh our God.'

**4** 'If you come back, Yisra'el (Yahweh's
      declaration),
    come back to me.
If you remove your abominations from before me
    and don't flit,
²But swear "As Yahweh lives",
    in truth and in the faithful exercise of authority,
Nations will pray to be blessed by him,
    and will exult in him.'

³Because Yahweh has said this to Yehudah's
people and to Yerushalaim:

Till the tillable land for yourselves,
    and don't sow among thorns.
⁴Circumcise yourselves for Yahweh,
    remove the foreskin from your mind,
People of Yehudah and inhabitants of Yerushalaim,
    so that my wrath doesn't come out like fire,
And burn up with no one putting it out,
    because of the bad nature of your practices.

⁵Tell out in Yehudah,
    make it heard in Yerushalaim,
Say, 'Sound the horn in the country',
    call out, fulfil it, say:
'Gather together, let's go into the fortified towns,
    ⁶raise a banner towards Tsiyyon, take refuge,
    don't stand still.'
Because I'm going to bring something bad from
    the north,
    a great breaking.

## The searing wind

⁷A lion has gone up from its thicket,
    a destroyer of nations has moved on.
He's gone out from his place
    to make your country a devastation.
Your towns will be wasted,
    without inhabitant.
⁸On account of this, wrap on sack,
    lament and howl:
'Yahweh's angry blazing
    isn't turning back from us.'
⁹On that day (Yahweh's declaration)
    the king's mind and the officials' mind will
    expire.

The priests will be devastated,
    the prophets will be dumbfounded.

¹⁰I said, 'Oh, Lord Yahweh,
    really you've totally deceived this people and
    Yerushalaim,
In saying "Things will be well for you",
    whereas the sword has reached as far as their
    throat.'

¹¹At that time it will be said
    concerning this people and concerning
    Yerushalaim:
On the way to the daughter of my people
    a searing wind comes,
From the bare places in the wilderness,
    not to winnow, not to fan.
¹²A wind too full for these things comes on my
    behalf;
    now I myself announce rulings against them.
¹³There, one will go up like clouds,
    his chariots like a whirlwind.
His horses are swifter than eagles –
    oh, alas for us, because we are destroyed.

¹⁴Wash your mind of what is bad, Yerushalaim,
    in order that you may find deliverance.
How long will you let your intentions to bring
    trouble
    lodge within you?
¹⁵Because a voice tells it from Dan,
    it lets trouble be heard from Mount Ephrayim.
¹⁶Make mention to the nations;
    there – make it heard against Yerushalaim.
Watchers are coming from a far-off country,
    they'll give voice against Yehudah's towns.
¹⁷Like people keeping watch on the fields
    they've come against it all round,
    because it has rebelled against me (Yahweh's
    declaration).

¹⁸Your way and your practices
    have done these things to you.
This is the bad fortune that's come to you, because
    it's bitter,
    because it's reached your heart.

## The empty void

¹⁹My pain, my pain, I writhe, the walls of my heart,
    my heart howls within me, I can't be still.

Because you've heard, my soul,
    the sound of the horn, the battle shout.
<sup>20</sup>Breaking meets with breaking,
    because the entire country is destroyed.
Suddenly my tents have been destroyed,
    in an instant my tent cloths.
<sup>21</sup>How long shall I see a banner,
    listen to the sound of the horn?

<sup>22</sup>Because my people are dense,
    they haven't acknowledged me.
They're idiotic children,
    they're not people who understand.
They're smart at doing what's bad,
    but they don't know how to do good.

<sup>23</sup>I looked at the earth and there – it was empty,
    void;
    and at the heavens – there was no light in them.
<sup>24</sup>I looked at the mountains and there – they were
    quaking,
    and all the hills were moving to and fro.
<sup>25</sup>I looked and there – no human being,
    and every bird in the heavens had fled.
<sup>26</sup>I looked and there – the farmland was
    wilderness,
    and all its towns were burned,
In the face of Yahweh,
    in the face of his angry blazing.

<sup>27</sup>Because Yahweh has said this:

'The entire country will become desolation
    (but I won't make an end).
<sup>28</sup>On account of this the earth mourns,
    the heavens are dark above.
Since I have spoken, I have made a scheme;
    I haven't relented, I won't turn back from it.'

<sup>29</sup>At the sound of cavalry and bowman
    the entire town is fleeing.
They've gone into the woods,
    climbed on to the rocks.
The entire town is abandoned,
    there's no inhabitant in it, not one.
<sup>30</sup>So you who are going to be destroyed,
    what do you do when you dress in scarlet,
When you adorn yourself in gold adornment,
    when you broaden your eyes with mascara?
It's with empty results that you look beautiful;
    your lovers have rejected you, they seek your life.
<sup>31</sup>Because I've heard a voice like someone in pain,
    distress like someone having her first baby,

The voice of Miss Tsiyyon –
    as she gasps, she stretches out the palms of her
      hands:
'Oh, me, please,
    because my life faints before my killers.'

## Can you find anyone?

**5** Explore Yerushalaim's streets, please look,
    and get to know,
    seek in its squares, if you can find anyone,
If there's someone exercising authority
    seeking truthfulness, and I'll pardon it.
<sup>2</sup>But even when they say, 'As Yahweh lives' –
    therefore they swear in falsehood.

<sup>3</sup>Yahweh, your eyes look for truthfulness, don't they;
    you struck them down but they didn't feel sick.
When you finished them off,
    they refused to accept discipline.
They made their faces stronger than a cliff;
    they refused to turn back.
<sup>4</sup>I myself said,
    'They're only the poor who act foolishly,
Because they don't acknowledge the way of
    Yahweh,
    the authority of their God.
<sup>5</sup>I'll go to the big people
    and speak with them,
Because those people acknowledge the way of
    Yahweh,
    the authority of their God.'
Yet those people had altogether broken the yoke,
    torn off the straps.
<sup>6</sup>That's why the lion from the forest has struck
    them down,
    the wolf from the steppes destroys them.
The leopard is lying by their townships;
    anyone who goes out from them will be torn
      to pieces.
Because their rebellions are many,
    their turnings away are numerous.

<sup>7</sup>For what reason should I pardon you? –
    your children have abandoned me and sworn
      by no-gods.
I filled them and they committed adultery;
    they troop off to the whorehouse.
<sup>8</sup>They were horses in heat, lusty;
    they were bellowing, each for his neighbour's
      wife.

⁹Shall I not attend to these things (Yahweh's
    declaration),
    or myself not take redress
    against a nation that's like this one?

¹⁰Go up among its vine-rows and destroy them,
    but don't make an end.
Remove its branches,
    because those people don't belong to Yahweh.
¹¹Because Yisra'el's household and Yehudah's
    household
    have totally broken faith with me (Yahweh's
    declaration).
¹²They've acted deceptively towards Yahweh,
    and said 'He isn't the one.
Bad fortune won't come upon us,
    we won't see sword or famine.
¹³The prophets – they'll be but wind,
    the word isn't in them; so it will be done to
    them.'

## Senseless people

¹⁴Therefore Yahweh, God of Armies, has said this,
    since you people have spoken this thing:

Here I am, putting my words in your mouth as
    fire:
    this people is the wood, and it will consume
    them.
¹⁵Here I am, bringing a nation from afar against
    you,
    Yisra'el's household (Yahweh's declaration).
It's an enduring nation,
    it's an age-old nation,
A nation whose tongue you don't know;
    you can't listen to what it speaks.
¹⁶Its quiver is like an open grave;
    all of them are strong men.
¹⁷It will consume your harvest and your bread;
    it will consume your sons and your daughters.
It will consume your flock and your cattle;
    it will consume your vine and your fig.
It will destroy your fortified towns,
    on which you rely, with the sword.

¹⁸But even in those days (Yahweh's
declaration) I won't make an end of you. ¹⁹And
when they say, 'On what account did Yahweh
our God do all these things to us?', you're to
say to them, 'As you abandoned me and served

alien gods in your country, so you'll serve
foreigners in a country that isn't yours.'

²⁰Tell of this in Ya'aqob's household,
    make it heard in Yehudah:
²¹Listen to this, please, idiotic people,
    without sense,
Who have eyes but don't look,
    have ears but don't listen.
²²It's me that you should be in awe of, isn't it
        (Yahweh's declaration),
    and before me that you should tremble,
The one who set the sand as a boundary for the
    sea,
    a permanent limit that it shouldn't pass over.
Its waves toss but don't overcome,
    they roar but don't pass over.
²³But this people has a defiant and rebellious mind;
    they've defied and gone.
²⁴They haven't said to themselves,
    'We must be in awe of Yahweh our God,
Who gives the rain, the early and later rain at its
    time,
    who keeps watch for us the weeks set for
    harvest.'
²⁵It's your wayward acts that have turned these
        things aside,
    your wrongdoings that have withheld good
        things from you.

## How to become sleek

²⁶Because faithless people were found among my
        people,
    like someone who watches in a bird-catchers'
    hide.
They've set up a means of destruction so they may
        capture people,
²⁷like a basket full of birds.
So their houses are full of deceit;
    that's how they've got big and rich.
²⁸They've become fat, become sleek;
    further, they've passed over words about bad
        dealing in giving judgement.
They haven't given judgement for the orphan, so
        that they might be successful;
    they haven't exercised authority for the needy.
²⁹Shall I not attend to these things (Yahweh's
        declaration),
    or myself not take redress against a nation that's
    like this one?

³⁰A devastating thing, a horrifying thing
    has happened in the country.
³¹The prophets prophesy falsely,
    the priests rule on the basis of their own
        capacity,
And my people like it so –
    but what will you do at the end of it?

**6** Take refuge, Binyaminites,
    from inside Yerushalaim!
Sound the horn in Teqoa,
    raise the signal at Bet Hakkerem!
Because something bad is looking out from the
       north,
    a big breaking.
²I'm terminating Miss Tsiyyon, lovely and refined:
    ³shepherds and their flocks will come to it.
They pitch their tents against it all round,
    they pasture each one his own responsibility.
⁴'Make battle sacred against it,
    set to, we'll go up at noon!'
'Oh, alas for us, because the day is declining,
    because the evening shadows get long.
⁵Set to, we'll go up at night
    and devastate its citadels.'

    ⁶Because Yahweh of Armies has said this:

Cut down the trees,
    heap up a ramp against Yerushalaim.
The town is appointed;
    within it, all of it is fraud.
⁷Like a well flowing with its water,
    so it flows with its bad dealing.
In it violence and destruction makes itself heard,
    sickness and wound are before me continually.
⁸Accept discipline, Yerushalaim,
    so that I myself don't withdraw from you,
So that I don't make you a devastation,
    a country not inhabited.

## Weary of holding in Yahweh's wrath

    ⁹Yahweh of Armies has said this:

Like a vine they are to glean and glean
    the remainder of Yisra'el.
'Put your hand again
    like a grape-picker over the branches.'
¹⁰To whom shall I speak,
    and testify so they listen?

There, their ear is foreskinned,
    they can't heed.
There, Yahweh's word has become for them
    a reviling; they don't delight in it.
¹¹So Yahweh's wrath – I'm full of it,
    I'm weary of holding it in.
'Pour it on the child in the street
    and on the group of young men, together.
Because both man and woman will be captured,
    the elder with the one full of years.
¹²Their houses will pass to other people,
    fields and wives together.
Because I shall stretch out my hand
    against the inhabitants of the country (Yahweh's
       declaration).
¹³Because from their smallest to their biggest,
    every one of them is greedy for loot.
Prophet and priest alike,
    every one of them is acting falsely.
¹⁴They've healed my people's break too lightly,
    saying, "Things are well, they're well",
    when they're not well.
¹⁵They've been shameful, because they've done
       something offensive;
    they neither manifest any shame
    nor do they know how to be disgraced.
Therefore they will fall among the people who
       fall;
    at the time when I attend to them, they will
       collapse
    (Yahweh has said).'

## The analyst

    ¹⁶Yahweh has said this:

Stand by the roads, and look,
    ask about the old paths.
Which is the road to good things? –
    walk on it, and find peacefulness for yourselves.
But they said, 'We won't walk',
    ¹⁷so I raised up lookouts for you.
'Heed the sound of the horn',
    but they said, 'We won't heed.'
¹⁸Therefore listen, you nations,
    and acknowledge, you assembly, what will be
       against them.
¹⁹Listen, earth:
    here am I.
I'm going to bring something bad on this people,
    the fruit of their intentions.

Because they haven't heeded my words,
  and my instruction – they've rejected it.
20What use to me is incense that comes from Sheba,
  or fine cane from a far-off country?
Your burnt offerings don't find acceptance,
  your sacrifices aren't pleasing to me.

21Therefore Yahweh has said this:

Here am I; I'm going to set for this people
  things to make them collapse, and they'll
    collapse because of them.
Parents and children together,
  neighbour and friend – they'll perish.

22Yahweh has said this:

There, a people is going to come from a northern
    country,
  a big nation will arise from earth's remotest
    parts.
23They take strong hold of bow and javelin;
  it's violent – they don't have compassion.
Their sound is like the sea that roars,
  they ride on horses.
It's lined up like a man for battle,
  against you, Miss Tsiyyon.
24'We've heard report of them, our hands go slack,
  pressure has taken strong hold of us, anguish
    like a woman giving birth.
25Don't go out into the fields, don't walk by the
    road,
  because the enemy has a sword, terror is all
    round.
26My dear people, wrap on sack, roll in the dust,
  make for yourself the mourning for an only
    child,
Bitter lament,
  because suddenly the destroyer will come upon
    us.'

27I made you an analyst among my people,
  a refiner, so you might know and analyse their
    way.
28All of them are the most defiant people,
  people who live by slander,
Copper and iron,
  all of them are people who devastate.
29The bellows are scorched by fire,
  the lead has come to an end.
With empty results the smelter smelted,
  and bad people were not separated out.

30Reject silver, people have called them,
  because Yahweh has rejected them.

## Remember Shiloh

**7** The word that came to Yirmeyahu from
Yahweh: 2'Stand at the gateway of Yahweh's
house and call out this word there. You're to
say, "Listen to Yahweh's word, all of Yehudah
who are coming through these gateways to bow
low to Yahweh. 3Yahweh of Armies, Yisra'el's
God, has said this: 'Make your ways and your
practices good, and I'll let you dwell in this
place. 4Don't rely for yourselves on words
of falsehood: "These buildings are Yahweh's
palace, Yahweh's palace, Yahweh's palace."
5Rather, make your ways and your practices
truly good. If you really exercise authority
between an individual and his neighbour,
6don't exploit alien, orphan and widow, don't
shed the blood of someone who is free of guilt
in this place, and don't follow other gods with
bad results for yourselves, 7I'll let you dwell in
this place, in the country that I gave to your
ancestors from of old, permanently.

8There, you're relying for yourselves on
words of falsehood that won't prevail. 9Is there
stealing, murder, adultery, swearing falsely and
burning sacrifices to the Master, and following
other gods that you didn't acknowledge, 10and
you come and stand before me in this house
over which my name has been called out and
say "We are rescued" – in order to do all these
offensive things? 11Has it become a cave for
thugs in your eyes, this house over which my
name has been called out? Yes, I myself, I've
been looking (Yahweh's declaration).

12Because you can go to my site that was
at Shiloh where I let my name dwell before,
and look at what I did to it in the face of my
people Yisra'el's bad dealing. 13So now because
of your doing all these things (Yahweh's
declaration), and I've spoken to you, starting
early, but you haven't listened, and I've called
you but you haven't answered, 14I shall do to
the house over which my name has been called
out, on which you're relying, the site that I
gave to you and your ancestors, as I did to
Shiloh. 15I'll throw you out from my presence
as I threw your brothers out, Ephrayim's entire
offspring."'

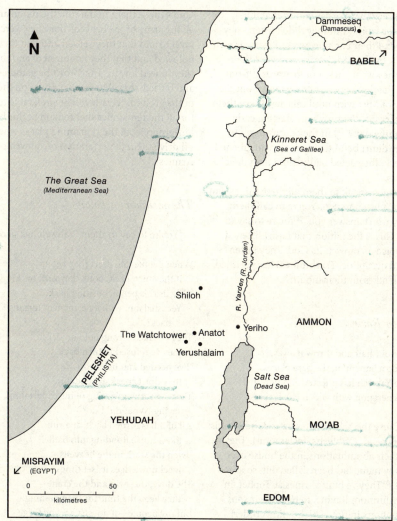

*Jeremiah 7: Yehudah (Judah) at the time of Yirmeyahu (Jeremiah)*

## The prophet forbidden to pray

[16]'You, don't plead for this people, don't lift up a cry or plea for them, don't intercede with me, because I'm not listening to you. [17]You see what they're doing in Yehudah's towns and in Yerushalaim's streets, don't you. [18]The sons are collecting wood, the fathers are lighting the fire and the women are kneading the dough, to make loaves for the Queen of Heaven and to pour libations to other gods, to provoke me. [19]Is it me they're provoking (Yahweh's declaration)? Is it not themselves, in order to bring shame on their faces?'

[20]Therefore the Lord Yahweh has said this: 'Here, my anger, my fury, is going to pour out on this place, on human beings, on animals, on the trees in the open country and on the fruit of the earth. It will burn up and not go out.'

[21]Yahweh of Armies, Yisra'el's God, has said this: 'Add your burnt offerings to your sacrifices, eat meat. [22]Because I didn't speak with your ancestors or order them on the day I got them out of the country of Misrayim regarding matters concerning burnt offering and sacrifice. [23]Rather I ordered them this thing: "Listen to my voice, and I'll be God for you and you'll be a people for me; walk

in every way that I order you so that it may
go well for you." ²⁴But they didn't listen, they
didn't bend their ear, they walked by their own
counsels, by the bad determination of their
mind. They went back, not forwards, ²⁵from
the day that I got your ancestors out from the
country of Misrayim until this day. I sent them
all my servants the prophets, starting early
and sending daily, ²⁶but they didn't listen to
me, they didn't bend their ear, they toughened
their neck; they acted badly more than their
ancestors.

²⁷You're to speak to them all these things, but
they won't listen to you. You're to call them
but they won't answer you. ²⁸You're to say to
them: "This is the nation that hasn't listened
to the voice of Yahweh its God. They haven't
accepted discipline. Truthfulness has perished,
cut itself off from their mouth.'"

## Slaughter Ravine

²⁹Shave your hair and throw it away,
    take up a lament on the bare places.
Because Yahweh has rejected and deserted
    the generation with which he's furious.

³⁰Because the Yehudahites have done what is
bad in my eyes (Yahweh's declaration). They've
set up their abominations in the house over
which my name has been called out, so as to
defile it. ³¹They've built shrines at Tophet, in
the Ben-hinnom Ravine, to burn their sons
and daughters in fire, which I didn't order;
it didn't come into my mind. ³²Therefore,
now, days are coming (Yahweh's declaration)
when it will no longer be said 'Tophet and
the Ben-hinnom Ravine' but rather 'Slaughter
Ravine'. They'll bury in Tophet because there's
no other place. ³³This people's carcases will
be food for the birds of the heavens and the
animals of the land, with no one making them
tremble. ³⁴I shall silence from Yehudah's towns
and from Yerushalaim's streets the joyful
voice, the rejoicing voice, the voice of groom
and the voice of bride. Because the country will
become a waste.

**8** At that time (Yahweh's declaration) people
    will take out the bones of Yehudah's
kings, its officials, the priests, the prophets and
Yerushalaim's inhabitants from their graves,

²and expose them to the sun, the moon and
all the army of the heavens that they were
loyal to and that they served and that they
followed and that they enquired of and that
they bowed low to. They won't be gathered up
and buried; they'll become manure on the face
of the ground. ³Death will be preferable to life
for all the remainder that remain of this bad
kin-group in all the remaining places where
I'll drive them (a declaration of Yahweh of
Armies).

## The misleading scholars

⁴You're to say to them, Yahweh has said this:

When people fall, don't they get up –
    if they turn back, don't they turn back?
⁵Why is this people turning back,
    Yerushalaim, with a permanent turning
        back?
They've taken strong hold on deceit,
    they've refused to turn back.
⁶I've heeded and listened;
    they don't speak dependably.
There's no one relenting of his bad dealing,
    saying 'What did I do?'
All of it has turned back, at a run,
    like a horse flooding into battle.
⁷Even the stork in the heavens –
    it acknowledges its set times.
The dove, the swift and the crane –
    they keep the time for their coming.
But my people – it doesn't acknowledge
    Yahweh's ruling.

⁸How can you say, 'We are smart,
    Yahweh's instruction is with us'?
Actually, there, the false pen of the scholars
    has made it into falsehood.
⁹The smart people have been shamed,
    they've shattered and been captured.
There, they've rejected Yahweh's word;
    what smartness do they have?

¹⁰Therefore I shall give their wives to other men,
    their fields to dispossessors.
Because from small to big,
    every one of them is greedy for loot.
Prophet and priest alike,
    every one of them is acting falsely.

[11]They've healed my dear people's break too
    lightly,
    saying, 'Things are well, they're well',
    when they're not well.
[12]They've been shameful, because they've done
    something offensive;
    they neither manifest any shame
    nor do they know how to be disgraced.
Therefore they will fall among the people who fall;
    at the time when I attend to them, they'll
    collapse (Yahweh has said).
[13]I shall totally gather them up (Yahweh's
    declaration):
    there'll be no grapes on the vine,
    no figs on the fig tree.
The leaves will wither,
    and what I have given them will pass away
    from them.

## No balm in Gil'ad?

[14]Why are we sitting? – gather up,
    we'll come into the fortified towns and be still
    there.
Because Yahweh our God is letting us perish
    and drink poisoned water,
Because we've done wrong to Yahweh,
    [15]hoping for things to go well but there's
    nothing good,
    for a time of healing but here – terror.
[16]From Dan its horses' snort has made itself heard:
    at the sound of the neighing of its sturdy ones
    the entire country has shaken.
They came and consumed the country and what
    fills it,
    the town and the people who live in it.
[17]Because here I am,
    sending off snakes against you,
Vipers for which there's no charming;
    they'll bite you' (Yahweh's declaration).

[18]You who cheer me in sorrow,
    my mind is sick.
[19]Here is the sound of my dear people's cry for help
    from the country far away:
'Isn't Yahweh in Tsiyyon,
    or isn't its King in it?'
'Why did they provoke me with their images,
    with hollow foreign beings?'
[20]Harvest has passed, summer is finished,
    but we ourselves haven't found deliverance.

[21]Because of my dear people's breaking I'm
    broken,
    I mourn, devastation has taken strong hold of
    me.
[22]Isn't there ointment in Gil'ad,
    or is there no healer there?
Because why has my dear people's restoration
    not developed?

# 9
    If only my head were water,
    my eye a fountain of tears.
I'd cry day and night
    for those who are run through among my dear
    people.

[2]If only I could have a travellers' lodge in the
    wilderness,
    and abandon my people, go from them,
Because all of them are adulterers,
    a pack of people breaking faith.
[3]They've directed their tongue, their bow has been
    falsehood;
    it's not on behalf of truthfulness that they've
    been strong in the country.
Because they've gone out from something bad, to
    something bad,
    and not acknowledged me (Yahweh's
    declaration).
[4]They should keep watch, each person, on his
    neighbour;
    don't rely on any brother.
Because every brother is totally crooked,
    and every neighbour goes about as a slanderer.
[5]Each one trifles with his neighbour;
    they don't speak the truth.
They've taught their tongue false speech;
    they've got tired being wayward.
[6]You [Yirmeyahu] have lived in the middle of
    deceit;
    in deceit they've refused to acknowledge me
    (Yahweh's declaration).

## Who is the smart person who understands all this?

[7]Therefore Yahweh of Armies has said this:

Here am I; I'm going to smelt them, test them,
    because how [else] can I act in the face of my
    dear people?
[8]Their tongue is a sharpened arrow,
    it's spoken deceit.

With his mouth someone speaks with his
    neighbour of how things will be well,
    but inside he lays an ambush for him.
[9]For these things shall I not attend to them
    (Yahweh's declaration),
    or on a nation that's like this shall I myself not
    take redress?
[10]For the mountains I shall take up crying and
    wailing,
    and for the wilderness pastures a lament.
Because they're laid waste, with no one passing
    through,
    and people don't hear the sound of livestock.
Both the birds of the heavens and the animals,
    they've fled; they've gone.
[11]I shall make Yerushalaim into heaps of rubble,
    the dwelling of jackals.
Yehudah's towns I shall make into a devastation,
    with no inhabitant.

[12]Who is the smart individual who understands this,
    to whom has Yahweh's mouth spoken so that he
    can tell of it?
On what account has the country perished,
    become wasted like a wilderness, with no one
    passing through?

[13]Yahweh said, 'Because they abandoned
my instruction which I put before them. They
didn't listen to my voice and they didn't walk
by it. [14]They followed the determination of
their mind and followed the Masters, as their
ancestors taught them.' [15]Therefore Yahweh of Armies, Yisra'el's God,
said this: 'Here am I; I'm going to make this
people eat bitter plants and make them drink
poisoned water. [16]I shall scatter them among
the nations that they and their ancestors
haven't known. I shall send off the sword after
them until I've finished them off.'

### The real circumcision

[17]Yahweh of Armies has said this:

Show some discernment, and call the lamenting
    women so they may come,
    send for the smart women so they may come.
[18]They must hurry and raise a wailing over us,
    so our eyes may run with tears,
    our pupils flow with water.

[19]Because the sound of wailing –
    it has made itself heard from Tsiyyon:
'How we are destroyed,
    we are very shamed.
Because we are abandoning our country,
    because they've overthrown our dwellings.'
[20]Because listen, women, to Yahweh's word;
    your ear must receive the word from his
    mouth.
Teach wailing to your daughters,
    lamentation one woman to her neighbour.
[21]Because death is climbing through our
    windows,
    coming into our citadels,
To cut off children from the streets,
    young men from the squares.

[22]Speak like this (Yahweh's declaration):

Human corpses will fall
    like manure on the face of the fields,
Like a sheaf behind the reaper
    with no one gathering it up.

[23]Yahweh has said this:

The smart person isn't to exult in his smartness,
    the strong person isn't to exult in his strength,
    the wealthy person isn't to exult in his wealth.
[24]Rather the person who exults is to exult in this:
    showing insight and acknowledging me,
That I am Yahweh,
    acting with commitment,
With authority and faithfulness in the country,
    because I delight in these things (Yahweh's
    declaration).

[25]There, days are coming (Yahweh's
declaration) when I shall attend to everyone
circumcised in the foreskin, [26]with Misrayim,
Yehudah, Edom, the Ammonites, Mo'ab, and
all the people shaved at the forehead who live
in the wilderness, because all the nations are
foreskinned, and Yisra'el's entire household –
foreskinned in mind.

### Facing the facts about images

**10** Listen to the word that Yahweh spoke
to you, Yisra'el's household. [2]Yahweh
has said this:

Don't learn the nations' way;
  don't shatter at signs in the heavens.
Because the nations may shatter at those,
  ³because the nations' laws are hollow.

Because someone cuts a tree from the forest,
  the work of a craftsman's hands, with an axe.
⁴With silver and gold he beautifies it,
  with nails and hammers he strengthens it, so it
    doesn't wobble.
⁵They're like a scarecrow in a melon patch;
  they don't speak.
They're carried, carried, because they don't walk;
  don't be in awe of them.
Because they don't do anything bad,
  nor is doing good with them.
⁶There is none like you, Yahweh;
  you are great and your name is great, with
    strength.
⁷Who would not be in awe of you, king of the
    nations,
  because it's fitting to you.
Because among all the nations' smart people
  and in all their dominion there's none like you.
⁸As one, they're stupid, dim-witted;
  the correction that comes from hollow beings
    is wood.
⁹Beaten silver is brought from Tarshish,
  gold from Uphaz,
A craftsman's work, a goldsmith's hands,
  their clothing blue and purple,
  the work of smart people, all of them.
¹⁰But Yahweh is the true God,
  he's the living God, the everlasting King.
At his fury, earth shakes;
  nations can't cope with his condemnation.

  ¹¹You're to speak in this way to them:

The gods that didn't make the heavens and the
    earth
  will perish from the earth and from under the
    heavens.

¹²One who made the earth by his energy,
  established the world by his expertise,
  by his understanding stretched out the
    heavens –
¹³At his giving voice there was a roar of water in
    the heavens,
  and he made clouds go up from the end of the
    earth.

He made lightning for the rain,
  made wind come out from his storehouses.

## Discipline with judgement

¹⁴Every human being proves stupid, without
    knowledge;
  every goldsmith is put to shame by the
    image,
Because his figure is a falsehood,
  and there's no breath in them.
¹⁵They're hollow, a work for mockery;
  at the time they're attended to, they'll perish.
¹⁶Not like these is Ya'aqob's share,
  because he's the former of everything.
Yisra'el is the clan that is his domain;
  Yahweh of Armies is his name.

¹⁷Gather up your baggage from the country
    [Yerushalaim],
  you who dwell under siege.

¹⁸Because Yahweh has said this:

Here am I, I'm going to fling away the people who
    dwell in the country,
  at this moment.
I shall pressure them
  in order that they experience it.

¹⁹Oh, alas for me, on account of my break,
  my wound is sickening,
Whereas myself I had said,
  'This is only a sickness, and I shall bear it.'
²⁰My tent is destroyed, all my tent cords have
    broken.
  my children have gone out from me, there are
    none of them,
No one spreading my tent again,
  hanging out my tent cloths.
²¹Because the shepherds are stupid,
  they haven't enquired of Yahweh.
That's why they haven't thrived,
  and all their flock has scattered.
²²A sound, a report – there, it's coming,
  a great shaking from a northern country,
To make Yehudah's towns a devastation,
  the abode of jackals.
²³I acknowledge, Yahweh,
  that an individual's road doesn't belong to
    him.

It doesn't belong to a person walking
    to set his step.
[24]Discipline me, Yahweh, only with judgement,
    not in your anger, so you don't make me small.
[25]Pour your wrath on the nations that haven't
    acknowledged you,
    on the kin-groups that haven't called out in
    your name.
Because they've consumed Ya'aqob,
    consumed him and finished him off, and
    devastated his abode.

## No shrugging of God's shoulders

**11** The word that came to Yirmeyahu
from Yahweh: [2]'You people, listen to
the words in this pact.'

'So you're to speak them to Yehudah's people
and against Yerushalaim's inhabitants, [3]and
say to them, "Yahweh, Yisra'el's God, has said
this: 'The person is cursed who doesn't listen
to the words in this pact [4]that I ordered your
ancestors on the day I got them out from the
country of Misrayim, from the iron smelter,
saying "Listen to my voice and act on them in
accordance with all that I order you, and you
will be a people for me and I will be God for
you", [5]in order to implement the oath that he
swore to your ancestors to give them a country
flowing with milk and syrup this very day.'"'

    I said, 'Yes, Yahweh.'

    [6]Yahweh said to me, 'Call out all these
words in Yehudah's towns and in Yerushalaim's
streets: "Listen to the words in this pact and act
on them. [7]Because I testified solemnly to your
ancestors on the day I got them out from the
country of Misrayim and until this day, starting
early to testify, saying 'Listen to my voice.' [8]But
they didn't listen or bend their ear but walked
each person by the bad determination of their
mind. So I brought on them all the words in
this pact that I ordered them to act on but they
didn't act on.'"

    [9]Yahweh said to me, 'A conspiracy can be
found among Yehudah's people and among
Yerushalaim's inhabitants. [10]They've turned
back to the wayward acts of their ancestors of
old, who refused to listen to my words. As those
people followed other gods, Yisra'el's household
and Yehudah's household have contravened my
pact that I solemnized with their ancestors.'

## Don't pray

[11]Therefore Yahweh has said this: 'Here am
I, I'm going to bring upon them bad fortune
from which they won't be able to get away.
They'll cry out to me but I won't listen to
them. [12]Yehudah's towns and Yerushalaim's
inhabitants will go and cry out to the gods
to whom they've been burning incense. But
they won't deliver them at all at the time when
the bad fortune comes to them. [13]Because
according to the number of your towns,
Yehudah, have been your gods, and according
to the number of your streets, Yerushalaim,
have you set up altars to Shame, altars to burn
incense to the Master.'

[14]And you, don't plead on this town's account,
    don't raise on its account a resounding shout
    or plea.
Because I won't be listening at the time when they
    call to me
    on account of the bad fortune that comes to
    them.
[15]What business does my beloved have in my
    house,
    as she acts on her strategy?
Many will make the sacred flesh pass from you,
    because you deal badly, then you exult.
[16]'Verdant olive, beautiful with shapely fruit',
    Yahweh named you.
To a big roaring sound he's set fire to it,
    and its branches have broken.
[17]Yahweh of Armies who planted you –
    he's spoken of bad fortune for you,
On account of the bad dealing of Yisra'el's
    household
    and Yehudah's household,
Which they did for themselves
    to provoke me by burning incense to the
    Master.

[18]When Yahweh made it known to me so that I
    might know –
    then you let me see their practices.
[19]And I myself had been like a docile lamb
    that's led to slaughter.
I didn't know that against me
    they'd thought up their intentions:
'Let's destroy the tree with its sap,
    let's cut him off from the land of the living,
    so that his name isn't mentioned any more.'

²⁰So, Yahweh of Armies, who exercises authority
  with faithfulness,
    who tests the inner being and the mind:
May I see your redress on them,
    because I've laid out my argument to you.

## Why do the faithless get away with it?

²¹Therefore Yahweh has said this:

'About the people of Anatot who are seeking
your life, saying "You will not prophesy in
Yahweh's name, then you won't die by our hand."'
²²Therefore Yahweh of Armies has said this:

Here am I; I'm going to attend to them;
    the young men will die by the sword.
Their sons and their daughters will die by famine;
  ²³there will be no remainder of them.
Because I shall bring bad fortune on the people
    of Anatot,
    the year when they're attended to.

**12** You'll be in the right, Yahweh, when I
        argue with you,
    yet I shall speak of your rulings with you.
Why does the way of the faithless succeed,
    why are all the people who break faith at ease?
²You plant them, yes they root;
    they go on, yes they produce fruit.
You're near in their mouth,
    but far from their inner being.
³But you, Yahweh, have acknowledged me and
    seen me,
    you've tested my mind in relation to you.
Drive them off like sheep to the slaughter,
    make them sacred for the killing day.

⁴How long will the country mourn,
    the grass in all the fields wither?
Through the bad action of the people who live in it,
    animals and birds come to an end,
Because people say,
    'He won't look at our future.'

⁵When you [Yirmeyahu] have run with people on
    foot and they've exhausted you,
    then how can you compete with horses?
If you're secure in a country where things are well,
    then how will you do in the Yarden [Jordan]
        jungle?

⁶Because yes, your brothers and your father's
    household –
    yes, those people have broken faith with you;
    yes, those people have called after you in full
        voice.
Don't trust them,
    when they speak good things to you.

## I have abandoned my household

⁷I have abandoned my household,
    I have deserted my domain.
I have given my dearly beloved
    into her enemies' fist.
⁸My domain has become to me
    like a lion in the forest.
She's given her voice against me;
    therefore I've been hostile to her.
⁹My domain is a coloured bird of prey;
    birds of prey are against her, all round.
Go, gather all the creatures of the wild,
    bring them to eat.
¹⁰Many shepherds have devastated my vineyard,
    trampled my share.
They've made my desirable share
    into a devastated wilderness.
¹¹Someone has made it into a devastation;
    it mourns before me, devastated.

The entire country is devastated,
    because there's no one taking it into their mind.
¹²Into all the bare places in the wilderness
        destroyers have come
    because Yahweh's sword consumes.
From one end of the country to the other end of
        the country
    there's no well-being for all flesh.
¹³They've sown wheat but reaped thorns,
    they've pained themselves but they don't
        prevail.
So be shamed by your yield
    because of Yahweh's angry blazing.

¹⁴Yahweh has said this: 'About all my
neighbours who deal badly, who touch the
domain that I gave to my people Yisra'el: here
am I, I'm going to uproot them from on their
land, and Yehudah's household I shall uproot
from among them. ¹⁵But after I've uprooted
them I shall again show compassion to them
and bring them back, each to his domain, each

to his country. <sup>16</sup>If they really learn the ways of my people, swearing by my name "As Yahweh lives" as they taught my people to swear by the Master, they'll be built up among my people. <sup>17</sup>But if they don't listen, I'll uproot that nation, uproot and destroy it (Yahweh's declaration).'

## A shorts story

**13** Yahweh said this to me: 'Go and get yourself a linen garment and put it round your hips, but don't let it come into water.' <sup>2</sup>So I got the garment in accordance with Yahweh's word and put it round my hips. <sup>3</sup>Yahweh's word came to me a second time: <sup>4</sup>"Take the garment that you got, which is round your hips, and set off for Perat. Hide it there in a crevice in the cliff.' <sup>5</sup>So I went and hid it at Perat as Yahweh ordered me. <sup>6</sup>After many days Yahweh said to me, 'Set off for Perat and get the garment from there that I ordered you to hide there.' <sup>7</sup>I went to Perat and dug, and got the garment from the place where I'd hidden it, and there, the garment was destroyed; it wouldn't be useful for anything.

<sup>8</sup>Yahweh's word came to me. <sup>9</sup>Yahweh said this: 'In this way I shall devastate Yehudah's majesty and Yerushalaim's majesty, which are great. <sup>10</sup>This people that deals badly, who refuse to listen to my words, who walk by the determination of their mind, and who follow other gods to serve them and bow low to them, will become like this garment that isn't useful for anything. <sup>11</sup>Because as a garment sticks to someone's hips, so I made Yisra'el's entire household and Yehudah's entire household stick to me (Yahweh's declaration) to be for me a people, a name, praise and splendour. But they didn't listen.

<sup>12</sup>So you're to speak this word to them. Yahweh the God of Yisra'el says this: "Every bottle should be full of wine." They'll say to you, "We know very well that every bottle should be full of wine, don't we." <sup>13</sup>You're to say to them, "Yahweh has said this: 'Here am I; I'm going to fill all the inhabitants of this country, the kings who sit on David's behalf on his throne, the priests, the prophets and all Yerushalaim's inhabitants – with drunkenness. <sup>14</sup>I shall smash them, one person against his brother, parents and children together

(Yahweh's declaration). I shall not pity and I shall not spare and I shall not have compassion so that I don't devastate them.""

## Can the people change?

<sup>15</sup>Listen, give ear, don't be superior,
    because Yahweh has spoken.
<sup>16</sup>Give honour to Yahweh your God
    before he brings darkness,
Before your feet stumble
    on the mountains at dusk,
And you hope for light but he turns it into deep
        darkness,
    makes it into dark gloom.
<sup>17</sup>If you don't listen to this, my soul will cry in
        hidden places
    before your majesty.
My eye will cry and cry, and run with crying,
    because Yahweh's flock has gone into captivity.

<sup>18</sup>Say to the king and to the queen mother,
    'Fall down, sit.
Because your headwear is coming down,
    your glorious crown.'
<sup>19</sup>The Negeb towns are closed,
    there's no one opening them.
Yehudah is taken into exile, all of it,
    taken into exile, completely.
<sup>20</sup>Lift up your eyes
    and look at the people coming from the north.
Where are the sheep that were given you
        [Yerushalaim],
    your glorious flock?
<sup>21</sup>What will you say when he appoints over you
    ones whom you trained for yourself,
    as allies, as your head?
Contractions will take hold of you, won't they,
    like a woman giving birth.
<sup>22</sup>And when you say to yourself,
    'Why have these things happened to me?' –
Because of the magnitude of your waywardness
    your skirts have been stripped off and your
        body has been violated.

<sup>23</sup>Does the Kushite [Sudanese] change his skin,
    the leopard his spots?
You people too can do good,
    you who have been taught to do bad.
<sup>24</sup>So I shall scatter them like chaff
    passing away before the wilderness wind.

<sup>25</sup>This will be your fate,
    your lot measured out from me (Yahweh's
      declaration),
In that you put me out of mind
    and relied on falsehood.
<sup>26</sup>Yes, I myself will lift up your skirts over your face,
    and your slighting will become visible,
<sup>27</sup>Your adulteries and your bellowings,
    your whorish scheming.
On the hills, in the open country,
    I've seen your abominable deeds.
Oh, alas for you, Yerushalaim, you're not clean –
    how much longer will it be?

## The God who doesn't answer prayer

**14** What came as a word from Yahweh to Yirmeyahu concerning the matter of the drought.

<sup>2</sup>Yehudah mourns,
    its settlements languish.
People look down to the ground,
    Yerushalaim's crying goes up.
<sup>3</sup>Their important people send their underlings for
      water;
    they come to the cisterns, they don't find water.
They return, their vessels empty;
    they're shamed, disgraced, they cover their head.
<sup>4</sup>On account of the fact that the ground has
      broken up,
    because there hasn't been rain in the country,
The farmers are shamed,
    they cover their head.
<sup>5</sup>When the hind in the open country, too, gives
      birth,
    it abandons, because there's been no grass.
<sup>6</sup>As the donkeys stand on the bare places,
    they gasp for air like jackals.
Their eyes fail,
    because there's no vegetation.

<sup>7</sup>If our wayward acts avow against us, Yahweh,
    act for the sake of your name.
Because our turnings away are many;
    we've done wrong to you.
<sup>8</sup>Yisra'el's hope,
    its deliverer in time of pressure,
Why should you become like an alien in the
      country,
    like a traveller who turns aside to lodge?

<sup>9</sup>Why should you become like someone
      bewildered,
    like a strong man who can't deliver?
But you're among us, Yahweh,
    your name has been called out over us, don't let
      go of us.

<sup>10</sup>Yahweh has said this to this people:

Yes, they've loved straying,
    they haven't restrained their feet.
Given that Yahweh doesn't accept them,
    he'll now be mindful of their waywardness
    and he'll attend to their wrongdoings.

## The encouraging prophets

<sup>11</sup>Yahweh said to me, 'Don't plead for good things on behalf of this people. <sup>12</sup>When they fast I won't be listening, when they make a burnt sacrifice or offering, I won't be accepting them, because by sword, by famine and by epidemic I'm going to finish them off.' <sup>13</sup>I said, 'Oh! Lord Yahweh! There, the prophets are saying to them, "You won't see a sword, famine won't happen to you, because I shall give you true well-being in this place."' <sup>14</sup>Yahweh said to me, 'It's falsehood that the prophets have prophesied in my name; I didn't send them, I didn't order them, I didn't speak to them. A false vision, divination and nothingness, their mind's deceit, is what those people are prophesying to you. <sup>15</sup>Therefore Yahweh has said this to the prophets who prophesy in my name when I didn't send them and they're saying, "Sword and famine won't happen in this country": by sword and famine those prophets will come to an end. <sup>16</sup>And the people to whom they're prophesying will be thrown out into Yerushalaim's streets because of famine and sword. There'll be no one burying them – them, their wives, their sons and their daughters. I'll pour out on them their bad fortune.

<sup>17</sup>And you're to speak this word to them.

My eyes run down with crying,
    night and day they won't stop.
Because with a great breaking
    the dear daughter of my people has broken,
    a very sickening wound.

¹⁸If I go out into the open country –
   there, people run through by the sword.
If I come into the town –
   there, sicknesses that come from famine.
Because both prophet and priest go round the
   country
     but don't acknowledge it.'

## No matter who prayed

¹⁹Have you totally rejected Yehudah,
   have you renounced Tsiyyon with your entire
     being?
Why have you struck us down
   and we have no one healing us? –
Hoping for things to go well, but there's nothing
     good,
   for a time of healing, but there – terror.
²⁰We acknowledge our faithlessness, Yahweh,
   our ancestors' waywardness.
Because we've done wrong to you,
   ²¹don't spurn us, for the sake of your
   name.
Don't disgrace your honoured throne;
   be mindful, don't contravene your pact with
     us.
²²Are there any among the nations' hollow beings
   who make it rain,
   or do the heavens give showers?
You're the one, Yahweh our God, aren't you,
   so we hope in you, because you made all these
     things.

**15** Yahweh said to me, 'If Mosheh [Moses] and Shemu'el [Samuel] were to stand before me, my soul wouldn't go out to this people. Send them away from my presence. They're to go away. ²When they say to you, "Where shall we go?", say to them, "Yahweh has said this:

Those who are for death, to death;
   those who are for the sword, to the sword;
Those who are for famine, to famine;
   those who are for captivity, to captivity.

³I shall appoint over them four species (Yahweh's declaration):

The sword to slay
   and the dogs to drag off,

The birds of the heavens and the animals of the
   earth
     to eat and to devastate.

⁴I shall make them a horror to all earth's kingdoms on account of Menashsheh ben Yehizqiyyahu king of Yehudah, because of what he did in Yerushalaim.'"

## I'm tired of relenting

⁵Because who will pity you, Yerushalaim,
   who will grieve for you,
Who will turn aside
   to ask about your well-being?
⁶You are one who has deserted me (Yahweh's
   declaration);
   you go backwards.
So I'm stretching out my hand against you and
   devastating you;
   I'm tired of relenting.
⁷I'm winnowing them with a pitchfork
   in the country's settlements.
I'm bereaving, I'm obliterating my people,
   because of their ways from which they wouldn't
     turn back.
⁸Their widows will be more numerous
   than the sand of the seas.
I shall bring to them (against mother, young man)
   a destroyer at noon.
I shall let shock and terror
   fall on them suddenly.
⁹One who has borne seven languishes,
   she's breathed out her life.
Her sun has set while it's still day;
   she's shamed and confounded.
Their remainder I'll give to the sword
   before their enemies (Yahweh's declaration).

¹⁰Oh, alas for me,
   my mother, that you gave birth to me,
An argumentative man and a disputatious man
   for the entire country.
Although I haven't lent and they haven't lent to me,
   everyone slights me.

¹¹Yahweh said:

If I do not free you for good things,
   if I do not get the enemy to intervene for you
   in a bad time and in a time of distress . . .

¹²Can one break iron,
iron from the north or copper?
¹³Your wealth [Yerushalaim] and your treasures I
shall give as plunder,
not for payment but for all your wrongdoings,
yes through all your territory.

¹⁴I shall make your enemies [Yirmeyahu] pass on
through a country they haven't known.
Because fire is blazing in my anger;
it will blaze against you all.

## You've been a deceiver

¹⁵You yourself acknowledge, Yahweh;
be mindful of me, attend to me.
Grant me redress from my persecutors;
don't let me be taken, because of your long-
temperedness.
Acknowledge my bearing of reviling because of
you;
¹⁶your words presented themselves and I
consumed them.
Your word became joy to me,
the rejoicing of my mind.
Because your name was called out over me,
Yahweh God of Armies.
¹⁷I haven't sat in the company of people having
fun, and exulted;
because of your hand I've sat alone,
because you'd filled me with condemnation.
¹⁸Why has my pain become endless,
my wound grave, refusing to heal?
You really have been to me a veritable
deceiver,
water that's not trustworthy.

¹⁹Therefore Yahweh has said this:

If you turn back, I'll let you come back;
you can stand before me.
If you let out what is valuable rather than what is
empty,
you can be my very mouth.
Those people will turn back to you,
but you yourself won't turn back to them.
²⁰To this people I shall make you
a copper wall, fortified;
They'll battle against you
but not prevail over you.
Because I shall be with you

to deliver you and to rescue you (Yahweh's
declaration).
²¹I will rescue you from the hand of people who
deal badly,
redeem you from the fist of the violent.

## Your marriage isn't your own

**16** Yahweh's word came to me: ²'You
will not get yourself a wife and you
will not have sons or daughters in this place.'
³Because Yahweh has said this about the
sons and the daughters that are born in this
place, and about the mothers who give birth to
them and about the fathers who father them in
this country: ⁴'Sickening deaths they will die.
They won't be lamented or buried. As manure
on the face of the ground they'll be. By sword
and famine they'll come to an end. Their
corpse will be food for the birds of the heavens
and for the animals of the earth.'

⁵Because Yahweh has said this:

Don't come to a house where there's a wake,
don't go to lament and grieve for them.
Because I have gathered up my well-being from
this people
(Yahweh's declaration), my commitment and
compassion.
⁶Big people and little people in this country will die;
they won't be buried.
People won't lament for them,
they won't gash themselves and they won't
shave their heads for them.
⁷They won't break bread for them in mourning
to comfort someone over a death.
They won't give them a cup of comfort to drink,
for his father or for his mother.
⁸And you're not to come to a house where there's
a banquet,
to sit with them to eat and drink.

⁹Because Yahweh of Armies, Yisra'el's God, has
said this:

Here am I – I'm going to make cease from this
place,
in front of your eyes and in your days,
The joyful voice and the rejoicing voice,
the voice of groom and the voice of bride.

*Fishers and hunters*

¹⁰"When you tell this people all these things, and they say to you, "Why has Yahweh spoken against us all this great bad fortune, and what is our waywardness and our wrongdoing that we've committed against Yahweh our God?" ¹¹you're to say to them, "Because your ancestors abandoned me (Yahweh's declaration) and followed other gods, served them and bowed low to them. They abandoned me and didn't keep my instruction. ¹²And you've dealt badly more than your ancestors. There you are, following each of you the bad determination of his mind, so as not to listen to me. ¹³So I shall hurl you from upon this country to a country that you haven't known, you or your ancestors, and there you will serve other gods, day and night, in that I won't show you grace."

¹⁴Therefore, here, days are coming (Yahweh's declaration) when it will no more be said, "As Yahweh lives, who got the Yisraelites up from the country of Misrayim", ¹⁵but rather, "As Yahweh lives, who got the Yisraelites up from the northern country and from all the countries where he'd driven them". I shall bring them back to their country, which I gave their ancestors.'

¹⁶Here am I; I'm going to send for many fishers
   (Yahweh's declaration), and they'll fish for
   them.
Afterwards I shall send
   for many hunters and they'll hunt for them,
From on every mountain and from on every hill
   and from the clefts in the cliffs.
¹⁷Because my eyes have been upon all their ways;
   they haven't hidden from my presence.
Their waywardness hasn't stayed concealed
   from in front of my eyes.
¹⁸So I shall make good to them first,
   double for their waywardness and their
   wrongdoing,
Because of their profaning my country
   with their abominable corpses;
   they filled my domain with their offensive
   practices.

¹⁹Yahweh, my vigour and my stronghold,
   my escape in the day of pressure,
To you nations will come
   from earth's ends and say,

'Our ancestors indeed had falsehood as their
   domain,
   hollowness, and there was nothing in them that
   would prevail.
²⁰Can a human being make himself gods? –
   but they're not gods.'

²¹Therefore here am I, I'm going to make them
   acknowledge it
   at this moment,
I shall make them acknowledge my hand and my
   strength,
   and they will acknowledge that my name is
   Yahweh.

*Yahweh tests the inner being*

# 17
   Yehudah's wrongdoing is written
      with an iron pen,
Engraved with a diamond point
   on their mind's tablet
And at the horns of their altars
   ²in accordance with their children's being
      mindful of their altars and their totem poles,
By a verdant tree and by high hills,
   ³the mountains in the open country.
Your resources, all your treasures, I shall give as
   plunder,
   the shrines for your wrongdoing, in all your
   territory.
⁴You'll forfeit hold (and by your own act)
   of your domain that I gave you.
I shall make you serve your enemies
   in a country that you haven't known.
Because you've lit a fire in my anger
   that will burn permanently.

⁵Yahweh has said this:

Cursed is the man
   who relies on human beings,
Makes flesh his strength,
   and his mind turns aside from Yahweh.
⁶He'll be like a shrub in the steppe;
   it can't see that good will come.
It dwells in parched places in the wilderness,
   salty land where no one lives.
⁷Blessed is the man who relies on Yahweh,
   and Yahweh is his reliance.
⁸He'll be like a tree planted by water;
   it sends out its roots by a channel.

It isn't afraid that heat will come;
  its foliage will be verdant.
In a year of drought it isn't anxious;
  it doesn't move away from producing fruit.
⁹The mind is more crooked than anything;
  it's grave – who can know it?
¹⁰I am Yahweh, searching the mind,
  testing the inner being,
To give to an individual in accordance with his
      ways,
  in accordance with the fruit proper to his
      practices.

¹¹A partridge hatching when it didn't give
      birth –
  someone who makes wealth but not by
      [proper] exercise of authority.
At the midpoint of his days it will abandon him,
  and at his end he'll be a villain.

¹²Splendid throne, on high from of old,
  our sacred place!
¹³Yisra'el's hope, Yahweh,
  all who abandon you will be shamed.
People who turn aside in the country will be
      written down,
  because they've abandoned
  the fountain of living water, Yahweh.

## Making the sabbath sacred

¹⁴Heal me, Yahweh, so I may find healing;
  deliver me, so I may find deliverance,
  because you're my praise.
¹⁵There, those people are saying to me,
  'Where is Yahweh's word? – yes, it should
      come.'
¹⁶I myself haven't hurried away from being a
      shepherd after you;
  I haven't longed for the grave day.
You yourself know what has come out from my
      lips;
  it's been in front of your face.
¹⁷Don't become a terror to me;
  you're my shelter on the day of bad fortune.
¹⁸My persecutors must be shamed;
  I myself must not be shamed.
They're the ones who must shatter;
  I myself must not shatter.
Bring upon them the day of bad fortune,
  break them with a double breaking.

¹⁹Yahweh said this to me: 'Go and stand
in the ordinary people's gateway by which
Yehudah's kings come in and by which they
go out, and in all Yerushalaim's gateways.
²⁰Say to them, "Listen to Yahweh's word,
Yehudah's kings and all Yehudah and all
Yerushalaim's inhabitants, who come in by
these gateways. ²¹Yahweh has said this: 'Keep
watch on yourselves, and don't carry a load
on the sabbath day or bring them through
Yerushalaim's gateways. ²²Don't take out a
load from your houses on the sabbath day or
do any work. Make the sabbath day sacred, as
I ordered your ancestors – ²³but they didn't
listen, they didn't bend their ear, but toughened
their neck so as not to listen and so as not to
accept discipline.

²⁴But if you really listen to me (Yahweh's
declaration) so as not to bring a load through
the gateways of this town on the sabbath day
but make the sabbath day sacred so as not
to do any work on it, ²⁵then there will come
through this town's gateways kings and officials
sitting on David's throne, riding on chariots
and horses, they and their officials, Yehudah's
people and Yerushalaim's inhabitants. This
town will stay permanently. ²⁶People will come
from Yehudah's towns, from Yerushalaim's
environs, from Binyamin's region, from the
foothills, from the mountains and from
the Negeb, bringing burnt offering, sacrifice,
grain offering and incense, and bringing a
thank-offering to Yahweh's house.

²⁷But if you don't listen to me by making
the sabbath day sacred and not carrying a
load, and you come through Yerushalaim's
gateways on the sabbath day, I shall set fire to
its gateways, and it will consume Yerushalaim's
citadels and not go out."'"

## Clay in the potter's hand

**18** The word that came to Yirmeyahu
from Yahweh: ²'Set off and go down
to a potter's house, and there I'll let you hear
my words.' ³So I went down to a potter's house,
and there, he was doing work at the stones. ⁴If
the object were to spoil that he was making
with clay, in the potter's hand, he'd make it
again into another object, as it was right in the
potter's eyes to do.

⁵Yahweh's word came to me: ⁶'Like this potter I can do to you, Yisra'el's household (Yahweh's declaration), can't I. There, like clay in the potter's hand, so are you in my hand, Yisra'el's household. ⁷Momentarily I may speak concerning a nation or kingdom about uprooting, demolishing and destroying, ⁸but that nation concerning which I've spoken may turn back from its bad dealing. I may then relent about the exile that I intended to do to it. ⁹But momentarily I may speak concerning a nation or kingdom about building and planting, ¹⁰and it may do what is bad in my eyes so as not to listen to my voice. I may then relent about the good that I said I'd do to it.

¹¹So now, say to Yehudah's people and Yerushalaim's inhabitants, please: "Yahweh has said this: 'Here, I'm shaping bad fortune for you. I'm thinking up intentions concerning you. Turn back, please, each person from his bad way, and make your ways and your practices good.'" ¹²But they'll say, "It's desperate, because we shall follow our intentions, and we shall act, each person by the bad determination of his mind."'

## Don't expiate their waywardness

¹³Therefore Yahweh has said this:

Ask among the nations, please:
   who has heard anything like this?
She's done something very horrible,
   Miss Yisra'el.
¹⁴Does Lebanon snow abandon
   the crags in the open country?
Or does foreign water,
   cool streams, uproot?
¹⁵Because my people have put me out of mind,
   so they may burn incense to something
      empty.
They've made them collapse on their ways,
   the age-old paths,
By walking on [other] tracks,
   a way not built up,
¹⁶To make their country a devastation,
   something to whistle at permanently.
Anyone who passes by it will be devastated
   and will shake his head.
¹⁷Like the east wind
   I shall scatter them in front of the enemy.

At their back, not their face,
   I shall look at them, on their day of disaster.

¹⁸People said, 'Come on, we'll think up some intentions against Yirmeyahu, because instruction won't perish from the priest, counsel from the smart person or word from the prophet. Come on, let's strike him down with the tongue, so we may not heed any of his words.'

¹⁹Heed me, Yahweh,
   listen to the voice of the people who argue with
      me.
²⁰Is someone to make good with bad, for good? –
   because they've dug a pit for me.
Be mindful of how I stood before you
   to speak good things concerning them,
   to turn away your wrath from them.
²¹Therefore give their children to famine,
   tip them out to the edges of the sword.
Their women should be bereaved of children and
      widowed,
   their men should be slain by death,
   their young men struck down by the sword in
      battle.
²²May an outcry make itself heard from their
      houses,
   when suddenly you bring a raiding gang on them.
Because they've dug a pit to capture me
   and laid snares for my feet.
²³Yahweh, you yourself know
   their entire counsel against me, for my death.
Don't expiate their waywardness,
   don't blot out their wrongdoing from before you.
They should become people caused to collapse
      before you;
   in the time of your anger, act against them.

## The pitcher that's to be pitched

**19** Yahweh said this: 'Go and get a potter's earthenware pitcher, and some of the elders of the people and some of the elders of the priests, ²and go out into the Ben-hinnom Ravine, which is at the entrance of the Potsherd Gate, and call out there the words that I shall speak to you. ³Say, "Listen to Yahweh's word, Yehudah's kings and Yerushalaim's inhabitants. Yahweh of Armies, Yisra'el's God, has said this: 'Here am I; I'm going to bring bad fortune on this place such that everyone who hears of it – his ears will ring, ⁴since they've abandoned me, made this place alien, burned sacrifices in it to other gods that they hadn't acknowledged, they, their ancestors and Yehudah's kings. They've filled this place with the blood of people free of guilt. ⁵They've built shrines for the Master for burning their children in fire as burnt offerings to the Master, which I didn't order or speak of; it didn't come up into my mind.

⁶Therefore days are coming (Yahweh's declaration) when this place will no longer be called Tophet or Ben-hinnom Ravine but rather Slaughter Ravine. ⁷I shall pitch out the counsel of Yehudah and Yerushalaim in this place. I shall make them fall by the sword before their enemies, by the hand of people who seek their lives, and give their corpse as food to the birds of the heavens and to the animals of the earth. ⁸I shall make this town into a devastation and something to whistle at; anyone who passes by it will be devastated and will whistle at all its wounds. ⁹I shall cause them to eat the flesh of their sons and the flesh of their daughters, and they'll each eat the flesh of his neighbour in the siege and in the straits that their enemies, the people who seek their lives, impose on them.'"

## Terror-Is-All-Around

¹⁰And you're to break the pitcher before the eyes of the men who go with you, ¹¹and say to them, "Yahweh of Armies has said this: 'In this way I shall break this people and this town, as one breaks a potter's article, which cannot be mended again. In Tophet they'll bury, because there'll be no place for burying. ¹²Thus I shall do to this place (Yahweh's declaration) and to its inhabitants, to make this town like Tophet. ¹³Yerushalaim's houses and the kings of Yehudah's houses will become like the place Tophet, defiled – that is, all the houses on whose roofs people have burned sacrifices to the entire heavenly army and poured libations to other gods.'"

¹⁴Yirmeyahu came from Tophet where Yahweh had sent him to prophesy, stood in the courtyard of Yahweh's house and said to the entire people: ¹⁵'Yahweh of Armies, Yisra'el's

God, has said this: "Here am I; I'm going to bring on this town and on all its towns all the bad fortune of which I've spoken concerning it, because they've toughened their neck so as not to listen to my words."'

# 20

Pashhur son of Immer, the priest (he was the leading appointee in Yahweh's house), heard Yirmeyahu prophesying these things. ²Pashhur struck the prophet Yirmeyahu down and put him in the stocks at the Upper Binyamin Gate, which is in Yahweh's house.

³Next day Pashhur let Yirmeyahu out from the stocks. Yirmeyahu said to him, 'Yahweh has named you not Pashhur but rather Terror-Is-All-Around. ⁴Because Yahweh has said this: "Here am I; I'm going to give you to terror, you and all your friends. They'll fall by the sword of their enemies, with your eyes seeing it. I shall give all Yehudah into the hand of the king of Babel and he'll exile them to Babel and strike them down with the sword. ⁵I shall give this town's entire wealth – all its profit, all its valuables and all the treasures of Yehudah's kings, I shall give into their enemies' hand. They'll plunder them, take them and carry them off to Babel. ⁶You, Pashhur, and all the people who live in your house – you'll go into captivity. You'll come to Babel, and there you'll die and there you'll be buried, you and all your friends to whom you've prophesied falsely."'

## Cursed be the day I was born

⁷You enticed me, Yahweh, I was enticed;
   you've taken strong hold of me and prevailed.
I've become an object of fun all the time,
   everyone ridicules me.
⁸Because every time I speak, I cry out,
   I call out violence and destruction.
Because Yahweh's word has become for me
   reviling and derision all the time.
⁹When I said, 'I won't make mention of him,
   not speak in his name any more',
It became in my mind like a raging fire,
   shut up in my bones.
I was weary of holding it in –
   I couldn't.
¹⁰Because I heard the murmuring of many:
   'Terror is on every side – tell of it, let's tell of it.'
Every person who was my friend –
   they're watching my step:

'Perhaps he can be trapped and we can prevail
      over him,
   and take our redress from him.'

[11]But Yahweh – he's with me as a violent strong man;
   therefore my persecutors will collapse and not
      win.
They're being utterly shamed, because they aren't
      thriving,
   with a disgrace for all time that won't be put
      out of mind.
[12]Yahweh of Armies, you who test the faithful
      person,
   who see inner being and mind,
May I see your redress on them,
   because to you I've rolled my argument.

[13]Sing for Yahweh,
   praise Yahweh.
Because he's rescued the life of a needy person
   from the hand of people who deal badly.

[14]Cursed be the day
   on which I was born.
The day when my mother gave birth to me –
   may it not be blessed.
[15]Cursed be the man
   who brought the news to my father,
'A male child has been born to you';
   he made him rejoice so much.
[16]That man will become like the towns
   that Yahweh overthrew and didn't relent.
He'll hear an outcry in the morning
   and a shout at noon time,
[17]The one who didn't kill me before birth,
   so that my mother became my grave,
   her womb pregnant permanently.
[18]Why then did I go out from the womb
   to see oppression and sorrow
   and so my days might consume themselves in
      shame?

## The way to life and the way to death

**21** The word that came to Yirmeyahu
from Yahweh when King Tsidqiyyahu
sent to him Pashhur ben Malkiyyah and
Tsephanyah ben Ma'aseyah the priest to say,
[2]'Enquire on our behalf of Yahweh, please,
because Nebukadre'tstsar king of Babel is doing
battle against us. Perhaps Yahweh will act with

us in accordance with his wonders, so that he
goes up from us.'
[3]Yirmeyahu said to them, 'You're to say this to
Tsidqiyyahu: [4]"Yahweh, Yisra'el's God, has said
this: 'Here am I; I'm going to turn back the battle
implements that are in your hand, with which
you're doing battle with the king of Babel and the
Kasdites who are besieging you from outside
the wall, and I shall gather them up into the
middle of this town. [5]I myself will do battle
against you with hand bent and strong arm, with
anger, with wrath and with great fury. [6]I shall
strike down this town's inhabitants, human beings
and animals; they'll die in a great epidemic.
[7]After this (Yahweh's declaration) I shall give
Tsidqiyyahu king of Yehudah and his servants
and the people, those who remain in this town
from epidemic, sword and famine, into the
hand of Nebukadre'tstsar king of Babel and
into the hand of their enemies, into the hand of
the people seeking their life. He'll strike them
down with the mouth of the sword. He won't
have pity for them. He won't have mercy. He
won't have compassion.'"

[8]And to this people you are to say, "Yahweh
has said this: 'Here am I, putting before you the
way to life and the way to death. [9]The one who
lives in this town will die by sword, by famine
or by epidemic. But the one who goes out and
goes over to the Kasdites who are besieging you
will live. His life will be his as a trophy. [10]Because
I have set my face against this town for bad
fortune and not for good fortune (Yahweh's
declaration). Into the hand of the king of Babel
it will be given, and he will burn it in fire.'"

## About false confidence

[11]And to the household of the king of
Yehudah, listen to Yahweh's word. [12]Household
of David, Yahweh has said this:

Judge with authority morning by morning,
   rescue the person who's been robbed from the
      hand of the oppressor,
So that my wrath doesn't go out like fire,
   and burn up with no one quenching it,
   because of the bad nature of your practices.
[13]Here am I towards you [Yerushalaim], you who
      dwell in the vale,
   a crag in the flatland (Yahweh's declaration).

People who say, "Who can come down against
us,
who can come into our abodes?",
¹⁴I shall attend to you
in accordance with the fruit of your practices
(Yahweh's declaration).
I shall set fire to its forest
and consume all that's round it.'

**22** Yahweh said this: 'Go down to the
house of the king of Yehudah and
speak there this word. ²Say, "Listen to Yahweh's
word, king of Yehudah, you who sit on David's
throne and your servants and your people who
come through these gateways. ³Yahweh has
said this: 'Exercise authority with faithfulness,
rescue the person who's been robbed from
the hand of the oppressor, don't wrong alien,
orphan and widow, don't be violent, don't
shed the blood of someone free of guilt in this
place. ⁴Because if you really do act on this
word, then through this house's gateways will
come David's kings sitting on his throne, riding
chariot and horses, he and his servants and his
people. ⁵But if you don't listen to these words,
I swear by myself (Yahweh's declaration) that
this house will become a waste.'"'

⁶Because Yahweh has said this concerning
the house of the king of Yehudah:

You are Gil'ad to me,
the top of Lebanon.
If I don't make you a wilderness,
towns that aren't inhabited . . .
⁷I shall make devastators sacred to go against
you,
each with his implements.
They'll cut the choicest of your cedars
and make them fall into the fire.

### How to evaluate a king

⁸Many nations will pass by this town and
will say, an individual to his neighbour, 'Why
did Yahweh act in this way to this great town?'
⁹And they'll say, 'On account of the fact that
they abandoned the pact of Yahweh their God
and bowed low to other gods and served them.'

¹⁰Don't cry for the one who is dead,
don't lament for him.

Cry and cry for the one who is going,
because he won't come back again
and see the country of his birth.

¹¹Because Yahweh has said this regarding
Shallum ben Yoshiyyahu king of Yehudah, who
was reigning in place of Yoshiyyahu his father,
who has gone out from this place: 'He won't
come back here again, ¹²because in the place
where they have exiled him, there he'll die. This
country he won't see again.'

¹³Hey, one who builds his house without
faithfulness,
his lofts without the [proper] exercise of
authority!
He makes his neighbour serve for nothing;
he doesn't give him his earnings.
¹⁴The one who says, 'I'll build myself a vast house,
spacious lofts.'
He cuts windows for it, panelled with cedar,
painted with vermilion.
¹⁵Are you a king
because you're competing in cedar?
Your father – he ate and drank, didn't he,
and acted in faithful exercise of authority.
Then things were good for him,
¹⁶when he gave judgement for the weak and needy.
Then things were good;
this is to acknowledge me, isn't it (Yahweh's
declaration).
¹⁷Because you have no eye or mind
except for loot,
For shedding the blood of the one free of guilt,
and for fraud and for extortion.

¹⁸Therefore Yahweh has said this concerning
Yehoyaqim ben Yoshiyyahu king of Yehudah:

They won't mourn for him,
'Oh my brother, oh my sister'.
They won't mourn for him,
'Oh my lord, oh His Majesty'.
¹⁹He'll be buried with a donkey's burial,
dragged and dumped outside Yerushalaim's
gateways.

### The despised potsherd

²⁰Climb the Lebanon and cry out [Yerushalaim],
in the Bashan lift your voice.

Cry out from Abarim,
>   because all your friends are broken.
²¹I spoke to you during your peaceful times;
>   you said, 'I won't listen.'
This was your way from your youth,
>   because you didn't listen to my voice.
²²All your shepherds – the wind will shepherd
>   them;
>   your friends will go into captivity.
Because then you'll be shamed and disgraced
>   because of all your bad dealing.
²³You who live in the Lebanon, nesting among the
>   cedars,
>   how needy of grace you'll be,
When contractions come to you,
>   labour like someone giving birth.

²⁴'As I live (Yahweh's declaration), if Konyah
ben Yehoyaqim king of Yehudah were the ring
on my right hand . . . Because from there I'd
tear you off. ²⁵I shall give you into the hand of
the people who seek your life, into the hand
of the people whom you yourself dread, into
the hand of Nebukadre'tstsar king of Babel,
into the hand of the Kasdites. ²⁶I'll hurl you
and your mother who gave birth to you into
another country where you were not born, and
there you'll die. ²⁷The country where people
will be lifting up their longing to come back:
they won't come back there.'

²⁸Is he a despised broken piece of pottery,
>   this man Konyahu,
>   or an implement in which there's no delight?
Why are they being hurled, he and his offspring,
>   thrown to a country that they don't know?
²⁹Country, country, country,
>   listen to Yahweh's word.
³⁰Yahweh has said this:
>   'Write down this person as childless,
A man who won't succeed in his time,
>   because not one of his offspring will succeed,
Sitting on David's throne
>   and ruling again in Yehudah.'

## A wicked play on words in a king's name

**23** 'Hey, shepherds who led astray
and scattered my flock (Yahweh's
declaration).' ²Therefore Yahweh, Yisra'el's
God, has said this about the shepherds who

shepherd my people: 'You – you've let my
flock scatter. You've driven them away and
not attended to them. Here am I; I'm going
to attend to you, to the bad nature of your
practices (Yahweh's declaration). ³And I
myself will draw together the remainder of my
flock from all the countries where I've driven
them. I'll take them back to their abode, and
they'll be fruitful and become many. ⁴I'll set
up shepherds over them and they'll shepherd
them, and they won't be afraid any more or
shatter or be missing (Yahweh's declaration).
⁵There, days are coming (Yahweh's
declaration) when I shall set up for David a
faithful branch. He will reign as king and show
insight and exercise authority and faithfulness
in the country. ⁶In his days Yehudah will
find deliverance and Yisra'el will dwell with
confidence. This is the name by which he'll
be called: "Yahweh Is Our Faithfulness"
[Yahweh Tsidqenu]. ⁷Therefore, here, days are
coming (Yahweh's declaration) when they will
no longer say "As Yahweh lives, who got the
Yisra'elites up from the country of Misrayim".
⁸Rather, "As Yahweh lives, who got up and
brought the offspring of Yisra'el's household
from the northern country" and from all the
countries where I will have driven them. And
they will live on their land.'

## False prophets

⁹Concerning the prophets.

My mind has broken within me,
>   all my bones have become weak.
I've become like someone drunk,
>   like a man wine has overcome,
Before Yahweh and before his sacred words,
>   ¹⁰because the country is full of adulterers.
Because the country mourns before a vow;
>   the wilderness pastures have dried up.
People's running has become something bad,
>   their strength not right.
¹¹Because both prophet and priest are impious;
>   'Even in my house I've found their bad dealing'
>   (Yahweh's declaration).
¹²Therefore their way will become for them like
>   slippery slopes,
>   they'll be driven into darkness and they'll fall
>   there.

Because I shall bring bad fortune upon them,
   the year when they're attended to (Yahweh's
     declaration).
¹³In Shomron's [Samaria's] prophets I saw
   corruptness:
   they prophesied by the Master and led my
     people astray.
¹⁴In Yerushalaim's prophets I saw a horror:
   adultery, walking by falsehood,
And they strengthen the hands of people dealing
   badly,
   so that no one may turn back from his bad
     dealing.
They've become like Sedom [Sodom] to me, all
   of them,
   its inhabitants like Amorah [Gomorrah].

¹⁵Therefore Yahweh of Armies has said this
concerning the prophets:

Here am I; I'm going to feed this people bitter plants
   and make them drink poisoned water.
Because from Yerushalaim's prophets
   impiety has gone out to the whole country.

¹⁶Yahweh of Armies has said this:

Don't listen to the words of the prophets
   who prophesy to you.
They're giving you something hollow;
   they speak a vision from their mind,
   not from Yahweh's mouth.
¹⁷They're saying to people who disdain Yahweh's
    word,
   'Things will go well for you.'
To everyone who's walking by the determination
    of his mind,
   they've said, 'Bad fortune won't come upon you.'

## Who has stood in Yahweh's council?

¹⁸Because who has stood in Yahweh's council,
   and seen and listened to his word –
   who has heeded his word and listened?
¹⁹There – Yahweh's hurricane,
   wrath has gone out.
The storm is whirling,
   on the head of the faithless it will whirl.
²⁰Yahweh's anger won't turn back until he's acted,
   until he's implemented the strategies in his
    mind.

At the end of the time
   you'll understand it fully.
²¹I didn't send the prophets, but those people ran;
   I didn't speak to them, but those people
    prophesied.
²²If they'd stood in my council,
   they'd have got my people to listen to my word.
They'd have turned them back from their bad way,
   from the bad nature of their practices.

²³Am I a God nearby (Yahweh's declaration),
   and not a God far away?
²⁴If a man hides in a hiding place,
   will I not see him (Yahweh's declaration)?
   I fill the heavens and the earth, don't I
    (Yahweh's declaration).

²⁵'I've listened to what the prophets who prophesy falsehood in my name say: "I've dreamed, I've dreamed." ²⁶How long? Is there in the mind of the prophets who prophesy falsehood, the prophets with deceit in their mind – ²⁷are they intending to get my people to put my name out of mind with their dreams that they recount, each to his neighbour, as their ancestors put my name out of mind because of the Master? ²⁸The prophet who has a dream with him should recount a dream, and the one who has my word with him should speak my word truthfully. What does straw have compared with grain (Yahweh's declaration)? ²⁹My word is like fire (Yahweh's declaration) and like a hammer that shatters a cliff, isn't it.

## Another wicked play on words

³⁰Therefore here am I, against the prophets (Yahweh's declaration), who steal my words each from his neighbour. ³¹Here am I, against the prophets (Yahweh's declaration), who take up their tongue and make a "declaration". ³²Here am I, against the prophets of false dreams (Yahweh's declaration) who recount them and lead my people astray with their falsehoods and their recklessness, when I didn't send them, didn't order them. In no way will they prevail for this people (Yahweh's declaration). ³³When this people or the prophet or the priest asks you, "What is Yahweh's burden?" you're to say to them, "You're the burden and

I shall desert you" (Yahweh's declaration). ³⁴As for the prophet and the priest and the people that says, "Yahweh's burden", I shall attend to that person and his household. ³⁵You're to say this, each to his neighbour, each to his brother: "What has Yahweh avowed?" or "What has Yahweh spoken?" ³⁶But don't make mention of Yahweh's burden any more, because the burden will belong to the person with his word, and you will overturn the words of the living God, Yahweh of Armies, our God.

³⁷You're to say this to the prophet: "What did Yahweh avow to you?" or "What did Yahweh speak?" ³⁸If you say "Yahweh's burden" – therefore Yahweh has said this: "Since you said this thing, 'Yahweh's burden', and I had sent to you saying, 'Don't say, "Yahweh's burden"', ³⁹therefore here am I: I shall simply forget you and desert you, you and the town that I gave you and your ancestors, from in front of my face. ⁴⁰I shall put upon you permanent reviling, permanent shame, which won't be put out of mind.'"

## Lucky figs and unlucky figs

**24** Yahweh showed me: there, two baskets of figs placed before Yahweh's palace (after Nebukadre'tstsar king of Babel exiled Yekonyahu ben Yehoyaqim king of Yehudah, Yehudah's officials, the craftworkers and the smiths, from Yerushalaim and brought them to Babel). ²One basket was very good figs, like early figs; one basket was very bad figs that couldn't be eaten because of being bad. ³Yahweh said to me, 'What are you looking at, Yirmeyahu?' I said, 'Figs – the good figs very good, the bad very bad, that couldn't be eaten because of being bad.'

⁴Yahweh's word came to me. ⁵Yahweh, Yisra'el's God, has said this: 'Like these good figs, so I shall mark down for good Yehudah's exile community that I've sent off from this place to the country of the Kasdites. ⁶I shall set my eye on them for good and bring them back to this country. I shall build them and not overthrow. I shall plant them and not uproot. ⁷I shall give them a mind to acknowledge me, that I am Yahweh. They will be a people for me and I shall be God for them, because they will turn back to me with their entire mind.

⁸But like bad figs that can't be eaten because of being bad (because Yahweh has said this), so shall I make Tsidqiyyahu king of Yehudah, his officials and the remainder of Yerushalaim who remain in this country and who are living in the country of Misrayim – ⁹I shall make them a horror, something bad, to all earth's kingdoms, an insult and an example, a taunt and a slighting, in all the places where I drive them. ¹⁰I shall send against them sword, famine and epidemic until they come to an end from on the land that I gave to them and to their ancestors.'

## Twenty-three years

**25** The word that came to Yirmeyahu concerning the entire people of Yehudah in the fourth year of Yehoyaqim ben Yoshiyyahu king of Yehudah (it was the first year of Nebukadre'tstsar king of Babel), ²which Yirmeyahu the prophet spoke to all Yehudah's people and all Yerushalaim's inhabitants: ³'From the thirteenth year of Yoshiyyahu ben Amon king of Yehudah, to this day, twenty-three years, Yahweh's word has come to me, and I've spoken to you, starting early and speaking, but you haven't listened. ⁴Yahweh has been sending to you all his servants, sending urgently, but you haven't listened. You haven't bent your ear to listen: ⁵"Please turn back each one from his bad way, from the bad nature of his acts, so you may live on the land that Yahweh gave you and your ancestors, from earliest ages to farthest ages. ⁶Don't follow other gods so as to serve them and bow down to them. Don't provoke me with the things your hands have made, and I won't bring bad fortune to you. ⁷But you didn't listen to me (Yahweh's declaration), so as to provoke me with the things your hands have made, to bring bad fortune to you."

⁸Therefore Yahweh of Armies has said this: "Since you haven't listened to my words, ⁹here am I; I'm going to send and get all the northern kin-groups (Yahweh's declaration) and Nebukadre'tstsar king of Babel my servant, and bring them against this country and against its inhabitants, and against all these nations round about. I shall devote them and make them a devastation, something to whistle at, a complete waste permanently. ¹⁰I shall

eliminate from them the sound of celebration and the sound of rejoicing, the sound of bride and the sound of groom, the sound of mill and the light of lamp. [11a]This entire country will become a waste, a desolation.

## Seventy years

[11b]These nations will serve the king of Babel for seventy years, [12]but when seventy years are fulfilled, I shall attend to the king of Babel and to that nation (Yahweh's declaration) for their waywardness, to the country of the Kasdites, and make it a desolation permanently. [13]I shall bring on that country all my words that I've spoken against it, all that's written in this book that Yirmeyahu prophesied against all the nations. [14]Because they, too, will serve many nations and great kings. I shall make good to them in accordance with their action and with the work of their hands."

[15]Because Yahweh, Yisra'el's God, has said this to me: "Take this chalice of wine (wrath) from my hand and get all the nations to which I'm sending you to drink it. [16]They will drink and throw up and go mad because of the sword that I'm sending among them.'"

[17]So I took the chalice from Yahweh's hand and got all the nations to which Yahweh sent me to drink: [18]Yerushalaim and all Yehudah's towns, its kings and its officials, to make them a waste, a desolation, something to whistle at, a slighting, this very day; [19]Par'oh [Pharaoh] king of Misrayim, his servants, his officials, all his people [20]and all the foreign group; all the kings of the country of Uts; all the kings of the country of the Pelishtites [Philistines], Ashqelon, Azzah [Gaza], Eqron and the remainder of Ashdod; [21]Edom, Mo'ab and Ammon; [22]all the kings of Tsor [Tyre], all the kings of Tsidon and the kings of the shore that's across the sea; [23]Dedan, Tema and Buz, and all the people shaved at the forehead; [24]all the kings of Arabia and all the kings of the foreign group who dwell in the wilderness; [25]all the kings of Zimri, all the kings of Elam and all the kings of Maday [Media]; [26]all the northern kings, near or far each to his brother; all the kingdoms of the earth that are on the face of the land; and the king of Sheshak will drink, as the last of them.

## The demon drink

[27]"You're to say to them: "Yahweh of Armies, Yisra'el's God, has said this: 'Drink, get drunk, throw up, fall down and don't get up again, because of the sword that I'm sending among you.'" [28]When they refuse to take the chalice from your hand to drink, you're to say to them, "Yahweh of Armies has said this: 'Drink, drink, [29]because here, in the town over which my name has been called out, I'm beginning to make bad things happen, and you, will you really be treated as free of guilt? You will not be treated as free of guilt, because I'm calling a sword against all earth's inhabitants (a declaration of Yahweh of Armies).'"

[30]You're to prophesy all these things to them, and say to them:

Yahweh roars from on high,
 from his sacred dwelling he gives voice,
 he roars and roars against his abode.
He chants a cry like grape-treaders
 to all earth's inhabitants.
[31]The din has come to the end of the earth,
 because Yahweh has an argument for the
  nations.
He's entering into judgement with all flesh;
 the faithless – he's giving them to the sword
  (Yahweh's declaration).'

[32]Yahweh of Armies has said this:

There something bad going out, from nation to
  nation;
 a great storm arises from earth's remotest
  parts.
[33]There will be people run through by Yahweh
 on that day
From the end of the earth
 as far as the end of the earth.
They won't be lamented
 and they won't be gathered up and they won't
  be buried;
 they'll become manure on the face of the
  ground.
[34]Howl, you shepherds, cry out,
 throw yourselves about, you who are eminences
  over the flock.
Because the days of your slaughter are fulfilled;
 I shall scatter you, and you will fall like a
  desirable bowl.

35Flight will perish from the shepherds,
   escape from the people who are eminences
      over the flock.
36The sound of the shepherds' cry,
   the howls of the people who are eminences
      over the flock!
Because Yahweh is destroying their pastures;
   37the meadows with their well-being will be still
   in the face of Yahweh's angry burning.
38He's abandoned his thicket like a lion
   because his country has become a desolation,
In the face of the oppressor's blazing,
   and in the face of his angry blazing.

## The threat of martyrdom

**26** At the beginning of the reign of
Yehoyaqim ben Yoshiyyahu king
of Yehudah, this word came from Yahweh:
2"Yahweh has said this: "Stand in the courtyard
of Yahweh's house and speak to all Yehudah's
towns, the people coming to bow low in
Yahweh's house, all the words that I'm ordering
you to speak to them. Don't omit a thing.
3Perhaps they'll listen and turn back, each from
his bad way, and I shall relent regarding the
bad things that I'm intending to do to them
because of the bad nature of their practices.
4You're to say to them, 'Yahweh has said this:
"If you don't listen to me by walking according
to the instruction that I've put before you,
5listening to the words of my servants the
prophets whom I've been sending to you,
starting early and sending them (but you
haven't listened), 6I shall make this house like
Shiloh, and make this town a slighting to all
the nations of the earth."'"

7The priests, the prophets and the entire
people listened to Yirmeyahu speaking
these words in Yahweh's house, 8and when
Yirmeyahu finished speaking all that Yahweh
had ordered him to speak to the entire people,
the priests, the prophets and the entire people
seized him, saying: 'You are definitely to die.
9Why have you been prophesying in Yahweh's
name, "This house will become like Shiloh, and
this town will be waste, without inhabitant"?'
So the entire people congregated against
Yirmeyahu in Yahweh's house. 10Yehudah's
officials heard these things and went up from
the king's house to Yahweh's house and sat

in the entrance of Yahweh's New Gate. 11The
priests and the prophets said to the officials
and to the entire people, 'A sentence of death
for this man, because he's prophesied against
this town, as you've heard with your own ears.'

## Remember Mikah

12Yirmeyahu said to all the officials and to
the entire people, 'It was Yahweh sent me
to prophesy to this house and to this town
all the words that you heard. 13So now make
your ways and your practices good and listen
to the voice of Yahweh your God, so Yahweh
may relent of the bad thing that he's spoken
of against you. 14And me – here am I in your
hand. Do to me in accordance with what is
good and right in your eyes. 15Yet you must
fully acknowledge that if you put me to death –
that you're putting on yourselves the blood of
someone who's free of guilt. Because in truth
Yahweh sent me to you to speak all these things
in your ears.'

16The officials and the entire people said to
the priests and to the prophets, 'There's no
sentence of death, because it was in the name
of Yahweh our God that he spoke to us.' 17Some
people from the country's elders got up and
said to all the congregation of the people,
18'Mikah the Morashtite was prophesying in the
days of Hizqiyyahu king of Yehudah. He said to
Yehudah's entire people:

"Yahweh of Armies has said this:
'Tsiyyon will be ploughed as open countryside.
Yerushalaim will become heaps of rubble,
   the mountain of the house shrines in the
      forest."

19Did Hizqiyyahu king of Yehudah and all
Yehudah put him to death at all? Was he not in
awe of Yahweh and did he not seek Yahweh's
goodwill, so that Yahweh relented of the bad
thing that he spoke against them? We're going
to do a great bad thing to ourselves.'

## Not always the Hollywood ending

20There was also a man prophesying in
Yahweh's name, Uriyyahu ben Shema'yahu

from Ye'arim Township. He prophesied against this town and against this people in accordance with all Yirmeyahu's words. [21]King Yehoyaqim, all his strong men and all the officials heard his words, and the king sent to put him to death. Uriyyahu heard and was afraid and fled, and came to Misrayim. [22]But King Yehoyaqim sent men to Misrayim, Elnatan ben Akbor and men with him, to Misrayim. [23]They got Uriyyahu out of Misrayim and brought him to King Yehoyaqim, and he struck him down with the sword and threw his corpse into the common graves. [24]However, the hand of Ahiqam ben Shaphan was with Yirmeyahu so as not to give him into the people's hand to put him to death.

**27** At the beginning of the reign of Yehoyaqim ben Yoshiyyahu king of Yehudah, this word came to Yirmeyahu from Yahweh: [2]Yahweh said this to me: 'Make yourself straps and bars and put them on your neck, [3]and send them to the king of Edom, the king of Mo'ab, the king of the Ammonites, the king of Tsor and the king of Tsidon, by the hand of the envoys who have come to Yerushalaim to Tsidqiyyahu king of Yehudah. [4]Order them regarding their lords: "Yahweh of Armies, Yisra'el's God, has said this: 'You're to say this to your lords: [5]"I'm the one who made the earth, the human beings and the animals that are on the face of the earth, by my great energy and by my bent arm, and I give it to whoever is right in my eyes. [6]So now, I'm giving all these countries into the hand of Nebukadne'tstsar king of Babel my servant. Even the creatures of the wild I'm giving him to serve him. [7]All the nations will serve him, his son and his grandson, until the time comes for his country, him too. Many nations and great kings will serve him. [8]The nation or kingdom that won't serve him (Nebukadne'tstsar king of Babel), that won't give its neck to the yoke of the king of Babel: I'll attend to that nation by sword, by famine and by epidemic (Yahweh's declaration) until I have brought them to an end by his hand.

## Don't listen to your prophets

[9]So you, don't listen to your prophets, to your augurs, to your dreams, to your mediums or to your diviners, who are saying to you,

'Don't serve the king of Babel.' [10]Because they're speaking falsehood to you, so he may take you far from your country, and I drive you out and you perish. [11]But the nation that brings its neck to the yoke of the king of Babel and serves him, I'll allow to stay on its land (Yahweh's declaration) and serve it and live on it."'"

[12]To Tsidqiyyah king of Yehudah I spoke in accordance with these words: 'Bring your necks to the king of Babel's yoke, serve him and his people, and live. [13]Why should you die, you and your people, by sword, by famine and by epidemic, as Yahweh has said regarding the nation that doesn't serve the king of Babel? [14]Don't listen to the words of the prophets who are saying to you, "Don't serve the king of Babel", because they're prophesying falsehood to you. [15]Because I didn't send them (Yahweh's declaration) and they're prophesying falsely in my name, so that I'll drive you out and you'll perish, you and the prophets who are prophesying to you.'

[16]And to the priests and to this entire people I spoke: 'Yahweh has said this: "Don't listen to the words of the prophets who are prophesying to you, 'There, the things from Yahweh's house are going to be brought back from Babel now, very soon', because they're prophesying falsehood to you. [17]Don't listen to them; serve the king of Babel and live – why should this town become a waste? [18]If they are prophets and Yahweh's word is with them, they should please intercede with Yahweh of Armies so that the rest of the things in Yahweh's house, in the house of the king of Yehudah and in Yerushalaim, don't come to Babel."

## Things have to get worse

[19]Because Yahweh of Armies has said this about the pillars, the Sea, the stands and the rest of the things that remain in this town, [20]which Nebukadne'tstsar king of Babel didn't take when he exiled Yekonyah ben Yehoyaqim king of Yehudah from Yerushalaim to Babel, with all the important people from Yehudah and Yerushalaim – [21]because Yahweh of Armies, Yisra'el's God, has said about the things that remain in Yahweh's house, in the house of the king of Yehudah and in Yerushalaim: [22]"To

Babel they will be brought, and there they will be, until the day when I attend to them (Yahweh's declaration) and take them up and bring them back to this place.'"

**28** That year, at the beginning of the reign of Tsidqiyyah king of Yehudah, in the fifth month of the fourth year, Hananyah ben Azzur the prophet, who was from Gib'on, said to me in Yahweh's house in the eyes of the priests and the entire people: ²'Yahweh of Armies, Yisra'el's God, has said this: "I am breaking the king of Babel's yoke. ³In yet two years' time I'm going to bring back to this place all the things from Yahweh's house that Nebukadne'tstsar king of Babel took from this place and brought to Babel. ⁴And I am going to return to this place Yekonyah ben Yehoyaqim king of Yehudah and all Yehudah's exile community who came to Babel (Yahweh's declaration), because I'm breaking the king of Babel's yoke."'

### Prophet confronts prophet

⁵Yirmeyahu the prophet said to Hananyah the prophet in the eyes of the priests and the entire people standing in Yahweh's house – ⁶Yirmeyahu the prophet said, 'Amen, so may Yahweh do. May Yahweh act on your words, which you've prophesied, bringing back the things from Yahweh's house and the entire exile community from Babel to this place. ⁷Nevertheless please listen to this word that I'm speaking in your ears and the ears of the entire people. ⁸The prophets who were before me and before you, from of old, prophesied against many countries and about great kingdoms, regarding battle, famine and epidemic. ⁹The prophet who prophesies of things going well – when the prophet's word comes about, he can be acknowledged as one whom Yahweh sent in truth.'

¹⁰Hananyah the prophet took the bar from on Yirmeyahu the prophet's neck and broke it. ¹¹Hananyah said in front of the entire people: 'Yahweh has said this: "In this way I shall break the yoke of Nebukadne'tstsar king of Babel, in yet two years, from on the neck of all the nations."'

Yirmeyahu the prophet went his way. ¹²But Yahweh's word came to Yirmeyahu after

Hananyah the prophet broke the bar from on Yirmeyahu the prophet's neck: ¹³Go and say to Hananyah, "Yahweh has said this: 'You broke bars of wood, but you're to make bars of iron.' ¹⁴Because Yahweh of Armies, Yisra'el's God, has said this: 'I'm putting an iron yoke on the neck of all these nations so that they serve Nebukadne'tstsar king of Babel. They will serve him; even the creatures of the wild I am giving him.'" ¹⁵And Yirmeyahu the prophet said to Hananyah the prophet, 'Please listen, Hananyah. Yahweh hasn't sent you, and you're one who has made this people trust in falsehood. ¹⁶Therefore Yahweh has said this: "Here am I; I'm going to send you off from on the face of the land. This year you're going to die, because you've spoken of defiance towards Yahweh."'

¹⁷Hananyah the prophet died that year in the seventh month.

### Settle down

**29** These are the words in a document that Yirmeyahu the prophet sent from Yerushalaim to the rest of the elders of the exile community, the priests, the prophets and the entire people that Nebukadne'tstsar had exiled from Yerushalaim to Babel ²(after King Yekonyah, the queen mother, the courtiers, the officials of Yehudah and Yerushalaim, the craftworkers and the smiths left Yerushalaim), ³by the hand of El'asah ben Shaphan and Gemaryah ben Hilqiyyah, whom Tsidqiyyah king of Yehudah sent to Babel to Nebukadne'tstsar king of Babel.

⁴'Yahweh of Armies, Yisra'el's God, has said this to the entire exile community that I exiled from Yerushalaim to Babel: ⁵"Build houses and live, plant gardens and eat their fruit. ⁶Take wives and have sons and daughters, take wives for your sons and give your daughters to husbands, so they may have sons and daughters. Become many there; don't become few. ⁷Seek the well-being of the town where I've exiled you; plead on its behalf with Yahweh, because in its well-being there will be well-being for you."

⁸Because Yahweh of Armies, Yisra'el's God, has said this: "Your prophets who are among you and your diviners must not deceive you.

You must not listen to your dreams that you're dreaming. [9]Because they're prophesying to you falsely in my name; I didn't send them (Yahweh's declaration)."

[10]Because Yahweh has said this: "At the bidding of the fulfilment for Babel of seventy years I shall attend to you, and act for you on my word about good things, bringing you back to this place. [11]Because I myself acknowledge the intentions that I'm formulating for you (Yahweh's declaration), intentions for your well-being and not for bad things, to give you a future, a hope. [12]You will call me and come and plead with me and I shall listen to you. [13]You will seek me and find me if you enquire of me with your entire mind, [14]and I'll be able to be found by you (Yahweh's declaration). I shall restore your fortunes, collect you from all the nations and from all the places where I've driven you (Yahweh's declaration), and bring you back to the place from where I've exiled you."

## The fate of false prophets

[15]Because you have said, "Yahweh has set up prophets for us in Babel." [16]Rather, Yahweh has said this regarding the king who sits on David's throne and the entire people that lives in this town, your brothers who haven't gone out with you into exile – [17]Yahweh of Armies has said this: "Here am I; I'm going to send off against them sword, famine and epidemic. I shall make them like horrible figs that may not be eaten because of being bad. [18]I shall pursue them with sword, famine and epidemic and make them a horror to all the kingdoms of the earth, a vow, a devastation, something to whistle at and a reviling among all the nations where I drive them out, [19]on account of the fact that they haven't listened to my words (Yahweh's declaration), in that I sent them my servants the prophets, starting early and sending. But you haven't listened (Yahweh's declaration). [20]So you people, the entire exile community that I sent off from Yerushalaim to Babel, listen to Yahweh's word."

[21]Yahweh of Armies, Yisra'el's God, has said this regarding Ah'ab ben Qolayah and regarding Tsidqiyyahu ben Ma'aseyah who are prophesying to you in my name: "Here

am I; I'm going to give them into the hand of Nebukadre'tstsar king of Babel. He will strike them down in front of your eyes. [22]A formula of slighting will be taken from them for the entire exile community of Yehudah in Babel: 'May Yahweh make you like Tsidqiyyahu and like Ah'ab, whom the king of Babel roasted in fire, [23]since they acted with villainy in Yisra'el and both committed adultery with the wives of their neighbours and spoke a word in my name that was false, which I hadn't ordered them.' I am the one who knows and who testifies (Yahweh's declaration)."

## Get a grip on that madman

[24]And regarding Shemayahu the Nehelemite you're to say: [25]"Yahweh of Armies, Yisra'el's God, has said this: 'Since you're the one who has sent documents in your name to the entire people in Yerushalaim, to Tsephanyah ben Ma'aseyah the priest and to all the priests, saying, [26]"Yahweh has made you priest instead of Yehoyada the priest, so that there might be appointees in Yahweh's house regarding anyone who's mad and is prophesying, and you're to put him into the stocks and into the neck iron: [27]so now, why have you not reprimanded Yirmeyahu from Anatot who's prophesying to you? [28]Because on account of this he's sent to us in Babel, saying, 'It will be a long time. Build houses and live [there], plant gardens and eat their fruit.'"" [29]Tsephanyah the priest read this document out in the hearing of Yirmeyahu the prophet, [30]and Yahweh's word came to Yirmeyahu: [31]"Send to the entire exile community, saying "Yahweh has said this regarding Shema'yah the Nehelemite: 'Since Shema'yah has prophesied to you and I myself hadn't sent him, and he's got you to trust in falsehood, [32]therefore Yahweh has said this: "Here am I; I'm going to attend to Shema'yah the Nehelemite and to his offspring. He won't have anyone living among this people and he won't see the good things that I'm going to do for this people (Yahweh's declaration), because he's spoken of defiance against Yahweh.""""

**30** The word that came to Yirmeyahu from Yahweh: [2]"Yahweh, Yisra'el's God, has said this: "Write down for yourself all the words that I've spoken to you in a document. ³Because there, days are coming (Yahweh's declaration) when I shall restore the fortunes of my people Yisra'el and Yehudah", Yahweh has said.'

## Is a man giving birth?

⁴So these are the words that Yahweh spoke concerning Yisra'el and Yehudah. ⁵Because Yahweh had said this:

We've heard the sound of trembling,
    dread, and lack of well-being.
⁶Please ask and see if a male is giving birth –
    why have I seen every man
With his hands on his stomach like someone
      giving birth
    and why have all faces turned to paleness?
⁷Hey, because that day is big,
    so that there has been none like it.
It will be a time of pressure for Ya'aqob,
    but from it he will find deliverance.

⁸On that day (a declaration of Yahweh of Armies):

I shall break his yoke from on your neck
    and tear off your straps.
They won't serve foreigners any more with it,
    ⁹but they will serve Yahweh their God,
And David their king,
    whom I shall set up over them.
¹⁰So you, don't be afraid, my servant Ya'aqob
    (Yahweh's declaration),
    don't shatter, Yisra'el.
Because here am I; I'm going to deliver you from
      far away,
    and your offspring from the country of their
      captivity.
Ya'aqob will again be calm,
    at peace with no one making him tremble.
¹¹Because I am with you (Yahweh's declaration) to
    deliver you,
    because I shall make an end among all the
      nations
    where I've scattered you,
Yet of you I won't make an end,
    though I discipline you in exercising
      authority
    and don't treat you as free of guilt.

¹²Because Yahweh has said this:

Your break is grave [Yerushalaim],
    your wound sickening.
¹³There's no one giving a judgement about
      treatment;
    there's no healing, growing back, for you.
¹⁴All your allies have put you out of mind,
    they don't enquire of you.
Because I struck you down with an enemy's blow,
    the discipline of someone violent,
On account of the magnitude of your
      waywardness;
    your wrongdoings were numerous.
¹⁵Why do you cry out because of your break,
    that your injury is grave?
It was on account of the magnitude of your
      waywardness,
    your wrongdoings were numerous,
    that I did these things to you.

## Compassion has the last word

¹⁶Therefore all the people who are consuming you
      will be consumed,
    and all your adversaries (all of them) will go
      into captivity.
Your despoilers will become spoil,
    and all who plundered you I'll give as plunder.
¹⁷Because I shall make restoration grow up for you
    and I shall heal you of your wounds (Yahweh's
      declaration).
Because they've called you 'Outcast',
    'It's Tsiyyon; there's no one enquiring about it.'

¹⁸Yahweh has said this:

Here am I, I'm going to restore the fortunes of
    Ya'aqob's tents,
    and on his dwellings I shall have compassion.
A town will be built on its tell;
    a citadel will sit on its authorized place.
¹⁹Thanksgiving will go out from them,
    and the sound of people having fun.
I shall make them many and they won't become
      few;
    I shall make them honourable and they won't
      become small.
²⁰Its children will be as of old,
    its assembly will stand established before me,
    and I shall attend to all its oppressors.

²¹Its august one will come from within it
   and its ruler will go out from within it.
I shall draw it near and it will come up to me,
   because who is the one
   who would have pledged his own mind to
      come up to me (Yahweh's declaration)?
²²So you will be a people for me
   and I shall be God for you.

²³There is Yahweh's hurricane,
   wrath has gone out.
A storm is raging,
   on the head of the faithless it whirls.
²⁴Yahweh's angry blazing won't turn back until he's
      acted,
   until he's implemented the strategies in his mind;
   at the end of the time you'll understand it.

# 31

At that time (Yahweh's declaration):

I shall be God for all Yisra'el's kin-groups
   and they'll be a people for me.

## Mourning becomes celebration

²Yahweh said this:

The people found grace in the wilderness,
   those who survived the sword.
As Yisra'el went to find its rest,
   ³'From afar Yahweh appeared to me.'
With permanent love I loved you;
   therefore I've drawn you out with commitment.
⁴I shall build you up again so that you are built up,
   Miss Yisra'el.
You will again deck yourself with your
      tambourine
   and go out in the dance of people having fun.
⁵You will again plant vineyards
   on Shomron's mountains;
   planters will have planted and will begin to
      have the use of them.
⁶Because there will be a day
   when lookouts call out on Ephrayim's highland,
'Set off so we may go up to Tsiyyon,
   to Yahweh our God.'

⁷Because Yahweh has said this:

Resound with rejoicing for Ya'aqob,
   bellow at the nations' crossroads.

Let them hear, exult and say,
   'Yahweh, deliver your people,
   the remainder of Yisra'el!'
⁸Here am I; I'm going to bring them
   from the northern country.
I shall collect them from the farthest reaches of
      the earth,
   among them blind and lame,
Pregnant and giving birth, together;
   a great congregation will come back here.
⁹With crying they'll come,
   and with prayers for grace I'll bring them
      along.
I shall lead them to streams of water
   by a straight way on which they won't collapse.
Because I've been a father to Yisra'el,
   and Ephrayim is my firstborn.

¹⁰Listen to Yahweh's word, you nations,
   tell of it on shores far away:
The one who scattered Yisra'el will collect it,
   and keep it like a shepherd his flock.
¹¹Because Yahweh is redeeming Ya'aqob,
   restoring it from a hand that's too strong for it.
¹²They will come and resound on Tsiyyon's
      height
   and shine because of Yahweh's good things,
Over grain and over new wine and over fresh oil,
   over newborn of flock and cattle.
Their entire being will become like a watered
      garden;
   they won't sorrow ever again.
¹³Then a girl will rejoice with dancing,
   young men and old together.
I shall turn their mourning into celebration,
   comfort them and let them rejoice after their
      grief.
¹⁴I shall saturate the priests' appetite with fat,
   and my people will be full of my good things
      (Yahweh's declaration).

## Rahel (Rachel) comforted

¹⁵Yahweh has said this:

A voice makes itself heard in Ramah,
   lamentation, bitter crying.
Rahel is crying over her children;
   she's refused to find comfort over her
      children,
   because they're not there.

¹⁶Yahweh has said this:

Restrain your voice from crying
    and your eyes from tears.
Because there will be a reward for your work
    (Yahweh's declaration);
    they will come back from the enemy's country.
¹⁷There is hope for your future (Yahweh's
    declaration);
    your children will come back to their territory.

¹⁸I've heard, I've heard Ephrayim lamenting:
    'You've disciplined me and I've undergone
        discipline
    like a calf that hadn't been trained.
Have me back and I'll turn back,
    because you are Yahweh my God.
¹⁹Because after I turned back I repented;
    after I came to acknowledge it I struck my
        thigh.
I was shamed, yes disgraced,
    because I bore the insult of my youth.'
²⁰Ephrayim is a dear son to me,
    or a child in whom I took pleasure, isn't he.
Because every time I speak against him,
    I'm so mindful of him again.
That's why my insides moan for him,
    I have deep compassion for him (Yahweh's
        declaration).

## Sour grapes

²¹Set up markers for yourself,
    put up signposts for yourself.
Give your mind to the causeway,
    the way you went.
Come back, Miss Yisra'el,
    come back to these towns of yours.
²²How long will you waver,
    daughter who's turned back?
Because Yahweh has created something new in
        the country:
    a woman surrounds a man.

²³Yahweh of Armies, Yisra'el's God, has said
this:

They will again say this thing
    in the country of Yehudah and in its towns,
    when I restore their fortunes:
'May Yahweh bless you,

faithful abode, sacred mountain.'
²⁴Yehudah and all its towns together will dwell in
    it as farmers,
    and people will go about with the flock.
²⁵Because I'm saturating the weary person
    and filling everyone who languishes.

²⁶Upon this I woke up and looked,
    and my sleep had been nice for me.

²⁷'There, days are coming (Yahweh's
declaration) when I shall sow Yisra'el's house
and Yehudah's household with human seed and
animal seed. ²⁸As I was watchful over them to
uproot, to demolish, to tear down, to obliterate
and to deal badly, so I'll be watchful over them
to build and to plant (Yahweh's declaration).'
²⁹In those days they will no longer say, 'The
parents ate sour grapes but the children's teeth
feel rough.' ³⁰Rather, each person will die for
his waywardness. Everyone who eats sour
grapes, his teeth will feel rough.

## The power of being forgiven

³¹'There, days are coming (Yahweh's
declaration) when I shall solemnize with
Yisra'el's household and with Yehudah's
household a new pact, ³²not like the pact that
I solemnized with your ancestors on the day I
took strong hold of them by the hand to get
them out of the country of Misrayim, my pact
which they contravened, though I was master
over them (Yahweh's declaration). ³³Because
this is the pact that I shall solemnize with
Yisra'el's household after those days (Yahweh's
declaration). I'm putting my instruction inside
them and I shall write it on their mind; and
I'll be God for them and they'll be a people for
me. ³⁴They will no longer teach each person
his neighbour and each his brother, saying
"Acknowledge Yahweh", because all of them
will acknowledge me from the least of them to
the biggest of them (Yahweh's declaration),
because I shall pardon their waywardness, and
their wrongdoing I shall not keep in mind any
more.'

³⁵Yahweh has said this
    (the one who gives the sun as light by day,
    the laws of the moon and stars as light by night,

Who stirs up the sea so that its waves roar –
   Yahweh of Armies is his name):

[36]If these laws move away from before me
   (Yahweh's declaration),
Yisra'el's offspring may also cease
   from being a nation for all time.

[37]Yahweh has said this:

If the heavens above may be measured
   and earth's foundations below be explored,
Also I may reject the entire offspring of Yisra'el
   for what they've done (Yahweh's declaration).

[38]There, days are coming (Yahweh's
declaration) when the town will be built up for
Yahweh from the Hanan'el Tower to the Corner
Gate, [39]and the measuring line will go out again
straight to Gareb Hill and turn to Go'ah. [40]The
entire vale (corpses and ashes) and all the open
country as far as Wadi Qidron and as far as
the Horses Gate on the east will be sacred for
Yahweh. It won't be uprooted or torn down
again ever.

*On putting your money where your
mouth is*

**32** The word that came to Yirmeyahu
from Yahweh in the tenth year of
Tsidqiyyahu king of Yehudah (it was the
eighteenth year of Nebukadre'tstsar). [2]The
king of Babel's force were then besieging
Yerushalaim, while Yirmeyahu the prophet was
confined in the prison courtyard at the king of
Yehudah's house, [3]where Tsidqiyyahu king
of Yehudah had confined him, saying 'Why
are you prophesying, "Yahweh has said this:
'Here am I; I'm going to give this town into
the hand of the king of Babel, and he'll capture
it. [4]Tsidqiyyahu king of Yehudah won't escape
from the hand of the Kasdites because he'll
definitely be given into the hand of the king of
Babel (his mouth will speak to his mouth, his
eyes will see his eyes). [5]He'll make Tsidqiyyahu
go to Babel, and he'll be there until I attend
to him (Yahweh's declaration). When you do
battle with the Kasdites, you won't succeed.'''

[6]Yirmeyahu said, 'Yahweh's word came to
me: [7]"Here, Hanam'el ben Shallum your uncle

is going to come to you, saying, 'Acquire for
yourself my field which is in Anatot, because
the ruling about restoration belongs to you, so
as to acquire it.'"

[8]So Hanam'el my uncle's son came to me in
accordance with Yahweh's word, to the prison
courtyard, and said to me, "Please acquire
my field which is in Anatot in the region of
Binyamin, because the ruling about possession
belongs to you and the restoration belongs to
you; acquire it for yourself." So I knew that it
was Yahweh's word. [9]I acquired the field from
Hanam'el my uncle's son, which is in Anatot,
and I weighed out the silver to him, seventeen
sheqels of silver. [10]I wrote in a document,
sealed it, got witnesses and weighed the silver
on scales. [11]I took the acquisition document,
the sealed one (the order and the laws) and the
open one, [12]and gave the acquisition document
to Baruk ben Nerayyah son of Mahseyah
before the eyes of Hanam'el my cousin and
of the witnesses inscribed in the acquisition
document and of all the Yehudahites sitting in
the prison courtyard.

*Are you asking something crazy of me?*

[13]I ordered Baruk before their eyes,
[14]"Yahweh of Armies, Yisra'el's God, has said
this: 'Take these documents, this acquisition
document (both the sealed one and this
open document) and put them in an earthen
container so that they may stand for a
long time.'" [15]Because Yahweh of Armies,
Yisra'el's God, has said this: "Houses, fields
and vineyards will again be acquired in this
country."

[16]I pleaded with Yahweh after giving the
acquisition document to Baruk ben Nerayyah:
[17]"Oh, Lord Yahweh! There – you made
the heavens and the earth by your great
energy and your bent arm. Nothing is too
extraordinary for you, [18]one who acts with
commitment to thousands but makes good
for the waywardness of parents into the lap
of their children after them: big strong man
God (Yahweh is his name), [19]big in counsel
and mighty in deed, you whose eyes are open
to all the ways of human beings to give to
each person in accordance with his ways and
in accordance with the fruit of his practices,

²⁰who put down signs and portents in the country of Misrayim to this day, and in Yisra'el and among humanity, and made a name for yourself this very day. ²¹You got your people Yisra'el out of the country of Misrayim with signs and portents and with a strong hand and a bent arm and with great fearfulness. ²²You gave them this country that you swore to their ancestors to give them, a country flowing with milk and syrup. ²³They came and possessed it, but they didn't listen to your voice or walk by your instruction.

All that you ordered them to do, they didn't do. So you've made all this bad fortune happen to them. ²⁴There – ramps have come to the town to capture it, and the town is being given into the hand of the Kasdites who are doing battle against it, in the face of sword, famine and epidemic. What you said has happened. There you are, looking.

²⁵And now you've said to me, Lord Yahweh, 'Acquire the field for yourself with silver and get witnesses', when this town is given into the hand of the Kasdites.'"

## Is anything too extraordinary for Yahweh?

²⁶Yahweh's word came to Yirmeyahu: ²⁷'Here am I, Yahweh, the God of all flesh. Is anything too extraordinary for me?' ²⁸Therefore Yahweh has said this: 'Here am I; I'm going to give this town into the hand of the Kasdites and into the hand of Nebukadre'tstsar king of Babel, and he will capture it. ²⁹The Kasdites who are doing battle against this town will come and set this town on fire and burn it, with the houses where people burned incense on the roofs to the Master and poured drink offerings to other gods, so as to provoke me. ³⁰Because the Yisra'elites and the Yehudahites have been doing only what is bad in my eyes from their youth, because the Yisra'elites have only been provoking me by the things that their hands made (Yahweh's declaration). ³¹Because this town became a cause of my anger and a cause of my wrath to me from the day that they built it until this day, so that I must remove it from before me, ³²on account of all the bad dealing of the Yisra'elites and the Yehudahites which they dealt so as to provoke me, they, their kings, their officials,

their priests, their prophets, Yehudah's people and Yerushalaim's inhabitants. ³³They turned their back and not their face to me; when I taught them, starting early and teaching, there were none of them listening so as to accept discipline.

³⁴They put their abominations in the house over which my name has been called out, to defile it, ³⁵and they built up the shrines of the Master in the Ben-hinnom Ravine to make their sons and their daughters pass through the fire to the Shameful King, which I didn't order them (it didn't come into my mind) to do this offensive thing, so as to cause Yehudah to do wrong.'

## Land will be acquired again

³⁶But now therefore Yahweh, Yisra'el's God, says this concerning this town of which you're saying, 'It's given into the hand of the king of Babel by sword, by famine and by epidemic': ³⁷'Here am I; I'm going to collect them from all the countries where I've driven them in my anger and wrath and great fury, and bring them back to this place and let them live with confidence. ³⁸They'll be a people for me and I'll be God for them. ³⁹I'll give them a single mind and a single way, to live in awe of me all the days, so that things will be good for them and for their children after them. ⁴⁰I shall solemnize for them a permanent pact that I won't turn back from them, and I shall do good to them. I shall put awe for me in their mind so that they don't turn away from me. ⁴¹I shall have delight towards them, in doing good to them. I shall plant them in this country in truth, with all my mind and soul.'

⁴²Because Yahweh has said this: 'As I have brought to this people all this great bad fortune, so I'm going to bring on them all the good things that I'm speaking about. ⁴³A field will be acquired in this country of which you're saying, "It's a desolation, without human being or animal; it's given into the hand of the Kasdites." ⁴⁴People will acquire fields for silver and write it in a document and seal it and get witnesses, in Binyamin's region, in Yerushalaim's environs, in Yehudah's towns, in the towns in the highland, in the towns in the foothills and in the towns in the Negeb.

Because I shall restore their fortunes (Yahweh's declaration).'

## Call me and I shall answer

**33** Yahweh's word came to Yirmeyahu a second time, while he was still detained in the prison courtyard: ²'Yahweh has said this (Yahweh is going to do it, he's going to form it, he is going to make sure of it – Yahweh is his name): ³"Call to me and I shall answer, and tell you great things, secret things that you haven't known."

⁴Because Yahweh, Yisra'el's God, has said this about the houses in this town and about the houses of Yehudah's kings that were torn down in connection with the ramps and the sword: ⁵"People are coming to do battle with the Kasdites – and to fill them with the corpses of the people that I will have struck down in my anger and my wrath, in that I've hidden my face from this town because of all their bad dealing.

⁶Here am I, I'm going to make recovery and healing grow up for it. I shall heal and reveal to them abundance of well-being and truth. ⁷I shall restore Yehudah's fortunes and Yisra'el's fortunes and build them up as before. ⁸I shall purify them from all their waywardness with which they did wrong to me, and I shall pardon all their wayward acts with which they did wrong to me and rebelled against me. ⁹For me it will mean a name to celebrate, and praise and splendour, for all the nations of the earth that hear of all the good things that I'm going to do with them, and they will be in awe and will shiver because of all the good things and all the well-being that I'm going to do for it."'

¹⁰Yahweh has said this: 'A voice will make itself heard in this place of which you're saying, "It's desolate, without human being, without animal, in Yehudah's towns and in Yerushalaim's devastated courtyards, without human being, without animal", ¹¹the voice of joy and of celebration, the voice of groom and of bride, the voice of people saying, "Confess Yahweh of Armies, because Yahweh is good, because his commitment lasts permanently", bringing a thank-offering to Yahweh's house, because I shall restore the country's fortunes as before (Yahweh has said).'

## Expect great things

¹²Yahweh of Armies has said this: 'In this place, desolate, without human being or animal, and in all its towns, there will again be an abode for shepherds resting a flock. ¹³In the mountain towns, in the lowland towns, in the Negeb towns, in Binyamin's country, in Yerushalaim's environs and in Yehudah's towns, sheep will again pass under the hands of the one counting (Yahweh has said). ¹⁴There, days are coming (Yahweh's declaration) when I shall act on the good word that I spoke concerning Yisra'el's household and Yehudah's household.

¹⁵In those days and at that time I shall grow for David a faithful branch, and he will implement authority and faithfulness in the country. ¹⁶In those days Yehudah will find deliverance, and Yerushalaim will dwell with confidence, and this is what it will be called: "Yahweh Is Our Faithfulness". ¹⁷Because Yahweh has said this: 'There will not be cut off from David someone sitting on the throne of Yisra'el's household. ¹⁸And from the priests, the Levites, there will not be cut off someone before me offering up the whole offering and burning the grain offering and performing the sacrifice, for all time.'

¹⁹Yahweh's word came to Yirmeyahu: ²⁰'Yahweh has said this: "If you people can contravene my pact about the day and my pact about the night so that there's no day and night at their time, ²¹also my pact with David my servant may be contravened so that there's no son for him reigning on his throne, and with the Levites, the priests, ministering to me. ²²As the heavens' army cannot be counted and the sea's sand cannot be measured, so I shall multiply the offspring of David my servant and the Levites who minister to me."'

²³Yahweh's word came to Yirmeyahu: ²⁴'You've seen what this people have spoken, haven't you: "The two kin-groups that Yahweh chose – he's rejected them." They've despised my people so that they are no longer a nation before them.' ²⁵Yahweh has said this: 'If I haven't laid down my pact about day and night, the laws about the heavens and the earth, ²⁶also the offspring of Ya'aqob and the offspring of David my servant may be rejected so as not to take from its offspring rulers for

the offspring of Abraham, Yitshaq [Isaac] and Ya'aqob. Because I shall restore their fortunes and have compassion on them.'

## A covenant for freedom

**34** The word that came to Yirmeyahu from Yahweh, when Nebukadre'tstsar king of Babel, and his entire force, and all the kingdoms of the earth ruled by his hand and all the peoples, were battling against Yerushalaim and against all its towns:

[2]'Yahweh, Yisra'el's God, has said this: "Go and say to Tsidqiyyahu king of Yehudah: 'Yahweh has said this: "Here am I, I'm going to give this town into the hand of the king of Babel, and he will burn it in fire. [3]You yourself won't escape from his hand, because you'll definitely be seized and be given into his hand. Your eyes will see the eyes of the king of Babel. His mouth will speak to your mouth. You will come to Babel." [4]Yet listen to Yahweh's word, Tsidqiyyahu king of Yehudah. Yahweh has said this about you: "You will not die by the sword. [5]You will die with things being well. In accordance with the burning [of incense] for your ancestors, the earlier kings who were before you, so people will burn it for you. 'Oh, lord', they will lament for you, because I myself have spoken the word (Yahweh's declaration)."''' [6]Yirmeyahu the prophet spoke all these words in Yerushalaim to Tsidqiyyahu king of Yehudah [7]while the king of Babel's force were battling against Yerushalaim and against all Yehudah's towns that were left, with Lakish and Azeqah, because these remained among Yehudah's towns as fortified towns.

[8]The word that came to Yirmeyahu from Yahweh after King Tsidqiyyahu solemnized a pact with the entire people that was in Yerushalaim to call to them for a release, [9]for each one to send off his servant and each one his maidservant, the Hebrew man and the Hebrew woman, as free persons, so that they wouldn't serve them, an individual Yehudahite his brother. [10a]All the officials and the entire people that came into the pact obeyed, by each one sending off his servant and each one his maidservant as free persons, so that they wouldn't serve them any more.

## The people who had prayed a dangerous prayer

[10b]So they obeyed and sent them off, [11]but afterwards they turned back and got back the servants and the maidservants whom they had sent off as free persons, and subjugated them as servants and maidservants.

[12]Yahweh's word came to Yirmeyahu from Yahweh: [13]'Yahweh, Yisra'el's God, has said this: "I myself solemnized a pact with your ancestors on the day I got them out of the country of Misrayim, out of a household of servants, saying, [14]'At the end of seven years you're to send off, each one, his Hebrew brother who has sold himself to you and served you for six years; you're to send him off as a free man from being with you.' Your ancestors didn't listen to me; they didn't bend their ear. [15]Just now you yourselves turned back and did what was right in my eyes by calling for a release, each one to his neighbour, and you solemnized a pact before me in the house over which my name has been called out. [16]But you've turned back and profaned my name; you've got back each one his servant and each one his maidservant whom you sent off as free persons to live their life, and you've subjugated them as servants and as maidservants to you."

[17]Therefore Yahweh has said this: "You haven't listened to me by calling for a release, each one to his brother, each to his neighbour. Here am I, I'm going to call for a release to you (Yahweh's declaration) – to sword, to epidemic and to famine. I'm going to make you a horror to all earth's kingdoms. [18]I'm going to make the people who are transgressing my pact, who haven't acted on the words in the pact that they solemnized before me, into the calf that they cut into two and passed between its parts: [19]Yehudah's officials and Yerushalaim's officials, the courtiers, the priests and the entire people of the country who passed between the parts of the calf.

## The tempting

[20]So I shall give them into the hand of their enemies, into the hand of those who seek their life. Their corpse will be food for the birds

of the heavens and for the animals of the earth. [21]Tsidqiyyahu king of Yehudah and his officials I shall give into the hand of their enemies, into the hand of those who seek their life, into the hand of the king of Babel's force who are pulling up from you. [22]Here am I, I'm going to give an order (Yahweh's declaration) and I shall bring them back to this town. They will do battle against it and capture it and burn it with fire, and Yehudah's towns I shall make a desolation without inhabitant.'"

# 35

The word that came to Yirmeyahu from Yahweh in the days of Yehoyaqim ben Yoshiyyahu king of Yehudah: [2]'Go to the Rekabites' house and speak with them, and bring them to Yahweh's house to one of the halls and get them to drink wine.'

[3]So I got Ya'azanyah ben Yirmeyahu son of Habatstsinyah, his brothers, all his sons and the entire household of the Rekabites [4]and brought them to Yahweh's house to the hall of the sons of Hanan ben Yigdalyahu, the supernatural man, which was near the officials' hall, which was above the hall of Ma'aseyahu ben Shallum, the guard of the threshold. [5]I put in front of the members of the Rekabites' household bowls full of wine and cups, and said to them, 'Drink wine.' [6]They said, 'We won't drink wine, because Yonadab ben Rekab our ancestor ordered us, "You're not to drink wine, you or your descendants permanently. [7]You're not to build a house, you're not to sow seed, you're not to plant a vineyard. They won't be for you. Rather, you're to live in tents all your days, so you may live for many days on the face of the land where you're residing."

## Witnessing by your obedience to your special vocation

[8]We've obeyed the voice of Yehonadab ben Rekab our ancestor regarding all he ordered us, not to drink wine all our days, we, our wives, our sons and our daughters, [9]and not to build houses for us to live in; and we don't have vineyard or field or seed. [10]We've lived in tents and obeyed, and acted in accordance with all that Yonadab our ancestor ordered us. [11]But when Nebukadre'tstsar king of Babel went up against the country we said, "Come on, we'll come into Yerushalaim in the face of the Kasdite force and in the face of the Aramite force." So we've lived in Yerushalaim.'

[12]Yahweh's word came to Yirmeyahu: [13]'Yahweh of Armies, Yisra'el's God, has said this: "Go and say to Yehudah's people and to Yerushalaim's inhabitants: 'Won't you accept discipline by listening to my words (Yahweh's declaration)? [14]It has been implemented, the words of Yehonadab ben Rekab which he ordered his descendants, not to drink wine. They haven't drunk up until this day because they've obeyed their ancestor's order. But I myself have spoken to you, starting early and speaking, but you haven't obeyed me. [15]I've sent to you all my servants the prophets, starting early and sending them, saying "Will you turn back, each one, from his bad way and make your deeds good, and not follow other gods so as to serve them, and you will live on the land that I gave to you and to your ancestors", but you haven't bent your ear, you haven't obeyed me. [16]Because the descendants of Yehonadab ben Rekab have implemented the order of their ancestor which he gave them, but this people – they haven't obeyed me.'"

[17]Therefore Yahweh, God of Armies, Yisra'el's God, has said this: 'Here am I, I'm going to bring to Yehudah and to all Yerushalaim's inhabitants all the bad fortune of which I spoke against them, since I spoke to them and they haven't listened, I called to them and they haven't answered.' [18]But to the household of the Rekabites Yirmeyahu said, 'Yahweh of Armies, Yisra'el's God, has said this: "Since you obeyed the order of Yehonadab your ancestor and kept all his orders and acted in accordance with all that he ordered you, [19]therefore Yahweh of Armies, Yisra'el's God, has said this: 'There shall not be cut off for Yonadab ben Rekab someone standing before me for all time.'"

## The scroll

# 36

In the fourth year of Yehoyaqim ben Yoshiyyahu king of Yehudah, this word came to Yirmeyahu from Yahweh: [2]'Get yourself a document scroll and write in it all the words that I've spoken to you about Yisra'el, about Yehudah and about all the nations from the day I spoke to you (from the days of Yoshiyyahu) until this day. [3]Perhaps Yehudah's household will listen to all the bad things that I'm intending to do to them, so they may turn back each one from his bad way and I may pardon their waywardness and their wrongdoing.'

⁴So Yirmeyahu called Baruk ben Neriyyah, and Baruk wrote from Yirmeyahu's mouth all Yahweh's words that he'd spoken to him, on a document scroll. ⁵Yirmeyahu ordered Baruk, 'I'm under constraint; I can't come to Yahweh's house. ⁶You're to come and read out, in the scroll that you've written from my mouth, the words from Yahweh, in the ears of the people at Yahweh's house on a fast day, and you're also to read them in the ears of all Yehudah who come from their towns. ⁷Perhaps their prayer for grace will fall before Yahweh and they'll turn back each one from his bad way, because Yahweh's anger and wrath are great, of which he's spoken concerning this people.'

⁸Baruk ben Neriyyah acted in accordance with all that Yirmeyahu the prophet ordered him, by reading out in the scroll Yahweh's words at Yahweh's house. ⁹In the fifth year of Yehoyaqim ben Yoshiyyahu king of Yehudah, in the ninth month, they called for a fast before Yahweh, the entire people in Yerushalaim and the entire people coming from Yehudah's towns into Yerushalaim. ¹⁰Baruk read in the scroll Yirmeyahu's words at Yahweh's house in the hall of Gemaryahu ben Shaphan the secretary, in the upper courtyard at the entrance of the new gateway of Yahweh's house, in the ears of the entire people.

## The bold miscalculation

¹¹Mikayehu ben Gemaryahu son of Shaphan listened to all Yahweh's words from the scroll, ¹²and went down to the king's house to the secretary's hall. There, all the officials were sitting there: Elishama the secretary, Delayahu ben Shema'yahu, Elnatan ben Akbor, Gemaryahu ben Shaphan, Tsidqiyyahu ben Hananyahu and all the officials. ¹³Mikayehu told them all the words that he'd heard when Baruk read out in the document in the people's ears.

¹⁴All the officials sent Yehudi ben Netanyahu son of Shelemyahu son of Kushi to Baruk, saying, 'The scroll in which you read out in the people's ears – will you get it in your hand and get going.' So Baruk ben Nirayyahu got the scroll in his hand and came to them. ¹⁵They said to him, 'Sit down, please, and read it out in our ears.' Baruk read it out in their ears. ¹⁶When they heard all the words, they were fearful, each towards his neighbour. They said to Baruk, 'We must definitely tell the king all these words.' ¹⁷They asked Baruk, 'Please tell us how you wrote all these words from his mouth.' ¹⁸Baruk said to them, 'From his mouth he called out to me all these words and I was writing them in the document in ink.' ¹⁹The officials said to Baruk, 'Go hide, you and Yirmeyahu. No one is to know where you are.' ²⁰They came to the king in the courtyard; the scroll they deposited in Elishama the secretary's hall, but they told in the king's ears all the words.

²¹The king sent Yehudi to get the scroll, and he got it from Elishama the secretary's hall. Yehudi read it out in the king's ears and in the ears of all the officials standing in attendance on the king. ²²The king was sitting in the winter house (in the ninth month) with the firepot before him, burning. ²³As Yehudi read out three or four columns, he would cut it with a secretary's knife and throw it into the fire that was in the firepot until the entire scroll was finished in the fire that was in the firepot.

## Yet more words

²⁴So they weren't fearful and they didn't tear their clothes, the king and all his servants who heard all these words, ²⁵even though Elnatan, Delayyahu and Gemaryahu entreated the king not to burn the scroll; he didn't listen to them. ²⁶The king ordered Yerahme'el the king's son, Serayahu ben Azri'el and Shelemyahu ben Abde'el to get Baruk the secretary and Yirmeyahu the prophet, but Yahweh hid them. ²⁷Yahweh's word came to Yirmeyahu after the king burned the scroll with the words that Baruk wrote from Yirmeyahu's mouth: ²⁸'Get yourself yet another scroll, and write on it all the earlier words that were on the earlier scroll that Yehoyaqim king of Yehudah burned. ²⁹About Yehoyaqim king of Yehudah you're to say, "Yahweh has said this: 'You – you burned this scroll, saying, "Why have you written on it, 'The king of Babel will definitely come and devastate this country and eliminate from it human beings and animals'?" ³⁰Therefore

Yahweh has said this about Yehoyaqim king of Yehudah: 'He will not have someone sitting on David's throne, and his corpse will be thrown out to the heat by day and to the cold by night. <sup>31</sup>I shall attend to their waywardness for him, for his offspring and for his servants, and bring on them, on Yerushalaim's inhabitants and on Yehudah's people all the bad fortune of which I spoke in connection with them, but they didn't listen."'"

<sup>32</sup>So Yirmeyahu got another scroll and gave it to Baruk ben Neriyyahu the secretary, and he wrote on it from the mouth of Yirmeyahu all the words on the document that Yehoyaqim king of Yehudah burned in the fire. There were also added to them many words like them.

## The king who vacillates

**37** King Tsidqiyyahu ben Yoshiyyahu became king in place of Konyahu ben Yehoyaqim; Nebukadre'tstsar king of Babel made him king in the country of Yehudah. <sup>2</sup>He didn't listen, he or his servants or the people of the country, to Yahweh's words which he spoke by means of Yirmeyahu the prophet.

<sup>3</sup>But King Tsidqiyyahu sent Yehukal ben Shelemyah and Tsephanyahu ben Ma'aseyah the priest to Yirmeyahu the prophet to say, 'Will you plead on our behalf with Yahweh our God?' (<sup>4</sup>when Yirmeyahu was coming in and going out among the people and they hadn't put him into a place of confinement, <sup>5</sup>and when Par'oh's force had come out from Misrayim, and the Kasdites who were besieging Yerushalaim had heard the report about them and had pulled up from Yerushalaim).

<sup>6</sup>Yahweh's word came to Yirmeyahu the prophet: <sup>7</sup>'Yahweh, Yisra'el's God, has said this: "This is what you people should say to the king of Yehudah who's sending you to me to enquire of me: 'There, Par'oh's force that are coming out to you to help you will go back to their country, to Misrayim. <sup>8</sup>The Kasdites will come back and will do battle against this town, capture it and burn it in fire.'"

<sup>9</sup>Yahweh has said this: "Don't deceive yourselves by saying, 'The Kasdites will certainly go from against us', because they won't go. <sup>10</sup>If you struck down the entire force of the Kasdites who are doing battle with you,

and people who were thrust through remained among them, each in his tent, they'd get up and burn this town in fire."'

## Until the bread runs out

<sup>11</sup>When the Kasdite force pulled up from Yerushalaim in the face of Par'oh's force, <sup>12</sup>Yirmeyahu went out from Yerushalaim to go to the region of Binyamin to divide a share there among the people. <sup>13</sup>When he was at the Binyamin Gate, a master over the appointment was there; his name was Yir'iyyah ben Shelemyah son of Hananyah. He seized Yirmeyahu the prophet, saying, 'You're going over to the Kasdites.' <sup>14</sup>Yirmeyahu said, 'It's a falsehood. I'm not going over to the Kasdites', but he didn't listen to him. Yir'iyyah seized Yirmeyahu and brought him to the officials. <sup>15</sup>The officials were furious at Yirmeyahu, struck him down and put him in the prison house, the house of Yehonatan the secretary, because they had made it into the jail.

<sup>16</sup>When Yirmeyahu had come to the cistern house and to the cells, and Yirmeyahu had lived there for many days, <sup>17</sup>King Tsidqiyyahu sent and got him, and the king asked him in his house in secret, 'Is there a word from Yahweh?' Yirmeyahu said, 'There is', and said, 'You'll be given into the hand of the king of Babel.' <sup>18</sup>And Yirmeyahu said to King Tsidqiyyahu, 'What have I done wrong to you, to your servants and to this people, that you've put me into the jail? <sup>19</sup>And where are your prophets who prophesied to you, "The king of Babel won't come against you or against this country"? <sup>20</sup>So now listen please, my lord king; may my plea for grace please fall to you. Don't send me back to the house of Yehonatan the secretary, so I don't die there.' <sup>21</sup>King Tsidqiyyahu gave an order and they placed Yirmeyahu in the prison courtyard, and gave him a loaf of bread per day from the bakers' street until all the bread came to an end from the town. So Yirmeyahu lived in the prison courtyard.

## The king can't prevail

**38** Shephatyah ben Mattan, Gedalyahu ben Pashhur, Yukal ben Shelemyahu and Pashhur ben Malkiyyah heard the words that Yirmeyahu was speaking to the entire people: ²'Yahweh has said this: "The person who lives in this town will die by sword, by famine or by epidemic, but the one who goes out to the Kasdites will live. His life will be his as a trophy. He'll live." ³Yahweh has said this: "This town will certainly be given into the hand of the king of Babel's force and he'll capture it."'

⁴The officials said to the king, 'This man should please be put to death, because by this means he's slackening the hands of the men of battle who remain in this town, and the hands of the entire people, by speaking to them in accordance with these words, because this man isn't seeking the well-being of this people, but something bad.' ⁵King Tsidqiyyahu said, 'There, he's in your hand, because the king can't prevail against you in a thing.' ⁶So they got Yirmeyahu and threw him into the cistern of Malkiyyahu the king's son, which was in the prison courtyard. They put Yirmeyahu in with ropes. There was no water in the cistern, but only mud. So Yirmeyahu sank into the mud.

⁷Ebed-melek the Kushite, a courtier who was in the king's household, heard that they'd put Yirmeyahu in the cistern. The king was sitting at the Binyamin Gate, ⁸so Ebed-melek went out from the king's house and spoke to the king: ⁹'My lord king, these men have dealt badly in all they've done to Yirmeyahu the prophet, whom they've thrown into the pit. He's dead in this place from hunger, because there's no more bread in the town.' ¹⁰So the king ordered Ebed-melek the Kushite, 'Get thirty people from here with you and pull Yirmeyahu the prophet up from the cistern before he dies.'

## The rescue

¹¹Ebed-melek got the men with him and came to the king's house to below the treasury. He got from there old rags and old clothes and sent them to Yirmeyahu in the pit by the ropes. ¹²Ebed-melek the Kushite said to Yirmeyahu, 'Put the old rags and clothes under your armpits, please, under the ropes.' Yirmeyahu did so. ¹³They drew Yirmeyahu up by the ropes and got him up from the cistern. So Yirmeyahu lived in the prison courtyard.

¹⁴King Tsidqiyyahu sent and got Yirmeyahu the prophet to him at the third entrance in Yahweh's house. The king said to Yirmeyahu, 'I'm going to ask you something; don't hide anything from me.' ¹⁵Yirmeyahu said to Tsidqiyyahu, 'When I tell you, won't you definitely put me to death? And when I counsel you, you won't listen to me.' ¹⁶King Tsidqiyyahu swore to Yirmeyahu in secret, 'As Yahweh lives, who made this life for us, if I put you to death or if I give you into the hand of these people who are seeking your life . . .'

¹⁷So Yirmeyahu said to Tsidqiyyahu, 'Yahweh, God of Armies, Yisra'el's God, has said this: "If you do go out to the king of Babel's officers, you yourself will live, and this town won't be burned with fire. You and your household will live. ¹⁸But if you don't go out to the king of Babel's officers, this town will be given into the hand of the Kasdites. They will burn it with fire and you won't escape from their hand."' ¹⁹King Tsidqiyyahu said to Yirmeyahu, 'I'm afraid of the Yehudahites who've submitted to the Kasdites, in case they give me over into their hand and they deal abusively with me.'

## Don't tell anyone

²⁰Yirmeyahu said, 'They won't give you over. Please listen to Yahweh's voice, to what I'm speaking to you, so he may do good things for you and you yourself may live. ²¹But if you refuse to go out, this is the word that Yahweh has shown me. ²²There – all the women who remain in the king of Yehudah's household are going to be taken out to the officers of the king of Babel, and there, they're going to say,

The people who were your friends
    have incited you and prevailed over you.
Your feet are stuck in the mire;
    they've turned away back.

²³They're going to take out all your women and children to the Kasdites, and you won't escape from their hand, because you'll be seized by the king of Babel's hand, and you will burn this town in fire.'

²⁴Tsidqiyyahu said to Yirmeyahu, 'No one is to know of these words, and you won't die.

<sup>25</sup>But when the officials hear that I've spoken with you and they come to you and say to you, "Tell us, please, what you spoke to the king. Don't hide it from us and we won't put you to death. And what did the king speak to you?", <sup>26</sup>you're to say to them, "I was letting my plea for grace fall before the king, not to send me back to the house of Yehonatan to die there."'

<sup>27</sup>All the officials came to Yirmeyahu and asked him, and he told them in accordance with all these words that the king had ordered him. So they left off from speaking with him, because the thing hadn't been audible. <sup>28a</sup>Yirmeyahu lived in the prison courtyard until the day when Yerushalaim was captured.

## The grimmest scene in the First Testament?

<sup>28b</sup>When Yerushalaim was captured.

**39** In the ninth year of Tsidqiyyahu king of Yehudah, in the tenth month, Nebukadre'tstsar king of Babel and his entire force came to Yerushalaim and besieged it. <sup>2</sup>In the eleventh year of Tsidqiyyahu, in the fourth month, on the ninth of the month, the town was broken open. <sup>3</sup>All the officers of the king of Babel came and sat in the Middle Gate – Nergal Sar-etser, Samgar-nebu, Sar-sekim the head courtier, Nergal Sar-etser the head official and all the remainder of the king of Babel's officers.

<sup>4</sup>When Tsidqiyyahu king of Yehudah and all the men of battle saw them, they fled. They went out by night from the town by the king's garden road, through the gateway between the double wall. He went out on the steppe road. <sup>5</sup>The Kasdite force pursued after them and overtook Tsidqiyyahu in the Yeriho [Jericho] steppes. They captured him and took him up to Nebukadre'tstsar king of Babel at Riblah in the country of Hamat, and he announced rulings with him. <sup>6</sup>The king of Babel slaughtered Tsidqiyyahu's sons at Riblah before his eyes, and the king of Babel slaughtered all the important people in Yehudah. <sup>7</sup>He blinded Tsidqiyyahu's eyes and shackled him in copper chains to bring him to Babel.

<sup>8</sup>The king's house and the people's housing the Kasdites burned in fire, and Yerushalaim's walls they demolished. <sup>9</sup>The rest of the people who remained in the town and the people who had submitted to him and the rest of the people who remained, Nebuzar'adan the head of the guards took into exile to Babel. <sup>10</sup>Some of the people who were poor, who had nothing, Nebuzar'adan the head of the guards left remaining in the country of Yehudah, and gave them vineyards and fields on that day.

## What will happen to Ebed-melek?

<sup>11</sup>Nebukadre'tstsar king of Babel gave order regarding Yirmeyahu by means of Nebuzar'adan the head of the guards: <sup>12</sup>'Get him and keep your eyes on him and don't do anything bad to him. Rather, as he speaks to you, so do with him.' <sup>13</sup>Then sent Nebuzar'adan the head of the guards, Nebushazban the head courtier, Nergal Sar-etser the head officer and all the heads of the king of Babel – <sup>14</sup>they sent and got Yirmeyahu from the prison courtyard and gave him over to Gedalyahu ben Ahiqam son of Shaphan to let him go out to a house. So he lived among the people.

<sup>15</sup>A word from Yahweh had come to Yirmeyahu while he was confined in the prison courtyard: <sup>16</sup>'Go and say to Ebed-melek the Kushite: "Yahweh of Armies, Yisra'el's God, has said this: 'Here am I, I'm going to bring about my words regarding this town for bad fortune and not for good. They will come about before you on that day. <sup>17</sup>But I shall rescue you on that day (Yahweh's declaration) and you will not be given into the hand of the people that you're afraid of. <sup>18</sup>Because I shall definitely save you. You will not fall by the sword. Your life will be yours as a trophy, because you've relied on me (Yahweh's declaration).'"'

**40** The word that came to Yirmeyahu from Yahweh after Nebuzar'adan the head of the guards sent him off from The Height, where he'd taken him (he was shackled in chains) among the exile community from Yerushalaim and Yehudah, who were being exiled to Babel. <sup>2</sup>The head of the guards took Yirmeyahu and said to him, 'It was Yahweh your God who spoke of this bad fortune for this place, <sup>3</sup>and he's brought it about. Yahweh has done as he spoke, because you people did wrong to Yahweh and didn't listen to his voice. So this thing has happened to you.

## What will happen to Yirmeyahu?

⁴But now, here: I'm releasing you yourself today from the chains that are on your hand. If it's good in your eyes to come with me to Babel, come, and I'll have my eye on you. But if it's bad in your eyes to come with me to Babel, leave off. Look, all the country is before you. Regarding what is good and what is right in your eyes to go, go there.' ⁵Still he wouldn't go back. 'Or go back to Gedalyah ben Ahiqam son of Shaphan whom the king of Babel has appointed over Yehudah's towns and live with him among the people. Or go anywhere that's right in your eyes to go.' The head of the guards gave him provisions and goods and sent him off. ⁶So Yirmeyahu came to Gedalyah ben Ahiqam at The Watchtower and lived with him among the people who remained in the country.

⁷All the officers in the forces that were in the open country, they and their men, heard that the king of Babel had appointed Gedalyahu ben Ahiqam over the country and that he'd appointed with him the men, the women, the children and those of the poor people of the country who hadn't been exiled to Babel. ⁸They came to Gedalyah at The Watchtower – Yishma'e'l ben Netanyah, Yohanan and Yonatan the sons of Qareah, Serayah ben Tanhumet, the sons of Ephay the Netophatite, and Yezanyahu the son of the Ma'akatite, they and their men. ⁹Gedalyahu ben Ahiqam son of Shaphan let it be heard by them and by their men, 'Don't be afraid of serving the Kasdites. Go back into the country and serve the king of Babel and things will be good for you. ¹⁰I, here am I, I'm going to live in The Watchtower to serve before the Kasdites who come to us. You, gather up wine, summer fruit and oil, put them in your containers and live in the towns that you'll have seized.'

## The fugitives return

¹¹All the Yehudahites who were in Mo'ab, among the Ammonites, in Edom, and those who were in all the countries also heard that the king of Babel had granted a remainder group to Yehudah and that he'd appointed over them Gedalyahu ben Ahiqam son of Shaphan, ¹²and all the Yehudahites came back from all

the places where they had been driven. They came to the country of Yehudah to Gedalyahu at The Watchtower and gathered up wine and summer fruit, very much.

¹³Yohanan ben Qareah and all the officers in the forces that were in the open country came to Gedalyahu at The Watchtower ¹⁴and said to him, 'Do you actually know that Ba'alis king of the Ammonites has sent Yishma'e'l ben Netanyah to strike down your life?' But Gedalyahu ben Ahiqam didn't believe them. ¹⁵Yohanan ben Qareah said to Gedalyahu in secret at The Watchtower, 'I shall go, please, and strike down Yishma'e'l ben Netanyah, and no one will know. Why should he strike down your life and scatter all Yehudah who've collected to you, and the remainder of Yehudah perish?' ¹⁶But Gedalyahu ben Ahiqam said to Yohanan ben Qareah, 'Don't do this thing, because you're speaking falsehood about Yishma'e'l.'

**41** But in the seventh month Yishma'e'l ben Netanyah son of Elishama, of the royal line, and the king's commanders and ten men with him, came to Gedalyahu ben Ahiqam at The Watchtower. They ate bread there together at The Watchtower, ²and Yishma'e'l ben Netanyah and the ten men who were with him got up and struck down Gedalyahu ben Ahiqam son of Shaphan with the sword and put him to death, the man whom the king of Babel had appointed over the country. ³And all the Yehudahites who were with him (with Gedalyahu at The Watchtower) and the Kasdites who were present there, the men of battle, Yishma'e'l struck down.

## The luckless penitents

⁴On the second day after they put Gedalyahu to death, when no one knew, ⁵some people came from Shekem, Shiloh and Shomron, eighty people, shaved bare, clothes torn, bodies gashed, grain offering and incense in their hand to bring to Yahweh's house. ⁶Yishma'e'l ben Netanyah went out from The Watchtower to meet them, crying as he went. When he reached them, he said to them, 'Come to Gedalyahu ben Ahiqam.'

⁷When they came inside the town Yishma'e'l ben Netanyah slaughtered them, into a cistern,

he and the men who were with him. ⁸But ten people were present among them who said to Yishma'e'l, 'Don't put us to death, because we have stores in the open country, grain, barley, oil and syrup.' So he held back and didn't put them to death among their brothers.

⁹The cistern where Yishma'e'l threw all the corpses of the people whom he struck down by the side of Gedalyahu, it was the one that King Asa had made on account of Ba'asha king of Yisra'el; Yishma'e'l ben Netanyah filled it with people who had been run through.

¹⁰Yishma'e'l took captive all the remainder of the company that was at The Watchtower, the king's daughters and all the people who had remained at The Watchtower over whom Nebuzar'adan the head of the guards had appointed Gedalyahu ben Ahiqam. Yishma'e'l ben Netanyah took them captive and went to cross over to the Ammonites. ¹¹But Yohanan ben Qareah and all the officers in the forces that were with him heard all the bad things that Yishma'e'l ben Netanyah had done, ¹²and they got all the people and went to do battle with Yishma'e'l ben Netanyah. They found him by the great pool that's at Gib'on.

¹³When all the company that was with Yishma'e'l saw Yohanan ben Qareah and all the officers in the forces that were with him, they rejoiced. ¹⁴All the company that Yishma'e'l had taken captive from The Watchtower turned round and went back and went to Yohanan ben Qareah.

## Turning to God?

¹⁵But Yishma'e'l ben Netanyah, with eight men, escaped from Yohanan and went to the Ammonites. ¹⁶Yohanan ben Qareah and all the officers in the forces that were with him took all the remainder of the company that he brought back from being with Yishma'e'l ben Netanyah from The Watchtower, after he struck down Gedalyah ben Ahiqam (men, men of battle, women, children and courtiers, whom he had brought back from Gib'on). ¹⁷They went and lived at Kimham Khan which is near Bet Lehem, going so as to come to Misrayim ¹⁸on account of the Kasdites, because they were afraid of them because Yishma'e'l ben Netanyah had struck down Gedalyahu ben Ahiqam

whom the king of Babel had appointed over the country.

**42** All the officers in the forces, Yohanan ben Qareah, Yezanyah ben Hosha'yah and the entire company, big and small, came up ²and said to Yirmeyahu the prophet, 'May our prayer for grace please fall before you; plead on our behalf with Yahweh your God on behalf of all this remainder, because we remain a few out of many, as your eyes see us. ³May Yahweh your God tell us the way by which we should go and what we should do.'

⁴Yirmeyahu the prophet said to them, 'I've listened. Here am I, I'm going to plead with Yahweh your God in accordance with your words. Everything that Yahweh will answer you, I shall tell you. I won't withhold anything from you.' ⁵They themselves said to Yirmeyahu, 'May Yahweh be a true and truthful witness against us, if we don't act in accordance with everything that Yahweh your God sends you for us. ⁶Whether good or bad, we'll listen to the voice of Yahweh our God to whom we're sending you, for the sake of what will be good for us when we listen to the voice of Yahweh our God.'

## Stay, don't go

⁷At the end of ten days Yahweh's word came to Yirmeyahu. ⁸He called to Yohanan ben Qareah, to all the officers in the forces that were with him and to the entire company, to big and small, ⁹and said to them: 'Yahweh, Yisra'el's God, to whom you sent me to let your prayer for grace fall before him, has said this: ¹⁰"If you again live in this country, I will build you up and not tear you down, I will plant you and not uproot, because I regret the bad things that I did to you. ¹¹Don't be afraid of the king of Babel, of whom you are afraid; don't be afraid of him (Yahweh's declaration) because I am with you to deliver you and to rescue you from his hand. ¹²I shall give you compassion, and he will have compassion towards you and take you back to your land."

¹³But if you're going to say, "We won't live in this country" (so as not to listen to Yahweh your God's voice), ¹⁴saying, "No, rather we'll come to the country of Misrayim, where we won't see battle or hear the sound of the

horn or be hungry for bread, and live there":
¹⁵now therefore listen to Yahweh's word, you
remainder of Yehudah. Yahweh of Armies,
Yisra'el's God, has said this: "If you do set your
faces to come to Misrayim, and you come to
reside there, ¹⁶the sword that you're afraid
of will overtake you there in the country of
Misrayim and the famine that you fear will
stick close to you there in Misrayim, and you'll
die there. ¹⁷All the people who set their faces
to come to Misrayim to reside there will die by
sword, by famine or by epidemic. There won't
be anyone surviving or escaping in the face of
the bad fate that I'm going to bring upon you."

### An ambassador in chains

¹⁸Because Yahweh of Armies, Yisra'el's God,
has said this: "As my anger and my wrath
poured out on Yerushalaim's inhabitants, so my
wrath will pour out on you when you come to
Misrayim. You'll become a vow, a devastation,
a slight and a reviling, and you won't again
see this place." ¹⁹Yahweh has spoken against
you, remainder of Yehudah. Don't come to
Misrayim. Acknowledge clearly that I've
testified against you this day. ²⁰Because you
were deceitful in your entire beings when
you yourselves sent me to Yahweh your God,
saying "Plead on our behalf to Yahweh our
God, and in accordance with all that Yahweh
our God says, so tell us and we will act." ²¹I've
told you this day, but you haven't listened to
the voice of Yahweh your God, even regarding
anything with which he sent me to you. ²²So
now you must really acknowledge that you'll
die by sword, by famine or by epidemic in the
place where you want to come to reside.'

**43** When Yirmeyahu finished speaking
to the entire people all the words of
Yahweh their God with which Yahweh their
God had sent him to them, all these words,
²Azaryah ben Hosha'yah, Yohanan ben Qareah
and all the assertive people were saying to
Yirmeyahu, 'You're speaking falsehood.
Yahweh our God hasn't sent you to say, "You're
not to come to Misrayim to reside there."
³Because Baruk ben Neriyyah is inciting you
against us in order to give us into the hand of
the Kasdites to put us to death or take us into
exile in Babel.'

⁴So Yohanan ben Qareah, all the officers in
the forces and the entire people didn't listen
to Yahweh's voice so as to stay in the country
of Yehudah. ⁵Yohanan ben Qareah and all the
officers in the forces took the entire remainder
of Yehudah that had come back to reside in
the country of Yehudah from all the nations
where they had been driven – ⁶men, women,
children, the king's daughters and every person
whom Nebuzar'adan the head of the guards
had set down with Gedalyahu ben Ahiqam son
of Shaphan, and Yirmeyahu the prophet and
Baruk ben Neriyyahu. ⁷ªThey came to Misrayim
because they didn't listen to Yahweh's voice.

### No escape from Nebukadre'tstsar

⁷ᵇThey came as far as Tahpanhes, ⁸and
Yahweh's word came to Yirmeyahu at
Tahpanhes: ⁹"Take some big stones in your
hand and bury them in clay on the pavement
that's at the entrance to Par'oh's house at
Tahpanhes, before the eyes of the Yehudahites.
¹⁰You're to say to them, "Yahweh of Armies,
Yisra'el's God, has said this: 'Here am I, I'm
going to send and get Nebukadre'tstsar king
of Babel my servant, and I shall set his throne
above these stones (that I've buried) and he will
spread his canopy over them. ¹¹He will come
and strike down the country of Misrayim:
the people destined for death, to death, the
people destined for captivity, to captivity,
the people destined for the sword, to the sword.
¹²I shall set fire to the houses of the gods of
Misrayim and he will burn them and take them
captive. He'll delouse the country of Misrayim
as a shepherd delouses his coat, and he'll go out
from there with things being well. ¹³He'll break
up the columns in Sun House which is in the
country of Misrayim, and he'll burn the houses
of Misrayim's gods with fire.'"'

**44** The word that came to Yirmeyahu
regarding all the Yehudahites who
were living in the country of Misrayim,
living in Migdol, in Tahpanhes, in Memphis
and in the country of Patros. ²'Yahweh of
Armies, Yisra'el's God, has said this: "You've
seen all the bad fortune that I've brought
on Yerushalaim and on all Yehudah's towns.
There they are, a waste this day, with no one
living in them, ³in the face of the bad dealing

that they did, so as to provoke me by going to burn incense to serve other gods that they hadn't acknowledged – they or you or your ancestors. [4]I sent to you all my servants the prophets, starting early and sending them, to say, 'Please don't do this offensive thing, to which I am hostile.' [5]But they didn't listen, they didn't bend their ear, so as to turn back from their bad dealing, so as not to burn incense to other gods. [6]So my wrath and my anger poured out and burned against Yehudah's towns and against Yerushalaim's streets, and they've become a waste, a desolation, this very day."

## Things can't get worse, can they?

[7]So now, Yahweh, God of Armies, Yisra'el's God, has said this: "Why are you going to do something that's so bad for yourselves, by cutting off for you man and woman, child and infant, from within Yehudah, so as not to leave a remainder for you, [8]by provoking me by the practices of your hands, by burning incense to other gods in the country of Misrayim to which you're coming to reside there, in order to cut them off for you and in order to become a slighting and a reviling among all the nations on earth? [9]Have you put out of mind the bad dealings of your ancestors, the bad dealings of Yehudah's kings, the bad dealings of its wives, your own bad dealings and the bad dealings of your wives, which they did in the country of Yehudah and in Yerushalaim's streets? [10]They were not crushed until this day, they didn't live in awe, they didn't walk by my instruction and by my laws that I put before you and before your ancestors."

[11]Therefore Yahweh of Armies, Yisra'el's God, has said this. "Here am I, I'm going to set my face against you for bad fortune and to cut off all Yehudah. [12]I shall take the remainder of Yehudah who have set their face to come to the country of Misrayim to reside there, and they will all come to an end in the country of Misrayim. They will fall by the sword and come to an end by famine. Big and small, by sword and by famine they will die. They will become a vow, a devastation, a slighting and a reviling. [13]I shall attend to the people living in the country of Misrayim as I attended to Yerushalaim, by sword, by famine and by epidemic. [14]There will

be no escapee or survivor of the remainder of Yehudah who are coming to reside there in the country of Misrayim, or to go back to the country of Yehudah when they are lifting up their longing to go back to live there, because they won't go back (except escapees).'"

## No, no turning to God

[15]All the men who knew that their wives burned incense to other gods, and all the wives standing by, a big congregation, and the entire company who were living in the country of Misrayim at Patros, answered Yirmeyahu, [16]'The word that you've spoken to us in Yahweh's name – we aren't listening to you. [17]Rather, we'll definitely act on every word that's gone out of our mouth, burning incense to the Queen of Heaven and pouring libations to her, as we and our ancestors, our kings and our officials, did in Yehudah's towns and in Yerushalaim's streets, and had our fill of bread and were finding things good, and saw no bad fortune. [18]But from when we left off burning incense to the Queen of Heaven and pouring libations to her, we've lacked everything and we've come to an end by sword and by famine. [19]And when we were burning incense to the Queen of Heaven and pouring libations to her, was it without our husbands that we made cakes to image her and poured libations to her?'

[20]Yirmeyahu said to the entire company, to the men, to the women and to the entire company who were giving him an answer: [21]'The incense you burned in Yehudah's towns and in Yerushalaim's streets, you and your ancestors, your kings, your officials and the people of the country – hasn't Yahweh been mindful of them and brought them to mind? [22]Yahweh could no longer bear it, in the face of the bad nature of your practices, in the face of the offensive acts that you committed, so that the country became a waste and a devastation and a slighting, so that there's no inhabitant, this very day. [23]In the face of the way you burned incense and in that you did wrong to Yahweh and didn't listen to Yahweh's voice and didn't walk by his instruction, his laws and his affirmations, that's why this bad fate has happened to you this very day.'

²⁴Yirmeyahu said to the entire company and to all the women, 'Listen to Yahweh's word, all of Yehudah in the country of Misrayim. ²⁵ᵃYahweh of Armies, Yisra'el's God, has said this: "You and your wives – you've spoken by your mouth and with your hands you've fulfilled it, saying 'We'll definitely act on our vows that we made, to burn incense to the Queen of Heaven and pour libations to her.'

## A promise for Baruk

²⁵ᵇYou may indeed implement your pledges. You may indeed act upon your pledges." ²⁶Therefore listen to Yahweh's word, all Yehudah who live in the country of Misrayim. 'Here am I: I am swearing by my great name (Yahweh has said), if my name will any more be called out in the mouth of anyone from Yehudah, saying 'As the Lord Yahweh lives', in all the country of Misrayim. ²⁷Here am I: I'm going to watch over them for bad things, not for good things. They will come to an end, every individual from Yehudah who's in the country of Misrayim, by sword and by famine, until they're finished off. ²⁸The people who escape the sword will go back from the country of Misrayim to the country of Yehudah few in number, and all the remainder of Yehudah who are coming to the country of Misrayim to reside there will acknowledge whose word will be implemented, mine or theirs. ²⁹This will be the sign for you (Yahweh's declaration) that I'm going to attend to you in this place, so that you may acknowledge that my words against you for bad fortune will indeed be implemented. ³⁰Yahweh has said this: 'Here am I; I'm going to give Par'oh Hophra king of Misrayim into the hand of his enemies and into the hand of the people who are seeking his life, as I gave Tsidqiyyahu king of Yehudah into the hand of Nebukadre'tstsar king of Babel his enemy and one seeking his life.'"

**45** The word that Yirmeyahu the prophet spoke to Baruk ben Neriyyah when he wrote these words in a document from Yirmeyahu's mouth in the fourth year of Yehoyaqim ben Yoshiyyahu king of Yehudah: ²"Yahweh, Yisra'el's God, has said this to you, Baruk: ³"You said, 'Oh, me, please, because

Yahweh has added sorrow to my pain. I'm weary with my groaning. I haven't found a settled place.'" ⁴You're to say to him, "Yahweh has said this: 'Here, what I built, I'm tearing down; what I planted, I'm uprooting (i.e. the entire country). ⁵You, do you seek big things for yourself? Don't seek them, because here am I, I'm going to bring bad fortune on all flesh (Yahweh's declaration), but I shall give you your life as a trophy in all the places where you go.'"

## Par'oh full of talk

**46** Things that came as Yahweh's word to Yirmeyahu the prophet about the nations.

²Regarding Misrayim.

About the force of Par'oh Neko king of Misrayim, which was at the River Euphrates at Karkemish, which Nebukadre'tstsar king of Babel struck down in the fourth year of Yehoyaqim ben Yoshiyyahu king of Yehudah:

³Get ready hand-shield and body-shield;
  go up to battle!
⁴Harness the horses;
  get up, cavalry!
Take your position with your helmets,
  polish lances, put on armour!
⁵Why have I seen – they're shattered,
  they're turning back!
Their strong men are struck down, they've fled,
    fled,
  they haven't turned round, terror is all round
    (Yahweh's declaration).
⁶The swift is not to flee,
  the strong man is not to escape.
To the north, by the side of the River Euphrates,
  they've collapsed and fallen.

⁷Who is this rises like the Ye'or,
  like streams whose water surges?
⁸It's Misrayim that rises like the Ye'or
  and like streams whose water surges.
It said, 'I'll rise, I'll cover the earth,
  I'll obliterate a town and the people who live
    in it.'
⁹Rise, horses, rage, chariotry,
  strong men are to go out,

Seba and Put seizing shields,
  Ludites seizing and directing bows.

[10]That day belongs to the Lord Yahweh of Armies,
  a day of redress, for taking redress from his
    adversaries.
The sword will consume, be full,
  will soak in their bloodshed.
Because the Lord Yahweh of Armies has a
    sacrifice
  in the northern country by the River Euphrates.
[11]Go up to Gil'ad and get balm,
  young Miss Misrayim.
To empty results you're multiplying healings –
  there's no growing back for you.
[12]Nations have heard your slighting;
  the earth is full of your scream.
Because strong man has collapsed on strong man;
  the two of them have fallen down together.

## Par'oh helpless

[13]The word that Yahweh spoke to Yirmeyahu
the prophet regarding the coming of
Nebukadre'tstsar king of Babel to strike down
the country of Misrayim:

[14]Tell it in Misrayim, make it heard in Migdal,
  make it heard in Memphis and in Tahpanhes.
Say, 'Take your position, prepare yourself,
  because the sword is consuming all round you.'
[15]Why has your champion been swept away?
  – he didn't stand, because Yahweh thrust him
    down.
[16]He's made many people collapse,
  yes, each one has fallen into his neighbour.
They said, 'Set to,
  let's turn back to our people,
To the country of our birth,
  from before the oppressor's sword.'
[17]There they called Par'oh king of Misrayim,
  'A din who has let the appointed time pass'.
[18]As I live (a declaration of the King,
  Yahweh of Armies is his name):
Like Tabor among the mountains,
  and like Carmel at the sea, one will come.
[19]Make for yourself things for exile,
  you who sit as Miss Misrayim.
Because Memphis will become a desolation,
  burned, without inhabitant.
[20]Misrayim is a beautiful, beautiful heifer;

a wasp from the north is coming, coming.
[21]Her mercenaries within her, too,
  are like well-fed bullocks.
Yet they're turning round, too,
  they're fleeing together, they're not taking a
    stand.
Because their day of disaster has come upon
    them,
  the time when they're attended to.
[22]Her sound will be like a snake when it goes,
  with a force they will go.
With axes they're coming to her,
  like fellers of trees.
[23]They're cutting down her forest (Yahweh's
    declaration)
  when it cannot be explored,
Because they're more than locusts;
  there's no numbering of them.
[24]Miss Misrayim is being shamed,
  given into the hand of the northern people.

## But of you I won't make an end

[25]Yahweh of Armies, Yisra'el's God, has said:

Here am I, attending to Amon of Thebes
and to Par'oh, to Misrayim, to its gods, to its
kings – to Par'oh and to the people who rely
on him. [26]I shall give them into the hand of
the people who seek their life, into the hand
of Nebukadre'tstsar king of Babel and into
the hand of his servants. But afterwards it will
dwell as in former days (Yahweh's declaration).

[27]But you, don't be afraid, my servant Ya'aqob;
  don't shatter, Yisra'el.
Because here am I, I'm going to deliver you from
    far away,
  and your offspring from the country of their
    captivity.
Ya'aqob will again be calm,
  at peace with no one making him tremble.
[28]So you, don't be afraid, my servant Ya'aqob
  (Yahweh's declaration),
  because I'm with you.
Because I shall make an end among all the nations
  where I've driven you,
But of you I won't make an end,
  though I discipline you in exercising
    authority,
  and don't treat you as free of guilt.

# 47

Something that came as Yahweh's word to Yirmeyahu the prophet regarding the Pelishtites, before Par'oh struck down Azzah.

²Yahweh has said this:

There, water is rising from the north,
 and it will become an overwhelming wadi.
They'll overwhelm the country and what fills it,
 the town and the people who live in it.
People will cry out,
 all the country's inhabitants will howl,
³At the sound of the pounding of his sturdy
 steeds' hooves,
 at the noise of his chariotry, the clatter of its
 wheels.
Fathers are not turning their faces to children
 because of the slackening of their hands,
⁴Because of the day that's coming
 for the destroying of all the Pelishtites,
For cutting off every helper who survives
 for Tsor and Tsidon.
Because Yahweh is going to destroy the
 Pelishtites,
 the remainder of Kaphtor's shore.
⁵The shaved head is coming to Azzah,
 Ashqelon is being terminated.
You remainder of their vale,
 how long will you gash yourself?
⁶Hey, sword of Yahweh,
 for how long will you not be calm? –
Gather up into your sheath,
 rest, be still.
⁷How can you be calm
 when Yahweh is ordering it?
For Ashqelon and for the seacoast
 he has set its appointment.

## Mo'ab broken

# 48

Regarding Mo'ab.

Yahweh of Armies, Yisra'el's God, has said this:

Hey for Nebo, that it's destroyed,
 Qiryatayim is shamed, captured.
The stronghold is shamed and it has
 shattered.
²Mo'ab's praise is no more.

In Heshbon they intended something bad against
 her:
 'Come, let's cut her down from being a
 nation.'
Madmenah, you'll be still, too;
 the sword will follow you.
³The sound of an outcry from Horonayim,
 destruction and great breaking.
⁴Mo'ab is broken,
 its little ones have let the outcry be heard.
⁵Because the ascent to Luhit –
 with crying one ascends, with crying.
Because on the Horonayim descent
 people have heard the crying distresses about
 the breaking.
⁶Flee, save your life,
 be like Aro'er in the wilderness!
⁷Because on account of your reliance on what
 you've made,
 and on your treasures, you too will be
 captured.
Kemosh will go out into exile,
 his priests and his officials together.
⁸The destroyer will come to every town,
 no town will escape.
The vale will perish,
 the flatland will be desolate, because Yahweh
 has said.
⁹Give wings to Mo'ab,
 because it's to fly, go out.
Its towns will be for desolation,
 with no inhabitant in them.
¹⁰Cursed is the one who does Yahweh's work
 deceitfully;
 cursed is the one who holds back his sword
 from blood.
¹¹Mo'ab has been at peace from its youth;
 it's been still on its lees.
It hasn't been poured from bowl to bowl;
 it hasn't gone into exile.
Therefore its taste has stayed in it,
 its bouquet hasn't changed.
¹²Therefore there – days are coming (Yahweh's
 declaration)
 when I'll send off decanters to it.
They'll decant it and empty its bowls
 and smash its jugs.
¹³Mo'ab will be shamed because of Kemosh
 as Yisra'el's household was shamed
 because of Bet El, the object of their reliance.
¹⁴How can you say, 'We are strong men,
 forceful men for the battle'?

¹⁵Mo'ab is destroyed, people have gone up to its
    towns,
  the choicest of its young men have gone down
    to the slaughter
(The declaration of the King,
  Yahweh of Armies is his name).


## A long quiet disturbed

¹⁶Mo'ab's disaster is near to coming,
  its bad fate is hurrying quickly.
¹⁷Condole with it, all you who are round it,
  all you who acknowledge its name.
Say, 'How has the vigorous club broken,
  the splendid mace.'
¹⁸Come down from honour, sit on the thirsty
    ground,
  you who sit as Miss Dibon.
Because Mo'ab's destroyer has come up against you;
  he's devastated your fortifications.
¹⁹Stand by the road and look out,
  you who live in Aro'er.
Ask the man who flees and the woman who
    escapes,
  say 'What's happened?'
²⁰Mo'ab is shamed, because it has shattered –
  howl and cry out;
Tell at the Arnon
  that Mo'ab is destroyed.

²¹A ruling has come for the flatland region,
  for Holon, for Yahtsah,
On Mepha'at, ²²on Dibon, on Nebo,
  on Bet Diblatayim, ²³on Qiryatayim,
On Bet Gamul, on Bet Me'on,
  ²⁴on Qeriyyot, on Botsrah,
On all the towns in the country of Mo'ab,
  far and near.

²⁵Mo'ab's horn is cut off,
  its arm broken (Yahweh's declaration).
²⁶Get it drunk, because it's made itself big against
    Yahweh;
  Mo'ab will wallow in its vomit.
It will be an object of fun, too:
  ²⁷wasn't Yisra'el an object of fun to you?
Was it found among robbers,
  that when you speak of it you shake your head?

²⁸Abandon the towns, dwell in the cliff,
  inhabitants of Mo'ab,

Be like a pigeon that nests
  in the sides of the mouth of a chasm.
²⁹We've heard of Mo'ab's majesty
  (it's very majestic),
Its height and its majesty and its exaltation,
  and the loftiness of its mind.
³⁰I myself know (Yahweh's declaration) its fury;
  its empty talk is not upright, they haven't acted
    uprightly.

³¹Therefore I will howl for Mo'ab,
  I will cry out regarding Mo'ab, all of it,
  concerning the people of Qir-heres I will murmur.
³²With more crying than for Ya'zer I'll cry for you,
  vine of Sibmah.
Your tendrils crossed the sea,
  to the sea of Ya'zer they reached.
On your summer fruit and on your grapes
  a destroyer has fallen.
³³Rejoicing and celebration gather up from the
    farmland
  and from the country of Mo'ab.
I've made wine cease from the presses;
  no one treads with a shout;
  the shout is no shout.


## My heart moans for Mo'ab

³⁴From the outcry of Heshbon as far as Ele'aleh,
  as far as Yahats, they're giving their voice,
From Tso'ar as far as Horonayim, Eglat Shelishiyyah,
  because the water of Nimrim, too, will become
    a great desolation.
³⁵I shall stop for Mo'ab (Yahweh's declaration)
  anyone ascending to the shrine,
  anyone burning incense to its gods.
³⁶Therefore my heart for Mo'ab
  moans like a flute.
My heart for the people of Qir-heres
  moans like a flute.
Therefore the profit it made –
  they've perished, ³⁷because every head is shaved,
  every beard cut off.
On all hands there are gashes,
  on hips there's sack.
³⁸On Mo'ab's roofs and in its squares,
  all of it, is lamentation,
Because I've broken Mo'ab
  like a jar no one wants (Yahweh's declaration).
³⁹How it has shattered – wail;
  how Mo'ab has turned its back in shame.

Mo'ab will be an object of fun,
 something to shatter all the people round it.

⁴⁰Because Yahweh has said this:

There, one swoops like an eagle
 and spreads his wings towards Mo'ab.
⁴¹Qeriyyot has been captured,
 the strongholds have been seized.
The mind of Mo'ab's strong men will be
 like the mind of a woman in labour on that day.
⁴²Mo'ab has been destroyed from being a people
 because it made itself big against Yahweh.
⁴³A terror and a pit and a trap
 are against you who live in Mo'ab (Yahweh's
  declaration).
⁴⁴The one who flees from the face of the terror
 will fall into the pit.
The one who climbs out of the pit
 will be captured by the trap.
Because I'll bring to it, to Mo'ab,
 the year of my attending to it (Yahweh's
  declaration).
⁴⁵In Heshbon's shade
 people who are fleeing stop, being out of energy.
Because fire has gone out from Heshbon,
 a flame from within Sihon,
Consumed Mo'ab's forehead,
 the skull of Sha'on's people.
⁴⁶Oh, alas for you, Mo'ab,
 the people of Kemosh have perished.
Because your sons have been taken into captivity,
 your daughters into captivity.

⁴⁷But I shall restore Mo'ab's fortunes
 at the end of the time (Yahweh's declaration).

 As far as here is the ruling about Mo'ab.

## The wisdom that fails

# 49  Regarding the Ammonites.

 Yahweh has said this:

Does Yisra'el have no sons,
 or no one entering into possession?
Why has Malkam dispossessed Gad
 and its people lived in its towns?
²Therefore – there, days are coming (Yahweh's
 declaration)

when I shall make the battle alarm heard
 for Rabbah of the Ammonites.
It will become a desolate tell;
 its daughter-townships will be set on fire.
Yisra'el will dispossess
 the people who dispossessed it (Yahweh has said).

³Howl, Heshbon,
 because Ai is destroyed!
Cry out, daughter-townships of Rabbah,
 wrap on sack, lament.
Run to and fro in the enclosures,
 because Malkam is to go into exile,
 his priests and his officials together with him.
⁴Why do you boast of your vales? –
 your vale is flowing away,
Miss-who-turns-back, you who rely on your
  treasures,
 'Who will come against me?'
⁵Here am I, I'm going to bring a terror against you
 (a declaration of the Lord Yahweh of Armies)
  from all those round you.
You'll be driven off, each one straight ahead;
 there'll be no one collecting the fugitive.

⁶But afterwards I shall restore
 the fortunes of the Ammonites (Yahweh's
  declaration).

⁷Regarding Edom.

 Yahweh of Armies has said this:

Is there no longer smartness in Teman,
 has counsel perished from the discerning,
 has their smartness gone stale?
⁸Flee, turn round, lie low,
 inhabitants of Dedan.
Because I'm going to bring Esaw's disaster upon
  him,
 the time when I attend to him.
⁹If grape-pickers came to you,
 would they not let gleanings remain?
If robbers [came] by night
 they'd devastate what they needed.
¹⁰But it's I who've stripped Esaw,
 bared his hiding place.
He can't conceal himself; his offspring is destroyed,
 his brothers and his neighbours, and there is
  no one.
¹¹Abandon your orphans, I'll keep them alive;
 your widows may rely on me.

## Strong men emasculated

<sup>12</sup>Because Yahweh has said this: 'The people for whom there has been no ruling that they should drink the glass: if they'll certainly drink it, are you one to go totally free of guilt? You won't go free of guilt, because you will certainly drink it. <sup>13</sup>Because by myself I have sworn (Yahweh's declaration) that Botsrah will be for desolation, for reviling, for wasting, for slighting, and all its towns will be for total waste permanently.'

<sup>14</sup>I have heard a report from Yahweh,
 and an envoy is sent among the nations.
Collect together and come to it,
 set to for battle!
<sup>15</sup>Because there – I'm going to make you small
  among the nations,
 despised among people.
<sup>16</sup>Your dreadfulness has deceived you,
 the assertiveness of your mind.
You who dwell in the clefts of the cliff,
 you who seize the height of the hill,
If you make your nest high like an eagle,
 I will get you down from there (Yahweh's
  declaration).

<sup>17</sup>Edom will become a desolation,
 everyone who passes by it will be desolate
And will whistle at all its wounds,
 <sup>18</sup>as at the overthrow of Sedom and Amorah
  and their neighbours (Yahweh has said).
No one will live there,
 no human being will reside there.

<sup>19</sup>There, it will be as when a lion comes up
 from the Yarden jungle into an enduring abode,
Because in a moment I shall run him out of it,
 and whoever is chosen for it I shall appoint.
Because who is like me, who can make me testify,
 who is the shepherd who can stand before me?
<sup>20</sup>Therefore listen to Yahweh's counsel
 which he's devised for Edom,
His intentions which he's formulated
 for the inhabitants of Teman.
If the flock's boys don't drag them away,
 if the abode isn't desolate at them . . .

<sup>21</sup>At the sound of their fall the earth shakes,
 the outcry makes its sound heard at the Sea of
  Reeds.

<sup>22</sup>There, like an eagle he goes up and swoops,
 spreads his wings against Botsrah.
The mind of Edom's strong men will be
 like the mind of a woman in labour on that day.

## The promise of a future

<sup>23</sup>Regarding Dammeseq [Damascus].

Hamat and Arpah are shamed,
 because they've heard a report of something
  bad.
They toss like the sea with anxiety;
 it cannot be calm.
<sup>24</sup>Dammeseq is weak,
 she's turned her face to flee.
Panic has taken strong hold of her,
 pressure and contractions have grasped her like
  a woman giving birth.
<sup>25</sup>How has the praiseworthy town not been
  abandoned,
 the town I celebrated?
<sup>26</sup>Therefore its young men will fall in its squares
 and all its men of battle will become still on
  that day (a declaration of Yahweh of Armies).
<sup>27</sup>I shall set fire to the wall of Dammeseq;
 it will consume the citadels of Ben-hadad.

<sup>28</sup>Regarding Qedar and the kingdoms of Hatsor, which Nebukadre'tstsar king of Babel struck down.

 Yahweh has said this:

Set to, go up to Qedar,
 destroy the Qedemites!
<sup>29</sup>They will take their tents and their flocks,
 their tent cloths and all their things.
They'll carry off their camels for themselves;
 they'll call out against them, 'Terror is all
  round.'
<sup>30</sup>Flit, go way away, lie low,
 inhabitants of Hatsor (Yahweh's declaration).
Because Nebukadre'tstsar king of Babel
 has devised counsel against you,
 has formulated an intention against you.

<sup>31</sup>Set to, go up, to a nation at peace,
 living in confidence (Yahweh's declaration).
It has no gateways and no bars;
 they dwell alone.

³²Their camels will become plunder,
　　their horde of livestock, spoil.
I shall scatter to every wind the people shaved at
　　the forehead,
　　from all sides I shall bring about their disaster
　　　(Yahweh's declaration).
³³Hatsor will become an abode for jackals,
　　a desolation permanently.
No one will live there;
　　no human being will reside there.

### An unexpected vulnerability

³⁴What came as Yahweh's word to Yirmeyahu
the prophet regarding Elam at the beginning
of the reign of Tsidqiyyah king of Yehudah.

　³⁵Yahweh of Armies has said this:

Here am I, I'm about to break Elam's bow,
　　the first principle of their strength.
³⁶I shall bring to Elam four winds
　　from the four corners of the heavens.
I shall scatter them to these four winds;
　　the nation won't exist
　　where Elam's fugitives don't come.
³⁷I shall shatter Elam before its enemies,
　　and before the people who seek their life.
I shall bring bad fortune on them,
　　my angry blazing (Yahweh's declaration).
I shall send the sword off after them
　　until I've finished them off.
³⁸I shall put my throne in Elam
　　and obliterate king and officials from there
　　　(Yahweh's declaration).

³⁹But at the end of the time
　　I shall restore Elam's fortunes (Yahweh's
　　declaration).

**50** The word that Yahweh spoke
regarding Babel, regarding the
country of the Kasdites, by means of
Yirmeyahu the prophet:

²Tell among the nations, make it heard;
　　lift a banner, make it heard.
Don't hide it, say, 'Babel is captured,
　　Bel is shamed, Merodak has shattered.'
Its idols are shamed,
　　its fetishes have shattered.

³Because a northern nation has gone up against it,
　　it will make its country a desolation.
There will be no one living in it;
　　both human being and animal – they have
　　flitted, gone.

⁴In those days and at that time (Yahweh's
declaration):

The Yisra'elites will come,
　　they and the Yehudahites together.
They'll go, and cry as they go,
　　and seek Yahweh their God.
⁵They'll ask the way to Tsiyyon,
　　and their faces will be towards there.
'Come, join yourselves to Yahweh
　　by a permanent pact that won't be put out of
　　mind.'
⁶My people were a flock that were lost;
　　their shepherds had led them astray.
On the mountains they turned them back,
　　from mountain to hill they went.
They put their resting-place out of mind;
　　⁷all the people who found them consumed them.
Their adversaries said, 'We won't incur liability,
　　on account of the fact that they did wrong to
　　Yahweh,
　　the faithful abode, their ancestors' hope, Yahweh.'

### Flit from within Babel

⁸Flit from within Babel,
　　get out of the country of the Kasdites,
　　be like the he-goats before the flock.
⁹Because here, I'm going to arouse,
　　and get to go up, against Babel
A congregation of great nations
　　from a northern country.
When they line up against it,
　　from there it will be captured.
Its arrows like those of an insightful strong man
　　won't turn back empty.
¹⁰The Kasdites will become spoil;
　　all its despoilers will be full (Yahweh's
　　declaration),
¹¹Because you rejoice, because you exult,
　　plunderers of my domain,
Because you jump like a heifer with grain;
　　you bellow like sturdy ones.
¹²Your mother is very shamed,
　　the one who gave birth to you is confounded.

There is the end of the nations:
wilderness, dry land and steppe.
[13]Because of Yahweh's fury it won't be inhabited,
it will become a desolation, all of it.
Everyone who passes by Babel will be desolate
and will whistle at all its wounds.

[14]Line up against Babel round about,
all you who direct a bow.
Shoot at it, don't hold back with an arrow,
because it's done wrong to Yahweh.
[15]Shout against it round about, it's giving its hand,
its towers are falling,
Its walls are being torn down,
because that is Yahweh's redress.
Take redress upon it;
as it has done, do to it.
[16]Cut off sower from Babel,
and seizer of sickle at harvest time.
Before the oppressor's sword
they'll turn, each one, to his people,
they'll flee, each one to his country.

## The superpower that thought it was safe

[17]Yisra'el is scattered sheep
that lions have driven away.
As first the king of Ashshur consumed him,
then as last Nebukadre'tstsar king of Babel
crushed his bones.

[18]Therefore Yahweh of Armies, Yisra'el's God,
has said this:

Here am I, I'm going to attend
to the king of Babel and to his country
as I attended to the king of Ashshur.
[19]And I shall take Yisra'el back to its abode,
and it will pasture in the Carmel and the
Bashan.
In the highland of Ephrayim and Gil'ad
its appetite will eat its fill.

[20]In those days and at that time (Yahweh's
declaration):

Yisra'el's waywardness will be looked for, and
there'll be none;
Yehudah's wrongdoings – and they won't be
found,
because I shall pardon the people I let remain.

[21]Against the country of Double Rebellion,
go up against her, and to the inhabitants of
Attention.
Put to the sword and devote the last of them
(Yahweh's declaration),
do in accordance with all that I've ordered
you.
[22]The sound of battle in the country,
a great breaking.
[23]How the hammer of the entire earth
has severed and broken!
How Babel has become
a desolation among the nations!
[24]I trapped you and yes, you were captured,
Babel,
and you didn't know it.
You were found and also caught,
because you challenged Yahweh.
[25]Yahweh opened his storehouse
and got out the instruments of his
condemnation,
Because that's the work
of the Lord Yahweh of Armies
in the country of the Kasdites.

[26]Come to it from afar, open its granaries,
pile it up like heaps,
devote it, there must be no remainder of it.
[27]Put to the sword all its bullocks,
they must go down for slaughter.
Oh, alas for them, because their day is coming,
the time when they're attended to.
[28]The sound of fugitives and escapees
from the country of Babel,
To tell in Tsiyyon
of the redress of Yahweh our God,
redress for his palace.

## Death and life interweave

[29]Make it heard to the archers against Babel,
all those who direct a bow!
Camp against it round about,
there must not be people who escape.
Make good to it for its action,
do to it in accordance with all that it did,
Because it asserted itself against Yahweh,
Yisra'el's sacred one.
[30]Therefore its young men will fall in the squares,
and all its men of battle will become still
on that day (Yahweh's declaration).

³¹Here am I regarding you, assertive one (a
    declaration of the Lord, Yahweh of Armies).
  because your day is coming,
  the time when I attend to you.
³²The assertive one will collapse and fall,
  and there will be no one raising him up.
I shall set fire to his towns
  and it will consume all round him.

³³Yahweh of Armies has said this:

The Yisra'elites and the Yehudahites
  are oppressed together.
All their captors have taken strong hold of them
  and refused to send them off.
³⁴Their restorer is strong,
  Yahweh of Armies is his name.
He will argue their case strongly
  in order that he may quieten the country
  and shake up Babel's inhabitants.

³⁵A sword against the Kasdites (Yahweh's
    declaration),
  for Babel's inhabitants, its officials and its experts!
³⁶A sword for the diviners so they become fools,
  a sword for its strong men so they shatter!
³⁷A sword to its horses and for its chariotry,
  and for all the foreign group that's within it,
  so they become women!
A sword to its storehouses, so they're plundered,
  ³⁸a drought to its water, so it dries up!
Because it's a country of images,
  and through their dreadful objects they'll go
    mad.
³⁹Therefore wildcats will live with jackals,
  and ostriches will live in it.
It won't be lived in again permanently,
  it won't dwell for generation after generation.
⁴⁰Like God's overthrow
  of Sedom, Amorah and their neighbours
    (Yahweh's declaration),
No one will live there,
  no human being will reside in it.

## Hands go limp

⁴¹There, a people is coming from the north;
  a big nation and many kings
  are aroused from earth's farthest reaches.
⁴²They take strong hold of bow and spear;
  they're violent and they don't show compassion.

Their sound is like the sea that rumbles;
  they ride on horses,
As someone lined up for battle,
  against you, Miss Babel.
⁴³The king of Babel has heard the report of them,
  his hands have become slack.
Pressure has taken strong hold of him,
  labour like a woman giving birth.
⁴⁴There, it will be as when a lion goes up
  from the Yarden jungle into an enduring
    abode,
Because in a moment I shall run him out of it,
  and whoever is chosen for it I shall appoint.
Because who is like me, who can make me testify,
  who is the shepherd who can stand before me?
⁴⁵Therefore listen to Yahweh's plan
  which he's devised for Babel,
His intentions which he's formulated
  for the country of the Kasdites.
If the flock's boys don't drag them away,
  if the abode isn't desolate at them . . .
⁴⁶At the sound of the seizing of Babel
    the earth shakes,
  the outcry makes itself heard among the
    nations.

# 51  Yahweh has said this:

Here am I, I'm rousing against Babel
  and for the inhabitants of The-Mind-of-One-
    Who-Rises-Against-Me a devastating wind.
²I shall send strangers off to Babel
  so they'll winnow it and strip its country,
Because they're against it all round,
  on the day of bad fortune.
³The one who directs his bow isn't to direct it
  and isn't to stand in his armour.
Don't spare its young men;
  devote its entire army.
⁴People are to fall run through in the country of
    the Kasdites,
  thrust through in its streets.

## Don't get caught

⁵Because Yisra'el and Yehudah were not widowed
  by its God, Yahweh of Armies.
Rather their country was full of liability
  because of Yisra'el's sacred one.
⁶Flee from inside Babel;
  each of you, save his life.

Don't be still because of its waywardness,
    because this is the time of redress for Yahweh;
he's making good with his dealings to it.
⁷Babel was a gold chalice in Yahweh's hand,
    making the entire earth drunk.
From its wine nations drank;
    therefore nations go mad.
⁸Suddenly Babel has fallen and broken;
    howl over it.
Get balm for its injuries,
    perhaps it may heal.
⁹"We're healing Babel but it hasn't healed;
    abandon it, let's go each to his country."
Because the ruling for it has reached to the
        heavens,
    lifted to the skies.
¹⁰Yahweh has brought out faithfulness for us;
    come, let's recount in Tsiyyon
    the action of Yahweh our God.

¹¹Polish the arrows, fill the quivers,
    Yahweh has aroused the spirit of Maday's
    [Media's] kings.
Because his strategy against Babel
    is to devastate it.
Because it's Yahweh's redress,
    redress for his palace.
¹²To Babel's walls lift up a banner,
    make a strong watch,
    set up watchmen, prepare ambushes.
Because Yahweh is both scheming and acting on
    what he spoke regarding Babel's inhabitants.
¹³You who dwell by much water, abundant in
        storehouses,
    your end has come, the time for your cutting off.

¹⁴Yahweh of Armies has sworn by his life:

I'm filling you with people like a locust swarm;
    they'll chant a shout over you.
¹⁵One who made the earth by his energy,
    established the world by his smartness,
    by his understanding stretched out the heavens:
¹⁶At his giving voice
    there was a rumble of the water in the heavens.
He brought up clouds from the end of the earth;
    made lightning for the rain,
    brought out wind from his storehouses.

¹⁷Every human being proves dense, without
        knowledge;
    every goldsmith is put to shame by the image,

Because his figure is a falsehood,
    and there's no breath in them.
¹⁸They're hollow, a work for mockery;
    at the time when they're attended to, they'll
        perish.
¹⁹Not like these is Ya'aqob's share,
    because he's the one who formed everything.
And it is the clan that is his domain;
    Yahweh of Armies is his name.

## You were my club

²⁰You were my club,
    my battle instruments.
I clubbed nations with you,
    I devastated kingdoms with you.
²¹I clubbed horse and its rider with you,
    I clubbed chariot and its rider with you.
²²I clubbed man and woman with you,
    I clubbed elder and youth with you.
I clubbed young man and girl with you,
    ²³I clubbed shepherd and his flock with you.
I clubbed ploughman and his pair with you,
    I clubbed governors and overseers with you.
²⁴But I shall make good to Babel
    and to all Kasdim's inhabitants
For all their bad dealing,
    which they did in Tsiyyon before your eyes
        (Yahweh's declaration).

²⁵Here am I in relation to you,
    mountain of the devastator (Yahweh's
        declaration),
Destroyer of the entire earth;
    I'm stretching out my hand against you.
I shall roll you from the cliffs
    and make you a burnt mountain.
²⁶They won't get from you
    a cornerstone or foundation stone,
    because you'll be a total desolation
        permanently (Yahweh's declaration).

²⁷Lift up a banner in the earth,
    sound a horn among the nations.
Make nations sacred against it,
    make it heard to kingdoms against it,
    Ararat, Minni, Ashkenaz.
Appoint a marshal against it,
    bring up horses like swarming locust.
²⁸Make nations sacred against it,
    the kings of Maday,

Its governors, all its overseers,
 every country it rules.

<sup>29</sup>The earth is shaking and writhing
 because Yahweh's intentions are implemented
  against Babel
To make the country of Babel
 a desolation without inhabitant.
<sup>30</sup>Babel's strong men are holding back from doing
  battle;
 they're sitting in the fortresses.
Their strength has failed,
 they've turned into women.
People have set fire to its dwellings,
 its gateway bars have broken.
<sup>31</sup>Runner runs to meet runner,
 messenger to meet messenger,
To tell the king of Babel
 that his town has been captured at one end.
<sup>32</sup>The fords have been seized,
 people have set the marshes on fire,
 the men of battle are fearful.

## Yahweh takes on Bel

<sup>33</sup>Because Yahweh of Armies, Yisra'el's God,
has said this:

Miss Babel is like a threshing-floor
 at the time of its treading:
Yet a little while
 and the time of its harvest will come.
<sup>34</sup>'He consumed me, crushed me,
 did Nebukadre'tstsar king of Babel,
 put me down an empty dish.
He swallowed me like a dragon,
 filled his belly with my tasty things, threw me up.
<sup>35</sup>The violence done to me and my body be on
  Babel'
 says the inhabitant of Tsiyyon.
'My blood be on Kasdim's inhabitants'
 says Yerushalaim.

<sup>36</sup>Therefore Yahweh says this:

Here am I, arguing your case.
 I'll exact redress for you.
I'll wither its sea and dry up its spring.
<sup>37</sup>Babel will become heaps of rubble,
The abode of jackals, a desolation,
 something to whistle at, with no inhabitant.

<sup>38</sup>Together, like cougars they roar,
 they've growled like the whelps of lions.
<sup>39</sup>When they've been made hot I'll set out their
  drink banquet,
 and get them drunk in order that they may
  exult,
And sleep an everlasting sleep
 and not wake up (Yahweh's declaration).
<sup>40</sup>I'll take them down like lambs to slaughter,
 like rams along with goats.
<sup>41</sup>How Sheshak has been captured,
 the praise of the entire earth has been seized.
How Babel has become
 a desolation among the nations.
<sup>42</sup>The sea has gone up over Babel;
 it's covered by the rumble of its waves.
<sup>43</sup>Its towns have become a desolation,
 its country desert and steppe,
A country where no one lives in them,
 where a human being doesn't pass through
  them.
<sup>44</sup>I shall attend to Bel in Babel
 and make what he's swallowed come out of his
  mouth.
Nations will no more flood to him;
 even Babel's wall is falling.

## An everlasting sleep

<sup>45</sup>Get out from inside it, my people;
 each of you save his life
 from Yahweh's angry blaze.
<sup>46</sup>Beware that your mind doesn't become soft or
  you become afraid
 at the report that makes itself heard in the
  country.
A report will come during the year
 and afterwards a report may come during the
  next year,
Violence in the country,
 ruler against ruler.
<sup>47</sup>Therefore, now, days are coming
 when I shall attend to Babel's images.
Its entire country will be shamed;
 all its people who are run through will fall
  within it.
<sup>48</sup>The heavens and the earth and all that's in
  them
 will resound over Babel,
 because from the north the destroyers will
  come to it (Yahweh's declaration).

⁴⁹Yes, Babel, for the falling of those of Yisra'el who
    have been run through;
yes, for Babel all in the earth who have been
    run through have fallen.
⁵⁰Survivors of the sword, go,
    don't stand there.
Be mindful of Yahweh from afar;
    Yerushalaim is to come up into your mind.
⁵¹'We were shamed, because we heard
    reviling,
    disgrace covered our faces.
Because strangers came
    into the sacred places in Yahweh's house.'

⁵²Therefore, there, days are coming (Yahweh's
    declaration)
    when I shall attend to its images
    and in the entire country the person who has
      been run through will groan.
⁵³When Babel goes up to the heavens,
    when it fortifies its strong height,
    destroyers will come to it from me (Yahweh's
      declaration).

⁵⁴The sound of a cry from Babel,
    a great breaking from the country of the
      Kasdites.
⁵⁵Because Yahweh is destroying Babel,
    eliminating the loud voice from it.
Their waves are rumbling like much water;
    the din of their voice gives out.
⁵⁶Because there is coming against it
    a destroyer, against Babel.
Its strong men will be captured;
    their bows will shatter.
Because Yahweh is a God of dealings;
    he really makes good.
⁵⁷I shall make its officials and its experts drunk,
    its governors and overseers and strong men.
They will sleep an everlasting sleep
    and not wake up (a declaration of the King,
      whose name is Yahweh of Armies).

## In the interests of the living

⁵⁸Yahweh of Armies has said this:

Babel's wall, broad, will be totally levelled,
    its high gateways burned with fire.
Peoples will have toiled for emptiness,
    nations will have got weary for fire.

⁵⁹The word that Yirmeyahu the prophet
ordered to Serayah ben Neriyyah son of
Mahseyah when he went with Tsidqiyyahu
king of Yehudah to Babel in the fourth year of
his reign; Serayah was accommodation officer.
⁶⁰Yirmeyahu wrote down all the bad fortune
that would come to Babel on a document, all
these words that are written concerning Babel.
⁶¹Yirmeyahu said to Serayah, 'When you
come to Babel, you're to see that you read out all
these words. ⁶²And you're to say, "Yahweh, you
yourself have spoken concerning this place that
you'll cut it off, so that there won't be anyone
living in it, human being or animal, because it's
to be a great desolation permanently."
⁶³When you've finished reading out this
document, you're to tie a stone to it and throw
it into the middle of the Euphrates. ⁶⁴You're to
say, "In this way Babel will sink and not rise
up because of the bad fortune that I'm going to
bring on it. They'll have got weary."'

As far as here it is the words of Yirmeyahu.

## The horrifying coda

**52** Tsidqiyyahu was twenty-one years
of age when he began to reign and
he reigned eleven years in Yerushalaim. His
mother's name was Hamutal bat Yirmeyahu,
from Libnah. ²He did what was bad in Yahweh's
eyes in accordance with all that Yehoyaqim had
done, ³because of the fact that Yahweh's anger
was against Yerushalaim and against Yehudah
until he threw them out of his presence.
Tsidqiyyahu rebelled against the king of
Babel, ⁴and in the ninth year of his reign, in
the tenth month, on the tenth of the month,
Nebukadne'tstsar king of Babel came against
Yerushalaim, he and his entire force. They
camped against it and built blockades all
round. ⁵The town came under siege until
the eleventh year of King Tsidqiyyahu. ⁶In the
fourth month, on the ninth of the month,
the famine had become overwhelming in the
town and there was no bread for the people of
the country. ⁷The town broke open, and all the
men of battle fled; they got out of the town in
the night by way of the gateway between the
double wall which was by the king's garden,
while the Kasdites were all round the town.

They went by the steppe road, [8]but the Kasdite force pursued after the king. They overtook Tsidqiyyahu in the Yeriho steppes when his entire force had scattered from him. [9]They captured the king and took him up to the king of Babel at Riblah in the region of Hamat, and he announced rulings with him. [10]The king of Babel slaughtered Tsidqiyyahu's sons before his eyes, and also slaughtered all the Yehudahite officials at Riblah. [11]Tsidqiyyahu's eyes he gouged out, and he bound him with copper chains. The king of Babel brought him to Babel and put him in the guard house until the day of his death.

## Yirmeyahu horribly vindicated

[12]In the fifth month, on the tenth of the month (i.e. the nineteenth year of King Nebukadne'tstsar king of Babel), Nebuzar'adan the chief of the guards stood before the king of Babel in Yerushalaim [13]and burned Yahweh's house, the king's house and all the houses in Yerushalaim. Every house of a big person he burned in fire. [14]All the walls round Yerushalaim, the entire Kasdite force that was with the chief of the guards demolished. [15]Some of the poorest elements of the people, and the rest of the people who remained in the town, and the people who had submitted (who had submitted to the king of Babel), and the rest of the horde, Nebuzar'adan the chief of the guards took into exile, [16]but some of the poorest elements in the country the chief of the guards let remain as vinedressers and farmworkers. [17]The copper pillars that belonged to Yahweh's house, and the stands and the copper sea that was in Yahweh's house, the Kasdites broke up. They carried all their copper to Babel. [18]The buckets, the shovels, the snuffers, the ladles, the sprinklers and all the copper articles with which they ministered, they took. [19]The basins, the pans, the sprinklers, the pots, the candelabra, the ladles, the bowls, whatever was of gold and whatever was of silver, the chief of the guards took. [20]The two pillars, the one sea and the twelve copper cattle that were under the stands, which Shelomoh [Solomon] made for Yahweh's house – there was no weighing the copper in all these articles. [21]The pillars: the height of one pillar was nine metres; a line of six metres

would go round it, and its thickness was four fingers, hollow, [22]with a copper capital on it; the height of the capital was one and a half metres, with a net with pomegranates on the capital all round, all of it copper; like these was the second pillar with pomegranates. [23]There were ninety-six pomegranates towards the wind: all the pomegranates were a hundred above the net all round.

## Is it the end or is there hope?

[24]The chief of the guards took Serayah the head priest, Tsephanyah the number two priest and the three keepers of the threshold, [25]and from the town he took a courtier who was appointee over the men of battle, and seven people from the heads who were before the king, who were found in the town, the secretary of the army officer who mustered the people of the country, and sixty individuals from the people of the country who were found inside the town. [26]Nebuzar'adan the chief of the guards took them and made them go to the king of Babel at Riblah. [27]The king of Babel struck them down and put them to death at Riblah, in the region of Hamat.

So Yehudah went into exile from upon its land.

[28]This is the company that Nebukadre'tstsar exiled in the seventh year: 3,023 Yehudahites;

[29]in Nebukadre'tstsar's eighteenth year: 832 people from Yerushalaim;

[30]in Nebukadre'tstsar's twenty-third year, Nebuzar'adan the head of the guards exiled 745 Yehudahites.

All the people were 4,600.

[31]But in the thirty-seventh year of the exile of Yehoyakin king of Yehudah, in the twelfth month, on the twenty-fifth of the month, Ewil Merodak king of Babel, in the year he began to reign, lifted up the head of Yehoyakin king of Yehudah and got him out of the prison. [32]He spoke of good things with him, gave him his seat above the seat of the kings who were with him in Babel [33]and changed his prison clothes. He ate a meal before him regularly for all the days of his life, [34]and his provision was given him as a regular provision from the king of Babel, a day's allocation on its day, until the day of his death, for all the days of his life.

# LAMENTATIONS

These five prayer-poems grieve over a great disaster that has happened to Yerushalaim. The poems presumably relate to the destruction of Jerusalem by Nebuchadnezzar in 587 BC, though the book doesn't make any concrete references that make that link explicit. But if that disaster is the one Lamentations refers to, it is appropriate that the book thus follows the account of this event in Jeremiah. Tradition identifies Jeremiah as the author, though the poems themselves are anonymous.

Each poem comprises twenty-two verses (except the middle one, with sixty-six), which is the number of letters in the Hebrew alphabet, and the first four poems are alphabetical – that is, the verses begin with the successive letters of the alphabet. They express grief, protest and prayer from A to Z.

The Hebrew Bible has the books of the Bible in a different order from that in the English Bible (which follows the order in the Greek translation of the Bible). The Hebrew Bible groups Lamentations with some other shorter books (Song of Songs, Ruth, Ecclesiastes and Esther) that are used once a year in Jewish communities. Lamentations is used on the sixth day of the month Ab, which overlaps with July–August, to mark the anniversary of the fall of Jerusalem in 587 and in AD 70.

## The town bereft

**1** Oh! – the town sits alone
  that abounded with a people.
She became like a widow,
  she who was great among the nations.
She who was a queen among the provinces
  became a slave.
² She cries and cries in the night;
  there are tears on her cheeks.
She has no comforter
  from all her allies.
All her friends broke faith with her;
  they became enemies to her.
³ Yehudah went into exile after humbling
  and a great amount of servitude.
When she went to live among the nations
  she didn't find a settled place.
All her pursuers caught up with her
  amid her pressures.
⁴ The roads to Tsiyyon [Zion] are mourning,
  because of the lack of people coming for the
    set times.
All her gateways are desolate,
  her priests are groaning.
Her girls are suffering,
  and her – it's hard for her.
⁵ Her adversaries became her head,
  her enemies are at peace.
Because Yahweh made her suffer
  on account of the great number of her rebellions.
Her infants went into captivity
  before the adversary.
⁶ From Miss Tsiyyon
  all her glory went away.
Her officials became like deer
  that had found no pasture.
They walked without energy
  before the pursuer.
⁷ Yerushalaim has been mindful,
  in her days of humbling and wandering,
Of all the desirable things she had,
  which there were from days before.
When her people fell into the hand of the adversary
  and there was no one helping her,
The adversaries saw her,
  made fun of her coming to an end.
⁸ Yerushalaim did wrong and did wrong;
  therefore she became taboo.
All the people who had honoured her treated her
    as wretched
  because they saw her exposure.

Yes, she groaned
  and turned backwards.
⁹ Though her uncleanness was in her skirts,
  she hadn't been mindful of her future.
She went down in extraordinary ways;
  she had no comforter.
'Yahweh, look at my humbling,
  because the enemy has got big.'
¹⁰ The adversary laid his hand
  on all her desirable things.
Because she saw nations
  that came into her sanctuary,
Who you ordered should not come
  into your congregation.
¹¹ All her people are groaning,
  looking for bread.
They have given their desirable things
  for food to bring life back.
'Look, Yahweh, heed,
  because I've become wretched.'

## It's nothing to you who pass by, is it?

¹² Though it's nothing to you, all you who pass
    along the road,
  heed and look.
Is there any pain like my pain,
  which was dealt out to me,
When Yahweh made me suffer
  on the day of his angry blazing?
¹³ From on high he sent fire,
  into my bones, and it held sway over them.
He spread a net for my feet;
  he turned me backwards.
He made me a desolation,
  faint all day long.
¹⁴ The yoke of my rebellions was bound on,
  they interweave by his hand.
They came up on to my neck;
  he made my energy collapse.
The Lord gave me
  into the hands of people before whom I cannot
    stand.
¹⁵ The Lord within me threw aside
  all my sturdy men.
He called for a set time against me
  to break my young men.
The Lord trod in a press
  young Miss Yehudah.
¹⁶ 'On account of these things I'm crying;
  both my eyes are going down with water.

Because a comforter is far from me,
   someone bringing my life back.
My children have become desolate,
   because an enemy was strong.'
¹⁷Tsiyyon spread out her hands;
   she has no comforter.
Yahweh ordered to Ya'aqob [Jacob]
   the people round him as his adversaries.
Yerushalaim became
   something taboo among them.
¹⁸'Yahweh is in the right,
   because I rebelled against his bidding.
Listen, please, all you peoples,
   see my pain.
My girls and my young men
   went into captivity.
¹⁹I called to my friends;
   those people beguiled me.
My priests and my elders
   perished in the town,
When they looked for food for themselves
   so they might bring their life back.
²⁰See, Yahweh, how there was pressure on me;
   my insides churned.
My heart turned over within me,
   because I had rebelled and rebelled.
Outside, the sword bereaved;
   at home, very death.
²¹People heard that I was groaning;
   I had no comforter.
When all my enemies heard of my bad fortune,
   they were glad
   that you yourself had acted.
You brought about the day you called for –
   they should be like me.
²²All their bad action should come before you –
   deal with them,
As you dealt with me
   on account of all my rebellions.
Because my groans are many,
   and my heart is faint.'

## Anger

**2** Oh! – with his anger the Lord clouds
    over
  Miss Tsiyyon.
He threw down Yisra'el's glory
   from the heavens to the earth.
He was not mindful of his footstool
   on his day of anger.

²The Lord swallowed up all Ya'aqob's pastures
   and didn't spare.
In his fury he tore down
   Miss Yehudah's fortifications.
He brought right to the earth, made ordinary,
   the kingdom and its officials.
³He cut off every horn of Yisra'el
   in his angry blazing.
He turned backwards his right hand
   from before the enemy.
He burned up against Ya'aqob like a flaming fire
   consuming all round.
⁴He directed his bow as an enemy,
   took his stand with his right hand as an
    adversary.
He killed everyone
   who was desirable to the eye.
In Miss Tsiyyon's tent
   he poured out his wrath like fire.
⁵The Lord became like an enemy;
   he swallowed up Yisra'el.
He swallowed up all her citadels,
   devastated her fortifications.
He made great in Miss Yehudah
   mourning and moaning.
⁶He violated his shelter like a garden,
   destroyed his set place.
Yahweh caused set time and sabbath
   to be put out of mind in Tsiyyon.
In his angry condemnation he spurned
   king and priest.
⁷The Lord rejected his altar,
   abandoned his sanctuary.
He gave over the walls of her citadels
   into the enemy's hand.
They gave voice in Yahweh's house
   as on the day when it was a set occasion.
⁸Yahweh intended to devastate
   Miss Tsiyyon's wall.
He stretched out a line,
   he didn't turn back his hand from swallowing
    up.
He made rampart and wall mourn;
   together they languished.
⁹Her gateways sank into the earth;
   he obliterated and broke up her bars.
Her king and her officials are among the nations;
   there is no instruction.
Her prophets, too, found
   no vision from Yahweh.
¹⁰Miss Tsiyyon's elders
   sit on the earth, they're silent.

They've taken up earth on their head,
   they've wrapped on sack.
Yerushalaim's girls
   have lowered their head to the ground.
¹¹My eyes are spent with tears,
   my insides churn.
My heart has poured out to the earth
   on account of the breaking of my dear people,
While infant and suckling faint
   in the township's squares.
¹²To their mothers they say,
   'Where are grain and wine?',
As they faint like someone run through
   in the town's squares,
As their life pours out
   in their mothers' arms.

## Is this the town called 'The Joy of All the Earth'?

¹³What can I avow, what can I liken to you,
   Miss Yerushalaim?
What can I compare with you so I may comfort
      you,
   fair Miss Tsiyyon?
Because your breaking is as big as the sea;
   who can heal you?
¹⁴Your prophets beheld for you
   things that were empty and arid.
They didn't reveal your waywardness
   so as to restore your fortunes.
They beheld for you
   empty prophecies and seductions.
¹⁵All the people who pass your way
   have clapped the palms of their hands at you.
They've whistled and shaken their head
   at Miss Yerushalaim:
'Is this the town of which they used to say,
   "Complete in beauty, a joy to the entire earth"?'
¹⁶Against you all your enemies
   have opened their mouth wide.
They've whistled and ground their teeth,
   they've said, 'We've swallowed her up.
Indeed this is the day that we hoped for;
   we've found it, we've seen it.'
¹⁷Yahweh did what he schemed,
   he accomplished his word,
Which he ordered long ago;
   he tore down and didn't spare.
He let an enemy rejoice over you,
   exalted the horn of your adversaries.

¹⁸Their heart cried out to the Lord;
   Miss Tsiyyon's wall,
Make your tears go down like a wadi,
   day and night.
Don't give yourself respite;
   your dear eye must not stop.
¹⁹Get up, resound at night,
   at the beginning of the watches.
Pour out your heart like water
   in front of the presence of the Lord.
Lift up the palms of your hands to him
   for the life of your infants,
Who faint with hunger
   at the top of all the streets.
²⁰Look, Yahweh, heed
   the one with whom you've dealt like this.
Do women eat their fruit,
   the babies they dandle?
Are priest and prophet killed
   in the Lord's sanctuary?
²¹Young person and old
   lay on the ground in the streets.
My girls and my young men
   fell by the sword.
You killed them on your day of anger,
   you slaughtered them, you didn't spare.
²²You call (as on the day of a set occasion) –
   for terrors for me from all round.
On Yahweh's day of anger
   there was no one escaping or surviving.
Those whom I dandled and raised –
   my enemy finished them off.

## The man who saw humbling

**3** I am the man who saw humbling,
   by his furious club.
²He drove me and made me go
   in darkness and not light.
³Yes, against me
   repeatedly he'd turn his hand all day long.
⁴He wore away my flesh and my skin,
   he broke my bones.
⁵He built up against me and surrounded me
   with poison and weariness.
⁶He made me live in darkness,
   like those long dead.
⁷He walled me in and I couldn't get out,
   he made my chains heavy.
⁸Even when I'd cry out and call for help,
   he shut out my plea.

⁹He walled in my ways with stonework,
   twisted my paths.
¹⁰He was a lurking bear to me,
   a lion in hiding.
¹¹He diverted my ways and mangled me,
   made me desolate.
¹²He directed his bow and set me up
   as the target for his arrow.
¹³He made the shafts from his quiver
   come into my inner being.
¹⁴I became an object of fun to all my people,
   their song all day long.
¹⁵He filled me with bitter herbs,
   saturated me with vinegar.
¹⁶He broke my teeth on the gravel,
   bent me down in the ashes.
¹⁷My soul gave up on well-being,
   I forgot good things.
¹⁸I said, 'My distinction has perished,
   and my waiting for something from Yahweh.'
¹⁹To be mindful of my humbling and my wandering
   was vinegar and poison.
²⁰My spirit is mindful, so mindful,
   and it bows down within me.

### They are new every morning

²¹This I bring back to my mind,
   therefore I shall wait:
²²Yahweh's acts of commitment, that we're not
      finished,
   that his compassion isn't ended.
²³They're new each morning;
   his truthfulness is great.
²⁴'Yahweh is my share', my entire being said;
   therefore I shall wait for him.
²⁵Yahweh is good to people who hope in him,
   to the person who enquires of him.
²⁶It's good that one waits and keeps still
   for Yahweh's deliverance.
²⁷It's good for a man
   that he carries a yoke in his youth.
²⁸He should sit alone and be still
   when he's put it on him.
²⁹He should put his mouth in the dirt;
   perhaps there's hope.
³⁰He should give his jaw to the one who strikes
      him down,
   become full of reviling.
³¹Because the Lord
   doesn't reject permanently.

³²Rather he brings suffering, but has compassion,
   in the greatness of his acts of commitment.
³³Because it's not from his heart that he humbles
   and brings suffering to human beings,
³⁴Crushing under his feet
   all earth's prisoners,
³⁵Turning aside the exercise of authority for a
      man
   in front of the presence of the One on High,
³⁶Putting someone in the wrong in his argument
   when the Lord didn't look.

³⁷Who is it who said and it happened,
   when the Lord didn't order?
³⁸From the mouth of the One on High
   do not the bad things and the good things issue?
³⁹Of what should a living person complain,
   a man in connection with his wrongdoings?
⁴⁰Let's search out and examine our ways
   and turn back to Yahweh.
⁴¹Let's lift up our mind with the palms of our hands
   to God in the heavens.
⁴²When we ourselves rebelled and defied,
   you yourself didn't pardon.
⁴³You wrapped yourself in anger and pursued us,
   you killed and didn't spare.
⁴⁴You wrapped yourself in your cloud
   so that a plea didn't pass through.

### Yahweh's shadow side

⁴⁵You make us trash and refuse
   among the peoples.
⁴⁶Against us all our enemies
   have opened their mouth wide.
⁴⁷Terror and trap have become ours,
   ruin and breaking.
⁴⁸My eye flows with streams of water
   because of the breaking of my fair people.
⁴⁹My eye has poured and won't stop,
   without respite,
⁵⁰Until Yahweh looks down
   and sees from the heavens.
⁵¹My eye has dealt hard to my entire being
   because of all the girls in my town.
⁵²My enemies hunted me relentlessly
   like a bird for no reason.
⁵³They put an end to my life in a pit
   and threw stones at me.
⁵⁴Water flowed over my head;
   I said, 'I'm lost.'

⁵⁵I called on your name, Yahweh,
   from the deepest pit.
⁵⁶You listened to my voice, 'Don't close your ear
   concerning my relief, to my cry for help.'
⁵⁷You came near on the day when I would call on
   you;
   you said, 'Don't be afraid.'
⁵⁸You pressed the arguments for me, Lord,
   you restored my life.
⁵⁹You've seen the wrong done to me, Yahweh:
   exercise authority with a ruling for me.
⁶⁰You've seen all their redress,
   all their intentions for me,
⁶¹You've listened to their reviling, Yahweh,
   all their intentions against me,
⁶²The lips of the people who rise up against me
   and their murmuring against me all day long.
⁶³Look at them sitting and rising;
   I'm their song.
⁶⁴Give back their dealings to them, Yahweh,
   in accordance with the action of their hands.
⁶⁵May you give them a covering over their mind,
   your vow for them.
⁶⁶May you pursue them in anger and annihilate them
   from under Yahweh's heavens.

## What happened to loving mothers

**4** Oh! – gold tarnishes,
   fine gold changes.
Sacred stones pour out
   at the top of every street.
²Tsiyyon's precious children,
   worth their weight in pure gold –
Oh, they're thought of like clay vessels,
   a potter's handiwork.
³Even jackals offer the breast,
   nurse their young.
My dear people has become cruel,
   like ostriches in the wilderness.
⁴The suckling's tongue sticks
   to the roof of its mouth, for thirst.
Infants ask for bread;
   there's no one offering it to them.
⁵People who ate gourmet food
   are desolate in the streets.
People brought up in purple
   cling to rubbish heaps.
⁶The waywardness of my dear people had become
   bigger
   than the wrongdoing of Sedom [Sodom],

Which was overturned in a moment,
   though hands didn't whirl at it.
⁷Her consecrated people were purer than snow,
   whiter than milk.
Their frame was redder than coral,
   their body was sapphire.
⁸Their appearance became blacker than soot;
   they weren't recognized in the streets.
Their skin shrivelled on their frame;
   it became dry like wood.
⁹The people run through by the sword were better
   off
   than the people run through by famine,
Those who slip away, thrust through,
   for lack of the produce of the field.
¹⁰The hands of compassionate women
   cooked their children.
They became food for them
   through the breaking of my dear people.
¹¹Yahweh finished up his wrath,
   poured out his angry blazing.
He kindled a fire in Tsiyyon;
   it consumed its foundations.

### Yahweh's anointed captured

¹²The kings of the earth didn't believe,
   or all the world's inhabitants,
That adversary or enemy would come
   through Yerushalaim's gates.
¹³Because of her prophets' wrongdoings,
   her priests' wayward acts,
People who shed within her
   the blood of the faithful,
¹⁴They wandered blind through the streets,
   they were defiled with blood,
Without people being able
   to touch their clothes.
¹⁵'Go away, polluted', they called to them,
   'Go away, go away, don't touch.'
When they fled and wandered, people said among
   the nations,
   'They must be resident no longer.'
¹⁶Yahweh's presence divided them up,
   he no longer looks to them.
They didn't honour the face of priests,
   they didn't show favour to elders.
¹⁷Our eyes still spend themselves
   looking for help for ourselves, in vain.
On our watchtowers we watched
   for a nation that wouldn't deliver.

<sup>18</sup>People hounded our steps
so that we didn't walk in our squares.
Our end was near, our days were full,
because our end had come.
<sup>19</sup>Our pursuers became swifter
than the eagles in the heavens.
They chased us on the mountains,
they lay in wait for us in the wilderness.
<sup>20</sup>The breath of our lungs, Yahweh's anointed,
was captured in their traps,
The one of whom we had said, 'In his shade
we will live among the nations.'
<sup>21</sup>Celebrate and rejoice, Miss Edom,
you who live in the country of Uts.
To you, too, the chalice will pass;
you'll get drunk and you'll strip naked.
<sup>22</sup>Your waywardness is complete, Miss Tsiyyon;
he will no longer exile you.
He's attending to your waywardness, Miss Edom;
he's exposing your wrongdoings.

## Have you totally rejected us?

**5** Be mindful, Yahweh, of what happened to us;
look, and see our reviling.
<sup>2</sup>Our domain was turned over to strangers,
our homes to foreigners.
<sup>3</sup>We became orphans with no father,
our mothers actual widows.
<sup>4</sup>We drank our water for money;
our wood comes for payment.
<sup>5</sup>We were pursued, at our neck;
we were weary, but there was no settling down
for us.

<sup>6</sup>We've put out our hand to Misrayim [Egypt],
to Ashshur to get a fill of bread.
<sup>7</sup>Our parents did wrong and are no more,
and we were the ones who carried their
wayward acts.
<sup>8</sup>Servants have ruled over us;
there's no one freeing us from their hand.
<sup>9</sup>It's at the risk of our lives that we bring our bread,
because of the sword in the wilderness.
<sup>10</sup>Our skin was as hot as an oven,
because of the fever of famine.
<sup>11</sup>They humbled women in Tsiyyon,
girls in Yehudah's towns.
<sup>12</sup>Officials were hung up by their hand;
elders weren't respected.
<sup>13</sup>Young men carried a millstone,
boys collapsed with wood.
<sup>14</sup>Elders turned back from the gate,
young men from their music.
<sup>15</sup>The joy of our heart ceased;
our dancing was turned to mourning.
<sup>16</sup>The crown on our head fell;
oh, alas for us, because we did wrong.
<sup>17</sup>Because of this, our heart has become sick,
because of these things, our eyes become dark,
<sup>18</sup>Because of Mount Tsiyyon, which is desolate;
jackals have walked about on it.
<sup>19</sup>You, Yahweh, sit permanently,
your throne endures through the generations.
<sup>20</sup>Why do you put us out of mind permanently,
abandon us for length of days?
<sup>21</sup>Bring us back to yourself, Yahweh, so we may
come back;
make our days new, as before.
<sup>22</sup>But you have totally rejected us,
you have been utterly furious with us.

# EZEKIEL

Ezekiel [Yehezqe'l] was a member of the priestly clan in Israel, but before he was old enough to be a priest he was taken off into exile in Babylon with other priestly families in 597 BC. In Babylon he was given a vision of Yahweh and was summoned to be a prophet there to the exiles. The beginning of his prophetic work thus coincided with the last years of Jeremiah's prophetic work. Like Jeremiah, his messages brought much critique of the Jerusalem community and many warnings about disaster coming to it, but also brought promises of a more positive future the other side of the trouble. But whereas Jeremiah delivered the warnings and the promises in Jerusalem itself, Ezekiel delivered his warnings and promises in Babylon. The reason was that the future of Jerusalem was of decisive importance to people who had been taken off from there into exile. They were inclined to think that they would soon be going back home. Yahweh needs to get them to see that they will not soon be going home, because the conduct of priests, prophets, other leaders and ordinary people back home is such (perhaps worse than that of the people in exile) that Yahweh has to bring more chastisement upon them. On the other hand, when the axe has fallen, it will be possible for restoration to happen.

The book of Ezekiel divides neatly in accordance with this profile.

- In chapters 1—3 Ezekiel gives us an account of the vision Yahweh gave him that commissioned him as a lookout-prophet. It is a great vision of Yahweh himself, whose appearing in Babylon indicated that he had not abandoned the people who had been taken off into exile.
- In chapters 4—24 Ezekiel relates a series of visions of what is going on in Jerusalem. He portrays the goings on in Jerusalem as vividly as if he were actually there. No doubt his envisioning was facilitated by the knowledge of things in Jerusalem that he would have gained before he was taken into exile. He portrays the pagan practices that characterized the worship in the Jerusalem temple and the oppressive practices that characterized the life of the city, and he acts out the fall of the city and the exile of its inhabitants. His rhetoric and his acting out are exotic, picturesque, horrifying and not for the squeamish. Everything is subordinate to breaking through the consciousness of his audience.
- In chapters 25—32 Ezekiel begins the transition to the hopeful half of the book. Chapter 24 has referred to the beginning of the city's final siege, whose success (from the Babylonians' perspective) will open up the way to a more hopeful message. The transition lies in prophecies about Judah's neighbours who were often its adversaries (Ammon, Moab, Edom and Philistia), about the great regional trading nation Tyre, and about the nation that Judah often relied on as an ally, Egypt.
- Chapters 33—48 constitute Yahweh's direct promises about Judah's future. They begin with a renewed summons to Ezekiel to act as a watchman-prophet and with the arrival in Babylon of the news that Jerusalem has fallen. Yahweh now commissions Ezekiel to promise Israel's renewal. The promises constitute a series of declarations that Yahweh will take up and be faithful to his long-standing commitments. The people will be properly shepherded, by Yahweh and by a new David. Incursions from a people such as Edom will be stopped and the land that such peoples occupied will be Israel's again. The exiles will be brought back, cleansed and given a new spirit. The nation that feels reduced to dry bones will be brought back to life. The divided people will become one. Renewed threats from strange northern peoples will lead to their elimination. A remarkable new temple will be built and Yahweh will once again dwell there. The country itself will be physically transformed and reallocated. A river will flow from the temple to bring fruitfulness to hostile parts of the country. The city will be renamed 'Yahweh-Is-There'. This last section of the book makes clear that we should not be literalistic in interpreting Ezekiel, and this consideration undermines any suggestion that Ezekiel is referring to Middle Eastern events in our own time or that he is indicating that we should expect or plan for the rebuilding of the Jerusalem temple. But neither should we underestimate the wonder of what Yahweh promises.

## God appears in Babel

**1** In the thirtieth year, in the fourth, on the fifth of the month, when I was among the exile community by the River Kebar, the heavens opened and I saw a great appearance of God. ²On the fifth of the month (it was the fifth year of King Yoyakin's exile), ³Yahweh's word came to Yehezqe'l ben Buzi, the priest, in the country of the Kasdites by the River Kebar. Yahweh's hand came on him there.

⁴I saw: there, a hurricane wind came from the north, a great cloud, with fire consuming itself, with its brightness all round, with a very gleam of electrum from inside it, from inside the fire, ⁵and from inside it the form of four creatures. This was their appearance. They had human form, ⁶but they had four faces each and four wings each. ⁷Their feet: a straight foot, but the sole of their feet was like the sole of a calf's foot, and they were sparkling like the gleam of burnished copper. ⁸Human hands were under their wings on their four quarters.

Their faces and their wings belonging to the four of them: ⁹their wings touched each other. They wouldn't turn as they went; they'd go, each in the direction of its face. ¹⁰The form of their faces: a human face, but the four of them had a lion's face on the right, and the four of them had an ox's face on the left, and the four of them had an eagle's face. ¹¹So their faces. Their wings were stretching upwards, two belonging to each touching each, and two covering its body. ¹²They'd go each in the direction of its face; to wherever the wind was to go, they'd go. They wouldn't turn as they went.

¹³So the form of the creatures. Their appearance was very coals of fire burning, the very appearance of torches. It was going about between the creatures. The fire had a brightness, and from the fire lightning was coming out. ¹⁴The creatures were running and coming back, the very appearance of lightning-flashes.

## The creatures powering the chariot

¹⁵I looked at the creatures. There, one wheel on the earth beside the creatures with its four faces. ¹⁶The wheels' appearance and

their construction: the very gleam of topaz. The form of each of the four of them: their appearance and their construction were like a wheel inside a wheel. ¹⁷When they went, they'd go in the direction of their four quarters; they wouldn't turn as they went. ¹⁸Their rims were high and awe-inspiring. Their rims were full of eyes all round, belonging to the four of them. ¹⁹When the creatures went, the wheels would go, beside them. When the creatures lifted above the earth, the wheels lifted. ²⁰Wherever the wind was to go, they'd go there, with the wind going. The wheels would lift alongside them, because the creature's spirit was in the wheels. ²¹When they went, they'd go; when they stopped, they'd stop; when they lifted from on the earth, the wheels would lift alongside them, because the creature's spirit was in the wheels.

²²A form was above the creature's heads, a platform, the very gleam of crystal, awe-inspiring, spread out over their heads, above. ²³Under the platform their wings were straight towards each other. Each had two covering their bodies on one side, and each had two covering on the other side. ²⁴I heard the sound of their wings, the very sound of much water, the very sound of Shadday, when they went, the sound of a tumult, the very sound of an army. When they stopped, they'd relax their wings.

²⁵There was a sound above the platform that was over their head (when they stopped, they'd relax their wings). ²⁶Above the platform that was over their head was the very appearance of sapphire, the form of a throne, and above the form of the throne a form that was a very human appearance on it, above.

## A rebellious household

²⁷I saw the very gleam of electrum, the very appearance of fire within it all round, from the appearance of his hips upwards and from the appearance of his hips downwards I saw the very appearance of fire. His brightness was all round. ²⁸The very appearance of the bow that comes in the cloud on a rainy day, such was the appearance of the brightness all round. That was the appearance of the form of Yahweh's splendour.

I saw it and fell on my face, and I heard a voice speaking.

**2** He said to me, 'Young man, stand on your feet, so I may speak with you.' ²A wind came into me as he spoke to me. It stood me on my feet and I listened to him speaking to me.

³He said to me, 'Young man, I'm sending you to the Yisra'elites, nations that rebel, who've rebelled against me. They and their ancestors have defied me right up to this day. ⁴The descendants are tough-faced and strong-minded. I'm sending you to them, and you're to say to them, "The Lord Yahweh has said this." ⁵Whether they listen or refuse (because they're a rebellious household), they will acknowledge that a prophet's been among them. ⁶So you, young man, don't be afraid of them and don't be afraid of their words, when thistles and thorns are with you and you're living with scorpions. Don't be afraid of their words, don't shatter because of them, because they're a rebellious household. ⁷You're to speak my words to them whether they listen, or whether they refuse because they're rebellious. ⁸You, young man, listen to what I'm speaking to you. Don't become rebellious like the rebellious household. Open your mouth and eat what I'm going to give you.'

⁹I saw: there, a hand put out to me, and there, in it a document scroll. ¹⁰He spread it out before me. It was written on front and back. Laments, muttering and groaning were written on it.

### Strong-headed and tough-minded

**3** He said to me, 'Young man, eat what you find. Eat this scroll, and go speak to Yisra'el's household.' ²I opened my mouth and he got me to eat this scroll. ³He said to me, 'Young man, get your stomach to eat, fill your insides with this scroll that I'm giving you.' I ate, and in my mouth it became like syrup for sweetness.

⁴He said to me, 'Young man, go, come to Yisra'el's household and speak with my words to them. ⁵Because not to a people unfathomable of speech and difficult of language – you're sent to Yisra'el's household, ⁶not to many peoples unfathomable of speech and difficult of language whose words you can't listen to. If I didn't send you to them . . .

Those people would listen to you. ⁷But Yisra'el's household won't be willing to listen to you, because they're not willing to listen to me, because Yisra'el's entire household are strong-headed and tough-minded. ⁸There, I'm making your face strong over against their face and your head tough over against their head. ⁹Like a mineral harder than flint I'm making your head. You will not be afraid of them, you will not shatter before them, because they're a rebellious household.'

¹⁰Then he said to me, 'Young man, receive into your mind all my words that I speak to you. Listen with your ears ¹¹and go, come to the exile community, to the members of your people, and speak to them. Say to them, "The Lord Yahweh has said this", whether they listen or refuse.'

¹²Then a wind lifted me, and I heard behind me a great quaking sound: 'Yahweh's splendour be blessed from his place', ¹³and the sound of the creatures' wings beating against each other and the sound of the wheels alongside them: a great quaking sound. ¹⁴When a wind lifted me and took me, I went, bitter and in wrath of my spirit, with Yahweh's hand strong on me.

### I shall look for his blood from your hand

¹⁵I came to the exile community at Tel Abib living by the River Kebar. I lived where they were living, lived there desolate for seven days, ¹⁶and at the end of the seven days Yahweh's word came to me: ¹⁷'Young man, I'm making you a lookout for Yisra'el's household. You're to listen to the word from my mouth and warn them from me.

¹⁸When I say about the faithless person, "You will definitely die", and you don't warn him and don't speak to warn the faithless person from his faithless way, to keep him alive: he, the faithless person, will die for his waywardness, but I shall look for his blood from your hand. ¹⁹But you – when you warn the faithless person and he doesn't turn back from his faithlessness, from his faithless way: he will die for his waywardness, but you will have saved your life. ²⁰And when a faithful person turns back from his faithfulness and does what is evil and I put an obstacle before him, he will die, because you didn't warn him. For his

wrongdoing he will die, and his faithful acts that he has done won't be borne in mind, but I shall look for his blood from your hand. <sup>21</sup>But you, when you warn him (the faithful person) that the faithful person shouldn't do wrong, and he doesn't do wrong, he will definitely live because he let himself be warned, and you yourself will have saved your life.'

<sup>22</sup>Yahweh's hand came on me there and he said to me, 'Set off, go out to the valley, and I shall speak with you there.' <sup>23</sup>So I set off and went out to the valley, and there – Yahweh's splendour was standing there, like the splendour that I saw at the River Kebar. I fell on my face, <sup>24a</sup>but a wind came into me and stood me up on my feet.

## Acting out a siege

<sup>24b</sup>He spoke with me and said to me, 'Come, shut yourself inside your house. <sup>25</sup>You, young man, there – they're putting ropes on you and tying you up with them. You're not to go out among them. <sup>26</sup>I shall make your tongue stick to your palate and you'll be dumb. To them, you won't be someone who reproves, because they're a rebellious household. <sup>27</sup>But when I speak with you, I shall open your mouth and you will say to them, "The Lord Yahweh has said this." The one who listens may listen and the one who refuses may refuse, because they're a rebellious household.

**4** You, young man, get yourself a brick, put it before you, and engrave a town on it: Yerushalaim. <sup>2</sup>Prepare a siege against it. Build a tower against it. Heap up a ramp against it. Make a camp against it. Set up battering rams against it all round. <sup>3</sup>And you, get yourself an iron plate and place it as an iron wall between you and the town, and set your face towards it. It will be under siege; you're to lay siege against it. It will be a sign for Yisra'el's household.

<sup>4</sup>You yourself, lie on your left side and on it put the waywardness of Yisra'el's household. The number of the days that you lie on it, you will carry their waywardness. <sup>5</sup>I myself am giving you the years of their waywardness, in number 390 days; you will carry the waywardness of Yisra'el's household. <sup>6</sup>You will finish these, then lie on your right side, a second time, and carry the waywardness of

Yehudah's household. Forty days, a day for each year, I'm giving you.

## Defiled bread

<sup>7</sup>And towards Yerushalaim's siege you're to set your face and your bared arm, and prophesy against it. <sup>8</sup>There, I'm putting ropes on you, and you aren't to turn from side to side until you've finished your days of siege. <sup>9</sup>You're to get yourself wheat, barley, beans, lentils, millet and spelt, put them into a jar and make them into bread for yourself. For the number of days that you're lying on your side, 390 days, you're to eat it.

<sup>10</sup>The food that you eat, by weight, twenty sheqels a day, you're to eat at the regular times, <sup>11</sup>and water by measure you're to drink, a sixth of a gallon you're to drink at the regular times. <sup>12</sup>You're to eat it as a barley cake. Cook it on human excrement in their sight.' <sup>13</sup>Yahweh said, 'In this way the Yisra'elites will eat their bread, defiled, among the nations where I'm driving them.'

<sup>14</sup>I said, 'Oh, Lord Yahweh, here, my person hasn't been defiled. I haven't eaten anything found dead or torn by an animal, from my youth until now. Impure meat hasn't come into my mouth.' <sup>15</sup>So he said to me, 'See, I'm going to give you cattle dung instead of human excrement. You can make your bread on that.' <sup>16</sup>But he said to me, 'Young man, here am I, I'm going to break the bread supply in Yerushalaim. They will eat bread by weight in anxiety, and drink water by measure in desolation, <sup>17</sup>so that they run out of bread and water and are desolate in relation to one another, and waste away because of their waywardness.'

## Among the nations

**5** 'You, young man, get yourself a sharp sword. You're to get it for yourself as a barber's razor and pass it over your head and over your beard. Get yourself weighing scales and divide them [the hairs]. <sup>2</sup>You're to burn a third in fire inside the town when the days of the siege are fulfilled. Take a third and strike down all round it with the sword. And scatter a third to the wind; I shall draw a sword after them. ³But you're to get from there a few and bind them into the folds of your clothes. ⁴Get some of them again and throw them into the middle of the fire. Burn them in the fire. From this a fire will go out against the entire household of Yisraël.'

⁵The Lord Yahweh said this: "This Yerushalaim I put among the nations, with countries round it. ⁶But it rebelled against my rulings with more faithlessness than the nations, and against my laws more than the countries round it. Because people rejected my rulings, and my laws – they didn't walk by them.'

⁷Therefore the Lord Yahweh said this: 'Since you've been more turbulent than the nations that are round you – you haven't walked by my laws, you haven't acted on my rulings and you haven't acted in accordance with the rulings of the nations that are round you'; ⁸therefore the Lord Yahweh said this: 'Here am I over against you, yes, I myself. I shall act on rulings among you before the eyes of the nations. ⁹I shall do in you what I haven't done and the like of which I won't do again, on account of all your offensive practices.

¹⁰Therefore within you parents will eat children and children will eat their parents. I shall execute acts of authority against you and scatter your remainder to every wind. ¹¹Therefore as I live (the Lord Yahweh's declaration) if I don't, because you defiled my sanctuary with all your abominations and all your offensive practices – yes, I myself will shave you, my eye won't spare you, and I myself won't pity you. ¹²A third of you will die in an epidemic or be finished off through famine within you. A third will fall by the sword all round you. And a third I shall scatter to every wind, and draw a sword after them.

## About intolerance

¹³So my anger will finish itself up and I shall set down my wrath on them. I shall find relief, and they will acknowledge that I, Yahweh, have spoken in my passion, when I've finished up my wrath against them. ¹⁴I shall make you a waste and an object of reviling among the nations that are round you, in the sight of everyone passing by. ¹⁵It will be a basis for reviling and ridicule, for discipline and

desolation, to the nations that are round you, when I execute acts of authority against you in anger, in wrath and in wrathful reproofs. I, Yahweh, have spoken.

¹⁶When I send off the bad arrows of famine on the people who were due for devastating, which I shall send off to devastate you, I shall add to the famine upon you and break the bread supply for you. ¹⁷I shall send off against you famine and bad creatures, and they will bereave you; epidemic and bloodshed will pass through you, and I shall bring the sword against you. I, Yahweh, have spoken.'

**6** Yahweh's word came to me: ²'Young man, set your face towards Yisraël's mountains and prophesy towards them. ³You're to say, "Yisraël's mountains, listen to the Lord Yahweh's word. The Lord Yahweh said this to the mountains and to the hills, to the canyons and to the ravines: 'Here am I, I'm going to bring a sword against you, and I shall obliterate your shrines. ⁴Your altars will become desolate, your incense stands broken. I shall make those of you who are run through fall before their lumps. ⁵I shall put the Yisraëlites' corpses before their lumps and scatter your bones round your altars ⁶in all your settlements. The towns will be laid waste and the shrines desolate, in order that your altars may be laid waste and may make restitution, your lumps break and cease, your incense stands be cut down and what you've made be wiped out, ⁷and the person who is run through may fall among you. And you will acknowledge that I am Yahweh.

## I shall let some be left

⁸But I shall let some be left. When you have people who have escaped the sword among the nations, when you're scattered among the countries, ⁹those of you who escape will be mindful of me among the nations where they've been taken captive, that I've been broken with their whorish mind that turned away from me and with their eyes whoring after their lumps. They'll feel a loathing towards their own selves concerning the bad things that they've done, regarding all their offensive practices. ¹⁰And they will acknowledge that I am Yahweh. Not for

nothing did I speak about bringing all this bad fortune to them.'

[11]The Lord Yahweh said this: 'Clap with the palm of your hand, stamp with your foot. Say, "Aagh" about all the offensive bad practices of Yisra'el's household, who will fall by sword, by famine and by epidemic. [12]The person who's far away will die by the epidemic, the one who's near will fall by the sword, and the one who remains and is preserved will die by the famine. I shall finish up my wrath on them. [13]And you will acknowledge that I am Yahweh when those of them who are run through are among their lumps round their altars towards every high hill, on all the tops of the mountains, under every verdant tree and under every leafy oak, the site where they presented a pleasing fragrance to all their lumps. [14]I shall stretch out my hand against them and make the country desolation and devastation, from the wilderness to Diblah, in all their settlements. And they will acknowledge that I am Yahweh."'

## The club has blossomed

**7** Yahweh's word came to me: [2]'You, young man – the Lord Yahweh has said this to Yisra'el's land: "An end! The end is coming upon the four corners of the country. [3]The end is now upon you. I shall send off my anger against you, and I shall exercise authority over you in accordance with your ways. I shall put all your offensive practices upon you. [4]My eye won't spare you, I shall not have pity, because I shall put upon you your ways and your offensive practices that are within you. And you will acknowledge that I am Yahweh."'

[5]The Lord Yahweh said this: 'A singular bad event, a bad event – there, it's coming. [6]An end is coming, it's coming. The end is rousing itself against you, there, it's coming. [7]The doom is coming upon you, you who inhabit the country. The time is coming. The day is near, tumult not cheering on the mountains. [8]Now it's near.

I shall pour out my wrath on you and finish up my anger against you. I shall exercise authority over you in accordance with your ways, and put all your offensive practices upon you. [9]My eye will not spare, I shall not have pity. When in accordance with your ways I put them upon you, your offensive practices that

are within you, you will acknowledge that I am Yahweh, the one who strikes down.

[10]There, the day, there, it's coming. The doom is coming out. The club has blossomed, assertiveness has flourished, [11]violence has arisen with a faithless club. Nothing comes from them, not from their horde, not from anything of theirs; there's no distinction in them. [12]The time is coming, the day is coming close. The buyer shouldn't rejoice, the seller shouldn't mourn, because wrath is upon its entire horde. [13]Because the seller won't turn back to what he sold, even though their life is still among the living, because the vision about the entire horde won't turn back. Each in his waywardness – they won't keep strong hold on their life.

## They'll throw their silver into the streets

[14]They've sounded the horn and made everything ready, but there's no one going to the battle, because my wrath is against its entire horde. [15]The sword is in the street, the epidemic and the famine in the house. The person who's in the field will die by the sword, and the person who's in the town – famine and epidemic will consume him.

[16]Those of them that escape – they'll escape but be in the mountains like the pigeons in the ravines, all of them moaning, each in his waywardness. [17]All the hands will go slack, water will go down all the knees. [18]They'll wrap on sack, and shuddering will cover them, with shame on all faces and shornness on all their heads.

[19]They'll throw their silver into the streets; their gold will become taboo. Their silver and their gold won't be able to rescue them on the day of Yahweh's outburst, they won't satisfy people's desire or fill their stomachs, because their waywardness has become the cause of their collapse.

[20]Its jewelled splendour that he set in majesty, with it they made their offensive images, their abominations with it. Therefore I'm making it taboo for them. [21]I shall give it into the hand of strangers as plunder, as spoil for the faithless of the earth, and they'll treat it as ordinary. [22]I shall turn away my face from them, and people will treat my treasured place

as ordinary – intruders will come into it and treat it as ordinary.

## Inflammatory images

²³Make a chain, because the country is full of bloody exercise of authority, the town is full of violence. ²⁴I shall bring the nations that deal most badly and they will take possession of their houses. I shall put a stop to the majesty of the vigorous. Their sanctuaries will be made ordinary.

²⁵Calamity is coming. People will seek well-being but there will be none. ²⁶Disaster will come upon disaster, report will follow upon report. They will seek a vision from a prophet, but instruction will perish from priest and counsel from elders. ²⁷The king will mourn, the ruler will put on desolation as clothing, the hands of the country's people will tremble. According to their way I shall act with them, and on the basis of their acts of authority I shall exercise authority over them. And they will acknowledge that I am Yahweh.'

**8** In the sixth year, in the sixth, on the fifth of the month, I was sitting in my house and the Yehudahite elders were sitting before me, and the hand of the Lord Yahweh fell on me there. ²I looked, and there, a form with a fiery appearance. From the appearance of his hips and downwards there was fire, and from his hips and upwards, a gold appearance, the very gleam of electrum. ³He put out the form of a hand and took me by the hair of my head, and a wind lifted me between the earth and the heavens and brought me to Yerushalaim with a great appearance of God, to the entrance of the gateway to the inner courtyard that faces north, where was the seat of the inflammatory image, which inflames. ⁴There, the splendour of Yisrael's God was there, like the appearance that I saw in the valley.

⁵He said to me, 'Young man, raise your eyes northward, please.' I raised my eyes in the northward direction, and there, north of the altar gateway, was this inflammatory image, at the entrance. ⁶He said to me, 'Young man, do you see what they're doing, great offensive things that Yisrael's household are doing here, so that I shall go far from my sanctuary? You will see further great offensive things.

## Religion and violence

⁷He brought me to the entrance of the courtyard. I looked, and there, a hole in the wall. ⁸He said to me, 'Young man, break through the wall, please.' I broke through the wall, and there, a door. ⁹He said to me, 'Come in, look at the offensive bad things that they're doing here.' ¹⁰I came and looked, and there, every form of abominable reptile and animal and all the lumps of Yisrael's household, carved on the wall all the way round. ¹¹Seventy individuals of the elders of Yisrael's household, with Ya'azanyahu ben Shaphan standing among them, were standing before them, each with his censer in his hand. The richness of the incense cloud was going up. ¹²He said to me, 'Young man, have you seen what the elders of Yisrael's household are doing in the dark, each in his image-covered rooms? Because they're saying, "Yahweh isn't looking at us. Yahweh's abandoned the country."'

¹³He said to me, 'You will again see further great offensive things that they're doing.' ¹⁴He brought me to the entrance of the gateway of Yahweh's house that's to the north. There, the women were sitting there, bewailing Tammuz. ¹⁵He said to me, 'Young man, have you seen? You will again see further greater offensive things than these.' ¹⁶He brought me to the inner courtyard of Yahweh's house. There, at the gateway of Yahweh's palace, between the portico and the altar, some twenty-five men, their backs to Yahweh's palace and their faces to the east, and they were bowing low to the east, to the sun.

¹⁷He said to me, 'Young man, have you seen? Is it too slight for Yehudah's household to do the offensive things that they've done here? Because they've filled the country with violence and again provoked me. There they are, putting the branch to their nose. ¹⁸Yes, I myself will act in wrath. My eye won't spare and I shall not pity. They will call in my ears in a loud voice but I shall not listen to them.'

## Who are the people who groan and moan?

**9** He called in my ears in a loud voice, 'Come near, you who have appointment over the town, each of you with his implement of devastation in his hand.' ²And there – six individuals coming by way of the upper gateway that faces north, each with his implement of demolition in his hand, and an individual among them dressed in linen, with a writing case at his hips. They came and stood beside the copper altar. ³Now the splendour of Yisra'el's God had gone up from on the sphinx on which it had been, to the house's terrace. He called to the one dressed in linen, at whose hips was the writing case. ⁴Yahweh said to him, 'Pass through the middle of the town, through the middle of Yerushalaim, and put an X on the foreheads of the people who are groaning and who are moaning over the offensive things that are done in the middle of it.'

⁵To the others he said in my ears, 'Pass through the town after him and strike down. Your eye must not spare. You must not pity. ⁶Elder, young man, girl, little one, women, you're to kill outright. But any individual on whom is the X – don't go up to them. Start from my sanctuary.' So they started with the men who were the elders who were before the house. ⁷He said to them, 'Defile the house. Fill the courtyards with the people run through. Go out.' They went out and struck the town down.

⁸While they were striking down, I myself remained alone. I fell on my face and cried out and said, 'Aagh, Lord Yahweh, are you going to devastate all that remains of Yisra'el by pouring out your wrath on Yerushalaim?' ⁹He said to me, 'The waywardness of the household of Yisra'el and Yehudah is very, very great. The country is full of bloodshed. The town is full of injustice. Because they've said, "Yahweh has abandoned the country. Yahweh isn't looking." ¹⁰I, too – my eye won't spare and I won't pity. I'm putting their own way on their head.' ¹¹And there – the one clothed in linen, at whose hips was the writing case, was bringing back word: 'I've acted in accordance with all that you ordered me.'

## Take fire

**10** I looked, and there – on the platform that was over the head of the sphinxes was an actual sapphire stone; the appearance of the form of a throne appeared on it. ²He said

to the man clothed in linen, 'Come in between the whirling, underneath the sphinx, fill the hollow of your hands with burning coals from between the sphinxes, and scatter them over the town.' He came in before my eyes. ³The sphinxes were standing at the right of the house when the man came in, and the cloud was filling the inner courtyard.

⁴Yahweh's splendour lifted from above the sphinx above the house's terrace, the house filled with the cloud, and the courtyard was full of the brightness of Yahweh's splendour. ⁵The sound of the sphinxes' wings made itself heard as far as the outer courtyard, like the voice of God Shadday when he speaks. ⁶When he ordered the one dressed in linen, 'Take fire from between the whirling, from between the sphinxes', he came in and stood beside the wheel. ⁷The sphinx put out its hand from between the sphinxes to the fire that was between the sphinxes, took some up and put it into the hollow of the hands of the one dressed in linen. He took it and went out. ⁸(The form of a human hand belonging to the sphinxes appeared under their wings.)

⁹I looked, and there – four wheels beside the sphinxes, one wheel beside one sphinx, another wheel beside another sphinx. The appearance of the wheels: the very gleam of beryl stone. ¹⁰Their appearance: the four of them had one form, as if one wheel were inside another wheel. ¹¹When they went, they'd go in the direction of their four quarters. They wouldn't turn as they went, because the place that the head faced, they'd follow it. They wouldn't turn as they went.

## Yahweh leaves

¹²Their entire body – their backs, their hands and their wings – and the wheels were full of eyes all round (the wheels belonging to the four of them; ¹³these wheels had been called 'the whirling' in my ears). ¹⁴Each had four faces. Face one was the sphinx's face. Face two was a human face. The third was a lion's face. The fourth was an eagle's face.

¹⁵The sphinxes lifted; it was the creature that I'd seen by the River Kebar. ¹⁶When the sphinxes went, the wheels would go beside them. When the sphinxes raised their wings to

lift from on the earth, the wheels wouldn't turn from beside them, too. [17]When they stopped, they'd stop, and when they lifted, they'd lift with them, because the creature's spirit was in them.

[18]Yahweh's splendour went out from above the house's terrace and stood above the sphinxes. [19]The sphinxes raised their wings and lifted from the earth before my eyes as they went out, with the wheels alongside them. It stood at the entrance of the east gateway of Yahweh's house, with the splendour of Yisra'el's God over them, above. [20]It was the creature that I saw below Yisra'el's God at the River Kebar. So I recognized that they were sphinxes. [21]Each had four faces and each had four wings, with the form of human hands under their wings. [22]The form of their faces – they were the faces that I saw by the River Kebar, their appearance and themselves. They'd each go in the direction of its face.

## The pot and the meat

**11** A wind lifted me and brought me to the east gateway of Yahweh's house, which faces east. There, at the entrance of the gateway, were twenty-five men. I saw among them Ya'azanyah ben Azzur and Pelatyahu ben Benayahu, officials of the people. [2]He said to me, 'Young man, these are the men who think up trouble and formulate bad counsel in this town, [3]who say, "The building of houses isn't near. That's the pot, and we're the meat." [4]Therefore prophesy against them. Prophesy, young man.'

[5]Yahweh's spirit fell on me, and he said to me, 'Say, "Yahweh has said this: 'This is what you've said, Yisra'el's household; I myself know what's come up into your spirit. [6]You've multiplied the people run through by you in this town. You've filled its streets with people run through.'

[7]Therefore the Lord Yahweh has said this: 'The people run through by you whom you've put in the middle of it: they're the meat. That's the pot, but he's making you go out from the middle of it. [8]You're afraid of a sword, but I shall bring a sword upon you (the Lord Yahweh's declaration). [9]I shall make you go out from the middle of it and give you into the hand of strangers. I shall execute acts of authority against you. [10]By the sword you will fall. At Yisra'el's border I shall exercise authority over you, and you will acknowledge that I am Yahweh. [11]It won't be a pot for you nor will you be the meat in the middle of it. At Yisra'el's border I shall exercise authority over you, [12]and you will acknowledge that I am Yahweh, whose laws you didn't follow and whose rulings you didn't act on, but acted in accordance with the rulings of the nations that are round you.'"'

[13]As I prophesied, Pelatyahu ben Benayahu died. I fell on my face and cried out in a loud voice, 'Aagh, Lord Yahweh, you're finishing off the remainder of Yisra'el.'

## A small sanctuary

[14]Yahweh's word came to me: [15]'Young man, your brothers, your brothers who are the people in your extended family, Yisra'el's entire household, all of it, are the people of whom Yerushalaim's inhabitants have said, "Get far away from Yahweh. It's being given to us, the country, as a possession." [16]Therefore say, "The Lord Yahweh has said this: 'Because I've made them go far away among the nations and because I've scattered them among the countries but become a small sanctuary for them in the countries where they've come'", [17]therefore say, "The Lord Yahweh has said this: 'I shall collect you from the peoples, gather you from the countries in which I scattered them, and I shall give you Yisra'el's land.' [18]They will come there and remove all their abominations and their offensive practices from them, [19]and I shall give them one mind. I shall put a new spirit within you. I shall remove the mind of stone from their flesh and give them a mind of flesh, [20]so that they will follow my laws, and keep my rulings and act on them. They will be a people for me and I shall be God for them. [21]But the people whose mind is walking after the mind of their abominations and their offensive practices, I'm going to put their way on their own head (a declaration of the Lord Yahweh).'"'

[22]The sphinxes lifted up their wings, with the wheels alongside them and the splendour of Yisra'el's God over them, above. [23]Yahweh's

splendour went up from over the middle of the town and stood over the mountain that's on the east of the town, ²⁴while a wind lifted me up and brought me to Kasdim to the exile community, by the appearance from God's spirit, and the appearance that I'd seen went up from over me. ²⁵I spoke to the exile community all Yahweh's words that he'd shown me.

## Dramatizing exile

**12** Yahweh's word came to me: ²'Young man, you're living in the middle of a rebellious household, who have eyes for seeing but don't see, ears for hearing but don't hear, because they're a rebellious household. ³You, young man, prepare things for exile for yourself and go into exile by day before their eyes. Go into exile from your place to another place before their eyes. Perhaps they will see that they're a rebellious household.

⁴You're to take your things out like things for exile by day, before their eyes, and you yourself are to go out in the evening, before their eyes, like people going out into exile. ⁵Before their eyes, break through the wall for yourself and take them out through it. ⁶Before their eyes, you're to lift them on to your shoulder. You're to take it out in the dark. You're to cover your face and not look at the land, because I'm making you a sign for Yisra'el's household.'

⁷I did just as I was ordered. I took my things out by day, like things for exile, and in the evening I broke through the wall for myself with my hand. In the dark I took them out. I lifted them on my shoulder before their eyes.

⁸Yahweh's word came to me in the morning: ⁹'Young man, Yisra'el's household (a rebellious household) said to you, "What are you doing?", didn't they. ¹⁰Say to them, "The Lord Yahweh has said this: 'This pronouncement: the ruler in Yerushalaim and all Yisra'el's household that are among them.'" ¹¹Say, "I'm a sign for you. As I've done, so it will be done to them. They will go into exile, into captivity. ¹²The ruler who's among them will lift them on to his shoulder in the dark. He'll go out through the wall. They'll break through in order to take them out through it. He'll cover his face, because he won't look at the land with his eye. ¹³But I shall spread my net over him, and he'll be caught

in my trap. I shall bring him to Babel, to the country of the Kasdites, but he won't see it, and he'll die there. ¹⁴Everyone who's round him, his support staff and all his legions, I shall scatter to every wind, and draw a sword after them.

## God won't let things drag on

¹⁵They will acknowledge that I am Yahweh when I scatter them among the nations and disperse them among the countries. ¹⁶But I shall let a few of the people be left from sword, from famine and from epidemic, in order that they may recount all their offensive practices among the nations where they come. And they will acknowledge that I am Yahweh.'"

¹⁷Yahweh's word came to me: ¹⁸'Young man, you're to eat your food with trembling and drink your water with shuddering and with anxiety, ¹⁹and say to the country's people, "The Lord Yahweh has said this concerning Yerushalaim's inhabitants in the land of Yisra'el: 'They will eat their bread with anxiety and drink their water in desolation, in order that their country may be desolate of what fills it because of the violence of all the people who live in it. ²⁰The inhabited towns will be wasted and the country will become a desolation. And you will acknowledge that I am Yahweh.'"'

²¹Yahweh's word came to me: ²²'Young man, what's this saying that you have in the land of Yisra'el, "Days grow long and every vision perishes"? ²³Therefore say to them, "The Lord Yahweh has said this: 'I shall make this saying stop. They won't say it any more in Yisra'el.'" Rather, speak to them: "The days are drawing near, and the thing in every vision." ²⁴Because there won't any more be empty vision or deceptive divination within Yisra'el's household. ²⁵Because I Yahweh shall speak the word that I speak and it will be done. It won't drag on any more. Because in your days, rebellious household, I shall speak a word and do it (a declaration of the Lord Yahweh).'

²⁶Yahweh's word came to me: ²⁷'Young man, there, Yisra'el's household are saying, "The vision that he sees is for many days and he prophesies for far-off times." ²⁸Therefore say to them: "The Lord Yahweh has said this: 'None of the words that I speak will drag on any

more. The word that I speak will be acted on (a declaration of the Lord Yahweh)."'"

## About building a wall

**13** Yahweh's word came to me: ²'Young man, prophesy against Yisra'el's prophets, who are prophesying. Say to the prophets of their own mind, "Listen to Yahweh's word. ³The Lord Yahweh has said this: 'Hey, against the villainous prophets who follow their own spirit and have seen nothing. ⁴Your prophets have been like jackals among wastes, Yisra'el. ⁵You didn't go up into the breaks and build up the barrier round Yisra'el's household so it would stand in the battle on Yahweh's day. ⁶They saw emptiness and lying divination, those who say "Yahweh's declaration" when Yahweh hadn't sent them, and people expected the implementing of the word. ⁷It was an empty vision that you saw and lying divination that you uttered, wasn't it, saying "Yahweh's declaration" when I myself hadn't spoken.'"

⁸Therefore the Lord Yahweh has said this: "Because you spoke emptiness and saw lies, here am I towards you (a declaration of the Lord Yahweh); ⁹my hand will be against the prophets who see emptiness and who divine lies. They won't be in my people's council. They won't be recorded in the record of Yisra'el's household. They won't come into Yisra'el's land. And you will acknowledge that I am the Lord Yahweh.

¹⁰Because, yes because they've misled my people, saying 'Things will be well', when things won't be well, and 'He's building a divider', and there – they're coating it with paint: ¹¹say to the people coating it with paint, 'It will fall. Pouring rain is coming and I shall send hailstones that will fall, and a hurricane wind will break it up. ¹²There, the wall is falling. It will be said to you, won't it, "Where's the coating that you put on?"'"

¹³Therefore the Lord Yahweh has said this: "I shall make a hurricane wind break out in my wrath, and pouring rain will come in my anger and hailstones in my wrath, to a finish. ¹⁴I shall tear down the wall that you've coated with paint, bring it close to the earth, and its foundation will become visible. When it falls, you will come to a finish within it. And you will acknowledge that I am Yahweh.

## Trapping people's lives like birds

¹⁵I shall finish up my wrath on the wall and on the people who coat it with paint, and I shall say to you, 'There's no wall and there are no painters of it, ¹⁶Yisra'el's prophets who prophesy about Yerushalaim and see a vision of things being well for it when things aren't going to be well (a declaration of the Lord Yahweh).'"

¹⁷And you, young man, set your face against your people's daughters, who prophesy out of their own mind. Prophesy against them. ¹⁸You shall say, "The Lord Yahweh has said this: 'Hey, to the women who sew straps on any wrists and make veils for the head of someone of any height, to trap their lives. Should you trap my people's lives but keep yourselves alive for yourselves? ¹⁹You've treated me as ordinary to my people, for handfuls of barley and for crumbs of bread, so as to put to death people who shouldn't die and to keep alive people who shouldn't live, with your lying to my people who listen to lying.'"

²⁰Therefore the Lord Yahweh has said this: "Here am I, against your straps, where you're [like people] hunting the lives of flying creatures. I shall tear them off from your arms and send off [free] the lives that you're hunting, [like] the lives of flying creatures. ²¹I shall tear off your veils and rescue my people from your hand. They will no longer be an object for hunting in your hand. And you will acknowledge that I am Yahweh.

²²Because of your saddening the heart of the faithful person with falsehood when I myself hadn't hurt him, and for your strengthening the hands of the faithless person so that he wouldn't turn back from his bad way so as to stay alive, ²³therefore you won't see emptiness and you won't practise divination any more. I shall rescue my people from your hand. And you will acknowledge that I am Yahweh.'"

## Shall I really let myself be enquired of by them?

**14** People from among Yisra'el's elders came to me and sat before me, ²and Yahweh's word came to me: ³'Young man, these people have taken up their lumps into their mind and set their waywardness as an obstacle in front of their faces. Shall I really let myself be enquired of by them? [4]Therefore speak to them: "The Lord Yahweh has said this: 'Any individual from Yisra'el's household who takes up his lumps into his mind and places his waywardness as an obstacle in front of his face, and comes to the prophet, I make an answer to him through it (through the great number of his lumps), [5]in order to lay hold of Yisra'el's household through its mind, because they've become estranged from me through their lumps, all of them.'"

[6]Therefore say to Yisra'el's household, "The Lord Yahweh has said this: 'Turn back, turn yourselves back from your lumps, turn back your faces from your offensive practices. [7]Because any individual from Yisra'el's household or from the aliens residing in Yisra'el who becomes estranged from following me and takes up his lumps into his mind and sets his waywardness as an obstacle in front of his face, and comes to the prophet to enquire of him with me – I Yahweh will make an answer to him by myself. [8]I shall set my face against that individual and make him a sign and a saying. I shall cut him off from among my people. And you will acknowledge that I am Yahweh.'"

[9]When a prophet is enticed and speaks a word, I Yahweh will have enticed that prophet, and I shall stretch out my hand against him and annihilate him from among my people Yisra'el. [10]They will carry their waywardness. The enquirer's waywardness and the prophet's waywardness will be the same, [11]in order that Yisra'el's household may not wander again from following me and may not defile itself again with all its rebellions. They will be a people for me and I shall be God for them (a declaration of the Lord Yahweh).'

## Noah, Dan'el and Iyyob (Job)

[12]Yahweh's word came to me: [13]'Young man, when a country does wrong to me by committing a trespass, and I stretch out my hand against it, and I break its bread supply and send famine against it and cut off from it human beings and animals, [14]were these three people within it, Noah, Dan'el and Iyyob, by their faithfulness they would save their own

lives (a declaration of the Lord Yahweh). [15]If I let bad creatures pass through the country, and they leave it childless and it becomes a desolation without anyone passing through in face of the creatures, [16]were these three people within it, as I live (a declaration of the Lord Yahweh), neither sons nor daughters would they save. They'd save themselves alone. The country would become a desolation.

[17]Or I might bring a sword against that country and say, "A sword is to pass through the country, and I shall cut off from it human beings and animals"; [18]were these three people within it, as I live (a declaration of the Lord Yahweh) they wouldn't save sons or daughters, but would save themselves alone.

[19]Or I might send off an epidemic to that country and pour out my wrath on it in bloodshed, cutting off from it human beings and animals; [20]were Noah, Dan'el and Iyyob within it, as I live (a declaration of the Lord Yahweh) they wouldn't save a son or a daughter. These people would save themselves alone by their faithfulness.'

[21]Because the Lord Yahweh has said this: 'How much more when I've sent off my four bad judgements – sword, famine, bad creature and epidemic – to Yerushalaim, to cut off from it human beings and animals.

[22]But there – an escape group is being left in it, people who are being taken out, sons and daughters. There they are, coming out to you. You will see their way and their deeds, and be comforted about the bad fate that I shall have brought upon Yerushalaim, all that I've brought upon it. [23]They will comfort you because you will see their way and their deeds and you will acknowledge that it was not without reason that I did all that I did against it (a declaration of the Lord Yahweh).'

## The useless vine wood

**15** Yahweh's word came to me: [2]'Young man, how will the vine's wood be better than the wood of any branch that's among the trees of the forest? [3]Will wood be taken from it to make anything? Will they take a peg from it to hang an object on? [4]There, it's put in the fire to be consumed. If the fire consumes the two ends of it and the middle of it is burned, is it useful for anything? [5]There, when it was whole, it couldn't be made into anything. How much less when the fire consumes it, and it burns, can it be made into anything.

[6]Therefore the Lord Yahweh says this: "As the wood of the vine among the trees of the forest that I gave to the fire for consuming, so I'm giving Yerushalaim's inhabitants. [7]I'm setting my face against them. They got out from the fire, but the fire will consume them. And you will acknowledge that I am Yahweh when I set my face against them. [8]I shall make the country a desolation because they committed trespass (a declaration of the Lord Yahweh).'"

**16** Yahweh's word came to me: [2]"Young man, get Yerushalaim to acknowledge its offensive practices. [3]You're to say, "The Lord Yahweh has said this to Yerushalaim: 'Your origin and your birth were from the Kena'anites' [Canaanites'] country – your father an Amorite and your mother a Hittite. [4]Your birth: on the day you were born, no one cut your cord and you weren't washed in water for cleansing. You weren't rubbed with salt at all and you weren't wrapped up at all. [5]No eye cared about you so as to do one of these things for you to express compassion for you. You were thrown on to the face of the open country in loathing for you on the day you were born. [6]But I passed by you and looked at you kicking about in your bloodiness and I said to you in your bloodiness, "Live." Yes, I said to you in your bloodiness, "Live."

### You're just a whore

[7]I made you big like a plant in the open country, and you grew big. You grew up and came to full loveliness; your breasts formed, your hair flourished, but you were naked, bare. [8]I passed by you and saw you – there, your time was time for love. I spread my robe over you and covered your nakedness. I took an oath to you and came into a pact with you (a declaration of the Lord Yahweh) and you became mine.

[9]I washed you in water and sluiced off the blood from on you and poured oil over you. [10]I clothed you with embroidery and gave you leather footwear. I wrapped you round in fine linen and covered you in silk. [11]I adorned you with jewellery and put bracelets on your hands and a necklace on your neck. [12]I put a ring on your nose, earrings on your ears and a splendid crown on your head. [13]So you adorned yourself with gold and silver, and your clothing was of fine linen, silk and embroidery, your food was choice flour, syrup and oil, and you became more and more beautiful, and attained a royal position. [14]Your fame went out among the nations for your beauty, because it was complete through the splendour that I put on you (a declaration of the Lord Yahweh).

[15]But you relied on your beauty and whored on the basis of your fame. You poured your whorings on every passer-by. It could become his. [16]You took some of your clothes and made yourself colourful shrines, and whored at them (not things to come, and they will not be). [17]You took your splendid things of gold and of silver that I gave you and made yourself male images and whored with them. [18]You took your embroidered clothes and covered them and offered my oil and incense before them.

### Yes, just a whore

[19]My food that I gave you, fine flour, oil and syrup that I let you eat, you gave before them as a pleasing fragrance, and so it became (a declaration of the Lord Yahweh). [20]You took your sons and your daughters to whom you gave birth for me and sacrificed them to them to eat: were your whorings trivial? [21]You slaughtered my children and gave them to them by making them pass through [fire].

[22]With all your offensive practices and your whorings, you weren't mindful of your young days when you were naked and bare, kicking about in your bloodiness. [23]After all your bad dealing (hey, hey, to you: a declaration of the Lord Yahweh) [24]you built yourself an enclosure and made yourself a platform in every square. [25]At the top of every street you built your platform and made your beauty something offensive. You spread your legs to every passer-by and multiplied your whorings. [26]You whored with the Misrayimites [Egyptians], your neighbours with their big members. You multiplied your whoring to provoke me. [27]So there, I'm stretching out my hand to you and

cutting your maintenance. I'm giving you over to the will of people who are hostile to you, the Pelishtite [Philistine] women, who are ashamed of your deliberately wicked way.

²⁸You whored with the Ashshurites because you weren't full. You whored with them, but you were still not full. ²⁹You multiplied your whoring with the trader country, Kasdim, but you were still not full with this. ³⁰How feeble was your mind (a declaration of the Lord Yahweh) when you did all these things, the action of a whorish, powerful woman.

## But a strange kind of whore

³¹When you built your enclosure at the top of every street and made your platform in every square, you were not like a whore in scorning a "gift", ³²you adulterous wife who accepts strangers instead of her husband. ³³To all whores men give a fee, but you – you've given fees to all your lovers, and paid them to come to you from all round for your whorings. ³⁴With you it was the opposite from other women, in your whorings. Whoring wasn't done by going after you but through your giving a "gift". A "gift" was not given to you. You were the opposite.

³⁵Therefore listen to Yahweh's word, whore. ³⁶The Lord Yahweh has said this: "Since your copper poured out and your nakedness exposed itself in your whorings with your lovers and with all your offensive lumps, and in accordance with the bloodshed of your children whom you gave to them, ³⁷therefore here am I, I'm going to collect all your lovers to whom you were sweet, each one whom you loved, as well as each one to whom you were hostile. I shall collect them against you from all round and expose your nakedness to them. They will see all your nakedness ³⁸and I shall make for you the judgements appropriate for women who commit adultery or pour out blood. I shall make you an object of the blood of wrath and passion. ³⁹I shall give you into their hand and they will tear down your enclosure and break down your platforms. They will strip you of your clothes, take your splendid things, and leave you naked and bare. ⁴⁰They will bring up a congregation against you, pelt you with stones and cut you down with their

swords. ⁴¹They will burn your houses with fire and execute acts of authority against you before the eyes of many women. I shall make your whoring stop. You will no more give 'gifts', either. ⁴²I shall set down my wrath with you and turn away my passion from you, and be calm and not vexed any more.

## Yerushalaim, her mother and her sisters

⁴³Since you weren't mindful of your young days and you infuriated me with all these things, I myself shall also – yes, I shall put your way on your own head (a declaration of the Lord Yahweh). You acted on your deliberate wickedness with your offensive practices, didn't you.

⁴⁴There, everyone who quotes sayings will quote this saying with regard to you: 'Like mother, like daughter'. ⁴⁵You're your mother's daughter, renouncing her husband and her children. You're the sister of your sisters, who renounced their husbands and their children. Your mother was a Hittite, your father an Amorite. ⁴⁶Your big sister was Shomron [Samaria], she and her daughters who were living to the north of you. Your little sister who was living to the south of you was Sedom [Sodom] and her daughters. ⁴⁷You walked in their ways and acted by their offensive practices, didn't you. In a very short while you became more devastating than them in all your ways. ⁴⁸As I live (a declaration of the Lord Yahweh), if Sedom your sister, she and her daughters, had acted as you and your daughters acted . . .

⁴⁹There, this was the waywardness of Sedom your sister: she and her daughters had majesty, plenty of bread, and calm peacefulness, but they didn't take the hand of the humble and needy. ⁵⁰They were lofty and they did something offensive before me. So I removed them, as you have seen. ⁵¹Shomron – she didn't commit half your wrongdoings; you've multiplied your wrongdoings more than her. You made your sisters seem faithful with all your offensive deeds that you did. ⁵²You, too, carry your shame, you who've pleaded for your sisters with your wrongdoings with which you've acted more offensively than them.

They're more faithful than you. Yes, you – be shamed. Carry your disgrace in your making your sisters seem faithful.

## But whoring will not be the end of the story

⁵³I shall restore their fortunes, the fortunes of Sedom and her daughters and the fortunes of Shomron and her daughters, and the fortunes of your captivity among them, ⁵⁴in order that you may carry your disgrace and feel disgraced for all that you've done in enabling them to take comfort. ⁵⁵Your sister Sedom and her daughters will go back to what they were before, Shomron and her daughters will go back to what they were before, and you and your daughters will go back to what you were before. ⁵⁶Your sister Sedom was a topic of talk in your mouth in the day of your majesty, wasn't she, ⁵⁷before your bad dealing became open, at the very time of the reviling of the daughters of Aram and all the peoples round her, the daughters of the Pelishtites, who jeer at you from all round. ⁵⁸Your scheming and your offensive deeds – you are going to carry them (Yahweh's declaration).'"

⁵⁹Because the Lord Yahweh has said this: 'Yes, I shall act with you as you've acted, in that you've despised the vow, in contravening the pact. ⁶⁰But I – I shall be mindful of my pact with you in your young days. I shall implement for you a permanent pact. ⁶¹You will be mindful of your ways and feel disgrace when you receive your sisters, the ones who are bigger than you and the ones who are younger than you. I shall give them to you as daughters, though not on the basis of your pact. ⁶²I – I shall implement my pact with you. And you will acknowledge that I am Yahweh, ⁶³in order that you may be mindful and feel shame. It won't be for you to open your mouth again in the face of your disgrace, when I make expiation for you for all that you've done (a declaration of the Lord Yahweh).'"

## A tale of two eagles

**17** Yahweh's word came to me: ²'Young man, unveil a conundrum, tell Yisra'el's household a parable. ³Say, "The Lord Yahweh has said this: 'A big eagle, big-winged, long-feathered, full-plumaged, with colouring, came to the Lebanon and took the top of a cedar. ⁴He broke off the highest of its shoots, brought it to a merchant country and put it in a traders' town. ⁵He took some of the country's seed and put it in a seed field; he placed it by plentiful water, a willow. ⁶It grew and became a spreading vine, low in height, its branches to turn to him, its roots being beneath it. So it became a vine, produced limbs and sent out shoots.

⁷But there was another big eagle, big-winged, much-plumaged. There – this vine turned its roots towards it and sent out its branches to it for it to water it, away from the beds where it was sown, ⁸though it had been planted in a good field by plentiful water so as to produce boughs, bear fruit, and become an impressive vine.'"

⁹Say, "The Lord Yahweh has said this: 'It may flourish, but he will tear up its roots and strip off its fruit so that it withers, won't he. All the leaves of its growth will wither (not by means of a big arm or by means of a large company) to carry it off by its roots. ¹⁰There, though planted, will it flourish? It will totally wither when the east wind touches it, won't it. It will wither on the beds where it grew.'"

¹¹Yahweh's word came to me: ¹²'Say to the rebellious household, please: "You acknowledge what these things are, don't you." Say: "There, the king of Babel came to Yerushalaim, took its king and its officials, and brought them to him, to Babel. ¹³He took someone from the royal offspring and solemnized a pact with him and put him under a vow, but he took the leaders of the country ¹⁴so that it might be a lowly kingdom and not exalt itself, keeping his pact so as to stand.

## A tale of two trees

¹⁵But he rebelled against him by sending his envoys to Misrayim so it would give him horses and a large company. Will he flourish? Will the one who does these things escape? Will he contravene a pact and escape? ¹⁶As I live (a declaration of the Lord Yahweh), if he doesn't die in the place belonging to the king who

made him king, whose vow he despised and
whose pact he contravened, inside Babel . . .

<sup>17</sup>Par'oh [Pharaoh] won't act towards
him with a big force, with a numerous
congregation – with battle, with the heaping up
of a ramp and with the building of a tower, to
cut down many lives. <sup>18</sup>He despised a vow by
contravening a pact. There – he gave his hand,
but he did all these things. He won't escape.
<sup>19</sup>Therefore the Lord Yahweh has said this: 'As I
live, if I don't put on his own head my vow that
he despised and my pact that he contravened . . .
<sup>20</sup>I shall spread my net over him, and he'll be
caught in my trap. I shall bring him to Babel
and enter into judgement with him there for
the trespass that he committed against me.
<sup>21</sup>All the fugitives in all his legions will fall by
the sword and the remainder will scatter to
every wind. And you will acknowledge that I
Yahweh have spoken.'''

<sup>22</sup>Yahweh has said this: 'And I myself shall
take from the top of a tall cedar, and put from
the highest of its shoots a tender one that I
shall break off and myself plant on a lofty, tall
mountain. <sup>23</sup>On Yisra'el's high mountains I shall
plant it. It will bear boughs and produce fruit,
and become an august cedar. Every bird of
every wing will dwell beneath it; in the shade
of its branches they will dwell. <sup>24</sup>All the trees of
the field will acknowledge that I am Yahweh. I
shall have brought low the exalted tree, exalted
the lowly tree, withered the green tree and
made the withered tree flourish. I am Yahweh.
I have spoken and I shall act.'

## Father and son

**18** Yahweh's word came to me: <sup>2</sup>'What
is it to you people using this saying
on Yisra'el's land, "Parents eat sour grapes,
but children's teeth feel rough"? <sup>3</sup>As I live
(a declaration of the Lord Yahweh), if you have
any more using of this saying in Yisra'el . . .
<sup>4</sup>Here, all lives are mine. As the parent's life,
so the child's life, they're mine. The person who
sins, he will die. <sup>5</sup>When an individual is faithful
and exercises authority with faithfulness:
<sup>6</sup>he hasn't eaten on the mountains;
nor raised his eyes to the lumps of Yisra'el's
household;
nor defiled his neighbour's wife;

nor does he draw near a woman who's taboo;
<sup>7</sup>nor does he oppress an individual;
he gives back the pledge given him for a debt;
nor does he commit robbery;
he gives his bread to the hungry person;
he covers the naked with clothes;
<sup>8</sup>he doesn't give on the basis of earning
interest nor take a profit;
he turns his hand back from what is evil;
he makes a truthful judgement between one
individual and another:
<sup>9</sup>he walks by my laws and has kept my rulings
by exercising truthfulness. He's faithful. He
will definitely live (a declaration of the Lord
Yahweh).

<sup>10</sup>But he fathers a violent son, a shedder
of blood, who does one or another of these
things, <sup>11</sup>when he himself did none of
these things. Rather he
has eaten on the mountains;
has defiled his neighbour's wife;
<sup>12</sup>has oppressed the humble and needy;
has committed robbery;
doesn't return a pledge;
has raised his eyes to the lumps;
has done an offensive thing;
<sup>13</sup>has given on the basis of earning interest
and taken a profit:
is he to live? He won't live. One who has done
any of these offensive things will definitely die.
His bloodshed will be against him.

## Do I really want the death of a faithless person?

<sup>14</sup>But there, he fathers a son, and he sees all
his father's wrongdoings that he committed.
He sees, and he doesn't act in accordance with
them:
<sup>15</sup>he hasn't eaten on the mountains;
he hasn't raised his eyes to the lumps of
Yisra'el's household;
he hasn't defiled his neighbour's wife;
<sup>16</sup>he hasn't oppressed anyone;
he hasn't exacted a pledge;
he hasn't committed robbery;
he has given his bread to a hungry person;
he has covered a naked person with clothes;
<sup>17</sup>he has turned his hand back from the
humble;
he hasn't taken interest or profit:

he has acted on my rulings; he has walked by my laws. He won't die because of his father's waywardness. He will definitely live. ¹⁸His father, because he practised fraud, committed robbery against his brother and did what was not good among his people: there, he will definitely die for his waywardness.

¹⁹You say, "Why has the son not carried any of the father's waywardness?" But the son has exercised authority with faithfulness, kept all my laws and done them. He will live. ²⁰The person who does wrong, he will die. A son doesn't carry any of the father's waywardness and a father doesn't carry any of the son's waywardness. The faithfulness of the faithful person belongs to him and the faithlessness of the faithless person belongs to him. ²¹But the faithless person when he turns back from all his wrongdoings that he's committed and keeps all my laws and exercises authority with faithfulness, he will definitely live. He won't die. ²²None of the rebellions that he's committed will be kept in mind for him; through the faithfulness with which he's acted, he will live. ²³Do I really want the death of the faithless person (a declaration of the Lord Yahweh) and not his turning back from his ways so that he lives?

### Produce yourselves a new mind and a new spirit

²⁴But when the faithful person turns back from his faithfulness and does what is evil in accordance with all the offensive things that the faithless person did, and does them, is he to live? None of his faithful acts that he's done will be kept in mind because of the trespass that he's committed and the wrongdoings that he's done. Through them he will die. ²⁵You say, "The Lord's way isn't just." Listen please, Yisra'el's household. Is it my way that isn't just? It's your ways that aren't just, isn't it. ²⁶When a faithful person turns back from his faithfulness and does what is evil and dies for them, he dies for the wrong that he's done. ²⁷And when a faithless person turns back from his faithlessness that he's done and exercises authority with faithfulness, he keeps himself alive. ²⁸He's seen and turned back from all his rebellions that he's done. He will definitely live. He won't die.

²⁹Yisra'el's household say, "The Lord's way isn't just." Is it my ways that are not just, Yisra'el's household? It's your ways that aren't just, isn't it. ³⁰Therefore I shall exercise authority over you, Yisra'el's household, over each person in accordance with his ways (a declaration of the Lord Yahweh). So turn back, turn yourselves back from all your rebellions, and they won't become a wayward obstacle to you. ³¹Throw away from you all your rebellions that you've committed. Produce yourselves a new mind and a new spirit. Why should you die, Yisra'el's household? ³²Because I don't want the death of the person who dies (a declaration of the Lord Yahweh). So turn back and live!'

### A dirge for a nation's rulers

**19** 'And you, take up a dirge for Yisra'el's rulers. ²Say:

What was your mother? –
   a lioness among lions.
She bedded down among the great cougars,
   reared her cubs.
³She brought up one of her cubs,
   he became a cougar.
He learned to hunt prey,
   he ate human beings.
⁴Nations heard about him,
   he was caught in their pit.
They brought him with hooks
   to the country of Misrayim.

⁵She saw that she'd expected,
   whereas her hope had perished.
She got another of her cubs,
   made him a cougar.
⁶He went about among the lions;
   he became a cougar.
He learned to hunt prey,
   he ate human beings.
⁷He had sex with their widows,
   wasted their towns.
The country and what filled it were desolate
   at the sound of his roaring.
⁸But nations set against him
   from provinces all round.
They spread their net over him;
   he was caught in their pit.
⁹They put him in a cage with hooks,

brought him to the king of Babel.
They brought him into a great stronghold,
  in order that his voice wouldn't make itself
    heard
  any more on Yisra'el's mountains.

¹⁰Your mother was a real vine (with your blood),
  planted by water.
It became fruitful and green
  because of the abundant water.
¹¹It had vigorous boughs
  fit for the clubs of rulers.
The stature of one grew high, among the clouds,
  and it was visible by its height, by the number
    of its branches.
¹²But it was uprooted in wrath, thrown to the
    earth,
  and the east wind withered its fruit.
They broke and withered;
  its vigorous bough – fire consumed it.
¹³So now it's planted in the wilderness,
  in a dry, thirsty country.
¹⁴Fire came out from its bough,
  consumed its branches with its fruit.
It didn't have a vigorous bough,
  a club for ruling.'

  It's a dirge. It became a dirge.

## When you can't enquire of God

**20** In the seventh year, in the fifth,
on the tenth of the month, some
Yisra'elite elders came to enquire of Yahweh,
and sat before me. ²Yahweh's word came to me:
³'Young man, speak to Yisra'el's elders: "The
Lord Yahweh has said this: 'Is it to enquire of
me that you're coming? As I live, if I shall let
myself be enquired of by you (a declaration of
the Lord Yahweh) . . .'"

⁴Will you exercise authority over them, will
you exercise authority over them, young man?
Get them to acknowledge their ancestors'
offensive practices. ⁵Say to them, "The Lord
Yahweh has said this: 'On the day when I
chose Yisra'el, I raised my hand [to swear] to
the offspring of Ya'aqob's [Jacob's] household,
and when I made myself known to them in
the country of Misrayim, I raised my hand to
them, saying "I am Yahweh your God." ⁶On
that day I raised my hand to them to get them

out of the country of Misrayim to a country
that I'd sought out for them, flowing with
milk and syrup; it was the most splendid of all
countries. ⁷I said to them, "Each person, throw
away the abominations before your eyes. Don't
defile yourselves with Misrayim's lumps. I am
Yahweh your God." ⁸But they rebelled against
me. They wouldn't listen to me. Each person,
they didn't throw away the abominations
before their eyes and abandon Misrayim's
lumps.
  I said I'd pour out my wrath on them, to
finish up my anger against them within the
country of Misrayim. ⁹But I acted for the sake
of my name, so that it might not be treated
as ordinary in the eyes of the nations among
whom they were, before whose eyes I'd caused
myself to be acknowledged by them in getting
them out of the country of Misrayim.

## They treated the sabbath as ordinary

¹⁰So I got them out of the country of
Misrayim and brought them into the
wilderness. ¹¹I gave them my laws and made
known to them my rulings, which a person
may act on and live by. ¹²I also gave them my
sabbaths, to become a sign between me and
them, so that they might acknowledge that I
am Yahweh, who makes them sacred. ¹³But
Yisra'el's household rebelled against me in the
wilderness. They didn't walk by my laws. They
rejected my rulings, which a person may act on
and live by, and they quite treated my sabbaths
as ordinary.
  I said I'd pour my wrath on them in the
wilderness, so as to finish them off. ¹⁴But I
acted for the sake of my name so that it might
not be treated as ordinary in the eyes of the
nations before whose eyes I got them out.
¹⁵But I did also raise my hand to them in the
wilderness not to bring them into the country
that I'd given them, flowing with milk and
syrup, the most splendid of all countries,
¹⁶because they'd rejected my rulings and not
walked by my laws, and treated my sabbaths
as ordinary, because their mind was following
their lumps.
  ¹⁷But my eye had pity on them so as not to
devastate them. I didn't bring them to a finish
in the wilderness. ¹⁸I said to their children in

the wilderness, "Don't follow your parents' laws and don't keep their rulings, and don't defile yourselves with their lumps. ¹⁹I am Yahweh your God. Walk by my laws and keep my rulings and do them, ²⁰and make my sabbaths sacred so that they're a sign between me and you, so that you acknowledge that I am Yahweh your God." ²¹But the children rebelled against me. They didn't walk by my laws and they didn't keep my rulings by acting on them, which an individual may act on and live by. They treated my sabbaths as ordinary.

I said I'd pour my wrath on them to finish up my anger against them in the wilderness. ²²But I held back my hand and acted for the sake of my name so that it might not be treated as ordinary in the eyes of the nations before whose eyes I'd got them out.

### The shrine (bamah): come to what (ba' mah)?

²³I did also raise my hand to them in the wilderness to scatter them through the nations and disperse them through the countries, ²⁴because they didn't act on my rulings but rejected my laws and treated my sabbaths as ordinary, and their parents' lumps were before their eyes. ²⁵I myself also gave them laws that weren't good and rulings they couldn't live by. ²⁶I defiled them by their gifts when they made every firstborn of the womb pass through [fire], so that I might desolate them, in order that they might acknowledge that I am Yahweh.'"

²⁷Therefore speak to Yisra'el's household, young man, and say to them, "The Lord Yahweh has said this: 'Your ancestors further insulted me with this, by committing trespass against me. ²⁸I brought them into the country that I'd raised my hand to give them. But they looked at every high hill and every leafy tree and slaughtered their sacrifices there, made the provocation of their offering there, produced their pleasing fragrance there and poured their libations there. ²⁹I said to them, "What [mah] is the shrine [bamah] that you're coming to [ba]?" (and they've named it bamah until this day).'"

³⁰Therefore say to Yisra'el's household: "The Lord Yahweh has said this: 'Are you defiling yourselves in the manner of your ancestors and whoring after their abominations, ³¹and

in presenting your gifts by making your children pass though fire defiling yourselves in connection with all your lumps, until this day? And shall I let myself be enquired of by you, Yisra'el's household? As I live (a declaration of the Lord Yahweh), if I let myself be enquired of by you . . .

³²What comes up into your spirit will simply not happen, that you're saying, "We'll be like the nations, like the countries' kin-groups, in ministering to wood and stone." ³³As I live (a declaration of the Lord Yahweh), if I don't reign over you with a strong hand and with an arm stretched out and with wrath poured out . . .

### Then I will accept you

³⁴So I shall get you out from the peoples and collect you from the countries among whom you're scattered, with a strong hand and with an arm stretched out and with wrath poured out. ³⁵I shall bring you into the wilderness of the peoples and enter into judgement with you there face to face. ³⁶As I entered into judgement with your ancestors in the wilderness of the country of Misrayim, so I shall enter into judgement with you (a declaration of the Lord Yahweh). ³⁷I shall get you to pass under a club and bring you into a pact bond. ³⁸I shall purge out from you the people who rebel and revolt against me; while I shall get them out from the country where they're residing, they will not come into the land of Yisra'el. And you will acknowledge that I am Yahweh.

³⁹You, Yisra'el's household: the Lord Yahweh has said this: "Each person, go, serve his lumps, and afterwards, if you don't listen to me. But you won't treat my sacred name as ordinary any more with your gifts and your lumps. ⁴⁰Because on my sacred mountain, on Yisra'el's high mountain (a declaration of the Lord Yahweh), there Yisra'el's entire household, all of it, will serve me in the country. There I shall accept them and there I shall ask after your donations and the finest of your offerings with all your sacred things. ⁴¹With your pleasing fragrance I shall accept you when I get you out from the peoples and collect you from the countries in which you're scattered. I shall make myself sacred through you in the eyes of the peoples.

⁴²You will acknowledge that I am Yahweh when I bring you into Yisra'el's land, into the country that I raised my hand to give your ancestors. ⁴³You will be mindful there of your ways and all your deeds by which you defiled yourselves. You will be loathsome in your own sight for all your bad dealings that you've done. ⁴⁴You will acknowledge that I am Yahweh when I deal with you for the sake of my name, not in accordance with your bad ways and your devastating deeds, Yisra'el's household (a declaration of the Lord Yahweh).'"'

## Slaughter from south to north

⁴⁵Yahweh's word came to me: ⁴⁶'Young man, set your face towards Teman, preach against Darom, prophesy against the open forest of the Southland. ⁴⁷You're to say to the Southland forest, "Listen to Yahweh's word. The Lord Yahweh has said this: 'Here am I, I'm going to light a fire in you. It will consume every green tree and every dry tree in you. The burning flame won't go out. Every face from south to north will be scorched by it. ⁴⁸All flesh will see that I, Yahweh, lit it; it won't go out.'" ⁴⁹But I said, 'Oh, Lord Yahweh, they're saying of me, "Isn't he a teller of parables?"'

**21** Yahweh's word came to me: ²'Young man, set your face against Yerushalaim. Preach against the sanctuaries, prophesy against Yisra'el's land. ³You're to say to Yisra'el's land, "Yahweh has said this: 'Here am I towards you. I shall get my sword out of its sheath and cut off from you faithful and faithless person. ⁴Since I'm going to cut off from you faithful and faithless person, therefore my sword will come out from its sheath against all flesh from south to north, ⁵and all flesh will acknowledge that I, Yahweh, got my sword out of its sheath; it won't go back again.'"

⁶So you, young man, sigh. With a breaking in your hips and with anguish you're to groan before their eyes. ⁷When they say to you, "Why are you groaning?", you're to say, "On account of the report, because it's coming. Every heart will melt. All hands will go limp. Every spirit will faint. Water will go down all knees. There, it's coming, it will happen (a declaration of the Lord Yahweh)."'

⁸Yahweh's word came to me: ⁹'Young man, prophesy: "The Lord Yahweh has said this: 'Say, "A sword, a sword sharpened, yes, and polished, ¹⁰sharpened in order that it can bring slaughter, polished in order that it can be a lightning-flash. Otherwise, could we celebrate the club of my son, which rejects every tree? ¹¹Someone gave it for polishing and for grasping in the fist. The sword is sharpened and polished, for putting into the hand of a killer."'"

## The fork in the road

¹²Cry and howl, young man, because it will happen among my people, among all Yisra'el's rulers. They're going to be tossed to the sword, with my people. Therefore strike your thigh. ¹³Because there's going to be a testing, and what if it scorns the club? Will it not happen? (a declaration of the Lord Yahweh).

¹⁴So you, young man, prophesy, clap palm against palm. The sword will come twice, a third time it will be the sword for people run through, a sword of someone run through, the great one who surrounds them, ¹⁵in order that the heart may melt and the fallings be many. At all their gateways I have set the sword's slaughter. Aagh, it's made to be a flash of lightning, sharpened for slaughter. ¹⁶Slash to the right, set yourself to the left, wherever your edges are appointed. ¹⁷I too will clap palm against palm and set down my wrath. I Yahweh have spoken.'

¹⁸Yahweh's word came to me: ¹⁹'You, young man, set for yourself two roads for the king of Babel's sword to come. They'll go out from one country. Choose a place; choose it at the beginning of the road to the town. ²⁰You're to set a road for the sword to come to Rabbah of the Ammonites, and [one] to Yehudah against fortified Yerushalaim. ²¹Because the king of Babel is standing at the split on the road, at the top of the two roads, to perform divination. He's shaking arrows, he's asking effigies, he's looking at a liver.

²²In his right hand was the divination for Yerushalaim, for setting battering rams, for giving the word for murder, for lifting up the voice in the battle shout, for setting battering rams against the gateways, for heaping up a

ramp, for building a tower. ²³To them it will be like empty divination, in the eyes of the people who've been sworn with oaths. But he is one who causes waywardness to be kept in mind, so that they will be taken.'

## The sword unsheathed and sheathed

²⁴Therefore the Lord Yahweh has said this: 'Since you've caused your waywardness to be kept in mind, as your rebellions reveal themselves, as your wrongdoings become visible, in all your doings – since you've caused it to be kept in mind, you will be taken in [his] fist.

²⁵And you, Yisra'el's slain, faithless ruler, whose day has come at the time of final waywardness, ²⁶the Lord Yahweh has said this: "Remove the mitre, lift off the crown. It won't stay like this. Exalt the lowly, lower the exalted. ²⁷Ruin, ruin, ruin, I shall make it (indeed, this hasn't happened) until the one comes to whom authority belongs, and I shall give it to him."

²⁸And you, young man, prophesy: "The Lord Yahweh has said this about the Ammonites and about their reviling." You're to say, "Sword, sword, unsheathed for slaughter, polished for finishing off, so as to be a flash of lightning. ²⁹Because of beholding something empty for you, because of divining lies for you, they will give you to the necks of the people run through, faithless people whose day has come at the time of final waywardness.

³⁰Put it back into its sheath. In the place where you were created, in the country of your origin, I shall exercise authority over you. ³¹I shall pour out my condemnation upon you. With my furious fire I shall blow on you. I shall give you into the hand of brutal people, craftsmen in devastation. ³²You will be for fire to consume. Your blood will be in the middle of the country. You won't be remembered. Because I, Yahweh, have spoken.'"

## Unfaithfulness to people and unfaithfulness to God

**22** Yahweh's word came to me: ²'You, young man, will you exercise authority, will you exercise authority, over the bloodshed town, and get it to acknowledge all its offensive practices? ³You're to say, "The Lord Yahweh has said this: 'Town that sheds blood within it, so that its time is coming, and makes lumps for itself, so that it becomes defiled! ⁴Through your blood that you've shed, you've incurred liability, and through the lumps that you've made, you're defiled. You've brought your days near; you've come to your years.

Therefore I'm making you an object of reviling for the nations, an object of scorn for all the countries. ⁵The ones near and the ones far away from you will scorn you, defiled of name, abounding in tumult.

⁶There, Yisra'el's rulers were in you, each one with his powerful arm, in order to shed blood:

⁷people have slighted father and mother in you;
towards the alien they've acted with fraud within you;
orphan and widow they've oppressed in you;
⁸you've despised my sacred things and treated my sabbaths as ordinary;
⁹people who spread lies have been in you in order to shed blood;
in you they've eaten on the mountains;
they've acted on their scheming within you;
¹⁰in you a man has exposed his father's nakedness;
they've raped a woman defiled by taboo;
¹¹an individual has done something offensive with his neighbour's wife;
another individual has defiled his daughter-in-law by scheming;
in you an individual has raped his sister, his father's daughter;
¹²in you they've taken a bribe so as to shed blood;
you've taken interest and profit;
you've looted your neighbours by fraud.
You've put me out of mind (a declaration of the Lord Yahweh). ¹³So here, I am clapping my palm about your loot that you've made and over your bloodshed that there's been within you. ¹⁴Will your mind stand firm or your hands be strong for the days when I'm dealing with you? I Yahweh have spoken and I shall act. ¹⁵I shall scatter you among the nations and disperse you among the countries. I shall consume your defilement out of you. ¹⁶You will be treated as ordinary in yourself before the

eyes of the nations. And you will acknowledge that I am Yahweh.""

## Smelting and slag

[17]Yahweh's word came to me: [18]"Young man, Yisra'el's household has become slag to me. All of them are copper, tin, iron and lead inside a furnace. Silver has become slag. [19]Therefore the Lord Yahweh has said this: "Because all of you have become slag, therefore here am I, I'm going to collect you into the middle of Yerushalaim. [20]The collecting of silver, copper, iron, lead and tin inside the furnace, for blowing fire on it to smelt it: so I shall collect you in my anger and wrath, and lay you down, and smelt you. [21]I shall collect you and blow on you with my furious fire and you will be smelted inside it. [22]Like the smelting of silver inside a furnace, so you will be smelted inside it, and you will acknowledge that I, Yahweh, have poured out my wrath upon you.""

[23]Yahweh's word came to me: [24]"Young man, say to it: "You're a country that's not been cleansed, and it's not to be rained on in the day of condemnation:

[25]its conspiracy of prophets within it is like a roaring lion tearing prey, they've consumed human beings, taken riches and wealth, made many widows within it;

[26]its priests have violated my instruction and treated my sacred things as ordinary, they haven't distinguished between sacred and ordinary, they haven't enabled people to know the difference between clean and defiled, they've closed their eyes to my sabbaths, and I'm treated as ordinary among them;

[27]its officials within it are like wolves tearing prey, shedding blood to destroy lives for the sake of gaining loot;

[28]its prophets have coated them with paint, seeing emptiness and divining lies for them, saying, 'The Lord Yahweh has said this' when Yahweh hasn't spoken;

[29]the country's people have practised fraud and committed robbery, they've oppressed the humble and needy, and they've defrauded the alien without the proper exercise of authority.

[30]I sought from them someone constructing the wall or standing in the breach before me on behalf of the country, so I might not devastate it, but I didn't find anyone. [31]So I'm pouring out my condemnation on them. In furious fire I'm finishing them off. I'm putting their way on their head (a declaration of the Lord Yahweh).'"

## A pornographic story begins

**23** Yahweh's word came to me: [2]"Young man, there were two women, the daughters of one mother. [3]They whored in Misrayim. They whored in their youth. Their breasts were pressed there. There men squeezed their girls' nipples. [4]Their names: the older one was Oholah, and her sister was Oholibah. They became mine, and they gave birth to sons and daughters. Their names: Oholah was Shomron and Oholibah was Yerushalaim.

[5]Oholah whored when under me. She doted on her lovers, towards Ashshur, guardsmen [6]clothed in blue, governors and overseers, all of them desirable young men, cavalry riding horses. [7]She gave her whorings to them, all of them the choicest of the Ashshurites, and with each one on whom she doted, with all their lumps, she defiled herself. [8]She didn't abandon her whorings from Misrayim, because men had slept with her in her youth, when they'd squeezed her girl's nipples and poured out their whoring on her. [9]Therefore I gave her into the hand of her lovers, into the hand of the Ashshurites on whom she'd doted. [10]When they had exposed her nakedness, they took her sons and daughters and killed her with the sword. When they implemented rulings against her, she became well known to women.

[11]Her sister Oholibah saw, but her doting was more devastating than hers, and her whorings than her sister's whorings. [12]She doted on Ashshurites, governors and overseers, guardsmen clothed in fullness, cavalry riding horses, all of them desirable young men. [13]I saw that she defiled herself. The two of them had one way, [14]but she increased her whorings. She saw men engraved on the wall, images of Kasdites engraved in vermilion, [15]girded with a belt round their hips, flowing turbans on their heads, all of them with the appearance of officers, the form of Babelites, Kasdim the country of their birth.

## The two sisters

¹⁶So she doted on them on their appearing before her eyes. She sent envoys to them to Kasdim, ¹⁷and the Babelites came to her to her love bed. They defiled her with their whoring. She defiled herself with them, then tore herself away from them. ¹⁸So she exposed her whorings and revealed her nakedness, and I tore myself away from her, as I'd torn myself away from her sister. ¹⁹She multiplied her whorings, being mindful of her young days when she whored in the country of Misrayim. ²⁰She doted on their concubinage, whose flesh was the flesh of donkeys, and their emission the emission of horses. ²¹You attended to the scheming of your youth, when men from Misrayim squeezed your nipples for the sake of your young breasts.'

²²Therefore, Oholibah, the Lord Yahweh has said this: 'Here am I, I'm going to arouse your lovers against you, the ones from whom you tore yourself away. I shall bring them against you from all round: ²³the Babelites, all the Kasdites, Peqod, Shoa, Qoa, all the Ashshurites with them, desirable young men, governors and overseers all of them, officers and men of renown, riding horses all of them. ²⁴They will come against you, armoury, chariot and wheel, and with a congregation of peoples. They will set body-shield, hand-shield and helmet against you all round. I shall put the exercise of authority before them and they will exercise authority over you with their acts of authority.

²⁵So I shall set my passion against you, and they will deal with you in fury. They will remove your nose and your ears, and the last of you will fall by the sword. Those people will take your sons and your daughters, and the last of you will be consumed by fire. ²⁶They will strip you of your clothes and take your majestic things. ²⁷I shall make your scheming cease from you, and your whoring from the country of Misrayim. You won't lift up your eyes to them. You won't be mindful of Misrayim any more.'

## Drunkenness and sorrow

²⁸Because the Lord Yahweh has said this: 'Here am I, I'm going to give you into the hand of the people to whom you are hostile, into the hand of the people from whom you tore yourself away. ²⁹They will act towards you with hostility and take all you've toiled for and abandon you naked and bare. The nakedness of your whorings will be visible, your scheming and your whorings. ³⁰They will do these things to you because of your whoring after the nations, on account of the way you defiled yourself with your lumps. ³¹You've walked in the way of your sister, so I shall put her chalice into your hand.'

³²The Lord Yahweh has said this:

'You're to drink your sister's chalice,
    deep and wide;
    it will bring laughter and scorn.
It contains much;
    ³³you will be full of drunkenness and sorrow,
A chalice of desolating and desolation,
    your sister Shomron's chalice.
³⁴You will drink it and drain it,
    and break it into shards
And tear your breasts,
    because I have spoken (a declaration of the
        Lord Yahweh).'

³⁵Therefore the Lord Yahweh has said this: 'Since you've put me out of mind and thrown me behind your back, you yourself indeed – carry your scheming and your whoring.'

³⁶Yahweh said to me, 'Young man, will you exercise authority over Oholah and Oholibah. Tell them of their offensive practices. ³⁷Because they've committed adultery and there's blood on their hands. They've committed adultery with their lumps and also made their children, to whom they gave birth for me, pass through [the fire] as food for them. ³⁸Further, they've done this to me: defiled my sanctuary and treated my sabbaths as ordinary. ³⁹When they'd slaughtered their children for their lumps, they came into my sanctuary that day, to treat it as ordinary. There, that's what they did within my house.

## Worn out by adultery

⁴⁰Furthermore you would send for men coming from afar, to whom an envoy was sent. There, they came, men for whom you bathed, painted your eyes and donned jewellery. ⁴¹You

sat on an elegant couch with a table spread before it, and you put my incense and my oil on it. ⁴²The sound of a horde feeling at peace was in it, with men from the human mass brought in, drunkards from the wilderness. They put bracelets on the women's hands and a majestic crown on their heads.

⁴³I said of one worn out by adulteries, "Even now they can engage in whorings with her, and she herself", ⁴⁴and they've had sex with her. As men have sex with a whore, so they've had sex with Oholah and Oholibah, scheming women. ⁴⁵But faithful men – they will exercise authority over them, a ruling for women who commit adultery and a ruling for women who've shed blood, because they're women who commit adultery and with blood on their hands.'

⁴⁶Because the Lord Yahweh has said this: 'Take up a congregation against them, give them over to terror and to plunder. ⁴⁷The congregation is to pelt them with stones and cut them down with their swords. They're to kill their sons and their daughters and burn their houses in fire. ⁴⁸I shall put a stop to scheming from the country, and all the women will accept discipline and won't act in accordance with your scheming. ⁴⁹They'll put your scheming upon you. You will carry the wrongdoings involved in your lumps. And you will acknowledge that I am the Lord Yahweh.'

## The cooking pot

**24** Yahweh's word came to me in the ninth year, in the tenth month, on the tenth of the month: ²'Young man, write for yourself the date today, this very day. The king of Babel is leaning on Yerushalaim on this very day. ³And tell a parable to the rebellious household: "The Lord Yahweh has said this:

'Put the pot on, put it on,
    and pour water into it, too.
⁴Gather its pieces into it,
    every good piece.
Leg and shoulder,
    the choicest of the bones, fill it.
⁵Get the choicest of the flock,
    pile the bones under it, too.
Get it to boil;
    its bones are to cook inside it, too.'

⁶Therefore the Lord Yahweh has said this:

'Oh, town of bloodshed,
    pot in which there's rust,
    whose rust hasn't gone out from it!
Piece by piece get it out
    no lot has fallen on it.
⁷Because the blood she shed was inside her;
    she put it on the face of a cliff.
She didn't pour it on the ground
    to cover over it with earth.
⁸To arouse wrath
    to take redress,
I put the blood she shed on the face of a cliff
    so that it wouldn't be covered.'

⁹Therefore the Lord Yahweh has said this:

'Oh, town of bloodshed,
    I shall make the pile big, too.
¹⁰Get much wood, light the fire,
    cook the meat through.
Mix the spices;
    the bones must burn.
¹¹Stand it on the coals empty,
    in order that it may get hot and its copper
    burn,
So its defilement may smelt inside it,
    its rust be consumed.
¹²It has wearied the trouble;
    the abundance of its rust doesn't come out
    from it,
    the rust in the fire.'

¹³Your scheming is your defilement, since I would have cleansed you, but you wouldn't be clean from your defilement. You won't be clean again until I've set down my wrath on you. ¹⁴I Yahweh have spoken. It's coming about and I shall do it. I won't hold back. I won't spare. I won't relent. In accordance with your ways and in accordance with your deeds they are exercising authority over you (a declaration of the Lord Yahweh)."'

## The bereavement

¹⁵Yahweh's word came to me: ¹⁶'Young man, here am I, I'm going to take from you the desire of your eyes through an epidemic. But you're not to mourn, you're not to cry, your

tears aren't to come. <sup>17</sup>Groan quietly. Don't make mourning for the dead. Put on your hat. Put your boots on your feet. Don't cover your lips. Don't eat people's food.'

<sup>18</sup>I spoke to the people in the morning, and my wife died in the evening. I did in the morning as I'd been ordered, <sup>19</sup>and the people said to me, 'Won't you tell us what these things mean for us, that you're acting so?'

<sup>20</sup>I said to them, 'Yahweh's word came to me: <sup>21</sup>"Say to Yisra'el's household: 'The Lord Yahweh has said this: "Here am I, I'm going to treat my sanctuary as ordinary, the pride of your vigour, the desire of your eyes, the object of your heart's pity. Your sons and your daughters whom you abandoned will fall by the sword. <sup>22</sup>You will do as I've done. You won't cover your lips. You won't eat people's food. <sup>23</sup>Your hat on your heads, your boots on your feet, you won't mourn and you won't cry. You will waste away because of your wayward acts and you will groan one to another. <sup>24</sup>So Yehezqe'l is to be a sign for you. In accordance with all that he's done, you will do, when it comes about. And you will acknowledge that I am the Lord Yahweh."'

<sup>25</sup>You, young man, on the day I take from them their stronghold, their splendid object of celebration, the desire of their eyes, the longing of their heart, their sons and their daughters – <sup>26</sup>on that day someone who has escaped will come to let you hear it with your ears, won't he. <sup>27</sup>On that day your mouth will open to the one who has escaped, and you will speak and no longer be dumb. You will be a sign to them. And they will acknowledge that I am Yahweh."'

## Redress is mine: Ammon and Mo'ab

**25** Yahweh's word came to me: <sup>2</sup>'Young man, set your face against the Ammonites and prophesy against them. <sup>3</sup>Say to the Ammonites, "Listen to the word of the Lord Yahweh. The Lord Yahweh has said this: 'Because you said "Ah" about my sanctuary when it was treated as ordinary, and about Yisra'el's land when it became desolate, and about Yehudah's household when they went into exile, <sup>4</sup>therefore, here am I, I'm going to give you to the Qedemites as a possession.

They will set up their encampments in you and put their dwellings in you. Those people will eat your fruit. Those people will drink your milk. <sup>5</sup>I shall make Rabbah an abode for camels and the Ammonites a fold for sheep. And you will acknowledge that I am Yahweh.'"

<sup>6</sup>Because the Lord Yahweh has said this: "Since you clapped your hand and stamped your foot and rejoiced with all your contempt in your soul about Yisra'el's land, <sup>7</sup>therefore here am I, I'm going to stretch out my hand against you, and I shall give you as plunder to the nations. I shall cut you off from the peoples, obliterate you from the countries, annihilate you. And you will acknowledge that I am Yahweh."'

<sup>8</sup>The Lord Yahweh has said this: 'Because Mo'ab and Se'ir said, "There – Yehudah's household is like all the nations", <sup>9</sup>therefore here am I, I'm going to open up Mo'ab's flank from the towns, from its towns on its extremity, the country's splendour – Bet Yeshimot, Ba'al Me'on and Qiryatayim – <sup>10</sup>to the Qedemites, along with the Ammonites. I shall give it as a possession, so that the Ammonites may not be remembered among the nations <sup>11</sup>and I shall execute acts of authority against Mo'ab. And they will acknowledge that I am Yahweh.'

## Redress meets redress: Edom and Peleshet (Philistia)

<sup>12</sup>The Lord Yahweh said this: 'Because of Edom's action in exacting redress on Yehudah's household and incurring liability when they took redress against them', <sup>13</sup>therefore the Lord Yahweh has said this: 'I shall stretch out my hand against Edom and cut off from it human being and animal. I shall make it a waste from Teman to Dedan. They will fall by the sword. <sup>14</sup>I shall inflict my redress on Edom by the hand of my people Yisra'el. They will act against Edom in accordance with my anger and with my fury, and they will acknowledge my redress (a declaration of the Lord Yahweh).'

<sup>15</sup>The Lord Yahweh has said this: 'Because of the Pelishtites' action in taking redress and because they've exacted redress with personal contempt in devastating with ancient enmity', <sup>16</sup>therefore the Lord Yahweh has said this:

'Here am I, I'm going to stretch out my hand against the Pelishtites and cut off the Keretites, and obliterate what remains of the seacoast. ¹⁷I shall execute great acts of redress against them with acts of wrathful reproof, and they will acknowledge that I am Yahweh when I impose my redress on them.'

### Tsor (Tyre): just a place for spreading nets

**26** In the eleventh year on the first of the month, Yahweh's word came to me: ²'Young man, since Tsor has said about Yerushalaim, "Ah, the people's gateway has broken, it has turned round to me, I shall be full now it's been laid waste", ³therefore the Lord Yahweh has said this: "Here am I against you, Tsor; I shall make many nations go up against you, like the sea making its waves go up. ⁴They will devastate Tsor's walls and tear down its towers. I shall scrape off its soil and make it into the face of a cliff. ⁵It will become a place for spreading nets in the middle of the sea: because I have spoken (a declaration of the Lord Yahweh). It will become plunder for the nations. ⁶Its daughter-townships that are in the open country will be killed by the sword. And they will acknowledge that I am Yahweh."

⁷Because the Lord Yahweh has said this: "Here am I, I'm going to bring against Tsor from the north Nebukadne'tstsar king of Babel, king of kings, with horse, chariotry, cavalry, a congregation, a great company. ⁸Your daughter-townships in the open country he will kill with the sword. He will build a tower against you, heap up a ramp against you and set a body-shield against you. ⁹He will set his opposing force against your walls and demolish your towers with his axes. ¹⁰From the profusion of his horses their dust will cover you. From the sound of the cavalry, wheel and chariot, your wheels will shake, when he comes through your gateways like people coming into a breached town. ¹¹With the hoofs of his horses he will trample all your streets. He will kill your people with the sword. Your strong columns will descend to earth. ¹²They will plunder your wealth and loot your merchandise. They will tear down your walls and demolish your desirable houses. Your

stones, your wood and your soil they will put in the middle of the water.

### The sound of music stops

¹³I shall put a stop to the uproar of your songs, and the sound of your guitars will make itself heard no more. ¹⁴I shall make you into the face of a cliff. You will become a place for spreading nets. You won't be built up any more. Because I, Yahweh, have spoken (a declaration of the Lord Yahweh)."

¹⁵The Lord Yahweh has said to Tsor: "At the sound of your downfall, at the groan of the people run through, at the instigation of killing within you, will foreign shores not shake? ¹⁶All the sea's rulers will descend from their thrones. They will remove their robes, strip off their embroidered clothes and put on great trembling. They will sit on the ground and tremble at every moment and be desolate because of you.

¹⁷They will take up a dirge over you and say to you:

Oh, you've perished,
    you who were peopled from the seas,
The renowned town,
    one that was strong on the sea,
It and its inhabitants,
    people that put their terror on all its
      inhabitants.
¹⁸Now the foreign shores tremble,
    on the day of your downfall.
The foreign shores panic,
    they that are by the sea, at your passing."

¹⁹Because the Lord Yahweh has said this: "When I make you a wasted town, like towns that are not inhabited, when I take up the deep over you and the mighty water covers you, ²⁰I shall make you descend with the people who descend to the Pit, to the people of old, and I shall make you live in the world deep below, like the wastes from of old, with those who descend to the Pit, in order that you won't be inhabited. I shall make 'Splendour in the Country of the Living' – ²¹I shall make you a great horror. There will be nothing of you. You will be sought out, but you won't be found again, ever (a declaration of the Lord Yahweh).'"

## Tsor, perfect in beauty?

**27** Yahweh's word came to me: [2]'You, young man, take up a dirge over Tsor. [3]You're to say to Tsor, which lives at the entrance to the sea, trading with the peoples at many foreign shores: "The Lord Yahweh has said this:

Tsor, you said,
  'I am perfect in beauty.'
[4]Your borders were in the heart of the seas;
  your builders perfected your beauty.
[5]With juniper from Senir
  they built all your planks.
They got a cedar from Lebanon
  to make a mast for you.
[6]With oaks from Bashan
  they made your oars.
Your boarding they made of ivory inlaid in cypress
  from the shores of Kittim [Cyprus].
[7]Linen with embroidery from Misrayim became
    your spread,
  to be an ensign for you.
Blue and purple from the shores of Elishah
  became your covering.
[8]The inhabitants of Tsidon and Arvad
  were your rowers.
Your experts, Tsor, were within you;
  they were your sailors.
[9]The elders of Gebel and its experts were within you,
  strengthening your cracks.

All the ships of the sea and their mariners
  were in you to deal in your merchandise.
[10]Paras [Persia], Lydia and Put were in your force,
  your men of battle.
They hung shield and helmet in you;
  those men gave you your splendour.
[11]People from Arvad and Helek
  were on your walls all round.
Gammadites were in your towers,
  they hung their quivers on your walls all round;
  those men perfected your beauty.

## The dealer

[12]Tarshish was your dealer because of the quantity of all your wealth; they gave your wares in exchange for silver, iron, tin and lead. [13]Yavan [Greece], Tubal and Meshek were your traders; they gave your merchandise in exchange for human life and things of copper. [14]From Bet Togarmah they gave horses, cavalry and mules in exchange for your wares. [15]The Dedanites were your traders. Many foreign shores were dealers under your control. They brought back to you ivory tusks and ebony as your payment. [16]Aram was your dealer because of the quantity of your products; they gave your wares in exchange for turquoise, purple, embroidery, fine linen, coral and ruby.

[17]Yehudah and the country of Yisra'el were your merchants; they gave your merchandise in exchange for wheat from Minnit and Pannag, syrup, oil and balm. [18]Dammeseq [Damascus] was your dealer because of the quantity of your products, because of the quantity of all your wealth, in wine of Helbon and white wool. [19]Vedan and Yavan gave yarn in exchange for your wares; there was wrought iron, cassia and cane among your merchandise. [20]Dedan was your trader in saddlecloths for riding. [21]Arabia and all Qedar's rulers were dealers under your control in lambs, rams and goats, as your dealers in these.

[22]The traders of Sheba and Ra'amah were your traders; they gave your wares in exchange for the finest of all spice and for all precious stone and gold. [23]Haran, Kanneh and Eden, the traders of Sheba, Ashshur and Kilmad, were your traders. [24]Those were your traders in fine things, in blue embroidered cloths, and in coloured rugs bound with cords and preserved with cedar, in your market. [25]Tarshish ships were your ministers for your merchandise.

## The wreck of the Titanic

You were full and very heavy
  in the heart of the seas.
[26]Into the mighty water
  the rowers brought you.
The east wind broke you
  in the heart of the seas.
[27]Your wealth and your wares, your merchandise,
  your mariners and your sailors,
The men who strengthened your cracks,
  and the people who handled your merchandise,
All your men of battle who were in you,
  and in all your congregation that was within
    you,

Will fall in the heart of the seas
  on the day of your downfall.
²⁸At the sound of your sailors' cry,
  the shorelands will shake.
²⁹All the oarsmen
  will come down from their ships.
The mariners, all the sailors of the sea,
  will stand on the earth.
³⁰They will let their voice be heard concerning you,
  and cry in distress.
They will take up earth on to their head,
  and cover themselves in ash.
³¹For you, they will shave their head,
  and wrap on sack.
They will cry for you with bitterness of soul,
  with bitter lament.
³²For you they will take up a dirge as they groan,
  and lament for you:
'Who was like Tsor,
  like the one silenced in the middle of the sea?'
³³When your wares went out from the seas,
  you filled many peoples.
With the quantity of your wealth and your
    merchandise
  you enriched earth's kings.
³⁴The time when you broke because of the seas,
  in the depths of the water,
Your merchandise and all your congregation
  fell in the middle of it.
³⁵All the inhabitants of foreign shores
  are desolate over you.
Their kings bristled with horror,
  their faces went dark.
³⁶The dealers among the peoples whistled at you;
  you became a horror, and you're no more,
    permanently.'"

## Another king who thinks he's a god

**28** Yahweh's word came to me: ²'Young
man, say to Tsor's ruler: "The Lord
Yahweh has said: 'Because your mind has been
lofty and you've said, "I am a god, I am sitting
as a deity – I've taken my seat in the heart of the
seas"', when you're a human being and not God,
but you made your mind like a deity's mind:

³There, you're smarter than Dan'el;
  nothing hidden baffles you.
⁴Through your smartness and your discernment
  you've made wealth for yourself.

You've made gold and silver in your treasuries
  ⁵through the magnitude of your smartness and
    through your trading.
You've made your wealth great,
  but you've let your mind get lofty because of
    your wealth.

⁶Therefore the Lord Yahweh has said this:

Because of your making your mind
  like the mind of a deity,
⁷Therefore here am I, I'm going to bring against
    you
  strangers, the most violent of nations.
They will draw their swords against your smart
    beauty
  and run you through in your splendour.
⁸Down to the Pit they will make you descend;
  you will die the death of someone run through
  in the heart of the seas.
⁹Will you actually say 'I'm a deity'
  before your killers –
Given that you're a human being and not God –
  at the hand of the people who run you through?
¹⁰The death of the foreskinned
  you will die, at the hand of strangers,
  because I have spoken (a declaration of the
    Lord Yahweh)."'

## A dirge for a living king

¹¹Yahweh's word came to me: ¹²'Young man,
take up a dirge over the king of Tsor. You're to
say to him: "The Lord Yahweh has said this:

You were an exact seal,
  full of smartness, perfect in beauty.
¹³You were in Eden, God's garden,
  every precious stone your covering:
Carnelian, topaz and diamond,
  beryl, onyx and jasper,
Sapphire, turquoise and emerald,
  and gold, the work of your tambourines,
And your sockets in you,
  that were prepared on the day of your creation.

¹⁴You were a sphinx, anointed as the protector,
  and I placed you –
  you were on God's sacred mountain.
When you walked about among the fiery stones,
  ¹⁵you were a person of integrity in all your ways,

From the day of your creation,
  until evil appeared in you.
16Through the quantity of your trading,
  people filled the middle of you with violence.
You did wrong, and I am treating you as ordinary,
  away from God's mountain, and destroying you,
Sphinx the protector,
  from among the fiery stones.
17Your mind became lofty because of your beauty;
  you devastated your smartness, through your
    splendour.
I'm throwing you out on to the earth;
  before kings I'm making you something to
    stare at.
18Because of the quantity of your wayward acts,
  through the evil of your trading,
You've treated your great sanctuary as ordinary.
  I'm making fire go out from within you and it's
    devouring you.
I'm making you into ash on the earth
  before the eyes of all who look at you.
19All who acknowledge you among the peoples
  are becoming desolate at you.
You're becoming a horror,
  and you will be no more, permanently.'"

## No more prickling briar

20Yahweh's word came to me: 21"Young man,
set your face towards Tsidon and prophesy
against it. 22You're to say, "The Lord Yahweh
has said this:

Here am I against you, Tsidon;
  I shall get honour within you.
They will acknowledge that I am Yahweh,
  when I execute acts of authority against it.
I shall show myself sacred in it
  23and let loose epidemic in it and blood in its
    streets.
The run through will fall within it
  by the sword that's against it from all round,
  and they will acknowledge that I am Yahweh.

24No more will there be for Yisra'el's
household prickling briar and piercing thorn
from all the people round them who treat them
with contempt. And they will acknowledge that
I am the Lord Yahweh.'"
  25The Lord Yahweh has said this: 'When I
have collected Yisra'el's household from the

peoples among whom they're dispersed and
I've shown myself sacred among them before
the eyes of the nations, they will live on their
land that I gave my servant Ya'aqob, 26and live
on it with confidence. They will build houses
and plant vineyards and live with confidence,
when I have executed acts of authority on all
the people who treat them with contempt, who
are round them. And they will acknowledge
that I Yahweh am their God.'

## The Ye'or (Nile) is mine: I made it

29 In the tenth year, in the tenth, on the
twelfth of the month, Yahweh's word
came to me: 2"Young man, set your face against
Par'oh king of Misrayim, and prophesy
against him and against Misrayim, all of it.
3Speak: "The Lord Yahweh has said this:

Here am I against you,
  Par'oh king of Misrayim,
Big monster stretching out
  in the middle of its channels,
That said, 'My Ye'or is mine;
  I'm the one who made it.'
4I shall put hooks in your jaws
  and make the fish in your channels stick to
    your scales.
I shall get you up from the middle of your
    channels,
  with all the fish in your channels that stick to
    your scales.
5I shall leave you to the wilderness,
  you and all the fish in your channels.
You will fall on the face of the open country;
  you won't be gathered and you won't be
    collected.
I'm giving you as food to the creatures of the
    earth
  and to the birds of the heavens.
6And all the inhabitants of Misrayim
  will acknowledge that I am Yahweh.
Since they were something to lean on that was
    made of reed
  for Yisra'el's household,
7When they grasped you in their fist, you would
    fracture,
  and tear their entire shoulder.
When they leaned on you, you'd break,
  and make their entire hips collapse."

[8]Therefore the Lord Yahweh has said this: "Here am I, I'm going to bring a sword against you. I shall cut off from you human being and animal. [9]The country of Misrayim will become desolation and waste. And they will acknowledge that I am Yahweh.

Because he said, 'The Ye'or is mine; I'm the one who made it', [10]therefore here am I towards you and towards your channels: I shall make the country of Misrayim an utter waste and desolation, from Migdol to Seweneh, as far as the border with Kush [Sudan]. [11]Human foot won't pass through it and animal foot won't pass through it. It won't be inhabited for forty years.

## Misrayim as compensation

[12]I shall make the country of Misrayim a desolation in the middle of desolate countries, and its towns in the middle of ruined towns will be a desolation for forty years. I shall scatter the Misrayimites among the nations and disperse them among the countries.'"
[13]Indeed the Lord Yahweh has said this: 'At the end of forty years I shall collect the Misrayimites from the peoples where they've scattered. [14]I shall restore the fortunes of the Misrayimites and bring them back to the country of Patros, on to the country of their origin. They will be a lowly kingdom there. [15]It will be the lowliest of the kingdoms; it won't arise again over the nations. I shall make them small so they don't have dominion over the nations. [16]It won't again be an object of reliance for Yisra'el's household, making it mindful of its waywardness in turning its face after them. And they will acknowledge that I am the Lord Yahweh.'
[17]In the twenty-seventh year, on the first of the first month, Yahweh's word came to me: [18]'Young man, Nebukadne'tstsar king of Babel has made his forces serve with great servitude against Tsor. Every head is rubbed bare. Every shoulder is scraped. But he and his forces have no wages from Tsor for the servitude with which they have served on it.'
[19]Therefore the Lord Yahweh has said this: 'Here am I, I'm going to give the country of Misrayim to Nebukadne'tstsar king of Babel. He will carry off its wealth, take spoil from it and seize plunder from it, and it will be the

wages for his force. [20]As his compensation for which he served, I'm giving him the country of Misrayim, because they acted for me (a declaration of the Lord Yahweh).
[21]On that day I shall make a horn grow for Yisra'el's household, and to you I shall give an opening of your mouth among them. And they will acknowledge that I am Yahweh.'

## The day of the Lord for Misrayim

**30** Yahweh's word came to me: [2]'Young man, prophesy. "Yahweh has said this:

Howl, aagh for the day,
   [3]because Yahweh's day is near.
A day of cloud,
   a time for nations, it will be.
[4]A sword will come upon Misrayim,
   anguish will fall upon Kush,
When people fall, run through, in Misrayim,
   and people take its wealth, and its foundations
      are torn down.
[5]Kush, Put, Lydia, the entire foreign group,
   Cyrenaica, and members of the country in the
      pact
   will fall by the sword with them.

[6]Yahweh has said this:

The people who support Misrayim will fall;
   its vigorous majesty will go down.
From Migdol to Seweneh
   they will fall there by the sword (a declaration
      of the Lord Yahweh).

[7]They will be desolate among desolate countries, and its towns will be among wasted towns. [8]And they will acknowledge that I am Yahweh when I put fire in Misrayim, and all its helpers break. [9]On that day envoys will go out from before me in ships to make confident Kush tremble. Anguish will be upon them on Misrayim's day, because there, it's coming."
[10]The Lord Yahweh has said this: "And I shall put a stop to Misrayim's horde by the hand of Nebukadne'tstsar king of Babel. [11]He and his company with him, the most violent of nations, are going to be brought to devastate the country. They will draw their swords against

Misrayim and fill the country with the people run through. ¹²I shall make the channels dry ground and sell the country into the hand of bad people. I shall desolate the country and everything in it by the hand of strangers. I, Yahweh, have spoken."

## Acts of authority on Misrayim

¹³The Lord Yahweh has said this: "I shall obliterate the lumps and make the non-entities cease from Memphis. There will no longer be a ruler from the country of Misrayim. I shall put fear in the country of Misrayim. ¹⁴I shall desolate Patros. I shall put fire in Tso'an. I shall execute acts of authority in Thebes. ¹⁵I shall pour out my fury on Pelusium, Misrayim's stronghold. I shall cut off the horde of Thebes. ¹⁶I shall put fire in Misrayim. Pelusium will writhe and writhe. Thebes will be torn apart. Memphis: adversaries daily. ¹⁷The young men of Heliopolis and Pi-beset will fall by the sword. Those – they will go into exile. ¹⁸In Tehaphnehes the day will be dark when I break Misrayim's yokes there, and its vigorous majesty comes to a stop in it. Cloud will cover it and its daughter-townships will go into captivity. ¹⁹I shall execute acts of authority in Misrayim, and they will acknowledge that I am Yahweh.'"

²⁰In the eleventh year, in the first, on the seventh of the month, Yahweh's word came to me: ²¹"Young man, I'm breaking the arm of Par'oh king of Misrayim. There, it's not bound up so as to give healing, by putting a bandage to bind it up to strengthen it for grasping a sword.' ²²Therefore the Lord Yahweh has said this: 'Here am I towards Par'oh king of Misrayim. I shall break his arms, the strong one and the broken one. I shall make the sword fall from his hand. ²³I shall scatter the Misrayimites among the nations and disperse them among the countries. ²⁴I shall strengthen the arms of the king of Babel and put my sword in his hand. I shall break the arms of Par'oh. He will groan before him with the groans of someone run through. ²⁵I shall strengthen the arms of the king of Babel, but Par'oh's arms – they will fall. And they will acknowledge that I am Yahweh, when I put my sword into the hand of the king of Babel and he stretches it out against the country of Misrayim. ²⁶I shall scatter the Misrayimites among the

nations and disperse them among the countries, and they will acknowledge that I am Yahweh.'

## An empire on which the sun never sets?

**31** In the eleventh year, in the third, on the first of the month, Yahweh's word came to me: ²"Young man, say to Par'oh king of Misrayim and to his horde: "To whom are you like in your greatness?

³There, Ashshur was a cedar in Lebanon,
  beautiful in boughs, and a shady thicket,
Lofty in height,
  and its top was among the clouds.
⁴Water made it big, the deep made it high,
  going with its rivers round its plantation.
It sent its channels
  to all the trees of the open country.
⁵As a result its height was loftier
  than all the trees of the open country.
Its branches abounded, its boughs extended,
  because of the abundant water in its channel.
⁶All the birds of the heavens
  nested in its branches.
All the animals of the open country
  gave birth under its boughs.
All the great nations
  were living in its shade.
⁷It was beautiful in its great size, in the length of
    its branches,
  because its root was by abundant water.
⁸Cedars in God's garden didn't overshadow it,
  junipers didn't equal its branches,
  plane trees didn't compare with its boughs.
No tree in God's garden
  equalled it in its beauty.
⁹I made it beautiful
  in the number of its branches.
All the trees of Eden were jealous of it,
  the ones that were in God's garden."

## Learn from its fall

¹⁰Therefore the Lord Yahweh has said this: "Since you were lofty in height – and it put its top into the middle of the clouds, and its mind became exalted in its loftiness, ¹¹I gave it into the hand of the leader of the nations so he'd deal effectively with it. In accordance with its

faithlessness I dispossessed it. ¹²Strangers, the most violent of nations, cut it down and left it. Its branches fell on the mountains and in all the ravines, and its boughs broke into all the canyons in the earth. All the peoples of the earth went down from its shade and left it.

¹³Upon it, fallen, all the birds of the heavens dwell, and to its boughs came all the animals of the open country – ¹⁴in order that no trees by water should become lofty in their height or put their top among the clouds, nor should any of their mighty ones, drinkers of water, stand up in their loftiness, because all of them were given over to death, to the country below, among all human beings, with the people who go down to the Pit."

¹⁵The Lord Yahweh has said this: "On the day it went down to She'ol, I caused mourning, I closed the deep over it. I held back its rivers; the abundant water held back. I made Lebanon grieve over it. All the trees of the open country languished over it. ¹⁶At the sound of its fall I made the nations shake, when I made it go down to She'ol with the people who go down to the Pit. In the country below, all the trees of Eden, the choicest and best of Lebanon, all the drinkers of water, found consolation. ¹⁷They also went down with it to She'ol, to the people run through by the sword, and its [supporting] arm, the people who had lived in its shadow among the nations.

¹⁸To whom are you thus like, in honour and in greatness among the trees of Eden? You will be brought down with the trees of Eden to the country below. Among the foreskinned you will lie, with the people run through by the sword. That is Par'oh and his entire horde (a declaration of the Lord Yahweh).'"

## The dragon caught

**32** In the twelfth year in the twelfth month on the first of the month, Yahweh's word came to me: ²'Young man, take up a dirge over Par'oh king of Misrayim:

Lion of the nations, you are being terminated, though you are like the dragon in the water.
You've thrust forth with your rivers,
you've stirred up the water with your feet,
you've muddied their rivers.

³The Lord Yahweh has said this:

And I shall spread my mesh over you
in a congregation of many peoples.
I shall lift you up in my net ⁴and leave you on the earth;
I shall throw you on the face of the open country.
I shall get all the birds of the heavens to dwell on you;
I shall get the animals of the entire earth to be full from you.
⁵I shall put your flesh on the mountains
and fill the ravines with your height.
⁶I shall drench the earth
with the flow of your blood on the mountains,
and canyons will fill from you.
⁷I shall cover the heavens when I put you out,
and make their stars dark.
I shall cover the sun with cloud,
and the moon won't give its light.
⁸All the bright lights in the heavens
I shall make dark above you.
I shall put darkness on your country
(a declaration of the Lord Yahweh)
⁹and vex the mind of many peoples,
When I bring you broken among the nations,
to countries that you haven't known.
¹⁰I shall make many peoples desolate because of you;
their kings will bristle with horror because of you.
When I whirl my sword in their faces,
they will tremble at every moment,
Each for his own life,
on the day of your fall.

## The great leveller

¹¹Because the Lord Yahweh has said this:

The king of Babel's sword will come to you;
¹²by strong men's swords I shall make your horde fall,
the most violent among the nations, all of them.
They will destroy Misrayim's majesty;
its entire horde will be annihilated.
¹³I shall obliterate all its cattle
from beside abundant water.
Human feet will no more muddy them,
and animal hoofs won't muddy them.
¹⁴Then I shall settle their water,
make their rivers go like oil (a declaration of the Lord Yahweh).

<sup>15</sup>When I make the country of Misrayim a
   desolation
and the country is desolate of what filled it,
When I strike down all the people who live in it,
   they will acknowledge that I am Yahweh.

<sup>16</sup>That is a dirge, and people will lament with it;
   the nations' daughters will lament with it.
Over Misrayim and over its entire horde
   they will lament with it (a declaration of the
   Lord Yahweh).'

<sup>17</sup>In the twelfth year, on the fifteenth of the
month, Yahweh's word came to me: <sup>18</sup>'Young
man, wail for Misrayim's horde. You're to send
them down, it and the daughter-townships of
mighty nations, to the country deep below,
with the people who go down to the Pit.
<sup>19</sup>"Than whom are you more beautiful? Go
down and be laid down with the foreskinned."
<sup>20</sup>They will fall among people run through
by the sword. The sword has been given over.
They're dragging it off with all its hordes. <sup>21</sup>The
mightiest of strong men speak to him from
within She'ol, with his helpers. The foreskinned,
people run through by the sword, have gone
down and lain down. <sup>22</sup>Ashshur is there, and all
its congregation, round him his graves, all of
them run through, fallen by the sword, <sup>23</sup>whose
graves were put in the Pit's far parts, and its
congregation was round its grave, all of them
run through, fallen by the sword, people who'd
spread terror in the country of the living.

### The strange consolation

<sup>24</sup>Elam is there, and all its horde, round its
grave, all of them run through, fallen by the
sword, people who went down foreskinned
to the country deep below, people who had
put their terror in the country of the living
but carried their shame with the people who
go down to the Pit. <sup>25</sup>Among the run through
they've given it a bed, with all its graves round
it, all of them foreskinned, run through by
the sword. Because their terror was put in the
country of the living, they carried their shame
with the people who go down to the Pit; among
the run through, he is put.
<sup>26</sup>Meshek and Tubal and its entire horde
are there. Its graves are round it, all of them

foreskinned, run through by the sword, because
they put their terror in the country of the living.
<sup>27</sup>They don't lie with the fallen strong men of the
foreskinned, who went down to She'ol with their
battle equipment and put their swords under
their heads. Their wayward acts were upon their
frames, because the strong men's terror had been
in the country of the living. <sup>28</sup>And you yourselves
will break among the foreskinned and will lie
down with people run through by the sword.
<sup>29</sup>Edom is there, its kings and all its rulers,
who despite their strength are put with
the people run through by the sword. Those
people lie with the foreskinned and with
the people who go down to the Pit. <sup>30</sup>The
leaders of the north, all of them, are there, and
all the Tsidonites, who went down with the
people run through despite their terror that
issued from their strength, disgraced. They lie
foreskinned with the people run through by
the sword. They carried their shame with the
people who go down to the Pit.
<sup>31</sup>These Par'oh will see, and he will be
consoled over his entire horde, Par'oh's people
who were run through by the sword, all his
force (a declaration of the Lord Yahweh).
<sup>32</sup>Because I'm putting my terror in the country
of the living. He will be laid down among
the foreskinned with the people run through
by the sword, Par'oh and his entire horde
(a declaration of the Lord Yahweh).'

### The lookout

**33** Yahweh's word came to me: <sup>2</sup>'Young
man, speak to the members of your
people: "Regarding a country: when I bring
the sword against it, and the country's people
take someone from their number and make
him into their lookout, <sup>3</sup>and he sees the sword
coming against the country and blows the horn
and warns the people, <sup>4</sup>and someone hears the
sound of the horn but doesn't take warning
and the sword comes and takes him – his
blood will be on his own head. <sup>5</sup>He heard the
sound of the horn but didn't take warning; his
blood will be on him. Had that person taken
warning, he'd have saved his life. <sup>6</sup>But should
the lookout, when he sees the sword coming,
not blow the horn, and the people don't take
warning, and the sword comes and takes one

of them, that person gets taken because of his own waywardness, but I shall require his blood from the lookout."

⁷So you, young man, I've made you a lookout for Yisra'el's household. You will hear a word from my mouth, and you're to warn them from me. ⁸When I say to the faithless person, "Faithless one, you shall definitely die", and you haven't spoken to warn the faithless person from his way, that faithless person will die because of his waywardness, but I shall require his blood from your hand. ⁹But you – when you've warned the faithless person from his way, to turn back from it, and he hasn't turned from his way, he will die because of his waywardness, but you will rescue your life.

¹⁰But you, young man, say to Yisra'el's household: "You've said this: 'Our rebellions and our wrongdoings rest upon us. Because of them we're wasting away, and how can we live?'" ¹¹Say to them, "As I live (a declaration of the Lord Yahweh), if I want the death of the faithless person . . . rather that the faithless person should turn back from his way and live. Turn back, turn back, from your bad ways. Why should you die, Yisra'el's household?"

## The news arrives

¹²So you, young man, say to the members of your people: "The faithfulness of the faithful person won't rescue him on the day of his rebellion, and the faithlessness of the faithless person – he won't fall because of it on the day he turns back from his faithlessness. So the faithful person won't be able to live because of it on the day he commits wrongdoing. ¹³When I say of the faithful person, 'He will indeed live', but he trusts in his faithfulness and does evil, none of his faithful deeds will be kept in mind. Because of the evil that he's done – he will die because of it. ¹⁴And when I say to the faithless person, 'You will definitely die', and he turns back from his wrongdoing and exercises authority faithfully ¹⁵(the faithless person gives back a pledge, makes good for what was stolen, walks by the laws of life, so as not to do evil), he will definitely live, he won't die. ¹⁶None of his wrongdoings that he's committed will be kept in mind for him. He's exercised authority faithfully. He will definitely live."

¹⁷The members of your people say, "The Lord's way isn't right." But they – their way isn't right. ¹⁸When a faithful person turns from his faithfulness and does evil, he will die because of them. ¹⁹When a faithless person turns from his faithlessness and exercises authority faithfully, on account of them that person will live. ²⁰And you say, "The Lord's way isn't right." I exercise authority over each person in accordance with his ways, Yisra'el's household.'

²¹In the twelfth year of our exile, in the tenth, on the fifth of the month, somebody who'd escaped from Yerushalaim came to me, saying, 'The town's been struck down.' ²²Yahweh's hand had come upon me in the evening before the person who'd escaped came, and he'd opened my mouth, before he came to me in the morning. So my mouth had opened. I was no longer dumb.

## On how not to listen to a preacher

²³Yahweh's word came to me: ²⁴"Young man, the people living in these wastes on Yisra'el's land are saying, "Abraham was one man, but he came to possess the country, whereas we're many. The country is given to us as a possession." ²⁵Therefore say to them, "The Lord Yahweh has said this: 'You eat with the blood, you raise your eyes to your lumps and you shed blood – and you will enter into possession of the country? ²⁶You've stood by your sword, you've done an offensive thing and you've each defiled his neighbour's wife – and you will enter into possession of the country?'"

²⁷You're to say this to them: "The Lord Yahweh has said this: 'As I live, if the people in the wastes don't fall by the sword and I don't give the people in the open country to the animals for them to eat, and the people in the strongholds and in the caves don't die in an epidemic . . .

²⁸I shall make the country desolating and desolation. Its vigorous majesty will cease, Yisra'el's mountains will be desolate, with no one passing through, ²⁹and they will acknowledge that I am Yahweh, when I make the country desolating and desolation because of all their offensive deeds that they've done.'"

³⁰But you, young man: the members of your people are speaking about you by the walls and in the entrances of the houses. One speaks to

another, a man to his brother: "Come, please, listen to what word is coming out from Yahweh." [31]They will come to you like a people coming, and sit before you, my people, and listen to your words. But they won't do them, because while they're making amorous sounds with their mouths, their mind is going after their loot. [32]And there are you, like a singer of amorous sounds to them, beautiful in voice and doing well in playing, and they listen to your words but none of them are doing them. [33]But when it comes about (there, it's coming), they will acknowledge that a prophet's been among them.'

## The self-indulgent shepherds

**34** Yahweh's word came to me: [2]'Young man, prophesy against Yisra'el's shepherds. Prophesy and say to them, "About the shepherds, the Lord Yahweh has said this: 'Hey, Yisra'el's shepherds, who've been shepherding themselves: isn't it the flock that shepherds shepherd? [3]You eat the fat and clothe yourselves in the wool, you sacrifice the fatlings; you don't shepherd the flock. [4]You haven't strengthened the weak, nor healed the sick, nor bandaged the broken, nor brought back the scattered, nor sought the missing, but ruled them with harshness and cruelty. [5]They scattered for lack of a shepherd, and they became food for any animal of the open country when they scattered. [6]My flock wanders through all the mountains and on every high hill. My flock scattered over the face of the country. There's been no one seeking and no one looking.'''

[7]Therefore, shepherds, listen to Yahweh's word. [8]'As I live (a declaration of the Lord Yahweh), since my flock's become plunder and my flock's become food for any animal of the open country through the lack of anyone shepherding, and my shepherds haven't sought my flock, but the shepherds have shepherded themselves and not shepherded my flock, if I don't . . .'

[9]Therefore listen, you shepherds, to Yahweh's word. [10]The Lord Yahweh has said this: 'Here am I towards the shepherds. I shall require my flock from their hand. I shall make them stop shepherding the flock, and the shepherds won't shepherd themselves any more. I shall rescue my flock from their mouth. They won't be food for them.'

## The good shepherd

[11]Because the Lord Yahweh has said this: 'Here am I, I myself, and I shall enquire after my flock and search for them. [12]Like a shepherd searching after his herd when he's among his dispersed flock, so I shall search for my flock and rescue them from all the places where they've scattered on the day of cloud and gloom. [13]I shall get them out from the peoples, collect them from the countries and bring them to their land. I shall shepherd them on Yisra'el's mountains by the canyons and by all the country's settlements. [14]I shall shepherd them on good pasturage; their abode will be on Yisra'el's high mountains. There they will lie down in a good abode, and they will pasture on rich pasturage on Yisra'el's mountains. [15]I myself shall shepherd my flock and I myself shall get them to lie down (a declaration of the Lord Yahweh). [16]I shall seek the missing, bring back the scattered, bandage the broken and strengthen the weak. But the fat and the strong I shall destroy. I shall shepherd with authority.

[17]And you, my flock (the Lord Yahweh has said this): here am I, I'm going to decide between one animal and another. About rams and he-goats: [18]is it too little for you that you pasture on good pasturage, but you trample with your feet what's left of your pasturage, and that you drink the clearest of the water, but muddy what's left with your feet, [19]so that my flock pastures on what your feet have trampled and your feet have muddied?'

[20]Therefore the Lord Yahweh has said this to them: 'Here am I, and I shall decide between fat animal and thin animal. [21]Since you were pushing with flank and shoulder, and butting with your horns against all the sick, until you scattered them abroad, [22]I shall deliver my flock, and it will no longer be plunder. I shall decide between one animal and another.

## The Davidic shepherd

[23]And I shall set up over them one shepherd and he will shepherd them, my servant David. He's the one who will shepherd them. He'll be their shepherd. [24]I, Yahweh, will be their God, with my servant David ruler among them. I Yahweh have spoken. [25]I shall solemnize a

pact of well-being for them. I shall stop bad creatures from the country, and they will live in the wilderness with confidence and sleep in the forests.

²⁶I shall make them and the environs of my hill a blessing. I shall make the rain come down in its season; they will be showers that bring blessing. ²⁷The trees of the open country will give their fruit; the earth will give its produce. People will be on their land with confidence, and they will acknowledge that I am Yahweh, when I break the bars of their yoke and rescue them from the people who make them serve them. ²⁸They will no longer be plunder for the nations. The country's creatures won't eat them and they will live in confidence with no one disturbing them.

²⁹I shall set up for them a plantation of renown, and they will no longer be carried off by famine in the country. They will no longer bear the nations' shame. ³⁰And they will acknowledge that I am Yahweh their God with them and they, Yisra'el's household, are my people (a declaration of the Lord Yahweh). ³¹You, my flock, the flock I shepherd, you're human, and I am your God (a declaration of the Lord Yahweh).'

## The two peoples

**35** Yahweh's word came to me: ²'Young man, set your face against Mount Se'ir and prophesy against it. ³You're to say to it: "The Lord Yahweh has said this: 'Here am I towards you, Mount Se'ir. I shall stretch out my hand against you and make you desolating and desolation. ⁴Your towns I shall make into a waste and you will be a desolation, and you will acknowledge that I am Yahweh.

⁵Since you had an ancient enmity and you hurled the Yisra'elites into the power of the sword at the time of their calamity, at the time of their final waywardness, ⁶therefore, as I live (a declaration of the Lord Yahweh), I shall make you into blood; blood will pursue you. Given that you were not hostile to blood, blood will pursue you. ⁷I shall make Mount Se'ir desolation and desolating, and I shall cut off from it anyone passing by and anyone coming back. ⁸I shall fill its mountains with its people run through. Your hills, your valleys

and all your canyons – people run through by the sword will fall in them. ⁹I shall make you a permanent desolation, your towns won't be inhabited and you will acknowledge that I am Yahweh.

¹⁰Since you said, "The two nations and the two countries will be mine, and we shall possess them" (but Yahweh was there), ¹¹therefore as I live (a declaration of the Lord Yahweh), I shall act in accordance with your anger and with your passion with which you acted out of your hostility to them. I shall cause myself to be acknowledged among them as I exercise authority over you. ¹²You will acknowledge that I Yahweh have heard all your insults, which you've uttered about Yisra'el's mountains: "They're desolate, they've been given to us as food." ¹³You acted big against me with your mouth and you made your words proliferate against me. I myself heard."'

¹⁴The Lord Yahweh has said this: 'In accordance with the rejoicing over the entire country, I shall make you a desolation. ¹⁵In accordance with your rejoicing over the domain that belonged to Yisra'el's household, because it became desolate, so I shall act towards you. You will become a desolation, Mount Se'ir and all Edom, all of it. And they will acknowledge that I am Yahweh.'

## The mountains renewed

**36** 'And you, young man, prophesy towards Yisra'el's mountains: "Mountains of Yisra'el, listen to Yahweh's word. ²The Lord Yahweh has said this: 'Since the enemy said over you, "Ah", and "The ancient shrines have become ours as a domain", ³therefore prophesy: "The Lord Yahweh has said this: 'Since, yes since they made you desolate and trampled you all round, so that you became the possession of the remaining nations, and you were taken up on to the lip of the tongue and the slur of the people, ⁴therefore, Yisra'el's mountains, listen to the Lord Yahweh's word.

The Lord Yahweh has said this to the mountains, to the hills, to the canyons, to the ravines, to the desolate wastes, and to the abandoned towns that have become plunder and derision to the remaining nations that are all round – [5]therefore the Lord Yahweh has said: "If I haven't spoken in my passionate anger against the remaining nations and against Edom, all of it, which made my country a possession for itself with wholehearted rejoicing, with contempt of soul, for the sake of pastureland, as plunder . . .'"'

[6]Therefore prophesy about Yisra'el's land. You're to say to the mountains, to the hills, to the canyons and to the ravines, "The Lord Yahweh has said this: 'Here am I, I'm going to speak in my passion and in my fury, since you've carried the nations' shame.' [7]Therefore the Lord Yahweh has said this: 'I myself have raised my hand [to swear]: if the nations that are from all round you don't carry their shame . . .

[8]But you, Yisra'el's mountains, will produce your boughs and bear your fruit for my people Yisra'el, because they're near coming. [9]Because here am I towards you, and I shall turn my face to you, and you will be served and sown. [10]I shall make the people on you abundant, Yisra'el's entire household, all of it. The towns will be inhabited, the wastes built up. [11]I shall multiply on you human beings and animals; they'll be many and they'll be fruitful. I shall cause you to be inhabited as you were before and I shall make things good for you, better than before for you, and you will acknowledge that I am Yahweh. [12]I shall get people, my people Yisra'el, to walk upon you. They will come to possess you and you will be their domain. You won't bereave them ever again."'

## Yahweh takes pity on his name

[13]The Lord Yahweh has said this: 'Since they're saying to you, "You've been one who devours human beings, who bereaves your nations", [14]therefore you will no more devour human beings, you will not bereave your nations again any more (a declaration of the Lord Yahweh). [15]I shall not let you hear the nations' shaming any more. You will no more carry the peoples' reviling. You will no more make your nations collapse (a declaration of the Lord Yahweh).'

[16]Yahweh's word came to me: [17]'Young man, when Yisra'el's household were living on their land, they defiled it with their way and with

their deeds. In my eyes their way was like the defilement of a woman who's taboo. [18]So I poured out my fury on them because of the blood they had poured out on the earth, and they had defiled it with their lumps. [19]I scattered them among the nations and they were dispersed among the countries. In accordance with their way and with their deeds I exercised authority over them.

[20]They came to the nations, wherever they came, and treated my sacred name as ordinary, in that people said of them, "These are Yahweh's people, but they went out of his country." [21]But I have taken pity on my sacred name, which Yisra'el's household caused to be treated as ordinary among the nations where they came.

[22]Therefore say to Yisra'el's household: "The Lord Yahweh has said this: 'It's not for your sake that I'm going to act, Yisra'el's household, but for my sacred name, which you've caused to be treated as ordinary among the nations where you came. [23]I shall make my great name sacred, which has been treated as ordinary among the nations among whom you have caused it to be treated as ordinary, and the nations will acknowledge that I am Yahweh (a declaration of the Lord Yahweh) when I show myself sacred through you before their eyes.

[24]I shall take you from the nations, collect you from all the countries and bring you to your land. [25]I shall toss clean water over you and you'll be clean. From all your defilements and from all your lumps I shall cleanse you.

## The gift of a new mind and a new spirit

[26]I shall give you a new mind and I shall put a new spirit inside you. I shall remove the stony mind from your flesh and give you a fleshy mind, [27]and I shall put my spirit inside you. I shall make it so that you walk by my laws and keep my rulings and do them. [28]You will live in the country that I gave your ancestors, and you will be my people and I shall be your God. [29]I shall deliver you from all your defilements. I shall call for the grain and make it abundant, and not put famine upon you. [30]I shall make the fruit of the trees and the produce of the fields abundant, so that you no more receive reviling because of famine among the nations. [31]You will be mindful of your bad ways and

your practices that were not good, and you will be loathsome in your own sight because of your wayward acts and because of your offensive practices. ³²It's not for your sake that I'm going to act (a declaration of the Lord Yahweh), be it known to you. Be disgraced and ashamed because of your ways, Yisra'el's household.'"

³³The Lord Yahweh has said this: 'On the day I cleanse you from all your wayward acts, I shall cause your towns to be inhabited, the wastes will be built up, ³⁴and the desolate country will be served instead of being a desolation in the sight of every passer-by. ³⁵People will say, "That country which was desolate has become like Eden Garden, and the towns that were wasted and desolate and torn down, people live in, fortified." ³⁶The nations that remain all round you will acknowledge that I Yahweh have built up the wastes; I have planted the desolations. I Yahweh have spoken and I shall act.'

³⁷The Lord Yahweh has said this: 'Further, in this I shall let myself be enquired of by Yisra'el's household, to act for them. I shall make people as abundant as a flock. ³⁸Like the flock of sacred ones, like the Yerushalaim flock at its set occasions, so the wasted towns will be full of a human flock, and they will acknowledge that I am Yahweh.'

## Dem bones, dem bones, dem dry bones

**37** Yahweh's hand came on me and took me out by Yahweh's wind, and set me down in the middle of a valley. It was full of bones. ²He got me to pass through them, all the way round. There, they were very many on the face of the valley. And there, they were very dry. ³He said to me, 'Young man, could these bones come to life?' I said, 'Lord Yahweh, you know.'

⁴He said to me, 'Prophesy to these bones: "You dry bones, listen to Yahweh's word. ⁵The Lord Yahweh has said this to these bones: 'Here, I'm going to make breath come into you, and you will come to life. ⁶I shall put muscles on you, make flesh go up on you, spread skin on you and put breath into you, and you'll come to life, and you will acknowledge that I am Yahweh."'"

⁷I prophesied as I was ordered, and a sound came as I prophesied, and there – a shaking,

and the bones drew near bone to its bone. ⁸I looked, and there, muscles were on them, and flesh went up, and skin spread on them above. But there was no breath in them. ⁹He said to me, 'Prophesy to the breath, prophesy, young man. You're to say to the breath, "The Lord Yahweh has said this: 'Come from the four winds, breath, and breathe into these people who are run through, so that they come to life.'"'

¹⁰So I prophesied as he ordered me, and the breath came into them. They came to life and stood on their feet, a very, very great force. ¹¹He said to me, 'Young man, these bones are Yisra'el's entire household. There, they're saying, "Our bones are dry, our hope has perished, we're totally finished." ¹²Therefore prophesy and say to them, "The Lord Yahweh has said this: 'Here, I'm going to open your graves and get you to go up from your graves, my people, and bring you to Yisra'el's land. ¹³You will acknowledge that I am Yahweh when I open your graves and get you to go up from your graves, my people. ¹⁴I shall put my spirit in you and you will come to life and I shall settle you down on your land, and you will acknowledge that I Yahweh have spoken and acted (Yahweh's declaration).'"'

## The two become one

¹⁵Yahweh's word came to me: ¹⁶'And you, young man, get yourself a piece of wood and write on it, "Belonging to Yehudah and to the Yisra'elites who are its associates", and get a piece of wood and write on it, "Belonging to Yoseph (Ephrayim's piece of wood) and all Yisra'el's household that are its associates". ¹⁷Bring them close one to the other so they become one piece of wood. They're to become one in your hand.

¹⁸When members of your people say to you, "Tell us what these things of yours are, won't you", ¹⁹speak to them: "The Lord Yahweh has said this: 'Here am I, I'm going to take Yoseph's piece of wood that's in Ephrayim's hand, and the Yisra'elite clans that are his associates, and I shall put them on it (Yehudah's piece of wood), and make them one piece of wood. They will be one in my hand."'

²⁰The pieces of wood on which you've written are to be in your hand before their

eyes, [21]and you're to speak to them, "The Lord Yahweh has said this: 'Here am I, I'm going to get the Yisra'elites from among the nations where they've gone, collect them from all round and bring them to their land. [22]I shall make them into one nation in the country, on Yisra'el's mountains. One king will be king for all of them. There won't be two nations again. They won't divide into two kingdoms ever again. [23]And they won't defile themselves again with their lumps and their abominations and all their rebellions. I shall deliver them from all their settlements in which they did wrong and cleanse them, and they will be my people and I shall be their God.

[24]My servant David will be king over them and they will all have one shepherd. They will walk by my rulings and keep my laws and do them. [25]They'll live in the country that I gave to my servant, to Ya'aqob, in which your ancestors lived. They'll live in it, they and their children and their grandchildren, permanently, with David my servant as their ruler permanently.

[26]I shall solemnize a pact of well-being for them. It will be a permanent pact with them. I shall give it to them and multiply them, and I shall put my sanctuary among them permanently. [27]My dwelling will be with them. I shall be their God and they will be my people. [28]And the nations will acknowledge that I am Yahweh, the one who makes Yisra'el sacred, when my sanctuary is among them permanently.'"

## Gog and Magog

**38** Yahweh's word came to me: [2]'Young man, set your face towards Gog, in the country of Magog, the highest ruler in Meshek and Tubal. You're to prophesy against him: [3]"The Lord Yahweh has said this: 'Here am I towards you, Gog, highest ruler in Meshek and Tubal. [4]I shall turn you back and put hooks in your jaws and make you go out, with your entire force, horses and cavalry, clothed in fullness all of them, a great congregation, with body-shield and hand-shield, grasping swords, all of them. [5]Paras, Kush and Put are with them, all of them with shield and helmet, [6]Gomer and all its legions, Bet Togarmah in the far parts of the north

and all its legions – many peoples with you. [7]Be ready, get yourselves ready, you and your entire congregation who are forming round you. You're to be a watch for them. [8]After many days you will be appointed; at the end of the years you will come to a country restored from the sword, collected from many peoples – against Yisra'el's mountains, which have been a waste continually. But it will have been taken out from the peoples, and they will be living with confidence, all of them. [9]When you go up, you will come as devastation; you will be like a cloud to cover the country, you and all your legions and many peoples with you.'"

[10]The Lord Yahweh has said: 'On that day, things will come up into your mind. You will think up a bad plan. [11]You will say, "I shall go up against a country of open villages. I shall come to quiet people living in confidence, all of them, living without walls and without bars or gateways, [12]to take plunder and seize spoil", to turn your hand against wastes that have become inhabited, and upon a people gathered from the nations, making livestock and possessions, living at the centre of the earth. [13]Sheba and Dedan, the traders of Tarshish and all its lions will say to you, "Is it to take plunder that you're coming? Is it to seize spoil that you've formed your congregation, to carry off silver and gold, to get livestock and possessions, to take much plunder?"'

## The last great battle

[14]Therefore prophesy, young man, and say to Gog: 'The Lord Yahweh has said this: "On that day, when my people Yisra'el are living with confidence, you will acknowledge it, won't you, [15]and come from your place, from the far parts of the north, you and many peoples with you, riding horses all of them, a great congregation, a huge force. [16]You'll go up against my people Yisra'el like a cloud to cover the country. At the end of the time it will come about. I shall bring you against my country in order that the nations may acknowledge me when I show myself sacred through you before their eyes, Gog."

[17]The Lord Yahweh said this: 'Are you the one of whom I spoke in earlier days by means of my servants Yisra'el's prophets,

who prophesied in those days for years that I would bring you against them? ¹⁸On that day, on the day Gog comes against Yisra'el's land (a declaration of the Lord Yahweh), my wrath will go up into my nostrils. ¹⁹In my passion, in my furious fire, I have spoken. If on that day a great earthquake doesn't happen in Yisra'el's land . . .

²⁰Before me things will quake: the fish in the sea, the birds in the heavens, the animals of the open country, everything that moves on the ground and all the human beings that are on the face of the ground. The mountains will be toppled, the cliffs will fall, every wall will fall to the earth.

²¹I shall call for a sword against him through all my mountains (a declaration of the Lord Yahweh). One person's sword will be against his brother. ²²I shall enter into judgement with him by epidemic and by bloodshed, and I shall pour torrential rain, hailstones, fire and sulphur, on him, on his legions and on the many peoples that are with him. ²³I shall show I am great and show I am sacred and cause myself to be acknowledged before the eyes of many nations. And they will acknowledge that I am Yahweh.'

## The peace dividend

**39** And you, young man, prophesy against Gog: 'The Lord Yahweh has said this: "Here am I towards you, Gog, the highest ruler of Meshek and Tubal. ²I shall turn you back. I shall lead you along and get you to go up from the far parts of the north and bring you against Yisra'el's mountains. ³But I shall strike down your bow from your left hand and make your arrows fall from your right hand. ⁴You will fall on Yisra'el's mountains, you and all your legions and the peoples that are with you. I shall give you as food to birds of prey of every kind and to the animals of the open country ⁵when you fall on the face of the open country, because I have spoken (a declaration of the Lord Yahweh).

⁶I shall send off fire on Magog and on the people who live with confidence on foreign shores, and they will acknowledge that I am Yahweh. I shall cause my sacred name to be acknowledged among my people Yisra'el and

not let my sacred name be treated as ordinary any more, and the nations will acknowledge that I Yahweh am sacred in Yisra'el.

⁸There, it's coming, it's happening (a declaration of the Lord Yahweh). It's the day of which I have spoken. ⁹The inhabitants of Yisra'el's towns will go out and make a fire and burn the weaponry, hand-shield and body-shield, bow and arrows, hand pike and spear. They'll make a fire with them for seven years. ¹⁰They won't carry wood from the open country and they won't cut it from the forests, because they'll make a fire with the weaponry. They'll plunder their plunderers and despoil their despoilers (a declaration of the Lord Yahweh).

## Proper burial

¹¹On that day I shall give Gog a place where there will be a grave in Yisra'el, Travellers' Ravine, east of the sea. It will obstruct travellers; they'll bury Gog and his entire multitude there. They'll call it Gog's Multitude's Ravine. ¹²Yisra'el's household will bury them to cleanse the country, for seven months; ¹³the entire people of the country will bury them. It will mean renown for them, the day I show my splendour (a declaration of the Lord Yahweh). ¹⁴They will set apart permanent people as travellers in the country, burying (the travellers) ones that remain on the face of the country, to cleanse it. At the end of seven months they'll search. ¹⁵As travellers travel in the country and see human bones, one is to build a marker by it, until the buriers have buried it in Gog's Multitude's Ravine ¹⁶(the name of the town will also be Multitude) and cleansed the country."

¹⁷And you, young man (the Lord Yahweh has said this), say to birds of every kind and to every animal of the open country, "Collect yourselves and come, gather from all round to my sacrifice that I'm going to make for you, a great sacrifice on Yisra'el's mountains. You'll eat flesh and drink blood. ¹⁸You'll eat strong men's flesh and drink the blood of earth's rulers: rams, lambs, goats, bulls, Bashan fatlings, all of them. ¹⁹You'll eat fat until you're full and drink blood until you're drunk from my sacrifice that I shall have made for you. ²⁰At my table you'll

become full of horses, chariotry, strong men, every man of battle (a declaration of the Lord Yahweh).

## I shall not hide my face any more

²¹I shall put my splendour among the nations, and all the nations will see my authoritative decision that I've made and my hand that I've set against them. ²²Yisra'el's household will acknowledge that I Yahweh am their God, from that day onwards. ²³And the nations will acknowledge that Yisra'el's household went into exile for their waywardness, because they trespassed against me. I hid my face from them and gave them into the hand of their adversaries, and all of them fell by the sword. ²⁴It was in accordance with their defilement and with their rebellions that I dealt with them and hid my face from them."

²⁵Therefore the Lord Yahweh has said this: 'Now I shall restore Ya'aqob's fortunes and have compassion on Yisra'el's entire household, and be passionate about my sacred name. ²⁶They will carry their shame and all their trespass that they committed against me when they live on their land with confidence, with no one disturbing them, ²⁷when I bring them back from the peoples and collect them from their enemies' countries and show myself sacred among them before the eyes of many nations. ²⁸They will acknowledge that I Yahweh am their God, when I've exiled them to the nations but gathered them on their land. I shall leave none of them there any more. ²⁹I shall not hide my face from them any more when I've poured out my spirit on Yisra'el's household (a declaration of the Lord Yahweh).'

## A town on a mountain

**40** In the twenty-fifth year of our exile, at the beginning of the year, on the tenth of the month, in the fourteenth year after the town was struck down, on this very day Yahweh's hand came upon me, and he brought me there. ²In a great appearance of God he brought me to the country of Yisra'el and set me down on a very high mountain. On it

was the very structure of a town to the south. ³He brought me to it, and there – a man, his appearance the very appearance of copper, a linen cord in his hand, and a measuring rod. He was standing in the gateway. ⁴The man spoke to me: 'Young man, look with your eyes, listen with your ears and set your mind on everything that I'm going to show you, because you've been brought here in order to show you. Tell Yisra'el's household everything you see.'

⁵There – a wall outside the house, all the way round. In the man's hand was a six-cubit measuring rod, by the cubit-plus-a-handbreadth [three metres]. He measured the structure's width – one rod, and the height – one rod. ⁶He came to the gateway whose face was towards the east, and went up its steps. He measured the gateway's threshold – one rod in depth (the one threshold – one rod in depth). ⁷Each alcove – one rod in length and one rod in width. Between the alcoves – five cubits.

The gateway's threshold next to the gateway's porch, facing the house – one rod. ⁸He measured the gateway's porch facing the house – one rod. ⁹He measured the gateway's porch – eight cubits, and its columns – two cubits; the gateway's porch was facing the house. ¹⁰The gateway alcoves towards the east were three on one side and three on the other side, one measurement for the three of them and one measurement for the columns on each side.

## Gateways (1)

¹¹He measured:
the width of the gateway opening – ten cubits;
the gateway's length – thirteen cubits;
¹²the barrier in front of the alcoves – one cubit, so the barrier was one cubit on each side;
the alcove – six cubits on one side and six cubits on the other side.
¹³He measured the gateway from the back of an alcove to the back of the other; the width – twenty-five cubits, opening to opening. ¹⁴He made columns – sixty cubits, and next to the column was the gateway courtyard all the way round. ¹⁵Starting at the front of the outer gateway to the front of the inner gateway's porch – fifty cubits. ¹⁶There were narrow windows to the alcoves and to their columns inside the

gateway all the way round, and similarly to the porches there were windows all the way round on the inside, with palms on a column.

¹⁷He brought me to the outer courtyard, and there – halls, and a pavement made for the courtyard all the way round, 30 halls to the pavement. ¹⁸The pavement was by the side of the gateways, alongside the length of the gateways (the lower pavement). ¹⁹He measured the width from in front of the lower gateway to the front of the outer courtyard – a hundred cubits, east and north.

²⁰The gateway whose face was towards the north, belonging to the outer courtyard – he measured its length and its width, ²¹its three alcoves on one side and three on the other side, its columns and its porches. Like the measurement of the first gate, its length – fifty cubits, and the width – twenty-five cubits. ²²Its windows, its porches and its palms were like the measurement of the gateway that faced towards the east. By seven steps people would go up on to it, and its porch would be in front of them. ²³There was a gateway to the inner courtyard facing the northern gate as well as the east; he measured from one gateway to the other gateway – a hundred cubits.

## Gateways (2)

²⁴He took me towards the south. There – a gate towards the south. He measured its columns and its porches, in accordance with these measurements. ²⁵It and its porches had windows all the way round like these windows; the length – fifty cubits, and the width – twenty-five cubits. ²⁶There were seven steps up to it. Its porch was in front of them. It had palms, one on one side and one on the other side, on its columns. ²⁷The inner courtyard had a gateway towards the south. He measured from the gateway to the gateway on the south – a hundred cubits.

²⁸He brought me to the inner courtyard through the southern gateway and measured the southern gateway in accordance with these measurements. ²⁹Its alcoves, its columns and its porches were in accordance with these measurements. It and its porches had windows all the way round. The length – fifty cubits, and the width – twenty-five cubits ³⁰(the porches

all the way round, the length – twenty-five cubits, the width – five cubits). ³¹Its porch was towards the outer courtyard. There were palms on its columns and eight steps in its staircase.

³²He brought me to the inner courtyard towards the east and measured the gateway in accordance with these measurements. ³³Its alcoves, its columns and its porches were in accordance with these measurements. It and its porches had windows all the way round. The length – fifty cubits, and the width – twenty-five cubits. ³⁴Its porch was towards the outer courtyard. There were palms on its columns, on one side and on the other side, and eight steps in its staircase.

³⁵He brought me to the northern gateway and measured it in accordance with these measurements – ³⁶its alcoves, its columns and its porches, and its windows all the way round. The length – fifty cubits, and the width – twenty-five cubits. ³⁷Its columns were towards the outer courtyard. There were palms on its columns, on one side and on the other side, and eight steps in its staircase.

## Provision for the priests and the singers

³⁸There was a hall and its entrance in the porch at the gateways, where they would wash the burnt offering. ³⁹In the gateway porch were two tables on one side and two tables on the other side for slaughtering the burnt offering, the purification offering and the restitution offering on them. ⁴⁰On the outer side wall for someone going up to the entrance of the northern gateway were two tables and on the other side wall in relation to the gateway's porch were two tables, ⁴¹four tables on one side and four tables on the other side at the side wall of the gateway, eight tables on which they would slaughter things. ⁴²The four tables for the burnt offering were of hewn stone. The length – a cubit and a half, the width – a cubit and a half, and the height – a cubit. On them they'd set down the things with which they would slaughter the burnt offering and the sacrifice. ⁴³There were ledges – one handbreadth, fixed inside all the way round. The flesh of the offering was on the tables.

⁴⁴Outside the inner gateway were the singers' halls in the inner courtyard, one that was on

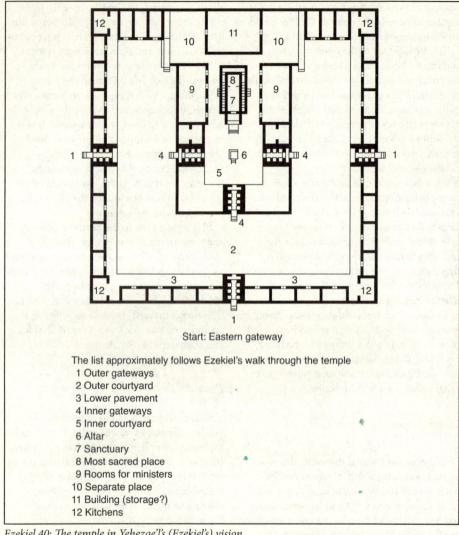

*Ezekiel 40: The temple in Yehezqe'l's (Ezekiel's) vision*

the side wall of the northern gateway with their face towards the south, one on the side wall of the eastern gateway facing towards the north. ⁴⁵He spoke to me: 'This, the hall that faces towards the south, is for the priests having charge of the house. ⁴⁶The hall that faces towards the north is for the priests having charge of the altar. They are the Tsadoqites, who of the Levites draw near Yahweh to minister to him.'

⁴⁷He measured the courtyard. The length – a hundred cubits, the width – a hundred cubits, foursquare. The altar was before the house. ⁴⁸He brought me to the house's porch

and measured a porch column – five cubits on one side and five cubits on the other side. The width of the gateway – three cubits on one side and three cubits on the other side. ⁴⁹The length of the porch – twenty cubits, and the width – eleven cubits. It was by steps that people would go up to it. There were pillars by the columns, one on one side, one on the other side.

## *Yahweh's palace (1)*

**41**    He brought me into the palace and measured the columns – six cubits the width on one side, six cubits the width on the other side (the width of the tent). [2]The width of the entrance – ten cubits, and the side walls of the entrance – five cubits on one side and five cubits on the other side. He measured its length – forty cubits, and the width – twenty cubits. [3]He came inside and measured an entrance column – two cubits, the entrance – six cubits, and the entrance's width – seven cubits. [4]He measured its length – twenty cubits, and the width – twenty cubits, before the palace. He said to me, 'This is the especially sacred place.'

[5]He measured the wall of the house – six cubits, and the width of a side room – four cubits, round the house, all the way round. [6]The side rooms – side room above side room, thirty-three-fold. There were insets in the wall that belonged to the house for the side rooms all the way round, to be supports but so that they wouldn't be supports in the wall of the house. [7]It widened as it went round higher and higher to the side rooms. Because the house's surrounding went higher and higher all the way round the house, consequently the width of the house went higher, and one would go up from the lowest to the highest via the middle.

[8]I saw belonging to the house a raised area all the way round, the foundations of the side rooms. Its height – the full length of a rod, six cubits, to the joint. [9]The width of the wall of a side room on the outside – five cubits. What was left clear between the side rooms of the house [10]and between the halls, the width – twenty cubits round the house, all the way round. [11]The entrance of a side room towards what was left clear, one entrance towards the north, one entrance to the south, and the width of the place that was left clear – five cubits all the way round. [12]The building that was towards the front of the separate place at the corner towards the west: the width – seventy cubits. The wall of the building: the width – five cubits all the way round, and its length – ninety cubits.

## Yahweh's palace (2)

[13]He measured the house:
the length – a hundred cubits;
the separate place, the building and its walls:
the length – a hundred cubits;

[14]the width of the front of the house and the separate place on the east – a hundred cubits.

[15]He measured the length of the building facing the separate place that was at the back of it, and its galleries on one side and on the other side – a hundred cubits. The palace inside, the courtyard porches [16](the thresholds), the narrow windows, and the galleries round the three of them by the threshold, they were panelled with wood all the way round. The ground up to the windows, and the windows, they were covered, [17]above the entrance and as far as the house, inside and outside.

On the entire wall, all the way round, inside and outside, was a measured area. [18]Sphinxes and palms were made, a palm between sphinx and sphinx. A sphinx had two faces, [19]a human face towards the palm on one side and a lion face towards the palm on the other side. It was made for the entire house all the way round. [20]From the ground to above the entrance the sphinxes and the palms were made, and the palace wall.

[21]The palace: there was a square door frame, and facing the sacred place something with an appearance like the appearance of [22]a wood altar. The height – three cubits, its length – two cubits. It had corners, and its length and its walls were wood. He spoke to me: 'This is the table that's before Yahweh.' [23]The palace had double doors, and the sacred place [24]had double doors. The double doors had double doors that could be turned, two doors for one and two doors for the other. [25]Sphinxes and palms were made for them (for the palace doors) as they were made for the walls. There was a wood canopy in front of the porch, on the outside. [26]There were narrow windows and palms on one side and on the other, on the porch's side walls and the side rooms of the house and the canopies.

## The halls

**42** He took me out into the outer courtyard by the way towards the north and brought me into the hall that was opposite the separate place and that was opposite the northern building. [2]Facing the length – a hundred cubits – was the northern entrance. The width – fifty cubits. [3]Opposite the twenty of the inner courtyard, and opposite the pavement of the outer courtyard, one gallery was facing another gallery in threes.

⁴Facing the halls was a walkway (the width – ten cubits, on the inside; a path – one cubit), with its entrances to the north. ⁵The upper halls were cut back, because galleries had an effect on them, more than the lowest and the middle ones in the building, ⁶because they were divided into three, and they had no pillars like the pillars in the courtyards. Therefore it got narrower from the lowest and from the middle, from the ground.

⁷There was a wall outside, alongside the halls, towards the outer courtyard facing the halls. Its length – fifty cubits, ⁸because the length of the halls belonging to the outer court was fifty cubits. So there, in front of the palace, it was a hundred cubits. ⁹From below these halls was the passageway from the east when someone comes here from the outer courtyard.

¹⁰In the width of the wall towards the east, facing the separate place and facing the building, there were halls. ¹¹Towards the front of them was a similar appearance of halls that were towards the north. Corresponding to their length, so was their width. All their exits were in accordance with the prescriptions for them and in accordance with their entrances. ¹²Like the halls' entrances that were towards the south was the entrance at the head of the path, the path in front of the wall going towards the east, as one comes into them.

## Separating between the sacred and the ordinary

¹³He said to me, 'The northern halls, the southern halls, that are facing the separate place, are the sacred halls where the priests who come near Yahweh will eat the most sacred things. They will set down the most sacred things there (the grain offering, the purification offering and the restitution offering), because the place is sacred. ¹⁴When the priests come in, they won't go out from the sacred place to the outer courtyard. They'll set down their garments in which they minister there because it's sacred, and put on other garments and go near the people's area.'

¹⁵He finished measuring the inner house and took me out towards the gateway that faces

towards the east, and measured all the way round.

¹⁶He measured the eastern side with the measuring rod – 500 (in rods) with the measuring rod, all round.

¹⁷He measured the northern side – 500 (in rods) with the measuring rod, all round.

¹⁸He measured the southern side – 500 (in rods) with the measuring rod.

¹⁹He turned to the southern side and measured – 500 (in rods) with the measuring rod.

²⁰Four sides he measured it. It had a wall all the way round (the length – 500; the width – 500) to separate between the sacred and the ordinary.

## Yahweh's splendour is returning

**43** He took me to a gateway, the gateway that faces towards the east. ²There – the splendour of Yisra'el's God was coming from the eastern direction, its sound like the sound of much water. The earth was lit up by his splendour. ³The appearance was like the appearance that I saw, like the appearance that I saw when I came to devastate the town, and the great appearance was like the appearance that I saw at the River Kebar. I fell on my face.

⁴Yahweh's splendour came into the house by way of the gateway whose face is towards the east. ⁵A spirit lifted me up and brought me to the inner courtyard. There, Yahweh's splendour was filling the house. ⁶I heard someone speaking to me from the house, while the man was standing next to me. ⁷He said to me, 'Young man: the place for my throne and the place for the soles of my feet, where I shall dwell among the Yisra'elites permanently – Yisra'el's household shall not defile my sacred name any more, they and their kings by their whoring and by their kings' corpses, their mounds. ⁸When they put their threshold with my threshold and their door frame next to my door frame with a wall between me and them, they would defile my sacred name with their offensive deeds that they did, and I consumed them in my anger. ⁹Now they are to put their whoring and their kings' corpses far away from me, and I shall dwell among them permanently.

¹⁰You, young man, tell Yisra'el's household about the house. They're to be ashamed of their wayward acts, but they're to measure out the plan. ¹¹When they're ashamed of all that they did, make known the house's form, its plan, its exits, its entrances, all its forms, all its laws, all its forms and all its instructions. Write it down before their eyes so they may keep its entire form and all its laws, and act on them. ¹²This is the instruction for the house on the mountain top. Its entire boundary all the way round is most sacred. Here, this is the instruction for the house.'

## The altar

¹³These are the measurements of the altar in cubits (a 'cubit' is a cubit plus a handbreadth):
the base – a cubit, and the width – a cubit;
its rim at its lip all round – one hand span; this is the altar's mound;
¹⁴from the base in the ground to the lower ledge – two cubits, and the width – one cubit;
from the small ledge to the big ledge – four cubits, and the width – a cubit;
¹⁵the hearth – four cubits, and from the hearth upwards, four horns;
¹⁶the hearth: the length – twelve, the width – twelve, made square on its four sides;
¹⁷the ledge: the length – fourteen, with the width – fourteen, on its four sides;
the rim round it – half a cubit;
the base to it – a cubit round it, with its steps facing east.

¹⁸He said to me, 'Young man, the Lord Yahweh has said this: "These are the laws for the altar on the day it's built, for offering the burnt offering on it and tossing blood on it. ¹⁹You're to give to the Levitical priests who are of the offspring of Tsadoq, who come near to me (a declaration of the Lord Yahweh) to minister to me, a bullock from the herd as a purification offering. ²⁰You're to get some of its blood and put it on its four horns and towards the four corners of the ledge and towards the rim round, and purge it and expiate it. ²¹And you're to get the purification offering bullock and burn it in the appointed place in the house, outside the sanctuary. ²²On the second day you're to present a male goat, whole, as a purification offering.

They're to purge the altar as they purged it with the bull. ²³When you've completed the purging, you're to present a bullock from the herd, whole, and a ram from the flock, whole. ²⁴You're to present them before Yahweh, and the priests are to throw salt on them and offer them as a burnt offering to Yahweh.

## Preparations for the splendour's return

²⁵For seven days you're to prepare a goat as a purification offering, daily, and they're to prepare a bullock from the herd and a ram from the flock, whole. ²⁶For seven days they are to expiate the altar, purify it and commission it. ²⁷They're to complete these days, and on the eighth day and onwards the priests are to make your burnt offerings and your fellowship sacrifices on the altar. And I shall accept you (a declaration of the Lord Yahweh)."'

**44** He took me back towards the sanctuary's outer gateway that faces east. It was shut. ²Yahweh said to me, 'This gateway is to be shut. It's not to be opened. No one is to come through it, because Yahweh, Yisra'el's God, came through it. It's to be shut. ³As for the ruler, the ruler himself will sit in it to eat bread before Yahweh. By way of the gateway's threshold he may come in and by way of it he may go out.'

⁴He brought me by way of the northern gateway to the front of the house. I looked, and there – Yahweh's splendour was filling Yahweh's house. I fell on my face. ⁵Yahweh said to me, 'Young man, apply your mind, look with your eyes, listen with your ears to all that I'm going to speak with you regarding all the laws for Yahweh's house and all the instructions for it. Set your mind on the entrance into the house with all the exits from the sanctuary. ⁶You're to say to the rebellious, to Yisra'el's household: "The Lord Yahweh has said this: 'You have plenty of all your offensive deeds, Yisra'el's household, ⁷in that you brought foreigners, foreskinned in spirit and foreskinned in flesh, to be in my sanctuary, to make my house ordinary when you present my meal, the fat and blood. You contravened my pact with all your offensive deeds. ⁸You didn't kept the charge of my sacred things; you appointed them as people to keep my charge in my sanctuary for you."'

## Who can properly minister?

⁹The Lord Yahweh has said this: 'No foreigner, foreskinned in spirit and foreskinned in flesh, is to come into my sanctuary, of any foreigner who's among the Yisra'elites. ¹⁰Rather, the Levites who went far from me when Yisra'el went astray (when they went astray from me, following their lumps) will carry their waywardness, ¹¹but in my sanctuary they will be ministering with oversight at the gateways of the house and ministering to the house. They will slaughter the burnt offering and the sacrifice for the people and they will stand before them to minister to them.

¹²Because they used to minister to them before their lumps, and to Yisra'el's household they were obstacles that tripped them into waywardness, therefore I've raised my hand [to swear] concerning them (a declaration of the Lord Almighty) that they will carry their waywardness. ¹³They're not to come near me to act as priests to me or to come near to any of my sacred things, to the most sacred things. They're to carry their shame, the offensive deeds that they did. ¹⁴But I shall make them guards in charge of the house, for all its service and for all that's done in it.

¹⁵But the Levitical priests who are descendants of Tsadoq, who kept the charge of my sanctuary when Yisra'el's household went astray from me, they may draw near to me to minister to me. They may stand before me to present fat and blood to me (a declaration of the Lord Yahweh). ¹⁶They're the ones to come into my sanctuary. They're the ones to draw near to my table to minister to me, and they will keep my charge.

¹⁷When they come to the gateways of the inner courtyard they're to wear linen garments. They're not to put wool on themselves when they minister in the gateways of the inner courtyard and inside. ¹⁸Linen attire is to be on their head and linen pants round their hips; they're not to wrap on anything sweaty. ¹⁹When they go out to the outer courtyard (to the outer courtyard to the people) they're to take off their garments in which they were ministering, set them down in the sacred halls, and put on other garments, and not make the people sacred by their garments.

## Priests

²⁰They're not to shave their head or grow long hair, but definitely to trim their heads. ²¹They're not to drink wine, any priest, when they go into the inner courtyard. ²²They're not to take a widow or a divorcee for themselves as wives, but rather to take a girl from the offspring of Yisra'el's household or a widow who's a priest's widow.

²³They're to teach my people between sacred and ordinary and to enable them to know between clean and defiled. ²⁴In connection with an argument, they're the ones to stand to give a ruling; they're to give a rule by my rulings. They're to keep my instructions and my laws regarding all set occasions, and to keep my sabbaths sacred.

²⁵An individual isn't to go in to someone dead, except that he may defile himself for father or for mother, for a son or for a daughter, for a brother or for a sister who hasn't come to belong to a man. ²⁶After his cleansing they're to count seven days for him, ²⁷and on the day he comes into the sacred place, into the inner courtyard, to minister in the sacred place, he's to present his purification offering (a declaration of the Lord Yahweh).

²⁸They're to have as a domain: I am their domain. You're to give them no holding in Yisra'el; I am their holding. ²⁹The grain offering, the purification offering and the restitution offering – they're the ones to eat them. Everything devoted in Yisra'el will be theirs. ³⁰The first of all the first fruits of everything and every donation of anything, of all your donations, will be the priests'. The first of your dough you're to give to the priest, to make a blessing set down on your house. ³¹The priests aren't to eat anything that's died naturally or any prey, bird or animal.

## Constraining the ruler

**45** When you allot the country as a domain:

You're to raise a donation for Yahweh, a sacred area of the country: the length – 25,000 in length; the width – 10,000. It's to be a sacred area in its entire border, all round.

²Of this, there's to be 500 by 500 squared all round for the sacred place, and fifty cubits as an open space all round. ³From this measurement you're to measure 25,000 in length and 10,000 in width; in it is to be the sanctuary, the most sacred place. ⁴It will be the sacred area of the country, for the priests, the sanctuary ministers, who draw near to minister to Yahweh. It will be a place for homes for them, and a sanctuary for the sanctuary. ⁵25,000 in length and 10,000 in width will be for the Levites, the ministers of the house, for them as a holding, twenty halls. ⁶The town's holding: you're to give 5,000 in width, and in length 25,000, alongside the sacred donation. It will belong to Yisra'el's entire household.

⁷To the ruler there will belong on one side and on the other side of the sacred donation and of the town's holding, in front of the sacred donation and in front of the town's holding, on the west westwards and on the east eastwards, a length alongside one of the shares, from the western border to the eastern border ⁸of the country. It will be a holding for him in Yisra'el. My rulers are no more to oppress my people. They will give the country to Yisra'el's household, to their clans.'

⁹The Lord Yahweh has said this: 'There's plenty for you, Yisra'el's rulers. Remove violence and destruction. Exercise authority with faithfulness. Lift your expulsions of my people (a declaration of the Lord Yahweh). ¹⁰You're to have faithful balances, a faithful *ephah*, a faithful *bat*. ¹¹The ephah and the bat are to be one size. The bat is to contain a tenth of a *homer*, and the ephah a tenth of a homer. The size will be based on the homer. ¹²The sheqel is twenty *gerahs*. Twenty sheqels plus twenty-five sheqels plus fifteen sheqels are a *mina* for you.

### Responsibilities of people and ruler

¹³This is the donation that you're to raise: a sixth of an ephah from a homer of wheat; a sixth of an ephah from a homer of barley; ¹⁴the law for oil – oil by the bat: a tenth of a bat from a kor (ten bats or a homer, because ten bats make a homer);

¹⁵one sheep from the flock, out of 200, from Yisra'el's pastureland for a grain offering, for a burnt offering and for fellowship sacrifices, to make expiation for them (a declaration of the Lord Yahweh). ¹⁶The entire people of the country are to be involved in this donation to the ruler in Yisra'el, ¹⁷but the burnt offerings, the grain offering, the libation – at festivals, at new months and on sabbaths, on all set occasions for Yisra'el's household – are incumbent on the ruler. He is to make the purification offering, the grain offering, the burnt offering and the fellowship sacrifices to make expiation for Yisra'el's household.'

¹⁸The Lord Yahweh has said this: 'On the first of the first month, you're to get a bullock from the herd, whole, and purify the sanctuary. ¹⁹The priest is to get some of the blood of the purification offering and put it on the door frame of the house, on the four corners of the altar's ledge, and on the door frame of the gateway to the inner courtyard. ²⁰So you're to do on the seventh of the month, because of someone making a mistake or being ignorant; you're to expiate the house.

²¹In the first, on the fourteenth day of the month, it's to be Pesah [Passover] for you. For the seven-day festival, flatbread is to be eaten. ²²On that day the ruler is to make on his behalf and on behalf of the entire people a bull as a purification offering. ²³For the seven days of the festival he's to make a burnt offering for Yahweh, seven bullocks and seven rams, whole, daily for the seven days, and as a purification offering a male goat, daily. ²⁴He's to make as a grain offering an ephah for the bullock, an ephah for the ram, and oil: a hin for the ephah. ²⁵In the seventh, on the fifteenth day of the month, during the festival, he's to make it in accordance with these for seven days, in accordance with the purification offering, with the burnt offering, with the grain offering and with the oil.'

### Daily, weekly, monthly, annually and spontaneously

**46** The Lord Yahweh said this: 'The gateway of the inner court facing east is to be shut for the six days of work, but on the sabbath day it's to be open, and on the new month day it's to be open. ²The ruler is to come in by way of the outer gateway's threshold and to stand at the door frame, and the priests are to make his burnt offering and his fellowship sacrifices. He's to bow low at the gateway's terrace and go out, but the gateway isn't to be shut until evening.

³The country's people are to bow low at that gateway door on sabbaths and on new months, before Yahweh. ⁴The burnt offering that the ruler presents for Yahweh on the sabbath day: six lambs, whole, a ram, whole, ⁵and a grain offering: an ephah for the ram, and for the lambs as a grain offering a gift from his hand, and oil: a hin for the ephah. ⁶On the day of the new month: a bullock from the herd, whole, six lambs and a ram; they're to be whole. ⁷He's to make an ephah for the bullock, an ephah for the ram as a grain offering, and for the lambs as his hand attains to, and oil: a hin for the ephah.

⁸When the ruler comes in, he's to come in by way of the gateway's threshold, and go out the same way. ⁹But when the country's people come in before Yahweh on the set occasions, someone who comes in by way of the northern gateway to bow low is to go out by way of the southern gateway, and someone who comes in by way of the southern gateway is to go out by way of the northern gateway. He isn't to go back by way of the gateway by which he came in but go out by the one opposite him.

¹⁰The ruler will come in among them when they come in, and go out when they go out. ¹¹On festivals and on set occasions the grain offering is to be an ephah for the bullock, an ephah for the ram, for the lambs a gift from his hand, and oil: a hin for the ephah.

## Preparations for sacrifices

¹²When the ruler makes a burnt offering as a voluntary offering or fellowship sacrifices as a voluntary offering to Yahweh, someone is to open the gateway facing east for him and he's to make his burnt offering and his fellowship sacrifices as he does on the sabbath day, and he's to go out. Someone is to shut the gateway after he goes out. ¹³With a lamb of the first year, whole, you're to make an offering for the day for Yahweh;

morning by morning you're to make it. ¹⁴You're to make a grain offering with it morning by morning: a sixth of an ephah and a third of a hin of oil to moisten the fine flour as a grain offering for Yahweh – permanent laws, regularly. ¹⁵They're to make the lamb, the grain offering and the oil morning by morning, a regular burnt offering.'

¹⁶The Lord Yahweh said this: 'When the ruler gives a gift to one of his sons, it will be his domain; it will belong to his sons. It will be their holding as a domain. ¹⁷But when he gives a gift out of his domain to one of his servants, it will belong to him until the year of release, and go back to the ruler. After all, his sons – his domain is to belong to them. ¹⁸But the ruler isn't to take from the people's domain, oppressing them out of their holding. From his own holding he may give a domain to his sons, so that my people may not be scattered, each person from his holding.'

¹⁹He brought me by the entrance that was by the side of the gateway to the sacred halls belonging to the priests, facing north. There, in the far parts to the west, a place was there. ²⁰He said to me, 'This is the place where the priests are to cook the restitution offering and the purification offering, where they're to bake the grain offering, so as not to have them go out into the outer courtyard and make the people sacred.' ²¹He took me out into the outer courtyard and got me to pass the courtyard's four corners. There, a courtyard in each courtyard corner: ²²in the four corners of the courtyard were enclosed courtyards: length – forty; width – thirty, one measurement for the four of them set in corners, ²³with a ledge all round them (all round the four of them), and cooking places made underneath the ledges all round. ²⁴He said to me, 'These are the kitchens where the ministers in the house will cook the people's fellowship sacrifice.'

## Life-giving water

**47** He took me back to the entrance of the house. There, water was going out from under the house's terrace, eastward, because the front of the house was to the east. The water was going down from under the right side of the house, south of the altar. ²He took me out by way of the northern gateway and took me round by way of the outside to the outer gateway, the way facing east. There, water was flowing from the right side. ³As the man went out eastward with a line in his hand, he measured 500 metres and got me to pass through the water, ankle-deep water. ⁴He measured 500 and got me to pass through the water, the water being knee-deep. He measured 500 and got me to pass through the hips-deep water. ⁵He measured 500, a wadi that I couldn't pass through because the water had risen, swimming water, a wadi that couldn't be passed through.

⁶He said to me, 'Have you seen, young man?', and got me to go and return to the wadi's bank. ⁷As I returned, there – on the wadi's bank, very many trees, this side and that. ⁸He said to me, 'This water is going out towards the eastern region, going down to the Steppe, and coming to the sea, to the sea of polluted water. The water will become healthy. ⁹Any living being that moves will live wherever the great wadi goes, and the fish will be very abundant because this water comes there. It will be healthy, and anything will live where the wadi comes. ¹⁰Fishermen will stand by it from Gedi Spring to Eglayim Spring, a place for spreading nets. In kind their fish will be like the fish of the Sea, very abundantly great. ¹¹But its swamps and marshes won't become healthy; they're given over to salt.

¹²By the wadi there will grow, on its bank this side and that, every tree for food. Their foliage won't wither, their fruit won't come to an end. By their months they will produce, because their water is going out from the sanctuary. Their fruit will be for food and their foliage for medicine.'

## The extent of the country

¹³The Lord Yahweh said this: 'This is the border by which you're to have the country as a domain for Yisra'el's twelve clans (Yoseph – holdings). ¹⁴You're to have it as a domain (each the same as his brother), that which I raised my hand [to swear] to give your ancestors. This country will fall to you as your domain. ¹⁵This is the border of the country:

On the northern side: from the Great Sea by way of Hetlon, Lebo, to Tsedad, ¹⁶Hamat,

Berotah, Sibrayim (which is between the border of Dammeseq and the border of Hamat), Hatser Hattikon (which is on the border of Havran). ¹⁷The border will be from the Sea to Hatser Enon, the border of Dammeseq and north, northward, and the border of Hamat: the north side.

¹⁸The eastern side: from between Havran and Dammeseq, and Gil'ad and Yisra'el's country, the Yarden [Jordan], you're to measure from the border to the Eastern Sea: the east side.

¹⁹The southern side: to the south from Tamar as far as the water at Meribot Qadesh, the Wadi, to the Great Sea: the southern side, to the south.

²⁰The western side: the Great Sea from the border as far as opposite Lebo Hamat: this is the western side.

²¹You're to share out this country for yourselves among Yisra'el's clans. ²²You're to allot it as a domain for yourselves and for the aliens residing among you who've had children among you. They're to be like natives among the Yisra'elites. With you they'll receive a domain in the property among Yisra'el's clans. ²³In the clan with which the alien resides, there you're to give him his domain (a declaration of the Lord Yahweh).'

## The clans

**48** 'These are the names of the clans. At the northern end, by the side of the Hetlon road to Lebo-hamat, Hatsar Enan, the border of Dammeseq to the north by the side of Hamat, from the eastern side to the Sea will belong to it: one, Dan.

²At Dan's border, from the eastern side as far as the western side: one, Asher.

³At Asher's border, from the eastern side as far as the western side: one, Naphtali.

⁴At Naphtali's border, from the eastern side as far as the western side: one, Menashsheh.

⁵At Menashsheh's border, from the eastern side as far as the western side: one, Ephrayim.

⁶At Ephrayim's border, from the eastern side as far as the western side: one, Re'uben.

⁷At Re'uben's border, from the eastern side as far as the western side: one, Yehudah.

⁸At Yehudah's border, from the eastern side as far as the western side, will be the donation that you raise, width and length – 25,000, like one of the holdings from the eastern side as far as the western side. The sanctuary will be in the middle of it. ⁹The donation that you raise for Yahweh: length – 25,000; width – 10,000. ¹⁰It will belong to these: the sacred donation to the priests, on the north – 25,000; on the west the width – 10,000; on the east the width – 10,000, and on the south the length – 25,000. Yahweh's sanctuary will be in the middle of it. ¹¹What is made sacred will belong to the priests, the Tsadoqites, who kept my charge, who didn't go astray when the Yisra'elites went astray, as the Levites went astray. ¹²It will belong to them as a donation out of the donation from the country, most sacred, at the Levites' border. ¹³The Levites, alongside the priests' border: length – 25,000, and width – 10,000 (the entire length – 25,000, and the width – 10,000). ¹⁴They're not to sell any of it. A person isn't to exchange or transfer the first fruits of the country, because it's sacred to Yahweh.

¹⁵The 5,000 in width by 25,000 in length that remain: it's ordinary land for the town, for dwelling and for pasture. The town will be in the middle of it. ¹⁶These are its measurements: the northern side – 4,500; the southern side – 4,500; the eastern side – 4,500; and the western side – 4,500. ¹⁷The pasture will belong to the town, northward – 250; southward – 250; eastward – 250; and westward – 250.

## Yahweh-Is-There

¹⁸What is left in the country alongside the sacred donation will be 10,000 eastward and 10,000 westward. It will be alongside the sacred donation, and its produce will be for food for the town's servants. ¹⁹One who serves the town – from all Yisra'el's clans they will serve it. ²⁰The entire donation, 25,000 by 25,000 square, you're to raise, the sacred donation with the town's holding. ²¹What is left will belong to the ruler, on this side and on the other of the sacred donation and the town's holding. In front of the 25,000 of the donation as far as the eastern border, and on the west in front of the 25,000 to the western border, alongside the shares, will belong to the ruler. The sacred donation and the sanctuary belonging to the house in the middle of it, ²²and apart from the Levites' holding and the town's holding within what belongs to the ruler, between Yehudah's border and Binyamin's border will belong to the ruler.

²³The rest of the clans:

from the eastern side as far as the western side: one, Binyamin;

²⁴at Binyamin's border, from the eastern side as far as the western side: one, Shim'on;

²⁵at Shim'on's border, from the eastern side as far as the western side: one, Yissakar;

²⁶at Yissakar's border, from the eastern side as far as the western side: one, Zebulun;

²⁷at Zebulun's border, from the eastern side as far as the western side: one, Gad;

²⁸at Gad's border, to the southern side, southward: the border will be from Tamar to the water at Meribat Qadesh, the Wadi, as far as the Great Sea.

²⁹This is the country that you're to allot as a domain to Yisra'el's clans. These will be the shares (a declaration of the Lord Yahweh).
³⁰These are the town's exits:

on the northern side, the measurement is 4,500 ³¹(the town's gateways will be by the names of Yisra'el's clans), three northern gateways: one the Re'uben gateway, one the Yehudah gateway, one the Levi gateway;

³²on the eastern side, 4,500, and three gateways: one the Yoseph gateway, one the Binyamin gateway, one the Dan gateway;

³³on the southern side, the measure is 4,500, and three gateways: one the Shim'on gateway, one the Yissakar gateway, one the Zebulun gateway;

³⁴on the western side, 4,500, their three gateways: one the Gad gateway, one the Asher gateway, one the Naphtali gateway.
³⁵All round – 18,000. The town's name from now on will be "Yahweh-Is-There".

# DANIEL

The book of Daniel [Daniyye'l] divides into two halves. The first half is a series of stories, amazing but easy to understand. They tell about a series of pressures that come on four Judahite boys taken off into exile in Babylon at the beginning of the sixth century, who are well-born and clever enough to get drafted into the Babylonian administration. The question is, can they survive the pressures as well as succeed there? Will God enable them to do so? God does, and the imperial authorities recognize it.

The second half is a series of dreams and visions (expanding on a first dream vision in chapter 2), amazing and hard to understand. Each of the dreams and visions tells the story from Daniel's own day up to a great crisis four centuries later. In the 160s BC Jerusalem was ruled from Syria as part of the Seleucid Empire, one of the entities into which Alexander the Great's empire split. Its current ruler, Antiochus IV, banned worship in accordance with the Torah and imposed alien forms of worship in Jerusalem. The dreams and visions in Daniel envisage the sequence of empires from Daniel's day up to Antiochus (Babylon, Medo-Persia, Greece, the Seleucids) and promise that at the end of this story God will put the empires down and bring in his own rule.

To judge from parallels with other dream visions from the cultural context, these stories expressed as depictions of the future are actually accounts formulated near the end of the story they tell. The actual future promise in them promises deliverance from Antiochus. And against all the odds the people of Jerusalem did get their freedom from Antiochus, and became masters of their own fate for the first time for many centuries. Of course it wasn't the final end, but it was a kind of anticipation of the final end, like the fall of Jerusalem in AD 70. The visions were thus vindicated and shown to be God-given. The pressures of the time, the persecution and the outrageous action on the part of the emperor recurred a century or two later when the Romans annexed Judea, and the portrait of events helped people in Jesus' day to understand what was going on and to live in hope.

## On drawing the line

**1** In the third year of the reign of Yehoyaqim king of Yehudah, Nebukadne'tstsar king of Babel came to Yerushalaim and besieged it. ²The Lord gave into his hand Yehoyaqim king of Yehudah and some of the articles from God's house, and he brought them to the country of Shin'ar, to his god's house. He brought the articles to his god's treasure house.

³The king said to Ashpenaz, the chief over his courtiers, to bring some of the Yisra'elites, both some of royal descent and some of the important people ⁴(young men in whom there was no defect, good in appearance, insightful in terms of all smartness, knowledgeable, discerning in knowledge and in whom there was capacity to stand in attendance in the king's palace), and to teach them the learning and the language of the Kasdites. ⁵The king assigned to them a daily allocation from the king's supplies and from the wine he drank, and to bring them up for three years and some of them would stand in attendance before the king.

⁶Among them were some Yehudahites, Daniyye'l, Hananyah, Misha'el and Azaryah, ⁷but the officer over the courtiers determined on names for them. For Daniyye'l he determined on 'Beltesha'tstsar', for Hananyah 'Shadrak', for Misha'el 'Meshack' and for Azaryah 'Abed Nego'.

⁸Daniyye'l determined in his mind that he would not defile himself with the king's supplies and with the wine he drank, and he asked the officer over the courtiers that he might not defile himself. ⁹God gave Daniyye'l commitment and compassion before the officer over the courtiers, ¹⁰but the officer over the courtiers said to Daniyye'l, 'I'm afraid of my lord the king, who assigned your food and your drink. What if he sees your faces thinner than the other young men of your generation and you risk my head with the king?'

## The test

¹¹So Daniyye'l said to the guard whom the officer over the courtiers had assigned over Daniyye'l, Hananyah, Misha'el and Azaryah, ¹²'Please test your servants for ten days.

They could give us some legumes to eat and water to drink, ¹³and our appearance and the appearance of the young men who eat the king's supplies will be visible before you. Deal with your servants in accordance with what you see.' ¹⁴He listened to them regarding this thing, and tested them for ten days. ¹⁵At the end of ten days their appearance looked better and they were heftier in body than all the young men who were eating the king's supplies. ¹⁶So the guard would carry away their supplies and the wine they were to drink, and give them legumes.

¹⁷These young men, the four of them: God gave them knowledge and insight in all writing and smartness, while Daniyye'l had discernment in all vision and dreams. ¹⁸At the end of the time that the king had said to bring them, the head of the courtiers brought them before Nebukadne'tstsar. ¹⁹The king spoke with them, and from all of them there was not found anyone like Daniyye'l, Hananyah, Misha'el and Azaryah. So they stood in attendance before the king. ²⁰Every matter of discerning smartness that he asked of them, the king found them ten times superior to all the diviners and chanters that were in his entire kingdom.

²¹Daniyye'l was there until the first year of Koresh [Cyrus] the king.

## Except the gods, whose home is not with humanity

**2** In the second year of Nebukadne'tstsar's reign, Nebukadne'tstsar had dreams. His spirit was agitated, but his sleep came over him. ²The king said to call the diviners, chanters, charmers and Kasdites to tell the king his dreams, and they came and stood in attendance before the king. ³The king said to them, 'I had a dream, and my spirit is agitated to know the dream.' ⁴The Kasdites spoke to the king (in Aramaic): 'Long live the king! Relate the dream to your servants and we'll explain its meaning.' ⁵The king answered the Kasdites: 'A firm decision has issued from me: if you don't make known to me the dream and its meaning, you'll be torn limb from limb and your houses turned into rubble. ⁶But if you explain the dream and its meaning, you'll receive a reward and gift and great honour from me. Now: explain to me the dream and its meaning.'

⁷They answered a second time, 'May Your Majesty relate the dream to his servants, and we'll explain its meaning.' ⁸The king answered, 'I know for sure that you're buying time, because you see that a firm decision has issued from me ⁹that if you don't make the dream known to me, there's a specific decree for you. You've arranged with each other to tell me something false and base, until the situation changes. Now: relate the dream to me, and I'll know that you can explain its meaning.' ¹⁰The Kasdites answered the king, 'There's no one on earth who can explain the thing for the king. Thus no great king or ruler has asked a thing like this of any diviner or chanter or Kasdite. ¹¹The thing that the king is asking is so daunting that there's no one else who can explain it to the king except the gods, whose home is not with humanity.' ¹²At this, the king became furious, very angry, and he said to put to death all Babel's experts.

## The God who changes times and eras

¹³So the decree went out and the experts were to be killed, and they looked for Daniyye'l and his companions, to kill them. ¹⁴Daniyye'l responded with shrewdness and judgement to Aryok, the king's chief of police, who had gone out to kill the experts in Babel. ¹⁵He answered Aryok, 'Royal marshal, why is there the severe decree from the king?' Aryok made the thing known to Daniyye'l, ¹⁶and Daniyye'l went and asked the king that he might give him a time, and he would explain the meaning to the king.

¹⁷Then Daniyye'l went to his house and made the thing known to his companions, Hananyah, Misha'el and Azaryah, ¹⁸for them to ask for compassion from the God of the heavens about this mystery, so that Daniyye'l and his companions might not be put to death, with the rest of the experts in Babel. ¹⁹Then the mystery was revealed to Daniyye'l in a vision by night. So Daniyye'l blessed the God of the heavens. ²⁰Daniyye'l avowed:

The name of God be blessed from age to age,
    because smartness and strength are his.

²¹He changes times and eras,
    removes kings and establishes kings.
He gives smartness to the smart,
    knowledge to the people who know
        discernment.
²²He reveals things that are deep and hidden;
    he knows what's in the dark, and light dwells
        with him.
²³God of my ancestors, I confess and praise you,
    because you've given me smartness and
        strength.
You've now made known to me what we asked of
        you;
    you've made known to us the thing that the
        king asked.

²⁴Thus Daniyye'l went to Aryok, whom the king had appointed to kill Babel's experts. He came and said this to him: 'Don't kill the experts in Babel. Take me to the king and I'll explain the meaning to the king.'

## The dream statue

²⁵With haste Aryok took Daniyye'l before the king and said this to him: 'I've found a man from the Yehudahite exiles who can make known the meaning to the king.' ²⁶The king answered Daniyye'l (whose name was Beltesha'tstsar), 'Can you make known to me the dream that I saw, and its meaning?' ²⁷Daniyye'l answered before the king, 'The mystery about which the king asked – experts, chanters, diviners and exorcists can't explain it to the king. ²⁸But there is a God in the heavens revealing mysteries, and he has made known to King Nebukadne'tstsar what will happen at the end of the time.

Your dream, the visions in your head in bed, was this. ²⁹Your Majesty, in bed your thoughts came concerning what will happen after this, and the one who reveals mysteries made known to you what will happen. ³⁰And I – not because of smartness that there is in me above any other human being has this mystery been revealed to me, but in order that the meaning should be made known to the king, and you may know the thoughts in your mind.

³¹Your Majesty, you were looking, and there – a large statue. This statue was big and its brightness extraordinary, standing in front

of you, an awe-inspiring sight. ³²That statue: its head was of fine gold, its chest and its arms of silver, its stomach and its sides of copper, ³³its legs of iron, its feet partly of iron and partly of pottery. ³⁴You watched as a stone broke off, not by hands, and hit the statue on its feet of iron and pottery, and shattered them. ³⁵All at once the iron, the pottery, the copper, the silver and the gold shattered. They became like chaff from a summer threshing-floor. The wind carried them. No place was found for them. But the stone that hit the statue became a big crag and filled the entire earth.

³⁶That was the dream. We will relate its meaning before the king.

## After Nebukadne'tstsar, what?

³⁷You, Your Majesty, king of kings, to whom the God of the heavens gave kingship, sovereignty, power and honour, ³⁸and gave into your hand, wherever they live, human beings, animals of the wild and birds of the heavens, and made you rule over all of them – you're the head of gold. ³⁹In your place another kingship will arise, inferior to you, and another, third kingship, of copper, which will rule over the entire earth. ⁴⁰The fourth kingship will be strong as iron, because iron shatters and smashes anything. Like iron that crushes, it will shatter and crush all these. ⁴¹In that you saw the feet and toes partly of clay pottery and partly of iron, it will be a split kingship, but some of the toughness of iron will be in it. Insofar as you saw iron mixed with earthen pottery, ⁴²and the toes of the feet were partly iron and partly clay, to some extent the kingship will be strong but in part it will be fragile. ⁴³In that you saw the iron mixed with earthen pottery, human beings will unite, but they won't stick with each other, as iron doesn't stick with pottery.

⁴⁴In the time of those kings, the God of the heavens will set up a kingship that won't be destroyed through the ages; the kingship won't pass to another people. It will shatter and terminate all these kingships, and it will stand through the ages, ⁴⁵insofar as you saw that a stone broke off from the crag, not by hands, and shattered the iron, the copper, the pottery, the silver and the gold.

The great God has made known to the king what will happen after this. The dream is true. Its meaning is reliable.'

⁴⁶King Nebukadne'tstsar fell on his face and bowed down before Daniyye'l. He said to present an offering and fragrant oblations to him. ⁴⁷The king answered Daniyye'l, 'Indeed your God is God of gods, Lord of kings, and revealer of mysteries, that you can reveal this mystery.' ⁴⁸The king elevated Daniyye'l and gave him many great gifts. He would have made him ruler over the entire province of Babel and chief officer over all the experts in Babel, ⁴⁹but Daniyye'l asked the king to appoint Shadrak, Meshak and Abed Nego over the administration of the province of Babel, with Daniyye'l at the king's court.

## On facing the music

3 Nebukadne'tstsar the king made a gold statue thirty metres in height, three metres in width. He set it up in the Dura Valley in the province of Babel. ²Nebukadne'tstsar the king sent to assemble the satraps, the governors and the commissioners, the counsellors, the treasurers, the judges, the officers, and all the provincial officials, to come for the dedication of the statue that Nebukadne'tstsar the king had set up. ³They assembled, the satraps, the governors and the commissioners, the counsellors, the treasurers, the judges, the officers and all the provincial officials, for the dedication of the statue that Nebukadne'tstsar the king had set up, and they stood in front of the statue that Nebukadne'tstsar had set up.

⁴The herald called out forcefully, 'To you it is being declared, peoples, nations and languages, ⁵at the time when you hear the sound of the horn, pipe, cithara, trigon, psaltery, ensemble and all types of music, you're to fall and bow down to the gold statue that Nebukadne'tstsar the king has set up. ⁶Anyone who doesn't fall and bow down will at that moment be thrown inside a red-hot blazing furnace.' ⁷So at that time when all the peoples heard the sound of the horn, pipe, cithara, trigon, psaltery and all types of music, all the peoples, the nations and the languages would bow down to the gold statue that Nebukadne'tstsar the king had set up.

[8]So at that time some Kasdites came and denounced the Yehudahites. [9]They avowed to King Nebukadne'tstsar: 'Long live the king! [10]Your Majesty, you gave notice that anyone who hears the sound of the horn, pipe, cithara, trigon, psaltery, ensemble and all types of music is to fall and bow down to the gold image, [11]and anyone who doesn't fall and bow down will be thrown inside a red-hot blazing furnace. [12]There are some Yehudahites whom you appointed over the business of the province of Babel, Shadrak, Meshak and Abed Nego. These men have not taken any notice of you, Your Majesty. They haven't revered your gods or bowed down to the gold image that you've set up.'

## But even if our God doesn't rescue us . . .

[13]Nebukadne'tstsar in rage and fury said to bring Shadrak, Meshak and Abed Nego, and these men were brought before the king. [1]Nebukadne'tstsar avowed to them: 'Shadrak, Meshak and Abed Nego, do you really not revere my gods and bow down to the gold statue that I've set up? [15]If you're indeed now ready, at the time when you hear the sound of the horn, pipe, cithara, trigon, psaltery, ensemble and all types of music, to fall and bow down to the statue that I've made . . .

But if you won't bow down, at that moment you'll be thrown inside a red-hot blazing furnace. And who is the god who could rescue you from my hand?' [16]Shadrak, Meshak and Abed Nego answered, 'King Nebukadne'tstsar, we don't need to make any response to this. [17]If our God, whom we revere, exists, he's able to rescue us from the red-hot blazing furnace, and he will rescue us from your hand, Your Majesty. [18]But if he doesn't, be it known to you, Your Majesty, that we won't revere your gods or bow down to the gold statue that you've set up.'

[19]Nebukadne'tstsar filled with wrath, and the expression on his face towards Shadrak, Meshak and Abed Nego changed. He avowed that they should heat the furnace seven times higher than it was customary to heat it. [20]He said to the strongest men in his forces to tie up Shadrak, Meshak and Abed Nego, to throw them into the red-hot blazing furnace. [21]These men were tied up in their trousers, shirts, headwear and other

clothes, and thrown inside the red-hot blazing furnace. [22]So because of the king's strict word, when the furnace was heated excessively, the flame from the fire killed those men who took up Shadrak, Meshak and Abed Nego.

## Four men walking free in the furnace

[23]So these three men, Shadrak, Meshak and Abed Nego, fell inside the red-hot blazing furnace, tied up. [24]Then Nebukadne'tstsar the king was startled and stood up in haste. He avowed to his advisers, 'Wasn't it three men, bound, that we threw inside the furnace?' They answered the king, 'Certainly, Your Majesty.' [25]He avowed, 'There, I see four men, free, walking about inside the fire. There's no effect on them. The appearance of the fourth is like a divine being.' [26]Nebukadne'tstsar went near the door of the red-hot blazing furnace. He avowed, 'Shadrak, Meshak and Abed Nego, servants of God on High, come out, come here.' Shadrak, Meshak and Abed Nego came out from inside the fire. [27]The satraps, the governors and the commissioners, and the king's advisers, assembled. They looked at these men, on whose bodies the fire had not had power and the hair on whose head was not singed. Their trousers were unaffected. The smell of the fire had not come on them.

[28]Nebukadne'tstsar avowed, 'The God of Shadrak, Meshak and Abed Nego be blessed, who's sent his envoy and rescued his servants who entrusted themselves to him. They defied the king's word and gave up their body so they might not revere or bow down to any god but their God. [29]Notice is given by me that any people, nation or tongue that says something remiss about the God of Shadrak, Meshak and Abed Nego will be torn limb from limb and his house turned into rubble, because there's no other god who can rescue like this.' [30]The king promoted Shadrak, Meshak and Abed Nego in the province of Babel.

## Nebukadne'tstsar gives his testimony

4 'Nebukadne'tstsar the king to all the peoples, the nations and the languages

that live in all the earth. May your well-being abound! [2]It has seemed good to me to relate the signs and wonders that God on High has done with me. [3]His signs – how great. His wonders – how mighty. His kingship is a kingship that lasts permanently, his rule continues generation after generation.

[4]I, Nebukadne'tstsar, was at peace in my house, flourishing in my palace. [5]I had a dream and it disturbed me, and images while I was in bed, visions that came into my head, alarmed me. [6]Notice was given by me to bring all Babel's experts so they could make known the dream's meaning. [7]The diviners, the chanters, the Kasdites and the exorcists came, and I related the dream before them, but they couldn't make its meaning known to me.

[8]Finally there came before me Daniyye'l, whose name is Beltesha'tstsar in accordance with my God's name, and in whom is the spirit of the sacred gods. I related the dream before him: [9]"Beltesha'tstsar, chief of the diviners, I know that the spirit of the sacred gods is in you and that no mystery defeats you. Tell me the visions in the dream that I had, and its meaning.

[10]The visions that came into my head: I looked, and there, a tree in the middle of the earth. Its height was big. [11]The tree grew and became mighty. Its height reached the heavens. It was visible to the end of the entire earth. [12]Its foliage was lovely, its fruit abundant, and there was food for everyone in it. Beneath it the animals of the wild sheltered. In its branches the birds of the heavens dwelt. From it all humanity fed.

### The dream should be for your enemy

[13]I looked in the visions that came into my head in bed, and there, a lookout, a sacred being, coming down from the heavens. [14]He called forcefully, 'Fell the tree, cut off its branches, strip off its foliage, scatter its fruit. The animals must flee from beneath it, the birds from its branches. [15]Yet leave its rooted stump in the earth. With a ring of iron and copper, with the grass of the wild, with the dew of the heavens he is to be watered, and with the animals his share will be in the plants of the earth. [16]His mind is to be changed from that of

a human being; the mind of an animal is to be given him. Seven periods are to pass over him.

[17]The decision is by the decree of the lookouts, the intent is by the word of the sacred ones, with the object that human beings may acknowledge that the One on High rules over human kingship. He can give it to whomever he wishes and set up over it the lowest of people.'"

[18]I, King Nebukadne'tstsar, had this dream. You, Beltesha'tstsar, tell me its meaning, since all my kingdom's experts can't make its meaning known to me. But you can, because the spirit of the sacred gods is in you.'

[19]Daniyye'l, whose name was Beltesha'tstsar, was overcome at that very moment. His thoughts alarmed him. The king avowed, 'Beltesha'tstsar, the dream and its meaning shouldn't alarm you.' Daniyye'l avowed, 'My lord, the dream should be for your enemy, its meaning for your foe. [20]The tree that you saw that grew and became mighty, its height reached the heavens and it was visible to the end of the entire earth, [21]its foliage was lovely, its fruit abundant, and there was food for everyone in it, beneath it animals of the wild sheltered, in its branches the birds of the heavens dwelt: [22]you, Your Majesty, are the one who's grown and become mighty. Your stature has grown and reached the heavens, your rule to the end of the earth.

### Break with your wrongdoings by faithfulness

[23]In that Your Majesty saw a lookout, a sacred one, come down from the heavens and say, "Fell the tree, destroy it, yet leave its rooted stump in the earth; with a ring of iron and copper, with the grass of the wild, with the dew of the heavens he's to be watered, and with the animals his share will be, until seven periods pass over him": [24]this is the meaning, Your Majesty.

It is the decision of the One on High that has befallen my lord the king. [25]They're going to lead you away from human beings, and your home will be with the animals of the wild. They'll feed you plants, like oxen, and water you with dew from the heavens. Seven periods will pass over you, until you acknowledge that the One on High rules over human kingship.

He can give it to whomever he wishes. <sup>26</sup>But in that they said to leave the rooted stump of the tree: your kingship is going to arise for you from when you acknowledge that the heavens rule.

<sup>27</sup>But, Your Majesty, may my counsel be pleasing to you. Break with your wrongdoings by faithfulness, your waywardness by grace to the humble, in case there may be an extending of your being at peace.'

<sup>28</sup>It all befell King Nebukadne'tstsar. <sup>29</sup>At the end of twelve months, he was walking on the royal palace in Babel. <sup>30</sup>The king avowed, 'This is great Babel, which I myself built as a royal home by my sovereign might and for my majestic honour.'

## A warning implemented

<sup>31</sup>The thing still on the king's lips, a voice fell from the heavens: 'To you they're saying, King Nebukadne'tstsar: your kingship has passed from you. <sup>32</sup>They're going to lead you away from human beings and your home will be with the animals of the wild. They'll feed you plants, like oxen. Seven periods will pass over you, until you acknowledge that the One on High rules over human kingship and can give it to whomever he wishes.'

<sup>33</sup>At that moment the thing was fulfilled upon Nebukadne'tstsar. He was led away from human beings, he ate plants, like oxen, and his body was watered with the dew of the heavens, until his hair had grown long like eagles and his nails like birds.

<sup>34</sup>'At the end of the time, I, Nebukadne'tstsar, raised my eyes to the heavens. My sanity came back to me and I blessed the One on High, praised and honoured the One Who Lives Permanently, whose rule is a rule that lasts permanently, whose kingship continues generation after generation. <sup>35</sup>All earth's inhabitants are counted as nothing. He acts in accordance with his wishes with the force in the heavens and the inhabitants of the earth. There's no one who can restrain his hand or say to him, "What have you done?"

<sup>36</sup>At that time, my sanity came back to me, and as for the honour of my kingship, my glory and my splendour came back to me. My advisers and my important people sought

audience with me. I was established over my kingdom, and exceeding power was added to me. <sup>37</sup>Now I, Nebukadne'tstsar, praise, exalt and honour the King of the Heavens, all of whose deeds are true and his ways just, and who can put down people who walk in pride.'

## A party interrupted

**5** Belsha'tstsar the king served a big dinner for his thousand important people, and in the presence of the thousand he was drinking wine. <sup>2</sup>Belsha'tstsar said, when he tasted the wine, to bring the gold and silver vessels that Nebukadne'tstsar his father had taken from the palace in Yerushalaim so they could drink from them – the king, his important people, his queens and his consorts. <sup>3</sup>The gold and silver vessels that had been taken from the palace in God's house in Yerushalaim were brought in, and they drank from them – the king, his important people, his queens and his consorts. <sup>4</sup>They drank wine and praised gods of gold and silver, copper, iron, wood and stone.

<sup>5</sup>At that moment the fingers of a human hand appeared and wrote, over against the lamp-stand, on the plaster of the wall of the king's palace. The king saw the palm of the hand that wrote. <sup>6</sup>The king – his face changed colour. His thoughts alarmed him. His hip joints went loose and his knees knocked one against the other. <sup>7</sup>The king called forcefully to bring the chanters, Kasdites and exorcists. The king avowed to the smart people of Babel, 'Anyone who can read this writing and tell me its meaning will wear the purple, and the gold chain on his neck, and will rule as Third in the kingdom.'

<sup>8</sup>All the king's smart people came, but they couldn't read the writing or make known its meaning to the king. <sup>9</sup>King Belsha'tstsar became very alarmed, his face changed colour further and his important people were put in turmoil.

## You can keep your rewards

<sup>10</sup>The queen – because of the words of the king and his important people, she came into the banquet hall. The queen avowed, 'Long

live the king! Your thoughts shouldn't alarm you or your face change colour. ¹¹There's a man in your kingdom in whom is the spirit of the sacred gods. In your father's days, illumination, insight and smartness like the gods' smartness was found in him. King Nebukadne'tstsar your father appointed him as chief of the diviners, chanters, Kasdites and exorcists – your father as king. ¹²Since a remarkable spirit, knowledge and insight – interpreting dreams, explaining puzzles and resolving enigmas – was found in him, in Daniyye'l whom the king named Beltesha'tstsar, Daniyye'l should now be called. He'll relate the meaning.'

¹³Daniyye'l was brought before the king. The king avowed to Daniyye'l, 'You are Daniyye'l, one of the exiles from Yehudah that my father as king brought from Yehudah. ¹⁴I've heard about you, that the spirit of the gods is in you, and illumination, insight and remarkable smartness are found in you. ¹⁵The smart people (the chanters) have now been brought before me so they could read this writing and make its meaning known to me, but they couldn't relate the words' meaning. ¹⁶I myself have heard about you, that you can explain meanings and resolve enigmas. If you can now read the writing and make known its meaning to me, you will wear the purple and the gold chain on your neck, and rule as Third in the kingdom.'

¹⁷Daniyye'l answered before the king, 'Your gifts can be for you; give your gifts to someone else. Nevertheless I'll read the writing for Your Majesty and make known the meaning to him.

## Weighed and found wanting

¹⁸You, Your Majesty – God on High gave kingship, greatness, majesty and honour to Nebukadne'tstsar, your father. ¹⁹Because of the greatness given him, all peoples, nations and languages trembled and feared before him. Whomever he wished, he killed, and whomever he wished, he kept alive. Whomever he wished, he elevated, and whomever he wished, he put down. ²⁰When his mind became elevated and his spirit arrogant, so that he became presumptuous, he was taken from his royal throne, and his honour was removed from him. ²¹He was led away from human beings, and his mind was made like an animal,

his dwelling with wild donkeys. They fed him grass like oxen and his body was watered with the dew of the heavens, until he acknowledged that God on High rules over human kingship and can set up over it whomever he wishes.

²²But you, his son, Belsha'tstsar, have not humbled your mind because you knew all this, ²³but have elevated yourself above the Lord of the Heavens. They brought the vessels from his house before you, and you, your important people, your queens and your consorts have drunk wine in them, and praised gods of silver and gold, copper, iron, wood and stone, that don't see, don't hear and don't know. But the God who has your breath in his hand, with all your ways, you haven't glorified.

²⁴From before him the palm of the hand was sent, and this writing inscribed. ²⁵This is the writing that was inscribed: "Counted at a mina, a teqel and two halves". ²⁶This is the meaning of the words: "A mina": God counted out [*mena*] the days of your kingship and handed it over. ²⁷"A teqel": you've been weighed [*teqal*] on the scales and found deficient. ²⁸"A half": your kingship has been broken in half [*peras*] and given to Maday and Paras [Media and Persia].'

²⁹Belsha'tstsar gave orders and they clothed Daniyye'l with the purple and with the gold chain on his neck and called out concerning him that he would rule as Third in the kingdom.

³⁰That night Belsha'tstsar the Kasdite king was killed, ³¹and Dareyavesh [Darius] the Maday acquired the kingship, as a man of sixty-two years.

## Standing firm in faith

**6** It seemed good to Dareyavesh to appoint over his kingdom 120 satraps who would be spread through the entire kingdom, ²and over them three supervisors, of whom Daniyye'l was one, to whom these satraps would give account, and the king would not be troubled. ³This man Daniyye'l distinguished himself above the other supervisors and satraps because of the remarkable spirit in him, and the king was inclined to appoint him over the entire kingdom.

⁴The supervisors and satraps were seeking to find some fault on Daniyye'l's part in the kingdom's affairs, but they couldn't find any

fault or corruption because he was trustworthy; no negligence or corruption could be found against him. [5]Those men said, 'We shall not find any fault in this Daniyye'l unless we find it regarding his God's law.'

[6]So these supervisors and satraps mustered to see the king and said this to him: 'Long live Dareyavesh the king! [7]All the supervisors of the kingdom, the governors, the satraps, the advisers and the commissioners have taken counsel about the setting up of a royal decree and the enforcing of an injunction that anyone who makes a petition of any god or human being for thirty days, except of you, Your Majesty, will be thrown into a lion pit. [8]Your Majesty, issue the injunction now and sign the document, so that it may not be changed, as a law of Maday and Paras, which won't pass away.' [9]So King Dareyavesh signed the document and the injunction.

[10]When Daniyye'l got to know that the document had been signed, he went to his house with its windows open at its top, facing Yerushalaim, and three times a day he'd get down on his knees and pray and give thanks before his God, because he'd been doing so before this.

## The frustrated king

[11]Those men mustered and found Daniyye'l petitioning and praying for grace before his God. [12]They came near and spoke before the king about the royal injunction: 'You signed an injunction, didn't you, that anyone who petitions any god or human being for thirty days except you, Your Majesty, will be thrown into the lion pit.' The king answered, 'The thing stands firm, as a law of Maday and Paras, which won't pass away.' [13]They answered before the king, 'Daniyye'l, one of the exiles from Yehudah, has not taken notice of you, Your Majesty, or of the injunction that you signed. Three times a day he makes his petition.'

[14]When he heard the thing, he was very displeased in himself, and regarding Daniyye'l he set his mind to delivering him. Until sunset he was working on rescuing him. [15]Then those men mustered and said to the king, 'Your Majesty, acknowledge that it is a law of Maday and Paras that any injunction or decree

that the king sets up cannot be changed.' [16]Then the king said, and they brought Daniyye'l and threw him into the lion pit.

The king avowed to Daniyye'l, 'Your God whom you revere continually must deliver you.' [17]A stone was brought and put on the mouth of the pit, and the king sealed it with his signet and with the signets of his important people, so that the intention regarding Daniyye'l might not be changed. [18]The king went off to his palace. He spent the night without food; nothing was brought before him. Sleep eluded him.

## Shutting the lions' mouths

[19]In the morning, the king got up at first light and went off in haste to the lion pit. [20]As he drew near to the pit, he cried in an anguished voice to Daniyye'l. The king avowed, 'Daniyye'l, servant of the living God, your God whom you revere continually – could he deliver you from the lions?' [21]Daniyye'l spoke with the king: 'Long live the king! [22]God sent his envoy and shut the lions' mouth. They haven't injured me, because before him innocence was found in me – and also before you, Your Majesty, I've done no injury.'

[23]The king was very glad about him, and said to get Daniyye'l up out of the pit. So Daniyye'l was got up out of the pit. No injury was found in him, because he had trusted in his God. [24]The king said, and they brought those men who had attacked Daniyye'l and threw them into the lion pit, them, their children and their wives. They hadn't reached the ground in the pit before the lions overpowered them and crushed all their bones.

[25]Then Dareyavesh the king wrote to all peoples, nations and languages that live in the entire earth: 'May your well-being abound! [26]From me notice is given that in every domain of my kingdom, people must tremble and fear before Daniyye'l's God, because he is the living God and he stands permanently. His kingship is one that will experience no injury, his rule will continue to the end. [27]He delivers and rescues and does signs and wonders in the heavens and in the earth. He rescued Daniyye'l from the hand of the lions.'

²⁸So this Daniyye'l flourished during the reign of Dareyavesh and during the reign of Koresh the Parsite [Cyrus the Persian].

## The four weird animals

**7** In the first year of Belsha'tstsar king of Babel, Daniyye'l had a dream, visions that came into his head in bed. He wrote the dream down.

The beginning of the account: ²Daniyye'l avowed, 'I looked in my vision during the night, and there, the four winds of the heavens stirring up the Great Sea, ³and four huge animals coming up out of the sea, each different from the others.

⁴The first was like a lion but it had an eagle's wings. I looked as its wings were plucked off and it was lifted up from the ground and set on its feet like a human being, and a human mind was given to it.

⁵And there – another, second animal. It was like a bear, but it was lifted up on one side, with three ribs in its mouth, between its teeth. They said this to it: "Get up, eat lots of meat."

⁶After that, I looked, and there – another, like a leopard, but it had four bird's wings on its back. The animal had four heads, and authority was given it.

⁷After that, I looked in the night visions and there – a fourth animal, fearsome, terrifying and extremely powerful. It had huge iron teeth, devouring, crushing and trampling what was left with its feet. It was different from all the animals that were before it. It had ten horns. ⁸I looked at the horns, and there – another small horn came up among them, and three of the first horns were uprooted before it. And there – something like human eyes in this horn, and a mouth speaking great things.

## A throne scene

⁹I looked as

Thrones were set in place,
    and someone advanced in years sat down.

His clothing was like white snow,
    the hair of his head like lamb's wool.
His throne was flashes of flame,
    its rings a blazing flame.
¹⁰A river of flame was flowing,
    coming out from before him.
A thousand thousands ministered to him,
    a myriad myriads stood in attendance before him.
The court sat,
    and books were opened.

¹¹I looked because of the sound of the great things that the horn was speaking. I looked as the animal was killed. Its body was destroyed and given to the burning fire. ¹²The rest of the animals: their authority was taken away, but an extension of their lives was given to them for a set time.

¹³I looked in my night visions, and there,

With the clouds in the heavens
    someone like a human being came.
He reached the one advanced in years
    and they presented him before him.
¹⁴To him was given authority, honour and kingship;
    all peoples, nations and languages were to revere him.
His authority is an authority that lasts permanently,
    that won't pass away,
    his kingship one that won't be destroyed.

¹⁵I (Daniyye'l) was disturbed in my spirit within me at this. The visions that came into my head alarmed me. ¹⁶I came near one of those standing in attendance and asked him the truth about all this. He told me and made known the meaning of the thing: ¹⁷"These huge animals, of which there were four: four kings will arise from the earth, ¹⁸but the sacred ones on high will acquire the kingship. They will take hold of the kingship permanently, lastingly and permanently."

## One who talks big is silenced

¹⁹I wanted to understand about the fourth animal which was different from all of them (extremely fearsome, its iron teeth, its copper

claws), devouring, crushing and trampling what was left with its feet, <sup>20</sup>and about the ten horns that were on its head, and the one that came up and three fell before it – and that horn had eyes and a mouth speaking great things, and its appearance was bigger than its companions. <sup>21</sup>I looked, and that horn made war with the sacred ones and prevailed over them, <sup>22</sup>until the one advanced in years came and judgement was given for the sacred ones on high, and the time arrived and the sacred ones took hold of the kingship.

<sup>23</sup>He said this:

"The fourth animal – there will be a fourth kingship in the earth that will be different from all the kingships. It will devour the entire earth, tread it down and crush it. <sup>24</sup>The ten horns – from that kingship ten kings will arise.

After them another will arise. He will be different from those before him. He will bring low three kings. <sup>25</sup>He will say things against the One on High and oppress the sacred ones on high. He will try to change times and a law. They will be given into his hand for a period, periods and half a period. <sup>26</sup>But the court will sit and take away his authority, to annihilate it and obliterate it permanently. <sup>27</sup>The kingship, the authority and the greatness of the kingships under the entire heavens will be given to the people of the sacred ones on high. Its kingship will be a kingship lasting permanently. All authorities will revere and bow down to it."

<sup>28</sup>That's the end of the account.

I Daniyye'l – my thoughts were very alarming to me. My face changed colour. I kept the thing in my mind.'

## A ram, a goat and the terminating of offerings

**8** In the third year of the reign of Belsha'tstsar the king, a vision appeared to me (me, Daniyye'l), after the one that appeared to me earlier. <sup>2</sup>I looked in the vision (when I saw it, I was in Shushan, the fortress town in Elam Province) – I looked in the vision and I was at the Ulay Gate. <sup>3</sup>I raised my eyes and looked, and there – a ram standing

before the gate. It had two horns. The horns were high, but the one was higher than the other. The high one came up later. <sup>4</sup>I looked at the ram charging west and north and south. No animals could stand before it. There was no one could rescue from its hand. It acted according to its wishes and got big.

<sup>5</sup>As I was considering it, there, a male goat coming from the west across the face of the entire earth, without touching the ground. The goat, a conspicuous horn between its eyes, <sup>6</sup>came to the ram that possessed the two horns, which I had seen standing before the gate, and ran at it in energetic wrath. <sup>7</sup>I looked at it reaching the ram. It raged at it, struck the ram down and broke its two horns. The ram didn't have the energy to stand before it. It threw it to the earth and trampled it. There was no one could rescue the ram from its hand.

<sup>8</sup>The male goat grew very big, but just when it had become so substantial, the big horn broke. Four conspicuous ones came up in its place, towards the four winds in the heavens. <sup>9</sup>From one of them came up a small horn. It grew abundantly towards the south and towards the east and towards the splendour. <sup>10</sup>It grew as far as the army of the heavens, and made some of the army, some of the stars, fall to earth, and it trampled them. <sup>11</sup>It grew as far as the officer over the army. By it the regular offering was removed and his sacred place and an army were overthrown. <sup>12</sup>It will be set over the regular offering in rebellion; it will throw truthfulness to the ground. It will act and succeed.

## The Greek king who goes too far

<sup>13</sup>I heard a sacred one speaking, and another sacred being said to the one who was speaking, 'How long will the vision be – the regular offering and the desolating rebellion, the giving of both the sacred place and the army to trampling?' <sup>14</sup>He said to me, 'For 2,300 evenings and mornings. But the sacred place will emerge in the right.'

<sup>15</sup>While I (Daniyye'l) was looking at the vision and seeking understanding, there – standing in front of me was a human-like person, <sup>16</sup>and I heard a human voice within Ulay. It called, 'Gabri'el, help this man

understand the vision.' [17]He came near where I was standing. When he came, I was overwhelmed and I fell on my face. He said to me, 'Understand, young man, that the vision relates to the time of the end.' [18]When he spoke with me, I fell into a trance, on the face of the ground, but he touched me and stood me up where I had been standing. [19]He said, 'Here am I, I'm going to make known to you what will happen at the conclusion of the condemnation, because it's for the time set for the end.

[20]The ram that you saw, having two horns, is the kings of Maday and Paras.

[21]The buck (the he-goat) is the king of Yavan [Greece].

The big horn between its eyes – that's the first king.

[22]The one that broke and four stood up in its place: four kingships will stand up from a nation, but not with its energy.

[23]At the conclusion of their kingship, when the rebels reach full measure, a king will arise fierce of face and understanding conundrums. [24]His energy will be substantial, but not by his own energy. He will perform extraordinary acts of devastation and he will succeed when he acts. He will devastate the substantial, and a people of sacred ones, [25]with his insight. He will succeed in deceit through his power, and through his mind he will get big. With ease he will devastate many, and he will stand against the officer-in-chief. But without a human hand he will break.

[26]The vision of evening and morning: what has been said is the truth. You, seal the vision, because it relates to many days.'

[27]I (Daniyye'l) fell ill for some days, but got up and performed the king's business. But I was overcome by the vision and there was no one could help me understand it.

## What happened to the seventy years of Jeremiah 29?

**9** In the first year of Dareyavesh son of Ahashverosh, of Maday birth, who was made king over the kingdom of the Kasdites – [2]in the first year of his reign, I (Daniyye'l) was considering in the Scriptures the number of years that were (Yahweh's word to Yirmeyah the prophet) to be fulfilled for Yerushalaim's wastes, seventy years.

[3]I set my face towards the Lord God, to make a plea and prayers for grace with fasting, sack and ash. [4]I pleaded with Yahweh my God and made confession: 'Oh, Lord, great and awe-inspiring God, who keeps pact and commitment to people who are loyal to him and keep his orders: [5]we did wrong, we were wayward, we were faithless, we rebelled, we turned aside from your orders and your rulings. [6]We didn't listen to your servants the prophets who spoke in your name to our kings, our officials and our ancestors, and to all the country's people.

[7]To you, Lord, belongs the right; to us, shame of face this very day, to Yehudah's people, to Yerushalaim's inhabitants and to all Yisra'el, near and far, in all the countries where you drove them because of their trespass that they committed against you. [8]Yahweh, to us belongs shame of face, to our kings, to our officials and to our ancestors, who did wrong to you. [9]To the Lord our God belong compassion and acts of pardon, because we rebelled against him [10]and didn't listen to the voice of Yahweh our God by walking according to his instructions that he set before us by means of his servants the prophets. [11a]All Yisra'el transgressed your instruction and turned aside so as not to listen to your voice.

## Lord, listen, Lord, pardon!

[11b]The vow and the oath that was written in the instruction of Mosheh [Moses], God's servant, overwhelmed us. Because we did wrong to him, [12]he confirmed his word that he spoke against us and against the people who exercised authority over us, by bringing great bad fortune upon us that hasn't been done under the entire heavens as it has been done in Yerushalaim.

[13]As it is written in Mosheh's instruction, all this bad fortune came upon us, but we didn't seek the goodwill of Yahweh our God by turning away from our waywardness and gaining insight through your truthfulness, [14]so Yahweh watched over this bad fortune and brought it on us, because Yahweh our God was in the right in all his actions that he undertook, and we didn't listen to his voice.

[15]But now, Lord our God, who got your people out of the country of Misrayim [Egypt] with a strong hand and made yourself a name this very day, we did wrong, we were faithless. [16]Lord, in accordance with all your faithfulness, please may your anger and your wrath turn back from your town, Yerushalaim, your sacred mountain, because through our wrongdoings and our ancestors' wayward acts, Yerushalaim and your people became an object of reviling to all the people round us.

[17]So now, listen, our God, to your servant's plea and to his prayers for grace, and shine your face on your desolate sanctuary, for the Lord's sake. [18]Bend your ear, my God, and listen, open your eyes and look at our desolations and at the town over which your name is called, because it's not on the basis of our faithful acts that we're letting our prayers for grace fall before you, but on the basis of your abundant compassion. [19]Lord, listen, Lord, pardon, Lord, heed and act, and don't delay, for your sake, my God, because your name is called over your town and over your people.'

### Seventy sevens until that king who goes too far

[20]I was still speaking, pleading, confessing my wrongdoing and the wrongdoing of my people Yisra'el, and letting my prayers for grace fall before Yahweh my God for my God's sacred mountain – [21]I was still speaking in my plea when Gabri'el, the person whom I saw in the vision I had before, tired and weary, reached me at the time of the evening offering [22]and enabled me to understand. He spoke with me: 'Daniyye'l, I have now come out to give you insight in understanding. [23]At the beginning of your prayers for grace a word went out, and I myself have come to relate it, because you're held in high regard. So understand the word and gain understanding into the vision. [24]Seventy sevens have been assigned for your people and for your sacred town to bring the rebellion to an end, to do away with wrongdoings, to wipe away waywardness, to bring permanent faithfulness, to seal vision and prophet, and to anoint a most sacred place.

[25]You're to acknowledge and perceive:
from the issuing of a word for restoring and
    building up Yerushalaim to an anointed, a
    leader, there are seven sevens;
for sixty-two sevens it will again be built up,
    square and moat;
but in the pressure of the times, [26]after the
    sixty-two sevens, an anointed will be cut
    off, and will have neither the town nor
    the sacred place; a leader to come will
    devastate a people and its end will come
    by a flood, but until the end of battle,
    devastations are determined;
[27]a pact will prevail for many people for one
    seven, for half the seven he will suspend
    sacrifice and offering, and upon a wing
    will be a great abomination, desolating,
    until a conclusion and something decreed
    overwhelms the desolator.'

### The last great vision

**10** In the third year of Koresh king of Paras, a word revealed itself to Daniyye'l who was called Beltesha'tstsar. The word was true: a great war. He understood the word; he had understanding through the vision.

[2]In those days I (Daniyye'l) was mourning for a period of three weeks. [3]I ate no food held in high regard; meat and wine didn't come into my mouth. I didn't put on make-up at all until the completion of the period of three weeks.

[4]On the twenty-fourth day of the first month I was on the bank of the big river (i.e. Hiddeqel [the Tigris]). [5]I raised my eyes and looked, and there, a man clothed in linen, his hips belted with pure gold, [6]his body like topaz, his face like the brightness of lightning, his eyes like fiery torches, his arms and his feet like the gleam of polished copper, and the sound of his words like the sound of thunder. [7]I (Daniyye'l) alone saw this vision. The people who were with me didn't see the vision, yet a great terror fell on them and they fled into hiding. [8]So I remained alone. I looked at this great vision. No energy remained in me. My vigour turned to devastation in me. I didn't retain any energy.

[9]I heard the sound of his words, but when I heard the sound of his words, I went into a trance on to my face, with my face to the

ground. ¹⁰But there, a hand touched me and shook me on to my knees and the palms of my hands. ¹¹He said to me, 'Daniyye'l, man held in high regard, understand the words that I'm going to speak to you. Stand up in your place, because I've now been sent to you.' When he spoke this word with me, I stood up, trembling.

## A battle in the heavens

¹²He said to me, 'Don't be afraid, Daniyye'l, because from the first day that you set your mind to understand and humble yourself before your God, your words were heard. I've come because of your words. ¹³The officer over the kingdom of Paras was standing over against me for twenty-one days, but there, Mika'el, one of the senior officers, came to help me. So I had remained there with the kings of Paras, ¹⁴but I've come to enable you to understand what will happen to your people at the end of the time, because there's yet a vision for that time.'

¹⁵While he spoke with me in accordance with these words, I put my face to the ground and kept silence. ¹⁶But there, someone with the likeness of human beings touched my lips, and I opened my mouth and spoke to the one standing over against me: 'My lord, because of the vision my convulsions have overthrown me. No energy has remained in me. ¹⁷How can this servant of my lord speak with this my lord when I – no energy now stays in me, no breath remains in me.'

¹⁸The one with a human appearance touched me again and strengthened me. ¹⁹He said, 'Don't be afraid, man held in high regard, things will be well for you. Be strong, be strong.' When he had spoken with me I asserted my strength and said, 'My lord may speak, because you've strengthened me.'

²⁰He said, 'You know why I've come to you, don't you. Now I shall go back to do battle with the officer over Paras. When I go off, there, the officer over Yavan is going to come. ²¹Nevertheless, I shall tell you what is inscribed in the truthful document. No one is asserting his strength with me against these except Mika'el, your [people's] officer.

**11** But I – in the first year of Dareyavesh the Maday, my place was to strengthen and fortify him.

## On earth as it is in the heavens

²Now I shall tell you some truth. There, three kings more are going to stand for Paras, and a fourth will possess great wealth, more than anyone. In accordance with the strength he gets through his wealth, he will stir up everyone against the kingdom of Yavan. ³A strong man king will arise, rule a great dominion and act in accordance with his will. ⁴But as soon as he arises, his kingdom will break and scatter to the four winds of the heavens, and not to his posterity nor in accordance with the dominion that he ruled, because his kingdom will uproot and belong to other people apart from these.

⁵The southern king will be strong, but one of his officers will be stronger than him, and he will rule a greater dominion than his dominion. ⁶At the end of some years people will make an alliance, and the southern king's daughter will come to the northern king to effect an agreement. But she won't retain the energy of her strength, nor will his strength stand. She will be given up, she and her escorts and the one who fathered her and the one who gave her strength.

In time ⁷one of the shoots from her roots will stand in his place. He will come against the force and come into the stronghold of the northern king. He will act against them and be strong. ⁸Also their gods with their images, with their articles held in high regard, gold and silver, he will take captive to Misrayim. For some years he will stand back from the northern king. ⁹He will come against the kingdom of the southern king but will go back to his own country. ¹⁰His sons will wage war and gather a horde of many forces. It will come repeatedly, and sweep and pass through, and again wage war as far as his stronghold.

## The meaningless to and fro

¹¹The southern king will rage and go out and do battle with him (with the northern king). He will raise a large horde, but the horde will be given into his hand. ¹²The horde will be carried off, but his mind will become superior. He will make myriads fall, but he won't prevail. ¹³The northern king will again raise a horde, greater than the first. At the end of a period of

years he will come repeatedly with a great force and with much equipment.

<sup>14</sup>In those times many will stand against the southern king. Wild men among your people will raise themselves, to confirm a vision, but they will collapse. <sup>15</sup>The northern king will come, heap up a ramp and capture a fortified town. The southern forces won't stand, even his company of picked soldiers. There will be no energy to stand. <sup>16</sup>The one who comes against him will act as he pleases, and there will be no one standing before him. He will stand in the splendid country, destruction in his hand. <sup>17</sup>He will set his face to come into control of his entire kingdom, but will make an agreement with him and give him a wife, in order to devastate it. But it won't stand, it won't come about for him. <sup>18</sup>He will set his face towards foreign shores and capture many, but a commander will stop his reviling for him so that he won't be able to turn back his reviling for him. <sup>19</sup>He will turn his face back to the strongholds in his own country. But he will collapse and fall and not be found.

<sup>20</sup>There will stand in his place one who sends round an oppressor of royal splendour. But in a few days he will break, not by anger or battle.

## People who break faith with the covenant

<sup>21</sup>There will stand in his place someone despised, to whom they've not given royal honour. He will come with ease and gain power over the kingdom by empty words. <sup>22</sup>Overwhelming forces will be overwhelmed before him and will break; so too a ruler of the pact. <sup>23</sup>Through the making of alliances with him, he will exercise deceit. He will arise and become substantial with a small group, <sup>24</sup>with ease. He will come against the richest of provinces and do what his father and forefathers didn't do. Plunder, spoil and wealth he will scatter among people. He will devise plans against fortresses, until a certain time. <sup>25</sup>He will assert his strength and his mind against the southern king with a large force. The southern king will do battle with a large and very substantial force, but he won't stand, because people will devise plans against him. <sup>26</sup>People who eat his provisions will break him. His force will be overwhelmed. Many will

fall, run through. <sup>27</sup>The two of them, the kings, their mind set on bad dealing, will speak lies at one table, but it won't succeed, because an end will yet wait for the set time.

<sup>28</sup>He will go back to his country with great wealth and with his mind against a sacred pact. So he will act and go back to his country. <sup>29</sup>At the set time he will come against the south again, but it won't be like the first and the second time. <sup>30</sup>Ships from Kittim will come against him, and he will cower and turn back. He will be condemning a sacred pact and he will act. He will go back and heed the people who abandon a sacred pact. <sup>31</sup>Forces of his will stand and treat the sanctuary, the fortress, as ordinary. They will remove the regular offering and set up the desolating abomination. <sup>32</sup>People who act faithlessly towards a pact he will make into apostates by empty words, but a people that acknowledge their God will be strong and will act. <sup>33</sup>The insightful among the people will help the multitude to understand, but they will fall by sword, by fire, by captivity and by becoming prey, for a time.

## The end approaches

<sup>34</sup>When they fall, they will receive a little help, but many will join them with empty words. <sup>35</sup>Some of the insightful people will fall, to refine them, to purify and to cleanse, until the time of the end, because it will yet wait for the set time.

<sup>36</sup>So the king will do as he pleases. He will exalt himself and magnify himself above every god, and against the God of gods he will speak extraordinary things. He will succeed until condemnation is complete, because what has been decreed has been done. <sup>37</sup>To his ancestors' gods he won't heed, nor to the one women hold in high regard. He won't heed any god, because over everything he will magnify himself. <sup>38</sup>A stronghold god he will honour in his place. A god whom his ancestors didn't acknowledge he will honour with gold and with silver, with precious stones and with things held in high regard. <sup>39</sup>He will attend to the securest of fortresses with the help of an alien god. To those whom he recognizes he will give great honour. He will let them rule over the multitude and divide up land as payment.

40At the time of the end the southern king will wrestle with him, but the northern king will storm against him with chariotry, with cavalry and with many ships. He will come against countries, sweep and pass through, 41and come against the splendid country. Many will fall, but these will escape from his hand: Edom, Mo'ab and the chief part of the Ammonites. 42He will put out his hand on other countries, and the country of Misrayim will not find escape. 43He will rule the treasuries of gold and silver and all the things held in high regard in Misrayim, with the Putites and Kushites [Sudanese] at his heel. 44But reports will alarm him from the east and from the north and he will go out in great wrath to destroy and annihilate many. 45He will pitch his royal tents between the seas and the splendid sacred mountain. But he will come to his end. There will be no helper for him.

## The people who will shine like stars

**12** At that time Mika'el will stand, the high officer who stands by the members of your people. There will be a time of pressure such as hasn't happened since it became a nation until that time. But at that time your people will escape, everyone who is found written in the book, 2and many sleeping in the earth country will wake up, some to permanent life, some to great reviling, to permanent abhorrence. 3The insightful people will be bright, like the sky's brightness, and the people who helped many to be faithful like stars, for ever and ever.

4You, Daniyye'l, close up the words, seal the book, until the time of the end. Many will run to and fro so that knowledge may increase.'

5I (Daniyye'l) looked, and there – two others standing, one on the riverbank this side, one on the riverbank the other side. 6Someone said to the man dressed in linen, who was above the water of the river, 'How long until the end of the extraordinary events?' 7I listened to the man dressed in linen who was above the water of the river. He raised his right hand and his left hand to the heavens and swore by the Ever-Living One, 'For a set time, set times and a half. When the shattering of the power of the sacred people ends, all these things will come to an end.'

8Though I listened, I didn't understand. I asked, 'My lord, what will be the final stage in these events?' 9He said, 'Go, Daniyye'l, because the words are closed up and sealed until the time of the end. 10Many will purify themselves, cleanse themselves and refine themselves, but the faithless will act faithlessly. None of the faithless will understand, but the people of insight will understand.

11From the time when the regular offering is removed and a desolating abomination put in place will be 1,290 days. 12The blessings of the one who waits and reaches 1,335 days! 13You, go to the end and settle down, so you may stand for your destiny at the end of the time.'

# HOSEA

Hosea [Hoshea] is the first of the twelve shorter prophetic books that close the First Testament. Chronologically, Hosea, Amos and Micah belong together, and they reflect a similar set of religious, social and political circumstances. They were all contemporaries of Isaiah ben Amoz. Hosea, however, worked in northern Israel, to which he often refers as Ephraim with its capital in Samaria, rather than in Judah with its capital in Jerusalem. His task was thus to seek to win Ephraim back to Yahweh in order to forestall Yahweh's taking action against it. Occasional references to Judah indicate that Judah needs to learn from Ephraim's bad example and its consequent fate.

Hosea's key image for portraying Ephraim's wrongdoing is that Ephraim is a whore in the sense of someone who is immoral and faithless to her husband, Yahweh. She expresses her whoring both in having recourse to other deities to get their help in making the land and its people fruitful, and also in having recourse to other political allies to get their help in standing up to Assyria as the threatening superpower. In the opening chapters Hosea's own marriage to someone who was unfaithful provides an acted parable of the nation's life.

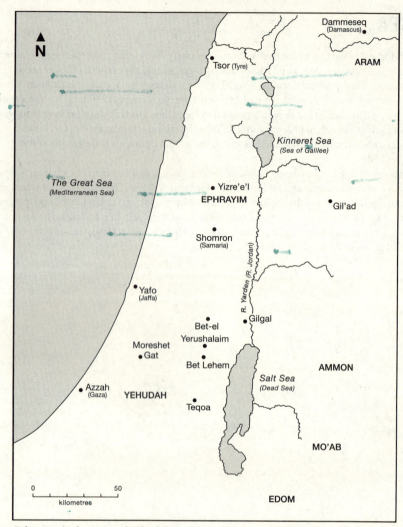

*Ephrayim (Ephraim) and Yehudah (Judah) at the time of Hoshea (Hosea)*

## The whore

**1** Yahweh's word which came to Hoshea ben Be'eri in the days of Uzziyah, Yotam, Ahaz and Yehizqiyyah, kings of Yehudah, and in the days of Yarob'am ben Yo'ash king of Yisra'el.

² As the beginning of Yahweh's word through Hoshea, Yahweh said to Hoshea, 'Go get yourself a whorish woman and whorish children, because the country is really whoring away from Yahweh.' ³ So he went and got Gomer bat Diblayim.

She got pregnant and gave birth to a son for him. ⁴ Yahweh said to him, 'Name him

"Yizre'e'l", because in yet a little while I shall attend to the bloodshed in Yizre'e'l upon Yehu's household. I shall stop the kingship of Yisra'el's household. ⁵ On that day I shall break Yisra'el's bow in Yizre'e'l Vale'.

⁶ She got pregnant again and gave birth to a daughter. He said to him, 'Name her "Not-Compassioned", because I shall no more have compassion again on Yisra'el's household, that I should carry them. ⁷ (But on Yehudah's household I will have compassion, and I will deliver them through Yahweh their God – I shall not deliver them through bow, through sword and through battle, through horses and through cavalry.)

⁸She weaned Not-Compassioned, got pregnant and gave birth to a son. ⁹He said, 'Name him "Not-My-People", because you're not my people and I – I shall not be God to you.'

¹⁰But the number of the Yisra'elites will be like the sand at the sea that cannot be measured or counted. In the place where it is said to them 'You are not my people' it will be said to them, 'Children of the living God'. ¹¹The Yehudahites and the Yisra'elites will collect together and make one head for themselves. They will go up from the country, because Yizre'e'l's day will be great.

**2** Say to your brothers, 'My people', and to your sisters, 'Compassioned'.

## Like mother, like sons and daughters

²Argue with your mother, argue,
 because she isn't my woman and I'm not her
  man.
She must put away her whoring from her face,
 her adultery from between her breasts.
³Otherwise I shall strip her naked,
 and turn her into like the day she was born.
I shall make her like the wilderness,
 change her into dry land, let her die of thirst.
⁴On her children I shall have no compassion,
 because they're whorish children.
⁵Because their mother has been whorish;
 the one who conceived them has acted
  shamefully.
Because she's said,
 'I'll go after my lovers,
The ones who give me my bread and my water,
 my wool and my linen, my oil and my drink.'

⁶Therefore, here am I,
 I'm going to hedge up your way with
  thorn-bushes,
And I shall build a wall for her,
 so she can't find her paths.
⁷She'll pursue her lovers but she won't catch them,
 she'll look for them but she won't find them,
And she'll say,
 'I'll go and return to my first man,
 because it was better for me then than now.'
⁸She – she hasn't acknowledged
 that I myself am the one who gave her
 the grain, the new wine and the fresh oil.

I produced an abundance of silver for her,
 and gold, which they used for the Master.
⁹Therefore, I shall take back
 my grain in its season and
 my new wine at its set time.
I shall rescue my wool and my linen
 for covering her nakedness.
¹⁰Now I shall uncover her villainy
 before her lovers' eyes.
No one will rescue her from my hand,
 ¹¹and I shall make all her celebrating stop,
Her festival, her new month, her sabbath,
 every set event of hers.
¹²I shall devastate her vine and her fig tree,
 of which she's said, 'It's my "gift",
 which my lovers gave me.'
I shall turn them into a forest;
 animals of the wild will consume them.
¹³I shall attend to her for the Masters' days
 when she burns incense for them.
She's decked herself with her ring and her
  jewellery,
 gone after her lovers,
 and put me out of mind (Yahweh's
  declaration).

## Trouble Vale can become Hope's Door

¹⁴Therefore, here,
 I'm going to charm her,
 and get her to go into the wilderness, and speak
  to her heart.
¹⁵I shall give her vineyards from there,
 Trouble Vale as Hope's Door.
She'll answer there as in her young days,
 as in the day she went up from the country of
  Misrayim [Egypt].
¹⁶On that day (Yahweh's declaration) she'll call,
 'My Man';
 she'll no more call me 'My Master'.
¹⁷I shall remove the Masters' names from her
  mouth;
 they'll be mentioned by their name no more.

¹⁸I shall solemnize a pact for them on that day
 with the creature of the wild,
With the bird in the heavens,
 and with what moves on the ground.
Bow and sword and battle
 I shall break from the country, and enable them
  to lie down in confidence.

¹⁹I shall marry you to me permanently,
marry you to me with faithfulness and with the
exercise of authority,
With commitment and with compassion,
²⁰marry you to me with truth.
You will acknowledge Yahweh,
²¹and on that day I shall answer (Yahweh's
declaration).
I shall answer the heavens,
and they will answer the earth.
²²The earth will answer
with grain, new wine and fresh oil,
Those will answer with Yizre'e'l,
²³and shall sow it for myself in the country.
I shall have compassion on Not-Compassioned,
and I shall say to Not-My-People 'My people'
and it will say 'My God'.

**3** Yahweh said to me further, 'Go, love a
woman who is loved by a neighbour and
who commits adultery – like Yahweh's love for
the Yisra'elites, though they're turning their
face towards other gods and loving raisin
slabs.' ²So I bought her for myself for fifte silver
pieces, a barrel of barley and half a barrel of
barley. ³I said to her, 'For a long time you're to
live for me. You will not go whoring; you will
not belong to a man. So also will I be for you.'
⁴Because for a long time the Yisra'elites are to
live with no king, no official, no sacrifice, no
pillar, no ephod or effigies. ⁵Afterwards the
Yisra'elites will turn back and have recourse to
Yahweh their God and David their king. They
will be in dread of Yahweh and of his goodness
at the end of the time.

## No acknowledgement

**4** Listen to Yahweh's word,
Yisra'elites:
Because Yahweh has an argument
with the country's inhabitants.
Because there's no truthfulness and no
commitment,
no acknowledging of God in the country.
²Vowing, deceit, murder,
robbery and adultery have spread out;
bloodshed follows on bloodshed.

³Therefore the country grieves,
everyone who lives in it languishes,

With the animal in the wild and with the bird in
the heavens –
even the fish in the sea are gathered up.

⁴Yet no one is to argue
no one is to reprove.
Your people are like people arguing with a priest,
⁵and you will collapse by day.
A prophet will also collapse with you by night,
and I shall terminate your mother.
⁶My people are terminated
for lack of acknowledgement.
Because you've rejected acknowledgement
I shall reject you from being a priest for me.
You've put out of mind your God's instruction;
I shall put out of mind your children, I too.
⁷As they became many, so they did wrong to me;
I shall exchange their honour for slighting.
⁸They feed on my people's wrongdoing;
they direct its appetite to their waywardness.
⁹So it will be: as the people, so the priest;
I shall attend to its ways for it.
I shall bring back its practices for it;
¹⁰they will eat but not be full.
They've whored but they won't spread out,
because they've abandoned Yahweh,
To keep watch ¹¹on whoring,
as wine and new wine takes away sense.
¹²My people asks things of its piece of wood;
its stick tells it.
Because a whorish spirit has led it astray;
they've whored from under their God.
¹³On the tops of the mountains they sacrifice,
on the hills they burn incense,
Under oak, poplar and terebinth,
because its shade is good.
That's why your daughters whore,
your brides commit adultery.
¹⁴I shall not attend to your daughters because they
whore,
or to your brides because they commit
adultery.
Because the men themselves consort with
whores
and sacrifice with hierodules,
and a people that doesn't understand comes to
ruin.
¹⁵(If you're whorish, Yisra'el,
Yehudah must not become liable.)
Don't come to Gilgal, don't go up to Bet Aven
['Trouble House'],
don't swear 'As Yahweh lives!'

## Malcontents have made deep slaughter

<sup>16</sup>Because like a defiant cow
  Yisraʾel has been stubborn.
Now Yahweh will pasture them
  like sheep on the range.
<sup>17</sup>Ephrayim is attached to images;
  leave him to himself.
<sup>18</sup>Their drink has gone as they've whored and
    whored;
  as they've loved and loved, slighting is its 'gift'.
<sup>19</sup>The wind has bound it up in its wings,
  so that they'll be shamed because of their
    sacrifices.

**5** Listen to this, priests;
  heed, Yisraʾelites.
Give ear, royal household,
  because authority belongs to you.
Because you've been a snare to The Watchtower,
  you've spread a net over Tabor.
<sup>2</sup>When malcontents have made deep slaughter,
  I was the correction for them all.
<sup>3</sup>I myself acknowledge Ephrayim;
  Yisraʾel has not eluded me.
Because you've now been whoring, Ephrayim;
  Yisraʾel has become defiled.
<sup>4</sup>Their practices don't allow them
  to turn back to their God.
Because there's a whorish spirit within them,
  and they don't acknowledge Yahweh.
<sup>5</sup>Yisraʾel's majesty will avow against it;
  so Yisraʾel and Ephrayim will collapse through
    their waywardness
  (Yehudah has fallen with them, too).
<sup>6</sup>They may go out with their flock and with their
    cattle,
  to seek Yahweh.
But they won't find him – he's withdrawn from
    them;
  <sup>7</sup>they've broken faith with Yahweh.
Because they've given birth to alien children,
  the new moon will now consume their shares.

<sup>8</sup>Sound a horn in Gibʾah,
  a trumpet in Ramah.
Raise a shout in Bet Aven,
  after you, Binyamin.
<sup>9</sup>Ephrayim will become a desolation
  on the day of reproof.
Against Yisraʾel's clans
  I've made known something truthful.

(<sup>10</sup>Yehudah's officials have become like people
    who move a boundary;
  on them I shall pour out my outburst like
    water.)

## What shall I do with you, Ephrayim?

<sup>11</sup>Ephrayim is oppressed, crushed by the exercise
    of authority;
  because he resolved to go after filth:
<sup>12</sup>I myself am like a moth to Ephrayim,
  like rot to Yehudah's household.
<sup>13</sup>Ephrayim saw its sickness,
  Yehudah its sore.
Ephrayim went to Ashshur,
  it sent to the king who would argue.
But that man won't be able to heal you;
  he won't cure you of a sore.
<sup>14</sup>Because I shall be like a lion to Ephrayim,
  like a cougar to Yehudah's household.
I, I myself, will tear,
  and as I go I shall carry, and there'll be no one
    to rescue.

<sup>15</sup>I shall go, I shall return to my place,
  until they make restitution,
And seek my face;
  in their pressure they'll seek me urgently:
**6** 'Come on, let's return to Yahweh,
  because he's the one who tore, but he can
    heal us,
He strikes down but he can bandage us;
  <sup>2</sup>he can bring us to life after two days.
On the third day he can raise us up,
  so we can live before him.
<sup>3</sup>When we acknowledge, pursue the
    acknowledging of Yahweh,
  like dawn his coming out is sure.
He'll come to us like rain,
  like spring rain that waters earth.'
<sup>4</sup>What shall I do with you, Ephrayim,
  what shall I do with you, Yehudah,
When your commitment is like morning cloud,
  like dew going early?

<sup>5</sup>That's why I hewed them down with my prophets,
  killed them with the words of my mouth;
  with rulings against you, light goes out.
<sup>6</sup>Because I wanted commitment not sacrifice,
  acknowledgement of God more than burnt
    offerings.

7But they – as at Adam they transgressed the pact;
  there they broke faith with me.
8Gil'ad is a township of people who bring trouble,
  trailed in blood.
9The company of priests
  is like gangs waiting for someone.
On the road to Shekem they commit murder,
  when they have committed deliberate wickedness.
10In Yisra'el's household I have seen something
    horrible:
  Ephrayim's whoring is there.
Yisra'el has become defiled 11a(Yehudah, too);
  he's appointed a harvest for you.

## A loaf not turned over

11bWhen I restore my people's fortunes,

**7** as I heal Yisra'el,
  Ephrayim's waywardness reveals itself,
    Shomron's [Samaria's] bad dealings.
Because people have practised falsehood, a thief
    enters,
  a gang has made a dash in the street.
2Their mind doesn't say,
  'I've kept in mind all their bad dealing.'
Now their practices have surrounded them;
  they've been in front of my face.
3They make a king rejoice, with their bad dealing,
  and officials, with their lies.
4All of them are committing adultery,
  like an oven burning without a baker.
He stops stirring
  from the kneading of the dough to its yeasting.
5On our king's day,
  officials got sick with the heat of wine.
He extended his hand to the arrogant 6when they
    came near,
  their mind like an oven with intrigue.
All night their baker slept,
  in the morning he's burning, like a flaming fire.
7All of them burn as hot as an oven,
  they consume their authorities.
All their kings have fallen;
  there's no one among them calling to me.

8Ephrayim among the peoples, he wastes away.
  Ephrayim has become a loaf not turned over.
9Strangers have consumed his energy,
  and he has not acknowledged it.
Yes, grey hair has spread over him,
  and he has not acknowledged it.

10Yisra'el's majesty avows against it,
  but they haven't turned back to Yahweh their
    God.
  they haven't sought him despite all this.

11Ephrayim has become like a simple pigeon,
  without sense.
They've called on Misrayim,
  they've gone to Ashshur.
12When they go,
  I shall spread my net over them.
Like a bird in the heavens, I shall bring them down;
  I shall correct them in accordance with the
    report of their assembly.
13Oh, these people, because they've strayed from
    me;
  destruction for them, because they've rebelled
    against me.
Whereas I'm the one who could redeem them,
  but they themselves have spoken lies about me.
14They haven't cried out to me in their heart,
  when they wail on their beds.
Over grain and new wine they quarrel;
  they turn against me.
15I myself corrected them, strengthened their arms,
  but they think up bad things against me.
16They turn back, not to the One on High;
  they've become like a false bow.
Their officials will fall by the sword
  because of the condemnation of their tongue
  (i.e. their jabbering in the country of
    Misrayim).

## They have made kings, but not through me

**8** Horn to your mouth,
  like an eagle over Yahweh's house!
Since they've transgressed my pact,
  rebelled against my instruction.
2To me they cry out,
  'My God, as Yisra'el we've acknowledged you.'
3Yisra'el has rejected what's good;
  an enemy pursues them.
4They've made kings, but not through me;
  they've made officials, but I haven't
    acknowledged them.
With their silver and gold they've made images
    for themselves,
  in order that [Yisra'el] may be cut off.
5He's rejected your bullock, Shomron;
  my anger burns against them.

How long will they be incapable of being free of
    guilt? –
    <sup>6</sup>because it was from Yisra'el.
That thing – a metal worker made it;
    it's not a god.
Because Shomron's bullock
    will be broken bits.

<sup>7</sup>Because they sow wind,
    they'll reap a hurricane.
A stalk that has no growth
    doesn't produce flour.
If perhaps it produces,
    strangers will swallow it;
<sup>8</sup>Yisra'el has been swallowed up
    and they have now become among the nations,
Like an object that no one wants,
    <sup>9</sup>because they've gone up to Ashshur.
A wild donkey on its own,
    Ephrayim has hired lovers.
<sup>10</sup>Even when they hire among the nations,
    now I shall collect them.
They've writhed for a while
    because of the burden (king, officers).
<sup>11</sup>Because Ephrayim has built many altars for
    wrongdoing;
    for it, they've become altars for wrongdoing.
<sup>12</sup>Though I write for it many things in my
    instruction,
    they've been thought of as alien.
<sup>13</sup>Though they offer sacrifices to me as gifts,
    and eat flesh,
Yahweh doesn't accept them;
    now he'll be mindful of their waywardness.
He'll attend to their wrongdoings;
    those people – they'll go back to Misrayim.
<sup>14</sup>Yisra'el has put out of mind its maker
    and built palaces,
    (and Yehudah has built many fortified towns).
I shall send off fire to its towns
    and it will consume its citadels.

## I found Yisra'el as like grapes in
the wilderness

**9** Don't rejoice, Yisra'el, with joy like the
    peoples,
    because you've gone whoring away from your
    God.
You have loved the 'gift'
    on every grain threshing-floor.

<sup>2</sup>Threshing-floor and winepress won't pasture
    them,
    new wine will deceive her.
<sup>3</sup>They won't live in Yahweh's country;
    Ephrayim will go back to Misrayim,
    in Ashshur they'll eat defiled food.
<sup>4</sup>They won't pour wine for Yahweh;
    their sacrifices won't please him.
Like mourners' bread to them,
    all who eat it will be defiled.
Because their bread will be for their own appetite;
    it will not come into Yahweh's house.
<sup>5</sup>What will you do for the set day,
    for the day of Yahweh's festival?
<sup>6</sup>Because there – when they have gone from
    destruction,
    Misrayim will collect them, Memphis will bury
    them.
Whereas high regard will attach to their silver,
    briar will dispossess them, bramble will be in
    their tents.
<sup>7</sup>The days of giving attention have come,
    the days of making good have come,
Yisra'el must acknowledge it, though the prophet
    is stupid,
    the person of the spirit is crazy,
On account of the abundance of your waywardness,
    your abundant animosity.
<sup>8</sup>A prophet, with my God,
    is a lookout over Ephrayim.
There's a hunter's snare over all his ways,
    animosity in its God's house.
<sup>9</sup>They've gone deep in devastation, as in the days
    at Gib'ah;
    he'll be mindful of their waywardness, he'll
    attend to their wrongdoings.

<sup>10</sup>I found Yisra'el
    as like grapes in the wilderness.
I saw your fathers
    as like the first fruit on a fig tree in its beginning.
When those people came to the Master of Pe'or,
    they dedicated themselves to Shame,
    and became abominations like the thing they
    loved.

## The King: what would he do for us?

<sup>11</sup>Ephrayim – their splendour will fly off like a bird,
    away from birth, from the womb, from
    conception.

¹²Even if they rear their children,
  I shall bereave them of people.
Because – oh they, indeed,
  when I turn away from them.
¹³Ephrayim – as I've seen with Tsor [Tyre],
  planted in a meadow,
    so Ephrayim is to take out its children to the
      killer.

¹⁴Give them: Yahweh, what are you to give? –
  give them a miscarrying womb, dry breasts.
¹⁵All their bad dealing was at Gilgal,
  because there I was hostile to them.
Because of the bad nature of their practices,
  I shall drive them from my house.
I shall not add to my love for them;
  all their officials are defiant.

¹⁶Ephrayim is struck down, their root withers,
  they won't produce fruit.
Even when they have children,
  I shall put to death the desired offspring of
    their womb.
¹⁷My God will reject them
  because they haven't listened to him;
    they'll become wanderers among the nations.

# 10

Yisra'el is a wasting vine;
  its fruit resembles it.
In accordance with the quantity of its fruit, it
    multiplied its altars;
  in accordance with the goodness of its country,
    they made good pillars.
²Because their mind was deceitful,
  now they are to make restitution;
He himself will break down their altars,
  destroy their pillars.
³Because they now say,
  'We have no king;
Because we do not live in awe of Yahweh,
  the King: what would he do for us?'
⁴They've spoken things with empty oaths
  in solemnizing a pact.
The exercise of authority has flourished like
    poisonous growth
  in the furrows of the field.

*Sow for yourselves for faithfulness*

⁵The population of Shomron fear
  for the bullock of Bet Aven,

Because its people and its priestlings are
    mourning over it
  whereas they celebrate over its splendour.
Because it's going into exile from it;
  ⁶it, too, will be brought to Ashshur,
    a gift to the king so he will argue.
Ephrayim will receive shame,
  Yisra'el will be shamed by its counsel.
⁷Shomron – its king is being terminated,
  like a twig on the face of water.
⁸The shrines of Aven will be annihilated,
  Yisra'el's wrongdoing.
Thorn and thistle
  will grow on their altars.
They will say to the mountains, 'Cover us',
  to the hills, 'Fall on us.'

⁹Since the days of Gib'ah you have done wrong,
  Yisra'el;
there they stood.
Will battle not overtake them in Gib'ah
  because of evildoers?
¹⁰When it's my desire and I correct them
  peoples will be gathered against them.
When they're disciplined for their double
    waywardness,
  ¹¹though Ephrayim was a trained bullock.
It loved threshing,
  and I – I passed over its good neck.
I shall drive Ephrayim, Yehudah will
    plough,
  Ya'aqob [Jacob] will harrow for itself.

¹²Sow for yourselves for faithfulness,
  reap in proportion to commitment,
    till the tillable ground for yourselves.
It's time for enquiring of Yahweh, until he
    comes,
  and showers faithfulness for you.
¹³You've ploughed faithlessness, you have reaped
    evil,
  you've eaten deceptive fruit.
Because you've relied on your way,
  on the number of your strong men.
¹⁴A din will arise against your people,
and all your fortifications will be
    destroyed.
Like Shalman's destruction of Bet Arbe'l on a day
    of battle,
  when mother smashed on children.
¹⁵Like this he is doing to you, Bet-el,
  in the face of your bad, bad dealing.

At dawn he's being terminated, being
    terminated,
    Yisra'el's king.

## *The unfailing nature of a mother's love*

**11** When Yisra'el was a boy I loved him;
    from Misrayim I called my son.
²I called them;
    thus they went from me.
They sacrifice to the Masters,
    burn incense to images.
³I myself taught Ephrayim to walk,
    lifted them into my arms.
But they didn't acknowledge
    that I healed them.
⁴With human cords I would lead them,
    with loving ties.
For them I was
    someone lifting a baby to the cheek,
    and I bent to him so that I might feed him.

⁵No, they'll go back to the country of
    Misrayim,
    or Ashshur will be their king.
    because they refused to come back.
⁶A sword will whirl against its towns,
    finish off its gate-bars, consume them because
    of their counsels.
⁷My people are bent on turning back from me;
    when they call to the One on High,
    he won't lift them up at all.

⁸How can I give you up, Ephrayim,
    hand you over, Yisra'el?
How can I make you like Admah,
    treat you like Tsebo'im?
My spirit turns round within me,
    my comfort warms all at once.
⁹I shall not act on my angry burning;
    I shall not again devastate Ephrayim.
Because I am God and not a human being,
    the sacred one among you,
    and I shall not come against the town.
¹⁰They will follow Yahweh;
    he will roar like a lion.
When he roars,
    children will come trembling from the west.
¹¹They will come trembling like a bird from
    Misrayim,
    like a pigeon from the country of Ashshur,

I shall let them live in their homes (Yahweh's
    declaration).

## *Fraud from the womb*

¹²Ephrayim has surrounded me with lying,
    Yisra'el's household with deceit.
(Yehudah still wanders with God,
    keeps faith with the sacred ones.)

**12** Ephrayim pastures the wind,
    pursues the easterly;
Continually it increases deception and destruction;
    they solemnize a pact with Ashshur,
    and oil is carried to Misrayim.
²Yahweh will argue with Yehudah,
    and attend to Ya'aqob in accordance with his
      ways;
    in accordance with his practices he will give
      back to him.
³In the womb he grabbed his brother,
    and in his strength he struggled with God.
⁴He struggled with the envoy and prevailed;
    he cried and sought grace from him.
He would find him at Bet-el,
    speak with him there,
⁵Yahweh, God of Armies –
    Yahweh is his name.
⁶So you yourself are to turn back to your God;
    keep watch on commitment in the exercise of
      authority,
    and wait for your God always.

⁷A trader in whose hand are deceptive scales
    loves to defraud.
⁸Ephrayim has said, 'Yes, I've become rich,
    I've acquired strength for myself.
In all that I've toiled for they won't find in me
    waywardness that amounts to wrongdoing.'

⁹I am Yahweh your God
    from the country of Misrayim.
I shall make you live in your tents again,
    as in the days of your set occasion.
¹⁰I spoke to the prophets
    and I – I gave many a vision;
    by means of the prophets I shall terminate.
¹¹Is Gil'ad trouble: yes, emptiness;
    in Gilgal did they sacrifice bulls?
Their altars, too,
    are like stone heaps [*gallim*] on the furrows of
    the field.

¹²Ya'aqob fled to the open country of Aram;
  Yisra'el served for a wife –
  for a wife he kept [sheep].
¹³Through a prophet Yahweh got Yisra'el up from
  Misrayim,
  and through a prophet he was kept.
¹⁴Ephrayim provoked with great bitterness;
  his Lord will leave his bloodshed on him,
  give back his reviling to him.

## Like the morning cloud

**13** When Ephrayim spoke, there was
         trembling,
  when he lifted [his voice] in Yisra'el,
  but through the Master he became liable and
  died.
²Now they commit more and more wrongdoing,
  and they've made themselves an idol,
Images from their silver in accordance with their
  insight,
  the work of craftsmen, all of it.
With regard to them people are saying,
  'Human sacrifices, they kiss bullocks.'
³Therefore they will be like the morning cloud,
  like the dew that goes early,
Like chaff that whirls from a threshing-floor,
  like smoke from a window.
⁴I am Yahweh your God
  from the country of Misrayim.
You will not acknowledge a god apart from me;
  there's no deliverer except me.
⁵I acknowledged you in the wilderness,
  in a country of droughts.
⁶When they pastured, they were full,
  when they were full, their attitude became
    superior;
  therefore they put me out of mind.
⁷So I've become like a cougar to them,
  like a leopard I shall lurk by the road.
⁸I shall attack them like a bereaved bear,
  rip open the cover of their heart.
I shall consume them like a lion;
  the animals of the wild will tear them apart.

⁹Your devastation, Yisra'el,
  because in me is your help.
¹⁰Where is your king, then,
  so he may deliver you in all your towns,
And your authorities, of whom you said,
  'Give me a king and officials'?

¹¹I'd give you a king in my anger
  and take him in my outburst.

## Birth and death

¹²Ephrayim's waywardness is preserved,
  his wrongdoings stored up.
¹³When the pains of giving birth come to him,
  he'll be a child who isn't smart.
Because at the time he won't stand
  at the breach for children.
¹⁴From She'ol's hand I could redeem them,
  from death I could restore them.
Where would be your scourges, death,
  where your destruction, She'ol?

Comfort will hide from my eyes,
  ¹⁵because he's fruitful among brothers.
An easterly will come, Yahweh's wind,
  coming up from the wilderness.
His fountain will dry up,
  his spring wither.
That will plunder the treasury,
  all the objects held in high regard.
¹⁶Shomron is liable,
  because it's rebelled against its God.
People will fall by the sword,
  their babies will be smashed,
  their pregnant women torn open.

**14** Turn back, Yisra'el,
         to Yahweh your God,
  because you've fallen through your
    waywardness.
²Take words with you,
  and turn back to Yahweh;
Say to him, 'Will you carry it all, the
    waywardness? –
  receive something good: for bulls we'll make up
  with our lips.
³Ashshur isn't to deliver us,
  we won't ride on horses.
We will no more say "our God"
  to something made by our hands,
  because in you the orphan will find
    compassion.'

⁴I shall heal their turning away, I shall love
    them freely,
  because my anger has turned back from
  me.

⁵I shall become like dew to Yisra'el;
   it will flourish like the lily,
It will strike roots like the Lebanon;
   ⁶its shoots will grow
Its splendour will be like an olive
      tree,
   its fragrance like the Lebanon.
⁷People who sit in its shade will again
      bring grain to life,
   and flourish like the vine,
   its fame like Lebanon wine.

⁸Ephrayim:
'What shall I have to do with idols any more? –
   I myself have answered and looked to him.
I myself am like a verdant juniper' –
   from me your fruit appears.

⁹Who is smart and discerning about these things,
   is discerning and acknowledges them?
Because Yahweh's ways are straight,
   and the faithful walk in them,
   but rebels collapse by them.

# JOEL

The first half of Joel [Yoel] comprises a double description of disaster: a locust epidemic that is portrayed as past and a military invasion that is portrayed as coming. Possibly one is a figure for the other. The book does not give any concrete indication of the century when the disaster(s) happened. Joel's task is to urge Judah to turn to Yahweh in this situation and to promise that Yahweh will then deliver and restore the country. Beyond this restoration, the second half of the book speaks of an unprecedented pouring out of Yahweh's spirit, which will also be associated with a day of world judgement and a final battle between forces of good and forces of wickedness. The natural and/or military catastrophe is an embodiment of 'Yahweh's day', which will come in its final form in those events.

## The disaster

**1** Yahweh's word that came to Yo'el ben Petu'el.

²Listen to this, you elders;
  give ear, all you inhabitants of the country.
Has this happened in your days,
  or in your ancestors' days?
³Recount it to your children,
  your children to their children,
  and their children to the next generation.

⁴What was left from the cutter, the locust has
    eaten;
  what was left from the locust, the grub has
    eaten;
  what was left from the grub, the hopper has
    eaten.
⁵Wake up, you drunks, and cry;
  howl, all you wine drinkers,
  about the new wine, because it's been cut off
    from your mouth.
⁶Because a nation has come up against my
    country,
  numerous, and beyond counting.
Its teeth are a lion's teeth,
  it has a lioness's fangs.
⁷It's made my vine into desolation,
  my fig tree into a stump.
It's stripped its bark and thrown it away;
  its branches have turned white.

⁸Wail like a girl wrapped in sack
  because of the husband of her youth.
⁹Offering and libation has been cut off
  from Yahweh's house;
The priests have mourned,
  Yahweh's ministers.
¹⁰The open country has been destroyed,
  the ground has mourned.
Because the grain has been destroyed,
  the new wine has withered,
  the fresh oil languishes.
¹¹Farmers, be ashamed,
  vinedressers, howl,
Over wheat, over barley,
  because the harvest of the field has perished.
¹²The vine has withered, the fig tree languishes,
  pomegranate, even palm, and apricot.
All the trees of the open country wither,
  because joy has withered from humankind.

## All you can do is pray

¹³Wrap on and lament, priests;
  howl, ministers of the altar.
Come, spend the night in sack,
  ministers of my God.
Because offering and libation
  have been held back from Yahweh's house.
¹⁴Declare a sacred fast, call an assembly,
  gather the elders,
  all the inhabitants of the country,
To the house of Yahweh your God,
  and cry out to Yahweh.

¹⁵Ah for the day,
  because Yahweh's day is near;
  it comes like destruction from Shadday
    ['Destroyer'].
¹⁶Food is cut off, isn't it,
  in front of our eyes,
Rejoicing and celebration
  from Yahweh's house.
¹⁷Seeds have shrivelled under their clods,
  storehouses are desolate.
Granaries are torn down,
  because grain has withered.
¹⁸How the animals have groaned,
  the herds of cattle have been befuddled.
Because they have no pasture,
  even the flocks of sheep suffer punishment.
¹⁹To you, Yahweh, I call,
  because fire has consumed
  the pastures in the wilderness.
Flame has burned
  all the trees in the open country.
²⁰Even the animals of the wild pant for you,
  because the canyons of water dry up.
Fire has consumed
  the pastures in the wilderness.

**2** Blow a horn in Tsiyyon [Zion],
  sound out on my sacred mountain.
All the country's inhabitants are to tremble,
  because Yahweh's day has come, because it's
    near,
²A day of darkness and gloom,
  a day of cloud and murk.

Like dawn spread over the mountains,
  a vast and numerous company.
Nothing like it has happened from of old,
  and it won't happen again after it,
  through the years of generation after generation.

³Before it fire has consumed,
  after it flame blazes.
Before it the country was like Eden Garden,
  but after it, desolate wilderness –
  indeed, no survivors have been left to it.

### Who knows, he may turn back

⁴Their appearance is like the appearance of horses;
  like steeds, so they run.
⁵Like the sound of chariots,
  on the tops of the mountains they leap.
Like the sound of a blazing fire
  consuming straw,
Like a numerous company
  lined up for battle.
⁶Before them, peoples shudder;
  all faces have collected a flush.
⁷Like strong men they run,
  like men of battle they climb a wall.
They go each of them on his ways,
  they don't deviate their paths.
⁸They don't jostle one another;
  they go each man on his causeway.
When they fall through the weaponry,
  they don't break off.
⁹They rush at the town,
  they run at the wall.
They climb on the houses,
  through the windows they come in like a robber.

¹⁰Before it earth has quaked,
  heavens have shaken.
Sun and moon have gone dark,
  stars have gathered up their brightness.
¹¹Yahweh – he has given his voice
  before his force.
Because his camp is very vast,
  because numerous is the one performing his
    word.
Because Yahweh's day is great,
  very extraordinary – who can endure it?

¹²But even now (Yahweh's declaration),
  turn back to me with your whole heart,
  with fasting, with crying and with lamenting.
¹³Tear your mind, not your clothes,
  and turn back to Yahweh your God,
Because he is gracious and compassionate,
  long-tempered and vast in commitment,
  and he relents of dealing badly.

¹⁴Who knows, he may turn back and relent,
  and let a blessing remain behind him,
  an offering and a libation for Yahweh your
    God?

¹⁵Blow the horn in Tsiyyon,
  declare a sacred fast, call an assembly.
¹⁶Gather the people, make the congregation
    sacred,
  collect the elders.
Gather the babies
  and those nursing at the breast.
The groom is to go out of his room,
  the bride out of her tent.
¹⁷Between the porch and the altar
  the priests, Yahweh's ministers, are to cry.
They're to say, 'Spare your people, Yahweh,
  don't give your domain to reviling.
  as a byword against them for the nations.
Why should they say among the peoples,
  "Where is their God?"'

### The years the locust has eaten

¹⁸So Yahweh became passionate about his country,
  and took pity on his people.
¹⁹Yahweh answered,
  and said to his people,
'Here I am, I'm going to send grain to you,
  new wine and fresh oil – you'll be full of it.
I shall not ever again give you over
  as an object of reviling among the nations.
²⁰I shall put the northerner far from you,
  thrust him into a dry and desolate country,
His face to the eastern sea,
  his rear to the western sea.
His smell will go up, his stench go up,
  because he has acted big.

²¹Don't be afraid, earth, celebrate and rejoice,
  because Yahweh has acted big.
²²Don't be afraid, animals of the wild,
  because the wilderness pastures are green.
Because the tree has borne its fruit,
  fig tree and vine have given their resources.
²³Members of Tsiyyon, celebrate,
  rejoice in Yahweh your God.
Because he's given you
  the autumn rain in faithfulness.
He's made rain come down for you,
  autumn rain and spring rain as before.

²⁴Threshing-floors will be full of grain,
   presses will abound in new wine and fresh oil.
²⁵I shall make good to you for the years
   that the locust and the grub have consumed,
The hopper and the cutter, my big force,
   which I sent off against you.
²⁶You will eat and eat and be full,
   and praise the name of Yahweh your God,
The one who acted in an extraordinary way with
   you;
   my people won't be ashamed permanently, and
   you will acknowledge it.
²⁷Because I will be within Yisra'el,
   and I am Yahweh your God.
And there is no other,
   and my people will not be ashamed,
   permanently.

## You can't control who receives God's spirit

²⁸After that, I shall pour my breath on all flesh,
   and your sons and your daughters will
     prophesy.
Your elderly will have dreams,
   your young men will see visions.
²⁹I shall also pour my breath
   on servants and maidservants in those days.

³⁰I shall put portents in the heavens and in the
   earth,
   blood, fire and columns of smoke.
³¹The sun will turn to darkness,
   the moon to blood,
Before Yahweh's day comes,
   great, extraordinary.
³²But anyone who calls
   in Yahweh's name will escape.
Because on Mount Tsiyyon and in Yerushalaim
   there will be an escape group,
As Yahweh has said,
   among the survivors whom Yahweh is going
     to call.

**3** Because there, in those days
   and at that time,
When I restore the fortunes
   of Yehudah and Yerushalaim,
²I shall collect all the nations
   and get them down to Yehoshaphat ['Yahweh
   has exercised authority'] Vale.

I shall enter into the exercise of authority with
     them there
   over my people, my domain, Yisra'el,
   whom they scattered among the nations.
They shared out my country.
   ³and for my people they cast the lot.
They gave a boy for a whore,
   sold a girl for wine and drank it.

⁴Now, what are you in relation to me, Tsor [Tyre]
     and Tsidon,
   and all you regions of Peleshet [Philistia]?
Are you making good to me with your
     dealings? –
   if you're dealing out me,
Swiftly, speedily,
   I shall give back your dealings on to your
     head.
⁵Because it was my silver and my gold you took,
   the good things that I held in high regard you
     brought into your palaces.
⁶Yehudahites and Yerushalaimites you sold to the
     Yavanites [Greeks],
   in order to send them far away from their
     territory.
⁷Here am I, stirring them up from the place to
     where you sold them,
   and I shall give back your dealings on to your
     head.
⁸I shall sell your sons and your daughters
   into the hand of the Yehudahites,
And they will sell them into captivity
   to a far-off nation (because Yahweh has
     spoken).

## Beat your hoes into swords

⁹Call out this among the nations,
   declare a sacred battle.
Stir up strong men so they draw near;
   all the men of battle are to go up.
¹⁰Beat your hoes into swords,
   your pruning hooks into spears;
The weakling is to say, 'I'm a strong man' –
   ¹¹hurry, come.
All you nations around, collect yourselves,
   make your strong men go down there, Yahweh.
¹²The nations are to stir themselves and go up
   to Yehoshaphat Vale,
Because there I shall sit to exercise authority
   over all the nations around.

<sup>13</sup>Put out the sickle,
because the harvest has ripened.
Come, tread,
because the vat is full.
The presses abound,
because their bad dealing is great.
<sup>14</sup>Hordes, hordes, in Verdict Vale,
because Yahweh's day is near in Verdict Vale.
<sup>15</sup>Sun and moon have gone dark,
stars have gathered up their brightness;
<sup>16</sup>Yahweh roars from Tsiyyon,
gives voice from Yerushalaim.
Heavens and earth tremble,
but Yahweh is a shelter for his people,
a stronghold for the Yisra'elites.
<sup>17</sup>You will acknowledge that I am Yahweh,
your God who dwells on Tsiyyon, my sacred
mountain.

Yerushalaim will be sacred;
strangers will no more pass through it.
<sup>18</sup>On that day
the mountains will drop sweet wine,
The hills will run with milk,
all Yehudah's canyons will run with water.
A fountain will go out of Yahweh's house
and water Acacias Wadi.
<sup>19</sup>Misrayim [Egypt] will become a desolation,
Edom will become a wilderness, a desolation,
Because of violence done to the Yehudahites,
in whose country they shed the blood of one
free of guilt.
<sup>20</sup>But Yehudah will live permanently,
Yerushalaim for generation after generation.
<sup>21</sup>I shall treat their bloodshed as free of guilt,
which I have not treated as free of guilt,
as Yahweh is dwelling on Tsiyyon.

# AMOS

Yahweh sent Amos from Judah to bring his message to northern Israel (Ephraim) at Bethel, at the southern end of the country. He was a contemporary of Hosea in Ephraim, though they may not have come into contact if Hosea was in the Ephraimite capital, Samaria. Compared with Hosea, Amos pays proportionately more attention to social ills than to religious ills, and he is a gifted communicator. The opening chapters win his audience's attention by lambasting other nations for their war crimes before turning to declare that Ephraim is worse because it had fuller revelation from God. He invites people to come to worship, but then tells them it's an act of rebellion that Yahweh hates. He sings a funeral lament that turns out to be a dirge for the coming demise of the nation itself. He declares that the day of Yahweh will be bad news, not good news. He tells people how he prayed successfully for Yahweh not to act in judgement but then indicates that he had to stop doing so. He warns people that they cannot escape Yahweh even by trying to hide in She'ol. But he also says that judgement will not be the end.

## Nations held responsible

**1** The words of Amos, who was among the sheep-breeders from Teqoa, which he saw concerning Yisra'el in the days of Uzziyyah king of Yehudah and in the days of Yarob'am ben Yo'ash king of Yisra'el, two years before the earthquake.

²When Yahweh roars from Tsiyyon [Zion],
    gives voice from Yerushalaim,
The shepherds' pastures will mourn,
    Carmel's head will wither.

³Yahweh has said this:

For three rebellions by Dammeseq [Damascus],
    for four I shall not turn it back,
    because of their threshing Gil'ad with iron
        sledges.
⁴I shall send off fire against Haza'el's house,
    and it will consume Ben-hadad's citadels.
⁵I shall break Dammeseq's bar,
    and I shall cut off inhabitants from Trouble
        Valley,
A sceptre-holder from Bet-eden,
    and the people of Aram will go into exile to Qir
        (Yahweh has said).

⁶Yahweh has said this:

For three rebellions by Azzah [Gaza],
    for four I shall not turn it back,
Because of their exiling a complete exile community,
    handing them over to Edom.
⁷I shall send off fire against Azzah's wall,
    and it will consume its citadels.
⁸I shall cut off inhabitants from Ashdod,
    a sceptre-holder from Ashqelon.
I shall turn back my hand against Eqron;
    the remainder of the Pelishtites [Philistines]
        will perish (the Lord Yahweh has said).

⁹Yahweh has said this:

For three rebellions by Tsor [Tyre],
    for four I shall not turn it back,
because of their handing over a complete exile
        community to Edom;
    they were not mindful of the brotherhood pact.
¹⁰I shall send off fire against Tsor's wall,
    and it will consume its fortresses.

## Yehudah too

¹¹Yahweh has said this:

For three rebellions by Edom,
    for four I shall not turn it back,
Because he pursued his brother with a sword,
    devastated his compassion.
His anger tore ceaselessly,
    his outburst kept watch continually.
¹²I shall send off fire against Teman,
    and it will consume Botsrah's citadels.

¹³Yahweh has said this:

For three rebellions by the Ammonites,
    for four I shall not turn it back,
Because of their ripping open pregnant women
        in Gil'ad,
    in order to enlarge their territory.
¹⁴I shall set fire to Rabbah's wall
    and it will consume its citadels,
With shouting on a day of battle,
    with a hurricane on a stormy day.
¹⁵Their king will go into exile,
    he and his officials together (Yahweh has
        said).

**2** Yahweh has said this:

For three rebellions by Mo'ab,
    for four I shall not turn it back,
    because of his burning the bones of the king of
        Edom to lime.
²I shall send off fire against Mo'ab,
    and it will consume Qeriyyot's citadels.
Mo'ab will die amid a din,
    amid shouting and the sound of a horn.
³I shall cut off the authority from within it,
    and kill all its officials with him (Yahweh has
        said).

⁴Yahweh has said this:

For three rebellions by Yehudah,
    for four I shall not turn it back,
Because of their rejecting Yahweh's instruction
    and not keeping his laws.
Their lies led them astray,
    which their ancestors followed.
⁵I shall send off fire against Yehudah,
    and it will consume Yerushalaim's citadels.

## And also Ephrayim

<sup>6</sup>Yahweh has said this:

For three rebellions by Yisra'el,
    for four I shall not turn it back,
Because of their selling a faithful person for
    silver,
    a needy person for a pair of boots.
<sup>7</sup>You who trample the head of poor people
    into the earth of the ground,
    and twist the way of humble people!
An individual and his father go to a girl,
    in order to treat my sacred name as
        ordinary.
<sup>8</sup>On garments given in pledge
    they lie down by every altar.
In their God's house they drink
    the wine of people who have been defrauded.

<sup>9</sup>And I'm the one who annihilated the Amorite
        before them,
    whose height was like the height of cedars,
    and who was as sturdy as oaks.
I annihilated his fruit above
    and his roots below.
<sup>10</sup>And I'm the one who took you up
    from the country of Misrayim [Egypt].
I enabled you to go through the wilderness for
        forty years,
    to take possession of the Amorite's country.
<sup>11</sup>I raised up prophets from your children,
    consecrated people from your young men.
It is indeed so, isn't it, Yisra'elites (Yahweh's
        declaration),
    <sup>12</sup>but you made the consecrated people drink
        wine
    and you ordered the prophets, 'You will not
        prophesy.'

<sup>13</sup>There, I'm going to make a split beneath you
        as a cart makes a split
    when full of its grain.
<sup>14</sup>Flight will perish from the swift,
    the strong won't firm up his energy.
The strong man won't save his life,
    <sup>15</sup>the one who wields the bow won't stand.
One swift on his feet won't save himself,
    one riding a horse won't save his life.
<sup>16</sup>The firmest of mind among the strong men
    will flee naked on that day (Yahweh's
        declaration).

## Do accidents happen?

**3** Listen to this word which Yahweh has
    spoken about you, Yisra'elites, about
the entire kin-group that I took up from
Misrayim:

<sup>2</sup>Only you did I acknowledge
    from all earth's kin-groups.
Therefore I shall attend to you
    for all your wayward acts.
<sup>3</sup>Do two walk together
    unless they've taken counsel?
<sup>4</sup>Does a lion roar in the forest
    and it has no prey?
Does a cougar give voice from its abode
    unless it has caught something?
<sup>5</sup>Does a bird fall in a trap on the earth
    and there's no snare there?
Does a trap come up from the ground
    and it hasn't actually caught something?
<sup>6</sup>If a horn sounds in a town,
    doesn't the people tremble?
And if something happens to a town,
    isn't it Yahweh who's acted?
<sup>7</sup>Because the Lord Yahweh does nothing
    except he has revealed his plan
    to his servants the prophets.

<sup>8</sup>A lion has roared,
    who would not be afraid?
The Lord Yahweh has spoken,
    who wouldn't prophesy?

<sup>9</sup>Make it heard in Ashdod's citadels,
    and in the citadels in the country of
        Misrayim.
Say, 'Gather on Shomron's [Samaria's]
        mountains,
    look at the great chaos within it,
    the oppressed within it.'
<sup>10</sup>They haven't acknowledged acting straight
        (Yahweh's declaration),
    the people who store up violence and
        destruction in their citadels.

<sup>11</sup>Therefore, the Lord Yahweh has said
this:

An adversary, round the country:
    he'll pull down your vigour from you,
    and your citadels will be plundered.

¹²Yahweh has said this:

As a shepherd rescues
   from a lion's mouth
Two shank bones
   or the tip of an ear,
So the Yisra'elites will escape,
   the people who live in Shomron,
   with the leg of a bed or the damask of a couch.

¹³Listen, and testify against Ya'aqob's [Jacob's]
   household
   (a declaration of the Lord Yahweh, God of
   Armies):
¹⁴On the day I attend to Yisra'el's rebellions
   for it,
   I shall attend to Bet-el's altars.
The altar's horns will be cut off,
   and will fall to the ground.
¹⁵I shall strike down the winter house
   as well as the summer house.
The ivory houses will perish,
   the great houses will come to an end (Yahweh's
   declaration).

*But you haven't turned back to me*

**4** Listen to this word,
   you Bashan cows,
You who are on Shomron's mountain,
   you who defraud the poor, who crush the
   needy,
Who say to their husbands,
   'Bring something so we can drink.'

²The Lord Yahweh has sworn by his
sacredness:

There, days are coming upon you
   when someone will carry you off with
   hooks –
   yes, the last of you with fish hooks.
³Through the breaches you'll go out, each woman
   straight ahead,
   and you'll be thrown out to Harmon (Yahweh's
   declaration).

⁴Come to Bet-el and rebel –
   to Gilgal, multiply the rebelling.
Bring your sacrifices every morning,
   your tenths every three days.

⁵Burn your thank-offering of leavened bread,
   call out voluntary offerings, make them heard,
   because so you love it, Yisra'elites (the Lord
   Yahweh's declaration).
⁶Even though I – I have given you
   emptiness of teeth in all your towns,
Lack of food in all your places,
   but you haven't turned back to me (Yahweh's
   declaration).
⁷Even though I – I have withheld the rain from you
   when it was still three months to the harvest.
I'd let it rain on one town
   but not let it rain on another town.
One plot would be rained on,
   but a plot on which it would not rain would
   wither.
⁸Two or three towns would wander
   to another town to drink water.
But they wouldn't be full,
   but you haven't turned back to me (Yahweh's
   declaration).
⁹I have struck you down with blight and with
   mildew,
   multiplying it on your gardens and your
   orchards.
The locust would eat your fig trees and olives,
   but you haven't turned back to me (Yahweh's
   declaration).
¹⁰I sent off an epidemic among you
   in the manner of Misrayim,
I killed your young men with the sword,
   with your captured horses,
Made the smell of your camps rise, even into your
   nostrils,
   but you haven't turned back to me (Yahweh's
   declaration).
¹¹I overthrew some of you
   like the supernatural overthrow of Sedom
   [Sodom] and Amorah [Gomorrah],
You became like a burning stick pulled out of the
   fire,
   but you haven't turned back to me (Yahweh's
   declaration).

*When authority becomes poisonous*

¹²Therefore this is what I shall do to you, Yisra'el;
   because I shall do this to you,
   get ready to meet your God, Yisra'el.
¹³Because there, one who shapes mountains,
   creates wind,

Tells human beings what his thinking is,
  makes dawn into darkness,
Treads on earth's high places –
  Yahweh, God of Armies, is his name.

**5** Listen to this word, which I'm taking up,
  a lament over you, Yisra'el's household.

²She's fallen, she won't get up again,
  Miss Yisra'el;
She's left on her land,
  there's no one to help her up.

³Because the Lord Yahweh has said this:

The town that goes out as a thousand
  will have a hundred remaining.
The one that goes out as a hundred
  will have ten remaining to Yisra'el's household.

⁴Because Yahweh has said this to Yisra'el's
household:

Enquire of me, and live,
  ⁵don't enquire of Bet-el,
Don't go to Gilgal,
  don't cross over to Be'er-sheba.
Because Gilgal is definitely to go into exile,
  and Bet-el is to become nothing.
⁶Enquire of Yahweh and live,
  so he doesn't break out like fire
On Yoseph's household, and consume,
  and there's no one to quench it for Bet-el.

⁷You who turn the exercise of authority to
  poison
  and set down faithfulness on the earth!
⁸He's the one who makes Pleiades and Orion,
  turns deep darkness to dawn.
He darkens day into night,
  the one who calls the water of the sea,
Pours it out on the face of the earth –
  Yahweh is his name –
⁹The one who flashes destruction on the vigorous,
  so that destruction comes on the fortification.

¹⁰They are hostile to the one who reproves in the
  gateway,
  they take offence at the one who speaks with
  integrity.
¹¹Therefore, because you tax the poor person,
  take a levy of grain from him:

You've built houses of square stone,
  but you won't live in them.
¹²Because I have got to know your many acts of
  rebellion,
  your numerous wrongdoings.
You adversaries of the faithful, takers of a bribe,
  who have turned aside the needy in the
  gateway.

## The day of the Lord as bad news

¹³Therefore the person of insight keeps silent at
  such a time,
  because it's a bad time.
¹⁴Enquire after what is good, not what is bad, in
  order that you may live;
  thus Yahweh, God of Armies, will be with
  you,
  as you've said.
¹⁵Be hostile to what is bad, be loyal to what is
  good,
  establish the exercise of authority in the
  gateway.
Perhaps Yahweh, God of Armies, will be gracious
  to what remains of Yoseph.

¹⁶Therefore Yahweh, God of Armies, the Lord,
has said this:

In all the squares lamenting,
  in all the streets they'll say, 'Oh, oh'.
They'll call the farmhand to mourning,
  and for lamenting to the people who know how
  to keen.
¹⁷In all the orchards lamenting,
  when I pass through the middle of you
  (Yahweh has said).

¹⁸Hey, you who wish
  for Yahweh's day.
What good really is Yahweh's day to you? –
  it will be darkness, not light.
¹⁹As when someone flees from before a lion
  and a bear meets him,
Or he comes home,
  leans his hand on a wall,
  and a snake bites him.
²⁰Yahweh's day will be darkness not light, won't it,
  gloom, with no brightness to it.
²¹I've been hostile, I've rejected your festivals;
  I don't savour your assemblies.

²²Even when you offer me burnt offerings,
  and your grain offerings, I shall not accept
    them.
To a fellowship offering of well-fed animals
  I shall not look.
²³Remove from me the noise of your songs;
  I shall not listen to the music of your
    mandolins.
²⁴The exercise of authority is to roll like water,
  faithfulness like a perennial wadi.
²⁵Was it sacrifices and an offering that you
    presented to me
  in the wilderness for forty years,
    household of Yisra'el?

²⁶You will carry Sikkut your king,
  and Kiyyun, your images, the star of your god,
That which you made for yourselves,
    ²⁷and I shall exile you beyond Dammeseq,
    (Yahweh whose name is God of Armies has
      said).

## A warning to people at peace

**6** Hey, you people who are at peace on
    Tsiyyon,
  who are confident on Shomron's mountain,
You notables of the first of the nations,
  to whom Yisra'el's household come.
²Pass over to Kalneh and look,
  go from there to Great Hamat,
  go down to Gat in Peleshet [Philistia].
Are these better than your kingdoms,
  or their territory than your territory,
³You who push away the bad day,
  but bring near the rule of violence,
⁴You who lie on ivory beds,
  lounging on their couches,
Eating lambs from the flock,
  bullocks from within the stall,
⁵Making music to the sound of the mandolin like
    David,
  people who have composed for themselves on
    musical instruments,
⁶Drink with bowls of wine,
  anoint themselves with the finest oils,
  but haven't got sick at the breaking of Yoseph?

⁷Therefore now:
  they will go into exile at the head of the exiles,
  and the revelry of the loungers will turn aside.

⁸The Lord Yahweh has sworn by himself
(a declaration of Yahweh, God of Armies):

I detest Ya'aqob's majesty,
  I'm hostile to its citadels,
  I shall deliver up the town and what fills it.
⁹If ten people are left
  in one house, they'll die.
¹⁰If someone's relative lifts him up (the person
      who burns spices for him)
  to take his bones out of the house,
And says to whoever is in the inner parts of the
      house,
  'Is anyone still with you?'
He'll say, 'Hush,
  because we're not to mention Yahweh's name.'
¹¹Because there, Yahweh is going to order,
  and he'll strike down the great house to pieces,
  the small house to bits.

¹²Do horses run on a cliff,
  or does one plough it with cattle?
Because you've turned the exercise of authority
    to venom,
  faithful fruit to poison,
¹³You who rejoice at No-thing,
  who say 'It was by our strength, wasn't it,
  that we took Qarnayim for ourselves?'
¹⁴Because here am I, about to raise up against
    you,
  Yisra'el's household (a declaration of Yahweh,
    God of Armies) –
A nation, and they'll afflict you
  from Lebo Hamat to Wadi Arabah.

## I wasn't a prophet

**7** The Lord Yahweh showed me this: there,
    he was forming a locust swarm at the
beginning of the growth of the spring crop.
There – the spring crop after the king's reaping.
²When it had finished consuming the grass
in the country, I said, 'Lord Yahweh, please
pardon, how can Ya'aqob stand, because it's
small.' ³Yahweh relented about this. 'It won't
happen', Yahweh said.
    ⁴The Lord Yahweh showed me this:
there, he was calling for an argument by
fire. It consumed the Great Deep and it was
consuming the plots. ⁵I said, 'Lord Yahweh,
please spare, how can Ya'aqob stand, because

it's small.' ⁶Yahweh relented about this. 'It won't happen either', the Lord Yahweh said.

⁷He showed me this: there, the Lord was standing by a lead-weight wall, and in his hand was a lead weight. ⁸Yahweh said to me, 'What are you looking at, Amos?' I said, 'A lead weight'. The Lord said, 'Here am I, I'm going to put a lead weight in the middle of my people Yisra'el. I shall not again pass over it any more. ⁹Yitshaq's [Isaac's] shrines will be desolate, Yisra'el's sanctuaries will be laid waste. I shall rise against Yarob'am's household with the sword.'

¹⁰Amatsyah the priest at Bet-el sent to Yarob'am king of Yisra'el to say, 'Amos has conspired against you within Yisra'el's household. The country can't endure all his words. ¹¹Because Amos has said this: "Yarob'am will die by the sword, Yisra'el will go into exile, exile away from its soil."' ¹²But Amatsyah said to Amos, 'Seer, go, flee for your life to the country of Yehudah, eat bread there, prophesy there. ¹³Don't prophesy again in Bet-el any more, because it's the king's sanctuary. It's the kingdom's house.'

¹⁴Amos answered Amatsyah, 'I wasn't a prophet and I wasn't a prophet's son; rather I was a cattleman and a dresser of sycamore figs. ¹⁵But Yahweh took me from following the flock, and Yahweh said to me, "Go, prophesy to my people Yisra'el."

¹⁶Now, listen to Yahweh's word. You're saying, "You shouldn't prophesy against Yisra'el. You shouldn't preach against Yitshaq's household." ¹⁷Therefore Yahweh has said this: "Your wife will whore in the town. Your sons and your daughters will fall by the sword. Your land will be shared out by measuring line. You yourself will die on unclean land. Yisra'el will go into exile, exile away from its land."'

## Amos isn't praying now

**8** The Lord Yahweh showed me this: there, a basket of ripe fruit. ²He said, 'What are you looking at, Amos?' I said, 'A basket of ripe fruit'. Yahweh said to me, 'The ripe time has come for my people Yisra'el. I shall not again pass over it any more. ³The palace singers will wail on that day (a declaration of the Lord

Yahweh): "He has thrown out many a corpse in every place – hush!"'

⁴Listen to this, you who trample the needy person,
  who make the humble people in the country
    cease,
⁵Saying, 'When will the new month be over,
  so we can sell wheat,
  and the sabbath, so we can lay out grain –
Making the barrel measure small but the sheqel
    big,
  falsifying the scales by deceit,
⁶Acquiring the poor people for silver,
  the needy person for a pair of boots,
  and selling sweepings as grain?'
⁷Yahweh has sworn by the Majesty of Ya'aqob,
  'If I ever put out of mind any of their doings ...'

⁸For this, the earth will shake, won't it,
  and everyone who lives in it mourn.
It will all rise like the Ye'or [Nile],
  surge and sink like Misrayim's Ye'or.

⁹On that day (a declaration of the Lord Yahweh),
  I shall make the sun set at noon,
  make the earth dark during daylight.
¹⁰I shall turn your festivals into mourning,
  all your songs into lamenting.
I shall put sack on all hips,
  shornness on every head,
I shall make it like the mourning for an only
    child,
  its end a truly bitter day.

## You can't get away from God

¹¹There, days are coming (a declaration of the
    Lord Yahweh)
  when I shall send famine through the country –
Not famine of bread, not thirst for water,
  but rather of hearing Yahweh's words.
¹²People will wander from sea to sea
  and roam from north to east,
To seek Yahweh's word,
  but they won't find it.
¹³On that day beautiful girls and young men
  will faint with thirst.
¹⁴People who swear by the liability of Shomron
  and say, 'As your god lives, Dan',
And 'As the way to Be'er-sheba lives',
  will fall and not rise again.

**9** I saw the Lord standing by the altar. He
said:

Strike down the capitals so the thresholds shake;
  break them off on to the head of all of them.
The last of them I shall kill with the sword;
  not one of them will flee as a fugitive,
  no escapee will survive.
[2]If they dig into Sheol,
  from there my hand will get them.
If they go up into the heavens,
  I shall get them down.
[3]If they hide on top of Carmel,
  from there I shall search them out and get them.
If they conceal themselves from in front of my eyes
  at the bottom of the sea,
From there I shall order
  the serpent and it will bite them.
[4]If they go into captivity before their enemies,
  from there I shall order the sword and it will
  kill them.
I shall set my eye on them for something bad,
  not for something good.

[5]The Lord Yahweh of Armies –
  he touches the earth and it melts,
  and all the people who live in it mourn.
All of it rises like the Yeor,
  and sinks like Misrayim's Yeor.
[6]He built his lofts in the heavens
  and founded his structure on the earth,
The one who calls the sea's water
  and pours it over the face of the earth –
  Yahweh is his name.

## The day of the Lord as good news again

[7]You're like the Kushites [Sudanese]
  to me, Yisraelites, aren't you (Yahweh's
  declaration).
I got Yisrael up from the country of Misrayim,
  didn't I –
  and the Pelishtites from Kaphtor, and the
  Aramites from Qir?

[8]There, the Lord Yahweh's eyes
  are on the kingdom that does wrong;
I annihilate it
  from on the face of the earth.
Except that I shall not totally annihilate
  Yaaqob's household (Yahweh's declaration).
[9]Because here I am, I'm going to give an order,
  and shake Yisrael's household among all the
  nations,
As someone shakes in a sieve,
  and no pebble falls to the earth.
[10]All the wrongdoers in my people
  will die by the sword,
The people who say, 'It won't reach,
  it won't come near us.'

[11]On that day:
  I shall raise David's fallen bivouac
  and repair its breaches,
I shall raise its ruins
  and build it up as in days of old,
[12]In order that they may enter into possession of
  what remains of Edom,
  and all the nations that were called by my
  name.
  (a declaration of Yahweh who is going to do
  this).

[13]There, days are coming (Yahweh's
  declaration):
  when the ploughman will reach the reaper,
  the treader of grapes the one trailing the
  seed.
The mountains will drop sweet wine,
  all the hills will flow.
[14]I shall restore the fortunes of my people
  Yisrael;
  they'll build up desolate towns and live there.
They'll plant vineyards and drink their wine,
  they will make gardens and eat their fruits.
[15]I shall plant them on their land
  and they won't uproot again
From on their land
  which I have given them (Yahweh your God
  has said).

# OBADIAH

Presumably Yahweh gave Obadiah [Obadyah] many other prophecies, but the Judahite community recognized this one as having long-lasting significance. It refers to Edom's involvement in the destruction of Jerusalem, particularly grievous because behind the relationship of Israel and Edom is the relationship between Jacob and Esau as brothers. One might guess that further background is the fact that Edom took over much of the territory Yahweh gave Judah in the centuries that followed.

## *Who could bring me down to earth?*

¹Obadyah's vision.

The Lord Yahweh has said this about Edom; we have heard a report from Yahweh:

An envoy has been sent out among the nations:
 'Rise up – let's rise up against it for battle!'
²Here, I'm making you small among the
   nations;
 you're going to be very despised.
³The arrogance of your mind has deceived you,
   you who dwell in the clefts of the crag, the
     height of its abode,
Saying within yourself,
 'Who could take me down to earth?'
⁴If you go up high like an eagle,
   if you put your nest among the stars,
   from there I could bring you down (Yahweh's
     declaration).

⁵If thieves came to you, if robbers came by night
   (how you are terminated!)
   they would steal what they needed, wouldn't
     they.
If grape-pickers came to you,
   they'd let gleanings remain, wouldn't they.
⁶How Esaw is being ransacked,
   its hidden treasures sought out!
⁷All the people you were in pact with
   are sending you off to the border.
The people you were in alliance with
   are deceiving you, prevailing over you.
The people who eat your bread set a trap beneath
     you
   (it has no understanding).

⁸On that day (Yahweh's declaration):

I shall eliminate the experts from Edom,
   shan't I,
   and understanding from Mount Esaw.
⁹Your strong men will shatter, Teman,
   in order that people will be cut off from Mount
     Esaw through slaughter.
¹⁰Because of the violence to your brother Ya'aqob
     [Jacob]
   shame will cover you, and you'll be cut off
     permanently.
¹¹On the day you stood aside,
   on the day foreigners captured his resources,

When aliens came into his gateways,
   and cast lots for Yerushalaim,
   you, too, were like one of them.

## *On gloating and taking advantage*

¹²You shouldn't have looked at your brother's day,
   the day this alien thing happened to him.
You shouldn't have rejoiced at the Yehudahites
   on the day of their perishing.
You shouldn't have talked big
   on the day of pressure.
¹³You shouldn't have come into my people's
     gateway
   on the day of their disaster.
You shouldn't have looked, you too, at his bad
     fortune
   on the day of his disaster.
You shouldn't have reached out at his resources
   on the day of his disaster.
¹⁴You shouldn't have stood at the crossroad
   to cut down his escapees.
You shouldn't have handed over his survivors
   on the day of pressure.
¹⁵Because Yahweh's day is near against all the
     nations;
   as you did, it will be done to you,
   when your dealings come back on your head.

¹⁶Because as you [Yehudahites] drank
   on my sacred mountain,
All the nations will drink continually,
   drink and swallow,
   and be as if they'd never been.
¹⁷But on Mount Tsiyyon [Zion] there'll be an
     escape group,
   and it will be sacred.
Ya'aqob's household will dispossess
   the people who dispossessed them.
¹⁸Ya'aqob's household will become a fire,
   Yoseph's household a flame,
Esaw's household straw,
   and they will burn among them, consume
     them.
Esaw's household
   will have no survivor (because Yahweh has
     spoken).

¹⁹The Negeb will possess Mount Esaw,
   the Lowland [will possess] the Pelishtites
   [Philistines].

They will possess the fields of Ephrayim,
    the fields of Shomron [Samaria],
    and Binyamin [will possess] Gil'ad.
²⁰This exile community force belonging to the
    Yisra'elites
    [will possess] what [belongs to] the Kena'anites
    [Canaanites] as far as Tsarepat.

The exile community from Yerushalaim which is
    in Sepharad
    will possess the towns of the Negeb.
²¹Deliverers will go up on Mount Tsiyyon
    to exercise authority over Mount Esaw,
    and the kingship will belong to
    Yahweh.

# JONAH

Yahweh used Jonah [Yonah] to promise Ephraim the recovery of territory from the Arameans (2 Kings 14.25). Thus it would not be surprising if he were unenthusiastic about preaching to the Assyrians because he knows that Yahweh will refrain from destroying them if they repent. The story about him thus warns prophets and other people about underestimating Yahweh's concern for other nations, even domineering superpowers. It thus complements Obadiah in illustrating the other side to Yahweh's attitude to oppressive nations. The story is full of humour and irony, which supports the idea that it is a parable rather than a historical story.

## The prophet who runs away

**1** Yahweh's word came to Yonah ben Amittay: ²'Set off, go to the great town of Nineveh and call out against it, because their bad dealing has come up before me.' ³But Yonah set off to flee to Tarshish from before Yahweh. He went down to Yafo [Jaffa], found a ship going to Tarshish, paid its fare and went down into it to go with them to Tarshish from before Yahweh. ⁴But Yahweh flung a great wind into the sea, there was a great storm in the sea, and the ship threatened to break up. ⁵The sailors were afraid and cried out each of them to his god. They flung the things that were in the ship into the sea to lighten it of them.

Yonah had gone down into the inmost parts of the vessel, lain down and gone to sleep. ⁶The captain went to see him and said to him, 'What are you doing, sleeping? Get up, call on your god. Perhaps the god will give a thought to us and we won't perish.'

⁷The men said to each other, 'Come on, let's make lots fall so we can know on whose account this bad fate has come to us.' They made lots fall, and the lot fell on Yonah. ⁸They said to him, 'Tell us, please, on whose account this bad fate has come to us. What's your work? Where do you come from? What's your country? What people are you from?' ⁹He said to them, 'I'm a Hebrew. I live in awe of Yahweh the God of the heavens, who made the sea and the dry land.'

¹⁰The men were greatly afraid, and said to him, 'What is this you've done?', when the men knew that he was fleeing from before Yahweh, when he had told them. ¹¹They said to him, 'What shall we do to you so that the sea quietens down from upon us?' (when the sea was growing stormier). ¹²He said to them, 'Lift me up and hurl me into the sea, and the sea will quieten down from upon you, because I acknowledge that it was on my account that this great storm has come upon you.'

## How to pray from inside a fish

¹³The men rowed to get back to dry land, but they couldn't, because the sea was growing stormier against them. ¹⁴They called to Yahweh, 'Oh, Yahweh, may we please not perish for this man's life. Don't put upon us the blood of someone free of guilt. Because you, Yahweh – as you wished, you have acted.' ¹⁵They lifted Yonah up and hurled him into the sea; and the sea stopped its raging. ¹⁶The men were in great awe of Yahweh. They offered a sacrifice to Yahweh and made pledges.

¹⁷Yahweh provided a big fish to swallow Yonah, and Yonah was in the fish's insides three days and three nights.

**2** Yonah prayed to Yahweh his God from the fish's insides:

²Out of my pressure I called
    to Yahweh and he answered me.
When I called for help from She'ol's belly,
    you listened to my voice.
³You threw me into the deep,
    into the heart of the seas.
The river surrounded me;
    all your breakers and your waves passed over me.
⁴I myself said, 'I've been driven away
    from in front of your eyes.'
Yet I shall again look
    towards your sacred palace.
⁵The water overwhelmed me, up to my neck,
    the deep surrounded me.
Reed was wrapped round my head
    ⁶at the roots of the mountains.
I went down into the earth,
    its bars were about me permanently.
But you got my life up from the Pit,
    Yahweh my God.
⁷When my life was ebbing away from me,
    I was mindful of Yahweh.
My plea came to you,
    to your sacred palace.
⁸People who keep watch for things that are empty
    and hollow
    forsake their commitment.
⁹But I – with a voice of thanksgiving I will
    sacrifice to you;
    for what I have pledged I shall make good –
    deliverance belongs to Yahweh.

¹⁰Yahweh spoke to the fish, and it vomited Yonah on to the dry land.

## The reluctant prophet does as he is told

**3** Yahweh's word came to Yonah a second time: ²'Set off, go to the great town of

Nineveh and call out to it the thing that I'm going to speak to you.' ³Yonah set off and went to Nineveh in accordance with Yahweh's word. Now Nineveh was an extraordinarily great town, three days walk through. ⁴Yonah started to go through the town, one day's walk. He called out, 'Forty days more, and Nineveh will be overthrown.' ⁵The Ninevites believed God, and called for a fast and put on sack, from the biggest of them to the least of them.

⁶The word reached the king of Nineveh, and he got up from his throne, took off his robe from upon him, covered himself with sack and sat on ash. ⁷He got people to cry out in Nineveh, by the decree of the king and his big people: 'Human being and animal (cattle and flock) are not to taste anything. They're not to pasture; they're not to drink water. ⁸They're to cover themselves in sack, human being and animal, and call on God strongly. They're to turn, each one from his bad way and from the violence that's in their fists. ⁹Who knows, God may turn back and relent, turn back from his anger, and we may not perish.'

¹⁰God saw their actions, that they turned back from their bad way, and God relented of the bad thing that he had spoken about doing to them. He didn't do it.

**4** But it seemed bad to Yonah, a very bad thing. He was enraged.

## I knew you'd do that

²He prayed to Yahweh: 'Oh, Yahweh, isn't this what I said when I was in my country? That's why I acted previously by fleeing to Tarshish, because I knew that you're a God gracious, compassionate, long-tempered, vast in commitment and relenting about something bad. ³So now, Yahweh, please take my life from me, because my dying will be good, better than my living.' ⁴Yahweh said, 'Was your rage good?'

⁵Yonah went out from the town and sat east of the town. He made a bivouac for himself there and sat under it in the shade until he could see what would happen in the town. ⁶Yahweh God provided a qiqayon vine and it grew up over Yonah so as to be a shade over his head to rescue him from what was bad for him. Yonah rejoiced greatly about the qiqayon. ⁷But God provided a worm when dawn came up next day and it struck down the qiqayon, and it withered; ⁸and when the sun rose, God provided a scorching east wind, and the sun struck down on Yonah's head. He grew faint and asked for his life, that he might die. He said, 'My dying will be good, better than my living.'

⁹God said to Yonah, 'Was your rage good about the qiqayon?' He said, 'It was good, my rage, to the point of death.' ¹⁰Yahweh said, 'You pitied the qiqayon, for which you didn't labour and which you didn't grow, which came into existence overnight and perished overnight. ¹¹Shouldn't I pity the great town of Nineveh, in which there are more than 120,000 human beings who don't know their right hand from their left, and many animals?'

# MICAH

Micah [Mikah] was a contemporary of Isaiah who worked in Jerusalem at about the same time and brought a similar message, though he originally came from the country rather than from the capital. Like Isaiah, he declares that Yahweh intends to take action against Jerusalem because of the way people with power and resources, and spiritual leaders, take advantage of their position. Like Isaiah, he has to deal with people who don't want prophets to say the kind of thing that as a prophet he says. But like Isaiah, he also looks beyond the coming disaster to Yahweh's restoring the city. It is he who asks what God requires, and answers the question in a powerful formulation (6.8).

## *Disaster reaches the very gateways*

**1** Yahweh's word that came to Mikah the Morashtite in the days of Yotam, Ahaz and Yehizqiyyah, kings of Yehudah, which he beheld concerning Shomron [Samaria] and Yerushalaim.

²Listen, peoples, all of you,
  heed, earth and what fills it,
So that the Lord Yahweh may be a witness against
    you,
  the Lord from his sacred palace.
³Because there – Yahweh is going to come out
    from his place,
  come down and tread on earth's heights.
⁴The mountains will melt beneath him,
  the vales split,
Like wax before the fire,
  like water propelled down a slope.

⁵All this is for Ya'aqob's [Jacob's] rebellion,
  for the household of Yisra'el's wrongdoings.
What is Ya'aqob's rebellion – it's Shomron, isn't it;
  and what is Yehudah's great shrine – it's
    Yerushalaim, isn't it.
⁶I shall make Shomron into a ruin in open country,
  plantations for a vineyard.
I shall propel its stones into the ravine,
  expose its foundations.
⁷All its images will be smashed,
  all its 'gifts' burned in fire.
All its idols I shall make into desolation.
  because it collected them from a whore's 'gift',
  and they will go back as a whore's 'gift'.

⁸Because of this I shall lament and howl,
  I shall go barefoot and stripped.
I shall make lament like the jackals,
  mourning like the ostriches.
⁹Because its wound is grave,
  because it's come right to Yehudah.
It's reached right to my people's gateway,
  right to Yerushalaim.
¹⁰Don't tell it in Gat, don't cry at all;
  in Bet Le'aprah roll in earth [*apar*].
¹¹Pass on,
  you inhabitants of Shapir, naked in shame;
The inhabitants of Tsa'anan
  have not gone out.
Bet Etsel is in lamentation;
  it will take its support from you.

¹²Because the inhabitants of Marot
  are sick for something good.
Because bad fortune has come down from
    Yahweh
  to Yerushalaim's gateway.
¹³Hitch the chariot to the steed,
  inhabitants of Lakish.
It was the beginning of wrongdoing for Miss
    Tsiyyon [Zion],
  because Yisra'el's rebellions were found in
    you.
¹⁴Therefore you will give parting gifts
  to Moreshet Gat.
The houses of Akzib will be a deception [*akzab*]
  to Yisra'el's kings.
¹⁵'I shall yet bring a dispossessor to you,
  inhabitants of Mareshah.
Yisra'el's splendour
  will come as far as Adullam.
¹⁶Shave your head, cut off your hair,
  for the children in whom you delighted.
Extend the shaving of your head like an eagle,
  because they've gone into exile from you.'

## *Don't preach?*

**2** Hey, you people thinking up trouble,
  doing something bad on their beds.
At morning light they do it,
  because it's in the power of their hand.
²They desire fields and steal them –
  houses, and take them.
They defraud a man and his household,
  an individual and his domain.

³Therefore Yahweh has said this:

Here am I, thinking up a bad fate for this kin-
    group
  that you won't move your neck away from.
You won't walk tall,
  because it will be a bad time.

⁴On that day,
  someone will lift up a poem against you,
  he'll wail with a wail, a wailing.
He's saying, 'We are destroyed, destroyed,
  he exchanges my people's share.
Aagh, he removes it from me,
  he shares out our fields to someone who turns
    away.'

⁵Therefore there will be no one for you
   casting the cord by lot
   in Yahweh's congregation.

⁶'Don't preach,' they preach,
   'people are not to preach about these things.
Disgrace won't turn away
   ⁷(should it be said, Ya'aqob's household?).
Has Yahweh's temper become short,
   are these things his acts?'
My words are good, aren't they,
   with someone who walks upright.
⁸But just now my people rises up as an enemy;
   you strip the mantle off the front of the coat
From people passing by with confidence,
   turning back from battle.
⁹The women among my people –
   you drive her out from the household in which
      she delights.
From her infants
   you take my glory permanently.
¹⁰Set off, go,
   because this won't be a place to settle,
On account of defilement that will destroy
   with a grave destruction.
¹¹If someone were going about
   with wind and deceptive falsehood,
'I shall preach to you about wine and about liquor',
   he'd be this people's preacher.

## Prophets who lead astray

¹²I shall definitely gather Ya'aqob, all of you,
   I shall definitely collect what remains of Yisra'el.
I shall put them together like a sheep in a fold;
   like a flock in the middle of its pasture,
It will be noisy with people;
   ¹³one who breaks out in front of them is going
      up.
They're breaking out, passing through the
      gateway,
   going out through it.
Their king passes through before them,
   Yahweh at their head.

3 I said, 'Listen, please, heads of Ya'aqob,
   rulers of Yisra'el's household:
It's for you to know how to exercise authority,
   isn't it,
   ²people who are hostile to what is good and
      loyal to what is bad,

Who tear the skin from on my people,
   their flesh from on their bones,
³Who eat my people's flesh
   and strip off their skin from on them,
Break up their bones,
   cut them up as in a pan,
   like meat inside a pot.'
⁴Then they will cry out to Yahweh,
   but he will not answer them.
He will hide his face from them at that time,
   as they've acted badly in their practices.

⁵Yahweh has said this:

About the prophets who lead my people astray,
   who chew with their teeth and call out that
      things will be well,
But someone who puts nothing in their mouths –
   they declare a sacred battle against him.
⁶Therefore there will be night for you, without
      vision,
   darkness for you, without divination.
The sun will set for the prophets,
   the day will be dark for them.
⁷The seers will be ashamed,
   the diviners confounded,
All of them will cover over their lip,
   because there's no answer from God.
⁸But as for me, I'm full of energy, with Yahweh's
      wind,
   and strong authority,
To tell Ya'aqob about its rebellion,
   Yisra'el about its wrongdoing.

## The new Jerusalem

⁹Listen to this, please,
   heads of Ya'aqob's household,
   rulers of Yisra'el's household,
You who take offence at the exercise of authority,
   and make what is straight crooked,
¹⁰One who builds Tsiyyon with bloodshed,
   Yerushalaim with evil.
¹¹Its heads exercise authority for a bribe,
   its priests teach for a fee.
Its prophets divine for money,
   but lean on Yahweh:
'Yahweh is among us, isn't he,
   bad fortune won't come upon us.'
¹²Therefore, on account of you,
   Tsiyyon will be a field that is ploughed.

Yerushalaim will become ruins,
  the house's mount a great shrine in a forest.

**4** But at the end of the time
  the mountain of Yahweh's house will be
Established at the head of the mountains,
  elevated above the hills.
Peoples will stream to it;
  ²many nations will go and say,
'Come, let's go up to Yahweh's mountain,
  to the house of Ya'aqob's God,
So he may teach us in his ways
  and we may walk in his paths.'
Because instruction will go out from Tsiyyon,
  Yahweh's word from Yerushalaim.
³He will decide between many peoples
  and issue reproof for numerous nations, even
    far away.
They'll beat their swords into hoes,
  their spears into pruning hooks.
Nation won't take up sword against nation;
  they will no more learn about battle.
⁴They will sit, each person
  under his vine and under his fig tree,
With no one disturbing –
  because the mouth of Yahweh of Armies has
    spoken.
⁵Because all the peoples walk,
  each in the name of its god,
But we ourselves will walk
  in the name of Yahweh our God lastingly and
    permanently.

⁶On that day (Yahweh's declaration):

I shall gather the lame, collect the ones driven out,
  and those to whom I've done something bad.
⁷I shall turn the lame into a remainder,
  the outcast into a numerous nation.
Yahweh will reign over them on Mount Tsiyyon
  from now and permanently.
⁸And you, watchtower of the flock,
  citadel, Miss Tsiyyon,
To you will arrive and come
  the former rule, the kingship of Miss
    Yerushalaim.

*Is there no king in you?*

⁹Now, why do you issue a shout,
  is there not a king in you?

Has your counsellor perished,
  that writhing has taken strong hold of you like
    a woman giving birth?
¹⁰Writhe and scream,
  Miss Tsiyyon, like a woman giving birth.
Because you will now go out from the township
  and dwell in the open country.
You will come as far as Babel,
  but there you will be rescued.
There Yahweh will restore you
  from the fist of your enemies.

¹¹But now many nations
  have gathered against you.
They're saying, 'It shall be profaned,
  our eye shall behold Tsiyyon.'
¹²But those people don't know
  Yahweh's intentions.
They don't understand his plan,
  that he's gathered them like sheaves on the
    threshing-floor.
¹³Rise up, thresh, Miss Tsiyyon,
  because I shall make your horn iron.
I shall make your hoofs copper,
  and you will crush many peoples.
They will devote their dishonest gain to Yahweh,
  their resources to the Lord of the entire earth.

**5** Now, you may form a gang, Miss Gang –
  someone has laid siege to us.
They strike down Yisra'el's authority
  on the cheek with a club.
²But you, Bet-lehem in Ephratah,
  small to be among Yehudah's clans,
From you will emerge for me
  someone to be a ruler in Yisra'el
  whose emerging is of old, of ancient days.
³Therefore he will give them up until the time
  when the one who is going to give birth has
    given birth,
And those who are left of his brothers
  come back to the Yisra'elites.
⁴He will stand and shepherd with Yahweh's
    vigour,
  in the majesty of the name of Yahweh his God.
They will live, because now he'll be great, as far as
    the ends of the earth,
  ⁵and this will mean things are well.
Ashshur, when it comes into our country,
  when it treads through our citadels:
We will set up over it seven shepherds,
  eight people as leaders.

⁶They will shepherd the country of Ashshur with
    the sword,
    the country of Nimrod with its entrances.
He will rescue us from Ashshur when it comes
    into our country,
    when it treads through our territory.

## What God looks for

⁷Ya'aqob's remainder will become,
    among many peoples,
Like dew from Yahweh,
    like showers on grass,
Which don't wait for people,
    don't look to human beings.
⁸Ya'aqob's remainder will become, among the
    nations,
    among many peoples,
Like a lion among the animals in the forest,
    like a cougar among the flocks of sheep,
Which, if it passes by, tramples and mauls,
    with no one to rescue.
⁹Your hand will rise over your adversaries,
    and all your enemies will be cut off.

¹⁰On that day (Yahweh's declaration):

I shall cut down your horses from among you
    and obliterate your chariots.
¹¹I shall cut down the towns in your country,
    and tear down all your fortresses.
¹²I shall cut down the charms from your hand,
    and you will have no chanters.
¹³I shall cut down your images
    and your pillars from among you.
You will not bow low any more
    to something made by your hands.
¹⁴I shall uproot your totem poles from among you
    and annihilate your towns.
¹⁵But I shall effect redress in anger and wrath
    on the nations that have not listened.

**6** Listen, please, to what Yahweh has said:

Get up, argue with the mountains;
    the hills must listen to your voice.
²Listen to Yahweh's argument, mountains,
    enduring ones, earth's foundations.
Because Yahweh has an argument with his people,
    with Yisra'el he issues a reproof.
³My people, what have I done to you,

how have I wearied you? – avow against me.
⁴Because I got you up out of the country of
    Misrayim [Egypt],
    redeemed you from a household of servants.
I sent before you
    Mosheh [Moses], Aharon [Aaron] and
    Miryam.
⁵My people, please be mindful
    of what Balaq king of Mo'ab counselled,
    and what Bil'am [Balaam] ben Be'or avowed
    with him,
From Acacias as far as Gilgal,
    for the sake of acknowledging Yahweh's faithful
    acts.'

⁶By what means shall I meet Yahweh,
    bow down to God on High?
Shall I meet him by means of burnt offerings,
    bullocks a year old?
⁷Would Yahweh accept thousands of rams,
    in myriads of streams of oil?
Should I give my firstborn for my rebellion,
    the fruit of my body for my own wrongdoing?
⁸He has told you, people, what is good,
    what Yahweh requires from you:
Rather, exercising authority and being loyal to
    commitment,
    and being diffident in how you walk with your
    God.

## Like the gleanings

⁹The voice of Yahweh calls to the town;
    awe for your name is good sense.
Listen to the club
    and the one who set it ¹⁰still.
'Shall I forget the faithless household,
    the faithless storehouses,
    the condemned short measure?
¹¹Would I be clean with faithless scales,
    with a bag of false weights? –
¹²Whose rich people are full of violence,
    whose inhabitants speak falsehood,
    and their tongue is deceit in their mouths?

¹³So I myself am indeed making you sick in
    striking you down,
    desolating you for your wrongdoings.
¹⁴You – you will eat but not be full,
    with your emptiness inside you.
You'll displace, but not save,

and what you save I shall give to the sword.
¹⁵You – you'll sow but not harvest;
    you – you'll tread olives, but not rub with oil,
    and grapes, but not drink wine.
¹⁶You've kept Omri's laws,
    every practice of Ah'ab's household.
You've walked by their policies,
    for the sake of my making you a desolation,
Your inhabitants a hissing,
    and you will bear the reviling of my people.'

**7** Aagh, me, because I've become
    like the gatherings of summer fruit,
    like the gleanings of the vintage.
There's no cluster to eat,
    or early fig that my appetite could fancy.
²The committed person has perished from the
      country,
    there's no one upright among the people.
All of them lie in wait for blood;
    one person hunts his brother with a net.
³Both fists are on what is bad, to do it well:
    the official asking, and the authority, with pay,
The big man speaking
    his appetite's desire, and they weave it together.
⁴The good one among them is like a briar,
    the most upright worse than a thorn hedge.
The day your lookouts described,
    the day when you're attended to, is going to
      come;
    now the disarray they described will happen.
⁵Don't believe a neighbour,
    don't rely on a friend.
From the one who sleeps in your embrace
    guard the opening of your mouth.
⁶Because son acts villainously to father,
    daughter rises up against her mother,
Daughter-in-law against her mother-in-law;
    a person's enemies are the people in his
      household.
⁷But I myself will look to Yahweh,
    I shall wait for my God who delivers me;
    my God will listen to me.

*Lament, prayer, expectation and worship for
the city*

⁸Don't rejoice over me, my enemy;
    when I've fallen, I'm getting up.
When I sit in darkness,
    Yahweh will be my light.

⁹I shall carry Yahweh's wrath
    when I've done wrong to him,
Until he gives judgement for me
    and exercises authority for me.
He will get me out into the light,
    I shall see his faithfulness,
¹⁰My enemy will see,
    and shame will cover it,
The one who says to me,
    'Where is he, Yahweh, your God?'
My eyes will look on it;
    now it'll be for trampling
    like mud in the streets.
¹¹A day for building up your walls –
    that will be a day when your boundary will be
      far away.
¹²That day one will come to you
    from Ashshur and the towns of Misrayim,
From Misrayim as far as the River,
    to sea from sea, to mountain from
      mountain.
¹³But the earth will become a desolation because
    of its inhabitants,
    as the fruit of their practices.

¹⁴Pasture your people with your club,
    the flock that's your domain,
Dwelling by itself in a forest
    in the middle of farmland.
May they pasture in Bashan and Gil'ad
    as in days of old,
    ¹⁵as in the days when you got out of the country
      of Misrayim.

'When I show it my wonders, ¹⁶nations will see
    and be ashamed of all their strength.
They'll put their hand to their mouth,
    their ears will go deaf.
¹⁷They'll lick earth like a snake,
    like things that crawl on the ground.'

May they come trembling out of their
    strongholds
    to Yahweh our God,
    may they be in dread and awe of you.
¹⁸Who is a God like you, one who carries
    waywardness,
    and passes over rebellion for the remainder of
      his domain.
He doesn't keep strong hold of his anger
    permanently,
    because he delights in commitment;

¹⁹When he has compassion on us again, he'll
   trample on our wayward acts;
   he'll throw all our wrongdoings into the depths
    of the sea.

²⁰You will show truthfulness to Ya'aqob,
   commitment to Abraham,
   as you swore to our ancestors from days of
    old.

# NAHUM

One can set Nahum, Habakkuk and Zephaniah alongside Jeremiah, in that they lived a century later than Amos, Hosea and Micah, in the time when Assyria was succeeded by Babylon as the world power. Nahum's vocation was to encourage Jerusalem when it was still under the domination of Assyria with its capital in Nineveh, by promising that Nineveh would be put down. Yahweh's promise through Nahum was fulfilled when Nineveh fell to the Babylonians in 612 BC. But there are few concrete references to Nineveh, so the promises (or warnings) can apply to other great imperial cities such as Babylon – or to Jerusalem itself.

## Yahweh the passionate God

**1** The pronouncement about Nineveh, the document with the vision of Nahum the Elqoshite.

[2]Yahweh is a God who is passionate and takes redress;
  Yahweh takes redress and is a possessor of wrath.
Yahweh takes redress on his adversaries,
  maintains it towards his enemies.
[3]Yahweh is long-tempered but big in energy,
  and certainly doesn't treat people as free of guilt.
Yahweh – his way is in whirlwind and in storm,
  the cloud is the dust from his feet.
[4]He reprimands the sea and withers it,
  dries up all the rivers.
Bashan and Carmel languish,
  Lebanon's blossom languishes.
[5]Mountains quake because of him,
  the hills melt.
The earth lifts from before him,
  the world and all the people who live in it.
[6]Before his condemnation, who can stand,
  and who can rise against his angry burning? –
His wrath pours out like fire,
  and crags shatter because of him.
[7]Yahweh is good, a stronghold on the day of pressure,
  and he acknowledges people who take shelter with him.
[8]With a flood passing
  he makes an end of [the city's] place,
He pursues his enemies into darkness;
  [9]what do you think up for Yahweh?
He makes an end;
  pressure doesn't rise twice.
[10]Because they're tangled among thorns,
  and drunk as with their drink,
  they're consumed like straw that is fully dry.

[11]From you [as a city] has gone out
  one who thinks up something bad against Yahweh,
  one who counsels wickedness.

[12]Yahweh has said this:

If they are allied and thus are many,
  even thus they're cut down and he passes away;

Whereas I afflicted you, I shall afflict you no more.
  [13]but now I shall break its yoke from on you,
tear off your shackles.

[14]Yahweh has given an order against you:
  nothing more from your name will be sown.
From your gods' house I shall cut off
  carved image and cast image.
I shall make your grave,
  because you are slight.
[15]There, on the mountains are the feet of a herald,
  letting people hear of well-being.
Observe your festival, Yehudah,
  make good your pledges.
Because he will no more pass through you:
  the scoundrel, all of him, is being cut off.

## The empire writes back

**2** A shatterer has gone up against you –
  guard the ramparts.
Watch the road, strengthen your hips,
  firm up your energy all you can.
[2]Because Yahweh is restoring
  Ya'aqob's [Jacob's] majesty like Yisra'el's majesty.
Because wasters have wasted them,
  devastated their branches.

[3]His strong men's shield is painted red,
  the men in the force clad in scarlet.
The chariotry is with flashing fire on the day it's made ready,
  the junipers are brandished.
[4]In the streets the chariotry race,
  they rush about in the squares,
Their appearance like torches,
  they speed like lightning streaks.
[5]Though he calls to mind his august men, they collapse as they go;
  they hurry to its wall, the shelter is made ready.
[6]The river gates open, the palace melts;
  [7]it's decreed: it's exiled, it's taken up.
Its handmaids lament like the voice of doves,
  beating on their chests.
[8]Nineveh was like a pool of water of old,
  but they're fleeing.
'Stop, stop,'
  but no one can turn them.

⁹Plunder silver, plunder gold,
 there's no limit to the things prepared,
 the splendour from all the things that people
  hold in high regard.

¹⁰Emptiness, just emptiness, waste;
 the mind melts, the knees knock.
All hips tremble,
 the faces of all of them have collected a
  flush.
¹¹Where is the lions' abode,
 the pasture for the cougars,
Where the lion walked,
 the lioness there,
The lion's cub, with no one disturbing,
 ¹²the lion tearing enough for its cubs,
And strangling for its lionesses –
 it filled its lairs with prey, its abodes with
  prey?
¹³Here am I towards you (a declaration of Yahweh
 of Armies):
 I shall burn up its chariotry in smoke.
The sword will consume your cougars;
 I shall cut off your prey from the earth.
Your envoys' voice
 will no more be listened to.

3 Hey, town of bloodshed,
 all of it deception,
Full of plunder,
 where prey doesn't depart.
²The sound of a whip,
 the sound of the rumble of a wheel,
A horse galloping,
 a chariot jumping,
³Cavalry going up, sword flashing,
 spear glittering, a multitude run through,
A heap of carcases, no end of the corpses,
 people collapse over their corpses.

## The invincible falls

⁴Because of the dimensions of the whore's
 whorings,
 the well-favoured expert in charms,
Who sells nations with her whorings,
 kin-groups with her charms,
⁵Here am I towards you (a declaration of Yahweh
 of Armies):
 I shall expose your skirts over your face.
I shall show the nations your nakedness,
 kingdoms your slighting.

⁶I shall throw abominations over you,
 demean you and make a spectacle of you;
⁷All who see you will flee from you
 and say, 'Nineveh is destroyed!
Who will mourn for her,
 where shall I seek for people to comfort
  her?'

⁸Are you better than Thebes of Amon,
 which was sitting on the Ye'or [Nile],
Water surrounding it,
 whose rampart was the sea, its wall made from
  the sea?
⁹Numerous Kush [Sudan]
 and Misrayim [Egypt] without end,
Put and the Lubites
 were your help.
¹⁰Even it was for exile, it went into captivity;
 even its babies were smashed at the head of
  every street.
For its honourable men people threw lots,
 and all its big people were bound in chains.
¹¹Even you will become drunk, you will be in
  hiding;
 even you will seek a refuge from the enemy.
¹²All your fortresses are fig trees, with the first
  fruits;
 if people shake them, they fall into the mouth
  of an eater.
¹³There, your company is women within you,
 to your enemies they are wide open,
The gateways of your country;
 fire is consuming your gate-bars.

¹⁴Draw siege water for yourself,
 strengthen your fortresses,
Tread the clay, trample the mud,
 take strong hold of the brick mould.
¹⁵Fire will consume you there,
 the sword will cut you off, consume you like the
  grasshopper.
Multiply like the grasshopper,
 multiply like the locust.
¹⁶You made your merchants more than the stars
 in the heavens;
 the grasshopper strips and flies.
¹⁷Your guards are like locusts,
 your officials like a pile of grubs,
That settle on walls
 on a cold day.
When the sun comes out, they flee;
 their place, where they are, isn't known.

¹⁸Your shepherds have gone to sleep, king of
    Ashshur;
  your august people settle down.
Your people have scattered over the
    mountains,
  and there's no one collecting them.

¹⁹There's no healing for your break;
  your wound is severe.
All who hear the report of you
  clap the palm of a hand at you,
Because to whom has bad fortune from you
  not passed, continually?

# HABAKKUK

The bulk of Habakkuk [Habaqquq] takes the form of questions and answers between the prophet and Yahweh. Like other prophets, Habakkuk is horrified at what he sees in Judah and he wants to know what Yahweh intends to do about it. Yahweh declares that he intends to bring the Babylonians to act against Judah. This idea horrifies Habakkuk; Yahweh adds that the Babylonians will get their own comeuppance in due course. The final chapter is a vision of Yahweh's coming to take action in this connection.

## Habaqquq protests, Yahweh answers, Habaqquq protests again

**1** The pronouncement that Habaqquq the prophet beheld.

²How long have I called for help, Yahweh,
    and you don't listen?
I cry out to you, 'Violence',
    but you don't deliver.
³Why do you make me see trouble,
    why do you look at oppression?
Destruction and violence are in front of me;
    there's been argument, and strife arises.
⁴Therefore instruction ceases,
    the exercise of authority never issues.
Because the faithless person encircles the faithful;
    therefore the exercise of authority issues
        deformed.

⁵Watch the nations,
    look, and be utterly astounded.
Because I'm going to do something in your days
    that you wouldn't believe when it was told.
⁶Because here am I, I'm going to raise up the
        Kasdites,
    the bitter, quick-moving nation,
That goes to the far reaches of the earth,
    to possess dwellings that don't belong to it.
⁷It's terrible and fearful;
    from itself its authority and its dignity issues.
⁸Its horses are swifter than leopards,
    keener than wolves at evening;
Its steeds gallop;
    its steeds come from afar.
They fly like an eagle hastening to devour;
    ⁹all of it comes for violence.
The thrust of their faces is forwards;
    it gathers captives like sand.
¹⁰It derides kings,
    rulers are fun to it.
It makes fun of every fortress,
    it fortifies earth and captures it.
¹¹Then the wind sweeps on and passes through,
    and it becomes guilty, because its energy is its
        god.

¹²You are from of old, Yahweh, are you not;
    my God, my sacredness, you don't die.
Yahweh, you've made it an authority;
    my crag, you have founded it to reprove.
¹³Your eyes are too pure to watch bad dealing,

you cannot look at oppression.
Why do you look at people who break faith –
        stay still,
    when the faithless person swallows one who is
        more faithful than him?
¹⁴You made humanity like the fish in the sea,
    like moving things that have no ruler.
¹⁵He's got all of it up with a hook,
    he drags it away in his net,
Gathers it in his trawl;
    that's why he rejoices and celebrates.
¹⁶That's why he sacrifices to his net,
    burns incense to his trawl.
Because through them his share is rich,
    his food luxuriant.
¹⁷Is he therefore to empty his net
    and continually to kill nations,
        not pity?

## Yahweh answers again

**2** On my watch I shall take my stand,
    station myself at my post.
I shall look to see what he'll speak through me,
    what I shall say back to the reproof that comes
        to me.

²Yahweh answered me:

Write the vision, make it plain on tablets,
    in order that someone who reads it out can run
        with it.
³Because there's yet a vision about a set time,
    it testifies about the end, and it won't deceive.
If it's slow, wait for it,
    because it will definitely come, it won't lag.
⁴There, his appetite within him
    is swollen, not upright,
    whereas the faithful person will live by his
        truthfulness.
⁵How much more does wine betray
    the arrogant man.
He won't abide,
    one who's let his appetite be as wide as She'ol.
The one who is like death,
    but he isn't full,
The one who gathers to himself all the nations,
    collects to himself all the peoples.
⁶These people, all of them,
    will raise a poem about him, won't they,
    mocking, conundrums, about him.

Hey, one who accumulates what's not his – how
long,
   one who makes debts heavy for himself?
⁷Your creditors will suddenly arise, won't they,
   the people who make you tremble will wake up,
   and you will turn into plunder for them.
⁸Because you're one who despoiled many nations,
   all that's left of the peoples will despoil you,
On account of the human bloodshed and the
      violence against the country,
   the township and all the people who live in it.

⁹Hey, one who makes dishonest gain,
   a bad thing for his household,
To set his nest on high,
   to escape from the fist of bad fortune.
¹⁰You've counselled shame for your household,
   cutting off many peoples and doing wrong to
      yourself.
¹¹Because a stone will cry out from a wall,
   and the beam from the wood will answer it.

¹²Hey, one who builds a town through bloodshed
   who establishes a township through evil
¹³(there, it's from Yahweh of Armies, isn't it?),
And peoples laboured for the fire,
   nations toiled for emptiness.
¹⁴Because the earth will be full
   so as to acknowledge Yahweh's splendour,
   as the water covers over the sea.

## The confrontation

¹⁵Hey, one who makes his neighbour drink,
   pouring out your wrath and your drunken anger,
   in order to look at their naked bodies.
¹⁶You're getting full of slighting rather than of
      splendour;
   drink, and show your foreskin, you too.
The chalice in Yahweh's right hand
   will come round to you,
   with slighting in place of your splendour.

¹⁷Because your violence to Lebanon will cover you,
   your destruction of animals, which terrifies them,
On account of human bloodshed and violence to
      the earth,
   the township and all who live in it.
¹⁸What use is a carved image when its carver has
      shaped it,
   an image, which teaches falsehood,

When the one who shaped it relies on it,
   in making dumb non-entities?

¹⁹Hey, one who says to wood, 'Wake up',
   'Get up', to dumb stone,
   so it may teach.
There, it's cased in gold and silver,
   but there isn't any breath within it.
²⁰But Yahweh is in his sacred palace –
   be silent before him, all the earth.

**3** A plea by Habaqquq the prophet; on
'Laments'.

²Yahweh, I've heard a report of you,
   I am in awe, Yahweh, of your action.
Within the years, bring it to life;
   within the years, cause it to be acknowledged;
   in the turmoil, be mindful of compassion.

³God comes from Teman,
   the sacred one from Mount Pa'ran. *(Rise)*
His majesty has covered the heavens,
   his praise has filled the earth.
⁴His brightness comes like dawn,
   its rays from his hand,
   and there is the hiding place of his vigour.
⁵Before him epidemic comes,
   plague comes out at his feet.
⁶He has stood and shaken the earth;
   he has looked, and agitated nations.
Ancient mountains have shattered,
   age-old hills sunk down.
The age-old ways are his,
   ⁷in place of the trouble that I have seen.
Kushan's tents shake,
   the dwellings of Midyan's country.

## A vision that God must and will turn to reality

⁸Are you wrathful at the Rivers, Yahweh,
   is your anger at the Rivers,
   is your wrath at the Sea,
When you mount on your horses,
   your chariots that bring deliverance?
⁹You totally bare your bow;
   your clubs are sworn, by your word. *(Rise)*
With the Rivers you split the earth;
   ¹⁰when they've seen you, mountains
      writhe.

A torrent of water has passed by,
  the Deep has given its voice.
The sun has raised its hands in the height,
  ¹¹the moon has stood on high.
Your arrows go to give light,
  the flash of your spear to give brightness.
¹²In condemnation you stride the earth,
  in anger you trample nations.
¹³You have gone out for the deliverance of your
    people,
  for the deliverance of your anointed.
You have shattered the head of the faithless
    household,
  laying it bare, foundation to neck. *(Rise)*
¹⁴You have pierced his head with his clubs
  when his strong men were storming out,
To scatter me in their exultation,
  like consuming a humble man in hiding.
¹⁵You have made your way through the sea with
    your horses,
  with a stirring of much water.

¹⁶I heard and my insides quaked,
  at the sound my lips quivered.
Rot comes into my bones;
  in my place I tremble,
While I settle for the day of pressure,
  for the people who invade us to go up.

¹⁷Because the fig tree may not bud,
  and there may be no produce on the
    vines,
The product of the olive may deceive,
  and the fields may not produce food,
Someone may cut off the flock from the fold
  and there may be no cattle in the stalls:
¹⁸Yet I shall exult in Yahweh,
  rejoice in the God who delivers me.
¹⁹The Lord Yahweh is my resource,
  he makes my feet like the deer's,
  enables me to tread on the high places.

  The leader's; with strings.

# ZEPHANIAH

The introduction to Zephaniah [Tsephanyah] makes him contemporary with the early years of Jeremiah's activity, when King Josiah engaged in a reform of Judah's religious life that for a while undid the apostasy of his grandfather Manasseh. The nature of the charges that Zephaniah issues indicates that any reform process is only partly under way. The threat of Yahweh's day thus hangs over Jerusalem, but it also hangs over the world. And the possibility of restoration holds for Jerusalem, and for the rest of the world. His distinctive declaration to Jerusalem in this connection is that Yahweh is 'within you'.

## A people that needs to change

**1** Yahweh's word that came to Tsephanyah
ben Kushi, son of Gedalyah son of
Amaryah son of Hizqiyyah, in the days
of Yoshiyyahu ben Amon, king of Yehudah.

<sup>2</sup>I shall totally gather up everything
from on the face of the ground (Yahweh's
declaration).
<sup>3</sup>I shall gather up human beings and animals;
I shall gather up the birds of the heavens and
the fish of the sea,
and the things that make the faithless collapse.
I shall cut off humanity
from on the face of the ground (Yahweh's
declaration).

<sup>4</sup>I shall stretch out my hand against Yehudah,
and against all the inhabitants of Yerushalaim.
I shall cut off from this place
the remainder of the Master,
the names of the priestlings with the priests,
<sup>5</sup>The people who bow low on the roofs
to the army in the heavens,
Who bow low, who swear, to Yahweh
and swear by Malkam,
<sup>6</sup>Who turn away from following Yahweh
and don't seek Yahweh nor enquire of him.

<sup>7</sup>Silence before the Lord Yahweh,
because Yahweh's day is coming near.
Because Yahweh has prepared a sacrifice,
made sacred the people he called.
<sup>8</sup>On the day of Yahweh's sacrifice
I shall attend to the officials,
To the king's sons,
and to all the people wearing foreign clothing.
<sup>9</sup>I shall attend to all the people who leap on the
threshold
on that day,
Who fill their lord's house
with violence and deceit.

<sup>10</sup>On that day there will be (Yahweh's declaration)
the sound of an outcry from the Fish Gate
A howl from the Mishneh,
a big breaking from the hills.
<sup>11</sup>Howl, you who live in the Maktesh,
because the entire trading people has perished,
all those who weigh out silver have been
cut off.

<sup>12</sup>At that time
I shall search Yerushalaim with lamps.
I shall attend to the people
who are relaxing on their lees,
Who are saying to themselves,
'Yahweh won't do something good and he won't
do something bad.'
<sup>13</sup>Their resources will be for plundering,
their houses will be for desolation.
They will build houses but not live [there],
plant vineyards but not drink their wine.

## Yahweh's day

<sup>14</sup>Yahweh's great day is coming near,
coming near very quickly.
The sound of Yahweh's day is bitter;
the strong man is going to shriek there.
<sup>15</sup>That day will be a day of outburst,
a day of pressure and distress,
A day of desolation and devastation,
a day of darkness and gloom,
A day of cloud and shadow,
<sup>16</sup>a day of horn blast and shout,
Against the fortified towns,
and against the lofty corner towers.
<sup>17</sup>I shall bring pressure to the people, they will
walk like the blind,
because they've done wrong to Yahweh.
Their blood will be poured out like earth,
their marrow like faeces.
<sup>18</sup>Neither their silver nor their gold
will be able to rescue them.
On the day of Yahweh's outburst,
in his passionate fire,
The entire country will be consumed,
because he will make an end, yes, how
terrible,
of all the people who live in the country.

**2** Pile together, pile it,
nation that isn't wanted,
<sup>2</sup>Before the decree's birth,
the day that passes like chaff,
Before Yahweh's angry blazing
doesn't come upon you,
Before Yahweh's angry day
doesn't come upon you.
<sup>3</sup>Seek Yahweh, all you humble people in the
country,
who have implemented his ruling.

Seek faithfulness, seek lowliness;
  perhaps you can hide on Yahweh's angry day.

## Where to look

⁴Because Azzah [Gaza] will become abandoned,
  Ashqelon a desolation.
Ashdod will be dispossessed at midday,
  Eqron uprooted.
⁵Hey, you people who live in the region by the sea,
  the nation of Keretites!
Yahweh's word is against you,
  Kena'an [Canaan], country of the Pelishtites
    [Philistines]!
I shall obliterate you, without inhabitant.
⁶The region by the sea will become abodes,
  shepherds' cisterns, pens for flocks.
⁷It will be a region
  for the remainder of Yehudah's household.
On these they will pasture;
  in Ashqelon's houses they'll lie down in the
    evening.
Because Yahweh their God will attend to them,
  and restore their fortunes.
⁸I have heard Mo'ab's reviling,
  the insults of Ammon,
Who have reviled my people,
  talked big over their territory.
⁹Therefore, as I live
  (a declaration of Yahweh of Armies, Yisra'el's
    God),
Mo'ab will become like Sedom [Sodom],
  the Ammonites like Amorah [Gomorrah]:
The domain of chickweed and a salt-pit,
  desolation permanently.
The remainder of my people will plunder them
  and what is left of my nation will have them as
    a domain.
¹⁰This is what they'll have instead of their majesty,
  because they reviled and talked big
  at the people belonging to Yahweh of Armies.
¹¹Yahweh will be fearsome against them,
  because he's reducing all earth's gods.
All the nations' shores will bow down to him,
  each from its place.
¹²You Kushites [Sudanese], too:
  run through by my sword.
¹³And he'll stretch out his hand against the north,
  and obliterate Ashshur.
He'll make Nineveh a desolation,
  dry like the wilderness.

¹⁴Flocks will lie down in the middle of it,
  every creature in the nation.
Both jackdaw and owl will lodge in its pillars,
  the sound will sing in the windows.
Waste will be on the threshold,
  because the cedar is stripped.
¹⁵This is the exultant town,
  one that sits in confidence,
Saying to itself,
  'I'm the one, there is no other.'
Aagh, it's become a desolation,
  a lair for creatures.
Everyone who passes by it hisses
  and shakes his hand.

## Wait for me

**3** Hey, rebellious and defiled one,
    oppressive town!
²It hasn't listened to a voice,
  it hasn't accepted correction.
It hasn't relied on Yahweh,
  it hasn't come near to its God.
³Its officials within it
  are roaring lions.
Its authorities are wolves at evening;
  they don't gnaw until morning.
⁴Its prophets are arrogant, people who break faith;
  its priests treat what's sacred as ordinary, they
    violate instruction.
⁵Yahweh is faithful within it;
  he doesn't do evil.
Morning by morning he gives his ruling,
  at daybreak he doesn't fail,
  but the evildoer doesn't acknowledge shame.

⁶I am cutting off nations, their corner towers are
    becoming desolate;
  I am wasting their streets, so that no one passes
    through.
Their towns are standing without people,
  with no inhabitant.
⁷I said, 'You'll surely be in awe of me,
  you'll accept correction.'
Then its abode wouldn't be cut off,
  all that I attended to for it.
On the contrary, they've been up early
  and made all their deeds devastating.

⁸Therefore wait for me (Yahweh's declaration),
  for the day when I rise as a witness.

Because it's my ruling to gather nations,
　for me to collect kingdoms,
To pour out on them my condemnation,
　all my angry blazing.
Because in my passionate fire
　the entire earth will be consumed.
⁹Because then I shall transform for the
　　peoples
　purified speech,
So that all of them call on Yahweh's name,
　so that they serve him shoulder to shoulder.
¹⁰From beyond Kush's rivers my suppliants,
　my scattered community, will bring my
　　offering.


## God among us

¹¹On that day,
　you [Yerushalaim] won't be ashamed of all your
　　deeds,
　with which you've rebelled against me.
Because then I shall remove from within you
　the people exulting in your majesty.
You'll no more be very superior
　on my sacred mountain.

¹²I shall leave remaining within you
　a humble, poor people,
　　and they will find shelter in Yahweh's name.
¹³The remainder of Yisra'el won't do wrong,
　and won't speak lies.
There won't be found in their mouth
　a deceitful tongue.
Because they are the ones who will pasture and
　　lie down,
　with no one disturbing.

¹⁴Resound, Miss Tsiyyon [Zion],
　shout, Yisra'el.
Rejoice and exult with all your heart,
　Miss Yerushalaim.
¹⁵Yahweh is turning aside the rulings about you,
　he's turning back your enemy.
Yahweh, Yisra'el's King, is within you;
　you needn't be afraid of bad things any more.

¹⁶On that day it will be said to Yerushalaim:

Don't be afraid, Tsiyyon;
　your hands shouldn't droop.
¹⁷Yahweh your God is within you,
　a strong man who delivers.
He'll celebrate over you with rejoicing,
　he'll hold his peace in his love,
　he'll be glad over you with resounding.
¹⁸The people who grieve on account of the set
　　occasions –
　I'm gathering them from you;
　upon you they've been a burden, a reviling.
¹⁹Here am I, I'm going to deal with all your
　　oppressors
　at that time.
I shall deliver the lame,
　collect the ones driven out.
I shall make them an object of praise and renown
　whose shame was in the entire earth.

²⁰At that time I shall bring you –
　yes, at the time I shall collect you.
Because I shall make you an object of renown and
　　praise
　among all the peoples of the earth,
　when I restore your fortunes before your eyes
　　(Yahweh has said).

# HAGGAI

On conquering Babylon, Cyrus the king of Persia permitted and encouraged Judahites who had been taken into exile there to return to Jerusalem to rebuild the temple. In the short term the work miscarried, and Haggai [Haggay], with whom Zechariah was contemporary, was involved in encouraging the people to take up the work again and complete it, in 520–516. It was apparently his vital role in connection with this crucial event that led to the preserving of his prophecies concerning it. The story, with an account of the role of Haggai and Zechariah, appears in Ezra 1—6.

*Concerning remodelling priorities*

**1** In the second year of Dareyavesh [Darius] the king, in the sixth month, on the first day of the month, Yahweh's word came by means of Haggay the prophet to Zerubbabel ben She'alti'el governor of Yehudah and to Yehoshua ben Yehotsadaq the big priest: ²'Yahweh of Armies has said this: "This people has said, 'The time hasn't come, the time for building Yahweh's house.'"

³Yahweh's word came by means of Haggay the prophet: ⁴'Is it the time for you yourselves to live in your panelled houses, and this house lies waste? ⁵So now Yahweh of Armies has said this: "Apply your mind to your ways. ⁶You've sown much but brought in little. You eat but without having enough. You drink but without getting drunk. You dress but without a person getting warm. And the people who earn wages earn them for a purse with holes."

⁷Yahweh of Armies has said this: "Apply your mind to your ways. ⁸Go up to the highland, bring wood and build the house, and I shall accept it and find honour", Yahweh has said. ⁹"You looked for much, but there – little. You brought it home, and I'd blow on it. On account of what (a declaration of Yahweh of Armies)? On account of my house that lies waste, and you're running each person to his own house. ¹⁰That's why above you the heavens have withheld dew, and the earth has withheld its produce, ¹¹and I've called for drought on the earth, on the mountains, on the grain, on the new wine, on the fresh oil, on all that the ground produces, on human beings, on animals and on all the labour of your fists."

¹²Zerubbabel ben She'alti'el, Yehoshua ben Yehotsadaq the big priest and all the remainder of the people listened to the voice of Yahweh their God, and because of Haggay the prophet, as Yahweh their God sent him. So the people were in awe of Yahweh, ¹³and Haggay, Yahweh's envoy in Yahweh's work, said to the people, 'I am with you (Yahweh's declaration).'

*A new splendour*

¹⁴So Yahweh aroused the spirit of Zerubbabel ben She'alti'el governor of Yehudah, the spirit of Yehoshua ben Yehotsadaq the big priest, and

the spirit of all the remainder of the people, and they came and did work on the house of Yahweh of Armies, their God, ¹⁵ᵃon the twenty-fourth day of the sixth.

**2** ¹⁵ᵇIn the second year of Dareyavesh the king, in the seventh, on the twenty-first of the month, Yahweh's word came by means of Haggay the prophet: ²'Say, please, to Zerubbabel ben She'alti'el governor of Yehudah, and to Yehoshua ben Yehotsadaq the big priest, and to the remainder of the people: ³"Who among you remains who saw this house in its former splendour? How do you see it now? In comparison with it, it's just nothing in your eyes, isn't it.

⁴But now, be strong, Zerubbabel (Yahweh's declaration), be strong, Yehoshua ben Yehotsadaq, big priest, be strong, all you people of the country (Yahweh's declaration). Act, because I am with you (a declaration of Yahweh of Armies), ⁵the thing that I solemnized with you when you got out of Misrayim [Egypt]. My spirit stays among you. Don't be afraid." ⁶Because Yahweh of Armies has said this: "Once more, shortly, I'm going to shake the heavens and the earth, the sea and the dry land. ⁷I shall shake all the nations, and the things held in high regard belonging to all the nations will come. I shall fill this house with splendour (Yahweh of Armies has said). ⁸Mine is the silver and mine is the gold (a declaration of Yahweh of Armies). ⁹The splendour of this later house will be greater than the earlier one (Yahweh of Armies has said). In this place I shall give you well-being (a declaration of Yahweh of Armies)."

*A renewed promise*

¹⁰On the twenty-fourth of the ninth in the second year of Dareyavesh, Yahweh's word came to Haggay the prophet. ¹¹Yahweh of Armies said this: 'Ask the priests for instruction, please: ¹²"If someone carries sacred meat in the fold of his garment and touches bread or stew or wine or oil or any other food with the fold, does it become sacred?"' The priests answered, 'No.' ¹³Haggay said, 'If someone taboo because of a body touches any of these, does it become taboo?' The priests answered, 'It becomes taboo.' ¹⁴Haggay responded, 'So is this

people, so is this nation before me (Yahweh's declaration) and so is the action of their hands. What they present there is taboo.

¹⁵But now, apply your mind, please, from this day and onwards. Before the setting of stone on stone in Yahweh's palace, ¹⁶from when these things happened, someone came to a twenty-measure heap, and there'd be ten; someone came to the wine vat to skim off fifty measures, there'd be twenty. ¹⁷I struck you down with blight, with mildew and with hail, in all the action of your hands, but you were not with me (Yahweh's declaration). ¹⁸Apply your mind, please, from this day and onwards, from the twenty-fourth day of the ninth, from the day when Yahweh's palace was founded. Apply your mind: ¹⁹is there still seed in the barn? Whereas until now the vine, the fig tree, the pomegranate and the olive tree have not borne, from this day I shall bless.'

²⁰Yahweh's word came a second time to Haggay on the twenty-fourth of the month. ²¹"Say to Zerubbabel governor of Yehudah: "I'm going to shake the heavens and the earth, ²²overturn the throne of the kingdoms, destroy the strength of the nations' kingdoms, and overturn chariotry and its drivers. Horses and their riders will come down, each by his brother's sword.

²³On that day (a declaration of Yahweh of Armies), I shall take you, Zerubbabel ben She'alti'el my servant (Yahweh's declaration), and make you like a signet, because I've chosen you (a declaration of Yahweh of Armies).'"

# ZECHARIAH

Zechariah [Zekaryah] was a contemporary of Haggai, associated with him in the story of the rebuilding of the temple in Ezra 1—6. While Haggai was the bad cop who confronted the people about their failure, Zechariah was the good cop who encouraged them with Yahweh's promises in chapters 1—8, a series of visions and exhortations. Zechariah 9—14 comprises a series of prophecies without concrete indications of a context.

## A world at peace

**1** In the eighth month in the second year of Dareyavesh [Darius], Yahweh's word came to Zekaryah ben Berekyah, son of Iddo, the prophet. ²Yahweh felt a great fury with your ancestors. ³You're to say to them, "Yahweh of Armies has said this: 'Turn back to me (a declaration of Yahweh of Armies) and I shall turn back to you (Yahweh of Armies has said). ⁴Don't become like your ancestors, to whom the earlier prophets called out, "Yahweh of Armies has said this: 'Turn back, please, from your bad ways and from your bad practices'", but they didn't listen or heed me (Yahweh's declaration). ⁵Your ancestors: where are they? The prophets: do they live permanently? ⁶Yet my words and my laws that I ordered my servants the prophets: they overtook your ancestors, didn't they, and they turned back and said, "As Yahweh of Armies schemed to do to us in accordance with our ways and with our practices, so he has done with us."'"

⁷On the twenty-fourth day of the eleventh month (i.e. the month of Shebat) in the second year of Dareyavesh, Yahweh's word came to Zekaryah ben Berekyah, son of Iddo:

⁸I saw by night: there, a man riding on a red horse. He was standing among myrtle trees that were in the deep. Behind him were red, brown and white horses. ⁹I said, 'What are these, my lord?' The envoy who was speaking with me said, 'I'll show you what those are.' ¹⁰The man who was standing among the myrtle trees answered, 'These are ones that Yahweh sent to go round in the earth.' ¹¹They answered Yahweh's envoy who was standing among the myrtle trees, 'We've been going round in the earth. There, the entire earth is living quiet.'

## Too peaceful

¹²Yahweh's envoy answered, 'Yahweh of Armies, how long will you not have compassion on Yerushalaim and on Yehudah's towns, which you've been condemning these seventy years?' ¹³Yahweh answered the envoy who was speaking with me with good words, comforting words. ¹⁴The envoy who was speaking with me said to me, 'Call out: "Yahweh of Armies has said

this: 'I have felt a great passion for Yerushalaim and for Tsiyyon [Zion], ¹⁵and I – I have been feeling a great fury with the nations that are peaceful, because I was a bit furious, but they helped it become bad fortune.' ¹⁶Therefore Yahweh has said this: 'I'm turning back to Yerushalaim in compassion. My house will be built up in it (a declaration of Yahweh of Armies), and a cord will be stretched over Yerushalaim.'" ¹⁷Call out further: "Yahweh of Armies has said this: 'My towns will again flow with good things. Yahweh will again comfort Tsiyyon and again choose Yerushalaim.'"

¹⁸I lifted my eyes and looked: there, four horns. ¹⁹I said to the envoy who was speaking with me, 'What are these?' He said to me, 'These are the horns that scattered Yehudah, Yisra'el and Yerushalaim.' ²⁰And Yahweh showed me four smiths. ²¹I said, 'What are these coming to do?' He said, 'These are the horns that scattered Yehudah to such an extent that no one lifted his head. But these have come to disturb them by throwing down the horns of the nations that lifted a horn against the country of Yehudah, to scatter it.'

## You can't measure Yerushalaim (Jerusalem)

**2** I lifted my eyes and looked: there, a man, with a measuring line in his hand. ²I said, 'Where are you going?' He said to me, 'To measure Yerushalaim, to see exactly what is its breadth and its length.' ³But there, the envoy who was speaking with me was going out, and another envoy was going out to meet him. ⁴He said to him, 'Run, speak to that young man: "Yerushalaim will be inhabited as unwalled villages because of the number of people and animals within it. ⁵And I myself shall be for it (Yahweh's declaration) a wall of fire round, and I shall be splendour within it."'

⁶'Hey, hey, flee from the northern country (Yahweh's declaration), because I'm scattering you like the four winds of the heavens (Yahweh's declaration).' ⁷Hey, Tsiyyon, escape, you who live in Miss Babel. ⁸Because Yahweh of Armies has said this (after splendour sent me) regarding the nations who plundered you: the one touching you was touching the apple of his eye. ⁹'Because here am I, I'm going to shake my hand against them. They will become spoil for

their servants.' And you will acknowledge that Yahweh of Armies sent me. [10]'Resound, rejoice, Miss Tsiyyon, because here am I – I'm coming to dwell within you (Yahweh's declaration). [11]Many nations will attach themselves to Yahweh on that day and will become my people, and I shall dwell within you.'

And you will acknowledge that Yahweh sent me to you. [12]And Yahweh will have Yehudah as his domain on the sacred ground, and will again choose Yerushalaim.

[13]Hush, all flesh, before Yahweh, because he has roused himself from his sacred abode.

## Guilt is not the end

**3** He showed me Yehoshua the big priest standing before Yahweh's envoy, and the adversary standing at his right to act as his adversary. [2]Yahweh said to the adversary, 'Yahweh reprimand you, adversary, Yahweh who chose Yerushalaim reprimand you. Isn't this a burning stick snatched from the fire?' [3]Yehoshua was wearing filthy clothes as he was standing before the envoy.

[4]He avowed to the beings who were standing before him, 'Take the filthy clothes off him', and he said to him, 'Look: I've made your waywardness pass on from you, and you may wear fine robes. [5]And I've said, "They should put a pure turban on his head."' They put the pure turban on his head and dressed him in clothes as Yahweh's envoy was standing by.

[6]Yahweh's envoy testified against Yehoshua: [7]'Yahweh of Armies has said this: "If you walk in my ways and keep my charge, you yourself will both judge my house and also keep watch on my courtyards, and I shall give you movement among these who are standing in attendance. [8]Listen, please, Yehoshua, senior priest, you and your fellows who are sitting before you, because they are people who constitute a sign. Because here am I, I'm going to bring my servant, Branch. [9]Because here's the stone that I've put before Yehoshua. On one stone are seven eyes. Here am I, I'm going to make its engraving (a declaration of Yahweh of Armies), and I shall remove this country's waywardness in one day.

[10]On that day (a declaration of Yahweh of Armies) you will call, each person his

neighbour, under his vine and under his fig tree.'"

## A candelabrum and a promise

**4** The envoy who was speaking with me came back and woke me up like someone who wakes up from his sleep. [2]He said to me, 'What are you looking at?' I said, 'I looked, and there – a candelabrum of gold, all of it, with its bowl on top of it, and its seven lamps on it, seven spouts each for the lamps that were on top of it, [3]and two olive trees by it, one to the right of the bowl and one to its left.' [4]I avowed to the envoy who was speaking with me, 'What are these, my lord?' [5]The envoy who was speaking with me answered me, 'Don't you know what these are?' I said, 'No, my lord'. [6]He answered me . . .

'This is Yahweh's word to Zerubbabel: "Not by resources, not by energy, but by my spirit", Yahweh of Armies has said. [7]'Who are you, big mountain, before Zerubbabel? Into flatland. He will take out the top stone, with shouts of "Grace, grace to it!"'

[8]Yahweh's word came to me: [9]'Zerubbabel's hands have founded this house and his hands will finish it off.' And you will acknowledge that Yahweh of Armies sent me to you. [10]Because who despises the day of little things? They will rejoice when they see the metal stone in Zerubbabel's hand.

. . . 'These seven are Yahweh's eyes ranging through the entire earth.' [11]I avowed to him, 'What are these two olive trees on the right of the candelabrum and on its left?' [12]And I avowed to him a second time, 'What are the two ears [of grain] of the olive trees that pour out gold from themselves by means of the two gold pipes?' [13]He said to me, 'Don't you know what these are?' I said, 'No, my lord'. [14]He said, 'These are the two sons of fresh oil who stand by the Lord of the entire earth.'

## A flying scroll and a flying container

**5** I again lifted my eyes and looked – there, a flying scroll. [2]He said to me, 'What are you looking at?' I said, 'I'm looking at a flying scroll. Its length is ten metres and its width five metres.' ³He said to me, 'This is the vow that's going out over the face of the entire country. Because everyone who steals (from this side, according to it) has gone free of guilt, and everyone who swears (from the other side, according to it) has gone free of guilt. ⁴I'm causing it to go out (a declaration of Yahweh of Armies) and it will come into the thief's house and the house of the person who swears by my name for falsehood. It will lodge inside his house and consume it, both its timbers and its stones.'

⁵The envoy who spoke with me went out and said to me, 'Lift up your eyes, please, and look. What's this going out?' ⁶I said, 'What is it?' He said, 'This is the barrel that's going out.' And he said, 'This is their appearance in the entire country.' ⁷And there, a lead disc lifted, and it was a woman sitting inside the barrel. ⁸He said, 'This is Faithlessness.' He thrust her inside the container and thrust the lead disc to its mouth. ⁹I lifted my eyes and looked, and there – two women going out with wind in their wings (they had wings like a stork's wings). They carried the barrel between the earth and the heavens. ¹⁰I said to the envoy who was speaking with me, 'Where are they making the container go?' ¹¹He said to me, 'To build it a house in the country of Shin'ar, which will be established, and it will be settled down there on its established place.'

### Settling Yahweh's spirit and making crowns

**6** I lifted my eyes again and looked, and there – four chariots going out from between two mountains; the mountains were mountains of copper. ²In the first chariot the horses were red, in the second chariot the horses were black, ³in the third chariot the horses were white, in the fourth chariot the horses were dappled, strong.

⁴I avowed to the envoy who was speaking with me, 'What are these, my lord?' ⁵The envoy answered me, 'These are the four winds of the heavens, going out after standing by the Lord of the entire earth.' ⁶The one where the black horses are – they were going out to the northern country. The white left after them. The dappled went out to the southern country.

⁷So the strong went out. When they sought to go, so as to go about through the earth, he said, 'Go, go about through the earth.' So they went about through the earth. ⁸He cried out to me and spoke to me: 'Look, the ones going out to the northern country have settled my spirit in the northern country.'

⁹Yahweh's word came to me: ¹⁰'Receive from the exile community, from Helday, from Tobiyyah and from Yeda'yah, and you yourself are to come on that day, to come to the house of Yo'shiyyah ben Tsephanyah, when they've come from Babel: ¹¹you're to receive gold and silver and make crowns and put them on the head of Yehoshua ben Yehotsadaq the big priest, ¹²and say to him, "Yahweh of Armies has said this: 'There is the man whose name is Branch. From his place he will branch out and build Yahweh's palace. ¹³He's the one who'll build Yahweh's palace. He's the one who'll put on majesty, and sit and rule on his throne. A priest will be by his throne, and there'll be peaceful counsel between the two of them.' ¹⁴For Helem, for Tobiyyah, for Yeda'yah and for Hen ben Tsephanyah, the crowns will be a memorial in Yahweh's palace. ¹⁵Distant people will come and build in Yahweh's palace, and you will acknowledge that Yahweh of Armies sent me to you. It will happen if you really do listen to the voice of Yahweh your God.'"

### Who are you fasting for?

**7** In the fourth year of Dareyavesh the king, Yahweh's word came to Zekaryah, on the fourth of the ninth month, in Kislev. ²Bet-el Sar-ezer and Regem Melek and his men sent to seek Yahweh's goodwill ³by saying to the priests who were at the house of Yahweh of Armies and to the prophets, 'Should I cry in the fifth month, consecrating myself, as I have done these how many years?'

⁴A word from Yahweh of Armies came to me: ⁵'Say to all the people of the country and to the priests, "When you fasted and lamented in the fifth and in the seventh even these seventy years, did you really fast for me? ⁶When you eat and when you drink, it's you who eat and you who drink, isn't it. ⁷They're the words that Yahweh called out by means of the earlier prophets, aren't they, when Yerushalaim

was peopled and peaceful, and its towns round it, and the Negeb and the Lowland were peopled?'"

[8]Yahweh's word came to Zekaryah: [9]Yahweh of Armies has said this: "Exercise truthful authority, exercise commitment and compassion each person with his brother. [10]Don't oppress widow and orphan, alien and humble. Don't think up bad dealings each person against his brother in his mind." [11]But they refused to heed and presented a defiant shoulder. They stopped their ears from listening. [12]They made their mind concrete so as not to listen to the instruction and the words that Yahweh of Armies sent by his spirit by means of the earlier prophets, and great wrath came from Yahweh of Armies. [13]As he called but they didn't listen, "so they'll call and I shall not listen", Yahweh of Armies said. [14]"And I blasted them away to all the nations that they hadn't known. The country was desolate behind them from anyone passing through or coming back. They made a country that was held in high regard into a desolation.'"

## I will make you a blessing

**8** A word from Yahweh of Armies came. [2]Yahweh of Armies has said this: "I feel a great passion for Tsiyyon. I feel a fierce passion for it." [3]Yahweh has said this: "I'm coming back to Tsiyyon and I shall dwell within Yerushalaim. Yerushalaim will be called 'Truthful Town', and the mountain of Yahweh of Armies 'Sacred Mountain.'"

[4]Yahweh of Armies has said this: "Old men and old women will again sit in Yerushalaim's squares, each with his cane in his hand because of the great number of his days. [5]The town's squares will be full of boys and girls having fun in its squares."

[6]Yahweh of Armies has said this: "Because it will be fantastic in the eyes of the remainder of this people in those days, will it also be fantastic in my eyes (a declaration of Yahweh of Armies)?"

[7]Yahweh of Armies has said this: "Here am I, I'm going to deliver my people from the eastern country and from the western country, [8]and bring them, and they will dwell within Yerushalaim. They will be a people for

me and I shall be God for them, in truth and faithfulness."

[9]Yahweh of Armies has said this: "Your hands are to be strong, you who are listening to these words in these days from the mouth of the prophets who [were there] on the day when the house of Yahweh of Armies was founded, for building the palace. [10]Because before those days there were no wages for a human being and there were no wages for an animal. For anyone going out or coming in, there was no peace from the adversary. I set all human beings one against his neighbour. [11]But now I'm not acting towards the remainder of this people as in earlier days (a declaration of Yahweh of Armies), [12]because the sowing will be in peace, the vine will give its fruit, the earth will give its produce, the heavens will give their dew, and I shall let the remainder of this people have all these things as a domain. [13]As you became a slighting among the nations, Yehudah's household and Yisra'el's household, so I shall deliver you and you will become a blessing. Don't be afraid. Your hands are to be strong."

## Make me a blessing

[14]Because Yahweh of Armies has said this: "As I schemed to do something bad to you when your ancestors infuriated me (Yahweh of Armies said) and didn't relent, [15]so I have again schemed in these days to do good to Yerushalaim and to Yehudah's household. Don't be afraid. [16]These are the things that you're to do. Speak the truth each to his neighbour. Exercise authority with truthful authority that makes for peace in your gateways. [17]Don't think up something bad in your mind each person against his neighbour. Don't love a false oath. Because all these are things to which I'm hostile (Yahweh's declaration).'"

[18]The word of Yahweh of Armies came to me. [19]Yahweh of Armies has said this: "The fast of the fourth, the fast of the fifth, the fast of the seventh and the fast of the tenth will become for Yehudah's household celebration and rejoicing, good set occasions. So love truthfulness and peace."

[20]Yahweh of Armies has said this: "Peoples and inhabitants of many towns will yet come, [21]and the inhabitants of one will go to

one another saying, 'Let's go, let's go to seek Yahweh's goodwill and seek Yahweh of Armies. I myself intend to go, yes.' ²²Many peoples will come, numerous nations, to seek Yahweh of Armies in Yerushalaim and to seek Yahweh's goodwill."

²³Yahweh of Armies has said this: "In those days, when ten people from all the nations' tongues will take hold, they'll take hold of the hem of a Yehudahite individual's coat, saying 'We want to go with you, because we've heard that God is with you.'"

## The king on a donkey

# 9 A pronouncement.

Yahweh's word against the country of Hadrak,
　　and Dammeseq [Damascus] its place of settling.
Because people's eye will be towards Yahweh,
　　all Yisra'el's clans.
²Hamat, too, which borders on it;
　　Tsor [Tyre], and Tsidon because it's very smart.
³Tsor has built itself a stronghold,
　　it has heaped up silver like earth,
Gold like the mud in the streets;
　　⁴there, the Lord Yahweh will dispossess it.
He'll strike down its resources at sea;
　　it will be consumed by fire, itself.
⁵Ashqelon will see and be afraid,
　　Azzah [Gaza] will writhe much,
　　and Eqron, because its reliance will have
　　　withered.
King will perish from Azzah,
　　Ashqelon won't be inhabited.
⁶A mongrel will live in Ashdod;
　　I shall cut off the majesty of the Pelishtites
　　　[Philistines].
⁷But I shall remove the blood it has shed from its
　　　mouth,
　　and its abominations from between its teeth.
What remains of it, too, will belong to our God,
　　and become like a clan in Yehudah,
　　while Eqron will be like the Yebusites.
⁸I shall camp for my house as a garrison
　　against anyone passing through or coming
　　　back.
No oppressor will pass through against them
　　again,
　　because now I shall have looked with my eyes.

⁹Celebrate greatly, Miss Tsiyyon;
　　shout, Miss Yerushalaim.
There, your king will come to you;
　　he'll be faithful and one who finds deliverance,
Humble and riding on a donkey,
　　on an ass, the child of a she-ass.
¹⁰I shall cut off chariotry from Ephrayim
　　and horse from Yerushalaim.
The bow of battle will be cut off;
　　he will speak of peace to the nations.
His rule will be from sea to sea,
　　from the River to the ends of the earth.

## Crown jewels glittering on his land

¹¹Yes, you [Yerushalaim], by the blood of your
　　　pact:
　　I'm sending off your captives.
From the pit where there's no water,
　　¹²get back to the fortress, hopeful prisoners.
Yes, today I'm going to announce:
　　I shall give back double to you.
¹³Because I'm directing Yehudah for myself as a
　　　bow,
　　I'm loading Ephrayim.
I shall arouse your sons, Tsiyyon,
　　against your sons, Yavan [Greece],
　　and make you like a strong man's sword.

¹⁴Yahweh – he'll appear over them,
　　his arrow will go out like lightning.
The Lord God will sound on the horn
　　and go in southern hurricanes.
¹⁵Yahweh of Armies will shield over them;
　　sling stones will consume and tread down.
They will drink, make a noise as with wine,
　　be full like a bowl, like the altar's corners.
¹⁶Yahweh our God will deliver them
　　on that day, like a flock, his people.
Because they are crown jewels glittering on his
　　　land,
　　¹⁷because how good they are and how beautiful
　　　they are.
Grain will make the young men flourish,
　　new wine the young women.

# 10 Ask for rain from Yahweh
　　at the time of the spring rain;
Yahweh is the one who sends lightning flashes,
　　gives them a downpour of rain,
　　growth in the fields for each one.

²Because the effigies have spoken trouble,
   the diviners have beheld falsehood.
They speak lying dreams,
   they comfort with hollowness.
Therefore people have strayed like a flock,
   they suffer because there's no shepherd.
³Against the shepherds my anger has blazed,
   I shall attend to the big guys.

Because Yahweh of Armies is attending to his
      flock,
   Yehudah's household.
He will make them
   like his majestic horse in battle.
⁴From it cornerstone, from it tent peg,
   from it battle bow,
From it will go out
   every overseer, together.
⁵They'll be like strong men,
   trampling the mud of the streets, in battle.
They'll do battle, because Yahweh will be with
      them;
   they'll shame the people riding horses.

### Yehudah's household become strong men

⁶So I shall make Yehudah's household strong
      men,
   and I shall deliver Yoseph's household.
I shall restore them, because I've had compassion
      on them;
   they'll be as if I had not rejected them.
Because I am Yahweh,
   their God, and I shall answer them.
⁷Ephrayim will be a veritable strong man;
   their heart will rejoice as with wine.
Their children will see and rejoice;
   their heart will be joyful in Yahweh.
⁸I shall whistle to them and gather them,
   because I have redeemed them.
They will become many, as they were many,
   ⁹though I sowed them among the nations.
In far-off places they will be mindful of me;
   they will live with their children, and come
      back.
¹⁰I shall bring them back from the country of
      Misrayim [Egypt],
   collect them from Ashshur.
Though I bring them to the country of Gil'ad and
      Lebanon,
   room won't be found for them.

¹¹He will pass through the confining sea,
   he will strike down the sea of waves.
All the Ye'or's [Nile's] deeps will dry up,
   and the majesty of Ashshur will be put down.
Misrayim's club will pass away,
   ¹²and I shall make them strong men through
      Yahweh,
   and in his name they'll go about (Yahweh's
      declaration).

# 11
Open your doors, Lebanon,
   so fire can consume your cedars.
²Howl, junipers, because the cedar is falling,
   when the august are being destroyed.
Howl, Bashan oaks,
   because the fortified forest is going down.
³The sound of the shepherds' howling,
   because their eminence is destroyed.
The sound of the lions' roar,
   because Yarden's [Jordan's] majesty is
      destroyed.

### Lying, neglectful, loathsome and stupid shepherds

⁴Yahweh my God said this: 'Tend the flock to be killed, ⁵whose acquirers will kill them and won't be liable, whose sellers will say, "Yahweh be blessed! I shall be rich", and whose shepherds won't have pity on them. ⁶Because I shall no more have pity on the country's inhabitants (Yahweh's declaration). There, I'm going to make people vulnerable, each to his neighbour's hand and to his king's hand. They will crush the country, and I shall not rescue it from their hand.'
⁷So I pastured the sheep to be killed, therefore the lowliest of the flock. I got myself two staffs, I called one 'Beauty', and the other I called 'Binders', and I pastured the sheep. ⁸I disposed of the three shepherds in one month. With my whole being I lost patience with them, and with their whole being they loathed me, too. ⁹So I said, 'I shall not pasture you. The one who dies may die and the one who gets disposed of may get disposed of, and the ones who remain, each may eat the flesh of her neighbour.'
¹⁰I got my staff 'Beauty' and broke it, contravening my pact that I had solemnized with all the peoples. ¹¹So it was contravened

on that day, and the lowliest of the sheep, who were keeping watch towards me, thus acknowledged that it was Yahweh's word. [12]I said to them, 'If it's good in your eyes, give me my pay; if not, withhold it.' They weighed out my pay, thirty silver pieces. [13]Yahweh said to me, 'Throw it to the potter' (the worthy magnificence that I was worth to them). So I took the thirty silver pieces and threw them to the potter in Yahweh's house. [14]And I broke my second staff, 'Binders', to contravene the brotherhood between Yehudah and Yisra'el.

[15]Yahweh said to me again, 'Get yourself the implements of a stupid shepherd. [16]Because here I am, I'm going to raise up a shepherd in the country who won't attend to the ones who are disposed of or seek the young one or heal the injured or sustain the one who stands firm, but will eat the flesh of the fat one and tear off their hoofs.

[17]Hey, non-entity shepherds,
    abandoning the flock:
A sword on your arm
    and on your right eye!
May his arm quite wither,
    his right eye go quite blind!'

## A chalice that causes reeling

**12** A pronouncement. Yahweh's word concerning Yisra'el.

A declaration of Yahweh,
    the one who stretched out the heavens,
Who founded the earth,
    who shaped the spirit of humanity within it.

[2]'There, I'm going to make Yerushalaim a chalice that causes reeling to all the peoples around. It will also be against Yehudah during the siege against Yerushalaim.

[3]On that day, I shall make Yerushalaim a stone hard to lift for all the peoples. All who lift it will seriously injure themselves when all the nations of the earth gather against it.

[4]On that day (Yahweh's declaration), I shall strike down every horse with panic and its rider with madness. Over Yehudah's household I shall open my eyes, but every horse belonging to the peoples I shall strike with blindness.

[5]Yehudah's clans will say to themselves, "Yerushalaim's inhabitants are my strength, through Yahweh of Armies, their God."

[6]On that day, I shall make Yehudah's clans like a firepot among trees, like a fiery torch among sheaves. They will consume all the peoples around, to the right and the left. And Yerushalaim will again live in its place, in Yerushalaim. [7]Yahweh will deliver Yehudah's tents first, so that the glory of David's household and the glory of Yerushalaim's population will not be greater than Yehudah.'

[8]On that day Yahweh will shield over Yerushalaim's population. Someone among them who is liable to collapse will be like David on that day, and David's household will be like gods, like Yahweh's envoy going before them.

[9]'On that day I shall seek to annihilate all the nations that come against Yerushalaim, [10]but I shall pour out on David's household and on Yerushalaim's population a spirit of grace and of prayers for grace. They will look to me concerning someone they've thrust through, and they will lament over him with the lamentation for an only son, and express distress for him like the distress over a firstborn.

## The sword against the shepherd

[11]On that day the lamentation in Yerushalaim will be great, like the lamentation for Hadad-rimmon in Megiddo Valley. [12]The country will lament, kin-group by kin-group by itself, the kin-group of David's household by itself and their women by themselves, the kin-group of Natan's household by itself and their women by themselves, [13]the kin-group of Levi's household by itself and their women by themselves, the kin-group of the Shim'ites by itself and their women by themselves, [14]all the remaining kin-groups kin-group by kin-group by itself and their women by themselves.

**13** On that day there will be a fountain opened for David's household and Yerushalaim's inhabitants, for purification and for cleansing.

[2]And on that day (a declaration of Yahweh of Armies) I shall cut off the names of the images from the country. They won't be mentioned

again. Also the prophets and the defiled spirit I shall cause to pass away from the country. ³When someone prophesies again, his father and his mother, who brought him to birth, will say, "You will not live, because you've spoken falsehood in Yahweh's name." His father and his mother, who brought him to birth, will thrust him through when he prophesies.

⁴On that day the prophets will be ashamed, each one, of his vision when he prophesies. They won't wear a garment of hair so as to deceive. ⁵He will say, "I'm not a prophet, I'm a man who works the ground, because a man acquired me from my youth." ⁶If someone says to him, "What are these wounds between your hands?" he will say, "I was wounded in my friends' house.'"

⁷Sword, rouse yourself against my shepherd,
  against a man who is my envoy (a declaration
    of Yahweh of Armies).
Strike down my shepherd, the flock is to scatter;
  I shall turn back my hand against the little
    ones.
⁸In all the country (Yahweh's declaration)
  two parts in it will be cut off, will perish.
A third will be left in it.
  ⁹but I shall bring the third into the fire.
I shall smelt them as one smelts silver,
  test them as one tests gold.
It will call in my name
  and I myself shall answer it,
I shall have said, "It is my people",
  and it will say, "Yahweh is my God."

## Yahweh stands on the Mount of Olives

**14** There, a day of Yahweh is coming, and your spoil [Yerushalaim] will be shared out within you. ²I shall gather all the nations to Yerushalaim for battle. The town will be captured, the houses will be plundered, the women will be ravished and half the town will go out into exile. But the rest of the people will not be cut off from the town, ³and Yahweh will go out and do battle against those nations, as he does battle on a day of engagement.

⁴On that day his feet will stand on the Mount of Olives which faces Yerushalaim to the east. The Mount of Olives will split in half from

east to west, a very big ravine; half of the mountain will move away northward, half of it southward. ⁵You people will flee by the ravine between my mountains, because the ravine between the mountains will reach to Atsal. You will flee as you fled from before the earthquake in the days of Uzziyah king of Yehudah. But Yahweh my God will come – all the sacred ones will be with you.

⁶On that day there won't be light from the glorious ones; they will dwindle. ⁷There'll be one day (it is known to Yahweh), not day and not night; at evening time it will be light.

⁸On that day living water will go out from Yerushalaim, half of it to the eastern sea, half of it to the western sea. It will happen in summer and in winter. ⁹Yahweh will be king over all the earth.

## No more trader in Yahweh's house

On that day Yahweh will be one and his name one. ¹⁰The entire country will turn round [and be] like the steppe, from Geba to Rimmon south of Yerushalaim, but it [Yerushalaim] will rise up and stay in its place, from the Binyamin Gate to the place of the First Gate, to the Corner Gate, and from Hananel's Tower to the king's winepresses. ¹¹People will live in it, and devoting will not happen any more. Yerushalaim will live in confidence. ¹²But this will be the epidemic that Yahweh will impose on all the peoples that made war against Yerushalaim: making someone's flesh waste away while he stands on his feet, his eyes waste away in their sockets, and his tongue waste away in their mouth. ¹³On that day a great panic from Yahweh will come upon them. They'll take hold, each person, of his neighbour's hand, and his hand will rise against his neighbour's hand. ¹⁴Yehudah, too, will do battle at Yerushalaim. The resources of all the nations around will be gathered – gold and silver and clothing, a great quantity. ¹⁵Like this epidemic, so will be the epidemic affecting horse, mule, camel, donkey and every animal that will be in those camps. ¹⁶But everyone who is left from all the nations that come against Yerushalaim will go up year by year to bow low to the King, Yahweh of

Armies, and to observe the Sukkot Festival. <sup>17</sup>Whichever does not go up from the kingroups of the earth to Yerushalaim to bow low to the King, Yahweh of Armies, there'll be no rain on them. <sup>18</sup>If Misrayim's kin-group doesn't go up and doesn't come, there'll be none on them; there'll be the epidemic that Yahweh imposes on the nations that don't go up to observe the Sukkot Festival. <sup>19</sup>This will be [the penalty for] the wrongdoing of Misrayim and

the wrongdoing of all the nations that don't go up to observe the Sukkot Festival.

<sup>20</sup>On that day, upon a horse's bells will be 'Sacred to Yahweh'. The pots in Yahweh's house will be like the basins before the altar. <sup>21</sup>Every pot in Yerushalaim and Yehudah will be sacred to Yahweh of Armies. All the people who offer sacrifice will come and take some of them and cook in them. There'll be no more trader in the house of Yahweh of Armies on that day.

# MALACHI

The location of Malachi [Mal'aki] in the First Testament invites us to infer that it belongs, with Haggai and Zechariah, in the period after exiled Judahites were free to return to Jerusalem. The temple is functioning, so it presupposes the completion of their work, while the variety of problems it seeks to handle then fit with the pressures of the subsequent time of Ezra and Nehemiah. It proceeds mostly by means of a to-and-fro argument in which Yahweh or the prophet confronts the community over a series of issues. Its ending with the prospect of Yahweh sending a new Elijah or the old Elijah recommissioned, to herald Yahweh's day, makes it an appropriate close to the Prophets. Also, its ending the old covenant Scriptures as a whole (in the Christian ordering of the First Testament) makes for a deft transition to the New Testament.

## Easy-going priests

1 A pronouncement. Yahweh's word to Yisra'el by means of Mal'aki.

²'I've been loyal to you', Yahweh said. But you say, 'How have you been loyal to us?' 'Esaw was Ya'aqob's [Jacob's] brother, wasn't he (Yahweh's declaration). But I was loyal to Ya'aqob ³and I was hostile to Esaw. I'm making his mountains a desolation, his domain to belong to wilderness jackals.' ⁴Because Edom says, 'We've been crushed, but we'll build the wastes again', Yahweh of Armies has said this: 'Those people may build, but I myself will tear down.' They will be called 'Faithless Territory' and 'the people Yahweh has condemned permanently'. ⁵Your own eyes will see it. You yourselves will say, 'Yahweh is great, beyond Yisra'el's territory.'

⁶"A son honours his father, a servant his lord. If I'm a father, where's the honour for me? If I'm a Lord, where's the awe for me?" Yahweh of Armies said to you, priests who disdain my name. You say, "How have we disdained your name?" ⁷You're presenting defiled food on my altar. You say, "How have we defiled you?" By your saying, "Yahweh's table can be disdained." ⁸When you bring up something blind for sacrifice, there's nothing bad. When you bring up something lame or sick, there's nothing bad. Present it to your governor, please. Will he accept you? Will he have regard to you? (Yahweh of Armies has said).' ⁹Now, please seek Yahweh's goodwill so that he shows favour to us. This has come from your hand. Will he have regard to any of you? (Yahweh of Armies has said).

¹⁰"Who indeed is there among you who'll shut the doors, and not light a fire on my altar to no end! I find no delight in you (Yahweh of Armies has said) and I shall not accept an offering from your hand.

## A priest's lips keep watch on knowledge

¹¹Because from the sun's rising to its setting my name is great among the nations and in every place incense is offered to my name, and a pure offering, because my name is great among the nations (Yahweh of Armies has said). ¹²But you're treating it as ordinary when you say, "The Lord's table is defiled, and its fruit, its food, can be disdained", ¹³or say, "This is a weariness", and blow it off (Yahweh of Armies has said), or bring something stolen or lame or sick, and bring it as the offering. Should I accept it from your hand (Yahweh has said)? ¹⁴Cursed is the cheat when there's a male in his flock but he pledges and sacrifices to the Lord something devastated. Because I am a great king (Yahweh of Armies has said) and my name is held in awe among the nations.

2 So now to you priests, this order. ²If you don't listen and don't receive it into your mind to give honour to my name (Yahweh of Armies has said), I shall send off a curse among you. I shall curse your blessings. Indeed, I have cursed it, because you don't receive it into your mind. ³Here am I, I'm going to reprimand your seed. I'm going to spread faeces on your faces, the faeces from your festival sacrifice. Someone will carry you out to it. ⁴And you will acknowledge that I have sent off this order to you so that my pact with Levi might exist (Yahweh of Armies has said). ⁵My pact with him was life and well-being, and I gave them to him, with awe. He was in awe of me. He was in dread of my name.

⁶True instruction was in his mouth;
   evil wasn't found on his lips.
In well-being and in uprightness he walked with
      me,
   and he turned many back from waywardness.
⁷Because a priest's lips keep watch on knowledge;
   people seek instruction from his mouth,
   because he's an envoy of Yahweh of Armies.

⁸But you've turned aside from the way. You've made many people collapse through your instruction. You've devastated Levi's pact (Yahweh of Armies has said). ⁹I myself in turn am making you shameful and low to the entire people, on account of the fact that you don't keep watch on my ways but you show regard in the instruction.'

## A broader neglected covenant

¹⁰We all of us have one father, don't we. One God created us, didn't he. Why do we break faith, each with his brother, in treating our

ancestors' pact as ordinary? ¹¹Yehudah has broken faith. An offence has been committed in Yisra'el and in Yerushalaim, because Yehudah has treated as ordinary what is sacred to Yahweh, to which he is loyal, and has married the daughter of a strange god. ¹²May Yahweh cut off the person who does this (anyone who arises and anyone who responds) from Ya'aqob's tents, even one who presents an offering to Yahweh of Armies.

¹³And you do this second thing, covering Yahweh's altar with tears, crying and wailing because he's no longer regarding the offering or receiving it with acceptance from your hand, ¹⁴and you've said, 'On account of what?' On account of the fact that Yahweh is a witness between you and the wife of your youth, with whom you've broken faith, when she was your partner and your covenanted woman. ¹⁵Didn't One make us, and isn't the remainder of the spirit his? And what is the One seeking? Godly offspring. So you will guard yourself in your spirit. Someone is not to break faith with the wife of your youth. ¹⁶When he's hostile so as to divorce (Yahweh the God of Yisra'el has said), he makes violence a cover over his clothing (Yahweh of Armies has said). So you're to keep watch for yourself in your spirit and not break faith.

¹⁷You've wearied Yahweh with your words. You've said, 'How have we wearied him?' When you say, 'Everyone who does something bad is good in Yahweh's eyes. In them he takes delight.' Or 'Where is the God who exercises authority?'

**3** 'Here am I, I'm going to send my envoy, and he'll clear the way before me.' Suddenly there will come to his palace the Lord for whom you are looking.

## A full and frank exchange of views

¹ᵇSo the envoy of the pact whom you want – there, he's coming (Yahweh of Armies has said). ²But who's going to endure the day of his coming? Who's going to stand when he appears? Because he'll be like a smelter's fire or like launderer's soap. ³He'll sit smelting and purifying silver. He'll purify the Levites and refine them like gold and silver, and they'll be Yahweh's, people who take up an offering

in faithfulness. ⁴The offering of Yehudah and Yerushalaim will please Yahweh as in the days gone by, in former years.

⁵So I shall come near to you to exercise authority and be an eager witness against the diviners, the adulterers, the people who swear falsely, the people who defraud the employee of his wages, the widow and orphan, and those who turn aside the resident and who are not in awe of me (Yahweh of Armies has said). ⁶Because I am Yahweh, I haven't changed, and you're Ya'aqob's descendants, you haven't come to an end. ⁷Given that from your ancestors' days you've turned aside from my laws and not kept them: come back to me and I'll come back to you (Yahweh of Armies has said).

You'll say, "How shall we come back?" ⁸Does a person cheat God? Because you're cheating me. You'll say, "How have we cheated you?" In tithe and contribution. ⁹You're subjected to a curse, and you're cheating me – the nation, all of it. ¹⁰Bring the entire tithe into the storehouse, so that there may be food in my house, and test me by this, please (Yahweh of Armies has said), if I don't open the heavens' floodgates and empty out blessing on you until there's no need. ¹¹I'll reprimand the devourer for you, and it won't destroy the fruit of the ground for you, and the vine in the open country won't miscarry for you (Yahweh of Armies has said). ¹²All the nations will count you fortunate, because you'll be a delightful land (Yahweh of Armies has said).

## A faithful sun with healing in its rays

¹³You've made your words strong against me (Yahweh has said). You'll say, "What have we spoken to ourselves against you?" ¹⁴You've said, "Serving God is empty in results. What was the gain when we kept his charge and walked in gloom before Yahweh of Armies? ¹⁵So now we count the arrogant fortunate. The people who act in faithlessness have both been built up and have also tested God and escaped.'"

¹⁶Then the people who were in awe of Yahweh talked, each with his neighbour, and Yahweh heeded and listened, and a remembrance scroll was written before him regarding the people who were in awe of Yahweh and who esteemed his name. ¹⁷'For me

they will be a special possession (Yahweh of Armies has said) for the day that I'm preparing. I shall have pity on them as someone has pity on his son who serves him. ¹⁸You'll again see the difference between the faithful and the faithless, between the one who serves God over against the one who has not served him.

4 Because there – the day is coming, burning like an oven, when all the arrogant and all the people who act in faithlessness will be stubble, and the day that's coming will burn them up (Yahweh of Armies has said) so that it doesn't leave them root or branch. ²But there will rise for you who are in awe of my name a faithful sun with healing in its rays. You'll go out and jump like well-fed bullocks. ³You'll trample the faithless, because they'll be ashes under the soles of your feet, on that day that I'm making (Yahweh of Armies has said).

⁴Be mindful of Mosheh [Moses] my servant's instruction, which I ordered him for all Yisra'el at Horeb, laws and rulings. ⁵There, I'm sending you Eliyyah [Elijah] the prophet before the coming of the great and awe-inspiring day of Yahweh. ⁶He will turn back the mind of parents to children and the mind of children to parents, so that I don't come and strike down the country with "devoting".

# GLOSSARY

**Abaddon**
One of the First Testament's words for the place where dead people are, like **She'ol**. The ordinary word is similar to a Hebrew word meaning 'perish', which may well not be a coincidence. Indeed, the verb can suggest 'destroy', and people might make a link with the fact that death does mean that our bodies decay. But the texts do not make anything of this. The word is simply a name.

**affirmation**
In the context of expressions such as '**affirmation chest**' or 'affirmation dwelling', affirmation refers to the things **Yahweh** has affirmed as his expectations of **Yisra'el (Israel)** – namely, the Ten Commandments.

**affirmation chest**
The '**affirmation** chest' is a box a bit more than a metre long, a bit more than half a metre wide and high. The King James Bible (KJV) refers to it as an 'ark', but the word means a box, though it is only occasionally used to refer to chests used for other purposes. It is the *affirmation* chest because it contains the stone tablets inscribed with the Ten Commandments, key expectations God affirmed in connection with establishing the Sinai covenant. It is regularly kept in the sanctuary, but there is a sense in which it symbolizes God's presence (given that **Yisra'el (Israel)** has no images to do so), and in that capacity the Israelites sometimes carry it with them. It is sometimes referred to as the pact chest, with the same meaning.

**altar**
A structure for offering a sacrifice (the Hebrew word for altar comes from the word for sacrifice), made of earth or stone. An altar might be relatively small, like a table, and the person making the offering would stand in front of it. Or it might be higher and larger, like a platform, and the person making the offering would climb on to it.

**Amorites**
A term for one of the original ethnic groups in **Kena'an (Canaan)**, though also used to refer to the people of that country as a whole. Genesis 15.16 and 21 illustrates the two uses of the word in close proximity. Indeed, outside the First Testament 'Amorites' refers to a people living over a much wider area of Mesopotamia. 'Amorites' is thus a little like the word 'America', which commonly refers to the USA but can denote a much broader area of the continent of which the USA is part.

**ancestral heads**
The heads of the (very) extended families within the twelve clans of **Yisra'el (Israel)**, a family unit rather larger than the household.

**Aram, Aramaic, Arameans, Aramites**
In the period to which Genesis refers, the Arameans (or Aramites) were a people living in Syria and northern Mesopotamia. Aram later became the name for a more defined political entity in Syria, **Ephrayim's (Ephraim's)** big north-eastern neighbour; English translations then often refer to it as Syria. The Aramaic language, a sister language of **Hebrew** somewhat in the way Spanish is a sister language of Portuguese or Italian, became the international language of the Middle East. Parts of Ezra, Jeremiah and Daniel are in Aramaic, and it was the everyday language of Palestine in Jesus' day.

## Asherah, Ashtar

The word is used both to signify the name of a deity and the name of an aid to worship (the two meanings come close together in 1 Kings 14—15). In **Kena'anite (Canaanite)** religion and elsewhere, strictly Asherah was a particular goddess, but the name came to be used in the plural as a general term for a goddess. As a word for an aid to worship, it denotes something that can be 'erected', 'planted' and 'burned', which suggests a tree-like column or pillar that represented and suggested the presence of the deity.

## Ashshur (Assyria)

The first great Middle Eastern superpower, the Assyrians spread their empire westward into Syria-Palestine in the eighth century BC, the time of Amos and Isaiah. They first made **Ephrayim (Ephraim)** part of their empire; then when Ephraim kept trying to assert independence, they invaded Ephraim, destroyed its capital at **Shomron (Samaria)**, transported its people and settled people from other parts of their empire in their place. They also invaded **Yehudah (Judah)** and devastated much of the country, but did not take Jerusalem. Prophets such as Amos and Isaiah describe how **Yahweh** was thus using Assyria as a means of disciplining **Yisra'el (Israel)**.

## assistant

These are the *netinim*, people who played a support role in the temple. Etymologically their name implies they are people who were 'given', dedicated to the service of God, or given to the priests and **Levites** as their assistants in fulfilling menial tasks. The people of Gibeon (Josh. 9.27) are not called *netinim*, but the role ascribed to them as water carriers and woodchoppers for the sanctuary conveys an idea of these assistants' work. The assistants came to be treated as among the Levites.

## authority

People such as Eli, Samuel, Samuel's sons and the kings 'exercise authority' over **Yisra'el (Israel)** and for Israel. The Hebrew word for someone who exercises such authority, *shopet*, is traditionally translated 'judge', but such leadership is wider than this. In the book called Judges, these **leader**s are people who have no official position like the later kings, but who arise and exercise initiative in a way that brings the people **deliverance** from the trouble they get into. It is a king's job to exercise authority in accordance with **faithfulness** to God and people.

## awe

**Hebrew** uses the same words for being afraid of someone fearful and for respecting someone whom it's appropriate to revere. Occasionally it's hard to be sure which sort of attitude is designated by the word. I have used 'awe' where the context implies the second sort of attitude, which also implies submission and obedience. In the wisdom books, awe is seen as a key aspect of a relationship with God, of crucial importance to understanding God and life. Awe for God has been described as the First Testament expression for spirituality.

## Azazel

The word comes only in the expression 'for Azazel' in Leviticus 16; it might be a deserted and/or rocky place or it might be a demonic power.

## Babel (Babylon)

A minor power in the context of **Yisra'el's (Israel's)** early history, in the time of Jeremiah they took over the position of superpower from **Ashshur (Assyria)** and kept that for nearly a century until conquered by **Paras (Persia)**. Prophets such as Jeremiah describe how **Yahweh** was using them as a means of disciplining **Yehudah (Judah)**. Their creation stories, law codes and more philosophical writings help us understand aspects of the First Testament's equivalent writings, while their astrological religion also forms background to aspects of polemic in the Prophets.

## bad
The First Testament uses this word in a similar fashion to the way English uses the word 'bad' –
it can refer both to the bad things that people do and the bad things that happen to us, both to
morally bad actions and to bad experiences. Sometimes prophets use the word with both
connotations in the same context, pointing towards the fact that bad things often happen because
people do bad things – though they know that this is not invariably so. They can thus speak of
God doing bad things in the sense of bringing calamity to people.

## Beliyya'al
A personification of death, which swallows (*bala*); the word became a term for Satan.

## brother
The Hebrew word can refer to blood relatives in a broader sense than the English word – both
male and female.

## Cistern
A term that can denote the grave as the place where dead people are (see **She'ol**).

## commitment
The word corresponds to the Hebrew word *hesed*, which translations render by means of
expressions such as 'steadfast love' or 'loving kindness' or 'goodness'. It is the First Testament
equivalent of the special word for love in the New Testament, the word *agapē*. The First
Testament uses this word to refer to an extraordinary act whereby someone pledges himself
or herself to someone else in some act of generosity, allegiance or grace when there is no prior
relationship between them and therefore no reason why they should do so. Thus in Joshua 2,
Rahab appropriately speaks of her protection of the Israelite spies as an act of commitment. It
can also refer to a similar extraordinary act that takes place when there is a relationship between
people, but one party has let the other party down and therefore has no right to expect any
**faithfulness** from the other party. If the party that has been let down continues being faithful,
they are showing this kind of commitment. In their response to Rahab, the Israelite spies declare
that they will relate to her in this way.

## cry, cry out
In describing the Israelites' response when they are oppressed by enemies, Judges uses the word
that the First Testament uses to describe Abel's blood crying out to God, the outcry of the people
of Sodom under their oppression, the Israelites' crying out in **Misrayim (Egypt)** and the outcry of
people who are unfairly treated within **Yisra'el (Israel)** in later centuries. It denotes an urgent cry
that presses God for **deliverance**, a cry that God can be relied on to hear even when people deserve
to be having the experience that is assailing them.

## cubit
Half a yard or just under half a metre (I usually translate cubit measurements into metres).

## day of the Lord
The oldest occurrence of the expression 'the day of the Lord', 'Yahweh's day', comes in Amos 5,
which indicates that people saw it as a time when **Yahweh** would bring great blessing on them.
Amos declares that the opposite is the case. Henceforth the expression always has sinister
connotations. Yahweh's day is a day when Yahweh acts in decisive fashion. It doesn't happen
just once; there are various occasions that the First Testament describes as Yahweh's day, such as
Jerusalem's fall in 587 BC and **Babel's (Babylon's)** fall in 539. In Isaiah, Sennacherib's devastation
of **Yehudah (Judah)** was such an embodiment of Yahweh's day (22.5).

### decontamination

A sacrifice that removes the **taboo** that comes from contravening **Yahweh**'s rulings for life.

### deliver, deliverance, deliverer

In the First Testament, modern translations often use the words 'save', 'saviour' and 'salvation', but this gives a misleading impression. In Christian usage, these words commonly refer to our personal relationship with God and to the enjoyment of heaven. The First Testament does speak of our personal relationship with God, but it does not use this group of words in that connection. They refer rather to God's practical intervention to get **Yisra'el (Israel)** or the individual out of a mess of some kind, such as false accusations by individuals within the community or invasion by enemies.

### devote, devotion

Devoting something to God means giving it over to God irrevocably. Translations use words such as 'annihilated' or 'destroyed', and that is often the implication, but it does not convey the word's distinctive point. You could devote land, or an animal such as a donkey, and in effect Hannah will devote Samuel; the donkey or the human being then belongs to God and is committed to God's service. In effect the Israelites devoted many **Kena'anites (Canaanites)** to God's service in this way; they became people who chopped wood and drew water for the **altar**, its offerings and the rites of the sanctuary. Devoting people to God by killing them as a kind of sacrifice was a practice known from other peoples, which **Yisra'el (Israel)** takes over on its own initiative, but which God validates. Israel knows this is how war works in its world and it assumes it is to operate the same way, and God goes along with that.

### disciples of the prophets

Literally, these are the 'sons of the prophets'. The books of 1 and 2 Kings mention communities of such prophets in various places in **Ephrayim (Ephraim)** in the time of Elijah and Elisha. They lived together and apparently made their services available to people who needed guidance from God on some matter. They would be dependent on donations from people who sought their help in this way; the stories indicate that this made them vulnerable to poverty.

### Edom, Edomites

Edom is **Yehudah's (Judah's)** south-eastern neighbour, occupying an area to the south-east of the Dead Sea. As **Yisra'el (Israel)** traces its ancestry back to Jacob, it traces Edom's ancestry back to Jacob's brother Esau. The First Testament critiques Edom in particular for its inclination to take advantage of Judah's vulnerability and its support of the Babylonians when they captured Jerusalem. Subsequently the Edomites occupied considerable parts of southern Judah.

### effigies

The Hebrew word for these is *teraphim*. In 1 Samuel 15.33 the text presupposes a link between the *teraphim* and divination, which involves techniques (like those of astrology) for trying to discover things about the future so that we can make sensible decisions or safeguard against trouble that might come. One form of divination involves consulting the dead. The effigies would be images of family members who had passed (a little like family photographs), whom people would seek to consult on the assumption that they might now know things that their relatives who were still alive could not know. **Yisra'el (Israel)** was not supposed to be involved in such procedures because it was expected to rely more directly on God for guidance.

### envoy

A supernatural agent through whom God may appear and work in the world. Standard English translations refer to them as 'angels', but this is inclined to suggest ethereal figures with wings, wearing diaphanous white dresses. Envoys are human-like figures; hence it is possible to give them hospitality without realizing this is who they are (Heb. 13). And they have no wings; hence their need of a stairway or ramp between heaven and earth (Gen. 28). They appear in order to act or speak on God's behalf, and so fully represent God that they can speak as if they *are* God (Gen. 22). They thus bring the reality of God's presence, action and voice, without bringing such a real presence that it would electrocute mere mortals or shatter their hearing.

### ephod
In some passages the First Testament implies that an ephod is a kind of vestment worn by a priest, but in some passages it at least incorporated something that contained the **Urim and Tummim**.

### Ephrayim (Ephraim)
After the reign of David and Solomon, the nation of **Yisra'el (Israel)** split into two. Most of the twelve Israelite clans set up an independent state in the north, separate from **Yehudah (Judah)** and Jerusalem and from the line of David. Because this was the bigger of the two states, politically it kept the name Israel, which is confusing because Israel is still the name of the people as a whole as the people of God. In the Prophets, it is sometimes difficult to tell whether 'Israel' refers to the people of God as a whole or just to the northern state. But sometimes the state is referred to by the name of Ephraim as one of its dominant clans, so I use this term to refer to that northern state, to try to reduce the confusion.

### exile
At the end of the seventh century **Babel (Babylon)** became the major power in **Yehudah**'s (**Judah**'s) world but Judah was inclined to rebel against its authority. As part of a successful campaign to get Judah to submit properly to its authority, in 597 and in 587 BC the Babylonians transported many people from Jerusalem to Babylon. They made a special point of transporting people in leadership positions, such as members of the royal family and the court, priests and prophets (Ezekiel was one of them). These people were thus compelled to live in Babylonia for the next fifty years or so. Through the same period, people back in Judah were also under Babylonian authority. So they were not physically in exile but they were also living *in* the exile as a period of time. A number of books in the First Testament indicate that one of the issues they are handling is the pressure this experience brings to people.

### expiation
A key concern in Exodus and Leviticus is keeping the sanctuary pure. While God may be able to tolerate a small amount of impurity there (as we can tolerate a small amount of dirt), if the place people have made as a home for God becomes too much affected by things that are alien, then God can hardly carry on living there. So it is important to deal with impurity that comes on the sanctuary through the infringement of **taboo**s. One way of conceiving this is to speak in terms of atonement (at-one-ment), which suggests the healing of a relationship. Another is to speak of propitiation, which suggests the mollifying of someone who was angry. In contrast, expiation relates to the thing that has caused the problem rather than to the person. It suggests the removal or wiping away of a stain. Of course the removal of the stain does mean that the threat to the relationship is gone and it is now possible for God to be in easy relationship with the people; in this sense expiation and at-one-ment are closely related. On the other hand, 'propitiation' is a more questionable idea in connection with Leviticus; while it does imply that God is offended by people and unwilling to associate with them, it does not speak of God being angry with them because of their offences.

### faithfulness
In English Bibles this Hebrew word (*tsedaqah*) is usually translated 'righteousness', but it denotes a particular slant on what we might mean by righteousness. It means doing the right thing by the people with whom one is in a relationship, the members of one's community. Thus it is really closer to 'faithfulness' than 'righteousness'.

**faithlessness**
A word for sin that suggests the opposite of **faithfulness**, an attitude to God and to other people that expresses a contempt for what right relationships deserve.

**flatbread**
Bread made without being yeasted and allowed to rise.

**Greece**
In 336 BC, Greek forces under Alexander the Great took control of the **Parsite (Persian)** Empire, but after Alexander's death in 333 his empire split up. The largest part, to the north and east of Palestine, was ruled by one of his generals, Seleucus, and his successors. **Yehudah (Judah)** was under its control for much of the next two centuries, though it was at the extreme south-western border of this empire and sometimes came under the control of the Ptolemaic Empire in **Misrayim (Egypt)** (ruled by successors of another of Alexander's officers).

**Hebrew**
Oddly, whereas this word became the term for the language of the Jewish people, it seems not to be an ethnic term in the First Testament. 'Hebrew' is not the same as 'Israelite'. While Abraham can be designated a Hebrew (Gen. 14.13) and the Israelites might be termed Hebrews, they were not the only Hebrews. Other languages have related words, and all seem to be more sociological terms than ethnic ones, a little like the word 'gypsy'. They suggest people who do not belong to a regular recognized political community. In the New Testament, the Hebrews are Hebrew-speaking **Jew**s as opposed to Greek-speaking Jews. So it's confusing to refer to First Testament Israelites as 'Hebrews'.

**hierodule**
A type of temple servant, possibly involved in sexual rites.

**Jew**
The word is a shortened version of the word *yehudi*, which thus denotes a member of the clan or province of **Yehudah (Judah)**. As Judah became the heart of **Yisra'el (Israel)** in the Second Temple period, *yehudim* or 'Jews' became a term for all members of the people of Israel and became a regular term for members of a religious community rather than members of an ethnic group. But this usage mostly belongs to post-First Testament times, and in the First Testament the word *yehudim* or 'Jews' would exclude most Israelites. So it's confusing to refer to First Testament Israelites as 'Jews'.

**Kasdites**
People from an area within Babylonia who came to rule Babylonia, so that it became a term for Babylonians in general (also sometimes for their expert advisers); an alternative form of the word is Kaldites (hence the traditional English term Chaldeans).

**Kena'an, Kena'anites (Canaan, Canaanites)**
As the biblical terms for the land of **Yisra'el (Israel)** as a whole and for its indigenous peoples, 'Canaan' and 'Canaanites' are not so much names that refer to a particular ethnic group as shorthand terms for all the peoples native to the land. See also **Amorites**.

**leader**
The book of Judges is named after the leaders whose stories appear in the book. The traditional term is 'judge', so that they are people who also give their name to the period of time between Joshua and Saul, the 'Judges Period'. But these 'judges' do not usually operate in connection with sorting out legal cases, and 'leaders' gives more the right idea concerning their role. They are people who have no official position like the later kings, but who arise and exercise initiative in a way that brings the clans **deliverance** from the trouble the clans get into.

## Levites

Within the clan of Levi, the descendants of Aaron are the priests, the people who have specific responsibilities in connection with offering the community's sacrifices and helping individuals to offer their sacrifices by performing some aspects of the offering such as the sprinkling of the animal's blood. The other Levites fulfil a support and administrative role in the temple and are also involved in teaching the people and in other aspects of leading worship.

## Livyatan (Leviathan)

A sea monster who is an embodiment or symbol of tumultuous power asserted against God and the world.

## Maday and Paras, Parsites (Media and Persia, Medo-Persia, Persians)

Media lies between Mesopotamia and Persia. In the 550s Cyrus the Great gained control of Media and also of Persia, and turned Medo-Persia into the third Middle Eastern superpower. Cyrus took control of the Babylonian Empire in 539 BC, which opened up the possibility of Judahites returning from **Babel (Babylon)** after the **exile**. **Yehudah (Judah)** and surrounding peoples such as **Shomron (Samaria)**, Ammon and Ashdod were then Persian provinces or colonies. The Persians stayed in power for two centuries until defeated by **Greece**.

## Master, Masters

The word *ba'al* is an ordinary Hebrew word for a master or lord or owner, but the word is also used to describe a **Kena'anite (Canaanite)** god. It is thus parallel to the word 'Lord' as used to describe **Yahweh**. Further, in effect 'Master' can be a proper name, like 'Lord'. To make the difference clear, the First Testament generally uses 'Master' for a foreign god and 'Lord' for the real God, Yahweh. Like other ancient peoples, the Canaanites acknowledged a number of gods, and strictly the Master was simply one of them, though he was one of the most prominent. In addition, a title such as 'The Master of Pe'or' suggests that the Master was believed to be manifest and known in different ways and different places. The First Testament also uses the plural 'Masters' to refer to Canaanite gods in general.

## Misrayim, Misrayimites (Egypt, Egyptians)

The major regional power to the south of **Kena'an (Canaan)** and the country where Jacob's family had found refuge, where they ended up as serfs, and from which the Israelites then needed to escape. In Moses' time Egypt controlled Canaan; in subsequent centuries it was sometimes a threat to **Yisra'el (Israel)**, sometimes a potential ally.

## name

The name of someone stands for the person. The First Testament talks of the temple as a place where God's name dwells. It's one of the ways it handles the paradox involved in speaking of the temple as a place where God lives. It knows this is a nonsense: how could a building contain the God who could not be contained by the entire heavens, no matter how far you could travel across them? Yet **Yisra'el (Israel)** knows that God does in some sense dwell in the temple. They know they can talk with God when they go there; they are aware that they can talk with God anywhere, but there is a special guarantee of this in the temple. They know they can make offerings there and that God will receive them (supposing they are made in good faith). One way they try to square the circle in speaking of the presence of God in the temple is therefore to speak of God's name being present there, because the name sums up the person. Uttering the name of someone you know brings home his or her reality to you; it's almost as if the person is there. When you say someone's name, there is a sense in which you conjure up the person. When people murmur 'Jesus, Jesus' in their prayer, it brings home the reality of Jesus' presence. Likewise, when Israel proclaimed the name **Yahweh** in worship, it brought home the reality of Yahweh's presence.

**non-entity**
A pejorative term, especially for gods other than **Yahweh**; it resembles the word for God but also a word for 'useless'.

**Paras, Parsites (Persia, Persians)**
See **Maday and Paras**.

**peace**
The Hebrew word *shalom* can suggest peace after there has been conflict, but it often points to a richer notion, of fullness of life. The KJV sometimes translates it 'welfare', and modern translations use words such as 'well-being' or 'prosperity'. It suggests that everything is going well for you.

**Pelishtites (Philistines)**
The Philistines were people who came from across the Mediterranean to settle in **Kena'an (Canaan)** at the same time as the Israelites were establishing themselves in Canaan, so that the two peoples formed an accidental pincer-movement on the existing inhabitants of the country and became each other's rivals for control of the area.

**Pesah**
A festival in spring commemorating the exodus (commonly rendered in English as Passover).

**purification, purification offering, purify**
A major concern of the Torah is dealing with the **taboo** that can come on people and places through the effect of something that is alien to who God is, such as contact with death. There is nothing wrong with being involved in burying someone, but you have to give the taint of death time to dissipate or have it removed before coming into God's presence. A purification rite can bring that about.

**Rahab** (not the woman Rahab in Joshua)
Another name for the creature also called **Livyatan (Leviathan)**.

**Reed Sea**
Literally 'sea of rushes'; the word is the one that came in Exodus 2 where Miriam left Moses in the reeds by the Nile. It might be one of the northern arms of what we call the Red Sea, either side of Sinai, or it might be an area of marshy lakes within Sinai.

**remainder**
The Prophets warn that **Yahweh**'s chastisement will mean **Yisra'el (Israel)** (and other peoples) being cut down so that the 'remainder' of them, what 'remains', the 'remnant', will be small. But at least some remainder of Israel will survive – so the idea of a 'remainder' can become a sign of hope. It can also become a challenge – the few that remain are challenged to become a faithful remainder, a faithful remnant.

**reside, resident**
Verb and noun refer to someone living in a country other than their own, who therefore cannot own land.

**restore, restorer**
A restorer is a person who is in a position to take action on behalf of someone within his extended family who is in need in order to restore the situation to what it should be. The word overlaps with expressions such as next-of-kin, guardian and redeemer. 'Next-of-kin' indicates the family context that 'restorer' presupposes. 'Guardian' indicates that the restorer is in a position

to be concerned for the person's protection and defence. 'Redeemer' indicates having resources that the restorer is prepared to expend on the person's behalf. The First Testament uses the term to refer to God's relationship with **Yisra'el (Israel)** as well as to the action of a human person in relation to another, so it implies that Israel belongs to God's family and that God acts on its behalf in the way a restorer does.

### rise
This term (*selah*) comes at the end of a number of lines in the Psalms (and in Habakkuk). We do not know what it refers to.

### scaliness
A skin condition traditionally translated 'leprosy' and carrying a **taboo**.

### secondary wife
Translations use the word 'concubine' to describe people such as Abimelek's mother, but the term used of them does not suggest that they were not properly married. Being a secondary wife rather means that a woman has a different status from that of other wives. It perhaps implies that her son had fewer or no inheritance rights. It may be that a wealthy or powerful man could have several wives with full rights and several secondary wives, or just one of each, or just the former, or even just a secondary wife.

### Shabu'ot
'Weeks', a harvest festival in May or June (commonly transliterated as Shavu'ot, and rendered in English as Pentecost).

### Shadday
El Shadday (or simply Shadday) is a name for God that the First Testament especially associates with the time when the name **Yahweh** would not have been known and with people who would not have known that name. Thus it comes in Genesis and it is used in connection with non-Israelites such as Balaam and Job. We do not know the meaning of the name. There are similar-looking words that mean destruction and breast and – in a sister language of **Hebrew** – mountain, so it could originally have meant destructive God or nourishing God or mountain-like God, but we have little evidence that people made any of those connections in the First Testament. The Greek translation of the First Testament often rendered it 'Almighty', and this also became the convention in English translations. But the significance of the word is rather that it indicates that we are talking about the true God but talking about this God in a way that people who do not know the name Yahweh could use.

### The Shameful King
The **Kena'anite (Canaanite)** god whose name means 'the king'. The name is altered in **Hebrew** by combining it with the word for 'shameful'.

### She'ol
The most frequent of the Hebrew names for the place where we go when we die (see also **Abaddon**). In the New Testament it is called Hades. It is not a place of punishment or suffering but simply a resting place for everyone, a kind of non-physical analogue to the tomb as the resting place for our bodies.

### sheqel
About half an ounce or ten grams.

## Shomron (Samaria)

The city of Samaria was the capital of **Ephrayim (Ephraim)**; it fell to the Assyrians in 722 BC. Many people were then transported there by the Assyrians. Samaria later became the name of the Babylonian and **Parsite (Persian)** province in the area, and for a while its governor had authority over **Yehudah (Judah)**. In the Second Temple period the Judahites were thus ethnically, politically and religiously suspicious of the Samarians. But many of the Samarians were actually more conservative than the Judahites; as their Scriptures they accepted only the Torah.

## soul

'Soul' in the English Bible usually represents Hebrew *nephesh* or Greek *psuche*. It can denote the inner person distinguishable and separable from the body but not independent of it; or the inner being of the whole person, their heart or deeply felt emotions; or the whole person comprising physical body plus divine breath; or the life of the person ('her soul was departing'). It does not mean the real person for which the body is a dispensable outward shell.

## spirit

The Hebrew word for spirit is also the word for breath and for wind, and the First Testament sometimes implies a link between these. Spirit suggests dynamic power; God's spirit suggests God's dynamic power. The wind in its forcefulness with its capacity to fell mighty trees is an embodiment of the powerful spirit of God. Breath is essential to life; where there is no breath, there is no life. And life comes from God. So human breath and even animal breath is an offshoot of God's breath.

## Sukkot

The word means 'shelters' and refers to the festival in September/October that marks the end of the harvest and also commemorates the way the Israelites had to live in makeshift shelters on the way from **Misrayim (Egypt)** to **Kena'an (Canaan)** (the term is commonly rendered in English as tabernacles or booths).

## taboo

I use the word 'taboo' to render the Hebrew word often translated 'impure' or 'unclean', because the Hebrew word suggests a positive quality rather than the absence of purity. There are certain things that are mysterious, extraordinary, perplexing and a bit worrying. Among these are menstruation and childbirth, because they suggest both death and life. These are opposites, and God is the God of life and not of death, yet menstruation (with its association of blood and life) and giving birth (which is both life-giving and very dangerous) bring them into close connection. So contact with them makes people taboo; they cannot go into God's presence until they are purified (see **purification**).

## talent

About 40 kilograms or 90 pounds.

## trespass

A term to describe sin or wrongdoing. It suggests the idea that in varying ways people owe it to one another to respect the rights that the other person has. So married people owe each other **faithfulness**, and unfaithfulness involves failure to respect that right. Unfaithfulness to **Yahweh** by serving other gods has similar implications; it fails to respect Yahweh's right to allegiance and trust. Devoting to God the plunder from a war means that someone who appropriates some of the plunder fails to respect God's right to it (1 Chron. 2.7). For a king to act as if he was a priest involves similar failure (2 Chron. 26.16).

## Tsiyyon (Zion)

The word is an alternative name for the city of Jerusalem. Jerusalem is more a political name; other peoples would refer to the city as 'Jerusalem'. Zion is more a religious name, a designation of the city that focuses on its being the place where **Yahweh** dwells and is worshipped.

## Urim and Tummim

The First Testament never describes the nature of these, but they were somehow means of God's guiding **Yisra'el (Israel)**. It seems they were something like two rocks that had marks on them signifying yes and no. You could ask God a question and if you got two yeses or two nos, God's answer was clear; if you got a mixed message, that meant God was not answering.

## Yah

Either an earlier version of the name of God, of which **Yahweh** is then an elaboration (cf. the story in Exod. 3), or an abbreviation of the longer name.

## Yahweh

In most English Bibles, the word 'LORD' often comes in all capitals like that, as does also sometimes the word 'GOD' in similar format. These actually represent the name of God, Yahweh. In later First Testament times, Israelites stopped using the name Yahweh and started to refer to Yahweh as 'the Lord'. There may be two reasons. They wanted other people to recognize that Yahweh was the one true God, but this strange foreign-sounding name could give the impression that Yahweh was just **Yisra'el's (Israel's)** tribal god. A term such as 'the Lord' was one anyone could recognize. In addition, they did not want to fall foul of the warning in the Ten Commandments about misusing Yahweh's **name**. Translations into other languages then followed suit and substituted an expression such as 'the Lord' for the name Yahweh. The downsides are that this obscures the fact that God wanted to be known by name, that often the text refers to Yahweh and not some other (so-called) god or lord, and that the practice gives the impression that God is much more 'lordly' and patriarchal than actually God is. (The form 'Jehovah' is not a real word but a mixture of the consonants of 'Yahweh' and the vowels of that word for 'Lord', to remind people in reading Scripture that they should say 'the Lord', not the actual name.)

## Yahweh of Armies

This title for God usually appears in English Bibles as 'the LORD of Hosts', but it is a more puzzling expression than that implies. The word for LORD is actually the **name** of God, **Yahweh**, and the word for Hosts is the regular Hebrew word for armies; it is the word that appears on the back of an Israeli military vehicle. So more literally the expression means 'Yahweh [of] Armies', which is just as odd in **Hebrew** as 'Goldingay of Armies' would be. Yet in general terms its likely implication is clear; it suggests that Yahweh is the embodiment of or controller of all war-making power, in heaven or on earth.

## Yahweh's day

See **day of the Lord**.

## Yehudah (Judah)

One of the twelve sons of Jacob, then the clan that traces its ancestry to him, then the dominant clan in the southern of the two states after the time of Solomon. Later, as a **Parsite (Persian)** province or colony, it was known in **Aramaic** as Yehud. Later still, the Roman province known as Judea also included much of the area of **Ephrayim (Ephraim)/Shomron (Samaria)**. In the context of the First Testament, it's thus less confusing to refer to Judah and to Judahites, not Judeans.

## Yisra'el (Israel)

Originally, 'Israel' was the new name God gave Abraham's grandson, Jacob. His twelve sons were then forefathers of the 12 clans that comprise the people Israel. In the time of Saul and David these twelve clans became more of a political entity. So Israel was both the people of God and a nation or state like other nations or states. After Solomon's day, this state split into two separate states, **Ephrayim (Ephraim)** and **Yehudah (Judah)**. Because Ephraim was far the bigger, it often continued to be referred to as Israel. So if one is thinking of the people of God, Judah is part of Israel. If one is thinking politically, Judah is not part of Israel. Once Ephraim has gone out of existence, then for practical purposes Judah *is* Israel, as the people of God.